COMPANION ENCYCLOPEDIA OF ASIAN PHILOSOPHY

COMPANION ENCYCLOPEDIA OF ASIAN PHILOSOPHY

EDITED BY

BRIAN CARR
and INDIRA MAHALINGAM

ROUTLEDGE
London and New York

First published 1997
by Routledge
11 New Fetter Lane, London EC4P 4EE

29 West 35th Street, New York, NY 10001

Typeset in Ehrhardt by
Florencetype Limited, Stoodleigh, Devon

Printed and bound in Great Britain by
TJ Press (Padstow) Limited, Padstow, Cornwall

British Library Cataloguing in Publication Data
A catalogue record for this book is available from the British Library

Library of Congress Cataloging in Publication Data
Companion encyclopedia of Asian philosophy/
edited by Brian Carr and Indira Mahalingam.
Includes bibliographical references and index
(hb: alk. paper)
1. Philosophy, Oriental–Encyclopedias. I. Carr, Brian. II. Mahalingam, Indira
B121.C66 1997 96–29027
181–dc20 CIP

ISBN 0–415–03535–X

CONTENTS

NOTES ON CONTRIBUTORS

MASAO ABE is a graduate of Kyoto University in Japan. He studied and practised Zen Buddhism with Shin-ichi Hisamatsu while also studying Western philosophy. He was Professor of Philosophy at Nara University of Education from 1952 to 1980 where he is now Emeritus Professor. From 1955–7 he studied Christian theology at Union Theological Seminary and Columbia University as a Rockefeller Foundation research fellow. Since 1965 he has served as Visiting Professor of Buddhism and philosophy at Columbia University, the University of Chicago, Princeton University, University of Hawaii, and other universities in the United States. He has published widely including *Zen and Western Thought*, a collection of essays. He also edited *A Zen Life: D. T. Suzuki Remembered* and translated Kitarō Nishida's *An Inquiry in the Good* with Christopher Ives. His most recent book is *A Study of Dōgen: His Philosophy and Religion*.

VIJAY BHARADWAJA is a Professor in Philosophy at the University of Delhi. His major publications include *Naturalistic Ethical Theory* (1978) and *Form and Validity in Indian Logic* (1990). His current interests are Indian logic, epistemology, and moral philosophy. He is currently working on a book on Indian Ethics.

SIDDHESHWAR BHATT is Professor and Head of the Department of Philosophy and co-ordinator of the U.G.C. Special Assistance Programme, University of Delhi. Previously Professor and Head of the Department of Philosophy at M.S. University, Baroda, his research interests include Indian philosophy, logic and epistemology, philosophy of religion, social and political philosophy, and philosophy of education. His publications include *The Philosophy of Pancaratra, Studies in Ramanuja Vedanta, Knowledge, Value and Education*. He is the editor of *Knowledge, Culture and Value, Glimpses of Buddhist Thought and Culture* and *Reality, Thought and Value* as well as numerous research papers in English and Hindi.

BRIAN BOCKING has been Head of the Department of the study of religions at Bath College of Higher Education since 1986. Previously he was a lecturer in Japanese religions at the University of Stirling and in 1981–2 he was Visiting Lecturer in the Institute of Philosophy and Thought, University of Tsukuba, Japan. His main research interests are Japanese religions, Chinese and Japanese Buddhism, mysticism and comparative religion. His publications include 'Reflections on Soka Gakkai' in the *Scottish Journal of Religious Studies* (1981); 'Comparative Studies of Buddhism and Christianity' in the *Japanese Journal of Religious Studies* (1983); 'The Japanese Religious Traditions in Today's World' in *Religion in Today's World* (1987) and 'Factionalism in Japanese Religion' in *Japan Forum* (1989).

BEATRICE M. BODART-BAILEY is a Visiting Research Fellow at the Institute of Social Science of the University of Tokyo. Her publications include *Kenperu to Tokugawa Tsunayoshi* and *The Furthest Goal, Engelbert Kaempfer's Encounter with Tokugawa Japan.* She has also completed a new English translation of Kaempfer's *History of Japan.*

HARRY BONE studied Arabic and Islamic Studies at the University of Exeter and the University of Aleppo, Syria and specializes in medieval Arabic history and philosophy. He was lecturer in Arabic and Islamic Studies at the University of Exeter and is currently preparing a doctorate in the Department of Near Eastern Studies, Princeton University.

JOHN BOUSFIELD is lecturer in Theology and Religious Studies and a member of the Centre of Southeast Asian Studies, University of Kent. Previously he was lecturer in Philosophy and Southeast Asian Studies, also at the University of Kent. His research interests include theoretical problems arising at the interface between philosophy and social anthropology, the ethnography of indigenous philosophy in Southeast Asia, and Islamic and related mysticism in Indonesia and Malaysia.

MARY BOYCE received her PhD in Oriental Studies from Cambridge University. She was appointed lecturer in Iranian Studies at the School of Oriental and African Studies, London University, in 1947 and became professor in 1963. She has specialized in Manichaeism and Zoroastrianism, her major publication being a history of Zoroastrianism, of which three volumes have appeared.

JOHN BROCKINGTON is Reader in Sanskrit and head of the Sanskrit department at the University of Edinburgh. He has published *The Sacred Thread: Hinduism and its Continuity and Diversity* (1981), *Righteous Rāma: The Evolution of an Epic* (1985), *Hinduism and Christianity* (1992) and numerous journal articles. His research interests include The Rāmāyaṇa in all its versions, the history of Vaishnavism and manuscript studies. He has also catalogued part of the Chandra Shum Shere manuscript collection in the Bodleian Library, Oxford.

BRIAN CARR studied at London University (Imperial, King's and Birkbeck Colleges) and lectured in philosophy at the University of Exeter until 1988 when he moved to a Senior Lectureship in Philosophy at the University of Nottingham. His previous published works include *Bertrand Russell* (1975), *Introduction to the Theory of Knowledge* (with D. J. O'Connor) (1982), *Metaphysics* (1987) and *Logical Foundations* edited with Indira Mahalingam (1991). In 1991 he and Indira Mahalingam co-founded the Carfax journal *Asian Philosophy*, and together they work as general editors of the *Curzon Studies in Asian Philosophy* series. He is the founder and co-ordinator of the European Society for Asian Philosophy, and director of the Research Centre for Asian Philosophy at the University of Nottingham. He was elected a Fellow of the Royal Asiatic Society in 1994.

SARASVATI CHENNAKESAVAN was the first woman professor at Pachaiyappas College, Madras University and the Chairman of the Department of Philosophy at Sri Venkateswara University. She was a visiting professor at Southern Illinois University and a cultural delegate to the USSR and British Council Visitor to the United Kingdom. Her doctoral thesis was on Indian psychology from a philosophical point of view. She has written books and articles on mind, perception, Hinduism, and concepts of Indian philosophy. A dictionary of Indian philosophical terms is currently in preparation. She is now retired from professional life.

CHUNG-YING CHENG is Professor of Philosophy at the University of Hawaii at Manoa. He received his PhD from Harvard University in 1964. He has published widely on Chinese philosophy including *Modernization and Globalization of Chinese Philosophy* (1985), *Inquiries into Harmony, Truth & Justice* (1986) and *Chu Hsi and Neo-Confucianism* (1986) as well as numerous journal articles.

MICHAEL COMANS has had a long interest in the Vedānta traditions, especially the Advaita Vedānta. After graduating with an MA in Religious Studies from the University of Sydney he undertook a careful study over a number of years, first in the United States and later in India, of the Advaita Vedānta and Sanskrit. In 1986 he received his PhD at the Australian National University under the supervision of Professor J. W. de Jong. He intends to continue his research and teaching in Indian philosophy, religion and Sanskrit.

ARIF DIRLIK is a Professor of History at Duke University, Durham, N.C. His works include *Revolution and History: Origins of Marxist Historiography in China, 1919–1937* (1978, 1989); *The Origins of Chinese Communism* (1989); *Marxism and the Chinese Experience: Issues in Contemporary Chinese Socialism* (ed. with Maurice Meisner) (1989, 1990); *Anarchism in the Chinese Revolution and Fields* (1991), and (with Ming K. Chan) *Schools into Fields and Factories: Anarchists, the Guomindang and the Labor University in Shanghai, 1927–1932* (1991).

CHARLES WEI-SHUN FU is Emeritus Professor of Buddhism and East Asian Thought in the Department of Religion, Temple University and Professor of Philosophy, Fo-Kuang University, Taiwan. He previously taught at Taiwan University and Ohio University. His publications include *Zen Master Dogen* (1996), *From Hermeneutics to Mahayana Buddhism* (1990), *'Cultural China' and Chinese Culture* (1988), *On the Critical Inheritance and Creative Development of Chinese Thought and Culture* (1986), *From Western Philosophy to Zen Buddhism* (1986), *Guide to Chinese Philosophy* (1978), and *A Critical History of Western Philosophy* (13th edn) in addition to numerous English, Chinese and Japanese articles in the fields of Buddhism, Chinese Philosophy, Marxism, existential philosophy, and comparative philosophy and religion. He has also edited *Postwar Movements and Issues in World Religions* (1987), *Postwar Religious Issues and Interreligious Dialogues* (1989), *Buddhist Ethics and Modern Society* (1991) and *Buddhist Behavioral Codes in the Modern World* (1993). He is currently the editor of several series and has lectured extensively throughout Asia. His current writing projects include three volumes of *A History of Japanese Thought and Culture* and four volumes on the development of Buddhist thought in Asia.

LENN E. GOODMAN received his DPhil in Islamic Philosophy at Oxford University where he was a Marshall Scholar. He has written on most of the classic Muslim and Jewish philosophers and has published book length translations and commentaries on major Arabic texts by Ibn Tufayl, the Ikhwân al-Safâ, Maimonides and Saadiah Gaon. His original philosophical writings include *Monotheism* (1981), *On Justice* (1991), and *Avicenna* (1993). He is Professor of Philosophy at Vanderbilt University, and previously was Professor of Philosophy at the University of Hawaii.

HASSAN HANAFI is Professor of Philosophy at Cairo University. He received his doctorate from the University of Paris, Sorbonne. Amongst his many well known works are *Religious Dialogue and Revolution, From Dogma to Revolution* (in Arabic) and *Introduction to the Science of Westernization* (in Arabic).

JOHN R. HINNELLS is Professor of Comparative Religion in the University of London at the School of Oriental and African Studies. His original research was in ancient Zoroastrian teaching and its influence on Judaism and Christianity. He has also published on Roman Mithraism. Since 1973 he has specialized on the Parsis in British India and from 1985 on the modern Parsi diaspora around the world, publishing *Zoroastrians in Britain* (1995). In the wider field of the study of religions he edited the *Penguin Dictionary of Religion* (1984) 2nd much enlarged edn (1996), the *Handbook of Living Religions* (1985) 2nd much enlarged edn (1995) and *Who's Who of World Religions* (1991). After 23 years at the University of Manchester where he was Professor of Comparative Religion he moved to London in 1993.

FRANK J. HOFFMAN has taught at universities in Hawaii, England, Japan, West Germany and the United States and is currently in the Department of Philosophy at West Chester University in Pennsylvania. He received a PhD in philosophy of religion from King's College, University of London. Recipient of teaching assistantships in Philosophy and in Asian Studies, an East–West Center grant and the Tutorial Studentship in philosophy of religion, he has directed five public humanities *colloquia*, and participated in five NEH Summer projects. His publications include *Rationality and Mind in Early Buddhism* (1987), a chapter in *Traditional Hermeneutics* (1990), *Pali Buddhism* co-edited with Bhikkhu Deegalle Mahinda (1996) as well as numerous journal articles and book reviews.

MANJU, a Research Fellow in Philosophy at the University of Delhi, specializes in Indian Philosophy. She has written various papers on aspects of Indian philosophy in Hindi.

HUANG NANSEN is Professor of Philosophy at the University of Peking, Beijing. He has written numerous articles and books in the Chinese language on various aspects of Chinese philosophy.

ROGER R. JACKSON is Professor of Religion at Carleton College, Northfield, Minnesota. He has also taught at the University of Michigan and Fairfield University, Connecticut. He received his PhD in Buddhist Studies from the University of Wisconsin–Madison in 1983. He is the author of *Is Enlightenment Possible? Dharmakīrti and rGyal tshab rje on Knowledge, Rebirth, No-self and Liberation*, co-author of *The Wheel of Time: Kalachakra in Context*, and co-editor of *Tibetan Literature: Studies in Genre*. His most recent research concerns the understanding of the nature of mind in the *mahāmudrā* traditions of Indo-Tibetan Buddhist meditation.

TAKASHI KOIZUMI was previously Professor of Philosophy at Keio University, Tokyo and is now Professor of Intellectual History of Modern Japan at International Christian University, Tokyo. His major specialism is utilitarianism. He has written a number of books and articles on central utilitarian thinkers such as John Stuart Mill.

PHILIP G. KREYENBROEK studied Iranian Languages and History of Religions in The Netherlands and Great Britain and taught Persian and Iranian Studies at the University of Utrecht, The Netherlands from 1973 to 1988. In that year he took up a lectureship in Modern Iranian Languages at the School of Oriental and African Studies, London University where he also teaches Zoroastrianism. He has published widely on Zoroastrianism, including *Sraoša in the Zoroastrian Tradition*. He has also written on modern Iranian languages, literature and religion. Since then, Reader in Iranian Languages and Religions, University of London, Professor of Iranian Studies, University of Göttingen, Germany.

WHALEN LAI received his PhD from Harvard University in 1975. In 1986 he was Guest Professor at the University of Tübingen where he worked with Hans Küng. He co-edited with Lewis Lancaster *Early Ch'an in China and Tibet* (1983) and has published numerous articles in academic journals. He is Professor and Chair of the Program in Religious Studies at the University of California, Davis. His research interests include Chinese Buddhism, Chinese thought and society.

OLIVER LEAMAN teaches Philosophy at Liverpool John Moores University and is the author of *An Introduction to Medieval Islamic Philosophy* (1985), *Averroes and his Philosophy* (1988) and *Moses Maimonides* (1990). He is co-editor (with S. H. Nasr) of *History of Islamic Philosophy* (1996), co-editor (with D. H. Frank) of *History of Jewish Philosophy* (1996) and editor of *Friendship East and West* (1996).

CHRISTIAN LINDTNER was born in 1949. He studied Greek, Latin, Tibetan, Sanskrit and Philosophy at the University of Copenhagen. He spent several years teaching and studying in Germany and the United States. After some years at the University of Copenhagen he is now with the Danish Ministry of Research. He has published numerous editions and translations of Hindu, Jain and Buddhist texts, including *Nagarjuniana: Studies in the Writings and Philosophy of Nāgārjuna*.

TREVOR LING (deceased) was Visiting Fellow of the Institute of South East Asian Studies from 1988 to 1990. Previously he was Fellow of the Institute of East Asian Philosophy and he has held positions at the National University of Singapore, Manchester University, and Leeds University. His publications include *A History of Religion: East and West* (1968), *The Buddha* (1973), *Karl Marx and Religion* (1980), *A Dictionary of Buddhism* (1981) and *The Buddha's Philosophy of Man* (1981).

DONALD S. LOPEZ, JR is Professor of Buddhist and Tibetan Studies at the University of Michigan. His recent books include *Buddhism in Practice* (editor) and *Elaborations on Emptiness, Uses of the Heart Sutra* (author).

STEWART MCFARLANE lectures in Religious Studies at the University of Lancaster. He is also Visiting Professor at the Chung Hwa Institute of Buddhist Studies, Taiwan. He has contributed to a number of publications including, *Religion, World Encyclopedia of Peace*, *Penguin Dictionary of Religions* and the *British Journal of Religious Education*. He is currently working on a volume on the religious and philosophical implications of eastern martial arts.

INDIRA MAHALINGAM is a Senior Lecturer in Law at the University of Exeter, and a Special Lecturer in Indian Philosophy at the University of Nottingham. She co-founded and co-edits *Asian Philosophy* with Brian Carr, and has written widely in both law (international trade and information technology) and in philosophy (Western and Asian). She is a Fellow of the Royal Asiatic Society and a member of the Royal Institute of International Affairs. She edits the journal *Information and Communications Technology Law*.

JOHN C. MARALDO is Professor of Philosophy at the University of North Florida, Jacksonville and was Guest Professor at Kyoto University in 1987–8 while a Fellow of the Social Science Research Council, and Guest Scholar in 1984–5 while a fellow of the Japan Foundation. He is the author of *Der hermeneutische Zirkel: Untersuchungen zu Schleiermacher, Dilthey und Heidegger*, co-author (with James G. Hart) of *The Piety of Thinking: Essays by Martin Heidegger with Notes and Commentary*, co-editor (with James W. Heisig) of *Rude Awakenings: Zen, the Kyoto School and the Question of Nationalism*, and co-editor (with Heinrich Dumoulin) of *Buddhism in the Modern World*. He has published articles on Nishida Kitarō, Japanese Philosophy, Zen Buddhism and the methodology of Buddhist studies, and has translated several books and articles relating to Zen Buddhism and to the Buddhist–Christian dialogue.

HAJIME NAKAMURA is Professor Emeritus of the University of Tokyo and Director of The Eastern Institute. He is a member of the Academy of Japan, and an Honorary Fellow of the Royal Asiatic Society. He was awarded the honorary degree of Vidya-Vacaspati by the President of the Republic of India, Dr Sarvepalli Radhakrishnan. He has published widely in both English and Japan including *A Comparative History of Ideas*, *Indian Buddhism* and *History of Early Vedanta Philosophy*.

IAN RICHARD NETTON teaches Islamic philosophy and theology in the Department of Arabic and Middle Eastern Studies, University of Leeds where he is Head of the Department and Professor of Arabic Studies. His books include *Muslim Neoplatonists* (1982), *Middle East Materials* (1983), *Arabia and the Gulf* (editor) (1986), *Allāh Transcendent: Studies in the Structure and Semiotics of Islamic Philosophy, Theology and Cosmology* (1989) and *Al-Fārābī and his School* (1992) as well as numerous articles on Islamic philosophy and theology, medieval Arab travellers and comparative religion.

DANIEL JOHN O'CONNOR is Emeritus Professor of Philosophy at the University of Exeter where he was Professor from 1957 to 1979. Before that he held positions at the University of Natal, University College of North Staffordshire, and the University of Liverpool. He has published widely on a variety of philosophical subjects including *John Locke* (1957), *Introduction to Symbolic Logic* (with A. H. Basson) (1953), *Introduction to the Philosophy of Education* (1957), *Aquinas and Natural Law* (1968), *Free Will* (1971), *The Correspondence Theory of Truth* (1973), *Elementary Logic* (with Betty Powell) (1980) and *Introduction to the Theory of Knowledge* (with Brian Carr) (1982). He also edited and contributed to *A Critical History of Western Philosophy*.

R. C. PANDEYA was Professor of Philosophy at the University of Delhi. He is the author of *Problem of Meaning in Indian Philosophy* and *Panorama of Indian Philosophy*.

KARL H. POTTER is Professor of Philosophy and South Asian Studies at the University of Washington, Seattle. He is the editor of the *Encyclopedia of Indian Philosophies*, an ongoing series of works on each of the systems of Indian thought, edited by renowned scholars, in which summaries of all available works of the system are prepared by scholars throughout the world.

K. VASUDEVA REDDY is a distinguished alumnus of Andhra University where he received the Dr S. Radhakrishnan Prize for Philosophy in 1996. He joined Sri Venkateswara University to do research in social philosophy in ancient India under the guidance of Professor Sarasvati Chennakesavan. After completing his PhD he obtained a U.G.T. fellowship for work on the preparation of the Dictionary of Indian Philosophical Terms. He continued to work as a research assistant at the university and was made a lecturer in the philosophy department in 1975. Currently he is the administrative head of the department. His special interests are social and political philosophies of India.

ARCHANA ROY taught philosophy at the University of Delhi. She has published three books; *A Short Commentary on Gilbert Ryle's 'The Concept of Mind'*, *Western Philosophy from Descartes to Kant* and *Metaphysics and Epistemology*. She has published articles in philosophy journals including the proceedings of the Indian Philosophical Congress in 1964. Her subjects of interest include epistemology, analytic philosophy, contemporary British and European thought, including phenomenology and existentialism.

PADMASIRI DE SILVA is currently a Research Fellow at Monash University. He was previously Professor and Head of the Department of Philosophy, University of Peradeniya, Sri Lanka. He is presently Senior Teaching Fellow at the National University of Singapore. From 1987 to 1989 he was Visiting Fulbright Professor at the University of Pittsburgh, Visiting Professor ISLE Programme in 1984 and Senior Research Fellow and Co-ordinator of the Philosophy Programme IFS in Sri Lanka. He is the author of a number of books and articles.

NINIAN SMART is J. F. Rowny Professor of Comparative Religions in the University of California, Santa Barbara. He founded the University of Lancaster's pioneering Department of Religious Studies, and is the author of numerous books including *Buddhism and Christianity: Rivals and Allies* (1993).

FRANCIS Y. K. SOO received his MA in political science at the University of the Philippines, his MA in Asian studies in Harvard University and his PhD from Boston

College. His major publications include *Mao Tse-tung's Theory of Dialectic* (1981), *Marriage and the Family: Their Values* (1987) and *Contemporary American Philosophy* (1990, in Chinese). Since 1987, he has been the director of the China Project at Boston College which aims to promote critical study of Western Philosophy among Chinese scholars.

WANG RUI SHENG is Professor in the Institute of Philosophy, Chinese Academy of Social Science and has held positions in the Graduate School of the Chinese Academy of Social Science, at Beijing Teachers' College and is Vice-president of the Union of Historical Materialism of China. His major publications include *Theory of Man in Marx* (1984), *Commodity Economy and Mental Civilization* (1987), *On Style of Life* (1989) and *An Introduction to Social Philosophy* (1994).

WILLIAM MONTGOMERY WATT is Professor Emeritus at the University of Edinburgh where he was Head of the Department of Arabic and Islamic Studies from 1947 to 1979. He has written a large number of books on Islamic subjects, of which the most important are: *Muhammad at Mecca* (1953), *Muhammad at Medina* (1956), *Islam and the Integration of Society* (1961), *The Formative Period of Islamic Thought* (1973), *Islamic Fundamentalism and Modernity* (1988) and *Muhammad's Mecca: History in the Qur'ān* (1988).

KAREL WERNER was born in 1925 in Czechoslovakia and appointed lecturer in Sanskrit and Indian civilization at the University of Olomouc in 1948. Banned from academia in 1951 by the Communist regime he spent several years in the coal mines and other manual jobs following an investigation into his publishing activities abroad. Able to leave the country in 1968 after the Soviet invasion he worked at Cambridge University Library while teaching part-time at Churchill College. In 1969 he was Spalding lecturer in Indian philosophy and religion at the School of Oriental Studies, University of Durham where he worked until his retirement in 1990. He is now Professor in the Institute of the Study of Religions, Masaryk University, Czech Republic, and honorary professional research associate in the Department of the Study of Religions, SOAS, London University. His publications include *Hatha Yoga* (1969, 1971), *Yoga and Indian Philosophy* (1977, 1980), *The Yogi and the Mystic* (1989, 1994), *Symbols in Art and Religion* (1991), *Love Divine* (1993), and *A Popular Dictionary of Hinduism* (1994).

ALAN WILLIAMS is lecturer in Comparative Religion in the Department of Religions and Theology at the University of Manchester. He read Literae Humaniores and Persian and Arabic at the University of Oxford and gained his PhD in Iranian Studies at the School of Oriental and African Studies, London University. He has published a two-volume edition and exegesis of medieval Zoroastrian text, *The Pahlavi Rivayat* (1990) and articles on Zoroastrianism and comparative religion.

LI XI is Research Professor at the Institute of Philosophy, Chinese Academy of Social Sciences and Associate Secretary-General of the Learned Society of the History of Chinese Philosophy. From 1982 to 1986, he was the Chief Editor of the philosophy volume of *The China Great Encyclopedia*. He was also a member of the editorial board of *The Subject of History in Chinese Philosophy* and wrote chapters on Confucius, Guyuanwu, Lizhi, Huhong, Wanguowei and others. From 1986 to 1987 he was Secretary-General of the Academic Commission of the China Confucius Foundation and an editor of Studies on Confucius. He has published numerous articles and is currently working on a book on Mongzi and Xunzi.

ZHANG JIALONG is Research Professor at the Institute of Philosophy, Chinese Academy of Social Sciences. His publications include *The Principles of Formal Logic* (1982), *Axiomatics, Metamathematics and Philosophy* (1983), *Research into History of Western Logic* (1984) and numerous articles. He is the Secretary-General of the Logical Society of China.

ZHUANG CHUNPO (deceased) was born in 1930. After completing his graduate studies at the People's University of China he studied foreign languages at the Institute of Diplomacy. During this time he studied Chinese and Indian Philosophy. From 1961 to 1965 he studied Buddhism under Lyu Cheng, a Buddhist master. He held positions as Lecturer, Associate Professor and Professor at the Institute of Philosophy, Chinese Academy of Social Sciences. He has published widely and written on the lives of Huineng, Zongmi and others.

PREFACE

The idea of producing this work grew out of a conversation with Jonathan Price, then at Routledge, at the celebration of the launching of the Routledge *Encyclopaedia of Philosophy* at Reading University in 1988. That work was edited by Professor G.H.R. Parkinson of Reading, and he made the point that his project had proved to be far bigger and much more time-consuming than he had ever imagined. We can duly report that his warning was very accurate indeed. Jonathan has since moved on to other publishing ventures, but we owe him an enormous debt of gratitude for his support, encouragement and good-natured indulgence and appreciation of the complexities involved in working with fifty other writers from the four corners of the world.

The project then fell into the hands of Seth Denbo, and we could not have hoped for a better pair of hands to take over the project at Routledge. Seth also must be heartily thanked for his support throughout the remaining years it has taken to bring this encyclopedia to completion.

The spur to produce this work was the launching, by Carfax in Abingdon, Oxfordshire of the academic journal *Asian Philosophy* under our joint editorship. Roger Osborne King had the courage to invest in this publishing venture, and we remain extremely grateful for his support. Roger has also now moved on to found a new company, but Carfax did us very proud indeed by putting that journal into the hands of David Green. Under David's stewardship the journal has gone from strength to strength and looks set for a very long and very prosperous future. David has moreover played an important role in helping us to bring into existence the European Society for Asian Philosophy, a society which has so far organized two international conferences and is enthusiastically planning a third. The society's conferences have attracted delegates from many European countries, but also from very many other nations.

One final offshoot of this encyclopedia project (and of the journal) has been the recent creation, at the University of Nottingham, of a Research Centre for Asian

Philosophy within the Philosophy Department. The role of this centre will be to encourage further growth in interest in this area among philosophers in Europe, and continue our collaboration with other philosophers world-wide.

B.C. and I.M., Exeter 1996

GENERAL INTRODUCTION

This collection of some fifty essays on Asian philosophy is designed as a reference volume for students, scholars and others who require more than just a simple sketch of 'oriental' ideas. It has been complied with the intention of doing justice to the arguments, ideas and presuppositions of philosophers working largely outside the confines of western philosophical traditions.

The volume engages in a unique project, that of bringing together scholars from institutions world-wide in an exploration of the great diversity of the philosophical traditions of Asia. These traditions are of quite widespread interest in the West, but their general appreciation falls far short of their vitality, their rigour and their immense contemporary relevance to the established practices of western philosophy. It is hoped that this volume will also prove useful to those working within any one of the Asian traditions who wish to acquire a foundation in other such traditions.

The choice of the title 'Asian philosophy' might give the misleading impression that the ideas discussed in this volume have a natural home only within a limited part of the globe. But the distinction between Asian and western philosophical traditions is a blurred one. Japanese philosophy, for example, has for a century or so had a very deep interest in the philosophers of Germany and of France; before that, Japanese philosophers had found their inspiration in systems of thought that had come from India and China. Chinese philosophy, as another example, is far from ignorant of and uninspired by the philosophers of Europe and of America. And contemporary Indian philosophers are just as at home with Russell, Frege, Wittgenstein and Quine as with Śaṅkara or Aurobindo. Even geographically the term 'Asian' is somewhat misleading, for though Islamic philosophers have the source of their tradition in the Middle East, they are as much involved with the ideas of Plato and Aristotle, and some of them have worked geographically as far west as Spain. The tradition of ancient Persian thought is, surprisingly to some, still alive and well among the Parsi thinkers of present-day Canada.

It cannot be denied that the philosophical styles of Asian philosophers are quite varied, though many of them bear more than a passing resemblance to the 'critical analytic' style of Anglo-American philosophy. We have not tried to force upon our contributors a standard style of presentation. On the contrary, we have encouraged our writers to work within the styles which best suit them, since the volume then stands as a representative sample of the way philosophers work and have worked in China, in India, in Japan and so forth. Readers will find that the chapters are even so quite accessible and can be readily appreciated for their academic rigour. We have indeed included chapters written by philosophers within and outside the countries in which the Asian traditions have their roots, with the intention of providing a diversity of treatment of those traditions. There is, therefore, no attempt to suggest an 'orthodoxy' in the present perspective on their histories, or in the current practice of Asian philosophy.

The chapters have – again a little artificially – been gathered into six parts, under the headings Persian, Indian, Buddhist, Chinese, Japanese and Islamic. The artificiality is most pronounced in the case of Buddhist philosophy, since Buddhism as a religion and as a philosophical movement began in India, spreading north and south, then further east through China, Korea and Japan and even west through Europe and North America. The division between the Buddhist and the Indian, Chinese and Japanese parts of the collection may be excused, nevertheless, by the fact that Buddhism has seen such a variety of manifestations in different areas of the globe. On its journey outside India it has found renewed vigour from its meetings with other indigenous systems of thought – as they have from it in their turn.

Within each part some chapters are devoted to individual philosophers who have played a seminal role in that tradition. Such chapters are few, however, all the others having a wider focus on ideas and debates. Each part begins with a chapter devoted to the origins of the tradition in question, and ends with a chapter which sketches the contemporary philosophical preoccupations of the descendants of that tradition. These latter chapters bring out quite vividly the extent to which contemporary philosophers world-wide are ready and able to learn and absorb from, and to contribute afresh to, the discussions which have been taking place elsewhere.

The other chapters are focused on broad philosophical areas, grouped together as the philosophy of knowledge and reality, of language and logic, and of morals and society. There is, of course, again an appearance of artificiality in such divisions, since, for example, the nature of reality and the nature of moral values are hardly distinct questions. Nevertheless, marking out these areas under such headings is a well-established practice in western philosophical circles even though it is at the same time recognized that they are intimately interconnected. We do not think, therefore, that we are forcing an unnatural structure on to the Asian traditions themselves.

Each part of the encyclopedia begins with a very brief sketch of the relevant tradition, which we hope will provide some pointers to the most prominent features of the terrain. Such sketches are no more than simple and simplistic maps which make no claim to anything more than that; and an exploration of the chapters that follow will soon indicate that alternative maps could and would have been drawn by other writers. In their turn, a serious reader will wish to treat those chapters as only the start of a journey into the Asian traditions, and our contributors have therefore been encouraged to give fairly substantial lists of further reading.

The encyclopedia includes a fairly extensive Glossary of Asian philosophical terms, which has been divided into sections relating to each of the six traditions. This has led to a certain degree of repetition, but it is hoped that such a division will prove helpful to the reader. Cross-referencing has been given where appropriate to other sections of the Glossary. We have tried, as far as possible, to take note of the diverse comments of our contributors in compiling this Glossary.

Romanization of Asian terms and names has been standardized, again as far as possible given the different practices of different scholars. Diacritics have been used in as simplified a form as possible, and we have chosen to adopt the newer Pinyin romanization system instead of the Wade–Giles system for Chinese.

B.C. and I.M.

Part I

PERSIAN PHILOSOPHY

INTRODUCTION

The dates of Zarathushtra, the prophet and founder of the religious philosophy Zoroastrianism (after the Greek version of his name, Zoroaster) are still strongly contested by modern scholarship, and possible dates vary from about 1400 BC to 500 BC. He is generally regarded to have lived in what is now north or east Iran. The religious tradition of Zoroastrianism is widely spread, represented in greatest numbers by the Parsis of the Indian sub-continent.

The ancient text, the *Avesta*, is divided into the *Yasna* (liturgy), the *Yashts* (sacrificial hymns) and the *Videvdat* (ritual purification). Included in the *Yasna* are the *Gāthās*, that portion of the *Avesta* which scholarship and religious tradition tend to proclaim as the essential teaching of the prophet Zarathushtra himself.

The history of Zoroastrianism can be roughly divided into three phases. The first, including the time of Zarathushtra himself, ended with the conquest by Alexander of the ancient Persian Empire in the late fourth century BC. The second phase was that of the Sasanian Empire. Zoroastrianism flourished as a state religion and saw the composition (in the Pahlavi language) of rich philosophical texts, which attempted a reclamation and reinterpretation of the ancient Avestan inheritance with a certain emphasis on the social dimension. This period ended with the Muslim conquests of the seventh century AD, and the final phase in its history began with migration of Zoroastrians to the Indian sub-continent, where they came to be known as 'Parsis' or people from Persia. Since that time Zoroastrianism has undergone a dynamic process of adjustment to the rival religious, philosophical and social traditions it has lived within and alongside of – from the Hindu and Muslim to the Protestant British culture of the nineteenth and early twentieth century.

In essence a religious philosophy, Zoroastrianism focuses on the problem of the moral and spiritual nature of man. Though it is often chastised by its opponents – and sometimes lauded by its proponents – as a ditheistic or even polytheistic system, the stronger emphasis seems to have been on developing a monotheism which yet resolves the problem of evil and gives freedom of moral choice to men. The cosmogony and eschatology trace the history of the world from its creation by the one god, Ahura Mazdā (in Pahlavi, Ohrmazd), through a struggle between goodness and evil personified by Angra Mainyu (in Pahlavi, Ahriman) to a state where man is rewarded by eternal happiness on earth. Zurvanism, with its emphasis on fate, is an atypical deviation from the essentially libertarian metaphysics. The moral and social philosophy is founded on the place of man within this struggle.

Of epistemological issues the most fundamental must be the prophetic status of Zarathushtra himself, in which his authority on his god's words is secured by their direct communication to him. But no less pressing, in the light of its history, are questions of the authenticity of those words in the varied attempts at reclamation and reconstruction within the tradition itself. Indeed, modern scholarship – from a neutral position outside the tradition – exhibits a lively disagreement over such fundamental questions as the authentic or core teaching of Zarathushtra, and the boundaries between its adaptation and relinquishment.

B.C. and I.M.

1

THE ORIGINS OF ZOROASTRIAN PHILOSOPHY

Mary Boyce

ZARATHUSHTRA'S DATE AND LAND

The Iranian religion variously known as Mazdaism, Magism, Parsism, 'the Persian religion' and Zoroastrianism is the oldest of the credal (as opposed to ethnic) faiths. It was founded in a region where there was then no knowledge of writing, and no long-lived kingdoms or other chronological markers by which to date events. The only dates assigned in antiquity to its founder Zarathushtra – better known in the West by a Greek form of his name, Zoroaster – were both invented by Greeks. One set him 5,000 years before the Trojan War, i.e. at *c.*6000 BC, the other at '258 years before Alexander', that is, before the Seleucid era which began in 312 BC, i.e. at 600 BC. The first, fantastically too early, was proposed by disciples of Plato; the second was evolved in the Hellenistic period on the basis of the fiction that Pythagoras had studied in Babylon with the great oriental sage (Kingsley 1990). This second one was adopted by Magian scholastics, doubtless to supply what they felt to be a lack in their own tradition, and so gained some credence among western academics in modern times. Thanks to finding distinguished and eloquent champions, this date became widely accepted as indicating approximately when Zarathushtra lived; but gradually the majority of scholars working in the field came to agree with what some had always maintained, that it is far too late to be reconciled with other data. It was therefore dismissed by most specialists as worthless even before its fictional origin was clearly demonstrated. Their conclusions have, however, been slow to filter through to the larger circle of those generally interested in the subject.

With both these dates rejected, Zarathushtra's time can be reckoned only approximately from the evidence of the *Avesta*, the collection of Zoroastrian holy texts. These, composed orally over generations, are in an otherwise unknown eastern Iranian language, called therefore simply Avestan. In it two stages are clearly distinguishable, of which Old Avestan is represented by only a small corpus of texts. These include the all-important *Gāthās*, seventeen hymns attributed to the prophet himself. They were strictly memorized by his followers and, arranged according to metre, were transmitted as *manthras*, inspired utterances, recited to form a protective frame round the rites of the *yasna*. This is the main Zoroastrian act of worship, whose liturgy was later extended around them, so that they are now cited as *Y(asna)* 28–34, 43–51, 53. The rites themselves were accompanied by the other main group of Old Avestan texts, the *Yasna Haptanhaiti*, a short liturgy almost certainly composed by Zarathushtra (*Y*. 35–42. Narten 1986, Boyce 1992: 87–94).

Old Avestan is very close to the language of the *Rig Veda* (held to have been composed between *c*.1500 and 900 BC), but is in some respects the more archaic (Kellens and Pirart 1988: 13). A considerable time is thought to have been needed for Old Avestan to develop into early Young Avestan, and Young Avestan then evolved further before the canon of the holy texts was closed. This, as their contents show (being related solely to eastern Iran), took place before Zoroastrianism, which had spread among eastern Iranian peoples, was adopted in western Iran by the Achaemenian royal family and became the state religion of the first Persian Empire (539–331 BC). So if the latest Young Avestan texts belong to the sixth century or earlier, the earliest probably go back to at least the eighth or ninth centuries, with the *Gāthās* being very considerably older. One of the first scholars to attempt to date them on the linguistic evidence set them at *c*.1400 BC (Geldner 1885: 653–4), and such a date remains possible in the light also of the social conditions reflected in them. Gathic society appears simpler than that of the Young Avesta, a pastoral one whose members were mostly herdsmen living close to their cattle, so that a single word, *pasu-vīra*, 'cattle-(and)-men', described their community. The only distinct professional group appears to be that of priests. The horse-drawn chariot was known (first attested on the Inner Asian steppes around 1500 BC (Gening 1977), but there is no evidence that a class of 'chariot riders', i.e. a warlike aristocracy, had yet evolved (Boyce 1987). Young Avestan society is formally divided into three groups: priests, 'chariot riders', and peasant-farmers, with agriculture, instead of cattle-herding, playing a large role. This more complex social structure may reasonably be supposed to have evolved in consequence of the great migrations (Polomé 1982: 170). The Iranians then followed their Indo-Aryan cousins south off the steppes into Soviet Central Asia, and then, branching westward, made themselves masters of what came to be called after them Iran. This movement is generally thought by archaeologists to have been at its peak around 1200–1000 BC. The indications thus all point to Zarathushtra having lived before then, sometime between perhaps 1400 and 1200 BC (*c*.1000 BC according to Gnoli 1980: ch. 5).

The tradition preserved in the *Young Avesta* about his homeland is that it was called *Airyana Vaejah*, 'The Aryan (or Iranian) Expanse', with fainter indications (Boyce

1992: ch. 1) that it lay far to the north of Iran. Presumably it was a region on the steppes once claimed as their own by his people, whose exact location was forgotten after they moved away; and in time it became for them a semi-mythical holy land lying at the centre of the world, not only the home of the prophet but the scene of all the great mythical and legendary events in their prehistory.

THE OLD IRANIAN RELIGION

The Old Iranian religion in which Zarathushtra was trained as a priest can be partially reconstructed from those elements in Zoroastrianism which are to be found also in the Vedic religion of India, since these can reasonably be presumed to be a common inheritance from the time when the Iranians and Indo-Aryans were one people. Their evolution linguistically into two distinct groups is generally thought to have taken place *c.*2000–1800 BC.

A dominant concept of the Old Iranian religion is thus known to have been *asha* (Vedic *ṛta*), the principle of order, that which ought to be, which is right. This should rule all aspects of existence. It was in accord with *asha* that the sun rose and set, the seasons changed, and rain fell and made the grasses grow and the creatures flourish. It was also through observing *asha* that humans throve, living thus in accord with their true nature: upholding justice, truth and fidelity, fulfilling family and tribal duties, and giving due worship to the gods. The opposite to *asha* was *drug* (Sanskrit *druh*), 'that which is crooked, deceiving'; but this is not prominent in Vedic thought, and was probably less vividly apprehended than *asha* by the proto-Indo-Iranians, whose outlook seems on the whole to have been positive and optimistic.

The gods whom they worshipped were many, for they were animatists, believing that all things, whether tangible or intangible, animate or inanimate, possessed an invisible inner power which they perceived as sentient spirit, *mainyu*. Probably most *mainyu* were thought to be *spenta*, a word which basically meant 'possessing power', and which, used of divinities, implied 'having power to aid, furthering, supporting, benefiting'. (For references see Boyce 1975:196 n. 26.) Attempts to render this adjective more exactly include 'bounteous' and 'incremental', but these lack the religious overtones which *spenta*, which is roughly the equivalent of 'holy' in its original sense, had probably already acquired by Zarathushtra's day; and 'holy' is accordingly often used to translate it.

Some concepts of *mainyu* – for example those of 'nature' gods, such as the spirits of the sky and earth, sun, moon and stars – remained simple ones, spirit and physical phenomenon being conceived as always in union. Others gathered complexity and evolved into great gods with manifold aspects and powers. Lesser divinities then became associated with them, for the Indo-Iranians characteristically saw their gods as collegial beings, acting in groups or at least amicably associated. The pantheon was thus not static, but continually if slowly evolving through priestly thinking about, and evocation of, the gods. (This process can be observed taking place in the Vedic religion.) In general the divinities were thought of as cosmic beings, without links to any particular places, a consequence presumably of the Indo-Iranians living on the vast plains of Inner Asia, where man had built no cities and raised no temples to house the gods.

The most important group of divinities in the pre-migration days appears to have been the trinity of *Ahuras*, 'Lords', who were the especial guardians of *asha*. Pre-eminent among them was Mazdā, by origin the spirit of wisdom; and beneath him were a close fraternal pair, Mithra and Vouruna Apąm Napāt, respectively by origin the spirits or forces inherent in the solemn pact or covenant, and the formally declared oath. (The name 'Varuṇa' does not appear in Iranian usage, in which this divinity is called simply by cult epithets.) Their Vedic equivalents appear to have been the Asura, Mitra and Varuṇa Apąm Napāt (Thieme 1957: 406–10; Boyce 1975: 40–8; 1986: 148–50; 1993, 35–40). Another Indo-Iranian god who was prominent at the time of the migrations was Indra. His original concept may have been that of the spirit or force which inspired the valiant herdsman when he was called upon to fight; but (to judge from the Vedic evidence) he evolved from a heroic into a virtually amoral war god (see Benveniste and Renou 1934: 189–95), delighting in combat for its own sake and granting favours in return for lavish offerings.

The gods, it was believed, had made the world, it seems from pre-existing materials (Boyce 1975: 131; 1992: 57) with Varuṇa apparently regarded as a chief actor in this, perhaps because of the power attributed to the truly spoken word. The world was held to be composed of seven separate 'creations': the 'sky' of stone (the literal meaning of the word for it, Avestan *asman-*, Vedic *aśman-*), that is, a hard shell enclosing all the rest; water in the lower part of this shell; earth as a round, flat disk lying on the water; and at its centre a plant, an animal (the 'Uniquely created Bull'), and a man. Seventh and last there was fire, which gave warmth and life to the rest. The Vedic cosmogony is rather different; but it can be reasonably assumed that the Old Iranian scheme had evolved to this point before Zarathushtra's lifetime (Boyce 1975:146). The gods then sacrificed the plant, animal and man, which, thus consecrated, generated in dying all plants, animals and peoples of the world. They also set in motion the sun, the greatest manifestation of the creation of fire, which began to regulate life according to *asha*.

Man had the duty, through worship, to strengthen the gods and so help them to maintain the world. As long as he performed this duty, and himself lived according to *asha*, he could expect the world to continue, and the generations of men. Among these he could hope would be the line of his own descendants, maintaining annual offerings for the benefit of his soul. At death a few – probably only leading men – could look forward to escaping the common fate of descent into a shadowy, joyless underworld, and to ascending instead to the realm (*khshathra*) of the gods, a radiant place of all delights, set above the solid sky. To enjoy its pleasures fully the soul needed to be again incarnated; and this, it was believed, would be done from the bones of its former body. The Indo-Aryans rid these bones of flesh by cremation and then buried them; the Iranians may already before Zarathushtra's day have exposed the corpse for the flesh to be devoured by dog and bird. To judge from Indian evidence the union of soul and recreated body was held to take place about a year after death.

Forces of evil were perceived, malevolent beings which inhabited this earth. Although they could do harm, they were thought of as less than the gods, and the individual could seek to propitiate or ward them off with offerings and spells.

ZARATHUSHTRA AND THE *GĀTHĀS*

Zarathushtra, it is evident from the *Gāthās*, was a qualified and practising priest, and according to Indo-Iranian custom he would have begun his training in childhood, learning about the gods and the rituals for their proper worship, and being taught myths and legends, priestly lore and the craft of composing religious verses, which if inspiration came could become *manthras*, holy words of power. For some pupils with especial gifts – which the prophet undoubtedly possessed – there was probably also training in the techniques of attaining mantic experience.

The *Gāthās* suggest that Zarathushtra grew up in a stable pastoral society, whose chief worship was offered to the *Ahuras*, and that he became deeply imbued with the values of its ordered ways; but that he then experienced ruthless raids on that society by predatory bands – 'non-herdsmen among herdsman' (*Y.* 49.4) – who carried off cattle and goods with shedding of blood. These raiders were evidently fellow-Iranians; and their activities seem to belong to a turbulent time on the steppes which preceded the migrations. Some men then, having abandoned traditional ways, sought apparently to live by preying off their fellow-tribesmen until eventually the chiefs of their war-bands led them south off the steppes to find richer plunder elsewhere.

The experience of such raids, and the contrast between the law-abiding herdsmen and the greedy predators, evidently had a profound effect on Zarathushtra and was a vital factor in the evolution of his new beliefs, by which he sought to account for the human predicament and the encounters of good and evil. Having failed to persuade his own community to accept these beliefs (*Y.* 46.1), he left it, and gained a hearing for them from Vishtaspa, the chieftain of another tribe, who brought all his people to adopt the new faith. According to the tradition (Jackson 1899:chs 8–10), Zarathushtra lived long after this, married and had children; and so he was presumably able himself to establish his religion firmly, linking beliefs to observances in ways that enabled it to endure, despite harsh vicissitudes, from those distant preliterate times down to the present day.

Part of the enormous strength of this religion lies in the logic and comprehensiveness of its doctrines. Once its premisses are granted, the whole system coheres in an intellectually satisfying way, and its doctrines, although complex, can be made accessible through observances to its simplest adherents. Moreover, its teachings satisfy human hopes, offering not only explanation and coherence, but also closure, a final blessed ending; and the actions which they require, though morally demanding, lie within the scope of ordinary human endeavour. But though Zarathushtra's ethical teachings can be applied in modern life, and though his doctrines are in some measure generally familiar (through borrowings by Judaism, Christianity and Islam) (Boyce and Grenet 1991: ch. 11), in other respects they are immensely strange and difficult for modern urban man to comprehend, fashioned as they were by a prophet who, though one of the great innovators in man's religious history, was himself nurtured in archaic ways of thought.

These difficult elements in his doctrines remained significant for his own community, and have continued to shape their lives because of an unbroken tradition of belief and practice; but Western scholars necessarily approached them mainly through texts alone, especially the *Gāthās*. These short hymns are subtle, passionate, personal utterances, many of their verses being addressed to Ahura Mazdā himself. In them there is no question of a full or systematic exposition of doctrine, but the whole essential Zoroastrian theology, as known from the later literature and living faith, appears assumed there, and some crucial beliefs are conveyed with poetic and visionary power.

These hymns present enormous difficulties for the translator, and probably even when they were first composed were fully understood only by the learned and the already enlightened. Layers of meaning appear present in their densely packed, richly allusive verses; and since the corpus of Old Avestan texts is small, they contain for the modern student the added difficulties of unknown words and intricate problems of syntax. Without the help of the later Zoroastrian literature and living tradition they would have been baffling in the extreme; but with it, many verses can be essentially understood. Others are likely to continue to defy satisfactory interpretation, although new light is being steadily shed on these texts through close comparisons with Rig Vedic vocabulary and usages. They present a major challenge and source of interest to students of Vedic and Old Avestan, and the most recent translations of them have all been made by scholars whose primary interest is language, and who tend to treat the *Gāthās* as a closed corpus, thus avoiding the need to consider them seriously in relation to the Zoroastrian religion. H. Humbach (1959) offered valuable identifications of ritual terms and allusions, previously misunderstood, but made little attempt to elucidate a system of doctrine; S. Insler (1975), in contrast treated all ritual and many doctrinal allusions allegorically, seeking throughout a lofty, somewhat vague theism; and J. Kellens and E. Pirart (1988) produced an idiosyncratic and over-sceptical rendering of what they maintained were no more than very restricted ritual texts, composed by a group of working priests. These translations need therefore to be used with caution and preferably together, with reference also to some earlier, more conservative ones, for example those of J. Darmesteter (1892–3), C. Bartholomae (1905),

H. Lommel (published posthumously, 1971) and J. Duchesne-Guillemin (1952), which, if outdated linguistically, pay more respect not only to Zoroastrian exegesis and later literature, but also to the actual beliefs and practice of the community – a *magisterium* which has only slowly been impaired in modern times. For the Zoroastrians themselves the *Gāthās* had become with the passage of time great sacred *manthras*, whose meaning it was not necessary to comprehend; and modern translations by them have either depended closely on western ones (principally Bartholomae's) or have been idealistically free renderings (for example Taraporewala 1951).

ZARATHUSHTRA'S TEACHINGS

Among the essential elements in Zarathushtra's thinking appear his love for this world and his conviction of its goodness when ordered by *asha*. Looking at it in this respect with the same eyes as his ancestors, he apprehended spirit, *mainyu*, in all things, to be revered and cherished. Those spirits which were *spenta* were perceived by him as upholding *asha*, and man's own aim should be to live according to *asha* and thus to become *ashavan*, 'possessing *asha*'. This is the central moral precept of Zoroastrianism, and it implies living an ordered purposeful life in 'thought, word and act'. This series of words recurs, with subtle variations, throughout the *Gāthās* (Humbach 1959:I.55–6), and it seems probable that Zarathushtra's emphasis on the need for all-embracing moral activity in these three ways reflects the pattern of his own training as a priest, which required that the gods should be worshipped with right intention, right invocation and right rituals. Living according to *asha* meant that the individual strove to acquire the virtues believed to be proper to a human being, notably wisdom, justice, truthfulness, loyalty, valour. These were thought of not as inherent qualities to be cultivated, but as external forces or spirits, *mainyu*, which through rightly directed endeavour might be brought to dwell within one.

Part of *ashavan* activity was offering regular worship to the gods at the traditional times of dawn, noon and eve (*Y.* 44.5). Priests would naturally have been engaged more often and longer in worship, and so have had constant occasion to fix their thoughts on the divine. Zarathushtra himself had evidently been brought up deeply to venerate the trinity of *Ahuras*, whom he twice names in the *Gāthās* by an evidently ancient formula, 'Mazdā – (and-the-other) Ahuras' (*Y.* 30.9; 31.4; Boyce 1975:225). This formula shows that pre-eminence among the *Ahuras* was attributed to Mazdā before Zarathushtra's day, a fact attested also for the Old Persian religion, in which for him alone title and name became fused through constant evocation, so that he was worshipped as Ahuramazda (Middle Persian Ohrmazd). To Zarathushtra himself, however, can be attributed the development of this veneration of Mazdā to the point where he saw him not only as greatest of the *Ahuras* but greatest of all the gods, in fact God himself in the sense of the one immortal eternal divine Being. This was such a huge theological step that it inevitably invites speculation as to how he came to make it. There is no evidence for the existence of a supreme ruler among the Iranian steppe-dwellers to provide an earthly model for a king of the gods. On the contrary, the *Gāthās* indicate a turbulent society with a number of chieftains, many of whom the prophet fiercely condemned (for example *Y.* 32.11; 46.11). It seems more likely, therefore, that he reached his lofty new concept of Mazdā through meditating on priestly speculations about the origins of life; for if in the beginning there had been one plant, one animal and one man from which all the rest had sprung, why should matters not have been similar in the divine sphere, with one original *spenta* God who brought into being from his own essence all other *spenta* divinities?

Zarathushtra must have meditated deeply on these matters before reaching his new concept of Mazdā, which his own words show rested also on mystical experience, on the conviction that he had seen and spoken with him. In accord with Indo-Iranian tradition, he perceived him anthropomorphically, with mouth and tongue, eye and hand (*Y.* 28.11; 31.3, 13; 43.4), but also as majestic beyond common imagining, wearing the sky as garment (*Y.* 30.5). Nevertheless he was Spirit, *Mainyu*, the 'most *spenta*' of all spirits, Spenishta Mainyu (*Y.* 30.5). This transcendent Being the prophet perceived as acting, and being at will immanent, through a power or force which he termed his spirit, naming this the Holy but also the Holiest Spirit, Spenta Mainyu, Spenishta Mainyu. The use of the latter term reflects the fact that Zarathushtra apprehended Mazdā's spirit sometimes as a distinct force, sometimes as virtually identical with Mazdā himself. This perhaps mystical blurring of concepts was logically clarified in the Young Avesta, where Spenishta Mainyu is reserved for Ahura Mazdā as one of his regular invocations (*Vendidad*, *passim*; *Y.* 1.1; *Yasht* 1.1, 12) and Spenta Mainyu is kept for his Holy Spirit (with an exception in *Yasht* 19.44, 46).

Zarathushtra further perceived Mazdā as possessing six other great *spenta* forces to which he had given existence as separate spirits, but which remained part of his being in ways that distinguished them from other gods. These formed with him or his Holy Spirit a divine Heptad, a concept which is at the heart of Zoroastrian moral and dogmatic theology (Jackson 1904: 161; Lommel 1959, 1964), but which is difficult for non-Zoroastrians to grasp. One of the greatest of these beings, ethically and doctrinally, is (Vohu) Manah, whose name is variously rendered as '(Good) Thought' or 'Purpose'. (With the names of members of the Heptad epithets occur in the *Gāthās* which become fixed only in the tradition.) In one of the *Gāthās* Zarathushtra speaks allusively of his enlightenment (*Y.* 43.7ff.), and there it is Vohu Manah who comes to him with Spenta Mainyu. It seems that he then actually 'saw' these two great beings with inward, visionary eye. Also one of the greatest of the six is Asha, once (*Y.* 28.8) called Vahishta, 'Best', which became his fixed epithet. He is the hypostasis of the principle of *asha*, and his name as ethical divinity is usually rendered as 'Righteousness' or 'Truth'. He has great importance, appearing often with Vohu Manah, but invoked even more frequently. Their closeness to Mazdā is brought out by the fact that although Zarathushtra usually addresses his god with the singular 'Thou', sometimes when he invokes him with members of the Heptad, or, as it seems, with them in mind, he uses the plural, 'You'. For example, against 'Tell me the things which Thou knowest, Ahura' (*Y*. 48.2) there is 'With Asha do You, O Mazdā, acknowledge me. . . . Approach now, Ahura, through our gift to You' (*Y*. 29.11).

A second pair within the Heptad are linked through having a complementary character and moral status. These are (Spenta) Armaiti and Khshathra (Vairya). Armaiti's name is usually rendered as '(Holy) Devotion' or 'Obedience', Khshathra's as '(Desirable) Dominion'. The latter concept is the more complex, since the noun *khshathra* can mean not only dominion but, secondarily, the place where dominion is exerted, realm, kingdom. Vedic *kṣatra* has the same range of meanings, and in both languages the word is used for the kingdom of the gods on high. As ethical divinity, Khshathra embodies the power of *spenta* authority, which almost all can exert in one way or another (Lommel 1959 apud Schlerath:257–8).

The last pair of the great six are Haurvatat, 'Wholeness, Health' and Ameretat, '(Long) Life, Immortality'. They have no epithets and are less prominent than the others, presumably because what they hypostatize is less immediately obtainable through moral striving. Their concepts appear to have evolved from Zarathushtra's deep sense of the positive good of health and life. Like the others', their names recur in the *Gāthās* and all six are named together, with Spenta Mainyu, in *Y*. 47.1: 'Through the Holy Spirit and Best Purpose, by act and word in accord with Truth, They shall grant him [i.e. the just man] Wholeness and Immortality – Lord Mazdā together with Dominion and Devotion.'

It would be possible in this verse to render *haurvatat-* and *ameretat-* as common nouns, and this is often the case with names of members of the Heptad in the *Gāthās*, for the virtues or qualities which they hypostatize not only belong to God and are divine but can be brought to dwell in men. There is, it must be admitted, a logical problem here, for presumably to entertain Asha within oneself one must already be partly, or at least striving to be, *ashavan*; but this perhaps accounts for the great importance of Vohu Manah, Good Purpose, in what is essentially a religious, not a philosophical, system.

Since, as the tradition establishes, Zarathushtra held that Mazdā brought all *spenta* divinities into existence from his own originally unique selfhood, it seems natural that he should use the metaphor of fatherhood in speaking of Mazdā's relationship with members of the Heptad, i.e. of Asha (*Y*. 44.3; 47.2), Vohu Manah (*Y*. 31.8; 45.4; 47.8) and Armaiti (*Y*. 45.4). The prophet calls him also the creator (*dąmī-*) of Asha (*Y*. 31.8); and using a synonym, *dātar-*, declares him further to be 'Creator of all things by the Holy Spirit' (*Y*. 44.7). How he was held to have performed the act of creation is perhaps indicated in a verse where Zarathushtra says to him: 'In the beginning Thou didst fashion for us by Thy thought creatures and inner selves (*daēnā-*) and intelligences. . . . Thou didst create corporeal life' (*Y*. 31.11).

The world which Ahura Mazdā created was that of the seven separate creations described above; and by another remarkable step in thought, Zarathushtra saw each of these seven creations as having one of the Heptad as its protector, dwelling within it. The transcendent creator was thus immanent through his hypostatized powers in the good world of his creation, which he helped in this way to sustain and defend. The links (in the order of creation) are as follows (Zaehner 1956:32–3; Boyce 1975:205ff.): Khshathra, strong Dominion, is guardian of the sky of stone; Haurvatat, Wholeness, of health-giving water; Obedience of the patient earth that bears all; Ameretat of life-sustaining plants; Good Purpose of the beneficent cow; the Holy Spirit of the *ashavan* man, who with his capacity for wisdom and exercising choice is the nearest of the creations to God; and Asha of fire, which through the sun regulates the natural world, and through the fire of the ordeal helped to administer justice. The concept of members of the Heptad being present in the seven creations has been perceptively analysed in the following words:

> For us . . . Good Purpose and the tending of cattle are admittedly two wholly different things. But must it always have been so? Could not at a certain epoch abstract and concrete have appeared to the human spirit as of unified being, the abstract as the inner reality of the concrete? So that, for instance, Pious Devotion and the earth were the spiritual and material aspects of the same thing. A division of this kind in general goes very deep in the Avestan concept of the world, and if this touches on 'speculation', I do not know why this word so readily attracts the adjectives 'learned, priestly, theological', whereby apparently it is intended to characterize a secondary development – secondary in opposition to the way of thought of a creative time or personality. I do not believe that speculation was solely or even predominantly a matter for theologians as distinct from the creative prophets, who were able to unite visionary perception with meditative speculation. Or do we consider something which is strange to us, and therefore appears artificial, as speculation, when it is unsought primary intuition?'
>
> (Lommel 1926:31–2 *apud* Schlerath 1970)

Such intuitions could have come to Zarathushtra the more readily because this manner of perceiving reality was not new for his people. For example, since proto-Indo-Iranian times both lesser *Ahuras* had themselves been associated with two of the creations, in which they also were believed to dwell at will – Mithra in fire, Varuna in water (hence his ancient epithet of Apąm Napāt, 'Son of the Waters'). In their case these associations appear to have been perceived because of the use of fire and water in judicial ordeals, presided over by these divinities as guardians of *asha* (Meillet 1907:156–8, Lüders 1951:655–74). Belief in the immanence of the Heptad was reached by Zarathushtra most probably through meditation on the priestly act of worship, the *yasna*. Since its rituals are essentially those of the Brahmanic *yajña*, the *yasna* evidently goes back to proto-Indo-Iranian times. At it three main offerings were made: a blood sacrifice devoted to one of the divine beings, an oblation to fire from that sacrifice, and a libation to water, the *parahaoma*, from the expressed juice of the *haoma* mixed with water and milk. The intention of the service appears to have been to gratify and strengthen the divinity to whom it was offered, and to purify and strengthen the life-giving creations of fire and water and through them the whole natural world. As priest, Zarathushtra speaks of sacrifice (*izhā-*) and of the spirit or power within the sacrifice, Izhā (Vedic Iḍā). 'In the famed footsteps of Izhā I shall circumambulate You, O Mazdā, with hands outstretched' (*Y.* 49.10). At the *yasna* the divinity invoked was believed to descend, seating himself on herbage strewn to receive him; and these words suggest how vividly the prophet apprehended the real presence there of his God. Further, all the Heptad could be thought of as present regularly, at every service, through the things which there represented their creations: Khshathra, of the sky of stone, through the stone pestle and mortar for crushing the *haoma*; Haurvatat through the pure water for the *parahaoma*; Armaiti through the earth of the ritual precinct; Ameretat through the *haoma*; Vohu Manah through the sacrificial beast; Spenta Mainyu through the officiating *ashavan* priest; and Asha through the ritual fire. Zarathushtra could thus be profoundly aware of the immediate presence of the Heptad within and around him as he worshipped, strengthening him with their powers while he consecrated their creations by consecrating the ritual precinct and the objects in it, and so in turn strengthened them. (The Indo-Iranians conceived of even their great gods as powerful but not all-powerful, and not without need of men's worship to give them added strength. So Zarathushtra addressed Mazdā himself: 'Arise . . . take to thyself might through devotion', *Y.* 33.12.) To judge from the tradition, the prophet taught his followers to be aware thus of the Heptad in their acts of worship, in the world around them, and, ideally and as a spiritual and ethical goal, as indwelling in themselves through their own strivings. This was not pantheism, for the members of the Heptad personify distinct powers, emanating from and of the same essence as the one eternal Being, but existing as separate divinities through his creative act.

Although the doctrine of the Heptad is at the heart of Zoroastrian theology, forming an essential element in its coherent system, and also in Zoroastrian devotional and ethical life, a number of scholars have denied that it is to be found in the *Gāthās*. The reasons for this are multiple. One is that there is a widely held theory that Zarathushtra taught not merely an original but an enduring and absolute monotheism, denying the existence of any beneficent divine being other than Ahura Mazdā. Even apart from the many invocations of members of the Heptad (seen by such scholars as mere abstractions), there is a whole range of other data in the *Gāthās* to disprove this theory; but it has been repeated so often since it was first advanced (before the *Gāthās* were known in the West) that it has gained academic respectability and survives against the evidence. There appears, moreover, to be a fairly general assumption, especially perhaps among those with a Christian background, that a complex theology is likely to have evolved over centuries in religious schools rather than being created by the founder of a faith. But Zarathushtra, trained from childhood in matters of religion, was uniquely qualified among the great prophets to evolve a completely thought out and coherent system, one which bears the imprint of a single, highly gifted mind and spirit.

A more scholarly reason for not attributing the full doctrine of the Heptad to Zarathushtra is that the relations of only five of them with their creations is attested in the *Gāthās*, those of Spenta Mainyu and Khshathra being lacking; and so it is argued that the full system evolved only later. But since the *Gāthās* are hymns, not theological treatises, gaps must be expected in the attestation of doctrine there. Moreover, belief in the Heptad not only appears to be an integral part of Zarathushtra's theology but is archaic in character; and no satisfactory explanation has ever been offered as to why such a doctrine should have been evolved in later times and have become part of the very essence of his religion. (On the weaknesses of the solitary attempt by Narten 1982:25–7 see Boyce 1984:160.)

That this doctrine was based on apprehensions reached by the prophet through meditating on the *yasna* is borne out by the fact that other *spenta* divinities named in the *Gāthās* have links with the cult (Boyce 1975:195). Of these the one who was later to gain most prominence was Sraosha, the spirit or force within hearkening, by which men hear and obey divine commands, and gods listen favourably to men's prayers (Kreyenbroek 1985:7ff.). His was a concept evolved, it is suggested, by Zarathushtra himself (Spiegel 1873: vol. II, 90; Kreyenbroek 1985: 164–5, 169) through meditation on a traditional ritual phrase that is closely paralleled in Vedic: *səraošō iδā astū*, 'may hearkening be here' (*Y*. 56.1), cf. Vedic *astu śrauṣaṭ* (*Rig Veda* 1.139.1). Sraosha is linked in the *Gāthās* with 'great-gifted Ashi' (*Y*. 43.12), probably in the old religion a goddess of fortune, but in Zarathushtra's highly ethical one the spirit of recompense bringing to each his deserts. Recompense for the *ashavan* was not perceived by the prophet as solely spiritual, for he thought that this good world of Mazdā's creation was to be enjoyed. So the acquiring by the 'herdsman' of the 'joy-bringing cow in calf' (*Y*. 44.6) is probably not to be taken merely metaphorically. Cattle-imagery in the *Gāthās*, like sheep-imagery in the Bible, is undoubtedly rich in symbolic, religious overtones, but appears to have its basis in the solid realities of stock-keeping life.

This cattle-imagery is used impressively in one of the most difficult of the *Gāthās*, *Y*. 29, where the prophet appears to speak of his own mission, appointed by Mazdā for all his lack of worldly power to bring aid to the upright man and helpless cattle. Here underlying a sense of cosmic sorrow and suffering appears to be harsh experience of the cattle-raid, by which the bloodthirsty and wicked (*Y*. 48.11) cruelly injured 'cattle-and-men' (*Y*. 31.15), i.e. ordered pastoral society. These marauders Zarathushtra saw as directly opposed in their lawlessness and greed to the *ashavan* herdsman, patiently tending the *spenta* cow; and he declared them to be *dregvant*, that is, attached to the principle of *drug*, 'crookedness', 'that which is contrary to *asha*. This principle, as we have seen, was probably only vaguely apprehended in the old Iranian religion, as in the *Rig Veda*; and its perception as an active aggressive force, an evil *mainyu*, is generally attributed to the prophet himself, as based on the most personal experiences he has had. . . . He himself has seen into Asha's order, and he proclaims it for him who will hear. But he who has heard must choose whether he will fight with thought, word and deed on Asha's side for the life-strengthening powers, or will follow the Drug.

(Barr 1945 : 134)

In the old Iranian religion, as in the Vedic, all men are likely to have venerated all gods, and it seems to have been part of Zarathushtra's new demands on his followers that they should venerate only those beings whom he saw as *spenta* and 'created' by Mazdā, wholly rejecting those especially worshipped by the *dregvant* (*Y*. 49.4), whom he called *daēvas*. *Daēva*, an ancient word for 'god' (cognate with Latin *deus*), was restricted by him to a group of divinities whom presumably the war-bands and their chieftains most frequently invoked. He names none of them individually, but in the Young Avesta (*Vendidad* 10.9) martial Indra is repudiated, together with Sarva (Indian Śarva, equivalent in later texts to the violent Vedic Rudra), and Nanhaithya (cf. the Vedic Nāsatyas). The *daēvas*, the prophet declares, had 'chosen the worst purpose' and had 'rushed to Wrath with whom they afflicted the world and mankind' (*Y*. 30.6). Such beings could not be of the same divine essence as Mazdā, like the *spenta* divinities, and he came to apprehend a wholly different origin for them. They were of the race or nature (*chithra-*) of Bad Purpose (Aka Manah) and *drug* (*Y*. 32.3), and had been deluded by the Deceiver (*Y*. 30.6), elsewhere (*Y*. 45.2) called by him the Evil Spirit, Angra Mainyu. Even as he had come to believe in a self-existent, original, *spenta* Spirit, Mazdā, so, logically and analogically, Zarathushtra came to postulate also a self-existent, original Spirit who is opposed to what is *spenta*, one who is bad, destructive, a negating force. In two *Gāthās* this doctrine is declared in terms which suggest that, perhaps after logic had guided his thinking, the prophet saw these Spirits with visionary eye as they first encountered, before the world was made.

'Then shall I speak of the two primal Spirits (*Mainyū*) of existence, of whom the One more *spenta* spoke thus to the Evil One: neither our thoughts nor teachings nor wills, neither our choices nor words nor acts, not our inner selves (*daēnā*) nor our souls agree'.

(*Y*. 45.2)

Truly there are two primal Spirits, twins. . . . In thought and word, in act they are two: the better and the bad. And those who act well have chosen rightly between these two, not so the evildoers. And when these two Spirits first came together they created life and not-life, and how at the end Worst Existence shall be for the *dregvant*, but (the House of) Best Purpose for the *ashavan*. Of these two Spirits the Dregvant chose achieving the worst things, Spenishta Mainyu, who is clad in hardest stones, chose *asha*, and (so do those) who shall satisfy Lord Mazdā continually with true acts.

(*Y*. 30.3–6)

The tradition unequivocally identified the two opposed Spirits of these verses as Ahura Mazdā and Angra Mainyu (Ohrmazd and Ahriman). But since the prophet, characteristically, varied his terms (Holier, Holiest Spirit for Mazdā, Evil, Bad Spirit for his adversary), scope exists for those who reject the tradition to interpret the doctrine otherwise. This goes back to Martin Haug, the brilliant nineteenth-century scholar who identified the *Gāthās* for the West as Zarathushtra's own words. He came to their study with knowledge of the Zurvanite heresy (see Chapter 2 below), and a heritage of Christian abhorrence of dualism, which to him and others after him appeared unworthy of the great Iranian prophet. Accordingly he took Spenishta Mainyu to stand here for Spenta Mainyu, and the word *yema*, 'twins', to mean not 'pair' but 'born of the same birth', arguing from this an implication that Mazdā was 'father' of both the Holy and Evil Spirits, good and evil having thus a single source, as in the three Semitic monotheisms. There is no trace of such a doctrine anywhere in orthodox Zoroastrianism before the nineteenth century, when some reformist Parsis, living under Christian rule and anxious to rid their faith of the slur (as Christian missionaries presented it) of dualism, adopted Haug's interpretation (see Chapter 4 below). This interpretation, put forward when the scholarly study of the *Gāthās* had just begun, flatly contradicts the burning conviction of the 'absolute heterogeneity' of good and evil which imbues them (Corbin 1951: 163, cf. Lommel 1930: 27–8. Bianchi 1958: ch. 5; further references *apud* Boyce 1975: 194). This well-intentioned imposition of an alien theology on Zarathushtra still has, however, its academic supporters (among them Gershevitch 1964: 32–3; Gnoli 1980: 213; Gnoli 1987: 581), and has come to be widely accepted by his own reformist followers.

The Gathic passages show that Zarathushtra apprehended the differences between the two Spirits as essential, not accidental: they were by nature opposed. Yet though according to *Y.* 31.8 Mazdā is creator of Asha, in *Y.* 30 he chooses *asha*, as if the principle already existed. This anomaly is explicable by the fact that Zarathushtra, although a thinker, was primarily a prophet, one who sought to win his hearers to act upon his words. If they and the world were to be saved from evil, they must be inspired to choose to uphold *asha*, not *drug*; and the myth of the primeval choices of the two Spirits, so powerfully conceived by him, gave his teaching dramatic force. The *spenta* divinities did not, it appears, repeat Ahura Mazdā's choice: they were of his essence, innately *ashavan*; but the *daēvas*, who once, it seems, despite their bad nature, acknowledged Mazdā's pre-eminence (*Y.* 32.1), were deluded by Angra Mainyu into choosing 'Worst Purpose' (*Y.* 30.6); and they then themselves deluded their worshippers, depriving them of good life on earth and of immortality (*Y.* 32.3–5).

With regard to the hereafter, Zarathushtra, as we have seen, inherited beliefs in two possible fates for the soul: a blissful, reincarnated one on high with the gods, or a joyless disembodied one in the underworld kingdom of the dead. There was thought to be a crossing place between this world and the next, perhaps originally a ford or ferry to the underworld, but a bridge to heaven, reaching from earth to sky. This is called in the *Gāthās* the Chinvat Bridge. Probably according to the old religion heaven was to be reached only by great men, but Zarathushtra taught that it was attainable by all who accepted his teachings and were *ashavan*, while the underworld kingdom was to him a place of retributive punishment, the worst existence, that is, hell, which awaited the *dregvant*.

> Whosoever, Lord, man or woman, will grant me those things Thou knowest best for life – recompense for truth, power with good purpose – and those whom I shall bring to Your worship, with all these shall I cross the Chinvat Bridge. False priests and princes by their powers yoked mankind with evil acts to destroy life. But their own soul and Inner Self tormented them when they reached the Chinvat Bridge – guests for a long lifetime in the House of Drug.
>
> (*Y.* 46.11)

> Heavenly glory shall be the future possession of him who comes (to the help of) the *ashavan*. A long life of darkness, foul food, the crying of woe – to that existence, O *dregvants*, your Inner Self shall lead you by her actions.
>
> (*Y.* 31.20–1)

The inner self, *daēnā*, also rendered as 'conscience', was a powerful concept apparently evolved by Zarathushtra from a myth that the soul of a man destined for heaven would be met at the bridge by a beautiful girl, thereafter to be his guide and companion. This hedonistic belief Zarathushtra transformed into an ethical one. What met people there was their own *daēnā*, the hypostasis of an inner self which they had made beautiful or ugly by their own conduct, and which then took them up to heaven or down to hell (cf. *Y.* 49.10–11). The word *daēnā* has been derived from the verbal root *dāy*, 'see', with implication of an inner or mental vision (Gnoli 1980: 195 n. 70), by which was gradually formed 'the sum of the spiritual and religious qualities of a person, his spiritual and religious individuality' (Bartholomae 1904: 666). 'He who makes better or worse his thought, O Mazdā, he by act and word (makes better or worse) his *Daēnā*; she follows his leanings, wishes and likings. At Thy will the end shall be different (for each)' (*Y.* 48.4). This end was to be decided by weighing each person's good thoughts, words and acts against the bad, the soul's fate being decided by how the scales tipped. There will then be unswerving justice 'for the *dregvant* as well as for the *ashavan*, and for him whose falsehood and honesty are assessed as equal' (*Y.* 33.1). It is part of the practical strength of Zarathushtra's teachings that evil thoughts, words and acts can be directly compensated for in this life by good ones, and so need not form a long-lasting burden of guilt.

The references to the Chinvat Bridge and *daēnā* can only be fully comprehended through the tradition, and the tradition has also to be drawn on to explain the recurrent allusions in the *Gāthās* to a decision to be made through 'bright blazing fire and molten metal . . . to destroy the *dregvant*, to save the *ashavan*' (*Y.* 51.9; cf. *Y.* 31.19, 43.4, 34.4). The doctrine behind the words is that when Mazdā and the *spenta* powers and creations finally defeat evil, and Angra Mainyu and his forces have been destroyed, souls will be brought back to earth from heaven and hell and enter their resurrected bodies, so that with those still living they can undergo the last judgement physically. (This doctrine of the 'future body', as it is called in later Zoroastrian creeds, appears to be a modification by Zarathushtra of the earlier concept of a resurrected body to be enjoyed soon after death by the fortunate in heaven on high.) The universal judgement will be by an ordeal analogous to that by molten metal which was part of ordinary Indo-Iranian judicial processes. In it, as in the judicial ordeal, the guilty will perish, and the just be saved by divine intervention (Lommel 1930: 219ff; Boyce 1996: 23–4). The last vestiges of evil will thereby be destroyed. Then the world will be made 'wonderful', an approximate rendering of *fareša* (*Y.* 30.9; 34.15), restored, that is, to its pristine state of wholeness and goodness. The resurrected bodies of the righteous will be made immortal, and they will live for ever joyously in the kingdom (*khshathra*) of Ahura Mazdā to be established here on earth. This will be stable, enduring, with no more mutability or corruption. The concept of an absolute end to the processes of birth and death and change is not the least radical and influential of Zarathushtra's innovative thoughts; and it appears to have been wholly original, not traceable anywhere in the world before his time (Cohn 1993). It is of profound importance in his teachings, which are essentially concerned with salvation and an end to evil; and it forms the concluding belief in a system which unites in a remarkable way some notably archaic elements (animatism, the strong sense of man's fellowship with the beasts, ancient cosmogonic ideas) with powerful new doctrines and a noble theology.

REFERENCES

Barr, K. (1945) 'Principia Zarathustriaca', in *Øst og Vest, Afhandlinger tilegnede A. Christensen*, Copenhagen: Munksgaard.

Bartholomae, C. (1904) *Altiranisches Wörterbuch*, Strasburg: K. J. Trübner.

—— (1905) *Die Gāthā's des Awesta*, Strasburg: K. J. Trübner.

Benveniste, E. and Renou, L. (1934) *Vṛtra et Vṛθragna, étude de mythologie indo-iranienne*, Paris: Imprimerie nationale.

Bianchi, U. (1958) *Zamān i Ōhrmazd, Storia e scienza delle religioni*, Turin: Societa Editrice Internazionale.

Boyce, M. (1975) *A History of Zoroastrianism*, vol. I, *The early period, Handbuch der Orientalistik*, ed. B. Spuler, Leiden: Brill. Revised repr., 1989, 1996.

—— (1984) Review of J. Narten, *Die Aməša Spəṇtas im Avesta, BSOAS* 47: 158–61.

—— (1986) 'Apąm Napāt', in *Encyclopaedia Iranica*, ed. E. Yarshater, vol. III, London: Routledge & Kegan Paul, pp. 148–50.

—— (1987) 'Priests, cattle and men', *BSOAS* 50: 508–26.

—— (1992) *Zoroastrianism: Its Antiquity and Constant Vigour*, Columbia Lectures on Iranian Studies 1992, Costa Mesa: Mazda Publishers.

—— (1993) 'Great Vayu and greater Varuna', *Bulletin of the Asia Institute*, n.s. 7: 35–40

—— (1996) 'On the orthodoxy of Sasanian Zoroastrianism' *BSAOS* 59: 11–28

Boyce, M. with Grenet, F. (1991) *A History of Zoroastrianism*, vol. III, *Under Macedonian and Roman Rule*, *Handbuch der Orientalistik*, Leiden: E. J. Brill.

Cohn, N. (1993) Cosmos, Chaos and the World to Come, The ancient roots of apocalyptic faith, Yale University Press, New Haven and London.

Corbin, H. (1951) 'Le Temps cyclique dans le mazdéisme et dans l'ismaélisme', *Eranos-Jahrbuch* 20: 149–217.

Darmesteter, J. (1892–3) *Le Zend-Avesta*, *Annales de Musée Guimet* 21, 22, 24, repr. Paris, A. Maisonneuve, 1960.

Duchesne-Guillemin, J. (1952) *The Hymns of Zarathushtra*, trans. M. Henning, Wisdom of the East Series, London: John Murray.

Geldner, K. (1885) 'Persian (Iranian) language and literature', *Encyclopaedia Britannica*, 9th edn, vol. XVIII, Edinburgh: A. & C. Black.

Gening, V. F. (1977) 'Le Champ funéraire de Sintachta et le problème des anciennes tribus indo-iraniennes', *Sovetskaja Arxeologija*, 1977(4):53–73 (Russian with a French summary). Eng. trans. by W. A. Brewer, 'The cemetery at Sintashta and the early Indo-Iranian peoples', *J. of Indo-European Studies* 7: 1979, 1–29.

Gershevitch, I. (1964) 'Zoroaster's own contribution', *JNES* 23: 12–38.

Gnoli, G. (1980) *Zoroaster's Time and Homeland*, Seminario di Studi Asiatici, Series Minor VII, Naples: Instituto Universitario Orientale.

—— (1987) 'Zoroastrianism', in *The Encyclopaedia of Religion*, ed. M. Eliade, vol. XV, New York: Macmillan, 579–91.

Haug, M. (1884) *Essays on the Sacred Language, Writings and Religion of the Parsis*, London: Trübner. 3rd edn, repr. Amsterdam, 1971.

Humbach, H. (1959) *Die Gathas des Zarathustra*, 2 vols, Revised Eng. transl., 2 vols, 1991, Heidelberg: C. Winter.

Insler, S. (1975) *The Gāthās of Zarathustra*, *Acta Iranica* 8, Leiden: Brill.

Jackson, A. V. W. (1899) *Zoroaster, the Prophet of Ancient Iran*, New York: Macmillan. Repr. 1965.

—— (1904) 'Khshathra Vairya, one of the Zoroastrian archangels', in *Avesta, Pahlavi and Ancient Persian Studies in honour of . . . P. B. Sanjana*, Strasburg: K. J. Trübner.

Kellens, J. and Pirart, E. (1988). *Les Textes vieil-avestiques*, vol. I, text and trans., Wiesbaden: Reichert.

Kingsley, P. (1990) 'The Greek source of the dating of Zoroaster', *BSOAS* 53(2): 245–65.

Kreyenbroek, G. (1985) *Sraoša in the Zoroastrian Tradition*, Leiden: Brill.

Lommel, H. (1926) 'Review of B. Geiger, Die Aməša Spəṇtas, ihr Wesen und ihre ursprungliche Bedeutung', *Anzeiger für indogermanische Sprach- und Altertumskunde* 43: 29–36; repr. in B. Schlerath (ed.) *Zarathustra, Wege der Forschung* 169, Darmstadt: Wissenschaftliche Buchgesellschaft, 1970, 20–32.

—— (1930) *Die Religion Zarathustras nach dem Awesta dargestellt*, Tübingen: J. C. B. Mohr. Repr. 1971.

—— (1959) 'Symbolik der Elemente in der zoroastrischen Religion', in *Symbolon* 2: 108–20; repr. in B. Schlerath (ed.) *Zarathustra, Wege der Forschung* 169, Darmstadt: Wissenschaftliche Buchgesellschaft, 1970, 253–69.

—— (1964) 'Die Elemente im Verhältnis zu den Ameša Spəntas', in *Festschrift für A. E. Jensen*, part I, 365–77; repr. in Schlerath (ed.) *Zarathustra, Wege der Forschung* 169, Darmstadt: Wissenschaftliche Buchgesellschaft, 1970, 377–96.

—— (trans.) (1971) *Die Gathas des Zarathustra*, ed. posthumously by B. Schlerath, Basle/Stuttgart: Schwabe.

Lüders, H. (1951, 1959) *Varuna*, ed. posthumously by L. Alsdorf, 2 vols, Göttingen: Vandenhoek and Ruprecht.

Meillet, A. (1907) 'Le Dieu indo-iranien Mitra', *Journal asiatique*, 143–59.

Narten, J. (1982) *Die Aməṣ̌a Spəṇtas im Avesta*, Wiesbaden: Harrassowitz.
—— (ed. and trans.) (1986) *Der Yasna Haptanhāiti*, Wiesbaden: L. Reichert.
Polomé, E. C. (1982) 'Indo-European culture, with special attention to religion', in Polomé (ed.) *The Indo-Europeans in the Fourth and Third Millennia*, Ann Arbor, Mich.
Spiegel, F. (1871, 1873, 1878) *Eranische Alterthumskunde*, 3 vols, Leipzig: W. Engelmann.
Taraporewala, I. J. S. (1951) *The Divine Songs of Zarathushtra*, Bombay: D. B. Taraporevala Sons & Co.
Thieme, P. (1957) *Mitra and Aryaman*, *Transactions of the Connecticut Academy of Arts and Sciences* 41.
Zaehner, R. C. (1955) *Zurvan, a Zoroastrian Dilemma*, Oxford: Clarendon Press. Repr. New York, 1972.
—— (1956) *The Teachings of the Magi*, Ethical and Religious Classics of East and West, London: Allen & Unwin. Repr. 1976.

FURTHER READING

Boyce, M. (1979) *Zoroastrians, their Religious Beliefs and Practices*, London: Routledge & Kegan Paul, 3rd revised repr., 1987.
—— (ed. and trans.) (1984) *Textual Sources for the Study of Zoroastrianism*, Manchester: Manchester University Press. Paperback, Chicago University Press.
Christensen, A. (1928) *Etudes sur le zoroastrisme de la Perse antique*, Copenhagen: Høst & Son.
—— (1941) *Essai sur la démonologie iranienne*, Copenhagen: Munksgaard.
Duchesne-Guillemin, J. (1948) *Zoroastre, étude critique avec une traduction commentée des Gāthā*, Paris: A. Maisonneuve.
—— (1962) *La Religion de l'Iran ancien*, Paris: Presses Universitaires de France (includes an interpretation of Zarathushtra's teachings according to the controversial theories of G. Dumézil). Eng. trans. by K.M. Jamaspasa, Bombay, 1973.
Gershevitch, I. (1959) *The Avestan Hymn to Mithra*, Cambridge: Cambridge University Press, repr. 1967 (the introduction includes learned but over-ingenious arguments for Zarathushtra's rigid monotheism).
Henning, W. B. (1951) *Zoroaster, Politician or Witch-doctor?*, Ratanbai Katrak Lectures 1949, Oxford: Oxford University Press (contains penetrating criticisms of the interpretations of Zarathushtra's teachings by E. Herzfeld and H. S. Nyberg).
Humbach, H. (1984) 'A western approach to Zarathushtra', *Journal of the K. R. Cama Oriental Institute* (Bombay) 51: 1–56 (controversial but with some illuminating matter).
Jackson, A. V. W. (1928) *Zoroastrian Studies, the Iranian Religion and Various Monographs*, New York: Macmillan, repr. 1965 (outdated but still in many respects sound).
Malandra, W. W. (1983) *An introduction to ancient Iranian religion, Readings from the Avesta and Achaemenid Inscriptions*, University of Minnesota Press, Minneapolis.
Meillet, A. (1925) *Trois conférences sur les Gāthā de l'Avesta*, Paris: P. Geuthner (outdated but in parts still valuable).
Molé, M. (1963) *Culte, mythe et cosmologie dans l'Iran ancien*, Paris: Presses Universitaires de France (a massive, controversial study of Zoroastrianism treated phenomenologically, with many citations of texts).

Moulton, J. H. (1913) *Early Zoroastrianism*, London: Williams & Norgate, repr. 1972 (much of it outdated, but with an English trans. of the *Gāthās*, pp. 344–90, based on that of C. Bartholomae).

Nyberg, H. S. (1938) *Die Religionen des alten Iran*, German trans. by H. H. Schaeder, Leipzig: J. C. Hinrichs, repr. 1966 (much learned matter, but a generally rejected interpretation of Zarathushtra's teachings: see Henning 1951 above).

Pavry, J. D. C. (1926) *The Zoroastrian Doctrine of a Future Life from Death to the Individual Judgment*, New York: Columbia University Press, 2nd edn 1929.

Schlerath, B. (ed.) (1970) *Zarathushtra*, *Wege der Forschung* 169, Darmstadt: Wissenschaftliche Buchgesellschaft (a valuable collection of articles, in or trans. into German, including, pp. 336–59, the editor's 'Die Gathas des Zarathustra').

Schmidt, H. P., Lentz, W. and Insler, S. (1985) *Form and Meaning in Yasna 33*, New Haven, Conn.: American Oriental Society.

Widengren, G. (1965) *Die Religionen Irans*, Stuttgart: W. Kohlhammer (contains a blend of the theories of G. Dumézil and H. S. Nyberg, and many inaccuracies, but also much useful information).

Zaehner, R. (1961) *The Dawn and Twilight of Zoroastrianism*, London: Weidenfeld & Nicolson, repr. 1975 (puts forward theories which have proved unacceptable, but has theologically valuable observations, more especially in the second part, and many citations of texts).

2

LATER ZOROASTRIANISM

Alan Williams

INTRODUCTION

It is not intended in this chapter to summarize the long history of Zoroastrianism after the Gathic period, but rather to sketch a picture of some of the main features of Zoroastrian thought as found in its theological and philosophical texts. The task of providing a historical survey of the several millennia of development of the religion has been attempted several times by Iranologists. Too often, however, because the period of the most coherent systematization of Zoroastrian theology, in the ninth to tenth centuries AD, coincided with the era of the religion's numerical decline, the strong character of that expression has been diminished by equating it with a supposed intellectual decline. Thus the religious thought of the later, i.e. Sasanian and post-Islamic, period has been depicted by some western scholars as a twilight (for example Zaehner 1961) or swansong of scholasticism and priestly apologetics. More sadly, as a consequence of their exposure to western scholarly preoccupations, but also for other reasons, even Zoroastrians of the modern community have tended to look down on the Pahlavi books as representing a medieval deviation from the true spirit of their prophet's ancient teachings. A more positive impression of Zoroastrian thought is obtained once it is acknowledged that the priests of the ninth century were neither composing a new philosophy nor trying to embalm a dead one: rather they wrote to record and defend the religious values of their old tradition in the fullest possible way. They accomplished this in a corpus of philosophical and theological as well as liturgical and mythological writings, in the Middle Persian language known as Pahlavi; happily these texts remain as testimony to the wide range of Zoroastrian religious thought which survived even after the waves of conversion to the new religion of Islam had swept over Iran, which had, since the mid-seventh century AD, drastically reduced the physical presence of the older religion there.[1]

Zoroastrian thought has been expressed, almost always and everywhere until the nineteenth century, in terms of the opposition and conflict of two utterly irreconcilable principles. One is divine in origin and is good, the source of creation in spiritual and physical states, and is embodied most completely in physicality by the *ashavan*, the man of righteousness who nurtures the purity and wisdom of the divine source. The other is demonic in origin, evil, chaotic and parasitic upon all existence; it is the antithesis of reality: it is described, in the most ancient texts and in the ensuing tradition, as 'the Lie'. The Good Religion (Pahlavi *weh dēn*) is governed by another characteristic which runs through all its writings – one which is found, usually with less emphasis, in other religious teachings which purport to liberate humanity from suffering in mortal existence, but which is most originally and dramatically represented in Zoroastrianism – namely the drive towards an eschatological and soteriological resolution of strife by the defeat of evil *in the world*. Although at times in the history of the faith external influences and circumstances of the day have coloured Zoroastrian thought, it was always distinguished by these two features: (1) the dialectical structure of existence, wherein humankind, along with the divine agencies, plays a decisive role in bringing about (2) the promised triumph of goodness and the final annihilation of evil in the world. Such an eschatological imperative is conveyed in many and various genres of Zoroastrian literature down to the last century, written in Avestan, Pahlavi, Persian and Gujarati languages respectively: namely in prophetic revelation, priestly-liturgical lore, mythology (especially of cosmology, eschatology and soteriology), heroic legend, ritual and purity codifications and, lastly, in theological and philosophical form in apologetic and encyclopaedic works. In the following discussion the focus will be on this latter philosophical and theological expression, but not without a summary first of the mythological landscape, for this is as ancient as the philosophy, and more enduring than the theological formulation.

SOURCES OF LATER ZOROASTRIAN THOUGHT

The source of all cosmological and eschatological lore is held to be the *Avesta*, the corpus of Mazdean holy writ, and the *Zand*, the accompanying exegetical literature. It is not certain exactly when the *Avesta* was first committed to writing. The fact of a long, but faithful, oral transmission has given rise to the phenomenon of relatively late texts representing much more ancient oral works, since in some of the most important cases they were written down only long after their original composition. This is most emphatically true of the *Gāthās* of the prophet Zarathushtra, as discussed in Chapter 1 above; the problem of the original date and location of those definitive texts has been shown to be acute, since they were transmitted orally, in the context of a liturgy recited daily for hundreds of years before first being written down in a script specially devised for that purpose, in the Sasanian period.[2] The *Gāthās* are part of the canon, known collectively as the *Avesta*, of twenty-one divisions (Avestan *nask*). This was a large body of writings, similarly transmitted for centuries in oral form; it is now estimated that only one-fifth of the *Avesta* is preserved, extant in the east Iranian language referred to by Iranologists as Avestan. It appears that during the Sasanian period, *c.* the fourth or fifth century AD, the whole corpus was committed to writing and translated literally into Pahlavi, by Zoroastrian priests who often seem hardly to have understood the old Avestan, i.e. Gathic, well, since that language had long since ceased to be a spoken tongue and had been preserved as a liturgical and mantric medium. Modern scholars have observed that the Pahlavi rendition of the *Gāthās* is a word-by-word translation. They were required for recitation in Avestan in the conduct of the daily round of liturgical and priestly life. An oral tradition of religious learning must have endured alongside the texts, however, down into the Sasanian period: from summaries in other Pahlavi texts it is known that the *Avesta* also included long works on cosmogony, eschatology, law and natural and religious philosophy. These have not survived in Avestan, though it is clear that several of the Pahlavi texts, to which the modern reader turns for an account of such material, are derived from Avestan originals. Similarly, the *Zand*, 'elucidation', survives only in Pahlavi and takes the form of glosses in the translated text of the *Avesta* or independent expository works which are compilations of *Zand* on various subjects. There were presumably other such *ad hoc* exegetical passages in other Middle Iranian languages, but these have not survived.

The most important work of this mythological, expository type is a text in Pahlavi called the *Bundahishn*, 'The creation', known also as *Zand Āgāhīh* 'The knowledge of the *Zand*'. The *Bundahishn* is concerned with, among other things, the themes of the creation of the world, the order of things, and the eschatological destiny of both the individual soul and the world at large. The material is clearly much older than the date of the last major recension of the text, which is thought to have been made at the end of the ninth century AD. Indeed it has been said:

> Here is preserved an ancient, in part pre-Zoroastrian picture of the world, conceived as saucer-shaped, with its rim one great mountain-range, a central peak thrusting up, star-encircled, to cut off the light of the sun by night; a world girdled by two great rivers, from which all other waters flow; in which yearly the gods fight against demons to end drought and famine, and to bring protection to man.[3]

In addition to such an ancient, mythological picture, the catalogues of species of living things and natural features of the physical universe provide a mythological taxonomy of the old and medieval Iranian world-view which is of far more than merely antiquarian interest. The account of the divine creation and demonic invasion of the world, however, has all the features of a living myth, intended to embody and amplify contemporary religious teaching in an imaginative form: thus its content is our legitimate concern here in describing later Zoroastrian thought. The mythological narrative of the *Bundahishn*, which accounts for the creation of a limited time of 12,000 years of existence in the spiritual and material worlds, is given in condensed form in the following section.

COSMOGONY AND ESCHATOLOGY IN THE *BUNDAHISHN*

According to the *Bundahishn*, and other similar texts, Ohrmazd (the Pahlavi spelling of Ahura Mazdā, 'Lord of Wisdom') existed in a pre-eternal state of omniscience and goodness, called 'Endless Light'. Ahriman (Avestan Angra Mainyu, 'Hostile Spirit', also called Gannāg Mẹnōg, 'Evil Spirit' in Pahlavi) lurked[4] in 'slowness of knowledge' in 'Endless Darkness'. The problem of conceiving of two infinite forces in pre-eternity is dealt with in the following passage:

> They were both limited and limitless: for that which was on high, which is called Endless Light . . . and that which is abased, which is Endless Darkness – those were limitless. [But] at the border both were limited, in that between them was emptiness. There was no connection between the two.[5]

Ohrmazd was omniscient, and thus knew also of what lay beyond the Light and of what Ahriman was plotting, i.e. the destruction of the world Ohrmazd was to create. For a period of 3,000 years of limited time Ohrmazd's first creation was of spiritual beings in a purely spiritual state (Pahlavi *Mēnōg*). Because of his slowness of knowledge, for a long time, it is said, Ahriman was aware neither of Ohrmazd nor of his spiritual creations. Once he saw the 'intangible light' of Ohrmazd, however, he rose to attack it, but 'he saw valour and supremacy greater than his own and he crawled back to darkness and shaped many demons, the destructive creation. And he rose for battle.'[6] Ahriman's insatiable lust for destruction was motivated by jealousy of the good creation, and Ohrmazd knew that the only effective response to this eternally destructive force was to set a finite time of battle between the forces of good and evil, even though in that time Ahriman would be able to lead the creatures astray and might make them his own. Yet Ohrmazd knew that through the setting of the time he would destroy the Evil Spirit. Ohrmazd established that for 3,000 years existence would proceed according to his will, then there would be 3,000 years of the 'mixed state' (Pahlavi *gumēzishn*) according to the will of both Ohrmazd and Ahriman, and finally 3,000 years which would end in the utter defeat of Ahriman and his legions for all eternity. Ohrmazd confronted Ahriman with a vision of the victorious end and his eventual powerlessness, and Ahriman fell prostrate and impotent for 3,000 years.

Ohrmazd became Lord of the Universe when he created the creatures: first he created the *yazads*, i.e. the beings 'worthy of worship', which are powerful spirits of goodness 'whereby He made Himself better, since His lordship was through creation'.[7] Creation was the only means by which the assault of the Evil Spirit could be overcome; but, as Ohrmazd knew, the creation of time would also allow the development of Ahriman's creation. Ahriman created the essence of the demons, namely his own wickedness, from his own darkness, ignorant, however, that it was 'that creation whereby he made himself worse since through it (i.e. in the end) he will become powerless'. The first six of Ohrmazd's spiritual beings are called *Amahraspands*, 'Blessed Immortals', whose names in Pahlavi translate spiritual perfections held as supreme virtues in the religion: Wahman, 'Good Mind'; Ardwahisht, 'Best Righteousness'; Shahrewar, 'Good Dominion'; Spendarmad, 'Blessed Devotion'; Hordād, 'Wholeness'; Amurdād, 'Immortality', and a seventh was himself, 'Ohrmazd'. Meanwhile Ahriman creates an opposite spiritual pandemonium of chief demons. During Ahriman's 3,000 year powerless prostration, Ohrmazd makes a physical creation (Pahlavi *Gētīg)* in seven elemental forms: sky, as a primary defence around the world; water, to defeat the demon of thirst; the all-solid earth; the plant, to help the fifth creation, the beneficent animal, which itself is made to help the sixth, the righteous man, 'to smite the Evil Spirit together with the demons and to make them powerless'. Fire, the seventh element of the *Gētīg*, was fashioned with its brilliance linked to the Endless Light, and was distributed within the whole creation in order to serve humankind during the Assault which will follow. This fire will become the iconic representation of the essential truth and order of Ohrmazd, and a focus of worship in the tradition. A synergic relationship between the spiritual Blessed Immortals and the physical creations is established when each of the Immortals takes one of the physical creations for its own for mutual protection. Ohrmazd (Wise Lord) takes humankind; Wahman (Good Mind), the cow, beneficent animal; Ardwahisht (Best Righteousness), fire; Shahrewar (Good Dominion), metal; Spandarmad (Blessed Devotion), earth; Hordād (Wholeness), water Amurdād (Immortality), plant. The synergic relationship between these spiritual powers and physical elements is a central point of Zoroastrian thought, in both mythological and philosophical-theological expressions. It is flanked by the creation of many other spiritual beings: 'Innumerable beings of creation were arrayed to help them', some of whom are specifically attached as 'helpers' of the Blessed Immortals, others acting independently.

Ohrmazd also created the *frawahr*, the higher spiritual part of every human. Ohrmazd challenges the *frawahrs* of men in the following words, in a passage of great significance in the *Bundahishn*, having bestowed the wisdom of all knowledge upon (the *frawahrs*) of men:

> 'Which seems to you the more profitable, that I should fashion you for the material world, and that you should struggle, embodied, with the Demon, and destroy the Demon; and that in the end I should restore you, whole and immortal, and recreate you in the physical state, for ever immortal, free from enemies; or that you should be protected forever from the Assault?' And the *Frawahrs* of men saw by the wisdom of all knowledge the evil which would come upon them in the world through the Demon and Ahriman; yet for the sake of freedom, in the end, from the enmity of the Adversary, and restoration, whole and immortal, in the future body for ever and ever, they agreed to go into the world.[8]

This text has much of the ancient spirit of Zoroaster's religious message in it. An unbreakable bond of trust is made between humankind and the creator Ohrmazd, wherein the act of divine creation is linked to a common purpose, i.e. *to be* is *to struggle against* the forces of evil. Moreover, it indicates that this is the rational choice by the human spirit in a pre-incarnate state, not a divine command, made in the knowledge that evil and suffering may be overcome only through heroic and painful resistance.

The account of the process of physical creation continues in the *Bundahishn* with the cataclysmic events of the assault of the Evil Spirit as he rushed with his demons: 'Like a snake he rushed upon the Sky . . . and sought to cleave it . . . and the Sky feared him as the sheep the wolf.' Ahriman attacks each of the seven elemental creations, corrupts all of them, 'and he made the world at midday quite dark, as if it were black night'. With Ahriman death enters the world: the earth is polluted with noxious creatures, the waters, plant and beneficent animal are poisoned and fire is darkened with smoke. When the primal man, Gayōmard (lit. 'mortal life') is killed, before he passes away he emits his seed and it is received by the *Amahraspand* of earth, Spandarmad; the seed is preserved for forty years in the earth. Thereafter the first human couple were born out of the earth 'and that glory which is the soul entered invisibly into them'. Just as Ohrmazd regenerates humankind in multiplicity from the demonically induced death of his first created man, so he brings to life the earth, waters, plants, beneficent animals and fires, now in the fullness of multiplicity – and this is a miracle of divine goodness – yet all are now mortal in duration and must all perish when their term of life runs out.

This is one of the accounts of the story of creation, and although there are others which differ in matters of detail, it summarizes not only the myth of the divine act of creation but also the purpose and structure of physical existence.

The destiny of the individual human soul and of the cosmos of Ohrmazd's creation is directly and coherently related to this beginning. During a Zoroastrian's lifetime each of the good deeds he or she performs accrues to an account in the spiritual world, as do all his or her acts of sinfulness. At death the soul ascends to a place where it is judged, called the Činwad Puhl, 'Bridge of the Separator'. This is an original doctrine of the faith, and expresses the belief that, although all Zoroastrians acknowledge their fealty to their creator, Ohrmazd the Lord of Wisdom, their souls are in fact personally accountable to themselves as regards their future spiritual existence: for the judgement made upon them requires neither grace nor mercy: the soul whose merit outweighs its sin passes onwards and upwards to paradise to abide with the *Yazads* and with Ohrmazd himself; the soul with a heavier burden of wickedness in its account falls from the bridge to hell to spend the rest of time with the demons in a miserable state of suffering.

According to the developed mythology of the Pahlavi books, all humankind will be recreated in bodily and spiritual form, and will undergo a last judgement whereby evil and wickedness will be purged. Thereafter existence will continue in what is known as the 'future body' (Pahlavi *tan ī pasēn*), which is at once spiritual and physical. The end of history will be 12,000 years after the beginning: the narrator of the myth places the 'now' of this world towards the end of the flow of time, as the following chart shows:

0–3000	Ohrmazd gives form to the *Mēnōg*, 'spiritual' creation. Ahriman reciprocates with an evil *Mēnōg*.
3000–6000	Ahriman falls unconscious. Ohrmazd creates the prototype *Gētīg*, 'material' world. The world according to the will of Ohrmazd.
6000–9000	Ahriman invades the prototype *Gētīg* and 'kills' it, but it is regenerated in multiplicity as the actual *Gētīg*. This is now the *Gumēzishn*, 'mixed state', as the *Gētīg* is open to the wills of both Ohrmazd and Ahriman.
9000–10000	Zarathushtra receives his revelation and teaches humankind. The myth speaks from the 'now' of this millennium, for though Zarathushtra himself has returned to the *Mēnōg*, Zoroastrians await the coming of the first of three saviours who will lead the *Gētīg* towards the final victory.
10000–11000	The millennium of the first saviour, Hushēdar.
11000–12000	The millennium of the second saviour, Hushēdarmāh.
11943	Birth of the saviour who will lead those of the Good Religion in the final struggle towards a period called *Frashegird* in the following fifty-seven years. All the dead, both good and evil souls, will be resurrected in their reconstituted *Gētīg* bodies. The last judgement and final spiritual battle when Ahriman and all his brood of demons are utterly annihilated.
12000	Time ends. The kingdom of Ohrmazd reigns eternally on earth as *Gētīg* and *Mēnōg* worlds coalesce in an unprecedented state of perfection in the fullness of physical multiplicity.

With its symmetry and congruence, this eschatological scheme has all the characteristics of a developed mythological narrative such as are found in other religions. It should not be taken as being merely a naive survival from a more archaic age of the faith which might have embarrassed the theologians and philosophers of the urbane and cultured milieu of Sasanian Iran: the mythology ran in parallel with doctrine, ritual and metaphysics, at different levels of Zoroastrian religious life.

THEOLOGICAL AND PHILOSOPHICAL THOUGHT

The reason for the above excursion into mythology is that such narratives served as an underpinning and popular expression of vital characteristics of Zoroastrian thought, which also took philosophical form when the need arose. By the same token, although the philosophical thought of the Pahlavi books is more abstract in character than the religious expression of the *Gāthās* and other older texts, it does not follow that such philosophy departs from the spirit and principle of Zarathushtra's original vision. For all Zoroastrians the visible, material world is apprehended as being alive with powerful invisible forces. Like the visual art of a religion, the mythological narrative illuminated and enlivened the doctrinal and ritual life of Zoroastrians, and the philosophical and theological texts explored and systematized religious meaning, in order to defend it against attacks from alien systems of thought.

The sources of a coherent Zoroastrian philosophy and systematic theology are principally those which were committed to writing by priests in Fars in south–west Iran in the ninth and tenth centuries AD in apologetic and exegetical works. This literature in Pahlavi presents to the modern translator problems of a kind hardly encountered by students of western philosophy, and indeed more intractable than the most difficult passages of comparable Jewish and Islamic texts. The orthography of Pahlavi is a cryptic medium for even the simplest forms of religious expression, since it is written in a combination of Aramaic ideograms and Iranian phonetic spellings, in an alphabet of only fourteen elements which served to render a much larger complement of transcribed letters. Also, the grammar of Pahlavi is best described as anarchic: in the case of the denser philosophical prose of the compendious *Dēnkard*, the translator cannot be sure that even the general meaning has been rendered, let alone the nuances of a technical and somewhat esoteric medieval disquisition.

The *Dēnkard*, 'Acts of the Religion', is an encyclopedic work of the ninth/tenth century AD in Pahlavi, of which six 'books' are extant, attributed to two priestly writers, Ādufarnbag ī Farroxzādān and Ādurbād ī Ēmēdān. The third book, running to approximately 170,000 words, by Ādurfarnbag, contains much material that may be called theological or philosophical. It is concerned with two main themes: (1) the theory of dualism and the transcendent and physical coexistence of opposites; (2) the search for a physics integrated into the dualist metaphysics of the religion. It is thus an apologetic, rational demonstration of Zoroastrian thinking, rather than a description of the religious faith as received revelation. This feature distinguishes it from other Pahlavi works, such as the *Bundahishn*, as has been observed:

> these two works are clearly from the same period, both after the Muslim conquest; it is the method, the intention, and also the audience which differ.[9]

The author's purpose, as the same scholar has observed elsewhere, is to systematize the religion, and to bring out the (metaphysical) principles that give force and life to its structure.[10] Certain passages in this part of the *Dēnkard* contain much older material, from the *Avesta* and the *Zand* of the Sasanian era and before; on the other hand, some of the metaphysical doctrines are Neoplatonic in origin, having been 'blended to various degrees with the indigenous Mazdean principles'.[11] Such passages are easy to identify, even if their interpretation has caused difficulty, and they may be excluded from this discussion.

Many of the chapters of the third book of the *Dēnkard* take the form of a refutation of the doctrines of the *kēshdārān*, the 'ideologues' of Christianity, Judaism, Manichaeism and, above all, of Islam (though for the sake of caution the latter is not mentioned by name). Several doctrines of these religions were flatly contradictory of

Zoroastrian principles: for the most part the authors need have recourse only to doctrines well known from the rest of the *Avesta* and *Zand*, but here such doctrines are interpreted from scripture and are affirmed in a challenging, apologetic discourse addressed to other theologians.

DUALISM

The most vehement offensive by the authors of the *Dēnkard*, which is echoed in other Pahlavi works, is on the truth of the doctrine of dualism, which was, and has throughout history continued to be, misunderstood and misrepresented by theologians and philosophers outside the religion. As has been acutely observed,[12] the Zoroastrian view is that the misapprehension of dualism has as its basis a sensual, not an intellectual, view of things. A purely sensual view of reality, when wisdom is weak, will never attain to the play of first principles which can be perceived clearly only beyond appearances, through empowering wisdom, as the *Dēnkard* expresses it:

> These many things made the ideologues of undiscerning belief say that all this is alike, when they said that ignorance and non-law and other manifest evils are from the same source as wisdom, and non-law and goodness are from the same source, from the all wise and all containing God.[13]

This passage accords with the theme in the *Dēnkard* that 'concupiscence is the contrary of the innate intellect, conjoins men to sin and throws them to the demons'.[14] Concupiscence is the principle of ignorance which is opposed by the principle of the intellect innate in the human soul and of the virtues, none other than Ohrmazd the creator.[15] The Good Religion is equated with this innate intellect (Pahlavi *asn xrad*), which is seen as the manifestation of two Blessed Immortals:

> the body (of the Good Religion) is the virtues (which are) the co-offspring of the Innate Intellect, the Innate Intellect and its body the virtues which are the offspring of Good Mind (Wahman), the Holy Spirit (Spanāg Mēnōg). The Evil Religion is concupiscence, its body is the vices, (which are) the co-offspring of the filthy concupiscence, filthy concupiscence and its body the vices of the filthy concupiscence are the co-offspring of Evil Mind and Evil Spirit.[16]

Concupiscence is no mere moral disorder: it is the inversion of the truth created by God. As such it is

> the most terrible adversary which comes from the assault in overturning the *gētīg* creatures: on account of it men are prevented from knowing the creator and in their deviation they see god as demon and the demons as god, the lie as the true and the true as the lie, the sinful act as meritorious and the meritorious act as sinful . . . etc[17]

Thus it is said that the concupiscence of the Evil Mind (personified in Akōman) is the cause of sinful acts of wickedness, harm and suffering: these are done by man through another principle which has made in him a character contrary to the character of the principle which has made the wisdom of Good Mind (Wahman), the cause of the meritorious acts of righteousness, an advantage and joy in man. The Zoroastrian writer thus affirms that there are two principles, the one the cause of righteousness, the other the cause of wickedness and suffering. As is usual in the *Dēnkard*, this section concludes with a refutation:

> The teachers whose doctrine is that there is only a single principle attribute to this unique principle of existence the origin and cause of sinful acts, of wickedness, of harm, of suffering and of man's misery and of the existence of the antagonist of the creatures, and they deny in him his divinity and his creatorship and friendship to the creatures.[18]

The dualism which the *Dēnkard* defends, therefore, so far from being a ditheistic theology, is in fact a doctrine of one creator God whose worshippers are not confounded by the otherwise universal stumbling block of theodicy, i.e. the problem of a loving, compassionate, good being from whom, as the source of all, evil and suffering ultimately originate. Such is the argument of another *Dēnkard* passage:

> And among the teachers those whose doctrine is that evil proceeds from the will and the commandment of God, their doctrine is thus that God is worse than all malice and is harmful to His own creatures. As to those whose doctrine is that God has no will, since he has no will there is thus ignorance in Him who they hold as God but they refuse the imbecility which goes with the absence of will.[19]

As well as the refutation of the consequences of the doctrine according to which God is the principle of evil, the text refutes also those who, like the Muʿtazilites of Islam, reject the divine attributes, and among those the will (of God).[20]

It emerges that one of the pre-conditions of understanding Zoroastrian theology on its own terms is the fact that the notion of will (Pahlavi *axw*, also rendered by *manah*, 'mind', and related concepts), both good and evil, is what constitutes the transcendent and immanent forces of Ohrmazd and Ahriman, rather than the notion of 'being'. Ohrmazd *is*, and he bestows being as the creator: Ahriman, exactly defined, *is not*, but is self-constituted as the will to negate all being. Ohrmazd's will is tantamount to his divinity, and the alignment of the human soul, through choice of that which Ohrmazd wills, is tantamount to its own humanity:

> those teachers who deny the will of God speak of his non-knowledge and of his absence of the logical faculty and deny in him divinity.[21]

In the Zoroastrian scheme of things the knowledge, will and power of God are explained in an important text which addresses the problem of a God who is opposed by an external evil force of limitation:

> The first principle of good beings who has no principle is Ohrmazd the Creator, omniscient, all powerful and lord of all. There is nothing, neither will be nor has been anything,

> which escapes the power of him whose will is best and beneficent. And it is revealed that seeing that the power is entirely comprised in the possible, God, who is the common principle of all, has power over the possible.[22]

Ahriman, as an impossible being (i.e. as that utter negation of being) has entered the possible world in order to destroy its possibility. The eschatological vision of the religion, from the *Gāthās* onwards, affirms the principle, put into philosophical terms in the *Dēnkard*, that the human will (or soul, since this is the moral and eschatological locus of the will) is central to the fulfilment of the will of Ohrmazd:

> What is in the course of limited time unchangeable is he who is in the state of non-opposition (i.e. Ohrmazd) and he who desires otherwise (Ahriman). . . . What is changeable is the conduct of time and of actions, multiplicity in the same person. . . . The teachers whose doctrine is that the will of God turns every day towards another opinion . . . deny in him divinity in saying that he wishes benevolence but tomorrow his will will have been repented, even though today it is benevolent.[23]

Thus the dualism of the religion is not conceived as an easy escape from the fact of evil in the world, but is rather a development of Zarathushtra's own well-known teaching that man is a moral being who must choose between good and evil: in choosing good he helps to bring about a remaking of a world afflicted by titanic forces of disorder. According to the later theological development of Zarathushtra's thought evil is neither human nor divine, but a 'will to smite' which derives from a principle of pure negativity having no existence of its own and which is, ultimately, only darkness, ignorance and concupiscence.

ZURVANISM

Here brief mention must be made of a strain of thought which has recurred in different forms in the ancient and modern history of Zoroastrianism. In its older form it is referred to by modern scholars as Zurvanism; in recent times it has been the root of a radical reinterpretation of Zoroastrian doctrine, influenced by both Christian and Islamic monotheism, and also by Hindu and Theosophical monism (on which see Chapter 4 below). In the past thirty years certain scholars have argued at length that there was a religion of Zurvanism which flourished from within Zoroastrianism and which came to be bitterly opposed to it. The figure of Zurvān and his attendant mythology were from time to time popular as a rival and independent movement alongside Zoroastrianism from the fifth or fourth century BC until *c.* the twelfth century AD.[24] Just as there have been movements within Islam and Christianity, arising from social circumstances and theological variegation, so Zurvanite tendencies, expressed in mythology, may be understood as a reaction to the orthodox dualism of Zoroastrianism when the religion was subjected to certain internal and external pressures. However, it does not seem to be the case that there was ever a cult of Zurvān, since we have no record of a separate ritual and liturgical cycle.

Zurvān, 'Time', is mentioned as a minor divinity in the *Avesta*. In the Zurvanite heresy, which some scholars think dates back to the late Achaemenian period,[25] Zurvān was elevated to the position of ultimate source of everything. He was posited as an all-powerful sentient divinity who was father of Ohrmazd and Ahriman, yet he is clearly felt to be a *deus otiosus*, since his twin offspring are left to fight over the world until the eventual triumph of Ohrmazd. The evidence for Zurvanism is mostly late, i.e. Sasanian and post-Sasanian, but the scriptural justification seems to have been a literalistic interpretation of the ancient, Gathic *Yasna* 30.3: 'Truly there are two primal spirits, twins, renowned to be in conflict', whereby as twins in the generic rather than metaphorical sense, they must have had a father, who was identified as Zurvān. Zurvanism is thus a type of monism, which appears in varying strengths in a few mythological texts in Pahlavi and in certain accounts by Christian writers.[26] Zurvān was hypostatized as a quaternity of four beings, himself Time, as well as Growth, Maturity and Decay. In Sasanian society Zurvanism seems to have been a prevalent theme which actually weakened Zoroastrianism against its Christian and latterly Islamic enemy. Its mythological and theological vocabulary was that of a crude ditheism, and since Ohrmazd was therefore reduced to a created entity, who was not primary in the order of things, it was an easy target for Christian and Islamic polemics. It was a religious form favoured by a complex and self-confident Sasanian society, whose absolute monarch corresponded to the high god Zurvān: the king's power was, like Zurvān's, absolute and beyond good and evil. In short, the moral and social basis of Sasanian society was in a process of decline and disintegration, brought about by the struggle for power between the Sasanian state and church. In the Syriac Christian martyrologies and other similar hostile accounts which refer to the Iranian religion, Christian caricatures of Zoroastrianism portray a Zurvanite ascendancy, most notably at the court of Shabuhr II (AD 309–79). Zurvanism was more vulnerable than Orthodox Zoroastrianism to the attacks of polemicists because it tended towards gnosticism and fatalism, and because its doctrine of God was, from the monotheistic point of view, fatally flawed. Ohrmazd could be dismissed as being a feeble, created being since, after all, he was the brother of Satan, sprung from a god of fate.

Zurvanism did not vanish when the Sasanian state was overthrown by the Islamic conquest, as we know from Muslim polemics against Zorastrianism, which were often directed at a Zurvanite rather than a Zoroastrian theology.[27] However, the ninth-century Pahlavi books give a picture of a religion which has returned to the old, orthodox theology and mythology of the Zarathushtra's original dualism, wherein Ohrmazd had to be the uncreated source of Good, and wherein the good creator was superior to any notion of fate and predestinationism. The reason for such a return appears to be that, having been deprived of their former autonomy and sovereignty as the state church of the Iranian Empire, Zoroastrians found themselves, as of old, struggling to maintain themselves against powerful aggressors *within their own land*. There is no trace of Zurvanite sympathies in the most authoritative Pahlavi sources: in fact it is attacked as being a theological impossibility, just like Christian trinitarianism and Islamic monotheism.

In modern times a tendency towards a kind of Zurvanite ditheism and overarching fatalistic monism reappeared as a result, principally, of the influence of the German scholar Martin Haug and the Parsi scholar M. Dhalla. Haug was attempting to reconcile the Zoroastrian scriptures with Christian monotheism, and like the Zurvanites of many centuries before, he posited the two spirits of the *Gāthās* as co-equals under a higher, omnipotent divinity, thus making evil a necessary part of the divine plan, and also as originating from the one source.[28] Certain modernist Parsi groups favoured Haug's reinterpretation of dualism as the original Zoroastrian doctrine, whereby Ohrmazd became above and beyond good and evil, the virtual equivalent of the Christian God and the Hindu ultimate reality.[29] Unwittingly they were resurrecting the old god Zurvān in the name of Ohrmazd. Even though every Pahlavi work contradicted such monism and modernist anti-ritualism, this was all dismissed, together with the testimony of the younger *Avesta*, as a corruption of the primitive faith. As Boyce has said,

> However one may refine the interpretation, it remains doctrinally utterly alien to the *Gāthās* and to the whole orthodox Zoroastrian tradition that evil should in any way originate from Ahura Mazdā.[30]

THE CONCEPTS OF *MĒNŌG* AND *GĒTĪG*

Although the doctrine of metaphysical dualism is a constant theme of the *Dēnkard* in the polemic against the false teachings of Islam, Judaism and Christianity, it is by no means the only one. An equally important notion, which is formulated as a philosophical given of the tradition, not as a separate doctrine, is that the universe exists in both *mēnōg* and *gētīg* worlds. The terms *mēnōg* and *gētīg* have two usages in the Pahlavi texts: (1) as adjectives or abstract nouns, when they denote the cosmological categories of spiritual, ideal, invisible, non-material on the one hand and actual, visible, and physical on the other; (2) as substantives, when they denote classes of beings: spiritual being and being of the physical world.[31] Although the *mēnōg* world was created prior to the *gētīg* world (see above), and although the term *mēnōg* signifies a complex of meanings concerned with religious values as opposed to the secular values of the *gētīg*, which has been subsequently attacked by evil, in the philosophical texts the former term denotes no moral superiority over the latter, only logical and chronological priority: the struggle against evil is ultimately for the *Frashegird*, the

'Renovation', of the *gētīg*. Even now the *gētīg* is not said to be evil in itself: it is full of sorrow and affliction, but this has come from outside the *gētīg* and has no reality of its own. Shaked's explanation is worth quoting at some length:

> the object of the material creation is to serve as the battle-ground for the fight against evil. It is in fact the only plane on which the struggle can at all be favourably decided. It is for this reason that it is crucially important to have a continuous existence of the material world, and for this reason it is also promised that there never will be a period in which man will not exist in the material world,[32] man being the main carrier of the battle against the evil spirits. We thus see here a certain dialectic relationship obtaining between the *mēnōg* and the *gētīg*. *Mēnōg* is the primary existence, but as it is invisible and immovable, it lacks an aspect of reality. The real clash between the good *mēnōg* and the evil *mēnōg* can only occur on a *gētīg* level. At the same time, however, the fight which takes place between the two parties is not conceived to be a straightforward war between equal rivals. Only Ohrmazd and his creations 'really' exist in *gētīg*, while Ahreman and the demons have no *gētīg* at all, and they only participate in the life of *gētīg* in a secondary way, parasitically, as it were.[33]

An ancient, indeed Gathic, doctrine of the faith is that man's choice for good or evil is preceded by a comparable pre-eternal choice of the *mēnōg* beings themselves.[34] By conforming itself to the wise choice for good made by the *mēnōg* beings of Ohrmazd's creation, the individual soul helps to speed the progress towards the Renovation of the *gētīg*. Man, endowed with human soul and physical nature, is said to be the embodiment of Ohrmazd, the Lord of Wisdom:

> By the fact of the creation by the creator the aspects of all the creatures are found in man who is the *Gētīg* form of Ohrmazd.

The religion teaches that the righteous man conforms his will to that of Ohrmazd, which is explained as follows:

> The proper nature of the Mazdean religion is the wisdom of Ohrmazd. And its wisdom is devised in knowledge and action. And its matter is knowledge of all, truth on the subject of all, the fact of foreseeing the need of everything, what is the proper character of Ohrmazd. Its function is to bring remedy to the creatures . . . And by all this knowledge of the power which is in things, brought into operation, and by the action, the healing of all the creatures freed from the Assault, to place them always in perfection, sanctity and complete, eternal happiness.[35]

Such ideas are, however, properly internal to the religion: without a philosophical argumentation they would have remained ineffective, in an apologetic work such as *Dēnkard* III, against the doctrines of other faiths. Theological explanations had to be accompanied by rational arguments, with little or no direct reference to scriptural authority, and the focus of this had to be through an examination of philosophical, psychological and ethical subjects. The focus of such considerations was the human soul and its relationship to the non-material principles of existence.

THE DOCTRINE OF THE EVIL ANTAGONIST

Since the dualism of Ohrmazd and Ahriman is a pervasive theme in the *Dēnkard* (because of its theological distinctiveness *vis-à-vis* the other religions), the problem of the nature of evil has a prominent place there. Many chapters take the form of an explanation of good actions, beings and qualities, followed by an equal and opposite treatment of evil doctrines and demonic beings – which are attributed polemically to the ideologues of the other religions. Men themselves cannot be wholly evil, just as even the most righteous may be only god-like:

> It is revealed that men resemble the gods and the demons. In the state of the mixture there are no pure gods or pure demons among men, but in the measure of their wisdom and other virtues men resemble the gods, and in the measure of their ignorance and other vices they resemble demons.[36]

Evil has, however, a 'purer' form, both in the *mēnōg* and the *gētīg*, and as such the religion affirms the reality of palpable spiritual malevolence, not merely human wickedness (which is really a perversion by such an extrinsic malevolence). Absolute evil is, however, unthinkable by definition, and even theologians may only describe it in terms of its opposition to the good. Good is defined as

> that whose movement is spontaneous; and non-movement comes from the outside; thus life is in its essence, desirable and praiseworthy . . . the cause of good among creatures is the good and the generosity inherent in the father and king of creatures, Ohrmazd the Creator. . . . And the summation of good is the Measure and its offspring the Law. The components of this offspring are wisdom, character, modesty, love, generosity, veracity, knowledge and the other virtues of which is made the essence of the *Amahraspands* and all the *mēnōg Yazads*, and as for men, life, holiness, prosperity, royalty, wisdom of the Religion, meritorious acts, justice and all the good things of the good creatures of the *gētīg*.[37]

Evil is defined as

> what is in itself without movement, and whose movement comes from outside: thus death, which is by itself undesirable and unpraiseworthy, it is not desirable and praiseworthy only extrinsically, thus illness, decrepitude, old age, misery and misfortune of unhappiness come to him from death. The cause of evil among the creatures of the *gētīg* and from the *mēnōg* is the principle of all malice, the Assault and Gannāg Mēnōg. The motive for which the calamity of the assault reaches to the good of the creatures is the will of these demons to destroy, because what is vulnerable, the creatures of Spenāg Mēnōg, they who by the principle of the evil, become the cause of all calamity.[38]

Such quasi-philosophical definitions of the nature of evil are inversions of the nature of good, since although evil stems from a wholly alien will, evil has no existence to be defined, only a denial and falsehood, which cannot be defined independently in language in this 'mixed state'. Other, more popular, genres of Zoroastrian literature gave much greater freedom to the religious imagination when depicting the terrors of evil powers in this world and the next. The descriptions of hellish afflictions for the wicked in a text such as the *Book of the Righteous Wīrāz* are quite as lurid as those of the visions of Dante's *Inferno*. In priestly, legalistic literature the punishments for ritual and criminal offences against the religious law indicate how cruelly the demonic agencies were believed to affect the wicked now and in the hereafter. Even in the more measured tones of *Dēnkard* III, however, the virulence of the Zoroastrian notion of evil forces is eloquently conveyed. There are said to be three species of antagonists to the creatures of Ohrmazd:

1 the adversaries who invade them through the *Mēnōg*: they are the demons and the *mēnōg drujs* ('devils'). They are to be defeated through the prayer formulae of the good religion, through sacrifices, and through the accomplishment of other acts of the good practice. Their power comes from the evil religions, from the cult of the demons and from other acts of bad practice.
2 The adversaries which invade them through their own nature are covetousness and envy and the other natures which are opposed thereby to virtue. One defeats them through *asn xrad*. . . . Their power comes from the predominance of concupiscence and other *drujs* in the nature.
3 The adversaries which invade them through the body are the *mar*, the adorers of the demons, corrupters of the world, the wolves and the monsters. . . . Their power stems from the defenders of wolves and monsters, adorers of the demons and many heretics which are throughout the world.[39]

Zoroastrian notions of wisdom and knowledge are concerned with the correct recognition of the above adversaries of the divine and human conditions. Knowledge of the distinction between the two powers, Ohrmazd and Ahriman, and the resultant opposing forces in the world is thus the basis of religion. In texts such as the third and sixth books of the *Dānkard*, instruction on such matters is conducted at a relatively high level of theological sophistication, so much so that some writers have sensed in it a kind of esotericism verging on the mystical.[40] However, such strands of religious thought, which gave fuller expression to the figurative and spiritualized interpretation of Zoroastrian ideas, can be shown to conform with the greater doctrinal, liturgical and ritual content of Zoroastrianism represented in other Pahlavi texts.[41] When the texts advocate human self-knowledge, they are upholding the old Zoroastrian teaching about the true origin and duty of the soul in its embodied state in the *gētīg*. This is to be distinguished from those gnostic, contemplative schemes of self-knowledge and self-perfectability which purport to lead to a perfected, interiorized, supreme intelligence, such as we find in certain Indian philosophies (for example Yoga, Advaita Vedānta) or in the Neoplatonic theosophical systems of Islamic Sufism in writers such as the thirteenth-century Ibn 'Arabī of Murcia. As Marijan Molé has said,

> It is not at all a question here of moral asceticism, but of the explanation of the situation of man in the world which has been polluted, in which malice and misery are strangers to its true nature. It can equally be shown how deliverance from bondage will be effected, not

> from matter as such, but from matter polluted by evil. . . . There is a point of vital optimism here: it is not a 'yes' to the material world, but rather a 'yes, but . . .': yes to the essence of the *gētīg* world, not to the pollution of the assault which, at present, is the rule there.[42]

> In the eschatological perspective, Zoroastrianism is an optimistic religion. The salvation that it preaches is not uniquely spiritual, it will be the flowering of life as we know it here, but transformed and transfigured, freed from the bondage of death and from the servitude which weighs on it at present. . . . The Zoroastrian ethic is an ethic of 'even when', of 'in spite of everything'. Even though the earth might be scorched, life continues, thanks to several places where the forces of evil have not been able to triumph. Even though death had invaded the entire world, life is perpetuated until the Renovation. Even though the Evil Spirit had submitted men to hunger and to thirst, they will not die from it because Ohrmazd has put at their disposal food and drink.[43]

Many of these principles are summed up in the Zoroastrian doctrine of the good measure (Pahlavi *paymān, paymānīgīh*, i.e. middle way, moderation or mean), which avoids either excess or deficiency (see Zaehner 1956) in all things. There is one exception to the rule of good measure, as a Pahlavi text says:

> Moderation is he who plans everything according to the right measure, so that there is no 'more' and 'less', for the right measure is the completeness of everything, except those things in which there is no need for moderation: knowledge and love and good deeds.[44]

PURITY AND THEOLOGY

It is well known that Zoroastrians were scrupulous in maintaining a code of purity rules which were quite as strict as those of Orthodox Judaism and Brahmanism, comprehensive of life from birth to death and beyond. Whilst the *Gāthās* themselves and the most ancient Avestan texts do not give details of purification and pollution, the foundation of the traditional observances is clearly established in the prophet Zarathushtra's own vision of a world which has been sullied by overpowering forces of evil, where the righteous must fight against the adversary in spiritual, moral and bodily form. In the foregoing discussion of how the spiritual world of Ohrmazd is embodied in the present state of *gētīg*, the physical state which is the battleground of the conflict of good and evil, the purity rules, routines and ritual activities of the righteous have not been mentioned, just as they are not described in the texts which give the most complete account of the theological system. This fact does not imply that the theology of texts such as the *Dēnkard* had dispensed with the traditional scheme of purification; in fact the whole theological system, from its doctrine of creation to its eschatological resolution in the concept of *Frashegird*, is built upon the principle of purification at all levels. The cosmic struggle of good against evil is dramatically enacted in the individual's struggle against impurity of thought, word and deed in the most mundane bodily, psychological and social encounters. The body is said to be one of the outer walls of defence against the adversary:

> Being on one's watch is this, one who makes his body like a fortress, and who places watch over it, keeping the *Yazads* inside and not letting the demons enter.[45]

The body of the righteous Zoroastrian was seen as being vulnerable to the constant attacks of evil, for the evil spirits are without a body of their own and so crave to be materialized. The purpose of personal, physical purification is explained by the *Dēnkard* as follows:

> It is possible to put Ahriman out of the world in this manner, namely, every person, for his own part, chases him out of his body, for the dwelling of Ahriman is in the bodies of men. When he will have no dwelling in the bodies of men, he will be annihilated from the whole world; for as long as there is in this world even a single person for a small demon, Ahriman is in the world.[46]

Although such explanations may be seen as a conscious rationalization of the ritual life, they are in accord with the original rationale of Zoroastrian purification, as mentioned before, i.e. that evil is extrinsic to the human condition, and indeed alien to the principle of life itself. Therefore the rigorous personal and social purity code delineated in the Avestan *Vīdaēvo dātəm* and the Pahlavi and Persian books, which extended to all matters of conduct, was no more and no less than a procedure of enactment of the original religious ethos in a highly ramified religious symbolism. The symbolism of purification extends to the highest level in the liturgical rites of cosmic purification of the great *Yasna* service and other rituals, which enact the drama of world renewal. This is analogous to the symbolism of similar rites in Judaism, Christianity, Brahmanism and other sacramental religions. The Zoroastrian's role as agent of God is to unmix the mixed world of good and evil and to maintain, as far as possible, discrete boundaries within which goodness may thrive and from which evil is excluded.[47]

For centuries the rituals and codes of rules about purification and pollution have been matters of internal, private relevance to Zoroastrians alone: this is why they do not feature in works which addressed issues of wider, inter-religious, theological concern such as the *Dēnkard* and similar texts. The Zoroastrian community in Islamic Iran, and later in India, was able to use its purity rules as a more or less effective means of perpetuating its identity, if not of sealing itself off entirely, in close proximity to the unsympathetic Muslim majority in Iran and the Hindu caste system in India.[48] As a minority community which was often brutally abused under Iranian Islamic rulers, Zoroastrians became inward looking, both socially and theologically, so that religious dialogue and apologetics fell into disuse as irrelevant to the major concern of survival as a community. The theological works of the ninth and tenth centuries were the last great expression of the working out of Zoroastrian spirituality in intellectual terms, until writers in the modern period took up the task against the new challenge of Christian missionizing and western secularism. Unfortunately the only other major texts which survive from the later medieval period, the Persian *Rivāyats* ('traditions') sent by priests from Iran to India to instruct the community there on points of religion, have nothing new to say on theological matters. They are concerned almost entirely with the explanation of matters of ritual, custom, institution, and other traditional lore. When the Persian *Rivāyats* do touch upon theological subjects, their treatment is either derived entirely from the Pahlavi books or is coloured by the experience of having had to compromise with the pressures of Islam upon their own religion.

CONCLUSION: THE PROBLEM OF THE MISREPRESENTATION OF ZOROASTRIAN THOUGHT

For over 150 years, since Christian missionaries in India and Iranologists in Europe both independently reinterpreted and re-evaluated Zoroastrianism, the theology of the Pahlavi books has been more or less misrepresented. The Zoroastrian doctrine of God is different in fundamental respects from that of classical theism in Christian theology. This fact seems often to have been overlooked by modern writers who have attempted to give an account of Zoroastrian thought. Amongst the nineteenth-century Christian missionaries in India such a bias is understandable as part of their polemic against a religion which, they assumed, was altogether inferior to their own. Amongst scholars the tendency may be attributed to the limitation of their own unacknowledged epistemological and theological categories, derived ultimately from the legacy of Platonism and of the classical theism of Catholic and Protestant Christianity. The stumbling blocks of this classical Christian theism for a correct understanding of the Iranian religion have in some instances been the self-same obstacles which have impeded modern western theologians in their attempt to represent Christianity to the contemporary audience. The Zoroastrian God is omniscient and all good. Yet he is opposed by another entity, an evil principle, Ahriman. Monotheists of the classical theistic tradition in western theology jumped to the conclusion that such a God must therefore be impotent and that the Zoroastrian theology was incurably ditheistic: thus such a doctrine of God must be inadequate and feeble. In fact, in the context of the larger whole of Zoroastrian thought and practice the Zoroastrian system is theologically highly plausible, but it may require a radical adjustment of theological assumptions for this to become apparent to the Christian thinker. Such an adjustment has already been announced for Christianity itself by theologians such as Charles Hartshorne and Schubert Ogden, who have developed a 'Process Theology', following on from the philosophical lead given by A. N. Whitehead.[49] It may be that the old Zoroastrian doctrines of the nature of Ohrmazd and his Immortals, the attribution of evil to an alien and impossible will, the dynamic role of the human will, and the nature of the states *mēnōg* and *gētīg* will be better understood from a vantage point of such a Process Theology. Such a re-evaluation of the old Iranian religion is no more than Jewish thinkers have asked for from their Christian counterparts, and Jewish theology has in some respects anticipated Process Theology in its rejection of the shackles of classical Christian theism. A similar reappraisal of Zoroastrian theology on its own terms is called for, which would accommodate the prophet Zarathushtra's own vision of the dynamic relationship between God and man, good and evil, spirit and matter.

NOTES

1 The most up to date scholarly study of the history of Zoroastrianism, with bibliographies of other works on the subject, is Boyce 1975, 1982 and (with F. Grenet) 1991. The same author has produced a one-volume history of the faith, Boyce 1987.

2 On the *Avesta* see K. Hoffman, J. Kellens in the entry 'Avesta' in Yarshater 1988–; Gershevitch 1968; and Boyce 1968.

3 Boyce 1968:41.

4 In Zoroastrian texts it was usual to use a different vocabulary when describing Ahriman and other demonic forces from that used of Ohrmazd and his good creations. The demonic vocabulary has a philosophical significance in that Ahriman, as the denial of existence, cannot be said to 'exist', just as the destroyer of all being can never be said to 'be', and so his demons, who are the corrupters of life, cannot be said to 'live', 'eat', 'speak', but rather 'lurk', 'devour', 'gabble'. The very name of Ahriman is written upside down in Pahlavi script so that the reader and writer are reminded that he is the inversion of reality and an altogether unnatural entity.

5 *Greater Bundahishn* (*GBd.*), ch. 1, trans. Boyce 1984: 45ff.

6 ibid.

7 ibid.

8 ibid., 50.

9 De Menasce 1958:17

10 De Menasce 1975:554. De Menasce gives an excellent brief description of the *Dēnkard* and other Pahlavi works in this article.

11 Shaki 1970:277. Shaki's is an excellent technical study of the Greek ancestry of certain cosmological and ontological doctrines in four passages of the third book of the *Dēnkard*. It should be pointed out that in spite of the interest of modern scholars in such foreign influences in the *Dēnkard*, these elements should be seen in their context as having formed a part, but by no means a major one, in the apologetic efforts of the authors; the indigenous Mazdean theology and metaphysics remain the dominant mode of the *Dēnkard*'s apologetics.

12 De Menasce 1975:22.

13 *Dēnkard*, ed. Madan (*DkM.*), 264.6ff.: also translated by De Menasce 1973:ch. 240. pp. 251ff.

14 *DkM.* 68.15–16, trans. De Menasce 1973:82.

15 *DkM.* 104.14–15, trans. De Menasce 1973:111.

16 *DkM.* 117.10–15, also trans. De Menasce 1973:123.

17 *DkM.* 69.1–7, also trans. De Menasce 1973 : 82.
18 *DkM.* 362.10–14, also trans. De Menasce 1973 : 341f.
19 *DkM.* 142.22–143.3, also trans. De Menasce 1973 : 144.
20 So observes De Menasce, 1973 : 399.
21 *DkM.* 149.11, trans. De Menasce 1973 : 150.
22 *DkM.* 198.22–199.4, also trans. De Menasce 1973 : 193.
23 *DkM.* 375.19–376.18, trans. De Menasce 1973 : 353.
24 See M. Boyce's arguments for a reappraisal of the independence of the Zurvanite cult from mainstream Zoroastrianism in Boyce 1990.
25 Following the original theory of Spiegel 1873 : 4–12, 182–7.
26 e.g. Eznik of Kołb, the Armenian apologist, translated, along with similar polemical passages, in Zaehner 1972.
27 See Boyce 1990 : 26.
28 Haug 1971 : 303ff., also cited in Boyce 1984 : 133ff.; see also Dhalla 1914.
29 See Williams 1986.
30 Boyce 1975 : 194
31 See the exhaustive treatment of these and related terms in Shaked 1971 : 59–107.
32 *Dādestān ī Dēnīg*, question 34, 2, trans. M. Molé 1959a:157ff.
33 Shaked 1971 : 69, and see also his detailed essay, Shaked 1967 : 227–34.
34 *Yasna* 30, quoted in the chapter on Zarathushtra's teachings above.
35 *DkM.* 329.14–330.6, also trans. De Menasce 1973 : 313.
36 *DkM.* 386.15–387.13, trans. De Menasce 1973 : 362.
37 *DkM.* 222.7–19, trans. De Menasce 1973 : 213f.
38 *DkM.* 223.10–19, trans. De Menasce 1973 : 214f.
39 *DkM.* 39.13–40.3, trans. De Menasce 1973 : 58f.
40 See, for example, Shaked 1979a.
41 See Shaked's discussion of the contents of *Dēnkard* VI in his introduction to his translation of that work, Shaked 1979b : xxivff.
42 Molé 1959b : 182.
43 Molé 1959b : 189–90.
44 *Pahlavi Rivāyat*, Williams 1990 II : 108.
45 *DkM.* 583.5–7, trans. Shaked 1979b : 203, §E34a.
46 *DkM.* 530.20–531.3, trans. Shaked 1979b : 103, §264.
47 See further Williams 1989.
48 See further Williams 1986.
49 Principally Whitehead 1978. See also Hartshorne 1984; Ogden 1967: Pailin 1972–3 and 1989.

REFERENCES

Anklesaria, B. T. (1956) *Zand-Ākāsīh Iranian or Greater Bundahišn*, Bombay: Rahnumae Mazdayasnan Sabha.

Boyce, M. (1968) 'Middle Persian literature', in *Iranistik, Handbuch der Orientalistik*, Abt. I, Bd IV, Abschn. 2, Lfg. I, Leiden: E. J. Brill.

—— (1975) *A History of Zoroastrianism*, vol. I, *The Early Period, Handbuch der Orientalistik*, Leiden: E. J. Brill.

—— (1982) *A History of Zoroastrianism*, vol. II, *Under the Achaemenians*, *Handbuch der Orientalistik*, Leiden: E. J. Brill.

—— (1984) *Textual Sources for the Study of Zoroastrianism*, Manchester: Manchester University Press.
—— (1987) *Zoroastrians: Their Religious Beliefs and Practices*, 3rd revised repr., London: Routledge & Kegan Paul.
—— (1990) 'Further reflections on Zurvanism', in *Iranica Varia: Papers in Honour of Professor Ehsan Yarshater*, Leiden: E. J. Brill.
Boyce, M. and Grenet, F. (1991) *A History of Zoroastrianism*, vol. III, *Under Macedonian and Roman Rule*, *Handbuch der Orientalistik*, Leiden: E. J. Brill.
Dēnkard (1911), ed. D. M. Madan, Bombay: Society for the Promotion of Researches into the Zoroastrian Religion (*DkM.*).
Dhalla, M. N. (1914) *Zoroastrian Theology*, New York: Oxford University Press.
Gershevitch, I, (1968) 'Avestan literature', in *Iranistik, Handbuch der Orientalistik*, Abt. I, Bd IV, Abschn. 2, Lfg. I, Leiden: E. J. Brill.
Hartshorne, C. (1984) *Omnipotence and Other Theological Mistakes*, New York: Albany.
Haug, M. (repr. 1978) *Essays on the Sacred Language, Writings and Religion of the Parsis*, New Delhi: Cosmo Publications; 1st edn 1862, 3rd edn, London: Trübner, 1884.
Menasce, J. P. de (1958) *Une Encyclopédie Mazdéenne: Le Dēnkart*, Paris: Presses Universitaires de France.
—— (1973) *Le Troisième Livre du Dēnkart, traduit du pehlevi*, Paris: Librairie C. Klincksieck.
—— (1975) 'Zoroastrian literature after the Muslim Conquest', *Cambridge History of Iran*, vol. IV, ed. R. N. Frye, Cambridge: Cambridge University Press, 543–65.
Molé, M. (1959a), 'Le Problème zurvanite', *Journale asiatique* 247 : 431–69.
—— (1959b) 'Un ascétisme moral dans les livres pehlevis', *Revue de l'histoire des religions* 155 : 145–90.
Ogden, S. M. (1967) *The Reality of God and Other Essays*, London: SCM Press.
Pailin, D. A. (1972–3) 'Process Theology – why and what?', *Faith and Thought* 100(1) : 45–66.
—— (1989) *God and the Processes of Reality*, London: Routledge.
Shaked, S. (1967) *Studies in Mysticism and Religion presented to G. Scholem*, Jerusalem.
—— (1971) 'The notions *mēnōg* and *gētīg* in the Pahlavi texts', *Acta Orientalia* 33 : 59–107.
—— (1979a) 'Esoteric trends in Zoroastrianism', *Proceedings of the Israel Academy of Sciences and Humanities* 3 : 175–221.
—— (1979b) *The Wisdom of the Sasanian Sages*, Persian Heritage Series, Boulder, Colo.: Westview Press.
Shaki, M. (1970) 'Some basic tenets of the eclectic metaphysics of the *Dēnkart*', *Archiv Orientalni* 38.
Spiegel, F. (1873) *Eranische Alterthumskunde*, vol. II, Leipzig.
Whitehead, A. N. (1978) *Process and Reality*, New York: Free Press.
Williams, A. V. (1986) 'The real Zoroastrian dilemma', in Victor C. Hayes (ed.) *Identity Issues and World Religions, Selected Proceedings of the Fifteenth Congress of the International Association for the History of Religions*, Adelaide: AASR.
—— (1989) 'The body and the boundaries of Zoroastrian spirituality', *Religion* 19 : 227–39.
—— (1990) *The Pahlavi Rivāyat Accompanying the Dādestān ī Dēnīg*, 2 vols, Copenhagen: Royal Danish Academy of Sciences.
Yarshater, E. (1988—) *Encyclopaedia Iranica*, London and New York: Routledge & Kegan Paul.
Zaehner, R. C. (1956) *The Teachings of the Magi*, London: George Allen & Unwin.
—— (1961) *The Dawn and Twilight of Zoroastrianism*, London: Weidenfeld & Nicolson.
--- (1972) *Zurvan: A Zoroastrian Dilemma*, Oxford: Oxford University Press, 1955, reprinted with new Introduction, New York: Biblo & Tannen, 1972.

3

MORALS AND SOCIETY IN ZOROASTRIAN PHILOSOPHY

Philip G. Kreyenbroek

INTRODUCTION

If philosophy is defined as the 'investigation of the nature of being, and of the causes and laws of all things', Zoroastrianism could be said to be a strongly philosophical religion. In the extant tradition, however, only a few texts of a predominantly philosophical nature are preserved. An important reason for this is undoubtedly to be sought in the fact that, until well into the Sasanian era, the religious tradition of the Zoroastrians was largely an oral one. Children of priestly families began to memorize Avestan texts at an early age. Some priests, the intellectuals of their societies, then went on to study exegesis, pondering the meaning and implications of the sacred texts. It was among such scholar-priests, it seems, that the body of doctrines and ideas developed which could be said to constitute Zoroastrian philosophy. Comparatively few of their insights and conclusions, however, were later recorded in writing. The teaching of exegesis, moreover, took place largely in the form of questions and answers about individual topics and, as a result, the extant tradition shows a greater preoccupation with concrete answers than with the reasoning behind these. In analysing the nature and history of Zoroastrian thought in the field of social and moral philosophy, it will therefore be assumed that the relatively meagre range of data available to us represents a far richer vein of oral teaching, whose contents can legitimately be deduced from the extant sources.

In studying the material it seems possible to discern a link between historical realities and the philosophical attitudes and ideas of the period concerned. In discussing the evidence, a roughly historical approach will therefore be followed here, based on the 'classical' Zoroastrian tradition: i.e. the *Avesta*, the Old Persian inscriptions, the Middle Persian, and to a lesser extent the early New Persian Zoroastrian texts. The theories about morals and society current among Indian and Iranian Zoroastrians of the nineteenth and twentieth centuries, being heterogeneous and in part strongly influenced by non-Zoroastrian (notably western) systems of thought, can hardly be regarded as a coherent and recognizable branch of Zoroastrian philosophy.

THE PRE-ZOROASTRIAN BACKGROUND

The strong links which exist in Zoroastrian thought between concepts of morality and views on the nature and purpose of society probably have their origin in the pre-Zoroastrian 'Indo-Iranian' religion. The ancient Indo-Iranians had no written tradition, however, and much of what follows is therefore necessarily speculative.

One of the fundamental concepts of the Indo-Iranian religion, and also of Zoroastrian moral and social philosophy, was *asha* (Vedic *ṛta*), an all-pervading principle which is perhaps best understood as 'right order', or indeed 'moral order'. All things that were true and right, and all processes evolving in the proper way, were held to be in harmony with this universal law: the seasons changed because of *asha*, and the man who spoke the truth acted in accord with it. The liar, the contract-breaker and the thief, on the other hand, were thought to violate *asha*. Infringements of the laws of *asha* were held to provoke the wrath of the gods who guarded that principle, especially Mithra and Varuna (on whom see further below). There is no indication that the Indo-Iranians believed that punishment for sins or wicked deeds would follow after death. Retribution, therefore, was presumably expected in this life. Since sinful acts were both infringements of the laws of society and offences against gods, concepts of justice and punishment were an integral part of religious thought. Priests, it seems, had judicial as well as ritual functions, and thus acted as human representatives of the divine powers guarding order. Ordeals by fire and water (elements which were particularly connected with Mithra and Varuna) probably played an important role in such judicial processes.

An important aspect of Indo-Iranian thought concerning order and justice may have been that sinful words, thoughts and deeds were held to weaken *asha*, and the forces of good generally. Such good acts as prayers and rituals, on the other hand, were necessary to strengthen the forces of good, which would in turn benefit the world generally, and the righteous community in particular. An ancient Iranian prayer to the sun (*Nyāyesh* 1.11f.), which is almost certainly of pre-Zoroastrian origin, implies that without prayer the sun might not come up, and light might not come to the world, which would then be left in the power of evil and darkness. Acts of devotion, and righteous acts generally, are plainly indispensable for the proper functioning of the world; the obligation on individuals to fulfil their role in society, and to carry out the duties imposed by their religion, could therefore be defined as a moral one.

The links between the divine sphere, social obligations and morality are further illustrated by the concepts of some Indo-Iranian divinities. The most prominent of these in the Zoroastrian tradition is Mithra (Vedic Mitra). Mithra, one of the guardians of *asha*, protects righteous individuals and communities, and punishes offenders (for example *Yasht* 10.28: 'You, Mithra, are both wicked and very good to countries; you, Mithra, are both wicked and very good to men'). Mithra's name, it seems, originally meant 'covenant, contract, compact', and the god's original concern may have been with obligations arising out of solemn agreements between societies or individuals (see *Yasht* 10.116–17; Gershevitch 1967 : 130ff.; Thieme 1957). Similarly, the Indo-Iranian god Varuna (Vedic Varuna; the Avestan form of the name, which is not attested, would have been Vouruna) is believed to have embodied the power inherent in the oath; the god Aryaman had special connections with the laws of hospitality (Thieme 1957). The role of the vow in the social life of the ancient Indo-Iranian peoples has been studied by Schmidt (1958 : 143ff.), who points out that the leader of society held a special position in this sphere.

The special role of leaders of society, or rulers, in the religious thought of the Indo-Iranians is also reflected by the myths surrounding *khvarenah*, an ancient and prominent concept in the Iranian tradition which has no obvious counterpart in the Vedas. *Khvarenah* may originally have been a force which brought fertility, growth, and perhaps general well-being: it was closely connected with light, sun, fire and water (Duchesne-Guillemin 1963). *Khvarenah* is said to be brought down from heaven each dawn by the divinities, and distributed over the earth (*Nyāyesh* 1.11). This clearly implies that it is expected to benefit all men. The tradition also suggests, however, that kings and leaders of society had particularly close links with *khvarenah*, and that its presence or absence – with all this implied for the community – was dependent upon the moral qualities of the ruler (the first person to 'possess' *khvarenah* was the mythical King Yima, from whom *khvarenah* fled when he spoke an untruth. *Yasht* 19.34). In the later, Zoroastrian tradition, the links between *khvarenah* and kings are very pronounced, and it may be significant that in some Middle Persian texts, the concept of *khvarenah* is closely linked to that of *khvēshkārīh*, 'fulfilling one's proper function in life (and thus in society)' (Dhabhar 1949: glossary, 54, s.v. *khvēshkārīh*). It would seem, therefore, that a hierarchical model may have played a part in Iranian thought from pre-Zoroastrian times onwards: society as a whole was believed to benefit if its leader was virtuous; the good ruler – no doubt advised by priests – then had the responsibility of ensuring that all members of society could carry out their proper duties.

If this partial reconstruction of Indo-Iranian ideas is valid, these ideas would appear to reflect the morals and ethics of a stable society. It is widely held, in fact, that this view of the world evolved over the centuries or millennia when the Indo-Iranians lived as pastoralists on the central Asian steppes. The concept of *asha* may well have been inspired by the strong awareness these herdsmen had of the recurring rhythms of life. Such divine figures as Mithra and Varuna, lords of the compact and the oath, seem to reflect the awe in which they held the implicit or explicit laws which governed their societies.

Both the Indian and the Iranian traditions suggest, however, that a different ethos gained prominence amongst the Indian and some of the Iranian peoples at some stage. This new ethos seems to be epitomized by the god Indra, an amoral, warlike divinity of relatively late origin (see Benveniste and Renou 1934; Thieme 1960). The cult of Indra may perhaps reflect the new social conditions obtaining at the time of the Indo-Iranian migrations, when the earlier centuries of stability were replaced by a heroic age. Unlike such gods as Mithra and Varuna, Indra was not bound by the laws of *asha* (see Boyce 1975:53–4). He is called the god 'by whom all things have been made unstable' (*Rig Veda* II.12.4). His favour, it seems, was most likely to be secured by sacrifices (*Rig Veda* II.12.14,15), on a scale which may have seemed excessive to those who held more traditional views. One might conjecture, therefore, that the new social conditions which affected the Indo-Iranian peoples gave rise in some milieux to a novel concept of morality, in which strength, might, riches and the ability to feast the gods played a more important role than they had done in earlier stages of the religious life of these communities.

EARLY ZOROASTRIANISM

Morals and society in the *Gāthās*

It seems likely that Zoroastrianism represents a 'moral' reaction against the ethos of a heroic age. Zarathushtra – a priest trained in the religious traditions of his people – accepted most of the teachings of the ancient faith relating to *asha*. The evil forces which were opposed to that principle, however, played a far more central role in his thinking than they appear to have done in the religious thought of an earlier and more peaceful age (on Zarathushtra's teaching see more fully Chapter 1 above).

Zarathushtra held that a number of moral forces (such as *asha*, 'right order', *Vohu Manah*, 'good thought', etc.) were operative in the universe both at the macrocosmic and microcosmic level, and that these were opposed by evil powers. The leader of these, the Evil Spirit (*Angra Mainyu*), has 'ruined' the world (see *Y.* 45.1), causing it to lapse from its original ideal state into a condition of instability and strife. This state of 'mixture', in which the world now finds itself, is to be brought to an end at some future time, when the forces of evil will finally be defeated by those of righteousness.

Both the Good and Evil Spirits have acquired their moral character through choice: 'Of these two Spirits the Evil One chose the worst action, the Bounteous Spirit . . . chose *asha*, and likewise those who . . . satisfy *Ahura Mazdā* with proper acts' (*Y.* 30.5). The concept of a conscious choice between good and evil is the basis of Zoroastrian moral philosophy. The choice of the divinities and *daēvas*, it seems, was made when the two spirits created the foundations of existence (*Y.*30.4,5,6; some translations, for example Humbach 1959:85, imply that Zarathushtra regarded their choice as a continuing process, but since there is no evidence that Zarathushtra or any Zoroastrian ever sought to influence the choice of the *daēvas*, this seems unlikely). All creations except man were probably held to share their moral nature with the spirit who created them, and to have made their choice accordingly. Man, on the other hand, is the only creation in the universe whose present and individual choice can influence the balance between the opposing forces, and hasten or delay the defeat of evil. The choice for righteousness, it seems, implied a conscious effort on the part of the individual to realize in his or her own life the moral forces personified by the Gathic Entities (see above, Chapter 1, and Kreyenbroek 1985:7–30). After death the men and women who choose righteousness will be rewarded by a blissful existence, while those who choose evil will dwell in the realms of darkness (*Y.* 31.20; see also Chapter 1 above). Unlike the ancient Indo-Iranian religion, Zoroastrianism thus teaches that the individual soul will be rewarded or punished for its words, thoughts and deeds in an afterlife; this does not imply, however, that society was no longer responsible for the behaviour of its members; although there appears to be no evidence of this in the *Gāthās*, the Zoroastrian tradition as a whole clearly demonstrates that the priesthood continued to fulfil its ancient judicial functions.

The *Gāthās* show that it was not only the choice of individuals which exercised the prophet's mind; the concept of society also played an important role in his teachings. The links he perceived between society, priests and the divine sphere are aptly illustrated by a well-known Gathic verse: 'They [lit. "one"] keep me away from family and tribe. The community to which I would belong does not accept [lit. "satisfy"] me, nor the evil rulers of the land; how, then, can I satisfy Thee, o Lord Wisdom?' (*Y.* 46.1). It is not just individual lives which the powers of evil seek to destroy, but the very structure of society, which enables men to live in accord with *asha*; members of the Zoroastrian community should therefore fight these forces by all possible means:

> Let no one belonging to the Evil one (be allowed to) listen to your powerful utterances and teachings, for they will deliver the house, the settlement, the district and the country up to evil and death: therefore ward them off with (your) weapon.
>
> (*Y.* 31.18)

In order to function effectively and withstand the onslaughts of evil, society needs a leader; Zarathustra's awareness of this is suggested by *Y.* 31.16:

> This I ask, what of him, the blessed one, who will strive (?) to increase the power of the (righteous) house, the district and the land. One resembling Thee, Lord Wisdom: when and through what action shall he appear?

Rulers, in turn, needed the guidance of a righteous priest, just as priests could not fulfil their function in society without the protection and patronage of rulers or powerful men. Righteous priests were mediators between society and the gods, instructing both the ruler and the community at large as to the wishes of the divine beings, and seeking to restore harmony between the divine and human spheres when sinners had provoked the divine wrath: 'As I shall turn away from Thee both disobedience and Evil Thought, o Wisdom; the arrogance of the family and the deceit which is very near to the community, and the scoffers among the tribe' (*Y.* 33.4).

If some of the later legends about Zarathushtra's life – which seem to find some confirmation in the *Gāthās* – are based on fact, Zarathushtra eventually found the patronage of a ruler, Kavi Vishtaspa. In one of the *Gāthās* (*Y.* 46), Zarathushtra depicts himself in the process of celebrating a ritual on behalf of this righteous ruler and prominent members of his court, and states that he will pronounce 'verses, not un-verses' (*Y.* 46.16) – i.e. effective utterances, such as only a righteous priest can pronounce, rather than the powerless mumblings of the priests of false cults. The ruler's patronage of a priest therefore results in benefit for himself, and so for the community as a whole. This passage could thus be said to illustrate the Zoroastrian view that members of a righteous society who perform their proper duties (in later terms, their *khvēshkārīh*) will benefit themselves, those they serve or befriend, the rest of their community, and ultimately the entire good creation. Zoroastrianism, it seems, recognized from its very beginning that men have different functions in society, and therefore different spheres of competence.

The passage *Y.* 46.6: 'for that (man) is wicked who is very good to the wicked one; that (man) is righteous to whom the righteous one is dear' may well sum up the essence of early Zoroastrian social morality as far as most laymen were concerned. In accepting Zarathushtra's message of a fundamental and universal ethical dualism, and in rejecting the amoral but undoubtedly powerful *daēvas* – which they can hardly have done without trepidation – they made an essentially moral choice, and learned to understand their lives in moral terms. Because of their choice, their efforts to realize the moral qualities represented by the Gathic Entities in their own lives, and because they shared their views on the nature of reality with the other followers of Zarathushtra, they belonged to the 'righteous', Zoroastrian community. In matters involving questions of greater complexity, however, they were expected to obey the authority of the prophet. In fact the concept *s(e)raosha*, 'hearkening, obedience', which links the prophet to the divine sphere, is also used to describe the relations between the prophet (or priest) and his followers (see Kreyenbroek 1985:7–30).

The early centuries

That membership of and loyalty to the Zoroastrian community played an extremely important part in the early Zoroastrian concept of morality is suggested by the 'Confession of Faith' (*Fravarānē*). After a formal rejection of the *daēvas*, and proclamation of one's faith in Ahura Mazdā and other good divinities (*Yazata*), a Zoroastrian vows (*Y*. 12.2–4):

> I renounce the theft and raiding of cattle, and harm and destruction for Mazdā-worshipping homes. To those who are worthy I shall grant movement at will, and lodging at will, those who are upon this earth with their cattle. With reverence for *Asha*, with offerings lifted up, that I avow: Henceforth I shall not, in caring for either life or limb, bring harm or destruction on Mazdā-worshipping homes. I forswear the company of the wicked *daēvas* . . . and the followers of the *daēvas*, of demons and the followers of demons.
>
> (Boyce 1984: 57)

Many older parts of the *Yashts* show a marked preoccupation with battle, victory, protection of the righteous and defeat of the followers of evil (for example *Yasht* 10.8,9,11,23,26; *Yasht* 14, *passim*; *Y*. 57.10,15,29, etc.), and there are occasional descriptions of non-Zoroastrian communities and their wicked practices (*Yasht* 14.54–6). This suggests that, for earlier Zoroastrian thinkers, the cosmic opposition between good and evil found its clearest and most immediate expression in the conflicts between Zoroastrian communities and their pagan foes, so that the fact of belonging to the community of the righteous was in itself felt to be morally significant. The moral and physical efforts required of members of early Zoroastrian communities, and their expected rewards, are aptly summed up in the following passage, *Y*. 68.12–13:

> Grant, o good Waters, to me, the celebrant priest, and to us, the loudly worshipping Mazdā-worshippers . . . priestly teachers and disciples, and men and women, boys and girls, and those who practise husbandry; (we) who stay in our places in order to overcome anxiety, to overcome the hostilities and famines caused by the army, or stemming from hostile enemies, (grant us) the seeking and finding of the straightest path, which leads most directly to *asha*, and to the existence of the righteous (i.e. paradise), the brilliant, offering all bliss.

The structure of society clearly continued to play a part in early Zoroastrian thought. As in the *Gāthās*, the territorial hierarchy of 'house, village or settlement, district and country' is frequently mentioned in Young Avestan texts. The *Gāthās*, it seems, only distinguish between two social groups, 'priests' and 'men' (see Boyce 1982b, 1987). Most later texts, however, recognize three or four social classes: priests, warriors, husbandmen and sometimes artisans (three classes: for example *Y*. 11.6; *Yasht* 19.8, 13.88; *Visparad* 3.2,5; four: *Y*. 19.17). Such is the proper structure of a stable and righteous society, a structure which was held to have its origin in the implications of the *Ahunvar* prayer, which Ahura Mazdā pronounced before he created the world: 'And this Mazdā-spoken word has three verses, four classes, five *ratus* [on which see below]. . . . Which are the classes? The priest, the warrior, the cattle-breeding farmer, and the artisan' (*Y*. 19.16–17).

Of these classes, it is the priesthood whose activities are most fully described in the *Avesta*. Apart from the general Avestan word for 'priest', *athaurvan*, terms often used in Young Avestan texts for members of the priesthood are *tkaēsha*, 'teacher' (for example *Yasht* 13.151), and *ratu*, a word analysed as cognate with *asha*. The term *ratu* can be used for a divine or human being who is responsible for the proper development of a given phenomenon, group or species, and is in authority over it. Thus it can be used of Ahura Mazdā, of lesser divine beings appointed by him (see *Yasht* 8.44), and also of Zarathushtra and of the living Zoroastrian priests, who derive their authority from that of the prophet. The passage *Y.* 19.18, 'Who are the *ratus*? The one of the house, the one of the village, the one of the district, the one of the land, Zarathushtra is the fifth', probably refers to priestly authorities (Gershevitch 1967:265–6, 296ff.) The fact that *Y.* 19.18 names Zarathushtra as the head of the priestly hierarchy suggests that the authority of the individual priest was held to be derived from that of the prophet and, through him, from the *Yazatas* (a similar passage, *Yasht* 10.115, implies that supreme authority could also be attributed to Zarathushtra's ideal representative on earth, the *Zarathushtrōtema*). Although such passages cannot be taken as proof that a unified, formal hierarchy actually existed in pre-Achaemenian times, they do suggest that the ideal of a priestly hierarchy was present in Zoroastrian thought at an early age.

The extent of the authority of a local *ratu* over his followers is illustrated by a prayer presumably of partly pre-Achaemenian origin, the *Āfrīnagān ī Gāhāmbār*: if those under his authority failed to contribute fittingly to the expenses of the obligatory religious gatherings (*Gāhāmbār*), the *ratu* could deny them the right to conclude a contract (*Āfrīnagān* 3.8) or the right to undergo a fire-ordeal (3.9); he could impose fines (3.10), declare their possessions forfeit (3.11), or deny them 'the *ahurian* teaching' (3.12). The latter punishment, implying no doubt that the *ratu* refused to accept the culprit as a member of his congregation, meant that such a person was outlawed, and could be driven away from the community (3.13). Another – possibly later – Avestan text (*Vendīdād* 16.18) states that those who do not recognize the authority of a priestly teacher are in a state of mortal sin.

According to early Zorastrian philosophy, the local priest thus played a central role in the leadership of society: he must ensure that those under his authority obeyed the laws and fulfilled the requirements of the religion. His followers owed him obedience, and he was entitled to impose drastic penalties if they disregarded his authority. Society, it seems, was defined by the concept of territorial hierarchies (there are several references to both spiritual leaders and secular masters of house, village, district and country), and its spiritual and moral guidance was held to be assured by the chain of authority whose last link was the local priest, and which derived ultimately from Ahura Mazdā's revelation to Zarathushtra.

THE ACHAEMENIAN PERIOD

It has been convincingly shown that members of the family of the Achaemenians, who ruled over the first Persian Empire from 550 until 331 BC, were Zoroastrians before they came to imperial power (Boyce 1982a:41ff.). It seems possible that religious issues played a role in a propaganda-campaign on their behalf which may have been conducted by Zoroastrian priests (Boyce 1982:41ff.). From a struggling faith intent upon survival, Zoroastrianism under the Achaemenians became virtually a state religion, upheld by a powerful dynasty whose legitimacy was thought to derive in part from its righteousness in matters of religion. Such close links between dynasty, state and religion may help to explain Herodotus' statement (*Historiai* I.132) that a Persian offering sacrifice should always pray for the well-being of 'all the Persians and the King'.

The philosophy reflected by the inscriptions of the Achaemenian kings – particularly those of Darius I (521–486 BC) and Xerxes I (486–465 BC) – appears to be based largely on the concepts and ideas of early Zoroastrianism, which in some cases are rooted in pre-Zoroastrian thought. The antithesis between good and evil (called 'the Lie': Old Persian *drauga*, Avestan *drug*) is central in the world-view expressed there. The Achaemenians, it is said, have come to bring stability and order to the Iranian realms:

> Saith Darius the king: Much which was ill-done, that I made good. Provinces were in commotion; one man smote the other. This I brought about by the favour of Ahuramazda, that the one does not smite the other at all, each one is in his place. My law – that they fear, so that the stronger does not smite nor destroy the weaker.
>
> (*DSe*. 30–41; Kent 1953:142)

It is further claimed that the King's rule has established a just law which rewards the virtuous and punishes the wicked. It has respect for truth, ensures the rights of each individual to contribute to society according to his capacity, and is thus in accord with the ordinances of Ahura Mazdā; the King, moreover, is temperate and virtuous, as a Zoroastrian should be:

> Saith Darius the King: By the favour of Ahuramazda I am of such a sort that I am a friend to right, I am not a friend to wrong. It is not my desire that the weak man should have wrong done to him by the mighty; nor is that my desire, that the mighty man should have wrong done to him by the weak. What is right, that is my desire. I am not a friend to the man who is a Lie-follower. I am not hot-tempered. What things develop in my anger, I hold firmly under control by my thinking power. I firmly rule over my own (impulses). The man who cooperates, him I reward according to his cooperative action. Who does harm, him I punish according to the damage. It is not my desire that a man should do harm; nor indeed is that my desire, that he should not be punished if he should do harm. What a man says against a man, that does not convince me, until he satisfies the Ordinance of Good Regulation. What a man does or performs (for me) according to his (natural) powers, (therewith) I am satisfied, and my pleasure is abundant, and I am well satisfied.
>
> (*DNb*. 5–11; Kent 1953:140)

Achaemenian rule is aided by the divine beings because it represents stability and right order (Old Persian *arta*, Avestan *asha*):

> Saith Darius the King: for this reason Ahuramazda bore aid, and the other gods who are, because I was not hostile, I was not a Lie-follower, I was not a doer of wrong – neither I

nor my family. According to righteousness I conducted myself. Neither to the weak nor to the powerful did I do wrong. The man who cooperated with my house, him I rewarded well; whoso did injury, him I punished well.

(*DB*. IV. 61–7; Kent 1953:132)

The opponents of the Achaemenians, whose defeat is achieved with Ahura Mazdā's help, are followers of the Lie; they are in fact characterized by their lies (compare the Avestan myth about Yima, from whom *khvarenah* fled, and who was therefore ruined, when he spoke an untruth – see above):

Saith Darius the King: this is what I did by the favour of Ahuramazda in one and the same year after I became king. Nineteen battles I fought; by the favour of Ahuramazda I smote them and took prisoner nine kings. One was Gaumata by name, a Magian; he lied, saying: I am Smerdis, the son of Cyrus; he made Persia rebellious. One, Açina by name, an Elamite; he lied, saying: I am king in Elam; he made Elam rebellious to me. One, Nidintu-Bel by name, a Babylonian; he lied, saying: I am Nebuchadnezzar, the son of Nabonidus; he made Babylon rebellious. [Here follows a further enumeration of rebellious leaders and their lies.]

(*DB* IV:2–31; Kent 1953:131; see also *DB*, *passim*)

While Darius repeatedly speaks of 'my law' (see above, and *DNa*. 21), an inscription of his son, Xerxes I, seems to imply that human law has its origin and foundation in divine law (*arta*, Avestan *asha*):

Thou who (shalt be) hereafter, if thou shalt think: happy may I be when living, and when dead may I be blessed, have respect for that law which Ahuramazda has established; worship Ahuramazda and Arta reverently. The man who has respect for the law which Ahuramazda has established, and worships Ahuramazda and Arta reverently, he becomes happy while living and blessed when dead.

(XPh. 46–56; Kent 1953:152)

This passage forms part of an inscription describing the destruction of a place where 'false gods' had been worshipped, and this may be the main reason for speaking of 'the law which Ahuramazda has established'. The passage cannot therefore be regarded as proof of a development in the understanding of the nature and origin of law in Achaemenian times; it does suggest, however, that those who composed the inscription regarded divine law as the ultimate source of the laws by which society was governed.

The Achaemenian inscriptions are presumably to be regarded as statements of the official ideology of the times, reflecting a dominant philosophy. There are no further sources dealing directly with the philosophy of the period (as opposed to reports of attitudes and practices reflecting views on ethics, on which see Boyce 1982a:300, s.v. 'ethics'). It seems likely, however, that the new status of the faith as the dominant religion of the Empire must to some extent have affected the social and moral philosophy of the times. Since non-Zoroastrians no longer posed a major threat to most communities, unbelievers may not have seemed to them the most obvious representatives of the powers of evil. Moreover, the Achaemenian period witnessed such novel phenomena as a temple cult and religious endowments, and influential positions were created for some priests, as representatives of the dominant religion of the Empire. All these factors may have had the effect of separating the lives of many influential members of the priesthood from those of the laity, whereas in earlier times the interdependence between the two groups must have been almost complete.

It may be due to such factors that a tendency can be observed in post-Achaemenian Zoroastrianism to define goodness increasingly in terms of ritual purity, orthopraxy and similar priestly concerns, and evil in terms of pollution and of sins whose seriousness would have been particularly apparent to the priesthood. The development of the *Yazata Sraosha* – who originally protected believers from the attacks of evildoers through the power of their righteousness, but later came to be associated increasingly with matters of priestly authority, orthopraxis and ritual purity – is only one example of this tendency (see Kreyenbroek 1985:164ff.).

It has been argued that the origins of Zurvanism go back to Achaemenian times (Boyce 1982a:239f.). If this is so, such apparently Zurvanist traits as fatalism and a belief in astrology may also have affected the understanding of the Zoroastrian ethos in some circles from the Achaemenian era onwards. Since, in the Zoroastrian tradition, Zurvanite tenets are most fully attested in the Pahlavi books, their implications for the moral and social philosophy of the faith will be briefly discussed in that context.

THE SASANIAN AND EARLY POST-SASANIAN PERIODS

Social philosophy

Most Pahlavi books were written down in their final redaction in the post-Sasanian period, and some of them go back to an oral tradition which had its roots far back in pre-Sasanian times. However, the evidence of these texts suggests that Sasanian theorists greatly advanced the development of Zoroastrian thought, particularly in the field of ethics and social philosophy. One of the main reasons for this can be sought in the fact that religious propaganda played an important role in the policies of the early Sasanians. Tansar (or Tosar), the chief priest and propagandist of Aradashir I, claimed that the faith had decayed as a result of Alexander's conquest of Iran five centuries earlier, and needed to be restored by 'a man of true and upright judgment'; Ardashir's virtues, moreover, were held to be such as to justify any departures he might make from established tradition (Boyce 1968; 1979:102–3).

As in earlier Zoroastrian thought, the King's virtue is represented in the Pahlavi books as being crucial for the welfare of his country. Kingship is frequently associated there with *khvarenah* (Pahlavi *khvarrah*; for example *Dēnkard* III.37,134,283; see De Menasce 1973). In another source (al-Biruni *apud* Sachau 1879:215), the story is told that, during a period of drought, the Sasanian King Peroz I made a pilgrimage to a fire-temple, and vowed to abdicate if a sign was given that he was the cause of the predicament of his country. The King's task is, first and foremost, to protect the good and prevent the wicked from doing harm (*Dēnkard* VI.117; Shaked 1979:49; *Dēnkard* III.46; De Menasce 1973:57; *Mēnōg ī Xrad* 15.16ff.); in other words, he must establish the rule of law: 'The domain of kingship is wisdom, truth and goodness. . . . Its manifestation is the expansion of the Law in the world, and the prosperity and well-being resulting from this' (*Dēnkard* III.96; De Menasce 1973:101). The law, it is held, is of divine origin; just as the light we see on earth is a dim reflection emanating from the pure light on high, so the pure, divine law can only be realized to a limited extent in the world of mixture (*Dēnkard* III.78; De Menasce 1973:83–4). The concepts of law (*dād*) and religious tradition (or 'religion', *dēn*), were closely connected in Zoroastrian thought, and kingship and religion were therefore held to be interdependent:

> Essentially, royal authority is religion and religion is royal authority. On this matter, which is set out in the teaching of the Good Religion, even those who are of a hostile religion are in agreement, saying that their kingship is based on religion, and religion on kingship. . . . Through the union of royal authority with the Good Religion, royal authority is just, and through its union with the Good Religion, just royal authority and Good Religion speak with one voice. Thus, since royal authority is essentially religion, and religion (is) royal authority, it follows that anarchy is evil religion, and evil religion is anarchy.
>
> (*Dēnkard* III.58; cf. De Menasce 1973:65)

Royal authority, therefore, is necessary (*Dēnkard* III.273; De Menasce 1973:274–5), and subjects owe absolute obedience to their sovereign. This takes precedence over every other consideration:

> When a lord and ruler has given an order not to perform even the greatest work of virtue, one should not perform it. A man who does perform it should desist. For it is not an act of virtue but a grievous sin. . . . When a ruler asks, 'Ought one to perform the *drōn* ritual [i.e. a meritorious rite] or not', one ought not to tell him not to perform it. . . . When, however, a ruler gives an order to a man: 'Do not perform the *drōn* ritual', if he does so, it is not (considered) worship but a sin. In the same manner as with *drōn*, so it is with regard to other good deeds.
>
> (*Dēnkard* VI. 232–3; Shaked 1979:91)

Such views on the functions of the king in society undoubtedly go back to pre-Sasanian theories of kingship; however, the great emphasis laid in the later Zoroastrian tradition on the need for obedience to the ruler may reflect a strong tendency, in Sasanian times, towards acceptance of the *status quo*. This is confirmed by the positive view Sasanian and later religious thinkers took of the traditional class-structure (Tansar *apud* Boyce 1968:37ff.; on the social classes in the Young Avesta see above). The *Škand-gūmānīg Vizār* (I.16–17, De Menasce 1945:25) refers to 'the four classes of the religion, by which the religion and the world are arranged, namely priesthood, warriors, husbandmen and artisans'. For the sake of their souls, all men must contribute to the proper functioning of society in the station to which they are born (*Dēnkard*

III.54; De Menasce 1973:63; on the link between *khvēshkārīh* and *khvarenah* see above). The interdependence of the classes is symbolized by comparing them to parts of the body: the priesthood to the head, the warrior-class to the hands and the husbandmen to the stomach (*Dēnkard* III.42; De Menasce 1973:54. Cf. *Dēnkard* III.69; De Menasce 1973:75, and *Dēnkard* III.335; De Menasce 1973:310). Ideally, the poor man should be neither angry towards nor contemptuous of one who is wealthy, but realize that both have their part to play in society: 'My poverty exists together with the wealth and richess of that man. After all, we are the same, he and I' (*Dēnkard* VI.143; Shaked 1979:59).

The understanding of society as a hierarchical structure of interdependent elements finds a parallel in the Sasanians' organization of the religion into a 'church', with a hierarchically ordered priesthood. Curiously, however, Zoroastrian theorists who discuss religious authority seldom use the titles of the actual Sasanian hierarchy, but prefer a terminology hallowed by older usage: *rad* and *dastvar*, terms which are regularly used to render Avestan *ratu* (on which see above). Like Avestan *ratu*, these words can be used of divinities, of Zarathushtra, and of human 'authorities' of different grades. This is aptly illustrated by a ritual formula, the *Dastūrī*, which priests recite to claim authority from Ahura Mazdā, from the Amesha Spentas, from Sraosha (who links the divine sphere with this world), from Zarathushtra or the sage Adurbad i Mahraspandan, and then from the 'Dastvar of the Age' (Kreyenbroek 1985:151). The concept of religious authority is of fundamental importance in post-Achaemenian Zoroastrianism, for it is repeatedly stated in texts of Sasanian and post-Sasanian origin that it is incumbent on each layman to choose a *dastvar* (Madan 1911:784.19), without whose authority the merit from his good deeds would not accrue to him: 'He who does not have a *dastvar*, as is prescribed by law, (his) possession of any good deeds which he performs will not reach Paradise' (Madan 1911:793.6ff.).

It would seem that, according to the religious thought of the age, a layman could not act in matters of religion without consulting the *dastvar* whom he had chosen as his spiritual leader. The latter, in turn, must recognize the authority of a superior *dastvar*: 'Those are suitable for leadership and religious authority (*dastvarīh*) who, besides their other virtues on account of which lordship and *dastvarīh* are theirs, themselves also recognise a lord and *dastvar*' (Madan 1911:822.11ff.; cf. 784.19ff).

The layman's *dastvar* was thus the last link in a chain of authority emanating ultimately from Ahura Mazdā and Zarathushtra: 'On choosing and obeying a *dastvar* who recognises a Lord and a *Ratu* [i.e. a higher *dastvar*], and being linked through him with the authority of Ahura Mazdā' (Madan 1911:855.8f.). Some thinkers, it seems, held that the choice of one's *dastvar* was as important as the choice between good and evil itself:

> For the one who loves the soul and has a wicked *dastvar* may come to salvation because of his love for the soul, and the one who loves the body and has a good *dastvar* may do so because of having a good *dastvar*.
>
> (*Dēnkard* III.97; cf. De Menasce 1973 : 102)

There appear to be no fundamental differences between these views on man's role in society and those postulated for early Zoroastrianism, but the later sources undoubtedly show a shift in emphasis, laying greater stress on the concept of authority and limiting the scope of individual choice and responsibility.

Ethics

Likewise, in later Zoroastrian thought the basis of individual morality was evidently the same as it had been since the foundation of the faith: the need to do good for the sake of one's soul (*Dēnkard* VI.32, Shaked 1979:15). After death, a man's good and wicked thoughts, words and deeds would be weighed, and the fate of the soul was held to depend on the outcome of this trial. In most cases, one could counteract the adverse effect of one's sins by repenting and performing meritorious acts. (The effects of some grave sins, including those which affected society, could be mitigated or neutralized by punishment imposed by the authorities, or by heavy voluntary penalties on earth: see *Dēnkard* III.175, De Menasce 1973:184–5.) Although all acts which benefited the good creations were regarded as meritorious, the Pahlavi books lay special emphasis on the need to take care of one's fellow-man: 'These two instruments are best for men: to be oneself good and do good to others' *Dēnkard* VI.116, Shaked 1979:49). This often takes the form of charity:

> It is necessary to keep the door open to people. For when a man does not keep the door open to people [who presumably need 'bread', see below], people do not come to his house. When people do not come to his house, the gods do not come to his house. When the gods do not come to someone's house, no fortune [*khvarrah*, Avestan *khvarenah*] adheres to him. For people are after bread, gods are after people, and fortune follows the gods.
>
> (*Dēnkard* VI.187, Shaked 1979:75)

Meritorious acts will benefit both the recipient and the soul of the benefactor, and also the divine beings and all good creations. Sins of omission or commission, on the other hand, may harm the entire world:

> When *myazd, gāhāmbār* [i.e. ritual acts], and acts of charity to good people diminish, there is increase of evil government for men, pain for corn plants, bad husbandry, diminution of the fertility of the land, and bad rains. When the virtue of consanguine marriage diminishes, darkness increases and light diminishes. When worship of the gods and the protection and advocacy of good people diminish, the evil government of rulers, and unlawful action increase, and evil people gain the upper hand over the good.
>
> (*Dēnkard* VI.C82, Shaked 1979:173)

Moral goodness does not, however, merely consist in taking care of the creations guarded by the Heptad (i.e. Ahura Mazdā and the six Amesha Spentas); by realizing the qualities represented by the divinities, and by the Amesha Spentas in particular, the believer should allow these to dwell in his own being as 'guests' (*mehmān*, see

Kreyenbroek 1985:125f.). There does not appear to have been a consensus among Sasanian thinkers as to the human qualities and characteristics connected with each divinity (Kreyenbroek 1985 : 125f.), but the following enumeration – where the word 'law' (*dād*) is used for the 'spheres' of the divine beings – may be representative:

> The law of Ahura Mazdā is love of men; the law of Vohu Manah is desire for peace; the law of Asha Vahishta is truthfulness; the law of Khshathra Vairya is support of one's kinsmen; the law of Spenta Armaiti is reverence and humility; the law of Haurvatat is generosity and gratitude; the law of Ameretat is consultation and keeping the measure [*paymān*: see below].
>
> (*Dēnkard* VI.114, cf. Shaked 1979 : 47, 215, E45h)

If the moral philosophy of Zoroastrianism thus shows a remarkable degree of continuity and consistency, there was also development and change. Because such elements as fatalism and a belief in astrology had come to be accepted as part of Zurvanite Zoroastrian teaching, for instance, the perception of the Zoroastrian ethos must have undergone considerable changes in Zurvanist circles. Theories about destiny, it seems, merely postulated that one's efforts are not always rewarded by success in this life, although they will 'go to one's account' in heaven (*Mēnōg ī Xrad*, XXII, cf. XXIII, LI). This is not formally in contradiction to the older view that positive efforts in this world may be thwarted by the powers of evil, but the concept of moral choice, for example, can hardly occupy the same place in a system of ethics based on a preoccupation with fatalism and astrology as it might in one that is founded on a pure ethical dualism.

Similarly, while the opposition between good and evil remained a central doctrine in Sasanian religious thought, in defining these concepts later moralists appear to have laid increasing emphasis on matters of ritual and purity (see above). One source, it is true, states:

> Keep further away from causing harm and affliction to people than from the corpses of men, because it is easier to wash and cleanse the filth and pollution which attaches itself to the body than that which comes to the soul.
>
> (*Dēnkard* VI.E31b, Shaked 1979 : 199)

The general tone of the Pahlavi books, however, suggests that a system of ethics which regarded harm to sentient beings as graver than sins against purity may not have been common to all Sasanian thinkers. In answer to the question 'which sin is the most heinous?', for example, the *Mēnōg ī Xrad* (XXXVI) first mentions two forms of forbidden sexual activity, and the murder of a righteous man as the third; this is followed by such sins against the religion as ending a consanguineous marriage, upsetting the arrangements for an adoption, extinguishing a sacred fire and killing a beaver. According to the same source (XXXVII), the most meritorious virtues are generosity, righteousness, gratitude and contentment. While Zoroastrians of an earlier age would presumably have agreed with the *Mēnōg ī Xrad* in regarding such deeds and qualities as sinful or virtuous, the order of priorities found there seems to reflect the concerns of a social establishment which valued stability, and in particular those of the priesthood.

As far as sinners or members of different faiths are concerned, the entirely hostile attitude implicit in Zarathushtra's statement: 'for that (man) is wicked who is very good to the wicked one' (*Y.* 46.6) is occasionally found in the later tradition (see Boyce 1970:337); however, in the more complex society reflected by the Pahlavi books, some thinkers evidently attached greater importance to the concept of charity: 'One ought not to withhold from people of bad repute and all other people who are to be regarded as heretics the material elements (which are) for using and possessing' (VI:288, Shaked 1979:111), and: 'Even if a poor man is of bad religion or not of righteous behaviour, one ought to give him something' (VI. 292, Shaked 1979:113).

The concerns of the age also appear to be reflected by the debate about the moral implications of wealth. Fundamentally, Zoroastrianism holds that the 'right measure' (*paymān*) is to be observed in all things, and that excess and deficiency are generally sinful: 'Religion is the right measure.' 'Sin mostly consists in excess and deficiency. Virtuous work mostly in right measure' (VI. 39, 38, cf. Shaked 1979:17). Where wealth was concerned, however, a generally accepted definition of what constitutes the right measure was evidently lacking. According to the *Mēnōg ī Xrad* (XV), poverty through honesty is better than ill-gotten opulence, but lawfully acquired wealth, if spent in proper pursuits, is best of all. A *Dēnkard* passage, however, states:

> Unless a man be examined and known in the most important things, one should not deny him goodness solely because of his wealth and opulence, and one should not thus praise a man for goodness because of his paucity of wealth and indigence.
>
> (VI.71, Shaked 1979:27)

Elsewhere in the same text it is said:

> Poverty is best. . . . A man who stands in poverty not out of constraint but solely because of the goodness and praise of poverty, banishes Ahriman and the demons from the world.
>
> (VI.141, Shaked 1979:57)

Both passages implicitly or explicitly suggest approval of at least a moderate form of asceticism–an impression which is confirmed by a group of stories extolling the virtue of priests who live in extreme poverty (*Dēnkard* D2,3,5, Shaked 1979:177–83).

Although the extant evidence suggests that during most of its history Zoroastrianism did not encourage asceticism, the concept of the pious poor man (Avestan. *drig(h)u*, Pahlavi *driyōsh*, New Persian *darvīsh*) goes back to the *Gāthās*, where Zarathushtra uses it of himself (*Y.* 34.4, cf. 53.9); it occurs in the most sacred prayer of Zoroastrianism (*Y.* 27.13), and it is found throughout the *Avesta* (*Y.* 57.10, 10.13, *Yasht* 10.84, 11.3). It seems likely that it came to play a more prominent role in Zoroastrian philosophy at a time when, for whatever reasons, some believers were attracted to an ascetic way of life.

The interest which the Sasanian books show in the moral aspects of poverty may perhaps serve as a final illustration of the fact that, whenever circumstances allowed thinkers to formulate a Zoroastrian philosophy, the latter tended to reflect the current concerns of the faithful. Zarathushtra's rejection of the dominant religious ideas of his time, which led him to formulate tenets of great philosophical depth, may have been prompted in part by social injustice. Early Zoroastrian moral and social philosophy appears to reflect the deeply felt but simple values of a struggling community forced to withstand the onslaughts of the powers of evil in their daily lives. When outside pressures grew less, the central opposition between good and evil was increasingly held to manifest itself in matters of ritual and purity. The later preoccupation with poverty in turn suggests that, in the course of time, some believers may have felt the need for a more tangible expression of their struggle to achieve righteousness, and turned towards some form of asceticism. Although the centuries following the Islamic conquest of Iran may well have made heavier demands than any other age on the philosophical skills and learning of those Zoroastrian priests who attempted to define and defend their ancient faith, these were not primarily concerned with the issues discussed in this chapter; few new insights in this field can therefore be attributed to the post-Sasanian period. By the tenth century, moreover, the Zoroastrian communities had clearly become too poor, and in many cases too oppressed, to take an active interest in questions of social and moral philosophy.

REFERENCES

Benveniste, E. and Renou, L. (1934) *Vrtra et Vərəθragna: étude de mythologie indo-iranienne*, *Cahiers de la Société Asiatique III*, Paris: Société Asiatique.

Boyce, M. (1968) *The Letter of Tansar*, Rome: Istituto Italiano per il Medio ed Estremo Oriente.

—— (1970) 'Toleranz und Intoleranz im Zoroastrismus', *Saeculum* 21(4): 325–43.

—— (1975) *A History of Zoroastrianism*, vol. I, Handbuch der Orientalistik I. viii, 1, Leiden/Cologne: Brill.

—— (1979) *Zoroastrians: Their Religious Beliefs and Practices*, London: Routledge & Kegan Paul.

—— (1982a) *A History of Zoroastrianism*, vol. II, *Handbuch der Orientalistik* I. viii, 2, Leiden/Cologne: Brill.

—— (1982b) 'The bipartite society of the ancient Iranians', in M. A. Dandamayev *et. al.* (eds) *Societies and Languages of the Ancient Near East: Studies in Honour of I. M. Diakonoff*, Warminster: Aris & Phillips, pp. 33–7.

—— (ed. and trans.) (1984) *Textual Sources for the Study of Zoroastrianism*, Manchester: Manchester University Press.

—— (1987) 'Priests, cattle and men', *BSOAS* 50: 508–26.

—— (1988) 'The religion of Cyrus the Great', in A. Kuhrt and H. Sancisi-Weerdenburg (eds) *Achaemenid History III: Method and Theory*, Leiden: Nederlands Instituut voor het Nabije Oosten, pp. 15–31.

Dhabhar, B. N. (1949) *Pahlavi Yasna and Visperad*, Bombay: S. F. Desai for the Trustees of the Parsi Punchayet Funds and Properties.

Duchesne-Guillemin, J. (1963) 'Le X^{u}arənah', *Annali dell'Istituto Orientale di Napoli*, sez. Linguistica V:19–31.
Gershevitch, I. (1967) *The Avestan Hymn to Mithra*, Cambridge: Cambridge University Press.
Humbach, H. (1959) *Die Gathas des Zarathustra*, 2 vols, Heidelberg: Carl Winter.
Kent, R. G. (1953) *Old Persian: Grammar, Texts, Lexicon*, New Haven: American Oriental Society.
Kreyenbroek, G. (1985) *Sraoša in the Zoroastrian Tradition*, Leiden: Brill.
Madan, D. M. (1911) *The Complete Text of the Pahlavi Dînkard*, 2 vols, Bombay: Fort Printing Press.
Menasce, J.-P. De (1945) *Škand Gumānīk Vicār: Solution décisive des doutes*, Fribourg: Librairie de l'Université.
—— (1973) *Le Troisième Livre du Dēnkart*, Paris: C. Klincksieck.
Sachau, C. E. (1879) *The Chronology of Ancient Nations*, London: William H. Allen & Co.
Schmidt, H.-P. (1958) *Vedisch vratá und awestisch urvata*, Hamburg: Cram, de Gruyter & Co.
Shaked, Sh. (trans.) (1979) *The Wisdom of the Sasanian Sages: Dēnkard* VI. Persian Heritage Series 34, Boulder: Westview Press.
Thieme, P. (1957) *Mitra and Aryaman*, Transactions of the Connecticut Academy of Arts and Sciences, New Haven.
—— (1960) 'The "Aryan" gods of the Mitanni Treaty', *Journal of the American Oriental Society* 80:301–17.
Wolff, F. (1910) *Avesta, die heiligen Bücher der Parsen*, Leipzig: Karl J. Trübner.
Zaehner, R. C. (1955) *Zurvan: A Zoroastrian Dilemma*, Oxford: Clarendon Press.

FURTHER READING

Boyce, M. (1970) 'Toleranz und Intoleranz im Zoroastrismus', *Saeculum* 21(4):325–43.
—— (1975, 1982) *A History of Zoroastrianism*, 2 vols, Leiden: Brill.
Humbach, H. (1959) *Die Gathas des Zarathustra*, 2 vols, Heidelberg: Carl Winter.
Insler, S. (1975) *The Gāthās of Zarathustra*, *Acta Iranica* 8, Leiden: Brill.
Kreyenbroek, G. (1985) *Sraoša in the Zoroastrian Tradition*, Leiden: Brill.
—— (forthcoming) 'On the concept of spiritual authority in Zoroastrianism', *Jerusalem Studies; Arabic and Islam* 17:1–15 .
Lommel, H. (1930) *Die Religion Zarathustras: nach dem Awesta dargestellt*, Tübingen: J. C. B. Mohr (Paul Siebeck), repr. 1971.
Menasce, J.-P. De (1973) *Le Troisième Livre du Dēnkart*, Paris: C. Klincksieck.
Shaked, Sh. (trans.) (1979) *The Wisdom of the Sasanian Sages: Dēnkard* VI. Persian Heritage Series 34, Boulder: Westview Press.
Thieme, P. (1957) *Mitra and Aryaman*, Transactions of the Connecticut Academy of Arts and Sciences, New Haven.

4

CONTEMPORARY ZOROASTRIAN PHILOSOPHY

John R. Hinnells

A religion is what it has become. Historians too often describe what the religion was at a given period in past history which they think represents the 'real' religion. Theologians commonly depict an idealistic picture of the 'true' faith and describe all variations as heresies or the falling away from 'the valid' or 'core' teaching as lesser manifestations of the religion. The truth is, of course, that all religions change as they evolve and must do so if they are to continue to be meaningful to the practitioner in a changing world. Religious philosophies cannot remain uninfluenced by the environment in which they are practised. This chapter will examine the various influences upon, and forms of, Zoroastrian philosophy in the nineteenth and twentieth centuries, specifically those within the Indian or Parsi community. This is a very literate community (with a literacy rate of 99 per cent for males and 97 per cent for females: Karkal 1984) and consequently produces countless books. This study cannot, therefore, be comprehensive; rather the aim has been to identify major themes and trends.

The history of Zoroastrianism is a long one, stretching from the end of the Stone Age on the inner Asian steppes through to the great Iranian Empire described in the previous chapters. But from that imperial stature it became the religion of an oppressed minority in Islamic Iran following the Arab invasion in the seventh century AD. There followed a millennium of pressure to convert to the new faith, of oppression and persecution. Zoroastrians were forced to retreat to the security of remote villages and the desert cities of Yazd and Kerman, in an inhospitable region where Muslims did not choose to live. The survival of Zoroastrianism for 1,300 years in such conditions is a great tribute to the determination, courage and commitment of its followers. At the end of the nineteenth century conditions began to ease slightly for them, although they still did not have equality before the law, were banned from the highest positions of state and were people who were thought to make unclean whatever they touched. Simple conversion to Islam could change all this and enable the convert to inherit the whole of the family estate, whatever their position in the family. Conditions eased further under the Pahlavi regime (1925–79) (Boyce 1979). Under the Islamic Republic they have not faced the fierce persecution that has been experienced by the Baha'i but living again under Muslim law they are restricted at work and treated unequally under Islamic law, and there is fear of what might happen at any time of social upheaval.

The setting for the faith and practice of Zoroastrians has undergone yet further dramatic changes. In the tenth century a small group of the faithful set out to find a new land of religious freedom and settled in north-west India, where they became known as 'the people from Pars' or the Parsis. The story of their journey is contained in 'The tale of Sanjan' or *The Qissa-i Sanjan* (Boyce 1984:120–3). It relates that the travellers were guided in their journey by a wise astrologer-priest and that when they were at sea they were threatened by a great storm, but in answer to their prayers, and after they had vowed to build a great Fire Temple (an *Ātash Bharām*) if they were safely delivered, the storm subsided and they landed safely in India. There the local prince gave them permission to settle providing they observed minimal restrictions (to speak the local language – Gujarati; to perform marriages at night as was the Indian practice; and, in the case of the men, not to carry weapons). The new settlers gave the prince a series of statements of their faith (*shlokas*) in which they stressed the common elements between their religion and Hinduism, for example respect for the cow and for purity laws. They were then given land on which to build a new temple. This, Parsis believe, characterizes their experiences in Hindu India, namely a freedom to practise their religion untroubled, providing that they observe minimal conditions of good citizenship.

The Parsis lived in relative obscurity until the arrival of European traders in the seventeenth century. As the British developed Bombay as a base from which to expand their trade in western India the Parsis migrated there in relatively large numbers. In the eighteenth and nineteenth centuries they rose to positions of considerable economic and political power in Bombay, the commercial capital of India to this day. First they prospered as builders and managers of the Bombay dockyard (the very reason for which Bombay was being developed), then they were pioneers as middle men in the trade with China and East Africa. When western-style education became available in the 1820s Parsis, consistently with their traditional respect for learning, seized the opportunity to a greater degree than did any other community. Thus in 1860 they occupied half of all the places in Bombay's educational system, although they represented only 6 per cent of the population. The result was that they went on to flourish in the various spheres which required an education, such as medicine, law, engineering and technology. As Indians began to involve themselves in politics at the end of the nineteenth century so Parsis came to the fore, particularly at the turn of the century, notably Sir Pherozeshah Mehta (1845–1915), often alluded to as the 'uncrowned king of Bombay'; Sir

Dinshah Wacha (1844–1936), for many years the Secretary of the Indian National Congress; but above all Dadabhoy Naoroji, 'the Grand Old Man of India', the first Indian to be elected an MP at Westminster (1892–5). He was succeeded in the House of Commons by two more Parsis, Sir Muncherji Bhownagree (1895–1906) and then from 1923 to 1929 Shapurji Saklatvala. In India, banking, insurance, the steel industry, airlines, social reform and science were all areas in which Parsis led the way (Kulke 1974; Hinnells 1978a). As Indian Independence approached and the battles between Muslims and Hindus became increasingly violent, so Parsis began to fear for their safety as a vulnerable minority in what threatened to be two militantly religious nations, India and Pakistan. Some, therefore, migrated westwards. But the majority stayed. Both in India and in Pakistan they have in fact remained secure and held positions of political influence as well as achieving significant commercial success.

As a result of their economic and political enterprise the Parsis have migrated to many parts of the globe. There are formal Zoroastrian Associations in Hong Kong, Singapore, Australia, Kenya, France, England, America and Canada. Typically these diaspora groups are composed mainly of young people, well educated, 'high flyers' in their careers (business, law, medicine, accountancy, engineering, the pharmaceutical industry). Since the fall of the Shah they have been joined by a number of Iranian Zoroastrians; again it has been mainly the well-educated and well-placed families, mostly from cosmopolitan Tehran, who have migrated. They have settled in Canada (especially Vancouver, but also Toronto) and America (mainly California and New York) (Hinnells forthcoming). Although the various communities typically have a low birth rate so that absolute numbers are declining (Karkal 1984), the dispersion means that Zoroastrianism is now practised in more countries around the world than at any other time in its history. These transformations in Parsi fortunes both in their homeland and in migration first to a continent of greatly contrasting philosophies and from there to a global dispersion are the background to an explosion of philosophical thought, a fragmentation and a rich diversification of interpretations of the tradition. Just as Christianity has assumed very different forms in the modern world, from American television evangelism to the Eastern Orthodox churches, from the liberation movements in Latin America to Indianized or Africanized forms, all of which are very distinct from, say, the Church of England, so too has Zoroastrianism been diversified, though not to the same extent as Christianity.

ZOROASTRIANISM IN BRITISH INDIA

As in ancient times Zoroastrianism had evolved as it became the religion of three world empires (see Chapter 3 above), so too in the nineteenth century it grew to meet the new intellectual stimuli of life in the British Empire. Until the renewal of the East India Company's Charter in 1813 only Company officials and related traders were allowed entry into India. It was established Company policy not to 'interfere with the religion of the natives' in case any unrest should interrupt the smooth flow of business. Partly as a result of this, and partly because the majority of Parsis were then still living in rural Gujarat, Zoroastrian beliefs were subject to little external influence. Some Indian customs, such as the decoration of homes at the time of weddings, had been incorporated, but the basic world-view does not seem to have changed dramatically. There was some ignorance of detailed ritual practice which led to an exchange of 'messages' – the Indian Zoroastrians sent queries to the Iranian priests, who replied in a series of *Rivāyats* (or treatises) – but custom and practice led to a general orthopraxy, and in so far as we can reconstruct the doctrine it had changed little over the centuries (Paymaster 1954; Seervai and Patel 1899).

Until the arrival of western traders Parsis were mostly poor. Their life style was not such that they could found priestly seminaries to facilitate a large body of professional theologians. There were, of course, some very learned priests, for example Neryosang Dhaval in the twelfth and thirteenth centuries, who laboured to produce editions and translations of texts (Boyce 1979:168ff.). But there are indications that the emphasis continued to be on the good formless God who created both the spiritual and material worlds, who was worshipped through the *kiblāh* of fire, on whose side men and women must undertake a daily battle with the forces of evil and impurity, and who was to be worshipped through the daily prayers and the great festivals. The great life-cycle rites of birth, initiation, marriage and death reaffirmed for all in the community the conviction that God could be experienced in and through the world in which they lived. In view of the onslaught which Wilson waged on Zoroastrian teaching it is worth quoting the account he himself gives of the theology of the high priest Dastur Edalji Sanjana:

> The one holy and glorious God, the Lord of the creation of both worlds, and the Creator of both worlds, I acknowledge thus. – He has no form, and no equal; and the creation and support of all things is from that Lord. And the lofty sky, and the earth, and light and fire, and air, and water, and the sun, and moon, and the stars, have all been created by him and are subject to him. And that glorious Master is almighty, and that Lord was the first of all, and there was nothing before him, and he is always, and will always remain. And he is very wise and just; and worthy of service, and praise. . . . God has no form or shape; and he is enveloped in holy, pure, brilliant, incomparable light. Wherefore, no one can see him. . . . We are able to inquire into that Lord by the light of the understanding, and through means of learning. We constantly observe his influence, and behold his marvelous wonders. This is equivalent to our seeing that Lord himself. . . . That God is present in every place, in heaven, earth, and the whole creation; and whithersoever thou dost cast thine eyes, there he is nigh and by no means far from thee.
>
> (Wilson 1843: 108ff.)

> We Zoroastrians reckon fire, and the moon, and other glorious objects filled with splendour and light, centres of worship (*kiblāh*); and in their presence we stand upright and practise worship.
>
> (Wilson 1843: 198)

Clearly the doctrine and practice of devotion to the Good Lord and his Good Creation was part of the Gathic and Pahlavi teaching which was strong long before any western influence.

With the renewal of the East India Company's Charter in 1813 missionaries were allowed into India as a result of evangelical lobbying of the British Parliament. The first missionary to turn his attention to the Parsis was the Revd John Wilson. He started his mission in 1829 and opened a school near to the main centre of the Parsi community because he was aware of the characteristic Parsi desire for education. He converted and baptized two Parsi youths, an event which caused a great uproar in the community. But from the perspective of philosophical development his major work was the publication of a book entitled *The Parsi Religion: as contained in the Zand-Avesta and propounded and defended by the Zoroastrians of India and Persia, unfolded, refuted, and contrasted with Christianity*, which was published in Bombay in 1843. His onslaught on Zoroastrianism, through articles in the press, sermons and that book, came as a massive cultural shock to the Parsis. They had typically regarded themselves as the most westernized and 'civilized' community in the subcontinent and were accustomed to westerners perceiving them to be such (Firby 1988). What compounded the Parsi distress was that because their priests had not had a western-style education they were unable to refute his attack. In one sense many members of the community spent the following hundred years seeking to refute his charges. In order to understand some of the later developments it is first necessary to outline his arguments briefly. Wilson focused his writings on the liturgical text the *Vendidad* (a text concerned mainly with purity laws), the Greek and Roman accounts of Zoroastrianism he had studied in Classics and some Arabic works. The words of the prophet, as outlined by Boyce in Chapter 1 above and the more philosophical Zoroastrian texts, discussed by Williams in Chapter 2 above, had not been identified as significantly distinct, readily available sources. On this basis he argued that Zoroastrianism was a dualism, because it propagated the belief in two gods (Ahura Mazdā and Angra Mainyu); that indeed it was polytheistic because of the worship of the Amesha Spentas; that Zoroastrians thereby robbed God of the honour and glory due to the creator; that the *Avesta* was 'a monument to human error'; that Zarathushtra was not the author of the whole *Avesta* and his religious authority cannot be great because he did not perform miracles. Because the Parsi leaders were not at that time well versed in western-style study of the ancient texts, their priests were not generally effective in their intellectual response to this onslaught. Henceforth Parsis were to have as a doctrinal priority the rejection of the charges of dualism and polytheism, and were concerned to validate the religious authority of their prophet and holy book.

Support for the Parsi cause so conceived came from two western scholars, Haug and Maulton (1917). Haug in lectures, articles and a book (1862) argued that only the *Gāthās* were the teaching of Zarathushtra. If the Parsis rejected the later 'priestly speculation' and returned to the pure teaching of the prophet, they would see that theirs was originally a monotheistic faith, in which evil was due to one of the twin spirits created by Ahura Mazdā, who stood above the divide of good and evil. Thus, he argued, they had a philosophical monotheism and an ethical dualism. The prophet, he maintained, did not propound a ritualistic superstitious religion, and they should abandon those parts of the religion which owed nothing to Zarathushtra. Coming after the onslaught of Wilson here was an exposition which meant that the community could believe that it truly had a philosophical system which was respectable in the eyes of modern, westernized people. Haug, like other commentators, also found much to praise in Zoroastrianism, for example its characteristic virtue of charity.

There was another path of western learning which stimulated Parsi thought, namely scientific discoveries connected with the positive and negative poles of magnetism and with electricity and the whole range of science concerned with unseen sound and light waves. It is difficult for readers at the end of the twentieth century to appreciate how exciting these discoveries were at first. One of the writers who applied them to Zoroastrian teachings, particularly ideas associated with the positive and negative forces in the world, was Samuel Laing, a finance minister in British India but also an author of several books in which he tried to apply 'modern' science to religion. One of these (1890) was specifically on Zoroastrianism. In it he argued that the polarity of the life-giving positive force of good and the negative destructive force of evil which Zoroastrians saw underlying all life (see Williams on 'dualism' in Chapter 2 above) was in fact a philosophical form of the latest scientific discovery, with its ideas of positive and negative forces and the polarity of matter in molecules and atoms. He also demonstrated how polarity could be seen in all forms of life in animals and plants and in the gender differences of the human species. Zoroastrianism he accordingly presented as the earliest religion to discover the truth about the duality inherent in the nature of existence.

Laing also argued (1890:ch. 14) that the 'sweet reasonableness' of Zoroastrianism was manifest also in its forms of worship, quoting extensively from Andrew Carnegie's description of Parsis praying before the sacred creations of fire and waters on Bombay beach at sunset:

> as the sun was sinking in the sea, and the slender silver thread of the crescent moon was faintly shining on the horizon, they congregated to perform their religious rites. Fire was there in its grandest form, the setting sun, and the water in the vast expanse of the Indian Ocean outstretched before them. The earth was under their feet, and wafted across the sea the air came laden with the perfumes of 'Araby the blest'. Surely no time or place could be more fitly chosen than this for lifting up the soul to the realms beyond sense. I could not but participate with these worshippers in what was so grandly beautiful. There was no music save the solemn moan of the waves as they broke into foam on the beach. But where shall we find so mighty an organ, or so grand an anthem?

Zoroastrian purity laws Laing interpreted as sound ideas of hygiene and fire as the ideal symbol of him who is pure undefiled light. Coming after the Muslim taunts of fire worshippers and Wilson's attack on the doctrines, these arguments regarding Zoroastrianism and science, and also the stress on the poetic beauty of the religion, came to play a central part in future Zoroastrian expositions of the faith. The arguments that the purity laws which Wilson scoffed at were in accord with the modern practice of hygiene were something which gave intellectual self-respect to many Zoroastrians.

One of the earliest pioneers in Zoroastrian doctrinal reform was K. R. Cama (Hinnells 1983), who started classes for adults and encouraged the study of Avestan and Pahlavi so that the priests might be better equipped to withstand missionary onslaughts on the faithful. But the man whose philosophy was more influential was M. N. Dhalla (1875–1956). Dhalla was born into a poor priestly family and grew up as a staunch Orthodox Zoroastrian in Karachi (Dhalla 1975). His lectures drew him to the attention of Cama, who arranged for the youth to study in Bombay. Then in 1905 he travelled to New York to study at Columbia University under the distinguished Iranist, and devout Protestant, A. V. W. Jackson. While in the States, Dhalla studied comparative religion. It is probably significant that he attended the lectures of Spencer, one of the pioneers in the theory of the evolution of religion from a crude animatism through animism to polytheism to henotheism and finally to the peak of the spiritual ladder, an ethical monotheism. It is worth quoting Dhalla's own account of his experience, for it articulates clearly how the western-educated Zoroastrian came to see his own personal religious development:

> By reading books on anthropology and sociology I began to examine scientifically, questions relating to superstition, magic, customs, ceremonies, prayer, priesthood, society, marriage and other allied subjects. I studied their origins historically, and, for the very first time I began to see vividly how they have progressed from the primitive stage to their present condition. My three years and nine months of scientific and critical study at Columbia University . . . eradicated religious misconceptions that had gathered in my mind due to my blinded mental vision, traditional beliefs and up-bringing. As the clouds of superstition dispersed, the mist of mental darkness was rent asunder. I was free of the religion of fear that was the belief of infant humanity and turned towards the pure religion of love, the religion as preached by the prophets and uncorrupted by their fanatical followers. Now that I had been enlightened by scientific study, and now that I had come to know and gain so much, I no longer adhered to old ideas. My thinking, my outlook, my ideals and my philosophy of life changed. The purpose and meaning of life changed – everything changed. I was now eager to become the thinker of new thoughts, the student of new ideas and the propagator of new concepts. In 1905 I had set foot on American soil as an orthodox. Now in 1909 I was leaving the shores of the New World as a Reformist.
>
> (Dhalla 1975 : 157ff.)

In a succession of books (notably in this context 1914 and 1938) Dhalla increasingly stressed that Zoroastrianism was the high point of the spiritual evolutionary ladder, in which the world's first ethical monotheism was revealed to Zarathushtra, but that his followers, who were not as spiritually exalted, could not live up to the ideals of the prophet and so reintroduced the ancient nature worship and polytheism of former times; and that thereafter Zoroastrianism became encrusted with superstitious and magical beliefs by the priesthood. It was only now, in the early twentieth century, that western scholarship had laid bare this historical corruption of the pure prophetic philosophy, and thereby the modern Zoroastrian could return to the original revealed message of the prophet. This is, of course, a perspective characteristic of Protestant Biblical scholarship of the day, with its quest for the historical Jesus separated from the later changes imposed by the church with its elaborate rituals and its priests who corrupted the pure, abstract, demythologized teaching of the founder.

Just how did Dhalla expound his religion under these influences? Consistently with contemporary liberal Protestant thought, Dhalla rejected the 'medieval mythology'. It is as much what he does *not* refer to as the new ideas he articulated which is significant for an appreciation of his religious philosophy. He did not refer, in his devotional works, to any of the mythology of creation, the concept of a personal evil being, Angra Mainyu, or the renovation of the universe. In particular he ignored the cosmic myths of creation and eschatology and the dualism which lay behind them (as described in Chapter 2 above). This presented substantial theological problems for Zoroastrian teaching, since Angra Mainyu is seen in it as the source of death and all evil. That belief was no longer available to Dhalla. In some of his devotional writings (1942), therefore, he speaks of death as Ahura calling men back to himself. In explaining the death of children he taught that they were so good that they could not live upon earth but returned to their heavenly abode (Hinnells 1978). Hell he interprets as a state of mind. His presentation of the image of Zarathushtra is clearly influenced by that of Jesus, meditating in the wilderness.

Dhalla was referred to by his Zoroastrian opponents as 'the Protestant Dastur', and in part at least one can see why. In his personal life Dhalla was a deeply devotional priest and he maintained throughout his life a commitment to the rituals, albeit somewhat modified (the traditional laws of purification, for example, were not stressed). Others who grew up at the same time, and some who were influenced by him, rejected the whole liturgical tradition, but in particular the preservation of prayers in the 'scriptural' but 'dead' language of the *Avesta*. Prayers, it was said, had to be understood if they were not to become 'mumbo jumbo'. The traditional idea, and one widely accepted in India, that prayers were holy *mantras*, words of power and spritual force, was not acceptable, as it might have been had the foreign influence been a Roman Catholic rather than a Protestant Christian one. Similarly the attitude to the authority of priests and the 'church' as the interpreter of 'holy writ' would almost certainly have been different. Undoubtedly the devotional importance of complex liturgies as the medium through which the 'real' presence of the divine is encountered would have been more acceptable under such an influence. As it was, the 'Protestantized' reformers emphasized the abstract nature of worship of the spirit as described by Laing above. Of all western writers Laing is probably the most frequently quoted by the reformists. The spirit of rationalism was so widespread that one writer, D. F. Madan (1909), argued that since in life we assume that knowledge gained for oneself is better than that imposed by an outsider, so revelation was an educationally and spiritually lower level of religion than that which had been thought through rationally. One result, therefore, of the onslaught of Wilson was the development of a westernized, specifically Protestant-type religious philosophy among the Parsis.

ZOROASTRIANISM AND THE OCCULT

It was inevitable that the westernizing trend among Indian Zoroastrians at the turn of the century would provoke a conservative backlash. For many, what was termed 'the Protestant party' went much too far in rejecting respected traditions and cherished practices. There was, for example, a real sense of loss at the proposed abandonment of the Avestan prayers. Parsis were not alone among sections of the various Indian religious groups who felt that their religious heritage was being rashly dispensed with. Mythologies are powerful forms of religious teaching, and what was needed after the rejection of the traditional myths was a new and powerful cosmology which related to the ideas of the day.

The answer for many educated groups in India at the turn of the century, including a number of Parsis, was the teaching of the Theosophical Society. This was started by Helena Blavatsky (1831–91) in New York in 1875 in conjunction with Henry Olcott. Her teaching was a mixture of Neoplatonism and Jewish and Indian mystical beliefs. She claimed that her authority was based on messages she received from Tibetan Masters, highly evolved human beings who had outgrown their need for bodies but remained on earth to help others (Barker 1991). She taught that the world is a many-tiered layering of spiritual and earthly reality which parallels the nature of the human self. The ultimate is not a deity but one's higher self, and the religious quest is to evolve into a state of spiritual perfection. Rebirth, *karma* and vegetarianism are essential steps on this path. The Society's base was moved from New York to Bombay in 1879, and there many Parsis became involved. The centre was transferred to Madras in 1907, and it came under the leadership of Annie Besant, who identified Theosophy strongly with the Home Rule League. At that point many Parsis drifted away from the Society. But during those twenty-eight years a number of Parsis had been deeply involved in the Society, holding between them at various times the posts of president, secretary, librarian and treasurer (Wadia 1931). There were also some noted Zoroastrian expositors of Theosophical belief (for example Vimadalal 1904; Bilimoria n. d.; Sorabji 1922).

The interaction between the Parsis and the Theosophical Society was a two-way process. Many Parsis were influenced by Theosophical teaching. In a lecture in 1882 in Bombay Town Hall, before more than 700 Parsis, including some leading teachers such as J. J. Modi and K. R. Cama, Olcott pressed the Zoroastrians to preserve their ancient rites because Zarathushtra and his ancient successors

> have transmitted their thoughts to posterity under the safe cover of an external ritual. They have masked them under a symbolism and ceremonies, that guard their mighty secrets from the prying curiosity of the vulgar crowd, but hide nothing from those who deserve to know all.

Olcott proceeded to warn the Zoroastrians that western-educated scholars failed to see the profound truth which lay at the heart of Zoroastrian prayer and practice. He said 'But I am to show you that your religion is in agreement with the most recent discoveries of modern science. . . . And I am to prove to you that your faith rests upon the rock of truth, the living rock of Occult Science.' He made several references to secret collections of teaching in Armenian or Iranian mountain caves (pp. 12, 14, 39 and 48).

> Some of the facts given in the Secret Records . . . are very interesting. They are to the effect that there exists a certain hollow rock of tablets in a gigantic cave bearing the name of the first Zarathust . . . and that the tablets may yet be rescued some day.

The lecture was privately published and achieved a wide circulation.

After the Theosophical Society moved its headquarters to Madras and the Parsis became less involved, the religious needs which Theosophy had met did not disappear. In its place there developed a 'Zoroastrianized Theosophy'. The leader was Behramshah Naoroji Shroff (1858–1927) (Hinnells 1988). He was brought up in Surat, where he received only an elementary education in Gujarati. At the age of 18, the tradition relates, he left home and travelled north. He met a caravan of secret Zoroastrians and was taken by them to a hidden colony of Zoroastrian spiritual masters hidden in caves in Mount Demavend, near Tehran, apparently thus fulfilling the forecasts of Olcott. This is said to have been one of three such 'mazdaznian' (= worship of Mazdā) monasteries, one on the European–Russian border, one subterranean colony near the Caspian Sea and the one in Mount Demavend visited by Shroff. His later followers believe that only three persons have ever been allowed to enter these hidden monasteries: one was an Iranian astrologer, Rustom Nazoomie, about whom nothing is known; a second was Revd Dr Otoman Zardusht, the prophet for America, whose Mazdaznian group still continues in Oregon, and the third was Shroff. Shroff entered 'Firdaus' (i.e. paradise) virtually illiterate, a hesitant speaker who stammered badly. He emerged a fiery orator claiming deep occult knowledge and a practitioner of Ayurvedic medicine, having been taught, he said, by the Grand Chief (Ustad Saheb). In Firdaus the hidden Zoroastrians dwell in a paradisal state, amid streets of rock-hewn caves with streams of nectar in an agricultural paradise where all is peace, prosperity and contentment. There, the spiritual and material treasures of ancient Iran are carefully preserved (Mama 1944; Tavaria 1971; Moos 1981 and 1983).

On Shroff's return to India he spent ten years (*c.*1881–91) travelling around India learning from spiritual leaders of various religions, but he remained silent about his own experiences until 1907, when he began teaching first in Surat, then in Bombay under the auspices of the Parsi Vegetarian and Temperance Society (PVTS) and the Theosophical Lodge. He did not start any separate cult but delivered numerous lectures on Fire and related topics. He wrote ten pamphlets for circulation, and his teaching was set out in the monthly magagazine of the PVTS, *Frashogard*. The movement he thus started is known as Ilm-i Khshnoom, 'the path of spiritual satisfaction'. Broadly the teachings are very similar to Theosophy in the emphasis on the occult significance of Avestan prayers and their vibrations, on rebirth, on vegetarianism, on the distinct mystical 'aura' surrounding each person. What is distinctive is the attribution of spiritual authority not to Theosophy's Tibetan Masters, but to hidden Iranian Zoroastrian Masters who appeared to fulfil what Olcott had indicated, the preservation of hidden teachings in an Iranian cave. These developments also coincided with contemporary political trends. From the early part of the twentieth century religious tensions were increasing in India as Hindu fought Muslim, and contemporary with this was the easing of conditions for Zoroastrians in Iran (as discussed above). The result was a trend towards a yearning for ancient Iran and speculation among some about a return to the homeland.

There have been various developments of Shroff's teaching. The first publication in English was Masani's (1917). It began by defending the integrity of the whole *Avesta* as the word of Zarathushtra *pace* Dhalla. Zoroastrianism, he argued, 'is nothing but the Natural Law of Evolution or Unfoldment of Soul' (p. 37). On earth, he writes, there are different levels of souls according to their development, and 'the different religions are necessary for different souls in various stages of their spiritual and mental development . . . the Zoroastrian religion . . . can only be followed by the . . . souls that have already reached the foremost stage of spiritual human progress' (p. 78). The great prayers of the religion, offered in purity by the necessarily advanced soul, have 'their great vibrationary effects in removing and annhilating all the major evil forces in nature' (p. 84). The religious path is for the soul to unfold itself from the lower levels of physical matter and for it to develop its latent higher spiritual powers. This unfoldment takes many ages, or births. The esoteric teaching of Zoroastrianism leads to knowledge of all the laws of the universe (notably what he refers to as 'the laws of polarity and duality'), to an appreciation of the forces seen and unseen. The rituals, not least the purity laws, help souls 'onward in their march in the unseen world' (p. 133). The understanding of science, especially the polarity of 'magnetism' and electricity outlined by Laing (see above), is used to explain how rituals work on unseen spiritual forces which the soul encounters as it progresses in the unseen world (p. 135). Part of the discipline required for the progress of the soul is the need to be vegetarian, otherwise the person swallows dead matter, which is against the moral order and thus inhibits the unfoldment of the soul (p. 208). The ideas of involution, enfoldment in matter and spiritual unfoldment strongly recall the teaching of Sri Aurobindo (Minor 1989). Similarly the emphasis on *mantras* whose efficacy depends on the holiness of the reciter's physical, mental, moral and spiritual constituents recalls much contemporary Indian thought. The traditional Zoroastrian philosophy of dualism is being recast in a form which 'speaks' to the Indian situation of the day, and in terms evoking contemporary science and therefore rational for the people of the time.

The Zoroastrian occult science has been developed by many authors since Masani, for example Chiniwalla (1942), who was a close personal friend and supporter of Shroff, and Tavaria (1971). In the 1980s there have been several widely popular interpreters of the Khshnoomic message. One (Dastoor 1984) presented what has become a fairly common Parsi conviction, that Zarathushtra was not an ordinary mortal: rather, Dastoor argued, he was a heavenly, or worshipful, being, a 'descent' from God. The idea that Zarathushtra was a *yazata*, a being worthy of worship (Hinnells 1985b:92–7) because he was chosen by God as the prophet to whom he revealed his message, was an old one. What is happening here is that this traditional teaching is being understood in the light of contemporary Indian philosophy, specifically the doctrine of the *avatara*. Another author who has written much is Adi Doctor (especially in the columns of the journal *Dharma Prakash* and whose writings are made available among American Zoroastrians by S. and F. Mehta in their newsletter, the *Mazdayasni Connection*). But perhaps the most prolific, and in some ways the most controversial, is Mrs Meher Master-Moos. She claims to have discovered trunks full of unpublished manuscripts written by Shroff. These she presents in English translation in a stream of books (for example 1981, 1984a) or in occasional collections of newsletters (for example 1984b). Common to all these writers is the emphasis on the occult knowledge which lies at the heart of true Zoroastrian teaching: the idea of a personal aura or magnetism which surrounds every individual, which is affected by actions and prayers and which can be characteristic of different races. For this Mrs Master-Moos places great emphasis on Kirlean photography, which shows the heat/energy output of a person's body, what is for her, their aura. It is on this latter basis that many Khshnoomists argue against any conversion of non-Zoroastrians and that they consider it totally wrong for a non-Zoroastrian to enter a fire temple. Not only would they disturb and defile the aura of the temple, but they themselves would not be suitably protected by the appropriate aura from the spiritual power of the fire and could thereby suffer harm. In short, a different cosmology has replaced that put forward in the Middle Persian literature, one which harmonizes contemporary occult or mystical thought with the deeply revered traditional devotional life and the ancient conviction regarding the uniqueness of Zoroastrianism.

There has been only one attempt to build a temple specifically for Khshnoomic ideals, at the holy village of Udwada, where the fire which was consecrated soon after the arrival of the Parsis in India now burns. Essentially Ilm-i Khshnoom is an interpretation of modern Zoroastrianism, not a separate cult. Indeed many Orthodox

Zoroastrians accept part of the teaching, not least on the purity laws, without considering themselves followers of Behramshah Shroff. The astrology which appeared in the earlier forms of Zoroastrianism has been developed both by Khshnoomic and Theosophical writers.

There has been one well-known Zoroastrian writer in recent times who openly proclaimed himself a Theosophist, namely Dastur (a high priestly title) Khurshed S. Dabu. One part of his popularity was, undoubtedly, that he was evidently a profoundly sincere, truly good man, of an ascetic leaning which was consistent with the ideas of a holy man which many had in mid-twentieth-century India. His teachings on vegetarianism and rebirth and his symbolic interpretations of the Middle Persian myths provided many with a Zoroastrian philosophy they could accept in the light of current knowledge. Thus (in 1956:12) he interprets the creation story of the *Bundahisn* (see Chapter 2 above) to indicate that Angra Mainyu is 'the destructive and ephemeral principle in the Cosmos', who is permitted a limited time in which to fulfil his role; he 'does unpleasant work assigned to him, under the supreme authority of God'. He argues that all forces need opposites: 'In electricity and hydraulics there is a law: "The greater the resistance, the greater the pressure." ' Angra Mainyu is not, he argues, to be understood as a being, Satan, but as a negative force which has its temporary necessary role of opposition to the force of good. Although Zoroastrianism has not generally been an ascetic tradition, there were clear antecedents for such an interpretation. Another aspect of Dabu's person and teaching was his devotion to a personal God (not for him the Impersonal Absolute of much Theosophical teaching). A number of his teachings were consistent with traditional Indian approaches to religion, not only the ideas of rebirth, asceticism and vegetarianism but also his ideal of celibacy for the truly religious life and his interpretation of prayers as *mantras* (1969:32ff.) which used ideas and language from ancient Indo-Iranian times. He stressed that because of the Indo-Iranian ancestry of both Zoroastrianismn and Hinduism the two were 'cousins' (1969:36ff.). He has not been alone in offering a parallel between Zoroastrianism and Hinduism: indeed this so much a theme of some Zoroastrian writing that it is worthy of a section on its own.

ZOROASTRIAN PHILOSOPHY IN A HINDU SETTING

It is not surprising that as the rule of the British in India was coming to an end, and even more so after Independence, the intellectual framework within which Zoroastrian philosophy functioned became that of Hinduism. Mention has already been made of the acquisition of some Hindu customs over the hundreds of years in which Zoroastrianism has coexisted with Hinduism. One obvious superficial example is the use of the red *kumkum* mark on the forehead on auspicious occasions. Perhaps the most fundamental impact has been that of caste on traditional Zoroastrian perspectives of the different classes in society (see Chapter 3 above). There has been little or no trend towards internal sub-caste groups (though a potential for that may be seen in the division between layman and hereditary priest), but the Parsis have often been seen by others and by themselves as an endogamous caste group in Indian society. In the twentieth century the process of interaction has been at a more philosophical level than before.

There has been the occasional Hindu author who writes about Zoroastrianism, most notably Jatindra Mohan Chatterji; he has written eight books on Zoroastrianism, the most popular among Parsis being one written in 1967, the main thrust of which is to interpret the *Gāthās* in the light of the *Vedas* and *Upaniṣads*. The reverse process has been far more common: many Parsis have sought to expound their philosophy in terms of the dominant Indian philosophy. The central themes underlying most of these expositions are the understanding of the interaction between the world of the spirit and the world of matter, an attempt to interpret the ancient teachings on *mēnōg* and *gētīg*, and the interaction between divine and human nature, specifically the Gathic idea that the world and mankind embody in some sense the divine world of the Amesha Spentas (see Chapter 1 above).

Some Parsi writers explicitly state their indebtedness to Hindu teachers, for example Wadia (1968) to Swami Virjananda and Jhabvala (n.d.), who quotes Aurobindo Ghose. It is not surprising that Parsis should turn to such teachers, partly because of their consciousness of the shared Indo-Iranian heritage, partly because of their perception of their history in India and partly because of the overwhelming presence of Hindu thought there. Increasingly in the twentieth century Zoroastrian writers have looked to Hindu ideas in order to elaborate their own beliefs. Thus in 1926 Taraporewala used Hindu ideas of *puruṣa* and *prakrti* to explain ideas on good and evil, and set forth his belief in the idea of *karma* and rebirth (1926:43 and 52).

There have been a number of writers on the periphery of the community who have written for a wider non-Parsi audience, for example Jal. K. Wadia (1968) and P. D. Mehta (1976). Wadia, for example, uses Hindu terms more than Zoroastrian ones in what he describes as his attempt to 'penetrate into the very depth of man' to understand the different 'Flows of Conscious Energy' constituted of consciousness (*Chit*) and energy (*Ānanda*). But the reader of his chapters on, for example, 'The Sanskaric elements' may be inclined to interpret his work as that of an Indian, not a Zoroastrian, writer. There has been little reaction to his book within the community. Both he (1973) and Mehta (1985) later wrote books with a more explicit Zoroastrian emphasis. Indeed the very purpose of Wadia (1973) was to explain the main Zoroastrian prayers in a 'meaningful' way for his readers. He writes on the subject of the Amesha Spenta, *Asha*, which it is the duty of every Zoroastrian to embody, that 'it is only on the light of Divinity penetrating through the veil of *Māyā* that man gets into a state of *Ashem*'. The use of the concept of the veil of *Māyā* or illusion is a very Hindu way of interpreting the Zoroastrian conception of evil blinding men to the good in creation. But it is not only a simple exchange of words from another language: something of the associated ideas comes with the vocabulary imported from outside Zoroastrianism. Thus Wadia, like a number of Indian Zoroastrians, believes in rebirth and so reinterprets the traditional explanation for the cause of suffering. Physical and worldly sufferings are traditionally in Zoroastrianism the assaults of evil, but Wadia interprets them as being the natural impurities of man and of the *karmas* which developed these impurities. Later he writes about the forces, what others may describe as the 'aura', in terms of the 'Shaktis' of Hinduism. In the concluding chapter of the book he gives an exposition of the role of fire in Zoroastrian worship in which fire is referred to as 'a valuable gift' to 'the larger Aryan community' and explained in terms not only of the fire in the sanctuary but also the fire within man. He writes of a 'certain kind of Shakti which can awaken inner spiritual or Divine Fire within man' (Wadia 1973:29).

A speaker and writer whose Hindu-influenced teachings have been at once controversial and influential within the Zoroastrian community, not least the Zoroastrian communities outside India, is the high priest Dastur Framroze Bode (who died in 1989). His lectures in India and on visits to London and America were commonly well attended. The book which sets out most clearly his use of Hindu terms and ideas was published in 1978 and is a collection of essays and lectures. In an article reprinted from the *American Theosophist* in 1968, he writes on 'the Seamless Web of Consciousness'. The theme of his paper is in one sense very Zoroastrian, namely how to embody the divine forces (the Amesha Spentas) and reject evil, but the language and imagery is very much that of the Hindu environment in which he lived in Bombay. Thus on p. 98: 'Our present state of consciousness is the result of ignorance (*avidyā*), bewildered limited consciousness (*māyā*) and form-creating karmic activities (*saṃskāra*). All appearances are *māyā* when seen from the universality of consciousness.' He then turns to what he calls

> the coiled serpent-power, the *Kundalini Shakti*, in the unfoldment of consciousness. To awaken this 'sleeping power', control, raise, and unite it with its Master Consciousness at the summit, to merge the psychic energies of the body into the power of the Soul is the goal of *Kundalini* Yoga. This union results in an ecstatic *Samadhi* in which the whole system is flooded with *Anand* and the individual consciousness becomes one with the Supreme Consciousness.

Although he thus uses Hindu terminology, and occasionally Buddhist phrases, he wishes to argue that such teachings are true to the deeper meaning of the words of Zarathushtra, whom he describes as 'the Founder of the Mystical Magian Brotherhood . . . the Master Adept in the science of spiritual Self-Unfoldment, who mystically apprehended all the Divine Laws governing the Universe. He was a Ratu – Illustrious Master of Spiritual Wisdom' (Bode 1978:30).

It is not possible for a historian to see this as consistent with traditional Zoroastrian teaching. It is also a philosophical system at complete variance with that expounded by Dhalla. It is, however, an attempt to interpret the meaning of life for people brought up in a Hindu environment where such ideas are not so much abstruse philosophy as the common assumptions (for example rebirth) of most religious people with whom Bode's followers met. The westernized, Protestantized Zoroastrianism 'does not speak to them in their situation'. From an external perspective it might be said that what Bode was doing was using contemporary language and idioms to convey the idea of the *Gāthās* that one should make the divine powers, the Amesha Spentas, indwell in oneself. What is worth emphasizing is that the vocabulary and imagery used by these various authors was not simply accidental. What they were each trying to do in their own way was to make the Zoroastrian philosophy from another age and another culture powerful in the lives of the followers they knew.

There are countless small ways in which Indian Zoroastrians are affected by or follow Hindu teachings. At a personal level many practise *yoga*. Many visit the shrines of popular holy men, most of all the Babas (Sai Baba of Shirdi and Satya Sai Baba in particular). In Bombay many will go to public lectures given by Indian religious teachers of various types. In one sense what is happening is that Parsis are being drawn into 'the new religious movements' of India. Academic studies of western new religious movements suggest that the membership is drawn mainly from the young to middle-aged, middle-class, urbanized, reasonably well-educated people who come from a religious background but are not finding satisfaction in the received wisdom of their tradition. Many such Parsis follow the equivalents of these 'new movements' in India. The common feature of those movements which Parsis tend to join is that they do not involve a rejection of the old religion in order to be converted to the new, unlike Christianity and Islam. Each of these new movements exhorts followers to see mystical truth in their own religion. Parsis do not, therefore, have to reject their community membership.

THE 'MIDDLE GROUND' AND MODERN ZOROASTRIAN PHILOSOPHY

Written expositions do not necessarily reflect the ideas of most Zoroastrians. Although Khshnoomic writing is fairly widely respected, relatively few would call themselves Khshnoomists. Although Bode's audiences were quite large, not many followed his Hindu interpretations. No single author or even 'school' reflects the philosophy of the majority of Indian Zoroastrians. What follows is a subjective assessment of the sections of various writings which reflect the broad beliefs of most Zoroastrians.

One of the most 'traditional' writers in the twentieth century was Dastur Rustom Sanjana, a Bombay high priest. His two main books were written in 1906 and 1924 and were, therefore, contemporary with the work of Behramshah Shroff and with the early years of Dhalla's writing. He asserted (1924) the divine inspiration of the whole

Avesta, not just of the *Gāthās*. He attacked agnosticism and scepticism and emphasized the link between religion and morals (1924:I). He attacked Theosophy for its belief in an impersonal God and in reincarnation (1924:51ff.). He was the last writer, until the 1980s, to assert belief in resurrection (1924:V). Salvation in a blessed hereafter is dependent upon observation of the purity laws, self-love, happiness and marriage but also upon a very strict moral code. What he is interesting for, and where he is characteristic of many writers who came after him, is in what he does not refer to. He does not allude to the mythology found in the Pahlavi literature regarding creation (though he does stress that Ahura Mazdā is the good creator (1924:167ff.)) or to the renovation. In particular he does not expound the idea of Angra Mainyu as an independent evil being; rather he believes that 'Angramainyu denotes nothing but the evil spirit or thought of man' (1906:142). The doctrine of the twin spirits he interprets as 'the two principles of volition within man. Man has a dual mind, that is, a mind capable of presenting to itself everything in its opposite aspects, good and evil' (1924:210). In this he reflects a belief found in Dhalla. Both writers consequently struggle to find a logical explanation for the suffering of the innocent and the death of children. He acclaims Zarathushtra not only as the first but as the greatest prophet in the history or religion (1924:II).

> Indeed, Zoroaster was the greatest spiritual force produced by our world. He was a colossal religious genius. He was the greatest Law-giver, the greatest Teacher, the greatest of prophets, the unique Prophet who revealed perfectly the Mind and Will of of Ahura Mazdā. (1924 : 87)

The emphasis of the prophet's teaching, he declared, was that 'men should believe in one God, Ahura Mazdā, and honour and glorify Him'. Zarathushtra also taught a doctrine of immortality and a code of ethics 'the fundamental principles of which were universal charity and peace of mankind' (1924:93). 'The Religion of Zoroaster is superior to all other religions of the world in its intense sense of Righteousness (*Asha*) and its conviction of a Righteous Personal God' (1924:135). He then proceeds to argue that unlike most religions Zoroastrianism, while stressing the goodness of God, does not teach a crude anthropomorphism. His attack on Christianity was strong, presumably because he felt that Christian teachings were deflecting his co-religionists from their true path. In particular he attacks the Christian doctrine of salvation as 'the bargain of the believed and saved, which leaves little room for the individual to do', and so he concludes that the Christian doctrine is for parasites (1924:297–9). One of the fundamental divides between many forms of Christian teaching and Zoroastrian doctrine is that the latter assumes that the sole basis on which an individual is sent to heaven or hell is the balance of good and evil thoughts, words and deeds. Sanjana was a priest, and his devotional emphasis was an important dimension of his teaching. Inner and outer purity, he argued, are interrelated. Nature, he said, never produces a tree without bark, or a fruit without a skin. Ceremonies and rites are the bark and skin of all inner purity. If one takes off the bark the result will be quick decay and corruption. 'The exterior is the index of the interior' (1924:302). For Sanjana external purity had to be balanced by inner (or moral) purity and a life of devotion.

There are several themes in Sanjana's writings that characterize much of popular Zoroastrian literature. The reverence for the prophet is an obvious one. One of the most widely read accounts of the life of the prophet, his miracles and stalwart fight for good in the face of evil onslaughts, as the ideal model for his followers to emulate, is in Rustomjee (1961), a story often seen as a parable or allegory for the difficulties individuals must follow in their daily lives (Hinnells 1985b:92–7). A characteristic feature of Sanjana and of other writers is to 'demythologize' the received tradition. Few 'ordinary' Zoroastrians know of the myths in the Pahlavi literature, as outlined by Williams in Chapter 2 above, just as few westerners know or understand the doctrinal formulations of the various Councils of the church on the subject of the Trinity. Even the scholarly Parsi writers who do know them rarely expound them: rather they emphasize the religious and moral messages implied by the myths; they handle the tradition by demythologizing. Perhaps the best of many examples is J. J. Modi in a catechism for children (1962). Modi was a widely respected Parsi scholar indeed he was awarded a doctorate by Oxford University and knighted for his services to scholarship. He took care not to take sides in the public disputes between 'Orthodox' and 'reform' teachers, largely confining himself to historical and literary studies. His scholarly studies included Middle Persian literature, but in the widely used catechism he produced in 1911, none of the myths appear. He asserts simply (1962:6) that Ahura Mazdā 'has brought the whole Universe into existence. Whatever we see in this world has been created by Him. He is the Source of the existence of all.' Similarly he refers in general terms to a belief in an afterlife without any discussion of heaven or hell:

> All who are born will one day die and will have another life hereafter. . . . After old age comes death. Sometime a person dies earlier without attaining to old age. All then go in the presence of their Creator in the invisible world. They live there. The body perishes but the soul lives on. . . . As, when we were born, we had our being from Ahura Mazdā, so, when we die, we shall go back to Him.
>
> (1962:11)

The extent to which Modi 'demythologizes' the tradition is evident in the following extract from the question and answer style of catechism:

> Q. – What do you mean by 'Responsibility'?
> A. – We shall be judged properly in the court of God, for all that we think, for all that we speak, for all that we do in this world.
> Q. – What do you mean by saying that 'we shall be judged properly in the court of God'? Do you mean that we shall be judged after our death?
> A. – No. We have learnt that God exists everywhere and at all times. So His court exists everywhere and at all times. We are therefore judged by him on all proper occasions. We shall be requited for our deeds in this life or in the life hereafter.
>
> (1962:12)

His catechism does not provide any cosmological explanation for the place of fire in Zoroastrian worship. It is explained simply in the following terms:

> We look to fire generally with reverential feelings, as the manifested form of the power of heat and light permeating this world and also as a symbol of the splendour and glory of the Creator. Then in the case of the Fire-temples, the religious ritual in its concentration adds some elements of moral thoughts and spiritual value. Hence it is, that we look to this consecrated fire with greater reverence.
>
> (1962 : 38)

Instead of explaining suffering as the weapon of an alien external force of evil he says 'We should affirm our faith in God, and bear those sufferings with a confident hope, that those sufferings are a trial for us and that everything will be right in the end' (1962:40). In this catechism he says virtually nothing on ritual purity, but that topic is taken up in his larger, more scholarly work (1922) describing and explaining the various Parsi rituals. It was written mainly with a western audience in mind, which is why the purity laws are consistently explained as being important for reasons of hygiene and keeping at bay 'the germs of impurity' (1922:64, 70). Keeping separate from what is impure is described as keeping away 'infection' (1922:49, 71). Living writers who also present this abstract interpretation are Sidhwa (1985) and Shahzadi (1986).

One group of writings which requires comment is that produced by a number of the high priests, *dasturs*, in the last few years. Led first by Dastur H. D. K. Mirza, the three high priests living at the time of writing (in the early 1990s) have all produced scholarly works of reference, largely but not exclusively concerned with editions and translations of liturgical texts: Kotwal (1969a and b); JamaspAsa (1969; 1971; 1982). The former has also worked with an American academic, James Boyd, to try to explain rituals both in detail and with their theological significance (1977). Another recent publication to try and explain the thinking behind Zoroastrian rituals, this time by a layman, is Choksy (1989). Kotwal and Boyd have also collaborated on a translation of a nineteenth-century Gujarati catechism with a modern commentary by Dastur Dr Firoze Kotwal (1982). Dastur Dr JamaspAsa has edited a substantial library of editions of Pahlavi texts. Dastur Dr Mirza has also been responsible for a historical survey of the religion (1974) and pamphlets (1980 and 1983) giving an overview of the historical position of the community. In one sense the works referred to in this paragraph do not belong in this chapter as they are textual and historical studies, but it is important to take note of how the priestly leaders have fulfilled their perceived role of the pursuit of scholarship and the obligation to disseminate this in publications. Some lay people have also been engaged in this work, notably B. T. Anklesaria (Boyce 1986) and T. R. Sethna (1975; 1976; 1977).

There is another strand of modern Zoroastrian literature which seeks to emphasize the rational, reasoning nature of Zoroastrianism, ignoring the myths and explaining away much of the ritual (Kapadia 1905; Wadia 1912; Masani 1938). With such a perspective there is relatively little cosmology or cosmogony, but rather Zoroastrianism is presented as an ethical monotheism, an abstract moral philosophy, centred on the exhortation to practise good thoughts, good words and good deeds. What constituted 'the good' was largely left unsaid: instead there was a bland ethical code thought likely to attract the western reader, for whom these books were mostly written. But there are two publications from the 1980s which have sought to do more than present this greatly simplified non-mythological picture. One is Mistree (1982), the other Motafram (1984). Both seek to explain a more Orthodox Zoroastrian perspective to co-religionists searching for spiritual guidance.

Mistree's book is of particular importance because the author is a charismatic teacher who has had a significant impact on the community, not only in the Indian sub-continent but also on his 'missions' to his fellow-Zoroastrians who have migrated overseas to America, Australia, Britain and Canada. His teaching has proved popular in various sections of the community but particularly with the educated youth. Mistree studied at Oxford and later under Mary Boyce of the School of Oriental and African Studies, London. In some circles he is bitterly criticized for what is seen as his input of western-influenced academic scholarship. His approach adheres closely to the *Gāthās* as expounded by Boyce in Chapter 1 above, and similarly his views on the doctrines of good and evil are taken directly from the Pahlavi books described by Williams in Chapter 2 above. His teaching is consistent with that of Boyce (1975) in his emphasis on the great continuity of the Zoroastrian tradition. Thus the Pahlavi texts, in Mistree's view, are not expositions of priestly corrupted superstitions, but are seen rather as invaluable guides to the heart of Zoroastrian spirituality, cosmology as well as ethics. At the same time that he believes in a separate force of evil he is also concerned to present Zoroastrianism as a monotheistic religion. It is because they think that he weakens the monotheistic emphasis with the teaching of dualism that some oppose him. Mistree thus expounds the view that God is not yet all powerful, but is rather 'latently omnipotent' (1982:28). He emphasizes that this does not mean that Ahriman is equal to, or as powerful as, God.

> It is empirically verifiable that the will of Ahura Mazdā continues to overwhelm the imperfections and inequalities in this world. The process of 'creative evolution' is an ongoing one, for it is within the cumulative power of man [the chosen soldier of God] to rid the world of disorder, poverty, misery, pain, suffering and eventually death.
>
> (1982 : 29)

He goes on to affirm the Orthodox position: 'In Zoroastrianism, an absolute distinction is maintained between the origin of good and its antithesis, evil.' He then explains this in the following words:

> In other words, the factor of separation results in the relative world in which existence mirrors its antithesis, non-existence. Non-existence on its own cannot exist; and that which cannot exist on its own cannot create, and that which cannot create knows not how to affirm, and that which cannot affirm is devoid of wisdom, and therefore is deemed to be

> the postulated nature of evil. Evil therefore clearly cannot come from God, as it is devoid of wisdom. Thus, there is a fundamental duality which absolves God from any taint of evil . . . Evil in Zoroastrianism is not a reality in itself, but is an existential paradox experienced by man, through the imbalance reflected in the physical world. It is only in the relative world that the states of excess and deficiency are observable and discernible, thereby giving an apparent existence to evil which does not and, in fact, cannot stem from any other source. . . . Evil only mirrors a denial of that which is existent and intrinsically good. Being parasitic, it does not and, in fact, cannot exist on its own. In other words, evil is *ex nihilo*; i.e. it arises from and out of nothing, and therefore has no real existence.
>
> (Mistree 1982:29)

Whereas some authors who have studied, or been heavily influenced by, western thought have played down the importance of rituals, Mistree sees these as a vital part of spiritual practice and progress towards a mystical experience. Ritual he defines as

> the medium through which a person is able to relate to the unseen spiritual world. It is through a ritual that an individual existentially experiences a link between the physical and spiritual worlds. A ritual also enables one to maintain a continuity of religious experience with the past. . . . Upon the proper enactment of a ritual, a qualitative appreciation of the goodness of God begins to emerge, which in turn generates an inexplicable harmony that momentarily brings the participant in contact with the divine centre – the the source of all reality! . . . The priests will be able to generate the ritual power . . . necessary to transpose the physical experience of the ritual into a spiritual reality, only if the recitation of the prayers is accompanied by the right intention balanced with a virtuous mind.
>
> (Mistree 1982:60)

Rituals he sees operating at three levels:

> i. the physical sensate world which is represented by the materials and implements (*alat*) used;
> ii. the psychological world within which are involved the emotions, feelings and participation of the celebrant;
> iii. the spiritual world within which the celebrant becomes aware of an intangible, experiential dimension of reality.
>
> (Mistree 1982:61)

Rituals, he explains, give joy and strength to the spiritual beings and in the physical world 'increased purity, goodness, strength, peace and prosperity leading to the quicker destruction of Angra Mainyu'.

A more recent publication is Motafram (1984). This work consists of three books offering an 'Elementary', an 'Intermediate' and an 'Advanced Course'. They were commissioned and published by the Bombay Parsi Punchayet, which is nowadays largely a body administering substantial charitable trust funds, but its status as a paternalistic body concerned to oversee the welfare and property of the community means that it is the nearest institution in the Indian sub-continent to a 'governing body' for Zoroastrians. These books do therefore have certain authority, although it may be doubted whether they have quite the widespread acceptance of (or provoke the strong adverse reaction against) Mistree's. Motafram's 'Elementary Course' presents a doctrinally 'bland' picture of the religion. His starting point is the picture of Zarathushtra, whose life provides the role-model and moral lessons which his followers should emulate, for example to reform the religion form the ignorance and superstitious beliefs which had developed; to be determined and resolute in the face of strong opposition; to practise an unflinching pursuit of duty; to remain steadfast in the faith and to follow the noble ideals of the religion. Motafram then proceeds to draw out the theme of two worlds, the spiritual and the material, re-expressing the ideas of *mēnōg* and *gētīg* of the Pahlavi literature. Much, he argues, lies beyond the material world that we cannot see. 'We can see light rays, but the high frequency radiations as cosmic rays, gamma rays, X-rays, ultraviolet rays are not visible to the naked eye. Shall we say they do not exist?' (1984:9). From the example of these unseen vibrations and colours Motafram draws the conclusion that there is much in the spiritual world which we cannot see but with which man must be 'in tune'. There is a heavy emphasis (1984:13ff.) on the practice of good thoughts, words and deeds, and the consequences of such a practice, but the terms 'good' and 'evil' are not defined: only their destination is pointed out, to the best or the worst existence in the hereafter. Essentially he is returning to the traditional picture of heaven and hell in contrast to the number of modern authors who have tried to explain these ideas away. He distinguishes between the purity of the body and that of the soul. The former is elucidated in terms of avoiding putrefaction, but the latter is said to be the more important and consists of keeping away from evil propensities like lust, anger, avarice, temptation, pride and jealousy. Although these 'definitions' of evil are consistent with modernizing tendencies to make the religion more 'abstract' (or utilitarian), at this point the interpretation is consistent with the abstract dimensions of the ancient Iranian teachings as elucidated in Chapter 1 above. Family and social duties are stressed and the characteristic Zoroastrian virtue of charity is heavily emphasized (1984:24ff.) However the Zoroastrian cosmology is interpreted, the practical moral philosophy has hardly changed over the centuries and continents. But it is interesting to note that some of the traditional mythology (for example the bridge of judgement) is included, and, remarkable among recent Zoroastrian writers, he states that resurrection is part of the Zoroastrian heritage (1984:42). It could be misleading to describe Mistree and Motafram as Zoroastrian 'fundamentalists' because that term has in the modern world taken on connotations of aggressive extremism, when used, for example, in connection with Christians, Jews and Muslims. But the term is appropriate in that they are both returning to what, from the historian's perspective, is the original or the fundamental (in the sense of 'foundational') tradition.

In Motafram's 'Intermediate Course', as well as referring to western philosophers and occasionally to Hindu teachers, he makes more reference to the traditional Middle Persian texts and myths than does any other author, except perhaps Mistree. One example of a Hindu idea that is taken over is the teaching on the saviours. These are part of traditional teaching in that the term is used of Zarathushtra and his three posthumous sons to be born in successive millennia as history approaches its climax, but Motafram's account is adapted to the idea of the *avatāra*. For example, he writes 1984:59):

> Whenever evil reigns supreme on the face of the earth and the moral fabric of mankind in general disintegrates, the law of *Asha* comes into operation and the Supreme God with the intention of saving mankind from the intensity of the worsening situation, sends saviours and benefactors.

The *Upaniṣads* and Swami Vivekananda are quoted in an exposition of the threefold path that the worshipper should follow, that of work, devotion and knowledge 1984:86ff.). Introspection is presented as a necessary first step on the path to disciplining the mind:

> Beginning should, however, be made by withdrawing the mind from sense objects for a while, and making it steady. Day by day, the mind will be trained to reflect upon itself, and will reveal its secrets, and a man will learn gradually to control, and skillfully manage the internal forces, and be in tune with the external ones which are the gross counter parts of the former. . . . One who calls himself a Raj Yogi proposes to do the same.
>
> (1984 : 65)

The theme of prayer and vibrations is pressed much further in this book (ch. 7): thus he refers not only to the vibrations associated with the sacred prayers but also to the 'fact that the law of vibrations can be experienced in everyday life as each individual whose mental and soul vibrations are properly attuned exudes a kind of magnetic influence. He has an aura round his face as in the case of prophets' (1984:49). Motafram also expounds an idea accepted by many who follow an esoteric Zoroastrian teaching, namely that of the ethereal body: 'Surrounding our physical body there is an envelope of very subtle and tenuous material. This is the so-called ethereal body which is rendered impure by the impurities given off by the physical body and a man's aura is defiled' (1984 III:50). The *sudre*, or sacred shirt, he believes 'absorbs these impurities, it helps to keep the ethereal body clean. It also acts as a protection from the power of external evil forces' (1984 III : 51). Thus on this level of teaching the sacred shirt and cord are seen not merely as symbols but also as spiritual, or occult, armour.

Motafram is but one example of a number of Parsis who thus offer a 'demythologized' ethical monotheism as the popular exposition of their religion but then give a more esoteric interpretation which blends together occult, Hindu and 'scientific' strands of thought at what is seen as a 'higher' level. Such teachers offer to 'spiritually developed' souls a new mythology, but it is one which continues to focus on the issue of the fundamentally opposed powers for good or ill, for life-giving and life-denying, positive and negative forces. The various expositions of modern Zoroastrian philosophy wrestle in different ways with the challenge posed to them by Wilson with his accusations of dualism and polytheism. Despite the variety of teachings in the modern period there is in fact a common thread and a continuity of basic convictions, however different their presentations. In each form of Zoroastrian teaching there is a fundamental assumption that unseen spiritual forces are interwoven with the material world so that the latter must be protected and respected. Parsis rarely accept the Hindu view of the material world as *māyā* or illusory. It is much more common for them to emphasize the teaching that man must care for the world because of the doctrines that the material world is God's creation and that the Amesha Spentas are represented by, or present in, the different creations. Hence, many now add, Zoroastrianism is in harmony with current ecological thinking.

ZOROASTRIAN PERCEPTIONS OF RELIGIOUS TRUTH AND RELIGIOUS AUTHORITY

Implied in many of the differences between Zoroastrian writers are contrasting perceptions of religious authority. Thus for many westernized Zoroastrians there was an emphasis on the authority of western-style scholarship and reason; the Theosophists looked to the teaching of Blavatsky and Olcott; the Khshnoomists turned to Shroff and the esoteric teaching said to emanate from hidden Zoroastrian groups in Iran; for others a valid spiritual insight is found in the writings of Hindu holy men. It is possible to indicate in very general terms how these perceptions of authority have changed from one period to another. Langstaff (1983) demonstrated how twentieth-century Indian Zoroastrian philosophy can be seen to pass through three historical periods: (a) before the First World War, when western (Protestant) thought was dominant, though challenged by occult teachings; (b) the inter-war years, when western influences declined, the occult teachings remained but Hindu influences began to emerge, as did the calls to return to the Iranian homeland as conditions there eased and concurrently communal tensions erupted in India; (c) post-Independence India, when western influences declined and Hindu influences increased. Again the occult tradition continues through the period. Religion is not a static phenomenon; any religion, including Zoroastrianism, must change to some degree if it is to remain meaningful to its adherents who live under very different conditions in different intellectual 'environments' and with different 'peer-group pressures'. This is particularly so in the rapidly changing scene of twentieth-century India. Motafram also offers a different perspective on the various teachings, seeing them as different levels each appropriate to the different spiritual development of individuals.

One reason for this variety of modern Indian Zoroastrian religious philosophies is that there is no widely recognized centre of religious authority which determines what is 'the true faith'. For 'the Protestant Party', authority rests simply in the *Gāthās*, the words of the prophet stripped of all later corruptions. This is true also for many Zoroastrians living in Islamic Iran (with its attitude to the authority of the written revealed word from God through the prophet). In the Hindu environment of India others emphasize more the authority of the priest as a man of spiritual power, whose words and acts, when recited with devotion and in purity, convey a spiritual force or power which results in the 'real' presence of the heavenly beings (Kotwal and Boyd 1977). For yet others, notably Mistree and Motafram, the Middle Persian texts are also sources of authority. For some the word of the various Hindu holy men, for others the scholarly conclusions of western academics carry weight.

A focal point of debates on the locus of religious truth and experience tends to be the attitude to conversion. For some the belief that Zoroastrianism teaches a special religious truth means that the possibility of conversion from another religion to Zoroastrianism is possible, indeed desirable. The most prolific speaker and writer on this theme is Dr Ali Jafary (who himself comes from a Muslim background), who works as religious teacher in one of the Zoroastrian Associations in California (1976 and 1988). The issue of whether Zoroastrians should actually seek converts is discussed mainly among the diaspora groups in America. More widely discussed there, but also in Britain and Australia, is the question of whether the community should 'accept' the offspring or spouses in a mixed marriage where the partner agrees. Without such an acceptance many see the religion dying out as numbers diminish in India (Karkal 1984) and intermarriage increases. Among traditional Zoroastrians in the diaspora, but especially in the 'old countries' of India and Pakistan, there is widespread feeling, led by the high priests (notably, K. M. JamaspAsa, F. M. Kotwal and H. D. K. Mirza – see Hinnells 1987), against the acceptance of anyone either of whose parents has married out of the religion. The arguments are, briefly, that a person is born into a particular religion because that is God's will and that to change religion is going against 'fate', and because it results in a conflict between upbringing and the developed self, it is likely to lead to psychological damage (Antia 1985). This argument hinges upon the conviction that there is valid religious truth in all religions (Dhalla 1950), and that any individual should be religious in the tradition into which they are born. There is, therefore, the acceptance of the relative truth of any religion, since none contains a unique truth which alone is required for salvation. One further element in the argument is that proselytism has been the biggest single cause of oppression and persecution throughout human history, hence conversion is an evil which should be consistently repudiated (Dadachanji, quoted in Hinnells 1987). Khshnoomists believe that Zoroastrianism has a special place because it is, in their teaching, the religion into which the souls are born of those who have reached their last birth before release from the round of rebirth (Masani 1917). For them, therefore, Zoroastrianism is not a possibility for 'outsiders' in this life, but is rather a state into which they will be born when their souls have progressed further on the spiritual path.

CONCLUSION

While Zoroastrians have wrestled with the challenges to their religious philosophy, with the idea of good and evil, with the interconnectedness of the spiritual and material worlds, what has remained constant is their moral philosophy. What in practice constitute the good thoughts, words and deeds have changed but little over millennia and continents. Foremost is the duty to care for the Good Creation, humanity, the physical and animal worlds. Truth and honesty, industry and learning, traditionally respected by Zoroastrians, are the very qualities which contributed to the Parsi rise to wealth and influence in British India. They are also characteristic of the Diaspora communities. The virtue they are probably best known for in India is charity. Indeed there is a saying 'Charity, thy name is Parsi; Parsi thy name is Charity', and Gandhi once commented that the best protection of the Parsis in the turbulent times of pre-Independent India is their record of cosmopolitan charity (Hinnells 1985a). However Zoroastrians may philosophize, what they practise has remained constant. The moral philosophy and the daily practices have remained undimmed from the early times down to the present.

(Note: I wish to record my sincere thanks to my colleague Dr A. Williams for his constructive comments on an early draft of this chapter, though the responsibility for any errors remains wholly mine.)

REFERENCES

(Note: Most Indian publications cited are privately printed; hence a publisher is not listed.)

Antia, B. H. (1985) *'Acceptance' – Never Ever! Conversion in Zoroastrianism: A Myth Exploded*, Bombay.

Barker, E. (1991) 'Helena Blavatsky', in John R. Hinnells (ed.) *Who's Who of Religions*, London: Macmillan.

Billimoria, N. F. (n.d.) *Zoroastrianism in the Light of Theosophy*, Bombay and Madras.

Bode, F. A. (1978) *Sharing the Joy of Learning*, Bombay.

Boyce, Mary (1975) *A History of Zoroastrianism*, vol. I, Leiden: Brill.

—— (1979) *Zoroastrians: Their Religious Beliefs and Practices*, London: Routledge.

—— (1984) *Sources for the Study of Zoroastrianism*, Manchester: Manchester University Press.

Boyce, Mary and JamaspAsa, K. M. (1986) 'Anklesaria', in *Encyclopaedia Iranica*, ed. E. Yarshater, London: Routledge, vol. II, fasc. 1, pp. 96f.

Chatterji, J. M. (1967) *The Hymns of Atharvan Zarathushtra*, Bombay.

Chiniwalla, F. S. (1942) *Essential Origins of Zoroastrianism*, Bombay.

Choksy, J. K. (1989) *Triumph over Evil: Purity and Pollution in Zoroastrianism*, Austin: University of Texas Press.

Dabu, K. S. (1956) *Message of Zarathushtra*, Bombay.

—— (1966) *Zarathushtra and his Teachings*, Bombay.

—— (1969) *Handbook of Information on Zoroastrianism*, Bombay.

Dastoor, K. N. (1984) *Zarathushtra the Yazata*, Bombay.

Dhalla, M. N. (1914) *Zoroastrian Theology, From the Earliest Times to the Present Day*, Oxford.
—— (1938) *History of Zoroastrianism*, Oxford.
—— (1942) *Hommage unto Ahura Mazda*, Karachi.
—— (1950) *Mankind – Whither Bound?*, Karachi.
—— (1975) *Dastur Dhalla: The Saga of a Soul, an Autobiography*, English trans. by G. and B. S. H. J. Rustomji, Karachi.
Firby, N. K. (1988) *European Travellers and their Perceptions of Zoroastrians in the 17th and 18th Centuries*, Berlin: German Archaeological Institute of Tehran.
Haug, M. (1862) *Essays on the Sacred Language, Writings and Religion of the Parsis*, repr. Amsterdam: Philo Press, 1971.
Hinnells, John R. (1978a) 'Parsis and the British', *Journal of the K. R. Cama Oriental Institute* 46:1–92.
—— (1978b) *Spanning East and West*, Milton Keynes: Open University Press.
—— (1983) 'Social change and religious transformation among Bombay Parsis in the early twentieth century', in P. Slater and D. Wiebe (eds) *Traditions in Contact and Change*, Winnipeg: Wilfred Laurier University Press.
—— (1985a) 'The flowering of Zoroastrian benevolence: Parsi charities in the 19th and 20th centuries', in *Papers in Honour of M. Boyce, Acta Iranica* 24(I): 261–326.
—— (1985b) *Persian Mythology*, 2nd edn, London: Hamlyn Press.
—— (1987) 'Parsi attitudes to religious pluralism', in H. Coward (ed.) *Modern Indian Responses to Religious Pluralism*, New York: State University of New York Press, pp. 195–233.
—— (1988) 'Behramshah Shroff', in *Encyclopaedia Iranica*, ed. E. Yarshater, vol. III(iv), pp. 109f.
—— (forthcoming) *The Modern Zoroastrian Diaspora*, Ratanbai Ktrak Lectures, Oxford: Oxford University Press, 1987.
Jafarey, A. A. (1976) *Good Conscience: The Rational Religion of Zarathushtra*, Lahore.
—— (1988) *Fravarane: I Choose for Myself the Zoroastrian Religion*, Westminster, Calif: California Zoroastrian Center.
JamaspAsa, K. M. J. (1982) *Aogəmadaēcā: A Zoroastrian Liturgy*, Vienna: Osterreichischen Akademie der Wissenschaften.
JamaspAsa, K. M. J. and Humbach, H. H. (1969) *Vaeθā Nask*, Wiesbaden: Harrassowitz.
—— (1971) *Pursišnīhā: A Zoroastrian Catechism*, Wiesbaden: Harrassowitz.
Jhabvala, S. H. (n.d.) *Catechism on Zoroastrianism*, Bombay.
Kapadia, S. A. (1905) *The Teachings of Zoroaster*, London: John Murray.
Karkal, M. (1984) *Survey of Parsi Population of Greater Bombay – 1982*, Bombay: Parsi Punchayet.
Kotwal, F. M. P. (1969a) *The Supplementary Texts to the Šāyest Nē-Šāyest*, Copenhagen: Royal Danish Academy of Sciences and Letters/Munksgaard Publishers.
—— (1969b) *Vaethā Nask*, Bombay.
Kotwal, F. M. P. and Boyd, J. W. (1977) 'The Zoroastrian paragṇā', *Journal of Mithraic Studies* 2(i): 18–52.
—— (1982) *A Guide to the Zoroastrian Religion*, Chico, Calif: Scholars Press.
Kulke, E. (1974) *The Parsees in India: A Minority as Agent of Social Change*, Munich: Weltforum Verlag.
Laing, S. (1890) *A Modern Zoroastrian*, London: Chapman & Hall.
Langstaff, H. (1983) 'The impact of Western education and political changes upon the religious teachings of Indian Parsis in the twentieth century', unpublished PhD thesis, University of Manchester.

Madan, D. M. (1909) *Revelation Considered as a Source of Religious Knowledge, with Special Reference to Zoroastrianism*, Bombay.
Mama, N. F. (1944) *A Mazdaznan Mystic, Life-sketch of the late Behramshah Naoroji Shroff*, Bombay.
Masani, P. S. (1917) *Zoroastrianism, Ancient and Modern*, Bombay.
Masani, R. P. (1938) *The Religion of the Good Life*, London: Allen & Unwin.
Mehta, P. D. (1976) *The Heart of Religion*, London: Compton Russell.
—— (1985) *Zarathushtra: The Transcendental Religion*, London: Element Books.
Minor, R. N. (1989) 'Sri Aurobindo and experience: yogic and otherwise', in R. D. Baird (ed.) *Religion in Modern India*, New York: South Asia Publications, pp. 421–54.
Mirza, H. D. K. (1974) *Outlines of Parsi History*, Bombay.
--- (1980) *Some Religious Problems Facing the Parsi Community*, Bombay.
—— (1983) *Zoroastrianism*, Religions of India Series, Delhi: Clarion Books.
Mistree, K. (1982) *Zoroastrianism: An Ethnic Perspective*, Bombay.
Modi, J. J. (1922) *The Religious Ceremonies and Customs of the Parsees*, Bombay; enlarged 2nd edn, 1937.
—— (1962) *A Catechism of the Zoroastrian Religion* (1st edn 1911), Bombay.
Moos, Meher Master (1981) *Life of Ustad Saheb Behramshah Nowroji Shroff*, Bombay.
—— (1983) *125th Birth Anniversary Celebration of Late Ustad Saheb Behramshah Nowroji Shroff*, Bombay.
—— (1984a) *Ustad Saheb Behramshah Nowroji Shroff on Asho Sarosh Yazad and the Divine Universal Natural Laws of Ecology*, Bombay.
—— (1984b) *Mazdayasnie Monasterie, Collection of Newsletter-articles, 1981–84*, Bombay.
Motafram, R. R. (1984) *Zoroastrianism* (in three volumes entitled *Elementary Course: Elements of Zoroastrianism*; *Intermediate Course: Salient Features of Zoroastrianism*; and *Advanced Course: Light on Zoroastrianism*), Bombay.
Moulton, J. H. (1917) *The Treasure of the Magi*, London.
Naoroji, D. (1862) 'The Parsi religion', *Proceedings of the Liverpool Literary and Philosophical Society*, London, 1–31.
Paymaster, R. B. (1954) *Early History of the Parsees in India*, Bombay.
Rustomjee, F. (1961) *The Life of Holy Zarathushtra*, Colombo.
Sanjana, R. E. D. P. (1906) *Zarathushtra and Zarathushtrianism in the Avesta*, Bombay.
—— (1924) *The Parsi Book of Books: The Zand Avesta*, Bombay.
Seervai, K. N. and Patel, B. B. (1899) 'Gujarat Parsis', in *Gazetteer of the Bombay Presidency*, 9(ii), Bombay.
Sethna, T. R. (1975) *Khordeh Avesta, Prayers in Roman Script and Translation in English*, Karachi.
—— (1976) *Yashts in Roman Script with Translation*, Karachi.
—— (1977) *Yasna (excluding the Gathas), Visparad, Marriage Blessings, Afringans, Afrins*, Karachi.
Shahzadi, B. (1986) *Message of Zarathushtra*, 2nd edn, Westminster, Calif.: California Zoroastrian Center.
Sidhwa, G. (1985) *Discourses on Zoroastrianism*, 2nd edn, Karachi.
Sorabji, J. (1922) *The Eternal Pilgrim and the Voice Divine*, ed. I. J. S. Taraporevala and M. K. Vesavala, Bombay.
Taraporewala, I. J. S. (1926) *The Religion of Zarathushtra*, Bombay (revised edn, 1965).
Tavaria, P. N. (1971) *A Manual of Khshnoom: The Zoroastrian Occult Knowledge*, Bombay.
Vimadalal, J. (1904) 'The principles of theosophy', *East and West*, 69–78, 154–60, 261–8.
Wadia, A. S. N. (1912) *The Message of Zoroaster*, London: Dent.

Wadia, J. K. (1968) *The Inner Man*, Calcutta.
—— (1973) *A Few Zoroastrian Fundamentals*, Calcutta.
Wadia, K. J. B. (1931) *Fifty Years of Theosophy in Bombay, 1880–1930*, Madras.
Wilson, J. (1843) *The Parsi Religion as Contained in the Zand-Avasta, and Propounded and Defended by the Zoroastrians of India and Persia, Unfolded, Refuted, and Contrasted with Christianity*, Bombay.

Part II

INDIAN PHILOSOPHY

INTRODUCTION

India has long been the recipient of religious and philosophical ideas from migrating or invading peoples from the North and the West. It is not, therefore, surprising that India is the birthplace of one of the most sophisticated and diverse philosophical traditions in Asia. What is perhaps the most striking feature of this tradition is its originality and rigorous development of themes ranging from social and political philosophy to abstract metaphysics and philosophical logic. Ideas and traditions were absorbed from outside, but Indian philosophers built upon them and adapted them into a structured and lively debate which lasted more than two thousand years.

Influences from outside India have been quite diverse. During the period 2000–1000 BC the indigenous population saw a continual influx of Āryan people, people coming out of the culture of central Asia. This was probably the most significant stage in the foundational development of the religious tradition of Brāhmanism or early Hinduism, for it was during this time (and the five hundred years that followed) that the four Vedas were composed. A further influx of people was to follow in 600–500 BC, this time the Zoroastrian (or Parsi) people, who found a congenial refuge in India's tolerant society.

Alexander's invading forces brought Greek culture into India, especially in the North, for the period 300–100 BC. The extent to which Alexander's invading forces brought with them Greek philosophy is still much debated. From AD 800 to AD 1800 the most important migrating and invading people were from Islamic cultures. From AD 1800 to India's independence in 1946 British culture left its mark on many aspects of social life which are vitally relevant to philosophical enquiry: education and its curriculum, the political and legal systems, and the preferred language of the scholars and political leaders. It says much for the vitality of India's own indigenous social and religious traditions that they have been able to absorb and assimilate many features of such diverse influences.

Towards the end of the composition of the Vedas – at around 800–500 BC – came the composition of the *Upaniṣads* as both a reflection on the Vedic tradition and the introduction of some strikingly new ideas concerning the nature of the individual soul (*ātman*) and its connection with the ultimately real (*Brahman*). The *Upanisads* introduced also the doctrine of the cycle of birth–death–rebirth (*saṁsāra*) and the hope of an escape from this cycle into *mokṣa* or *mukti*. The *Bhagavadgītā* attempted a synthesis of previous Vedic and Upaniṣadic ideas, whereas many rival systems of thought flourished at the same time. Of these latter, the two most durable have proved to be Buddhism and Jainism.

From that time to about AD 1800 the philosophical community took the form of schools, both orthodox (following or at least in theory consistent with the teachings of the Vedas) and non-orthodox (where Buddhism manifested the most extreme variations on possible implications of the teachings of the Buddha). After the formulation of the original *sūtras* of the six orthodox schools, there soon emerged a pairing of these schools as Sāṅkhya-Yoga, Nyāya-Vaiśeṣika and Mīmāṁsā-Vedānta, and a large corpus of works followed which were commentaries and sub-commentaries on the *sūtras*. These texts developed and defended their school's major tenets against the developing texts of rival schools.

From the latter part of the nineteenth century, Indian philosophers have attempted an accommodation with western thought. This has taken two forms, represented in the cases of Radhakrishnan and some contemporary scholars. Radhakrishnan found inspiration in Vedānta philosophy and in Kantian and post-Kantian philosophy of the eighteenth and nineteenth centuries, and sought to combine these traditions with his own thinking. Contemporary philosophers in India take a different approach. Working in university departments where the emphasis has been very heavily on the analytic tradition of the west, some leading scholars are attempting a recovery of the indigenous philosophical tradition, yet with an analytical approach. Though Indian philosophy has its mystical side, and though the general setting of the philosophical schools is within the soteriological context of seeking *mokṣa* by way of *jñāna* or intellectual knowledge, there is much in the Indian tradition which may fairly be called analytic philosophy.

B.C. and I.M.

5

THE ORIGINS OF INDIAN PHILOSOPHY

John Brockington

The Vedas have generally been regarded as the ultimate authority in Hinduism, both by those who belong to that religion and by others from the outside. The same is broadly true for Hindu systems of philosophy. So much is this the case that non-orthodox systems of thought are in large measure defined as those that reject the authority of the Vedas. It is therefore appropriate to begin an examination of the origins of Indian philosophy with the Vedas, while not overlooking the fact that there were other, though less immediately obvious, sources for Indian thought.

The religion that is recorded in the Vedic hymns is an élite form of that brought into India by the Āryans who began to settle in north India soon after the middle of the second millennium BC, and has recognizable affinities with the early religion of other Indo-European-speaking peoples; indeed, in some respects it shows greater similarity to such religions than to developed Hinduism. These hymns, the *saṃhitās*, form the first of the four categories which evolved within the Vedic literature (the whole of which is for Hindus 'the Vedas', although western writers tend to use the term to denote these hymns alone). They were grouped into four collections, of which the oldest in terms of compilation is the *Ṛg Veda*, which can be assigned to around 1200 BC on the basis of its language and also of its clear links with the Iranian religion, especially in the form which precedes Zarathushtra's reforms, so far as we can discern it from the Avesta. Probably the next is the *Sāma Veda*, although the *Yajur Veda* cannot be much later, and finally comes the *Atharva Veda*.[1] It must be emphasized that this order is based on the date of compilation and that individual hymns may be much older than that. The Vedic literature was then further developed, also over an extended period, by the group of texts known as the *Brāhmaṇas*, which differ from the hymns by their prose form, their later language and their more elaborate ritual; they form the second category. Within the *Brāhmaṇas* is contained the third category, the *Āraṇyakas*, of which the *Upaniṣads* were in their origin a further development, although they became increasingly independent later.

The hymns of the *Ṛg Veda* are thus our earliest textual evidence for the religious beliefs of the Āryans. They were transmitted orally for many centuries, initially because this was the way that they were composed but subsequently because they were regarded as too sacred to be reduced to writing, but the hymns have nevertheless been preserved with remarkable accuracy as a result of elaborate methods of recitation introduced to safeguard their exact wording. The picture that they give us of the religious thought and practices of their time is hardly complete, however, for they reflect the interests of the priestly group concerned with the ritual worship of the major gods, while the total length of the collection (just over a thousand hymns, containing in all a little over ten thousand verses) means that there is not in any case the space for a comprehensive picture, given the nature of the hymns as primarily poems of praise and petition to the various deities.[2]

The collection is divided into ten books, each of which is a separate grouping. The earliest block seems to consist of books 2–7, each containing the hymns composed by one family of seers and all following the same arrangement of their hymns by deity addressed and by length of hymn. These were then bracketed (probably in a two-stage process) by the first and eighth books. The ninth book consists exclusively of hymns to Soma, collected together here because of the importance of Soma in the ritual, as we shall see shortly. The hymns of the tenth book were then the last to be added and, while a few of them are as early as any in the other books, they are in general distinctly later, as their language and metre reveal quite as obviously as their content.

Indra was clearly the most popular deity in the pantheon for the poets of the *Ṛg Veda*, for nearly a quarter of all its hymns are addressed to him. He is also described in more anthropomorphic terms than the other deities, with his bodily strength, his great size and his weapons being often alluded to, for he is clearly the apotheosis of the Āryan warrior. His conflict and victory over the serpent Vṛtra is frequently mentioned in the hymns and this is now usually regarded as a creation myth (one of several that we find in the hymns), but the style of the allusions to it tends to stress Indra's martial character. More generally, he appears as the king of the gods (paralleling the way that the Āryan chief was both leader in battle and head of his clan). Nevertheless, although the order of the hymns in the 'family' books 2–7 generally reflects the relative ranking of the deities (as shown by the number of hymns addressed to them), the hymns to Indra follow those to Agni, reflecting one of the major constraints on the nature of the collection as it has come down to us: its use in the ritual.

Agni's prominence in the *Ṛg Veda* (*ṚV*), where he is invoked in over two hundred hymns, is based essentially on his character as the sacrificial fire. He is the actual fire on the altar (his name is also the standard term for 'fire') and in that capacity conveys the sacrifice to heaven and brings the other gods down to the sacrifice. He is therefore the mediator between men and gods and so the counterpart among the gods of the priests among men. His linking with the human priests leads to his being credited with other aspects of their role, so that he is regarded as poet, sage and seer, as well as attending Indra in much the same fashion as a priest accompanying a human chief and using his weapons of incantations and rites against a common enemy. On the other hand, the fact that he is at the same time both one, as the god, and many, as the individual fires, both immortal and reborn daily from the kindling sticks, leads in one of the latest hymns in the collection to speculation on the relationship between the one and the many (*ṚV* 10.88.17–19).

The importance of the ritual to the selection of the hymns actually represented in the *Ṛg Veda* is still more clearly seen in the figure of Soma, the deified personification of a plant which was central to Vedic ritual (just as the equivalent *haoma* was of great importance in early Iranian religion). The physical basis of both Agni and Soma was a major restriction on the growth of any mythology associated with them, and Soma's exploits, such as they are, are derived almost entirely from Indra, because he is the great *soma* drinker, and from Agni, because he is also a god of ritual. The elaboration of imagery in the hymns, gathered together almost entirely in the ninth book, is in fact centered on the pressing and straining of the juice from this plant. The exhilaration produced by drinking the resulting liquid is clearly indicated: it is a divine drink, which confers immortality (*amṛta*) on gods and men, and Indra needs to be invigorated by it before performing his major exploits. It is a relatively easy progression from here to the idea that Soma is necessary to Indra's activity and so is some kind of cosmic power, who produces the world and wields universal sway; this appears to underlie the claims that Soma is not only lord of plants but also king of the gods, of the whole earth and of men.

The identity of the *soma* plant has still not been conclusively established, with many different candidates having been put forward over the years.[3] What is clear is that, because of where it grew (both the Avesta and the Vedas state that the plant grew on the tops of mountains, while details of the Vedic Soma ritual indicate that it had to be bought from outsiders some distance away), there were increasing difficulties over time in obtaining it and eventually substitutes began to be used. Over the same period the ritual was steadily becoming more elaborate as the priestly influence, with which the emphasis on Soma is so closely linked, became more and more dominant. The two developments may, indeed, be interconnected, for it is not unlikely that the ineffectiveness of a substitute in producing the effects of Soma was compensated for by the elaboration of the ritual producing its own exhilaration, in such a way that the sense of ecstasy and communion with the gods was now produced by purely ritual means. In the still longer term, this may have contributed to the emphasis in later stages of Hinduism on the achievement of certain states by manipulation of one's own consciousness.

These three gods are the most prominent among the pantheon of the gods, the Devas, who were traditionally numbered as thirty-three. Among these the most significant single grouping is that of the Ādityas, the twelve sons of Aditi ('boundlessness, freedom'), who is one of the few goddesses of any significance in this overwhelmingly male pantheon. Alongside the *Devas* are another group, the *Asuras*, although at this stage both terms can be applied to the same individual and there is little sign of the structural opposition between the two groups which characterizes the next stage of the religion. However, one of the figures most often called *asura* is Varuṇa, a more remote figure than Indra (who has perhaps replaced him as the most important of the gods) and the guardian above all of *ṛta*, the principle of order in the universe in both its natural and its moral aspects.

Even within the period represented by the composition of the hymns of the four Vedas, there were significant developments. The tenth book of the *Ṛg Veda* presents a considerably different picture from the earlier books,[4] and this is supplemented by the material of the *Atharva Veda*, which was in all probability compiled at a later date than the other three Vedas and, because of its general lack of connection with the sacrificial ritual, was only with some reluctance accepted as authoritative alongside them.

The earlier books of the *Ṛg Veda* present their cosmological views in mythological form on the basis of analogies with procreation or with the craftsman's activity. Although such views are still found in the tenth book, there is a definite trend there towards philosophical rather than mythological speculation. The two may well, of course, be combined at this stage; a good example is hymn 10.72, in which the poet declares that he will proclaim 'the births of the gods', then goes on to assert that: 'In the first age of the gods, being was born from non-being', but ends the hymn again on a more mythological note. Both in this hymn (Bṛhaspati, 'the lord of ritual power', in verse 2) and elsewhere terms that were in origin epithets, often of Indra, are turned into independent but more abstract deities. Another example is found in the pair of hymns 10.81–2, where Viśvakarman, 'the maker of all', is represented as creating the world through sacrifice and as having on all sides eyes, faces, arms and feet, but where another explanation is also given in terms of a 'first embryo', a world egg floating on the waters of chaos, out of which Viśvakarman emerges.

The image of an original sacrifice is much more forcefully presented in hymn 10.90, to *puruṣa*, the cosmic person. The poet first describes this *puruṣa* as having a thousand heads, eyes and feet (much as Viśvakarman in 10.81.3) and then declares that only a quarter of him is manifest in creation – a clearly panentheistic approach. When the gods performed a sacrifice with this *puruṣa* as the victim, there were produced birds and animals (the material for sacrifice), the hymns, the classes of mankind, Indra, Agni, the wind-god Vāyu, the atmosphere, heaven and earth. Noteworthy are the problems that the poet has in expressing his ideas: the gods are there to perform the sacrifice (since an act requires an agent, a verb requires a subject), but the major gods including Indra are produced from it, and 'Virāj was born from him and Puruṣa was born from Virāj', where the poet is no more ignorant of basic biology than was the poet of 10.72 (who similarly declares that Dakṣa was born from Aditi and Aditi from

Dakṣa) but rather both are struggling to say that the creative power and the created world are interdependent.

A still more pointed expression of dissatisfaction with existing explanations for the origin of the world is seen in hymn 10.121, where impressive definitions of a creator deity in each verse end with the question, 'to which god shall we offer worship with an oblation?', implicitly suggesting that none of the existing pantheon measures up to such a description while at the same time affirming the efficacy of the ritual. Admittedly, the hymn as it is recorded goes on to answer its question in the last verse by naming Prajāpati, 'the lord of creatures', but this verse is a later addition and the deity himself otherwise unknown to the *Ṛg Veda* though frequent in the *Brāhmaṇas*. This trend of rejection culminates in hymn 10.129, which begins: 'Non-being did not exist, nor did being at that time; there was no atmosphere nor firmament beyond it. What enveloped it, where, whose the protection? Was there water, profound and deep?' After declaring explicitly within the hymn that the gods are later than creation (cf. 10.90 above), the poet ends on a note of agnosticism: 'he who is its overseer in the highest firmament, he no doubt knows or else he does not.' No longer are the gods or even one creator deity seen as agents of creation, but we now have *asat*, non-being or the unreal, and *sat*, being or the real, evolving together – a further shift in thinking from 10.72.2–3.

Such trends are not exclusively confined to the tenth book of the *Ṛg Veda*, of course. A close parallel to the statement in *ṚV* 10.90 that only one-quarter of Puruṣa is manifest is found in 1.164.45–6, where Vāc, 'speech', but especially 'sacred speech', similarly has only one-quarter manifest and is declared to be That One, which seers speak of variously as Indra, Mitra, Varuṇa, Agni and so forth. The context is again a ritual one and the form is that of the riddling contests (*brahmodya*) in which the nature of *brahman* was enigmatically revealed as underlying such rituals. Interestingly, this hymn recurs in the *Atharva Veda*, while one of its motifs, that of the two birds perching on the same tree (1.164.20–2), is found in the *Upaniṣads* and later.

The *Atharva Veda* (*AV*), despite its more popular character (seen in the lack of connection with the ritual on the whole and in the proliferation of spells instead), does in fact contain a greater number of speculative hymns than the *Ṛg Veda*.[5] It is interesting to note that it uses the term *brahman* to denote both its own incantations (in itself a shift in emphasis from the other Vedas' use for the power underlying the sacrificial ritual) and the universal principle, or more exactly the term now covers both meanings at the same time, as when *Brahman* is the origin of both *sat* and *asat* and is also connected with Vāc (*AV* 4.1.1–2). It also makes use of various other images of the ultimate cosmic principle, of which several are material and even mechanical in nature. There are a couple of hymns to Virāj, the principle of extension (*AV* 8.9–10, cf. *ṚV* 10.90.5, quoted above), and one on the creation of *puruṣa* (*AV* 10.2, while *ṚV* 10.90 recurs as *AV* 19.6). A pair of hymns (*AV* 10.7–8) contain the glorification of *skambha*, 'support', a form of the cosmic tree, seen as the framework on which the universe is erected and within which exist both the non-existent and the existent; the second hymn of the pair concludes with a declaration of *ātman*, here still apparently 'the breathing one', as the cosmic principle, while another hymn (*AV* 11.4) regards *prāṇa*, 'breath', as both the breath of life in the individual and the wind animating the universe. The next hymn (*AV* 11.5) then celebrates the *brahmacārin*, the Vedic student, who is treated as an incarnation of *Brahman* and is said to fill his teacher with *tapas*. One line that was not developed subsequently is that seen in a pair of hymns (19.53–4, in fact one hymn arbitrarily divided) in which *kāla*, 'time', is celebrated as the first principle, by which everything has been created and set in motion, from the sun's course down, including Prajāpati, 'the lord of creatures'; they include the striking image of immortality as the axle around which everything revolves.

The presence in the *Atharva Veda* of this larger element of philosophical speculation in comparison with the other three Vedas is explicable in terms of the practical orientation that continues to be a feature of philosophy in India. Knowledge of the true nature of things was viewed as being not only a liberating force for the individual concerned but also a way of acquiring power over others, especially his enemies, and so of gaining success. However, despite the somewhat more speculative aspect of such hymns, the ritual emphasis was still the dominant one in the Vedic tradition and was tending, as we have already seen to a limited extent, towards a more impersonal view.

The dominance of ritual is particularly obvious in the next category of the Vedic literature, the *Brāhmaṇas*, whose name derives from *Brahman*, the sacred power now linked especially with the sacrificial ritual, which it is the task of the *Brāhmaṇas* to expound. In contrast to the hymns, which are relatively brief, poetic and allusive, the *Brāhmaṇas* are voluminous prose works which aim to include everything relevant to their central theme of the ritual and are in consequence often extremely discursive. Indigenous tradition divides their contents into the two categories of rules (*vidhi*) and explanations (*arthavāda*), the rules being the prescriptions for the performance of the individual sacrificial rites and the explanations being the mass of mythology and legend, etymology and speculation by which the authors of the *Brāhmaṇas* seek to explain the origin, purpose and meaning of the rituals and so to establish their validity and importance. While from one angle such explanatory material is peripheral to the prime focus of the *Brāhmaṇas*, it does in fact bear witness to a significant strand in their authors' thinking. In Vedic thought, as in the Iranian tradition, we find the view that the world is not due to chance in any sense but governed by an objective order, inherent in the nature of things. In the *Brāhmaṇas* these basic laws of the world have come increasingly to be identified with the laws of sacrifice; thus *dharma* (the term which now replaces the older *ṛta*, the cosmic law guarded by Varuṇa) denotes especially the sacrificial act which controls and maintains the cosmic order.

The idea already found in a few of the later hymns of the *Ṛg Veda* that sacrifice created the world evolves in the *Brāhmaṇas* into the view that the correct performance of sacrifice regulates the maintenance of the world through the power inherent in it, *Brahman*, by a direct cause–effect relationship. The result of concentrating on the sacrificial act itself was to make the gods to whom it had originally been directed less and less relevant, for if the ritual was so potent in itself it was the mechanisms involved and not its nominal recipient which were significant, while those who officiated at it also became more important still. Systems of classification became even more important in consequence, for it was thought that knowledge of the relevant interrelationships between superficially diverse phenomena enabled the extension of influence or control from one category to another.

This trend does not see the elimination of the deities but rather a shift of emphasis, whereby the older gods as recipients of the sacrifice decline in importance as those more closely connected with the ritual and its symbolism gain prominence. Prajāpati, 'the lord of creatures', thereby becomes in some ways the main deity, whose role, however, is completed in the act of creation, and Viṣṇu comes to be regarded as the personification of the sacrifice and to be equated with both Prajāpati and Puruṣa (developments which may well be significant in his rise to become one of the two contenders, along with Śiva, for the position of supreme deity in classical Hinduism). In some later parts of the *Brāhmaṇas*, indeed, this trend goes a stage further and a growing preoccupation among their composers with the ultimate basis of this ritually maintained cosmos is discernible. This ultimate is identified either with certain ritualistic principles (such as Vāc or Agni) or with a divine creator embodied in the sacrifice, by some authors named as Prajāpati but increasingly identified directly with the creative principles of the ritual and thus with *Brahman*. Despite their ritualism and formalism, the *Brāhmaṇas* can be seen as having more in common with the *Upaniṣads* than with the *Ṛg Veda* to the extent that they emphasize the importance of a full understanding of the inner meaning of the matters discussed, in effect of knowledge. Their extensive debates on the ritual and its significance, cluttered though they are with so much that strikes the outsider as tedious and repetitive, nevertheless should be seen as the forerunners of the cosmic and metaphysical speculations of the *Upaniṣads*.

Between the *Brāhmaṇas* and the *Upaniṣads* comes the third category of the Vedic literature, the *Āraṇyakas*, which form the concluding sections of several *Brāhmaṇas*. Their name, meaning literally 'belonging to the forest', has commonly been interpreted to mean that they were not for general circulation and were studied outside the normal limits of society, whether because of their esoteric nature or their mystical power; this is broadly valid, provided that it is not taken to mean that they were specifically related to the third stage of life, that of retirement to the forest, in the system of the four stages of life that only later evolves in orthodox thought. Most of the *Āraṇyakas* are in reality composite works, containing material appropriate to the other three categories of Vedic literature, but they do form something of a transition between the mainly ritualistic *Brāhmaṇas* and the mainly speculative *Upaniṣads* (some of which are embedded within *Āraṇyakas* in the same way that the *Āraṇyakas* are incorporated within the *Brāhmaṇas*). The overall message of the *Āraṇyakas* is an admission that by no means everyone could take part in the expensive and complex ritual which forms the subject matter of the *Brāhmaṇas*, for they largely ignore the practical detail of the ritual in favour of its symbolism. Meditation on the inner meaning of the sacrifice rather than its performance is thus their keynote, and in line with this they tend to substitute a simpler ritual; the *Kauṣītaki Āraṇyaka*, for example, expounds the *prāṇāgnihotra*, 'the fire oblation through one's breath', as a replacement for the basic ritual.

By this time the traditions recorded for us in the Vedic literature must already have been considerably influenced by interaction with the ideas and beliefs of indigenous groups with whom the Āryans came into contact after their arrival in India. It is therefore tempting and plausible to see some of the major innovations that are found in the *Upaniṣads* as springing from such sources. The problem is that the hypothesis is incapable of verification or falsification in the absence of any really firm evidence. There are a number of features of, for example, the Indus Valley Civilization, the highly urbanized culture preceding the Āryan arrival (*c*.2500–1700 BC), which may well survive to reappear in later Indian culture, but these can only be presented in broad terms in the absence of any readable records; when it comes to the transmission of ideas, inference is a rather hazardous process.[6] The presence of the Great Bath complex on the citadel of one of the two largest cities of this Indus Civilization, Mohenjo-daro, no doubt points to the centrality of water in the people's lives and may well prefigure the emphasis on ritual purity and bathing in tanks attached to temples in more recent Hinduism, but it may well also have been influenced by the importance of water for the arable farming on which the rise of this culture is based. From the finds of figurines of various sorts it can be inferred that the people had a cult of a mother goddess as well as of male deities, but it seems doubtful whether this is the source of the goddess cult in later Hinduism when one takes into account the relatively late emergence of that cult. None the less, it remains highly likely that the religion was affected by a large influx of deities or spirits and of new concepts from non-Vedic sources during and after the Vedic period, with a substantial amount first attested in the *Upaniṣads*. The earliest term to denote such often localized beings, occurring already in the *Ṛg Veda*, is *yakṣa*, denoting basically some kind of apparition of whatever sort. Both these strands come together in one well-known passage of the *Kena Upaniṣad*, noted below.

In terms of the categorization of Vedic literature the *Upaniṣads* are, as we have seen, the fourth of the groupings and tied to the *Brāhmaṇas* through the *Āraṇyakas*. In reality, the older *Upaniṣads* have as much in common with the speculative hymns of the tenth book of the *Ṛg Veda* and parts of the *Atharva Veda*, although the closeness of their connection with the preceding Vedic literatures varies. The name *Upaniṣad* is interpreted as meaning either 'a sitting down near', in the way that pupils would sit around their teacher, or as 'a setting alongside', that is, the making of connections and equivalences (in a more sophisticated version of the *Brāhmaṇas* quest for control through categorization). The oldest *Upaniṣads*, which may date from the eighth century BC, are truly Vedic in being closely linked with their *Brāhmaṇas* and in being written in the same prose style, though with occasional verses. These are the *Bṛhadāraṇyaka*, *Chāndogya*, *Aitareya*, *Taittirīya* and *Kauṣītaki Upaniṣads*; the first two in particular were formed by the fusion of several texts which were perhaps once separate *Upaniṣads*, and what is essentially the same text is sometimes found in several of them. They contain the teachings of about a hundred individuals, who seem from the links between them to cover a period of rather over a century.[7]

The next group consists of *Upaniṣads* which are also linked to *Brāhmaṇas* but by a less integral connection. They are the *Kena*, *Īśa*, *Kaṭha*, *Śvetāśvatara*, *Praśna*, *Muṇḍaka*, *Mahānārayaṇa*, *Māṇḍūkya and Maitrī Upaniṣads*; the earliest in this group are metrical in form, but this gives way to a mixture of prose and verse and then prose. These two groups contain the major early *Upaniṣads*, but there are many more *Upaniṣads* with a purely nominal or totally non-existent connection with Vedic schools and the title has been taken by many works right up to modern times if their authors wished to lay claim to esoteric knowledge.

The *Upaniṣads* are mostly in dialogue form and in some instances record great set debates reminiscent of the debating contests (*brahmodyas*) found earlier. Perhaps the best known instance is that where King Janaka of Videha performs a sacrifice and organizes a debating contest with an enormous prize, to which the sage Yājñavalkya stakes his claim even before the start of the contest. Janaka himself appears more directly elsewhere as a participant in discussion and he is, in fact, only one of a number of protagonists in the *Upaniṣads* who come from *kṣatriya*, aristocratic, backgrounds; theological and philosophical speculation was evidently by no means limited at this period to the professionals from among the *Brāhmans* and indeed, since some of the greatest innovations found in the *Upaniṣads* occur in passages linked with the *kṣatriyas*, it has been argued that they were the means by which ideas from outside the Āryan community were penetrating into the literature.[8] Equally, such occasions demonstrate that participants in *Upaniṣadic* debates were still very much part of society, although, for example, Yājñavalkya is recorded as having subsequently retired to the forest, when his intention to distribute his property between his two wives leads one of them, Maitreyī, to demand and receive instruction on the nature of the self as being what leads to immortality (*Bṛhadāraṇyaka Upaniṣad* 4.5).[9]

Nevertheless, the context of the earlier speculation in the *Upaniṣads* is still very much the ritual world of the *Brāhmaṇas* modified by the shift in emphasis already started in the *Āraṇyakas* towards what underlies the sacrifice rather than the sacrifice in itself. Hence speculation now focuses at the cosmic level on the nature and identity of *Brahman*, the sacred power operative through the sacrifice and now regarded as the power underlying the cosmos. Hence, too, the earliest speculation in the

Upaniṣads on the nature of *Brahman* is basically materialistic, with this principle identified either as food or as breath or as both. Yet this ritually derived type of speculation leads in due course to the more characteristically *Upaniṣadic* view that the world has *Brahman* as its inner essence and emanates from *Brahman*.

Paralleling this cosmic speculation and quite possibly springing from the same sense that there must be more than could be found in the sacrifice, there also emerges the concept of the *ātman* as the permanent self or soul within the individual. Originally the term was probably synonymous with *prāṇa*, 'breath', and thus denoted the vital force in an individual, but in the *Upaniṣads* it comes to be used increasingly for the inner spiritual principle. Certainly, *prāṇa* is also used in the same sense and in fact several *Upaniṣadic* passages talk about *prāṇa* or its relationship to the organs of the self (speech, breath, sight, hearing and thought), corresponding to the five forces of nature (fire, wind, sun, the directions and the moon). Such correspondences are still important to the compilers of the *Upaniṣads*, who continue to some extent to embrace the logic behind such identifications in the *Brāhmaṇas*, and must underlie that further leap of thought which is so often considered the most important innovation of the *Upaniṣads*: the identification of the basic principle in man with the basic principle of the universe, of *ātman* with *Brahman*. Within the *Upaniṣads* themselves this equation is connected especially with the name of *Śāṇḍilya*, who first declares it in the *Chāndogya Upaniṣad* (3.14).

No less important an innovation, however, is the concept of rebirth, which appears first in a passage found both in the *Bṛhadāraṇyaka Upaniṣad* (6.2) and, in a slightly fuller form, in the *Chāndogya Upaniṣad* (5.3–10). The setting for this is the inability of the young Śvetaketu, son of Uddālaka Āruṇi, either to answer the five questions put to him by the Pañcāla prince, Pravāhana Jaivali, about an individual's fate at death or to get an answer from his father; the instruction subsequently given by the prince to Uddālaka puts forward a theory of rebirth in which the conditions of rebirth are determined solely by one's knowledge, according to the *Bṛhadāraṇyaka Upaniṣad* version, or by *karma* (literally 'action', but usually used in the religious context to mean the results of one's actions), according to the *Chāndogya Upaniṣad* version. A more developed view is found already in another passage in the *Bṛhadāraṇyaka Upaniṣad* where a different thinker, Yājñavalkya, unequivocally asserts that rebirth is determined by one's actions (*karma*) and that release is achieved through knowledge (4.4). The rapidity with which this revolutionary concept became accepted is remarkable and it is quite plausible that this idea of selves entrapped in a cycle of rebirth but capable of liberation from it is a contribution to Indian thought from non-Āryan sources, especially when one considers that it is taken as axiomatic in both Buddhism and Jainism; but when this concept is related to the other speculation of the *Upaniṣads* in the *Brahman–ātman* equation, it leads ultimately to the belief that there is only one *ātman* as later propounded by the Vedāntins, while the Sāṅkhya system retains the more archaic emphasis on a plurality of selves.

Although *Brahman* and *ātman* are the main focus of attention in the *Upaniṣads*, there are many other speculations put forward and there is nothing like the uniformity of outlook that is asserted by later orthodoxy, and especially by the Vedānta system (which by its very name claims to be the continuation of the *Upaniṣads*, which form the 'end of the Veda' or Vedānta). A brief look at some of the individual *Upaniṣads* and at the figures appearing in them will illustrate this variety.

The *Bṛhadāraṇyaka Upaniṣad*, which is the largest and probably the oldest of the *Upaniṣads*, reveals its composite character in the way that its first part looks to Śāṇḍilya as its great teacher and opens with the themes of the symbolism of the horse sacrifice and of death (building on the view, first found in the *Brāhmaṇas*, that repeated death is an evil that can be warded off), whereas its central part has Yājñavalkya as its main authority. Yājñavalkya, a great intuitive and mystical thinker, appears only in the *Bṛhadāraṇyaka* and *Chāndogya Upaniṣads*, whereas his teacher Uddālaka, a more critical and analytical thinker, occurs also in the *Kauṣītaki Upaniṣad*. He is, as we have seen, linked with Janaka of Videha, and on another occasion he explains to Janaka about the three states of the self (*BĀU* 4.3). In its normal waking state the self participates in the everyday world, where it is most influenced by externals; in the dreaming state, the self projects and operates in its own interior world; but beyond these two and more basic than them is the state of deep sleep, for here the dichotomy of experience into a conscious subject and an external object is replaced by a unitary and blissful state. This unitary state also forms the climax to his discourse with his wife Maitreyī, already mentioned, where he concludes:

> For where there is indeed duality, there one smells another, there one sees another . . . there one knows another; but where the whole of this has indeed become the *ātman*, then how and what would one smell, then how and what would one see . . . then how and what would one know? How would one understand him through whom one knows all this? How assuredly can one know the knower?
>
> (*BĀU* 2.4.14, cf. 4.5.15)

The best-known part of the *Chāndogya Upaniṣad* is undoubtedly Uddālaka's teaching to his son Śvetaketu on the *sadvidyā*, 'the knowledge of the existent', contained in the sixth chapter. Uddālaka begins by declaring that individual objects are only the matter of which they are made and that only formless matter is real, and goes on to challenge the view of *Ṛg Veda* 10.72 that in the beginning being emerged from non-being; these first two sections may well be one source of the later Sāṅkhya theory of causation that the effect pre-exists in its substantial cause. He next expounds this being, *sat*, as first the essence of the universe and then the essence of man. In the second half of the chapter Uddālaka then drives home his views with a series of illustrations drawn mostly from the natural world; for example, he tells Śvetaketu to split a banyan fruit and then to split one of the seeds inside and declares that the subtle principle inside the seed which he cannot perceive is the essence of the tree. Each of these illustrations culminates in his 'great saying' (*mahāvākya*): 'You are that' (*tat tvam asi*). Although Uddālaka does not use the term '*Brahman*', talking here about this being which is identified with the *ātman* and with *satya*, 'truth', the Vedānta later uses this as one of the key texts for the absolute identity of *ātman* with *Brahman*.

The three chapters of the brief *Aitareya Upaniṣad* each examine a different facet of the *ātman*: the first consists of a cosmogony with *ātman* as the creator rather in the *Brāhmaṇa* style, the second deals with the triple origin of the *ātman*, and the third defines the *ātman* as intelligence. The second section of the *Taittirīya Upaniṣad*, the best-known of its three parts, defines *Brahman* as truth, knowledge and infinity, and then analyses man on five levels – the five sheaths – from the physical, vital, mental and intellectual up to the blissful aspect of the true self, which is ultimately identical with *Brahman*. The *Kauṣītaki Upaniṣad*, the last of the five *Upaniṣads* that are fully integral to their *Brāhmaṇas*, is less original and indeed reproduces a considerable amount of material from the *Bṛhadāraṇyaka Upaniṣad*, though with some development of the ideas.

The *Kena Upaniṣad* is notable on the one hand for the emphasis in its first half on the inscrutability of *Brahman*, which is nevertheless everywhere, and on the other for an extensive allegory in the second half of how even the gods are ignorant of *Brahman*. *Brahman* appears to the gods, who do not understand what this apparition (*yakṣa*) is, and so Agni and Vāyu go out to challenge it with their powers of burning and blowing, but to no avail (since in challenging *Brahman*, they are cutting themselves off from the power that underlies everything). When Indra finally goes out to discover what the *yakṣa* is, *Brahman* has gone and instead Umā, daughter of the Himālaya (and later wife of Śiva), reveals to him that it was *Brahman*.

The brief *Īśa Upaniṣad* (so called from its opening word, *īśāvasya*, 'enveloped by the Lord') reveals even in its name the new emphasis which begins to be apparent in this second group of *Upaniṣads*, while in the extent of its quotations from the *Bṛhadāraṇyaka Upaniṣad* it provides the first example of what becomes a standard device within the Hindu tradition, a definite appeal to tradition precisely at the point of any innovation, in this instance the more theistic approach in contrast to the more impersonal tendencies of the previous *Upaniṣads*. As always, of course, the shift to a new outlook did not occur all at once, and some later *Upaniṣads* continue the more impersonal outlook of the earlier ones, for example the three *Upaniṣads* that are assigned to the *Atharva Veda*, the *Praśna*, *Muṇḍaka* and *Māṇḍūkya Upaniṣads*. The last of these is notable for developing the older notion of the three stages of waking and sleep by the addition of a fourth stage, which is both the sum of the other three and at the same time opposed to them. These four stages are also identified with the four quarters of the sacred syllable *oṃ* and with the three times and what transcends temporality; thus, after successively realizing the correspondences of the first three quarters, one arrives at a fourth state (which is also the whole) and merges the immanent with the transcendent. Incidentally, it may be noticed that this exactly reverses the proportions that are immanent and transcendent from the quarters of Puruṣa or Vāc in the *Ṛg Veda*.

The *Kaṭha Upaniṣad* is noteworthy for the mythological framework that it shares with the *Taittirīya Brāhmaṇa*, in which the pious young *brāhman* Naciketas goes voluntarily to the abode of Yama and is then granted three boons by his host in recompense for having been kept waiting three days. Naciketas' third boon is to ask about man's destiny after death, and Yama's eventual reply concerns the *ātman* which is not born and does not die, but is eternal and indestructible, and it includes a series of stages in the ascent to the final goal, which places the *puruṣa* beyond the unmanifest (*avyakta*, a state of non-differentiation, which is equivalent to Brahman), thus incorporating a personal element, even if not a strongly theistic one.

The *Śvetāśvatara Upaniṣad*, again quoting extensively from older Vedic literature (as does the *Mahānārāyaṇa Upaniṣad*), is clearly theistic, being intent on establishing the existence and supremacy of the Lord, whom equally clearly its author regards as Śiva. It seeks to demonstrate that Śiva is the one meant by older references, for example in the tenth book of the *Ṛg Veda*, to Prajāpati and so forth as the creator whose face, eyes, arms and feet are everywhere. In a similar fashion the *Mahānārāyaṇa Upaniṣad* uses such quotations to reinforce its belief in a personal supreme deity, who is for it, however, the Nārāyaṇa of its title, a name of Viṣṇu, also identified with the Puruṣa of *ṚV* 10.90. Perhaps because of the focus on Viṣṇu with his earlier links with the sacrifice, the *Mahānārāyaṇa Upaniṣad* presents a slightly archaic picture, with its attempt to harmonize the ritual and reflective ways of life and the prominence given to the 'fire-oblation with breath' (*prāṇāgnihotra*), both reminiscent of the *Āraṇyakas*. We see here no doubt the influence of more popular religious attitudes, for which in some ways fuller evidence comes before long from the two Sanskrit epics, the *Mahābhārata* and the *Rāmāyaṇa*. Similarly, Buddhist influence has frequently been detected in the latest of these major *Upaniṣads*, the *Maitrī Upaniṣad*, for it begins with an expression of world-weariness that is similar to Buddhist meditations on the loathsomeness of the human body and with a grim picture of cosmic dissolution. There was clearly a continuing inflow of ideas and attitudes from non-Vedic sources into the orthodox tradition that did not cease with the innovations of these major early *Upaniṣads* but was to influence both the religious and philosophical expressions of Hinduism profoundly.

Not only do the epics provide much evidence for the next stages in the growth of Hinduism as a religion, but the *Mahābhārata* also includes the *Bhagavadgītā* (*Mbh.* 6.23–40), a text which has come to be in more modern times their main religious text for many Vaiṣṇavas and indeed many other Hindus, a text which also lays claim to the status of an *Upaniṣad* and is regularly, almost obligatorily, commented on by Vedāntin teachers. As we have seen, the somewhat earlier *Mahānārayaṇa Upaniṣad* makes Nārāyaṇa the supreme deity, but Kṛṣṇa, the expounder of the *Bhagavadgītā*, presents himself as the supreme, identical to or more often superior to *Brahman*, and sets forth a way to liberation and a view of life with which the ordinary man in the world can identify. He starts from Arjuna's dilemma as he faces the prospect of fighting relatives and so begins with the concept of the *ātman* as eternal and indestructible, so that it does not die with the body but transmigrates from body to body until it achieves liberation; hence Arjuna will not be killing what really matters, the *ātman*. Throughout the *Bhagavadgītā* Kṛṣṇa draws heavily on the *Upaniṣads* (quoting, for example, in this part from the *Kaṭha Upaniṣad*) as well as on other parts of Vedic literature and on less easily identifiable strands of thought, in order to combine and synthesize into an overall theistic framework the various ideas then current. The result is not a completely consistent work, but one that as a work of popularization has gained wide currency.[10]

Kṛṣṇa goes on to suggest that all activity is a sacrifice provided that it is undertaken in the right spirit of detachment, which is specifically an absence of selfish motivation. He thereby provides at the same time a reinterpretation of sacrifice and of the renunciatory way of life, which had obviously become substantially more popular in the interval between the early *Upaniṣads* and the time of the *Bhagavadgītā* (which is often assigned to the second century BC but is probably rather later than that), as among other things the rise of Buddhism, Jainism and other unorthodox movements testifies. He argues that withdrawal into inactivity is not the answer, but rather, following the example of the deity himself, all have the duty to maintain the world order, and in particular to perform the activities for which their particular position in society has fitted them. Since desire is more basic than action, actions as such have no particular effect, provided that the individual acts unselfishly: disinterested action, rather than mere inactivity, is the true spirit of renunciation. Kṛṣṇa is thus also providing a new aspect to the doctrine of *karma* by stressing the motivation involved. Although there had already been suggestions in the *Upaniṣads* that it is desire that leads to actions, such views are more prominent in Buddhism, and in part the message of the *Bhagavadgītā* seems designed to counter the popularity of the heterodox movements by providing a more accessible religious text for the ordinary person; its inclusion within the *Mahābhārata* with its massive audience is no coincidence.

Having examined the way of activity (*karmamārga*), Kṛṣṇa then moves on to the way of knowledge (*jñānamārga*), the type of intuition that can be traced as far back as the speculative hymns of the *Ṛg Veda* but which he carefully defines as knowledge of the deity, before reverting for a while to the topics of *Brahman* and *ātman* and to ideas of meditation as the means to achieve insight. The middle third of the *Bhagavadgītā* is then taken up mainly with the nature of the supreme deity and his attributes, of which the high point is Kṛṣṇa's revelation to Arjuna of his universal form, which produces in Arjuna a spirit of humble adoration, summed up as the way of devotion (*bhaktimārga*). The concept of *bhakti* is further developed in the last third of the *Bhagavadgītā*, but the form of such devotion consists mainly of the loyal service and subservience of the devotee to the supreme, without any real hint of the intimacy which was to mark the *bhakti* movement at a much later date. This way of devotion is open to all and is ranked higher than the way of knowledge, open only to a few because of its difficulties, and to the way of activity; the other two ways are not rejected but are definitely placed at a lower level – one of the earliest uses of the principle of ranking to avoid confrontation between potentially opposing views, while ensuring that the favoured view is supreme.

In many respects the *Bhagavadgītā* marks the start of the period of development of classical Hinduism, with its accommodation of many different trends and emphases into an overall framework provided by the *brāhmans* as the great guardians of tradition within the Indian context. The first phase of innovations in thought marked by the later stages of the Vedic literature and by the emergence of Buddhism, Jainism and the other heterodox movements is over; religious life is entering a period of rapid growth of sects centring around the worship of Viṣṇu or Śiva (or a little later of the goddess) and developments in philosophical thought are beginning to find expression in the basic texts of the six systems, to be examined in Chapters 7–11 below.

NOTES

1 Since a substantial part of the text of both the *Sāma Veda* and the *Yajur Veda* is drawn from the *Ṛg Veda*, they are of less interest in tracing the history of ideas. Indeed, the main interest of the *Sāma Veda* lies in its form rather than its content (of which over 95 per cent is taken directly from the *Ṛg Veda*), for it consists of a handbook of the chants or *sāmans* used by one set of priests in the sacrifice along with the musical notation. While the *Yajur Veda* is partly drawn from the *Ṛg Veda*, there is also new material composed directly for the ritual context, which was the *raison d'être* for the compilation of all three collections. By contrast, the *Atharva Veda* is much more independent (although even so about a seventh of its hymns come from the *Ṛg Veda*).

2 The character of the collection as a whole is well presented in the extensive selection of hymns contained in W. D. O'Flaherty, *The Rig Veda* (Harmondsworth: Penguin Books, 1981); another recently published selection is W. H. Maurer, *Pinnacles of India's Past*, University of Pennsylvania Studies on South Asia 2 (Amsterdam: John Benjamins, 1986).

3 Suggested identifications in the past have been Sacrostemma species, Ephedra species, rhubarb, millet, hops and cannabis (in fact well known in the Indian tradition as *bhaṅg*), among others. Somewhat more recently, R. G. Wasson put forward the proposal that it was Amanita muscaria, the fly agaric, a hallucinogenic mushroom growing in the mountains of Afghanistan, in his *Soma: Divine Mushroom of Immortality* (New York: Harcourt Brace Jovanovich, 1968). The most recent attempts to identify the *soma* plant that I am aware of are those by Harry Falk in his 'Soma I and II' (*Bulletin of the School of Oriental and African Studies* 52 (1989), 77–90) and by D. S. Flattery and Martin Schwartz in their *Haoma and Harmaline: The Botanical Identity of the Indo-Iranian Sacred Hallucinogen 'Soma' and its Legacy in Religion, Language, and Middle Eastern Folklore*, University of California Publications, Near Eastern Studies 21 (Berkeley: University of California Press, 1989). Falk puts forward a number of cogent arguments in favour of the traditional identification as Ephedra, while Flattery argues on botanical and pharmacological evidence that

> harmel or wild rue, *Peganum harmala* L. (Zygophyllaceae), a common weed of the Central Asian Steppes, the Iranian Plateau, and adjacent areas, was the original intoxicant plant

represented in the Iranian religious tradition by the term *haoma* and in the religious tradition of India by the etymologically identical term *soma*.

4 This is especially true of the third of the units into which it can be divided, from 10.85 onwards, but also to some extent of the second unit, 10.61–84.

5 The *Atharva Veda* is extant in two recensions, the *Śaunakīya* and the *Paippalāda* recensions, which vary considerably in their arrangement and to some extent in their content; it is the *Śaunakīya* recension which is usually meant when the *Atharva Veda* is cited, and references here are to that recension.

6 The Indus Valley Civilization or Harappa Culture was clearly literate, as is shown by the brief inscriptions on the enormous numbers of seals discovered at its sites, but so far no attempt at decipherment has achieved general acceptance. It remains plausible that the language represented is an ancient form of Dravidian. Asko Parpola, who has been active in attempts to decipher the script, has recently examined the religion in his 'The Sky-Garment: a study of the Harappan religion and its relation to the Mesopotamian and later Indian religions', *Studia Orientalia* 57 (1985), 1–216.

7 Such is the calculation of Walter Ruben in his *Die Philosophen der Upanischaden* (Bern: A. Francke, 1947), where he suggests that they represent about five generations in time, covering very approximately the period from the mid-ninth century to the mid-eighth century BC.

8 We may even be able in part to distinguish this material by its form if we are to accept Paul Horsch's suggestion (in his *Die vedische Gāthā- und Śloka-Literatur* (Bern: Francke Verlag, 1966) that *gāthās* and *ślokas* – verses quoted in the Vedic prose and explicitly distinguished from the *mantras* by these terms – are of anonymous origin but come mainly from *kṣatriya* circles. He notes that the term *gāthā*, which goes back to Indo-Iranian times, was gradually replaced by the word *śloka* in the *Brāhmaṇas*, the process being completed by the *Upaniṣads*, and he argues that this corresponds to a brahmanical reaction against the *gāthā* tradition as impure and profane.

9 The most accessible translations of the *Upaniṣads* are those by Sarvepalli Radhakrishnan, *The Principal Upaniṣads* (London: Allen & Unwin, 1953, frequently reprinted), and Patrick Olivelle, *Upaniṣads*, World's Classics (Oxford and New York: Oxford University Press, 1966); but selections can be found in most of the anthologies of Hindu religious or philosophical literature.

10 Translations of the *Bhagavadgītā* abound. One of the best, which also includes a study of the text, is that by Franklin Edgerton, *The Bhagavad Gītā translated and interpreted*, Harvard Oriental Series, 38–9 Cambridge, Mass.: Harvard University Press, 1944 (reprinted 1952). Some worthwhile recent ones are those by W. J. Johnson (World's Classics; Oxford and New York: Oxford University Press, 1994), Barbara Stoler Miller (New York: Columbia University Press, 1986) and Robert Minor (Columbia, MO: South Asia Books, 1982).

FURTHER READING

Bowes, Pratima (1978) *The Hindu Religious Tradition, A Philosophical Approach*, London: Routledge & Kegan Paul.

Brockington, J. L. (1996) *The Sacred Thread: Hinduism in its Continuity and Diversity*, Edinburgh: Edinburgh University Press (chs 1–3).

Brown, W. Norman (1966) *Man in the Universe: Some Continuities in Indian Thought*, Berkeley: University of California Press.
—— (1978) *India and Indology – Collected Papers*, ed. Rosane Rocher, Delhi: Motilal Banarsidass.
Deutsch, E. and Buitenen, J. A. B. van (1971) *A Source Book of Advaita Vedānta*, Honolulu: University of Hawaii Press (chs 1–2).
Edgerton, Franklin (1965) *The Beginnings of Indian Philosophy*, London: Allen & Unwin.
Gonda, Jan (1963) *The Vision of the Vedic Poets*, Disputationes Rheno-Trajectinae 8, 's-Gravenhage: Mouton & Co.
—— (1975) *Vedic Literature (Saṃhitās and Brāhmaṇas)*, A History of Indian Literature I.1 Wiesbaden: Harrassowitz.
—— (1978) *Die Religionen Indiens I*, Die Religionen der Menschheit 11, 2nd edn, Stuttgart: W. Kohlhammer.
—— (1980) *Vedic Ritual, The Non-Solemn Rites*, Handbuch der Orientalistik 2.4.1, Leiden: E. J. Brill.
Hanefeldt, Erhardt (1976) *Philosophische Haupttexte der älteren Upaniṣaden*, Freiburger Beiträge zur Indologie 9, Wiesbaden: Harrassowitz.
Keith, A. B. (1925) *The Religion and Philosophy of the Veda and Upanishads*, Harvard Oriental Series 31–2, Cambridge, Mass.: Harvard University Press.
Knipe, David M. (1975) *In the Image of Fire: Vedic Experiences of Heat*, Delhi: Motilal Banarsidass.
O'Flaherty, W. D. (trans.) (1988) *Textual Sources for the Study of Hinduism*, Textual Sources for the Study of Religion, Manchester: Manchester University Press.
Panikkar, Raimundo (1977) *The Vedic Experience: Mantramañjarī*, London: Darton, Longman & Todd.
Renou, Louis (1953) *Religions of Ancient India*, Jordan Lectures 1951, London: Athlone Press (University of London). First and Second Lectures.
Rodhe, Sten (1946) *Deliver us from Evil: Studies on the Vedic Ideas of Salvation*, Lund: C. W. K. Gleerup.
Staal, J. F. (ed.) (1983) *Agni: The Vedic Ritual of the Fire Altar*, 2 vols, Berkeley: Asian Humanities Press.
Tull, H. W. (1989) *The Vedic Origins of Karma*, Albany, N.Y.: State University of New York Press.

6

NON-ORTHODOX INDIAN PHILOSOPHIES

Karel Werner

Besides philosophies derived from or developed within the mainstream of the orthodox Vedic tradition in ancient India there were trends of thought in existence from earliest times which originated outside Vedic orthodoxy and were cultivated in parallel with it. They seem originally to have thrived predominantly in the eastern parts of northern India (today's West Bengal and Bihar, known in later Vedic times as Magadha) and therefore away from or on the fringe of the early Vedic civilization which flourished in the ancient land of Saptasindhu (extending from the territory of the old Punjab, now in Pakistan, to the upper Ganges and Jumna). The ancient Magadha was the domain of Vrātyas, a loose confederation of tribal Āryan fraternities with their own religious, mythological and philosophical tradition only partly overlapping with the Vedic one. Because of the absence of an organized priestly class among Vrātyas there was more variety and freedom in the approach to questions of a religious and philosophical nature and most of the later recorded non-orthodox teachings originated or were first documented in their area. As well as the Vrātya philosophy there developed schools of thought which can be classified as various forms of scepticism, relativism, agnosticism, materialism, and deterministic and voluntaristic salvationism. The most notable among them were Lokāyata, Jainism and Buddhism.

VRĀTYA PHILOSOPHY

With the spread of Vedic orthodoxy, the bulk of the Vrātya lore was absorbed into it in a brahmanized form, influencing it in turn and substantially contributing to the blossoming of Upaniṣadic philosophy. The sources for Vrātya teachings are the *Atharva Veda* and scattered references in the other three Vedas and in later Vedic and Brahmanic literature.

The mystical philosophy of Vrātyas can be classified as metaphysical monism expressed in the imagery of cosmogony, which was reflected in the communal ritual and in salvationist aspirations. The term 'Vrātya' referred originally to a primordial cosmogonic power which manifested itself in the individualized form as Ekavrātya, also called Mahādeva, the great god. From him emanated the cosmic Brahmacāri (divine wanderer), who established the Earth, thus producing polarity, and by impregnating her gave rise to multiplicity. This cosmogonic drama produced by the divine trinity (Vrātya, Ekavrātya and Earth) was re-enacted in the social context in fertility rites by a Vrātya team of three (a master called *māgadha*, a young pupil or *brahmacāri* and a female attendant, *puṁścalī*, in ritual cohabitation, *maithuna*), which ensured the duration of the universe and life in it and the continuity of the community. At the individual level the aspiration of reaching the status of the cosmic Ekavrātya, often referred to as the achievement of immortality, led to the renunciation of worldly life. The aim was the individual reversal of the cosmogonic process and the return to the primeval cosmic transcendence. In practice this meant that one became a celibate *brahmacāri* and, when one became accomplished, one was known as *ekavrātya* or *arhat*, and also as *keśin*, 'the long-haried one' (Hauer 1927; Werner 1989). The line employing esoteric magic rites with sexual elements continued in obscurity and re-emerged in some varieties of later Tantrism.

LOKĀYATA MATERIALISM

The emergence of materialist philosophy in India was preceded by religious and philosophical scepticism. Already some verses in the *Ṛg Veda* have been interpreted as expressing doubts about the existence of gods since it was not certain that anybody had ever seen them. The *Upaniṣads* testify that some people denied survival after death and the existence of the other world (*Kaṭha* 1,20; 2,6). Buddhist and Jainist sources have preserved a story about King Pāyāsi, who was doubtful about life after death because none of those he had asked before their death to come back and tell him that they were alive elsewhere did so and he could not detect a soul leaving the body by observation or by weighing the body before and after death. The Pali canon (especially *Dīgha Nikāya* 1,2) gives the names and summaries of teachings of heads of six 'heretical' schools. Philosophical scepticism in the form of radical epistemological and logical agnosticism is attached there to the name of Sañjaya Belaṭṭha, who abstained from making any definite statement about anything because it was not possible to guarantee its truth. Ethical scepticism or relativism, with a touch of naturalist determinism, was advocated by Pūraṇa Kassapa, who denied the validity of the concepts of merit in doing good and of guilt in performing evil deeds. Good and evil were not results of ethical causation, but just happened (as natural processes).

Fully fledged materialism is ascribed to Ajita Kesakambali, who denied life after death and the validity of any transcendental knowledge claimed by allegedly perfect teachers. A human being is a product of the four elements, which dissolve after death; the person ceases to exist. The early existence of materialist philosophy as a school of thought advocated on the grounds of logical argument may be further inferred from the *Maitrī Upaniṣad* (7,8) which is probably slightly post-Buddhist. It warns against contacts with those who use false logic and confusing arguments to press believers in the Vedas; their doctrine, denying the existence of the self or soul (*ātman*), supported by false proofs, puzzles people, who then cannot distinguish Vedic lore from ordinary human knowledge. This warning could be equally applied to Buddhists, with their *anātman/anatta* doctrine. However, the *Upaniṣad* further says (7,9) that the false doctrine was, in fact, taught by Bṛhaspati, the teacher of gods, to demons to bring about their destruction. Whatever the merit of this story, a work called *Bṛhaspatisūtras*, now lost, must have existed, since several quotations from it have been preserved by later authors and it was widely referred to as the source of materialist philosophy.

References to popular as well as philosophical materialism can be found also in Jainist scriptures, Buddhist *jātakas* (stories of the former lives of the Buddha), the epics, the writings of the Chinese Buddhist pilgrim Hiuen Tsang, who travelled in India during the years 530–45, and even in dramatic literature, for example in the philosophical drama *Prabodhacandrodaya* (*The Rise of the Moon of Awakening*) by Kṛṣṇa Miśra (probably from the eleventh century). The crucial tenets of the doctrine of materialism were philosophically attacked even by the great Śaṅkara in his commentary to the *Brahma Sūtras* (3,3,53). Before refuting them he summarized them with competence and without the denigrating remarks which were usual with many other opponents of materialism.

The most extensive and systematic source of Lokāyata philosophy is the work *Tattvopaplavasiṁha* (*The Lion of Annihilation of Principles*) by Jayarāśi (dated around the year 700), which frequently draws on the lost *Bṛhaspatisūtras*. Some believe that it is the one and only surviving truly Lokāyata text, but doubts have recently been expressed about this view. Although Jayarāśi proclaims himself to be a follower of Bṛhaspati, his argumentation often brings him close to the position of a sceptic if not an agnostic (Franco 1987, Introduction). Other systematic expositions of Lokāyata philosophy can be found in philosophical manuals which undertake to summarize the doctrines of several philosophical schools, both orthodox and non-orthodox. A short account of Lokāyata philosophy appeared in the manual *Ṣaddarśanasamucchaya* (*A Collection of Six Doctrines*) by Haribhadra (ninth century), which is supplemented by a more extensive and reasonably accurate summary in Guṇaratna's commentary. But the most comprehensive and systematic treatise can be found in the work called *Sarvadarśanasaṅgraha* (*A Compilation of All Doctrines*) by Mādhava (fourteenth century) under the heading 'Cārvākadarśaṇa' ('The doctrine of Cārvāka'). At the end he quotes eleven stanzas from the lost work of Bṛhaspati.

The name of the school – Lokāyata – means 'worldly' or 'concerned with the world', i.e. the world accessible to the senses, which is regarded as the only real one. The followers of the school are sometimes referred to as Bārhaspatyas after the above-mentioned mythical teacher of materialism, Bṛhaspati. Another name for them is Cārvākas, the followers of Cārvāka. Mādhava mentions that Cārvāka followed the teachings of Bṛhaspati and was the jewel of all *nāstikas*. His reputation as a great Lokāyata teacher is testified to by the fact that his name became virtually synonymous with the doctrine. The expression *nāstika* means 'the one who says "is not" ' (i.e. denies the existence of something). It frequently denotes Lokāyatas and others who deny or doubt the existence of other worlds, but it is also applied to all non-orthodox doctrines which deny the authority of the Vedas such as Jainism and Buddhism.

Lokāyata ontology is determined by what can be called its radical epistemological empiricism, which recognizes sensory perception as the only valid avenue of our knowledge of reality and, indeed, as the only valid proof of the existence of anything. Whatever cannot be perceived does not exist. Talk of higher invisible worlds, of an afterlife with its rewards and punishments, and of God as the highest ruler of the world, is a product of fantasy or an invention of deceitful priests in order to gain comfortable livelihoods out of a credulous populace. Logical proof (in the form of a syllogism) for the existence of the unseen is invalid, because the validity of the general premiss is only assumed and cannot be proved unconditionally. This rules out not only what in Europe is known as the ontological proof of God, but also the acceptance of inference as a valid source of new knowledge, since inference is a process perceived in the mind, which is, however, fully dependent on sensory input for its material, a view reminiscent of Locke and Hume. Opponents pointed out that Lokāyatists themselves used inference in refuting other doctrines, but from at least one fragment it transpires that the Lokāyata rejection of inference was not so absolute. Purandara (dated to the seventh century) admitted the validity of inference within the perceptible world if verification by sensory perception was at least conceivable. But he rejected its use and validity wherever the conclusion pointed towards the assumption of some transcendent worlds beyond sensory perception (Dasgupta 1940: 536–7; Chattopadhyaya 1968: 28–30). However, this explanation does not deal with the obvious difficulty that the Lokāyatas themselves derive their dogma of the non-existence of the unseen transcendent from an inference in which the general premiss (what cannot be perceived does not exist) itself cannot be proved, but is a metaphysical postulate.

A further problem arises with Lokāyata metaphysics when we consider its basic tenet that the world, which is purely material, is composed of a combination of four elements, namely earth, water, air and fire. All things in the world, including man, are the result of different patterns in which the elements combine to produce them. Traces of the doctrine of four elements forming the foundation of the material world can be found as far back as the *Ṛg Veda*, but it may be of older (Indo-European) origin as it existed also in ancient Greece (and, of course, in medieval alchemy), unless we assume a traffic of ideas between India and Greece in antiquity. It is fully spelled out in the Upaniṣads, with a fifth element, ether, added (*Bṛhadāraṇyaka* 4,4,5; *Taittirīya* 2,1). This doctrine then became accepted by virtually every school of Indian philosophy with various other elements added by different schools to account for mental phenomena. The Lokāyata school, of course, rejected all additional non-material elements, but accepted the four 'material' ones while further rejecting ether on the grounds that it cannot be perceived by the senses and therefore it does not exist. The difficulty here is that the four material elements cannot be perceived in their pure form either. This objection was not raised by the opponents of Lokāyata, no doubt because of the universal acceptance of the doctrine of the elements. These elements were, in fact, understood in most systems not as some kind of dead building stones of the world, but as dynamic natural forces or categories of material existence. Thus Buddhism explains earth as solidity, water as liquidity, air as vibration and fire as heat/light (and, like Lokāyata, excludes ether). While no detailed explanation of the Lokāyata views of the four elements has been preserved, it could be that they understood them in a similar way to Buddhism and regarded them as perceivable.

There is some evidence that Lokāyata accepted the atomic theory (Dasgupta 1940: 540), although doubts have been expressed on the matter. Either it regarded atoms (unlike Nyāya and Vaiśeṣika) as the smallest perceptible particles or concluded that, while atoms were not perceivable, it was enough that their conglomerates were.

Lokāyata psychology does not accept the existence of a soul or self (*ātman*) separate from the body. The proof is seen in statements in which one clearly identifies oneself with the body, such as 'I am fat' or 'I am thin.' At the same time it is asserted that the expression 'my body' does not prove the existence of a separate, immaterial owner of the body, but is only figurative. The emergence of consciousness is explained by the use of an analogy. When elements combine in a certain configuration to produce a person, consciousness emerges, as does the power of intoxication in a mixture of appropriate ingredients through fermentation. When eventually the elements forming the body dissolve at the death of a person, his or her consciousness disappears and he or she is gone for good.

It would seem that some Lokāyatists were not satisfied with the simple identification of the individual with his or her body because of the complexity of the vital and mental processes regarded by some other schools of Indian philosophy as independent cosmic forces of a higher order. Therefore one can assume that there were several schools of Lokāyata, some of which may have been influenced by these other philosophies. An Advaitic work of the fifteenth century, Sadānanda's *Vedāntasāra* (verses 121–4), enumerates four schools of Lokāyata. The first of them is identical with the one just described and its view is illustrated by a reference to the teaching on different levels or sheaths of self in the *Taittirīya Upaniṣad* (section 2), which was embraced and further elaborated particularly by the system of Advaita Vedānta. This first school of Lokāyata limits the person to the level called in the *Upaniṣad* 'the self made of the essence of food' (*annarasamaya ātman*). The second school identifies the self with the power of sensory perception (*indriya*), which is supported by such sayings as 'I am blind' or 'I am deaf.' Senses do figure as cosmic forces or independent intelligences in most other Indian systems and *Vedāntasāra* here refers, somewhat unphilosophically, to the story about the quarrel of the senses in the *Chāndogya Upaniṣad* (5,1,7). There is no corresponding level in the Advaitic teaching, because it regards the senses as being derived from the vital force which is manifested in breath (*prāṇa*). The third Lokāyata school is said to identify the self with this vital force, since as it ceases to function, the senses also cease to perform and the person is gone, even though the body may still be seen for a time. One experiences oneself as the vital force when one realizes that one is hungry, thirsty, etc. This school would seem, therefore, to have believed in the existence of a 'vital self' (*prāṇamaya ātman*). The fourth school is even credited with the acceptance of the existence of the mind (*manas*) as the real, although – of course – perishable, self. It corresponds on the Advaitic level to the mental or 'mind-made' self (*manomaya ātman*). In modern English one would probably use, for the purposes of the fourth Lokāyata school, the expression 'brain' rather than 'mind'. The proof of the existence of mind is seen in Cartesian-like statements such as 'I am considering this or that' and in the fact that when the mind is in deep sleep, the vital force does not manifest itself in sensory perception, which does not operate in deep sleep. In the absence of other sources for the existence of differing schools of Lokāyata philosophy it is impossible to assess the reliability of Sadānanda's account or to imagine the type of arguments which may have been conducted within the Lokāyata school when it embarked on elaborating its tenets in detail and started splitting in consequence.

The ethics of Lokāyata follow from its basic tenet, which denies any form of individual survival after death. The logical conclusion is that one should live as agreeably as possible. The aim of life is to experience pleasure, which should not be rejected just because it is often associated with hardship or suffering. One ought to enjoy pleasure in the highest measure while thoughtfully avoiding or removing accompanying hardships and evils, just as one removes bones when eating fish. There is no reward or punishment beyond death. The highest bliss comes from the embrace of a beautiful woman. Hell is only pain caused by hardship in this world, like swallowing a fishbone. Final liberation comes with the death of the body, and it is not necessary to seek it through the acquisition of special knowledge. Performing sacrifices, learning Vedas, asceticism and applying ashes to one's body is the way of life of those who lack intelligence and manliness.

Although the hedonistic aspect of the Lokāyata ethics was often overemphasized in the preserved accounts which come invariably from opponents, and granted that there must have been some realistic grounds for the exaggeration, it is nevertheless also clear that, as in the case of the Greek equivalent of Lokāyata, the philosophy of Epicurus, there were also positive aspects to Lokāyata. There is some evidence that intellectual pleasures were also prized and that the pursuit of sensory pleasures was incompatible for many with perceiving, let alone causing, suffering to others, especially by killing. Hence a further reason for the Lokāyata condemnation of animal sacrifices. Some Lokāyatists seem even to have condemned war for the same reason (Chattopadhyaya 1968: 31–5).

As the preoccupation with refuting Lokāyata philosophy in orthodox and other philosophical writings in India lasted for several centuries, it has to be assumed that it must have had a significant following during that time and that it must have reached a considerable degree of theoretical elaboration, especially in the field of logical argument. The fact that Lokāyata original sources have not been preserved is probably due to the circumstances after Indian creative philosophizing passed its peak and India concentrated under Islamic and other foreign domination on preserving, in the first place, her orthodox religious heritage and those philosophies which were compatible with it.

JAINA PHILOSOPHY

Besides its own tradition of a succession of teachers Jainism had some historically proven links to the teachings called Ājīvika whose main protagonist, known from Pali Buddhist sources as Makkhali Gosāla, is regarded by some as a *māgadha* (Basham 1981: 8) so that a Vrātya connection could be assumed. In its elaborated form, pieced together from fragmentary quotations, the Ājīvika philosophy can be described as a kind of fatalistic optimism or salvationist determinism. Fate or destiny (*niyati*) governs the world process (*saṁsāra*) as well as individual lives. In the end each individual will reach salvation (*mokṣa*) after a very long, though fixed, period of purification in the course of transmigration through all forms of life, of which there is a large, though again fixed, number in *saṁsāra*. Some Ājīvika sects seem to have conceived the state of liberation (*nirvāṇa*) as not necessarily final, since some souls could again get contaminated by passions and return to *saṁsāra*. Nothing is known about the Ājīvika ontology of the early period, but later sources indicate that seven elements or categories of being were accepted: in addition to the four material elements there were the non-material elements of joy, sorrow and life (or soul, *jīva*); the teaching of elements was also somehow combined with the atomic theory. In Ājīvika epistemology and logic there are overlaps with Jainism and to a minor degree also with Buddhism, but a consistent picture can hardly be reconstructed.

Jainism perceives itself as an eternal teaching brought to mankind periodically by accomplished teachers called *tīrthaṅkaras* (ford-makers: for crossing the stream of *saṁsāra* to the safe shore of *nirvāṇa*). There have been twenty-four of them and the name of the first one, Ṛṣabha, is mentioned in the Vedic *Kalpasūtras* in connection with radical teaching on non-violence. Some measure of historicity is ascribed to the twenty-third one, Pārśva, believed to have lived in the eighth century BC, but the actual historical personage to whom the known Jaina teachings are ascribed is the last *tīrthaṅkara*, Vardhamāna, called Mahāvīra ('great hero') or Jina ('victor'), of the sixth century BC. In the Pali canon he was named Nigaṇṭha Nātaputta, and it transpires that he was an older contemporary of the Buddha and died some years before him. Jainism as a doctrine is geared to individual salvation and its philosophy serves that ultimate purpose, but it has elaborated some of its philosophical tenets in great detail, often eclectically borrowing from other schools of thought. Because Jaina sources were codified relatively late, influences from later developments in Buddhist and Hindu teachings were considerable and therefore make a reliable reconstruction of original Jaina views rather difficult and in some respects uncertain.

Jaina ontology is based on the assertion of a plurality of substances. A substance (*dravya*) is an eternal entity which possesses unchangeable characteristics or qualities (*guṇas*), but on which certain changeable modes, modifications or states (*paryāyas*) can occur. The highest substance is *jīva* (animate substance, soul, spirit-monad), and there is an infinite number of them. By itself, in its pure form, a *jīva*, often called also *ātman*, is perfect, omniscient, eternal, formless and in possession of unlimited energy and infinite bliss. When subject to influences (*āśravas*) from the phenomenal world of modalities (*saṁsāra*), the *jīva* takes shape, assuming a body born from his or her actions (*karmaśarīra*), loses his or her perfection and becomes a mundane pilgrim (*saṁsāri*) through innumerable forms of life which are determined by his or her desires and actions. These forms include not only higher and lower celestial beings and inhabitants of invisible worlds, humans, animals and all forms of organic life, plants and even invisible micro-organisms, but also minerals and elements (units of fire, water or air). The phenomenal world of *saṁsāra*, inhabited by bound *jīvas*, is composed of *ajīvas*, inanimate substances of two kinds: (1) the formless (*arūpi*) ones, namely time (*kāla*), which governs its sequential nature, space (*ākāśa*), in which everything is contained, motion (*dharma*), or the power of attraction and repulsion, and rest (*adharma*), or the power of inertia; and (2) the kind of substance which has form (*rūpi*) and is called *pudgala*, usually translated as 'matter', sometimes as 'body'. It would seem that *pudgala* in the singular refers sometimes to the abstract notion of matter and at other times to a particular material entity or body, while *pudgalas* in the plural always denotes concrete bodies or material objects and diverse stuffs. The smallest, imperceptible particle of matter is an atom (*aṇu*, or *paramāṇu*); there are four kinds of atoms: of air, fire, water and earth; and their combinations produce aggregates or compounds (*skandhas*, or *saṅghātas*), thus forming objects and fine and gross stuffs. The *saṁsāric* world process is beginningless and eternal and in its totality unchanging as it comprises the whole of time. In detail, however, for the bound individual consciousness, it unfolds in the flow of time in ever-recurring world periods of evolution and devolution reflected in human history as periods of progress and degeneration.

As a salvationist doctrine Jainism aims at providing means for the development of the highest knowledge or omniscience, the natural property of the soul in its pure state. Jaina epistemology is therefore subject to the metaphysical stance which postulates such a state. However, its pragmatic starting point is the everyday *saṁsāric* situation of a soul bound by the limitations of a human body. It therefore pays due attention also to the normal epistemological and logical procedures. The two levels of Jaina epistemology are, of course, intermingled, and there is some development of views in evidence without a sufficiently coherent theory being presented. Basically, Jaina epistemology accepts two kinds of cognition (*jñāna*), direct (*pratyakṣa*) and indirect (*parokṣa*), each being fivefold. Direct cognition includes (1) the fivefold sensory cognition (*matijñāna*) and also, unusually, the so-called (2) auditory cognition (*śrutajñāna*), which means cognition through understanding verbal messages, signs and symbols by way of the cognitive capacity of the mind (*manas*); these two kinds of direct cognition are possessed by all. Next comes (3) limited clairvoyant cognition (*avadhijñāna*) of spatially distant and past and future objects and events which some people have in differing measure. A yogi can develop (4) cognition of the contents of other minds than his (*manaḥparyāyajñāna*), and the liberated soul gains (5) the direct cognition of everything or absolute omniscience (*kevalajñāna*).

Each act of direct cognition is preceded by a kind of indeterminate or general awareness of the existence of the object to be cognized. It is termed 'viewing' (*darśaṇa*). This can be taken in the context of sensory cognition as sensory perception preceding the clear cognizance of the object, but Jaina epistemology accepts this kind of preliminary viewing or 'dawning' of knowledge as preceding all direct cognitions, including the transcendental kinds.

Indirect cognition includes (1) recollection (*smṛti*) or the capacity to invoke in one's mind objects of past experience; next is (2) recognition (*pratyabhijñā*), which is a kind of combination of perception and memory, as when we see an object and recognize that we saw it yesterday also; then there is (3) inductive reasoning (*tarka*) and (4) inference (*anumāna*), which deal mainly with syllogistic operations extended to five parts instead of the usual three, but more sophisticated logical operations were also developed over the centuries; and last there is (5) trustworthy testimony (*āgama*), which comes from a liberated omniscient person and can be verbal if such a person is encountered (for example a *tīrthaṅkara*) or written; only Jaina scriptures are recognized as true *āgama*; this channel of cognition provides indirect knowledge of truth to faithful followers who have not yet developed higher direct cognition.

Since transmitting absolute knowledge by an omniscient person on to the level of indirect cognition, verbal or scriptural, cannot be adequately accomplished in conceptual terms, Jaina logic developed for the purpose the doctrine of relative pluralism or multiple modalities (*anekānta*) and the method of conditioned predication (*syādvāda*).

Basically, *anekānta* translates the totality of omniscient knowledge into the notion of the complexity of reality which cannot be expressed in terms of one or other of the possible modalities or standpoints (*nayas*) and therefore it, in a way, accepts and respects them all, thereby providing a synoptic instead of a one-sided view of reality. This is illustrated by the well-known story of blind men inspecting an elephant. The method of *syādvāda* gives expression to the doctrine of *anekānta* in predicative form. Jainism uses this method when dealing with metaphysical entities such as the soul, but it can be well enough illustrated in the context of subatomic physics. An electron is said to be a particle from one point of view and a quantity of energy behaving like waves from another angle and it can, in a way, be described or defined, yet what it is like by itself cannot be explained.

Because of the salvationist character of Jainism, its metaphysics is closely connected with its ethics. Its main concern is the soul, whose existence needs no proof because it is directly experienced in every process of cognition as the conscious subject. Because the soul in its pure state is omniscient, its consciousness is infinite. In *saṁsāra* the consciousness is obscured or limited by the soul's actions (*karmas*), which stick to it like dust particles to the body and burden it so that it sinks to the appropriate position within the universe and takes an incarnation which is determined by the ethical quality of its past actions. Liberation (*mokṣa*) is achieved when the soul rises above involvement in actions and all actions accumulated from the past are exhausted. Good actions promote the soul's temporary well-being in *saṁsāra*, but do not lead to liberation. Of bad actions injury to life is the most detrimental one. Jaina ascetics take great pains to practise non-injury (*ahiṁsā*), to the point of straining their drinking water to avoid swallowing small organisms, and sweeping the footpath before them to avoid treading on small insects. In the last stages of the path abstention from action may extend to stopping the intake of food and drink to the point of starving to death, at which liberation is reached. But one may reach it during one's lifetime as well, thus becoming a perfect one (*siddha*) or a *tīrthaṅkara*. Jainism developed an elaborate methodical path to liberation which overlaps in many respects with the Buddhist one and with Patañjali's Yoga.

Discarnate *siddhas* in the state of *nirvāṇa* enjoy four infinite accomplishments: infinite knowledge, infinite vision, infinite strength and infinite bliss.

AN INTRODUCTION TO BUDDHIST PHILOSOPHY

Buddhism emerged, like Jainism, out of the background of Magadhan non-orthodox philosophical and ascetic movements. Unlike Jainism, it cannot be linked to any historically known predecessors except those referred to by the Buddha himself, as is reported in the Pali canon; they can be regarded as representatives of what later became known as Yoga, and traces of their teachings can be found not only in

Buddhism, but also in later *Upaniṣads*, in Patañjali's Yoga and even in Advaita Vedānta.

Buddhism, again like Jainism, regards itself as an eternal teaching (*dhamma*, Sanskrit: *dharma*). It is rediscovered from time to time by an individual striving for truth and salvation who, on reaching this goal, becomes a *buddha* (an awakened one or enlightened one) and assumes the task of a universal 'teacher of gods and men'. The names of several previous *buddhas* are given in the Pali canon, but only the last one is a historical personage. His real name was Siddhattha Gotama Sakya (Sanskrit: Siddhārtha Gautama Śākya), and he became known as *the* Buddha. The chief method he used for teaching was discourse (*sutta*). Memorized versions of his discourses were recorded in the Pali language, which may be near to the language he actually spoke, in what became known as the Pali canon, together with materials on the discipline (*vinaya*) of his monks and also with records of analytical texts on what can be termed early Buddhist philosophy and psychology (*abhidhamma*). The Pali canon was written down in the middle of the first century BC in Sri Lanka by monks of the Theravāda school of Buddhism. Other versions of the Buddhist canon were recorded in northern India in Sanskrit, adopted some time after the Buddha's death to facilitate discourse with Hindu opponents, but only fragments have been preserved. They show considerable agreement with Pali *sutta* and *vinaya* texts, while the Sanskrit *abhidharma* texts, which are preserved in several versions and much more fully, all differ substantially from the stance of the Pali *abhidhamma* and from each other, thus suggesting a later, sectarian, origin for this analytical type of texts. By the same token, the agreement within the scope of the *sutta* texts suggests a measure of reliability for them as being near to what the Buddha actually taught and therefore as preceding sectarian divisions.

Basically, the Buddha appears to have discouraged philosophizing and taught a practical way to salvation or liberation, refusing to give a direct answer to questions of a metaphysical character on subjects beyond ordinary experience. Conceptual preoccupation with those questions only hinders progress to liberation, which, when achieved, will have solved them by direct insight. Nevertheless, in expounding his practical doctrine, the Buddha gave enough away for a basic philosophical picture of reality both at the ordinary and the transcendental level to emerge, although its tenets are not always directly formulated and often have to be construed from a type of didactic rather than informative statements.

With respect to epistemology it can be said that the Buddha stressed direct personal knowledge accompanied by rational evaluation and reasoned understanding. At the ordinary level of knowledge it means direct sensory perception by the five senses and the mind (regarded as the sixth sense), which mediates a reasonably reliable cognition of the outer world and the perceiving subject's own situation. Claims for both the existence and non-existence of realities beyond normal sensory perception and the mind's grasp made by various spiritual teachers are to be rationally evaluated as to their plausibility and likely effect on one's life and taken on trust only if there is a way to verify them, which would, of course, mean developing a higher (supra-sensory and supra-rational) cognitive capacity culminating in enlightenment (*bodhi*). In the case of the Buddha, and those who manage to emulate his achievement, this amounts to a global vision or universal knowledge of the phenomenal world (*saṁsāra*) and the ultimate reality (*nirvāṇa*, Pali: *nibbāna*), but not to complete omniscience as is claimed in Jainism. Buddhist epistemology thus does accept higher direct cognition as most other Indian systems do, but insists also that it be accompanied by higher rational analysis. This is illustrated by the story of the Buddha's meditations for some weeks under various trees after his enlightenment when he pondered over what became known as his teaching of *paṭiccasamuppāda* (dependent origination). Out of such meditative musings grew the later structures of the analytical philosophy and psychology of *abhidhamma*, but early Buddhism did not develop a systematic theory of knowledge and formal logic; both were pursued by later schools of Buddhist thought.

The early Buddhist ontology pieced together from the *sutta* literature has some elements in common with Jainism and also with the Brahminic thought of the time, but differs from them radically in some particulars. In the first place, it views reality, at least in its phenomenal aspect, as an unceasing process reminiscent of the Heraclitean flux. It is a global flow (this, in fact, is what *saṁsāra* literally means) of events. The material reality is constituted by the interaction of four elements or elemental forces (*dhātus*): earth (solidity), water (liquidity), air (vibration) and fire (heat and light). This process of interaction takes place within the element of space. (Time is implicit in the concept of flux.) This process is accompanied by the elemental force of consciousness (*viññāṇa-dhātu*), although it is not quite clear from the texts whether this is the case throughout, so that some form of consciousness could also be ascribed, as in Jainism, to the elemental forces and even their conglomerates such as minerals, or whether it joins only the higher, 'sentient', combinations or organisms. The ultimate reality is also referred to as an element, namely *nibbāna-dhātu*, and it is clearly regarded as being beyond time. The world process, on the other hand, is subject to the march of time, but it has no conceivable beginning or end and is viewed as being cyclic, with the implicit understanding of time as being also in a way cyclic or circular.

The psychology of early Buddhism has as its starting point the analysis of the human personality in self-experience, without any direct reference to an assumed or postulated core, substance or soul. It arrives at five constituents, groups or aggregates (*khandhas*) which form a person's self-experience. One identifies oneself with them and clings to them and therefore they are termed 'groups of clinging' (*upādānakkhandhas*). They are: (1) bodily awareness or the experience of having a form (*rūpa*); this is the material group of the four elemental forces which form the physical body. They are then joined or saturated with various forms of consciousness represented by the four remaining groups. (2) The experience of feeling (*vedanā*) is the next, and it may be pleasant, unpleasant or neutral; this group is further differentiated according to the association of the feeling experience with the sixfold sensory input. (3) The process of perception (*saññā*) is experienced through six channels, the five senses and the mind, the latter having a co-ordinating function responsible for the fact that one not only perceives sensory data, but conceives a group of them as an object. (4) The experience of inner dynamism of volitional character is represented by the group of mental coefficients (*saṅkhāras*) which have also the sixfold sensory orientation and range from instincts and urges to desires, wishes, decisions and aspirations. (5) The group of consciousness (*viññāṇa*) is the direct awareness of the concrete process of being conscious of visual and other sensory objects and of mental images and concepts. The group of consciousness (*viññāṇakkhandha*) is therefore different from the element of consciousness (*viññāṇadhātu*), which is the basis for all other *khandhas* and suffuses them as the element of space does with respect to material elements and their conglomerates.

The five groups of clinging form a structural unity called *nāmarūpa* ('name and form'), a psycho-physical dynamic entity experiencing itself as a person, with a vacillating sense of self-identity in that one identifies oneself, in turn, with one's body, feelings, volitional and other mental processes, while on analysis one has to admit that none of the *khandhas* can really be one's own self (*atta*, Sanskrit: *ātman*); they are all said to be *anatta*. The Pali *sutta* literature does not make any statement about the absolute nature of *atta* and whether it ultimately does or does not exist, in keeping with the Buddha's avoidance of any intellectual discussion of metaphysical questions. But some later schools, including the Theravāda, went a step further and produced an elaborate *anatta* doctrine which fully denies the existence of any self, whether within the phenomenal world of *saṁsāra* or within the absolute element of *nibbāna*, apparently in conscious contradistinction to the Brahminic-Hindu *ātman* doctrine derived from the *Upaniṣads*.

The constituents of the personality (the *khandhas* forming the *nāmarūpa*) constantly change so that there can be no question of identity, not even in two consecutive moments, but its continuity as a structural unity is assured by the volitional dynamism of the *saṅkhārakkhandha*: as long as there is desire to go on, the person continues despite all the changes in its material and mental formations and survives even the total change of its bodily form, i.e. physical death and a rebirth into another life. In this way all beings within *saṁsāra* continue from life to life, without a conceivable beginning and also without end as long as they do not make a determined effort to liberate themselves from this continuous round of existences.

The quality and status of each life of the individual being depend on his or her actions (*kamma*, Sanskrit: *karma*), which brings us to the sphere of Buddhist ethics, but some further insights into early Buddhist ontology also transpire in the context. As clinging to the variety of experiences obtained through the functioning of *khandhas* is what keeps the personality or *nāmarūpa* going, it is desire which is the main force and motivation for acting in a being's life. It is termed *taṇhā* (thirst; often translated as 'craving'), and it is said to manifest itself chiefly in three varieties: (1) *kāmataṇhā* (sensual craving) indicates that there is constant pursuit of sensual satisfaction and fear of sensory deprivation; (2) *bhavataṇhā* (craving for existence) suggests that, in addition to the instinct for survival, there is also a conscious desire to continue existing as a person; and (3) *vibhavataṇhā* (craving for prosperity) refers to the desire to prosper by expansion: by creating a family, building an empire or enhancing the sense and size of one's self-importance in any other way; an alternative interpretation, given by the other meaning of the term *vibhava*, which is 'annihilation', is craving for non-existence, said to be the case with suicides; although adopted by many interpreters, including the Theravāda school, it appears unlikely, since suicides normally desire to escape from a particular stressful or hopeless existence rather than from existence altogether. Further, more detailed, classifications of craving, often also referred to as *lobha* (greed), are derived from the type of object or existence desired.

When the satisfaction of a desire is blocked by something or someone, hate (*dosa*) may arise, which is also a powerful force in individuals' lives, motivating many of their actions. Craving and hate are unwholesome forces in one's life and lead to dire consequences. Their functioning is enabled by delusion (*moha*) or ignorance (*avijjā*) as to what constitutes real good and leads to lasting happiness – which can come only with the achievement of *nibbāna*. While desire is allowed to operate, it is always directed to values within the *saṁsāric* realm out of ignorance of their essential unsatisfactoriness and sometimes even of their overt detrimental character. This is because it is in the nature of *saṁsāra* that all things and experiences within it have the characteristic of *dukkha*, suffering, which may be direct and immediate or delayed until the satisfaction from them vanishes and has to be struggled for again or is no longer within one's reach, or because one has become saturated with one particular type of satisfaction, previously seen as highly desirable, and has to look for other varieties. This is the case because of the second characteristic of *saṁsāra*, namely impermanence (*anicca*), and the third one, lack of substance within it (*anatta*). The unsubstantiality of *saṁsāric* experiences or things and events is the objective equivalent of the subjective experience of the impossibility of finding a self, a soul or a permanent substance in the constituents of one's phenomenal personality, *nāmarūpa*, as was explained above.

While succumbing to the pursuit of desires one is tied to *saṁsāric* existence in consecutive lives on this earth, in lower worlds of woe ('hells') or in higher abodes of bliss ('heavens'), as a certain type of being (human, animal, 'devilish' or 'angelic', etc.) with a temporary life span and varying fortunes, depending on the quality of one's previous volitions and actions. Basically, the clarity, degree of intelligence and moral quality of mind which one develops determine one's position on the ladder of beings in the next life. Being and remaining human is therefore dependent on maintaining such qualities of mind as enable one to handle a human type of organism and environment. In philosophical terms one can say that, unlike in Thomism, in which beings are created as essentially human or otherwise before they start their existence, in Buddhism existence precedes essence, because by the quality of their existence all beings determine what type of being they will essentially become in future. But no type is fixed for ever, and there is potential in everybody to become anybody or any type of being in the endless round of rebirths by slow evolution or degeneration or, more quickly, by determined effort or utter carelessness and depravity. A process of upward evolution is initiated when the amount of experienced suffering awakens a yearning for brighter circumstances in life rather than bitterness or further hardening of one's attitude. It would seem that a certain amount of discretion is always involved in the way a being acts upon or reacts to suffering, except perhaps when the bottom of existence has been arrived at, from where there is only a way upwards, however slow, although discretion can again speed it up from a certain point – or again slow it down and reverse it. But no amount of evil can bring about eternal damnation. Similarly, no amount of merit can secure eternal bliss, only temporary enjoyment of divine status in higher worlds or good fortune on earth. Morality does not lead to *nibbāna* or final liberation and is in this sense just as binding to life in *saṁsāra*, however pleasant it may be for a time, as is immorality, which, of course, leads to greater suffering.

The mechanism of *saṁsāric* life is described by the formula of dependent origination (*paṭiccasamuppāda*), a kind of structural causal chain which has twelve links. Its crucial link is (1) *avijjā*, because it is out of ignorance that beings act out their desires, thus producing (2) *saṅkhāras* or the whole range of volitional coefficients which are the conditioning factors for the functioning of (3) *viññāṇa*, the concrete consciousness or awareness of desired objects and experiences which are accessible to it through (4) *nāmarūpa*, the psycho-physical personality structure with its apparatus of (5) *saḷāyatana*, six bases of experience, i.e. five sensory organs with their corresponding objects and the mind with its contents; the resulting experience of coming together of the perceptors and their objects is (6) *phassa*, contact, and it produces (7) *vedanās*, the various feelings described earlier, which in turn lead to the second crucial link, namely to the arising of (8) *taṇhā*, or craving for more pleasant feelings and avoidance of unpleasant ones; craving is the condition for the arising of the basic frame of mind of beings, namely (9) *upādāna*, or clinging to the whole complex of life so that (10) *bhava*, existence, is assured and with it comes the inevitable recurring experience of (11) *jāti*, birth, and its concomitants (12) *jarāmaraṇa*, i.e. ageing and death.

Whatever cosmic and metaphysical views have been later read into or developed from the scheme of *paṭiccasamuppāda*, it would seem that in early Buddhism it was understood more or less as a psychological process, largely accessible to individual rational scrutiny in introspection. It does not suggest any beginning and should most probably be looked at as a complex and repetitive, circular progression of psycho-physical processes governed by the principle of causality. But it is obvious that it is meant also to make it logically understandable how various mental conditions and volitional states of mind lead to further lives. Although presented in succession, all the links are operative simultaneously, so that, for example, ignorance accompanies death and leads inevitably to a new birth and so on. Contemplation of the chain can start with any of its links and progress in a circle, and it is said that it can be breached anywhere by removing or overcoming a chosen link, but the best line of attack is at the two crucial links. This is then the beginning of the process of gaining enlightenment by removing ignorance and of liberating oneself from the bondage of *saṁsāra* into the freedom of *nibbāna* by overcoming craving.

The possibility of breaching the chain of causation is given by the fact of discretion, which also exists to a limited degree within the processes of *saṁsāra*, allowing one to steer one's lives to brighter realms in it and consequently to longer-lasting and more pleasant experiences than can be had without such conscious effort. But repeated frustrations caused by the *anicca/dukkha/anatta* nature of *saṁsāra*, when understood, may provide enough motivation for using one's discretion to escape from it altogether. The method of achieving it was described by the Buddha in the framework of the so-called Four Noble Truths. The first three of them present the Buddhist philosophy of life in a nutshell and have already been dealt with, namely (1) that phenomenal existence is of the nature of suffering; (2) that the cause of suffering is craving; and (3) that it ceases when craving is overcome or dropped. The fourth truth describes in eight steps the way to the cessation of suffering. (1) *Sammā diṭṭhi*, right viewing, is looking at things, events and oneself without the usual attitude of self-interest; it is seeing things 'as they really are' or, to employ a European phrase, *sub specie aeternitatis*, instead of in the light of temporary aims within an individual life. From this follows logically (2) *sammā saṅkappa*, right resolution or right thought, in agreement with the attitude of right viewing. When perfected, the achievement stemming from these two capabilities is regarded as the possession of true wisdom (*paññā*). The new frame of mind is then incorporated in practical life into three steps which represent Buddhist ethics (*sīla*). They are (3) *sammā vācā*, right speech, which involves abstaining from lying, tale-bearing, harsh speech and vain talk; (4) *sammā kammanta*, right action or abstaining from killing and harming (cf. *ahiṁsā*), from stealing and from improper sex; and (5) *sammā ājīva*, right livelihood, gained in a way which does not harm others. The last three steps are concerned with mind training and the development of transcendental vision (*samādhi*): (6) *sammā vāyāma*, right endeavour, expresses the early Buddhist stance on the role of free will in achieving liberation: only if one makes the choice and puts in the effort can one reach it, not by evolution or through the grace of a divine agent; (7) *sammā sati*, right mindfulness, is a training in consistent and constant goal-directedness of the mind, with the help of elaborate techniques; and lastly (8) *sammā samādhi*, right absorption, describes and instructs in methods of developing progressively more and more refined states of higher consciousness up to the threshold of enlightenment.

The state of liberation (*nibbāna*) is described only negatively as the overcoming of *saṁsāra* and metaphorically as the highest bliss. Those who 'thus arrived' (*tathāgatas*), i.e. the Buddha and the *buddhas* of the past as well as their accomplished disciples (*arahats*), cannot be defined in terms of ordinary existential logic (whether, after the physical death, they exist; do not exist; both exist and do not exist; or neither exist nor do not exist); their metaphysical status is beyond the grasp of an unenlightened mind. The Theravāda school treats it in terms suggesting that their personalities have been dissolved. Some *suttas* report that even in the Buddha's time the 'heresy' of viewing *nibbāna* on physical death as total annihilation occurred, and it was so viewed also by some western interpreters (Welbon 1968). But popular worship has always implied some form of continuation of the Buddha and the *arahats*, and so later did some schools even of pre-Mahāyāna Buddhism such as Pudgalavāda. The latest research suggests that a positive view of some form of transcendental existence of the liberated ones can be ascertained even from the Pali *sutta* sources (Johansson 1969; Harvey 1983, 1986; Werner 1988). The controversy surrounding this question contributed, among other problems, to the rise of different sects and schools in the early centuries of Buddhist history, but was more or less positively resolved in the Mahāyāna schools of Buddhist thought.

REFERENCES

Basham, A. L. (1981) *History and Doctrines of the Ājīvīkas*, Delhi: Motilal Banarsidass (1st edn: London, 1951.)

Chattopadhyaya, D. (1968) *Lokāyata: A Study in Ancient Indian Materialism,* New Delhi: People's Publishing House (first published in 1959).

Dasgupta, S. (1940) *A History of Indian Philosophy,* vol. III, Cambridge: Cambridge University Press.

Franco, E. (1987) *Perception, Knowledge and Disbelief: A Study of Jayarāśi's Scepticism*, Stuttgart: Franz Steiner Verlag Wiesbaden.

Harvey, Peter (1983) 'The nature of the Tathāgata', in P. Denwood and A. Piatigorsky (eds) *Buddhist Studies, Ancient and Modern*, London: Curzon.

—— (1986) 'The between-lives state in the Pāli Suttas', in P. Connolly (ed.) *Perspectives on Indian Religion: Papers in Honour of Karel Werner*, Bibliotheca Indo-Buddhica 30, Delhi: Sri Satguru Publications.

Hauer, J. W. (1927) *Der Vrātya: Untersuchungen über die nicht-brahmanische Religion Altindiens*, Stuttgart: Kohlhammer.

Johansson, R. (1969) *The Psychology of Nirvana*, London: Allen & Unwin.

Werner, K. (1988) 'Indian concepts of human personality in relation to the doctrine of the soul', *Journal of the Royal Asiatic Society* 1988 (1): 73–97.

—— (1989) 'The longhaired sage of Ṛg Veda 10, 136: a shaman, a mystic or a yogi?', in K. Werner (ed.) *The Yogi and the Mystic*, London: Curzon.

FURTHER READING

Conze, Edward (1962) *Buddhist Thought in India*, London: Allen & Unwin.

Glasenapp, H. von (1964) *Der Jainismus: Eine indische Erlösungsreligion*, Hildesheim: Georg Olms Verlagsbuchhandlung (first published in 1925).

Govinda, Lama Anagarika (1961) *The Psychological Attitude of Early Buddhist Philosophy*, London: Rider & Company.

Guenther, Herbert V. (1972) *Buddhist Philosophy in Theory and Practice*, Harmondsworth: Penguin Books.

Jayatilleke, K. N. (1963) *Early Buddhist Theory of Knowledge*, London: Allen & Unwin.

Kalghatgi, T. G. (1969) *Jaina View of Life*, Sholapur: Lalchand Hirachand Doshi.

—— (1984) *Jaina Logic*, Delhi: Shri Raja Krishen Jain Charitable Trust.

Keith, A. B. (1923) *Buddhist Philosophy in India and Ceylon*, Oxford: Clarendon Press.

Ñāṇananda, Bhikkhu (1971) *Concept and Reality in Early Buddhist Thought*, Kandy: Buddhist Publication Society.

Nyanaponika Thera (1965) *Abhidhamma Studies: Researches in Buddhist Psychology*, 2nd revised and enlarged edn, Kandy: Buddhist Publication Society.

Shastri, D. (1951) *A Short History of Indian Materialism*, Calcutta: Bookland Private Ltd.

Stevenson, S. (1915) *The Heart of Jainism*, Oxford: Oxford University Press.

Webb, Russell (1975) *An Analysis of the Pāli Canon*, Kandy: Buddhist Publication Society.

Welbon, G. R. (1968) *The Buddhist Nirvāṇa and its Western Interpreters*, Chicago/London: The University of Chicago Press.

7

NYĀYA-VAIŚEṢIKA

S. R. Bhatt

INTRODUCTION

Historically the Nyāya and Vaiśeṣika schools are different. They had separate origins and developed differently in the early phases of their existence and also had different spheres of interest and expertise. However, on account of their common philosophical standpoints and methodology a link seems to have existed between the two quite early in their history which during the course of their development brought them closer, resulting in their subsequent amalgamation into a single syncretic system.

Roughly speaking the history of the Nyāya-Vaiśeṣika system extends over a period of twenty-four centuries, i.e. from about the fourth century BC, till modern times. Like Vedānta, it has been one of the living systems of philosophy. Redaction of the Nyāya doctrines in the form of *sūtras* was done by Gautama around the fourth century BC. He was succeeded by an array of illustrious commentators and exponents like Vātsyāyana (about AD 400), Uddyotakara (about AD 650), Vācaspati (about AD 840), Bhāsarvajña (about AD 860), Udayana (about AD 984), Jayanta (about the tenth century AD) and many others. The *sūtras* of the Vaiśeṣika school were formulated by Kaṇāda, about one century prior to Gautama, and he was followed by thinkers like Praśastapāda (about the sixth century AD), Śrīdhara (about AD 990 and Śaṁkara Miśra (about the fifteenth century AD).

As stated above, the Nyāya and Vaiśeṣika schools had more or less the same sort of philosophical orientation and presuppositions; however, their interests were most pronounced in the fields of epistemology and metaphysics respectively. They borrowed from and leaned upon each other so heavily that they could not afford to remain separate for long. Though the synthesis of the two schools began appearing in Udayana, it was Gaṅgeśa (about the twelfth century AD) who is to be given the credit of forging the unity of the two schools. He is regarded as the founder of the syncretic school known as the Navya-Nyāya (Neo-Nyāya) school. The Navya-Nyāya school firstly brought about a synthesis of the two schools by placing metaphysical reflections in an epistemic setting following their basic commitment that epistemology is the gateway to metaphysics. It also provided an 'epistemic-linguistic turn' in so far as it made subtle, sharp and exquisitely minute distinctions in the connotations of philosophical terms. In conformity with its objectives, it gave rise to a new mode of thinking and a new style of expression, the impact of which went beyond the frontiers of the Nyāya-Vaiśeṣika system and affected all the then prevalent schools of philosophy and grammar. The Navya-Nyāya school transformed the character of philosophical reflections from empirical and practical to formal and analytical.

Though the Nyāya-Vaiśeṣika system has a galaxy of brilliant thinkers, it will not be possible to discuss all their contributions in this chapter. Only general positions on different philosophical issues will be stated in order to provide a holistic picture of the system.

The Nyāya-Vaiśeṣika system begins with a thoroughgoing empiricist stance and builds theories regarding reality, thought and language on this basis. The concept of *padārtha*, ('category') which provides the starting point of Nyāya-Vaiśeṣika thought, results in a 'compatibility-thesis' with regard to the interrelations between reality, thought and language, as is evident from the very definition of *padārtha* as that which has existence (*astitva*), knowability (*jñeyatva*) and expressibility in language (*abhidheyatva*). The empiricist orientation of the Nyāya-Vaiśeṣika system finds its expression in the system's characteristic boldness in maintaining that our experience is the sole criterion for determining the nature of reality. It analyses experience and evolves a coherent system of logic, language, ontology and value-theory based on this analysis.

As a corollary to the empiricist commitment, the Nyāya-Vaiśeṣika system puts forward a vigorous substantialist-realist ontology in contrast to the event-ontology of the Buddhists or the idealistic ontology of the Vedānta. Its naïve realism also offers a bold antithesis to the subjective idealism of the Yogācāra Buddhists. In this venture it derives substantial support from the system of Pūrva Mīmāṁsā, which also presents a scheme of realist categories.

The empiricist-realist bias of the Nyāya-Vaiśeṣika system provides the philosophical base for accommodating scientific insights in the form of an empiricist theory of causation, an account of which will be given later. Its metaphysical pluralism, admitting a number of categories of different types, is also due to its empiricist bias.

The Nyāya-Vaiśeṣika system is basically *mokṣa*-oriented emphasizing the absolute cessation of all sorts of suffering as a *summum bonum* of all living existence. But it also emphasizes that this goal is possible only after the attainment of material prosperity (*abhyudaya*). It further believes that a reflective life is a means to the good life and that understanding of the true nature of reality alone leads to *mokṣa* which is termed *niḥśreyas*, meaning attainment of fullness of life in all its aspects. It argues that nothing can be accomplished without proper effort and that effort is proper only if it is in accordance with reality. Hence there is a need for true knowledge of reality. The metaphysical categories are seven in number. They are substance (*dravya*), quality (*guṇa*), action (motion, *karma*), class character (universal, *sāmānya*), individual character (unique character, *viśeṣa*), inseparability (inherence, *samavāya*) and non-existence (absence, *abhāva*). A detailed account of these categories is given subsequently. They are intended to provide an exhaustive catalogue of all the things that need to be known. The Nyāya list of categories, which includes the Vaiśeṣika one, ranges wider inasmuch as apart from metaphysical categories it comprises those which deal with logic, epistemology and many other modes of thought connected with discovery of truth through discussion and debate. The underlying idea is that intellectual deliberation and discussion can also pave the way for spiritual realization. Thus the Nyāya-Vaiśeṣika system comprises both the science of reasoning (*ānvikṣakī*) and spiritual discipline (*adhyātma vidyā*).

THE NATURE OF REALITY

According to Nyāya-Vaiśeṣika, reality is a totality of substratum (*dharmin*), properties (*dharma*) and relations (*sambandha*). The minimum real or atomic fact given in experience consists of a substratum related to a property by a relation. It classifies the entire reality into seven types of basic categories which correspond to the constituents of language and thought. This is why all these constituents of reality, thought and language are commonly designated as *padārtha* or categories which are existent, which are knowable and which are expressible in language. It is a postulate of the Nyāya-Vaiśeṣika pluralistic metaphysics that there cannot be a simple entity. The very logical necessity of a real being possessing distinctive and inalienable identity (*anyonyābhāva*), the forfeiture of which will make it cease to be real, presupposes that this self-identity must have a definitive qualificative content. The real, thus, by the very force of its nature, has to be a complex entity, and nothing real has a simple constitution. Thus the substratum–property–relation distinction is a basic plank on which the entire Nyāya-Vaiśeṣika system rests. In this context it is interesting to note that for Advaita Vedānta only substratum is real and all properties and relations are phenomenal (*māyā*). For Buddhism all three are phenomenal (*vikalpa*) since something real is a pure momentary state of existence (*dharma* or *svalakṣaṇa*). For Nyāya-Vaiśeṣika, however, all three are real and intimately interrelated. It is significant also that in the Nyāya-Vaiśeṣika system all three are distinct and different entities with separate essences and real objective existence. Of course substratum alone is independent, and both properties and relations depend on it.

Substance

All seven metaphysical categories admit of inter-categorial and intra-categorial differences which impart a pluralistic character to the Nyāya-Vaiśeṣika ontology. A brief account of these categories is helpful in understanding their nature and role in the scheme of reality. Among them substance is the first and foremost category in so far as it is the constitutive cause of things which are in the form of products. The world of our experience is a totality of such things. Substance is a substratum of qualities, action, etc. It is also the inherent cause of conjunction and disjunction of substances. In its original form substance is devoid of qualities and action, and it acquires them adventitiously in the process of creation. So substance can be conceived of as existing in two states: i.e. as original, in which it is pure, and relational, in which it gets associated with other substances, qualities and action.

The substances are of nine types. They are earth (*pṛthivī*), water (*jala*), fire (*tejas*), air (*vāyu*), space (*ākāśa*), direction (*dik*), time (*kāla*), mind (*manas*) and self (*ātman*). Of these, the first four and mind are infinitesimal (*paramāṇu*) in size and the rest are ubiquitous (*vibhu*). The first five substances constitute the physical world. Direction (*dik*) makes movement possible, and time (*kāla*) is the substratum and one of the causal factors of all psycho-physical products and worldly behaviour.

The atoms of earth, water, fire and air are substances having respectively the qualities of smell (*gandha*), taste (*rasa*), colour (*rūpa*) and touch (*sparśa*). All these four kinds of substances, which are innumerable, have two modes of existence namely eternal in infinitesimal form and non-eternal when a product. In the form of a product they can be classified as body, sense-organ and mass. Body is the medium through which the self acquires experiences. It is also an instrument of activity. A sense-organ also acts as an instrument of experience. A mass of matter constitutes inorganic substances, which are the objects of experience and not the instruments. The proof for the existence of infinitesimal elements is divisibility of matter up to a logical limit in order to avoid the predicament of an infinite regress. The ultimate, irreducible and indivisible element of matter is known as *paramāṇu*. All material entities have *paramāṇus* as their ultimate components. The process of combination of *paramāṇus* is in the form of geometrical progression. These *paramāṇus* constitute the material cause of the physical world. The entire physical world is created out of them.

Space, direction and time are all-pervading and eternal. Space is a medium through which light and sound traverse. Direction is an instrumental cause of the cognition of directions like east, west, etc. It is known by subjective experience only. Time is the instrumental cause of cognitions like priority and posteriority, simultaneity, slowness and quickness. Some Naiyāyikas regard time as a collection of moments (Athalye and Bodas 1974: 131).

Mind (*manas*) is the instrument of experience. It is infinitesimal, eternal and distinctive to each individual self. It has a double character. It is an organ of sense itself as all internal experiences are acquired through it, but it is also an accessory to other cognitive senses, which are known as the external senses. Athalye and Bodas (1974: 147–9) describe the theory of *puritat* (an organ of the body), according to which *puritat* is an intestine somewhere near the heart and conceived as a sort of fleshy bag in which the mind remains during sleep.

The last substance is self (*ātman*), which is twofold – individual self and Supreme Self (God). The individual self is a simple, permanent, ubiquitous, spiritual substance which exists by itself. Each individual self is a unique centre of experience having an inalienable existence. It is the fundamental ground of all mental functions – cognitive, volitional and affective. All experiences belong to the self and inhere in it. Body, senses and mind cannot function without the self. It is their controlling, guiding and animating principle. It is the substratum of properties like pleasure, the possessor of generated knowledge and the subject of bondage and liberation. In the early Nyāya-Vaiśeṣika tradition it is taken to be devoid of consciousness in the original form but acquires consciousness as its adventitious property. But in the Navya-Nyāya tradition, particularly according to Raghunātha (AD 1475–1550), self is conscious and self-conscious essentially and remains so even in the state of *mokṣa*.

The existence of self is a matter of immediate experience and therefore some Naiyāyikas maintain that the self is perceived through *mānasa pratyakṣa* (mental perception) as the 'I' in cognitions like 'I am happy'. But it is perceived only as related to some perceptible attribute like cognition and pleasure. Vātsyāyana distinctly states that the pure self, which is unrelated to a body or to attributes like consciousness, can never be perceived in a normal way, although it can be perceived in a supra-normal (*yogaja*) way. Even though it may be admitted that one's own self can be perceived through mental or internal perception, the existence of other selves can only be inferred from their bodily actions. The self is to be inferred, for instance, as an animating principle of the sense-organs, and as an agent of knowledge. It is the self which imparts sentiency to sense-organs and body. The body has no sentiency, for it is not found in dead bodies. The sense-organs also do not have it, otherwise recollection, for example, could not have taken place when there is loss of organs. The mind too does not have it, as it is atomic and cannot have experience of composite objects.

According to the Nyāya-Vaiśeṣika tradition, the self is different from body, senses and mind. That it is different from the body is proved by the fact that the self remains the same in spite of the changes in the body and we feel no diminution of self even if parts of body such as legs or arms are cut off. Moreover, awarenesses like 'my body' or 'my hand' prove their separateness. The self is also not identical with the senses, and this is proved by the fact that the deprivation of any sense-organ does not injure the self. Further, the multiplicity of senses would imply multiplicity of selves in the same body, and also multiplicity of experiences would not result in identity of consciousness. The self is different from the mind also because mind, being atomic, is incapable of simultaneously apprehending many objects.

According to the Nyāya-Vaiśeṣika system, the individual selves are innumerable because of the fact that they are experienced to be so on account of the multiplicity of bodies with inalienably distinct experiences. However, the same individual self gets associated with different bodies in different births. This belief in transmigration and rebirth is based on the ground that there are certain impressions and habits which are derived from our experiences in previous births. From this phenomenon of transmigration it follows that the individual self is eternal and immutable, for otherwise it cannot pass through several births without losing its identity. The ultimate destiny of the self is to attain *mokṣa* by acquiring true knowledge of reality and by performing right actions (*dharma*).

The other type of self is the Supreme Self, God. The Nyāya-Vaiśeṣika system assigns an important role to God in its cosmology and ethics. God is the instrumental cause of the world who supervises and controls the world process.

Though the existence of God can be known through transcendental perception and scriptures, the Naiyāyikas also adduced rational arguments to prove His existence. The basic argument advanced by them is a cosmological proof based on the universally accepted principle of causality. The argument can be analysed as follows:

1 Every effect must have an agent.
2 The universe is an effect.
3 Therefore it must have an agent.
4 This agent is called God.

According to Athalye this argument is founded on four assumptions:

1 that the relation of causality is universal;
2 that every product must have a sentient producer;
3 that this world is such a product; and
4 that its producer must be an extraordinary Being such as God.

According to the Naiyāyikas the first assumption is a self-evident axiom, known to us intuitively, as it were, and corroborated by experience. The second one is proved by daily observation: we see that a jar is made by a potter, without whom it could not have been produced. Creation results from some kind of motion in the atoms, and motion requires previous volition and effort. This last being the quality of a sentient being only, it follows that no creation is possible unless there is a sentient being pre-existing to set the particles of matter in motion. The third assumption, that the world is a product, is also based on observation. The objects of the world are products because we see their origin, growth and decay. These occurrences cannot be spontaneous, and there must be some hidden agency to prompt them. Besides, they happen with such remarkable regularity that one is forced to think that the agency directing them must be an intelligent one and not simply the unseen retributive or *karmic* force (*adṛṣṭa*) of fate or destiny.

The last assumption necessarily follows from the preceding ones because a creator of this multifarious universe must be omniscient and omnipotent, and in fact must possess all the attributes usually ascribed to God, otherwise he will be either incapable of creating or be himself liable to creation and destruction. The foregoing chain of reasoning is, of course, ineffective against an opponent who denies any one of the above assumptions or the validity of the common sense on which these are founded. The weakness of the argument to prove a creator God lies mainly in the third and fourth assumptions, which are not accepted by many. For instance, it may be asked how we know that this universe is a product. Individual things in the world may be products, but that does not necessarily prove that the whole is also a product. The whole does not always share the nature of the parts. Second, our human experience being limited, how can we conclude that everything in this world is a product and that there is nothing which is not produced? Third, Naiyāyikas themselves accept several eternal things. Being eternal, they are not products and can have no creator. Fourth, since every intelligent agent must have a will, God must also have a will and consequently feelings of pleasure and pain. He cannot therefore be much better than frail mortals. Lastly, to call this world a product or effect is begging the whole question. Cause and effect being merely correlative terms, a thing cannot be called an effect unless and until its cause is proved. The world, therefore, cannot be called a product unless the existence of its creator is proved independently.

Apart from the cosmological argument, a few additional arguments are to be found in Udayana's *Nyāya Kusumāñjali*. One of the arguments is similar to the teleological argument put forward in western philosophy. The other argument is that the world depends upon some Being who is its support or sustaining principle. Likewise, consummation of the world process presupposes a final end which is God. Another argument is based on linguistic usage. The word 'God' has a meaningful usage and its meaningfulness lies in its correct reference. So God must exist as a referent of the word 'God'. The next argument is based on the authoritativeness of the Vedas, which implies God, who alone can impart that quality as their author. Another argument which appears circular with the preceding one is based on the Vedic statements which declare that God exists. The last proof is based on our conception of number. Finite numbers are conceived by finite minds, but for conceiving an infinite number God must exist. There is still another argument advanced by Udayana which is comparable to the moral argument of western philosophy. He first attempts to prove that there is necessary and inevitable retribution for all actions performed by human beings. There is a force generated by every action which causes and ensures retribution. Udayana then argues that this force being inanimate must have some intelligent being to regulate it, so God must exist.

Quality

The second category in the Nyāya-Vaiśeṣika metaphysics is quality or attribute (*guṇa*). A quality depends for its existence on some substance and is a non-inherent cause of things in so far as it determines their nature and character but not their existence. There are twenty-four qualities, which stand to substance in one–one, one–many, many–one and many–many relations.

According to the Nyāya-Vaiśeṣika system, qualities like numbers other than oneness and remoteness or nearness in space or time are both mind-dependent and object-dependent. These qualities are present in the objects and are cognized by the mind. However, they do not exist permanently in those objects. They are produced only at the time of their cognition.

> The process of the production of the quality of duality (*dvitva*) is still more striking. According to the Nyāya-Vaiśeṣika the quality of oneness (*ekatva*) resides in every object permanently. When, however, we see two objects simultaneously, we have a collective perception of two onenesses. On account of this collective perception (*samuccaya-buddhi*), which itself is one and which is technically called *apekṣā-buddhi*, there is produced an external objective quality (called *dvitya*) jointly, i.e. one quality residing simultaneously in the two objects – each of which is the abode of the quality of oneness separately. Only after the production of the objective quality of duality in the two objects, can we have a perception of the same. It is pointed out that the collective notion (*samuccaya-buddhi*) of two onenesses cannot cause the perception of duality, because we see duality externally and therefore it must exist externally in the objects themselves. We have here a striking illustration of the principle that our mind can have no perception of which the counterpart reality does not exist in the external world. Where a reality corresponding to our perception cannot be accepted as existing permanently in the external world it must be assumed to have come into existence even for a few moments in order to serve as a counterpart of the perception.
> (Shastri 143–4)

Action

The third category is action (*karma*), which is also understood as motion. Action, like quality, is a property inherent in substance. However, unlike quality, which is enduring, action is dynamic. While quality is passive and does not take us beyond the things it belongs to, the latter is a transitive process by which one substance reaches another. Action is regarded as an independent, direct and immediate cause of conjunction and disjunction.

In the Nyāya-Vaiśeṣika system motion is not inherent in matter. It is extrinsic and is imparted from outside. In the beginning an unseen retributive force (*adṛṣṭa*) was regarded as motion-giver, but later on God was accepted to be the unmoved mover. Like substance and quality, action is also regarded as objectively real. The three are said to be existents (*sattā*) in distinction from the next three categories, which are only subsistents (*bhāva*).

Class character

The next category is class character or universal (*sāmānya*). Universal and its cognate concept class (*jāti*) play a very significant role in Nyāya-Vaiśeṣika metaphysics and epistemology. Though the exact meaning and relationship between the two has not been uniform, they may be used interchangeably inasmuch as every case of the presence of one is the case of the presence of the other. Class character can be understood as the differential property commonly shared by some individuals. Class can be regarded as a collection of the individuals sharing that property. Every class character/class is an objective entity distinct from those individuals with which it is inseparably associated. Not only is it distinct from them, but it may also be present, though potentially, independently of and in spite of the individuals. We experience similarity and dissimilarity among individual things. Class character is the cause of the conception of similarity among them, which is present in them wholly and inseparably, say the Naiyāyikas. From this two important features of class character follow. First, class character inheres in many individuals, but in spite of this it preserves its unitary character, which is why, though the individuals are multiple, the class character inhering in them is one. Second, it is never the case that class character inheres partially in its multiple individuals. However, it has been a matter of great controversy how in spite of being unitary it can inhere in multiple individuals without an affect on its unitary character.

The Naiyāyikas point out that not all notions of similarity are based on class character, but only those where certain constitutive and regulative conditions are fulfilled. We do have notions of similarity as cooks, teachers, etc., but at the basis of these notions there are no universals. On the other hand, in notions like cowness, potness, etc. we have the corresponding universals like cowness, potness, etc. This led the Naiyāyikas to draw a distinction between class character and imposed characters (*upādhi*). Cooks, teachers, etc. are only imposed characters.

Following Uddyotakara, Viśvanātha points out three essential conditions of a class character/class inasmuch as all three are equally essential and inevitable for any entity to be so. These three are eternality (*nityatva*), commonness (*anekavṛttitva*) and inseparability (*samavetatva*). The first constitutive condition is that class character is not a mental construct or a subjective characterization imposed by the knowing mind, which can only be cognized but not created by the latter. Not only is it independent of the knowing mind, but it is also independent of the individuals in which it inheres. Individuals are subject to origin and annihilation and hence are temporal, but the class character is eternal. The individual comes and goes, but this does not affect its being. It may be that at a particular point of time a class character may not have any actual individual as its locus and may thus be empty or potential, but this does not imply its cessation. In this sense it is eternal. The second constitutive condition is commonness, which can be variously described as occurrence of class character in multiple loci or as having multiple membership. The basic idea is that nothing can be a class character unless and until it is present in more than one individual. This follows from the fact that class character is characterized by commonness, and there cannot be commonness unless a common property is shared by two or more individuals.

The third constitutive condition is inseparability (*samavetatva*). As distinct from the accidental properties, which have the relation of separability (*saṃyoga*) with their loci, class character, being an essential property, stands in the relation of inseparability (*samavāya*). To be a member of any class is to be inseparable from it. This means that any and every individual cannot be and can cease to be a member of any and every class. The class or class character constitutes the essential character (*svabhāva*) of its individual members and therefore, though it may exist without its individual members, the latter cannot exist without the former. There is an essential dependence of the individual members upon their respective class.

As a corollary to the above-stated constitutive conditions some regulative conditions can also be put forward, the presence of which impedes or precludes a property from being a class character. The enumeration of these conditions is necessary because we have not only to draw a distinction between separable and inseparable properties, but within the inseparable properties again a distinction needs to be drawn between that which is inseparable and essential and that which is inseparable but not essential. Udayana discusses six such regulative conditions known as impediments to class-formation (*jāti bādhakas*), which can best be understood by using the terminology of class-calculus.

The first impediment pertains to non-shareability of a property or unitarity of membership. If a property exclusively belongs to one single individual, it disqualifies itself from being a class character. In other words, unitarity is a hindrance to class-formation. The second impediment states that two synonyms do not refer to two different individuals. Multiplicity of members should not be just linguistic but ontological. Similarly, if two properties completely coincide so that the loci of one are the same as, and neither more nor less than those of the other, then the two properties cannot be said to constitute two different class characters. They stand for one and the same class character. The third impediment is cross-division. According to some Nyāya-Vaiśeṣika thinkers, the relation between class character and its individual members should be such that if any individual possesses one class character, then it cannot possess another class character. To be a member of one class is to be completely included in it, which means that the individual should be completely excluded from all other classes. This implies that no two or more classes can intersect or coincide. There has been much controversy in the Nyāya-Vaiśeṣika tradition as to whether or not cross-division is a fallacy. The fallacious character of the other impediments is quite evident, but there does not seem to be any absurdity in regarding two classes as partially overlapping. Those who do not regard cross-division as a fallacy argue that in experience we do find objects possessing more than one class character. However, this much must be said in favour of the proponents of cross-division as a fallacy: if one cares for a neat classification, it has to be dichotomous, and in that case cross-division should be regarded as a fallacy.

The fourth impediment is infinite regress (*anavasthiti*). It stipulates that membership of a class is open only to individual entities and never to a class. However, one class can be said to be included in another class. A lower class is included in a higher class. Thus a distinction can be drawn between class membership and class inclusion. Class inclusion is a relation between a lower class and a higher class, whereas class membership is a relation between a class and its individual members. The basis of class inclusion is extension and not similarity, which is the basis of class membership. The reason why one class cannot be a member of another class is that this would lead to an infinite regress: there would be class over class *ad infinitum*, and so no finality. The basic consideration in denying class membership to classes is that the necessary condition of class membership is commonness of property, which cannot exist between any two classes, which have to be mutually exclusive. If two or more classes were taken to have a common property, this would amount to their sameness (*tulyatva*).

The fifth impediment is loss of nature (*rūpahāni*). It regulates that class membership is not possible in those cases where such membership would result in annihilation of the nature of the entities which were to be the members. Such a regulation is needed to exclude individual character, the ultimate principle of differentiation accepted in Nyāya-Vaiśeṣika pluralistic metaphysics. The ultimate entities are differentiated from one another on the basis of individual character which is unique to them. Every individual character is solely and exclusively present in one and altogether absent in the rest of the entities. Since every individual character is unique unto itself and absolutely dissimilar from the rest, whereas it is similarity of nature which is the basis of class membership, to regard individual characters as constituting a class would amount to saying that absolutely dissimilars are similar, which is a patent contradiction.

The sixth and the last impediment is absence of relationship (*asambandha*). One of the basic conditions for class membership is the relation of inseparability obtaining between a class and its members. In the absence of such a relationship, class membership is not possible. So, wherever such a relationship of class membership is not possible, class formation also is not possible. Relation itself is not a relatum and therefore does not admit of class membership. Likewise, absences do not constitute a class, simply because the positive relation of inseparability is not possible among non-existent facts.

Individual character

The fifth category is that of individual character (*viśeṣa*), which stands for the unique individual character residing in eternal elements on the basis of which their inalienable identities are preserved (perhaps the Vaiśeṣika school was named after this category, which is exclusively advocated by it). The differences among composite things are based on their component parts, but the differences among the simple substances are due to individual characters (*viśeṣas*). All eternal (*nitya*) and ultimate (*anitya*) substances, both infinite and infinitesimal, have their own individual characters (*viśeṣas*). This helps in maintaining their identity and provides a ground for pluralism and atomism. The uniqueness of individual character lies in the fact that it performs the double function of differentiating one ultimate and eternal substance from all others and also that of differentiating itself from other individual characters and everything else.

The theory of individual character (*viśeṣa*) has not found favour with other schools of philosophy in India, and even some of the Nyāya-Vaiśeṣika thinkers like Varadarāja have not accepted it. The main objection is that if individual characters are needed to distinguish ultimate individuals, there must be something else to distinguish the individual characters from others. If, however, it is said that the latter function is performed by the individual characters themselves by some peculiar inherent faculty, why not then attribute this inherent faculty to the ultimate individuals themselves. In other words, if the individual characters are regarded as self-individuating, then why not regard the simple substances themselves as self-individuating?

Inseparability

The next category is the relation of inseparability (*samavāya*), which is another peculiar concept of the Nyāya-Vaiśeṣika system. The problem of relations has been of great interest to the Nyāya-Vaiśeṣika thinkers because of its deep involvement in most metaphysical, epistemological and logical reflections. Broadly speaking three types of relations can be classified in the Nyāya-Vaiśeṣika system, namely conjunction (*saṃyoga*), inseparability (*samavāya*) and self-identity (*svarūpa*). Conjunction is an intra-categorial relation pertaining to the category of substance. It is one of the qualities which stand for the conjunction between one substance and another. This relation has a key role to play in Nyāya-Vaiśeṣika ontology inasmuch as all creation or production is due to conjunction among ultimate elements. It is a separable relation in which two or more substances existing independently of one another become so contiguous that there seems to be no intervening space between them. It is an accidental, non-eternal, external and separable relation.

Conjunction is defined as contact between two or more initially separate things. Therefore there cannot be any contact between all-pervading things which are never apart from each other. This relation is perceived as an attribute of the things related by it. So long as it exists it is a property of the things conjointed, but it does not affect their independent existence. Absence of conjunction is disjunction. It is a quality but not a relation. It is due to a state of isolation or an act of separation. Conjunction is regarded as of two kinds, namely born of action and produced by another conjunction. The former are again of two types, namely where there is motion in one relatum only and where there is motion in both the relata.

Different from conjunction is the relation of inseparability (*samavāya*), which is a relation of distinguishability. Kaṇāda defines it as the cause of the notion of 'here' in a locus and connects it to causality. Praśastapāda improves upon this by defining inseparability (*samavāya*) as a relationship that subsists between two inseparable (*ayutasiddha*) entities related to each other as substrate and its content and which is the cause of the notion 'This subsists in this locus.' It is a relation which makes two different entities blend together, giving up their separate existence. This relation obtains (a) between substance on the one hand and quality, action and universal on the other; (b) between universal on the one hand and quality and action on the other; (c) between whole and its parts, etc.

Some Nyāya-Vaiśeṣika thinkers take inseparability (*samavāya*) to be one and eternal. They do so, perhaps, to avoid the possible difficulties in accepting it as multiple and non-eternal. Inseparability is accepted as an independent category because (1) it is not a substance as it has no qualities, (2) it is not a quality or action as it is not limited to substances, and (3) it is not universal (*sāmānya*) or individual character (*viśeṣa*) as it is neither the common essence of things nor the individual differential character of anything. The Naiyāyikas have struggled hard to justify the relation of inseparability. Jayanta does so in answering an opponent who declares that the very idea of a relation between two inseparables is self-contradictory. How can inseparability and relation be reconciled? Jayanta points out in reply that inseparability as a relation of distinguishability distinct from that of separability is incontrovertibly given to us in our experience. Inseparability is an inter-categorial relation, and the necessity of its acceptance arises from the conception of a thing as a complex of different categories. Earlier Vācaspati Miśra also pointed out that parts and whole, qualifiers and qualified, motion and moving entities, universals and their substrata are experienced as related to one another. Otherwise, there cannot be any cognition of expressions like 'It is a white cloth.'

In Nyāya-Vaiśeṣika metaphysics the world is taken to be a composition of heterogeneous entities which have independent ontological reality, and hence conjunction and inseparability are both external relations. Inseparability is a relation of locus-locatedness (*vṛttiniyāmaka*) in which one relatum is the substratum and the other is the superstratum. The superstratum wholly pervades the substratum (*vyāpya vṛtti*). Inseparability (*samavāya*) subsists in its substratum and relates the superstratum to it. But in itself it is self-relating (*svatantra*) and needs no other relation to relate it. As Śrīdhara puts it, 'Being independent it does not subsist in any other relation as conjunction (*saṃyoga*) does' (*Nyāya Kanādalī*, p. 780). The third variety of relation is named self-identity (*svarūpa*), mainly because it is one with its locus. It is a basis of qualificative cognition. The self-identity (*svarūpa*) relation can be either positive or negative. The negative one is between an absence and its locus. In the Navya-Nyāya quite a large number of positive self-identity (*svarūpa*) relations have been accepted. Ingalls and Guha have discussed some of them. As Ingalls has rightly pointed out, perhaps the most interesting and philosophically significant relation is that of *paryāpti*, which is similar to the concept of number as a class of classes. It is the relation by which numbers like twoness, threeness, etc. reside in the classes rather than in the individual members of the classes.

The phenomenon of causation can also be viewed as a relation. In fact in the Nyāya – Vaiśeṣika tradition it is treated as a form of inseparability (*samavāya*) relation. The theory of causation has been put forward to explain change experienced in the world, but its significance can be gauged by the fact that it has provided a base for the metaphysical structure and for the conception of reality of every school of Indian philosophical thought.

The Nyāya-Vaiśeṣika thinkers define a cause as an invariable and unconditional antecedent condition. In other words, cause is that which regularly and unconditionally precedes its effect. The concepts of invariability (*niyatatva*) and unconditionality (*ananyathāsiddhatva*) have been analysed in great depth by the later Nyāya-Vaiśeṣika thinkers keeping in view their specific ontology. An effect is defined as the counter-positive of its prior non-existence. That is to say, an effect is what begins to be and thereby negates its antecedent non-existence. A cause stands for a sum total of positive and negative conditions (*kāraṇa sāmagrī*) consisting of inherent (*samavāyi*), non-inherent (*asamavāyi*) and efficient (*nimitta*) *kāraṇas* called causal factors. The distinction between inherent and non-inherent conditions is based on the distinction between properties and their substratum. The same word *kāraṇa* is used both for the sum total of the causal conditions and for the individual causal conditions. The inherent cause is the constituent stuff in which the effect inheres, for example threads in respect of a cloth. The inherent cause is in the form of parts while the effect is a whole. The whole, however, is not a mere aggregate of the parts but a new entity altogether different from its parts. A whole emerges as residing in its parts by inherent relation. The non-inherent cause is the mediate causal stuff. It determines the effect only in so far as it stands as an inherent attribute of the inherent cause. Its causal efficiency is mediated through its intimate relation to the inherent cause. The efficient cause is different from the two. It is the agency that acts on both and makes them produce the effect. In the case of cloth, for example, threads are the inherent cause, colour of the threads is the non-inherent cause and loom, weaver, etc. are the efficient cause. An interesting distinction is drawn by the Naiyāyikas between most efficient causal condition (*karaṇa*) and general causal condition (*kāraṇa*). The general causal condition (*kāraṇa*) stands for any condition which possesses causal potency or causal efficiency. The condition which possesses not only causal efficiency but also causal sufficiency is said to be the most efficient condition (*karaṇa*). The moment the most efficient condition (*karaṇa*) becomes a part of the causal collocation, the effect necessarily takes place. The most efficient condition (*karaṇa*) is thus a necessary guarantee for the occurrence of the effect. The differential character of the most efficient condition (*karaṇa*) is its operational capacity, which brings about the effect.

Consistently with its realistic stance the Nyāya-Vaiśeṣika system maintains that cause and effect are both objectively real. Rejecting the Sāṃkhya view that the effect is potentially pre-existent in the cause and that there is identity of essence between cause and effect, it holds the view that the effect is a new creation, that it has a new beginning by cancelling its prior non-existence and that the causal-essence gives rise to the effect-essence and yet retains its distinctness. In other words, the cause continues to exist in the effect even after the emergence of the effect, simultaneously and side by side with the effect. If it were not so, then the ultimate elements would not be eternal. And if they were not eternal, they would not be *ultimate* and thus the very foundation of Nyāya-Vaiśeṣika realistic pluralism would be demolished.

Non-existence

Our experience consists of apprehension of the presence or absence of an entity or event. Just as presence of an entity is taken to be a fact, its non-existence should also be reckoned to be a fact. Thus we can talk of two types of facts – positive and negative. The Nyāya-Vaiśeṣika thinkers, therefore, assign the status of objective fact to non-existence and elevate it to a category of reality, i.e. *padārtha*. As stated earlier, a *padārtha* has to fulfil the three requirements of existence, knowability and linguistic expressibility, and non-existence does that.

The category of non-existence plays a pivotal role in Nyāya-Vaiśeṣika epistemology, logic, metaphysics and theory of values. Its pervasive nature can be grasped from the fact that without postulating non-existence no pluralism and realism can be maintained.

Non-existence is basically relational in nature, and it can be in the form either of denial of identity or of denial of relationship. The former can be expressed as 'A is not B' and the latter as 'A is not on B.' The former is named as mutual absence and the latter as relational absence. Mutual absence is reciprocal. So to say that 'A is not B' is also to say that 'B is not A', but with the transposition of the relata the nature of the relation and the content of the relation-apprehending cognition change. So to say that 'A is not B' is to say that B is absent as A. It is B which is negated and therefore it is adjunct (*pratiyogi*). B is negated in respect of A and therefore A is subjunct (*anuyogi*); by transposition the adjunct becomes subjunct and vice versa, and this changes the nature of the relationship. Mutual absence is non-temporal. It is a relation of other-than-ness which holds good irrespective of time factor. The relational absence is a denial of togetherness. It is a temporal relation, and therefore it is of four types as follows:

1 Non-existence of a thing prior to its production. It pertains to the past. It is beginningless but has an end.
2 Non-existence of a thing after its destruction. It pertains to the future. It has a beginning but no end.
3 Absolute non-existence. It is not like that of a 'square circle' but like 'absence of colour in air'. It pertains to the past, present and future. It is beginningless and endless.
4 The fourth type is that of temporal absence, consisting in the absence of an object in relation to a particular locus at a given point of time. It can be illustrated by the example of the absence of a flower-pot on a particular table at a particular time. This absence refers to the non-existence of an object in the present. It is having a beginning and also having an end.

The Nyāya-Vaiśeṣika thinkers argue that in every case of absence the adjunct stands related to the subjunct by the relation of qualification, which is a variety of the self-identity (*svarūpa*) relation discussed earlier, in such a way that the absence of adjunct qualifies the subjunct. Rejecting the view of Prabhākara of the school of Pūrva Mīmāṁsā that non-existence is not a separate category existing apart from its locus and also rejecting the view of Kumārila of the same school that non-existence constitutes an additional characteristic of the locus and therefore there has to be another means of knowing the non-existence named as non-apprehension (*anupalabdhi*), the Nyāya-Vaiśeṣika thinkers maintain that negative characterizations are as descriptive of the locus as the positive characterizations. So to apprehend an object or a locus is to apprehend it along with its positive or negative or both positive and negative characterizations, and there is no need to postulate non-apprehension (*anupalabdhi*) as a separate mode of knowing an absence or non-existence.

THEORY OF KNOWLEDGE

Consistent with its metaphysics, the Nyāya-Vaiśeṣika system presents a realistic epistemology which provides a foundation for its metaphysics. Knowledge is understood in this system as a true awareness, the truth of which is well evidenced. Every awareness has a built-in intentionality towards an object (*arthaprakāśakatvam*) in the sense that it consists in revealing an object. But in order to acquire the status of knowledge an awareness has to be true (*yathārtha*). The term *yathārtha* literally means 'as is the object, so should be the knowledge'. Gaṅgeśa understands it as *tadvati tatprakārakatva*, which means that all the knowledge-content must be determined by the object-content. The Nyāya-Vaiśeṣika system adopts a causal approach to knowledge and accordingly it would mean that all the knowledge-content should be caused by the object-content and nothing should be an element in the knowledge-content which is not caused by the object-content. Objective reference (*arthaprakāśakatva*) and truth (*yathārthatva*) are necessary conditions of knowledge. The sufficient condition is indubitability (*asaṃdigdhatva*). A knowledge not only has to be true but should also be evidenced to be so. Here comes the role of *pramāṇa*, which, apart from being an originating condition, is also an evidencing condition. On the basis of its cognitivity-claim knowledge is distinguishable, though not separable, from volition and feeling. Within the cognitive domain, again, knowledge is differentiated from memory, doubt, error, hypothetical judgement or conjecture.

According to the Nyāya school knowledge cognizes objects that are distinct from and outside itself. It cannot turn back on itself and cognize its own existence, far less its own validity. Truth, therefore, cannot be self-evident in any knowledge. Truth is a property of knowledge in relation to its object. Knowledge is not true or false in itself, but only through certain extraneous factors. Falsity is due to certain vitiating factors, and truth is due to certain positive factors which ensure conformity of knowledge to its object. Thus Naiyāyikas draw a distinction between those conditions which give rise to knowledge and those conditions which impart truth to it. According to them the awareness of knowledge and the awareness of its truth are different phenomena and are given to us only in post-reflection. Knowledge is needed to guide our behaviour. In fact on the basis of awareness all living beings deal with the objects of the surrounding world. For the attainment of the *summum bonum* of life a true knowledge of objects is the sure and indispensable means. With this end in view the Nyāya school deals with all the processes and methods that are involved, directly or indirectly, in the right and consistent knowledge of reality.

Methods of knowing

The role of the methods of knowing (*pramāṇas*) has been given great significance in the Nyāya-Vaiśeṣika tradition. Truth or objective validity of knowledge is due to the methods of knowing. The methods of knowing not only give rise to knowledge but also ensure its truth. They are a *karaṇa*, i.e. most efficient or unique operative cause of knowledge. This uniqueness consists in its evidential role in respect of the truth of knowledge.

According to this tradition there are four methods of knowing, namely perception (*pratyakṣa*), inference (*anumāna*), verbal testimony (*śabda*) and comparison (*upamāna*). All that is real is knowable, and it can be known by any of the methods of knowing under different conditions. Perception is the first and the foundational method of knowing. It is the direct and immediate mode of knowing. It gives us knowledge of what is directly present to the senses. It is the basis of the remaining three methods of knowing inasmuch as all three derive their starting points from perceptual cognition. It may also be regarded as the final test of the truth of all knowledge in so far as perceptual verification is the most handy and reliable mode of confirmation.

The word *pratyakṣa* is used for both the method of knowing and the resultant knowledge. It consists of two types, or rather two stages, namely indeterminate (*nirvikalpaka*) and determinate (*savikalpaka*). Indeterminate perception is pure unverbalized experience. It is a conscious but not a self-conscious state in the sense that there can be no direct awareness of it. Its existence is known inferentially. In determinate perception an object is known as related to its qualifications. This is possible only if the object and its qualities are first known separately prior to being related. This indeterminate stage is presupposed as the ground of the determinate cognition.

Determinate perception is cognition of an object as qualified by certain properties. It is a judgemental cognition in which the object of perception is known as characterized by certain qualities and relations. It consists in apprehending an object along with its differentiating characteristics. It is, therefore, defined as a cognition apprehending the qualifiers of a qualificand or as a cognition apprehending the relation between the qualificand and its qualifiers. The contents of indeterminate and determinate perceptions are the same. The only difference is that in the latter they are judged and verbalized. While in an indeterminate perception the object is apprehended as an undifferentiated whole of universal and particulars, in a determinate perception they are analysed and organized into a substantive–adjective relationship. Thus they differ not in terms of content but in the way they are ordering. To cognize a thing once again, to know it as that which was known before, is also a part of determinate perception. It is an awareness of a common reference to one and the same object by the previous and the present cognition. Perceptual knowledge is an outcome of sense–object contact. This contact may be normal or supra-normal depending upon the way in which senses come into contact with their objects. Normal perception is again of two types, namely external and mental. It is the self which is the knower, and it needs mind to perceive mental facts just as it needs senses to perceive external facts.

In supra-normal perception the objects are not actually present to the senses but are conveyed to it through an extra-ordinary medium giving rise to a special kind of sense–object contact. It is of three types. The first and most significant variety is named *sāmānya lakṣaṇa*, which pertains to perception of classes. As Chatterjee (1965: 20 9–10) puts it,

> *Sāmānya lakṣaṇa* is the perception of a whole class of objects through the generic property (*sāmānya*) perceived in any individual member of that class. Thus when we perceive something as a pot we judge it as belonging to the class of pots. But to know that the thing belongs to the class of pots is also to know all other pots belonging to the same class. . . . But the other pots are not present. . . . It is the perception of this universal 'potness' in the present pot that serves the purpose of contact (*āsatti*) between sense and all other pots.

Here only one member is perceived as having both specific and generic properties, while the other members are known as possessing the generic property. Without accepting such a type of perception generalization is not possible. The second variety, known as *jñāna lakṣaṇa*, is the perception of an object which is in contact with a self. Here past experience serves as a medium of contact between sense and the perceived objects. The visual perception of distance and the cognition of ice looking cold are examples of this type. Illusory experiences can also be explained on this basis. The third kind of supra-normal perception is *yogaja*. It is intuitive perception like that of a mystic, a seer or a saint. It is comparable to omniscience inasmuch as it is instantaneous knowledge of all things – past, present or future – due to supernatural powers.

Inference

The second method of knowing is *anumāna*, i.e. inference. All Indian systems, except Cārvāka and a few individual thinkers, accept it as a valid means of acquiring knowledge. The word *nyāya* stands for a logical theory, and ascription of this name to this school indicates that the classical Indian intellectuals looked to the school as the authority pertaining to matters of detail connected with logic.

The theory of inference (*anumāna*) is not a system of formal logic in the strict sense, and constants like *pakṣa*, *hetu* and *sādhya* employed in it are not terms but things and properties. Yet it is formal in the sense that its central concern is 'what follows from what'. It takes both truth and validity into account and its format is a combination of deductive and inductive elements. Inference (*anumāna*) is resorted to for acquisition of knowledge, as also for demonstration of a known truth.

Etymologically, *anumāna* means knowledge which is based on or which follows previous knowledge. It is knowledge of an object on the basis of the knowledge of its mark, which is invariably associated with it. Inference (*anumāna*) as a method of knowing, therefore, stands for knowing an object on the basis of the knowledge of the mark which is known to be invariably associated with it. Thus in inference (*anumāna*) an object is known through the medium of two sorts of knowledge which may be taken to be the premisses.

Among the constituents of inference (*anumāna*) three terms and two relations are basic. The object of inferential enquiry, that which is to be inferred or proved, is known as *sādhya* (major term). The reason or the ground of inference is called *hetu*, *liṅga* or *sādhana* (middle term). That in respect of which the major term (*sādhya*) is inferred on the basis of the middle term (*hetu*) and which is a common locus of the two is called *pakṣa* (minor term). The relation between middle term (*hetu*) and major term (*sādhya*) is that of invariable concomitance, and it is known as *vyāpti* (pervasion). It is the logical ground and the very nerve of the process of inference (*anumāna*). The relation between middle term (*hetu*) and minor term (*pakṣa*) is known as *pakṣadharmatā*, which is the starting point of this process. Both *pakṣadharmatā*, i.e. the relation between middle and minor terms, and *vyāpti*, i.e. the relation between middle and major terms, may be said to be the premisses.

When the knowledge of *pakṣadharmatā* is characterized by the knowledge of *vyāpti*, the synthetic product, known as *parāmarśa*, becomes the actual complex premiss which alone entails the inferential conclusion. *Parāmarśa* is knowledge of the relation of middle and minor terms along with the knowledge of that middle term with the major term. There are two more complex terms which play a vital role in the inferential process. They are homologues (*sapakṣa*) and heterologues (*vipakṣa*), which stand for positive and negative trilateral relations involving minor term (*pakṣa*), middle term (*hetu*) and major term (*sādhya*). Homologue (*sapakṣa*) stands for a positive instance in which the major term (*sādhya*) is decisively proved to be present. The implicit idea here is that the major term (*sādhya*) is present along with the middle term (*hetu*) in a locus which is similar to the instance where the presence of the major term is intended to be proved on the basis of the presence of the middle term. Heterologue (*vipakṣa*) is that locus which is definitely known to be characterized by the absence of the major term (*sādhya*) and hence by implication that of the middle term (*hetu*) as well. In the process of inference (*anumāna*) the transition from the knowledge of the middle term (*liṅga* or *hetu*) to that of the major term (*sādhya*) is made possible on the ground of a universal relation of concomitance known as *vyāpti*. The Naiyāyikas have done a good deal of hairsplitting in discussing the nature of *vyāpti*. Ingalls and Goekoop have given a good account of it. The relation between middle and major terms is an invariable and unconditional one. In the language of Navya-Nyāya it is such a relation of coexistence of the middle and the major terms that the major term is not a counter-entity to any absence abiding in the middle term. In other words, the middle term can be present only in the presence of the major term, and if the major term is absent, the middle term (*hetu*) must also be absent. Thus the invariable relation (*vyāpti*) can be of two types – affirmative and negative. The invariable relation can also be understood as a relation of pervasion, i.e. correlation between two terms/facts of which one is the pervader and the other the pervaded. A term or fact is said to pervade another when it always accompanies the other. In this extensional sense invariable relation can be of equal or inequal extension.

As regards the method of apprehending the invariable relations, the Naiyāyikas resort to uncontradicted uniform experience of concomitance. On the basis of observation, single or repeated, of uncontradicted agreement in presence and/or absence and by further verification of this uniformity by an indirect method of *tarka*, i.e. *reductio ad absurdum*, invariable relation is established.

Another important ground of inference is *pakṣatā*, which is the relation between middle and minor terms. It regulates the occurrence of the minor term (*pakṣa*). The minor term is that about which something is inferred. Validity of inference depends on invariable relation, and its possibility depends on the relation between middle and minor terms (*pakṣatā*). The process of inference takes place when (1) there is absence of certainty and (2) there is a will to infer. The Naiyāyikas point out three possibilities which are conducive to inference and are known as *pakṣatā*. They are:

1 absence of certainty and presence of will to infer;
2 absence of both certainty and will to infer;
3 presence of both certainty and will to infer.

One possibility prevents inference: presence of certainty and absence of will to infer.

The logical form of the process of inference consists of five steps, all of which are constituents of the same process. They are named statement of thesis (*pratijñā*), reason (*hetu*), example (*udāharaṇa*), application (*upanaya*) and conclusion (*nigamana*). This can be illustrated as follows:

> There is fire on the hill.
> Because there is smoke there.
> And because wherever there is smoke there is fire, as in a kitchen.
> The hill is such.
> Therefore, there is fire on the hill.

The entire process of inference centres around the middle term, on which depends its validity or invalidity. A proper or legitimate middle term has to fulfil five conditions, the violation of which leads to fallacy. The five conditions are:

1 The middle term must be present in the minor term as its property.
2 The middle term must be distributively related to the major term.
3 The middle term must be absent in all those cases where the major term is absent.
4 The middle term must not be contradictory of the major term.
5 The middle term must not be contradicted by some other middle term.

Comparison and verbal testimony

The third method of knowing is named comparison (*upamāna*). It is knowledge through description based on knowing the relation between a word and its meaning coupled with actual observation of the referent. The process of comparison consists of four stages as follows:

1 receiving of reliable information or description;
2 observation of an object agreeing with the description;
3 recollection of description;
4 identification of the object as the one agreeing with the description.

Since the knowledge here is mainly based on comparison, the Naiyāyikas insist that one has to be very careful in the observation of similarity and dissimilarity because sometimes comparison may be misleading, however accredited it may be.

The fourth and final mode of knowing is verbal testimony (*śabda*), which stands for language-generated knowledge. More particularly, it is knowledge based on understanding the meaning of the statement or assertion of a trustworthy person. Language is a significant means of communication, but it is also a generator and repository of knowledge. The heritage of knowledge is handed down to posterity only through language.

In a sense all determinate and judgemental knowledge is language-embedded. The validity of language-generated knowledge depends upon the trustworthiness of the person or source from where communication is received. Its possibility depends on the rapport between speaker and hearer or writer and reader on the basis of a common linguistic framework. Exact communication, proper apprehension and correct interpretation are its presuppositions.

According to the Nyāya-Vaiśeṣika tradition the word, and not the sentence, is the lowest unit of language. The essential nature of a word lies in its meaning, and its meaningfulness consists in its referential capacity. The meaning of a word is sometimes directly given and sometimes by implication. The relation between a word and its meaning is conventional and not natural. This accounts for varied usages of one word. As regards import, a word refers to an individual through a universal or as characterized by a universal.

In language-composition, which is basically sentence-formation, the sentential meaning is secondary and construed. There are four syntactical, semantic and pragmatic rules of sentence-formation and interpretation of its meaning. Though word is a basic unit of language, a word by itself cannot convey a complete meaning and must be brought into relation with other words in a sentence. Thus words in a sentence should 'expect' or imply one another. This is technically known as expectancy (*ākāṃkṣā*) Any incompatibility between the meanings of different words renders the whole sentence meaningless. So mutual compatibility and meaning-yielding support is another condition, known as *yogyatā*. Proximity between different words of a sentence is the third condition, known as *sannidhi*. The last condition is due consideration of the meaning intended to be conveyed by a sentence, known as *tātparya*.

The other modes of knowing accepted in the schools of Vedānta and Pūrva Mīmāṃsā have been reduced to these four by the Naiyāyikas.

REFERENCES

Athalye, Y. S. and Bodas, M. S. (eds) (1974) *The Tarkasaṃgraha of Annaṃ-Bhaṭṭa*, Poona: Bhandarkar Oriental Research Institute.

Chatterjee, S. C. (1965) *The Nyāya Theory of Knowledge*, University of Calcutta.

Madhavanand, Swami (trans.) (1940) *Bhāṣā-pariccheda of Viśvanātha*, Calcutta: Advaiton Ashrama.

Mohanty, Jitendranath (1966) *Gangeśa's Theory of Truth*, Santiniketan.
Shastri, D. N. (1976) *The Philosophy of Nyāya-Vaiśeṣika and its Conflict with the Buddhist Dignāga School*, Delhi: Motilal Banarsidass.

FURTHER READING

Bhaduri, S. (1947) *Studies in Nyāya-Vaiśeṣika Metaphysics* Poona: Bhandarkar Oriental Research Institute.
Bhattacharya, Chandrodaya (1975) *Elements of Indian Logic and Epistemology*, Calcutta.
Bhimacharya, J. (1928) *Nyāya-Kośa*, Poona: Bhandarkar Oriental Research Institute.
Jha, Ganganatha (trans) (1916) *The Padārthadharmasaṁgraha of Prasastapāda*, Allahabad: E. J. Lazarus & Co.
Jha, Ganganatha (trans) (1939) *Nyāya Sūtra of Gautama*, Poona: Oriental Book Agency.
Guha, D. C. (1968) *Navya-Nyāya System of Logic*, Varanasi.
Halbfass, Wilhelm (1992) *On Being and What There Is*, Albany: SUNY Press.
Ingalls, D. H. H. (1951) *Materials for the Study of Navya-Nyāya Logic*, Harvard Oriental Series 40, Cambridge, Mass.: Harvard University Press.
Potter, Karl (1977) *The Encyclopaedia of Indian Philosophies: Nyāya-Vaiśeṣika up to Gaṅgeśa*, Vol. II, Delhi.
Potter, Karl H. and Bhattacharyya, Sibajibhan (1992) *Indian Philosophical Analysis: Nyāya Vaiśeṣika from Gaṅgeśa to Raghunātha Śiromaṇi*, Vol. 6, Princeton NJ: Princeton University Press.
Sinha, Nandalal (trans) (1923) *Vaiśeṣika Sūtra of Kaṇāda*, in *The Sacred Books of the Hindus*, Vol. 6, 2nd edn, Allahabad: The Panini House.

8

SĀṄKHYA-YOGA

Indira Mahalingam

INTRODUCTION

This chapter will consider two closely associated orthodox schools of Indian thought – Sāṅkhya and Yoga. Sāṅkhya concentrates its efforts primarily on providing an account of reality, and Yoga, which accepts the Sāṅkhya account of the nature of reality, provides a detailed description of the practical steps to be taken by the individual in attaining liberation from the world of suffering. Because of the closeness of the intellectual positions of these two schools, they are traditionally viewed as one. The close alliance of the schools does not mean that there are no divergencies in their views. One important difference is that Yoga is theistic whereas Sāṅkhya is atheistic.[1]

Since the greater emphasis of Sāṅkhya is on the theoretical and that of Yoga on the practical, the section in this chapter on Saṅkhya will examine, in some detail, its epistemology and metaphysics and that on Yoga will deal briefly with spiritual discipline.

SĀṄKHYA

Historical background

The Sāṅkhya school is often regarded as one of the oldest schools of Indian philosophy for a number of reasons:

- The *Śvetāśvatara Upaniṣad* refers to Kapila *ṛṣi* (Kapila, the seer), who is regarded by tradition as the founder of the school.
- The *Śvetāśvatara Upaniṣad*, the *Mahābhārata* and the *Bhagavadgītā* refer to *sāṅkhya*.
- *Prakṛti* (matter) and *puruṣa* (consciousness) – core concepts in Sāṅkhyan metaphysics – are found in the *Mahābhārata* and in the *Bhagavadgītā*. Also, central

ideas of Saṅkhya such as the distinction of *prakṛti* and *puruṣa* as object and subject and the evolution of *prakṛti* are found in these texts.

Modern scholarship, however, regards the evidence as insufficient to establish a link. 'Kapila' is taken to mean 'red wizard' and hence as a reference to a mythical being rather than a reference to the founder of the school. The reference to *sāṅkhya* in these works is regarded as a use of the term in its lexical sense – i.e. knowledge or wisdom – and not as a reference to the school.[2] And doubt is cast on the view that the presence of ideas central to the school in the epics is supportive of a relationship to the school since these ideas are developed against a theistic backdrop. Furthermore, who is to say that Sāṅkhya did not borrow these ideas and doctrines from the ancient texts and develop them further?

Tradition, as stated earlier, regards Kapila (100 BC–AD 200?) as the founder of the Sāṅkhya school. It is difficult to back this claim with evidence since his works remain untraced. A work commonly attributed to him – *Sāṅkhyapravacana Sūtra* – is thought by modern scholars to have been composed in the fourteenth century AD.

The earliest available work of the school is Īśvara Kṛṣṇa's *Sāṅkhya Kārikā*. Composed probably during the fifth century AD, it provides a terse account of the system. There are a number of commentaries on the *Sāṅkhya Kārikā*, the best known of which are Gauḍapāda's *Bhāṣya* (AD 500–600), *Yuktidīpikā* (AD 600–700) by an unknown author and Vācaspati Miśra's *Sāṅkhyatattvkaumudī* (AD 850–975?).

Philosophical background

Like the other Indian philosophical schools the object of Sāṅkhya's philosophical enquiry is to alleviate human suffering caused by the three miseries – (1) misery due to intrinsic influences such as anger and desire (*ādhyātmika*), (2) misery caused by others such as friends, enemies, relatives and animals (*ādhibhautika*) and (3) misery caused by the supernatural influence of spirits in natural disasters and extreme weather conditions (*ādhidaivika*).[3] To this end Sāṅkhya offers an account of the true nature of reality, knowledge of which is said to result in liberation. Any account of reality, however, must make certain assumptions about the means by which we come to have knowledge of the world around us and the nature of the process that brings the world as we know it into being. It will therefore be useful to give a brief overview of Sāṅkhya epistemology and theory of causation, since these are the basic tenets on which the school's account of reality is founded.

Theory of knowledge

The Sāṅkhya school accepts three means of right knowledge (*pramāṇa*) – perception (*dṛṣṭa*), inference (*anumāna*) and reliable verbal testimony (*āptavacana or śruti*).[4]

Perception (*dṛṣṭa*)

Perception, according to Sāṅkhya, takes place through images or ideas (*ākāra*) of objects. As for the mechanics, during perception the intellect (*buddhi*), upon stimulation by an object through the sense-organs, undergoes a modification (*buddhivṛtti*). In other words, intellect assumes the form of the object that stimulates it. Accordingly, when I perceive a cow I do not perceive the cow directly but perceive only a representation of the cow. That is, I am not directly aware of the cow but am aware of it through the image – the mental construct – I have of the cow.

Such an account raises some interesting questions. If what I perceive is a representation of the cow and not the cow itself, what status does the cow – that which is represented – have? Does it exist *only* as an image, an idea, a mental construct, or does it have an independent existence? That is, does it exist independently of the perceiver?

In response to the above questions a number of moves are possible. One could, for instance, adopt the view that all we perceive and are capable of perceiving are mental constructs, and that the existence of the world cannot be independently and reliably established since we can never go beyond the mental constructs. Alternatively, one could adopt the view that that which is represented exists independently of the representation since the image must have been produced by an object that exists in the external world. It is the latter view that is adopted by Sāṅkhya.

In adopting this view the Sāṅkhyan seems to be committing himself to holding that all images have objects that exist independently of the object. Such a stance, however, could cause problems when it comes to hallucinations. For instance, do pink elephants perceived by an individual under the influence of alcohol exist independently of the perceiver? The position adopted by Sāṅkhya – which could be termed representational realism – can easily explain away pink elephants and similar hallucinations and illusions. Since perception is not the result of a direct confrontation with the external world but takes place indirectly through a medium, perceiving objects that are not there or perceiving objects differently from what they are must be due to defects in that medium. Just as a short-sighted person sees a rope lying at a distance as a snake because of defects in the visual organ, so an intoxicated person sees pink elephants when there are none because of the effects of alcohol on the visual organ and the intellect.

However, a persistent problem with a representational realist account, for which there is no adequate solution other than a shift in the fundamental stance, is that we can never know whether objects exist independently since there is no means of comparing the objects with the ideas of the objects: all that we perceive are ideas. Reports and descriptions of objects seen by others or the behaviour of others based on their perceptions could provide the required comparisons. In other words, others' private sensations and their responses to those private sensations allow one to conclude that objects exist independently of the perceiver. However, reliance on what others see and their behaviour in relation to what they see makes a number of assumptions. For instance, it assumes that others exist independently of our perceptions of them, that they are like me in having private sensations, and that their private sensations are like mine.

A possible (but, I believe, an unsatisfactory) solution would be to take refuge in epistemological solipsism – to say that all that I perceive are private sensations and the independent existence of objects can never be inferred from the private sensations alone. But then, for a solipsist, philosophical debates about the nature of reality, the nature of human suffering, liberation, etc. are all meaningless since others do not exist! To move from representational realism to epistemological solipsism seems at best a move from the sublime to the ridiculous.

An alternative solution would be to adopt a variant of realism known as direct realism – where material objects exist independently of our sense-experience and our perception is a direct contact with the external object, and where properties such as shapes, colours, hardness, etc. are intrinsic properties of things outside us as well as objective. The direct realist account has the advantage of getting rid of the notion of a mental construct, thus avoiding the problem of transcending the idea for the purpose of comparison. But direct realism has problems of its own. If shapes and colours are intrinsic properties and objective, then, according to a direct realist, a table could be both round and elliptical since X, who looks at the table from the top, sees a round shape and Y, who looks at the table from a distance, sees an elliptical shape. But is this not self-contradictory? The problem could be resolved by refining the direct realist account. One could say that the table is both elliptical and round but that the individual sees only one aspect of the table because of the disposition of the nervous system to select one property from the set of properties. Such an account, however, would be unable to explain illusions or errors in perception – for instance the rope that is perceived as a snake.

The problem of illusions and hallucinations could be resolved satisfactorily by refining the direct realist account further – by taking the view that objects do not possess the sensible qualities themselves but that sensible qualities are perceived from some perspective – for example a spatial perspective, a temporal perspective, and so on. In other words, all properties are relative. However, it seems that according to a relative or perspective realist account perception could never be erroneous!

All in all, the Sāṅkhya version of representational realism seems to be a better alternative. Of course, one can never transcend private sensations to establish whether images of objects are like objects in the external world. But there is nothing stopping me from inferring from my private sensations and others' reports of their private sensations that our ideas are approximations of the objects in the external world. Moreover, the distinction established at the epistemological level between subject and object, perceiver and perceived, knower and known helps underpin the distinction between *puruṣa* (consciousness) and *prakṛti* (matter) – the two ultimate realities of Sāṅkhyan metaphysics.

Inference (*anumāna*)

Sāṅkhya, by and large, accepts the Nyāya account of inference.[5] What is interesting, however, is the use made by Sāṅkhya of a variety of inference known as *sāmānyatodṛṣṭa*[6] (analogical reasoning) in its account of reality, since it allows the possibility of moving from the perceptible to the imperceptible – as where the movement of the sun (which is imperceptible) is inferred by analogy with Rāma, who comes to occupy different positions in the room as a result of moving from one part of the room to the other (which is perceptible). It is largely through this type of reasoning that Sāṅkhya provides its account of causation, and the existence of *prakṛti* (materiality) and *puruṣa* (consciousness) – the mainstays of Sāṅkhyan metaphysics.

Though *sāmānyatodṛṣṭa* plays an important role in providing an account of reality, the nature of analogical reasoning is hardly discussed by Sāṅkhya. The analogies used by Sāṅkhya are capable of supporting alternative explanations, and this raises questions about the effectiveness of analogy as a form of reasoning: its central use in the Sāṅkhya method is therefore open to serious doubt. For instance, Sāṅkhya uses the lame man–blind man analogy to establish the association between *prakṛti* and *puruṣa* and purposive activity of *prakṛti* for the sake of *puruṣa*'s release. This analogy would work if both *prakṛti* and *puruṣa* were intelligent like the lame man and blind man, who use their intelligence for a common purpose. *Prakṛti*, however, is unintelligent (without intelligence).

Valid testimony (*śruti, āptavacana*)

Like the other Indian orthodox schools Sāṅkhya accepts valid testimony (knowledge from scriptures such as the Vedas) as a source of correct knowledge. According to Sāṅkhya this means of knowledge comes into its own where knowledge of objects beyond the senses cannot be obtained by *sāmānyatodṛṣṭa* (inference by analogy).[7] It is, however, highly questionable whether Sāṅkhyans did in fact make much use of scriptural knowledge since they rely largely on *sāmānyatodṛṣṭa* to provide their account of reality as apparent from the sections on causation, *prakṛti* and *puruṣa*. As Radhakrishnan correctly observes,

> Sāṁkhya avoids the appearance of being an innovation by its acceptance of the Veda as a means of knowledge. But . . . it discards many an old dogma and silently ignores others. It, however, never openly opposes the Vedas but adopts the more deadly process of sapping their foundations.[8]

And it is this lack of reliance on the scriptures and the extensive use of inference to provide an account of reality which led Śaṅkara to launch his vehement attack on Sāṅkhyan philosophy.[9]

Causation

Sāṅkhyans' account of causation plays a principal part in their account of reality since it is on the basis of this that they argue for the existence of *prakṛti*, out of which the world of our experience has evolved. As opposed to regarding cause as an antecedent of effect and each effect as a new beginning (*ārambhavāda*), Sāṅkhya regards cause and effect as essentially identical in that the cause and effect are two states – the implicit and the explicit or the undeveloped and developed – of the same substance. Accordingly, Sāṅkhya views the effect as pre-existing in the cause (*satkāryavāda*). That is to say, the effect is not a new coming into being but is a manifestation – a different form – of that which already exists. So for Sāṅkhya the pot (effect) exists in the mud (material cause) in a potential form at time t_1 and does not come into existence when the pot is made by the potter at time t_2. What happens at time t_2 is simply an actualization of the potential – a manifestation – brought about by the efficient cause – in the case of the pot, the potter.

In support of the view that the effect already exists in the cause[10] Sāṅkhya provides the following argument:

- Since no amount of effort could bring about an effect which is non-existent, the effect must exist in the cause. For instance, the effort of even a thousand artists cannot produce blue out of yellow or oil from sand. Moreover, people seek only those material causes that are capable of producing particular effects – a person who wants to produce curd seeks milk rather than water.
- There must be an invariable connection between the effect and the cause, for if the effect is not connected to the cause, it will make no sense to talk of the cause at all. If the cause and the effect are connected, then both of them must exist since sense can be made of the relationship only if both the cause and the effect exist.
- Experience shows us that it is not possible to produce anything from anything. For instance, blue cannot be produced from yellow or cloth from reeds, which suggests that the effect exists before it comes into being in the material cause.
- An efficient cause can make manifest that which is potent in the material cause. If this were not so, it would be possible to produce oil from sand.
- The non-difference of the cause and the effect shows that the effect is of the same nature as the cause. For instance, the cloth is non-different from the threads and the pot is non-different from the mud since they are neither brought together nor separated (i.e. they coexist). The cloth is simply a different state of the threads and the pot that of mud.

The existence of a close connection between cause and effect cannot be denied since in the absence of a connection it would be possible to make wine out of water or silk from sand – in other words, to produce anything from anything. If the cause and the effect were regarded as totally distinct, one would be hard put to find a principle that related the two. A contentious issue, however, is the extent of the close connection of cause and effect. Are they so connected that there is no difference between cause and effect (for example threads and cloth) as the Sāṅkhyans claim? If the cloth is non-different from the threads, then why cannot one simply wear the threads? By weaving the threads into cloth are we not bringing into being something new – something that did not exist in the threads? If that is the case, then how can the effect be said to pre-exist in the cause? Besides, there are differences between the cloth and the threads – amongst others, we know that cloth provides better covering and protection against the elements than the threads, and the consistency and feel of the cloth is not the same as those of the threads. Surely, the cloth must be different from the threads.

It would indeed be surprising if the Sāṅkhyans were to deny that there are differences that exist between the cloth and the threads at the practical level: that the cloth is of a different consistency from the threads and can be used in a variety of ways unlike the threads and so on. What they are insisting on is that the properties exhibited by the cloth must exist potentially in the threads; otherwise the cloth could not have the properties it has. Against this context it cannot be denied that cloth and threads are in essence identical; the threads have the disposition, the potential to become cloth if certain conditions are present – for instance a loom and a weaver. So when the threads are woven into cloth, the cloth is but an actualization of the potential that exists in the threads. The efficient cause facilitates this manifestation. The threads take a different form through the actions of the weaver, but the cloth and the threads are simply different states of the same substance.

The illustration of threads and cloth fits well with the Sāṅkhyan claim for the sameness of cause and effect since it is possible, on close scrutiny, to see individual threads in the cloth. But the same cannot be said of milk and curd since there is no milk to be seen when the curd is produced. Does this mean that the milk is destroyed? If there is total destruction of the milk it is difficult to envisage how the curd could have been produced in the first place, since there would be no milk to produce it from. This seems to reinforce the Sāṅkhya view that cause and effect are simply different states of the same substance.

Account of reality

The Sāṅkhyans' account of reality is a natural progression from their epistemology and theory of causation. Sāṅkhyans, as we saw earlier, are epistemological realists who accept a distinction between the knower and the known. Comparable to the distinction of the knower and the known they posit two ultimate realities – *puruṣa* (consciousness) and *prakṛti* (matter). And in accordance with their theory that cause and effect are the developed and undeveloped states of the same substance, the world with its many forms, shapes, colours that we experience is regarded as implicit in *prakṛti* and made explicit in the process of evolution. Upon dissolution the world that we experience returns to *prakṛti*.

Prakṛti (matter)

Prakṛti is the first principle – the root cause – out of which the world of our experience evolves. All objects are present in *prakṛti* in a latent form, and the world around us with its diversities is the product of *prakṛti*. In other words, the world is a manifest state of the unmanifest *prakṛti* (also known as *pradhāna*).

Prakṛti is composed of three *guṇas* (strands or ropes) – *sattva*, *rajas* and *tamas* – which are responsible for imparting various characteristics according to their preponderance in the products of evolution. These *guṇas* are not qualities that *prakṛti* possesses but are the constituents of *prakṛti*. The *guṇas* themselves possess qualities that are at variance, but they function together like the wick, oil and fire to produce light. *Sattva* (real, existent) is illuminative and at the epistemological level results in reflection and at the psychological level produces pleasure, happiness and bliss. *Rajas* (foulness) is active and is responsible for restless activity at the epistemological level and pain at the psychological level. *Tamas* (darkness) is responsible for resistance or inertia and at the epistemological level produces ignorance and uninterestedness and at the psychological level indifference or apathy.

Our knowledge of the *guṇas* is obtained on the basis of the effects they produce in all things – pleasure, pain and indifference experienced by the things in the world around us. The manifest *prakṛti*, according to Sāṅkhya, is manifold, limited in space and time, and caused.[11] In contrast, *prakṛti* in its unmanifested state is one, complex, independent, eternal, infinite, uncaused and dynamic, but unconscious, unintelligent, imperceptible.[12] Its imperceptibility is due to its subtle nature, but its existence none the less is established on the basis of our experience of the objects around us and inference:[13]

- The limited, dependent and finite objects we experience around us cannot be the cause of the universe; so there must be an infinite cause out of which this finite world has evolved.
- The common characteristics that produce pleasure, pain and indifference shared by all things in the universe indicate that there must be a source composed of pleasure, pain and indifference.
- Since the effect differs from the cause, the effect cannot be its own cause, which means that there must be a cause in which effects exist in their potential form.
- The unity of the world points to the existence of a single cause.

Puruṣa (consciousness, pure spirit)

The other entity in Sāṅkhyan metaphysics, other than matter (*prakṛti*), is *puruṣa* (consciousness or pure spirit). As opposed to *prakṛti*, *puruṣa* as the self, the subject, the knower is intelligent and makes all knowledge possible. It is not to be confused with the mind, ego or intellect, since these, as evolutes of *prakṛti*, are material. *Puruṣa*, according to Sāṅkhya, is eternal, free, beyond space and time, neutral and a non-agent.[14]

The existence of *puruṣa*, like the existence of *prakṛti*, is arrived at through a number of arguments based on inference:[15]

- Just as a bed is assembled for the use of a man who sleeps on it, so the world constituted of the five elements must be for the enjoyment of another; that other must be the self or *puruṣa*.
- The world of knowable objects, constituted of the three *guṇas* – *sattva*, *rajas* and *tamas* – presupposes a self, a seer of the *guṇas*.
- Just as a chariot requires a charioteer, co-ordination of our experiences reveals a consciousness which makes that co-ordination possible. (The use of the chariot–charioteer analogy is a figurative one and does not suggest that *puruṣa* extends the kind of active control exercised by the charioteer since *puruṣa* is non-active.)
- There must be a subject that is affected by pleasure, pain and indifference – the three constituents of *prakṛti*. It cannot be intellect or ego since these are evolutes of *prakṛti*, which suggests that there must be a self or an experiencing subject.
- Constant talk of striving for liberation, freedom from this world of suffering makes sense only if there is an experiencing subject capable of obtaining release.

Puruṣa, unlike *prakṛti*, is manifold. Our knowledge of the plurality of selves is gained, as before, through a combination of experience and analogical reasoning.[16] The dissimilarities in people's moral outlooks, intellectual abilities, etc. suggest that there are different witnessing selves; if this were not the case, everyone would be alike. Likewise, the many births and deaths also point to the existence of many *puruṣas*. Moreover, if there were only one *puruṣa*, the release or bondage of that *puruṣa* would mean the release or bondage of all, but experience shows that this is not so.

The individual (*jīva*) according to Sāṅkhya is *puruṣa* in conjunction with ego or *ahaṅkāra* (an evolute of *prakṛti*), senses and the body. As long as *jīva* through ignorance regards itself as the reflection of *puruṣa* in *ahaṅkāra*, it enjoys and suffers the pleasures and pains of life. However, when the *jīva* discriminates between *prakṛti* and *puruṣa* and realizes that it is *puruṣa* – eternal, free, a non-agent, etc. – it achieves liberation.

Evolution

The entire world of objects, with their diverse qualities, is a consequence of the evolution of *prakṛti*. Like Darwin, who explains the evolution of the diverse organic world in terms of a few simple life-forms through a process of mutation and adaptation, Sāṅkhya traces the world of our experience in its entirety to *prakṛti*; the world as we know it exists in *prakṛti* in a potential form. The similarity with Darwin stops here, however. Unlike Darwin, who provides an account of organic evolution in linear terms, Sāṅkhya regards evolution as a cyclical process such that evolution (*sarga*) is followed by dissolution (*pralaya*) and dissolution by evolution and so on. Evolution occurs when the constituents (*guṇas*) of *prakṛti* are in a state of disequilibrium, and dissolution occurs when the *guṇas* return to a state of equilibrium. This cycle of evolution and dissolution continues till all the selves (*puruṣas*) are freed from this world of suffering.

Sāṅkhya provides a detailed list of the products that evolve from *prakṛti*.[17] The first product to evolve is *mahat* (great) at the cosmic level or *buddhi* (intellect) at the individual level. Intellect is made of fine matter, giving it the capacity to reflect consciousness or *puruṣa*, and it is due to this reflection that intellect acquires intelligence and consciousness and is capable of ascertainment and decision. Intellect in turn produces *ahaṅkāra* (ego-sense, self-sense or individuation), which is responsible for the sense of I-ness or selfhood. At the psychological level *ahaṅkāra* is responsible for self-love and agency. *Ahaṅkāra* in turn, depending on the preponderance of a particular *guṇa*, produces further evolutes. The *sattvika ahaṅkāra* produces mind or *manas* responsible for synthesizing sense-data, the five sensory organs (*jñānendriya*) of sight, smell, taste, touch and sound and the five motor organs (*karmendriya*) of speech, handling, movement, excretion and reproduction. The *tāmasa ahaṅkāra* produces the five subtle elements (*tanmātra*) or essences of sound, touch, sight, taste and smell, and these in turn produce the five gross elements of ether, air, light, water and earth. The things of our everyday experience such as hills, insects, animals and human beings are a result of various combinations of the *mahābhūtas* or gross elements. The evolutionary story of Sāṅkhya can be diagrammatically expressed as shown in *Figure 8.1*.

The evolution of *prakṛti* is for an end, and that end is *puruṣa*. Just as unintelligent milk flows out of the cow to nourish the calf,[18] *prakṛti* evolves so that *puruṣa* can know about the true nature of *prakṛti* and *puruṣa* and be liberated from this world of suffering.

The process of evolution begins when the equilibrium of the *guṇas* is disturbed. This is a result of the association of *prakṛti* and *puruṣa*. Their association is like the partnership of a lame man and a blind man – the lame man like *puruṣa* is capable of sight but cannot act (i.e. walk), and the blind man like *prakṛti* can act (i.e. walk), but cannot see. Their cooperation, however, enables them to transcend their weaknesses, thus allowing them to travel.

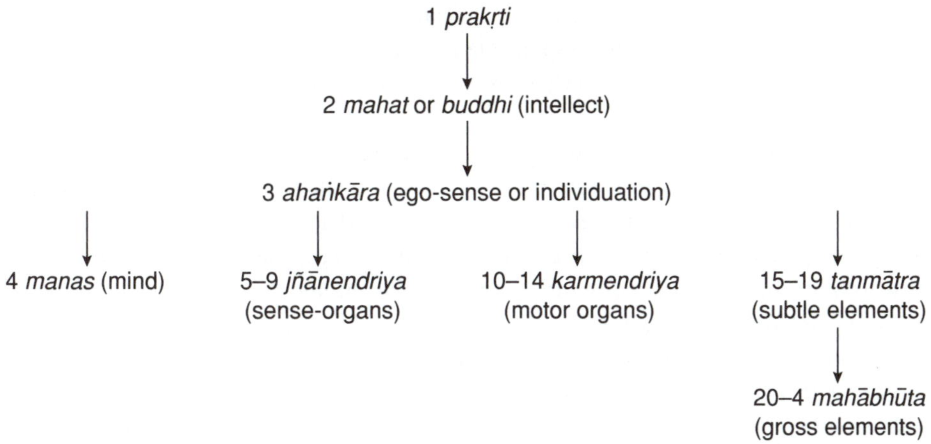

Figure 8.1

The Sāṅkhya account of evolution is a perplexing one. It raises a number of questions, some specific to the system and others inevitable consequences of a dualistic account. The first issue relates to the order of the evolutes of *prakṛti*. The significance of the order is unclear since no explanation is provided in support of the order in the evolution of matter – surprising since the system prides itself on providing reasons. One possible view is that the evolutes are ordered in terms of temporal priority. This, however, does not make much sense. For instance, to say that intellect is temporally prior to self-sense or that sense-organs are temporally prior to sensation is meaningless since there must be a physical being made up of gross elements in terms of which one could talk sensibly of intellect, sense-organs, ego and so on. In other words, the evolutes of *prakṛti* seem to make more sense if viewed bottom up rather than top down – that is, from gross elements upwards rather than intellect downwards. A possible alternative would be to view the order in terms of conceptual priority and to say that an earlier evolute is essential to make sense of a later evolute. For instance, to make sense of self-sense or *ahaṅkāra* (evolute 3) one needs *buddhi* or intellect (evolute 2); similarly essences such as colour and sound (15–19) do not make sense without the sense-organs of sight and hearing (evolutes 5–9).[19]

The next criticism of the Sāṅkhya account of evolution is the one put forward by Śaṅkara,[20] who, while agreeing with Sāṅkhya that there is a single cause, disagrees on the question of whether this cause could be unintelligent *prakṛti*. According to Śaṅkara evolution makes sense only if the cause is intelligent. He tries to show that analogies such as that of the cow and the calf and the lame man and the blind man used by Sāṅkhya, if anything, establish intelligence as a central feature. For Śaṅkara, it is the combined intelligence of the lame man and the blind man which results in the pursuit of a purpose. Likewise, milk flows from the cow because of the cow's maternal feelings for the calf. To some extent Śaṅkara is correct in saying that conditions in the cow are responsible for the flow of the milk – for instance hormonal changes in the cow. The sucking action of the calf is also responsible for the flow of the milk. But Śaṅkara's view that milk flows because of the cow's volition or will and therefore intelligence is totally incorrect.

An interesting consequence of Śaṅkara's alternative explanation to the analogies used by Sāṅkhya is that it affects the reliability of analogy as a form of reasoning – on which the Sāṅkhyans rely heavily. The other drawback is the association of *prakṛti* and *puruṣa*, which is essential for evolution to take place. The manner in which these two absolute and independent entities – one intelligent and immobile, the other unintelligent and dynamic – are brought together seems to undermine their account of evolution as a cyclical process. According to Sāṅkhya the mere presence of *puruṣa* is sufficient to bring about evolution. If this is the case, then it raises an insurmountable problem for Sāṅkhya since *puruṣa*, being static or immobile, will always be present near *prakṛti*, in which case evolution could never have begun and can never cease – in other words, evolution cannot be followed by dissolution and dissolution by evolution as Sāṅkhya claims.

Liberation

Prakṛti, as stated earlier, continues to go through periods of evolution and dissolution till all the *puruṣas* are liberated. There is bondage as long as a *puruṣa* mistakenly identifies itself with *buddhi*, *ahaṅkāra* and *manas* (the internal organ) in which it is reflected. As soon as the *puruṣa* realizes that it is not the intellect or ego or mind – that it is not *prakṛti* – it is liberated.

As for the individual soul (*jīva*), it attains liberation as soon as it discriminates between *puruṣa* and *prakṛti*. The acquisition of discriminative knowledge does not, however, immediately result in release of the *puruṣa* from the body. The body continues to exist till the impressions of past *karmas* which took effect prior to discriminative knowledge cease like the potter's wheel that continues to spin for a time because of the original momentum.[21]

A criticism that can be raised at this stage is that it is not very clear from the Sāṅkhya account whether there is one cosmological evolution of *prakṛti* or whether there are as many evolutions of *prakṛti* as there are *puruṣas*. If it is the latter, then *prakṛti* must be at different stages of evolution at the same time. If it is the former, then the evolution or dissolution of *prakṛti* must affect all *puruṣas* equally. This is a problem that is created by the Sāṅkhyan ambition to provide an explanation at the cosmic and at the individual level with the same story.

The discriminatory knowledge which makes liberation possible is obtained through right knowledge, reflection and spiritual discipline. As for spiritual discipline, Sāṅkhya relies on the practical steps developed fully in Yoga.

YOGA

Historical background

The idea that *yoga* (discipline, mental and physical) is a way of achieving release from suffering is found in the ancient texts. The texts which refer to *sāṅkhya* (i.e. the *Śvetāśvatara Upaniṣad* and the *Bhagavadgītā*) refer to *yoga* as well. The question whether the references are to Yoga as expounded by Patañjali (200 BC–AD 400?) is open to doubt. Patañjali's *Yoga Sūtra* is the oldest text of the Yoga school, and the best-known commentary on it is Vyāsa's *Yogasūtrabhāṣya* (AD 400). Some scholars believe that Patañjali, the author of *Yoga Sūtra* and Patañjali the grammarian (200 BC) are one and the same on the basis that Bhoja, a later commentator on the *Yoga Sūtras*, refers to the contributions made to grammar by Patañjali. Modern scholars, however, do not perceive a strong link between the Patañjali of grammar and the Patañjali of Yoga.

Philosophical background

Yoga, as stated earlier, accepts by and large the epistemology and metaphysics of Sāṅkhya. The distinctive feature of Yoga is that, unlike Sāṅkhya, it accepts God or *Īśvara*. God's existence is established on the basis of the law of continuity – i.e. on the reasoning that where there is a great and a greater there must be a greatest. The argument goes like this: we see that people possess different qualities such as knowledge and power in different strengths; so there must be a Being who possesses these excellent qualities at the highest strengths.

Yoga's *Īśvara*, however, is a *puruṣa* among other *puruṣas*. He is eternal, omniscient and omnipresent, but is not the creator of the world; the world of our experience, for Yoga, evolves out of *prakṛti*. God, however, brings about the association of *prakṛti* and *puruṣa* which starts the process of evolution in *prakṛti*. The introduction of God by Yoga gets round the problem of cooperation between an intelligent *puruṣa* and an unintelligent *prakṛti* faced by Sāṅkhya. However, as Hiriyanna correctly observes, 'such an assumption is against the very fundamentals of the doctrine, at all events, of the Sāṅkhya phase of it'.[22]

Īśvara plays an important role in the realm of spiritual discipline. Devotion to *Īśvara* is a necessary part of the eightfold discipline prescribed by Yoga that makes liberation possible.

Spiritual discipline

Puruṣa, according to Yoga, realizes its nature when there is cessation of the modifications of *citta* (Yoga's collective term for the internal organs of *buddhi*, *ahaṅkāra* and *manas*).[23] This cessation is brought about through spiritual discipline. Yoga recommends an Eightfold Path[24] (*aṣṭāṅga yoga*) aimed at moral discipline, physical discipline and mental discipline. For Yoga the control of the physical body is a prerequisite for controlling the mind.

Moral discipline

The first two stages of the Eightfold Path, *yama*[25] (abstention) and *niyama* (observances), deal with the moral well-being of the individual and reflect pursuit of the good. Under *yama* the individual is advised to refrain from (a) causing injury through thought, word or deed (*ahiṁsā*), (b) falsehood (*satya*), (c) stealing (*asteya*), (d) sensual pleasures (*brahmacārya*) and (e) avarice or greed (*aparigraha*). *Niyama*[26] prescribes that individuals should (a) purify themselves internally as well as externally (*śauca*), (b) be content (*saṅtoṣa*), (c) practise austerity (*tapas*), (d) study philosophical texts (*syādhyāya*) and (e) devote themselves to God (*Īśvara-praṇidhāna*).

Physical discipline and mental discipline

The control of the physical body is achieved through a combination of (a) right posture or *āsana*, (b) regulation of inhalation, retention and exhalation of breath (*prāṇāyāma*) and (c) withdrawal of the senses (*pratyāhāra*).

The next stage is mental discipline, which consists of (a) *dhāraṇa* or fixing the mind on an object of meditation like an image, (b) *dhyāna* or contemplation and (c) *samādhi* or meditative trance.

In *samādhi*, the final step in the eightfold discipline, the individual's mind is totally immersed in the object of meditation. *Samādhi* is of two kinds – *saṁprajñāta samādhi* and *asaṁprajñāta samādhi*. In *saṁprajñāta samādhi* the individual though absorbed or immersed in the object of meditation is still conscious or aware of the object of meditation. What the individual has at this stage is intuitive knowledge of the truth. In *asaṁprajñāta samādhi* the individual is no longer conscious of the object of meditation and there is total immersion – a condition often described in the texts as sleepless sleep. And it is at this level, since there is no modification of *citta*, that liberation is attained.

During the course of practising the Eightfold Path the individual is likely to be rewarded with other powers including supernormal powers – for instance knowledge of the past, present and future. Though the supernormal powers are perfections (*siddhis*), Yoga regards them as a hindrance to *samādhi*. Liberation can be gained only by disregarding these powers that one obtains on the journey to freedom.

CONCLUSION

A full appreciation of Sāṅkhya, reputed to be the oldest Indian philosophical system, is not possible, partly because of missing literature. The commentaries are not of much help in putting a systematic philosophy together. Īśvara Kṛṣṇa's *Sāṅkhya Kārikā*, as the oldest text, is comparable to an intricate jigsaw puzzle with central pieces missing. For instance, epistemology is sketchily discussed in the text, with the result that readers are forced to rely on their own ingenuity or on the commentaries (which more than occasionally are at variance) to construct a plausible account of perception for the system. At times Sāṅkhya exhibits glimpses of a grandiose metaphysics aimed at explaining the nature of reality and human phenomena at different levels, for example cosmic and individual, epistemological and psychological; at other times it comes across as a not so well-thought-out philosophy meant to confound and frustrate the reader at every turn. Whatever guise Sāṅkhya takes, it cannot be denied that it demands attention from the reader at every stage. As for Yoga, Sāṅkhya's sister school, it has had a profound influence on philosophy in India since most Indian philosophical schools (including Buddhism) endorse the importance of physical and mental discipline besides moral discipline in attaining freedom from the world of suffering.

NOTES

1 There are a few proponents of later Sāṅkhya who accept theism – for example Vijñānabhikṣu (AD 1550–1600), author of *Sāṅkhyapravacanabhāṣya*.

2 See Gerald James Larson and Ram Shankar Bhattacharya, (eds) *Sāṁkhya: A Dualist Tradition in Indian Philosophy* (*Encyclopaedia of Indian Philosophies Vol. IV*) (Delhi: Motilal Banarsidass, 1987), pp. 1–14 for an account of the history of the tradition.

3 'From the torment by three-fold misery (arises) the inquiry into the means of terminating it' (*Sāṅkhya Kārikā*, verse I).

4 'Three varieties are recognised of the means of correct knowledge being comprehended (in these); for the establishment of what is to be known depends on the means of correct knowledge' (*Sāṅkhya Kārikā*, verse IV).

5 According to Vātsyāyana, a Nyāya commentator, there are three different classes of inference: *pūrvavat* (inference from prior perception), *śeṣavat* (inference by exclusion) and *sāmānyatodṛṣṭa* (inference by analogy). Vācaspati Miśra, the Sāṅkhya commentator, accepts these three types of inference but classifies them differently. He divides inference into *vīta* (inference based on positive concomitance) and *avīta* (inference based on negative concomitance) and includes *pūrvavat* and *sāmānyatodṛṣṭa* under *vīta* and *śeavat* under *avīta*. See Chapter 7 above for the five-step syllogistic reasoning developed by Nyāya.

6 'Knowledge of objects beyond the senses comes from inference based on analogy' (*Sāṅkhya Kārikā*, verse IV).

7 'What (knowledge) is obscure and not attainable even thereby [inference based on analogy] is gained by valid testimony' (*Sāṅkhya Kārikā*; verse IV).

8 S. Radhakrishan, *Indian Philosophy* (2 vols, London: George Allen & Unwin, 1966), vol. II, p. 302.

9 See Chapter 10 below.

10 'The effect exists (even prior to the operation of the cause) since what is non-existent cannot be brought into existence by the operation of a cause, since there is recourse to the (appropriate) material cause, since there is not production of all (by all), since the potent (cause) effects (only) that of which it is capable, and since (the effect) is non-different from the cause' (*Sāṅkhya Kārikā*, verse IX).

11 'The evolved is caused, non-eternal, non-pervasive, mob[i]le, manifold, dependent, mergent, conjunct and heteronomous; the unevolved is the reverse (of all these)' (*Sāṅkhya Kārikā*, verse X).

12 'The non-perception of that (Primal Nature) is due to its subtlety, not to its non-existence, since it is cognised from its effects' (*Sāṅkhya Kārikā*, verse VIII).

13 'The unevolved exists as the cause of the diverse, because of the finitude, and homogenous nature (of the latter), because of its proceeding from the potentiality (of the cause), and because of there being in respect of the variegated world both the emergence of effect from causes as also their merger; it (the unevolved) functions through their combination being modified like water, by the specific nature abiding in the respective constituents' (*Sāṅkhya Kārikā*, verses XV, XVI).

14 'And from the contrast with that (which is composed of the three constituents etc.) there follows for the Spirit, the character of being a witness, freedom (from misery), neutrality, percipience and non-agency' (*Sāṅkhya Kārikā*, verse XIX).

15 'Spirit exists (as distinct from matter), since collocations serve a purpose of some (being) other than themselves, since this other must be the reverse of (what is composed of) the three constituents and so on, since there must be control (of the collocations), since there must be an enjoyer and since there is activity for the purpose of release (from three fold misery)' (*Sāṅkhya Kārikā*, verse XVII).

16 'The plurality of Spirits certainly follows from the distributive (nature of the) incidence of birth and death and of (the endowment of) the instruments (of cognition and action), from (bodies) engaging in action, not all at the same time, and also from the differences in (the proportion of) the three constituents (in different entities, like sages, ordinary morals and beast)' (*Sāṅkhya Kārikā*, verse XVIII).

17 'From Primal Nature proceeds the Great One (intellect), thence individuation, thence the aggregate of the sixteen and from five out of these sixteen, the five gross elements' (*Sāṅkhya Kārikā*, verse XXII).

18 'As non-intelligent milk functions for the nourishment of the calf, even so does Primal Nature function for the liberation of the Spirit' (*Sāṅkhya Kārikā*, verse LVII). 'Just as (in) the world (one) undertakes action in order to be rid of desire (by satisfying it), even so does the unevolved function for the release of the Spirit' (*Sāṅkhya Kārikā*, verse LVIII).

19 One of the later proponents of the system, Vijñānabhikṣu (AD 1550–1600), in *Sāṁkhyasāra* accepts the order of the evolutes on scriptural authority.

20 See Brian Carr's chapter on Śaṅkara (Chapter 10 below) for a more detailed appraisal of the criticisms.

21 'Virtue and the rest having ceased to function as causes, because of the attainment of perfect wisdom, (the Spirit) remains invested with the body, because of the force of past impressions, like the whirl of the (potter's) wheel (which persists for a while by virtue of the momentum imparted by a prior impulse)', (*Sāṅkhya Kārikā*, verse LXVII).

22 M. Hiriyanna, *Essentials of Indian Philosophy* (London: George Allen & Unwin, 1985), p. 125.

23 '*Yoga* is the restraint of mental modifications' (*Yoga Sūtra* 1:2).

24 'Restraint, observance, posture, regulation of breath, abstraction [of the senses], concentration, meditation, and trance are the eight accessories of *yoga*', (*Yoga Sūtra* 2:29).

25 'Of these, the restraints (*yama*) are: abstinence from injury (*āhiṃsā*), veracity, abstinence from theft, continence, and abstinence from avariciousness' (*Yoga Sūtra* 2:30).

26 'The observances (*niyama*) are cleanliness, contentment, purificatory action, study and the making of the Lord the motive of all action' (*Yoga Sūtra* 2:32).

REFERENCES

Hiriyanna, M. (1932) *Outlines of Indian Philosophy*, London: George Allen & Unwin.

—— (1985) *Essentials of Indian Philosophy*, London: George Allen & Unwin (first published 1949).

Larson, Gerald James and Bhattacharya, Ram Shankar (eds) (1987) *Sāṁkhya: A Dualist Tradition in Indian Philosophy* (*Encyclopaedia of Indian Philosophies Vol. IV*), Delhi: Motilal Banarsidass.

Radhakrishnan, S. (1966) *Indian Philosophy*, 2 vols, London: George Allen & Unwin (first published 1923).

Radhakrishnan, Sarvepalli and Moore, Charles A. (eds) (1957) *A Sourcebook in Indian Philosophy*, Princeton: Princeton University Press (for extracts of Patañjali's *Yoga Sūtra*).

Sastri, S. S. Suryanarayana (ed. and trans.) (1948) *The Saṅkhyakārikā of Īśvara Kṛṣṇa*, University of Madras.

FURTHER READING

Bastow, David (1978) 'An attempt to understand Sāṁkhya-Yoga', *Journal of Indian Philosophy* 5:191–207.

Conger, George P. (1953) 'A naturalistic approach to Sāṁkhya-Yoga', *Philosophy East and West* 3:233–40.

Coward, Harold (1979) 'Mysticism in the analytical psychology of Carl Jung and the Yoga Psychology', *Philosophy East and West* 29:323–36.

Dasgupta, Surendra Nath (1924) *Yoga as Philosophy and Religion*, London: Kegan Paul.

Feuerstein, Georg (1980) *The Philosophy of Classical Yoga*, New York: St Martin's Press.

—— (1987) 'The concept of God ("Īśvara") in classical Yoga', *Journal of Indian Philosophy* 15:385–97.

Kesarcodi-Watson, Ian (1982) ' "Samādhi" in Patañjali's "Yoga Sūtras" ', *Philosophy East and West* 32:77–90.

Larson, Gerald James (1983) 'An eccentric ghost in the machine: formal and quantitative aspects of the Sāṅkhya-Yoga dualism', *Journal of Indian Philosophy* 33:219–34.

Podgorski, Frank R. (1994) 'Paths to perfection: Yoga and Confucian', *Asian Philosophy* 4(2):151–64.

Schweizer, Paul (1993) 'Mind/consciousness dualism in Sāṅkhya-Yoga philosophy' *Philosophical and Phenomenological Research* 53(4):845–59.

Whicher, Ian (1995) 'Cessation and integration in classical Yoga', *Asian Philosophy* 5(1):47–58.

9

PŪRVA MĪMĀṀSĀ AND VEDĀNTA

R. C. Pandeya and Manju

INTRODUCTION

In the Indian philosophical tradition the word *Mīmāṁsā* is used to signify repeated contemplation of the import of the texts of the entire Veda, including the hymns, the Brāhmaṇa books and the *Upaniṣads*. The word also carries with it the sense of 'sacred' inasmuch as a philosophical system associated with the Vedas it has also assumed the sense of sacredness. Apart from its etymological and religious senses it also, in a philosophical sense, stands for a distinct methodology, which has been spelled out at the very beginning of both parts of the Mīmāṁsā. Both Bādarāyaṇa and Jaimini call their work an enquiry (*jijñāsā*). Thus the system of Mīmāṁsā concerns itself with an enquiry into the significance and purport of the Vedic text of all kinds, as is evident from the study of the Mīmāṁsā work in its entirety.

PŪRVA MĪMĀṀSĀ

Traditionally the Mīmāṁsā system has been divided into prior (*Pūrva*) and later (*Uttara*) Mīmāṁsās: the first is commonly known as Pūrva Mīmāṁsā and the second as Vedānta. The older tradition uses the terms Dharma Mīmāṁsā and Brahma Mīmāṁsā for Pūrva Mīmāṁsā and Vedānta respectively. These names reflect the respective subject matter of the two systems enunciated in the very first statements of the two parts. Jaimini begins with the statement 'Henceforth begins the enquiry into the nature of *dharma*',[1] and Bādarāyaṇa likewise starts his work with the statement 'Henceforth begins an enquiry into the nature of Brahman.'[2] The terms '*dharma*' and '*Brahman*' assume crucial importance as far as the subject matter of enquiry of the two systems is concerned. The word *dharma* has been used by Pūrva Mīmāṁsā to mean an act enjoined by the Vedic texts.[3] The term '*Brahman*', on the other hand, is used by Bādarāyaṇa for the ultimate cause of all that exists.[4] Accordingly Jaimini addresses himself exclusively to the understanding of what actions ought to be performed in keeping with the purport of the Vedic text. The sense of 'ought' which is associated with any philosophical and religious enquiry concerning action can be sustained only in terms of some infallible authority, like the command of the supreme being, God, reason, and revealed texts. On the other hand the enquiry into the ultimate cause proceeds along similar lines except that it takes into account not human conduct but an ultimate entity which is the cause of all, yet itself remains without all causation. Such a reality obviously can be accepted not on the basis of any authority, because any such authority would itself be caused, but on the basis of some source which is revealed simultaneously with the ultimate reality itself. Thus in both the cases the authority has to be accepted as impersonally revealed (*apauruṣeya*).

The division of Mīmāṁsā into earlier and later is linked solely with *dharma* and *Brahman*, and should not be construed in a chronological sense. Both these systems hold that the revealed text of the Veda, having no connection with any person and being without any reference to temporal events, is ahistorical. It is only as a matter of convenience that action gets priority over philosophical contemplation. Thus the part of the Veda dealing with human action of various kinds, known as *dharma*, is earlier than that part which deals with human and worldly existence which come later in life. Apart from this reason the division of earlier and later, as far as the two systems are concerned, cannot be established on the basis of usual historical method. In fact there is ample evidence to suggest that the 'later' Mīmāṁsā of Bādarāyaṇa, in chronological terms, is earlier than the 'earlier' Mīmāṁsā of Jaimini. These authors mention each other in their texts, but internal evidence reveals that Jaimini is presupposing Bādarāyaṇa.[5] In both cases, however, there is an indication of a long unrecorded tradition of scholars prior to the final composition of the two *sūtras*. It is, however, not possible to precisely fix the dates of these two authors other than to state that they might have flourished between 200 BC and AD 200.

The book of Jaimini called the *Mīmāṁsā sūtra* (*MS*) consists of sixteen chapters, of which the first twelve deal with the problem of interpretation of Vedic texts and the last four, in the form of an appendix, address themselves to the discussion concerning various deities.[6] Since the main Vedic text is primarily concerned with rituals, sacrifices and elaborate discussions given in the Brāhmaṇa texts, forming a supplement to the main Vedic texts, the *MS* takes into account both the nature of sacrifices and their elaborate procedures and the roles of different categories of persons and things employed in the rituals. Since the extensive literature of the Veda contains statements, recommended procedures and interpretations of various statements that are contradictory, the *MS* tries to remove these contradictions by means of establishing cogent rules of textual interpretation, with a view to arriving at uniformity of the Vedic procedures and texts. The *MS* therefore, being concerned mainly with the problem of textual interpretation and performance of rituals, propounds a comprehensive philosophical position in the first section of the text itself. In order to understand the philosophical view of Pūrva Mīmāṁsā this section only is relevant; the other sections are mainly devoted to the discussion of sacrifices and rituals.[7]

Since the *sūtras* written by Jaimini are in the form of cryptic statements, the text of the *MS*, without any explanatory aid, cannot be properly understood. The tradition records a long list of commentators who attempted elaboration and exposition of the *sūtras* of the *MS*. Of many such comments only one commentary called the *Bhāṣya* of Śabara (*SB*) is available today, and it is the sole guide to our understanding of the *MS*. In fact the entire Mīmāṁsā literature written after Śabara takes the *Bhāṣya* as its basis. We find references in the *SB* to various philosophical views of other schools of Indian philosophy, on the basis of which the date of Śabara could be said to fall within the range of the third and fourth centuries AD.[8]

Three different schools grew within the Mīmāṁsā system, differing on the basis of the contending philosophical positions adopted. Prabhākara, Kumārila Bhaṭṭa and Murāri Miśra were the founders of these schools; the works of only the first two are available. The works of Murāri Miśra are not traceable. His views are known only through stray references found in the works of various subsequent authors. The tradition is contradictory as far as the relative historical priority of Prabhākara and Kumārila is concerned. According to one tradition Prabhākara was the pupil of Kumārila, but because in some cases Prabhākara corrected his teacher, he was given the name of Guru, as his views are also known as Gurumata. On the basis of internal evidence one can say that Prabhākara is familiar with the views of Kumārila, but Kumārila does not show acquaintance with the position of Prabhākara. Both these authors established their own schools of thought, and very important philosophical works were written on their philosophical positions. Notable among those who propounded the views of Kumārila were Pārthasārathi and Gāgā Bhaṭṭa, and those of Prabhākara, Śālikanātha.[9]

In keeping with the basic idea that philosophy is concerned with human conduct and that infallible guidance for the conduct is provided by the Vedas, the Pūrva Mīmāṁsā system considers the Vedas as a set of imperative statements. Descriptive statements found in the Vedas are construed as statements eulogizing actions to be performed.[10] In order to support the view that descriptive statements are subservient to prescriptive statements, the system proposed a theory of meaning which allows meaningfulness only to prescriptive sentences.

According to the Mīmāṁsakas the meaning of descriptive sentences depends on verification of facts of various kinds. Since facts are perceivable and unperceivable and belong to past, present or future, they are not available for immediate verification leading to a conclusive truth of descriptive statements. Moreover, the idea of description is related to linguistic convention, which must have a beginning in history. This would go against the basic assumption that the Vedas are eternal. Therefore, the Pūrva Mīmāṁsā, in order to overcome the difficulties of verification and allied matters, proposed that meaningfulness would belong only to prescriptive sentences in the sense that they express the idea of human Good to be realized. The question of verification in this case does not arise. This being the case, any descriptive sentences to be found in the body of the Veda, consisting of predominantly prescriptive statements, would have to be relegated to a secondary position and their meaning has to be explained in relation to some relevant prescription.[11]

The view of the Pūrva Mīmāṁsā outlined above is further strengthened by eliminating any reference to particulars from the purview of meaning. Meaning consists in being related to the universals, which are eternal and participate in particulars. Words relate to it and convey to the listeners the meaning, as particulars figure only by courtesy.[12] In this sense what words mean are entities not occurring in space and time. The relation between words and what they mean (universals) is considered to be natural towards themselves. Thus there is no artificiality in all meaning situations so far as the Vedas are concerned. Common language spoken outside the context of the Vedas derives its meaningfulness from its close resemblance to the Vedic language. Languages further removed from the standard Vedic language, thus, are imitations of the Vedic language and their true meaning would be revealed by translating them into the standard Vedic form. Moreover all the non-Vedic languages are also subject to human mentality, thereby demanding conventions and rules which have evolved in the course of human history.[13]

The nature of words is a subject of controversy in the school of Mīmāṁsā. The dominant position is that the syllables which constitute words are eternal and that a word is a combination of them. Unlike the grammarians, Mīmāṁsā does not hold the eternality of words to be a fact. The unity of a word and the order of words in a sentence are to be accountable in terms of the impressions they create on the human mind. This is because the Mīmāṁsā is averse to according a special status to structure over and above the elements constituting it. The relation of *samavāya* or inherence, as accepted by the Nyāya-Vaiśeṣika, is rejected on the grounds that discrete elements, being discernible in structure, cannot contribute anything beyond their own inherent character. In other words, a forest has no identity of its own beyond particular trees.[14]

Śabara holds that the last letter of a word along with the impressions of each of the preceding letters is the cause of verbal knowledge. Kumārila thinks that it is what a word means (an entity) which is the cause of our knowledge of words. Prabhākara holds on the other hand that the meaning of a sentence is the direct outcome of the meaning of the words constituting it.

In the Mīmāṁsā system three factors are recognized as making a sentence meaningful, namely *ākāṅkṣā*, *yogyatā* and *āsatti*.

(a) *Ākāṅkṣā* provides syntactical unity to a sentence. Each word in a sentence being related to other words cannot convey full meaning in the absence of its relation with others. An isolated word does not convey full meaning, and the listener is desirous of other words to be brought in.

(b) *Yogyatā* is the logical compatibility of words in a sentence as far as their mutual relation is concerned. In other words, *yogyatā* demands competence for mutual relation from words in a sentence.

(c) *Āsatti* requires that words in a sentence are continuous and proximate in time.

There are two major theories concerning the meaning of linguistic expression in the Pūrva Mīmāṁsā school. These are the *abhihitānvaya* and *anvitābhidhāna* theories. The former theory is advocated by Kumārila and the latter by Prabhākara. The *abhihitānvaya* theory holds that words convey their own individual meanings and these become mutually related in a sentence. The meanings of individual words are comprehended separately and the meaning of the sentence is obtained from the association of word meanings. The *anvitābhidhāna* theory advocated by Prabhākara on the other hand holds that a word expresses its meaning being in conjunction with an act to be done (*Niyoga*). Words in a sentence convey their meanings only in relation to the meaning of other words. Words in a sentence have the double function of giving their individual as well as conjoined meanings. Individual word meanings as well as their mutual relation constitute a sentence.

Apart from the meaning situations, the Mīmāṁsā also propounds a view concerning the truth of a sentence. As stated above, the procedure of verification is ruled out because it does not apply to sentences of an impersonal nature. But at the same time, in any given situation of meaning, a procedure for ensuring the truth of a sentence has to be evolved. The question that the Mīmāṁsā raises is not whether a statement is true or false but whether a sentence being true what is it that the truth consists in. For example, if a sentence enjoins some sacrifice to be performed, we should ask how this is to be performed correctly and not whether its performance would give the results envisaged. Therefore, for the Mīmāṁsā, truth consists in being a part of Vedic injunction, but the procedure for performing the act strictly in accordance with the intent and purport of the Vedic statement is to be decided by means of certain *pramāṇas*. Thus, so far as truth is concerned *pramāṇa* is self-evident in the case of the Vedic statement, but it plays the role of confirming the truth self-evidently given. *Pramāṇa* is thus *svataḥ* (by itself), and no further proof is required for it as in the case of Nyāya; it only confirms, but does not prove anything.[15]

For Mīmāṁsā knowledge is self-evident in the sense that its emergence in the human mind carries with it a guarantee of its validity. In other words, at this initial stage no extraneous factors are required to make it valid. It is, however, a different story when this self-evident knowledge meets with failure in subsequent human transactions. It appears that invalidity depends upon external factors, which can render invalid what was initially valid. The question of validity seems, in the Mīmāṁsā system, more of a psychological phenomenon than the logical one, because in keeping with the logic of truth a valid cognition cannot be rendered invalid subsequently.[16] We can see here that the Mīmāṁsā in order to maintain consistency with the theory of the impersonal character of the Vedas has no other option than to hold all cognition, particularly the verbal cognition arising from the Vedas, to be self-evident. It is only in the Vedic context of injunction that the question of invalidity of what the Vedas say cannot be settled during one's lifetime. The theory of *apūrva* (unseen force), examined below, is also an outcome of the unfailing character of the Vedic injunction.

The character of knowledge as self-evident is based, as Prabhākara thinks, on the conception of knowledge as self-luminous.[17] Along with the revelation of the object of cognition the knowledge also reveals itself, leading to the position that in all knowledge, self-consciousness is given. Thus no other effort is needed to make man self-conscious. This eliminates the possibility of raising a further question: how does one know that one knows? All knowledge is both self-evident and self-aware of an object given to it. The status of the object, apart from our knowledge of it, cannot be established in any manner other than its status of givenness of knowledge. Knowledge is, however, incapable of creating an object and giving it to itself. In this sense the Mīmāṁsā is committed to the position of realism of the extreme form where the knowing subject is totally barren and sterile so far as creating an object is concerned. Even in the case of illusion, the object of illusory cognition is not accepted as a creation of mind. According to both Prabhākara and Kumārila error is totally due to abnormality in the functioning of mind. The *akhyāti* theory of Prabhākara explains error mainly as a creation of truncated memory.[18] In the *anyathākhyāti* theory of Kumārila, error is conceived as misplaced perception of an object.[19] Therefore, the Mīmāṁsā is averse to any attempt to hold the view that a given object is the creation of mind. Strict duality and irreducibility of the cognizing mind and the cognized object as given in knowledge is maintained at all levels.

Prabhākara, following Śabara's statement, holds that the resultant comprehension of an object is revealed along with the object of knowledge. No other comprehension (*saṁvit)* is needed to comprehend the original comprehension.[20] There is no manifestation of an object in the absence of this comprehension, and no second manifestation for the original manifestation is needed. Prabhākara holds that in every cognition three factors are necessarily manifest, namely the cognizer, the object cognized and the cognition. Thus in every cognition situation we have a tripartite consciousness (*tripuṭī-saṁvit*). At the level of linguistic expression we have the object of knowledge (accusative case), the knower (nominative case) and awareness of the object (verb). The awareness as an act while revealing the first two reveals itself as well.

Kumārila, however, does not agree with this view because for him the statement 'This is a book' is quite different from the statement 'I know this book.' In the former case we have a judgement of perception, but in the latter we infer the givenness of a book on the basis of self-reflection.[21] For Kumārila the relation between the cognition and an object of this cognition is that of givenness (*viṣayatā*) and not of identity.

This is a special kind of causal relation involving reciprocity. Cognition being caused in a cognitive situation has sense-object contact as its cause. But the object in its turn being in contact with sense-organs causes cognition, and this cognition becomes the cause of manifestedness (*bhāsana*) of the object. Though cognition arises before the consciousness of an object, this cognition, however, is not known at the time when it arises. This cognition is not self-luminous, because the function of cognition is restricted to revealing the given object. It cannot be expected to have two functions simultaneously, that is, revealing the object as well as revealing itself. Thus the immediate knowledge of this supposedly self-luminous cognition is not possible. Nor can the cognition be cognized subsequently, because being momentary it can only be presumed (*arthāpatti*) from the fact of givenness of the object. It is further held that there arises in the object cognized a special property called givenness or cognizedness (*jñātatā*).[22]

The above-mentioned view of knowledge in the Mīmāṁsā system is reflected in its theory of *pramāṇas*. Thus perception for them is immediate awareness of an object, where the object is initially comprehended as undifferentiated and subsequently fully differentiated. Differentiation among various aspects of object is done by mind but not created by it.[23] Even in the case of inference the Mīmāṁsakas believe that inferential knowledge is the result of the knowledge of *vyāpti*. *Vyāpti* has been defined as the co-presence of the two related things in all the positive instances, thereby negating the inferential knowledge based on the observation of the absence of two things together.[24] Knowledge by comparison (*upamāna*) is obtained in the form of one thing being similar to the other. Mīmāṁsā believes in *arthāpatti* as a separate *pramāṇa* where one has to posit an unknown factor in order to explain an otherwise unexplainable known phenomenon. For example, if someone is well-built but is known to avoid eating during the daytime, according to *arthāpatti*, he is supposed to eat during the night. *Anupalabdhi* (non-apprehension) is another *pramāṇa* held by Kumārila peculiar to Mīmāṁsā whereby the absence of a thing is known.[25] Verbal testimony as a *pramāṇa* is, of course, the very foundation of this system.

Being an enquiry into the nature of *dharma* the Mīmāṁsā addresses itself to an investigation into the nature of *dharma*. Here *dharma* is used in a special sense which is quite different from the meanings given to this word by other Indian systems of thought. According to the Mīmāṁsā, *dharma* is that entity which is characterized by imperative statements.[26] Imperative statements are necessarily Vedic statements, as that entity which is meant by non-Vedic statements cannot enjoy the status of *dharma*. The idea behind this view is that the human mind is likely to be partial, biased, motivated and mistaken at times. The Vedic imperative statements, being free from all the impediments mentioned above, aim at the ultimate Good of human life. Someone following these injunctions in the prescribed order of procedure is bound to achieve the Good. The belief in the efficacy of the enjoined act is an outcome of people's firm faith in the Vedas. This belief is so strong that the Mīmāṁsā goes to the extent of holding that if the envisaged result of an action does not come in this life, it is bound to come in a life hereafter; because the action which has not yielded the intended result will create another life to get the result for the person who has performed an action. Thus we see here that the concept of *dharma* is linked with transmigration of the soul to a body reborn, which is another way of stating the law of *karma*.

Dharma leading to rebirth where the result of an enjoined action performed in the previous life is bound to come is based on faith and belief. Here the link between an action performed and the result to come after a long gap is explained in terms of an unseen force or *apūrva*. *Apūrva* means that which did not exist before: the idea being that any action is undertaken for the achievement of a result which is not available at the time the action is performed. Thus the result of an action is a new product dependent upon the quality of an action done. Action and the result are therefore interlinked as cause and effect through that unseen force. That force will cease working only when the result is fully generated.[27] In this philosophy a kind of determinism is present because it seeks to explain any new occurrence in life in terms of the result of the forces generated by the past act done, not only in this life but even in lives before this.

There are different categories of forces generated by actions:, the forces which are still in store lying dormant, the forces which are still in the process of being generated by continuing actions, and the forces which are in the process of giving shape to the result. Likewise there are forces which are totally exhausted after completely presenting the result.[28]

It would be wrong to suppose that all actions alike produce results. There are mandatory actions depending upon the status and station of a person in life, which when performed do not give any result, but if not performed give adverse results. Similarly, there are actions depending upon special occasions which when performed give good results, but non-performance of them gives adverse results. There is a third category of actions which aim at expressly desired goals. These actions when performed would accomplish the goals; the non-performance has no effect, because the person has no desire for the goal.[29]

The Mīmāṁsā school has nothing significant to contribute to ontology. Kumārila holds that there are five categories, namely substance, quality, motion, universal and absence. Prabhākara does not recognize absence as a separate category; instead he adds four more to the list proposed by Kumārila, namely power, similarity, number and inherence. God is not recognized as a distinct factor for our knowledge of *dharma* based on the Vedas or for the explanation of ontology.

Right from the time of Śabara, Mīmāṁsā has taken up the task of providing intellectual and philosophical strong base for the forward march of the Brahmanical philosophy. In this process it had to meet vigorously the attacks on Brahmanical philosophy by Buddhist and Jaina thinkers. Kumārila's contributions in this respect are noteworthy inasmuch as it is through his and his followers' intellectual efforts that Brahmanism developed a new kind of philosophical vigour in response to challenges posed by Vasubandhu, Diṅnāga, Dharmakīrti, Śāntarakṣita and so on. It is only at a later stage that this task was taken up by Nyāya.

Another significant contribution made by the Mīmāṁsā has been in the field of ancient and medieval Hindu law. The entire *smṛti* literature bases its rules of interpretation of civil and criminal laws, procedure and applications on the Mīmāṁsā discussions embodied in its maxims or *nyāyas*, as they are called. Thus this system was guiding the secular, religious and philosophical destiny of Brahmanical India till the beginning of the present day.

THE VEDĀNTA PHILOSOPHY

The term 'Vedānta' means the end of the Veda or the culmination of the Vedic thinking or the goal towards which the Vedas lead, i.e. the *Brahman*, as set forth in the *Upaniṣads*. The *Vedāntasūtra* is called *Brahmasūtra* because it contains the exposition of the Upaniṣadic doctrine of *Brahman*; it is also called *Śārīrakasūtra* because it deals with that which resides in the body. The Vedānta is also known as Uttara Mīmāṁsā, in contrast to the Pūrva Mīmāṁsā of Jaimini. The subject matter of the Pūrva Mīmāṁsā is *dharma*, whereas the Uttara Mīmāṁsā in its *sūtras* gives a systematic account of various views contained in the *Upaniṣads*.

The *Upaniṣads* contain insightful statements of truths viewed from different standpoints. But these statements are not systematic in our sense of the term. Being the parts of the Veda, the *Upaniṣads* contain revealed, eternal truth; so it is necessary to present the teachings of the *Upaniṣads* in a systematic form. Bādarāyaṇa, the author of the *Vedāntasūtra*, attempts a kind of systematic presentation of thoughts revealed in the *Upaniṣads*. It enquires into the nature of *Brahman*, God, the world and soul, in the states of both bondage and liberation. It seeks to remove apparent contradictions in the Upaniṣadic doctrines, binding them together in a system and defending them against the attacks of opponents.

There are 555 *sūtras* in which the Vedānta system is developed. They in themselves are not clear; they require interpretation. Thus these are subjected to diverse interpretations which are very often opposed to each other. These *sūtras* have been commented upon by Śaṅkara, Bhāskara, Yādavaprakāśa, Rāmānuja, Mādhva, Vallabha and others whose commentaries are available to us. There were, however, many commentators before Śaṅkara, who are known only through references, such as Śuka, Upavarṣa, also known as Bodhāyana, Bhartṛprapañca and Bhartṛhari. The *sūtras* contain references to other teachers also who might have interpreted the *Upaniṣads* before Bādarāyaṇa. Bādarāyaṇa records in his *sūtras* differences of opinion about the characteristics of the liberated soul, the relation of the individual soul and so on. According to Āśmarathya the soul is neither different nor non-different from *Brahman*.

According to Auḍulomi the soul is altogether different from *Brahman* before it is liberated, but it merges in *Brahman* thereafter. According to Kārśakṛtsna, the soul is identical with *Brahman* in the final analysis. These various interpretations indicate that before Bādarāyaṇa there were considerable discussions on various aspects of *Upaniṣads*. Thus Bādarāyaṇa's work is the culmination of extensive discussions of the Upaniṣadic doctrines which flourished before him.[30]

According to tradition the *Vedāntasūtra* is attributed to Bādarāyaṇa. However, his name is mentioned in the *sūtras* in the third person, which, as has been the practice in India, is not uncommon and thus need not imply a different authorship. Bādarāyaṇa is identified with Vyāsa. Sometimes Vyāsa is called the author of these *sūtras*.[31]

Jaimini and Bādarāyaṇa, each of whom quotes both himself and the other, were most probably contemporaries. There are allusions to the views of Sāṅkhya, Vaiśeṣika, Jaina and Buddhist philosophers. The *Bhagavadgītā* is also referred to. Many names mentioned in the *sūtras* are also found in the *Śrautasūtras*: Āśmarathya, Bādari, Kṛṣṇājini, Kārśakṛtsna, Ātreya and Auḍulomi. *Garuḍapurāṇa*, *Padmapurāṇa*, *Manusmṛti* and *Harivaṁśa* contain references to it. In all probability the author Bādarāyaṇa must have flourished at any time between 500 BC and AD 200.[32]

The *Vedāntasūtra* has four chapters, each further divided into four parts. The *sūtras* in each part are arranged in groups called *adhikaraṇas*. The first chapter deals with the theory of *Brahman* as the basic reality. This chapter aims at *samanvaya* or reconciliation of different Vedic statements. There is an account of the nature of Brahman and its relation to the world and the individual soul. This is based on the experiences of the sages of the past, which are recorded in the *Upaniṣads*. Apparent contradictions in these experiences are sought to be resolved and reconciled in this chapter. The second chapter considers objections to the theory of *Brahman* and criticizes those theories which go against the Vedāntic position. This chapter also shows the nature of dependence of the world on *Brahman* as well as the evolution of the world from *Brahman* and devolution of it into him. There are discussions about the nature of soul, its attributes, its relation to *Brahman*, the body and *karma*. The third chapter discusses the ways and means of attaining knowledge of Brahman. There is an account of rebirth as well as some discussion of psychological and theological matters. The fourth chapter deals with the result of knowledge of *Brahman* and describes in detail the theory of the departure of the soul after death along the two paths of Gods and Fathers. It also deals with the nature of release from bondage from where there is no return (*mokṣa*).

In the opinion of Bādarāyaṇa the Veda is eternal and is the final authority. The ultimate truth cannot be known by means of reasoning and logic. According to him there are two sources of knowledge, *śruti* and *smṛti*, which roughly correspond to perception and inference. Inference is based upon perception, but the perception is self-revealed and self-evident. Thus for Bādarāyaṇa the *Upaniṣads* are the records of direct perception or *śruti*. The *Bhagavadgītā*, the *Mahābhārata* and the *Manusmṛti* are authentic sources of knowledge in so far as they depend on *śruti*. There are two spheres of existence: the thinkable and the unthinkable. The first is the sphere of *prakṛti* containing elements, mind, intellect and egoity, and the second is the sphere of *Brahman*, where *śruti* alone is the guide. Reasoning is guided by marks or *liṅgas*, but *Brahman* is free from all attributes, having no mark for the reasoning to comprehend it. Thus *Brahman* can be known only through devotion and meditation.

Puruṣa and *prakṛti* of the Sāṅkhya are regarded by Bādarāyaṇa as two modifications of one reality, *Brahman*. *Brahman* is the origin, support and end of the world as well as its efficient and material cause. The proof for the existence of *Brahman* is provided by *śruti* and the evidence of dreamless sleep. He is omniscient, omnipotent and the guide of the inner law. He is also the light of the soul. *Brahman* himself, being eternal, is the cause of the whole universe. After creating the elements constituting the universe he enters them and keeps on guiding them throughout. *Brahman* is the creator of all things by transforming himself into them. Bādarāyaṇa brings out that in an ultimate analysis there is an identity of cause and effect. Thus *Brahman* and the world are not different. Bādarāyaṇa does not have recourse to *avidyā* (ignorance) as Śaṅkara does later on. Other commentators view the world as the transformation of *Brahman*, meaning that finite things are real determinations or modifications of the substance of *Brahman*. The author of the *sūtra* also believes that the power of creation belongs to *Brahman*, who for his sport (*līlā*) develops himself into the world without undergoing any change. Bādarāyaṇa does not explain how this could happen. Thus from a logical and consistent philosophical point of view the position of Bādarāyaṇa is not substantiated.[33]

According to Bādarāyaṇa the soul is both intelligence and a knower; it is also an agent, without beginning, eternal; birth and death do not affect it. The individual soul is said to be atomic in size. *Brahman* exists in individual souls but without being influenced by the character of the individual souls. They differ in the same way as the light of the sun and the sun. The embodied soul acts and enjoys, acquires merits and demerits and is affected by pleasure and pain, while *Brahman* in it is free from all this. It is not clear in what manner the individual soul and *Brahman* are related. Bādarāyaṇa relates several opinions of ancient thinkers on this point, but he does not give his own view on it. It seems that according to Bādarāyaṇa the difference between *Brahman* and the individual soul is ultimate and continues even after the soul is released from bondage.

The world is due to the will of God and is his play or *līlā*, but the sufferings of individuals and their diversity in the world are not due to God; they are determined by the *karma* of the individuals. God is limited by the necessity of taking into account the *karma* done in previous life, but at the same time God is supposed to be the causal agent of right and wrong conduct. The *sūtra* does not attempt to give any cogent view on the contradiction involved in holding God to be both the agent of action and the individual soul undergoing suffering for action.

According to the *Vedāntasūtra* moral life leads to the knowledge of *Brahman*. Active service of God and renunciation of the world lead to supreme knowledge. Action done out of ignorance arrests knowledge of *Brahman*. Knowledge of *Brahman* gives liberation in this life (*jīvanamukti*). A liberated soul on attaining *mokṣa* gets exalted qualities as well as the power of infinite form. But none of them will get the powers of creating, preserving and destroying the universe which belong to God alone.[34]

PRE-ŚAṄKARA EXPOSITIONS OF THE ADVAITA PHILOSOPHY

Gauḍapāda[35] is one of the well-known exponents of the Advaita philosophy before Śaṅkara. In the Advaitic tradition he is known as the teacher of Śaṅkara's teacher Govindapāda. There is no certainty about his date. According to some of the works of Gauḍapāda known as *Gauḍapāda-kārikā* or the *Māṇḍūkya-kārikā*, consisting of four chapters, his period is later than the *Brahmasūtra*. But others hold that since there is no reference to the *Brahmasūtra* in this work and the ideas of the *Brahmasūtra* are also not reflected in it, it must be earlier than the *Brahmasūtra*. However, on the basis of the quotation of one *kārikā* in the Mādhyamika work of Bhāvaviveka, *Tarkajvālā,* Gauḍapāda may be earlier than AD 550. He is also known as the commentator on the *Uttaragītā*.

The *Kārikā* work of Gauḍapāda starts with a commentary on the *Māṇḍūkya Upaniṣad*. The first chapter, called *Āgama*, is basically an exposition of the mystical sound *Om* and its correlation with experience. Some scholars believe that this chapter is the basis for the reconstruction of the *Māṇḍūkya Upaniṣad* at a later date. In the second chapter, called *Vaitathya*, the world is analysed as appearance because it involves duality and contradictions. The third chapter is devoted to the establishment of the non-dual character of reality. The ideas of the third chapter are further elaborated in the fourth and last chapter, called *Alātaśānti*. As a stick burning at one end when whirled around produces the illusion of circular fire, so it is with the plurality of the world. It is full of the ideas developed in the Yogācāra Buddhist philosophy and mentions the name of the Buddha several times. It seems that in this work Gauḍapāda attempts to arrive at a synthesis of the doctrines developed in Mahāyāna Buddhism and the Upaniṣadic philosophy of the Advaita type.[36]

The basis of Gauḍapāda's attempted synthesis of Buddhism and Vedānta is the analysis of experience into waking, dreaming and dreamless sleep. In the spirit of Vasubandhu's *Vijñaptimātratā* theory he tries to put waking and dreaming experiences on the same level and concludes that as in dreams so in waking the objects seen are unreal. In the spirit of Nāgārjuna he further tries to find out the real nature of a thing or its identity (*svabhāva*) and concludes that nothing in the world of experience can really have this *svabhāva*.[37] But he parts company with Nāgārjuna when he asserts that such an identity would belong only to *ātman*, the basis of all experiences. Taking his stand on the immutable character of *ātman* he denies even the possibility of causation (*ajāti*). Production and destruction are, according to him, mere appearances. In reality nothing is produced or destroyed. From this point of view no distinction of any kind can be made between truth and falsity of experience, as it is a natural manifestation of *ātman*, which is given in almost objectless state of existence in dreamless sleep. But it would be wrong, according to Gauḍapāda, to equate a negative blank state of dreamless sleep with ever-conscious objectless pure state of cognition, which is real *ātman*, or the Upaniṣadic *Brahman*. Thus, we find a cogent and convincing attempt made by Gauḍapāda to combine the negative logic of the Mādhyamika, idealism based on the transitory nature of mind of the Vijñānavāda and the absolutistic idealism of the *Upaniṣads*. This is what he does by positing the fourth state of existence of pure consciousness, the *turīya*.

Bhartṛhari[38] is acknowledged as another important writer on Vedānta before Śaṅkara. But no work on Vedānta by Bhartṛhari is available to us. He is reported to have propounded an interpretation of Vedānta on the Advaitic line; but his Advaitism must have been different from what Śaṅkara projected afterwards. It is not possible to fix the exact date of Bhartṛhari, first, because there are at least two Bhartṛharis, if not three, known in the history of Indian literature, and second, because there are conflicting evidences available for his date. There is one Bhartṛhari who is a logician and grammarian and is the author of the *Vākyapadīya*, a work dealing mainly with the syntactical and semantic meaning of language. In all probability the author of the *Vākyapadīya* could also be a writer on Vedānta. Since his views are quoted in the works of Dignāga, a famous Buddhist logician, he must have flourished in the early part of the fifth century. There is another Bhartṛhari, the poet, whose three collections of one hundred stanzas each (*śatakatraya*) on different aspects of human life are available to us. According to the general opinion of historians the poet must be different from the philosopher-grammarian. Another Bhartṛhari figures in the legends associated with Gorakhanātha and others.

In his *Vākyapadīya* Bhartṛhari starts with the statement that *Brahman* is of the nature of word (*śabdabrahma*) and that the entire world is a manifestation of this *śabdabrahma*. The kind of manifestation that he is talking about is closer to the Sāṁkhya idea of modification (*pariṇāma*) than to the appearance idea of Śāṅkara Vedānta. This *Brahman* is one without a second, and with the help of his time-power (*kālaśakti*), which is non-different from him, he manifests different facets (*kalā*) of the multifarious world. Not only is *Brahman* manifesting himself ontologically; his world-nature is immanent in knowledge situation as well. Thus Bhartṛhari holds that no knowledge is possible which is devoid of language comprehension. Every knowledge is, as it were, impregnated by word. This view rules out the possibility of indeterminate knowledge and goes against the indescribability view of *Brahman*, which was one of the main planks of Śaṅkara's Advaita Vedānta.

Bhartṛhari's view of *Brahman* as word, in both its ontological and epistemological senses, is propounded in his theory of *sphoṭa*.[39] The language that we use, itself a manifestation of *Brahman*, is in essence one unanalysable mental or conceptual sentence unit, being given gross auditory form by the vocal chords. Sentence is the primary meaningful unit of language for the speaker, giving rise to unitary form of consciousness of meaning in the listener. Thus a sentence and what it means are only two aspects of the supreme manifestation of *Brahman* called *sphoṭa*.

Bhartṛhari's theory of *sphoṭa* or *Śabdabrahma* has become a target of attack by almost all Brahmanical, Buddhist and Jaina philosophers.[40] Even Śaṅkara did not approve of this theory, though he appreciated Bhartṛhari's efforts to establish non-dualistic absolutism. In his extensive exposition and argumentation Bhartṛhari takes into account the entire gamut of Vedic literature. He does not approve of that logic which is not guided by scriptures. He says that a logician not taking the support of scriptures is like a blind person who gropes with his hands to find his way. Such a person is bound to fall down. Thus for his philosophy the Veda is the main guide. In this enterprise Bhartṛhari not only shows his deep and extensive knowledge of the Vedas, the *Brāhmaṇas* and the *Upaniṣads* but also exhibits his close acquaintance with the Pūrva Mīmāṁsā system.

Bhartṛprapañca is known as another exponent of Vedānta before Śaṅkara. Unfortunately his works are not known; only stray references are available. He is an exponent of the philosophy of identity-in-difference. According to him *Brahman* is both one and dual. *Brahman* as the cause is different from *Brahman* as effect, but the effect *Brahman* subsequently returns back to the original *Brahman*. In this kind of interpretation the philosophy of Bhartṛprapañca can be supported by many statements in the *Upaniṣads* and the *Bhagavadgītā*. To some extent the Vedāntic philosophy of Rāmānuja also takes the help of the line of thought propounded by Bhartṛprapañca.

The relation between the Pūrva and Uttara Mīmāṁsās is a matter of controversy in the history of Indian philosophy. As has been stated earlier, both the schools embark on *jijñāsā* or enquiry, which according to the grammatical structure of the word means 'a desire to know' (*jñātumicchā*). It is pertinent to ask as to the genesis of this desire. For the Pūrva Mīmāṁsā it is not difficult to relate this desire to the study of the Vedas. According to the ancient tradition a child, at about the age of 8, is given initiation (*upanayana*) and sent to the school of a teacher for acquiring the knowledge of the Vedas. Kumārila thinks that the study of the Vedas is an injunction prescribed by the Vedas to everyone who is entitled to receive initiation. This is what is called *adhyayana vidhi* (injunction concerning the study).[41] Prabhākara, on the other hand, thinks that the injunction is applicable primarily to the teacher who imparts initiation. It is the duty of the teacher to teach because he is the person who knows the meaning and purport of this Vedic injunction, rather than that of the pupil as at the time of the initiation he is ignorant about the nature and importance of the Vedic injunction.[42] However, in either case a desire to know will arise when a person has already learned the text of Vedas and having learned it wants to know the meaning of the text. The desire to know is therefore related to the prior learning of the Vedas.

In the case of Pūrva Mīmāṁsā, as Kumārila puts it, in course of knowing what one ought to do (*dharma*) along with the path suggested by the Vedas, the Mīmaṁsā provides the necessary knowledge of how one should proceed (*iti kartavyatā*) to accomplish what one ought to do. Thus, Mīmāṁsā as a branch of knowledge has the clear purpose of providing instruments to achieve the result, as envisaged in the Vedas.[43] The word *Atha* at the beginning of the first *sūtra* of Jaimini's *MS* indicates the point suggested above.

In the case of the *Brahmasūtra* the word *Atha* at the beginning of the first *sūtra* has no such clear significance. The word cannot refer to any injunction as to the study or teaching of the Veda, as the same is already covered by the general injunction which includes, among others, the study of the *Upaniṣads*, which form an integral part of the Vedic literature. Here injunction, if any, would relate to the desire to know Brahman. Brahman is on the one hand a subject matter of the *Upaniṣads* and on the other hand, on the evidence of the *Upaniṣads* themselves, the innermost knower himself. This would then mean that Vedānta would aim at knowing the knower along the path envisaged by the *Upaniṣads*. Thus some may hold that the knowledge of *Brahman* does not require any special preparation except the general study of the Vedas. On the other hand it may also be said that because the *Upaniṣads* form the last part of the Vedas, preparation of the kind prescribed by the Pūrva Mīmāṁsā must be a necessary presupposition. Thus here the word *Atha* assumes a crucial significance. On the one hand it may mean 'after the study and practice of what the Pūrva Mīmāṁsā says', and on the other hand it may also assert the independent status of Vedānta, having no concern with the injunctions of the Vedas. The first approach leads to the interpretation of the *Brahmasūtra* as a later branch of knowledge, blending knowledge with action (*jñānakarmasamuccaya*). The second interpretation, disregarding injunction as a necessary pre-condition for the knowledge of *Brahman*, has given rise to the philosophy of knowledge for the sake of it (*jñānamārga*). Moreover, this divergence in the interpretation of the word *Atha* also has an implication for the status of Pūrva and Uttara Mīmāṁsās. If injunction is associated with knowledge, the *Brahmasūtra* will not enjoy the independent status of a text; it will be a continuation of the text initiated by Jaimini. In the case of the second interpretation, however, the *Brahmasūtra* will assume the independent status of a *śāstra*, though allied to the Pūrva Mīmāṁsā in matters of methodology and the technique of the interpretation of Vedic text.

NOTES

1 'Athāto dharma-jijñāsā', *Mīmāṁsāsūtra* (*MS*) 1.1.1.
2 'Athāto Brahma-jijñāsā', *Brahmasūtra* (*BS*) 1.1.1.
3 Codanā-lakṣaṇa'rtha dharmaḥ, *MS* 2.
4 Janmādyasya yataḥ, *BS* 1.1.2.

5 See Hajime Nakamura, *A History of Early Vedānta Philosophy*, part I (Delhi, 1985), p. 423.
6 This part is called *Devatā-kāṇḍa* or *Saṁkarṣaṇa-kāṇḍa*.
7 *MS* has been translated into English by M. L. Sandal in *Sacred Books of the Hindus Series*, vol. I.
8 See V. A. Ramaswami Sastri, Old Vṛttikāras on the Pūrva-Mīmāṁsā-Sūtras, *Indian Historical Quarterly* Vol X (1934), pp. 449ff.
9 For a detailed discussion on historical issues concerning Prabhākara and Kumārila, see C. Kunhan Raja, Introduction to *Ślokavārtikavyākhyā Tātpar aṭīkā*, ed. S. K. Ramanatha Sastri (Madras, 1971).
10 *MS* 1.2, 1–53.
11 Cf. Gaurinath Sastri, *The Philosophy of Word and Meaning* (Calcutta, 1959), pp. 172–287.
12 R. C. Pandeya, *The Problem of Meaning in Indian Philosophy* (Delhi: Motilal Banarsidass 1963), ch. 8, pp. 193ff.
13 ibid., pp. 171–87.
14 For a detailed discussion on the nature of word see Gaurinath Sastri, op. cit., pp. 102–35.
15 *Śabara, Bhāṣya* on *MS* 1.1, section 5.
16 Jitendranath Mohanty, *Gaṅgeśa's Theory of Truth* (Santiniketan, 1966), Introduction.
17 Ganganathan Jha, *The Prabhākara School of Pūrva Mīmāṁsā* (Benares Hindu University, 1918) pp. 28ff.
18 ibid., pp. 28–9.
19 Govardhan P. Bhatt, *The Basic Ways of Knowing* (Delhi: Motilal Benarsidass 1989), pp. 96ff.
20 Śalikanātha, *Ṛjuvimalā* (Commentary on *Bṛhatī*) (Madras, 1934), p. 79.
21 Pārthasārathi Miśra, *Nyāyaratnākara* (Commentary on Kumārila *Ślokavārtika*), Śūnyavāda section, kārikā 72.
22 Kumārila, *Ślokavārtika*, Śūnyavāda section.
23 Bhatt, op. cit., pp. 145ff.
24 Kumārila, op. cit., Anumāna section.
25 Bhatt, op. cit., part II.
26 See *MS* 1. 1. 2 and Śabara *Bhāṣya* on it.
27 Kumārila, *Tantravārtika* (Poona, 1929), pp. 364–5.
28 Laugākṣi Bhāskara, *Arthasaṁgraha*, ed. and trans. A. B. Gajendrogadkar and R. D. Karmakar (Delhi, 1984).
29 ibid.
30 See Nakamura, op. cit., pp. 369–90.
31 However, Prof. Nakamura holds that Bādarāyaṇa and Vyāsa were different persons and that Bādarāyaṇa is not the original author of *VS*.
32 S. Radhakrishnan, *Indian Philosophy*, vol. II.
33 ibid.
34 For a detailed account of the *Vedāntasūtra* see Nakamura, op. cit., pp. 425–529.
35 For an extensive discussion on Gauḍapāda, his life, work and philosophy see Pandit Vidhushekhar Bhattacharya, *Āgama-śāstra* (University of Calcutta, 1943).
36 For a comprehensive discussion on the relation between Vedānta and Mahāyāna Buddhism see T. R. V. Murti, *The Central Philosophy of Buddhism* 2nd edn (London: Allen & Unwin 1960); R. C. Pandeya, *Indian Studies in Philosophy* (Delhi, 1977).
37 On Nāgārjuna's treatment of the concept of *svabhāva* see R. C. Pandeya and Manju, *Nāgārjuna's Philosophy of No-Identity* (Delhi, 1991).
38 For an extensive account of Bhartṛhari see K. A. Subramania Iyer, *Bhartṛhari* (University of Poona, 1969).

39 For a detailed exposition of the *sphoṭa* theory see Pandeya, op. cit.; Gaurinath Sastri, op. cit., pp. 102–5.
40 Pandeya (1963), op. cit., pp. 267–77.
41 Kumārila, *Ślokavārtika*, section I.
42 Śālikanātha, *Prakaraṇa-pancikā* (Varanasi, 1903, ch. 1).
43 Kumārila, *Ślokavārtika*, section I.

FURTHER READING

Bādarāyaṇa (1890, 1896) *Vedānta Sūtras*, translated by George Thibaut, *The Vedānta Sūtras with the Commentary by Śaṅkarācārya*, Sacred Books of the East Series, Vols XXXIV and XXXVIII, Oxford, The Clarendon Press.

Dwivedi, R.C. (ed) (1994), *Studies in Mīmāṁsā*, Delhi, Motilal Banarsidass.

Govindacarya, Alkondavilli (tr.) (1898) *Śrī Bhagavad-gītā with Śrī Rāmānujāchārya's Visishtādvaita Commentary*, Madras, Vaijayanti Press.

Hiriyanna, M. (1949) *Essentials of Indian Philosophy*, London, George Allen & Unwin, Chapters VI–VIII

Hiriyanna, M. (1932) *Outlines of Indian Philosophy*, London, Unwin Brothers, Chapters XII–XIV

Jaimini, (1933, 1934, 1936) *Mīmāṁsā Sūtra*, with commentary of Śabara, English translation, *Śabara-Bhāṣya*, by Ganganatha Jha, Gaekwad's Oriental Series, Vols LXVI, LXX, LXXIII, Baroda, Oriental Institute.

Jha, Ganganatha (1918) *The Prabhākara School of Pūrva Mīmāṁsā*, Indian Thought Series, No. VIII, Benares, Benares Hindu University.

Kumārila Bhatta (1909) *Ślokavārtika*, translated by Ganganatha Jha, Calcutta, Asiatic Society of Bengal.

Madhva (1936) *Brahma-sūtra-bhāṣya*, translated by S Subba Rao, *Vedanta-sutras with the Commentary by Sri Madhwacharya*, Tirupati, Sri Vyasa Press, 2nd edition.

Mahadeva Sastri, Alladi (trs) (1897), *The Bhagavad-gītā with the Commentary of Shri Shaṅkarāchārya*, Madras, Minerva Press.

Nakamura, Hajime (1985) *A History of Early Vedanta Philosophy*, Delhi, Motilal Banarsidass.

Radhakrishnan, S (1929) *Indian Philosophy*, Second Edition, London, George Allen & Unwin, Volume II, Chapters VI–IX

Rāmānuja (1904) *Śrī-bhāṣya*, translated by George Thibaut, *The Vedānta Sūtras with the Commentary of Rāmānuga*, Sacred Books of the East Series, Vol XL VIII, Oxford, The Clarendon Press.

Subba Rao, S (tr.) (1906) *The Bhagavad-gītā (Translation and Commentaries in English according to Sri Madhwacharya's Bhasya)*, Madras, Minerva Press.

10

ŚAṄKARĀCĀRYA

Brian Carr

ŚAṄKARA AND HIS TEXTS[1]

Śaṅkarācārya (or Master Śaṅkara) lived at a time when Hinduism was once more gaining ascendancy over Buddhism in India, and he is credited with a major role in that revival. Born in Kaladi in modern Kerala, Śaṅkara lived for only thirty-two years, but – if tradition is in any way a reliable guide – managed to produce in that short life a vast corpus of writings as well as founding important centres of Hindu learning in the four corners of India.

There are still no universally agreed dates for Śaṅkara's life, but modern scholarship places him between the start of the eighth century and the start of the ninth.[2] Moreover, the authenticity of the works which tradition has ascribed to him is a matter of great contemporary debate. As a member of the Vedānta school of Hinduism Śaṅkara would have found his inspiration in the *Upaniṣads*, in the *Bhagavadgītā* and in the *sūtra* written by Bādarāyaṇa, the *Brahmasūtra* or *Vedantasūtra* (the date of composition of this work is unknown, but usually placed sometime between 200 BC and AD 400). These three sources are known as the *prasthāna-traya*, or triple canon of the Vedānta school. Karl Potter, utilizing the recent scholarship of Paul Hacker and others, suggests that at least the commentaries on the *Bṛhadāraṇyaka Upaniṣad* and the *Chāndogya Upaniṣad* might be counted as authentic works of the author of the commentaries on the *Bhagavadgītā* and the *Brahmasūtra*. But by tradition, Śaṅkara also composed commentaries on all the major *Upaniṣads*, most of the minor *Upaniṣads*, on the *Bhagadvadgītā* and on the *Brahmasūtra*, and indeed composed a number of other works. What follows is largely based on the *Brahmasūtrabhāṣya*, Śaṅkara's commentary on Bādarāyaṇa's *sūtra*, which is of prime importance in the Indian philosophical tradition.

The role of the *Brahmasūtrabhāṣya* in that tradition is somewhat akin to the role of Kant's *Critique of Pure Reason* in western philosophy, serving as a watershed for philosophical enquiry and often as a way of mapping the shortcomings of earlier thinkers. Indeed, there are certain obvious similarities between the philosophies of Śaṅkara and of Kant which have sometimes tended to blind enthusiasts to their differences. Many standard works on Indian philosophy – for example Sharma's *A Critical Survey of Indian Philosophy*, Hiriyanna's *Essentials of Indian Philosophy* and *Outlines of Indian Philosophy*, and Radhakrishnan's two-volume *Indian Philosophy*[3] – manifest not only an obvious commitment to the main theses of Śaṅkara's position, but also a tendency to expound Śaṅkara in Kantian terminology. We should remember that Kant prohibited any claim about the nature of the noumenon, not because of its essential oneness but because we could have no knowledge of it; and Śaṅkara on the contrary emphasizes the knowledge we can have of *Brahman*, for this is his central theme.

Śaṅkara's interpretation of the essence of the *Bhagavadgītā* puts the emphasis on *jñāna yoga*, as opposed to *karma yoga* or *bhakti yoga*, and the legitimacy of such an interpretation is perhaps well founded on the ambiguities and rich complexities of that work. With the *Brahmasūtra* of Bādarāyaṇa we are faced with other problems, for that text is terse and opaque and clearly in need of exposition, explanation and defence. Thibaut makes a reasonable case for the thesis that Rāmānuja's commentary is closer to the intent of Bādarāyaṇa than Śaṅkara's, with Śaṅkara forcing interpretation beyond the obvious.[4] Be that as it may, Śaṅkara's commentary stands as a work of impressively coherent and strikingly ambitious metaphysics and epistemology. That it ultimately fails – even in its own terms – to provide a solution to all intellectual and religious questions is hardly a charge uniquely against Śaṅkara.

The story of the life of Śaṅkara is obscured by the mists of time. This is not inconsistent, of course, with a very rich and detailed tale available to those who ally themselves to the philosophy of Śaṅkarācārya.

WHAT IS OUR KNOWLEDGE OF *BRAHMAN* (REALITY)?

Śaṅkara's philosophy can be approached from two directions, both of which he adopts in the *Brahmasūtrabhāṣya* (*BSB*). The first concerns his emphasis on the texts of the Vedic tradition, and in particular the *Upaniṣads*. This emphasis, where Śaṅkara presents himself as offering a philosophy which is not only consistent with such texts but also interpretative of them, is what places Śaṅkara within the Vedānta tradition. The second approach concerns his critical assaults on the other systems of thought – both orthodox and non-orthodox – carried through with a combination of corrections to their scriptural interpretations and scripturally independent assessments of their coherence. It would be a mistake, nevertheless, to assume that it is only when Śaṅkara takes this second approach of critical demolition of opposing schools that he merits the title of original and outstanding thinker. His interpretation of the scriptural texts, on the contrary, contains much original thought and undoubtedly contentious rendering of their obscurities. In this and the following section we will concentrate of the first approach; the second approach will be explored later.

The *Upaniṣads* are discussions or contemplations of the nature of *Brahman*, Reality. It is Śaṅkara's most striking thesis that they constitute the *only* source of knowledge of *Brahman* available to those who aspire to it, for the normal means of gaining knowledge (perception, inference and so on) are applicable only within the empirical field of ordinary experience. The *Upaniṣads* contain the wisdom of those who have achieved a direct knowledge of *Brahman*. Śaṅkara sees no inconsistency here with imputing their origin to *Brahman* itself, for he defines *Brahman* as:

> That omniscient and omnipotent source . . . from which occur the birth, continuance, and dissolution of this universe that is manifested through name and form, that is associated with diverse agents and experiences, that provides the support for actions and results, having well-regulated space, time, and causation, and that defies all thoughts about the real nature of its creation.
>
> (*BSB*, p. 14)[5]

The *Upaniṣads* serve the function of providing direction for the full understanding and realization of this fact. Since *Brahman* is (though its efficient and material cause) so unlike the empirical world, with its complexity of objects, properties and changes through time, no access can be gained to *Brahman* through the use of sense-perception or of reasoning from such perception (see *BSB* I.i.3–4)[6]

Yet even without the *Upaniṣads* we are, every one of us, directly aware of *Brahman* in a limited way. Each of us is aware of the existence of consciousness within ourselves:

> The Self [*Brahman*] is not absolutely beyond apprehension, because It is apprehended as the content of the concept 'I'; and because the Self, opposed to the non-Self, is well known in the world as an immediately perceived (i.e. self-revealing) entity.
>
> (*BSB*, p. 3)

This awareness, however, does not involve a proper appreciation of the nature of consciousness, and therefore we must resort to the *Upaniṣads*.

Śaṅkara emphasizes, therefore, the role of meditation in moving from the limited and distorted awareness of consciousness to its full appreciation. But this must be understood in a philosophical sense, rather than in the sense usually meant in the Indian tradition. The latter kind of meditation – *upāsanā* as specified in the Vedic texts – focuses on one of the various properties of what Śaṅkara calls 'Qualified Reality' (*Saguṇa Brahman*), *Brahman* manifested, for example, as *prāṇa* (vital force), *jyotir* (light), *pañcāgni* (the five fires), or even on all taken together as *Īśvara* (God). These are but various conceptions of *Saguṇa Brahman* (*vijñānas*). When Śaṅkara speaks of meditation in the context of the *Brahmasūtrabhāṣya* itself he is implying a serious consideration of their import, a philosophical meditation on 'Unqualified Reality' (*Nirguṇa Brahman*). And such indeed is the nature of Śaṅkara's own text: it has the vital practical function of helping us to grasp the full import of the *Upaniṣads* and thereby move from our limited knowledge of the existence of consciousness within ourselves to an appreciation of the true nature of *Nirguṇa Brahman*.

The real nature of unconditioned *Nirguṇa Brahman* is distinguished from conditioned *Saguṇa Brahman* in *BSB* III.ii.11–22. *Nirguṇa Brahman* is impartite pure consciousness, bliss itself, the omnipresent Self of all. (In later Advaita texts, *Nirguṇa Brahman* is said to be 'being, consciousness, bliss' – *saccidānanda*.) But this does not mean that it has three distinct properties, for *Nirguṇa Brahman* is without distinctions within itself and without relation to any other thing (*BSB* III.ii.16). The apparently individual consciousness of which we are in ordinary life dimly aware is identical with this *Brahman*. 'Thou art that' (*Chāndogya Upaniṣad* VI.viii.7), 'I am Brahman' (*Bṛhadāraṇyaka Upaniṣad* I.iv.10), 'This Self is Brahman' (*Bṛhadāraṇyaka Upaniṣad* II.v.19) – all these passages teach this identity. The most we can impute to *Nirguṇa Brahman* by way of characteristics is its utter unity. It is *neti-neti* (not this, not that):

> Now therefore the description (of Brahman): Not so, not so. Because there is no other and more appropriate description than this 'Not so, not so'.
>
> (*BSB* p. 624, quoting *Bṛhadāraṇyaka Upaniṣad* II.iii.6)

Finally, knowledge of the true nature of *Nirguṇa Brahman* culminates in a direct experience of it, and one who has so experienced *Brahman* becomes an enlightened being (*jīvanmukta*) who achieves liberation (*mokṣa*) from ordinary experience and from rebirth (*saṁsāra*). (*BSB* IV.i.13).

Before leaving this brief exposition of Śaṅkara's account of our knowledge of *Brahman*, it is pertinent to ask (as in western discussions of God's attributes) whether those attributes ascribed to *Nirguṇa Brahman* have any similarity to those normally ascribed to human beings. Śaṅkara, of course, states that *Nirguṇa Brahman* is pure consciousness, but what is it conscious *of*? It is not self-aware, nor is there anything other than itself to be aware of, so we can conclude that it is utterly different from human consciousness. And what of bliss (*ānanda*), which Śaṅkara also ascribes to *Nirguṇa Brahman*? For humans, pleasure is a feeling accompanying activities and perceptions, yet for *Nirguṇa Brahman* there are no such activities or perceptions. Bliss must therefore be utterly different in the two cases.

Moreover, is there not an inconsistency in Śaṅkara's ascription of *any* attributes whatever to *Nirguṇa Brahman* – knowledge, intellect, consciousness, bliss, creatorship and so on? Some of those attributes can plausibly be taken as being ascribed to *Saguṇa Brahman* as God, so no inconsistency will then arise. But what of consciousness itself, bliss itself – whatever they come to as attributes of *Nirguṇa Brahman*?

Śaṅkara's thesis, that the *Upaniṣads* provide the only route to a full and proper knowledge of the nature of *Brahman*, clearly raises pressing questions. How, if this is so, can the authors of the *Upaniṣads* have come across that knowledge independently? Why, if this is so, do we need Śaṅkara himself to lead us through the message of those texts with the aid of the *Brahmasūtrabhāṣya*? And surely the *Upaniṣads* are thereby charged with an obscurity which needs all the normal means of acquiring knowledge from an authoritative source to overcome: we need to infer their meaning from their analogies and comparisons, and we need an independent source to validate their message when so interpreted. Śaṅkara, of course, believes that a final realization of the truth about Reality will itself do this validating; but the *Upaniṣads* as interpreted for us by Śaṅkara must until that time be taken on trust.

WHAT IS OUR 'KNOWLEDGE' OF SOUL AND NATURE?

Since *Nirguṇa Brahman* is pure, undifferentiated consciousness, it follows that our ordinary experience of the natural world is but mere appearance. Following a well-established criterion of validity, Śaṅkara sees this ordinary experience as acceptable – properly taken to be valid knowledge – until it is finally sublated (undermined) by a direct experience of *Nirguṇa Brahman* itself. At that moment the knower, through his realization of the true *Nirguṇa Brahman*, will have achieved the insight leading to the cessation of rebirth (*saṁsāra*) and so will have achieved *mokṣa*.

Śaṅkara needs to explain how *Brahman* can be manifested to us as something which it is not. For our ordinary experience, involving both an awareness of the individuality of our selves as conscious beings and an awareness of the complex physical world of objects undergoing cause and effect interactions in a spatial and temporal public world, is by definition something more objective than a mere phantasm or dream.

That something essentially singular can appear as multiple Śaṅkara illustrates with various analogies. One of these, the 'space in the pot' analogy, occurs at *BSB* I.i.5 (p. 51):

> Really speaking, there is no soul under bondage and different from God. Still just like the association of space with such conditioning factors as pots, jars, caves of mountains, etc., it is assumed that God has association with such limiting adjuncts as body, etc. And people are seen to use words and ideas based on that association, as for instance, 'The space in a pot' . . . though these are non-different from space. . . . Similarly in the case under consideration, the idea of difference of God and a transmigrating soul is false, it having been created by non-discrimination (i.e. ignorance) which causes the ascription of the limiting adjuncts – body and the rest.

Another analogy, of the 'sun on water', is found at *BSB* III.ii.19 (p. 615):

> Since the Self is by nature Consciousness Itself, distinctionless, beyond speech and mind, and can be taught by way of negating other things, hence in the scriptures dealing with liberation an illustration is cited by saying that it is 'like the sun reflected in water' . . . as is done in such texts, 'As this luminous sun, though one in itself, becomes multifarious owing to its entry into water divided by different pots, similarly this Deity, the birthless self-effulgent Self, though one, seems to be diversified owing to Its entry into the different bodies, constituting Its limiting adjuncts.'

But what is the mechanism by which such false appearance (from the standpoint of a direct knowledge of *Brahman*) comes about? In giving his explanation, Śaṅkara gives most prominence to the question of how *Brahman* appears to each of us as an individual *ātman*, saying hardly enough about the other pressing question of how *Brahman* appears falsely as the public natural world. This fits in, of course, with Śaṅkara's primary emphasis on changing the appreciation we have of the nature of our selves as conscious beings, yet leaves us to work out the details of the wider picture.

The mechanism of false appearance owes much to the Mīmāṁsā philosopher Prabhākara, whose extreme empiricist model of illusion Śaṅkara introduces in the first few pages of the *Brahmasūtrabhāṣya*. According to Prabhākara, we (falsely) see a rope as a snake because we are misled by the similarity of the rope and the snake into mixing up the perceived rope and the remembered snake. Both rope and snake are real objects, the one perceived and the other remembered, so Prabhākara avoids a wholly illusory private snake object in the mind of the experiencer. Prabhākara is therefore propounding an empiricist direct realist account of false appearance.[7]

In Śaṅkara's adaptation this theory is pressed into service to construct a very substantial metaphysical move. The opening preamble to *BSB* I.i.1 elaborates the theme that our 'knowledge' of our individual selves, embodied in the natural world of experience, is the outcome of a mixing up of our awareness of consciousness (our limited experience of *Brahman*) with what does not belong to consciousness. This latter is called a 'limiting adjunct' (*upādhi* – see *BSB* I.i.4 and III.ii.14–15), which by a false *superimposition* (*adhyāsa*) becomes confused with consciousness. And this confusion is the outcome of our ignorance (*avidyā*) of the true nature of *Brahman*:

> the superimposition of the object, referable through the concept 'you', and its attributes on the subject that is conscious by nature and is referable through the concept 'we' (should be impossible), and contrariwise the superimposition of the subject and its attributes on the object should be impossible. Nevertheless, owing to an absence of discrimination between these attributes, as also between substances, which are absolutely disparate, there continues a natural human behaviour based on self-identification in the form 'I am this' or 'This is mine.'
>
> (*BSB*, p. 1)

And Śaṅkara uses an analogy of a transparent crystal and a flower standing behind it to illustrate the false superimposition on to consciousness of the limiting adjuncts of ordinary experience:

> Before the dawn of discriminating knowledge, the individual soul's nature of Consciousness, expressing through seeing etc., remains mixed up as it were, with the body, senses, mind, intellect, sense-objects, and sorrow and happiness. Just as before the perception of distinction, the transparent whiteness, constituting the real nature of a crystal, remains indistinguishable, as it were, from red, blue, and other conditioning factors.
>
> (*BSB* I.iii.19 (p. 193))

A sublation (*bādha*) of this superimposition comes about when ignorance is replaced by knowledge (*vidyā*) of *Nirguṇa Brahman*, the pure, immediate consciousness (*cit, anubhava*) of *Brahman* itself:

> After the unreal aspect of the individual being, conjured up by ignorance etc., tainted by many such defects as agentship, experiencership, love, hatred, etc., and subject to many evils, has been eliminated, the opposite aspect, viz. the reality that is the supreme Lord, possessed of the characteristics of freedom from sin and so on, becomes revealed, just as the rope etc. are revealed after eliminating the snake etc. (superimposed on them through error).
>
> (*BSB* I.iii.19 (p. 195))

Śaṅkara's adaptation of Prabhākara's theory of false appearance is an outstandingly ambitious metaphysical theory, yet one which provides him with an essentially simple key for interpreting the obscure and diverse claims contained in the *Upaniṣads*. Yet it may fairly be said to be oversimplistic in that it leaves too many questions unanswered. One clear difference with Prabhākara's original theory is that in Śaṅkara's hands we no longer have a commitment to an empiricist direct realism. We have, instead, a treatment of the objects of experience as almost completely (except for consciousness) unreal.

Secondly, in Prabhākara's theory the directly experienced object (the rope) is conflated with a remembered object (the snake), yet in Śaṅkara's adaptation the directly experienced (consciousness) is conflated with something which *itself* is the outcome of another act of superimposition upon *Nirguṇa Brahman* – namely the complexities of the physical world. The superimposition theory at the very least needs a double application to achieve Śaṅkara's ends, and it is far from obvious that the mechanisms will work in the same way in both applications. Indeed, the rope/snake and shell/flower models of false identification clearly invite distinctions and hence constitute a complication to Śaṅkara's theory.

Moreover, where is the *source* of the *avidyā*, the individual's ignorance which is the root cause of *saṁsāra*? Once ignorance has led to the superimpositions producing our false awareness of consciousness through various limiting adjuncts, it can be allowed to continue to produce its effects through lives involving death and rebirth as the *saṁsāra* theory requires, assuming of course that the mechanisms of this causal chain can be worked out satisfactorily. But where does the original *avidyā* spring from?

Śaṅkara hesitatingly invokes a theory of *Māyā*, a *Saguṇa Brahman* conception of a force of illusion which has its basis somehow in *Nirguṇa Brahman* itself and is the origin of the individual's *avidyā* and so the individual's bondage to the physical world in *saṁsāra*:

> The supreme Lord is but one – unchanging, eternal, absolute Consciousness; but like a magician. He appears diversely through Maya, otherwise known as *Avidyā* (ignorance).
>
> (*BSB* I.iii.19 (p. 195))

And Śaṅkara compounds the obscurity of this *Māyā* theory by commiting himself to the thesis that the whole creation of the world of ordinary experience is as it were a game, a sport, on the part of *Brahman*:

> As in the world it is seen that though a king . . . who has got all his desires fulfilled, may still, without any aim in view, indulge in activities in the form of sports and pastimes, as a sort of diversion . . . so also God can have activities of the nature of mere pastime out of His spontaneity without any extraneous motive.
>
> (*BSB* II.i.33 (p. 361))

It must be pointed out, nevertheless, that Śaṅkara is clearly uncomfortable with this theory of *Māyā*, for it is after all applicable only at the level of *Saguṇa Brahman*. He immediately appends a disclaimer:

> it must not be forgotten that such a text is valid within the range of activities concerned with name and form called up by ignorance.
>
> (ibid.)

The two doctrines together, of *Māyā* and of individual *avidyā*, cosmic and individual ignorance, obviously confuse the issue of responsibility and add little clarification if any to the compounded double superimpositions which Śaṅkara wants to read into our limited awareness of consciousness. If *Nirguṇa Brahman* as the one Self (*Ātman*) has in some way the power of creating illusion, perhaps that power should be allowed in a suitably limited fashion to the individual self (*ātman*) which after all is but a reflection of It. Yet we saw at the end of the last section that the attributes of *Nirguṇa Brahman* can have little comparability to those of ordinary human consciousness, and that point must be extended to encompass too the notions of *Māyā* and *avidyā*.

ŚAṄKARA'S REFUTATION OF SĀṄKHYA-YOGA DUALISM

Śaṅkara devotes a good deal of space in the *Brahmasūtrabhāṣya* to refuting the views of the Saṅkhya-Yoga orthodox schools, particularly the metaphysical dualism of the Sāṅkhya. In many ways, this school holds views which come close to those of Śaṅkara himself – not surprisingly since it, too, bases its claims on what it finds in the Vedas and *Upaniṣads*. The most fundamental difference between Śaṅkara and the Sāṅkhya school is that the latter, rightly finding enormous obscurities in those texts as well as wishing to fill out the metaphysical and soteriological story, readily resorts to *inference* for its account of reality. Śaṅkara, as we saw above, has substantial reservations about the use of inference to achieve a knowledge of *Brahman*, taking the *Upaniṣads* to be its only proper source.

Śaṅkara therefore sees Sāṅkhya philosophy as not only mistaken but also, because of its closeness to his own, a dangerous variation on the truth. His vehement opposition to Sāṅkhya is well expressed in some biting opening remarks under *BSB* II.ii.1:

> there are some people of dull intellect who on noticing that the great scriptures of the Sankhyas and others are accepted by the honoured ones and that they proceed under the plea of bestowing the right knowledge, may conclude that these too are to be accepted as a means to right knowledge. Besides, they may have faith in these, since there is a possibility of weight of reasoning and since they are spoken by omniscient people. Hence this effort is being made to expose their hollowness.

Śaṅkara's attack on Sāṅkhya is multidimensional. Apart from arguing at some considerable length (beginning under *BSB* II.i.5) that the Śāṅkhya school has misinterpreted the import of various terms in the *Upaniṣads* (particularly concerning reference to the cause of the world), he tries to prove by arguments largely independent of reliance on these scriptures (a) that the Sāṅkhya view of causation, seeing effects as pre-existing potentially in their causes, does not go far enough and (b) that the Sāṅkhya use of inference by analogy is indefensible, and that its dualism is unproven and fundamentally incoherent. These two important arguments will be discussed in the following two subsections.

(a) The identity of cause and effect

According to Śaṅkara's interpretation of the *Upaniṣads, Brahman* is the (efficient and material) cause of the complex world of physical objects and their properties, properties which are changing and evolving and of which the individual soul or *ātman* has perceptual knowledge. But this must, on his interpretation, be handled very carefully indeed, for *Brahman* is at the same time the one real entity which is unchanging, unevolving and without diversity within itself. How can *Brahman* therefore be the cause of something other than itself? How can the diverse world of physical objects exist as well as *Brahman*? How can unity in *Brahman* exist alongside diversity in the physical world?

The answer, according to Śaṅkara, is that there is no *real* distinction to be drawn between *Brahman* and its creation. Śaṅkara proposes a quite general theory of causation as the *apparent* transformation of a cause into its effects (*vivartavāda*), a theory opposed to one of *real* transformation (*pariṇāmavāda*). And applying this general theory to the case (the one real case) of *Brahman* as the cause of the complex physical world, Śaṅkara holds that *Brahman* merely appears to evolve into that world. The appearance has its seat in our ignorance of the true nature of *Brahman*, its unity and utter unchanging simplicity as pure consciousness.

Modifications of substance have their origin in language, according to *Chāndogya Upaniṣad* VI.i.4: 'a modification has speech as its origin and exists only in name'. Śaṅkara explains that this is an analogy for *Brahman* and its apparent modifications:

> A modification, e.g. a pot, plate, or jar, etc. originates from speech alone that makes it current by announcing, 'It exists'. But speaking from the standpoint of the basic substance,

no modification exists as such (apart from the clay). It has existence only in name and it is unreal.

(*BSB* II.i.14)

One alternative to Śaṅkara's thesis of the reality of what is non-diverse and the merely apparent nature of the diverse is the thesis that *Brahman* has both unity and diversity. This, the *bhedābheda* thesis, was indeed adopted by some earlier Vedānta commentators (for example Bhartṛprapañca) in an attempt to make sense of the creation of the world by *Brahman*. On this view, *Brahman* as cause of the world is non-complex, a unity just as Śaṅkara supposes; but it is complex in that its effect is complex. By treating the effect as only an *apparent* modification of the cause Śaṅkara is able to avoid the inconsistency involved in ascribing both unity and diversity equally to *Brahman*.

Yet in this section of the *Brahmasūtrabhāṣya* (II.ii.14–20) Śaṅkara is engaging not only with other Vendānta philosophers but also, and more importantly, with the Sāṅkhya theses that the material cause of the physical world is insentient *prakṛti* and that *prakṛti* really evolves from a state of equipoise between the three *guṇas* into the diverse world which we perceive. Śaṅkara's opposition to the Sāṅkhyan *pariṇāmavāda* theory of real evolution goes beyond a straightforward appeal to scriptural interpretation and involves an independent analysis of the cause–effect relation.

To understand Śaṅkara's criticism of the Sāṅkhya theory we have first to note that in this passage he is dealing only with the *material* cause of the world: he will take up the question of the *efficient* cause of world in a later passage (see subsection (b) below). The analogies which he uses make this plain. Under *BSB* II.i.19 he writes:

> A piece of rolled up cloth is not recognised . . . but when it is spread out, its real nature becomes revealed through that spreading . . . Or even though it is cognized as cloth when remaining rolled up, its length and breadth are not definitely known . . . And yet it is never known to be something other than the rolled up piece of cloth. Similarly, such products as the cloth etc. are unmanifest so long as they remain latent in their causes, viz yarns etc.; but they are known distinctly when they become manifest as a result of the activity of such causal agents as the shuttle, loom, weaver etc.

These analogies would in fact be acceptable to the Sāṅkhya school, for they too treat the effect as the manifestation of what exists already potentially in the material cause. It is possible, on this model, to reject as irrelevant the efficient causal relation between fire and smoke, or between potter and pot. The relevant comparisons are with clay and the pot, and with yarn and the cloth.

But another point which must be grasped to understand Śaṅkara's opposition to Saṅkhya is that both his and their theories share even more in common than the analogies. In essence, Śaṅkara thinks that the rival theory makes a first good move, but does not go far enough. The first move is (i) to see that the effect already *pre-exists* in some way in the material cause, before it becomes manifest through the intervention of some efficient cause; the second move is (ii) to see that the effect is in fact *identical* with its material cause. The argument for Śaṅkara's conclusion comes under *BSB* II.ii.18.

Śaṅkara establishes (i) by a consideration familiar in Sāṅkhya texts. Why, he asks, is it possible to produce a given effect from only a particular material cause? Why are curds produced only from milk, or a pot from clay?

> If everything is to be equally non-existent everywhere before creation, why should curds be produced from milk alone and not from clay; and why should a pot come out of clay and not out of milk?
>
> (*BSB*, p. 339)

We need to say that milk has a special *potency* for curd, or equivalently that the curds are *latent* in milk. Curds therefore pre-exist in a latent form which is peculiarly suited to be their material cause. Moreover, we cannot say that the *potency* is a separate existence from either the milk or the curds: if milk exists independently of the potency, or the potency exists independently of the curds, why should the milk have a special tendency to give rise to that potency and no other, or the potency a special tendency to give rise to the curds and not something else? The existence of the milk, the potency and the curds must be an intimate one: 'the potency must be the very essence of the cause, and the effect must be involved in the very core of the potency' (*BSB*, p. 340). At least in this sense, therefore, the conclusion follows that the effect must pre-exist in the material cause, and become manifest through the activity of an efficient cause or agent.

The argument to establish (ii), the identity of the effect and the material cause, is more complex. Śaṅkara begins by pointing out that the very ideas of cause and effect are linked together, just as the ideas of substance and quality are linked, in contrast to the ideas of things which are at best conjoined. For example, our experience might provide the notion of the constant conjunction of two objects – say a horse and a buffalo – but the ideas of the two objects remain distinct. Not so in the case of cause and effect, any more than in the case of substance and quality. Such ideas suggest a special kind of relation between the two terms, the relation of *inherence* as opposed to *conjunction* (*BSB*, p. 340). But what sense can we make of this relation? Śaṅkara's answer is that the very idea of inherence leads to an infinite regress, and that it raises other intellectual puzzles which are insoluble.

Let us assume that the three things – cause (C), potency (P) and effect (E) – are linked by relations of inherence (^). We have therefore these two relations to begin with, C^P and P^E. But a connection between the *three* terms in each case has to be accounted for, and this leads us to suppose again the relation of inherence between each of the three terms. We now have these more complex five-term relations, C^^^P and P^^^E. Yet again, to avoid the supposition that the five terms in each case are disconnected, we must obviously join all five terms in each case with further inherence relations, giving us the even more complex nine-term relations C^^^^^^^P and P^^^^^^^E. And clearly this process can never stop:

> if a relation of inherence be postulated, it will lead to an infinite regress, since if the inherence has to be related to a thing in which it is to inhere by the assumption of another relation (between the inherence and the thing), one will be forced to fancy another relation to connect this one with inherence, etc., and still another relation to connect the new relation, and so on.
>
> (*BSB*, p. 340)

The implication is clear for Śaṅkara – the only acceptable relation between cause, potency and effect is one of identity, so the conclusion has been established that effects not only pre-exist in their causes but are also *identical* with their causes.

Among other arguments presented by Śaṅkara against the idea of inherence is one which asks how the effect is supposed to inhere in its cause. Does it inhere in *all* parts of the cause taken together, or in it *part by part*? Neither alternative will do. We do not perceive all the parts of a cause together, the first alternative therefore rendering the perception of the effect impossible. For example, our perception of the cloth cannot depend on our perception of each and every one of the fibres, since we are not aware of each and every one of them. And the second alternative leads to unacceptable consequences, for on the assumption that the effect inheres in each and every part taken separately we would have to say that each part is on its own sufficient for the production of the effect:

> if the whole (composite product) abides in its totality in each part, then since the whole has competence to perform its own functions, and since it is the same (even when existing separately on all the parts) it should perform the duties of the teats even through the horn (of the animal), and the duties of the back through the chest.
>
> (*BSB*, p. 341)

Śaṅkara's concern with the identity of material causes and their effects leads him back, of course, to his primary interest in the question of the origin of the world of experience and of our awareness of our selves within that world. If effect pre-exists in the cause, and indeed is identical with the cause, then the world as we experience it pre-exists in and is identical with *Brahman*:

> Similarly it is the primary cause (Brahman) Itself that like an actor evolves into the respective products up to the last one, and thus becomes the objects of all empirical dealings.
>
> (*BSB*, p. 345)

Any assessment of Śaṅkara's arguments leading to the conclusion that the effect is identical with the material cause must take objection to the idea that the effect must already exist to be acted upon. No new thing could ever, on that view, be brought into existence. Since this is indeed Śaṅkara's thesis, however, it hardly stands as a serious objection. More difficult for Śaṅkara is the issue of the function of the efficient cause in making what is latent in the cause become manifest in the effect. If the effect already pre-exists in the cause, and is identical with it, some account must be given of what work the efficient cause can do. Given the models which Śaṅkara adopts, of threads and cloth, for example, we might be tempted to agree that the manifestation of the effect is nothing other than a change of intellectual focus from the material ingredients to the final form of the effect, a perspective that is certainly in step with the *vivartavāda* or 'apparent change' thesis which he is using these arguments to support. But other examples do not lend themselves so readily to this thesis. The cloth has to be woven out of threads, the pot has to be thrown and fired by the potter, and the milk has to be heated and fermented to produce curds. Material cause alone is hardly sufficient for the effect. If it were, *Brahman* without *avidyā* would be sufficient to produce the world of ordinary experience.

The strong point in Śaṅkara's treatment of the cause–effect relation is nevertheless his recognition of the intimacy of the relationship between the nature of the cause and its potency to produce a given effect. This issue is still debated in contemporary western philosophy in terms of the difference or identity of the categorical properties a material possesses and the dispositional properties to which the categorical properties give rise. Is, for example, the peculiar molecular stucture of an elastic body the same as, or in some way simply the source of, the elasticity which the body manifests? The same issue arises too in contemporary philosophy of language, when we ask for the truth-conditions of a counterfactual sentence: what, for example, must be true of the world to make true the sentence that 'If this body had been stretched, it would have regained its original shape'? Perhaps Śaṅkara's thesis of *vivartavāda* echoes John Locke's claim that the knowledge of the primary qualities of a substance such as gold (and of the primary qualities of other substances with which it interacts) would enable us to conclude *a priori* the consequences of affecting the gold in various ways: we could know *a priori* that it would melt, for example, if placed in a hot furnace.

The infinite regress argument concerning the notion of inherence must, however, be challenged. Inherence gives rise to such a regress only on the assumption that it can be treated as a third term on a logical par with C and P, in such a relation as C^P. Perhaps the best way to bring this out is to consider the relation of inherence that holds between a substance and a property, rather than a cause and its potency. The categorial status of a substance and a property are different, since a substance is that which possesses a property and conversely a property is that which is possessed by a substance. A swan is white in so far as it possesses the property whiteness, and whiteness is a property which is manifested in, or possessed by, the swan. The swan and the whiteness are not like two objects that are placed beside each other, which acquire a relational property of 'being next to each other' by their proximity. Indeed, a similar point can be made concerning such a relational property, since the same mistake would be involved in seeing that relational property as a third term on a logical par with the two objects involved. The objects and the relational property would then seem to acquire further relations between each other, leading to an infinite regress of relations between relations. Frege made this point in terms of the 'unsaturated' nature of a function, and Strawson reiterated it in terms of the 'non-relational tie' between a substance and a universal.[8]

(b) The incoherence of Sāṅkhya dualism

In *BSB* II.ii Śaṅkara develops a series of critical assaults on the philosophy of Sāṅkhya. Here he claims to be showing, by arguments which are independent of any reliance on Vedic authority, both that the Sāṅkhya system is insupportable by the kind of reasoning adopted by Sāṅkhya philosophers – reasoning by analogy – and that the Sāṅkhya system constitutes an incoherent metaphysics.

Under *BSB* II.ii.1 Śaṅkara tries to bring out the weakness of argument by analogy by turning this kind of argument against his Sāṅkhya opponents. He sums up a major Sāṅkhya argument for the existence of *pradhāna* (the 'inferred one', *prakṛti* in its original state of equilibrium between the three *guṇas*) as follows:

> As it is seen in this world that the modifications like pots, plates, etc. which remain transfused with earth as their common substance, originate from the material cause earth, so all the different products, external or corporeal, which remain transfused with happiness, misery, and delusion, must spring from a material cause constituted by happiness, misery, and delusion. Now the material cause constituted by happiness, sorrow, and delusion is the same as Pradhāna, which is constituted by the three *guṇas* (*sattva, rajas*, and *tamas* – intelligence, activity and inertia), which is insentient like earth, and which engages in activity by undergoing diverse transformation under a natural impulsion for serving the sentient soul (by providing experience or liberation).
>
> (*BSB*, p. 368)

Śaṅkara responds equally by an argument from analogy:

> if this has to be decided on the basis of analogy alone, then it is not seen in this world that any independent insentient thing that is not guided by some sentient being can produce modifications to serve some special purpose of a man; for what is noticed in the world is that houses, palaces, beds, seats, recreation grounds, etc., are made by the intelligent engineers and others. . . . So how can the insentient Pradhāna create this universe, which cannot even be mentally conceived of by the most intelligent (i.e. skilful) and most far-famed architects?
>
> (*BSB*, p. 369)

For Śaṅkara, the universe has a conscious entity as its cause (both efficiently and materially). But more importantly, if analogical reasoning can be so easily used to establish contradictory conclusions about the nature of ultimate reality, what value can it have in this context? We can have recourse only to *śruti*.

Under *BSB* II.ii.2, Śaṅkara begins to develop his criticism of Sāṅkhya, again using their preferred kind of reasoning, that the efficient cause of activity must be a sentient being. The first argument above has been for the need of an *intelligent* cause of design, and now Śaṅkara argues for an intelligent cause of any activity:

> For neither earth etc. nor chariot etc. which are themselves insentient, are seen to have any tendency to behave in a particular way unless they are under the guidance of potters and others or horses and the like. The unseen has to be inferred from the seen.
>
> (*BSB*, p. 371)

Yet could not *pradhāna/prakṛti* act *spontaneously*? After all, and contrary to Śaṅkara's contentions above, the Sāṅkhya school may have recourse to the observed fact that there are indeed in nature various cases of spontaneous activity: Śaṅkara cites under *BSB* II.ii.3 on his opponent's behalf such cases as insentient milk flowing spontaneously to nourish the calf, and insentient water flowing spontaneously for the good of people. Yet Śaṅkara believes that these cases are misleading:

> we infer that even in those cases, the milk and water develop a tendency to act when they are under the guidance of some sentient beings. . . . It is logical to hold that milk is induced to flow under the affectionate desire of the cow: and it is drawn out by the sucking of the calf. Water too is not quite independent since its flow is dependent on the slope of the ground etc.
>
> (*BSB*, p. 373)

Would a fair retort be that the causal factors cited hardly constitute intelligence, even if they do imply that spontaneity is absent? But this is in fact Śaṅkara's point, merely at this stage of the debate to question the supposed experience of spontaneity. To bring this home he adds under *BSB* II.ii.5 the more subtle point that the non-observance of a cause cannot allow us to conclude that the activity is spontaneous. To the thought that *pradhāna* could change naturally into *mahat* etc. just as grass, leaves, water, etc. change naturally into milk without the help of any other factors, Śaṅkara replies:

> other causes are perceived. . . . For grass etc. eaten by a cow alone changes into milk; but not so when rejected or eaten by a bull etc. If this could happen without any cause, then grass etc. would also have become milk even without entering a cow's body. A thing does not become causeless just because men cannot manufacture it at will.
>
> (*BSB*, p. 375)

In other words, there must be a cause or causal factors involved even though not observed, for some indications of causal influence are observed.

Next Śaṅkara points out, under *BSB* II.ii.6, what he sees to be an unfortunate inconsistency developing in Sāṅkhya metaphysics, in consequence of this appeal to spontaneity. On the assumption that *prakṛti* acts spontaneously, it could have no purposes, he argues. Yet Sāṅkhya philosophers think that it does indeed have purposes, namely to engage *puruṣas* in *saṁsāra* (to provide psycho-physical organisms by which the *puruṣas* can become aware of the evolutions of *prakṛti*) and to provide the possibility of *puruṣas* achieving *mokṣa* through a correct discrimination of their difference from *prakṛti*.

On this point Śaṅkara himself seems wrong, since to say that some activity is spontaneous need only be to claim that it lacks an efficient cause. Śaṅkara assumes that some activity needs both a material cause and an efficient cause (and for him, of course, *Brahman* is both). But why believe that all activity takes place on this model? He clearly fails to appreciate the possibility of a teleological kind of activity as in Aristotle's philosophy of nature. For the Sāṅkhya school, the Aristotelian kind of explanation of *prakṛti* evolving is in terms of (a) itself as the material cause and (b) the ends to which it moves. Talk of *spontaneity* is consistent with ascribing purposes to *prakṛti* if spontaneity involves merely the absence of an efficient cause.

With this discussion of spontaneity Śaṅkara has in fact moved on to his second charge against the Sāṅhkya school. Śaṅkara's essential thought in this charge against Sāṅkhya is that the dualistic metaphysics of *prakṛti* and *puruṣas* contains a fundamental incoherence, one which in his eyes must be symptomatic of any such thoroughgoing dualism. The incoherence is that the dualism provides no basis for understanding the way in which the two sides may combine their efforts in producing the world as we experience it. Under *BSB* II.ii.7 Śaṅkara fairly easily demolishes the two analogies offered by his opponents which supposedly make sense of interaction between very different things. *Prakṛti* and *puruṣa* may, on one analogy, be likened to the lame yet sighted man riding on the shoulders of someone else who is blind yet capable of walking: together they act. Or, on the analogy of a loadstone whose simple presence makes a piece of iron move, the *puruṣa* could impel *prakṛti* to evolve. Śaṅkara's responses are simple and to the point. The two men clearly have the power of communication, yet what sense could we make of *puruṣas* communicating with *prakṛti*, since they are by definition actionless and without attributes? As for the loadstone analogy, *prakṛti*

> cannot stimulate movement like a loadstone by mere proximity, for proximity (between soul and Pradhāna) being eternal, the possibility will arise of such movement also becoming endless. In the case of a loadstone . . . there can be such an activity as the attraction (of the iron to itself), for the proximity is inconstant. Besides, the loadstone depends on cleaning etc. for its action. . . . Again, there can be no relation between the soul and Pradhāna, since Pradhāna is insentient, the soul is indifferent, and there is no third factor to bring them into relation.
>
> (*BSB*, p. 377)

But a defence of Sāṅkhya can be developed against Śaṅkara's second charge of incoherence. Śaṅkara is assuming – admittedly not without substantial evidence from many passages in the Sāṅkhya texts – that their metaphysical dualism is an extreme one. *Puruṣas* and *prakṛti* are independent entities, self-subsistent and possessing incommensurable properties: so far, this appears to be an extreme Cartesian dualism of soul and matter. And yet, while avoiding an over-simplistic attempt at an interactionist story, the Sāṅkhya dualism is developed in such a way that in the very elementary ingredients of *prakṛti* and in all its stages of evolution a link with *puruṣas* is insisted upon.

For what are *sattva*, *rajas* and *tamas*, the three *guṇas* or ingredients of *prakṛti*? They are not just material ingredients, but in their very essences are linked to *puruṣas* – for they are *essentially* and not just accidentally *puruṣa*-related. *Sattva* is the source of *consciousness* and of *pleasure*, which are properties not of *sattva* but of *puruṣas*; similarly, *rajas* is the source of *pain*, and *tamas* is the source of *confusion*.

And the stages of the evolution of *prakṛti* are equally essentially *puruṣa*-related. When *prakṛti* first moves out of the *pradhāna* stage of equilibrium between the three *guṇas*, the first evolute is *buddhi*, a word denoting *intellect*. This cannot be read as meaning that *prakṛti* itself evolves into intellect, but that it evolves in such a way as to provide a necessary condition for the emergence of awareness of itself by *puruṣas*. The next evolute is *ahaṅkāra*, which denotes *self-awareness*: again, not the self-awareness of *prakṛti* but a necessary condition for the self-awareness of *puruṣas* – a self-awareness involving, of course, a confusion of the true nature of *puruṣas* with the growing complexity of the purely material *prakṛti*. And the final stages of the evolution of *prakṛti*, the ultimate evolutes, are on the one side the organs of *sense* and of *motion*, and on the other the physical objects of which *puruṣas* may have knowledge through those organs.

At every stage, therefore, the story of the evolution of *prakṛti* relates it to *puruṣas*. The dualism of the Sāṅkhya school may fairly be said to avoid the extreme form which Cartesian dualism takes, and to avoid an oversimplistic causal interactionist theme. Whether the dualism can be charged with an incoherence in its details concerning the psycho-physical *ātman* is another matter: Śaṅkara's accusation that *prakṛti* and *puruṣas* are described in such fundamentally different terms that *no* account of their relationship can be offered appears to oversimplify both the intent and the content of Sāṅkhya metaphysics.

To conclude this section, on a careful assessment the individual moves which Śaṅkara makes in his criticism of Sāṅkhya involve him in suspicious shifts between ascribing to *Brahman* – which, on his own view, is both the material and the efficient cause of the world as experienced – such distinct features as consciousness, intelligence, design and purpose. What is more, he seems not to appreciate the power of a teleological explanatory style to compete with one of efficient causation. He may further be charged with representing Sāṅkhya dualism in an overly extreme form, which fails to appreciate the details of the evolutionary process of *prakṛti* which are fundamentally *puruṣa*-related.

There is, moreover, one point which Śaṅkara misses in his criticism of Sāṅkhya metaphysics, and this is that the evolution of *prakṛti* is described by them in ambiguous terms. Sometimes they are dealing with a single, cosmic evolution, yet at other times they are describing an individual evolution concerning each *puruṣa*. It is not clear how these two stories are to be made consistent with each other, and Śaṅkara might well have pointed this out – but perhaps he prefers not to explore this problem, for fear of opening up the same charge against his own metaphysics of cosmic *Māyā* and individual *avidyā*.

ŚAṄKARA'S REFUTATION OF OTHER SCHOOLS

Having disposed of the philosophy of Sāṅkhya dualism, Śaṅkara devotes the rest of *BSB* II.ii to refuting the other main rivals to his own view: (a) Vaiśeṣika atomism, (b)

Buddhism, (c) Jainism and (d) the view that God is merely a superintendent (the efficient cause but not the material cause of the world).

(a) A major assumption used by Vaiśeṣika for the conclusion that the world originates from atoms is that the qualities of a material cause are reproduced in its effects. If, therefore, intelligent *Brahman* were the material cause of the world, intelligence should be a quality of the world itself – a conclusion which experience of that world refutes. Śaṅkara's response is to question the assumption, pointing out that the Vaiśeṣika atomists' very own theory runs contrary to it. On that theory,

> when two (ultimate) atoms create a dyad, the colours, viz white etc., inhering in the atoms, produce a new whiteness etc. in the dyad. But the special characteristic of the atoms, viz their inextension (i.e. atomicity) does not produce a new inextension. . . . So also if the insentient universe emerges out of the intelligent Brahman, what do you lose?
>
> (*BSB*, pp. 384–5)

Śaṅkara adds to this *ad hominem* argument a stronger one concerning the origin of action. Before the world had any order – or at any time of ultimate dissolution – the atoms are presumed to exist in isolation. But then there is no possibility of action to bring about atomic combinations, since

> no effort, which (according to the atomist) is a quality of the soul, can be possible in the absence of a body; for effort springs up as a quality of the soul when a contact between the mind and the soul takes place in the mind having the body as its seat.
>
> (*BSB*, p. 389)

(b) Śaṅkara divides the schools of Buddhism into realist, idealist and nihilist (though he uses the term 'nihilist' also quite generally to cover all these schools). The first are the Sarvāstivādins, further divided into the Sautrāntikas and Vaibhāṣikas, who believe respectively in the inferential and perceptual existence of things in the world. The second are the Vijñānavādins (or Yogācāras), who believe in the existence of consciousness or ideas alone. The third are Sarvaśunyavādins (or Mādhyamikas), who deny the existence of everything.

Buddhist realism proposes a theory of physical atomism. This holds that atoms of earth and so on, with the characteristics of solidity, fluidity, heat and motion, come together to form the objects of perception and the sense-organs. Similarly, there are four other groups of cognitive, emotional, volitional and perceptual ingredients. The five *khandhas* (aggregates) are ever changing from moment to moment, and constitute all there is of what we designate as a person. Śaṅkara takes issue with this *khandha* theory, on the grounds that it provides nothing to hold together the various ingredients either at any one time or through progression in time:

> Because the components of such a combination are insentient and because consciousness can flash (from the contact between sense-organs and objects) only if a combination of things (forming the body etc) is already there, and because no other steady and independent entity is admitted which is sentient, an experiencer, and a ruler, which can bring about the combination.
>
> (*BSB*, p. 403)

The Buddhist reply, that at least ingredients within any one aggregate can give rise to successive ingredients of the same kind – so that 'these nescience and the rest go on revolving for ever like (the cups in) a Persian wheel, as cause and effect' (*BSB*, pp. 404–5) – is clearly inadequate. Nescience presupposes the existence of a combination in the form, at the very least, of a body, and cannot therefore be the source of that combination (*BSB*, p. 405). If the Buddhist realist holds, in response, that combinations simply exist and give rise to successive combinations without any experiencer behind them, only two dire options present themselves. Is the succession regular or irregular, Śaṅkara asks:

> If regularity be admitted, then a human body can have no possibility of being transformed into divine, animal or hellish bodies. And if irregularity be admitted, then a human body may at times turn momentarily into an elephant, and then be transformed again into godly or human form.
>
> (*BSB*, p. 406)

Śaṅkara takes exception, moreover, to the Buddhist realist's doctrine of the momentariness of all ingredients in the *khandhas*. If one such ingredient is supposed to give rise to a succeeding ingredient of the same kind, this requires the continued existence of the first into the moment of arising of the second. Should we adopt the Buddhist theory of causation, we are committed to the view that the first has become non-existent *before* the second arises: but how can what is now non-existent give rise to what is not yet existent either? (*BSB* p. 407.)

A final criticism is levelled by Śaṅkara against Buddhist realism under *BSB* II.ii.25. In the absence of a permanent throughout the successive *kandhas*, what sense can we make of memory and recognition?

> Remembrance means recalling to mind something after its perception, and that can happen only when the agent of perception and memory is the same. . . . How can there be an awareness of the form, 'I who saw earlier see now' . . . unless the earlier and later perceiver be the same?
>
> (*BSB*, p. 412)

And a similarity between the previous experience and the present experience will not do in either case,

> for the experience is of the existence of the entity itself (expressing itself as, 'I am that very person') and not of mere similarity with that (as would be expressed in, 'I am like that person').
>
> (*BSB*, p. 413)

The second school of Buddhism, the Buddhist idealists, rejects the existence of objects independent of subjective consciousness, for two reasons. First, such an object would be unknowable since the atoms could not be individually perceived and the resulting conglomeration of atomic parts is arguably neither different from nor identical with those parts. Second, from the fact of the simultaneous appearance of the knowledge and the object it follows that knowledge and object are identical. Perception is analogous to dreaming, and just as dreams exhibit a diversity due (as we normally say) to the diversity of individual experiences, so perceptions exhibit a diversity due to the diversity of previous perceptual states (*BSB*, p. 417).

Śaṅkara's refutation of this Buddhist idealism is a firm insistence on the real existence of external things,

> since the possibility or impossibility of the existence of a thing is determined in accordance with the applicability or non-applicability of the means of knowledge.
>
> (*BSB*, pp. 419–20)

And the regularity of the simultaneous appearance of the cognition and its object is, Śaṅkara argues, due not to their identity but to the relation of causality between them. Moreover, there is a world of difference between dreams and waking experience: dreams are subject to sublation by later cognitive events, whereas waking experiences are not; and dreams are a form of memory, whereas perceptions are new cognition and experienced as such (*BSB*, p. 423).

Of the third school of Buddhism, the Mādhyamikas, Śaṅkara is very dismissive indeed:

> As for the view of the absolute nihilist, no attempt is made for its refutation since it is opposed to all means of valid knowledge. For human behaviour, conforming as it does to all right means of knowledge, cannot be denied as long as a different order of reality is not realized; for unless there be an exception, the general rule prevails.
>
> (*BSB*, p. 426)

And commenting on the fact that there are all these competing schools of Buddhism, Śaṅkara says that Buddhist doctrine 'breaks down like a well sunk in sand' (*BSB*, p. 426).

(c) Śaṅkara shows little sympathy for the subtle metaphysical and epistemological views of the Jains. Rather than a careful analysis of the integrated theories of the multi-faceted nature of reality (*anekāntavāda*), the limited nature of much of human knowledge (*nayavāda*) and the idea of perfect knowledge (*kevala*) to be achieved by the liberated *jīva*, Śaṅkara chooses to level his criticisms at an impoverished version of Jainism. The obscure seven-step logic (*saptabhaṅgī*) is taken by Śaṅkara as a warrant for accusing Jains of contemplating the simultaneous possession by all things of inconsistent characteristics, forgetting the Jains' relativization of such ascriptions; and consequently further for accusing Jainism of ascribing an indefinite nature to its own instructions, means of knowing, objects of knowledge, the knower, and knowledge itself:

> if anyone should write a scripture of such indefinite significance, his words will be unacceptable like those of the mad or intoxicated.
>
> (*BSB*, p. 428)

And following Bādarāyaṇa's lead in the original *sūtra*, Śaṅkara makes much capital out of the peculiar Jain theory that the soul (*jīva*) expands to fill the space occupied by the body and so has different sizes as a man grows from boyhood, or transmigrates into a larger or smaller animal.

(d) Śaṅkara's final philosophical opponent is the philosopher who claims that God is the efficient cause of the world but not its material cause. This view, seeing God as a 'mere superintendent', Śaṅkara finds in the writings of the Mahesvaras (Śaivas and others), of some members of the Sāṅkhya and Yoga schools, and some members too of the Nyāya and Vaiśeṣika schools. (Clearly it was not an orthodox tenet of all such school members.) Śaṅkara finds that such a view imputes an imperfection to God:

> For a Lord who creates the various creatures by dividing them into grades of inferiority, mediocrity, and superiority will be open like ourselves to the charges of likes, dislikes, etc., so that He will cease to be God.
>
> (*BSB*, p. 434)

A God, moreover, who is driven to bring about rebirths according to merit and demerit is under a compulsion to act – which argues against his omnipotence. And a God presiding over a world of nature and souls independent of himself must, argues Śaṅkara in a brief but striking passage (*BSB*, pp. 438–9), lose either his omnipotence of his omniscience. Can the limits (in number and extension) of nature and souls be determined by God? If the answer is positive, this means that nature and souls must have a beginning and an end, and God will lose his directorship and divine power during their non-existence. If the answer is negative, then God will clearly lose his omniscience.

NOTES

1 I would like to thank Indira Mahalingam for her valuable help in the writing of this chapter. Her own chapter, on Sāṅkhya-Yoga (Chapter 8 above), relates closely to the fourth section of this one.

2 See K. H. Potter (ed.), *Encyclopaedia of Indian Philosophies*, vol. III (Delhi: Motilal Banarsidass, 1981), p. 116 for this scholarship.

3 See Further Reading for publication details.

4 G. Thibaut (trans.), *The Vedānta-Sūtras with a Commentary by Śaṅkarācārya* (2 vols, Delhi: Motilal Banarsidass, 1890, 1896), Sacred Books of the East Series 34, 38; G. Thibaut (trans.), *The Vedānta-Sūtras with a Commentary by Rāmānuja* (Delhi: Motilal Barnasidass, 1962), Sacred Books of the East Series 48 (first published Oxford: Oxford University Press, 1904).

5 All page references to Śaṅkara's *Brahmasātrabhāṣya* (hereafter *BSB*) are to the translation by Swami Gambhirananda, 2nd edn (Calcutta: Advaita Ashrama, 1972).

6 Śaṅkara's *BSB* commentary to part I, section i, *sūtras* 3–4.

7 For a discussion of this theory, see B. K. Matilal, *Perception* (Oxford: Oxford University Press, 1986), Ch. 6, section 4.

8 'For not all parts of a thought can be complete; at least one must be "unsaturated" or predicative; otherwise they would not hold together.' Quoted from G. Frege, 'On concept

and object', in P. Geach and M. Black, *Translations from the Philosophical Writings of Gottlob Frege* (Oxford: Blackwell, 1970), p. 54. See also P. F. Strawson, *Individuals* (London: Methuen, 1959), p. 171 for 'non-relational tie'.

FURTHER READING

Gambhirananda, Swami (trans.) (1965) *Brahmasūtrabhāṣya of Sri Śaṅkarācārya,* Calcutta: Advaita Ashrama (2nd edn 1972).

Hiriyanna, M. (1932) *Outlines of Indian Philosophy*, Woking: Unwin Brothers. See ch. 13.

— (1949) *Essentials of Indian Philosophy*, London: Allen & Unwin. See ch. 7.

Pande, G. C. (1994) *Life and Thought of Śaṅkarācārya,* Delhi: Motilal Banarsidass.

Potter, K. H. (ed.) (1981) *Encyclopaedia of Indian Philosophies*, vol. III, *Advaita Vedānta up to Śaṅkara and his Pupils*, Delhi: Motilal Banarsidass. See also Potter's introduction, pp. 3–102.

Radhakrishnan, S. (1923) *Indian Philosophy*, 2 vols, London: Allen & Unwin; Centenary Edition, Delhi: Oxford University Press, 1989. See vol. II, chs 7, 8.

Sharma, C. (1964) *A Critical Survey of Indian Philosophy,* Delhi: Motilal Banarsidass. See ch. 15.

Smart, N. (1967) 'Śankara', in P. Edwards (ed.) *The Encyclopaedia of Philosophy,* New York: Macmillan.

Thibaut, G. (trans.) (1890, 1896) *The Vedānta-sūtras with a commentary by Śaṅkarācārya*, 2 vols, Oxford: Oxford University Press. Sacred Books of the East Series, ed. F. Max Muller, 34 and 38.

— (1904) *The Vedānta-sūtras with a commentary by Rāmānuja*, Oxford: Oxford University Press (reprinted Delhi: Motilal Barnasidass, 1962). Sacred Books of the East Series, ed. F. Max Muller, 48.

11

LATER VEDĀNTA

Michael Comans

INTRODUCTION: THE 'VEDĀNTA'

The word 'Vedānta' means the 'end' or the 'culmination' of the Veda, and it specifically refers to the class of texts called *Upaniṣads* which constitute the final portion of the Vedic literature. The followers of the Vedānta rely upon the *Upaniṣad* texts as a means of knowledge concerning matters which do not fall within the scope of sense-based knowledge. Vedāntins argue that our usual means of knowledge, perception and inference, are valid for empirical operations, but are unable by themselves to discover metaphysical truth.[1] Vedāntins consider that answers to such questions as the existence and nature of God, the nature and destiny of the individual self and the reality or otherwise of the physical world are to be found only in the revelation of the *Upaniṣads* and they are therefore concerned, to a very large extent, with arriving at a systematic interpretation of the entire Upaniṣadic literature. Since the Vedāntins place such importance upon textual exegesis they can also properly be called 'Uttara Mīmāṁsakas', for they analyse the latter part of the Veda, the *Upaniṣads*, with the same care that the 'Pūrva Mīmāṁsakas' exhibited in their analysis of the earlier portion of the Veda, which has to do with ritual activity. The difference between the Pūrva and Uttara Mīmāṁsā is that the followers of the former were predominantly concerned with the interpretation of the injunctive statements in the Veda so that they could correctly perform the prescribed rituals, whereas the followers of the Uttara Mīmāṁsā, i.e. the Vedāntins, continue to find in the *Upaniṣads* not an injunction to action but a *knowledge* of the ever-existing, absolute truth.

From what has been said it could be thought that Vedāntins are solely concerned with the exegesis of scripture, but that is not so. Vedāntins rely upon scripture in their attempt to formulate a comprehensive, coherent and meaningful world-view and they also uphold that view against other schools of thought through argument. Thus Vedānta has an important philosophical dimension in that it possesses a coherent metaphysics, epistemology and ethics which it seeks to defend through argument, even without having recourse to scripture. This it must do when the opponents are those such as Buddhists who do not accept the authority of the Vedic scripture.

Six schools of Vedānta arose between the eighth and the fifteenth century, each basing itself upon different interpretations of the *Upaniṣads*, the *Bhagavadgītā* and the *Brahmasūtras* and holding, in some cases, vastly divergent views.[2] They are all still extant, but the most important in the history of Indian philosophical thought are the earlier three: Advaita, Viśiṣṭādvaita and Dvaita Vedānta. The school of Advaita looks to the *Upaniṣads* more exclusively than the other Vedāntic schools. The other schools have increasingly tended towards a wider interpretation of what constitutes authoritative scripture and, while paying formal homage to the *Upaniṣads*, have come to rely heavily on other literature such as the Epics and *Purāṇas* as their primary texts.

ADVAITA AFTER ŚAṄKARA

After Śaṅkara, the history of the Advaita school shows a trend towards greater systematization and dialectical complexity. Between the eighth and the twelfth century Advaitins were concerned with developing a systematic metaphysics and epistemology and with defending Advaita against the Buddhists, Pūrva Mīmāṁsakas and Nyāya-Vaiśeṣikas. During the twelfth and thirteenth centuries philosophical controversy was mostly with the Nyāya and the Vaiśeṣika schools and was dominated by considerations of logical formalism which had been developing since the tenth century.[3] During this period there was an overriding concern with the formation of precise definitions and proof through the use of syllogisms. The defeat of one's opponent was assured if one could demonstrate a defect in either the formation of the opponent's definition or in his use of syllogistic reasoning. From the thirteenth or fourteenth century the Advaitins were increasingly engaged in controversy with the followers of Rāmānuja and Madhva. The developments in logic made by the Naiyāyikas during this period were not overlooked, and all these Vedānta schools incorporated the increasingly sophisticated logical techniques into the disputations they conducted against one another.

To illustrate this increasing complexity in Advaita thought we shall take up two issues of fundamental importance for Advaita, the ascertainment of the true nature of the Self and the falsity of the world. We shall see how these issues are treated by three Advaita authors: Padmapāda, an immediate disciple of Śaṅkara, Ānandabodha at the end of the twelfth century and Citsukha in the thirteenth century.

The Self and self-luminosity

According to Advaita there is, underlying the diversity in the world, a single reality which is of the nature of Pure Consciousness which is Pure Being. Such a reality, designated in the *Upaniṣads* by the terms *Brahman* or *Ātman*, constitutes the fundamental 'Self' of everything. Thus all beings, including God (*Īśvara*), partake of the same essential Self which is Pure Consciousness identical to Pure Being. The multiplicity in the world and the difference between God and individual beings are empirically valid but not absolutely true, for ultimately everything is an appearance upon *Brahman* just as a film is played out upon a screen. According to Śaṅkara, the sorrows of our existence must finally be traced to an original ignorance of this underlying essential Self, and because of such ignorance there has occurred a fundamental mistake consisting of the mutual superimposition and erroneous identification of the two primary categories of experience: 'I' (*aham*) and 'this' (*idam*). The underlying Self, the I which is inherently free from all limiting conditions, has been identified with factors which are illumined by I and thereby must fall within the category of 'this'. Such factors are the physical body, the sense-organs and the mind itself, which consists of various types of cognitive activity. As a result of ignorance we are habituated to attributing the pure I, the Self, to its objects, the body, senses and mind, and to attribute the defects and problems of the latter to the subject, I, which is inherently free from the defects which belong to its objects.

In their endeavour to ascertain this essential Self, Advaitins have made a subtle distinction between Consciousness as Self and consciousness as the empirical ego, which is normally taken to be the Self. Padmapāda, in his commentary upon Śaṅkara's introduction to the *Brahmasūtras*, explains that there are two factors involved in the very notion of 'I': there is the 'not this' (*anidam aṁśa*) aspect which is the Self and there is the 'this' (*idamaṁśa*) or objectified aspect which is the ego and which consists of all cognitive states including the self-reflexive cognition of 'me', the historical person who has an identification with a set of memories, who has a particular personality and who carries a certain sense of self-worth, etc.[4] Padmapāda says that the idea of 'I', as consisting of both these aspects, is a matter for one's own careful consideration.[5] Thus in the Advaita of Śaṅkara and Padmapāda the ascertainment of the essential Self is not so much a matter of a 'mystical' experience occurring in time as a matter of enquiry consisting of the careful and concentrated inspection of and reflection upon one's ordinary experience. Through the discrimination of the outward or objectified factors from I, Advaitins conclude that the true Self can only be Pure Consciousness or Pure Experience (*anubhūtisvarūpa*). Thus there can be no 'objective' experience of the Self because Consciousness itself is Experience.

Advaitins consider that since the Self is Consciousness the Self must also be self-luminous, which means that the Self does not depend upon something other than itself in order to be manifest. Ānandabodha responds to the objection that the Self is not self-luminous since the Self is revealed by mental perception by saying that if it were the case that the Self could be revealed by mental perception, then the Self would be an object for itself. But the Self cannot become its own object just as the tip of the finger cannot touch itself. He says that if the Self is not the object of cognition, then it cannot be manifested by a cognition and must therefore be self-luminous. In support of this position he offers the following syllogism: 'The Self is not dependent upon cognition in order to be revealed. Because, like cognition, the Self is immediately evident (*aparokṣa*) without being an object of cognition.'[6] Ānandabodha's reasoning is that just as a cognition does not need to be revealed by a second cognition or else there would be an infinite regression, so too the Self is immediately evident without requiring something to reveal it. The statement that the Self is 'immediately evident' is given as the reason for its self-luminosity.

Citsukha, in the following century, utilized the idea of the Self's immediacy in presenting a formal definition of self-luminosity. He defines self-luminosity as 'what is capable of being immediately evident in empirical life while not being an object of knowledge'.[7] Citsukha has been careful to fulfil two criteria in formulating his definition. First, what is self-luminous cannot be an object of knowledge, for if something is an object of knowledge then it must have been revealed and cannot therefore be self-luminous. But there could be an objection that what cannot be an object of knowledge may as well be non-existent. To avoid this objection Citsukha has added the qualifying clause 'capable of being immediately evident in empirical life'. The immediacy of Consciousness is undeniable. And Consciousness is ultimately not an object of knowledge, for (a) everything is revealed as an object of Consciousness itself and (b) if Consciousness could be objectified, it would lead to an infinite regression. Therefore the Advaitins maintain that the essential Self is the non-objective I. This Self is of the nature of Pure Consciousness and is self-luminous because Consciousness, while not being an object of knowledge, is immediately present as the indispensable condition for any experience to be known.

The falsity of the world

If Pure, self-revealing Consciousness, identical to Pure Being, is the underlying reality of everything, then how do Advaitins respond when asked, 'How did everything come about?' Advaitins answer from either of two standpoints, that of absolute truth, or that of 'relative truth' when they are concerned with 'saving the appearances'. In absolute truth, nothing has truly come into being. All things, including the personal God, individual souls and the physical world, are merely an appearance in Consciousness itself, analogous to the inexplicable arising of dream phenomena in one's own consciousness.[8] But Advaita also takes a position on the standpoint of 'relative truth' and maintains that the personal God, individual souls and the physical world *do have* an empirical existence even though they do not have absolute reality. It is from this empirical position that Advaita seeks to account for the existence of God, the souls and the world through the explanation that Consciousness is as though associated with a Power known as *māyā* or *avidyā* which is indefinable as either absolutely real or absolutely unreal. Consciousness, when apparently conditioned by this Power, is the omniscient, personal God who then becomes both the efficient and the material cause of the world. Śaṅkara's disciple Padmapāda explicitly states that the appearance of the phenomenal world has to be traced to such a Power,[9] and this view has become the standard position in Advaita.

Other schools, such as Nyāya, did not accept such a Power, nor did they accept that the world has only an apparent reality. The followers of Nyāya maintained that the world is a real effect which has God as its efficient cause. In defending the Advaita position, Ānandabodha says that the existence of such a Power can be proved if it is held that the world is an effect.[10] He explains that an effect cannot originate from an efficient cause alone but requires both an efficient and a material cause. He argues that it would be incorrect to hold that something unreal has a real thing as its material cause. For if the material cause is real, then its effect too will be real. And it would be equally incorrect to hold that something which is purely fictitious, such as a rabbit's horn, could have any material cause at all. Because the world, which is an effect, is neither absolutely real nor entirely fictitious, it must be inferred from the evidence of the effect that the material cause too is something indeterminable as either absolutely real or absolutely unreal, and such a material cause is the Power known as *māyā*.

Against the Naiyāyika contention that the Advaitin is unable to demonstrate that the world is indeterminable as either real or unreal, i.e. that it is *mithyā*, Citsukha advanced the following definition of falsity: 'whatever is the counter-correlate of its absolute non-existence in its own locus' is *mithyā*.[11] That is to say, when a thing appears in a place where it does not actually exist, it is false. For instance, a cotton shirt must be false or *mithyā* because the shirt is the counter-correlate of its absolute non-existence in its locus, the cotton threads. The shirt does not exist *as a shirt* either in the threads taken singly or in the pile of threads taken as a whole. Yet the shirt appears there in the threads when the threads are arranged in a certain way. The appearance of the shirt is the counter-correlate of its absolute non-existence in the threads and so the shirt is *mithyā*. Śaṅkara's definition of falsity is simpler, though no less effective. He equates reality with permanence: what is truly real must not undergo change. It follows from this position that whatever is seen to undergo change cannot be truly real and must therefore be *mithyā*, and hence the changing world is *mithyā*.[12]

It can be seen that Advaitins after Śaṅkara met the new challenges of each period by reformulating fundamental Advaita views in new ways, utilizing the sophisticated logical techniques developed by the Naiyāyikas.

VIŚIṢṬĀDVAITA VEDĀNTA

The Viśiṣṭādvaita world-view

Viśiṣṭādvaita is a religious and philosophical tradition which upholds the full reality of a personal God, the real existence of individual selves and the objective reality of the physical world. The tradition of Viśiṣṭādvaita has its roots in the religious literature of the Tamil *bhakti* poets known as Āḷvārs. The south Indian Śrīvaiṣṇava community came to look upon the collection of the devotional hymns of the Āḷvārs, the *Divyaprabandham*, as constituting a 'Tamil Veda' equivalent in status to the Sanskrit Veda. However, the religious teachers (*ācāryas*) of this community equally affirmed the authority of the Vedic tradition and the importance of the *prasthānatraya* of the Vedānta, i.e. the *Upaniṣads*, the *Bhagavadgītā* and the *Brahmasūtras*, and in doing so they linked themselves to the pan-Indian Vedic heritage. Thus the followers of Viśiṣṭādvaita also refer to themselves as followers of 'Ubhaya Vedānta', or 'double Vedānta, since they base their doctrines upon the Tamil *Divyaprabandham* as well as upon the classical Sanskrit texts of the Vedānta. Among the religious teachers of the Śrīvaiṣṇava community three are especially notable: Yāmuna (918–1038[?]), Rāmānuja (1017–1137) and Vedānta Deśika (1268–1369). These teachers wrote extensively in Sanskrit and propounded and defended the philosophy and religion of Viśiṣṭādvaita.

The name 'Viśiṣṭādvaita' means 'the non-duality (*advaita*) of the One who is qualified (*viśiṣṭasya*)', and it refers to Brahman, who is none other than the personal Lord Viṣṇu and who is eternally qualified by individual selves and by physical matter. What is meant in this context by the term 'non-duality' is that nothing else exists other than the Lord qualified by all sentient and insentient things. Viśiṣṭādvaitins, while relying like other Vedāntins upon the revealed texts, seek to interpret the texts from the perspective of a common-sense realism. Consequently they maintain that reality contains three real categories: the Lord (*Īśvara*), the sentient individual souls (*cit*) and insentient matter (*acit*). The existence of the Lord is established solely on the basis of the scriptures, whereas the reality of the latter two categories is established in accord with ordinary sense-perception. A distinctive feature of the Viśiṣṭādvaita metaphysics is its explanation of the relation that exists between these three categories. Viśiṣṭādvaita seeks to explain this relation by drawing upon our common understanding of the relation that exists between a substance and its attributes. According to our ordinary experience the world contains substances as well as attributes: a rose, for example, can be considered as a substantive while its particular colour forms its attribute. There is no experience of an unqualified substantive or of an independently existing attribute, but rather a substantive is always seen to be qualified by some attribute or the other. Although the substantive and the attribute are distinct, since we can conceive of them separately, they always exist in an inseparable relationship since we cannot have a substance without its attribute or an attribute without its substance. According to Viśiṣṭādvaita, the Lord is the sole substantive while the individual souls and physical matter are in an attributive relation. The souls and matter are intrinsically other than the Lord, just as attributes are distinct from their substantive, but they are ontologically dependent upon the Lord and inseparable from him as attributes are dependent upon and inseparable from the substantive in which they inhere.

Viśiṣṭādvaita draws upon the analogy of the body and its indwelling soul (*śarīraśarīribhāva*) to help elucidate this relationship between the Lord, souls and matter. Rāmānuja defines a body as a dependent entity which exists for the sake of the indwelling self and is under the control of that self. While body and soul are essentially distinct, they can be seen to form a kind of organic unity. Likewise, souls and matter are the 'body' of the Lord and as such they exist for the sake of the Lord and are under the control of the Lord, who is their innermost Self. Although souls and matter are essentially distinct from the Lord, they form the 'body' while the Lord is their indwelling Self and thus the Lord, souls and matter together form a kind of organic whole.[13] It should not be thought that Viśiṣṭādvaita teaches a philosophy of simultaneous difference and non-difference (*bhedābheda*) between the self and the Lord. In Viśiṣṭādvaita the self is different from the Lord, but is dependent upon him as an attribute to a substantive or as a body to its indwelling soul.

Viśiṣṭādvaita accepts that the Lord is both the efficient and the material cause of the world, but it invests these terms with its own meaning. At the time of the periodic cosmic dissolution (*pralaya*), the primary matter (*prakṛti*) and the as yet unliberated souls remain in a subtle, almost undifferentiated, condition. When the Lord has as his body the primary matter and souls in this subtle condition, the Lord is said to be in a causal state. At the time of creation the Lord does not directly become the material of the universe, but he causes the ever-existent primary matter to evolve from its subtle condition into the physical world and he causes the bound souls to assume bodies appropriate to their former deeds (*karma*). Thus the Lord does not directly undergo change, but he can be said to be either the efficient or the material cause when his 'body' exists in a causal or in a manifest condition.[14]

The self and its consciousness

According to Viśiṣṭādvaita the self is distinct from the physical body, the senses, the mind, the vital-breath and consciousness. The self is other than the body because the consciousness of 'I' has only the 'I' as its referent. When a person has concentrated his mind and restrained the activity of his senses, he knows himself only as 'I' while the body and its various parts do not form the object of the consciousness of 'I'. Another reason for the difference between self and body is based upon the logical distinction between subject and object. Viśiṣṭādvaita argues, in the same manner as does Advaita, that while the self is the sole referent of the cognition 'I' (*aham*), the body is an object of the cognition 'this' (*idam*), and the referent of the cognition 'I' and the referent of the cognition 'this' cannot be identical.[15] The self is distinct from the senses because consciousness cannot be intrinsic to the senses either individually or collectively. If each sense-organ had its own consciousness, then what was apprehended by one sense would not be able to be recollected by another; but we do have recollections such as 'I am touching what I had previously seen.' Nor can the senses have consciousness collectively, because if that were the case an object would always be experienced by all of the five senses, which is not the case, and the loss of even one sense would result in death.

Viśiṣṭādvaita argues that the self is other than the mind because the latter is considered to be an instrument of cognition. The existence of the mind can be inferred from the fact that in spite of the simultaneous contact of the senses with their respective sense-objects, knowledge occurs in a successive manner rather than simultaneously. Here Viśiṣṭādvaita has relied upon the Nyāya explanation, though all Vedāntins would argue, on the basis of the *Upaniṣads*, that the self is other than the mind and the vital-breath.[16]

The self is also other than mere consciousness, whether consciousness is conceived as momentary and thereby impermanent as in Buddhist thought, or as changeless and hence permanent as in Advaita. Viśiṣṭādvaita argues that if the illusion of selfhood is due to the similarity of a momentary stream of cognitions, because each cognition is momentary and discrete, the Buddhists cannot account for the occurrence of recollection such as in the statement, 'I am the one who did this yesterday.' According to Viśiṣṭādvaita a recollection of this type demonstrates the presence of a conscious self who is the permanent locus of the stream of consciousness.[17]

Yāmuna, the predecessor of Rāmānuja, presents the following argument to prove that the individual knowing subject, the self-conscious 'I' who is directly evident in the first-person singular 'I know', is a self-evident entity. He says that: 'all things [A] are manifest without relying upon something of the same type [as A] or upon something which has already been manifested by those things [by A]. Therefore the self is self-evident without relying upon another thing.'[18] Yāmuna then explains that a material object, such as a pot, does not depend upon something of the same type (*sajātīya*) in order to be revealed but requires something dissimilar (*vijātīya*), namely a light. A light need not be revealed by another light, nor does it depend upon the pot whose manifestation itself depended upon the light. The manifestation of light requires the presence of something else, namely the visual sense-organ. The operation of the visual sense-organ depends neither upon another sense-organ nor upon what is revealed by the visual sense-organ, namely the pot and the light. But the operation of the visual sense-organ depends upon the presence of consciousness. Consciousness does not require another consciousness in order to be manifest, nor does its manifestation depend upon what it has manifested, i.e. the pot, the light and the sense-organ. Although consciousness is self-revealing, its function is to reveal its objects to its locus and so consciousness depends upon a locus which is the self, the knowing subject 'I'. The self does not depend upon another self in order to become manifest, nor does it depend upon what is dependent upon it, namely the light, the sense-organs and consciousness. Therefore the conclusion reached is that the self is self-revealing because it does not depend upon something else in order to be manifest.

According to Viśiṣṭādvaita the self is self-revealing because the self is of the nature of consciousness. Thus both Advaita and Viśiṣṭādvaita consider the self to be self-revealing precisely because it is of the nature of consciousness. However, the fundamental difference between these two Vedānta schools is that for Advaita the Self is nothing but Consciousness, whereas for Viśiṣṭādvaita the self is an eternal, individual, knowing subject.

A particular feature of Viśiṣṭādvaita is the distinction it makes between the consciousness which constitutes the essential nature of the knowing subject and the consciousness which is an essential attribute of that subject. The consciousness constituting the essence of 'I' (*dharmibhūtajñāna*) is the consciousness whereby the 'I' only knows itself to be an 'I'. The consciousness which constitutes an essential attribute (*dharmabhūtajñāna*) of the self has the function of revealing some object, whether it is a mental state or a physical object, to the self. Viśiṣṭādvaita uses the analogy of a light and its lustre to explain the distinction between consciousness as the essence of the self and consciousness as the intrinsic attribute of the self. A light reveals only itself while the lustre of the light reveals both itself and other things. Similarly, the self is like the self-revealing light and the attributive consciousness, like the lustre of a light, reveals both itself and other things to the self. Viśiṣṭādvaita argues against Advaita that the self cannot be mere consciousness because the self shines forth directly as 'I' whereas consciousness depends upon a locus who *has* consciousness and consciousness also requires an object. According to Viśiṣṭādvaita it is the attributive consciousness which depends upon the self and reveals all objects to the self. Attributive consciousness is capable of contraction and expansion; for example, when a person is in the state of deep sleep, the attributive consciousness is in a contracted condition and so in sleep the 'I' is only manifest to itself as 'I' but cannot know anything outside itself. In the state of liberation (*mokṣa*) the attributive consciousness is released from the shackles of *karma* and assumes its natural condition so that the soul becomes virtually all-knowing.

The reality of the world

Viśiṣṭādvaita upholds the common-sense view that the world is an objective physical reality. We have seen that the Advaita position is that the world cannot be categorically determined as either absolutely real or as entirely fictitious, and this is what is meant by the word *mithyā*. The world is therefore an unreal appearance. The Advaita view follows from their definition of reality: reality must be permanent; what is real cannot undergo change. What changes cannot therefore be fully real. To put the matter in a more technical manner, in Advaita the criterion for the reality of a thing is the ascertainment of its continued existence in the same manner, i.e. the fact that it persists (*anuvartamānatva*). Hence the criterion for the unreality of a thing is linked to the discontinuity of the thing, i.e. the fact that it has exclusion (*vyāvartamānatva*) from existing in the same manner. If a thing is so excluded its reality is thereby negated (*bādhita*). For example, in the case of a rope appearing to be a snake, the rope is real because it persists as a rope when the snake imagination has been excluded and thereby been negated. With regard to the reality of the world, Advaita maintains that ultimately mere Being, which is identical to mere Consciousness, alone is fully real because Being persists in all things: the pot *is*, the cloth *is*, etc. The particular objects such as the pot and the cloth cannot be fully real because they are excluded either on account of (a) the fact that they mutually exclude each other as in the case of potness and clothness, which exclude each other since the pot does not exist in the cloth and vice versa, or (b) because while the object changes, Being persists: the pot *is*, the broken piece *is*, the clay *is*, etc.[19] Thus Advaita reasons in this manner: 'Being is real because it persists, as proved by the case of the rope in the rope-snake; jars and similar things are non-real because they are non-continuous, as proved by the case of the snake which has the rope for its substrate.'[20]

Viśiṣṭādvaita does not accept the Advaita position. Rāmānuja argues that it is incorrect to hold that negation is the result of non-persisting. Instead Rāmānuja says that non-persisting is the result of a negation and that negation will occur only when there is contradiction between two cognitions which have the same object. For example, in the case of the rope appearing as a snake there is the contradiction of the two cognitions 'this is a snake' and 'this is not a snake', which have the same object, namely the rope. When there is such a contradiction the cognition which has been produced by a valid means of knowledge i.e. perception, negates the defective cognition, which is thereby excluded and admitted to be unreal. But when there is no such contradiction among cognitions having the same referent there is no negation and hence no exclusion and no unreality. So even though the pot and the cloth exclude each other, or even though they both undergo change, there is no contradiction of cognitions just on that account and hence the pot and the cloth, etc., though not eternal, are not unreal. Thus we can see how Rāmānuja has reorientated the Advaita argument along realistic lines and tried to uphold the common-sense view of the reality of the world.

DVAITA VEDĀNTA

The Dvaita world-view

The tradition of Dvaita Vedānta arose as a reaction against the school of Śaṅkara and to a lesser extent against the school of Rāmānuja. The historical founder of the Dvaita school, Madhvācārya (1238–1317), known also as Ānandatīrtha and Pūrṇaprajña, was initiated into the Śaṅkara order of renunciates and studied Advaita literature for some time before adopting a radically different position from that of Advaita. He composed commentaries upon the *Upaniṣads*, the *Bhagavadgītā* and the *Brahmasūtras* as well as a number of independent works. A community of followers grew up around his teaching with their monastic centre in Udipi in south-west Karnataka. Along with Madhva, the notable figures of the Dvaita tradition are Jayatīrtha (1345–88), who produced lucid commentaries on most of the writings of Madhva, and Vyāsatīrtha (1460–1539), who perfected the formidable dialectical skills of the followers of Madhva with his work *Nyāyāmṛta*, which contains a trenchant critique of Advaita.

There are numerous broad areas of agreement between Dvaita and Viśiṣṭādvaita: they both uphold the reality of a personal God, Lord Viṣṇu, who is endowed with infinite auspicious attributes; they uphold the real existence of finite individual selves and the real existence of an objective world; and they both share the belief that devotion (*bhakti*) is the indispensable requirement for spiritual liberation. Madhva, however, rejected Rāmānuja's method of harmonizing all the *Upaniṣad* texts on the basis of the analogy of the relationship between body and soul. Implicit in this was his rejection of the Viśiṣṭādvaita explanation that there is an 'inseparable existence' (*apṛthaksiddhi*) between substance and attributes, for if attributes are inseparably connected to a substance, the converse must also be true and the substance must be inseparably connected to its attributes. If souls and matter form the 'body' or the 'attributes' of God, then according to Madhva the concept of *apṛthaksiddhi* would seriously compromise the independence of God.

Instead of the Viśiṣṭādvaita conception of a threefold order of reality consisting of the Lord (*īśvara*), sentient selves (*cit*) and insentient matter (*acit*), Madhva sought to emphasize the complete independence of God by enunciating a twofold category: God who is the only Independent Real (*svatantra*) and everything else which is totally dependent (*paratantra*) upon him. Within this twofold conception of reality Madhva enumerated a realistic pluralism:

> The manifest world contains a fivefold difference. There is (a) a difference between the individual self and God. So too (b) there is a difference between matter and God. There is (c) a mutual difference between individual selves, and (d) a difference between individual selves and matter. And there is (e) a mutual difference in physical matter.[21]

However, Madhva's pluralism is not a pluralism of independently real entities as in Nyāya-Vaiśeṣika, for in Madhva's system all plurality depends for its continued existence upon the will of God. Although Madhva considered the individual selves and matter to be beginningless and eternal and to exist in their own right separately from God, he makes their existence dependent upon the will of God. Individual selves, whether in the state of bondage or liberation, and physical matter, exist only for the sake of God and through the grace of God, and everything would instantaneously cease to exist if God did not choose to will its continued existence.[22]

Madhva differs openly from the other Vedānta schools in maintaining that God is solely the efficient cause of the world and not also the material cause. Madhva argues that what is sentient cannot change into what is insentient and vice versa.[23] Therefore God, being sentient, cannot also be the material cause of the insentient world. Madhva accepts the Sāṅkhya concept of an eternal, insentient, subtle material called *prakṛti*, and his explanation of creation is that God originates each cosmic cycle by causing *prakṛti* to evolve into increasingly more complex forms. However, God should not be thought of as just the initiator of the creation process, for Madhva maintains that each and every successive distinction in the evolving matter is dependent upon the will of God. Madhva's explanation of creation, which he called 'the acquisition of new traits depending upon the will of the other [God]' (*parādhīnaviśeṣāpti*), is intended to emphasize both the immanence of God in the world and the continuing dependence of the primary material, throughout all its modifications, upon the will of God.

A unique feature of Madhva's thought is his doctrine that there is an intrinsic inequality among selves. In Viśiṣṭādvaita, the individual selves are fundamentally alike, and although some souls such as Śrī, Garuḍa and Ananta are considered to be eternally liberated, all other souls are capable of achieving liberation. Madhva, however, distinguishes three classes of selves: those who are fit for liberation, those who will always remain within the cycle of rebirth, and those who are condemned to eternal suffering. Such an unusual doctrine in Indian thought has led to the speculation that Madhva may have come under some influence of an early Christian community living in south India, but this issue has not been settled.[24] In putting forward the doctrine of the intrinsic difference (*svarūpabheda*) among selves Madhva is not content with the usual justification that the different condition among souls is brought about because each soul is experiencing the results of its own beginningless involvement in action (*karma*). While this explanation accounts for the diversity of life-experiences among souls, it does not necessarily point to the fact that souls are intrinsically different by disposition. According to Madhva, individuals must be intrinsically different in their disposition because otherwise it cannot be explained how a soul would originally have come to choose one course of action over another. The soul must have initially chosen to involve itself in some particular action according to its intrinsic disposition, and that action then set in motion the law of *karma*. Souls must therefore, by their very nature, be intrinsically different in disposition.

According to Madhva both bondage and liberation must ultimately be traced to the will of God. Bondage is the self's false presumption of its own independence. This false presumption is due to ignorance of the fact that the self is totally dependent upon the will of God. Liberation is acquired through devotion (*bhakti*), which eventually gives rise to the immediate knowledge (*aparokṣajñāna*) of one's essential dependence upon God. This direct knowledge leads to the gift of grace whereby God liberates the soul upon the termination of the remaining *karma* whose results have to be experienced in the present life (*prārabdhakarma*). Even after liberation the souls, though in communion with God, do not all experience either the same degree of proximity to God or the same degree of bliss, but they experience a gradation of proximity and bliss according to their previous spiritual practice which corresponds to their intrinsic spiritual capacity, and thus even in liberation Madhva maintains that there is an intrinsic gradation among souls.

The individual self

Madhva's explanation of the nature of the individual self is not fundamentally different from that of Viśiṣṭādvaita. The essential self is not other than the knowing subject who is directly revealed in the enunciation of the first-person singular 'I'.[25] The individuality of each self can be known from the uniqueness of experience, for a person's experience of happiness or sadness rests with that person alone and cannot be directly experienced by another. Madhva argues against the Advaita view that the difference between selves can be explained on the basis of the presence of limiting adjuncts (*upādhi*), such as the mind, which brings about an apparent difference in the non-dual Self. Madhva says that the concept of a limiting adjunct has serious difficulties, such as whether the limiting adjunct has contact with a part of the Self or with the whole Self. If the adjunct has contact with a part of the Self, then the Self will be composite and therefore non-eternal. If the adjunct is in contact with the whole Self, then the oneness of the Self cannot be differentiated by limiting adjuncts.[26] Like Rāmānuja, Madhva maintains that the self is intrinsically self-luminous, the possessor of agentship and the experiencer of happiness and sadness. Madhva, however, does not make explicit the distinction that is made in Viśiṣṭādvaita between the self having substantive consciousness (*dharmibhūtajñāna*) and attributive consciousness (*dharmabhūtajñāna*).

A distinctive feature of the Dvaita conception of the self is the explanation put forward about the relation between the self and God. Madhva uses the analogy of the relation between the original image and its reflection (*bimbapratibimbabhāva*) to characterize the relation between God and the soul. The Advaita tradition also uses the same analogy of the original (*bimba*) and the reflection (*pratibimba*) to illustrate the nature of the appearance of the conditioned self. In Advaita, the individual conditioned self is equivalent to the reflection of *Brahman*, i.e. Pure Being-Consciousness, in the limiting adjunct of the internal organ. In the Advaita analogy, the original face stands for *Brahman*, the mirror stands for the internal organ, and the reflection of the face in the mirror represents the conditioned self. The conditioned self is unreal since it depends upon the presence of the reflecting medium in order for the reflection to take place.[27] This is not what Madhva seeks to convey through his use of the analogy. He seeks to communicate the idea that the self has both similarity to God and dependence upon God, just as a reflection is both similar to the original and dependent upon it. According to Madhva this relationship of similarity and dependence between the soul and God should form the subject matter for devotional contemplation.

An analogy is useful to illustrate only those aspects where similarity is intended to be conveyed, and it is not meant to indicate that there is a complete correspondence between all respects of the analogy and what it refers to. Otherwise, the reality of the soul would have to be seriously questioned if it were thought to be some kind of reflection, since a reflection has no reality of its own as it depends upon proximity between the original and the reflecting medium. Just as Madhva criticized the Advaita explanation of individuality where there is a reflection of the Self in limiting adjuncts, the Advaitins could equally question how Madhva could uphold the real existence of an individual self while using the analogy of a reflection. In fact Advaita and Dvaita utilize the idea of the original and its reflection only to conceptually explicate their respective teachings as developed in their own contexts, and these ideas could not have been intended to be subject to scrutiny concerning the logical sustainability of the analogy in all its respects.

Epistemology

Dvaita, like Viśiṣṭādvaita, holds that perception, inference and verbal testimony constitute the means through which we are able to gather knowledge. Among the three, perception and inference are authoritative means of knowledge in empirical matters while the verbal testimony of the sacred texts is authoritative for those matters which fall within the domain of revelation, such as the existence and nature of God. If the evidence from ordinary perception appears to conflict with scriptural testimony, as in the case where the revelation 'you are That' (*tat tvam asi*) appears to conflict with our ordinary self-understanding, than both Dvaita and Viśiṣṭādvaita accept ordinary perception as the support (*upajīvya*) of scripture and the latter must be interpreted in such a way as to be in accord with ordinary perception. This shows the importance given to common-sense realism in both these traditions. Advaita, however, maintains that if the Vedic texts contradict something *established* by perception, such as that fire is hot, then scripture has to be interpreted to accord with our normal perception; but if scripture contradicts our dualistic *assumptions* made on the basis of perception, which it does when it reveals that there is ultimately non-duality, then scripture becomes the support (*upajīvya*) and the assumption of a real duality is falsified.

All Vedāntins hold that knowledge which is produced by a valid and non-defective means of knowledge is intrinsically valid (*svataḥ prāmāṇya*) and does not require further validation from another source in order to prove it valid, because that other source would itself require to be validated and this would lead to an infinite regression. Validity is thus intrinsic to knowledge and valid knowledge is what corresponds to its object just as that object really is.[28] However, we have to know that our knowledge does in fact correspond to its object. Viśiṣṭādvaita maintains that knowledge is shown to be valid when it accords with our practical life as it is ordinarily understood.[29] Advaita adopts the principle of the absence of negation in order to test validity. Knowledge is valid so long as it is not negated. When the knowledge of the silver seen in the oyster-shell is negated by the subsequent knowledge that there is no silver in the shell, the former knowledge is negated and thereby shown to be erroneous. The latter knowledge is true so long as it is not negated.[30] Dvaita maintains that the Advaita criterion for validity can only be provisional, for although one's knowledge of a thing may not be negated at the present time, there is no guarantee that such knowledge will not be negated at some time in the future.[31] Madhva, therefore, in an attempt to discover certitude, has posited a novel criterion in order to test validity. He maintains that the self has as an intrinsic attribute a faculty of knowing called the *sākṣin*. The functions of the *sākṣin* are two: 1 (a) it perceives the sense-objects as they are revealed through sense-contact and (b) it directly perceives mental objects such as pleasure and pain and intuits the concepts of space and time; 2 (a) it reveals the presence of knowledge so that when we know something we are able to know that we know it and (b) it validates our knowledge of things. However, when the natural capacity of the *sākṣin* to apprehend the validity of knowledge is obstructed by contrary cognitions in the mind, then an extrinsic means such as workability has to be employed to remove the doubt, and when the obstructing doubt is removed then the *sākṣin* validates the knowledge. Thus the school of Dvaita posits the existence of an intuitive faculty which operates as the unerring criterion for apprehending the validity of knowledge.

The world

Dvaita, like Viśiṣṭādvaita, upholds the full reality of the ordinary, common-sense understanding of the world against the Advaita position that the world is a superimposition upon *Brahman* and is non-different from *Brahman*, analogous to a dream event where the dream is a superimposition occurring in Consciousness and is itself nothing but Consciousness. Madhva argues that in order for an illusory superimposition to occur there is the twofold requirement of (a) a real prototype and (b) a real substratum. If the world is an illusory superimposition upon *Brahman*, then there will have to be a real world somewhere which is similar to the illusory one and there will have to be a real substratum on which the illusion can occur.[32] Madhva argues that Advaita cannot admit a real prototype and so this world cannot be an illusory superimposition. The world is fully real and this must be so because the world (a) is the object of a valid means of knowledge, namely perception; (b) exists in time and space; and (c) has practical efficiency, unlike an illusory thing such as the horn of a rabbit etc.

In reply to the Dvaita argument, Advaita would agree that a superimposition requires a real substratum but disagree that the prototype must be something real. For instance, the mental impressions gathered while watching a horror film may be sufficient to cause a nightmare. Further, while Advaita admits that there is a perception of difference, it denies the truth of that perception on the ground that the function of perception is only to reveal but it is not the function of perception to *distinguish* between what it reveals. The function of distinguishing is actually a mental operation subsequent to perception. Advaita also argues that the concept of difference is difficult to prove logically, for it depends upon the knowledge of the relation between two factors: (a) a thing (*dharmi*), such as a cloth, and (b) a counter correlate (*pratiyogi*), i.e. something other than the cloth such as a pot etc. If we take the statement 'the cloth is different from the pot', the difference belonging to the cloth, which distinguishes it from the pot, is either identical to the cloth or is an attribute of the cloth. If difference is the same as the cloth, then as soon as the word 'cloth' is uttered the difference of the cloth from every other thing should automatically be known and any subsequent statement of difference such as '(the cloth) is different from . . .' would be redundant. But we do make such statements as 'the cloth is different from the pot' etc. Nor can difference be an attribute of the cloth. If difference is an attribute, then it is not identical to the thing itself. In order to distinguish the attribute, difference (D), from the substantive cloth we must posit another difference (D1) which is an attribute of the first difference and which distinguishes that first difference from the substantive. Otherwise difference (D) would be identical with the substantive. So, too, it is necessary to posit another difference (D2) as an attribute of D1 in order to distinguish D1 from D. And to distinguish D2 from D1 it is necessary to posit yet another difference (D3) as an attribute of D2, and so there will be an infinite regression.

Madhva has attempted to 'save the appearance' of difference by formulating a new explanation which could side-step the difficulties put forward by Advaita. He agreed with the Prabhākara school of Mīmāṁsā that difference is the very nature of the object and he thought that while difference is identical to the object, it is a special type of identity which provides for an occasional distinction to be made between difference and the object. Madhva explains this relationship by proposing the concept of 'distinction' or *viśeṣa*. Every substance has the capacity to show distinctions within its own structure.[33] This is why we can speak of the weight of a coin even though there is no actual difference between the coin and its weight. According to Madhva, since difference is identical to an object, when we first see an object we immediately know its difference from everything else in a general way. The general notion can become specific when required to do so because every substance has the capacity of *viśeṣa*, i.e. the capacity to allow a distinction to be made within itself.

The polemical literature between the Dvaita and Advaita schools reached its height between the fifteenth and sixteenth centuries when the Dvaita author Vyāsatīrtha wrote his critique of Advaita, *Nyāyāmṛta*, which was responded to by the Advaitin Madhusūdana Sarasvatī (AD 1500) in his work *Advaitasiddhi*. These schools of Vedānta, the Advaita, Viśiṣṭādvaita and Dvaita, continue into the present time, each with its own orders of renunciates (*sannyāsin*), professional scholars (*paṇḍita*) and lay adherents, and the Vedānta traditions still have an important part to play in the spiritual, intellectual and cultural life of India.

NOTES

1 See the commentaries of Śaṅkara, Rāmānuja and Madhva on *Brahmasūtra* 1.1.3–4.

2 Śaṅkara (circa AD 788–820) is the most renowned teacher in the tradition of Advaita. The most renowned teacher in the Viśiṣṭādvaita tradition is Rāmānuja (1017–1137). Madhva (1238–1317) is the most renowned teacher in the Dvaita tradition. Nimbārka (thirteenth century) is the principal teacher in the Dvaitādvaita school. Vallabha (1478–1531) is the principal teacher in the school of Śuddhādvaita and Caitanya (1485–1533) is the principal figure in the school of Acintyabhedābheda.

3 S. N. Dasgupta, *A History of Indian Philosophy* (Delhi: Motilal Banarsidass, 1975), vol. II, p. 125.

4 'In the "I" there is a non-object portion (*anidamaṁśa*) which is of the nature of homogeneous Awareness. In that "I" there is the appearance, a union as it were, of the false presumption of being "such and such" (*manuṣyābhimāna*) which is an objective element (*yuṣmadartha*) as it has the characteristic of being illumined by the Awareness.' See S. Rama Sastri and S. R. Krishnamurthi Sastri (eds), *Pañcapādikā with Two Commentaries and Pañcapādikāvivaraṇa with Two Commentaries*, Madras Gov. Oriental Series (Madras, 1958), p. 22.

5 'The I-notion (*ahaṅkāra*) is what has the sense of "I". It is a matter of common experience that the I contains the elements "this" and "not this". Let the learned people, after looking into the I thoroughly with a concentrated mind like an examiner of coins, say, without concealing their own experience, whether the I has the above mentioned character or not.' Ibid., pp. 29–30.

6 Swami Balarama (ed.), *Nyāyamakaranda: A Treatise on Vedanta Philosophy by Ānanda Bodha Bhaṭṭārakācārya with a Commentary by Chitsukha Muni* (Benares: Chowkhamba, 1901–7), p. 135.

7 Pt. Kashinath Shastri (ed.), *Tattvapradīpikā of Chitsukhācārya with the Commentary Nayanaprasādinī*, (Delhi: Chaukhamba Sanskrit Pratishthan, 1987), p. 9.

8 See *Māṇḍūkya Kārikā* 2.31–2.

9 Rama Sastri, op. cit., pp. 26, 98–9.

10 Balarama, op. cit., pp. 122–3.

11 Kashinath Sastri, op. cit., p. 39.

12 'A thing is said to be real when it does not deviate from the nature that is ascertained to be its own. A thing is said to be unreal when it deviates from the nature that is ascertained to be its own. Hence something mutable is unreal.' Śaṅkara, *Taittirīyopaniṣad-bhāṣya* 2.1.1, in *Īśādidaśopaniṣadaḥ (Ten Principal Upaniṣads with Śāṅkarabhāṣya)* (Delhi: Motilal Banarsidass, 1978), p. 283.

13 The 'body–soul' analogy is the primary conceptual model in Viśiṣṭādvaita. Rāmānuja considers that all the major *Upaniṣad* texts can be harmonized on the basis of this model. When an objector enquires whether Rāmānuja holds the position of a dualist or a non-dualist, or accepts simultaneous duality and non-duality, Rāmānuja replies that all these views are valid since they can all be found in the Veda. Rāmānuja then proceeds to harmonize these divergent positions by showing how they correspond to a particular feature of the body–soul model. Non-difference is established when it is thought that *Brahman* alone

exists, having everything as his body. Difference and non-difference are established when it is considered that *Brahman*, though one, exists qualified by a plurality since he has all sentient and insentient things as his modes. Difference is established because the Lord, the sentient souls and insentient matter are all distinct both in essence and in attributes. See S. S. Raghavachar, *Vedārtha-Saṅgraha of Śrī Rāmānujācārya* (Mysore: Sri Ramakrishna Ashrama, 1978), p. 90; also, T. G. Mainkar (ed.), *Sarva-Darśana-Saṅgraha of Sāyana-Mādhava* (Poona: Bhandarkar Oriental Research Institute, 1978), p. 110.

14 See Swami Adidevananda (trans.), *Yatīndramatadīpikā of Śrīnivāsadāsa* (Madras: Sri Ramakrishna Math, 1967), p. 130.

15 This discussion is taken from the *Ātmasiddhi* of Yāmunācārya. See R. Ramanujachari and K. Srinivasacharya (trans.), *Siddhitraya of Yāmunācārya with the Commentary Gūḍaprakāśa by U. Viraraghavacharya* (Madras: Ubhaya Vedanta Grantha Mala, 1972), pp. 12ff. (text pp. 12ff.).

16 See *Nyāyasūtra* 1.1.16, also *Bṛhadāraṇyaka-Upaniṣad* 1.5.3, and Śaṅkara's commentary, op. cit., pp. 697ff.

17 Ramanujachari, op. cit., pp. 30ff. (text pp. 25ff.). Also R. D. Karmarkar (ed. and trans.), *Śrībhāṣya of Rāmānuja* (3 vols, Poona: University of Poona, 1959–64), p. 61.

18 Ramanujachari, op. cit., p. 88 (text p. 62).

19 See Śaṅkara on *Bhagavadgītā* 2.16, in *Śrībhagavadgītā (Bhagavadgītā with Śāṅkarabhāṣya)* (Delhi: Motilal Banarsidass, 1978), p. 14.

20 G. Thibaut (trans.), *The Vedānta-Sūtras with the Commentary by Rāmānuja*, Sacred Books of the East Series XLVIII, (Delhi: Motilal Banarsidass, 1984), p. 33; Karmarkar, op. cit., p. 39.

21 *Viṣṇutattvanirṇaya*, cited in B. N. K. Sharma, *Sri Madhva's Teaching in His Own Words* (Bombay: Bharatiya Vidya Bhavan, 1979), p. 78.

22 Madhva frequently refers to a verse from the *Bhāgavata Purāṇa* (2.10.12) to justify his belief that the existence of everything depends upon the will of God: 'Matter, action, time, the natural tendency of things, and individual selves exist because of Whose grace and they do not exist if He becomes indifferent.' See also *Anuvyākhyāna* as cited in Sharma, op. cit., p. 123.

23 'Nowhere can the insentient be a product of the sentient and at no time can the sentient be a product of the insentient', *Anuvyākhyāna*, in Sharma, op. cit., p. 128.

24 A. L. Basham, *The Wonder that was India* (London: Fontana, 1976), p. 336.

25 'The individual soul is the one who is known just as "I". That one is indeed the experiencer of both happiness and sadness and is eligible for bondage and liberation.' *Viṣṇutattvanirṇaya* in Sharma, p. 87.

26 ibid., p. 93.

27 Swami Jagadananda (trans.), *Upadeśasāhasrī of Srī Śaṅkarācārya* (Madras: Sri Ramakrishna Math, 1984), ch. 18, v. 43.

28 In respect of Śaṅkara see J. L. Shastri (ed.), *Brahmasūtra-Śaṅkarabhāṣyam* (Delhi: Motilal Banarsidass, 1980), p. 78; Swami Gambhirananda (trans.), *Brahma-Sūtra-Bhāṣya of Śrī Śaṅkarācārya* (Calcutta: Advaita Ashrama, 1977), p. 30. In respect of Rāmānuja see Karmarkar, op. cit., p. 183. For Madhva see Sharma, op. cit., p. 42.

29 'Valid knowledge is knowledge which is in accord with practical life just as it is.' U. Viraraghavacharya (ed.), *Nyāyapariśuddhi by Sri Vedanta Desika* (Madras: Ubhaya Vedanta Grantamala, 1978), p. 44. Also, Adidevananda, op. cit., p. 5.

30 See S. S. Suryanarayana Sastri (ed. and trans.), *Vedāntaparibhāṣā by Dharmarāja Adhvarin* (Madras: The Adyar Library and Research Centre, 1971), p. 3. Also Swami Swahananda

(trans.), *Pañcadaśī of Vidyāraṇya Swāmī* (Madras: Sri Ramakrishna Math, 1975), ch. 2, verses 108–9.

31 To this the Advaitin would reply that once duality has been falsified it is no longer able subsequently to negate the non-dual.

32 Sharma, op. cit., pp. 79–80.

33 T. P. Ramachandran, *Dvaita Vedānta* (Wiltshire: Compton Russell, 1977), p. 130.

FURTHER READING

Balasubramanian, R. (1988) *The Naiṣkarmyasiddhi of Sureśvara*, Madras University Philosophical Series 47, Madras: University of Madras.

Carman, J. B. (1974) *The Theology of Rāmānuja: An Essay in Interreligious Understanding*, New Haven: Yale University Press.

Comans, M. (1988) *Advaitāmoda by Vāsudevaśāstrī Abhyankar: A Study of Advaita and Viśiṣṭādvaita*, Delhi: Sri Satguru Publications.

Lipner, J. (1986) *The Face of Truth: A Study of Meaning and Metaphysics in the Vedāntic Theology of Rāmānuja*. Albany: State University of New York Press.

Mahadevan, T. M. P. (1977) *The Philosophy of Advaita*, Wiltshire: Compton Russell.

Ramachandran, T. P. (1977) *Dvaita Vedānta*, Wiltshire, Compton Russell, 1977.

Sharma, B. N. K. (1981) *History of the Dvaita School of Vedānta and its Literature*. Delhi: Motilal Banarsidass.

—- (1986) *Philosophy of Śrī Madhvācārya*, Delhi: Motilal Banarsidass.

Srinivasa Chari, S. M. (1987) *Fundamentals of Viśiṣṭādvaita Vedānta*. Delhi: Motilal Banarsidass.

12

LOGIC AND LANGUAGE IN INDIAN PHILOSOPHY

Vijay Bharadwaja

INTRODUCTION

Logic in Indian philosophy covers the study of the methodology of knowledge (*pramāṇa-śāstra*). *Hetu-vidyā* (the logic of justification), *ānvīkṣiki* (the science of enquiry) and *tarka-śāstra* (the study of reasoning) are the other common synonyms for it. Typical examples of items included in the study of logic are perception (*pratyakṣa*), inference (*anumāna*), analogy (*upamāna*) and verbal testimony (*śabda*). These are called sources, methods or criteria of knowledge (*pramāṇa*). Different Indian philosophical traditions accept different sets of *pramāṇas*, taking some to be primitive and others derivative and hence dispensable. In the materialistic (Lokāyata) tradition which subscribes to the naïve common-sense world-view of philosophy, perception alone is accepted as the primitive source of knowledge. Since no authentic texts of the tradition are available, it is not possible to say how they defined perception. Whatever account of the Lokāyata tradition we have is inadequately based on their critics' often derogatory statements about them. The Lokāyata thinkers are believed to have denied the possibility of the certainty and necessity of empirical knowledge and hence rejected the possibility of inference, which simply cannot take off without its relevant empirical generalization (*vyāpti*).[1]

Kumārilabhaṭṭa (who belonged to the Pūrva Mīmāṁsā tradition) accepts the framework of six *pramāṇas* as primitive – perception, inference, analogy, verbal testimony, presumption or contextual interpretation (*arthāpatti*), and negation (*abhāva*). He regards the other *pramāṇas* like inclusion (*sambhavam*) and tradition (*aitihyam*) as derivative and hence dispensable.

In the available discussions of the sources of knowledge, a large number of logical, linguistic, epistemological, ontological and scientific issues are involved. Questions like what are the criteria of a good, acceptable argument (*hetu*), what are the conditions which make communication possible, and how is the concept of knowledge to be analysed belong to the first three types. Whether the self and God exist, and how many elements, like earth, water, fire and air, and in what quantity or form these go into the making of this world belong to the last two types. In this chapter, we shall focus on the logical, linguistic and epistemological issues, and touch upon others only when they impinge upon this interest. Also, as far as possible, we shall keep from discussing the Buddhist views on these issues.

KNOWLEDGE

Factual beliefs

The Indian philosophers employed the concept of a source, method or criterion of knowledge (*pramāṇa*) in the context of beliefs (*jñāna*) and knowledge (*pramā*). The question of the kind of beliefs there are is decided from the source or the means through which they are acquired. Beliefs like 'This is a man' or 'This man is brown' are acquired from observation (*pratyakṣa*). The belief that there is fire on the hill is acquired on the basis of the empirical generalization 'where there is smoke, there is fire', and it falls within the scope of inference (*anumāna*). Similarly, for a Hindu the source of our knowledge of moral and religious concerns is the Veda, and such knowledge constitutes the proper jurisdiction of verbal testimony (*śabda pramāṇa*).

Not all beliefs (*jñāna*) are knowledge (*pramā*).[2] For a piece of information to count as knowledge it must meet two conditions, one internal and the other external to the source of knowledge. What we claim to know must tally with facts as they are; this is the external condition. Let us call it the condition of truth (*yathārthatā*). The internal condition consists in satisfying the conceptual requirements of *pramāṇa* relevant to the given belief (*jñāna*). A belief gained by inference, for example, must satisfy the defining conditions of inference and all the rules of its acceptability as a good inference. Similarly, a belief which falls within the jurisdiction of verbal testimony must satisfy the requirements of its acceptability as specified in the conceptual structure of verbal testimony (*śabda pramāṇa*). Let us call this the condition of justifiability (*prāmāṇya*). On this account (which is generally accepted by different Indian philosophers) knowledge by definition is justified true belief. This is to say that only a belief (*jñāna*) which satisfies the condition of justifiability (*prāmāṇya*) and also the condition of truth (*yathārthatā*) is to count as knowledge (*pramā*).

The Naiyāyikas accept the epistemological framework of four sources of knowledge, namely perception, inference, analogy and verbal testimony. Bhāsarvajña (who is regarded as a Naiyāyika) does not accept analogy as an independent, primitive source of knowledge. He analyses analogy in terms of inference. However, Bhāsarvajña is an exception in the Nyāya tradition. In general, both the traditionalist and the modern Naiyāyikas define verbal testimony in such a way that any belief whose source falls within its jurisdiction must satisfy the condition of justifiability and the condition of truth. They do not conflate these two; rather they differentiate them sharply. This is why they define an authority (*āpta*) as one who speaks the truth and not as one whose authority constitutes truth.[3] The Naiyāyika position can therefore be characterized as epistemological externalism (*parataḥ-prāmāṇyavāda*).

The Pūrva Mīmāṁsakas subscribe to a diametrically opposed view. Their main preoccupation is investigation (*jijñāsā*) into the nature of our moral and religious concerns (*dharma*),[4] into our duty or what one ought to do. This interest puts constraints on how they analyse knowledge. Besides, they accept the primacy of the scriptures (the Veda) as the sole source of our knowledge of moral and religious matters. Such knowledge on their view is not factual, and therefore is not a matter of perception or inference or any other means of knowledge except verbal testimony. It is this knowledge that tells us what one ought or ought not to do. It is made available to us in the form of Vedic injunctions and prohibitions. It does not consist in descriptions of what the case is. Whatever other forms of (linguistic) expressions occur in the Veda, the Pūrva Mīmaṁsakas interpret them as subsidiary to the Vedic injunctions and prohibitions.

Three features of moral and religious knowledge are worth noting. First, such knowledge is not factual. Second, there is no source of it except the scriptures. And third, since the Veda is not the work of human mortals or some divine being and is infallible, such knowledge is necessarily true and unquestionable. The first feature makes the condition of factual truth (*yathārthatā*) to this kind of knowledge inapplicable; the condition is relevant to the factual knowledge only. The second feature renders the distinction between (a) the *source* and (b) *knowledge* of moral and religious matters look unimportant. Rather, of the two senses of the word *pramāṇa* – (i) that which makes the formation of beliefs and also the criteria of their criticizability possible (*pramīyate jñāyate anena*), and (ii) that which provides us with the criteria of the criticizability of beliefs (*pramīyate yat*) – the first is assimilated to the second and the word is used in the second sense exclusively.[5] The third feature makes infallibility internal to the built-in structure of this kind of knowledge; as the Pūrva Mīmāṁsakas would say, whatever conditions make such knowledge possible make it infallible also. This is the thesis of self-evidence of knowledge (*svataḥ prāmāṇyavāda*) as opposed to the Nyaya thesis of epistemological externalism (*parataḥ prāmānyavāda*). I would call this position epistemological internalism with respect to our knowledge of moral and religious concerns (*dharma*). However weak their argument might be, the Pūrva Mīmāṁsakas extend this thesis to all the other types of knowledge including perception and inference.

Beliefs (*jñāna*) are expressed in statements which are said to be true or false. When justified and true they constitute knowledge (*pramā*). Epistemologically, the minimal structure of a statement is given by the rule that a certain predicate is affirmed or denied of some individual (*jātiviśiṣṭa vyakti*). We do not know individuals as 'x', 'y' or 'z' as such without reference to their properties and relations, nor do we know properties like 'being a man', 'being tall' and 'being a brahmin' by themselves, in isolation from the individuals who possess them. We know individuals as having certain properties and relations, and we know properties and relations as possessed by certain individuals. Affirmative statements like 'he is a man', 'he is tall' and 'he is a brahmin' fall within the scope of this analysis. Justification (*prāmāṇya*) of such statements comes from observation (*pratyakṣa*); and if true, their truth (*yathārthatā*) consists in their tallying with facts or how things are.

Negative sentences

The account of negative statements in Indian logic is very complex. Statements like 'there is no jar here (at this place)', 'there are no sky flowers' and 'the son of a barren woman does not exist' are negative statements. In the history of logic in India, philosophers have adopted three major epistemological strategies to explain the conditions of the possibility of true negative statements. (1) The Pūrva Mīmāṁsakas accept negation (*abhāva*) as an independent means of knowledge. On their view negative statements are the subject matter neither of perception nor of inference but of an independent means of knowledge called *negation*.[6] To say this is to say that we form such statements and also know them to be true in a direct way on a par with true affirmative statements. (2) A second strategy is adopted by the Buddhists.[7] On their view, our knowledge of true negative statements is strictly a matter of inference – that inference whose conclusion is a negative statement. (They call it *anupalabdhi*.) They see no need to envisage an independent means of knowledge to account for such statements. (3) The Naiyāyikas seek to explain the possibility of true negative statements within the framework of perception.[8] It is important to note that there is a common element in these strategies which constitutes the core of their analysis. Other things being equal, they employ the *reduction* pattern of argument central to which is a counterfactual conditional (*tarka*) of the form 'if such and such were the case, then such and such would have been the case'. Take, for example, the statement 'there is no jar here (at this place)'. The core argument in each one of these strategies runs as follows: other things being equal, for example the light is good, visibility is not poor, etc., if the jar were here, it would have been visible as the ground is visible. Since the jar is not visible, it is fair to conclude that there is no jar here (*yadi atra ghaṭo abhaviṣyat tarhi bhūtalam ivadrakṣyat*). Explanation of the other two examples, 'there are no sky flowers, and 'the son of a barren woman does not exist', is given along these lines; only in their case, the situation is a little more complex.

Generality sentences

Central to the Indian theories of reasoning is the concept of generality (*vyāpti*), as in 'wherever there is smoke, there is fire'. The Indian logicians differentiate several types of generalities and discuss in detail the epistemological problems concerning them – like how we come to form them and what conditions must be satisfied to make them reliable for purposes of justification of some other statements which are always singular in character. For example, if one seeks to justify the statement 'there is fire here', when the fire is not within one's field of vision, one justifies it by citing a statement 'there is smoke here' in conjunction with a generality sentence 'wherever there is smoke, there is fire'. Such justification also requires pointing to a paradigm case (*dṛṣṭānta*) exemplifying the relevant generality (*vyāpti*). The following are examples of generality expressing sentences discussed in Indian logical theory:

(1) Where there is smoke, there is fire, as in the kitchen.
(2) Where there is no fire, there is no smoke either, as in a lake.
(3) Where there is smoke, there is fire fed by wet fuel.
(4) Where there is fire fed by wet fuel, there is smoke.
(5) Whatever is produced is not eternal, like the pot.
(6) Whatever is knowable is nameable like cloth. (This generality sentence is used in the argument, as in 'pot is nameable because it is knowable like cloth'.)
(7) Whatever is not nameable is not knowable either.
(8) Whatever does not have the distinctive feature of earth – that it is different from all other substances, that thing does not have the characteristic of smell either, for example water. (This generality sentence is used in the argument: 'Earth differs from other things because it has smell; that which does not so differ has no smell, as water; this is not like it; and hence it is not so.' Other things being equal, the argument comes to this: if F is a differentiating feature of x, and if y is different from x, then y does not have F.)
(9) All of Maitreyi's children are dark-complexioned like Devadatta.
(10) All *śiṁśapās* (the Aśoka trees) are trees.
(11) The third of the lunar asterisms consisting of six stars (*Kṛttikas*) rise whenever they are in the proximity of the fourth lunar aṣterism containing five stars figured by a cart (*Rohiṇi*).

The Indian logicians, particularly the Naiyāyikas and the Pūrva Mīmāṁsakas, disagree whether each of the sentences is a reliable generality which could be legitimately used in the justification procedure. However, they all agree that (9) is not a reliable generality sentence, that it expresses an accidental, not a nomological, generalization. They observe that from the fact that all Maitreyi's children are dark-complexioned it does not follow that her next child will be dark-complexioned. Their argument is that 'being Maitreyi's child' and 'being dark-complexioned' are only accidentally connected.

These logicians also agree that (1) definitely is a reliable and not an accidental generalization, and therefore it is a fit candidate for use in the justification procedure.

A nomological generalization need not always be causal. For instance, the generality sentence (10), which asserts that the class of the Aśoka trees is a proper subset of the class of trees, is a nomological and not a causal generalization. Similarly, (11) is also a nomological generalization, though we do not know whether the relationship between 'being in the proximity of the fourth lunar asterism' and 'rising of the third lunar asterism' is causal. An interesting example is that of a weighing scale. The relationship between its two sides may not be said to be causal, yet the generality expressing the relationship must be regarded as nomological.

Though the Indian logicians differentiated causal from non-causal, and accidental from nomological, generalizations, they seem to have failed completely in distinguishing a definition, an axiom, or a presupposition fundamental to their conceptual frameworks, from an empirical generalization. They did not see, for instance, that (6) is a presupposition fundamental to someone's (in this case, the Naiyāyikas') conceptual framework, and that it is not a generalization on a par with the empirical generalizations expressed in (1) and (2). They regarded (1) as a generalization reached by the method of agreement (*anvaya vyāpti*), and (2) as a generalization reached by the method of difference (*vyatireka vyāpti*), because for both (1) and (2) a good paradigm or example could be shown.[9] For (1) an example showing the agreement – a positive example – could be given in which smoke is shown to be regularly associated with fire, for instance in the kitchen; and for (2) an example showing the difference – a negative example – could be presented in which absence of fire is shown to be regularly associated with absence of smoke, for instance in the lake. But on the Naiyāyikas' view, for (6) no negative example is conceptually possible; only a positive example can be given. They did not see that if a negative example is logically impossible, then giving a positive example has no meaning, because the very intelligibility of the one derives from its contrast with the other. If this is true, then saying that there is a paradigm or an example in such cases ceases to have meaning; for then the very notion of a paradigm or example is rendered conceptually otiose. The point I am making is that the notion of a paradigm or an example is not at all relevant to sentences of type (6). Sentence (6) is a presupposition or an axiomatic assumption which is fundamental to the Naiyāyika conceptual framework; it is only a gross misunderstanding of the nature of this presupposition that the Naiyāyikas go about looking for a paradigm or an example of it. In the nature of the case, either everything or nothing is an example of it, and both these alternatives are equally illusory. The same argument applies to sentence (5).

The Naiyāyikas' position becomes all the more untenable when we consider the generality sentence (7). Sentences (7) and (6) are equivalent; and as the Naiyāyikas view them, everything is an instance of (6) but nothing is an instance of (7), because there is nothing which could possibly be said to be an example of it. To my mind, it is simply mistaken to say of any two equivalent generalizations that there are instances of one but none of the other. The Naiyāyikas would not have made this mistake if they had cared to examine closely the nature of the sort of generality they were talking about in accepting (6) or rejecting (7).

The case of the generality sentence (8) is more complex. The sentence moves on the strength of the individuating feature of earth, namely that it has smell. Given this feature, it is an obvious truism that whatever else is different from earth does not have the differentiating feature of earth, namely smell. I do not quite see why the Naiyāyikas called (8) a generality sentence. More or less, (8) is an argument which gives the incorrect impression that it has a certain shared structure with the law of identity, that is, for all x and for all y, if F is a feature of x and x is identical with y, then F is a feature of y also; in symbols, $(x)\ (y)\ (Fx.\ (x = y) \rightarrow Fy)$. However, (8) is not a statement of the law of identity. What it says is that if F is a distinctive feature of x, and if y is different from x, then F is not true of y. As said earlier, (8) moves on the strength of the definition, in this case, of earth. The Naiyāyikas take (8) as a generalization which shows the exclusion of something from everything else (*kevala vyatireki vyāpti*), for which no positive example is conceptually possible. The situation here is similar to that we encountered in the case of the generality sentence (6). The Naiyāyikas misunderstood the nature of (8); they misconstrued it on the model of (1) and (2), taking it to be some sort of empirical generalization for which an exclusively negative example can be given. They failed to see that definitions could not be said to be empirical generalizations which have instances. It is possible, however, that some definitions are abstractions reached on the basis of empirical observation such that they have application to the empirical sphere.

In this light it is not surprising that the Pūrva Mīmāṁsakas and many other logicians did not share the Naiyāyika view that sentences (5), (6) and (8) express some sort of (empirical) generalizations which must have exclusively positive or exclusively negative examples. It is important to observe, however, that the Naiyāyikas had a point when they regarded (5), (6) and (8) as generality sentences. The role played by these sentences is that they make certain types of inferences possible and legitimate. Thus, on the Naiyāyika view, inferences based upon definitions, axioms and presuppositions fundamental to one's conceptual framework as exemplified in (5), (6) and (8) are valid at least within the specified conceptual scheme. This insight is illuminating with respect to the question of the validity of reasoning patterns within a given tradition. Several instances of extensive exploitation of this insight are available in the logical patterns developed by the Vedāntic thinkers, for example their arguments to justify the thesis that this world is not real.[10]

In the different traditions of Indian logic, the concept of generality has been analysed differently. In the Nyāya tradition it has been analysed as a regular association (*sāhacarya* or *sāhacarya niyama*) counter-instances of which are not known (*vyabhicāra jñāna viraha*). The Pūrva Mīmāṁsakas analyse it as a natural relationship (*svabhāvika sambandha*) which is not vitiated by some or other restriction, exception, or limiting condition (*upādhi*). One example of such a condition is provided by the following argument: 'Violence which is part of a Vedic sacrifice is wrong; for, it is violence like any other violence, etc.'[11] The context of this argument is this: the Veda enjoins the sacrifice (called *agniṣomīya*) the performance of which involves violence to certain animals (for example killing them). Violence involved in the performance of a sacrifice is known as sacrificial violence (*kṛatuhiṃsā*). What is enjoined by the Veda is morally right and what is forbidden by the Veda is morally wrong. Sacrificial violence is enjoined by the Veda, so it is morally right; on the contrary, killing a brahmin is forbidden by the Veda, so it is morally wrong. The argument is directed against the Pūrva Mīmāṁsakas, who accept the authority of the Veda in matters of moral and religious concerns. In this argument 'being forbidden' is the restriction, a limiting condition (*upādhi*). 'Being forbidden' is not applicable to sacrificial violence, though it is relevant to some other cases of violence, for example killing a brahmin. The argument illicitly conflates the sacrificial violence which is enjoined by the Veda and thus allowed with any other violence, like killing a brahmin, which is forbidden by the Veda.

The generality sentences (1) and (2) express empirical generalization, a regular association with no known counter-instances. When sentence (1), 'where there is smoke, there is fire, as in the kitchen', is true but its converse, 'where there is fire there is smoke', is false, it is a case of non-equivalent generality (*viṣama vyāpti*). However, it is possible to have a generality sentence like (3), 'where there is smoke, there is fire fed by wet fuel', or (4), 'where there is fire fed by wet fuel, there is smoke'. Sentences (3) and (4) are a pair of equivalent generality (*sama vyāpti*). The same is true of (5), 'whatever is produced is not eternal, like the pot'. Here also the class of things said to be produced is coextensive with the class of things said to be non-eternal; so the generality expressed in (5) is a case of equivalent generality; only it is not an empirical generalization as (3) and (4) are.

As remarked earlier, the Indian logicians do not seem to be clear regarding the nature of generality – whether in forming generalities they were formulating empirical generalizations, definitions or presuppositions fundamental to their conceptual frameworks. My feeling is that they viewed generalities as empirical generalizations. This feeling is confirmed by the methodology they adopted for forming generalizations. The most frequently used method is the repeated observation. Having repeatedly observed a regular association, say, of smoke with fire, we reach the generalization 'where there is smoke there is fire, as in the kitchen'. This is one half of the story. The other half consists in handling possible doubts about a given generalization. This is done by employing argumentation (*tarka*), particularly of the *reductio* type.[12] With its help, we are able to say that there are no known counter-instances. Yet the sceptic may argue that it is logically illegitimate to move from the observation of some instances, say, of smoke with fire to the generalization that 'where there is smoke there is fire'. To meet the sceptic's argument, the Indian logicians have taken two tacks. The Naiyāyikas have brought in the notion of an extraordinary perception (*sāmānya lakṣaṇa pratyāsatti*) whose function is to abstract the general features of what is observed to enable us to grasp the generality, as in 'where there is smoke there is fire, as in the kitchen'.[13] The Jaina thinkers followed a different tack.[14] They maintained that perception can give us knowledge of particulars only, not of generality. Nor can inference give us knowledge of generality; for it itself is parasitic on perception. So they accepted an additional independent means of knowledge called induction (*tarka*) and claimed that this alone can give us knowledge of generality. Their strategy was more like that of Bertrand Russell in the twentieth century of accepting induction as an independent principle of logic.

Besides the methods of repeated observation, extraordinary perception, and induction, the Indian logicians recognize a fourth way of forming generalities. It is the method of intuitive induction, that is, one can form a legitimate generalization in one single perception. This method is exploited mainly by the Vedanta Māmāmśakas in their arguments to show the illusoriness of this world on the strength merely of certain paradigms of visual illusions like nacre silver.[15] The Naiyāyikas and the Jaina philosophers, who are realists through and through, do not put much store by this method of forming and knowing generalities.

JUSTIFICATION

Patterns of arguments

The concept of generality is central to the Indian theory of inference and justification. The word *anumāna* has often been translated as 'inference'; and with this all sorts of assertions have been made about it: that *anumāna* is inference, that it is deductive and formal, that it could be said to be valid or invalid. Fortunately, these and similar characterizations of it have recently been challenged, and a new thinking is emerging.[16] In the relevant literature, the word *anumāna* has been used to describe a variety of reasoning patterns. In the *Nyāyasūtra* of Gotama, we find at least three different reasoning patterns. They are classified as inference. (1), inference may be justification of a prediction (*pūrvavat*). It is arguing from a cause to its effect by way of making a prediction. For example, a person observing clouds, other things being equal, is able to say that there will be rain. (2), inference may be an explanation (*śeṣavat*). It is arguing from an effect to its cause by way of explaining a phenomenon. For example, a person observing a swollen river, other things being equal, is able to say that there have been rains in the region. (3), inference may be a justification from the commonly seen (*sāmānyato dṛṣṭa*). If two things have been commonly observed to be regularly associated, then arguing from seeing one to the knowledge of the other is called inference or justification from the commonly seen. For example, a person observing an animal possessing horns is able to say that the animal also has a tail. Smoke and fire are observed to be regularly associated; so if one knows that there is smoke on the hill, one's argument then that there must also be fire would fall within the scope of inference from the commonly seen.

The structure of inference in Indian logic has followed three major patterns:

(A) (1) There is fire on the hill
(2) because there is smoke on it.

In this pattern, (1) is called the thesis to be justified (*pakṣa, ṣādhya*), and (2) is called the argument or reason (*hetu, sādhana*). Ordinarily, (2) is stated in conjunction with some observationally available paradigm or example (*udāharaṇa*) which shows that the reason statement is true and thus acceptable.

(B) (1) There is fire on the hill
(2) because there is smoke on it
(3) where there is smoke, there is fire, as in the kitchen
(4) this is so
(5) hence, this has fire.

In this pattern, (1) is called the thesis; (2) the reason or argument; (3) the paradigm or example stated in conjunction with its relevant generality; (4) the application (*upanaya*) which consists in thinking of (1), (2) and (3) together, and (5) the deduction (*nigamana*) or the result of (4). When inference has this structure, the Naiyāyikas call it fully formed reasoning (*nyāya*). This pattern is aimed at communicating and demonstrating to others how a given thesis is argued for, and it is technically classified as inference for the sake of others (*parārthānumāna*). In this pattern, (1) is the declaration of the thesis to be shown to be true, (2) to (4) consist of argument supported by observational evidence, and (5) is the declaration that (1) is shown to be true.

Inference for the sake of others has been differentiated from inference for oneself (*svārthānumāna*), in which the individual in the process of investigation himself reaches the truth of a given thesis. When required to show his reasoning, he exhibits it as inference for others, that is, by giving a full-blown account of his reasoning leading to the truth of the thesis.

The Pūrva Mīmāṁsakas find pattern (A) inadequate, for it does not explicitly include a generalization; and pattern (B) unnecessarily artificial, as it involves two superfluous statements. They suggest that a pattern (C) consisting of three statements, either a conjunction of (1), (2) and (3) or a conjunction of (3), (4) and (5), is good enough to qualify as a precise statement of inference.[17]

Another classification of inference is based on the type of generality used in it at step (3) in pattern (B). Thus, inference is said to be based on both agreement and difference (*anvaya-vyatireki*), based on agreement exclusively (*kevalānvayi*), and based on difference exclusively (*kevala vyatireki*) if it works with the type of generality exemplified in the generality sentences (1), (6) and (8) respectively. The Naiyāvikas broadly accept this threefold division of inference, but Kumārila Bhaṭṭa of the Pūrva Mīmāṁsaka tradition denies that inference based on difference exclusively really is inference. Instead he accepts an independent means of knowledge, namely presumption or contextual interpretation (*arthāpatti*), which he employs to handle 'inferences' based on difference exclusively. In general, those who do not accept patterns of inferences based on agreement exclusively or based on difference exclusively argue essentially from the logical fact that inferences based on agreement exclusively fail to satisfy the condition that a good reason or argument must not allow counter-examples (*vipakṣa*); and that inferences based on difference exclusively fail to satisfy the condition, namely that a good reason or argument must admit favourable examples (*sapakṣa*). This indeed is the case, because inferences based on agreement exclusively exclude the possibility of counter-examples, and similarly, inferences based on difference exclusively exclude the possibility of favourable examples. The logical fallacies committed in these inference patterns are extraordinary discrepancy and ordinary discrepancy respectively. None the less, the Naiyāyikas stuck to these inference patterns in spite of their logical fallacies.

I indicated earlier that the thesis to be justified is called *pakṣa*. For instance, in argument pattern (A), the statement (1) 'There is fire on the hill' is the thesis to be justified; so it is called *pakṣa* in that argument pattern. *Sādhya* is a term which is alternative to and synonymous with *pakṣa*. An argument or reason offered in support of the thesis to be justified is called *hetu* or *sādhana* for the thesis. The idea of a reason's being relevant to the thesis to be justified is called relevance (in Sanskrit, *pakṣadharmatā*).

When made explicit an argument consists of (i) a statement of observed condition(s), for example 'There is smoke on the hill', and (ii) a generalization including (iii) a relevant paradigm or example. Knowledge of the relevance of the reason to the thesis is called ratiocination or deliberation (*parāmarśa*).[18] On the Nyāya view, inferential knowledge is the result of inference; and since deliberation or ratiocination leads to such knowledge, the ratiocination itself is regarded as the same as inference.

The notions of *sapakṣa* and *vipakṣa* must be clarified. In the Indian logical literature, there are at least two different though related uses of these terms – (1) in relation to the thesis to be justified, and (2) in relation to the paradigm or example. In relation to the thesis to be justified, *sapakṣa* means the same as the thesis to be justified; and *vipakṣa* means any thesis other than the thesis to be justified. For instance, in a given argument, if *sapakṣa* is the thesis that sound is eternal, its *vipakṣa* would be a thesis other than or opposite to this thesis for example 'sound is audible' or 'sound is not eternal'. This usage is characteristic of Buddhist logic. The way the Naiyāyikas, for instance Annaṁbhaṭṭa (1623 AD) and Viśvanātha (1634 AD), employ these terms suggests their second use. Here the two terms are applicable to paradigms or examples. Thus, *sapakṣa* means a paradigm which exemplifies the applicability of its relevant reason and *vipakṣa* means a paradigm which exemplifies the inapplicability of its relevant reason. For instance, if the reason is the smoke–fire generality, then its *sapakṣa* paradigm is the case of the kitchen, where smoke connected to fire is observable; and its *vipakṣa* paradigm is the case of the lake, to which the relevant generality is inapplicable. The Indian logicians have not been very good at keeping these two uses of the term separate; often they have tended to blur the distinction.

Conditions of justification

The Nyāya thinkers in general have not paid much attention to formulating explicitly the conditions for a good argument; the Buddhists have done far better in this regard. Some discussion, however, is found in Nyāya works like *Tarkāmṛta* of Jagadīśa (1635 AD) and *Tarkakaumudi* of Laugākṣi Bhāskara (seventeeth century), and in Pūrva Mīmāṁsa works like *Manameyodaya* of Nārāyaṇa (AD 1587–1656). Most of these works belong to the later period of Nyāya and Pūrva Mīmāṁsa logic, and they show evidence of the Buddhist influence. According to these thinkers, the following are the five conditions which must be satisfied for a reason or an argument to be good:

1 The reason must be relevant to the thesis to be justified.
2 The reason must be true of the thesis to be justified.
3 The reason must not be applicable to a thesis other than the thesis to be justified.
4 The thesis to be justified must not be inconsistent with anything known by some other means of knowledge.
5 The argument must not leave open the possibility of a stronger reason which can be used to justify the opposite of the thesis to be justified.

Of these, the fourth is not really a condition for a good reason, but concerns the nature of the thesis to be justified. It specifies the requirement that the thesis to be argued for must not be inconsistent with anything known by some other means of knowledge. For instance, the statement 'Fire is not hot' is inconsistent with what we know by perception; hence this statement could not be a (legitimate) thesis for the purposes of inference. The Naiyāyikas called it a pseudo-thesis, that is, a statement which appears to be the thesis but in fact is not.

The fifth condition concerns neither the thesis nor the reason justifying it; it is more or less heuristic in intent for argumentation in general. It requires that an argument should be strong enough to prevent the opponent from justifying his thesis by a different set of argument. For instance, the argument

(a) Sound is eternal
because it is an exclusive characteristic of ether

is not strong enough to prevent an opponent from justifying his thesis that sound is not eternal by advancing the following argument:

(b) Sound is not eternal
because it is originated.

Conditions (1), (2) and (3) indeed concern the reason or argument. It we accept them as criteria of a good reason, then the Naiyāyikas land themselves in an unenviable position with respect to inference patterns based exclusively on agreement or exclusively on difference. The argument in the case of the former fails to satisfy the third condition, the negative example being impossible; and the argument in the case of the latter fails to satisfy the second condition, the positive example being impossible. So, the Naiyāyikas are faced with a dilemma: either accept (2) and (3) as the necessary conditions for a good, acceptable argument, and reject the inference patterns based exclusively on agreement or exclusively on difference as invalid; or retain the two inference patterns as acceptable and valid but say that (2) and (3) are not really the necessary conditions for a good reason or argument. Both these positions in one or another form have been adopted in the history of Indian logic. It is noteworthy that Annaṁbhaṭṭa (AD 1623) is apparently silent on the question of the conditions for a good argument, and he accepts the said inference patterns as good and acceptable forms of reasoning. A Pūrva Mīmāṁsa thinker, Nārāyaṇa (AD 1587–1656), formulates requirements (1) to (5) clearly, but restricts their application mainly to the pattern of inference based on both agreement and difference as illustrated in the smoke–fire example.[19]

Fallacies

Fallacious reasoning involves a pseudo-reason (*hetvābhāsa*). A pseudo-reason is something which appears to be a reason but really is not a (good) reason. There is no general agreement on the number of fallacies in Indian logic. Kaṇāda (AD 450), the author of *Vaiśeṣika-sūtra*, accepts three – discrepant, opposite, and irrelevant; Kumārilabhaṭṭa (AD 600–660), of the Pūrva Mīmāṁsa tradition, accepts four – irrelevant, opposite, uncertain, and extraordinary. The Jaina thinkers accept three – irrelevant, opposite, and uncertain; Gotama (AD 150), the author of *Nyāya-sūtra*, accepts five – discrepant, opposite, equipollent, circular, and untimely; so does Annaṁbhaṭṭa (AD 1623), the author of *Tarkasaṁgraha* and *Tarkadīpikā* – discrepant, opposite, counterbalanced, irrelevant, and futile. Often there is disagreement on the interpretation of these terms. However, we give here Annaṁbhaṭṭa's classification. Since the five criteria of a good reason or argument have been formulated earlier, it is convenient to discuss the fallacies in terms of these criteria.

One commits the fallacy of irrelevant reason (*asiddha hetu*) when (a) the thesis to be justified is about something which does not exist, or (b) when the reason advanced is irrelevant to the thesis, or (c) when the reason fails to specify the limiting condition or restriction which alone can make the reason relevant to the thesis. Consider the argument

(a) The sky lotus is fragrant
because it is a lotus like a lotus in a lake.

In this argument, the thesis is about the sky lotus. The sky lotus is a concept, and there is nothing in the world to which it is applicable. But the reason speaks of the real lotus. A statement about the real lotus is not relevant to justifying a statement about something which is unreal. Hence, the fallacy of irrelevant reason. Since in this argument there is no logical basis for advancing the reason, the type of irrelevance involved is called logical irrelevance.

(b) Sound is a quality
because it is ocular.

In this argument, the thesis is about sound, while the reason is about something relating to the eye. So, the reason is not relevant to the thesis to be justified; hence the fallacy of irrelevant reason. The type of irrelevance involved here is generated by confusion of logical types; for sound can be said to be audible or inaudible, and the ocular has nothing to do with it.

(c) There is smoke on the hill
because there is fire on it.

Since it is possible to have smokeless fire, the reason here is not relevant to the thesis to be justified unless it is explicitly specified which kind of fire is being talked about. This can be done by articulating the limiting condition or restriction, namely the contact (of fire) with wet fuel (which naturally produces smoke). Hence the fallacy of irrelevant reason. The type of irrelevance involved here is that the reason is too wide in its application; for, in the argument as stated, the reason is more general than the thesis to be justified, with the consequence that it is not strictly related to the thesis. It is to be noticed that in all these arguments (a), (b) and (c) the reason fails to satisfy condition (1) for a good reason or argument, namely the condition of relevance. For a reason to be good, it is essential that it is relevant to the thesis to be justified. If the reason is not relevant to the thesis, the fallacy of irrelevant reason is committed.

Consider the argument

(d) Sound is eternal
because it is produced.

In this argument, 'being eternal' and 'being a product' are mutually incompatible. So, the reason is inconsistent (*viruddha*) with the thesis. Hence, the fallacy of opposite reason is committed. In fact, 'being a product' could be cited as a good reason for saying that sound is not eternal. The thesis 'sound is not eternal' is the opposite (*vipakṣa*) of the thesis in (d), and the given reason is correctly applicable to it, resulting in the violation of the third rule, which says that the reason must not be applicable to the opposite thesis.

Sometimes, a fallacy is committed when the reason is discrepant (*savythhicāra*) with the thesis to be justified. In the following three arguments, the fallacy of discrepant reason is committed:

(e) There is fire on the hill
because it is knowable.
(f) Sound is eternal
because it is a sound.
(g) Nothing is eternal
because it is knowable.

In argument (e), the reason is applicable not only to the case of fire on the hill but also to the case of there being no fire on the hill; in fact it is applicable to whatever the case may be – it may be the opposite of the given thesis or it may be any other thesis; the reason would be equally applicable to it. This shows that the reason is too general to support the thesis. Since the claim made in the reason statement is quite at variance with the claim made in the thesis, the reason is said to be discrepant with the thesis. And, since the reason is too wide in its application, the specific discrepancy involved is called the ordinary or common discrepancy. Thus argument (e) involves the fallacy of common discrepancy.

The reason in argument (f) is discrepant because it makes a claim which is trivially true; no sane person would ordinarily advance it as a reason in support of the substantive claim made in the thesis in question. Hence, this reason is extraordinary. So, the fallacy committed is extraordinary discrepancy.

In argument (g) also, the reason is discrepant with the thesis. The claim in the reason statement that something is knowable is quite at variance with the claim in the thesis that nothing is eternal. Besides, no positive or counter-example is possible in the case of this argument. Thus the reason in this argument is discrepant: it is inconclusive, and does not clinch the issue.

A discrepant reason is also called uncertain (*anaikāntika*) – that which is vague and ambiguous, not precise, not pointed. It follows from the meaning of this word that a reason which commits this fallacy is a suspect (*sandigdha*) reason.

When a reason fails to satisfy the second or third condition for a good argument it is said to be a discrepant reason. The reason in argument (e) turns out to be applicable to the opposite thesis also, thus violating the third condition, namely that a good reason must not be applicable to the opposite thesis. In the case of argument (g), neither a positive nor a negative example is possible; thus it fails to satisfy both the second and the third condition. In argument (f) the claim made in the reason statement does not connect it to the thesis to be justified. So, the argument flouts the first rule, namely that the reason must be relevant to the thesis to be justified.

An example of an argument which involves the fallacy of futile (*bādhita*) reason is:

(h) Fire is not hot
because it is a substance.

In this argument, the thesis is inconsistent with what is known to be true by perception; in fact, the contradictory of the thesis, 'Fire is hot', is definitely known by perception to be true. So, the thesis is one which needs no inferential argument. When this is the case, the fourth condition for a good reason is not satisfied, and the resultant fallacy is called futile (that is, 'not allowed'). This fallacy properly belongs to the nature of the thesis to be justified and not to the reason justifying it.

Similarly, the fallacy of the counterbalanced reason (*satpratipakṣa*), which is illustrated by the following pair of arguments, is not a fallacy of the reason; it strictly pertains to the relative strength of any two arguments. Given the argument

(i) Sound is eternal
because it is the exclusive property of ether,

if an opponent can advance another argument,

(j) Sound is not eternal
because it is originated,

for his thesis that sound is not eternal, then we have what has been called the fallacy of the counterbalanced reason, since we have in (j) the contradictory of the thesis of (i) and at the same time a much stronger argument for it. The argument (i) leaves open the possibility of a stronger argument (j) which justifies the opposite of the thesis to be justified. Thus, in the case of the counterbalanced reason, the fifth requirement of a good reason is violated.

LANGUAGE

Meaning of words and sentences

A word is a sequence of letters in a certain order. Letters are regarded as forming a sequence only because they are so thought of; the number of letters forming one sequence is regarded as one word, another sequence as another word and so on. A sentence is a sequence of words in a certain order. (1) 'Bring the cow', (2) 'there is fire on the hill', (3) 'he is the same Devadatta', (4) 'the cottage is on the Ganges' are examples of sentences. In (1), there is a reference to performing an action; so, the meaning of such sentences consists in the action enjoined in them. In (2), something is said about something else; the meaning of such sentences consists in the ascription of a characteristic to the characterized. Sentence (3) is an example of an identity sentence; and (4) is a sentence which when taken literally could not be said to be true, but its use suggests metaphorically that the cottage built on the bank of the Ganges is cool in summer, etc.

A word has meaning (*śakti*, lit. 'power'), which may be literal (*abhidhā*) or metaphorical (*lakṣaṇā*). On the traditionalist Naiyāyika view, for instance Annambhatta's, it is God who ordains which word will mean what; though the modern Naiyāyikas underscore the role of man in giving meanings to words.[20] Since the Pūrva Mīmāṁsakas accept the Veda as the only source of knowledge in matters of moral and religious concerns (*dharma*), and since they regard the Veda as impersonal (*apauruṣeya*) with respect to its authorship, they reject the Nyāya view that it is God or man who gives meaning to the words in moral and religious matters.

The paradigm of a meaningful expression, I must add, in the context of the Veda is an injunction sentence, a sentence which enjoins one to do something (*vidhi vākya*), for example performance of a sacrifice. In their simplest form, injunction sentences follow the pattern shown in example (1), namely 'Bring the cow' or 'The cow ought to be brought'; in general they are grammatically in the imperative or potential mood. The life and soul of sentence (1) is the action of bringing the cow. The verb in it is the principal word; other words in the sentence have meaning in virtue of their relationship with it; standing alone they remain incomplete and cannot be regarded as meaningful. The words in such sentences have the power (*śakti*) of literal or metaphorical use, not because God or man has so willed it but because they are part of the impersonal and eternal Veda whose core constituents are injunction sentences. This is Prabhākaramiśra's (AD 600–650) theory of the primacy of the sentence for meaningfulness (*anvitābhidhānavāda*).[21] In the Veda, injunction sentences occur or can be shown (by contextual interpretation) to occur as complete sentences; the sentence, and not the word, being the unit of communication. Thus, Prabhākaramiśra gives primacy to the sentence and not to the individual words for purposes of communication; and his strategy for explaining the meaningfulness of words consists in showing the meaningfulness of sentences in terms of their core constituent word, i.e. the verb, the action word.

Not all the Pūrva Mīmāṁsakas, however, accept the theory of the primacy of the sentence for meaningfulness. Kumārilabhaṭṭa, for instance, does not agree that words standing alone are not meaningful. On his view, words *qua* words have (literal) meaning. When ordered to form syntactically complete sentences they express sentential meaning, i.e. one connected idea. Like Prabhākaramiśra he rejects the view that it is God or man who decides which words will mean what. Kumārila argues that Prabhākaramiśra seems to deny the very basis of meaningfulness of a sentence by denying meaningfulness to the individual words *qua* words. It is a necessary condition for understanding the meaning of a sentence that we understand the meaning of the words constituting it. The fact that different words are classified as nouns, adjectives and verbs, etc. shows that words *qua* words are meaningful. Further, sentence meaning cannot be said to be logically independent of word meanings. If they were, then any sentence could be said to mean anything. It follows, Kumārila argues, that sentence meaning is a function (*vyāpāra*) of the meanings of words which constitute the sentence. He maintains that at the basis of the meaning of a sentence lies the meaning of the words which make up the sentence. In a sentence, words perform a dual function: they have meaning *qua* words and they have meaning as a part of the sentence in which they occur. Consider the sentence 'Bring the cow.' In this sentence, both 'cow' and 'bring' have a dual function. The word 'cow' is really a predicate word, a class name, bearing the universal element in its meaning, and it has application to the individual cow specified by the context in which the sentence 'Bring the cow' is used. Similarly, the word 'bring' means 'the action of bringing' in general, and at the same time it means 'the particular act of bringing' as specified by the context of the use of the sentence 'Bring the cow.' This theory which insists on the dual function of words in the context of a sentence in which they occur is known as *abhihitānvayavāda* of Kumārilabhaṭṭa.[22]

We learn the literal and metaphorical meaning of words from different sources including dictionaries, grammar, usage, and the context in which a certain word has been used.[23] Sometimes, ostensive definition and gestures are also employed for learning the meaning of words.

Conditions of meaningfulness of sentences

As a sentence is a sequence of words in a certain order, understanding its meaning usually means understanding the words and the order in which they occur in the sentence. The traditionalist Naiyāyikas mention three conditions – the requirement that a sentence should be grammatically complete (*ākāṅkṣā*), semantical or logical compatibility (*yogyatā*) and spatio-temporal contiguity (*sannidhi*) – for the understanding of the meaning of a sentence; while the modern Naiyāyikas, the Mīmāṁsakas of all hues and the Grammarians, Bhartṛhari (AD 450–540), for instance do not find these three conditions sufficient, and therefore they add intention (*tātparya*) together with the context (*prasaṅga*) in which a sentence occurs as the fourth condition for understanding the meaning of a sentence.[24]

(a) A sentence must be a complete grammatical structure. This is the requirement of grammatical completeness (*akāṅkṣā*). For example, the word 'bring' standing alone and the sequence of words 'cow the bring' are grammatically incomplete and thus do not constitute sentences. The sequence of words 'Bring the cow' is grammatically complete: it satisfies the grammatical requirement; and hence it constitutes a sentence.

(b) A sequence of words may be grammatically complete, yet fail to communicate sense. For example, the sentence 'Moisten with fire' is grammatically complete, but it fails to communicate sense. Communication fails because the words used in this sequence are categorially incompatible; they belong to two different, logically incompatible types like the words involved in the question 'Is father the female parent?'

This sequence thus fails to satisfy the requirement of semantical or logical compatibility (*yogyatā*).

(c) In spite of satisfying conditions (a) and (b), a sequence of words may still fail to qualify as a sentence if the words occurring in it are written or uttered in such a way that they do not form one unified whole contiguous in space and time. The words occurring in a sentence must be so written or uttered that they form one unified whole. This is the requirement of spatio-temporal contiguity (*sannidhi*).

(d) It is possible for a sequence of words to satisfy the first three requirements and yet fail to communicate meaning or be ambiguous and vague. For example, the sentence 'The cottage is on the Ganges', taken literally, fails to communicate meaning; while the Sanskrit sentence '*saindhavamānaya*' may in one context mean 'Bring the salt' and in another 'Bring the horse', and thus taken alone in isolation from the context of its occurrence it is ambiguous. To eliminate both these possibilities it is required for understanding the meaning of a sentence that the intention of the speaker is made explicit by specifying the context in which the sentence is used to communicate.

NOTES

1 S. C. Vidyābhūṣaṇa, *A History of Indian Logic* (Calcutta: Calcutta University Press, 1921).
2 See *Tarka-saṁgraha* of Annaṁbhaṭṭa, trans. Y. V. Athalye and M. R. Bodas (Poona: Bhandarkar Research Institute, 1963 (repr.), pp. 21–4.
3 Ibid., p. 50: *āptastu yathārthavaktā* ('Authority is a person who speaks truth').
4 Ganganath Jha, *Pūrva-mīmāṁsā in its Sources*, (Varanasi: The Banaras Hindu University, 1964 (repr.)).
5 ibid., p. 69.
6 ibid., pp. 143–6.
7 F. Th. Stcherbatsky, *Buddhist Logic* (2 vols, New York: Dover, 1962 (repr.)).
8 *Tarka-saṁgraha*, op. cit.; *Maṇikaṇa* (A Navya-Nyāya manual), trans. E. R. Sreekrishna Sarma (Madras: The Adyar Library and Research Centre, 1977 (repr.)), pp. 22–6.
9 N. S. Junankar, *Gautama: The Nyāya Philosophy* (Delhi: Motilal Banarsidass, 1978).
10 *Vedāntaparibhāṣā* of Dharmaraja Adhvarin, trans. S. S. Suryanarayana Sastri (Madras: The Adyar Library and Research Centre, 1971 (repr.)).
11 *Mānameyodaya* of Nārāyaṇa, trans. C. Kunhan Raja and S. S. Suryanarayana Sastri (Madras: The Adyar Library and Research Centre, 1975 (repr.)), pp. 28–9.
12 Vijay Bharadwaja, *Form and Validity in Indian Logic* (New Delhi: Munshiram Manoharlal Publishers, 1990).
13 Satischandra Chatterjee, *The Nyaya Theory of Knowledge*: *A critical study of some problems of logic and metaphysics* (Calcutta: University of Calcutta, 1965).
14 *Jaina Tarkabhāṣā* of Yaśovijayagaṇi, trans. Dayanand Bhargav (Delhi: Motilal Banarsidass, 1975), pp. 10–11.
15 *Vedāntaparibhāṣā*, op. cit., p. 55.
16 Bharadwaja, op. cit.
17 *Mānameyodaya*, op. cit., pp. 65–7.
18 For an alternative interpretation of *parāmarśa* see S. S. Barlingay, *A Modern Introduction to Indian Logic* (New Delhi: National Publishing House, 1976).

19 *Mānameyodaya*, op. cit., p. 60.
20 *Tarka-saṁgraha*, op. cit., pp. 50–2; *Maṇikaṇa*, op. cit., pp. 68–71.
21 Jha, op. cit., pp. 113–26.
22 ibid., pp. 127–35.
23 *Tarka-saṁgraha*, op. cit., pp. 338–9.
24 Ibid., *Maṇikaṇa*, op. cit., *Mānameyodaya*, op. cit.

FURTHER READING

Sanskrit texts

Athalye, Y. V. and Bodas, M. R. (trans.) (1963) *Tarka-saṁgraha* of Annaṁbhaṭṭa, Poona: Bhandarkar Research Institute (reprint).
Bhargava, Dayanand (trans.) (1975) *Jaina Tarkabhāṣā* of Yaśovijayagaṇi, Delhi: Motilal Banarsidass.
Bhattacharyya, Janaki Vallabha (trans.) (1978) *Nyāya-mañjari* of Jayantabhaṭṭa, Delhi: Motilal Banarsidass.
Cowell, E. B. and Gough, A. E. (trans.) (1978) *Sarva-darśana-saṁgraha* of Madhava Āchārya, Varanasi: Chowkhamba Sanskrit Series Office (reprint).
Dhruva, A. B. (trans.) (1933) *Syādvādamañjari* of Malliṣena, Bombay: The Department of Public Instruction.
Iyer, K. A. Subramania (trans.) (1965) *The Vākyapadīya* of Bhartṛhari, chapter 1, Poona: Deccan College Postgraduate and Research Institute.
Jha, Ganganath (trans.) (1900–8) *Ślokavārttika* of Kumārilabhaṭṭa, Calcutta: Asiatic Society of Bengal Bibliotheka Indica, NS, nos 965, 986, 1017, 1055, 1091, 1157, 1183.
—— *Tarkabhāṣā* of Keśavamiśra, (1967) Poona: Oriental Book Agency.
—— *Śabara-bhasyam*, vol. I (*Adhyāya*-s I–III), 2nd edn, 1973; vol. II (*Adhyāya*s IV–VIII), 2nd edn, 1973; vol. III (*Adhyāya*-s IX–XII), 2nd edn, 1974, Baroda: Gaekwad's Oriental Institute.
Raja, C. Kunhan and Sastri, S. S. Suryanarayana (trans.) (1975) *Mānameyodaya* of Nārāyaṇa, Madras: The Adyar Library and Research Centre (reprint).
Sarma, E. R. Sreekrishna (trans.) (1977) *Maṇikaṇa* (a Navya-Nyāya manual), Madras: The Adyar Library and Research Centre (reprint).
Sastri, S. S. Suryanarayana (trans.) (1971) *Vedāntaparibhāṣā* of Dharmaraja Adhvarin, (1971) Madras: The Adyar Library and Research Centre (reprint).
Vidyabhusana, S. C. (trans.) (1975) *The Nyāya Sūtras of Gotama*, New Delhi: Munshiram Manoharlal (reprint).

Secondary Literature

Chatterjee, Satischandra (1965) *The Nyaya Theory of Knowledge*, A critical study of some problems of logic and metaphysics, Calcutta: University of Calcutta, 1965.
D'Sa, Francis X. (1980) *Śabdaprāmāṇyam in Śabara and Kumārila*: *Towards a study of the Mīmāṁsā experience of language*, Vienna: Indological Institute, University of Vienna.
Ingalls, D. H. H. (1951) *Materials on Navya-Nyāya Logic*, Harvard Oriental Series 40, Cambridge, Mass.: Harvard University Press.

Jha, Ganganath (1964) *Pūrva-Mīmāṁsā in its Sources*, Varanasi: The Banaras Hindu University (repr.).

Kunjunni Raja, K. (1977) *Indian Theories of Meaning*, Madras: The Adyar Library and Research Centre (repr.).

Matilal, B. K. (1968) *The Navya-Nyāya Doctrine of Negation*, Harvard Oriental Series 46, Cambridge, Mass.: Harvard University Press.

Potter, Karl H. (ed.) (1977) *Encyclopedia of Indian Philosophies*, vol. II, *Indian Metaphysics and Epistemology: The Tradition of Nyāya-Vaiśeṣika up to Gaṅgeśa*, Delhi: Motilal Banarsidass.

Randle, H. N. (1930) *Indian Logic in the Early Schools: A study of the Nyāyadarśana in its relation to the early logic and other schools*, London: Oxford University Press.

Staal, F. J. (1967) 'Sanskrit philosophy of language', *Current Trends in Linguistics* 5: 499–531.

Vidyābhūṣaṇa, S. C. (1921) *A History of Indian Logic: Ancient, Mediaeval, and Modern Schools*, Calcutta: Calcutta University Press.

13

KNOWLEDGE AND REALITY IN INDIAN PHILOSOPHY

Karl H. Potter

The Buddha, when asked questions that he deemed it unprofitable to try to answer, framed his response in what is known as the 'tetralemma' or fourfold negation (*catuṣkoṭi*). For example, asked whether the universe exists eternally he responded as follows (I paraphrase): I don't believe that the universe is eternal; nor do I believe that it is not eternal; or that it is both eternal and not eternal; or that it is neither eternal nor non-eternal. The implication is clear: for whatever reason, the Buddha did not believe it worth while to try to respond to such a puzzle; it is, to use a happy translation of the relevant Pali terms, a 'question not tending to edification'.

Obviously, if someone were to take this line with any and all questions he or she would not have anything very helpful to say. It is tempting, then, to try to capture the essence of Indian philosophy by judging which questions are so basic that any philosopher should view their answer as tending to edification, and ought to have views about them.

I suggest that there is at least one such question, consideration of which will lead us directly into the multifariousness of philosophical views in India. That question is: *Are there none, one, or more than one ultimate causes of the bondage that is this universe?* The relevance of this question should be evident. The purpose of mankind, Indians of this period assumed, is to gain release from bondage. Man needs to know what causes bondage, so that he may strive to eliminate its cause(s). Without such knowledge any striving is likely to be irrelevant. Conviction on this point appears to have the highest priority.

Just as there is a tetralemma generated by the Buddha's question about eternal existence, the question about ultimate causes can be viewed in terms of four alternative answers. One answer is surely this: there is precisely one ultimate cause of the universe. A second answer is: there are many conditions which conspire to cause the universe.

A third is: the cause of the universe is both one and many. And a fourth is: there is no cause of the universe at all. The systems of classical India all take a stance in favour of one or another of these answers.

'Philosophy' in classical India had as its fundamental problem how to flesh out an account of things consistent with the viability of attaining liberation. The problem for each philosophical system was to develop an account of things that fits the answer chosen among these four to the question of ultimate causation. Such an account must, of course, satisfy as well the normal requirements of system-making: adequacy, accuracy, consistency and simplicity. Thus detailed analysis of specific aspects of bondage is required as well as the general premisses of the system's response to fundamental questions.

THE FIRST ANSWER: PRECISELY ONE ULTIMATE CAUSE

This answer – like the others – operates as if moved by a fundamental metaphor – a 'world hypothesis', to borrow Stephen Pepper's useful notion. The metaphor latched on to by this first answer is the metaphor of transformation or manifestation of one thing as many. Illustrations of this fundamental metaphorical picture are to be found in the change of water into ice or vapour, of milk into curds, of seed into sprout, of an actual rope in the corner into an apparent snake, of a single face into many reflections in a mirror, of a whole into its parts. These metaphors actually pull in somewhat different directions, and the differences characteristically differentiate the several systems that propose this first answer.

The systems of Sāṅkhya and Yoga

These systems latch on to the first kind of metaphor – of milk and curds, seed and sprout. As these systems see it, the multiplicity of different things – objects, qualities, bodies, minds, selves – that appear to us as constituting our world is the result of a kind of evolutionary emanation of things from a primal category classically known as *prakṛti*. In fact, this emanation takes place periodically at the beginning of an era – a vast period of time, but only one of indefinitely many in the history of the Indian cosmos. At that moment from unmanifest *prakṛti* evolve minds, egoities, organs of sense and activity, and eventually bodies and the sense-objects of experience. Once the initial evolution has taken place, life, death and rebirth follow on, the specific forms of mind, organs, body and experience in each rebirth determined by a portion of one's stored-up *karma*.

But what is this 'one' that has stored up the *karma*? For Sāṅkhya and Yoga it is the individual's consciousness, called *puruṣa*. Each individual *puruṣa* is nothing but pure consciousness – the specificity of its experiences is entirely due to the forms of the *prakṛti* that are karmically activated at any time.

It must be emphasized that, for Sāṅkhya and Yoga, both *puruṣa* and *prakṛti* are real, as indeed are the evolutes of *prakṛti* – bodies, minds, objects and their experiences. What does it mean to say they are 'real'? That they actually come to pass in the way that curds are actual and not merely apparent transformations of milk. The actuality of the curds is evidenced by the fact that though the curds may be reduced to liquid, the result will be a different stuff from the original milk. When a seed becomes a sprout and the sprout sows a seed, it is a *different* seed that is sown. Thus the change from cause to effect is real, not illusory. One does not reproduce the original milk merely by realizing its basic identity with the curds; the original seed that produced a sprout is not regenerated merely by realizing that it was the producer. Primal *prakṛti* is the one ultimate cause of all evolutes, operating through the *karmic* process. *Puruṣa* is not a cause; it is merely the witness, providing the awareness that allows beings to experience the multifariousness of evolution. Liberation is possible, since it is possible to cut off the *karmic* seeds that cause *prakṛti* to sprout into its evolute. When for a *puruṣa* those seeds are anaesthetized by discipline (*yoga*) of body and mind, and the absolute otherness of *puruṣa* from *prakṛti* is fully appreciated, *prakṛti* ceases to operate for that *puruṣa*, 'the dancer desists from dancing', to allude to the powerful analogy of the basic Sāṅkhya text. All that remains is pure conciousness, witnessing but uninvolved.

Advaita Vedānta

This system, like Sāṅkhya and Yoga, views the universe as emanating from precisely one ultimate cause. The term Advaitins use for this ultimately single, partless reality is '*Brahman*'. In a number of Upaniṣadic passages this ultimate reality is identified with *ātman*, the self. Advaitins view this literally. There is only one *Brahman*; thus, there is only one real Self. Your individual self, as different from mine, is merely an appearance or projection of the one Self, just as the plurality of things – bodies, minds, objects – is an appearance or projection of *Brahman*. But since *Brahman* and the Self are identical, to view either of these pluralities as real is to be taken in by an illusion. Bodies, minds, objects, world – indeed, anything involving the imputation of real difference among things – signify this illusoriness. All difference is mere appearance.

Yet, as we are visited by these appearances, supposing we wish to be liberated from the frustrations arising from them, the problem seems to remain of explaining whence these illusions arise and how to stop them from doing so. Since *Brahman*, the only reality, is partless, *it* cannot undergo change. It follows that all plurality, all distinctions, all difference are *our* mistake. What occasions this mistake? Practically, the answer once again is *karma*, the proclivities to attraction and aversion, distinction and identification that have their origins in past actions born of desires. Theoretically, Advaita traces the source of diversity to ignorance (*avidyā*), also called *māyā*. What occasions our experience of plurality is our ignorance about ultimate matter, an ignorance fostered and nurtured by *karma*.

Ignorance is, of course, not real, since only Brahman is real. On the other hand it is not completely unreal either, since it occurs and occasions the frustration and misery we are subject to. Like all of what we ordinarily call 'real', ignorance, along with everything else except *Brahman*, occupies an in-between status of neither-real-nor-unreal.

Since *Brahman* is incapable of transformation, Advaita's favourite metaphors feature change as illusory appearance – the rope as snake, the face as many faces. Instead of actual transformation the model is apparent manifestation – the rope manifests itself as a snake, which though unreal can scare you to death! The analogy is with *karma*, which, though not real, brings about the appearance of the myriad features of experience, so it is not unreal either.

Our bondage consists in this entire world-show of illusory manifestation. To free oneself from the show one has to realize its illusoriness. Since no real bondage occurs, we are all intrinsically free, being in actuality nothing save *Brahman*, the One True Self. By meditation one may come to appreciate one's identity with that Self in this very lifetime. Conviction of the liberating insight does not result in immediate extinction of the appearance of differences, since the *karmic* mechanism determined to condition this life must run its course. At the conclusion of the present lifetime, though, unlike the conclusions of the indefinitely many previous lifetimes one has been through, one will no longer experience any further distinctions – one will be liberated.

Viśiṣṭādvaita Vedānta

Historically, Indian thought can be seen to have gone through at least three phases. Vedic tradition shows a period, in very ancient times, when liberation was unrecognized as the ultimate end, the supreme purpose of man being *dharma* or righteousness. The period of the classical Indian philosophies that we are discussing superimposed liberation on *dharma* as a superior aim. There will be, arising at the beginning of the second millennium AD, a third phase, usually known as the '*bhakti* period'. Eventually the aim of liberation becomes in the *bhakti* period overshadowed by theism and devotionalism. Instead of liberation the ultimate aim is now seen to be divinization, unity with the godhead.

Most of the myriad systems that fall under the general rubric 'Vedānta' belong to the *bhakti* period. Classical talk about liberation becomes incorporated into a basically different, religious orientation, though maintaining the classical terminology in which philosophical systems were broached during the classical period. A case in point is the Viśiṣṭādvaita system of the Śrīvaiṣṇavas, the vast Vaiṣṇavite sect of south India.

Essentially, the *bhakti* tradition reinterprets the abstract reality of classical systems (*prakṛti*, *Brahman*) as a personal God, identified with one of the members of the Hindu pantheon. In the case of Viśiṣṭādvaita this godhead is Viṣṇu – thus the sect is known as Vaiṣṇava. God, while supreme like Advaita's *Brahman*, can nevertheless be correctly cognized, unlike Advaita's *Brahman*. Since this is so, God must have, if not parts, at least aspects or features that can be correctly appreciated. In contrast to Sāṅkhya and Yoga, on the other hand, God is to be distinguished from his products, the evolutes of *prakṛti*.

Whereas for Sāṅkhya, Yoga and Advaita liberation is achieved by meditation leading to a *distinguishing* of one thing (*puruṣa*, Self) from others (*prakṛti*, *avidyā*), in *bhakti*-orientated Viśiṣṭādvaita the aim is rather *identification* of everything – selves and world – with the ultimate godhead. Rather than the karmically conditioned selves creating the world of our experiencing, God has that responsibility. Rather than an aim of elimination of the world of our experiencing, an acceptance of it or resignation to it is what is propounded. These are all characteristic of the later, devotional period in Hinduism.

THE SECOND ANSWER: MANY CAUSAL CONDITIONS

The second of our four views is easier for the modern West to appreciate since, in accord broadly with the attitude of empiricism, it views the causes of the universe as many and diverse.

Mīmāṁsā and Nyāya-Vaiśeṣika

As was pointed out a few paragraphs back, liberation was not always recognized as the ultimate end and value for man. The classical period, orientated towards liberation, was preceded by a Vedic period in which liberation was unrecognized and in which the highest purpose and value were found in the heavenly state attained by observance of *dharma*. This extroverted attitude of the Vedic period favoured positive activity (*pravṛtti*), directed towards the ultimate human purpose (*puruṣārtha*) by performance of ritual and other appropriate actions.

Acts (*karman*) are of three sorts: bodily, mental and vocal. The function of classical 'sciences' (*śāstra*) was to tell us how to act in these three ways in order to achieve prosperity, satisfaction and eventually, heaven. One may say that the fundamental sciences were *dharmaśāstra*, which tells us how to choose our overt actions, grammar (*vyākaraṇa*), which tells us how to speak properly, and 'logic' (*nyāya*), which tells us how to think clearly and cogently. Other sciences (for example astronomy, medicine, agriculture, architecture) develop understanding of the specific subject matter about which people with particular roles and concerns speak and think; these three are fundamental because they abstract from such specific subject matter and tell people in general how to use their bodies, minds and voices to maximal effect.

Thus, linguistic acts should be performed if they are conducive to *puruṣārtha*, and they are likely to be so if they utilize words which were originally established as useful in this respect, originally established either in the nature of things (as Mīmāṁsā doctrine has it) or by God or by the ancient *ṛṣis*, wise men of yore. Grammar tells us what right speech consists in; other *śāstras* tell us what it is good for. The feature which makes a word an appropriate one for discussing grammar is not its capacity for ranging over a precisely determined domain of objects. Rather, it is the word's function in guiding us to proper speech, a function whose evidence is just the fact that it is found in the oldest discussions. There may be differences of opinion over what such a word actually denotes or connotes, since people now do not always understand entirely clearly the precise intentions of the ancient sages or God or the impersonal source of language. But despite the differences of semantic meaning which different interpreters may attach to a traditional word, if they are in agreement about the pragmatic function of the word in guiding action, they are speaking to the same end, are all interpreters and are all practising the same science.

'Logic' (broadly conceived) is to be viewed in parallel fashion. Mental acts should be performed if they are conducive to *puruṣārtha*, and they are likely to be so if they measure things out in a fashion that fits the requirements of *puruṣārtha* as established by tradition, providing the understanding of tradition is not defective. The terminology for speaking correctly about mental acts is, once again, established by traditional authority, and, once again, it is not the semantic content of those words which fixes their function but rather their practical role in guiding people to the performance of mental acts, proper habits of thought which are conducive to *puruṣārtha*. Again, there may be differences of opinion over what such a word actually denotes or connotes, differences which arise because we do not now remember clearly what the semantic content (if any) of those words was according to the original intent (if any) of the first speaker. But again, despite wide divergences of interpretation, if the interpreters are in agreement about the practical role of the word in guiding mental activities, they are speaking to the same end, practising the same science.

All this makes excellent sense as long as we are assuming that positive activity (*pravṛtti*) is the purport of the sciences. And it appears that in the earliest Vedic period this was indeed so, that the attitude was extroverted and the concern was with achieving a better state ('heaven') through positive actions leading to such a state. All this was brought into question when a new *puruṣārtha* came to be recognized, the end of man which is liberation from existence altogether. This new aim of man is to be achieved, according to suggestions in the *Upaniṣads*, in various sectarian teachings such as those found taught by Gautama the Buddha, Mahāvīra the Jina, and an increasingly impressive number of teachers down through the centuries, not by positive activity but by what is precisely its opposite, withdrawal from action (*nivṛtti*). The new goal of liberation gradually came to be accepted as superior to the other three, and we enter the classical philosophical period.

Among the *darśanas* or systems of our classical period there is one known as Mīmāṁsā, whose origins can clearly be traced back to the earlier Vedic period just characterized. 'Mīmāṁsā' originally meant the science of Vedic interpretation. It is in the Vedas that one can find the means for gaining heaven. The Vedas are the handbook of *dharma*. On Mīmāṁsā interpretation all Vedic passages either explicitly or implicitly state or support injunctions to act. By their timeless, authorless purity they can be trusted to yield the necessary guidance to actions conducive to *dharma*, provided they are correctly understood. Mīmāṁsā gives rigorously scientific exegetical procedures for proper understanding of Vedic passages.

In India what is olden is golden. When the Vedic, *dharma*-orientated paradigm gave way to the classical, liberation-orientated paradigm, the attitudes, myths, texts and mystique of the Vedic period were not jettisoned. Rather, the old terminology was retained, but reinterpreted to fit the new paradigm. (The same procedure of reinterpretative retention marks the treatment of classical philosophy in *bhakti*-period literature.) So Mīmāṁsā, technically rendered *passé* since its purpose, *dharma*, was no longer primary, is reinterpreted as itself a philosophical system devoted to liberation. Indeed, there are several philosophical Mīmāṁsā systems, and a sizeable literature survives from at least two of them.

These Mīmāṁsā schools share their fundamental categories with two other systems, Nyāya and Vaiśeṣika. The resulting collection of systems took over the mantle of philosophical analysis offered by the many-one viewpoint. All these schools, though they differ among each other on many points of importance, share a set of systematic features. Basically, what they share derives from common assumptions about the causes of bondage.

All these systems believe that there are many causal conditions that conspire to produce bondage. Second, they all believe that some of these conditions are fleeting events, others enduring substances, and still others ubiquitous, atemporal entities. The philosophical problem according to these systems is to arrive at a set of categories which satisfies methodological criteria of adequacy, accuracy, consistency and simplicity while allowing for, and explaining the way to achieve, liberation.

In contrast to the first answer, which contended that there is only one real thing, this second answer admits a plurality of real entities. The fundamental metaphor here is exemplified in any standard case of material causation. Just as several actual entities – moisture, a seed, earth, a reasonable temperature (not too hot or too cold), absence of various mitigating circumstances – are required so that a sprout may grow, so many kinds of real things conspire to produce bondage. And just as to prevent a seed from sprouting one or more of these conditions must be prevented from doing their thing, to prevent more bondage and gain liberation one must discover one or more conditions whose non-occurrence results in the future non-arising of bondage. Since our interest is in finding the means to avoid rebirth, one such condition we want to find must be avoidable *by us*.

Attention is thus forcibly directed on what kinds of things there are and to how, if at all, they are caused to occur. What results, for all these systems, is the production of lengthy lists of categories, with accounts of what occasions the arising of each kind of thing categorized. Featured in these lists of actual entities are such staples of metaphysics as substances, qualities, universals and particulars, positive and negative entities, and various sorts of relations, with *causal* relations playing a prominent part in the proceedings.

All these systems in fact agree on the ultimate cause of bondage. That is ignorance, wrong understanding of how things are. Thus the philosopher's game of discovering the most theoretically satisfying account of what things there are becomes the key to the gaining of liberation. Since bondage results from ignorance, liberation results from knowledge. Philosophy is both the proper understanding of the problem and the solution to that problem.

To summarize all too briefly a complex story, that proper understanding which is the philosophy of Nyāya, Vaiśeṣika and Mīmāṁsā theorizes that each of us is a naturally eternal, ubiquitous, non-conscious entity, a self. A self is visited by fleeting awarenesses – awarenesses which are reactions to a real, external world but are also conditioned by *karmic* residues stored up from previous experiences. Specifically what these residues do is cause us to be attracted by certain aspects of our world and repelled by others. These attractions and repulsions cause us to perform actions to acquire some kinds of things and to avoid others. The key to liberation is to gain that understanding which will block these attitudes of acquisition and avoidance.

But how can mere understanding block the *karmic* process? These systems hypothesize that the awarenesses, attractions and repulsions are related to the self that experiences them in a non-essential way. *Karma*, and the resultant awarenesses and emotions, can be destroyed without the destruction of the self that experiences. The self is in fact indestructible. So, when one understands the nature of things, one's experiences become free from error, and as a result one no longer experiences desires or aversions, and breeds no more *karma*. Moreover, the remaining stored-up *karma* for that self is rendered inoperative, and since it is operative *karma* that causes rebirth, one is no more reborn, and the self becomes free from karmic baggage and reverts to its natural eternal, ubiquitous, non-conscious state, unconnected to any body or awarenesses.

Abhidharma and Vijñānavāda Buddhism

Buddhists, unlike the Nyāya-Vaiśeṣika and Mīmāṁsā philosophers, view practically everything as fleeting, following one of the Buddha's fundamental insights. Nothing persists; there are no objects, no bodies, no enduring selves. Our interpretation of our world as a mixture of enduring entities lasting for various lengths of time is a misinterpretation. Reality for the Buddhist, as for the contemporary physicist, is a flux.

Real entities in Buddhist accounts are called *dharmas*, factors. Each thing we identify in our experience as an external object is a series of momentary flashes of factors. It is we who interpret this series as constituting objects and selves. So the first problem for one who seeks to understand how things are – and in particular how to achieve liberation – is to recognize his or her own insubstantiality. Indeed, language itself, which breeds thoughts of ego, of ownership, can hardly occur except to those under the bonds of ignorance.

Nevertheless, the factors do occur; they are not imaginary. So realizing that there is no self does not terminate one's frustrations. Experience goes on as before. How, then, can one escape this persisting flux of momentary factors?

Well, what is it that fuels the flux, that causes it to occur at all? As we now realize, it is *karma*, past actions that occasion subsequent factors to flash in a stream of experiences. The problem is, again, to discover how to stop the *karmic* process.

The clue to how to do this comes in the recognition that there is no self that 'has' these experiences. Since that is so, there is no relationship between two things – self and experienced – that has to be broken. Rather, it is precisely our natural misapprehension on this point that fosters the karmic mechanism. While we think that we continue to exist, we shall naturally seek what we desire and avoid what we fear. Once convinced that I do not exist I shall no longer seek or fear anything, since I realize that there is no 'me' that can seek or fear, no entities to be sought or feared. Satisfying desires takes time; if what is desired is no longer there in the next instant, it is stupid to desire *it*.

Fundamental metaphors for Buddhists are the waves in the ocean or the circle of fire that results when one whirls a torch. Waves and circle are misinterpretations of flux. There are no waves or circles of fire. There are only momentary states of H_2O, momentary flashes of light.

Are there even momentary states or flashes? Early Buddhism, as found in Abhidiharma texts, assumes so. Later, some Mahāyāna schools began to doubt even this. Using arguments resembling those familiar to readers of Berkeley and Hume, Vijñānavāda teachers taught that nothing 'external' exists, that all that is real is the *experiences* of the flashes. A very large part of what we take for granted about ourselves and our world becomes mere illusion when viewed in this way. The *karmic* mechanism becomes rather mysterious too, and our ability literally to describe reality highly precarious.

Dvaita Vedānta

Analogously to Viśiṣṭādvaita for the first answer, one can locate *bhakti*-period developments for this second answer as well. Buddhism left India as *bhakti* arrived, but a bhaktized counterpart of the first – Nyāya/Vaiśeṣika/ Mīmāṁsā – sort can be found in the system called Dvaita Vedānta.

As with Viśiṣṭādvaita, the most notable feature ontologically in Dvaita is the God Viṣṇu. Unlike Rāmānuja's system, however, Madhva propounds a robust realism in which God, selves and objects are all real and distinct. God is fundamental not in the sense that everything is a part or aspect of him, as in Viśiṣṭādvaita, but rather in that everything is dependent on him, and so subservient to him. Since beings are different in nature from the godhead, as well as dependent on him, we find in Dvaita a position reminiscent of Calvinist Christianity, in which man's destiny is entirely dependent on God's will rather than on any efforts of his own. But again, with this sort of view we leave the period of our present discussion.

THE THIRD ANSWER: BOTH ONE AND MANY CAUSES OF THE UNIVERSE

The first two positions of our tetralemma both have their difficulties. The first answer tends to swallow up the diversity of things in a fundamental unity. In the second answer the connections of things fall apart into a universal diversity. Both the first and second answers can therefore be seen as unstable. One may suspect that they can be pushed into fatalism or scepticism by a clever critic. Perhaps, then, the answer is to have the best of both. This is what Jain philosophy attempts to do.

Fundamental to the Jains' methodology is their concept of viewpoints (*naya*). Everything may be seen from different viewpoints, and is shown to be different – indeed, opposed to itself – when viewed from different perspectives. Indeed, even to refer to a thing's nature is only a partial truth, for everything, though it has a single nature, also has a plural nature. Everything is both one and many: which you see depends on your selective interest, your point of view.

In keeping with this methodological stance the Jains subscribe to a view about causes and effects which is both monistic and pluralistic. The ultimate cause of the universe is from one point of view single, from another point of view many, from a third both, from a fourth neither. If one seeks the basic unity of things one must fail; however, one need not fall into desperate pluralistic confusion because of this.

The Jain view of bondage and liberation is very literal. We are really bound, and we can really be liberated. (One could argue, about the systems previously considered, that for each of them either we are not really bound or we are never really liberated!) *Karma*, the term used to identify the source of our bondage, is used by Jains to designate everything that constitutes a person and his or her environment. At any moment a person is acquiring *karma* and burning off other *karma*, rather as a very hot lamp attracts insects and burns them off at the same time. The problem of gaining liberation is just that of stopping the acquisition of *karma*. This can be done, Jainism holds, by stopping these responses of the person using yoga and meditational techniques conducive to development of dispassionateness. When one no longer has desires one no longer accretes *karmic* baggage, and the way to liberation is clear though not immediate – one must burn off the *karma* remaining from one's prior *karma*-producing efforts.

The (alleged) instability of the first and second answers is thus avoided, but at a price of its own: if everything is true only from a standpoint, liberation itself would seem to have to take place only from a standpoint. The liberated Jain person is held to ascend to the roof of heaven, where he or she hangs unsullied for ever after, since he or she no longer accretes any *karma*. Is this only one point of view? If so, it may be the case that from another point of view that self is still bound. If not, how to differentiate absolute truths from things true only from a standpoint?

THE FOURTH ANSWER: AN UNCAUSED UNIVERSE

Faced with the instability of the three views reviewed so far, the thoughtful philosopher may become convinced that something has gone wrong, that some assumption has been made generating these views which is confused. Our fourth answer adopts this stance. Specifically, what has gone wrong is the very assumption of causality.

Note, by the way, that this rejection of causality is not the most extreme negative attitude that can be taken towards what has been said so far. An even more extreme position will reject the entire paradigm by denying either the possibility of gaining liberation, the worth of attaining it, or both. Even at the height of the classical period such doubts existed, though it seems that the literature documenting this, if there was any, has been almost completely expunged from the historical record. One group, known as Cārvāka or Lokāyata, denied that liberation was possible on the ground that there was nothing we could do to escape the cycle of rebirths. The idea here was that the causal connections we would have to utilize to bring about release were too weak – if they existed at all – to ensure success in the venture. Another group, exemplified by fatalists such as the ancient Ājīvikas, felt by contrast that the relations between the causes of bondage and their effects were too strong to be broken. These traditions were anti-philosophical if by 'philosophy' we decide to mean the assumptions about bondage and liberation that governed the thinking of the systems we have been reviewing. That did not stop their arguments from being seriously considered by the philosophers proper, who understandably viewed these sceptical and fatalistic attitudes as the most fundamental attack of all on their position.

(Note, also, that one should not assume that these sceptical and fatalistic views are closer to western philosophy. The Cārvākas and Ājīvikas are still very Indian and non-western, in that they accept the *karmic* framework. Western philosophers, with rare exceptions, do not.)

The fourth answer we consider here, then, maintains liberation as a realizable goal and *karma* as the actual source of bondage. But it rejects the assumption of the other three answers, believing that gaining liberation is not achievable by bringing about causal factors sufficient to achieve it. Bondage is just not a cause–effect matter at all. What is it, then?

Mādhyamika Buddhism

The problematic of the previous answers turns on their assumption that something really causes something else. This is what the fourth answer rejects. To impose a causal model gives precedence to one phenomenon over another; it leads us to look for a way of dealing with the causes of bondage to bring about the eradication of their effects.

Suppose, instead, that nothing causes anything, that causation is a mistaken notion we impose on things. The entire show of objects, selves, minds, whatever – of any events viewed as causally prior or posterior to other events – is our mistake. *Karma*, too, is our mistake. We mistakenly believe ourselves bound; in fact we are free – our bondage is the result of misconception.

Even that way of putting it may be a source of confusion. This 'we' I speak of: it makes it sound as if there is myself and, a different thing, my ideas, my *karma*, my body, etc. No doubt (says Mādhyamika) these are all different, but this notion of ownership is what is at fault here. There is no 'I' that owns some ideas; no one possesses his *karma* or her body. The Buddha's warnings about grasping need to be read in the broadest possible way.

At the heart of the problem is a very convincing argument. It goes like this. Experience shows us that things are caused: *x* occurs when and only when *y* occurs. If *y* does not occur, *x* does not. But *x* does occur, and so does *y*. Therefore we can say that *y* is real; if it were not, *x* would not have occurred – but it did. Therefore, even if *x* might not be real, *y* must be – and even if, somehow, *y* is not actually real, there must be some *z* that caused *y* and is real – otherwise *y* would not have occurred. The only way to escape this argument is to deny that anything occurs at all – but this is nihilism, a repugnant view explicitly rejected (by the way) by the Buddha.

Now the criticism Mādhyamika has of this argument is against using the term 'real' to pick out some occurrences over others. Mādhyamika also cites the Buddha as authority. According to Mādhyamika the Buddha held that *everything* is conditioned, which is to say, everything is on a par as far as causation goes. If anything is a cause of *x*, everything is. Likewise, if anything is an effect of *y*, everything is. That leaves us no room for using the term 'real' to mean 'a cause that is not an effect'. But that is precisely what the argument of the previous paragraph does. So that argument is wrong.

To put it another way, it seems only common sense to suppose that if a thing were not real it could not really do anything. But either this is a truism, and does not tell us anything other than that real things (whatever they are) are real, or it is wrong. What is it to 'really do' something? An unreal thing can really do something, if 'really do' means to bring about a result – we are really scared by unreal ghosts, really moved by unreal stories, etc. So if 'real' only means 'does something' it does not effect any distinction – anything at all 'does something'! And to try to distinguish 'really does something' from 'only apparently does something' is to call for a distinction that cannot ultimately be found.

Thus causation, if it means elevating one or more events or things above the rest, is an illusion. Conditioning, by contrast, being all-pervasive, does not elevate anything. Where does that leave us? Right where we are, no doubt, but wiser – we no longer seek reality: we learn to accept all comers. We develop equanimity, compassion, insight – good qualities, these. Liberation is not something of a different order – it just is the possession of these good qualities at the expense of bad ones such as grasping.

From this standpoint the function of philosophical parlance is mainly negative; its function is to destroy the illusions fostered by the other three answers. In addition, it can function to indicate positive ethical attitudes – it is not so much philosophical as advisory. The dry abstractions of metaphysics give way to the inspirational, often humorous, literature of stories, jokes and poems – even to whacks on the head, as in Zen, the Japanese descendant of Mādhyamika.

'Leap' Advaita Vedānta

A Hindu analogue to Mādhyamika can be found in certain Advaita writers. Here too one finds an abandonment of causation as a basis for a philosophy. The attempt of first answer Advaitins to elevate *Brahman/Ātman* to the status of Supreme Reality becomes a metaphorical way of advising adepts to meditate. Liberation is no change of anything, other than a removal of a wrong way of conceptualizing things. As in Mādhyamika, philosophers deal with *karma* by accepting it rather than trying to find a way to reject or avoid it. Paradoxically, to accept *karma* and rebirth for what they are is to overcome them at one leap – they are only dangerous if distinguished conceptually from liberation. The descriptive function of philosophical terms is again essentially rejected in favour of an interpretation of philosophical texts as either destructive of wrong views or metaphorical expressions of good attitudes.

For these fourth answer philosophers knowledge and reality are notions that are dangerous. If anything is real, everything is; if anything is unreal, everything is. 'Reality', then, does not distinguish one kind of thing from another, unless it does so as a value judgement. Likewise with 'knowledge' the only proper use it might have is to indicate useful ways of thinking as opposed to bad ways. This is not scepticism or fatalism. Liberation is still aimed for and assumed possible. There *are* better and worse ways of thinking and acting. But terms like 'real' and 'know' are to be made evaluative. To call something 'real', to say one 'knows', should be to praise or accept it, to upgrade it as worthy of attention and respect – and that is all. Nothing is real – in the metaphysical sense – and no one knows anything – in the epistemic sense. Still, it is better to think, talk and act in some ways rather than others.

CONCLUSION

Our four answers make a kind of circle, as shown in Figure 13.1.

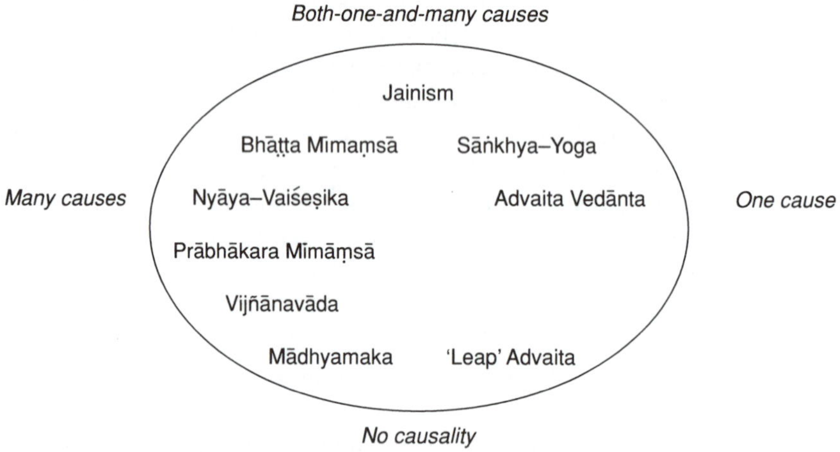

Figure 13.1

It has a certain rationale. None of the four answers is without difficulty, none without merit. As a group, the philosophical systems of India produced a kind of standoff, which may explain why its history proceeded into the *bhakti* period and a new paradigm.

FURTHER READING

Basham, Arthur L. (1951) *History and Doctrines of the Ājīvikas*, London: Luzac.
Dasgupta, Surendranath (1924) *Yoga as Philosophy and Religion*, London: Kegan Paul, Trench, Trubner.
—— (1952–5) *A History of Indian Philosophy*, 5 vols, Cambridge: Cambridge University Press.

Guenther, Herbert V. (1974) *Philosophy and Psychology in the Abhidharma*. Delhi: Berkeley.
Jha, Ganganatha (1942) *Pūrva-Mīmāṃsā in its Sources*, Benares: Benares Hindu University Press.
Larson, Gerald James (1969) *Classical Sāṃkhya: An Interpretation of its History and Meaning*, Delhi: Motilal Banarsidass.
Larson, Gerald James and Bhattacharya, Ram Shankar (eds.) (1987) *Sāṃkhya: A Dualist Tradition in Indian Philosophy. Encyclopedia of Indian Philosophies*, vol. IV, Delhi: Motilal Banarsidass and Princeton, N. J.: Princeton University Press.
Mookerjee, Satkari (1935) *The Buddhist Philosophy of Universal Flux*, Calcutta: University of Calcutta Press.
—— (1944) *The Jaina Philosophy of Non-Absolutism*, Calcutta: Bharata Jaina Parisat.
Murti, T. R. V. (1955) *The Central Philosophy of Buddhism*, London: Allen & Unwin.
Narain, K. (1962) *An Outline of Madhva Philosophy*, Allahabad: Udayana.
O'Flaherty, Wendy Doniger (ed.) (1980) *Karma and Rebirth in Classical Indian Traditions*, Berkeley and Los Angeles: University of California Press.
Potter, Karl H. (ed.) (1977) *Indian Metaphysics and Epistemology: The Tradition of Nyāya-Vaiśeṣika up to Gaṅgeśa. Encyclopedia of Indian Philosophies*, vol. II, Delhi: Motilal Banarsidass and Princeton, N.J.: Princeton University Press.
—— (ed.) (1981) *Advaita Vedānta up to Śaṃkara and his Pupils. Encyclopedia of Indian Philosophies*, vol. III, Delhi: Motilal Banarsidass and Princeton, N.J.: Princeton University Press.
Potter, Karl H. (comp.) (1995) *Bibliography*, 3rd edn. *Encyclopedia of Indian Philosophies*, 2 vols, Delhi: Motilal Banarsidass and Princeton, N.J.: Princeton University Press.
Radhakrishnan, Sarvepalli (1923) *Indian Philosophy*, 2 vols, London: Allen & Unwin.

14

MORALS AND SOCIETY IN INDIAN PHILOSOPHY

Sarasvati Chennakesavan and K. Vasudeva Reddy

MORALS IN INDIAN PHILOSOPHY

Indian moral philosophy is interested in pragmatic ideals such as bringing about a perfect society, a perfect person and finally personal liberation (*mokṣa*). Apart from the extreme materialist school, Cārvāka, all systems of Indian thought accept these ideals as the goal of human behaviour. Towards the achievement of this goal, the ancient seers evolved a code of conduct to be cultivated in a prescribed manner. As regards the more fundamental question of why these ideals should be accepted and acted upon, answers can be found from a study of the prescribed ideals right from the Vedic times to the present day. However, it must be emphasized that the validity and veracity of an ideal should not be judged from the way it is practised since no ethical ideal finds its fulfilment in practice. It gets either distorted by or mixed with other considerations and rarely reflects the fullness and richness of the ideal.

Vedic and Upaniṣadic thought

There are two distinct theories regarding ethical ideals. One equates the moral ideal with the universal law operating in nature and finds it operative in man as well, since he is a part of nature. The universal law of nature is awe-inspiring, never wavering, always systematic and all-pervading. Seasons follow each other without fail just as day follows night. Nature strikes fear in its awesome forms of storms and earthquakes which spare no one. It seems to be highly organized and systematic. The *Ṛg Veda* Indian named this order *ṛta*. This principle is active as much in the affairs of men as it is in nature. Since the Vedic man could not provide an explanation for this universal law, he devised a system of gods to explain each phenomenon. All Vedic gods were nature gods whose task was to maintain and protect *ṛta*. *Ṛta* was supreme and the gods, equally subject to this law, were merely its keepers. Man, however, found that he was capable of breaking this law. This breaking of the law came to be known as *anṛta* (the opposite of *ṛta*), and was considered to be untruth and evil. The ancient man thought he could be a truthful man only if he propiated the god in charge of a particular thing. Hence the performance of ritual sacrifices to gods came to be associated with a good act. Over time, in the *Brāḥmaṇa* literature of the Vedas *ṛta* came to be identified with the performance of ritual sacrifices and duties. Each ritual act had a set reward which brought about the welfare of man. Suffering, pain and distress were the result of non-performance of ritual acts and were thus *anṛta*. We thus find the beginnings of an identification of pleasure, happiness and worldly welfare with good acts and pain and unhappiness with bad acts.

Alongside the above view of moral law, a second strand of thought was also emerging. This was the belief that the sanctions for morality rested on the will of god – a belief that still persists in the modern-day India. The modern Indian's faith in the *bona fides* of the scriptures is strong. The Vedas are such scriptures. The relation between the gods and the Vedas is rather peculiar and significant in Indian thought. The Vedas are regarded as eternal sound and the spoken language of the gods – the first revelators of Vedic sound. The Vedas prescribe the sacrificial moral code and thus indirectly are the will of god, since it is the purpose of the gods to maintain both the moral laws and the natural laws. However, strangely enough, these gods themselves are the brain-children of the Vedic Indian. Hence it is said that the Vedas, which impart immemorial tradition, are preserved and handed down by gods to man during various spans of time (*yuga*). The gods are intermediaries where the Vedic word is concerned. Hence, though in a sense it is the will of god, the moral law is the word of the Vedas and is inviolable – a view found in later Indian thought when the moral ideal became more cogent and expansive.

In spite of such a rigorous explanation of the moral ideal, the approach to morality has never been static, as evidenced by the *Upaniṣads* and the historical and literary works of later years. As the philosophical ideals and practices were discussed, appraised and rationalized, the moral ideals enshrined in such philosophies took different forms in practice. The moral ideal as such, however, remains the same, even though its interpretation differs.

Very early the Vedic Indian came to the conclusion that mere threats of an unknown hell and rewards in heaven could not provide the basis for the 'oughtness' of moral judgements. The performance of the required sacrifices was insufficient as their rewards were limited. If a man regards his efforts at leading a moral life as having no goal other than the present, there could be no incentive for leading a sustained moralistic and ritualistic life. And in the *Upaniṣads* we come across the concept of an eternal soul (*ātman*). Whether this is a justifiable concept or not is disputable. None the less it performs a useful function in establishing the 'oughtness' of moral behaviour. It is this, combined with the Vedic idea of the inexorability of the causal principle, that has given rise to unique Indian notion of *karma* (action), from which arises the doctrine of rebirth (*saṁsāra*).

The main theme of the Upaniṣadic philosophy and consequently their ethical theory is that, as long as man remains attached to worldly possessions, without seeking to know the real nature of himself as an eternal soul (*ātman*), he is wasting his time. Someone who seeks to acquire knowledge about himself or herself and his or her true nature is truly the person who is seeking the way to *mokṣa* (liberation). Almost all the *Upaniṣads* stress this view. It is knowledge of *ātman* and not action in the form of various types of rituals (*yajña* and *yāga*) that leads man to ultimate bliss. The method of instruction adopted in the *Upaniṣads* is a dialectic one. Hence for instance, in the *Chāndogya Upaniṣad* we find Matreyi, the wife of Yājñyavalkya, asking him, 'If now, sir, this whole earth filled with wealth were mine, would I be immortal thereby?'[1] The answer that finally emerges after extensive discussion is that it is knowledge of the true nature of the soul that makes man immortal. This theme is constantly repeated in almost all the *Upaniṣads* through the use of different arguments. The idea of *mokṣa*, seen as immortality of the soul, is emphasized throughout and only that man is a good man who strives to understand this and acts accordingly. *Mokṣa* – release from sorrow and suffering, attainment of bliss – is seen as a corollary of the true knowledge of the self. The concept of evil that emerges from Upaniṣadic thought is that it is a metaphysical error, which lies in seeing the soul, which is the only immortal, as something other than it is. Again it is because each individual regards himself or herself as distinct and different from others that he or she becomes selfish and cruel. However, once unity is realized, there is no delusion, sorrow or misery.[2]

The Upaniṣadic period finally merged into intellectual activity enshrined in the *śāstras* and *smṛtis*. The most famous of these are the *Manusmṛti*, the *Mahābhārata* and Kautilya's *Arthaśāstra*, where the foundation for the fourfold moral ideals of life known as *puruṣārtha* is laid. The *puruṣārthas* maintained their status as ideals; but changed their content from time to time to reflect the changes in social organization. The saints called such codes of conduct *yugadharma*. This aspect of moral life, that is its flexibility and expediency *vis-à-vis* social needs, is brought out extremely well, for instance, in the *Mahābhārata* in connection with speaking the truth:

> It is said, 'To tell the truth is consistent with righteousness. There is nothing higher than truth. I shall now, O Bhārata, say unto thee that which is not generally known to men. . . . There where falsehood would assume the aspect of truth, truth should not be said. There again, where truth would assume the aspect of falsehood, even falsehood should be said.[3]

The moral ideals (puruṣārthas)

There are four moral ideals which are *dharma*, *artha*, *kāma* and *mokṣa*. These are elaborated in what is generally known as *Kalpa Sūtras*, the most important of which for our purposes are the *Dharma Sūtras*, which consider the social, legal and spiritual life of the people. Amongst these, *Manudharma Śāstra* (also known as *Manusmṛti*) is the most important source. Of the *puruṣārthas*, *dharma* is the supreme ideal. The word *dharma* is comparable to *ṛta* and means literally that which supports or upholds.[4] It is the governing principle, and stands for a way of life which upholds society. The actualizing of this principle leads not only to a stable society here and now, but to the much sought after release from sorrow and suffering resulting in *mokṣa*. These actions which help in maintaining society in the path of righteousness and which are not self-regarding form the legal code and the customary morality of the times.

It is in determining that which is beneficial to society while being at the same time non-violative of the harmony in one's life, that is called *dharma*. In the *Bhagavadgītā* this is called a *svadharma*. This concept of *svadharma* is important even today in Hinduism because it provides the practical meaning for *dharma*. There are four ways of determining *svadharma*, or *dharma* for one's own self. These are Vedas, *smṛtis*, *ācāra*, and most important of all, *conscience*. Of these the importance of the *Vedas* and the *smṛtis* have already been alluded to. *Ācāra* refers to the path trodden by the learned and has therefore become the customary mode of behaviour. Such customary morality is always in the form of restrictive commands, laying down the daily observations, and is most suited for those who have neither the time nor the inclination to study and practise what is given in the scriptures. However, not all may be prepared to accept the restrictive morality enshrined in *ācāra*. So, for those with a knowledge of the *śāstras* and an ability to meditate and ratiocinate, conscience becomes the guiding law. Since they have been nurtured by both traditional and Vedic thinking, their conscience does not lead them into selfish and self-maintaining decisions.

Moreover, they understand their *svadharma* as one which can never be against the welfare of the whole society (*lokasaṁgraha*). Much of modern-day reform of the Hindu religion and social-welfare ideals are results of implementing the ideal of *svadharma* to suit modern civilization by reformists such as Mahatma Gandhi and Raja Ram Mohan Roy.

Goals such as *dharma* and *mokṣa* may not appeal as ideals to all. It is often said that it is only when man's physical welfare is assured and psychological pressures are assuaged that he can even begin to think of his spiritual welfare and therefore of goals such as *dharma* and *mokṣa*. Hence, *artha* and *kāma* are also prescribed as moral ideals. *Artha* is economic welfare and *kāma* is sensuous experience. Pursuit of *artha* as a goal, however, does not permit anti-social activities such as cheating, corruption, hoarding and denying others what is due to them. These are all considered to be against *dharma*, which is the guiding principle. Similarly in the pursuit of *kāma* a sense of proportion and detachment is advised, since undue desire could lead to unhappiness and sorrow. *Kāma* and *artha* are enjoined because they make man's life composite out of which emerges a total man. In other words, riches and pleasures, though worldly ends, should make an individual a worthy member of society fulfilling his or her duties. These three, *dharma*, *artha* and *kāma*, are known as the *trivargas*, the three categories which make for the fullness of a person's life.

The ultimate goal of man's life is freedom from the dualities of life (*mokṣa*). All systems of Indian thought accept this. The nature of this goal, however, varies according to the school, since each school has its own conception of the nature of a soul. *Mokṣa*, though the highest ideal, is the last goal, since it is believed that man can contemplate *mokṣa* only after he has lived in society and realized its futility.

The prescribed practical methodology

In answer to the question why man should lead a moral life, it is not enough if an ideal is prescribed. An account of both the meaning and the content of a moral life needs to be provided. In Indian thought the purpose of a moral life is not so much to fulfil the will of god as to seek one's own salvation. Salvation is attaining freedom from sorrow and suffering. However, the intermediary purpose of a moral life is to achieve a just society. Man should not, by his voluntary actions, cause sorrow and suffering to others. To achieve this end two ways of life are prescribed. These are *nivṛtti mārga*, the path of renunciation, and *pravṛtti mārga*, where man is required to participate, with moderation and restraint, in all activities of life. The former requires that man should become a recluse (*sannyāsin*). This, however, is neither possible for everyone nor is it desirable. Hence in the latter way of life man should use his discrimination and practise renunciation in action: the *karma mārga* propounded in the *Bhagavadgītā*. *Karma mārga* requires man to carry out his responsibilities, but emphasizes that he should not become so involved in fulfilling his responsibilities and his role in life that he would go to any length to achieve this. Unbridled attachment leads only to sorrow and suffering. It has already been stated above how man, driven by his desires, loses even his intelligence. So the *Gītā* advocates not complete *sannyāsa* but *karma sannyāsa*, where man is exhorted not to shirk his responsibilities but act without attachment to the results of such action. Inevitably each action will produce results. The wise man, however, would not concern himself with such effects, but would carry out his duty to the best of his ability. But is it psychologically possible for man to act without the motivating force of achieving a desired goal? The *Gītā* answers this question by saying that by transubstantiating the goals it is possible to act without limited desires. That is, one should sublate a personal goal to the wider all-comprehensive goal of the welfare of society (*lokasaṁgraha*). *Dharma* is the ideal and *svadharma* is the means of achieving it. Motivated interpretations of *svadharma* are not wanting. The most important of them, held by staunch traditionalists, is that it means the duties enjoined by each caste upon its members. However, such an explanation would be absurd in present times since there are a multiplicity of castes and there are no prescribed rules for the behaviour of each caste. Moreover, in present-day India affected by scientific and technological advances it is impractical and impossible for the castes to be solely following vocations prescribed by the Vedas. This has resulted in a reinterpretation of *svadharma* as that which is suitable to an individual's capabilities, intelligence and inclination. Thus the Gītā says that it is better to do the things for which one is most suited even incompetently than aspire to do that for which one is neither trained nor competent psychologically. The end or *lokasaṁgraha* can be achieved only slowly and by deliberate cultivation of disciplined action. Certain practical steps which help its cultivation are given in the Yoga system.

The practical requirements for good conduct described in the Yoga system are accepted by the other classical orthodox systems of Indian philosophy. The principles consist of both negative and positive principles and are called *yama* and *niyama* respectively. These are to be observed daily. In addition there are two others, *āsana* and *prāṇāyāma*. *Āsana* is posture which is comfortable and leaves the mind to concentrate. *Prāṇāyāma* is controlled breathing which makes the mind and the internal organs calm and quiescent, thus leaving the self or *ātman* free to concentrate and fit to undertake the practice of *niyamas*. These are cleanliness of the body and surroundings, *śaouca*, contentment, *santoṣa*, purificatory mental concentration, *tapas*, studying together with fellow-aspirants (*svādyāya*) and devotion to god (*Īśvara praṇidhāna*). These are to be observed daily and by all people without any distinction of caste, creed or sex. The *yamas* are five in number, and they are negative commands to be observed just like *niyamas*. These are *ahiṃsā*, abstinence from causing any type of injury to all living beings, *satya*, speaking truth even if it is against one's own welfare, *asteya*, non-stealing, which means not taking that which is not one's own but belongs to others, *brahmacārya*, continence in all things which give rise to sensuous enjoyment, and *aparigraha*, abstaining from avarice.

The practice of *yamas* and *niyamas* helps in disciplining the body and mind, and achieving contentment. These are all social practices which help man to lead a comfortable and stable life, thereby making him fit to act for the welfare of humanity.

We have said that the final *puruṣārtha* is *mokṣa*. One way of attaining this is by following the *pravṛtti mārga*, which involves the doctrine of *svadharma*. But it is not everyone who can achieve this in his life. Human nature being what it is, to carry out one's duty irrespective of the results which follow is almost impossible for the majority. Hence the *Bhagavadgītā* prescribes two other modes of action known as *bhakti mārga* and *jñāna mārga*. One of the *niyamas* already mentioned is devotion to god (*Īśvara praṇidhāna*). *Bhakti mārga* is the same as devotion to god. However, according to the Yoga system devotion to god is one method by the practice of which man can lead a peaceful life. The principle stressed here is that since all are god's creation, what is harmful to one would also be harmful to others. While this principle is accepted in the *bhakti mārga* it goes one step further and maintains that all actions arising from greed, hatred, selfishness and unhealthy competition must be eschewed. Every action must be performed as an offering to god without burdening our minds about its results. Such devotion, however, is not easy to practise, as it requires utter selflessness.

The next path for the achievement of *mokṣa* is *jñāna mārga*, the way of knowledge. Here knowledge means not merely worldly knowledge but a knowledge of ultimate reality. It requires a rigorous training in logical thinking and a sustained faith that knowledge is attainable. This has to be cultivated as a prerequisite for following this route to attain *mokṣa*. This is perhaps the most difficult of all the routes, even though knowledge is a prerequsite for the other two routes. That is, one cannot act without desire unless one *knows* that what one desires is not ultimate; similarly, one cannot *love* that which one does not know. So knowledge is the basis. A rigorous training and an ardent desire to know that which is ultimate releases man from sorrow and suffering.

So far the discussion has centered around the fourfold ideals of *dharma*, *artha*, *kāma* and *mokṣa*. There are, however, two auxiliary theories, orientated towards the application of these ideals, that need to be considered. One is the socio-ethical-metaphysical principle of the doctrine of *karma* and *saṁsāra* (rebirth), and the other is the socio-ethical-economic doctrine of the theories of caste and the different stages of life. The first theory's contribution to a moral life will be considered briefly. A very tenacious and widespread aspect of Indian ethics, whether it be of the *āstika* (theistic) or *nāstika darśanas* (non-theistic philosophies), is the doctrine of *karma* and its consequent theory of rebirth. Both are often referred to as *saṁsāra*. The first and the most important is the law of *karma*. This maintains that the law of causation is effective not only in the natural world but also in the moral realm. Man reaps as he sows, not only in his life an earth but also in moral life. The beginnings of this idea are to be found in the concept of *ṛta* in the *Ṛg Veda*. When *karma* came to be interpreted in the *Brāhmaṇas* not merely as action, but as sacrificial rite, the results of actions were said to be reaped in heaven (*svarga loka*). The ancient Hindu, however, began to question how the results of ritual action performed here and now could be preserved during a considerable length of time by which a man could attain heaven, since this could happen only after a person was dead. The vehicle of such conveyance of the results of moral action was said to be *adṛṣṭa*, the unseen. It was thought that *adṛṣṭa* consisting of either good or bad deeds could not be exhausted in one lifetime. Good actions lead to a benevolent, pleasurable and economically viable rebirth, while bad actions lead to the opposite. In the light of this, the final purpose of man is to act in such a way that there is no accumulation of *adṛṣṭa* which is carried from life to life along with the soul. This in practice means acting in such a way that the self or *ātman* is not influenced by the results of its action. This theory of *adṛṣṭa* and the methodology to get rid of its existence was propounded by the Nyāya-Vaiśeṣika school and accepted by other systems since there is no refutation of it.

The *karma* theory outlined above seems to be a deterministic view of morality, binding man for ever to the fruits of his actions without any let up. However, human free will is affected if this *karma* doctrine is accepted. The Nyāya-Vaiśeṣika school tried to resolve this in the following way. Since all actions are in time, there must be a past, present and future for it. The fruits of actions whether in this life or in a past life, must be lived and experienced now, just as the results of actions performed now are preserved for future results. Thus while the results of the past cannot be escaped, the future can be controlled by controlling the present. Thus *prārabdha karma* refers to the results of the past, and *āgāmi karma* is that which refers to the future. The present is called *sañcita karma*. It must be controlled and prevented from accumlating, so that the future can be free from its results. It is here that man's efforts are necessary. Man is completely his own master. His future life depends upon what he does now and how he does it. God helps him in controlling his actions and redirecting them towards the cancellation of the *karmaphala*. Thus the *karma* doctrine absolves god from all responsibility for the sufferings of man and makes man himself responsible for his own sufferings. Determinism in human behaviour is absolved.

In spite of such a generous interpretation of *karma* and *karmaphala* by classical philosophers there is a vagueness regarding what is meant by *karmaphala*, the fruit of action. An ordinary action like giving charity benefits the person to whom the charity is given. This is the normal meaning of action. But we have to go beyond such a simplistic interpretation. The giver of charity also derives a satisfactory pleasure. Tradition, however, holds that *puṇya* and *pāpa* also are the results of such actions. These words do not stand for the right or the wrong. They signify the *merit* that comes from the performance of right actions and the *demerit* that comes from the performance of wrong actions. The perception of the difference between these two is the result of continuous self-discipline and the development of Yogic powers.[5] It is this that is required for our explanation of reincarnation together with the concept that the soul (*ātman*) is eternal and indestructible.

While the above explanation of *karma* and the eternality of the soul is accepted in various degrees and forms by almost all the schools of Indian philosophy, the one important exception is the Cārvāka school, which points out that there are lacunae in this theory. According to this school the law of causality is effective only in the empirical world. If the cause and effect are here and now, their counterparts cannot be somewhere else like another birth. If this is the case, it is difficult to see how the two could be connected. Moreover, the Cārvāka school points out that attribution of a transcendental cause to an empirical effect and vice-versa results in a category mistake. Besides, it is not possible to argue from effect to cause because of the multiplicity of possible causes.

Cārvāka, Bauddha and Jaina ethics

The Cārvāka, the oldest of the heterodox systems, rebelled against Upaniṣadic and Vedic thought. Perhaps the rebellion was motivated by the extreme form of renunciation advocated by the *Upaniṣads* and the ritualistic formalism which resulted from the Vedic stress on the performance of sacrifices. So, for the Cārvāka there is no all-controlling god, no conscience to guide, and it does not believe in life after death and *mokṣa*. Only sensations and happiness derived from sense-satisfaction are the ideal for human activity. *Dharma* is rejected, along with *mokṣa*, and only sensual pleasure, *kāma*, and the means of securing such pleasure, *artha*, are acceptable. No doubt there is pain along with pleasure; but according to the Cārvāka because of that, pleasure should not be neglected.[6] Hence traditional ethical principles are disregarded and hedonism accepted. While there are other materialistic and realistic schools in Indian philosophy, the Cārvāka is the only naturalist, *svabhāva vādin*). According to this school, the soul is the result of an interaction of the subjective and purely objective experiences, vanishing once the experiences vanish. Man is a creature of nature, and nature is neither good nor bad. It is only events that become good or bad inasmuch as they produce pleasure or pain. But events are not permanent.

The Jaina philosphy is also against the Vedic and Upaniṣadic traditions. They, however, posit the existence of a soul whose characteristic is consciousness. Each soul corresponds to the nature, size and structure of the body it occupies. This concept seems to have been derived from the etymological meaning of the word *ātman* ('what lives or is animate'). The intrinsic nature of the soul is perfection. To achieve this perfection while still embodied is the aim of the ethical teaching of Jainism. While the soul is transcendental in its true form, *karma*, which is flowing matter, binds it to the body. Freedom from such bondage can be achieved by leading a moral life. Moral life consists of observing the Three Jewels (*triratna*). These are right faith, right knowledge and right conduct. The former two form the basis for right conduct which are the fivefold virtues *pancaśīla*. These are (1) *ahiṃsā*, non-violence, (2) *satya*, not making wrong statements roused by the passions of anger, greed, conceit and others, (3) *asteya*, not taking anything that is neither yours nor given to you, (4) *brahmācarya*, chastity and continence, (5) *parigraha*, controlling all internal or external attachment. Of these the most important is *ahiṃsā*. Since soul is present in all living beings, *ahiṃsā* covers a large variety of actions. It is only when *ahiṃsā* in all its aspects is practised that one becomes a *jina* or a perfect man. This is not purely a negative concept as it does not mean only desisting from harming other living beings, but also rendering active service to others. Thus Jaina ethics does not neglect the social aspect of an ethical life. In both Buddhism and Jainism two-fold training is prescribed, one branch for the monks and the other for the householder. But unlike Buddhism, the Jainism permits a combination of the two disciplines, thus forming a graded system, different in degree at various levels.

Buddhism takes a different approach to the moral life altogether. While the Cārvāka said that soul is a manifestation of the combination of material things and Jainism maintained that soul was material but all-pervasive for the Buddhists soul is merely a name for a series of becoming. There is nothing permanent including the soul. The cause of sorrow and suffering is ignorance of this state (*avidyā*). The consequent desire (*tṛṣṇā*) is the thirst for possession of things. When these two are conquered man attains *nirvāṇa*, which is the equivalent of *mokṣa* in the orthodox systems. The method prescribed for attaining *nirvāṇa* is leading a moral life here and now. The system of morality prescribed is the Eightfold Path known as the middle way. It steers between the extreme asceticism of the Upaniṣadic teaching and the extreme indulgence taught by the Naturalists (*svabhāva vādins*), of whom Cārvāka is an example. The Eightfold Path consists of (1) right faith, (2) right resolve, (3) right speech, (4) right action, (5) right living, (6) right effort, (7) right thought and (8) right concentration. Right faith is to know that there is suffering and right resolve is to get rid of this. All the other principles strengthen this resolve. A moral life conducted along the recommended lines gets rid of *karma*, which causes dependent origination and which in turn causes suffering. The Buddha always insisted that one must accept only that which one realized was right. Salvation or *nirvāṇa* can be realized only through self-reliance and not by the grace of god. Even a teacher (*guru*) can only show the way. But a perception of truth can only come by right conduct (*śīla*), which includes veracity, non-injury and contentment.

The Buddhists believe in *karma* and rebirth. But these are not transcendental. The soul, which is not permanent but a stream of existence, is still the agent of action. Hence there can also be a transmigration without a transmigrating agent. Rebirth is not a post-mortem affair but something which takes place every instant. Like the flame of the candle which is ever changing though seemingly continuous, so also with the individual self. It is character that transmigrates by attaching itself to a new body-series. This process goes on till *tṛṣṇā* or desire is conquered and there is a cessation (*nirvāṇa*). Thus *karma* is an impersonal law and rebirth happens every moment (*kṣaṇa*).

SOCIETY IN INDIAN PHILOSOPHY

The foundations of the structure of Indian society are found in the theories of caste (*varṇa*) and stages of human life (*āśrama*). These theories are often justified on socio-economic grounds.

Caste (*varṇa*)

The earliest reference to the caste system is to be found in the Puruṣa Sūkta of the *Ṛg Veda*.[7] According to the Puruṣa Sūkta the four primary castes *brāhmin*, *rājanya*, *vaiśya* and *śūdra* emerged from the mouth, the two arms, the two thighs and the feet of Puruṣa respectively, and the functions of each correspond to the position they occupy in the body of Puruṣa. Since the mouth signifies teaching, *brāhmins* are scholars; since the arms signify offence and defence, the *rājanya* (also *kṣatriyas*) are warriors; since the thighs signify activity, the *vaiśyas* are traders, and since the feet serve the body in giving mobility, the *śūdras* are to render services. The origins of the caste system seem to be based on the nature of work to be done and its importance. The above account, however, is allegorical and mythical and provides an elusive origin for caste system.

The early Vedic texts suggest that the caste system may have had its origins in the two tightly demarcated groups of people based on their colour (*varṇa*): the fair-complexioned Āryan immigrants and the dark-complexioned inhabitants of the country, the *dāsa*. The Āryan as the conquerors devoted themselves to learning, fighting and trade, while the *dāsas* were relegated to manual labour and service. This is also claimed to be another factor in the constitution of caste or *varṇa*, as it came to be known later. Over the generations, however, birth began to play a pivotal role in the system, so that status was determined by birth. So a child born in a *brāhmin* family had the privileges of a *brāhmin* even though he may not have had the necessary qualities for that profession. However, there are no evaluative statements in the Vedas on the impact of this system on society or indeed the relation of this system to the monistic metaphysical philosophy to be found in the Vedas and the *Upaniṣads*. Indeed it would not be an exaggeration to say that the caste system is at variance with the Upaniṣadic philosophy which continuously equates the individual (*ātman*) with the Absolute (*Brahman*), thereby implying equality. Against this it is indeed difficult to see how the caste system could be rationally justified.

However, we do have a rising of a rebellion against both the metaphysical and social structure of the early people in the rising on the non-orthodox systems of Cārvāka and Buddhism. As stated above, while Cārvāka is purely hedonistic, the Buddhists, influenced by the ideal of *mokṣa*, sought to break the chain of *saṁsāra*. While the belief in *karma* made the Hindu maintain that the reward for a good action was birth in a higher place in society, Buddhism maintained that good actions led to a release from birth. It also emphasized the need for a change in the outlook of the socio-economic pattern, as evidenced by its Eightfold Path. The strength of Buddhism lies in its concern for the welfare of the common man and its emphasis on escaping from *saṁsāra*.

Responding to the new ideas introduced by non-orthodox schools, Hinduism tried to redraw its framework for social life by redefining the role of the individual and the social institutions to lend them clarity, consistency and viability. The *Dharma Sūtras*, *Arthaśāstra* and *Nīti Śāstras* are the results of this concern. All deal with the everyday life of people, thereby bearing testimony for their concern for social institutions. They not only emphasize the divine origin of the theory of caste system, but maintain that the prevailing castes denote the innate nature and intelligence of people. For instance, the *Bhagavadgītā* enunciates the characters of the four castes as follows:

> Serenity, self-restraint, austerity, purity, forgiveness, and also uprightness, knowledge, realization, belief in hereafter – these are the duties of Brāhmins born of their own nature. Heroism, vigour, firmness, resourcefulness, not flying from battle, generosity and lordliness are the duties of the Kṣatriyas born of their own nature. Agriculture, cattle-rearing, and trade are the duties of the Vaiśyas born of their own nature, and action consisting of service is the duty of śūdras born of their own nature.[8]

This idea seems at first sight to be meaningful. Birth itself is synonymous with the instrinsic nature of an individual and consequently his or her function in society. However, the *karma* theory maintains that it is possible to be born either on a higher or lower plane by controlling one's *sañcita karma*. Hence by controlling one's actions here and now it is possible to change the intrinsic nature in a future birth. Thus we have the story of Viswāmitra, born a *kṣatriya*, changing his nature into that of a *brāhmin* by performing austerities and attaining the privileges due to a *brāhmin*. Thus it is definitely stated that birth alone does not confer on one the status of any caste.[9] As this is an uphill task, the *Bhagavadgītā* exhorts everyone to stick conscientiously to their duties (*svadharma*). However, it is accepted that in a moment of crisis one is permitted to perform the duties of other castes. This type of *dharma* is called *āpadharma*. There is also the emphasis on *niṣkāma karma* (desireless action) to overcome the frustration that may spring up from adherence to *svadharma*. Since there is no restriction on the performance of *niṣkāma karma*, it enables one to achieve in one stage what is appropriate to another stage. Thus *śūdras* become entitled to *mokṣa* straight away irrespective of other considerations, since all their actions have been desireless.

It is thus that *varṇa* (caste) becomes a *dharma* (ordained duty). Though admixture of castes by marriage (*varṇasaṃkara*) was prohibited, a scheme was none the less devised to regulate it. A *brāhmin* could marry a woman from the three lower castes, and so on down the grades. However, there could be no upward marriages: a man could not marry a woman of a higher caste. Marriages were generally monogamous, but polygamy was not frowned upon.

All decision-making was a democratic process involving the entire family. The child's first education started at home, at the feet of his father, who initiated him into the skills of his calling. The importance of the family grew with each individual's dependence on the whole. Thus the family gained in importance and occupied foreground in all matters. The importance of the father or the oldest male member of the family gained in momentum, and he came to be designated the *kartā* or the responsible *doer* of the family.

During the Vedic and the Upaniṣadic period women enjoyed a status equal to that of men in all fields of activity. They excelled in Vedic and philosophical studies, as evidenced by the rigorous debates engaged in by women like Gargi and Maitreyi.

However, by the time of the *Dharma Sūtras*, specially Manu's *Dharma Śāstra*, a woman was regarded as unfit for Vedic studies. She became dependent on her father, husband and son during the different stages of her development. Though presence of a wife was necessary for the performance of all ritual acts by the husband, she could not perform the rites. Her duty was by the side of her husband.

Āśrama

Just as the *Varṇadharma* (the caste system) defines the role of the individual in society, *āśrama dharma* regulates the inner development of the individual, both biological and psychological. *Āśrama* means 'exerting oneself'. The *āśrama* theory charters the life of an individual into four different phases – *brahmacārya*, *gṛhasta*, *vānaprasta* and *sannyāsa* – on the basis of the varied emotional states and capabilities. At each stage, emotionally and psychologically an individual is deemed fit to take up a particular state of social life. During the first stage, *brahmacārya*, the individual should remain unmarried, observe celibacy and earnestly devote himself to the pursuit of knowledge. After the completion of learning, he moves on to the next stage and marries a suitable girl and performs the duties of a householder. This is *gṛhastāśrama*. *Vānaprasta* is the third stage, in which he avoids active social life and moves away from his house, invariably with his wife, to the forests, to live in peace and meditation. In *sannyāsa*, the last and final stage, he leads a life of renunciation. The householder is the centre of manifold activity, but the *sannyāsi*, on the contrary, is a detached, self-isolating individual. He is not attached to the family and all values are value-neutral to him. In fact, a *sannyāsi* is dead to society. He dramatizes this detachment from society by performing his own funeral rites, by distributing all his possessions and keeping away from the performance of any religious rites and social duties. Thus, according to the *āśrama* system an individual has to lead a life of activity for the major part of his life. He can switch over to a life of renunciation only in the last stages of his life. After becoming a *sannyāsi* one cannot return to the life of a householder. This division of a man's life into stages helps each individual to perform his duties diligently and to the satisfaction of all members of society. On account of the influence of family, custom and tradition, individuals adhered to *dharma* and life went on in society in an ordained manner.

The king and his *dharma*

A society was not governed merely by social norms as prescribed in the *varṇa* and the *āśrama dharma*. There was also a political angle. The authority of the state or the king was not limited to the economic and political aspects of people's lives, but extended to their social and private lives as well. The king was not merely a protector from aggression from outside but also a protector of a way of life ordained in the *Dharma Śāstras*. Hence the king's place was a very important one. The institution of kingship was instituted for the upholding of *dharma* because when people were allowed to deviate from *dharma* there was strife and uncertainty in society. Hence the duty of the king was to see that such a state of affairs did not develop. As the *Arthaśāstra* of Kautilya says, 'In the happiness of his subjects lies his happiness; in their welfare his welfare.[10] The king was not democratically chosen but chosen on the strength of the hereditary principle. As in the other professions the king was trained and prepared for his duties right from his childhood by a competent *guru* (teacher) who was invariably either a sage or a learned *brāhmin*. The king was divinely ordained and his word was the command of God. But like the gods he was trained to be generous and unattached.

The king was always assisted by a council of ministers chosen carefully 'whose character [had] been tested under the three pursuits of life, religion, wealth and love and under fear'.[11]

CONCLUSION

Though moral and social values in present-day India are still based on the traditions handed down by texts such as the *Bhagavadgītā* and *Manu Smṛti*, there are none the less continuous efforts at adapting the traditional values to suit the needs of modern-day society.

NOTES

1 *Chāndogya Upaniṣad* II.IV, verse 2 onwards.
2 *Īśa Upaniṣad* 7.
3 Śāntiparva 109 4–5 onwards. As quoted in S. Radhakrishnan and Charles A. Moore (eds), *A Source Book in Indian Philosophy* (Princeton, N.J.: Princeton University Press, 1957), p. 165.
4 *Dhārayāt dharmaḥ*.
5 The *Āpastambha Dharma Sūtra* maintains: 'He is gentle and serene. He exercises the highest self-control. He is modest and courageous. He has cast off all lassitude and is free from anger.' Mysore Oriental Library edition I.iii.17–24 (as quoted by M. Hiriyanna, *Outlines of Indian Philosophy* (London: George Allen & Unwin, 1932)).
6 'No body casts away the grain because of the husks'. Mādhava Ācārya, *Sarvadarśana Saṁgraha*, reprint (New Delhi: Cosmo Publishers, 1976), pp. 1–3.
7 Edward J. Thomas, *Vedic Hymns*, Wisdom of the East Series (London: John Murray, 1923), X, 90.
8 *Bhagavadgītā*, chapter 18, verses 42–4.
9 ibid.

10 Kautilya's *Artha Śāstra*, trans. R. Shama Sastry, 2nd edn (Wesleyan Mission Press, 1923), ch. 19, 'The duties of a king'.

11 ibid., ch. 10.

FURTHER READING

Brown, D. M. (1953) *The White Umbrella – Indian Political Thought from Manu to Gandhi*, Berkeley: University of California Press.

Chatterjee, S. (1950) *Fundamentals of Hinduism: A Philosophical Study*, Calcutta: Das Gupta.

Chennakesavan, Sarasvasti (1976) *Concepts in Indian Philosophy*, Madras: Orient Longman.

Heimann, Betty (1937) *Indian and Western Philosophy: A Study in Contrast*, London: George Allen & Unwin.

Hiriyanna, M. (1932) *Outlines of Indian Philosophy*, London: George Allen & Unwin.

Iyer, P. S. Sivaswami (1935) *Evolution of Hindu Moral Ideals*, Calcutta: University of Calcutta.

Kane, P. V. (1930–53) *History of Dharmaśāstra* (ancient and medieval religious and civil law in India), 4 vols, Bombay: Bhandarkar Oriental Research Institute.

Māhdhava Ācārya (1904) *Sarvadarśana Saṁgraha*, trans. E. B. Cowell and A. E. George, London: Kegan Paul, Trench, Trübner & Co.

Maitra, S. K. (1925) *The Ethics of the Hindus*, Calcutta: University of Calcutta.

Radhakrishnan, S. and Moore, Charles A. (eds) (1957) *A Source Book in Indian Philosophy*, Princeton, N.J.: Princeton University Press.

15

CONTEMPORARY INDIAN PHILOSOPHY

A. Roy

INTRODUCTION

Indian philosophy in the twentieth century is a reflection of ancient philosophical thoughts in the changing times of society. It is an expression of the eternal in the temporal, a reverberation of what is perennial of philosophic thoughts in the ever-changing social order of mankind. It implies quite a few factors which may not be apparent at first sight. When man lives in the world, he takes it to be as real as he experiences it. As experience grows deeper and man starts questioning some of the obvious incompatibilities of nature and the world, he realizes that all that he knows through sense-experience is not really real. Reality lies beyond the world of appearances; it is something constant and eternal; it always is. Man must turn himself in search of that reality. The search is eternal, true of mankind throughout the world and particularly true of the country in which it seems to have taken very deep root.

Philosophy in the West was initiated with the global interest of knowing the fundamental substance which constitutes the basic material of all things in the world. The Greek philosophers sought a speculative solution to their philosophic wonder. Thales wondered at the fundamental element from which everything in the world is evolved. In this philosophical wonder, he was a spectator who enquired about the reality that lay outside himself. A different attitude of wonder seemed to prevail in Indian philosophical thought. Philosophers enquiring about reality were not detached from the object of their enquiry. They were steeped in the very nature of reality they enquired about. It was a unique union of being with knowing that characterized their philosophical investigation in the earliest ages of Vedas. The Vedic hymns heard and subsequently sung resounded through the very length and breadth of the universe. When the ancient sages responded to the Vedic hymns, they did so in wonder but not with the detachment of a speculative thinker. In deep veneration of what they heard, they remained totally immersed in the echoing sound of *Om* (a unique sound of invoking God)[1] vibrating throughout the universe, and reminding the saintly hearers that peace is the abiding truth of reality and that all must strive towards that. The temporal and the transcendent, the material and the spiritual constitute the inseparable elements of that reality. Life needs to realize that simple reality. Here knowledge came as an intuitive insight to illumined souls who not only knew but identified themselves with the truth.

METAPHYSICAL FOUNDATION OF INDIAN PHILOSOPHY

Contemporary thought in India seems to be grounded in the metaphysics of Vedānta. The philosophical reflections of the *Upaniṣads* culminate in the ultimate union of *ātman* with *Brahman*. Vedānta, as the word indicates, is the end of philosophical deliberations carried on in the various *Upaniṣads* like the *Chāndogya*, *Māṇḍukya* and *Kaṭha* which dealt with the gradual evolution of the empirical self from its ever-changing nature to its eternal being of *Brahman*. The word *Brahman* is derived from the root *Bṛh*, meaning to grow or evolve. *Brahman* is that which bursts forth as nature and soul. It is the ultimate cause of the universe. In the *Chāndogya* it is cryptically described as *tajjalān* – as that (*tat*) from which the world arises (*ja*), into which it returns (*la*), and by which it is supported and it lives (*an*). In *Taittirīya*, *Brahman* is defined as that from which all things are born, by which they live and into which they are reabsorbed. Vedānta gives a unique interpretation to the three states of the self – its waking, dreaming and dreamless deep-sleep state. When life begins, the empirical self engaged in the everyday concerns of experience seems to be the sole reality. But the self which is awake is also the self which dreams and the self which sleeps deeply without ever being conscious either of itself or of the world in which it eventually awakes. In all three states the self that experiences, understands and realizes is not the self that can ever be the object of itself. It is the eternal subject, the spirit or the *ātman* which, remaining constant with itself, directs and envisions its ultimate unity with *Brahman*. 'In defining reality as that whose non-existence cannot be conceived, Śaṅkara identifies it with pure consciousness or the witness, not subject to change.'[2]

Such being the metaphysical foundation, most philosophical thought depends on the ancient thought of the Vedas, *Upaniṣads* and Vedānta for its main source of knowledge. However, contemporary thought is generally criticized as being merely interpretative and recasting the old in new modes of thought and expression. It does not impart anything new that would hold, guide and lead the nation to a better and more prosperous future. This criticism is not well founded since contemporary philosophy, even if it derives from ancient sources, is universal and perennial. It speaks the language of the spiritual consciousness of the individual, the unique search of the being of man. The man in India is the man in England, America, Europe, Asia and every other corner of the world. Indian philosophy today recasts the ancient idea of *saccidānanda* or *sat*, *cit* and *ānanda*, meaning pure existence, consciousness and bliss, in the contemporary socio-political and economic contexts of the country.[3] To emphasize the essence of the universal in the individual is to emphasize the essence of the universal in all human beings. It is with this idea in mind that Sri Aurobindo thought of liberating mankind by realizing the world soul or super-mind in himself. The same idea was expressed by Swami Vivekananda when he said that he would experience birth hundreds of times in the world and suffer the sufferings of millions till the whole human race was emancipated from the evils of life. Mahatma Gandhi fought for the freedom of the nation with the two universal weapons of *satyāgraha*, attachment to truth, and non-violence. It is only in the realization of the essential spiritual consciousness that Gandhi could combine philosophical knowledge with the political freedom of the country.

CONTEMPORARY PHILOSOPHICAL THOUGHT

All the contemporary philosophical knowledge of the world could be said to be interpretative of old thoughts of ancient times. Who can be original in the sense of Socrates or Plato or of the Āryans who heard the Vedic songs long before they could be rendered in language and later on in scriptures? To be original today means to take on the old, to assimilate and revive it in the mould of the new. Contemporary Indian philosophy can be said to be original in this sense. For all the contemporary thinkers whose contributions to present-day philosophy count most, the keynote has been the teachings of Advaita Vedānta. Life is spiritual and eternal; our search is for the realization of *ātman* or spirit, which is one with *Brahman*. Call it religious, call it philosophical or call it the message of spirituality in every living soul of the world, it is one and the same. The individual needs to realize his or her constant, unchanging, eternal self which is not the self of the material world, but the underlying self or spiritual consciousness pining to be one with *Brahman*. No wonder, then, that India is said to spiritualize the whole world. It is religious because here philosophy cannot be disassociated from religion, the way of knowledge from the way of life. Although Indian philosophy generally prescribes three paths (*mārgas*), according to different objectives pursued at different stages of life, namely duty (*karma*), devotion (*bhakti*) and knowledge (*jñāna*), no one way of life can be attained exclusively on its own without the others being pursued.[4] The *jñāna mārg* (path of knowledge) is supposed to lead to the highest knowledge of *Brahman*. It is knowledge attained not through scholastic learning and discursive reason but through the constant effort of the individual passing through the stages of *karma* and *bhakti* together. Knowledge of the unity of *Brahman* with *ātman* is enlightenment and realization of the soul in being truly itself. When harmonization of knowing with being is complete, man attains salvation, *mokṣa* or the state of *saccidānanda*. For the Greeks, philosophy meant love of wisdom; for the Indians, philosophy means love of wisdom that directs man to the true abode of eternity and universality. What should man do with knowledge or a storehouse of rich information which he does not experience personally in life and experiencing which he does not realize that wisdom carries the message of liberation of the soul from the shackles of bondage, pain and suffering of the entire human race?

Present-day philosophical thinking in India is a peculiar combination of ancient thoughts with the current socio-political and economic problems of life. There are quite a few twentieth-century thinkers whose contributions to present-day philosophical thinking count most. However, I shall be referring to only four, mentioning their heritage and relevance in modern India. In referring to the philosophies of Vivekananda, Mahatma Gandhi, Sri Aurobindo and Radhakrishnan I hope to show in what sense they can be said to be true representatives of contemporary Indian thought.

NINETEENTH- AND TWENTIETH-CENTURY THINKERS

Swami Vivekananda (1863–1902)

Vivekananda was the monastic name of Narendranath Datta, who was born on 12 January 1863 in an aristocratic family of Calcutta, the then capital of India. Brought up with western culture and literature, Narendranath continued to be sceptical regarding Ramakrishna's intensely personal experience of the transcendent till a glimpse of beatitude calmed his surging humanitarian instinct. He realized the immensity of the vision he had in front of him and wanted to merge his soul completely in the Absolute Reality through *nirvikalpa samādhi* (meditation of a nameless, formless and impersonal reality).[5] At this stage of spiritual ecstasy Ramakrishna[6] charged him with his life's mission. He was not to seek salvation for himself. The mission of his life lay in serving suffering mankind and seeking spiritual satisfaction in that service alone. Convinced by his own realization of the spiritual value of his master's injunction, he later combined the two ideals of individual salvation and universal well-being.

Vivekananda was a relentless seeker of the truth of God. His passionate zeal for realizing salvation for himself along with the well-being of his fellow-brethren kept him roaming from one part of the country to the other, from the Himalayas to Cape Comorin. Apart from what he learned in the company of sages and from his own reading of religious books, he drew valuable insight from the firsthand experience of the social, economic and cultural life of the people. Men belonging to different castes, sects and communities with different regional shades in their widely varying thoughts and ways of life proved to be a highly engrossing subject of study. By the time he reached the end of his journey in the South, he realized how myriad kaleidoscopic patterns of social life, scattered all over the country, were all ultimately based on the same spiritual foundation laid by the seers of old, the *ṛṣis* (sages) of ancient India. Thus his direct experience opened his eyes to the fact that a central unity could accommodate thousands of varieties on the surface.

While Vivekananda's intellect was busy acquiring knowledge, his heart sank at the sight of the miseries of masses in every part of the country through which he happened to pass. His direct experience of the appalling misery of the down-trodden people set his whole being on fire. With such a burning passion in his heart, he reached the southernmost tip of India, paid his homage to the goddess Kanya Kumari at Cape Comorin and swam across to a neighbouring rock entirely cut off from the mainland, now known as Vivekananda Rock. Sitting in complete solitude on the rock and surrounded by the dashing waves of the ocean all about him, he looked at the mainland and visualized the whole of India before him. The real self of India stood revealed before his eyes.

Hearing of the Parliament of Religions to be held in 1893 in Chicago, he decided to attend it in order to communicate the universality of Hindu philosophy. The questions he was going to put to the congregation were: 'Was not the world a sacred manifestation of the divine?' and 'Was not man behind all shades of complexion equally holy as an expression of the lord?' The Parliament of Religions commenced its first session on 11 September 1893. Before the final session of the Parliament on 27 September he had delivered ten to twelve speeches. Through them he acquainted the house with the lofty ideas and ideals connected with various aspects of Hinduism and also with his central theme of universal religion based on the findings of the Vedic seers. In the inspired utterance with which he concluded his address at the final session, one sees a revelation of the spirit of Ramakrishna, and gets the keynote of Vivekananda's message to the West. He declared with all emphasis:

> The Christian is not to become a Hindu, or a Buddhist, nor a Hindu or a Buddhist to become a Christian. But each must assimilate the spirit of the others and yet preserve his individuality and grow according to his own law of growth.[7]

In the same vein he proclaimed:

> If the Parliament of Religions has shown anything to the world, it is this: it has proved to the world that holiness, purity, and charity are not the exclusive possessions of any church in the world and that every system has produced men and women of the most exalted character. In the face of this evidence, if anybody dreams of the exclusive revival of his own religion and the destruction of others, I pity him from the bottom of my heart and point out to him that upon the banner of every religion will be written inspite of his resistance; 'Help and not fight', 'Assimilation and not destruction', 'Harmony and Peace and not Dissension'.[8]

Vivekananda spent some of the best years of his life in America and Europe. He explained to the audience the essentially impersonal character of the Hindu religion, its universal message of unbounded catholicism, its presentation of various readings of divinity, monistic, qualified monistic and dualistic. Further he observed different kinds of religious practice grouped under the fundamental types of *jñāna yoga*, *bhakti yoga* and *karma yoga* (meditation in knowledge, worship and work) covering the entire range of human tastes, temperaments and capacities. He explained to them the doctrine of *karma* (philosophy of action) and rebirth and enlightened them with the Hindu idea of salvation through realization of one's identity with the Absolute. Then by his rational exposition he showed how the Hindu view of religion could stand the severest scrutiny of reason and exist in perfect amity with the findings of science. Above all he laid special emphasis on the fact that the broad and liberal message of Vedānta contained the science of all religions, which might enable the world to realize the essential unity of all religions and stand united on the magnificent pedestal of universal religion. Vivekananda's definition of religion as the manifestation of the divinity that is already in man went surely to clear a mass of prejudices against religion. According to him religion is a growth from within till one reaches the last stage of human evolution. When man conquers his inner nature, he becomes perfect and finds God, the ever-free master of nature, the living ideal of perfection and absolute freedom. He said, 'Religion is neither in books nor in intellectual content, nor in reason. Reason, theories, documents, doctrines, books, religious ceremonies are all helps to religion; religion itself consists of realization.'[9] He pointed out further that religion is not only a normal and natural element, but also a universal phenomenon of human life. He said, 'It is my belief that religious thought is in man's very constitution, so much so that it is impossible for him to give up religion until he can give up thought and life.'[10]

In emphasizing the supreme importance of religion he did not suggest any seclusion of man from the context of society. On the contrary, the true religion goes hand in hand with universal brotherhood and cooperation of man with man. Vivekananda emphasized the fact that

> If Hindus could again live up to the ideals of their own original scriptures, the *Vedānta*, they might pull down all barriers that divided man from man, and by this process they might develop a gigantic power of cohesion that could integrate the various Indian sects and communities into one mighty passion.[11]

He pointed out further that the Vedāntic ideas about the divinity of the soul and the oneness of the universe and of consequent 'fearlessness' would not only unite the people of India but also infuse enormous strength into the nation and raise it from the slough of lethargy and despair.

'Arise, Awake' are the two touch-stones to inspire millions of Indians to work and cooperate in a universal brotherhood. Till today, towards the end of the twentieth century, the thinking community of India remember Vivekananda's sayings to inspire people to honest thought and action, sincerity of purpose and compassionate living together.

Mohandas Karamchand Gandhi (1869–1948)

Mohandas Karamchand Gandhi was born in a middle-class Vaiṣṇava family. In the absence of any formal training in philosophy, his early life was spent in deep faith in a transcendent God who created the world of things and beings. It is extremely difficult for a student of philosophy to reduce Gandhi's concept of God to any of the accepted philosophical theories. He did not have any training in academic philosophy; for him the distinction between theism and pantheism did not carry any meaning. His philosophy of religion was essentially theistic, believing in God, the creator and hence distinct from the created. Philosophers have differed widely in interpreting Gandhi's philosophy of religion as dualistic (*dvaita*) or non-dualistic (*advaitavāda*), whether he believed in the dualistic religion or in monistic religion advocated by Śaṅkara's Advaita Vedānta. If his early association with Vaiṣṇava (followers of Viṣṇu)[12] faith drew him towards dualistic religion, his personal reading and experiences seem to have led him to advocate a philosophy in which the finite souls are one with the universal soul or *Brahman*. For instance, some of the thoughts expressed in *Young India*, a monthly news magazine, quoted parts which gave a clear account of Gandhi's conception of Vedānta. He said, 'I believe in *Advaita*, I believe in the essential unity of man and for that matter of all that lives.'[13] 'I believe in absolute oneness of God, and therefore, also of humanity. What though we have many bodies? We have but one soul. The rays of the sun are many through refraction. But they have the same source.'[14] Further, the expressions that Gandhi used to indicate the plenary reality are closely similar to those that are employed in Advaita Vedānta. He said, 'The Vedas describe *Brahman* as not this, not this, "*neti*, *neti*". But if he or it is not this, he or it is.'[15]

It has been observed by some commentators that Gandhi being a Vaiṣṇavite could not have advocated monism (*advaitavāda*); rather that his belief in a personal God led him to accept the creatorship of God and the relative dependence of the world. He did not reject the world as illusory and seek salvation for himself. The suffering of millions of people in India was too deeply ingrained in his nature to think of individual enlightment and happiness. His strong sense of duty towards suffering fellow-beings stood in the way of dismissing this world as unreal. In *Harijan* he wrote:

> Joy or what men call happiness may be, as it really is, a dream in a fleeting and transitory world. But we cannot dismiss the suffering of our fellow-creatures as unreal and thereby provide a moral alibi for ourselves. Even dreams are true while they last and to suffer his suffering is a grim reality.[16]

When intellectual reconciliation between the reality of the phenomenal world and the absolute unity of *Brahman* becomes difficult, it comes as the most natural and inevitable manifestation to a thinker who practises philosophy at every instance of his life. The personal conviction of the unity in multiplicity was too deeply ingrained to allow any intellectual scepticism cross its way. In a similar vein he believed in the unity of all the basic religions of the world. As Vaiṣṇava theism resembles both Christianity and Islam, he realized the essential unity of all religions. He said:

> I have come to the conclusion that (i) all religions are true, (ii) all religions have some error in them, (iii) and all religions are dear to me as my own Hinduism, in as much as all human beings should be as dear to one as one's own close relatives.[17]

Although Gandhi began his life in an atmosphere of complete devotion to Lord Kṛṣṇa and believed that devotion and prayer would bring spiritual salvation to man, in later life he believed more and more in the non-duality of the universe. One of his early realizations was that God is truth, i.e. that to realize God in himself is to realize truth in himself. In his later reflections, he observed further that truth is God. Having explained how he arrived at this conclusion, Gandhi drew attention to the Sanskrit word *sat*, which literally means 'that which exists'. When truth exists, God exists. For these and various other reasons, Gandhi observed that his realization of the essence of truth and its identification with God gave him the greatest satisfaction. He could be said to be a philosopher who did not find any inconsistency between the plurality of the world order and its unity in the ultimate reality of *Brahman*. Advaita philosophy has no quarrel with any system of philosophy advocating theories of dualism, monism or pluralism. Hostility generally arises from partial views of the universe. When the whole truth is known, there is no hostility.

In deep veneration of the universality of truth, Gandhi fought the political battle with the two key tools of *satyāgraha* and *ahiṃsā* (non-violence). *Ahiṃsā* has both a positive and a negative meaning. Positively *ahiṃsā* means the largest love and the greatest charity. Followers of *ahiṃsā* should love their enemies. The active *ahiṃsā* includes truth and fearlessness. The ideal of non-violence makes us loving and compassionate towards others. The principle which includes all these vows and commitments is truth. Gandhi mentions three vows one must make in following the principles of *ahiṃsā*: (a) the vow of *swadeshi* (self-rule), (b) the vow of fearlessness and (c) the vow regarding the social equality of the untouchables. According to the vow of *swadeshi*, one should not support a merchant from any other part of the world when there is a merchant in one's neighbourhood. The vow of fearlessness declares that a God-fearing man is not afraid of any man or any earthly consequences. Gandhi believed that the practice of untouchability is not ancient and in all probability was evoked at a time when life was at the lowest ebb of awareness. He pointed out that castism arises when man ceases to be critical of his thought and action. The Hindu view of society is ingrained in three fundamental principles aiming at realizing the highest truth of life. Man's relation to society can be best brought out by reference to the synthesis and gradation of (1) the fourfold objects of life (*puruṣārthas*): *kāma*, desire and enjoyment; *artha*, interest in worldly possessions; *dharma*, ethical living; and *mokṣa*, or spiritual emancipation; (2) the fourfold order of society (*varṇaśrama*) (division of society according to profession): the man of learning, *brāhmin*; of power, *kṣatriya*; of skilled productivity, *vaiśya*; and of service, *sūdra*; (3) and the fourfold succession of the stages of life (*āśrama*): student, *brahmachāri*; householder, *gṛhasta*; forest recluse, *vānaprastha*; and the free supersocial man, *sannyāsin*. By means of the threefold disciplines in learning, service and ideals, an individual ascends gradually to the highest order of existence, a blissful consciousness of the ultimate reality. That the approach to this goal may not be too sudden and arbitrary, a gradual process of ascendance through self-realization is suggested at all stages of an individual's life in society. The *varṇaśrama dharma*, which was purely a means to bring about harmony in different classes of social order according to the nature of work performed, changed to the rigid caste system of the untouchables. Gandhi fought a relentless battle to fight this evil by bringing to consciousness the indignity thrust upon man for his labour and service to society. He wrote:

> Nothing in the world is wholly good or wholly evil and every action involves evil. The remedy for evil is self purification. When there exists one self in all, self-purification will contribute to the welfare of the whole world. Self purification is *tapas* or austerity.[18]

Satyāgraha, on the other hand, means attachment to truth. It implies unflinching adherence to a realization that can never be shaken by any external forces of the world. Gandhi believed that there are two forces at work in our nature: *satyāgraha*, the divine, and *durāgraha*, the devil. Both the methods are applied in attaining the various goals of life. It is worth while to remember that no one force works in exclusion of the other. It is only in the predominance of the one over the other that the driving force of action depends. Gandhi said, 'In *satyāgraha* there is always unflinching adherence to truth.' *Satyāgraha* presupposes the ultimate triumph of truth. It enkindles the freedom of the soul, whereas *durāgraha* has the opposite quality of thinking and doing evil. The literal meaning of *satyāgraha* is insistence on truth, and force derivable from such insistence in order to cure evil. It therefore means adherence to truth, and conduct based on truth is impossible without love; hence *satyāgraha* is the truth-force or the love-force. It is the force which when universally adopted would revolutionize social ideals and remove despotism and militarism. The principle of unity of truth with God seems to have been one driving force in Gandhi to inspire him to fight political battles and bring about social reform and radical changes in the education system. Education at the earliest stage of a child's life was what concerned him most. He believed that education should be given in the mother tongue and in the natural environment of village homes. The fundamental principle of such education is to build children's characters rather than equipping them with some foreign language, behaviour and ways of life. Gandhi's philosophy of education is inspired by the ideal of uniting body and mind and building up the foundation of being truly human.

Sri Aurobindo (1870–1950)

Aurobindo Ghose was the original name of Sri Aurobindo, who sought spiritual solution through realization of *Brahman* of Advaita Vedānta. After his education in the West, he came back to India and participated actively in the political activities of the country. However, he soon realized that his path was different. He could not seek the political independence of the country without realizing the spiritual emancipation of the nation and mankind. Aurobindo said that the Vedāntic message 'one without a second' must be interpreted in the light of the other truth, 'All this is *Brahman*.' His philosophy is generally known as integral non-dualism (*pūrṇa advaita*) or integral idealism. It is monism, but different in shades of meaning from Spinoza's neutral monism or Hegel's absolute idealism. In the system of both these western thinkers ideal reality is arrived at conceptually through logical reasoning. With Aurobindo non-dualistic monism is an intellectual insight which can be known only through intense realization. The personal experience of man is a necessity in such comprehension.

Aurobindo's conception of reality is spiritualistic, that which includes the notion of matter as an integral part of evolution of the entire system. He objected to the asceticism of ancient Indian thought which denied the reality of matter in realizing the reality of spirit. According to him, if reality is spiritual then even matter is spiritual. An outright rejection of matter and the material world is therefore evidently fallacious. The fact is that matter and spirit are the two inseparable aspects of the same reality. If matter is to ascend to the spirit, the spirit is to descend to matter. Where there is evolution, there is corresponding involution. The two processes work integrally together so that the mind or spirit aspiring towards higher realizations does so while living in the world of appalling miseries of mankind. Aurobindo's concept of a dual world order evolving towards a non-dual reality of super-mind greatly resembles the neutral monism of Spinoza. In the seventeenth century, Spinoza believed reality to be one substance or God which manifests itself in infinite attributes and modes. Of the infinite attributes, man is acquainted only with the attributes of thought and extension.

Spinoza spoke almost the same language as Sri Aurobindo when he observed that thought and extension are the two aspects of the same reality; viewed mechanically with the help of science it is material, while viewed mentally with the help of illumined intellect or insight it is ideal. The two philosophical theories, though similar, are not identical. One comprehends reality as a static exposition of reason; the other comprehends it as a constant resurgence of spirit in quest of the ultimate reality of *Brahman* or *gnosis*.

Reality, according to Aurobindo, has two aspects – nonbeing and being, the static and the dynamic. The former is the basis and support of the latter. There is one truth, one reality; the being and the many are his becomings. The truth behind all dualities, all contradictions, all variations perceived in the light of spiritual consciousness is *Brahman*, the omnipresent reality. Reality is *saguṇa* or with attributes, inasmuch as it is capable of manifesting qualities, and *nirguṅa* inasmuch as it is not marked or limited by any sum of qualities. The many or infinite multiplicity is one of the potentialities of the one which manifests itself in many but is more than the sum of its manifestations. Aurobindo held that 'the Divine is formless and nameless, but by that very reason capable of manifesting all possible names and shapes of being.'[19]

Aurobindo's concept of *Brahman*, though derived essentially from Śaṅkara's Advaita Vedānta, differs in its emphasis on the relation between matter and spirit. It is most important that one understands clearly Aurobindo's concept of *Brahman* as the ultimate reality of the universe. The ultimate reality evolves itself through different stages of evolution, from matter to life, to mind, to cosmic consciousness, and to transcendental consciousness of the unknowable. He felt that in cosmic consciousness there is a meeting place of matter and spirit where matter becomes real to the spirit and the spirit becomes real to matter. In this evolutionary state there is an attempt to rise above the separation of the material and the spiritual. But this cosmic consciousness tends towards a transcendental consciousness, which initially is nothing but consciousness of the unknowable. The unknowable, in spite of being incomprehensible to the limited consciousness of man, draws incessantly towards itself as something supreme, wonderful and ineffable. The unknowable is called the *Brahman* by Sri Aurobindo. The unknowable manifests itself partly in the world of multiplicity and partly remaining unmanifest in itself.

Aurobindo believed that creation is a movement between two involutions. The many involved in spirit evolve downwards to the other pole of matter. In matter too all is involved and evolves out of it upwards to the other pole of spirit. The formless has descended, taken form or manifested itself through two essential appearances, the universe and the individual. It is *līla* or a divine play of self-concealment and self-revelation. The infinite, the super-consciousness has gradually descended step by step, covering itself by veil upon veil, till it disappears completely under the mask of 'inconsciant matter'. It then traverses back step by step by removing veil after veil and thus waking up from its slumber of inconscience and proceeds towards self-revelation. Thus each step in the descent is necessarily a step in the ascent. The divine creation is as real as *Brahman* and is not an illusion. *Brahman* expresses himself in many forms of consciousness; instead of being given up, the previous form is taken up in the next step and is transformed. Thus life emerged from matter and mind and intelligence in human beings from life. In the emergence of life and mind, nature transformed matter into bodies and mind; the preceding form serves as the basis of the next dominant principle. This process of taking up and transforming the physical-vital-mental being proceeds integrally in order to serve the laws for the first dominant principle of super-mind. This force is eternal in existence and is its very nature. It may be in manifestation or non-manifestation.

The presence of the super-mind in the evolution of every form of being in the world does not cease to operate with the illumined consciousness of individual beings.

The evolution continues incessantly throughout the universe, and man must take yet another step to merge into cosmic consciousness or consciousness of the totality of being. There are four ascending steps of consciousness, through higher mind, illumined mind, intuitive mind and over mind. Beyond over mind consciousness undergoes certain changes to reach the summit, the supermind or divine *gnosis*. Man's ascent towards higher stages of consciousness is at once self-realization through self-surrender in the realm of gnosis or the world of light of the ancients. As Pearson pointed out, the emergent self in its higher stage of consciousness passes beyond its individual personality and merges in the higher status of reality of which it is an integral part. He said, 'But the spiritual element is not only emergent, a thing still to come; it is in its higher status a Reality above mind, eternally self-existent in the world of light or the Truth Plane.'[20]

A reference to the spiritual order of the universe along with the development of the empirical sciences accounts for the fact that scientific truths are not contradictory, but rather complementary to the spiritual evolution of the world order. The sciences seem to be aiming at a synthesis of the physical, biological and mental processes. There are no longer rigid divisions between or exclusive preoccupations of particular sciences which remain oblivious of the investigations of other branches of human knowledge. According to Pearson,

> Matter, as it is now being explained by physical sciences is not the whole but merely the surface of our existence, and so the material entity alone cannot give the real purpose and meaning of all the hidden complex movement that are being revealed in and beyond it. One is forced more and more to call in the other entities, either of life or mind, to explain many of the inconsistencies now being exposed therein.[21]

If all sciences must coordinate to provide a synthetic unity of the world, human consciousness strives to attain the significance of that unity in the total purpose of the universe, known as super-mind, *Brahman* or divine *gnosis*.

Aurobindo's account of the metaphysical reality of the universe cannot be understood fully without reflecting on its application to the political cause of the nation. He referred constantly to *saccidānanda* or the pure existence, consciousness and bliss of individual minds in realizing super-mind as the essence of their innermost nature. Whether he talked of the spiritualization of individual consciousness or of the entire human race, his emphasis remained the same. The world is spiritual and it must be attained through constant effort by individuals. It is worth while to remember that when Aurobindo talked about the process of integral evolution his aim was to emphasize the spirituality of the whole universe and not merely individual souls in the universe. It is only in the light of the spiritual reality of the universe that the enlightened consciousness of individuals carries any meaning. Moreover Aurobindo talked about the political independence of the nation in the higher independence of individual consciousness. At one stage he felt that realizing the super-mind in himself he would emancipate the entire nation of its slavery and dependence. A word or two on his political philosophy is a necessary prelude to understanding his spiritual philosophy.

The most important contribution of Sri Aurobindo as a political philosopher was advocating a responsible constitutional and popular government in India entirely free from alien control. He formulated his ideal for the country in the pages of *Bandé Mātaram* in 1907.[22] His assertion of complete *swarāj* (self-rule) was prophetic at a time when the Indian National Congress was thinking hard on the nature of self-determination of the country. Aurobindo gave a call for the Indianization of the political movement. He wanted to graft the freedom movement in the hearts and heritage of the people. In his celebrated 'Open letter to my Countrymen' written in 1909 he said:

> Our ideal of patriotism proceeds on the basis of love and brotherhood and it looks beyond the unity of the mankind. But it is a unity of brothers, equals and free men that we seek, not the unity of master and serf or the devourer and the devoured.[23]

It must be mentioned that Sri Aurobindo was one of the first Indian leaders to recognize the absolute necessity of generating mass enthusiasm and participation in the case of the nation. This factor of mass participation did not receive sufficient recognition amongst the leaders of the country. Aurobindo had the courage to declare *pūrṇa swarāj* (total independence) openly, not as a favour from the foreign rulers, but as an indispensible birth-right of Indians. His concept of the divinity of motherland led directly to his demand for political emancipation – a claim which he demanded with immense patriotic fervour. He not only advocated the cause of ideal independence of the nation, but also criticized most vehemently the cautious and constricted ideas of the moderates. He stressed the fact that India's freedom could be attained only through the 'fire and blood' of millions. Karan Singh, while emphasizing Aurobindo's concept of political struggle, pointed out that:

> His stress on the goal of complete independence, his theory of the divinity of the motherland and the most religious character of the liberation movement, and his emphasis upon the necessity of suffering and sacrifice to achieve the goal, all combined to impart charismatic, revolutionary spirit to the national movement against British domination.[24]

While Sri Aurobindo thought of the immediate end of securing the freedom of the nation, he aimed ultimately at the unity of mankind throughout the world. His belief in the unique role of independent India towards emancipation of mankind of the world led to his incessant search for the ultimate reality of super-mind or *Brahman*.

Among the theoretical considerations behind Aurobindo's political goal of complete independence was the underlying conviction that India must be free not only for herself but for the good of the entire human race. He felt that India had a spiritual message which was urgently needed in the world of the twentieth century. In fact his firm conviction was that India was destined to lead mankind up to the next step of spiritual evolution. Karan Singh referred to Aurobindo's message of spiritual consciousness as one of the reasons why he was so adamant that the political goal should be nothing less than complete independence, since only then could India fulfil her destiny of *swadharma* or the broader interest of the international community. This, it may be added, was one of the major motives of Indian Renaissance.[25]

Sarvepalli Radhakrishnan (1888–1975)

Sarvepalli Radhakrishnan was born in 1888 in a small town, Tirutani, in south India. From early childhood he was deeply influenced by Hindu religious beliefs and thoughts. His formal education by Christian missionaries together with their religious convictions developed in Radhakrishnan a mixed feeling of cultures of both sides. His wide knowledge of the works of Plato, Plotinus and Kant and his understanding of Christianity created a deep impression of combining eastern thoughts with western culture. Radhakrishnan's concept of metaphysical reality was based on the ancient thought of Advaita Vedānta and Hegel's notion of absolute idealism. He believed that the main function of philosophical enquiry lies in seeking an explanation of the nature of the universe as a whole. The metaphysical enquiry gives a teleological account of the world order in which the scientific explanation finds its relative position and relevance. The explanation is mechanistic, teleological and spiritual at the same time. It is mechanistic when philosophy aims at discovering the facts of life and reality, it is teleological when philosophy reads meanings and values in empirical experience, and it is spiritual when the entire span of experience points to a reality beyond phenomena and the ever-changing world order. In the mechanistic account the world is a conglomeration of physical units with no meaning or value attached to its existence. The immense variety of non-living and living matter experienced in life could be accounted for at best as 'chance variation' or accidental happenings of the world phenomenon. But meanings and values are evidenced in every object of nature. It needs only a discerning eye to see the world's teleological, valuational and purposeful direction to attain the Ultimate Reality – a non-dual unity in itself. Radhakrishnan's unique approach of harmonizing mechanism with teleology gives great significance to the world's mechanistic interpretation with the spiritual unity of the world order.

As Radhakrishnan observed, philosophy

> looks upon the world as a sort of an automatic machine which goes on working in a blind, haphazard way. It reduces the temporal world to unconscious forces, makes life, consciousness and value mere by-products. It believes that the world machine needs only to be taken to pieces to be comprehended.[26]

There was no accounting for values and religious experiences of life. These experiences would be considered as emotional reactions by individuals having no objective reality in the world order. As subjective experience all evaluations and religious concepts would have as many meanings and as much significance as individuals experiencing them. Such an account is naturalistic and positivistic, the world being limited strictly to explanation as can be known through natural sciences. On the other hand, philosophers comprehending reality from a wider perspective realize that the concept of *Brahman* or the Absolute is not a superimposition on the nature of things, but ingrained in the very constitution of reality as a whole. The world is teleological in the process of evolving itself, and man is spiritual by his inner consciousness of fullness or completeness. The two processes of evolution in the world order and in human beings is one single process of ideal reality manifesting itself at different stages of growth and development. Radhakrishnan feels that the qualities of existence, order, development and purposefulness that are noticed in the world order demand an ontological foundation which can be provided only by the Absolute. He wrote:

> Why is there existence? Why is there anything at all? If everything disappeared there would be utter nothingness. If that nothingness did not provide or was not itself the possibility of being, there could not have been anything at all. The existence of the world is imperfect and impermanent and nothing that is imperfect can subsist by itself or for itself, for in so far as it is imperfect, it is not. The *Upaniṣads* lead us from the imperfect existence in the world to the supreme and Absolute being . . . the existence of the world means the primacy of Being.[27]

In explaining the nature of the Absolute or *Brahman* and the gradual manifestation in the world order, Radhakrishnan referred to the significant contribution of religious faith in realizing reality. The function of religion is to further the evolution of man into his divine nature, develop increased awareness and understanding and bring about a deeper and more enduring adjustment to life. Religion commands man to change his own nature in order to let the divine essence manifest itself. For religious illumination, the discipline of the three facets of consciousness, that is, the cognitive, the conative and the affective, is absolutely necessary. Radhakrishnan pointed out that the purpose of life is not enjoyment of the world of things and events, but the education of the soul. The religious consciousness lies in turning inwards, deepening one's inwardness and developing a more meaningful attitude to life. He states that *śravana*, *manana* and *nidhidhyāsana* (hearing, reflecting and meditating respectively) are the three stages of religious consciousness and that one has to rise from one stage to another. In this connection he gives a comparative account of religion in the West and in the East. The religions in the East aim at cultivation of the interior life and at the attainment of spiritual freedom, which is the result of individual effort in solitude. In the West religion suffers from the misleading notion of 'national mysticism' – a feeling that aims at social security and freedom from domination by other religions. When religious consciousness tries to provide peace and security to man of the nation, it also makes man conscious of the exclusive superiority of his own religion compared to those of others. This leads Radhakrishnan to observe that 'Western religion is dominated by "this worldiness".' No religion, according to him, is perfect, as every religion is a growth or development. The different religions are like comrades in a joint enterprise for facing the common problem of peaceful co-existence, international welfare and justice, social equality and political independence'.[28] And a religion which does not seek the welfare of fellow-beings in search of self-realization is no religion at all.

Using metaphysics and religious experience as a basis Radhakrishnan tried to explain the main trends of the world community in the present century. His constant reference to western culture and civilization gave a global relevance to the problem of human salvation in spiritual realization. He talked about similar interests, humanistic values and the degeneration of the western world under the influence of science and technology. Modern civilization with its scientific temper and secular views of life was seen as uprooting the world over the customs of long centuries and creating a ferment of restlessness. The new world was perceived as a confused mass of needs and impulses, ambitions and materially orientated activities, lacking control and the guidance of the spirit. The void created by abandoned superstitions and uprooted beliefs required, according to Radhakrishnan, a spiritual filling. Physical unity and economic independence are not by themselves sufficient to create a universal human community, a sense of personal relationship among men. What is needed in sustaining the world community that is growing among nations of the world is spiritual awakening and keenness to uphold it. He saw the supreme task of this generation as giving a soul to the growing world consciousness; as developing ideals and institutions necessary for the creative expression of the world soul; as transmitting their loyalties and strivings to future generations and training them into world citizens. In emphasizing the need for cultivating a world soul, Radhakrishnan believed that the mind of the world needs to be pulled together and the present aimless state of dementia replaced by a collective rational purpose. He said, 'we are in search of a spiritual religion, that is universally valid, vital, clear-cut, one that has an understanding of the fresh sense of truth and the awakened social passion, which are the characteristics of the religious situation today'.[29]

In the western world the impact of scientific development was such that reason got dissociated from faith, and religious experience from the scientifically orientated experiences of life. From the eighteenth century onwards with Hume, Kant and Hegel, reason as a branch of theoretical science was supposed to make enquiries about the nature of reality independently of any other dimension of consciousness. While Hume and Kant were sceptical about the extent of theoretical reason, Hegel was confident that the system of metaphysical reality could be constructed solely on the foundation of absolute thought. In the late nineteenth century Husserl made a unique attempt to build up a presuppositionless philosophy based upon a pure description of noetic consciousness. The noetic consciousness, according to Husserl, is disclosed to pure reason when it has been disentangled from all associated beliefs of natural sciences and sense-experiences of everyday life. It is consciousness pure and simple, known to absolute reason itself. Like Kant, Husserl wanted to provide a radical beginning for philosophy. He desired to 'furnish philosophy with a scientific beginning'.[30] When reason seemed to have reached the apex of consciousness, it was reason alone that would comprehend reality as a whole. That the human consciousness may have an equally vital spiritual dimension was not considered in western philosophy. On the contrary, the truth is that intellectual height is not the goal but the medium which while transcending itself can reach the higher region of spiritual consciousness.

It seems that at this juncture of philosophical thinking Indian philosophy stands apart from western philosophy both in attitude and direction. Man is not either reason or faith but both reason and faith; his theoretical comprehension with the help of natural sciences goes hand in hand with the practical dealings of everyday life. He is a totality of all natural, biological and psychological sciences along with evaluational and religious experience. He moves ahead with everything in hand, not discarding or neglecting any part of living experience, but modifying, transforming it all into one single experience of merging in the ultimate reality of *Brahman*. The striving of the soul for the infinite is said to be *Brahman*. *Brahman* stands for the breath, 'the breath of the power of God'. It is man's sense of the divine, and divine reality itself – these two meanings must coalesce. As Radhakrishnan observed:

> The transcendental self stoops down, as it were, and touches the eyes of the empirical self, overwhelmed by the delusions of the world's work. When the individual withdraws his soul from all outward events, gathers himself inwardly and strives with concentration, there breaks upon him an experience, secret, strange and wondrous, which quietens within him, lays hold on him and becomes his very being.[31]

To say that God exists means that spiritual experience is attainable. The possibility of experience constitutes the most conclusive proof of the reality of God. In all this the greatest contribution of the contemporary philosopher lies in emphasizing the need to realize spirituality amidst the social well-being of mankind. The togetherness of the different nations of the world calls for building up a feeling of universal brotherhood and unity of mankind.

With time, Radhakrishnan's call for developing human interests, irrespective of national differences, became incessant and ever-demanding. As D. P. Chattopadhyaya said in the birth centenary lecture, 'Dr Radhakrishnan was looking for a deeper spiritual truth and his form of humanism was not at all opposed to scientific temper.'[32] His sense of humanism was one in which human individuality was consistent with social unity and harmony. He rejected the kind of humanism which he thought was a mere reaction against fascism or Communism. The kind of humanism in which individuals shed their egoism and transcend their narrow interests to find their larger self in society was what appealed to him most. It was humanism rooted in spiritual consciousness, having the widest meaning of the universal brotherhood and unity of mankind.

As stated in the Introduction to this chapter, much of contemporary Indian philosophy is founded on the teachings of the Vedas, *Upaniṣads* and Advaita Vedānta. However, the modern Indian thinkers have recast the old, spiritual unity of individual consciousness with the universal consciousness of *Brahman* in the socio-political context of man. Man is to seek self-realization not as a recluse or as a lonely sojourner, but necessarily as an active participant in the world order. He is to live with others and share their joys and sufferings to attain the ultimate reality of his life. The goal is spiritual; the means is the well-being of mankind as a whole.

Ātmano mokṣārtam jagat hitāya.

(Seek self-emancipation; do good to the world.)

NOTES

1 *Om* – invocation, *Iśa Upaniṣad.* The concept means fullness as 'That is full, this is full. This fullness is projected from that fullness. When this fullness merges into that fullness all that remains is fullness. Peace is the abiding truth of that fullness.'

2 Haridas Bhattacharya (ed.), *The Cultural Heritage of India*, vol. III (Calcutta: The Ramakrishna Mission Institute of Culture), p. 230.

3 *Sacchidānanda* – an unparalleled combination of pure existence, consciousness and bliss indicating the total emancipation of man.

4 The synthesis of three ways of life suggested in the *Bhagavadgītā* is indicative of three elements of the human mind, namely cognition, conation and affection. Synthesis is 'Yoga' as union of the different elements of mind striving towards realization of the ultimate truth in life.

5 *Nirvikalpa samādhi* – a state of intense meditation towards realization of a nameless, formless and impersonal reality of *Brahman.*

6 Ramakrishna was a devout follower of the Hindu religion and was deeply immersed in intense spiritual experiences of Kāli, goddess of power or Śakti.

7 Haridas Bhattacharya (ed.), *The Cultural Heritage of India*, vol. IV (Calcutta: The Ramakrishna Mission Institute of Culture), p. 708.

8 ibid., p. 709.

9 ibid., p. 712.

10 ibid.

11 ibid., p. 717.

12 *Vaiṣṇavism* – followers of Lord Viṣṇu, who is represented as one of the great gods in some sections of the *Ṛg-Veda.*

13 M. K. Gandhi, *Young India*, 4 December 1924.

14 ibid., 25 September 1924.

15 ibid., 31 January 1926.

16 M. K. Gandhi, *Harijan* (a local journal on untouchables), 21 July 1946.

17 N. K. Bose, *Selections from Gandhi*, 2nd revised edn (Ahmedabad Navjiuan Publishing House, 1957), pp. 258–9.

18 *The Collected Works of Mahatma Gandhi*, 2nd revised edn, vol. XLV (Government of India, Publications Division, Ministry of Information and Broadcasting, 1969), p. 113.

19 Sri Aurobindo, *Sri Aurobindo Birth Centenary Library*, vol. 18 (Pondicherry: Sri Aurobindo Ashram, 1972), p. 337.

20 Nathaniel Pearson, *Sri Aurobindo and the Soul Quest of Man* (London: George Allen & Unwin, 1952), p. 22.
21 ibid., p. 19.
22 *Bandé Mātaram* – a phrase for paying homage to mother India.
23 Aurobindo, *Speeches*, Collection of essays and speeches published in Bande Mataram, a daily newspaper edited by Sri Aurobindo, 1905–1908 p. 142.
24 ibid., pp. 54–5.
25 ibid., p. 57.
26 Radhakrishnan, *An Idealist View of Life* (London: George Allen & Unwin, 1932), p. 314.
27 Radhakrishnan, *The Recovery of Faith*, (London: George Allen & Unwin, 1956), p. 82.
28 T. M. P. Mahadevan and G. V. Saroja, *Contemporary Indian Philosophy* (New Delhi: Sterling, 1981), p. 248.
29 Paul Arthur Schilpp (ed.), *The Philosophy of Sarvepalli Radhakrishnan* (New York: Tudor, 1952).
30 E. Husserl, *Ideas*, trans. W. R. Boyce Gibson (London: George Allen & Unwin, 1939), pp. 27, 30.
31 S. Radhakrishnan, *Eastern Religions and Western Thought* (London: Oxford University Press, 1939), p. 22.
32 D. P. Chattopadhyaya, *The Statesman*, 17 December 1988.

REFERENCES

The Cultural Heritage of India (1956) Vols III and IV, Calcutta: The Ramakrishna Mission Institute of Culture.

Devaraja, N. K. (1975) *Indian Philosophy Today*, Meerut, India: The Macmillan Company of India.

Fischer, Louis (1982) *The Life of Mahatma Gandhi*, St Albans: Granada.

Gandhi, Kishore (1973) *Contemporary Relevance of Sri Aurobindo*, Delhi: Vivek Publishing.

Gandhi, M. K. (1927) *The Story of My Experiments with Truth*, vol. I., Ahmedabad: Navjiuan

—— (1969) *The Collected Works of Mahatma Gandhi*, 2nd revised edn, Government of India, Publications Division, Ministry of Information and Broadcasting.

Lal, B. K. (1973) *Contemporary Indian Philosophy*, Delhi: Motilal Banarasidass.

Mahadevan, T. M. P. and Saroja, G. S. (1982) *Contemporary Indian Philosophy*, Sterling.

Marlow, A. N. (1952) *Radhakrishnan: An Anthology*, London: George Allen & Unwin.

Muirhead J. H. (ed.) (1936) *Contemporary Indian Philosophy*, 1st edn, London: George Allen & Unwin.

Nikhilananda, Swami (1949) *Upanishads*, vol. I, London: Phoenix House.

Pearson, Nathaniel (1952) *Sri Aurobindo and the Soul Quest of Man*, London: George Allen & Unwin.

Radhakrishnan, S. (1927) *The Hindu View of Life*, London: George Allen & Unwin.

—— (1929) *Eastern Religions and Western Thought*, 2nd edn, London: Oxford University Press.

—— (1977) *Indian Philosophy*, vol. I, 10th impression, London, George Allen and Unwin.

The Religions of the World (1987) vol. II, Calcutta: The Ramakrishna Mission Institute of Culture.

Saksena, Kishore (1970) *Essays in Indian Philosophy*, Honolulu: University of Hawaii Press.

Schilpp, Paul Arthur (ed.) (1952) *The Philosophy of Sarvepalli Radhakrishnan*, New York: Tudor.

Sharma, Chandradhar (1976) *A Critical Survey of Indian Philosophy*, Delhi: Motilal Banarsidass.

Part III

BUDDHIST PHILOSOPHY

INTRODUCTION

Buddhism, as a religious tradition and an associated philosophy, has spread far from its original Indian soil into cultures as diverse as those of Sri Lanka, Japan and the United States. It is not surprising, therefore, that little can be said in general terms of what Buddhist thought amounts to. Within the philosophical tradition, indeed, it is possible to find a whole range of positions taken on a subject such as the nature of perception, or on the existence and nature of a persisting substratum behind the fleeting consciousness which is our ordinary life.

Buddhism can, however, be divided very roughly into two closely associated, but nevertheless competing, schools. These are the Theravāda and Mahāyāna schools, the 'way of the elders' and the 'Greater Vehicle'. Both schools, in all their divergent manifestations, claim the authority of the Buddha for their propositions; either in what is reported about him in the dialogues and associated interpretative texts known collectively as the Tripiṭaka, or more obviously much more contentiously in what he must have meant or must have believed but did not say to avoid confusing his hearers. There is, however, a strong strand of rationalism in Buddhism, in the sense that the ideas being propounded in its philosophical treatises are supposed to commend themselves – quite independently of the authority of the Buddha – to reason, to be consistent with what is actually observable of the world outside and (through introspection, aided by meditative skills) of the nature of human consciousness.

The Buddha (literally 'the Enlightened One') was born Siddhārtha Gautama in northern India in 563 BC. His ideas can best be appreciated against those of the traditional Hinduism of that time which had developed its own set of answers to the questions of human nature and spiritual salvation. Though the Buddha retained a commitment to the theory of *saṃsāra*, the cycle of birth–death–rebirth, he rejected almost all the central beliefs of Hinduism. Indeed, out must go any reliance on revelation and traditional authority, and in its place must be put outer and inner observation.

Whereas Hinduism saw reality as a *permanent being, consciousness and bliss*, for the Buddha the 'three marks of reality' are *impermanence, no consciousness and suffering.*

The second 'mark', the absence in what we can observe of ourselves of any permanent seat of our fleeting thoughts, feelings, volitions and so on, is fundamental in the Buddha's account of personhood. We are not permanent souls which travel through a succession of lives to an ultimate *mokṣa*, but no more than a flow of ever-changing thoughts, feelings, physical elements and so forth.

This analysis of the nature of human existence is thought to have major significance at the psychological level, and in consequence at the moral and social levels too. Primarily, once we have the insight that we are not permanent souls, we shall change our perception of ourselves quite generally – we shall lose our grasping attitudes and act unselfishly for the good of all. The end result will be the cessation of suffering which is the third 'mark' of reality, and the achievement of *nirvāṇa*.

Mahāyāna Buddhism represents a fundamental break with the traditional 'no-soul' position, under the influence of other religious and philosophical systems in India, China and elsewhere. A deeper persisting being is proposed, behind the individual person's consciousness, to be identified with the Buddha himself or the Truth of his teachings. Mahāyāna Buddhism also represents a more socially orientated system of ideas, with the compassion of saints (*boddhisattvas*) working towards the salvation of all.

This brief sketch does little justice to the sophistication of Buddhist thought, for both Theravāda and Mahāyāna Buddhism developed a rich appreciation of the functioning of language, of reason, and of human psychology. Many of these ideas found their way into orthodox Hindu philosophical systems, and into later Daoism and Confucianism in China, Korea and Japan.

B.C. and I.M.

16

THE BUDDHA

Ninian Smart

The Buddha is the typical title given to Siddhārtha Gautama, founder or re-founder of the Buddhist tradition. It is among a number of epithets assigned to Gautama and to some other spiritual leaders of the period. The term means 'awakened one' or 'enlightened one' and is related to the word *bodhi*, meaning 'awakening' or 'enlightenment'. The latter expression has become the favourite translation of the word in modern English.

Siddhārtha was his given name and Gautama his family or clan name. These spellings are the Sanskrit ones. In Pali the two names are Siddhattha and Gotama. Since the Theravāda canon is composed in Pali and in some ways reflects an earlier tradition than many of the Sanskrit texts of the Mahāyāna, it is quite common in English writings to see the Buddha's names rendered in their Pali version. However, the materials which we have on the life of the Buddha are heavily encrusted with legendary and mythic material, and as we shall see, it is hard to be sure of much in the actual life of the Buddha. The quest for the historical Buddha is even more arduous than the quest of the historical Jesus. The term 'Buddha' is the same in both Pali and Sanskrit, fortunately.

Because he came from a small people known as the Śākyas (Sanskrit; Pali: Sākya), he was also known as Śākyamuni, or sage of the Śākyas. Among other important epithets used of him are *jina* ('conqueror', 'victor'), *tathāgata* ('thus-gone'), *bhagavan* ('lord') and *sugata* ('well-gone'). *Jina* was also a favourite title of the contemporary movement known as Jainas ('followers of the *jina*'). In parallel the Buddhist followers came to be called *bauddhas*.

The term 'the Buddha' is usually taken to refer to the historical figure; but in the Buddhist tradition there has virtually always been a belief in earlier buddhas. In the Pali canon they are often simply referred to collectively. But in the *Mahāvadāna Sutta* they are listed as six. Later this number was expanded to twenty-four (in the Sri Lankan chronicle, the *Buddhavaṃsa*), no doubt under Jaina influence, since the Jains listed twenty-four *Tīrthaṇkaras* or 'makers of the ford' (across the stream of rebirth). There was also in the Pali tradition the notion of *paccekabuddhas*, who were human beings who could gain enlightenment but were incapable of teaching it. Perhaps this was a way to give recognition to other eminent and holy persons belonging to the various groups contemporary with the Buddha. In Greater Vehicle or Mahāyāna Buddhism the notion of buddhahood was greatly expanded, together with that of the buddha-to-be or *bodhisattva* (being of enlightenment, namely a person destined for buddhahood). There was in due course a doctrine of different levels of buddhahood, formalized in the doctrine of three bodies or aspects of the Buddha, dealt with below.

There is great debate about the dates of the Buddha. Based on the Sri Lankan tradition, there is the commonly accepted pair of dates for the birth and death of the Buddha, namely 563 and 483 BC. Other variants calculated by scholars are 484 and 485 as the death date. But such theories depend on Sri Lankan traditional calculations from the date of the accession of Aśoka, which is also in dispute. Another strategy is to take the northern tradition, which has a different view of the time between the death of the Buddha and the accession of Aśoka, namely 116 years instead of 218 according to Sri Lankan sources. This would have the Buddha die in 386 or 383. Recently Richard Gombrich has recalculated the Sri Lankan record, which would suggest that the Buddha would have died some sixty years later than the previous Sri Lankan calculations. So it may be that the Buddha died somewhere between about 400 and 385 BC. Most scholars agree with the tradition that the Buddha lived eighty years.

Let us now rehearse the legendary account of the life of the Buddha, and then estimate what of this is historically reliable. The legendary life is of course important, for it is that narrative that enters phenomenologically into the consciousness of most Buddhists up to modern times. He was born the son of Śuddhodana, the King of the Śākyans (who were ruled by a council of nobles and had a revolving kingship) and Mahāmāyā. Before his birth his mother dreamed that a beautiful white elephant passed through her side into her womb. This led to the prediction that when he grew up he would either be a universal monarch (*cakravartin*) or a spiritual *cakravartin*. His mother bore him at Lumbini in Nepal, as it is now, where in the third century BC the Emperor Aśoka would implant an inscribed pillar, rediscovered in 1896, and a *stūpa* or memorial shrine. A holy man called Asita, hearing of his birth, came down from the mountains and again predicted the dual choice in his destiny. A week after his birth his mother died, and he was raised by her sister. Because of the predictions he was treated to great luxury, fitting for a prince. His classification in accord with his tribal origins was as a *kṣatriya* or warrior: in his later teachings, however, he was to set himself against the *varṇa* system of ancient Aryan India, which assigned people to four classes, headed by the Brahmins. Possibly the system was not functioning among the Śākyans. When he was 12, he was found during a festival sitting alone under a tree, having attained the first stage of meditation (*dhyāna*, *jhāna*). At 16 he was married to Yaśodharā. It was not, however, till he was 29 that he made some harrowing discoveries which would impel him to leave home. These 'four signs' were the sight of an old man, bent and feeble; a sick man, stewing in his own excreta; a corpse; and a shaven-headed man wearing a robe who had left home, to wander. He shortly heard of the birth of his first and only son, Rahula. He decided to leave home, and slipped away in the middle of the night, making his great renunciation. His desire was to find the good, and during the early part of his search he sat at the feet of two notable teachers who taught him different stages of meditation (the sphere of nothing, and that of neither-perception-nor-non-perception), incorporated later into the ascending scale of stages of *dhyāna* in the Buddha's teaching. But both left him dissatisfied, and he tried to attain peace through the practice of severe self-mortification, in the company of five fellow-seekers. But in due course he came to reject the path of extreme austerity, and his companions left him, disillusioned with him. He accepted food from a young woman named Sujātā, and strengthened by this prepared to attain enlightenment, seated at the base of an *aśvattha* or *bodhi* tree (as it came to be called). During the night of the full moon during the month of Vaiśākha (April/May), at the age of 35, he attained the supreme vision and understanding – recalling his previous births, seeing the rebirth of others, and finally realizing that all his defilements had been removed. He had attained *bodhi*, and this despite the desperate attempts by his satanic adversary, Māra, who hoped to tempt him back to the world. But the Buddha 'saw through' Māra, who was both deceptive and ultimately powerless.

Gautama set forth to teach his former comrades, and delivered the first sermon in the deer park at a place called Sārnāth, close to Vāraṇāsi (Banaras). The rest of his life was devoted to teaching and to the founding and nurture of his order of monks (later nuns too), known as the *sangha*. Later formulations would sum up the creed of Buddhism as affirming that one went to the Buddha, the *dharma* and the *sangha* for refuge. These are the Three Jewels of Buddhism. The forty-five years of organizing and teaching involved his wandering over the Gangetic region, winding up in Kusinagara, a small town not far from his birthplace, where he died after a severe illness resulting from eating a meal given him by a smith called Chanda: probably of pork, though another translation of the once-used term is truffles. When he died his body was cremated and his ashes distributed to various sites, later important for pilgrimages. The most important pilgrimage locations, however, are the places associated with the crucial stages of his life – Lumbini, where he was born, Bodh Gaya, where he gained *bodhi*, Sārnāth, where he set the wheel of the *dharma* in motion, and Kusinagara, where he deceased and so gained ultimate *nirvāṇa*. Before his death he reminded his disciples that their teacher would not have disappeared but would live on in the teachings, and that they should diligently strive to attain liberation. Earlier he had remarked that he did not have the closed fist of the teacher, that is, he did not hold anything back: and so we may assume that he (or rather the Theravādins who recounted the text) thought that the *Dharma* was sufficient for salvation.

To these events may be added other legendary material relating to the extensive collection of stories of the previous lives of the Buddha, when he was *bodhisattva* or buddha-to-be, in various forms at varying times – as a king, a hare, and so on. Immediately before his birth he resided as a god in the Tuṣita heaven. But gods cannot attain *nirvāṇa* or the highest wisdom or insight, because their glorious life does not permit them to realize the urgency and nature of *duḥkha* (unsatisfactoriness or suffering). It is only humans who can gain the ultimate. In the Pali texts the Buddha is considered as superior to the gods – though somewhat hyperbolically he is also referred to as *devātideva* or a god above (beyond) gods. His status sometimes floats in the myths between the human and the divine. The various characteristic bodily features of a buddha, such as the circle of hair on the forehead, the raised crown of the skull, and the long earlobes, signify a somewhat supernatural status, and yet the Buddha is definitely human in the early scriptural accounts.

How much of all this can be taken literally? It is a fair presumption, first of all, that the sites associated with the Buddha are genuine enough – Kapilavastu, Lumbinī, Rājagṛha, Bodh Gayā, Sārnāth, Pātaliputra, Vaiśālī, Kusinagara, etc. It is no doubt true that he was a Śākyan, a rather peripheral people in terms of the growing mercantile economy of the Gangetic plain, based largely on rice-growing, with the Ganges and other rivers providing important arteries of trade. We do not have much in the way of archaeological remains, since early Buddhist meeting places and monastic settlements, primarily intended for the rainy season, were constructed of wood. When later Buddhist monuments appear, some of them betray their wooden prototypes. Among the peoples he associated with were the Vajjians and the Licchavis, who had republican-type constitutions, and they served as rough models for the constitution of the *sangha*, which was also, however, bound tightly by a rule or *vinaya*, later increasingly elaborated, which imposed upon monks and hermits rules designed to make them tread a middle path between luxury and harsh austerity.

We can assume that the Buddha did leave home after marriage and wander in search of truth. It was a classical mode of conduct for *śramaṇas* or recluses during the Buddha's period. How far the tales of his luxurious living when he was young correspond to any reality is open to doubt: after all, the Śākyans were peripheral, and his father was not an absolute monarch or grand lord such as were to be found in kingdoms like Magadha at its capital Rājagṛha. We may of course take the stories of his previous lives as edifying fiction. But no doubt we can accept as historical the bare bones of his story, including the account of his, for that time, unusually advanced age at death.

More can be gleaned from the discourses of the Buddha as to his originality as a teacher. Although there are certain ritual elements evident in early Buddhism, and though ultimately his teachings were something to be confirmed by direct experience (he referred to his teachings as *ehipassiko* in Pali, that is, 'come-and-see-ish'), it is in his philosophical and doctrinal teachings that his creativity shows through. There is a characteristic style about the Buddha's teachings as transmitted and of course greatly elaborated in the canonical texts which is striking: it is a style which is on the one hand highly analytical, and on the other hand full of metaphors, parables and illustrations.

It is very likely that the Buddha himself formulated early versions of some of the key ideas – the Four Noble Truths, the Eightfold Path, the doctrine of dependent origination, the analysis of the self into the five *skandhas* (*khandhas*), the Buddhist version of rebirth and *karma* doctrine, the rationalistic ethic, the rejection of the *varṇa* system, the critique of Brahmin claims about the gods and about creation, and the nature of the *sangha*. But it may be noted that he performed a degree of synthesis between the religious culture of the area in which he worked and the rather radical nature of his teachings. For instance, he did not meet the Brahmins in a head-on confrontation, but rather reinterpreted the Brahmin ideal in psychological and moral terms. So the Buddha, while belonging in a general sense to the group of movements prevalent among the *śramaṇas* of his time – and they tended to be non-Brahmin and even anti-Brahmin – provided teachings which could permeate a society in which Brahmin rituals remained important.

Perhaps the most original idea of the Buddha was his rejection of the permanent self, and more generally his analysis of the world without recourse to the idea of substance. This related, it seems, to a conventionalist account of language. The growing Sanskrit tradition of the period appealed to the everlasting and primordial character of the Sanskrit language, which in the form of the recited Veda formed the backbone of a revelatory ritual tradition. The banddhas were characteristically *nāstika* or non-orthodox, rejecting such a revelatory tradition. This goes back to the Buddha's having found the source of his knowledge from quite a different source, namely in inner contemplative experience. In addition he found it in analysis, not reliance on traditions handed down by sacred persons. There was an empiricist bent, no doubt, to the Buddha's outlook, although it was not a narrow empiricism he expressed which confines knowledge to what can be derived from the five senses, but included, importantly, yogic perception also. That is, he included a type of religious experience, which of course had to be cultivated through the practice of *dhyāna* and to be buttressed by some degree of moral development, as a source of empirical knowledge.

But he also perceived that from the empirical point of view it was not necessary to postulate permanent entities underlying the shifting phenomena which we encounter in experience. This fitted in with a conventionalist view of language, since language could be held to be up to a point misleading, in suggesting that there are permanent things, and in particular a self, underlying changes. It would seem to be these insights which led him to his interpretation of *nirvāṇa*, which is so crucial for understanding early Buddhist philosophy. If we do not need, for the purposes of analysis, to postulate a permanent soul, then the fact of liberation could, so to speak, take the place of the soul. It was sufficient to postulate a state beyond all states, namely a transcendental liberation, in place of the soul. Being critical of the notion of a creator, the Buddha had no call to associate salvation with divine activity or grace. Liberation is something a person could achieve on his or her own, provided, of course, he or she paid attention to the Buddha's analysis and sought the help of the environment provided by the *sangha*. So the Buddha postulated a *nirvāṇa* which meant the end of rebirth and which was virtually indescribable except in so far as during this life the liberated saint (*arhant*) displayed certain excellent behavioural patterns, such as peacefulness or equanimity, and showed insight. *Nirvāṇa* could be obliquely characterized too by glowing epithets, such as 'the immortal place' (*amataṃ padam*), 'the unborn' (*aja*) and so forth. Negatively it was no longer being reborn, and this of course entailed the end of unsatisfactoriness or suffering. In brief, the Buddha substituted the idea of a liberated state for the concept of a soul.

It was from this point of view that he was led to some other momentous ideas (whether set forth in their most elaborate form or not), namely the idea of the undetermined questions and the notion of the individual as a bundle of types of states or processes. The former questions relate above all to the status of the *Tathāgata* after his death. It is inappropriate to say that he does exist, or does not, or both does and does not, or neither does nor does not. The analogy is with the question of where a fire goes when it goes out. It does not make sense. In so far as the *Tathāgata* is defined by the empirical states which can be pointed to in this life, there is no *Tathāgata* to point to once he has deceased after attaining *nirvāṇa* in this life. Similarly the question of whether there is an end or boundary to the cosmos is unanswerable. In a certain sense there is, in so far as the saint ultimately disappears when he gains *nirvāṇa*, and here we are led back to the concept of *nirvāṇa*. It would seem that the fourfold negation (not without precedent among the Buddha's contemporaries) was used creatively by him to eliminate radically transcendental questions, as being metaphysically unanswerable, given the analysis of the world as a series of processes and without a characterizable creator standing behind it. The Buddha produced what might be called, maybe anachronistically, a non-substantialist variety of Sāṅkhya.

His original view of *nirvāṇa* led to his characterizing the individual as being made up of bundles of different kinds of processes, with nothing permanent or substantial underlying them. This doubtless is the root of the doctrine of *skandhas* (whether the Buddha formulated them as we now have them may be a question, but why should he have not?). We are made up of bodily processes, perceptions, feelings, dispositions and states of consciousness. The doctrine has a double effect: one is to make us see ourselves as composite beings, who are the result of different ingredients being put together; the other is to make us see ourselves as impermanent entities. The idea of us as a composite of ingredients has a typically Buddhist air, where so much is made of lists of ingredients and types of events. This itself indicates something else that we can perhaps trace back to the Buddha himself – the close relation between analysis and meditation. It is in meditating on ourselves as made up of ingredients that we help to throw off the sense that we are egos. So there is a double strategy in much of early Buddhist teaching – to make people use their minds to realize a philosophical truth, and to get people to *feel* the analysis through the cultivation of the contemplative method.

Another piece of originality seems to be the Buddha's reading of *karma* and rebirth. Generally speaking we may look on his doctrine of *karma* as being a psychological one. Sometimes, of course, it looks as if the whole of Buddhist teaching is psychological. But unlike the Jainas he did not see the effects of *karma* as being automatic given a certain external act, such as crushing an insect. The crucial thing, on the contrary, was the mental disposition of the actor. That is why the very first verse of the *Dhammapada* claims that whenever anyone acts with an impure mind *duḥkha* follows him or her as the plough follows the ox.

The Buddha accepted the notion of rebirth, though, rather originally, he dispensed with the notion of an underlying *jīva* or *ātman* carrying over from one life to the next. The causation of rebirth had to do with the dispositions of the individual. It looks as if he kept to the doctrine (which was a *śramanic* rather than a Brahminical one – for the belief in reincarnation scarcely appears in the Vedic hymn collections: there is rather little sign that the Buddha knew about Upanishadic teachings) because he believed that it was based on memory of previous lives, which he, it was claimed, possessed. The triad of rebirth, *karma* and yogic practice (accompanied sometimes by severely ascetic practice) seems to have belonged widely to *śramanic* religious movements of his time and no doubt had begun to penetrate Brahmins' thinking.

The Buddha's teaching also embraced a strong sense of causation. This was later fully elaborated in the doctrine known as *pratītyasamutpāda*, or dependent origination. Initially, no doubt, the Buddha considered causation from a purely pragmatic angle. If we suppose that he himself formulated the Four Noble Truths, then we may note (another piece of the Buddha's originality) that he used a medical formula to express them. First, we suffer from a condition, namely suffering or unsatisfactoriness (*duḥkha*). Second, the condition of suffering is thirst or grasping (*tṛṣṇā*). Third, there is the possibility of removing the cause. Fourth, the medicine to accomplish this is the Eightfold Path (the 'Noble' one – perhaps the Buddha's use of *ārya* or 'noble' here was used to reinforce the sense of synthesizing the *śramanic* and the Brahminical cultures, by claiming that his heterodoxies were nevertheless mainstream Aryan teachings). While it is clear that analysis was important to the Buddha, he underlined by his use of the medical analogy his pragmatic ultimate concern. The philosophy was important because it could help towards liberation.

Possibly because he came from a rather marginal area and group, the Buddha was critical of the social mores entrenched in the theory of the four classes or *varṇas*, which was the overall framework for and the precursor of the more elaborate *jāti* system which characterized classical Hinduism. His interpretation of rituals, which themselves were woven into the world-view and practice of Brahmin-dominated society, was, as would be expected, psychological and ethical. So the true Brahmin was not someone who had ritual endowments but someone who had moral qualities.

Similarly the true monk (who was the recipient of *pūjā* from lay people) was someone who obeyed the moral precepts. No doubt the rituals associated with the Buddha, at the places where his ashes had been distributed, were anticipated by him as conducing to the right state of mind which would help people to follow his teaching.

His rationalist ethic can be glimpsed in various primitive formulations of it as in the Five Precepts and the transcendental virtues (the *brahmavihāras*) of *maitrī* or kindliness; *karuṇā* or compassion; *muditā* or joy (in others' happiness); and *upekṣā* or equanimity. Ethics was of course a vital ingredient in the Eightfold Path, and is the necessary accompaniment to meditative accomplishment as represented in the last three stages or aspects of the path.

In a special way the Buddha's attitude towards the gods seems to have been sceptical. In regard to Brahmā he was ironic: Brahmā, creator and patron of Brahmins, was the first being to emerge after a period of cosmic repose: he then thinks that other beings, which come into being later than he, occur *because* of him. So he fallaciously supposes himself to be creator. The rest of the gods may be some sort of force within the cosmos, but Brahmā and they are all ultimately impermanent. Moreover the Buddha knows them in his own experience, but Brahmins rely upon a handed-down tradition, which is like a chain of blind persons hanging on to one another.

It is difficult to believe that the root ideas of all the above doctrines and attitudes do not go back to the Buddha himself. It is reasonable therefore to look upon him as an innovator of genius, who framed a world-view and a practice which were to permeate so much of Asian – and more recently world – civilization. Whether he would have approved of all the elaboration of ideas and behaviour which have followed on is open to doubt. But he did sow at least the germ of the method of *upāyakauśalya* or skill in means, that is, of teaching the path of Buddhism in a manner adapted to the varying conditions, both psychological and cultural, of people.

There were some paradoxes in his position which were to generate, fruitfully, some new developments. Thus there is an obscurity in the position as sketched above about the relation between ethics and the pursuit of salvation. The aim of the saint (*arhant*) to liberate himself or herself could be interpreted as being ultimately selfish, however heroically the saint might relinquish this-worldly aims. Is the pursuit of *nirvāṇa* not in the end a solitary one, and not integrated into the social demands implied by morality, and by the demand to be compassionate above all? As we know, this tension was overcome in the Mahāyāna by the ideal of the *bodhisattva*, who puts off his or her own liberation in order to work for the welfare of all living beings.

There were issues too about the scope of early Buddhist critique of language. It seems clear that some core of scepticism about ordinary language existed from the earliest teachings. How far should criticism be taken? The notion that all substance-talk is misleading would take us very far indeed in criticizing all nouns whatsoever. The extreme outcome of this extension of scepticism was found in the dialectic of Nāgārjuna.

There was also some ambiguity about the question of impermanence. Is it to be interpreted in the strongest possible way, which would reduce all events to a powder of instants? If so, then difficulties regarding causation will arise, if a given effect is to be explained by reference to an instantaneous cause that will already have gone out of existence before the effect arises.

The Mahāyāna development of a thoroughly critical philosophy based on these considerations supposed that it could be attributed to the Buddha himself. It seems more plausible to hold that there were as yet unexplored ambiguities in the Buddha's own actual position which were exploited by later thinkers. It would seem that the limitation of undetermined questions in the Theravāda does reflect something of the Buddha's original teaching, in which case he would not have progressed to the conclusion that all questions about reality are unanswerable.

Meanwhile the concept of buddhahood began to develop. The idea of previous buddhas arose because it was a commonplace of śramanic thinking to see teachers as restoring a prior truth. The notion of a future buddha, Maitreya, also became important. We have noted already the curious belief in *pratyekabuddhas* (*pacceka-buddhas*) or silent buddhas. The use of stories of the previous lives of the historical Buddha was also a fruitful source of ethical teaching. Moreover, it came to be held that the Buddha embarked on his very arduous and lengthy quest for enlightenment after hearing the teaching of a previous buddha called Dīpankara. Such a story highlighted the importance of the career of the *bodhisattva*. There were ample clues in the *Jātaka* or birth-story material for the later-developed ideal of the *bodhisattva*.

Another factor in the elevation and expansion of the concept of the Buddha was the elaboration of ritual directed towards the Buddha through *stūpas* or memorial mounds. These became integral parts of temple complexes, which came to include bas-reliefs and paintings of the Buddha's life, and also in due course (from the beginning of the first century AD at least) Buddha-statues. In the earlier representations the Buddha appears by his absence. His disciples and other characters are fully depicted or sculpted. The Buddha is marked by associated objects and the like – such as the wheel-shaped mark of his footprints, his throne, his begging-bowl, the *bodhi* tree and so on. The non-depiction of the Buddha was most probably a way of conveying his transcendental status, having disappeared into *nirvāṇa* (so to speak). It is possible that the transition to actual statues of the Buddha came under Indo-Greek influences, starting in Gandhāra in the North-West and at Mathurā. Under Mahāyāna influences such direct art spread to Sri Lanka and other Buddhist countries.

The use of Buddha-images both reflected and encouraged the growth of *bhakti* or devotion. As this became more intense and elaborate there evolved the worship of celestial buddhas, notably the great five buddhas: Vairocana, Akṣobhya, Ratnasambhava, Amitābha and Amoghasiddhi. Of these the most important, ultimately, was Amitābha, who became the focus of Pure Land piety. This stressed the grace of Amitābha (Chinese O-mi-t'o [Amituo]; Japanese Amida), who creates the

Pure Land as a heaven for the otherwise unworthy faithful who are translated thither if they call upon the Buddha in faith and who there enjoy not only a life of supreme enjoyment but also propitious conditions for the realization of *nirvāṇa*. The idea that buddhas could project *buddha-kṣetras* or buddhafields made them into semi-creators. A kind of Buddhist theism emerged, with many of the properties of Christian, especially post-Reformation, piety. The many buddhas were considered to be manifestations of the one Buddha as represented by his *dharmakāya* or *dharma*-body or aspect. We return to this idea below.

Buddhas did not merely blossom vertically, but horizontally, with the spread of the *bodhisattva* ideal and the implication that many, perhaps an infinite number of, persons attain buddhahood. Also, there was the realization of some implications of philosophical developments. The notion of emptiness was by no means absent from the Lesser Vehicle traditions, and is to be found in the Theravādin canon. It was used in relation to the practice of meditation. But it underwent an important transformation in the Mahāyāna. It was argued that everything lacks its own nature or *svabhāva* and is thus 'empty' or *śūnya*. At the same time *nirvāṇa* too was empty: it was through an 'empty' consciousness that the meditator progresses to the realization of the ultimate truth. Now, another factor in the Mahāyāna was the combination of a thorough critique of existing concepts and the adoption of ways of talking which used key expressions in a quasi-substantial way. Though it was not strictly right to do so, it was easy to think of ultimate reality as consisting in *śūnyatā* or emptiness. As a result of these developments the essence of *nirvāṇa*, which is emptiness, is identical with the essence of this world, which is also emptiness. All things are empty. All this could give the false impression that emptiness is a kind of thing, but it helped to express the Mahāyāna idea that we all in principle possess a transcendental nature, though we have to realize that in our own experience. It was a short step to saying that we all possess the buddha-nature. This could help to explain the universality of the call to be *bodhisattvas* and to take the path to the full realization of our innate buddhahood.

The identification of the transcendental aspect of the Buddha with emptiness was helped also by the *advaya* or non-dual nature of mystical experience. It is of course fairly common in all traditions to have mystics say or imply that the distinction between subject and object fades away in the mystical experience. Theistic mystics often write about the union (*unio mystica*) between the self or soul and the divine being. Strictly the notion of *unio* does not apply in the Buddhist case since there is nothing to be united with. But in the language of quasi-substances we can say that the mystic does unite himself or herself with transcendental emptiness. There could then be no essential difference between the emptiness of the Buddha and the emptiness of anyone else who attains to realization. This was a further motive for expanding the concept of buddhahood.

From another point of view, in the maze of Buddhist paradoxes, the Buddha continues after his decease in the form of the *Dharma*, the teaching. But this *Dharma* is not in the last resort to be identified with the words of the teaching. To concentrate on the words and to miss the reality of the teaching is like looking at the finger rather than at the moon to which it is pointing. So the meaning of the *Dharma* is to be found in what it points to. That is the transcendent truth of emptiness. It is for this reason that the higher nature of the Buddha came to be called the *Dharmakāya* or 'Truth-Body' ('Truth-Aspect'). This prepared the way for the summation of the high Mahāyāna doctrine of buddhahood as the *trikāya* or 'Three-Aspect' doctrine. According to this there are three levels. There is at the worldly level the *nirmāṇakāya* or 'Transformation-Aspect'. This refers to the historical Buddha and his predecessors, not to mention the future buddha Maitreya. It chimes in with the more magical idea of buddhahood which accompanied his becoming the focus of *bhakti*: as though his appearance on earth is a kind of conjuring-trick, to help living beings existing in ignorance. Then at a higher level there is the *sambhogakāya* or Enjoyment-Aspect. Buddhas at this level are the *foci* of worship, and will help the faithful in various ways. They also serve as objects of meditation. The five great ones listed earlier were identified also with the five *skandhas*, and so were present within the individual. All the celestial and earthly buddhas are united in the Truth-Aspect. This is in the language of substances the original Buddha and ultimate truth. This whole elaborate schema is a very rich universe for the exercise of piety and aids to calming and mystical attainment.

Though the development of these ideas was very rich and complex, part at least of them was based on conceptions observable within the Theravādin canon. The transition philosophically to the language of quasi-substances and the dialectical critique of notions such as causation and instantaneity – a critique issuing in the philosophy of emptiness – are in accord, in many ways, with the spirit of the Buddha's teaching as found in the more austere Theravādin accounts. The concept of the 'Truth-Aspect' of the Buddha is a natural deduction from some of his last words. What is new in the whole train of ideas and practices we have sketched above is the development of the cult of celestial buddhas. This may among other things have had to do with parallel movements in the Hindu tradition towards devotionalism focused on great gods such as Viṣṇu and Śiva, not to mention *avatārs* like Kṛṣṇa and Rāma. There were Iranian influences in the formation of the figure of Amitābha. Moreover, the pietism of Pure Land and other devotional kinds of Buddhism was highly acceptable and meaningful to many in Chinese, Korean and Japanese cultures, as well as in Tibet, when Indian Buddhism migrated thither. The absorbent character of later Hinduism meant that the Buddha himself came to be regarded as an *avatāra* of Viṣṇu, one of whose functions was to test the faith of Vaiṣṇavites. Also, it may be noted that the theory of periodic buddhas, whose job was to rediscover the *Dharma* and to preach it during a period of civilization when it was overlaid and forgotten, influenced the Hindu account of *avatārs*, who periodically restore the *Dharma*. Nevertheless, the two religions had different atmospheres. While numinous representations of buddhas occur in later

Buddhism, on the whole the icons of Buddhism tend to emphasize the calm and equanimity which remain at the heart of the Buddhist moral ideal: often the statues are sublime portrayals of moral qualities which combine with the life of contemplation and analysis.

It was therefore natural too that Buddhism should come to identify some this-worldly individuals as living buddhas, because of the way in which they express a buddha's quality of life – such as Padmasambhava (eighth century AD), the missionary who brought Buddhism to Tibet. There was also the notion of a person as being the incarnation or manifestation of a celestial buddha. Thus in medieval Cambodia the monarch was seen as an *avatār* of Bhaiṣajyaguru, a healing buddha. In Tibet the Panchen Lamas were seen as incarnations of Amitābha, and the Dalai Lamas as manifestations of the *bodhisattva* Avalokiteśvara.

It appears that a systematic biography of the Buddha within the tradition was rather late in coming (the *Mahāvastu* of about the first century AD). It has been argued by Frauwallner that there was an original biographical text which was composed about a century after the death of the Buddha and accepted at the Second Buddhist Council. It is more probable that there was only scattered material, such as we find in the Vinaya and Sutta sections of the canon. In the *Mahāparinibbāna Sutta* there is a somewhat continuous narrative of the last journey and decease of the Buddha. Most of the references to incidents in his life are there to illustrate doctrines. The best-known biographies or chronicles of the Buddha's life are the rather loose work already mentioned, the *Mahāvastu*; the *Lalitavistara*, translated into Chinese in AD 308, a Mahāyāna elaboration of a Sarvāstivādin ('realist') work; and the *Buddhacarita* of Aśvaghoṣa (died *c.*AD 150). In the Theravādin literature there is the *Nidānakathā*, which introduces the commentary on the *Jātakas* or birth-stories of the Buddha (that is, accounts of previous lives). The Sri Lankan chronicles also contain an account of the Buddha's life and include narratives of his miraculous journeys to Sri Lanka during his lifetime, which conferred upon the island its sacred status as protector of the *dhamma*. Since most of the biographies are so long removed in time from the life of the Buddha himself and typically in any case have pious and doctrinal intentions, it is better to rely more on the spirit of the teachings of the Buddha as they have come down to us to infer anything more than the bare bones of his biography that I have indicated at the beginning of this chapter. Naturally the later biographies are important phenomenologically in helping to shape Buddhist devotional practice, ethical ideals and art.

The originality and force of the Buddha's personality can be in little doubt. The power of his ideas has survived through many elaborations in the wide swathe of Asian civilization which his religion has penetrated. It was therefore not surprising that there was an increase in the tendency to deify him, from the time of the proto-Mahāyāna Lokottaravādins ('Transcendentalists'). It would seem, though, that in the earliest teaching the transcendent aspect of Buddhahood had simply to do with his capacity for *nirvāṇa*, and with the non-composite and non-important character of that ideal. This was indicated in that unrevealing title accorded to him, the *tathāgata* or 'thus-gone'.

FURTHER READING

Bareau, André (1963–71) *Recherches sur la biographie du Buddha dans les Sūtrapiṭaka et les Vinayapiṭaka anciens*, 2 vols, Paris: École Française d'Extrême-Orient.
Bechert, Hans (1982) 'The date of the Buddha reconsidered', *Indologica Taurinensia* 10 : 29–36.
Bechert, Hans and Gombrich, Richard (1984) *The World of Buddhism*, London: Thames & Hudson.
Conze, Edward (1967) *Buddhist Thought in India*, Ann Arbor: University of Chicago Press.
Dayal, Har (1932) *The Bodhisattva Doctrine in Buddhist Sanskrit Literature*, London: Kegan Paul.
Foucher, Alfred (1963) *The Life of the Buddha according to the Ancient Texts and Monuments of India*, Middletown, Conn.
Frauwallner, Erich (1956) *The Earliest Vinaya and the Beginnings of Buddhist Literature*, Rome.
Jaini, Padmanabh S. (1970) '*Sramaṇas*: their conflict with Brahmaṇical society', in Joseph W. Elder (ed.) *Chapters in Indian Civilization*, revised edn, Dubuque.
Kalupahana, David (1975) *Causality: The Central Philosophy of Buddhism*, Honolulu: Hawaii University Press.
Lamotte, Étienne (1958) *Histoire du bouddhisme indien*, Louvain: Université de Louvain.
Ling, Trevor (1973) *The Buddha*, London: Temple Smith.
Mus, Paul (1935) *Barabuḍur*, 2 vols, Hanoi: Impremerie d'Extrême Orient.
Reynolds, Frank (1976) 'The many lives of Buddha: a study of sacred biography and Theravada tradition', in Donald Capps and Frank Reynolds (eds) *The Biographical Process*, The Hague.
Smart, Ninian (1991) *Doctrine and Argument in Indian Philosophy*, Leiden.
Snellgrove, David (1978) *The Image of the Buddha*, Tokyo.
Streng, Frederick J. (1967) *Emptiness: A Study in Religious Meaning*, Nashville: Abingdon Press.
Thomas, Edward J. (1949) *The Life of Buddha as Legend and History*, revised edn, London: Routledge & Kegan Paul.
Warder, A. K. (1980) *Indian Buddhism*, revised edn, Delhi: Motilal Banarsidass.
Welbon, Guy (1968) *Buddhist Nirvāṇa and its Western Interpreters*, Chicago.

17

BUDDHISM IN INDIA

Roger R. Jackson

INTRODUCTION

Sources

In oral form, Indian Buddhist literature may date back to the fifth century BC, but the actual written texts in which we might find 'philosophy' were all composed between approximately the third century BC and the thirteenth century AD – when Buddhism effectively disappeared from India under an onslaught of Turkic Muslim invaders. The corpus is vast, running to several hundred volumes each in the partially overlapping Chinese and Tibetan canons that are the most complete extant record of Indian Buddhism's literary output. Perhaps half of the texts are not remotely philosophical, but that still leaves a large number that are. Many early texts were written in Pali, and preserved over the centuries outside India, in Sri Lanka, Burma and Thailand. The greatest number, both early and late, were written in one or another form of Sanskrit, and although the majority of the Sanskrit literature was lost when Buddhism disappeared from India, most of it is found translated into Chinese and/or Tibetan.

This poses a significant problem for any attempt to write a 'history' of Indian Buddhist philosophy: a complete account requires research in at least four different languages. Little of the material has yet been translated into western languages, and the linguistic and cultural barriers to translating it successfully are considerable. A further problem is posed by the fact that dating has always been an inexact science in India. As a result, both absolute and relative chronologies tend to be speculative at best. Also, authorship is a much more complex issue in India than in the West. Anonymity is often seen as valuable, because it allows one either to speak with the authority of timeless 'tradition' or to concoct such tradition: hence the many *sūtras* and *tantras* alleged to have been spoken by the Buddha. When they are identified, writers may take – or be assigned – the names of famous predecessors: hence the interminable debates both in and outside the tradition over how many Vasubandhus or Nāgārjunas or Candrakīrtis there were. Finally, the historian is faced by the relative paucity of Indian Buddhist writings that attempt systematically to describe philosophical schools or positions, and a complete absence of texts that purport to write a 'history of philosophy'. Tibetan scholars from the thirteenth century on wrote both on doxography and history of philosophy, but their efforts, like ours, are beset by ideological and historiographical constraints that limit their reliability.[1]

With the historiographical problems firmly in mind, we still can say some things about the texts in which we find Indian Buddhist philosophy. They are broadly divisible into *sūtras* (or *tantras*), texts allegedly spoken by the Buddha himself, and *śāstras*, which either comment upon *sūtras* or are independent treatises, and may themselves receive commentary, sub-commentary, and so forth. In general, *sūtras* are more 'literary' and 'rhetorical' in their philosophical passages, while *śāstras* tend to be more systematic – though their 'system' may vary from the exhaustive enumeration and classification of existents, to the critical analysis of opposing Buddhist or non-Buddhist positions, to the construction of speculative or inferential accounts of 'reality'. The authors of these texts, whatever their period or provenance, were by and large celibate males, most of them attached to one or another Buddhist monastery, and writing primarily for a like-minded audience. Though it is dangerous to speculate excessively about the 'social uses' of texts about which we have so little history, it nevertheless is important to keep in mind that most Buddhist literature arose within a monastic setting, and that this *does* entail certain perspectives and purposes that might be quite different had it been written by, say, lay females.

Purposes and problems

In a culture like that of ancient India, where asceticism and monasticism were widespread social phenomena, we must be wary of assuming that all monks thought alike or had the same purposes. Nevertheless, the monastic milieu of most Buddhist philosophy allows us to conclude, at least in principle, that philosophy was wedded to the ultimate purpose of monastic life, which was the production of enlightened individuals. Further, just as most Buddhist practitioners through the centuries have attempted to attain an enlightenment that they believe identical to that of the Buddha himself, so have most Buddhist philosophers, whether explicitly or not, attempted to forge, between 'extremes', a 'middle way' (*madhyama pratipad*) like that articulated by the Buddha in his 'first sermon' at Sārnāth, and in other, subsequent, discourses. Thus, the Buddhist middle way was seen as falling ethically between hedonism and asceticism, metaphysically between nihilism and eternalism, and causally between fatalism and indeterminism.

This middle way both presupposed and entailed certain assumptions about reality, which were formulated early on as the 'three characteristics' of existents: (1) 'all compounded phenomena are impermanent (*anitya*)', (2) 'all contaminated phenomena are suffering (*duḥkha*)', (3) 'all existents (*dharmas*) are without self (*anātman*)'. To this a fourth was sometimes added: '*nirvāṇa* is peace'. Equally fundamental was the assumption that all phenomena are subject to 'dependent origination' (*pratītyasamutpāda*), and hence causal, and that this ensures (a) the existence of past lives that cause, and future lives that result from, the present life, (b) the reality of a principle of moral causation, *karma*, and (c) the potential for the practices that comprise the Buddhist 'path' to result in *nirvāṇa*. These assumptions, in turn, generated certain problems that Buddhist philosophers were forced again and again to confront. Among these are: what ontological status to assign to the different *dharmas* that constitute the 'lexicon' of the Buddhist vision of reality; how to explain memory, karmic efficacy and personal continuity in the absence of a permanent self; how to evaluate knowledge and reason in a tradition that assumes that liberation must occur through trans-rational means; and how to relate an unconditioned, non-causal state like *nirvāṇa* to the dependently originated practices of the path and to basic ontological assumptions about impermanence and no-self.

Preview

Here, we can only suggest in the most general manner the variety of different Buddhist responses to these problems. Our primary purpose is to delineate broadly the major 'schools' that developed in the course of Buddhist philosophizing in India. There are many different lists of such schools, none of them without its difficulties, but at least some kind of division into schools is warranted by the Buddhist tradition itself. I have already alluded to the historiographical problems any such account faces, but I shall attempt nevertheless to reflect the present scholarly consensus on at least the relative chronology of these schools, and individuals where it is relevant. The major divisions I shall employ, and examine in turn, are (1) the *nikāya/āgama* tradition, (2) the Hīnayāna, and (3) the Mahāyāna. In discussing the *nikāyas* and *āgamas*, I shall analyse the problem of establishing either an *ur*-Buddhism or the philosophy of the Buddha himself. The Hīnayāna schools I shall examine are the (a) Sthaviravāda/Theravāda, (b) Mahāsāṃghika, (c) Pudgalavāda, (d) Sarvāstivāda/Vaibhāṣika and (e) Sautrāntika. The Mahāyāna schools I shall examine are the (a) early Madhyamaka, (b) Yogācāra, (c) Pramāṇavāda, and (d) later Madhyamaka. For each school, I shall describe (i) the historical and textual sources, (ii) the spiritual and philosophical problematic from which it probably arose, and (iii) the major perspectives that it offers. The latter will sometimes correspond closely to the issues cited in the previous section, and sometimes not; in all cases, I shall attempt to present the problematic and perspective as the school itself articulates them.

THE *ĀGAMA/NIKĀYA* TRADITION AND 'THE PHILOSOPHY OF THE BUDDHA'

Sources

Every Buddhist tradition, from Sri Lanka to Japan, asserts that its central ideas were taught by Śākyamuni, the Buddha of this historical epoch. His dates are in dispute, but he probably flourished sometime in the fifth century BC. There is little evidence that any of the discourses attributed to the Buddha really were delivered by him in the form in which we have them. Certainly, the Mahāyāna *sūtras*, which do not appear until the first century BC at the earliest (let alone the *tantras*, which appear even later), are unlikely to have been uttered by the historical Buddha. The more promising source for a reconstruction of the Buddha's 'original teaching' would seem to be the material contained in the Pali *nikāyas* preserved by the Theravāda tradition and their Sanskrit counterparts, the *āgamas*, which unfortunately are extant only in Chinese translation. The *nikāyas/āgamas* are five collections made up primarily of discourses attributed to the Buddha, the *Sūtra-piṭaka* that, together with collected texts on monastic conduct (*vinaya*) and ontological phenomenology (*abhidharma*), comprises the 'three baskets' (*Tripiṭaka*) that were canonical for the earliest Buddhist schools. There is undoubtedly much ancient material contained in the *nikāyas* and *āgamas*, but stratification is no easy matter, and the collections themselves were not completed until perhaps the first century BC, several centuries after the Buddha's final *nirvāṇa*. Thus, the material in the *nikāyas* and *āgamas* must also be regarded very cautiously; what the Buddha 'really taught' will probably elude historians – if not believers – for ever. Still, the *nikāya/āgama* textual tradition is the only one accepted as canonical by all Buddhists, both Hīnayāna and Mahāyāna, so, with these historical caveats in mind, we may nevertheless attempt to speculate about the problematic inherited by the historical Buddha and the philosophical perspectives he offered.[2]

Problematic

Regardless of his actual dates, we can be certain that the Buddha lived in an age of profound spiritual and philosophical turmoil. Social and religious changes in the first part of the first millennium BC had undermined the institutions and world-view brought by the Āryans to India centuries before, leading to what Joseph Campbell has referred to as a 'great reversal' of Indian values. Where the early Āryans had sought to maintain the orderly rhythm (*ṛta*) of the cosmos and the pleasures of this one life through ritual sacrifice, Indians after the great reversal increasingly viewed sacrifice as irrelevant or arcane and the rhythm of the cosmos as a vicious cycle of unstable events in an ultimately unsatisfying life that might itself merely be one of many into which one could be reincarnated. The problem of *saṃsāra* – of unwanted rebirth from unstable life to unstable life – became a concern of Indian thinkers as early as the time of the first *Upaniṣads* (*c.*800 BC), and, by the time of Buddha, it had come to dominate the philosophical and spiritual agenda of both Hindu (*brāḥmana*) and non-Hindu (*śramaṇa*) schools. Most schools agreed that *saṃsāra* was the essential problem of human existence, and most, too, agreed that the 'solution' to *saṃsāra* was the attainment of a condition of immutable release (*mokṣa* or *nirvāṇa*) outside the cycle of rebirths. There was, further, widespread agreement that our continued rebirth in *saṃsāra* was the natural result of actions (*karma*) that were motivated by such negative factors as desire and fear, which, in turn, were rooted in an ignorance of the true nature of reality. The chain of causes that resulted in *saṃsāra*'s perpetuation, then, could be undone by a correct understanding of reality, which, integrated radically enough via yogic meditation, would uproot the basic cause of our suffering. Not surprisingly, where Indian schools before and during the Buddha's time differed was in their vision of the ignorance that keeps us in *saṃsāra* and of the liberating knowledge that is its antidote.

If the spiritual problematic to which the Buddha responded was framed by what we might call the *saṃsāra–nirvāṇa* cosmology, the philosophical situation was defined by a variety of approaches, Hindu and non-Hindu, to the problem of ignorance, knowledge and liberation. Though there were many Hindus – the Buddha would criticize them – who continued to focus on ritual sacrifice as a key to happiness, the dominant Hindu approach, expressed in the *Upaniṣads*, was to view as the root of *saṃsāra* our ignorance of our identity with the immutable, blissful basis of both the cosmos and ourselves, the most important term for which is *ātman*. Casting aside our beguilement by the multiple, material, mutable reality we encounter in ordinary experience, we must, through analysis, meditation, or both, realize our identity with the *ātman*, that single, spiritual, unchanging reality that is the source and substratum of all things. Among non-Hindu schools, there are several that draw the attention of the Buddha of the *nikāyas* and *āgamas*. The Lokāyatas were naturalists and materialists, rejecting the *saṃsāra–nirvāṇa* cosmology and insisting on the centrality of this life, to which the pursuit of pleasure ought to be central. Philosophically, Lokāyatas were inclined to indeterminism, maintaining that entities acted not in a causally determined manner, but spontaneously, according to their own natures (*svabhāva*). The Ājīvikas adhered to a form of fatalism. They accepted the *saṃsāra–nirvāṇa* cosmology, but insisted that there was little one could do, either through knowledge or action, to pass from the former to the latter. Rather, one simply achieved liberation at the predetermined end of one's succession of rebirths. Jainas sought liberation through an ascetic shedding of the material accretions of *karma* on the soul (*jīva*). Philosophically, they were inclined to a relativism that accepted the partial truth of all views, the complete truth of none. The agnostics, who seem to have little interest in spiritual liberation, were sceptics and sophists who developed arguments through which they attempted to demonstrate the impossibility of any human knowledge.

Perspectives

Against the background of these competing schools, the 'middle way' of early Buddhism can be more clearly delineated. The middle way articulated by the Buddha in his first sermon was ethical, falling between the hedonism of the Lokāyatas and the extreme asceticism typical of the Jainas, and affirming an approach to spiritual life that stresses detachment, but not to the extent of self-mortification. At other places in the *nikāyas* and *āgamas*, the Buddha repudiates the causal extremes of Ājīvika fatalism and Lokāyata indeterminism, articulating the doctrine of dependent origination, whereby all events arise from preceding events, but in patterns complex and variable enough that there is some room for choice and chance. With regard to rebirth, the Buddha rejects both the eternalism of the Hindus, Jainas and Ājīvikas and the nihilism of the Lokāyatas, insisting that there is no permanent *ātman* or *jīva* that travels from life to life, but that rebirth nevertheless does occur, as the continuation of impermanent mental patterns. Epistemologically, the Buddha rejects both the common-sense empiricism of the Lokāyatas and the radical scepticism of the agnostics. He believes that certain questions (for example the existence or non-existence of an enlightened being after death) are best not asked, and he evinces considerable suspicion of testimony, pure reason or faith as a basis for knowledge, believing that one's own experience is the surest guide. His 'empiricism', however (if such it is), involves yogic as well as ordinary experience, and may be bolstered by reasoning – and even philosophizing – where appropriate. Finally, in the realm of ontology, the Buddha steers between the naïve realism of the Lokāyatas and the implicit nihilism of the agnostics, denying that 'persons' or 'things' exist substantially in the way we perceive them to, yet asserting that they may meaningfully be understood as constellations of impermanent events – *dharmas* – such as the five psycho-physical aggregates (*skandha*), the various sensory spheres and the physical elements.

If we return to the spiritual problematic that was the motive force for the Buddha's search and teaching, we see that he preached 'Four Noble Truths': (1) He accepted the reality of constant, unsatisfactory rebirth within *saṃsāra*, but did not accept any permanent principle that is reborn. (2) He believed that *saṃsāric* suffering, as all events, could be understood as originating in dependence on specific causes, i.e. desire and/or ignorance, which were linked to suffering through the predictable, if not inevitable, force of our various actions. (One implication of this was the denial of any God that created the cosmos: it is without beginning and karmically conditioned). (3) He believed that there existed beyond the fluctuations of *saṃsāra* a peaceful, liberated condition, *nirvāṇa* – attainment of which made one an *arhant* ('worthy one'). And, most importantly, (4) he proclaimed that there exists a path that leads to *nirvāṇa*, and that a crucial element of that path is the understanding that all things are impermanent and bereft of a substantial self – for it is precisely belief in such a self that entails the desire and fear that motivate most of our actions, ensuring that the results

– including rebirth – will be similarly negative. Of all the doctrines promulgated by the Buddha, it is this teaching of no-self (*anātman*) that was probably the most controversial and did most to delineate Buddhists philosophically from other Indian schools. Because of its antiquity and its psychological and spiritual importance, it became a doctrine that every Buddhist school would uphold, but it was susceptible of a variety of interpretations, and did not always mesh well with other elements of the Buddhist world-view, such as the belief in rebirth or the assertion of an immutable, peaceful *nirvāṇa*. It is an exaggeration to see the entire history of Buddhist philosophy after the Buddha as an attempt to articulate the implications of no-self, but we shall see, in what follows, that the doctrine was never far from the minds of Buddhist thinkers, as they struggled to reinterpret the 'middle way' in various times and situations.[3]

HĪNAYĀNA SCHOOLS

The term 'Hīnayāna' ('Lesser Vehicle') was coined in the early centuries AD in certain Mahāyāna ('Greater Vehicle') *sūtras*, where it is a pejorative designation for those Buddhist schools that accepted as canonical only the texts collected in the earliest *Tripiṭakas*, and whose practitioners were regarded as lacking sufficient wisdom or compassion to receive and practise the teachings contained in the Mahāyāna *sūtras* – which led beyond the goal of the *arhant*'s *nirvāṇa* to full buddhahood. Only one 'Hīnayāna' tradition, the Theravāda, still exists, and its adherents rightly insist that 'Theravāda' is the proper designation for the contemporary non-Mahāyāna Buddhist tradition. Historically, however, Theravāda was only one of many 'Hīnayāna' schools (the traditional number is eighteen, though there actually were between twenty and thirty),[4] so the term would be confusing if applied *a posteriori*. Thus, it is appropriate, if not ideal, to refer to the set of schools that follows as 'Hīnayāna', bearing in mind that their differences with the 'Mahāyāna' are ultimately reducible less to complete disagreement over doctrines than to a dispute over how extensive the Buddhist canon is.

Sthaviravāda/Theravāda

Sources

Sthaviravāda, the 'doctrine of the elders', refers to that tradition of Buddhism that maintained a conservative doctrinal stance in the face of the changes and charges proffered by the Mahāsāṃghikas at a council held at Pataliputra no earlier than 346 BC. In the next century, there branched off from the Sthaviravāda a number of other schools, including the Pudgalavāda and the Sarvāstivāda. The strand of thought that regarded these competing schools as aberrant came to be known as the Vibhajyavāda ('the distinctionist doctrine'). It, too, subdivided, and one of its sub-schools, whose canon was in Pali, and which was transplanted to Sri Lanka as early as the mid-third century BC, took as its name the Pali equivalent of 'Sthaviravāda', 'Theravāda'. Under that name (and with its own subsequent divisions), it became and has remained the dominant form of Buddhism throughout south-east Asia. Other Vibhajyavāda sub-schools, such as the Mahīśāsakas, Dharmaguptakas or Kaśyapīyas, might with equal conviction lay claim to preserving the 'doctrine of the elders', but they have perished where Theravāda has survived, so we shall use Theravāda as our major prism for viewing Sthaviravāda.

The basic sources of Theravāda tradition are the texts of the Pali *Tripiṭaka*, which was closed and committed to writing during the first century BC: the five *nikāyas* of the *Sutta-piṭaka*, the greater part of which are discourses attributed to the Buddha; the various regulations for and discussions of monastic life found in the *Vinaya-piṭaka*; and the ontological phenomenology that dominates the *Abhidhamma-piṭaka*. The *sutta* and *vinaya* portions of the Theravāda *Tripiṭaka* overlap considerably with those of other Hīnayāna schools. The doctrinal and philosophical material in the *suttas*, however, was vast and disparate, and there arose in the period after the Buddha's passing a need for a systematic, coherent elucidation of the essential teachings so that they could be mastered intellectually and meditatively as easily as possible. In response to this need, the texts that compose the *Abhidhamma-piṭaka* were written. They exhaustively enumerate, classify and analyse the different *dhammas* (Sanskrit: *dharmas*) that constitute reality. They appear bloodless and scholastic to the casual reader, but were understood by those within the traditions that developed them as necessary skeletons that could be filled out as needed by the philosopher or contemplative. For the historian, the most interesting of these texts is probably the *Kathāvatthu*, a record of third-century BC debates between the Sthaviravāda and such opponents as the Mahāsāṃghikas, Pudgalavādins and Sarvāstivādins. Outside the canon are found a number of crucial texts that have further helped to define the Theravāda standpoint: the *Milindapañhā*, a dialogue between an Indo-Greek king (perhaps Menander, first century AD) and a Buddhist monk on points of Buddhist doctrine; and the various commentaries and treatises of the fourth–fifth-century AD south Indian monk, Buddhaghosa, which have, above all, defined Theravāda orthodoxy.[5]

Problematic

Unlike the Buddha, who necessarily responded to an external problematic, Theravāda must be seen as responding primarily to problems generated within the evolving Buddhist tradition. Much of the literature cited above, from the *abhidhamma* writings, to the *Milindapañhā* and the works of Buddhaghosa, reflects the Theravādin response to the problem of elucidating basic doctrines so that practitioners might more easily grasp them. These are its positive contributions. In other ways, Sthaviravāda/Theravāda has defined itself reactively, as a particular strand of thought that finds a middle way among various spurious 'innovations' in the Buddhist tradition, such as the Mahāsāṃghika critique of the spiritual achievements of *arhants* (enlightened *sthaviras*) and its docetic speculations about the nature of the Buddha, the Pudgalavāda positing of a non-permanent and non-impermanent 'person' found neither within nor beyond the aggregates that continues from life to life, and the Sarvāstivāda insistence that all *dharmas* 'exist' in some ultimate sense. The implication of rejecting such 'innovation' is that Theravāda, uniquely, preserves the 'original teaching' of the Buddha. We have seen, of course, that establishing historically what such a teaching was is impossible. Still, if we do not regard the Theravāda 'reaction' as defining some original Buddhism, it nevertheless does express a distinctive point of view that – because of its conservatism – gives us a window on a relatively early Buddhist perspective, if not the earliest.

Perspectives

On a broad, affirmative plane, Theravāda asserts the reality of rebirth, *karma* and dependent origination; the transcendent nature of *nibbāna* (Pali for *nirvāṇa*); the absence of self in the 'person', who is seen as a mere convention, a designation of parts, like 'chariot'; and a threefold path to liberation consisting of morality, concentration and wisdom. More specifically, the *abhidhamma* literature contributes detailed analyses of *dhammas* and relations. The *Dhammasaṅgaṇi* of the *Abhidhamma-piṭaka* enumerates anywhere from 89 to 200 elements of existence. They are essentially divisible into categories corresponding to the five aggregates (*khandha*, Sanskrit: *skandha*) that make up the 'individual': (1) matter (*rūpa*), which includes the elements, physical organs, life, and so on, (2) sensation (*vedanā*), which includes pleasure, pain and indifference, (3) perception (*saññā*), which is the recognition of objects, (4) formations (*saṅkhāra*), which include a multiplicity of dispositions, attitudes, categories and so on and (5) consciousness (*viññāṇa*), which comprises visual, aural, olfactory, gustatory, tactile and mental awarenesses. In addition to these conditioned and impermanent (but not absolutely durationless) *dhammas*, there is one unconditioned *dhamma*: *nibbāna*. The *Paṭṭhāna*, also a part of the *Abhidhamma-piṭaka*, enumerates twenty-four relations, including a variety of causes and conditions, conjunctions and disjunctions, actions and results. Theravāda never developed 'logic' as systematically as later Indian schools would, but did derive certain basic forms of inference from the *Kathāvatthu*, and analogical styles of argument from the *Milindapañhā*. The tradition also developed – as would other schools – principles for the interpretation of scripture and for analysing existents as 'conventional' (*vohāra*) or 'ultimate' (*paramattha*). In its reaction to competing traditions, the Theravāda asserted against the

Mahāsāṃghikas that arhatship was the highest possible achievement and the historical Buddha a human being who at death completely transcended the world, in no way being projected by a supreme principle or continuing after his passing; against the Pudgalavādins that there exists no 'person' within or beyond the five aggregates that can explain continuity from life to life; and against the Sarvāstivādins that past and future *dhammas* do not 'exist' in the way that present *dhammas* do.[6]

Mahāsāṃghika

Sources

The Mahāsāṃghika (the 'greater community') was the opponent of the Sthaviravāda at the time of the Buddhist community's first serious schism, at a council held in Pataliputra no earlier than 346 BC. In subsequent centuries, the Mahāsāṃghika divided into a number of sub-schools, including the Lokottaravāda, Gokulika and Caitika, which themselves then further divided. The school seems to have persisted with diminishing strength until the Turkic invasions. I have characterized Sthaviravāda as a 'conservative' school, and, in the light of its views on the qualities of various spiritual practitioners and the Buddha, it is probably fair to describe the Mahāsāṃghika as 'innovative'. The term must be used cautiously, however, since the Mahāsāṃghikas undoubtedly believed as sincerely as the Sthaviravādins that they were the preservers of the original tradition. Since they are extinct, however, and most of their *Sūtra-piṭaka* is lost to us, it is impossible to assess the evidence on the basis of which they would support this belief. It has also been widely assumed that the Mahāsāṃghikas represent a doctrinal bridge between the early tradition and Mahāyāna. It is true that some doctrines attributed to the Mahāsāṃghikas are reflected in Mahāyāna texts, but many are not, and Mahāyānists obviously drew on a wide range of earlier sources in composing their texts. As hinted above, the major problem besetting our study of Mahāsāṃghika is the paucity of surviving original texts. Their *Ekottara-āgama* (equivalent to the Pali *Aṅguttara-nikāya*) survives in Chinese translation, and in Sanskrit we have the Lokottaravāda *Mahāvastu*, a great chronicle of the Buddha's life from which some doctrines may be gleaned. Beyond this, there is little, and most of our information about them is derived from accounts by non-Mahāsāṃghika Indian and Chinese writers.[7]

Problematic

Later accounts of the Pataliputra council indicate that the issue over which the Sthaviravāda and Mahāsāṃghika split was the contention by a Mahāsāṃghika named

Mahādeva that *arhats*, the enlightened beings revered by the *sthaviras*, were still subject to various worldly impulses, such as nocturnal emissions, ignorance, unintended verbalizations, etc. This is hardly a philosophical critique, yet it reflects a concern that must have arisen in the early community to the effect that 'enlightened beings' may not really be enlightened, and that criteria need to be developed for assessing enlightenment-claims. It is uncertain whether Mahādeva and his cohorts were rejecting the *arhat*-ideal as a whole or simply the claims of false *arhats*. A problem to which some later Mahāsāṃghikas responded was that of the nature of the Buddha, who was held by the Sthaviravādins to have been born a human being and at his final *nirvāṇa* to have passed completely beyond any involvement in the world. What this view failed to satisfy in some Buddhists was the sense that the Buddha must have been truly extraordinary, and thus that there must be some way in which he was eternally pure and existent, both before and after his earthly career. Another problem to which some Mahāsāṃghikas responded was that of the ontological status of worldly and trans-worldly entities. If, as implied by the Sthaviravādins, entities ('person', 'chariot') are understood merely to be fictions, designations or verbal conventions (*prajñapti*), then how much reality can we actually attribute to them?

Perspectives

It is unclear from the little remaining Mahāsāṃghika literature or from later accounts of their views whether they went so far as to replace the *arhant*-ideal with the *bodhisattva*-ideal that would become so important in Mahāyāna. What is clear is that the *bodhisattva* began to take on greater importance for the Mahāsāṃghikas. The term still referred primarily to a buddha before his enlightenment, but he was said to be remarkably pure and greatly compassionate, and the fact that he was discussed in such detail hints that he was emerging as an ideal that unenlightened beings might emulate. The Buddha himself was seen by most Mahāsāṃghikas (especially the Lokottaravādins) as utterly transmundane (*lokottara*); therefore, his birth, struggles, enlightenment and passing are merely projections of a completely purified being. This view represents a radical break with the Sthaviravāda view, and points towards the docetic speculations that would be so prevalent in the Mahāyāna. Finally, at least one Mahāsāṃghika tradition, the Prajñaptivāda sub-school of the Gokulika, seems to have asserted that all conditioned *dharmas* (including those of the present) or even all *dharmas* whatsoever (including *nirvāṇa*) must be understood – at least on an ultimate level – as fictions (*prajñapti*). This represents a radical extension of the early Buddhist rejection of self, and anticipates the sort of analysis to be found in later Mahāyāna literature, especially that of the Madhyamaka school.

Pudgalavāda

Sources

'Pudgalavāda' (the 'personalist doctrine') is not the name of a particular school, but is, rather, a designation used occasionally by later writers to refer to that group of schools that separated from Sthaviravāda in the third century BC over the question of the existence of a 'person' (*pudgala*) that assures continuity within and between one's lives. The original Pudgalavāda splinter group seems to have been designated the Vātsīputrīya (after its founder, Vātsīputra), but a number of sub-schools developed over the centuries, including the Dharmottarīya, Bhadrayānīya, Sammatīya and Ṣaṇṇagarika. The most important of these, the Sammatīya, was observed by the Chinese traveller Hsüan-tsang [Xuanzang] to be flourishing in the seventh century AD, and Tāranātha reports the persistence of Pudgalavāda in the period just before the Turkic invasions. Unfortunately, we have almost no literature from the Pudgalavādins themselves, and must content ourselves with reconstructing their doctrines largely from the accounts of later Indian and Chinese writers who opposed them.[8]

Problematic

The Pudgalavādins developed theses on any number of important points of Buddhist practice, but the doctrine that drew the greatest attention – not to mention ire – from other Buddhists was their assertion of a real 'person'. This distinctive theory was developed in response to one of the central problems of Buddhist philosophy: how to account for 'personal' continuity within and between lives when impermanence and no-self are the nature of all phenomena, including the aggregates that comprise the 'person'. Every school that attempted to construct a positive account of the categories and distribution of *dharmas* was forced to provide an explanation that somehow accounted for continuity without positing a permanent self. What set the Pudgalavādin answer apart from the others was the boldness with which it proclaimed the existence of a category that almost no one else would admit: a non-permanent, non-impermanent, non-identical, non-different 'person'. Given the choice between undermining continuity and risking assertion of a self, the Pudgalavādins chose the latter option, and no doubt felt that in doing so they had found a middle way between Hindu eternalism and the causal nihilism they saw implicit in Sthaviravāda.

Perspectives

Taking as their scriptural support passages where the Buddha talks of a 'person' being reborn, or makes a distinction between 'the burden' (the five aggregates) and 'the bearer of the burden' (a person), the Pudgalavādins asserted the existence of a 'person'. The person is that in a being that 'knows' *dharmas*, is the only factor that assures continuity within a lifetime, and is the only principle that survives death, to take rebirth with a new set of aggregates. The person's relation to the aggregates is neither identity nor difference, and its own nature is neither permanent nor impermanent, conditioned nor unconditioned. The Pudgalavādins no doubt felt that they had arrived at a satisfactory compromise between *ātman*-eternalism on the one hand and the utter discontinuity threatened by radical interpretations of the doctrine of impermanence on the other. In the eyes of most other Buddhists, however, the Pudgalavādins were quasi-heretical, having misconstrued the Buddha's conventional references to a person as somehow entailing a real principle beyond the mere name, 'person', and having implied, by their denial that the person is purely impermanent, that it must be permanent – for this is the only alternative in the two-valued logic favoured by most Buddhist thinkers. Thus, most other Buddhists regarded Pudgalavāda as a crypto-*ātman* view – though it is ironic (and unsurprising) that such views continued to appear in various guises in the course of Buddhist thought, whether as the 'matrix of enlightenment' (*tathāgatagarbha*) of Mahāyāna speculation, or the 'pure mind' (*cittaviśuddhi*) of the tantric tradition.

Sarvāstivāda/Vaibhāṣika

Sources

Sarvāstivāda (the 'doctrine that everything exists') separated from Sthaviravāda in the third century BC, sometime after the Pudgalavāda schism. It became influential in the north-west of India and Kashmir, whence it eventually spread via trade routes into China and Tibet; in Tibet, it (or, more properly, one of its sub-schools, Mūlasarvāstivāda) provided the *vinaya* that is the basis of Buddhist monastic life. It seems never to have existed as a separate philosophical school in Tibet, though it was well known there. In China, it was one of the first schools to be established, but it faded eventually in the face of Chinese enthusiasm for Mahāyāna and persecutions by anti-Buddhist emperors. In India, it seems to have persisted and flourished until the Turkic invasions. Like the other schools we have discussed, Sarvāstivāda developed contending sub-schools. The most important of these was the Vaibhāṣika, which arose in the first centuries AD among the exponents of the *Mahāvibhāṣa* a great *abhidharma* compendium. Vaibhāṣika is often treated as synonymous with Sarvāstivāda, and it is on Vaibhāṣika doctrines that we shall concentrate here, but technically, Vaibhāṣika must be regarded simply as the most influential later branch of the larger school that was Sarvāstivāda. Though only a few of its texts are extant in the original Sanskrit, the majority of Sarvāstivāda literature was preserved in Chinese and/or Tibetan, so we have more information on it than on other extinct schools. Preserved in Chinese are Sarvāstivāda's *Tripiṭaka*, as well as most of its later *abhidharma* literature, including the *Mahāvibhāṣa* and the writings of such luminaries as Vasumitra and Saṃghabhadra. The most important single work on Sarvāstivāda is probably the *Abhidharmakośa* of Vasubandhu (fourth–fifth century AD), which, together with its auto-commentary, is a lucid summary (and critique) of the Vaibhāṣika world-view. It is still studied by Tibetan Buddhists to this day.[9]

Problematic

Though they probably agreed with other Buddhists on the majority of doctrinal issues, the Sarvāstivādins distinguished themselves – and drew criticism – from other schools on the basis of their 'realism', their insistence that all (*sarva*) the *dharmas* into which the world could be analysed, whether conditioned or unconditioned, whether past, present or future, exist (*asti*) in a real, substantial sense. The problem to which such a view would seem to respond is similar to the one that vexed the Pudgalavādins: the doctrines of impermanence and no-self appear to entail both causal discontinuity and ontological nihilism. The Sarvāstivādins no doubt felt that such positions were philosophically problematic and spiritually dangerous, and that affirmation had to be permitted at a certain (if not commonsensical) level of analysis. They no doubt also felt that their analysis was a middle way between the 'nihilism' entailed, if not admitted, by Sthaviravāda views and the eternalism to which the Pudgalavādins were prey. Sarvāstivāda also introduced analyses of the nature of the Buddha and of the *bodhisattva* that address the same issues that centrally motivated the Mahāsāṃghika, namely how to conceive a being who has passed beyond the world, and what sort of spiritual models we who are left behind should emulate.

Perspectives

As expounded in the *Abhidharmakośa*, the Sarvāstivāda cosmology is essentially fivefold, being divided into (1) matter (*rūpa*), which is elevenfold: five types of sense-object, five types of sense-organ, and a type of subtle form, (2) mind (*citta*), which is the basic awareness brought to any cognitive situation, (3) forty-six types of mental factor (*caitta*), which are our various mental dispositions and qualities, (4) fourteen formations unassociated with either mind or matter (*rūpacittaviprayuktasaṃskāras*), including the phases through which entities pass in arising and ceasing and a glue-like 'obtainer' (*prāpti*) that assures karmic continuity and (5) unconditioned (*asaṃskṛta*) *dharmas*, which are three: space and non-analytical and analytical cessations (the latter include *nirvāṇa*). These seventy-five *dharmas* into which reality may be analysed are said by

Sarvāstivāda all to be existents (*bhāva*) that are real (*sat*), substantially established (*dravyasiddha*) and possessed of their own defining nature (*svabhāva*). Thus, a number of *dharmas* whose substantial existence was denied by other schools were admitted by the Sarvāstivāda: the past and future, *nirvāṇa* and negations, and the 'obtainer' of karmic results. Conditioned *dharmas* were said ultimately and 'really' to be atomic moments (*kṣaṇa*), which passed through phases of arising, subsisting, ceasing and non-existence. Sarvāstivāda was realistic in epistemology, too, asserting that a consciousness, whether mental or sensory, directly cognizes its objects. Soteriologically, Sarvāstivāda maintained the Hīnayāna emphasis on the achievement of *arhat* status. It articulated a framework consisting of five 'paths': accumulation, preparation, seeing, development and no-more-training; speculated on the possibility that the Buddha's '*dharma* body' (*dharmakāya*) might be an enduring principle beyond the mere 'body of texts' he left behind; and discussed the six 'perfections' (*pāramitā*: charity, morality, patience, zeal, concentration and wisdom) practised by the *bodhisattva*. Reorientated, the five-path system, *dharma* body and six perfections would all become focal points in Mahāyāna literature.

Sautrāntika

Sources

Sautrāntika ('*sūtra*-follower') is one of the most confusing names in Buddhist philosophy. It is used by scholars, both traditional and modern, to designate one, or a combination, of the following: (1) an anti-*abhidharma* school, of which no literature remains, that split off from Sarvāstivāda sometime in the first centuries AD, (2) the school reflected in many of Vasubandhu's criticisms of Sarvāstivāda in his commentary to his *Abhidharmakośa* and (3) the school of the great sixth- and seventh-century 'logicians', Dignāga and Dharmakīrti. Here, I shall apply the term only to the first two, which seem consistent, if not clearly contiguous, with each other. Dignāga and Dharmakīrti do reflect a number of ontological perspectives found in earlier Sautrāntika, but their sophisticated epistemological and logical analyses and their Mahāyāna context make them different enough from their predecessors for us to designate them separately, as Pramāṇavāda, and consider them later. Aside from Vasubandhu's *Abhidharmakośa* commentary, there is no Sautrāntika literature extant, and the school seems to have been absorbed in India by the Pramāṇavāda by the middle of the first millennium AD. Because of the influence of Vasubandhu and the logicians, however, Sautrāntika ideas gained wide currency, and it was enshrined by later Indian and Tibetan doxographers as one of the two standard Hīnayāna schools, the other being Vaibhāṣika.[10]

Problematic

Sautrāntika has sometimes been characterized as a school of 'critical realism', or even 'nominalism', and implicit in these names is a contrast with the sort of straightforward realism exemplified by Sarvāstivāda. The basic problem to which Sautrāntikas responded was the danger of absolutizing *dharmas* that is suggested by *abhidharma* analysis in general and Sarvāstivāda in particular. The Sarvāstivāda penchant for granting 'substantial reality' not only to impermanent *dharmas*, but also to rather more abstract concepts, such as space, cessations, the past and future, the phases of a 'momentary' entity, and the mysterious 'obtainer', was perceived by Sautrāntikas as starting down a road that led inevitably to eternalism, and hence to a form of the *ātman*-view that no Buddhist could countenance. Because the *ātman*-view was known to be the root cause of our suffering in *saṃsāra*, Sautrāntikas saw a need to counter Sarvāstivāda realism, and they called for a radical re-evaluation both of the ontology of *dharmas* and of the value of the *abhidharma* tradition itself. By rejecting Sarvāstivāda and much of the *abdhidharma*, Sautrāntikas no doubt saw themselves as having returned to the middle way preached by the Buddha in the *sūtras* (hence the name, 'Sautrāntika'): between eternalism (of which naïve realism is a precursor) and nihilism (which could never be accepted as long as dependent origination was presupposed).

Perspectives

As already indicated, one of Sautrāntika's important contributions was to question the validity, as the word of the Buddha, of the *abhidharma* tradition. Of greater philosophical interest, however, was the way in which Sautrāntika analysed and criticized the doctrines of the Sarvāstivāda. In ontology, Sautrāntika maintains first of all that unconditioned *dharmas*, such as space and *nirvāṇa*, exist only as designations or fictions (*prajñapti*), not as substantial entities. Further, they deny the existence of the 'obtainer' of karmic results, seeing in it a crypto-*ātman*. They explain continuity in general by the dependently originated co-ordination of momentary events of varying types, and the obtaining of karmic results in particular by the moment-to-moment 'perfuming' of the mental series by 'traces' (*vāsanā*) left by actions. They also reject the substantial existence of the past and future, accepting the reality only of present moments and entities, for only in the present can there be the 'efficiency' (*arthakriyatva*) that is the legitimate criterion of 'existence'. Present moments cannot, as Sarvāstivāda asserted, be analysed into phases of arising, subsisting, ceasing and non-existence, for each of these phases could be analysed in its own sub-phases, in a process that leads to an infinite regress. Rather, present momentary entities are virtually durationless, ceasing in the same instant in which they arise, lasting only long enough to effect subsequent, equally momentary entities. Continuous 'things', therefore, are an illusion, like a circle of fire seen when a torch is rotated swiftly. To this degree, even conditioned *dharmas* may be seen as 'fictions'. Epistemologically, Sautrāntika adopts what has been called a 'representational realism': a consciousness does directly perceive its object, but for so brief an instant that the awareness of a particular object actually is the perception of a remembered image of the object. Soteriologically, Sautrāntika differs little from Sarvāstivāda. Though its nominalist and representationalist tendencies still are rooted in a form of 'realism' – the reality of efficient entities – Sautrāntika very much echoes the radically critical spirit of Madhyamaka and the 'idealism' of Yogācāra, so it is not surprising that it would be adopted and adapted by later representatives of these Mahāyāna schools, and thus continue to influence Buddhist philosophy down to the present day, through the Tibetan tradition.

MAHĀYĀNA SCHOOLS

As noted earlier, Mahāyāna Buddhists are ultimately distinguishable from Hīnayānists essentially on the basis of their acceptance of a significantly larger collection of discourses attributed to the Buddha. Uniquely Mahāyāna *sūtras* (and *tantras*) have certain themes and emphases that differ from those of Hīnayāna *sūtras*, such as the quest for full buddhahood rather than arhantship, the skill and compassion of the *bodhisattva* as both saviour and model, and the doctrine of the emptiness (*śūnyatā)* of all entities. Among the earliest, and certainly the philosophically most important, Mahāyāna *sūtras* are the Perfection of Wisdom (*prajñāpāramitā*) scriptures, whose rhetorical exposition of the emptiness of all phenomena, conditioned and unconditioned, profane and sacred, sets the tone for much subsequent Mahāyāna philosophizing. Indeed, much of the Mahāyāna philosophy that I shall examine here must be seen as at least an implicit attempt to work out the full implications of the Perfection of Wisdom's unsystematic, but powerful, negative rhetoric. At the same time, we must recognize that 'Mahāyāna philosophy' drew also on insights developed in Hīnayāna schools, and may not mark a radical break so much as a shift along the same continuum.[11] Late Indian and Tibetan doxographers distinguished two Mahāyāna philosophical schools, Madhyamaka and Yogācāra. These terms, however, cover a multitude of viewpoints, and I shall distinguish here between early, critical Madhyamaka and its later ramification into the critical and synthetic sub-schools that the Tibetans came to call Prāsaṅgika and Svātantrika, and between those Yogācāras who were primarily concerned with metaphysics and psychology (those 'following scripture', according to Tibetans) and those – the Pramāṇavādins – concerned primarily with epistemology and logic (those 'following reasoning').

Early Madhyamaka

Sources

Madhyamaka (the 'middle' school) is traced primarily to the writings of Nāgārjuna, a south Indian of the first or second century AD, and secondarily to his disciple, Āryadeva. Its radically critical perspective on traditional Indian ontology attracted both supporters and virulent detractors almost immediately, and it flourished and grew in India right up to the Turkic invasions. In the mean time, it was exported to both China and Tibet, and so came to influence developments throughout the Mahāyāna world. Madhyamaka deeply (if not always directly) affected Chinese Ch'an and Japanese Zen, and it is nominally the philosophical school followed by almost all Tibetan Buddhists. There is much debate among both traditional and modern scholars as to which of the numerous works attributed to Nāgārjuna were actually written by him, and some modern scholars have questioned whether he really was a Mahāyānist. If one accepts the *śāstras* and tantric works attributed to him by Chinese and Tibetan tradition (these only partially overlap), then he was clearly a Mahāyānist, whose philosophical works may be seen as a commentary on the Perfection of Wisdom's concept of 'emptiness'. If one accepts only his most purely philosophical works, the *Madhyamakakārikā* (*Stanzas of the Middle School*) and the *Vigrahavyavārtanī* (*Turning Aside Objections*), then the absence of particular references to Mahāyāna *sūtras* can be used to argue that he was not a Mahāyānist. Unfortunately, there are no purely internal criteria for determining which texts are authentic, so decisions are made primarily on the basis of prior ideological commitment. The resulting hermeneutical circle cannot be broken, so we cannot decide the issue of Nāgārjuna's affiliation with certainty. What is certain, however, is that it is almost exclusively upon Mahāyāna that his thought has exercised influence, so the Madhyamaka school that he founded safely may be considered Mahāyānist.[12]

Problematic

Uniquely among the Buddhist schools that we have examined, Madhyamaka actually calls itself a 'middle way'. The middle way to which it refers is apparently the ontological middle between existence and non-existence referred to in the early *Mahākatyāyana Sūtra*, which Nāgārjuna cites. The rhetoric of early Madhyamaka literature, however, is almost relentlessly negative. Nāgārjuna prefaces his *Madhyamakakārikā* with the proclamation that the Buddha taught 'non-cessation and non-arising, non-destruction and non-persistence, non-identity and non-difference, non-coming and non-going', and in chapter after chapter of their treatises, he and Āryadeva attempt systematically to undermine – to show the 'emptiness' (*śūnyatā*) of

– the crucial concepts and categories of Indian philosophy: *ātman*, God, causality, motion, time, *karma*, the aggregates, the sensory spheres – even the Buddha and *nirvāṇa*. In early Madhyamaka (as in the Perfection of Wisdom *sūtras*), it is primarily *Buddhist* concepts and categories that are negated, and it seems fair to conclude that the central problematic to which Nāgārjuna was responding was the abhidharmist – especially Sarvāstivādin – tendency to see the various *dharmas* into which the cosmos may be analysed as 'substantially established' (*dravyasiddha*) or possessing some type of 'self-existence' (*svabhāva*). The concern with such views, in turn, would seem to be founded ultimately on spiritual considerations: belief in some type of self-existence – even of impermanent *dharmas* or conceptual categories – entails belief in a self, and that, Buddhists have insisted from the earliest times, is the basis of our suffering in *saṃsāra*. Thus, the Madhyamaka insistence that all entities and concepts are 'empty' may be seen as a radical, but logical, extension of the early Buddhist doctrine of no-self, rooted in the understanding that a permanent, independent, partless 'self' may be imputed not only to persons (their traditional locus), but to virtually any object of knowledge – including no-self or emptiness itself. Since every seedbed of a self-view must be destroyed, every entity or concept there is must be shown to be empty.

Perspectives

The way in which Madhyamaka demonstrates the emptiness of various entities and concepts is critical and dialectical rather than syllogistic. The basic technique is that of a fourfold *reductio ad absurdum* (*catuṣkoṭi*) in which, through a relentless application of the law of the excluded middle, entities and concepts are shown not to be expressible either as *x*, non-*x*, both *x* and non-*x*, or neither *x* nor non-*x*. Entities are shown to originate in dependence on other entities and concepts to be incomprehensible without reference to other concepts. If they are not independent, they cannot possess self-existence (*svabhāva*), and so must be considered empty, without true foundation. As noted above, this sort of analysis is applied not only to the concepts usually rejected by Buddhists, such as *ātman* and God, but also to key Buddhist concepts. Nāgārjuna argues, for instance, that an effect cannot be shown to originate from itself (for cause and effect must be distinguishable), something utterly different (for there must be some sort of connection), or both (two wrongs don't make a right), or neither (which begs the question). Similarly, *nirvāṇa* cannot be said to exist (if it does, it is permanent, hence a self), not-exist (if it doesn't, what are Buddhists striving for?), or both or neither (as before). Nāgārjuna also argues that the sources of epistemic authority (*pramāṇa*) on which we generally rely, such as perception and inference, turn out on examination to be self-referential and unfounded, hence themselves empty, too.

This thoroughgoing Madhyamaka critique was taken by many Indians, both Buddhist and non-Buddhist, to be sheer nihilism. It is evident from the crucial twenty-fourth chapter of the *Madhyamakakārika*, however, that this is not so. There, Nāgārjuna specifically refutes the charge of nihilism by invoking the concept of 'Two Truths' (*satyadvaya*). From the ultimate (*paramārtha*) perspective, all entities and concepts are empty, without foundation. From a conventional or phenomenal (*saṃvṛti*) perspective, however, entities and concepts do exist: there is cause and effect, bondage and liberation, etc. Indeed, were entities *not* empty (hence self-existent), we could not explain the phenomenal, changing world we know. It is precisely *because* they are empty ultimately (hence capable of change and relation) that entities and concepts can be said to exist conventionally. In sum, Nāgārjuna establishes an equivalency between dependent origination (a conventional account of how things exist) and emptiness (their ultimate nature): the one entails the other, and this equivalency is said to be 'the middle'. Indeed, it should be evident now why Madhyamaka is, as it proclaims, a 'middle way' between 'existence' and 'non-existence'. It denies that ultimately anything exists independently, by its own nature, but does not deny that, on a conventional level, entities and concepts do originate in dependence on one another. There is little explicit soteriology in early Madhyamaka, but the attainment of wisdom (*prajñā*) and the stilling of conceptual proliferation (*prapañca*) of which Nāgārjuna speaks evidently rest upon an ability to see that emptiness is the nature of all, and that there exists nowhere a self. However, emptiness itself must not be absolutized any more than other concepts, and conventionally, precisely because they are empty/dependently originated, the path-practices of which Buddhists have traditionally spoken may be pursued with confidence.

Yogācāra

Sources

Yogācāra (the 'yoga practice' school), known alternatively as Cittamātra ('mind-only') or Vijñānavāda ('consciousness-only'), arose in the early centuries AD as a constructive, metaphysically complex, philosophically 'idealist' alternative to Madhyamaka. It reached its apogee around the middle of the first millennium, then gradually lost ground among Mahāyānists to various later versions of Madhyamaka – some of which incorporated Yogācāra elements. Through the efforts of the great translator Hsüan-tsang, it exercised considerable influence on early Buddhist movements in China, and many of its treatises are still read by the Tibetans, who consider it second only to Madhyamaka in philosophical subtlety. Unlike Madhyamaka, it is clearly traceable not only to writers of *śāstras*, but to the Perfection of Wisdom and other Mahāyāna *sūtras*, in which many of its crucial concepts may first have appeared. Among these, the most important are probably the *Saṃdhinirmocana*, which discusses, *inter alia*, the theories of the three turnings of the *Dharma*-wheel, the three natures of existents, the world as 'concept only' (*vijñaptimātra*) and the storehouse consciousness (*ālaya-vijñāna*); and the *Laṅkāvatāra*, which discusses the theory of mind-only, as well the storehouse consciousness and the matrix of enlightenment (*tathāgatagarbha*) within each sentient being. At least as ancient as these *sūtras* are parts of the *Yogācārabhūmi*, an immense Yogācāra compendium of doubtful authorship. Aside from the *Yogācārabhūmi*, the most important Yogācāra *śāstra* sources are the works of Asaṅga (fourth century AD), who wrote several clearly attributable treatises, including a 'Mahāyāna *abdhidharma*', the *Abhidharmasamuccaya*, and a great compendium of Mahāyāna metaphysics, the *Mahāyānasaṃgraha*. He also (according to some traditions) 'transmitted' five texts received in visions from the buddha Maitreya: the *Abhisamayālaṃkāra* (a soteriological systematization of certain Perfection of Wisdom themes), *Madhyāntavibhāga* (on the Yogācāra 'middle way'), *Dharmadharmatāvibhāga* (on the true nature of *dharmas*), *Mahāyānasūtrālaṃkāra* (a metaphysical compendium) and *Ratnagotravibhāga* (on *tathāgatagarbha*, or, more properly, the pure 'element' [*dhātu*] within us). A number of philosophically sophisticated Yogācāra treatises were also written by Vasubandhu, including the *Viṃśatikā* (which seeks to establish 'concept only'), the *Triṃśikā* and a number of commentaries on earlier texts. Two great commentators later in the tradition (sixth century) were Sthiramati and Dharmapāla.[13]

Problematic

The problematic to which Yogācāra writers responded appears to have been twofold: the concern to assert a more positive vision in the face of the perceived nihilism of Madhyamaka, and a concern to explore to its limit the problem of the relation between consciousness and world. The first concern is expressed in the seventh chapter of the *Saṃdhinirmocana Sūtra*, where a 'history' of the Buddha's teachings (and a basis for later Buddhist hermeneutics) is given. The first time he turned the wheel of *Dharma*, he taught Sarvāstivāda-style realism. This was only provisional (*neyārtha*), however, and since it conduced to eternalism, he turned the wheel a second time, teaching the doctrine of emptiness. This, however, was also provisional, since it conduced to nihilism, so he turned the wheel a third time, imparting the definitive (*nītārtha*) teaching that discriminates among those entities that exist and those that do not. This 'middle way' between Sarvāstivādin eternalism and Madhyamaka nihilism was, of course, Yogācāra, especially its teaching of the three natures, which will be discussed below. The second concern, about the status of the external world, arose from a number of sources. Buddhists had maintained from the earliest times that much of what we think is 'real' and 'objective' is merely a result of our afflicted conceptualizations (*vikalpa*), and a number of *sūtras* had spoken of the 'dream-' or 'illusion-like' nature of the world. Hīnayāna epistemology had moved from the objective realism of

Sarvāstivāda to the representationalism of Sautrāntika. All of these trends tended to bring under suspicion the objective, external reality of the world and its objects – belief in which, after all, might in its own way lead to eternalism, hence to undermining the doctrine of no-self. Thus, Yogācāra took the final, logical step, and declared that the external world was no different from the consciousness that perceived it, was 'mind-only' (*cittamātra*).

Perspectives

The crucial doctrine in Yogācāra ontology was of the 'three natures' (*svabhāva*; alternatively, 'characteristics': *lakṣaṇa*) under which all existents could be found: (1) the dependent nature (*paratantra*) is the conditioned reality of entities, real in so far as it is comprehended, unreal in so far as it is misunderstood; (2) the imaginary nature (*parikalpita*) is the self-existence we wrongly impute to the dependent nature, utterly unreal; (3) the absolute nature (*pariniṣpanna*) is the complete absence of self-existence in the dependent nature. It is this willingness to affirm some entities while denying others that, in its own view, separates Yogācāra from Madhyamaka 'nihilism'. As Yogācāra thought develops, it is increasingly evident that the 'self-existence' that the dependent nature lacks is a self-sufficient *externality*, and so the absolute nature is expressed with increasing frequency as subject–object non-duality, or, more positively, mind-only, or concept-only. Whether we call it 'idealism' or 'phenomenalism', Yogācāra maintains that the 'triple world' of *saṃsāra* is merely a conceptual construct. Vasubandhu attempts to make the case in his *Viṃśatikā*: he argues that the criteria we use to assure externality in the waking state – three-dimensionality, temporal continuity, intersubjectivity and efficacy – can all be observed in dreams, and that just as dreams are sublated by waking, so is the externality of entities in the waking state sublated by a wisdom-consciousness. The psychological and metaphysical implications of the doctrine of mind-only were worked out primarily through the theory of the storehouse consciousness (*ālaya-vijñāna*), a neutral, momentary mental substrate that explains continuity and is the ultimate source of the traditional six consciousnesses and their (non-different) objects, as well as a 'defiled mind' that distorts our understanding. When the storehouse consciousness is purified by a 'basic transformation' (*āśraya-parāvṛtti*), the defiled mind disappears, and the world is seen as it is, with the mind of a buddha. Because of its systematic tendencies, it was Yogācāra that provided most of the framework for Mahāyāna soteriology: a version of the five-path system, an explication of the ten *bodhisattva* levels, a delineation of the three 'bodies' of a buddha, and the first explorations of the concept of the matrix of enlightenment, the *tathāgatagarbha* that is the pure element within us that assures our eventual enlightenment.

Pramāṇavāda

Sources

The term 'Pramāṇavāda' (the 'authority doctrine') is a neologism, invented to distinguish its approach to philosophy from that of the two major sources on which its proponents drew, Sautrāntika and Yogācāra. Sautrāntika, as we have seen, was a critical Hīnayāna school whose major contribution was an ontology of momentariness, while Yogācāra was a Mahāyāna school that emphasized the 'conceptual' nature of external reality. Pramāṇavādins incorporate these crucial elements from the two foregoing traditions, but add enough wrinkles of their own (including non-Buddhist influences) to warrant their designation by more than simply 'Sautrāntika Yogācāra', or, as the Tibetans identify them, 'Cittamātrins Following Reasoning'. What sets them apart as a '*pramāṇa*' school is that, whatever their views on momentariness or mind-only, their central concern is with the enumeration, delineation and detailing of the sources of epistemic authority, the *pramāṇas*, and then with applying those authorities to the adjudication of various philosophical disputes, both intra-and inter-traditionally. The works of both Vasubandhu and Asaṅga reveal at least an elementary interest in questions of *pramāṇa*, but their major interests, as we have seen, lie elsewhere. The first writer to make *pramāṇa* a central concern was Dignāga, a south Indian of the sixth century AD. In his various essays, and above all in his masterwork, the *Pramāṇasamuccaya*, Dignāga placed Buddhist theories of perception and inference on a firm footing, while at the same time attacking a variety of Buddhist (especially Sarvāstivādin) and non-Buddhist theories of reality. He was succeeded in the seventh century by Dharmakīrti, who, in such works as the *Pramāṇavārttika* and *Pramāṇaviniścaya*, refined many of Dignāga's theories on perception and inference, and sought to turn formal inference (*anumāna*) to the task of establishing the validity of various Buddhist metaphysical doctrines. Though he was perhaps less original than Dignāga, Dharmakīrti was a subtle and powerful thinker, and his works drew the admiring and critical attention of subsequent generations of philosophers. Among Buddhists, he became the primary inspiration for such later figures as Dharmottara, Jñānaśrīmitra and Ratnakīrti (and secondarily inspired many later Mādhyamikas), who carried the *pramāṇa* tradition to the final days of Buddhism in India. *Pramāṇa* was never a major topic of interest in China, but in Tibet, it became an important field of study, accepted as the basis for determining truth in conventional matters – and even some ultimate ones.[14]

Problematic

The issues that motivated the articulation of the Hīnayāna and early Mahāyāna schools were primarily intra-Buddhist: finding a middle way, explaining no-self *vis-à-vis* causal continuity, delineating what is real from what is not. Some thinkers, for example Vasubandhu, Nāgārjuna and Āryadeva, took time out to attack non-Buddhist schools, but were still animated essentially by problems generated within the Buddhist tradition of discourse. Towards the middle of the first millennium AD, however, there began to emerge among both Buddhist and non-Buddhist philosophers a rough consensus on certain crucial methodological issues, such as the rules of argumentation (*tarka*) and the structure of a formal inference, or 'syllogism'. These methodological advances, when fuelled by the heady cultural and religious atmosphere of the Gupta and post-Gupta ages, made possible for the first time a type of inter-traditional philosophical discussion that did not immediately collapse into the assertion of competing presuppositions. This, in turn, held out the promise (illusory or not) that reason might be able to adjudicate the great philosophical arguments that separated the traditions: the existence or non-existence of a self, the externality or internality of knowledge-objects, the relation between universals and particulars or words and objects, the validity of the Vedas, the existence of a creator God, etc. Dignāga and Dharmakīrti – the former more critically, the latter more constructively – both concerned themselves with these issues, and in so doing entered Buddhism into a philosophical fray that no subsequent Buddhist philosopher could really avoid. Pramāṇavādins placed a confidence in reason considerably beyond that evinced by the Buddha of the *nikāyas*, but they were not without their spiritual motives – the elucidation of *pramāṇa* turns out to be necessary because, as Dharmakīrti puts it (*Nyāyabindu* I, i), 'all human accomplishment is preceded by correct cognition'. Thus, in spiritual as in ordinary life, we must secure proper knowledge before succeeding in our projects. To do this, however, we must know how to distinguish between correct and incorrect, and we only can do this if we understand what is authoritative and what is not, i.e. we must know *pramāṇa*. Thus, Pramāṇavāda comes to be a middle way between an anti-rationalism so thoroughgoing that it rejects philosophy and a rationalism so uncompromising that it eliminates the spiritual life.

Perspectives

As already noted, Pramāṇavāda ontology combined a Sautrāntika insistence on the radically momentary, nominal nature of all conditioned phenomena with a Yogācāra denial that external reality was ultimately separable from the consciousness that perceives it. The doctrine of momentariness (*kṣaṇikatva*) entailed a Pramāṇavādin rejection of any theory (for example Sāṃkhya) that defined causality in terms of 'development' or 'manifestation'. Entailed by the tradition's nominalism was the reality only of that which is causally efficient; hence, Pramāṇavādins rejected the existence of 'universals' (*sāmānya*) like those posited by Vaiśeṣikas, affirming only concrete particulars, and explaining that we come to know 'classes' through a double-negative exclusion (*apoha*) of what is other than a member of a particular class. Their nominalism and idealism similarly led Pramāṇavādins to deny (contra the Nyāya) that a word and its referent are intrinsically related, since there exists no external referent that can finally be distinguished from the term that denotes it.

Pramāṇavādins accept two, and only two, epistemic authorities: perception (*pratyakṣa*) and inference (*anumāna*); this entails the subsumption of testimony under inference, robs it of its independence, and so vitiates the claim by Mīmāṃsā and other Hindu schools that the Vedas stand as an independent source of knowledge. Perception is for the Pramāṇavāda fourfold: sense-perception, which is direct for an instant, then representational; mental perception, which includes cognitions immediately subsequent to sense-impressions, as well as paranormal cognitions; yogic perception, which is a direct realization of a crucial soteriological principle, for example the Four Noble Truths or no-self; and apperception, which is an awareness simultaneous with any of the previous three, and is used (rather than a storehouse consciousness) to explain memory. Inference, as articulated by Dignāga and Dharmakīrti, involves deducing an unknown from commonly accepted, perceptually based knowns. Specifically, a subject (*dharmin*: for example a hill) is proven to possess a predicate (*sādhya*: for example fire) through the presence of a reason (*hetu*) or mark (*liṅga*: for example smoke). The reason must be found in the subject (there is smoke on the hill) and positively and negatively concomitant with the predicate (where there's smoke there's fire, as in a kitchen; where there's no smoke, there's no fire, as in a lake). The examples (kitchen and lake) are sometimes taken as superfluous elements of the inference, but they are the bedrock of Buddhist syllogism, and show the degree to which perception – even a thousand years after the Buddha – is still the ultimate basis of truth for Buddhists: an inference derives its 'force' from the actual, perceived nature of entities.

Most Pramāṇavāda writings focus on epistemological and logical problems, but soteriology is not forgotten. The most systematic soteriological arguments were proffered by Dharmakīrti, who attempted in the second chapter of the *Pramāṇavārttika* to use formal inference against a whole array of opponents to demonstrate that the essential doctrines of the Buddhist world-view – atheism, rebirth, the Four Noble Truths, the soteriological value of a realization of no-self – are true, and that the Buddha, uniquely, is an embodiment of *pramāṇa* (*pramāṇabhūta*). Whether or not his arguments succeeded, they became an important part of Pramāṇavāda tradition, along with the epistemological and logical theories on which they were based, though it is the latter that are certainly the school's unique and greatest contribution to Buddhist philosophy.

Later Madhyamaka

Sources

Around the middle of the first millennium AD, the various logical and epistemological currents sweeping the Indian philosophical world began to affect Madhyamaka, and a dispute arose within the school between those who believed that Madhyamaka analysis only could be carried out via a *reductio ad absurdum* (*prasaṅga*) like that employed by Nāgārjuna, and those who believed that it could be effected via independent (*svātantra*) inferences of the sort favoured by the Pramāṇavāda. The former group came to be designated later by Tibetan doxographers as the Prāsaṅgika, the latter as the Svātantrika. The dispute was inaugurated by the first Svātantrika, Bhāvaviveka (sixth century), who, in a commentary to Nāgārjuna's *Madhyamaka-kārikā*, criticized his older contemporary, Buddhapālita, for failing in *his* commentary on Nāgārjuna to take advantage of the full array of logical tools at his disposal, thus depriving Mādhyamikas of important ways of demonstrating the emptiness of all phenomena. Bhāvaviveka was attacked, and Buddhapālita defended, by Candrakīrti (seventh century), who is the great exponent of Prāsaṅgika. In such works as the *Prasannapadā* (his commentary on Nāgārjuna) and the *Madhyamakāvatāra*, he argued strongly against the use of independent inferences, as well as the Svātantrika suggestion that, conventionally, phenomena might be said to possess their own defining characteristics (*svalakṣaṇa*). After Candrakīrti, the Prāsaṅgika tradition was taken up in India by such figures as Śāntideva (eighth century) and Atīśa (eleventh century), and it became eventually the dominant philosophical perspective among Tibetan Buddhists – who would, of course, differ widely in interpreting it. The Svātantrika sub-school also continued to flourish. Such later works as the *Abhisamayālaṃkārāloka* of Haribhadra, *Tattvasaṃgraha* of Śāntarakṣita, the three *Bhavanākramas* of Kamalaśīla and the various writings of Jñānagarbha (all eighth century) extended Bhāvaviveka's synthetic tendencies by further incorporating Sautrāntika-based theories of momentariness, the Yogācāra theory of mind-only, and the logical techniques developed by Dignāga and Dharmakīrti.[15]

Problematic

Like the Pramāṇavādins, later Mādhyamikas found themselves in a wide-open philosophical world, in which debates between traditions were at least as common as those within traditions. Thus, we find that both Prāsaṅgikas and Svātantrikas trained their sights on non-Buddhist opponents, against whom they sought to uphold such essential doctrines as rebirth, no-self, momentariness, atheism, and the non-existence of universals. In their debates between themselves, Prāsangikas and Svātantrikas presupposed the truth of all these doctrines, but both claimed that their interpretation of them found the 'middle ground' perennially sought by Buddhists. Thus, Svātantrikas insisted that only by granting the value of independent inference and accepting that entities existed conventionally via their own characteristics could one preserve conventional discourse and conventional truth. Nāgārjuna, after all, had insisted that the ultimate truth depends on the conventional, and the Prāsaṅgika reliance only on the *reductio* and their denial of defining characteristics even conventionally would seem to negate the conventional, hence invite both an end to debate and a descent into nihilism. If the Svātantrikas were motivated by a fear of nihilism, it should not surprise us that the Prāsaṅgikas were responding to their own fear that the Svātantrikas risked eternalism, for by accepting the validity of independent inferences, especially when such inferences related to ultimate truth, they would have to concede to their opponents that the phenomena that served as terms in the inference were conventionally established by their own characteristics. By such a concession, however, they posited a version of conventional truth that radically contradicted, rather then harmonized with, the ultimate truth (as, for example, dependent origination harmonized with emptiness) and also risked the next logical step, the admission that phenomena are self-existent ultimately, the very antithesis of the Madhyamaka view. From the Prāsaṅgika perspective, it was better to let an opponent's position collapse under the weight of its own contradictions than to risk the admission of *any* hint of self-existence, even if one were thereby to gain use of powerful logical weapons.[16]

Perspectives

The basic perspectives of the Prāsaṅgikas and Svātantrikas should be evident from the foregoing. They were essentially in agreement on the nature of ultimate truth, which was any phenomenon's emptiness of self-existence. This entailed their rejection of any other Buddhist account of ultimacy, from Sarvāstivāda and Sautrāntika versions of realism to Yogācāra idealism. It was on the level of conventional truth that their differences were clearest: the Svātantrikas accepted, and the Prāsaṅgikas rejected, the notion that entities might be said to exist conventionally according to their own characteristics; and the former also accepted, while the latter rejected or ignored, the possibility that one might admit, and even argue for, the conventional validity of such concepts as mind-only and momentariness. Whatever their differences regarding conventional truth, however, most later Mādhyamikas were explicitly soteriological in ways that Nāgārjuna perhaps was not. They accepted that their philosophical analyses comprised only the wisdom half of the wisdom–method pairing that led a *bodhisattva* to buddhahood, and developed various methods of integrating the analysis and contemplation of emptiness with traditional schemata such as the five-path system, the six perfections, the ten *bodhisattva* grounds, and the two, three or four bodies of a buddha.

Thus, the later phase of Madhyamaka in India is marked (albeit more among Svātantrikas than Prāsaṅgikas) by a pronounced synthetic tendency, in which many of the most important developments of Buddhism's first millennium – *abhidharma* categorizations, the theory of momentariness, the mind-only perspective, various sophisticated epistemological and logical ideas, the all-important teaching on emptiness, and a number of soteriological schemes – are brought together into a more or less harmonious configuration. This configuration may be understood as defining a 'middle' – but it is a middle that, unlike so many we have examined, is inclusive rather than exclusive of the various elements whose tension it seeks to resolve. In establishing such an inclusive middle, it mirrors the approach taken by Chinese Buddhist scholiasts of the same period, and anticipates the style that would come eventually to dominate Buddhism in Tibet, too.

NOTES

1 Exceptions include the writings of Vasumitra (fourth century AD), Bhāvaviveka (sixth century), Śāntarakṣita (eighth century), Vinītadeva (eighth century) and 'Āryadeva' (eleventh century). On doxography, see Mimaki 1976 and 1987 and Sopa and Hopkins 1976. For traditional histories that discuss philosophers, see Obermiller 1931–2 and Chimpa and Chattopadhyaya 1972. The most valuable modern history of Indian Buddhist philosophy is probably Warder 1980. Other useful surveys are found in Lamotte 1967, Conze 1967, Prebish 1975, Kalupahana 1976 and Kitagawa and Cummings 1989. Works that deal with Buddhist philosophy in a broader Indian context include Potter 1976 and Matilal 1971 and 1986. Works that are primarily bibliographical in nature include Potter 1977 and 1988 and Reynolds 1981.

2 Here, and in the 'sources' notes that follow, only a few references can be given. For more information on editions and translations of authors and works cited, the reader should consult bibliographies in the works cited here. The standard translation of the five *nikāyas*, *Dīgha* (Sanskrit: *Dīrgha*), *Majjhima* (*Madhyama*), *Saṃyutta* (*Saṃyukta*), *Aṅguttara* (*Ekottara*) and *Khuddaka Kṣudraka*) of the Pali canon is that of the Pali Text Society (London). The most useful one-volume distillation of the canon probably remains that of Warren (1984). Unfortunately, little has yet been translated from the Chinese versions of the *āgamas* drawn from the Sanskrit canons of the Sarvāstivādins and Dharmaguptakas – which largely, but not entirely, overlap the Theravādin canon. The best overall discussion of the philosophical standpoint of the *nikāyas* remains Jayatilleke 1980, which is the classic statement of the 'Buddhist empiricism thesis'. For a contrasting interpretation, see Hoffman 1987.

3 The most interesting treatment of no-self in an early Buddhist context is Collins 1982.

4 On the various traditional ways of arranging the Hīnayāna schools, see Bareau 1955: 15–30, Dutt 1970: 51–9, Kitagawa and Cummings 1989: 197–201 and Hirakawa 1990: 105–26. The traditional division into eighteen may reflect the number of different Hīnayāna *Tripiṭakas* said to have existed. Because it fails to distinguish schools from sub-schools, it is not useful for our purposes. I shall distinguish here among five major *types* of schools, under one of which all of the traditional eighteen may be found.

5 On *abhidhamma*, see the Pali Text Society's translations of the various components of the Pali *Abhidhamma-piṭaka*, as well as Ñāṇatiloka 1957 and Guenther 1976; for the *Visuddhimagga*, arguably Buddhaghosa's masterpiece, see Ñāṇamoli 1976.

6 For accounts of Sthaviravāda Theravāda, see Bareau 1955: 110, 160–258, Dutt 1970: 227–33, Prebish 1975: 39–41 and Warder 1980: 295–326.
7 For accounts of Mahāsāṃghika doctrines, see Bareau 1955: 56–109, Dutt 1970: 60–128, Prebish 1975: 36–8 and Warder 1980: 212–18, 326–41.
8 For accounts of Pudgalavāda, see Bareau 1955: 114–30 and Dutt 1970: 194–226.
9 For a translation of the *Abhidharmakośa* and its commentary, see La Vallée Poussin 1971–80. For further information on the history and doctrines of Sarvāstivāda, see Stcherbatsky 1970, as well as Bareau 1955: 131–52, Dutt 1970: 134–83, Prebish 1975: 41–5, Sopa and Hopkins 1976: 70–91, Warder 1980: 341–7 and Hirakawa 1990: 105–219.
10 Among Tibetan doxographers, 'Vaibhāṣika' usually referred to Sarvāstivāda, but sometimes it was said to comprise 'eighteen schools', and thus to serve as a catch-all for any non-Sautrāntika Hīnayāna tradition. On Sautrāntika, besides La Vallée Poussin 1971–80, see Bareau 1955: 155–66, Dutt 1970: 186–9 and Mimaki 1976: 195–9.
11 On the Perfection of Wisdom literature, see Lancaster 1977. On Mahāyāna philosophy in general, see Dutt 1977 and Williams 1989.
12 On Madhyamaka in general, see especially Robinson 1967 and Ruegg 1981, as well as Streng 1967, Prebish 1975: 76–96, Warder 1980: 373–92, Lindtner 1982, Nakamura 1987: 235–80, Huntington 1989, Williams 1989: 55–76 and Garfield 1995. The most useful edition/translation of the *Madhyamakakārikā* is probably Inada 1970, and of the *Vigrahavyāvartanī*, Bhattacharya 1978.
13 On Yogācāra, see Lamotte 1935, Ruegg 1968, Sopa and Hopkins 1976: 107–21; Warder 1980: 423–47, Kochumuttom 1982, Anacker 1984, Nakamura 1987: 253–83, Schmithausen 1987, Williams 1989: 77–105 and Powers 1995.
14 On Pramāṇavāda, see Stcherbatsky 1962, Prebish 1975: 127–32, Sopa and Hopkins 1976: 92–106, Warder 1980: 447–74, Nakamura 1987: 294–312, Jackson 1993 and Dreyfus 1996.
15 On Prāsaṅgika and Svātantrika, see Sopa and Hopkins 1976: 122–45, Lopez 1987, Nakamura 1987: 284–9, Williams 1989: 57–60. For Svātantrika texts, see Jha 1937–9 and Eckel 1986. The tendency of Haribhadra *et al.* to accept the conventional validity or usefulness of the concept of mind-only has led to the later designation of their position as Yogācāra-Svātantrika-Madhyamaka, in contrast to the Sautrāntika-Svātantrika-Madhyamaka of Bhāvaviveka, who vigorously opposed Yogācāra on every level.
16 It should be noted that Prāsaṅgika Mādhyamikas in Tibet, such as the dGe lugs pas, came to accept the use of formal inference, but with the proviso that it was not conventional *truth* that was established thereby, but merely 'worldly conventions'.

REFERENCES

Anacker, S. (trans.) (1984) *Seven Works of Vasubandhu*, Delhi: Motilal Banarsidass.
Bareau, A. (1955) *Les Sectes bouddhiques du Petit Véhicule*, Saigon: Ecole Française d'Extrême-Orient.
Bhattacharya, K. (ed.) (1978) *The Dialectical Method of Nāgārjuna (Vigrahavyāvartanī)*, Delhi: Motilal Banarsidass.
Chimpa, L. and Chattopadhyaya, A. (trans.) (1972) *Tāranātha's History of Buddhism in India*, Simla: Indian Institute of Advanced Study.
Collins, S. (1982) *Selfless Persons*, Cambridge: Cambridge University Press.
Conze, E. (1967) *Buddhist Thought in India*, Ann Arbor: University of Michigan Press.
Dreyfus, G (1996) *Recognizing Reality: Dharmakīrti's Philosophy and Its Tibetan Interpretations*, Albany: State University of New York Press
Dutt, N. (1970) *Buddhist Sects in India*, Calcutta: Firma K. L. Mukhopadhyay.
—— (1977) *Mahayana Buddhism*, Calcutta: Firma KLM Private.
Eckel, M. D. (1986) *Jñānagarbha's Commentary on the Distinction between the Two Truths*, Albany, N.Y.: State University of New York Press.

Garfield, J. (ed.) (1995) *The Fundamental Wisdom of the Middle Way*, New York: Oxford University Press.
Guenther, H. V. (1976) *Philosophy and Psychology in the Abhidharma*, Berkeley: Shambhala.
Hirakawa, A. (1990) *A History of Indian Buddhism: From Śākyamuni to Early Mahāyāna*, trans. P. Groner, Honolulu: University of Hawaii Press.
Hoffman, F. J. (1987) *Rationality and Mind in Early Buddhism*, Delhi: Motilal Banarsidass.
Huntington, C. W., Jr (1989) *The Emptiness of Emptiness*, Honolulu: University of Hawaii Press.
Inada, K. K. (1970) *Nāgārjuna: A Translation of his Mūlamadhyamakakārikā*, Tokyo: The Hokuseido.
Jackson, R. R. (1993) *Is Enlightenment Possible? Dharmakīrti and rGyal tshabrje on Knowledge, Rebirth, No-Self and Liberation*, Ithaca, N.Y.: Snow Lion.
Jayatilleke, K. N. (1980) *Early Buddhist Theory of Knowledge*, Delhi: Motilal Banarsidass.
Jha, G. (trans.) (1937–9) *The Tattvasaṃgraha of Śāntarakṣita with the Commentary of Kamalaśīla*, 2 vols, Baroda: Oriental Institute.
Kalupahana, D. J. (1976) *Buddhist Philosophy: A Historical Introduction*, Honolulu: University of Hawaii Press.
Kitagawa, J. M. and Cummings, M. D. (1989) *Buddhism and Asian History*, New York: Macmillan.
Kochumuttom, T. J. (1982) *A Buddhist Doctrine of Experience*, Delhi: Motilal Banarsidass.
La Vallée Poussin, L. de (trans.) (1971–80) *L'Abhidharmakośa de Vasubandhu*, 6 vols, Brussels: Institut Belge des Hautes Études Chinoises.
Lamotte, E. (1967) *Histoire du bouddhisme indien*, Louvain: Université de Louvain.
Lamotte, E. (ed. and trans.) (1935) *Saṃdhinirmocana Sūtra: Explication des Mystères*, Louvain: Université de Louvain.
Lancaster, L. (ed.) (1977) *Prajñāpāramitā and Related Systems*, Berkeley: University of California Press.
Lindtner, Chr. (1982) *Nāgārjuniana*, Copenhagen: Akademisk Forlag.
Lopez, D. S., Jr (1987) *A Study of Svātantrika*, Ithaca, N.Y.: Snow Lion.
Matilal, B. K. (1971) *Epistemology, Logic and Grammar in Indian Philosophical Analysis*, The Hague: Mouton.
—— (1986) *Perception: An Essay on Classical Indian Theories of Knowledge*, Oxford: Clarendon Press.
Mimaki, K. (1976) *La Réfutation bouddhique de la permanence des choses*, Paris: Institut de Civilisation Indienne.
—— (1987) *Blo gsal grub mtha'*, Kyoto: Zinbun Kagaku Kenkyusyo.
Nakamura, H. (1987) *Indian Buddhism: A Survey with Bibliographical Notes*, Delhi: Motilal Banarsidass.
Ñāṇamoli, B. (trans.) (1976) *The Path of Purification*, Boulder: Shambhala.
Ñāṇatiloka Mahāthera (1957) *Guide Through the Abhidhammapiṭaka*, Colombo: Bauddha Sahityā Sabhā.
Obermiller, E. (trans.) (1931–2) *History of Buddhism by Bu-ston*, 2 parts, Heidelberg.
Potter, K. H. (1976) *Presuppositions of India's Philosophies*, Westport, Conn.: Greenwood Press.
—— (1977) *The Encyclopedia of Indian Philosophies: Bibliography*, revised edn. Princeton: Princeton University Press.
—— (1988) *Guide to Indian Philosophy*, Boston, Mass.: G. K. Hall.
Powers, J. (trans) (1995) *Wisdom of Buddha: The Saṁdhinirmocana Mahāyāna Sūtra*, Berkeley: Dharma Publishing.
Prebish, C. S. (1975) *Buddhism: A Modern Perspective*, University Park, Pa.: Pennsylvania State University Press.
Reynolds, F. J. (1981) *Guide to Buddhist Religion*, Boston, Mass.: G. K. Hall.
Robinson, R. H. (1967) *Early Mādhyamika in India and China*, Madison: University of Wisconsin Press.
Ruegg, D. S. (1968) *La Théorie du Tathāgatagarbha et du Gotra*, Paris: École Française d'Extrême-Orient.

Ruegg, D. S. (1981) *The Literature of the Madhyamaka School of Philosophy in India*, Wiesbaden: Otto Harrassowitz.
Schmithausen, L. (1987) *Ālayavijñāna: On the Origin and the Early Development of a Central Concept of Yogācāra Philosophy*, Tokyo: International Institute for Buddhist Studies.
Sopa, G. and Hopkins, J. (1976) *Practice and Theory of Tibetan Buddhism*, New York: Grove Press.
Stcherbatsky, F. Th. (1962) *Buddhist Logic*, 2 vols, New York: Dover.
—— (1970) *The Central Conception of Buddhism and the Meaning of the Word 'Dharma'*. Delhi: Motilal Banarsidass.
Streng, F. J. (1967) *Emptiness: A Study in Religious Meaning*, Nashville: Abingdon Press.
Warder, A. K. (1980) *Indian Buddhism*, 2nd edn, Delhi: Motilal Banarsidass.
Warren, H. C. (1984) *Buddhism in Translations*, New York: Atheneum.
Williams, P. (1989) *Mahāyāna Buddhism: The Doctrinal Foundations*, London New York: Routledge.

FURTHER READING

Bodhi, Bhikku (1978) *The Discourse on the All-Embracing Net of Views: The Brahmajāla Sutta and its Commentaries*, Kandy: Buddhist Publication Society.
Cabezón, J. I. (1994) *Buddhism and Language*, Albany: State University of New York Press.
Eckel, M. D. (1992) *To See the Buddha: A Philosopher's Quest for the Meaning of Emptiness*, San Francisco: HarperSanFrancisco.
Griffiths, P. J. (1994) *On Being Buddha: The Classical Doctrine of Buddhahood*, Albany: State University of New York Press.
Gyatso, J. B. (ed.) (1992) *In the Mirror of Memory: Reflections on Mindfulness and Remembrance in Indian and Tibetan Buddhism*, Albany: State University of New York Press.
Karunadasa, Y. (1967) *Buddhist Analysis of Matter*, Colombo: Department of Cultural Affairs.
Keith, A. B. (1923) *Buddhist Philosophy in India and Ceylon*, Oxford: Oxford University Press.
Keown, D. (1992) *The Nature of Buddhist Ethics*, New York: Curzon/St Martin's Press.
King, S. B. (1991) *Buddha Nature*, Albany: State University of New York Press.
King, W. (1964) *In the Hope of Nibbana: The Ethics of Theravada Buddhism*, La Salle, Ill.: Open Court.
Mookerjee, S. (1970) *The Buddhist Philosophy of Universal Flux*, Delhi: Motilal Banarsidass.
Murti, T. R. V. (1960) *The Central Philosophy of Buddhism: A Study of the Mādhyamika System*, London: George Allen & Unwin.
Nagao, G. M. (1991) *Mādhyamika and Yogācāra: A Study of Mahāyāna Philosophies*, Albany: State University of New York Press.
Saddhatissa, H. (1970) *Buddhist Ethics*, New York: George Braziller.
Thomas, E. J. (1933) *The History of Buddhist Thought*, New York: Barnes & Noble.

18

NĀGĀRJUNA

Chr. Lindtner

Nāgārjuna is the first outstanding figure in the long gallery of Indian Mahāyāna Buddhists, and the study of his works has many facets of interest. Recent research has shown that he is to be ranked with the greatest names in the history of philosophy. A knowledge not only of the man but also of his thinking is necessary for an understanding of the later developments of Mahāyāna in India, China and Tibet. Even certain currents in other Indian philosophical systems, especially Vedānta (Qvarnström 1989), and occasionally Nyāya and Jaina, are not seen in perspective unless one has Nāgārjuna and his pupils in mind.

Our main sources for an understanding of Nāgārjuna and his cultural background are his own works and the documents belonging to the tradition in which he was active as a creative writer. Nāgārjuna wrote in Sanskrit, and while some of his main works are still extant in that language, some are now only available in later Chinese and/or Tibetan translations.

Among the numerous works ascribed to Nāgārjuna the following can, on various internal and external grounds, be considered authentic (Lindtner 1982): *Mūlamadhyamakakārikā* (*MK*), *Śūnyatāsaptati* (*ŚS*), *Vigrahavyāvartanī* (*VV*), *Vaidalyaprakaraṇa* (*VP*), **Vyavahārasiddhi* (*VS*), *Yuktiṣaṣṭikā* (*YṢ*), *Catuḥstava* (*CS*), *Ratnāvalī* (*RĀ*), *Pratītyasamutpādahṛdayakārikā* (*PK*), *Sūtrasamuccaya* (*SS*), *Suhṛllekha* (*SL*) and **Bodhisaṃbhāraka* (*BS*). I also consider *Bodhicittavivaraṇa* (*BV*) authentic, but other scholars would disagree (Lindtner 1982).

Among the spurious, but for our understanding of Nāgārjuna's school, Madhyamaka, important documents are: **Mahāprajñāpāramitopadeśa* (Lamotte 1949–80), **Dvādaśadvāraka* (Cheng 1982, Lindtner 1986), and *Akutobhayā* (Huntington 1986).

Among the numerous dubious texts ascribed to Nāgārjuna may be mentioned in particular: *Mahāyānaviṃśikā* (Tucci 1978: 195–207), *Bhavasaṃkrānti*, *Daśabhūmikavibhāṣā*, **Upāyahṛdaya* and *Dharmadhātustava*. Indispensable for a proper understanding of Nāgārjuna's intellectual and religious background are some of the less philosophical of his writings, i.e. *ŚS* (Bhikkhu Pāsādika 1989), an anthology giving extracts from sixty-eight canonical texts, mainly Mahāyāna, supplemented by *CS*, *BS*,

SL and *RĀ*, all of which contain copious allusions to or quotations from a large number of holy scriptures, or *sūtras*, belonging to both vehicles.

MK, *ŚS* and *VV* are mostly purely philosophical and abstract in content. The basic idea in these writings is the emptiness (*śūnyatā*) of all phenomena, or concepts (*dharma*), and for this doctrine, which is, properly understood, not a doctrine but rather an attitude, Nāgārjuna is largely indebted to the vast teachings of the *Prajñā-pāramitā* scriptures (Conze 1978).

VP is conceived as a criticism of Nyāya philosophy and thus shows Nāgārjuna as a patriarch defending Buddhism against the infidel. Most probably we are justified in regarding Nāgārjuna as the founder of the Madhyamaka school. His pupil, Āryadeva is the author of *Catuḥśataka* (Lang 1986), and next in importance only to Nāgārjuna himself. His work is largely conceived as a criticism of various non-Buddhist schools left unattacked by Nāgārjuna, his teacher. Rāhulabhadra and Mātṛceṭa (Hartmann 1987) also belong to Nāgārjuna's school, and their celebrated hymns to the Buddha, in the tradition of Nāgārjuna's *CS*, display the devotional side of early Indian Madhyamaka. Without *faith* in the Buddha there is no Medhyamaka.

Most of the later representatives of Madhyamaka in India were authors of commentaries on the basic works of Nāgārjuna and Āryadeva. Those whose commentaries are still extant are *Piṅgala, or Ch'ing-mu, Buddhapālita, Bhavya, Avalokitavrata and Candrakīrti. Independent works on Madhyamaka were written by Bhavya (Lindtner 1984 and Lopez 1987) and, partly in opposition to Bhavya, by Candrakīrti (Huntington 1989). (The Sanskrit originals of some of these texts, formerly only available in Tibetan versions, have recently been discovered in Tibet, but are still awaiting publication.) Commentaries on Nāgārjuna and Āryadeva were also composed by Dharmapāla and Sthiramati, both of whom belong to the other important branch of Mahāyāna, Yogācāra. Their approach to the founding fathers was severely criticized by Bhavya (Lindtner 1986). While both schools developed from common roots, the controversy with the Yogācāra led to a schism in the sixth century AD. While not yet apparent in the work of Kambala (Lindtner 1985), the schism is undeniable in Śāntadeva's celebrated *Bodhi[sattva]caryāvatāra*, the most readable of all presentations (*avatāra*), or general introductions to Madhyamaka (Lindtner 1981a). Later Madhyamaka authors who tend to minimize the differences between the two schools, partly under the influence of Dharmakīrti (Lindtner 1989), include Śrīgupta (Ruegg 1981 : 67), Jñānagarbha (Eckel 1987), Śāntarakṣita (Ichigō 1985), Kamalaśīla and Atiśa (Lindtner 1981a).

Regarding the date, life and personal circumstances of Nāgārjuna little or nothing is known with certainty (Ruegg 1981 : 5). From the cocoon of legends surrounding the historical Nāgārjuna, the probable truth is that he must have been very active philosophically and also in practical affairs as an abbot and as court counsellor in south India in the second or third century AD.

The first solid foundation for Madhyamaka studies was laid with the great La Vallée Poussin's editions of *Mūlamadhyamakakārikās de Nāgārjuna avec le Prasannapadā*

Commentaire de Candrakirtī (St Petersburg, 1903–14), *Madhyamakāvatāra par Candrakīrti. Traduction tibétaine* (St Petersburg, 1907–12) and *Bodhicaryāvatārapañjikā. Commentary to the Bodhicaryāvatāra of Śāntideva* (Calcutta, 1901–14). These excellent editions are now in need of minor revision. Literal translations of the earliest commentary on *MK* were published by Max Walleser, *Die Mittlere Lehre des Nāgārjuna* (Heidelberg, 1912). All the English versions of *MK* are unreliable (Streng 1967, Inada 1970, Sprung 1979, Kalupahana 1986), and one still has to consult *MK* as found in the commentaries of Buddhapālita (Lindtner 1981b and Saitō 1984), Bhavya (Kajiyama 1989: 417–73 and Ames 1986) and Candrakīrti (Stcherbatsky 1927; Schayer 1931; Lamotte 1936 and de Jong 1949; in Lindtner 1982; May 1959). *ŚS*, *VV*, *VS*, *YṢ*, *CS*, *PK*, *BS* and *BV* have been edited and/or translated in Lindtner (Copenhagen, 1982). The edition and translation of *VV* in Bhattacharya, Johnston and Kunst (Delhi, 1978) is fairly reliable. *RĀ* was edited by Hahn (Bonn, 1982) and translated by Hopkins (London, 1975) and Lindtner (Copenhagen, 1979). There are several versions of *SL*, for example Jamspal *et al.* (Delhi, 1978) and Kawamura (Emeryville, 1975). A critical edition of the Tibetan version is still a desideratum (promised by S. Dietz). An excellent critical edition of *ŚS* was published by Bhikkhu Pāsādika (Copenhagen, 1989), who also promises an English translation.

Good editions and/or translations of later Madhyamaka texts include Lang (1986), Eckel (1987), Ichigō (1985) and Huntington (1989), to mention only a few of the most recent publications. There are several versions of *Bodhi[sattva]caryāvatāra*, for example La Vallée Poussin (Paris, 1906–7), Steinkellner (Düsseldorf/Cologne, 1981), Lindtner (Copenhagen, 1981). Matics (London, 1971) is totally unreliable. Classical works such as Stcherbatsky (Leningrad, 1927) and Murti (London, 1960) are now somewhat outdated. Quite useful for early Madhyamaka in India and China are Robinson (Madison, 1967) and Ramanan (Tokyo, 1966). Further references are to be found in Lindtner 1982: 282–6.

An enormous mass of scholarly literature is available in Tibetan, and much of it consists of commentaries and doxographical works in which Madhyamaka plays the most important role. In particular the works of Tsong Kha-pa and his followers have drawn the attention of translators, including Wayman, *Calming the Mind and Discerning the Real: Buddhist Meditation and the Middle Way. From the Lam rim chen mo of Tsoṅ-kha-pa* (New York, 1978), Thurman, *Tsong Khapa's Speech of Gold in the Essence of True Eloquence* (Princeton, 1984), Hopkins, *Meditation on Emptiness* (London, 1983), Lopez, *A Study of Svātantrika* Ithaca, N.Y., 1987), and Napper, *Dependent-Arising and Emptiness* (London, 1989). However, these translations tend to be either very inaccurate, very idiosyncratic or too literal to make much sense, and generally they lack a historical perspective. Mostly, the American translators of Tsong Kha-pa seem to have an apologetic rather than a scholarly concern. Quite apart from that, later Tibetan scholarly literature has a very limited value for a proper understanding of the Indian sources, but there is a general, but unhappy, tendency to overestimate its independent merits. Scholars must, of course, go directly *ad fontes* and leave later Tibetan literature aside. Each tradition should be studied in its own right.

There are undoubtedly several angles from which a systematic presentation of Nāgārjuna's religious philosophy may be undertaken. Also, if we use the term 'philosophy' in the sense of love of the result of wisdom, rather than in the sense of love of wisdom, we are justified in speaking of the philosophy of Nāgārjuna. What I mean to say is that his highest authority is never reason, but faith. In the case of Nāgārjuna (and most Indian philosophers, for that matter) reason is always ancillary to faith. None the less one may still speak of a system of philosophy. Only by seeing all the parts as a whole can one avoid emphases that would lead to contradictory conclusions about the author's intentions. The real task, as it is in any systematic research, is to determine the basic patterns that make the mass of isolated observations immediately comprehensible. Then the important factors can be sifted out, and a judgement made on Nāgārjuna's aims and achievements. Basically, Nāgārjuna is a yogin.

As a Buddhist Nāgārjuna regards ordinary experience as miserable, or unsatisfactory (*duḥkha*). By 'existence' is meant the five groups (*skandha*) which taken together form a 'person' or individual, the physical body (*rūpa*), feelings (*vedanā*), ideas (*saṃjñā*), the will to live and all its outward expressions (*saṃskāra*) and, finally, consciousness (*vijñāna*).

A careful observer will be able to confirm that our existence as individuals is characterized by three ineradicable traits: it is (1) conditioned and composite (*saṃskṛta*) and therefore (2) impermanent (*anitya*), which again implies that existence lacks any immutable, constant nucleus, and, as such, (3) it is without a self (*anātman*). These, in a nutshell, are the three aspects of *duḥkha*.

It may seem strange that the word *duḥkha*, literally 'unsatisfactory, painful', should be used for an objective relationship, but this is really just one of many instances in Buddhism where a basic concept has a double function, sometimes denoting a psychological condition, sometimes an objective fact. This ambiguity between (subjective) evaluation and (objective) denotation in key concepts like *dharma* (concept – thing), *karma* (manner of acting – action), *artha* (meaning – object), *saṃskāra* (volition – physical formations), *satya* (truth – reality), *vyavahāra* (use of language, usage – usual practice of Buddhism) and *prapañca* (linguistic concepts – the world objectively displayed) seems to have caused western scholars more trouble than anything else in their attempts to understand Buddhism on its own ground.

To return to the subject of *duḥkha*, one basic trait, the principle of inconstancy, unites its three aspects, and that provides the transition to the immediate cause of *duḥkha*. This is *karma*, literally 'work', a psychological concept corresponding to volition (*cetanā*), and also the deliberate decision to do something (*cetayitvā*). *Karma* is manifested in the individual's physical, verbal and mental acts of volition. It can be 'neutral', but in most cases it is positively or negatively charged. It is at the same time the functional and the material unique cause for the continuance of the individual's existence in the present and subsequent lives, and has been so since the beginning of time. *Karma* is the driving force that hustles the individual forward in the circuit of renewed birth and death (*saṃsāra*), and even if the individual by exerting his or her own will can guide the course of *karma* in a favourable or unfavourable direction, it is undoubtedly *karma* that binds him or her to *saṃsāra*, according not only to the Buddhists, but many other Indian philosophers also. Only diehard nihilists contest the reality, or efficiency, of *karma*. One is not even supposed to communicate with such vicious people. There is no sense in investigating the original cause of *karma*, the basic energy and matter of existence, because it has always been there, and 'Even the buddhas cannot fathom the might of *karma*.' However, the buddhas have their part to play. They have themselves acknowledged that there is a liberation (*mokṣa*) from the bonds of *karma*, and they have made a plan (*mārga*) to achieve it. As in other Indian systems liberation occurs with an intuitive realization (*jñāna*) of one or more fundamental facts (*tattva*). In Nāgārjuna's system, Madhyamaka, it occurs, as we shall see, with a full realization (*parijñāna*) of the 'law', or principle of conditioned co-origination (*pratītyasamutpāda*), which rules that everything lacks independent existence (*niḥsvabhāvatā*), is in fact empty (*śūnyatā*). This is equivalent to the cessation of *saṃsāra*; it is extinction (*nirvāṇa*, *nirodha*), where everything transitory comes to rest (*śānta*).

We still have to see the relation between *pratītyasamutpāda* and *karma*. According to Nāgārjuna, *karma* is by nature passion (*karma kleśātmakam*). There are three passions which tyrannically and unceasingly motivate people to committed action, or *karma*. Desire (*rāga*) leads one to the pursuit of pleasure (*śubha*), aversion (*dveṣa*) prompts one to shun what repels, and sheer stupidity (*moha*) involves mankind and other living creatures in all kinds of desperate ventures because it conceals from their vision the fundamental transitoriness, which is *duḥkha*.

The genesis of the passions is due to the notions of discursive thought (*vikalpa*), to evaluations (*saṃkalpa*) and abstract constructions (*kalpanā*) of the empirically perceived world (*prapañca*), that is, existence in all its variety.

If *karma* is due to passion, *kleśa*, and *kleśa* is due to *vikalpa* (which is accompanied by *saṃkalpa*, *kalpanā* and *parikalpa*, intellectual systematization), then the battle should be joined against *vikalpa*, and, indeed, philosophical activity enters into it here as well. In general, the purpose of yoga is to transcend discursive thought

Let us take a closer look at *vikalpa*, discursive thought. Its action is to separate things into constituent parts, and for this it needs an expanded substrate, undifferentiated before its operation, on which to build its compositions. The word *prapañca* means expansion, display, a sort of clean slate which holds the initial state of words or things at the moment *vikalpa* begins to function. *Vikalpa* automatically (i.e. nourished by karmic energy) classifies the material into all manner of categories: cause–effect, simultaneous–successive, substance–attribute, subject–predicate, short–long, subject–object, far–near, and all other conceivable spatial and temporal criteria (*padārtha*), all of them consisting of something that exists in a certain manner (*sat*), and its opposite or absence, which does not exist in that manner (*asat*).

As soon as *vikalpa* has differentiated the expansion, the living beings discriminate between the phenomena produced and select them in groups of things (*bhāva*) with specific forms of existence (*svabhāva*). After that, comparisons and evaluations are made, and things are assigned values. This brings about the misconceptions (*viparyāsa*), that something in itself should be attractive (*śuci*), good (*sukha*), durable (*nitya*), or anything in and by itself (*ātman*). Out of plain ignorance, one will not admit to oneself that in their true nature they are only abstractions (*kevala*) and empty hypostases.

As mentioned above, it is because of misconceptions that the *kleśas* urge the living beings to *karma*, which leads again to a new birth, the procedure being repeated to infinity, as it has always been. Most Indian philosophers would agree about this.

That is why philosophy enters the lists against the activity of *vikalpa*. Analytical insight (*prajñā*) performs the task of inspecting the differentiated multiplicity and revealing it to be the web (*jāla*) of the *vikalpas*. The philosophical examination begins by taking the premisses of the ignorant as given. After all, *they* are in the power of *karma* and the *kleśas*. Now, let us suppose, as is claimed, that there really is a multiplicity of independent entities (*svabhāva*): then that must imply that every single thing (*bhāva*) is cognizable in itself, that it is independent of anything else. It must naturally be unqualified, and as such immutable and a unity. It cannot be composite, for then it would be nothing in itself. As such it really exists nor does not exist, like an image.

It will soon appear that neither experience nor logic, two authorities that no realistic thinker can afford to ignore, will leave a foothold for the existence of an independent entity. Who has ever seen, or could visualize, anything absolutely unconditioned? (Naturally, Nāgārjuna does not pose this question of his own faith in *nirvāṇa*!) On the contrary, experience and reflection show clearly that things are only what they are in relation to something else, and so *ad infinitum*. Everything is conditioned co-originated, therefore void of 'own-being' (*svabhāva*), in other words, empty and non-originated. As such it really exists nor does not exist, like an image.

Thus the Madhyamaka has drawn the absurd implications (*prasaṅga*) with which experience and logic must confront the realistic world-view. Up to a point the philosophical aspect of Madhyamaka is patently simple, the psychological being more subtle, but the fact is that not only the untutored and the profane (*pṛthagjana*), but also the dogmatists, of whatever persuasion it might be, stand fast by the unconditional validity of their views (*dṛṣṭi*) as against that of others. That sets off the whole wretched process, for not only is the individual at the mercy of *kleśas* etc., but discontent spreads out implacably in the form of disagreement, conflict, hate and dissension.

This brings us to Nāgārjuna's conception of *nirvāṇa*, a conception which, quite naturally, forms the centre from which all his thinking derives its energy. Without faith in *nirvāṇa* no Buddhist philosophy or practice would be possible. The first thing that strikes us is how orthodox Nāgārjuna is in his attitudes and ideas. The possibility of realizing *nirvāṇa* is never questioned; it is an article of unshaken faith based on the Buddhist scriptures handed down by tradition.

Extinction, or *nirvāṇa*, is held out to be a 'psychological' state in which all our passions – and thereby suffering – disappear. From an 'epistemological' point of view it means the extinction of ignorance (*avidyā*). Ignorance is understood as clinging to ideas and dogmas, as sticking to concepts and beliefs in opposites. But *nirvāṇa* is, at the same time, an 'ontological' state, a *locus*, in which all the elements, earth, wind, etc., in a word, the universe, is no more present. Nāgārjuna is – to turn to grammar – very fond of using the locative case to indicate this state, which, owing to its 'confusion' of psychology, epistemology and ontology, must remain foreign to our way of thinking. Some references to his own writings may show this: thus in *RĀ* I 93–5, referring to a canonical passage corresponding to *Dīgha-Nikāya* I 223, he says that earth, water, fire, wind, long, short, fine, gross, good, bad, etc. are extinguished in consciousness, i.e. *in nirvāṇa*. He has the same passage in mind in *YṢ* 34 when saying that the Buddha has stated that the elements are absorbed *in* consciousness. This takes place *in* an act of cognition (*jñāna*) that shows them to have been falsely imagined. In *RĀ* I 41 it is stated that *in* liberation (*mokṣa*) there is no ego and no *skandhas*. And in *RĀ* I 98 that *in* the determination of the true meaning (*tattvārthanirṇaye*) one understands that everything is falsely imagined, that there is actually neither being nor lack of being. In another passage, *MK* XVIII 5, often misunderstood, it is said that *karma* and *kleśas* are due to *vikalpas*, and that *vikalpas* are due to *prapañca*, but *prapañca* ceases *in* emptiness (*śūnyatā*).

So, to some extent, *nirvāṇa*, or emptiness, is an empty *locus*, a blank, or Nothing. It does not leave any basis for further rebirth, surely. Nevertheless, Nāgārjuna links the concept of *nirvāṇa* with the concept of compassion, or responsibility (*karuṇā*). Let us for now just point out that this shows his Mahāyāna background very clearly. Apart from this rather irrational, or religious element, there is nothing new or original in Nāgārjuna's conception of *nirvāṇa*. What is new and original is the systematic way in which he employs 'wisdom' (*prajñā*) to show the emptiness of all phenomena.

It is commonly accepted by Buddhists that *prajñā*, the analytic comprehension of the true nature of things, can also be acquired, to different degrees. There are three phases. It can be acquired as knowledge through study (*śruta*), and it can crystallize by means of independent reflection (*cintā*). But practice and meditation over a long period are needed to develop *prajñā* to the stage where it brings about a thorough conversion of the adept. This is personal realization (*bhāvanā*).

Thus the first two phases are not of very much help, and this is why Nāgārjuna tirelessly applies the same logic of *pratītyasamutpāda* to all conceivable categories, limited only to the dictates of his time and environment. He is a master of *docta ignorantia*, learned, or conscious, ignorance.

The tradition that Nāgārjuna was an abbot with responsibility for the education of monks in his monastery is strengthened by the most reliable evidence we possess today, namely his own works. His philosophical works (especially *MK*, *ŚS* and *VV*) were obviously planned as textbooks for monks who had completed their courses in traditional Buddhist dogmatics (*abhidharma*). The verses were learned by heart, discussed, and their content acquired by solitary meditation. Not for nothing does his philosophical masterpiece, the *Fundamental Memorial Verses of the Middle Way* (i.e. *MK*), bear the appellation '*Prajñā*'.

Before we take a closer look at Nāgārjuna's three basic philosophical works, it will be useful to recall that *prajñā*, after all, only expresses one aspect of his thinking. In *RĀ* I 5 Nāgārjuna thus observes that *prajñā* is the most important thing, but it presupposes faith (*śraddhā*). In *BS* 6 it says that: 'Perfection in *prajñā* is the mother of bodhisattvas. Skill in means (*upāyakauśalya*) is their father, and compassion (*karuṇā*) is their daughter' (Lindtner 1982: 228). This image illustrates three features that belong naturally together in Mahāyāna.

As we have seen, *prajñā* is primary, but in Mahāyāna if one has come to realize emptiness through *prajñā* there is paradoxically no more pressing duty than to find ways of helping those who cannot share in it. It is exclusively a compassion, or sense of responsibility, born of a higher knowledge that motivates one to engage with all the means at one's disposal in the struggle to help those in adversity. In practice it is usual to spread the Buddhist doctrine (*Dharma*), to oppose bad influences, promote the good and help those in difficulties. It would, of course, also be the ultimate reason for writing textbooks for students, for example *MK*, *ŚS* and *VV*. With this background the question in *RĀ* IV 78 becomes more comprehensible: 'What reasonable person could sneer at Mahāyāna when it says that all actions are guided by compassion and purified by knowledge?'

When the monks in a south Indian monastery some 1,800 years ago were handed a few palm-leaves on which several of Nāgārjuna's works were written in Sanskrit, their background was quite different from that of a modern reader. Whether they had been ordained as young boys or converted later in life, they would certainly have had a good grounding in Buddhist dogmatics (*abhidharma*). Otherwise they could have stood no chance of understanding the works that were soon to make history.

It was almost seven hundred years since the death of the Buddha, and by far the most important developments in his doctrine had taken place in dogmatics. Already in the Founder's own time there were many attempts to systematize the basic concepts (*dharma*), but they were mostly stumbling and superficial. *Abhidharma* denotes a systematic arrangement of the recognized *dharmas* according to certain dominant criteria. The aim is to study the resulting lists and definitions, rather like a catechism, in order to determine, as methodically as possible, which *dharmas* are positive and which negative, and so regulate one's life style accordingly: practise good *karma*, avoid bad *karma*, and, finally, by yoga, transcend both!

The various sects of Buddhism developed their own *abhidharma*. The differences between the schools stem from the criteria used in the classification, in the number of *dharmas* in the scheme, and in their definition. Still, they have in common the vital factor, the soteriological purpose, that a searching analysis of the *dharmas*' nature and properties, accompanied by meditation, leads to liberation (*mokṣa*). One conquers by cognition, an axiom whose truth is not contested by Buddhists, or by many other Indian philosophers.

The historical development of *abhidharma* is in many respects not well understood. We limit ourselves here to the schools criticized in Nāgārjuna's polemic, the Sautrāntika, the Sāṃmitīya and the Sarvāstivāda. The first two play a minor role, and yet Nāgārjuna gives much emphasis to his rejection of the Sāṃmitīya's belief in the existence of an independent individual (*pudgala*) over and above the five *skandhas*.

It is quite different with Sarvāstivāda, the 'Everything exists' school, which not only marks the high point in *abhidharma*, but also made the greatest contribution of all to the Buddhist world-view. Although we have to admit that the precise stage of development reached by Sarvāstivāda in Nāgārjuna's time is not known, it is still possible, partly from Nāgārjuna's information, partly with the aid of the extraordinarily rich documentation bequeathed by the Sarvāstivādins, to present the main features. This is not to say that the study of the school's principal works does not present difficulties. Useful, general introductions are given, for instance, by Rosenberg (Heidelberg, 1924) and Stcherbatsky (London, 1923).

This school is characterized by the doctrine that all concepts or phenomena (*dharma*) exist in the right of their own special being (*svabhāva*) in all time. However, they manifest themselves only in individual concrete forms of existence (*bhāva*). 'Own-being' (*svabhāva*) is immutable and eternal, existing in all three periods of time, past, present and future. Its empirical form occurs in the present and is always composite and conditioned. It goes through a process of origination, duration and extinction. Thus things are 'waiting' in the future, appearing in the present and disappearing into the past. The 'existence' remains in all aspects of time. For example, fire will be hot, as it always has been. It is only in the present that it burns, depending on fuel.

It is thus postulated that phenomena, and concepts, occur with an eternal nature (*svabhāva*), but as impermanent apparitions. In the last analysis, the cause of their appearance at all is one's *karma*. There can be an individual ripening (of *karma*), for example a headache, or it can be collective, as in the case of a mountain. The *dharmas* do not originate at random, but are subject to strict causality. Before a *dharma*, psychical or physical, can occur in its specific *bhāva*, four conditions, or at least two of them, must be fulfilled:

1 a condition in the form of an efficient cause (*hetupratyaya*), which activates the process;
2 a related prior condition (*samanantarapratyaya*);
3 a condition in the form of a basis for each form of consciousness (*ālambanapratyaya*);
4 a decisive condition (*adhipatipratyaya*).

The effective cause can be further resolved into six causes:

1 accompanying (*saṃprayukta*);
2 coexisting (*sahabhū*);
3 related (*sabhāga*);
4 universal (*sarvatraga*);
5 retributory (*vipāka*);
6 instrumental (*kāraṇa*).

In this way the *karma* of the past is latent in the 'future' (*anāgata*, what has yet to come), waiting for the 'present' (*pratyutpanna*, what has come up), in which it can project itself as a phenomenon, then entering the 'past' (*atīta*, what has gone). All *dharmas* circulate like this, eternal in terms of *svabhāva*, transient in terms of *bhāva*, mode of being. One attains liberation by suppressing, or preventing their appearance. There is much more on causality and time in the Sarvāstivāda's own texts, but this will be sufficient for an understanding of the target of Nāgārjuna's criticism.

In Sarvāstivāda, as in all other forms of classical Buddhism, the karmic energy must be slaked, the method being, according to the *abhidharma*, to have full cognizance of all *dharmas*, in order to eliminate the *kleśas*, the immediate cause of *karma*, which relies exclusively on the hazy conceptions which untutored folk have about things. In the clear light of recognition the vices (*kleśa*) disappear like mists. The process can be described as one of gradual depersonalization, or prevention.

As mentioned above, we do not know which of Sarvāstivāda's handbooks Nāgārjuna consulted. The two passages that show most clearly his dependence on dogmatics are *RĀ* V 2–33 and the auto-commentary to *VV* 7. There are no absolutely identical lists elsewhere, so there is no definite answer to the two key criteria in the works of *abhidharma*, how many *dharmas* are included, and what principles determine the grouping.

On the authority of *BV* 66, and many canonical passages, it is: 'In brief, the five *skandhas* that are meant by the expression "all things" '. Exactly the same conclusion is the basis for classification of 'all things' in Candrakīrti's *Pañcaskandhaprakaraṇa*, composed some 350 years after Nāgārjuna, and, not counting the **Mahāprajñāpāramitopadeśa*, the most important source for our knowledge of the relationship between Madhyamaka and *abhidharma*. I shall list briefly the *dharmas* essential for our purpose.

There are five *skandhas*:

1 material form (*rūpa*);
2 feelings (*vedanā*);
3 ideas (*saṃjñā*);
4 volitions, karmic energies (*saṃskāra*);
5 consciousness (*vijñāna*).

Material form, or matter, is divided into two groups:

1 The basic elements, earth, water, fire and air (space not being counted as an element).
2 The three kinds of derived matter, i.e. (a) the sense-organs, eye, ear, nose, tongue, and the body (or skin) as the organ of touch, (b) sense-objects, shape-colour, sound, smell, taste, and what can be touched, and finally (c) 'non-expression' (*avijñapti*), being a positive or negative physical or verbal *karma* which, without attracting the attention of others, contains the elements of self-discipline or laxity (cf. *MK* XVII 4).

Feelings, the second *skandha*, can be bodily or mental. They can be pleasant, unpleasant or neither. Their further definition depends on the sense-organ they are associated with.

Ideas, the third *skandha*, mean the perception of anything that can be given a name. There are several sub-classes.

Karmic energy forms, or formations, the fourth *skandha*, consist of thirty-nine phenomena linked with a thought process and nineteen not linked to thought. The thirty-nine are volition, contact, attention, initiative, enthusiasm, faith, energy, memory, concentration, discernment, reflection, examination, slovenliness, persistence, loathing, exuberance, repose, vehemence, mildness, bashfulness, chastity, equanimity, freedom, three positive attitudes, three negative attitudes, three indeterminate attitudes, nine fetters, three bonds, six vices, six secondary passions, ten infatuations, three bad influences, four 'torrents', four 'yokes', four identifications, four 'knots', five 'veils', ten types of cognition, and ten types of patience.

The nineteen *dharmas* not linked to thought are: acquisition, loss, unconscious trance state, expiration trance state, absence of all notions, life-energy, fellowship, attainment of individuality, attainment of basis, birth, becoming old, duration, impermanence, labelling with names, word groups, phoneme groups, non-causal complex, and causal complex.

The fifth *skandha*, or consciousness, arises in connection with sense-organ and sense-object. There are six types, one for each sense-organ.

The twelve bases and the eighteen elements are subsidiary to the five *skandhas*. The bases are the six sense-organs with sense-objects, and eighteen elements add the corresponding consciousness to form six triplets (Lindtner 1979).

All these *dharmas* are *karmic* products, arising only when the prescribed conditions and causes are to hand. These concepts are discussed at great length in the *Mahāvibhāṣā*, *Nyāyānusāra*, *Abhidharmadīpa* and numerous other works. By the very fact of acknowledging their reality, belief in an individual, an ego, is excluded. Only the Sāṃmitīyas take an unorthodox position, as has already been seen.

Education in *abhidharma* was certainly central to the background of Nāgārjuna's first readers. In his *YṢ* 30 he even says that one can only understand his philosophy provided one has studied *abhidharma*. In one sense Nāgārjuna accepts *abhidharma*, but in another sense he does not. This brings us to the celebrated doctrine of Two

Truths, a relative (*saṃvṛti*) and an absolute (*paramārtha*), where the former serves as a means to the latter. In relative reality everything is conditioned and in constant ferment. The true Buddhist adopts the Mahāyāna doctrine of the *bodhisattva* ideal and the 'Hīnayāna' dogmas, without, however, considering them as anything more than means to an end, and that end is absolute reality (*paramārthasatya*), realized as emptiness. Material and ideological contacts, as we have seen, are the source of all misery. When reading Nāgārjuna one must keep the distinction between the Two Truths in mind – and remember that this distinction itself is relative!

Are these Two Truths really related in any way, or is there an unbridgeable chasm separating them? Nāgārjuna himself has pedagogically laid down the relation of means to an end, but in India there have been various theoretical objections to his separation of the Two Truths. Does the relative truth exist only relatively, or absolutely? Whatever alternative the Mādhyamika may choose, the conclusion will be that only the absolute exists, so that it is self-contradictory to talk about *two* truths. Another question is whether 'relative' is synonymous with 'false', which will imply that there is only one truth, the absolute. Finally there is the complaint that one and the same thing was relatively one thing, absolutely another, so how could *one* thing be *two* different things? Even if there is no documentation for Nāgārjuna's having foreseen all these objections, which are by no means irrelevant, it seems that he has anticipated them with the only possible defence, that the separation between the Two Truths works in practice. Moreover, the distinction is approved by the scriptures (Lindtner 1981a).

From this one can see the reason for the form in which Nāgārjuna usually presents his criticism. He will not be drawn into discussions on the relevance or the definition of individual concepts, but rejects them all at one stroke because they are not based on absolute reality. However useful they could turn out to be in practice, which Buddhist concepts are, in the most fundamental sense they are just gossamer of thoughts. This is the lesson he wants to emphasize in his philosophical works.

Nāgārjuna takes the offensive against 'rationalists' and 'realists' chiefly in three works, namely *MK*, *ŚS* and *VV*. First, he points out a number of absurd implications in his opponent's position. Because things always arise on the basis of conditions and causes, which no one would be prepared to contest, it is impossible that they should exist independently. They have no 'own-being' (*svabhāva*). They are what they are in mutual relation, like long and short. Therefore, in any real sense, they cannot be said to arise as genuine entities. He accepts the Sarvāstivāda term *svabhāva*, but gives it a new and deeper meaning. The basic flaw in the opponent's case is that on the one hand he advocates some sort of *svabhāva*, while on the other hand he must concede that neither experience nor logic support him when he accepts the existence of independent entities.

Nāgārjuna also produces some 'positive' arguments in favour of 'non-production'. In later terminology one speaks of the 'four great reasons for non-origination' (Lindtner 1982: 273–4):

1 Neither the existing, the non-existent, the existing-non-existent, nor the neither existing nor non-existent can arise.
2 A thing cannot arise of itself, of anything else, of both, or neither (that is also to say, without a cause).
3 Nothing can be proved to be either numerically 'one' or numerically 'more than one', or 'many'.
4 Everything is demonstrably 'conditioned co-originated'.

The objection to the Sarvāstivāda is that they ignore the fact that things are without own-being as a direct consequence of conditioned co-origination, in other words, they are empty, like illusions. Nāgārjuna, as said, calls to witness experience and logic, and also the warning from the Buddha himself to avoid extremes of absolute existence and absolute non-existence. His later adherents called themselves 'men of the middle way', Mādhyamika, because they claimed to steer a middle course between absolute existence and non-existence towards liberation, which follows on dissociation from being and non-being, morally as well as theoretically. Nāgārjuna and his followers choose mirages, delusions and dreams to represent what lies between existence and non-existence. They are naturally only models, but useful for what it is all about, the acknowledgement of universal emptiness, which is really not an acknowledgement of anything at all.

With this broad picture in mind we may now have a closer look at Nāgārjuna's three basic philosophical works, *MK*, *ŚS* and *VV*.

MK is Nāgārjuna's philosophical masterpiece, as proved by the work's scope and character. It consists of 448 verses divided into 27 chapters. Some of the verses (see I 1; II 1, 21; IV 6, 8, 9; V 8; VI 4; VII 34; IX 5; X 10, 11; XI 1; XIII 1, 8; XIV 5, 6, 7; XV 1, 2, 10; XXI 6, 12; XXII 12, 15, 16; XXIII 1; XXIV 8, 9, 10) are fundamental to the topic, or axiomatic, while the rest are mostly destructive argumentation. Chapters XVIII, XXVI and XXVII have a special role, as we shall see later.

The central position of this work is indirectly shown by the great influence it had in later times. In India alone at least ten commentaries and two sub-commentaries are known to have been composed, though several of these are no longer extant; and in China and Tibet numerous commentaries were written.

The overriding intention of the author of *MK* is evident from the introductory paean and the last verse of chapter XXVII. The Buddha has shown that the True Doctrine is conditioned co-origination, which points beyond the world of experience to an ineffable peace removed from all and every contradiction. *MK* sets out to prove that the correct understanding of *pratītyasamutpāda* is synonymous with the elimination of all the speculative views and dogmas (*dṛṣṭi*) that various Buddhists have permitted discursive thought to fabricate on the basis of *prapañca*.

With the exception of Chapters XVIII, XXVI and XXVII, the chapters are constructed as a critical investigation (*parīkṣā*) of one or more dogmas (*dṛṣṭi*) championed by one or more Buddhist schools. Even if the commentators, especially Bhavya and Avalokitavrata, occasionally make sallies against non-Buddhists, Nāgārjuna's own dialogues are always with Buddhists. It is important to note that the argumentation is strictly methodical throughout. Nāgārjuna can lead with a 'negative' proposition, or the opponent can submit a 'positive' view. Then the formal possibilities and alternatives are stated one by one, purely hypothetically. The inescapable conclusion is that neither the view that is being promoted nor its opposite can stand up to a critical scrutiny which avails itself of specific logical reasons for 'non-origination' as a means of forcing the opponent into absurdity.

The question of the topics and sequence of the chapters is interesting, but not quite straightforward. The Indian commentators have not paid it any attention, taking the chapters as they come, and leaving it up to an imaginary opponent to decide the next issue on the agenda. Can one see a progression in the work, or could one envisage a change in the argument or the chapter sequence without too much disturbance? Serious matters like momentariness and the independent existence of consciousness, discussed in some of the author's other works, could in my opinion well have had a chapter in *MK*, but the fact remains that they did not. As far as I can see there are intimations of a progression, in *MK* as in most other works by Nāgārjuna, but nothing more. A theme is dealt with, then you go on to a new one, and back to the old one again. On the other hand, one must not overlook the fact that topics dealt with only once are treated systematically and consistently. This is best seen in *MK* and *VV*, and also in *VP*, where the sixteen basic concepts of the Nyāya school are rejected step by step (Lindtner 1982: 87–93). My view of all this is that we have eight loosely connected 'clusters' of chapters.

Chapters I–II attack the two corner-stones of the ontology of the arch-enemy, the Sarvāstivāda, namely causality and the movement of the *dharmas*, which are the natural prerequisites for any sort of causality. The next three chapters belong together in that they deal with 'everything that exists', that is to say the five *skandhas* (IV), the twelve/eighteen bases (II), and the six elements (V). The eighteen elements were indirectly disposed of in ch. III. Chapter VI investigates the relation between desire and the desiring subject, but this is obviously an arbitrary choice, dictated by a 'rhetorical' motive. The real subject is coexistence (*sahabhāva*), a key concept in the Sarvāstivāda type of causal coexistence, whether, as in this instance, it is an action–agent relationship, or in any other way. Chapter VII disproves the three characteristics, origination, duration, and cessation, inseparable from anything causally created, that is, composite (*saṃskṛta*), and to that extent elaborates the discussion on causation. In addition, ch. VII has a long digression criticizing an auxiliary hypothesis of the Vātsīputrīya (Sāṃmitīya), a school that makes its first appearance here. One could say that VII 34 is a sort of preliminary conclusion to I-VII: objective multiplicity considered as a series of independent *dharmas* subjected to change according to a given causal pattern (namely that of Sarvāstivāda, in particular) is illusory.

Chapters VIII–X have a strong thematic connection, attacking the thesis peculiar to the Vātsīputrīya of the existence of a personal substance (a 'soul'), which is its own creative principle, and for which the physical and psychical components of the personality are merely instruments in *saṃsāra*. In ch. X, as in ch. VI, one concrete example is taken from the set to illustrate how an ontological entity is disproved.

Chapter XI brings us on to new ground, in my opinion connecting up with chs XII and XIII. Nāgārjuna discourses here on 'things' in their widest generality. The world of *saṃsāra* is limitless in space and time (ch. XI). Therefore everything bounded by *saṃsāra* is without a beginning and without limits. This is in fact the ontological *raison d'être* behind Nāgārjuna's attack on all the distinctions and entities of discursive thought. Chapter XI, though brief, is a vital part of the work. In ch. XII, with suffering as the particular case (as in chs VI and X), things in general are also shown to be indeterminate by the very fact that they are, to use a characteristic Mahāyāna term, 'unoriginated'. They cannot be created from themselves, from anything else, both or neither (without cause). The purpose of ch. XIII was evidently to forestall the objection that however Nāgārjuna may disprove things in general in chs XI and XII, is not the inconstancy of the empirical world a palpable fact that only a fool would deny? No, because alteration (*anyathābhāva*) is a logical impossibility.

In the next four chapters Nāgārjuna concentrates again on specifically Buddhist concepts. Chapter XIV resumes a theme from ch. III, which is also found in ch. VI: even admitting that the twelve bases and the eighteen elements existed, they could not possibly enter into combination. Chapter XIV establishes that Sarvāstivāda's belief in an immutable *svabhāva* is both illogical and unorthodox. Whereas ch. XI assumed the reality of *saṃsāra* (i.e. on the level of relative truth), transmigration is rejected in ch. XVI because neither the five *skandhas* nor the 'soul' (the Vātsīputrīya concept) can be said to migrate in any way. Therefore there is no *nirvāṇa* either, the idea of absolute truth that can hold only in contrast to *saṃsāra*. (For the Two Truths see ch. XXIV.) Chapter XVII is about *karma*, a central concept closely connected with that of *saṃsāra*. It begins (verses 1–20) with a very detailed account from the relative standpoint of *karma*'s nature and aspects in relation to the various schools of *abhidharma*. In the absolute sense there is nothing that can be called *karma* (verses 21–33).

Chapter XVIII is not very well arranged, but it does, in a very condensed manner, give a better idea of the essence of the author's own philosophy than any other chapter in *MK*. The belief in 'I' and 'mine' (i.e. the five *skandhas*) is due to discursive thought (*vikalpa*), which, again, is due to ignorance. These *vikalpas* produce the defilements (*kleśa*), which again activate *karma*, which in turn leads to rebirth. Emptiness is the weapon that destroys the expanded world (*prapañca*) forming the basis of the initial *vikalpas*. The absolute truth, liberation, is beyond *prapañca*, and therefore nothing can be said about it. So the buddhas can preach one doctrine at one time, or its exact opposite at another time, depending, not on the 'truth', but on the needs and presuppositions of their audience. There are three groups of Buddhists, and it is depth of insight that distinguishes them from one another.

Chapter XIX leads rather abruptly back to a typical Sarvāstivāda problem: the three periods of the *dharmas*, in one word, time. The same goes for chs XX and XXI, the critical examination of causality and of existence-cessation. They give an added emphasis to the criticism in ch. I, and together with ch. XIX they can be considered as a sort of appendix to ch. I.

Chapters XIX–XXI tolled the knell for the long-drawn-out refutation of the two major Buddhist dogmatic schools, Sarvāstivāda and Vātsīputrīya. All possible views were shown to be empty in the absolute sense. Chapters XXII–XXIV are coherent in the sense that they have no regard for the holiest of the holies for any Buddhist, the concept of Tathāgata, the Buddha himself (XXII), the four misconceptions, that is, the ignorance in which Buddha found the cause for the sufferings of existence (XXIII), the Four Noble Truths (XXIV), and even the highest goal for Buddhism, *nirvāṇa* (XXV), all so that Nāgārjuna could ram home his basic idea of the emptiness of things. These four chapters effectively conclude the author's rejection of all conceivable dogmas (*dṛṣṭi*).

The final two chapters in *MK* are not polemical in scope. On first reading it is rather an anti-climax because Nāgārjuna has obviously deigned to come down to the relative plane, without the rhetorical élan of the absolute. The role of these chapters is to show how important it was for the author to be considered a good and orthodox Buddhist. According to tradition, it was during the night of his enlightenment that the Buddha became aware of the twelve members, from whose activity suffering stemmed. The interpretation of this formula of the twelve members has always been regarded as problematic and crucial. Therefore, in ch. XXVI Nāgārjuna must emphasize in plain language that the realization of emptiness provides exactly the means desired to terminate the ignorance which, as the initial member of the formula, is at the bottom of the genesis of suffering. Moreover, in the oldest canonical texts, we sometimes see that the Buddha warns against the acceptance of sixteen dogmas which presuppose that either the 'soul' or the world should be finite or infinite with respect to time (eternal etc.). As announced in the two introductory couplets of *MK*, and in the final verse, it is precisely these two dogmatic extremes that Nāgārjuna has tried to avoid by enlisting emptiness. It is essential to embrace this doctrine if one wishes to understand the Buddha correctly. The purpose of the two final chapters, then, is immediately obvious once one remembers that *MK* is addressed to Buddhist monks, some of whom in the course of their study of this revolutionary manual of meditation may well have had their doubts about the orthodoxy of its author. Nāgārjuna very much wants to emphasize his orthodoxy.

The fact that Nāgārjuna soon had to write two supplements to *MK* – for this is how we have to regard his *ŚS* and *VV* – shows that *MK* did not meet with unconditioned approval in all quarters of Buddhism.

There can be no doubt that *ŚS*, *The Septuagint on Emptiness*, actually seventy-three verses with the author's own commentary in prose (Lindtner 1982: 31–69), was not only written later than *MK*, but was conceived as a sort of postscript to the main work. This is seen in the format, as there are several references back to what has already been said, i.e. in *MK*, and also in the content, as the verses of *ŚS* most often summarize a chapter of *MK*, or part of one, or go into a subject not dealt with or only partially treated in *MK* and therefore the cause for further comment.

Candrakīrti and a later commentator, Parahita, put it that *ŚS* is written to meet the criticism that could be levelled against *MK* VII 34. This may be correct, but sounds rather facile. The relationship to *MK* must have determined the composition of *ŚS*. The text consists of a number of independent chapters, the argument carried in verses that are so ambivalent that they need an oral or written commentary. One can imagine that the 'publication' of an original text of the standard of *MK* must have caused a good deal of bewilderment among readers. Some have asked for a straightforward, authentic prose commentary; others have raised objections on various points.

To meet these demands, Nāgārjuna could well have decided to write *ŚS* as a supplement. To prevent misunderstanding he set out his main thesis again, made good omissions, and provided the whole with a prose commentary that leaves nothing to be desired in completeness and clarity.

The main features of the argumentation in *ŚS* are as follows: all concepts in Buddhism have only relative practical validity (1), for in the absolute view they are empty (2), as properly speaking they lack an independent form of existence (3). One cannot, in other words, speak of anything 'arising' in the real sense. This can be proved in several ways (4–6).

The opponent is foiled in his attempt to abandon postulated entities such as numbers (7) and go over to the existence of things, thereby to disprove Nāgārjuna's claim that everything is empty. This concept too is conditioned co-originated (8). The same is true for ignorance etc. which is due to misconceptions (9–14). It is precisely because of this lack of own-being that the idea of relative (Buddhist) causality can be entertained at all. Compare *MK* XXIV (15–16). Every conceivable form of existence must, by the very fact that it is only possible in correlation, be empty (17–21). Nor can existence, non-existence, etc. form a continuum. Compare *MK* XVII 22–4 (22). Since no form of existence (*bhāva*) whatever exists in the real sense, *nirvāṇa* cannot be defined as the cessation of such an existence. Extinction, or *nirvāṇa*, is purely and simply Non-existence (23–4); only in that way can one avoid falling into the two heretical extremes (25–6).

The opponent, who is still not satisfied with Nāgārjuna's rejection of all forms of existence, tries to drop the existence of certain other postulated entities in favour of existence in general, but only to be rebuffed again. There is nothing which is in itself a characteristic or which characterizes (27). The existence of time as a basis for things cannot be substantiated (28). There are no composite things etc., because their postulated characteristics are in fact not demonstrable (30–1), and because they cannot be numerically determined (32). One cannot claim the existence of any form of being (*bhāva*) on these grounds either.

Next comes a long section on *karma*, an extension of *MK* XVII. *Karma*, the cause for the body, is due to passions (*kleśa*) which are stirred up by belief in the ego, a form of *vikalpa*. Since *karma* is thus conditioned co-originated, it is empty, that is, non-arisen and illusory. The agent likewise, naturally (33–43). This idea is in no way contrary to the Buddha's own words (44).

There follows a disproof of the *skandha* 'form' (*rūpa*), i.e. matter appearing as form and colour, which goes much further than *MK* IV. The elements, the presumed basis from which form is derived, do not exist (45–6); one cannot proceed logically to the existence of form (47), and form cannot be perceived, for several reasons (48–54). This emptiness of the *skandhas* provides the opportunity for showing that feelings (*vedanā*) (55) and consciousness (*vijñāna*) (56–7) are also conditioned co-originated.

The next section harks back to verses 9–26, in which ignorance (*avidyā*) was due to misconceptions (*viparyāsa*), which in the final analysis is based on an unfounded acceptance of some form of *bhāva*. The origination of *karma*-conditioned passions (*kleśa*) is now determined to be due to the stupefying misconceptions (*viparyāsa*) of things really existing that can be pleasant etc. (58–61). When one realizes the emptiness of the fictitious objects, the basic factor, ignorance, is brought to an end, and the other eleven follow. This is equivalent to the cessation of suffering. Compare *MK* XXVI (62–6).

In the conclusion it is stated that the absolute truth is emptiness, that is, no self-existence, conditioned co-origination, non-arising. The relative truth, that is, Buddhist dogma, is by no means excluded, as it is the essential means of realizing *nirvāṇa* (67–73). Compare *MK* XXIV and *RĀ* I 3–6.

This finally brings us to the *End to Discussions*, *VV*, which is in seventy plus two verses (*āryā*), with a detailed, almost too copious auto-commentary. *VV* is later than *MK*, which is cited in the text, and probably also later than *ŚS* (the stanzas of which were also composed in the *āryā* metre). The author's purpose in *VV* is indubitably to answer or forestall the objects that can be raised against Nāgārjuna's position from a logical and epistemological point of view. The opponent is an unidentified, possibly fictitious Buddhist logician, well versed, naturally, in *abhidharma*.

With this in view, *VV* proceeds according to the contemporary rules of debate (*vāda*). One tries to prove one's case (*sādhana*) by putting forth a proposition (*pratijñā*, *pakṣa*) accompanied by a logical reason (*hetu*), and exemplified with an analogy (*dṛṣṭānta*). In the same way one seeks to refute the opponent's point by proving standard-type errors or lacunae in his proof (*dūṣaṇa*). The theoretical justification for what is included as an integral part in the proof is fixed by the doctrine of means of cognition (*pramāṇa*). Four means are accepted for the cognition of a given object: perception, inference, scripture (*āgama*) and analogy (*upamāna*).

Nāgārjuna accepts this, but only on the relative plane. He is unusual in introducing his theory of the Two Truths into the debate. It happens that at one time he reasons on the relative plane, only to withdraw on to the absolute plane. We have no evidence for how the opponent reacted to the *VV*, but we can establish indirectly that it was not considered fair for him to have it both ways. Nāgārjuna and his sort were thought to be not much more than pettifoggers (*vaitaṇḍika*). It was left to Nāgārjuna's successors, Bhavya and Candrakīrti in particular, to confront the logical consequences of the doctrine of the Two Truths.

The 'opponent' sets out his criticism in *VV* 1–20, Nāgārjuna giving his answer in verses 21–70. His *pratijñā* (on the relative plane): all forms of existence are void of own-being, i.e. empty. His *hetu*: because they are conditioned co-originated. His analogy: like a phantom. The opponent now tries to point out various errors in Nāgārjuna's proof. Here, it is very important to note that the opponent works on the unspoken assumption that Nagarjuna's *pratijñā* (given above) implies a negation (*pratiṣedha*) of own-being. Nāgārjuna, however, does nothing about this misunderstanding until verse 63! He is not denying own-being, but merely pointing out that according to logic and experience a thing's own-being cannot be apprehended. That is, Nāgārjuna thinks, quite a different matter from denying an actual instance of own-being.

The opponent makes nine points in his *dūṣaṇa*:

1 If everything is empty, so must Nāgārjuna's words be empty, and thus they can deny nothing, or else Nāgārjuna's words must be an exception, but that is inconsistent with the claim that *everything* is empty (1–2).
2 Nāgārjuna's example, a prohibition against making noise, cannot really illustrate his *pratijñā* (3).
3 It is inconsistent when Nāgārjuna, who claims that everything can be negated, will not allow the opponent to deny Nāgārjuna's denials also (4).
4 Before Nāgārjuna can deny anything he must affirm one or more means of cognition (*pramāṇa*) as existing 'suppliers' of the things that Nāgārjuna is going to deny. By this reasoning he does not deny everything (5–6).
5 Nāgārjuna's *pratijñā* (above) is in conflict with scripture (*āgama*).
6 When Nāgārjuna ascribes own-being to things, that must presume that he affirms the existence of the things that are being deprived of a given form of self-existence (9–10).
7 Denial presumes the reality of what is being denied, otherwise denial would just be automatic, without there being any question of anything that is denied (11–12). Even if, as a hypothesis, one accepted the possibility of denying without there being anything to deny, then it would at least imply that the false belief that there was something to deny was indeed true (i.e. if there were no false belief to deny, there would be nothing to deny). Therefore own-being exists (13–16).
8 Nāgārjuna cannot claim that things are empty on the ground that they lack self-existence, for there exists no self-existence they can feel the loss of. If, on the other hand, he keeps on asserting his claim without giving a reason for it, then the

opponent can also permit himself to claim the opposite of Nāgārjuna without having to submit a ground for it (17–18). But if Nāgārjuna confirms his logical ground (that is, that there is an own-being to deny), this is again in conflict with his claim that everything lacks self-existence (19).

9 Finally, to turn one of Nāgārjuna's arguments against himself, Nāgārjuna cannot at any point of time establish a denial, whether of something that is denied, or of something that is not denied, or of something that is simultaneous with the denial. Therefore own-being is a fact (20).

Nāgārjuna's answer is as follows (21–70). He begins by repeating his *pratijñā* (21), his *hetu* (22) and an analogy (23), then replies to the separate points:

ad 1 There is no such inconsistency (24).

ad 2 Nāgārjuna does not recognize the adduced analogy (25–6), and introduces a satisfactory one (27). These seven verses (i.e. 21–7) have been on the relative plane. The argument continues on the absolute plane. Here no noise exists that can prevent anyone from making a noise (28).

ad 3 In the absolute sense Nāgārjuna cannot contradict his own *pratijñā*, because he has not got one (29).

ad 4 No, Nāgārjuna cannot, from the absolute point of view, recognize any *pramāṇa* (30), because it cannot be established (31) by any other *pramāṇas* (32) without *pramāṇas* (33) of its own right, partly because the analogy does not hold good (34–9), partly because the *pramāṇa* would then have to be dependent on objects of cognition (40–1). On the other hand objects cannot constitute *pramāṇa* (42–5), nor can they be mutually ascertained, like father and son (46–50). Thus *pramāṇa* cannot be established. Compare *pratijñā* and *hetu* in verses 30–1. *Quod erat demonstrandum* (51).

ad 5 There is no conflict with *āgama* because all *dharmas* are said to be empty (52–6).

ad 6 As far as Nāgārjuna is concerned, the thing referred to and the term that is used for it are equally empty (57). Besides, the opponent cannot speak of non-existing words (58). Names are, like everything else, empty (59). There is nothing behind the *dharmas* (60).

ad 7 If the opponent believes that denial must have something real to deny, he is thereby acknowledging emptiness (61), or else he must abandon his belief (62). Nāgārjuna denies nothing (63); he only *draws attention* to the lack of own-being (64–7).

ad 8 In the same way there is no own-being that serves as a logical ground (*hetu*) and that can be denied as a reason for Nāgārjuna's *pratijñā* (68).

ad 9 On the contrary, just because there is no own-being, Nāgārjuna's 'denials' will always be valid (69).

It has been shown that the doctrine of emptiness is perfectly compatible with sound logic and good Buddhism (70). Concluding homage to the Buddha.

There is, as said, undoubtedly more than one way to present Nāgārjuna's philosophical and religious views in a systematic manner. Nāgārjuna, too, is conscious of this state of affairs. The Buddhist teachings can be summarized under headings such as the five *skandhas*, the Two Truths, the Four Noble Truths (i.e. the four facts, suffering, etc., that the noble ones consider true), the thirty-seven *dharmas*, the six, or ten, perfections, etc. (Dayal 1932). In *Rā* I 3–4, adopting Vaiśeṣika terminology, Nāgārjuna speaks of 'high status' (*adhyudaya*) and *summum bonum* (*naiḥśreyasa*), i.e. happiness in this life, and final liberation; they mostly depend on faith and wisdom, respectively. Otherwise the main theme in *RĀ* and **BS* is the twofold collection for enlightenment (*bodhisaṃbhāra*). When a *bodhisattva*, i.e. a Mahāyānist, has collected an enormous mass of merit and insight he will come into possession of a physical and a spiritual body, together believed to constitute buddhahood, the ultimate ideal of Mahāyāna. Madhyamaka, in brief, is thus but a special Buddhist yogic form of moral and intellectual *purification*, i.e. a doctrine of a double *dharma* acknowledged, with individual differences, by virtually all classical Indian philosophers

REFERENCES

Ames, W. (1986) '*Prajñāpradīpa*, Chapters 3–5, 23, 26', Ph.D. dissertation, University of Washington, Seattle.

Bhattacharya, K. (trans.), Johnston, E. H. and Kunst, A. (eds) (1978) *The Dialectical Method of Nāgārjuna (Vigrahavyāvartanī)*, Delhi: Motilal Banarsidass.

Cheng, H. (1982) *Nāgārjuna's 'Twelve Gate Treatise'. Translated, with Introductory Essays, Comments, and Notes*, Dordrecht: Reidel.

Conze, E. (1978) *The Prajñāpāramitā Literature*, Tokyo: The Reiyukai.

Dayal, H. (1932) *The Bodhisattva Doctrine in Buddhist Sanskrit Literature*, London: Kegan Paul, Trubner, Trench & Co.

Eckel, M. D. (1987) *Jñānagarbha's Commentary on the Distinction between the Two Truths*, Albany: State University of New York Press.

—— (1992) *To See the Buddha*, New York: HarperCollins.

Ejima, Y. (1980) *Chūckan-shisō no tenkai: Bhāvaviveka kenkyū*, Tokyo: Shunjūsha.

Finot, L. (1987) *La Marche à la lumière*, Paris: Les Deux Océans.

Frauwallner, E. (1982) *Kleine Schriften*, Wiesbaden: Franz Steiner Verlag.

Hahn, M. (1982) *Nāgārjuna's Ratnāvālī*, Bonn: Indica et Tibetica.

Hartmann, J.-U. (1987) *Das Varṇārhavarṇastotra des Mātṛceṭa*, Göttingen: Vandenhoeck & Ruprecht.

Hopkins, J. (1975). *The Precious Garland and The Song of the Four Mindfulnesses*, New York: Harper & Row.

Huntington, C. W. (1986) 'The *Akutobhayā* and early Indian Madhyamaka', Ph.D. dissertation, University of Michigan.

—— (1989) *The Emptiness of Emptiness: An Introduction to Early Indian Mādhyamika*, Honolulu: University of Hawaii Press.

Ichigō, M. (1985) *Madhyamakālaṃkāra of Śāntarakṣita*, I–II, Kyoto: Buneido.

Jamspal, L. *et al.* (1978) *Nāgārjuna's Letter to King Gautamīputra*, Delhi: Motilal Banarsidass.

Kajiyama, Y. (1989) *Studies in Buddhist Philosophy: Selected Papers*, Kyoto: Rinsen Book Co.

Kawamura, L. (1975) *Golden Zephyr: Instructions from a Spiritual Friend*, Emeryville: Dharma Publishing.

Kawasaki, Sh. (1992) *Issai chi shisó no kenkyū*, Tokyo: Shunjūsha.

Lamotte, E. (1949–80) *Le Traité de la grande vertu de sagesse de Nāgārjuna (Mahāprajñāpāramitāśāstra)*, Louvain: Université de Louvain.

Lang, K. (1986) *Āryadeva's Catuḥśataka: On the Bodhisattva's Cultivation of Merit and Knowledge*, Copenhagen: Akademisk Forlag.
La Vallée Poussin, L. de (1923–31) *L'Abhidharmakośa de Vasubandhu*, I–VI, *Mélanges chinois et bouddhiques*, Paris: Geuthner.
Lindtner, C. (ed.) (1979) 'Candrakīrti's *Pañcaskandhaprakaraṇa*', *Acta Orientalia* 40: 87–145.
—— (1981a) 'Atiśa's introduction to the Two Truths, and its sources', *Journal of Indian Philosophy* 9: 161–214.
—— (1981b) 'Buddhapālita on emptiness', *Indo-Iranian Journal* 23: 187–217.
—— (1982) *Nagarjuniana: Studies in the Writings and Philosophy of Nāgārjuna*, Copenhagen: Akademisk Forlag.
—— (1984) 'On Bhavya's *Madhyamakaratnapradīpa*', *Indologica Taurinensia* 12: 163–84.
—— (1985) 'A treatise on Buddhist idealism: Kambala's *Ālokamālā*', in *Miscellanea Buddhica*, Copenhagen: Akademisk Forlag, pp. 109–221.
—— (1986) Review of 'Cheng (1982)', *Orientalistische Literaturzeitung* 81: 409–13.
—— (1989) 'The Yogācāra philosophy of Dignāga and Dharmakīrti, *Studies in Central and Eastern Religions* 2: 27–52.
May, J. (1959) *Candrakīrti: Prasannapadā Madhyamakavṛtti*, Paris: Adrien Maisonneuve.
Mimaki, K. (1982) '*Blo gsal grub mtha*', Kyoto: Zinbun Kagaku Kenkyusyo.
Murti, T. R. V. (1960) *The Central Philosophy of Buddhism: A Study of the Mādhyamika System*, London: George Allen & Unwin.
Nagao, G. M. (1991) *Mādhyamika and Yogācāra*, Albany: State University of New York Press.
Nakamura, H. (1980) *Indian Buddhism: A Survey with Bibliographical Notes*, Tokyo: Intercultural Research Institute.
Pāsādika, Bhikkhu (1989) *Nāgārjuna's Sūtrasamuccaya: A Critical Edition* of the *mDo kun las btus pa*, Copenhagen: Akademisk Forlag.
Qvarnström, O. (1989) *Hindu Philosophy in Buddhist Perspective: The Vedāntatattvaviniścaya Chapter of Bhavya's Madhyamakahṛdayakārikā*, Lund: Almqvist Wiksell International.
Ramanan, K. V. (1966) *Nāgārjuna's Philosophy as Presented in The MahāPrajñāpāramitā-Śāstra*, Tokyo: Charles E. Tuttle.
Robinson, R. H. (1967) *Early Mādhyamika in India and China*, Madison: University of Wisconsin Press.
Rosenberg, O. (1924) *Die Probleme der Buddhistischen Philosophie: Materialien zur Kunde des Buddhismus* Heidelberg: C. Winter.
Ruegg, D. S. (1981) *The Literature of the Madhyamaka School of Philosophy in India*, Wiesbaden: Otto Harrassowitz.
Saitō, A. (1984) '*Buddhapālita-mūlamadhyamaka-vṛtti*', Ph.D. diss., Canberra: Australian National University.
Schayer, S. (1931) *Ausgewählte Kapitel aus der Prasannapadā (V, XII, XIII, XIV, XV, XVI)*, Polska Akademja Umiejętności. Cracow.
—— (1988) *O filozofowaniu Hindusów*, Warsaw: Polska Akademia Nauk.
Scherrer-Schaub, C. A. (1991) *Yuktiṣaṣṭikāvṛtti*, *Mélanges chinois et bouddhiques* 25, Brussels: Institute Belge des Hautes Études Chinoises.
Stcherbatsky, Th. (1923) *The Central Conception of Buddhism and the Meaning of the Word 'Dharma'*, London: Royal Asiatic Society.
—— (1927) *The Conception of Buddhist Nirvāṇa*, Leningrad: Publishing Office of the Academy of Sciences of the USSR.
Steinkellner, E. (1981) *Sāntideva [sic!]: Eintritt in das Leben zur Erleuchtung: Poesie und Lehre des Mahayana-Buddhismus*, Düsseldorf Cologne: Eugen Diederichs Verlag.
Tillemans, T.J.F. (1990) *Materials for the Study of Āryadiva, Dharmapāla and Candrakīrti*, Wien: Arbeitskreis für tibetische und buddhistische studien Universität Wien.
Tucci, G. (1978) *Minor Buddhist Texts: Parts I & II*, Kyoto: Rinsen Book Company.
Tuxen, P. (1982) *Yoga: en oversigt over den systematiske yogafilosofi på grundlag af kilderne*, Copenhagen: Akademisk Forlag.

19

BUDDHISM IN TIBET

Donald S. Lopez, Jr

The influence of Buddhism on Tibet since its introduction in the seventh century has been profound, serving as a catalyst for developments in almost every facet of Tibetan culture: in art, with the development of the Tibetan painted scroll; in architecture, with the design of temples, monasteries and *stūpas*; in politics, with the institution of the Dalai Lama; in social structure, with a large segment of the male population becoming celibate monks; in language, with the creation of the Tibetan script for the apparent purpose of translating Buddhist scriptures; in literature, with the composition of thousands of Buddhist texts in a vast variety of genres; and, of course, in religion. To seek to isolate from Tibetan culture something called philosophy is to misrepresent the myriad uses to which Buddhist doctrine was put over the centuries of Tibetan history. If something that can be termed 'Tibetan Buddhist philosophy' exists, it is a complex phenomenon, not easily isolatable.

Buddhist thought was imported into Tibet beginning in the seventh century from the neighbouring cultures of China, central Asia and most importantly, India. From that point, Buddhism in Tibet developed rapidly, with the early centuries marked by contacts with influential Buddhist figures of Kashmir and Bengal. Tibetan Buddhist thought thus sees itself as an inheritance from India, with the notion of lineage playing a pre-eminent position, lineages that the Tibetans attempted to maintain in the centuries that followed the demise of Buddhism in India. Any evaluation of Tibetan Buddhist thought that does not pay due attention to its history must, therefore, very quickly prove inadequate, despite the claims to transhistorical truth made by the Tibetans themselves.

The ideas and doctrines inherited from India were elaborated upon and synthesized in Tibet, with schools of thought developing that were often at odds with each other. This chapter will consider how the term 'philosophy' might be rendered in Tibetan, and then provide a brief historical survey of the tradition, followed by an examination of Tibetan compendia of Indian Buddhist philosophy called doxographies (*grub mtha'*), an important genre of literature in which a wide range of philosophical positions are catalogued and evaluated. In addition, there will be an examination of the role of the monastic institution as the arena of philosophical discourse and an analysis of a major doctrinal controversy. This chapter will not deal specifically with the philosophy of Bön, a tradition often described as the pre-Buddhist religion of Tibet, but more accurately regarded, especially after the eleventh century, as a heterodox sect of Tibetan Buddhism.

The Tibetan Buddhist vocabulary has several terms that might be provisionally translated as 'philosophy'. One such term is *lta ba* (Sanskrit: *dṛṣṭi*), often translated as 'view'. The term most often means a school's or person's positions on a range of religious questions that are considered cardinal in Buddhism, concerning rebirth, the state of perfection and the nature of reality. The right view is always deemed to be that inherited from the Buddha or some other famous Indian master, and much of Tibetan Buddhist literature is devoted to the delineation of the right view from the wrong. To this extent, *lta ba* has a stronger connotation of belief than of knowledge or philosophy; a view is a point of doctrine to which one intellectually assents under instruction from a teacher, and which, in principle, eventually becomes confirmed through normative meditative experience. A second term that could be translated as 'philosophy' is *mtshan ñid*, meaning 'defining characteristic' or 'mark' and by extension, the field of knowledge that is concerned with identifying defining characteristics. It is the translation of the Sanskrit term *lakṣaṇa*, which is used in certain Indian Buddhist contexts to distinguish the more technical and literal delineations of doctrine found in the *abhidharma* (scholastic works dealing with psychology, epistemology and soteriology) from the more figurative language of the *sūtras* (works traditionally regarded as discourses of the Buddha). In common Tibetan parlance *mtshan ñid* connotes the various categories of Buddhist doctrine as contained in specific Indian treatises (see the section on monastic education below). It should be noted, however, that the study of *mtshan ñid* was not universally judged to be of primary importance for the acquisition of the salvific wisdom that is the goal of the Buddhist path. Even for those traditions that emphasized skill in *mtshan ñid*, such skill was considered not as an end in itself but as a prerequisite for deeper studies, in which whatever intellectual insight that might be gained through the study of *mtshan ñid* was to be raised to the level of direct experience through meditative exercises. Those who remained concerned merely with the precise verbal articulation of doctrine, however sophisticated such verbiage may be, are uniformly condemned as sophists in Tibetan literature of all sects.

Of greater significance for the consideration of what might be meant by the term 'Tibetan Buddhist philosophy' is the fact that the authors of philosophical treatises do not conform to our traditional image of the philosopher engaged in the description and analysis of certain fundamental states of affairs, the identification of problems, and the development and application of theories that address such problems, with an overarching concern with logic, rationality and theoretical consistency. While all of these enterprises find an important place in the Tibetan Buddhist tradition, it is also the case that for many Tibetan savants the faculty of reason provides a relatively superficial awareness, insufficient to the task of directly apprehending the truth. All endeavours in the realm of what might be termed 'philosophy' were theoretically subservient to the greater goal of enlightenment, and the ultimate task of the 'philosopher', at least in theory, was to attain that enlightenment, the state of buddhahood. The Tibetan authors who are regarded as pre-eminent scholars were in most cases Buddhist monks, much of whose lives was spent either in the performance of *tantric* ritual or in various sophisticated forms of meditation, in an effort to manifest a fantastic world of benign and malevolent forces, propitiating deities and repelling demons. What we might term 'philosophy' was but one concern of these authors; a perusal of the titles in the collected works of any of Tibet's most erudite thinkers reveals that among the commentaries on Indian logical treatises and expositions of emptiness are myriad works devoted to *tantric* ceremonies and visualizations, along with instructions on techniques for drawing *maṇḍalas*, making rain, stopping smallpox, and manufacturing magical pills.

For the traditional Tibetan scholar, unlike any supposed counterpart in the West, there is no graver sin than innovation. The venerated thinkers of the Tibetan tradition have always seen themselves as merely preserving and elaborating upon the rich philosophical heritage derived from India. (It would therefore be useful for the reader to consult Chapter 17 above on Indian Buddhism before proceeding.) Over a period of twelve centuries, Tibet produced generations of scholars of remarkable learning through an educational system centred in the Buddhist monastery. Here, and in mountain retreats, the tasks of preservation and elaboration were carried on with great diligence. At the same time, Tibetan thinkers, benefiting from the diachronic perspective afforded by their late and lofty vantage point, were able to synthesize chronologically discrete elements of the Indian tradition in ways both provocative and problematic, and contribute to the Buddhist philosophical heritage in ways that can only be judged as innovative.

THE FIRST DISSEMINATION OF BUDDHISM IN TIBET

Sustained Tibetan exposure to Buddhist thought began at the end of the eighth century, during the reign of King Khri-sroṅ-lde-btsan, when the renowned Indian scholar Śāntarakṣita was invited to the capital. Śāntarakṣita was the author of several important philosophical works, including the *Compendium of Principles* (*Tattvasaṃgraha*) and the *Ornament of the Middle Way* (*Madhyamakālaṃkāra*), the first of which catalogues the doctrines of the major Indian philosophical schools, both Hindu and Buddhist, while the second disputes the assertions of those schools in the light of Śāntarakṣita's own Mādhyamika (middle way) position. The Buddhist teachings that Śāntarakṣita brought to Tibet seem not to have gained the favour of a certain faction of the Tibetan aristocracy, who are said to have blamed a series of natural disasters on the introduction of the foreign faith. Śāntarakṣita was forced to retreat to Nepal, but before doing so he advised the king to invite the *tantric* master and magician Padmasambhava to Tibet. This was done, and according to chronicles written several centuries later, Padmasambhava converted the demons of Tibet to the Buddhist fold, enlisting their promise always to protect the new faith. With the impropitious elements duly subdued, Śāntarakṣita returned to Tibet, where he founded the first Buddhist monastery in Tibet at bSam-yas in 775 and ordained seven sons of noble families as the first Buddhist monks. Padmasambhava seems to have departed the scene, but remained as a strong mythic presence for Tibetan Buddhism. We have in Śāntarakṣita and Padmasambhava two paradigmatic figures of the Tibetan tradition, the scholar and the *yogin*. While each was presumably versed in Buddhist doctrine as well as in *tantra* (a complex programme of visualization and ritual designed to bestow enlightenment and supernormal powers with greater speed than is possible via the exoteric path), Śāntarakṣita appears as the reserved and methodical pundit, fully conversant with the assertions of the various schools, Buddhist and non-Buddhist. Padmasambhava is the more volatile figure, the *tantric* magician, expert in ritual and in meditation, employing the fantastic powers that result from their practice. These paradigms, often in stereotypic form, persist throughout the Tibetan tradition.

It was not long after the founding of the bSam-yas monastery that a politically charged doctrinal controversy erupted in Tibet. In addition to the Indian party of Śāntarakṣita, there was also an influential Chinese Buddhist contingent who found favour with the Tibetan nobility. These were monks of the Chan (Zen) school, led by one Ho-shang Mo-ho-yen [Heshang Moheyan]. According to traditional accounts, Śāntarakṣita foretold of dangers from the Chinese position and instructed that his student Kamalaśīla be called from India should the situation prove desperate. A conflict seems to have developed between the Indian and Chinese partisans (and their allies in the Tibetan court) over the question of the nature of enlightenment. The Indians held that enlightenment takes place as the culmination of a gradual process of purification, the result of combining virtuous action, meditational serenity and philosophical insight. The Chinese spoke against this view, holding that enlightenment was the intrinsic nature of the mind rather than the goal of a protracted path, so that one need simply to recognize the presence of this innate nature of enlightenment by entering what they deemed a non-conceptual state beyond distinctions; all other practices were superfluous. According to both Chinese and Tibetan records a debate was held between Kamalaśīla and Ho-shang Mo-ho-yen at bSam-yas *c.*797, with King Khri-sroṅ-lde-btsan himself serving as judge. Kamalaśīla was declared the winner and the Ho-shang and his party banished from Tibet, with the king proclaiming that thereafter the Mādhyamika position of Nāgārjuna would be followed in Tibet. It is unlikely that a face-to-face debate took place or that the outcome of the controversy was so unequivocal.[1] None the less, from this point Tibet turned for its Buddhism towards

India and away from China; no school of Chinese Buddhism had any further influence in Tibet. Indeed, the identification of one's opponent with the Chinese monk Mo-ho-yen was to become a stock device in polemical literature in Tibet.

The next few decades were a period of strong royal patronage for Buddhism, with the inception of an enterprise that stands as one of Tibet's great contributions to Buddhist philosophy, the translation of a vast Indian Buddhist literature from Sanskrit into Tibetan. Translation academies were established and standard glossaries of technical terms were developed during the ninth century. The relatively late date of the introduction of Buddhism to Tibet compared to China (first century AD) and Japan (fifth century) had important ramifications for the development of the Tibetan Buddhist tradition, the foremost being that the Tibetans had access to large bodies of Indian Buddhist literature that either never were translated into Chinese (and thus never transmitted to Japan) or had little influence in east Asia. This literature fell into two categories: *tantras* and *śāstras*. Tantric Buddhism seems to have developed in India beginning in the sixth century. Its literature, including all manner of ritual texts and meditation manuals, continued to be composed for the next six centuries. This literature purported to offer a speedy path to enlightenment, radically truncating the aeons-long path set forth in the earlier *sūtras*. To this end, the *tantric* literature set forth a wide range of techniques for the attainment of goals both mundane and supramundane, techniques for bringing the baroque worlds described in the Mahāyāna *sūtras* into actuality. Although *tantrism* was preserved in east Asia in the Shingon sect of Japan, hundreds of influential *tantric* texts, especially those associated with *Anuttarayoga* (Unsurpassed Yoga), were never translated into Chinese or Japanese.

A second body of literature, more important for Buddhist philosophy *per se*, was the *śāstras* (treatises). Buddhist literature is sometimes divided into *sūtras*, those texts traditionally held to be either the word of the Buddha or spoken with his sanction, and *śāstras*, treatises composed by Indian commentators. In the case of Mahāyāna literature, *sūtras* often contain fantastic visions of worlds populated by enlightened beings, with entrance to such a world gained through devotion to the *sūtra* itself. When points of doctrine are presented, it is often in the form of narrative, allegory, or the repetition of stock phrases. The *śāstras* are closer to what might be called systematic philosophy, with positions presented with reasoned argumentation supported by relevant passages from the *sūtras*. East Asian Buddhism was predominantly a *sūtra*-based tradition, with schools forming around single texts, as in the case of the *Lotus Sūtra* for T'ien-t'ai [Tiantai] and the *Avataṃsaka Sūtra* for Hua-yen [Huayan]. These *sūtras* were considered by their adherents to represent the supreme expression of the Buddha's enlightenment; it was in terms of the individual *sūtra* that all other Buddhist doctrine was to be understood, and the Chinese composed extensive commentaries on their chosen *sūtras* to demonstrate this. Some important *śāstras*, especially those of the Yogācāra, were translated. But the major project of translating into Chinese texts brought from India virtually ended with the work of Hsüan-tsang [Xuanzang] (596–664), by whose time the major east Asian schools were well formed. Consequently, works by such figures as Bhāvaviveka (*c.*500–70), Candrakīrti (*c.*600–50) and Dharmakīrti (seventh century), who flourished when the Chinese Buddhist schools had already developed, never gained wide currency in east Asia. And the transmission of Buddhism from India had effectively drawn to a close before some of the most influential treatises of late Indian Mahāyāna Buddhism were composed, works by such authors as Haribhadra (late eighth century), Śāntarakṣita (died 788), Kamalaśīla (*c.*740–95), Śāntideva (early eighth century) and Atīśa (*c.*982–1054). The works by these authors became the basis of the scholastic tradition in Tibet, which from the early period was a *śāstra*-based Buddhism. *Sūtras* were venerated but rarely read independently; the *śāstras* were studied and commented upon at great length.

The translation of Indian Buddhist literature, the *sūtras*, *tantras* and *śāstras*, from Sanskrit into Tibetan was interrupted by the suppression of Buddhist monastic institutions in 838. The Tibetan monarchy ended shortly thereafter.

THE SECOND DISSEMINATION OF BUDDHISM IN TIBET

The eleventh and twelfth centuries, the period of the second dissemination of Buddhism in Tibet, were a period of active translation of numerous philosophical texts and retranslation of texts, especially *tantras*, first translated during the period of the earlier dissemination. Apart from the Bsam-yas debate there were few developments in Buddhist philosophy during the first period of dissemination of Buddhism in Tibet. Much effort was devoted to the elucidation of basic Buddhist doctrines and the assimilation of a formidable technical vocabulary. If a particular philosophical position could be said to predominate, it would be that of Śāntarakṣita and his student Kamalaśīla, a school which later Tibetan doxographers retrospectively labelled the Yogācāra-Svātantrika-Mādhyamika. A second efflorescence of Buddhism occurred in the eleventh century, the key event of which is traditionally deemed the arrival of the Bengali scholar Atīśa in western Tibet in 1042. Of at least equal importance were the activities, both as a translator and as a builder of temples, of Rin-chen-bzaṅ-po (958–1055).[2] Atīśa was a proponent of the Mādhyamika and proclaimed in his *Satyadvayāvatāra* the primacy of Candrakīrti's exposition of Nāgārjuna's thought. Elsewhere, he relies heavily on the interpretations of Bhāvaviveka, suggesting that the distinction between the Candrakīrti's Prāsaṅgika and Bhāvaviveka's Svātantrika that came to be of major importance to Tibetan thinkers was not evident to Atīśa.[3] With Atīśa and his followers we note the formation of a Mādhyamika curriculum in Tibet centred around the works of Nāgārjuna; it is not until the beginning of the twelfth century and the translations of Candrakīrti's major works by Spa-tshab Ñi-ma-grags (b. 1055) that the so-called Prāsaṅgika reading of Nāgārjuna became the dominant Tibetan interpretation of Mādhyamika.

THE MAJOR SECTS

The period of the thirteenth through the fifteenth centuries was one of the most intellectually fertile in the history of Tibetan Buddhism. Here we see the rise of the major sects[4] of Tibetan Buddhism, each with its own literature. The period of translation and assimilation was for the most part over, and Tibetan scholars began to delineate philosophical positions based on their close analyses of Indian texts. A relatively small group of Indian works served both as the primary source of philosophical issues and as the primary subject of study, commentary and debate. In Mādhyamika philosophy, these works included Nāgārjuna's 'Collection of Reasoning' (*rigs tshogs*), Āryadeva's *Catuḥśataka (Four Hundred)* and Candrakīrti's *Prasannapadā* (*Clear Words*) and *Entry to the Middle Way* (*Madhyamakāvatāra*). In Yogācāra philosophy, the chief texts were those of Asaṅga (especially the *Yogācārabhūmi* and the *Mahāyānasaṃgraha*) and Vasubandhu (especially the *Viṃśatikā* and *Triṃśikā*). Logic and epistemology elicited particular attention from Tibetan scholars, whose primary Indian sources were the 'Seven Treatises on Valid Knowledge' (*tshad ma sde bdun*) of Dharmakīrti, with the majority of exegesis performed on his *Commentary on [Dignāga's 'Compendium on] Valid Knowledge'* (*Pramāṇavārttika*). For Hīnayāna doctrine the Tibetans relied heavily on Vasubandhu's *Treasury of Knowledge* (*Abhidharmakośa*). The topic of soteriology (to the extent that it can be separated from philosophy in the Buddhist context), especially as it pertains to the structure of the path to enlightenment and its praxis, was pursued via the study of the 'Five Works of Maitreya' (*byams pa sde lṅa*), especially the *Ornament of Realization* (*Abhisamayālaṃkāra*).

The thirteenth and fourteenth centuries saw the development of distinct sects that developed from the various lineages of teaching that had been initiated during the previous periods. These sects are traditionally divided under two major headings: those who base their tantric practice on texts translated during the period of the first dissemination and those who base their tantric practice on texts translated or retranslated during the period of the second dissemination. These two groups are referred to simply as the old (*rñiṅ ma*) and the new (*gsar ma*), with the old obviously including the Rñiṅ-ma-pa sect and the new including the Bka'-rgyud-pa, the Sa-skya-pa and the Dge-lugs-pa. The distinctive doctrines of each of these four will be briefly surveyed.

The Rñiṅ-ma-pa

The Rñiṅ-ma-pa sect traces its origins back to the teachings of the mysterious figure of Padmasambhava, who visited Tibet during the eighth century. 'Treasures' (*gter ma*), texts believed to have been hidden by him, began to be discovered beginning in the eleventh century and continue even into the twentieth century; the fourteenth century was an especially active period for the text discovers (*gter ston*).[5] According to their claim, these texts were sometimes discovered in physical form, often within stone, or mentally, within the mind of the discoverer. The Rñiṅ-ma-pa include a collection of *tantras* (the *Rñiṅ ma'i rgyud 'bum*) as well as these discovered texts in their canonical corpus, works that the other sects generally regard as apocryphal, that is, not of Indian origin.

The Rñiṅ-ma-pa produced many famous scholars and visionaries, such as Kloṅ-chen-rab-'byams (1308–63), 'Jigs-med-gliṅ-pa (1729–98) and 'Ju Mi-pham-rnam-rgyal (1846–1912). Rñiṅ-ma-pa identifies nine vehicles among the corpus of Buddhist teachings, the highest of which is known as *ati-yoga* or, more commonly, the Great Completeness (*rdzogs-chen*). The Great Completeness teachings are found in three collections of texts, known as the Section on the Mind (*sems sde*), the Section on the Primordial Sphere (*gloṅ sde*) and the Section on Quintessential Instructions (*man ṅag gi sde*). The Great Completeness teachings describe the mind as the primordial basis, characterized with qualities such as presence, spontaneity, luminosity, original purity, unobstructed freedom, expanse, clarity, self-liberation, openness, effortlessness and intrinsic awareness. It is not accessible through conceptual elaboration or logical analysis. Rather, the primordial basis is an eternally pure state free from the dualism of subject and object, infinite and perfect from the beginning, ever complete. The Great Completeness tradition shares with certain Indian Buddhist schools the view that mind (*sems*) creates the appearances of the world, the arena of human suffering. All of these appearances are said to be illusory, however. The ignorant mind believes that its own creations are real, forgetting its true nature of original purity. For the mind wilfully to seek to liberate itself is both inappropriate and futile because it is already self-liberated. The technique for the discovery of the ubiquitous original purity and self-liberation is to engage in a variety of practices designed to eliminate *karmic* obstacles, at which point the mind eliminates all thought and experiences itself, thereby recognizing its true nature. The teachings of the Great Completeness are shared with the non-Buddhist Bön religion (which has its own *rdzogs-chen* tradition). The Great Completeness doctrine does not seem to be directly derived from any of the Indian philosophical schools; its precise connections to the Indian Buddhist tradition have yet to be established.[6] Some scholars have claimed a historical link and doctrinal affinity between the Great Completeness and the Chan tradition of Chinese Buddhism, but the precise relationship between the two remains to be fully investigated. It is noteworthy that certain of the earliest extant Great Completeness texts specifically contrast their own tradition with that of Chan.

The Bka'-rgyud-pa

The Bka'-rgyud-pa sect derives its lineage from the visits to India by Mar-pa the Translator (1012–99), where he studied under several of the famous *tantric* masters of the day, including Nāropa and Maitrīpa. Mar-pa's disciple Mi-la-ras-pa is said to have achieved buddhahood in one lifetime (an achievement usually considered to require aeons of practice) through his diligent meditation practice in the caves of southern Tibet, despite having committed murder as a youth through the practice of black magic. His moving biography and didactic songs are among the most famous works of Tibetan literature.[7] Mi-la-ras-pa's most illustrious disciple was the scholar and physician Gam-po-pa (1079–1153), who gave a strong monastic foundation to the sect. His own disciples, in turn, are regarded as the founders of the four major schools and the eight minor schools of the Bka'-rgyud. Among the prominent philosophers of the Bka'-rgyud sect are Mi-bskyod-rdo-rje (1507–54), Padma-dkar-po (1527–92) and Koṅ-sprul Yon-tan-rgya-mtsho (1813–99).

The defining doctrine of the Bka'-rgyud-pa sect is the Great Seal (*phyag rgya chen po*, *mahāmudrā*), which they regard as the crowning experience of Buddhist practice. The Great Seal is a state of enlightened awareness in which phenomenal appearance and noumenal emptiness are unified. Like the Great Completeness of the Rñiṅ-ma-pas, it is considered to be primordially present, that is, not something that is newly created. The goal of the meditative practices of the Great Seal is called the union of the innate mind (*sems ñid lhan skyes*) and innate appearances (*snaṅ ba lhan skyes*), a natural state of mind free of discursive thought and unfettered by analysis. Rather than emphasizing the attainment of an extraordinary level of consciousness, the Great Seal literature exalts the ordinary state of mind as both the natural and ultimate state, characterized by lucidity and simplicity. In Bka'-rgyud literature, this ordinary mind is contrasted with the worldly mind. The former, compared to a mirror, reflects reality exactly as it is, simply and purely, whereas the worldly mind is distorted by its mistaken perception of subject and object as real. Rather than seeking to destroy this worldly mind as other systems do, however, the Great Seal values the worldly mind for its ultimate identity with the ordinary mind; every deluded thought contains within it the lucidity and simplicity of the ordinary mind. This identity merely needs to be recognized to bring about the dawning of wisdom, the realization that a natural purity pervades all existence, including the deluded mind.[8]

The Sa-skya-pa

The Sa-skya sect looks back to another translator, 'Brog-mi Śākya Ye-śes (993–1050), who studied in India under disciples of the *tantric* master Virūpa. A disciple of 'Brog-mi, 'Khon Dkon-mchog-rgyal-po, founded a monastery at Sa-skya ('grey earth') in 1073. This monastery became the seat of the sect, hence its name. The most influential scholars of the Sa-skya sect in the twelfth and thirteenth centuries were members of the 'Khon family, the most notable of whom was Kun-dga'-rgyal-mtshan (1181–1251), better known as Sa-skya Paṇḍita. He studied under the last generation of Indian Buddhist scholars to visit Tibet, notably Śākyaśrībhadra. Sa-skya Paṇḍita claims two important achievements in the history of Tibetan philosophy. First, he defeated the Hindu *paṇḍita* Harinanda in formal philosophical debate. Second, his master work on logic, the *Treasury of Reasoning* (*Rigs gter*) was so highly regarded that it is said to have been translated from Tibetan into Sanskrit and circulated in northern India.[9] Later Sa-skya scholars of particular distinction are Go-rab-byams Bsod-nams-seṅ-ge (1429–89) and Śākya-mchog-ldan (1428–1507).

The early Sa-skya tradition was concerned primarily with *tantric* practice, especially the 'path and fruition' (*lam 'bras*) tradition associated with the *Hevajra Tantra*, but there was very soon a move to balance and harmonize tantric studies with the study of scholastic philosophy (*mtshan ñid*). Sa-skya scholars wrote extensively on Mādhyamika philosophy, but are particularly famous for their work in logic and epistemology (*tshad ma*, *pramāṇa*). The seminal work on this topic is the *Treasury of Reasoning* by Sa-skya Paṇḍita mentioned above. This work inaugurated a new age in logic studies in Tibet by focusing attention on the most important of Dharmakīrti's works, the *Pramāṇavārttika*, which, in addition to technical issues of Indian logic, provides arguments for the existence of such crucial elements of Buddhist soteriology as liberation and omniscience. Up to this point in the Tibetan study of logic, Dharmakīrti had been primarily approached through composite summaries of his seven works, summaries which Sa-skya Paṇḍita showed to be fraught with problems. In his other writings, Sa-skya Paṇḍita insisted on rational consistency and fidelity to Indian sources in all branches of Buddhist theory and practice. This conviction resulted in often polemical evaluations of the doctrines of other sects, particularly the Bka'-rgyud.[10]

The Dge-lugs-pa

Unlike the other major sects of Tibetan Buddhism, the Dge-lugs-pas do not identify a specific Indian master as the source of their tradition, although they see themselves as inheriting the tradition of Atīśa, the Bengali scholar who arrived in Tibet in 1042. The pre-eminent figure for the sect (who may only retrospectively be identified as the 'founder') is Tsoṅ-kha-pa (1357–1419). While known in the West primarily as a reformer, apparently because of his commitment to monasticism, Tsoṅ-kha-pa was also a creative and controversial interpreter of Buddhist philosophy, especially of Mādhyamika. His stature, which seems to have been considerable during his lifetime, was only enhanced by the subsequent political ascendancy of his followers through the institution of the Dalai Lama, the first of whom (identified as such retrospectively) was Tsoṅ-kha-pa's disciple, Dge-'dun-grub (1391–1474). Tsoṅ-kha-pa founded the monastery of Dga'-ldan (named after the Buddhist heaven Tuṣita) outside of Lhasa in 1409, and his followers were originally known as the Dga'-ldan-pas. This eventually evolved to Dge-lugs-pa, the 'system of virtue'. The Dge-lugs-pa established large monastic universities throughout Tibet, one of which, 'Bras-spuṅ, was the largest Buddhist monastery in the world, with over 13,000 monks in 1959.

The hallmark of Tsoṅ-kha-pa's work is the pursuit of consistency among apparently disparate or contradictory elements within Buddhist doctrine. He sought to demonstrate a harmony between *sūtra* and *tantra*, between the logical system of Dharmakīrti and the Mādhyamika dialectic of Candrakīrti, between reasoned analysis and contemplative experience, between the conventional truth and the ultimate truth. He claimed that it could be logically established that there is no contradiction between the validity of worldly categories, especially in the ethical sphere, and the fact that those categories were empty, that is, utterly lacking in any kind of intrinsic nature. He also argued that the logical and systematic analysis of the constituents of experience is essential for the attainment of enlightenment. In his exegeses of Indian doctrine he championed Candrakīrti's interpretation of Mādhyamika, the so-called Prāsaṅgika-Mādhyamika school, as the most profound description of the nature of reality. In his less technical works, he said that all of Buddhist practice could be encompassed under the categories of renunciation, the compassionate aspiration to liberate all beings from suffering, and the understanding that all phenomena are devoid of substantial existence.[11]

DOXOGRAPHICAL LITERATURE

The Tibetans' access to centuries of Buddhist literature from India afforded them the opportunity not only to comment on individual texts but to construct synthetic expositions on a wide range of topics. One such genre of Tibetan literature, called the 'stages of the path' (*lam rim*) literature, sought to bring together in a single work all of the essential doctrines and practices required for progressing on the path to enlightenment. Such texts were common to all four of the major sects. Another, more philosophical genre of literature was the doxographies (*grub mtha'*), compendia of the doctrines of the various schools of Indian philosophy. There was a precedent for such works in India in Bhāvaviveka's *Blaze of Reasoning* (*Tarkajvālā*) and Śāntarakṣita's *Compendium of Principles* (*Tattvasaṃgraha*). Doxographies appear very early in the history of Tibetan literature: Dpal-brtseg's *Explanation of the Sequence of Views* (*Lta ba'i rim pa bśad pa*) and Ye-śes-sde's *Different Views* (*Lta ba'i khyad par*) date from around 800. Eventually, all the major sects were to produce important doxographies. Special mention may be made of the *Treasury of Tenets* (*Grub mtha' mdzod*) of Kloṅ-chen-pa of the Rñiṅ-ma sect, the Sa-skya scholar Stag-tshaṅ's (b. 1405) *Freedom from Extremes through Understanding All Tenets* (*Grub mtha' kun śes nas mtha' bral grub pa*), the *Thorough Pervasion of all Objects of Knowledge* (*Śes bya kun khyab*, an encyclopedia that contains a section on tenets) by the Bka'-rgyud scholar Koṅ-sprul Yon-tan-rgya-mtsho (1813–99), and the *Great Exposition of Tenets* (*Grub mtha' chen mo*) by the

Dge-lugs scholar 'Jam-dbyang-bźad-pa (1648–1721). While these texts contained summaries of the doctrines of non-Buddhist schools of classical Indian philosophy such as Jaina, Sāṅkhya, Nyāya, and Cārvāka, the bulk of the exposition was concerned with the Buddhist schools, which were generally numbered as four: the two Hīnayāna schools of Vaibhāṣika and Sautrāntika and the two Mahāyāna schools of Yogācāra (usually referred to as Cittamātra, 'mind only,' in the doxographical literature) and Mādhyamika. Some of the doxographies also contained expositions of the various Indian *tantric* systems, while certain later works, notably *The Crystal Mirror of Tenets* (*Grub mtha' śel gyi me loṅ*) by Thu'u bkwan Blo-bzaṅ Chos-kyi-ñi-ma (1737–1802), provided summaries of the tenets of the indigenous Tibetan sects.[12]

The Tibetans brought their own approach to the study of Buddhist philosophy. In addition to cataloguing the positions of the various Indian schools, they ranked them and compared their assertions on a wide range of topics. The hierarchy they established provides a further insight into the problems of Indian Buddhist philosophy. The hierarchy common to most of the doxographies ranks the Indian Buddhist schools in the following order (with outstanding representatives of each in parentheses):

Prāsaṅgika-Mādhyamika (Candrakīrti)
Sautrāntika-Svātantrika-Mādhyamika (Bhāvaviveka)
Yogācāra-Svātantrika-Mādhyamika (Śāntarakṣita)
Cittamātra (Yogācāra) Following Reasoning (Dharmakīrti)
Cittamātra (Yogācāra) Following Scripture (Asaṅga)
Sautrāntika Following Reasoning (Dharmakīrti)
Sautrāntika Following Scripture (Vasubandhu)
Vaibhāṣika (Vasumitra).

Despite the fact that Vaibhāṣikas and Sautrāntikas never had adherents in Tibet and the Cittamātra view was only occasionally espoused, studies that move upward through this hierarchy are considered, especially in the Dge-lugs sect, to have a strong pedagogic and even soteriological value; the exposition begins with Vaibhāṣika and moves towards Prāsaṅgika-Mādhyamika, with the assertions of one school serving as a propaedeutic for the next. Each school is considered to outshine the one below it in subtlety and sophistication so that each school is in principle able to defeat in debate the school below it while being refuted by the school above. Thus, the Vaibhāṣikas, while able philosophically to overpower any of the non-Buddhist schools, would be helpless against a Sautrāntika Following Scripture, for example, who would in turn have to capitulate to a Prāsaṅgika. The tenets of the lower schools are seen as stepping stones to the higher, as means of understanding increasingly subtle philosophical positions, providing an opportunity to discern a development and refinement of concepts and terminology that would be imperceptible if study were limited simply to what is judged by many to be the most profound, the Prāsaṅgika-Mādhyamika.

Following the exposition of the schools by 'Jam-byaṅs-bźad-pa, for example, we can note what is deemed an evolution on the topic of the nature of sense-experience as one moves through Buddhist schools listed above. Among the four major systems (Vaibhāṣika, Sautrāntika, Yogācāra and Mādhyamika) there are two theories as to how a sense consciousness comes to perceive its object. The Sautrāntika, Yogācāra and Mādhyamika assert that the object casts an image or aspect (*rnam pa*, *ākāra*) towards the perceiving consciousness. The Vaibhāṣikas hold that no such aspect exists. According to the other three schools, an eye consciousness perceives an object, such as a chair, because the eye consciousness is produced in the aspect of the chair, as a mirror assumes the aspect of the object reflected in it; the consciousness is said to become 'like the object'. In contrast, the Vaibhāṣikas claim that the eye consciousness goes out to the object so that there is no need for the object to be reflected in the consciousness. They do not therefore distinguish between the subjective aspect of the object and the object itself, as do the other schools; for the Vaibhāṣikas, the appearance of the object is the object itself.

The Buddhist schools' positions on what might be termed aspected (mediated) and aspectless (unmediated) sense-perception have correlates to the various types of realism elaborated in the West, with realism taken to mean the view that material objects exist externally and independently of sense-perception. In such a scheme, the Vaibhāṣika position represents a commonsensical form of realism, the view that sense-perception is a direct, straightforward and immediate contact of the consciousness and its object. The Vaibhāṣikas, however, do not represent the most simple form of realism, naïve realism, according to which things exist exactly as they are perceived, because the Vaibhāṣikas classify all gross objects, things that can be either physically or mentally broken into parts, as not ultimately real, but rather as conventional truths (*kun rdzob bden pa*, *saṃvṛti-satya*).

The Sautrāntikas criticize the Vaibhāṣika position, arguing that if sense-perception were not aspected, either objects could not be perceived at all because there would be no medium for perception, or it should be possible to see through walls because consciousness, being immaterial and moving out to its material object, would not be obstructed by it. The Sautrāntika introduction of the aspect (the image or representation of the object) into the process of sense-perception marks a development away from the Vaibhāṣika view towards what would be classed as a form of representative realism, that actual perception is perception of sense-data or sensa; to perceive an external object is to perceive the sensa caused by it, not the object itself. The Sautrāntikas indeed distinguish between the object and its aspect, but would not hold that sense perception is therefore somehow indirect. Despite their assertion that objects exist external to the mind perceiving them and that those objects produce the sensa or representations that are perceived, they appear not to be daunted by the dilemma of representative realism – if sense-experience is technically only of sensa and never of external objects, how are the objects to be known? They simply claim that the aspect is similar to the object, allowing the object to be directly perceived. The aspect is not mistaken for the actual object; it simply permits the object to be perceived.[13]

Persuaded apparently by the argument from illusion, that the same object often appears differently to different people, the Yogācāra severs the relationship between the external object and its aspect that the Sautrāntikas maintain, claiming instead that external objects do not exist and that the object is not the cause of the consciousness that perceives it. The Yogācāra holds that subject and object arise simultaneously, both arising from the same latency (*bags chags*, *vāsanā*) or seed (*sa bon*, *bīja*) that resides in the mental consciousness or the substratum consciousness (*kun gźi rnam śes*, *ālayavijñāna*). A seed is activated, causing at once both the appearance of the object and the consciousness perceiving it. For the Yogācāra, then, there are no objects that are not of the nature of consciousness; there are only sensa without originary objects; sensa are of the nature of the mind. Such a view approaches idealist empiricism or Berkeley's immaterialism, for the Yogācāra holds that material objects do not exist apart from perception.

The Prāsaṅgika, as rendered by Tsoṅ-kha-pa, incorporate elements of both realism and skepticism in their position on sense-experience. They are realists to the extent that they hold that external objects exist as distinct entities, separate from the perceiving consciousness. They are skeptics to the extent that they hold that objects appear falsely in sense-perception, that the senses are fundamentally deluded in their experience of objects. For the Prāsaṅgikas, external objects exist, but they do not exist as they appear. Objects appear to exist intrinsically, in and of themselves, and this false appearance is perceived by the senses. They claim that there are two factors present in any sense-perception by an unenlightened person, the false appearance, resulting from ignorance, of the object as an intrinsically existent entity, and the correct appearance of the object as imputedly existent. For those who have not understood emptiness, the absence of the intrinsic existence, the true and false aspects of sensa seem indistinguishably mixed in all cases of sense-perception. This inability to distinguish what is false from what is true in turn motivates desire and hatred, which, through *karma*, bring about suffering in the realm of rebirth. The Prāsaṅgikas prescribe the use of inference (here, arguments against the possibility of intrinsic existence) in order to reveal that objects do not exist in and of themselves but are empty of any intrinsic nature. When such revelation is deepened through meditation, it becomes salvific insight.[14]

This is one of many possible comparisons that can be drawn across the Buddhist philosophical schools using the doxographical literature. It is important to note when making such comparisons that the Tibetan doxographies are very much constructions of the Indian schools and, to that extent, artificial. They are, first of all, largely ahistorical, juxtaposing and amalgamating positions that were often separated by centuries. They are also synthetic, erecting 'schools' for which there is insufficient historical evidence in India. For example, Sautrāntika texts from India were never translated into Tibetan and hence were never studied in Tibet in their own right; doxographic 'presentations' of this school derive its tenets from references in various Yogācāra and Mādhyamika texts. Perhaps a more striking instance of such construction is the Svātantrika and Prāsaṅgika, terms that do not appear as the names of branches of Mādhyamika in any Indian text, but rather were coined in Tibet, probably in the late eleventh century. Later Tibetan scholars disagreed over what constituted the difference between the two sub-schools, which Indian figures belonged to which, and which of the two should be ranked above the other; Tsoṅ-kha-pa's reading was by no means universally accepted. The Indian schools of tenets were certainly not as coherent, self-conscious and monolithic as the Tibetan doxographies would suggest. Buddhist philosophy developed in India over many centuries, shaped by thinkers who thought of themselves simply as Buddhist, responding to developments and innovations in a fluid intellectual environment. They did not necessarily organize their positions along the lines described in the Tibetan doxographies, with the result that points of doctrine that do not fit into the philosophical schema of the Tibetan doxographer are often overlooked.

None of these qualifications, however, is meant to diminish the importance of Tibetan doxographical literature, which rather than being regarded as a flawless portrayal of Buddhist philosophy in India, deserves to be regarded as a significant development and contribution to Buddhist philosophy in its own right.

PHILOSOPHICAL EDUCATION

It may be useful to describe briefly the nature of philosophical training in Tibet. The greater part of such training took place within the monastery. Monasteries were often large and complex institutions serving many functions in traditional society, only one of which was the training of scholars. The majority of the monks in any given monastery were not actively engaged in philosophical training; even in the large teaching monasteries of the major sects, it has been estimated that only one-fourth of the monks undertook the study of the philosophical curriculum. The curriculum varied from sect to sect. Here we shall take the example of the curriculum of the monasteries called the 'three seats' of the Dge-lugs sect, Dga'-ldan, Se-ra and 'Bras-spung, all located in the vicinity of Lhasa, which together housed approximately 20,000 monks drawn from all regions of inner Asia.[15]

After learning to read and write (usually beginning between the ages of 7 and 12), a monk would study elementary textbooks on logic called *Collected Topics* (*bsdus grwa*) which introduced philosophical categories drawn largely from the works of Dharmakīrti and which provided numerous examples of the mechanics of logical statements that are roughly the equivalent of the syllogism.[16] This was followed by the study of basic epistemology through the study of textbooks called 'types of awareness' (*blo rigs*) and more advanced study of the mechanics of argumentation through works called 'types of reasons' (*rtags rigs*).[17] The formal curriculum entailed the study of five main texts. The first is the *Ornament of Realization* (*Abhisamayālaṃkāra*) attributed to Maitreyanātha, which delineates the various Hīnayāna and Mahāyāna paths to enlightenment. It is highly detailed, employing the famed eight subjects and seventy topics to reveal the so-called 'hidden teaching' of the Perfection of Wisdom (*prajñāpāramitā*) *sūtras*. Tibetan doxographers have classified this text as belonging to the Yogācāra-Svātantrika-Mādhyamika school, which asserts that external objects do not exist but also denies the ultimate existence of consciousness. Such issues are not of central importance in the *Ornament for Realization*, which offers a complex taxonomy of the Buddhist path. After completing the study of this text, the curriculum moved next to Candrakīrti's *Entrance to the Middle Way* (*Madhyamakāvatāra*), which is regarded as a supplement to Nāgārjuna's famous *Treatise on the Middle Way* (*Madhyamakaśāstra*) in that it provides the religious context to Nāgārjuna's exposition of emptiness. Candrakīrti's text is divided into ten chapters, each devoted to setting forth how the understanding of emptiness is to be integrated with the practice of one of the ten perfections (*pāramitā*), virtues cultivated by *bodhisattvas* on a ten-staged path to enlightenment. Over half of Candrakīrti's text is devoted to the sixth perfection, wisdom. This long discussion of the seminal topics of Mādhyamika philosophy, including emptiness, the Two Truths, a critique of the Yogācāra, and proofs for the selflessness of persons and other phenomena, is regarded by the Dge-lugs-pas as the *locus classicus* of Prāsaṅgika-Mādhyamika. Throughout the long course of study, there was time taken each year (often in the form of a communal retreat from the monastery) for the topic of logic and epistemology, represented by Dharmakīrti's *Commentary to [Dignāga's 'Compendium on] Valid Knowledge'* (*Pramāṇavārttika*). This text contains arguments for the existence of rebirth, for liberation from rebirth, and for the omniscience of a buddha, discussions of the two valid sources of knowledge (direct perception and inference), classifications of proof-statements and an analysis of the operations of thought. Written in a cryptic poetic style, this is considered one of the most difficult Indian *śāstras*.[18] The final two texts of the Dge-lugs curriculum are the *Discourse on Monastic Discipline* (*Vinaya Sūtra*) by Guṇaprabha, which is the source for the rules and regulations governing monastic life, and the *Treasury of Knowledge* (*Abhidharmakośa*) by Vasubandhu, a compendium of Vaibhāṣika and Sautrāntika tenets dealing with all the major categories of Hīnayāna doctrine, encompassing philosophy, soteriology and cosmology.

The successful completion of the entire curriculum took some twenty years of study. During this time, the educational techniques were two: memorization and debate. In addition to the Indian texts listed above, the monk would study extensive commentaries or textbooks (*yig cha*) on each work. Each college of the major monastic universities had its own textbooks on the Indian root texts. One type of textbook, called 'general meaning' (*spyi don*), were relatively straightforward prose commentaries that followed the sequence of the Indian text, offering what was considered by the college to be the correct interpretation. The other form of textbook was the 'analysis' (*mtha' dbyod*), which set forth the meaning of the text in the form of debates on each of the important points. Each section of the 'analysis' has three subsections: the refutation of wrong interpretations, the presentation of the correct position and the dispelling of any objections that might be raised about the correct position. It was customary for a monk over the course of his study to memorize the five Indian texts, his college's textbooks on the Indian text, and often Tsoṅ-kha-pa's major philosophical writings; it was not uncommon for an accomplished scholar to have several thousand pages of Tibetan text committed to memory.

This repository of doctrine was mined in the second educational technique of the monastic university, debate. The debate tradition in Tibet is said to have originated with Phya-pa-chos-kyi-seṅ-ge in the twelfth century and was adopted by all of the major sects. Debate took place in a highly structured format in which one monk defended a position that was systematically attacked by his opponent. Skill in debate was essential to progress to the highest rank of academic scholarship and was greatly admired. Particular fame was attached to those monks who were able to hold the position of one of the lower schools in the doxographical hierarchy against the higher. These debates were often quite spirited, and certain debates between highly skilled opponents are remembered with the affection not unlike that which some attach to important sporting events in the West. It is commonly the case that a monk, adept at the skills of memorization and debate, would achieve prominence as a scholar without ever writing a single word. Only a small percentage of the highly trained scholars of the Tibetan sects ever wrote anything. The motivation of those who did are not always clear. Judging from their colophons, texts were often written at the request of a student who wished for some record of his teacher's views on a particular topic. Texts were also written, of course, as a response to doctrinal controversies that occurred throughout Tibetan history, both within and between sects.

A CONTROVERSY

A persistent intersectarian doctrinal controversy centred on two of the most important questions in Mahāyāna Buddhist thought: the meaning of emptiness and the status of the buddha-nature. Surrounding this controversy are problems of interpretation concerning the Mahāyāna *sūtras* and a sectarian battle over who holds the legitimate claim as custodian of Nāgārjuna's final view. It is known in Tibetan as the controversy over *raṅ stoṅ gźan stoṅ*, literally 'self-empty, other-empty'. The opposing factions are the Dge-lugs-pas on one side and a now defunct sect called the Jo-naṅ-pa on the other, with support from certain of the Bka'-rgyud-pas. This controversy differs from that played out at Bsam-yas in the eighth century, where Indian and Chinese disputants argued the question of gradual versus sudden enlightenment. There, the Tibetans were for the most part onlookers to a debate the doctrinal antecedents and implications of which they did not fully comprehend. The *raṅ stoṅ gźan stoṅ* controversy also differs from the disputes that occur in the doxographical literature over the correct interpretation of the assertions of long dead Indian schools which had no adherents in Tibet. It was waged between Tibetan savants with knowledge of a vast literature, both Indian and Tibetan, who disagreed over issues fundamental to their understanding of what constituted enlightenment and the path to its achievement. As was inevitably the case in Tibetan Buddhism, however, the legitimation of arguments rested on an appeal to Indian sources.

The controversy can be traced in part to a hermeneutical dilemma that the Tibetans inherited from India. The Mahāyāna in India accepted a huge corpus of literature as the word of the Buddha, encompassing a wide variety of *sūtras* that were in no way philosophically or doctrinally consistent with each other. One such *sūtra*, the *Untying of the [Buddha's] Intention* (*Saṃdhinirmocana*), confronted the issue of interpretation by classifying the Buddha's teachings into three groups, called the three turnings of the wheel of doctrine. It was said that in his first teachings the Buddha taught that everything exists. The Hīnayāna *sūtras* are generally considered to fall into this category. In the second turning of the wheel, exemplified by the Perfection of Wisdom *sūtras*, the Buddha taught that nothing exists, that is, that everything is empty. In the third turning of the wheel, the Buddha taught that some things exist and some do not. Exactly which *sūtras* fall into this last category is itself a point of disputation. Both sides would place the *sūtras* that set forth the Mind Only doctrine into the third wheel as well as many of the *sūtras* that teach the existence of the buddha-nature (*tathāgatagarbha*). If the Buddha taught all of these positions, which is considered to represent his final opinion on the nature of reality? Here again, the two sides part, with the Dge-lugs-pa holding that the second wheel is definitive: that is, that it represents the Buddha's own view rather than an accommodation made for those incapable of understanding that view. The teachings contained in the other two wheels cannot be accepted literally, but require interpretation in order to discern the Buddha's intention in saying something that is not ultimately the case.

In the Dge-lugs-pa view, the first wheel was taught for those Hīnayāna disciples who could not fathom the doctrine of emptiness. Therefore, the Buddha explained to them that everything exists until they were sufficiently mature to understand emptiness. The third wheel was intended for those Mahāyāna disciples who could not benefit from being taught that nothing exists intrinsically. Instead, he taught them that external objects do not exist but that consciousness does. The Jo-naṅ-pa's disagree, claiming that it is the third wheel that is the definitive teaching while the first two wheels are not to be taken literally; it is necessary there to resort to interpretation to arrive at the Buddha's true meaning.

For the Dge-lugs-pas the highest of all Buddhist doctrines is that all phenomena in the universe are empty of an intrinsic nature (*raṅ bźin*, *svabhāva*), that the constituents of experience are not naturally endowed with a defining characteristic (*raṅ gi mtshan ñid kyi grub ba*). Emptiness for the Dge-lugs-pas is thus the fact that phenomena do not exist in and of themselves; it is the lack of substantial existence, literally of 'self-nature'. The Dge-lugs-pas, then, are proponents of 'self-emptiness', and argue that the hypostatized factor which an object in reality lacks (i.e. is empty of) is wrongly believed by the unenlightened to be intrinsic to the object itself. Everything, from physical forms to the omniscient mind of the Buddha, is equally empty. This emptiness is described by the Dge-lugs-pas as a non-affirming negation (*med dgag*, *prasajyapratiṣedha*), an absence with nothing else implied in its place. From this perspective, the Dge-lugs-pas judge the *sūtras* of the second wheel, typified by the *Heart Sūtra*, which states that 'in emptiness, there is no form, no feeling, no discrimination, no conditioning factors, and no consciousness', to contain the definitive expression of the Buddha's most profound intention.

The Jo-naṅ-pas look to the third wheel, especially to those statements that describe the non-duality of subject and object as the consummate nature (*yongs grub*, *pariniṣpanna*) and the understanding of that non-duality as the highest wisdom. They describe this wisdom in rather substantialist terms, calling it eternal, self-arisen and truly established. This wisdom consciousness exists autonomously and is thus not empty in the way that emptiness is understood by the Dge-lugs-pas. Instead, it is empty in the sense that it is devoid of all defilements and conventional factors, which are extraneous to its true nature. Hence, the Jo-naṅ-pas speak of the 'emptiness of the other', the absence of extrinsic and extraneous qualities. Their understanding of emptiness is almost certainly influenced by the *Kālacakra Tantra*, in which they specialized, which speaks of a divine body of empty form (*stoṅ gzugs*), that is, a body that is utterly immaterial.

The Dge-lugs-pas' critique of the Jo-naṅ-pas is quite vociferous, declaring that the Jo-naṅ-pa position has no antecedent whatsoever in the Indian Buddhist tradition, harsh criticism indeed. They furthermore point out the affinities that exist between the Jo-naṅ-pa view of permanent and independent consciousness and the heretical views of self propounded by the non-Buddhist Vedāntins and Sāṅkhyas. The Dge-lugs-pas cannot deny the presence of statements in the Mahāyāna canon that speak of the buddha-nature as permanent, pure, blissful and endowed with self. But they argue that such statements are provisional, another example of the Buddha's expedient means of attracting to the faith those who find such a description appealing. The true buddha-nature, they would claim, is the emptiness of the mind; it is this factor, present in all sentient beings, that provides the possibility of transformation into an enlightened buddha. This is the view of Candrakīrti, whom they regard as the supreme interpreter of the doctrine of emptiness.

The Jo-naṅ-pas (and certain Bka'-rgyud scholars) do not deny that this is Candrakīrti's view, but they do deny Candrakīrti the rank of premier expositor of Nāgārjuna's thought. For them, Candrakīrti teaches an emptiness which is a mere negation of true existence, which they equate with nihilism. Nor do they deny that such an exposition is also to be found in Nāgārjuna's philosophical treatises. But those texts, they claim, do not represent Nāgārjuna's final view, which is expressed instead in his devotional corpus (*bstod tshogs*), notably the *Praise of the Sphere of Reality* (*Dharmadhātustotra*). Here we find a more positive exposition of the nature of reality. How can it be possible that the highest wisdom is not ultimately real? Those who would deny its ultimate existence, such as Candrakīrti, they class as 'one-sided Mādhyamikas' (*phyogs gcig pa'i dbu ma pa*) as opposed to the Great Mādhyamikas (*dbu ma pa chen po*), among whom they would include the Nāgārjuna of the four hymns and Āryadeva as well as thinkers whom the Dge-lugs-pa class as Yogācāra or Svātantrika-Mādhyamika: Asaṅga, Vasubandhu, Maitreyanātha, Śāntarakṣita.

And so the argument continues, with the Dge-lugs-pas attempting to demonstrate that the nature of reality praised by Nāgārjuna in his hymns is exactly the emptiness that he derives in his philosophical writings.

The issue here is not to seek to determine who is 'correct'. There are precedents for both positions in the Indian canon. Indeed, in the Perfection of Wisdom literature, the Buddha's nature body (*ṅo bo ñid sku*, *svabhāvikakāya*), the highest form of the *dharmakāya*, is said to have two aspects, the emptiness of intrinsic nature and the emptiness of adventitious defilements. Should we adopt the terms of the controversy, it is thus both *raṅ stoṅ* (self-empty) and *gźan stoṅ* (other empty). And as is the case with any doctrinal controversy, the issues do not reside solely in the rarefied atmosphere of philosophy. There are historical factors to consider, such as the possible influence of Kashmiri and Nepali brahmanical teachings on some of the major figures of the Jo-naṅ-pa, as well as political factors, the most notable of which are the actions taken by the fifth Dalai Lama, who banned the Jo-naṅ-pa texts and ordered the forcible closing of the Jo-naṅ-pa monasteries, with their subsequent conversion to Dge-lugs-pa institutions.[19] Despite this suppression, the *gźan stoṅ* position has displayed considerable resilience and continues to hold an important place in Bka'-rgyud and Rñiṅ-ma.

Some scholars have been tempted to see such doctrinal controversies in Tibet, especially those which tend to place the 'scholastic' Sa-skya-pas and Dge-lugs-pas contra the 'yogic' Rñiṅ-ma-pas and Bka'-rgyud-pas, as representative of two general tendencies in Tibetan Buddhist philosophy, one in which the pre-eminent position is given to reason, to which reality must conform, and another in which the pre-eminent position is given to a meditative experience unmediated by ratiocination, such that philosophical consistency becomes of secondary interest. Such a characterization fails to take into account the range of opinion found in each of the major sects, representing both a variety of trends inherited from India and a complex matrix of lineages in Tibet. Each of the sects certainly upheld a vocabulary which to a large extent determined the content of its doctrine, but contained in that vocabulary is a wealth of significance that has only begun to be adequately studied.

Tibetan Buddhist thought has undergone a variety of representations in western scholarship. At the beginning of the current century, it was both condemned as a debased and demonic aberration of 'original Buddhism' (by figures such as L. Austine Waddell) and exalted as the fount of all esoteric wisdom (by figures such as H. P. Blavatsky). This latter tendency was only prolonged by the commentaries provided by the American Theosophist W. Y. Evans-Wentz in a series of popular translations of Tibetan texts, including the so-called *Tibetan Book of the Dead.* During the same period, Indologists valued the Tibetan translations of Indian Buddhist scriptures for their accurate rendition of numerous lost Sanskrit texts, but Tibetan Buddhist literature, including extensive commentaries on those Indian texts, was largely ignored. It is with the work of the Russian scholar E. Obermiller (1901–35) that Tibetan philosophical literature was studied in its own right and positively evaluated for its contributions to the Buddhist thought. With the Tibetan diaspora beginning in 1959, thousands of heretofore unknown or unstudied Tibetan texts became available in the West, largely due to the efforts of E. Gene Smith of the US Library of Congress. Since then, a new generation of scholars has devoted itself to Tibetan studies, and autochthonous Tibetan Buddhist literature is slowly being admitted into the domain of comparative philosophy. The next decades should increasingly see a turn towards understanding Tibetan Buddhist philosophy in the context of the religious and social climate in which it arose.

NOTES

1 The classic studies of the debate remain Demiéville 1952 and Tucci 1958. A more recent study and analysis of the debate is that by Gómez 1987. Gómez's extensive notes contain references to his previous work as well as the wealth of Japanese scholarship on the subject. See also Ruegg 1989.

2 On Rin-chen-bzaṅ-po see Tucci 1988.

3 For a biography of Atīśa, see Chattopadhyaya 1981.

4 I use the term 'sect' to translate the Tibetan *chos lugs*, literally 'religious system' or 'doctrinal system', because it seems more appropriate than the usual alternatives. One standard translation, 'order', connotes a group living under the same religious rules. In Tibet, all monks followed the Mūlasarvāstivādin *vinaya*, whether they were Bka'-rgyud or Dge-lugs. Hence, 'order' is misleading. Another alternative, 'school', suggests a group of scholars adhering to the same philosophical perspective, whereas it would not be correct to describe the majority of adherents of the various Tibetan *chos lugs* as scholars. 'Sect', as a group adhering to a distinctive doctrine or leader, despite certain negative connotations in English, appears to be the least misleading rendering.

5 For a traditional study of *gter-ma* literature, see Thondup 1986.

6 On the Great Completeness, see Karmay 1988, Thondup 1989 and Guenther 1975–6.

7 For the biography and songs of Mi-la-ras-pa, see Lhalungpa 1977 and Chang 1962.

8 On *mahāmudrā*, see Lhalungpa 1986.

9 On Sa-skya Paṇḍita, see D. Jackson 1987.

10 On the early study of Buddhist logic in India and Sa-skya Paṇḍita's contributions see van der Kuijp 1983.

11 For a life of Tsoṅ-kha-pa and a translation of one of his most important works, see Thurman 1984. Tsoṅ-kha-pa's perspective on emptiness has been examined by Napper 1989.
12 For a survey of Tibetan doxographical literature and a translation of portions of an early *grub mtha'* text, see Mimaki 1982. For a translation and commentary on a popular Dge-lugs-pa doxographical work, see Sopa and Hopkins 1990. For another translation of that same text as well as a translation of a Rñiṅ-ma-pa doxography, see Guenther 1972.
13 For a more detailed discussion of the mechanics of perception in Sautrāntika as set forth by Dge-lugs and Sa-skya doxographers, see Klein 1986 : 68–140.
14 The foregoing comparison of the positions of the various schools has been adapted from Lopez 1987 : 155–9.
15 For a detailed account of studies at Se-ra, see Sopa 1986.
16 For a translation and commentary on a *Collected Topics* text, see Perdue 1992.
17 For a translation and commentary on a 'types of awareness' text, see Lati Rinbochay and Napper 1980.
18 For a discussion of some of the issues raised in the Dge-lugs-pa exegesis of Dharmakīrti's work, see Klein 1986 and 1990 and R. Jackson 1993.
19 The best study of the *raṅ stoṅ gźan stoṅ* controversy remains the article by Ruegg 1963.

REFERENCES

Chang, G. (trans.) (1962) *The Hundred Thousand Songs of Milarepa*, 2 vols, Seacaucus, N.J.: University Press.

Chattopadhyaya, A. (1981) *Atisa and Tibet*, Delhi: Motilal Banarsidass.

Demiéville, P. (1952) *Le Concile de Lhasa*, *Bibliothèque de l'Institut des Hautes Etudes Chinoises* 7, Paris: Imprimerie Nationale de France.

Dudjom Rimpoche (1991) *The Nyingma School of Tibetan Buddhism: Its Fundamentals and History*, Boston, Mass.: Wisdom Publications.

Gómez, L. (1987) 'Purifying gold: the metaphor of effort and intuition in Buddhist thought and practice', in P. Gregory (ed.) *Sudden and Gradual: Approaches to Enlightenment in Chinese Thought*, Honolulu: University of Hawaii Press, pp. 67–145.

Guenther, H. (1972) *Buddhist Philosophy in Theory and Practice*, Baltimore: Penguin Books.

—— (trans.) (1975–6) *Kindly Bent to Ease Us*, 3 vols, Emeryville, Calif.: Dharma Publishing.

Hopkins, J. (1983) *Meditation on Emptiness*, London: Wisdom Publications.

Jackson, D. (1987) *The Entrance Gate for the Wise: Sa-skya Paṇḍita on Indian and Tibetan Traditions of Pramāṇa and Philosophical Debate*, Vienna: Arbeitskreis für Tibetische und Buddhistische Studien Universität Wien.

Jackson, R. (1993) *Is Enlightenment Possible?: Dharmakīrti and rGyal-tshab-rje on Mind and Body, No-Self, and Freedom*, Ithaca, N.Y.: Snow Lion Publications.

Karmay, S. G. (1988) *The Great Perfection: A Philosophical and Meditative Teaching of Tibetan Buddhism*, Leiden: E. J. Brill.

Klein, A. (1986) *Knowledge and Liberation*, Ithaca, N.Y.: Snow Lion Press.

—— (1990) *Knowing, Naming, and Negation*, Ithaca, N.Y.: Snow Lion Press.

Kuijp, L. van der (1983) *Contributions to the Development of Tibetan Buddhist Epistemology*, Wiesbaden: Franz Steiner Verlag.

Lati Rinbochay and Napper, E. (1980) *Mind in Tibetan Buddhism*, Ithaca, N.Y.: Snow Lion Press.

Lhalungpa, L. (trans.) (1977) *The Life of Milarepa*, New York: Dutton.

—— (1986) *Mahāmudrā: The Quintessence of Mind and Meditation*, Boston, Mass.: Shambala.

Lopez, D. S. Jr (1987) *A Study of Svātantrika*, Ithaca, N.Y.: Snow Lion Publications.

Mimaki, K. (1982) *Blo gsal grub mtha'*, Kyoto: Zinbun Kagaku Kenkyusyo.

Napper, E. (1989) *Dependent Arising and Emptiness*, London: Wisdom Publications.

Perdue, D. (1992) *Debate in Tibetan Buddhism*, Ithaca, N.Y.: Snow Lion Publications.
Ruegg, D. S. (1963) The Jo-naṅ-pas, a school of Buddhist ontologists', *Journal of the American Oriental Society* 83:73–91.
—— (1968) *La Théorie du tathāgatagarbha et du gotra*, Paris: École Française d'Extrême-Orient.
—— (1989) *Buddha-nature, Mind and the Problem of Gradualism in a Comparative Perspective: On the Transmission and Reception of Buddhism in India and Tibet*, London: School of Oriental and African Studies.
Snellgrove, D. (1987) *Indo-Tibetan Buddhism*, Boston, Mass.: Shambala.
Sopa, G. (1986) *Lectures in Tibetan Culture*, 2 vols, Dharamsala, India: Library of Tibetan Works and Archives.
Sopa, G. and Hopkins, J. (1990) *Cutting through Appearances: Practice and Theory of Tibetan Buddhism*, Ithaca, N.Y.: Snow Lion Publications.
Thondup, T. (1986) *Hidden Teachings of Tibet*, London: Wisdom Publications.
—— (1989) *Buddha Mind: An Anthology of Longchen Rabjam's Writings on Dzogpa Chenpo*, Ithaca, N.Y.: Snow Lion Press.
Thurman, R. (1984) *Tsong Khapa's Speech of Gold in the 'Essence of True Eloquence'*, Princeton, N.J.: Princeton University Press.
Tucci, G. (1958) *Minor Buddhist Texts. Part 2: First Bhāvanākrama of Kamalaśīla*, Rome: Istituto Italiano per il Medio ed Estremo Oriente.
—— (1988) *Rin-chen-bzaṅ-po and the Renaissance of Buddhism in Tibet around the Millennium*, New Delhi: Aditya Press.

20

BUDDHISM IN SRI LANKA AND SOUTH-EAST ASIA

Padmasiri de Silva and Trevor Ling

BUDDHISM IN SRI LANKA

Sri Lanka is often considered to be the homeland of 'Theravāda Buddhism', in other words, the 'religion of the elders'. In fact, the Buddhist traditions in Thailand and Burma, along with Sri Lanka, present the geographical and historical frontiers for the study of the emergence and development of the Theravāda Buddhist tradition. In this section, we are concerned with a critical survey and assessment of the Buddhist tradition in Sri Lanka, but we shall also attempt to integrate into the section any philosophical insights which can be generated within the socio-historical purview of the chapter.

Buddhism is one of the most distinctive philosophical systems found in the East, yet it has a strong practical focus, a basic concern with the human predicament of suffering, misery and tribulation. The socio-historical spectrum provides the clear setting in which systems of beliefs enter the arena of practical life. While critical studies of Buddhism have cited some of the distortions and reversals found in actual practice, a more interesting point is how the duality of the secular and the religious, the tensions, the conflicts and the dilemmas emerge as doctrinal resources, encounter problematic social realities, and are integrated and accommodated within the tradition of Buddhism. An interesting point, for instance, would be how the Theravāda tradition has a strong rational temper and analytical rigour but how in actual practice and expansion in Sri Lanka it has become interwoven into the very fabric of life, people's routine vocations, rituals, festivals and the contexts of social interaction. Some of the rituals and practices of Hinduism were integrated into Buddhism with very little conflict. Some see this as a process which generates certain contradictions within Buddhism, while others see the flexibility in Buddhist practice and its power to absorb and interpret incoming ideas.

In this section, we shall first make a brief sketch of the historical background of the emergence and the development of the Buddhist tradition; then we shall look at the growth of the strong institutional framework of Buddhism through the concept of the *sangha*, the order of the Buddhist monks, and its links with the concept of royal patronage and kingship; and third, at what may be called the dualities between the 'religious' and the 'secular': fourth, at the question of religion and nationalism; and conclude with a brief reference to the work of Buddhist scholars during recent times.

Historical background

Sri Lankan history is generally divided into ancient and modern, and the dividing line is taken to be the advent of the Portuguese in 1505; the country came in turn under Dutch rule in 1658 and British in 1796. Basically the European powers governed the coastal region of the country, and the Kingdom of Kandy remained autonomous till the British took it over in 1815. The emergence and development of Buddhism in the ancient period revolves around the history of the capitals Anuradhapura from the fourth century BC to the late ninth century AD and then that of Polonnaruwa up to the thirteenth century. The kings of the time gave royal patronage to Buddhism, and a prosperous civilization with a strong agricultural base flourished during this time. A visitor to Sri Lanka today will find the *dagabas*, the tanks and the network of irrigation schemes, the symbols of a civilization which flourished in these ancient capitals.

The chronicles *Mahāvamsa* and *Dīpavamsa* provide a very important source for the history of Sri Lanka, along with the Pali commentaries and ancient inscriptions. These chronicles deal with the history of Sri Lanka, from the arrival of Vijaya and his followers in the fifth century BC. The crucial event recorded in these works for the present section is the coming of the famous Buddhist missionary Mahinda, the son of the Emperor Aśoka of India. Mahinda came to Sri Lanka during the time of King Devanampiyatissa, who was the first formal convert to Buddhism.

The history of the time of Devanampiyatissa has to be gleaned from these chronicles, but it is a kind of history mixed with myth, legend and other literary embellishments, so that only a very critical reading will help us to infer the possible historical data. The Buddhism which was brought to Sri Lanka by Mahinda is Theravāda Buddhism, and that is why when Buddhism gradually ceased to be a strong force in India, Sri Lanka came to be considered as the homeland of Theravāda Buddhism. Of course, though Buddhism was officially introduced during the time of Devanampiyatissa, it is possible that there were followers of Buddhism as well as some of the pre-Buddhist religions like Brahmanism and different forms of spirit worship.[1] In fact, the chronicles even record three visits of the Buddha to Sri Lanka.[2] But all in all the history of Buddhism may be formally considered to have begun with the advent of Mahinda to Sri Lanka and later of his sister Sanghamitta, who established the order of nuns in Sri Lanka. The focus on the Theravāda tradition in Sri Lanka is important in many other ways. While all the three major Theravāda countries have the Pali canon as a unitary body of knowledge, unlike Thailand and Burma, Sri Lanka's insular position has made it possible to identify and isolate the many influences that entered its precints.[3] Its written chronicles and the commentaries help us to gather relevant information. Finally, the Sinhalese form a majority of the inhabitants, and the majority of the Sinhalese have been Buddhists. Thus it has been observed about Buddhism in Sri Lanka that there is a long and uninterrupted tradition of over two thousand years. It may also be mentioned that while Buddhism entered and remained in Sri Lanka as an oral tradition for many years, later the teachings of the Buddha were committed to writing at a temple in the vicinity of Matale, in the central province.

Anuradhapura was the centre of Buddhist activity. But in the second century BC Tamils from south India invaded and ruled over Anuradhapura. It is recorded that in the Sinhalese Kingdom of the South, there was a King Duthagamini who generated a national revival to preserve Buddhism, and killed the Tamil king in combat in Anuradhapura, and thus Anuradhapura regained its official position as the central capital of Ceylon. Hence the concept of the king as the defender and preserver of Buddhism and the issue of state patronage of Buddhism and nationalism which are being discussed today have their roots in a long history. Mahavihara was the chief centre of Buddhist monks, but forty years after the death of Duthagamini there were reversals again and King Vattgamini-Abhaya, who won over Anuradhapura from the Tamils, was instrumental in starting a new monastery called Abhayagiri. The rivalry between the two temples of the Mahavihara and Abhayagiri was the background for the emergence of the Schisms, and perhaps these factors made it imperative that at some later time the canon be put into writing. Next the centre of Buddhist activity shifted to Polonnaruwa; later, the Kandyan Kingdom became the formal guardian of Buddhism. The issues of Sinhala Buddhist nationalism, state patronage of religion and all that the cultural symbols of the Anuradhpura and Polonnaruwa civilizations stood for have always been factors with a strong 'political valence' in the history of Sri Lanka.

Sangha, the order of monks

The Buddha in his discourses often insisted that the best way of respecting him is to follow his doctrine (the *Dhamma*). Yet he established the monastic order so that the doctrine would be preserved in its pristine form. The Buddha also worked out a code of discipline (*vinaya*) for the monks. But over the passage of years the monk had to play many roles, as the changing socio-political climate made many demands on him, claims which were not incorporated into his traditional role. It has been observed that in ancient India the rules of the *vinaya* were established and codified, 'as part of the spiritual path of a small body of religious medicants, acquainted with each other face to face each seeking his own salvation'.[4] But as Buddhism developed in Sri Lanka with royal patronage, the doctrine and the discipline of the monks had to adapt to the needs of protecting the nation, the culture of the people and the development of a single polity within the region of Sri Lanka.

The monks had many roles to play: interpret and preach the *Dhamma*, become living examplars of the doctrine, advise the king, give direction to the material and spiritual life of the people, etc. In the villages of Sri Lanka, the temple became a centre of social activity, and as the receiver of regular alms from the people became the spiritual guide for the family. As the monk's meal became a source of 'merit', many important family occasions were preceded by the preaching of a sermon and by a meal. The chanting of *pirit* became one of their added functions. It has been observed that as the need increased for the monk to play the role of the specialist at family ceremonies there was a requirement for a more lasting arrangement for feeding and housing the *sangha*. Thus grew the group of householders who regularly saw to the comfort of the monks, and finally land was donated to the temple. It is in this context of the changing phases of the Buddhist monk that Michael Carrithers sees four basic roles for the monk: the monk as teacher, preacher, priest and ceremonial specialist; as landlord; as politician; and as a reforming forest dweller.[5] The political role of the monks assumed great importance in recent times. There has also been strong pressure for the reform of the *sangha*, and of course the concept of the forest-dwelling monk and the emphasis on the contemplative life come to the surface from time to time. While the *sangha* can be viewed from the bottom in relation to land and the village, we can also discern its power from the top, in relation to the king. In the long history of Buddhism the link between the king and the *sangha* has been a crucial and yet a complex one. In fact the institution of the kingship came to be legitimated by this most important relationship to the *sangha*. The ceremonials surrounding the kingship bear witness to this fact. On the one hand the link with the *sangha* gave the king a formal relation to Buddhism; on the other, as a 'wheel-turning monarch', he was expected to see that his regime manifested an expression of the *Dhamma* in the cosmos.

Kingship: the *Dhamma* and politics

It has been pointed out, that the link between the king and the *sangha* and then finally with the nation rests on two important ideas: first, like any other layman, the king earns merit by offering gifts to the *sangha* based on the concept of the moral superiority of the *sangha*; second, the king is the owner of all the land, all rights flow from him, and he has to preserve all the institutions of society. 'He is in other words the state. Hence the state, the entire Sinhalese nation owes obedience to the Sangha through the person of the king.'[6] It was the same idea which was established in the story pertaining to the conversion of King Aśoka. As Bardwell Smith has observed. 'The image of Aśoka loomed larger with time. Legends about the great king were circulated soon after his death (later collected in the Sanskrit *Aśokavadana*), but their full impact only hit Sri Lanka about the time chronicles were being written.'[7] The Sinhalese model of kingship derived inspiration from this image. The Aśoka image of kingship had many ingredients: the fusion of the Universal Monarch (*cakkavatti*) and the Great Man (*Mahāpurisa*), the idea of *dharma-vijaya* conquest through righteousness, and even the idea of religious tolerance which has been quoted extensively during recent times.

When the *secular* and the *spiritual* are thus brought together, there can be a blending of the two as well as inevitable tensions, and much of the critical literature which has emerged on the question about religion and politics in Sri Lanka has to be understood against the background of these concepts. It must be mentioned that these various ways in which the secular political power was legitimized by religious ceremonies, the creation of myths and the accommodations made at various levels to meet the needs of the laity, were not confined to Sri Lanka. In south and south-east Asian rural communities similar patterns emerged. A further factor was the establishment of Buddhism and its expansion in Asia as a whole. That is why Max Weber sees a transformation in ancient Buddhism 'from the position of a religious "technology" of wandering and intellectually schooled mendicant monks to that of a world religion commanding allegiance among large masses of laymen'.[8]

Bridge building across the stream of *saṃsāra*

There has been a great deal of discussion by Buddhist scholars, historians and sociologists about disparities between the theory and practice of Buddhism.[9] Of course all religions face this problem. We wish to focus attention on the question of how Buddhism dealt with the emerging dualities as religious involvement in society became necessary. The dualities of the secular and the religious are blended in different ways by different religious traditions, partly on reinterpreting their doctrines and the formal scriptures and the kind of weight given to different realms of discourse. These are also perhaps an aspect of the inbuilt dualities of human nature, and each age interprets them in terms of the issues of the times. Another sort of tension is caused by attempts to integrate religious traditions which have cultural affinities, like Hinduism and Buddhism. In contrast to the peaceful coexistence of Hinduism and Buddhism in Sri Lanka there have been times of great conflict between Christianity and Buddhism. The healing of the dualities or the bridge building across the stream of *saṃsāra* is a question of great thematic significance in the development of Buddhism in Sri Lanka. This question is important as there is some misunderstanding that Theravāda Buddhism has no basis for social ethics. Dualities between the secular and the religious, the phenomenal and the transcendental, the material and the spiritual, this-worldly and other-worldly have different meanings, and unless they are tied to special contexts, may lose meaning. There are more specific foci of opposition, such as that between worldly power (*anucakka*) and the power of righteousness (*dhammacakka*), as mentioned in Bardwell Smith's *Two Wheels of the Dhamma*,[10] and that between Nibbānic Buddhism and Kammic Buddhism, as discussed in Melford Spiro's *Buddhism and Society*.[11] Also some see it as an opposition between the active and the contemplative life and some others as an opposition between individual salvation and social change. We shall limit our discussion to the distinction between Kammic Buddhism and Nibbānic Buddhism, as it has direct relevance to the issues in this analysis. Spiro has observed that, 'involvement in the world is more than religiously neutral, it is religiously perilous. Even moral behaviour is an obstacle to salvation, since it leads to the accumulation of merit and hence the continuation of karma and the cycle of rebirth. The true Buddhist is one who abandons all ties and attachments and wanders alone like the rhinoceros.'[12] Spiro feels that this gap cannot be bridged. He sees a gap between the ideal of the *arahant* and a conceptualized world of 'social conduct'. Of course Spiro says that in actual practice people 'see no contradiction' in bridging the gap.

But even at the doctrinal level, Spiro has overdone the duality. The concept of *kamma* is associated in the popular mind and also by the scholars with a kind of 'judicial model' of rewards and punishments. In the *suttas* it is said that if an individual resorts to killing living creatures, steals, resorts to sexual misconduct, etc. he will be born in a sorrowful state of existence, but if he practises kindness to animals, is compassionate, etc. he will be born in a happy state or a heavenly world.[13] Thus even morally good actions on this model lead to the accumulation of merit and to the continuation of the cycle of rebirth. The process is like collecting fuel for a longer journey in *saṃsāra*. *Kamma* could also be viewed on the 'craftsmanship model'. In this context *kamma* is action which reflects the agent's character, and repeated actions tend to be repeated. *Kamma* is the development of a momentum or a disposition to do good or evil; it is building of character. When *kamma* is looked at this way, these two aspects may flow into each other or form aspects of the *nibbānic* quest. The greatest blessing of a good action is the development of good character, which may also be the only way of building a good society. A detailed analysis of the supposed dichotomies is found elsewhere.[14] A very special approach that is emphasized here is to say not only that a great many of these supposed dichotomies are reconciled in the routine lives of the Buddhists, but that doctrinal and conceptual backing may be found for the healing of the tensions between the secular and the spiritual.

Religion and nationalism

Apart from the tension between the secular and the religious, an area where a great deal of tension emerged between doctrinal perspectives and socio-political realities is that of inter-group conflicts and the need to generate relevant identity profiles.[15] Both Roman Catholic and Protestant Christianity came to Sri Lanka with the arrival of the Portuguese, Dutch and British. Though there was conflict between the Sinhala kings of the Anuradhapura and Polonnaruwa regimes and the Tamil kings who often owed allegiance to south India, not only were the Buddhist–Hindu relations cordial, but many Hindu rituals were integrated into the daily life of the Buddhist. In fact, many years later Robert Knox remarked that for the tribulations of the present life the Buddhists go to the *dēvāle*, and for the fears of this life they go to the Buddhist temple. In this sense inter-group conflict of a religious nature was basically contexualized by the state patronage given to Catholic and the Protestant versions of Christianity by these foreign rulers, the Portuguese, the Dutch and the British. There were both restrictions and penalities imposed on those who practised the traditional religions of Buddhism, Hinduism and Islam.[16]

The British had promised not to do away with the state patronage of Buddhism in 1815 when they took over the Kandyan Kingdom and the whole of Sri Lanka came under their rule. They did not do so, but they gradually announced a stand of neutrality regarding religion and thought that this should be advantageous to the Buddhists. There was, however, a strong Buddhist revival during the latter part of the nineteenth century as well as the early part of the twentieth century. With the gaining of independence under the leadership of the late D. S. Senanayake, the basis for a pluralist Sri Lanka encouraging inter-group harmony became a possibility. However, the Sinhala Buddhist majority which had stayed dormant emerged more vociferously in the elections of 1956, which brought the new Sri Lanka Freedom Party into power. The form of linguistic nationalism and the Sinhala-Buddhist identity which came to the surface during the elections remained through all the vagaries of time and change. It is unfortunate that this feeling of identity could not be used for a healthy revitalization of the cultural roots of the country as well as contributing to the making of a larger 'Sri-Lankan' identity. As has been mentioned elsewhere. 'the semantic bridge between healthy national pride and fanaticism becomes hazy and clouded and has to be penetrated by the process of self-criticism.'[17] Yet the doctrinal resources in Buddhism for moving from a healthy, critical and interim idea of personal identity to an equally provisional and critical and corporate identity are very rich.

> Somewhere within the narrow ridge between the paths of chaos and nihilism and the traps of identity illusions, one has to penetrate through a razor's edge, a realm of interim and critical identities, dissolving them as we cross them, transcending them as we cut across their inner dialectic.[18]

In spite of these rich doctrinal resources, the momentum of Sri Lankan history took a tragic turn. Insurgency and terrorism have clouded the scene and the context is too recent for a historian to generate the needed mellow and profound insights. It was a crisis of identity between communities which had 'mutually conflicting historical perceptions of each other's identity'.[19] As Bardwell Smith has pointed out, the question of identity, whether we are dealing with a person or community, is not merely social, political or ethnic; it is a deeply religious issue. Thus for a philosopher of Buddhism who delves into the historical setting of Buddhism in Sri Lanka an interesting focus is not just the gap between theory and practice which has been the subject of some studies, but more importantly, the conflict and tensions between doctrinal resources and socio-economic as well as political realities. The broad conflict between the secular and the religious looms large in the history of Buddhism in Sri Lanka, and the taxing of the doctrinal resources will always continue. But out of all these foci of tension and dilemmas, the focus on the issue of identity profiles is the central concern today. The malleability of identity as such means that it changes with changing historical currents. If a person as well as a group can contexualize their identities and treat them as provisional and interim, then identity conflicts can be minimized. Religion is like an instrument with a dual edge: a true believer can become either a fanatic or a person who believes in rational compromise.

Buddhist scholarship in a changing world

One of the beneficial aspects of the Buddhist revival that took place in Sri Lanka during the last five decades was the attempt to develop Buddhism on a modern footing. Even though some of the institutional provisions made for a revival of Buddhist learning lacked clear planning, in an overall impression we certainly see important contributions made in the field of Buddhist learning. During the last few decades, we have seen the initiation of the Buddhist encyclopedia project, the revival of the traditional seats of learning like the Vidyodaya and Vidyalankara Pirivena by granting them university status, and during more recent times the establishment of the Pali and Buddhist university and an institute of Buddhist studies within the university organization. The training of Sri Lankan scholars abroad in Buddhist studies and Buddhist philosophy had more tangible results, and there were important contributions made to the world of learning. There have also been useful studies with a sociological and historical orientation. It must be mentioned that some of the studies spilled over from academic circles to Buddhists in general. Buddhist academics did have a considerable role in the dissemination of knowledge by writing to popular journals and participating in public talks and seminars. But it is doubtful whether any intellectual leadership emerged from them that would have given some specific direction to the emerging Buddhist revival.

But learned Buddhist monks became an important factor in national politics and continued to wield a great deal of influence on successive governments. As Walpola Rahula remarks in *The Heritage of the Bhikkhu*,

> Bhikkhus who have acquired a good modern education have an insight into current problems and through their devotion to the country, their nation and their religion have come forward independently to tell the masses of their legitimate rights and privileges.[20]

A document released by the Vidyodaya Pirivena in 1946 formalizes the need for the Buddhist monks to play a central role in the political activities of the country.[21] There was also an expansion of Buddhist research into areas like Buddhism and social ethics and Buddhist economics. The application of Buddhist principles in areas of applied ethics is a major concern of Buddhist scholars in Sri Lanka today, and this is a product of the great need felt that Buddhism should have a relevant message for governmental and economic development issues. At a more abstract level scholars trained more exclusively in the traditions of western philosophy attempted to give a 'modern appeal' to Buddhism. It was an attempt to revive tradition but give it a more modernist appeal. In general there were three outstanding features in this modernist appeal: rationality and analytical rigour;[22] the possible coexistence with science; and the resources for strong social involvement.[23] Philosophy, science and social involvement were the norms for the new emphasis in Buddhist thought.

But intellectual fashions change, and within the same context emerged a profound interest in the existential and personal entry into the *Dhamma*,[24] the deep-meditative culture of the mind[25] and some interests in inter-religious dialogue. This diversity of appeals, whether we call them 'modernist' or 'traditionalist', is possible because the *Dhamma* is so rich, so flexible as far as appeals to different temperaments matter, and may be inexhaustible. Perhaps the *Dhamma* holds the key to understanding the more tragic aspects of the history of the country as well as its more satisfying achievements.

Concluding thoughts

Philosophical systems like Buddhism cannot be separated from their manifestation in history and culture. This is all the more true of Buddhism as it is not merely meant for intellectual debate and analysis but meant to enter integrally into the everyday lives of the adherents. But there are many dimensions to Buddhism, as text and doctrine: Buddhism as containing the kind of insights which can only be penetrated by the insights of meditation; Buddhism as an institution as seen in the institution of the *sangha* and the patronage of kings; and finally Buddhism as the ordinary person (who does not claim to be a part of the intelligentsia) applies it to the tribulations and the aspirations of daily living. Some see contradictions in these different aspects of Buddhism, while others see tensions and dualities which are integrated by a process of slow growth, but basically they are facets of a single universe. As Steven Collins, who attempts to see Buddhism as a single cultural world, says, 'the most abstract forms of its imaginative representation, what we call its "ideas", are intimately connected with and inextricable from the presuppositions and institutional framework of Buddhist culture and society'.[26]

BUDDHISM IN SOUTH-EAST ASIA

General features

In south-east Asia as elsewhere, what in modern terminology has come to be called 'Buddhism' consists of three specific and essential components: the Buddha, the *Dhamma* and the *Sangha*. Where the importance of all three is duly acknowledged, honoured and respected, *there* is Buddhism. 'The Buddha' means the historical human figure who is held to have lived in India in the sixth and early fifth centuries BC. 'The *Dhamma*' generally means the entire doctrine taught by the Buddha; the term also means the 'law of the universe', that which upholds all things. 'The *sangha*' means the order of the *bhikkhus* (or monks).

The type of Buddhism which has been predominant in south-east Asia since at least the middle of the eleventh century is of the kind which is generally described as Theravāda Buddhism (the doctrine of the elder monks, that is, the *thera*), the scriptures of which are in the Pali language. Not much is known with certainty concerning Buddhism in south-east Asia prior to that time, except that for some considerable period there had been what Professor Hla Pe has called 'a one way cultural traffic between India and Burma', as Indians who were visiting or migrating 'brought their religious cults with them . . . among which Mahayanism was certainly prominent'. Hla Pe adds, however, that 'the Ceylon Pali canon was in the ascendant', and in lower Burma Theravāda Buddhism predominated.[27]

It can safely be claimed that Buddhism is now the predominant form of institutionalized religion in most of the countries of mainland south-east Asia: that is, Burma, Thailand, Laos and Cambodia; it has its adherents in Vietnam also. Buddhism has been an important element in the traditions and national cultures of these countries for many centuries, and prior to the period of European colonial expansion in south-east Asia in the nineteenth century, it provided the major institutions of their national life. In addition to this, in the modern period the missionary activities of Buddhist monks from India and Sri Lanka have introduced a more specifically Buddhist element into the spectrum of broadly Chinese traditional religious institutions and the practices of Chinese immigrants in Malaysia and Singapore.

It is often claimed that Theravāda is the characteristic form or tradition of Buddhism found in south-east Asia. 'Theravāda' indicates a specific doctrinal emphasis: it claims to be the doctrine (*vāda*) of the elders (*thera*). It is the survivor from among what in the ancient period in India were eighteen specialized schools of Buddhist thought and doctrine. All these were distinguished from the one, simple 'broad-church' tradition which called itself the Mahāyāna: that is, 'the Great *Yāna* (or 'Vehicle', the one that can cope with a wide variety of tradition and practice, and carry large numbers to salvation. Anything other than this broad tradition was regarded (by the Mahāyāna) as 'Little Vehicle' or Hīnayāna. In south-east Asia the distinction between the

Hīnayāna (in the form of its now one surviving sect or school, the Theravāda) and the Mahāyāna largely reflects different geographical sources: the presence of the Hīnayāna is usually due to recent Indian or Sri Lankan influence, and the presence of Mahāyāna usually indicates Chinese or Tibetan influence, and even Japanese influence, as in one of Singapore's newer Buddhist sects.

By virtue of the almost unrivalled support the Theravāda commands throughout mainland south-east Asia it has, in the terms used in the sociology of religion, become virtually a 'church-type', and is no longer a 'sect-type'.

The basic scriptures of the Theravāda tradition, claiming to present the sayings and teachings of the Buddha, are preserved in an ancient Indian language, Pali, which has much similarity to some of the modern languages of south Asia, such as Hindi, Bengali, Marathi and Sinhalese. The ancient Buddhist documents which constitute its scriptures are by tradition arranged in three collections, or *piṭakas*, and hence are referred to collectively as the *Ti*-(three)*piṭaka*. They are distinct from the Mahāyāna collections of Buddhist teachings, which are generally in Sanskrit. Sanskrit is common both to the Buddhist scriptures and to the Brahmanical scriptures of Hinduism, the Veda. However, there is some difference between these two varieties of Sanskrit, that is, between Buddhist Sanskrit and Brahmanical Sanskrit. The Mahāyāna Buddhist scriptures, in Sanskrit, differ also from the other surviving Buddhist collection, the Theravāda scriptures (in Pali), in the generally more miraculous and spectacular (and thus, presumably, more popular) nature of the Buddhist stories they contain.

Pali Buddhist scriptures, originating in India, were carried to Sri Lanka, and from there, in various ways and at various times, to the countries of south-east Asia: Burma, Thailand, Cambodia and Laos. But something of the Sanskrit tradition was also known, and influential, in some of these countries.

What may seem, on the basis of these considerations, to be the extreme complexity of Buddhism in south-east Asia is compounded by another characteristic: that throughout south-east Asia each of the now recognized 'Buddhist' countries has developed its own specific Buddhist traditions and forms. In each country 'Buddhism' has become slightly different from the Buddhism of the neighbouring countries, in that each has developed its own 'country-specific' Buddhism in its history, forms of organization, practices, literature, political affinities, social structure, doctrine, and scriptural preferences and traditions. Such variations may be more marked in some cases than in others: clearer, for example, between Thai Buddhism and Burmese Buddhism than between Thai Buddhism and the Buddhism of Laos.

The differences between Thai Buddhism and Burmese Buddhism may be seen as partly due to the political history of the two countries. In Thailand the political tradition of the Buddhist state, with a Buddhist monarch, politically established *sangha* (that is, the totality of the Thai Buddhist monks) and a largely Buddhist lay population is in contrast with the situation in Burma, where the tradition of the Buddhist monarch and a politically established *sangha* was brought to an end by the British invasion and imperial occupation of Burma in the nineteenth century. This has had its effect, in part at least, in a much greater degree of sectarianism among the Buddhist monks of Burma than is found within the Thai *sangha*. Another well-known difference is in the prior concern of Thai monks with the *vinaya piṭaka*, the first division of the Pali Buddhist scriptures, which deals with the discipline and units of the Buddhist *sangha*, personal and collective; whereas in Burma the traditional concern of the most famous and learned monks is with the *abhidhamma piṭaka*, the third section of the Pali Buddhist scriptures, in which philosophical and doctrinal questions are dealt with in great detail and complexity. It is often noted that the first question asked by a Thai monk on hearing that a fellow-monk is proposing to visit a non-Buddhist country is: 'But how will you keep the *vinaya* there?' (that is to say: how will you as a monk be able to comply with the Buddhist *sangha*'s code of discipline in that non-Buddhist country where conditions are not conducive to the keeping of Buddhist norms as they are here in Thailand?). This indicates the priority which Thai Buddhism gives to conformity to Buddhist norms, and the correctness of a monk's conduct.

None of the south-east Asian countries where Buddhism is well established has gained a prominent reputation for special knowledge and learning in the third, and remaining *piṭaka*: the *sutta piṭaka*. This consists of stories concerning the Buddha himself and the early history of Buddhism in India. It is, of course, fully accepted and used in south-east Asia, but is also generally recognized as the section of the Pali Buddhist scriptures in which the monks of Sri Lanka have become most prominent for their knowledge and interpretation of the stories and general, popular teachings of the Buddha which it contains.

Buddhism in Burma

In a similar way the tradition has established itself that the monks of Burma have special prominence when it comes to proficiency in the understanding and teaching of the *abhidhamma piṭaka* and the practices of meditation which are based upon what may be called, broadly, the *abhidhamma* tradition of 'psychological' analysis. In the Buddhist context this means the analysis of mental states and their ways of changing, and of the nature of material and non-material entities and events. In the modern period, from the beginning of the nineteenth century especially, some of Burma's Buddhist monks (*sayadaws*) have been very famous in this respect, for example the Ledi Sayadaw, that is, the learned master of Leditawya Monastery, north of Monywa town, who is less well known by his personal name of Bhikkhu Nyana. Born in 1846, he died in 1923 at the age of 77, and his career was of a pattern followed by other less well-known Burmese monks. At the age of 20 he was ordained a *bhikkhu* and soon gained a reputation for his outstanding ability as a student in Pali and in Buddhist literature. He published his first Pali work, the *Manual of Perfections* (*Parami Dipani*), at the age of 35. In the course of his lifetime he wrote seventy-six Buddhist manuals, commentaries and essays altogether, some in Pali and some in Burmese. He was well known as a teacher of *abhidhamma* and the founder of meditation centres for lay Buddhist devotees. The quality of his scholarship was recognized by the University of Rangoon's conferring on him the degree of Doctor of Literature (*honoris causa*). He is best remembered in Burma for his emphasis upon the practice of meditation, and the exercises of insight which are necessary as a preliminary to meditation.[28] His life and work provide a good illustration of the way in which Burmese Buddhist monks have combined serious scholarship in Buddhist philosophy with personal practice of Buddhist meditation.

Up to this point our concern in Burma has been with the Burmese Buddhists only. However, considerable numbers of other ethnic communities in Burma are also Buddhists. These include the Shans, Chins, Kachins and Karens. So far as the Shans are concerned, a 'most important criterion of group identity is that all Shans are Buddhists'[29], 'and being a Buddhist is symbolically important as an index of Shan sophistication', since Shan settlements 'are always found associated with irrigated wet paddy land'. In Burma this indicates prosperity, compared with the generally less sophisticated life of those who live in mountainous country. Such prosperity in Burma also implies Buddhist culture.[30] The same is true in Thailand, formerly known as Siam, where the main ethnic group is Tai-speaking, Buddhist by religion and 'Shan' (or people of *Siam*) in terms of ethnicity.[31]

The broad generalization made by Edmund Leach, that the people of Burma are basically of two kinds, 'Hill People' and 'Valley People', with different modes of subsistence and hence different levels of prosperity, is used by him to emphasize the contrast in life styles between Buddhist and non-Buddhist. 'Valley People are all assumed to be wet rice cultivators living in conditions highly favourable to wet rice cultivation.'[32] 'Hill People', on the other hand, 'live in steep hill country' and 'enjoy a somewhat meagre standard of living sustained through the aid of shifting cultivation'. Among them 'there is a great range of variety both in language and tribal organisation'. Another fact concerning them, observed but not explained, is that 'true "Hill People" are never Buddhists', although, as Leach points out, many Hill People have become Christians during the past century (Leach was writing in 1960); there are other occasional exceptions. 'In general however it is only the true Valley People who can afford to be civilised and Buddhist.'[33] This appears to reflect the view that a basic desideratum for living as a Buddhist is a reasonable level of economic prosperity, a view which the history of Buddhism in India from the earliest days tends to support, where its growth was primarily and mainly among sophisticated urban dwellers. (And towns tend to be located in valleys and plains rather than on hill tops.) It is acknowledged that there are what appear to be exceptions, that is, Hill People who have become Buddhists. For example, Leach takes the case of 'the Palaung inhabitants of Tawnpeng in the Burma Shan State who are prosperous cultivators of tea'. They 'have become

Buddhists and have organised their Tawng Peng State in exact imitation of the political model provided by their Shan neighbours who are typical rice-growing Valley People'.[34] Broadly the same economic determinant appears to operate in Thailand between hill peoples and people of the irrigated lowlands.

Buddhism in Thailand

Thailand is sometimes regarded as an example of a country where 'normative' or 'traditional' Buddhism is to be found, supported by the state and 'undamaged' by the political intervention of European colonial rulers. As Heinz Bechert has pointed out, the 'notion that the state has a responsibility for the religious institutions had become an essential part of political thinking in Theravada Buddhist countries'. He comments that this notion has, in recent years, 'been one of the causes for the internal problems of Burma'. Nevertheless, he points out that 'from a study of the original Buddhist texts it is evident that this particular form of Sangha–state relations that has emerged in Southeast Asia is not at all based on canonical Buddhism and is not in any way a necessary part of a Theravada Buddhist structure'. Moreover, he cites evidence from his research in Theravāda Buddhism in East Bengal (now Bangladesh) to show 'that a non-governmental autonomous religious body could be as effective in preventing a decay of the Sangha as any state action in a Theravada society'.[35]

The problems that colonial rule are said to have brought upon Burma's Buddhism can thus be fully recognized without the conclusion necessarily being drawn that the best way forward for Burmese Buddhism is for it to become state-established once again, and without looking to Thailand's state Buddhism as necessarily the ideal example of normative Buddhism for south-east Asia. The question whether the close relationship between the Thai government and the Thai Buddhist *sangha* is one which favours normative Buddhism in that country is a matter which has, however, been largely passed over until recent times. The comparison with the case of Burma, where British colonial conquest and rule interfered very seriously with the condition of Buddhism as it had existed from the time of the Burmese kings, may be misleading, partly because of the hasty assumption that what existed in Burma under the Burmese kings was normative Buddhism. Such assumptions take some of their strength also from what is assumed to be the admirable example of Buddhism–state relations in Thailand. The Thai example is sometimes justified on the grounds that the relations between the secular government and the Buddhist *sangha* in Thailand reflect similar relations with the Buddhist *sangha* in India in the time of its emperor Aśoka, generally regarded as the upholder and defender of early Buddhism in India. Another possible model, possibly more relevant in the twentieth century, is that of the relation between institutional Buddhism, and what is by the Constitution the secular state in India since Independence, where 'secular' is understood to mean 'religiously non-committed'. On the other hand, and by way of contrast, when U Nu as Prime Minister of Burma, following tradition, tried to make Buddhism once again the state religion of Burma the attempt failed, as he was not able to control what had by then become 'the politically minded groups within the Sangha'.[36] Moreover, it has to be recognized that Thailand presents in its clearest form what appears to be the paradox of Theravāda Buddhism: this has been described not unfairly as 'a radically rationalistic doctrine . . . [Buddhism] . . . directed more to an intellectual elite than to the masses', having nevertheless been officially adopted as a national, indeed a mass religion.[37] The problem, as Yoneo Ishii observes, is 'to explain coherently the structure of this mass religion that rests on an elite-oriented doctrine'.[38] The answer, as appears from the evidence of Buddhist history, is that the early stage, when the first Buddhists 'wandered abroad seeking solitude far from human habitation, in mountain caves, forests, graveyards and like places', did not last for long. Such early practitioners began to form communities, while nevertheless remaining homeless and living as 'beggars of alms'. This means that the *sangha* is necessarily located physically within secular society,[39] and tension thus develops between the two; the history of Buddhism in the various countries in which it has existed illustrates the character of this tension. The history of Buddhism in Thailand shows particularly clearly the role which Buddhism has played in various other south-east Asian societies also in (a) the creation and preservation of culture and (b) the transmission of culture (i.e. the *sangha*'s role in south-east Asian societies seen in its educational functions). This has been the role of the Buddhist *sangha* in other south-east Asian countries, notably Burma, Cambodia and Laos, but it is in Thailand that it has continued with least interruption until recently. Formerly, as Somboon Suksamran points out, when 'the school system in the modern sense had not yet been set up, the monks were regarded as the most important teachers, and the *wat* [monastery] was the major educational institution, where both religious and secular subjects were taught'.[40] After the state educational system was set up in the 1870s and 1880s, however, the role of the monks in this respect declined, 'and the monks have lost their vital secular function as teachers of the young'.[41]

Cambodian Buddhists

Traditionally a Buddhist country, Cambodia had for many years until recently maintained a formal observance of the ritual practices of Theravāda Buddhism as part of the Khmer tradition. It is acknowledged, by a recent reviewer of Cambodia's past, that for the Khmers generally,

> those rituals provided them with the feeling of being protected by the supernatural power in the current life and of being promoted to better living conditions in the future life. That is why they used to attend ceremonial and religious gatherings or go to the pagoda offering food and other supplies to the Buddhist monks. . . . All those ritual practices were well

> accommodated to the Khmer tradition which has been moulded also, since the beginning of our history, by Brahminism, animism and by ancestor worship.[42]

However, since the invasion of Cambodia by neighbouring Vietnamese forces, many Cambodians have become refugees in the camps set up in Thailand, where, with some outside help, they have reconstructed certain elements of Cambodian life, and especially their Buddhist institutions:

> There has been a vigorous attempt by the Khmer under the leadership of Son Sann to preserve Khmer Buddhism in its original form. . . . Son Sann [the Prime Minister of the Coalition Government of Democratic Kampuchea] evidences a strong belief that Buddhism is the foundation of Khmer culture and way of life and could provide the most vital integrating force for Khmer unification.[43]

It is under the leadership of Son Sann that the Cambodian exiles along the Thai border have continued their determined efforts to preserve Khmer Buddhism, to scrutinize its past record, to assess its weaknesses and its strengths, and to consider how best it may be reconstituted in a future Cambodia, liberated from foreign rule.[44]

Buddhism in Vietnam

There has been a tendency in western accounts of Buddhism in south-east Asia to overlook Vietnam. One of the factors responsible for this may be that such accounts have tended to concern themselves mainly with the Theravāda form of Buddhism. Yet Buddhism was introduced into Vietnam towards the end of the second century of the Christian era, and has continued to be part of the history of that country. It suffered a decline during the second half of the nineteenth century, under French colonial rule and the privileged position of Roman Catholicism. But by 1920 'a new Buddhist movement was launched simultaneously in the three main regions of Vietnam: North, Centre, and South'.[45] This was a movement which aimed at a regeneration of Buddhism, and in 1931 an Association of Buddhist Studies was founded in Saigon. Similar associations were founded in Hue in 1932 and in Hanoi in 1934.

In 1951 Buddhists in Vietnam were sufficiently notable among the Buddhists of south-east Asia for the President of the World Fellowship of Buddhists, Dr Malalasekere, to make an official visit to Saigon and Hue and to receive an impressive welcome from Vietnamese Buddhists, including a large contingent of Buddhist youth.

Buddhism in Laos[46]

The Buddhism of Laos, like that of Burma, Thailand and Cambodia, is traditionally of the Hīnayāna form, and uses the Theravāda scriptures, in Pali. The period of its great expansion was in the sixteenth and seventeenth centuries. This was followed by a period of foreign invasions and internal warfare and the decline of Buddhism, particularly in the nineteenth century; with this went the destruction or the decay of many Buddhist monasteries. However, the national Buddhist Institute (L'Institute bouddhique du Royaume) and the French School of the Far East (L'Ecole Française d'Extrême-Orient) undertook the work of restoration and the revival of Buddhist studies.[47] The decline of Buddhism coincided with a resurgence of the cult of the *Phi*, an ancestor cult which has popular equivalents among the Vietnamese, the Cambodians and the Burmese, and is intended to deflect the displeasure of ancestors and the maladies which this entails. The result was a form of Lao popular religion in which Buddhist elements were combined with the local spiritual cults.

As elsewhere in south-east Asia, the monastery in Laos is the centre of Buddhist religious, educational and social activities, and often also of medical consultations.

The Buddhists of Laos have mainly inhabited the lowland areas; they are ethnically distinct from the hill- and forest-dwelling minorities who 'eked livings from unreported trade across the border with China, from cultivating opium, and in the 1960s and 1970s as mercenaries paid by the United States to fight Lao communist forces'.[48] The subordinate relationship with Vietnam which replaced what had been for the Lao the subordinate relationship with the French meant that, so far as Buddhism is concerned, 'the Buddhist Sangha seems to have operated more openly in Laos than in Cambodia', for the 'Vietnamese, in fact, had replaced the French as the patron of the Lao'.[49]

Buddhism in Malaysia and Singapore

Since about the beginning of the 1960s there has been a marked increase in the number of people in Malaysia and Singapore who have counted themselves as Buddhists, so far as official religious identity for Census purposes is concerned. With this, there has been also an increase in the number of Buddhist Associations. These exist mainly to provide a venue for meeting fellow-Buddhists, including members of the *sangha*, and for attending lectures and classes at which Buddhist methods of meditation are taught, as well as talks on various aspects of Buddhist philosophy and practice. The notable growth of this kind of constituency is of sufficiently general lay character (not only in south-east Asia but elsewhere) to be described as 'Associational Buddhism'. (One of its earliest manifestations in Europe was the Buddhist Society, founded by the late Christmas Humphreys.)

In Malaysia and Singapore, prior to the rise of such Buddhist Associations there was no particularly clear way of identification as a Buddhist; visits to a Chinese temple and the making of offerings could be counted as such, but were not necessarily so. With the emergence of the Buddhist Associations a more reliable and definite mode of identification as a Buddhist became available. A feature of these Associations which helps in this direction is the publication by the individual Association of collections of papers and essays on Buddhist subjects, often in the form of an annual. One example (among many) is *The Young Buddhist*, a two-hundred-page publication of the Singapore Buddha Yana Organization (SBYO). The 1979 issue, for example, carried greetings from a government Minister (Goh Chok Tong), and from Chan Chee Seng, a Parliamentary Secretary and a patron of the SBYO, and consisted otherwise of essays on Buddhism, its characteristic teachings and its local manifestations in Singapore. This example is chosen as representative of similar publications of contemporary Buddhist Associations and Societies in Singapore and Malaysia.

NOTES

1 See Adikaram 1953: pp. 43–9.
2 ibid.
3 Gombrich 1972: pp. 17–20.
4 Michael B. Carrithers, 'They will be lords upon the island: Buddhism in Sri Lanka', in Heinz Bechert and Richard Gombrich (eds), *The World of Buddhism* (London: Thames & Hudson, 1984), pp. 134–44.
5 ibid.
6 ibid., p. 141.
7 Bardwell L. Smith, 'The ideal social order as portrayed in the chronicles of Ceylon', in Smith 1978: p. 53.
8 Max Weber. *Religions of India*, quoted in Malagoda Kitsiri 1976: p. 1.
9 See Gombrich 1971.
10 Smith 1972.
11 Melford Spiro, *Buddhism and Society: A Great Tradition and its Burmese Vicissitudes* (Berkeley: University of California Press, 1971).
12 ibid., p. 427.
13 See the discussion in Padmasiri de Silva, *Value Orientations and Nation Building* (Colombo: Lake House Investments Ltd, 1976), pp. 12–13.
14 ibid., p. 12.
15 Padmasiri de Silva, 'The logic of identity profiles and the ethics of communal violence', in K. M. de Silva *et al.* 1988: pp. 14–26.
16 K. M. de Silva, 'Nationalism and the state in Sri Lanka', in K. M. de Silva *et al.* 1988: pp. 62–76.
17 Padmasiri de Silva, 'The logic', *op. cit.*
18 ibid., p. 17.
19 Godfrey Gunatilleke *et al.* (eds), *Ethical Dilemmas of Development in Asia* (Toronto: Lexington Press, 1983), p. 149.
20 Rahula 1974: pp. 128.
21 ibid., p. 131.
22 For a comprehensive analysis of the place of analysis and empiricism in Buddhism, see Jayatilleke 1963.
23 O. H. de A. Wijesekera. *Buddhism and Society* (Colombo: Baudha Sahitya Sabha Publications).
24 See Nanavira Thera, *Clearing the Path* (Colombo: Path Press, 1987); Padmasiri de Silva, *Tangles and Webs* (Colombo: Lake House Investments Ltd, 1976).

25 Nyanaponika Thera 1975.
26 Steven Collins, *Selfless Persons* (Cambridge: Cambridge University Press, 1982), pp. 265–6.
27 Hla Pe, *Burma* (Singapore: Institute of South East Asia Studies, 1985), p. 190.
28 See Mehathera Ledi Sayadaw, *The Manuals of Bon* (Rangoon: Union Buddha Sasana Council, 1965).
29 Edmund Leach, 'The frontiers of Burma', *Comparative Studies in Society and History* (1960–6), Vol III, p. 52.
30 ibid.
31 ibid.
32 ibid.
33 ibid., p. 53.
34 ibid.
35 Heinz Bechert, 'Buddhism in the modern states of South East Asia', in Bernard Grossman (ed.), *South East Asia in the Modern World* (Wiesbaden, 1972), p. 132.
36 ibid., p. 138.
37 Yoneo Ishii, *Sangha, State and Society: Thai Buddhism in History*, trans. Peter Hawkes (Honolulu: University of Hawaii Press, 1986).
38 ibid.
39 ibid., p. 8.
40 Somboon Suksamran, *Political Buddhism in South East Asia*, p. 11.
41 ibid., p. 12.
42 Ieng Mouly, in *Buddhists and the Future of Cambodia* (Rithisen: Khmer Buddhist Centre, 1986), p. 45.
43 Somboon Suksamran, in *Buddhists and the Future of Cambodia*, p. 125.
44 Author's personal contacts with Khmer Buddhists at Rithisen, 1986.
45 Mai-Tho-Truyen, *Le Buddhisme au Vietnam* (Saigon, 1962), p. 47.
46 This section is based on the contribution by Georges Condominas, 'Notes sur le bouddhisme populaire en milieu rural Lao', in *Aspects du Bouddhisme Lao* (Special Number, no. 9, 1973), pp. 27–115.
47 ibid., p. 31.
48 See D. J. Steinberg (ed.), *In Search of Southeast Asia* (1971, 1987), pp. 383, 386.
49 ibid., p. 386.

REFERENCES

Adikaram, E. W. (1953) *Early History of Buddhism in Ceylon*, Colombo: Gunasena.
Gombrich, Richard F. (1971) *Precept and Practice*, Oxford: Clarendon Press.
Jayatilleke, K. N. (1963) *Early Buddhist Theory of Knowledge*, London: George Allen & Unwin.
Malalgoda Kitsiri (1976) *Buddhism in Sinhalese Society*, Berkeley: University of California Press.
Rahula, Walpola (1974) *The Heritage of the Bhikkhu*, New York: Grove Press.
Silva, K. M. de *et al.* (eds) (1988) *Ethnic Conflict in Buddhist Societies*, London: Pinter.
Smith, Bardwell L. (ed.) (1972) *The Two Wheels of the Dhamma*, Chambersburgh: American Academy of Religion.
—— (1978) *Religion and Legitimation of Power in Sri Lanka*, Chambersburgh: Anima Books.
Thera, Nyanaponika (1975) *The Heart of Buddhist Meditation*, London: Rider.

FURTHER READING

Bechert, Heinz and Gombrich, Richard F. (eds) (1984) *The World of Buddhism*, London: Thames & Hudson.

Jayatilleke, K. N. (1974) *The Message of the Buddha*, ed. Ninian Smart, New York: Free Press.

Karunatilleke, H. N. S. (1976) *This Confused Society*, Colombo: Buddhist Information Centre.

Malalasekara, G. P. (1928) *The Pali Literature of Ceylon*, London: Royal Asiatic Society.

Obeyesekera, G. (1963) 'The great tradition and the little in perspectives of Sinhala Buddhism', *Journal of the Asiatic Society* 21(2):139–53.

Phra Prayudh Payutto (1995) *Buddhadhamma Natural Laws and Values for Life* (tr Oslon, Grant A), New York: State University of New York Press.

Rahula, Walpola (1956) *History of Buddhism in Ceylon*, Colombo: Gunasena.

Silva, Padmasiri de (1979) *An Introduction to Buddhist Psychology*, London: Macmillan Press.

—— (forthcoming) *Environmental Ethics in Buddhism*, Paris: UNESCO.

21

LOGIC AND LANGUAGE IN BUDDHISM

S. R. Bhatt

INTRODUCTION

Every school of philosophy in India has attempted a theory of knowledge in conformity with its theory of reality. Though the primary aim of all philosophizing is generally recognized as knowledge of the nature of reality (*tattva jñāna*), it is believed that a theory of knowledge is a necessary prerequisite to a theory of reality. This belief is grounded in the view that to philosophize is to reflect upon the nature of reality given in experience. But since every experience is inevitably a cognitive reference to an object, there is always a possibility of going astray in the objective reference. Though every experience has a built-in trans-phenomenality or intentionality consisting in a revelation of an object, it is not always guaranteed that it would adequately and faithfully reveal its object. This possibility of error in experience necessitates an enquiry into its veracity. In fact, the entire epistemological pursuit, whether for or against the possibility of acquiring knowledge, begins with and centres on this task.

In the non-Buddhist traditions of Indian philosophical thought, and perhaps also in early Buddhist thought, there appears to be a tacit acceptance of the possibility of acquiring knowledge of reality. However, Nāgārjuna (about AD 250), a later Buddhist dialectical thinker, raised serious doubts about the possibility of acquiring knowledge by pointing out the self-contradictory character of all means of acquiring knowledge. Nāgārjuna's objections stimulated and compelled all subsequent philosophers to provide a solid foundation to epistemology and logic before proceeding with the formulations of their philosophical positions.

In Buddhist circles Asaṅga (about AD 405) and Vasubandhu (about AD 410) made pioneering attempts to construct epistemology and logic on the Buddhist pattern. However, it was Dignāga (about AD 450) who put Buddhist epistemology and logic on a solid footing and gave them a distinctive character. He is, therefore, rightly regarded as the father of Buddhist epistemology and logic, and also of medieval Indian epistemology and logic in general, for he not only gave a precise formulation to Buddhist epistemology and logic but also imparted a new direction to Indian epistemology and logic by way of composing independent treatises on epistemology and logic and interspersing the treatment of metaphysical problems within them, a style which was later on followed by Gaṅgeśa (about the twelth century AD), the founder of the school of Navya-Nyāya.

Buddhist literature prior to Dignāga deals with the problem of knowledge and the means of knowing either very casually or not at all. There seems to be no work devoted to the problem. But Dignāga felt the necessity for a distinct treatise on epistemology and logic to establish the Buddhist doctrines in a logical manner. He explicitly mentions in the *Pramāṇa-samuccaya* that its composition was led by the need to establish the means of valid cognition.

The task initiated by Dignāga was brilliantly continued by Dharmakīrti (about AD 635), a doyen of Buddhist epistemology and logic. His *Pramāṇa-vārtika*, *Pramāṇa-viniścaya* and *Nyāya-bindu* are masterpieces of Buddhist epistemology and logic. When Dignāga undertook an examination of the logical tenets of other philosophical schools in his treatise there were reactions from the latter. For instance, Uddyotakara and Kumārila (about AD 500) tried to controvert the views of Dignāga. Dharmakīrti therefore defended and modified the views of Dignāga, thereby strengthening the foundations of Buddhist epistemology and logic. However, his exposition, which was intended to explain and defend the views of Dignāga, superseded and eclipsed the original by its superior merit. This tradition of Dharmakīrti was carried forward by Dharmottara (about AD 847) and subsequently by, amongst others, Jñānaśrīmitra (about AD 1040).

ANALYSIS OF KNOWLEDGE

'All successful human action is necessarily preceded by knowledge and therefore we are going to investigate it.' With this prefatory sentence Dharmakīrti defines the scope and aim of epistemology and logic in the *Nyāya-bindu*. Human action may be either purposive or instinctive. Human aims are either positive or negative, something either desirable or undesirable. Purposive action consists in attaining the desirable and avoiding the undesirable. Knowledge is efficacious in causing successful action in the sense that it is followed by successful action consisting in the attainment of the desirable aim or avoidance of the undesirable aim. A cause may be productive or informative. Knowledge is a cause of successful action in the latter sense only. It enables us to reach the reality which alone has practical efficiency.

Different from knowledge is false cognition. That cognition which makes us reach an object *different* from the one revealed in cognition is false. Objects differ on account of their form, or their spatio-temporal locations. Thus, cognition representing one form of the object is not to be considered as a true cognition when the real object has a different form. Likewise a cognition is not true if it wrongly represents the place or time of the object. Knowledge is defined by Dharmakīrti in the *Pramāṇa-vārtika* as that which is not in disagreement with its object. Knowledge thus stands for that cognition which is a faithful representation of reality. What it means is that in knowledge the object must be known as *it is* and not *other than what it is*. Since a non-deviating reference is the essential condition of a true cognition, which alone differentiates it from a false or erroneous cognition, the truth of knowledge about something consists in its accord with the object cognized. Dharmottara puts this characteristically as follows:

> In common life when we say that truth is being spoken what we mean is that it makes us reach an object. Similarly, that knowledge is true which makes us reach an object it points to. Indeed, knowledge does not create an object and does not offer it to us, but just makes us reach at it. By making us reach an object nothing else is meant than attending to the object.

Here Dharmottara points out three distinct successive stages involved in the process of apprehension of an object, each succeeding one resulting from the preceding. They are cognizing (*adhigati*), attending (*pravartana*) and reaching (*prāpaṇa*). But he makes it clear that the first stage alone is knowledge.

Knowledge being perfectly in agreement with the object must also be a cognition of an object not yet cognized. It is the first moment of cognition, the moment of the first awareness. Enduring cognition is recognition, but that is not to be regarded as knowledge. This is because of the momentary existence of the object and knowledge.

Knowledge is of two types. It is intuitive when it springs from insight. It is discursive when it is acquired by directing our attention towards an object with the help of the senses and the cognizing mind. Only discursive knowledge is analysed in epistemology.

Analysis of *pramāṇa*

The Indian thinkers generally adopt a causal approach to knowledge. Knowledge is taken to be an outcome of a particular causal complex in which the most efficient instrumental cause (*karaṇa*) is technically known as *pramāṇa*. The word *pramāṇa* literally means the most efficient instrumental cause of knowledge. In Buddhist tradition the word *pramāṇa* refers to both the mode of knowing and the knowledge acquired on that basis. The Buddhists do not entertain the distinction between the process of knowing (*pramāṇa*) and the outcome of this process (*pramāṇa phala* or *pramā*). The Naiyāyikas, on the other hand, insist that the mode of knowing as a process should be distinguished from the resulting knowledge. The Buddhists, however, maintain that no distinction can be possible between the noetic process and its outcome. The act of cognizing completely coincides with the cognition of an object. In fact the Naiyāyikas have to accept the distinction because for them the most efficient instrumental cause of knowledge not only gives rise to knowledge but also evidences the truth of knowledge. For the Buddhists knowledge is self-evidencing, and this consists in knowledge having accord (*sārūpya*) with the object. Thus the difference between the Naiyāyikas and the Buddhists is due to a difference in their understanding of the nature and role of *pramāṇa*. For the Naiyāyikas it stands for the most efficient instrumental cause of knowledge (*pramāyāḥ karaṇam*), whereas for the Buddhists it means that true cognition by which an object is known (*pramīyate anena*).

The role of *pramāṇa*

The problem of *pramāṇa* has given rise to much stimulating debate in the epistemological treatises of Indian origin. The problem is, in a way, that of evidencing the truth of a cognition. The question of evidencing of cognition arises because cognitions are unequal in their epistemic status. Some appear to be true and reveal their corresponding objects as they are, whereas there are others which seem to be erroneous and which misrepresent their objects. Had all cognitions been true, there would have been no need of evidencing them and the entire epistemological enquiry would not have arisen. But since some seem to lead us astray, no cognition prima facie can be said to be true. The very possibility of error in a cognition necessitates its subjection to a critical examination with a view to establishing its truth or falsity. If the truth or falsity of a cognition needs to be established, the question arises as to what sort of criterion has to be resorted to. The problem of *pramāṇa* has been raised and discussed by the Indian epistemological thinkers precisely against this background.

Maintaining a distinction between evidenced cognition (*pramā* or *pramāṇa phala*) and the evidence (*pramāṇa*), the Nyāya thinkers put forward the view that the truth of knowledge is to be established in terms of its being grounded in adequate and sufficient evidence. The Buddhist thinkers, on the other hand, argue that since knowledge is self-revelatory by its inherent nature its truth is to be determined in terms of itself, and since it is necessarily revelatory of its object, this determination should be with reference to its object. Such a position resulted in the advocacy of the doctrine of accord (*sārūpya*), which we shall discuss later.

The doctrine of the twofold form of knowledge

Now the question is: how is it that cognition cognizes itself and thus establishes itself as true? To answer this the doctrine of the twofold form of knowledge (*dvairūpya jñāna*) has been put forward. This doctrine advocates that every cognition is produced with a twofold form, namely that of itself (*svābhāsa*) and that of the object (*viṣayābhāsa*). In being of its own form (*svābhāsa*) it cognizes itself, and in being of the form of the object (*viṣayābhāsa*) it establishes its truthfulness because of its being in the form of the object. When a cognition possesses the form of its object it is a sufficient condition of its being true. From the former the Buddhist thinkers deduce the doctrine of the self-luminous nature of knowledge (*svaprakāśa*) and from the latter follows the doctrine of self-evidencing nature of knowledge (*svataḥ prāmāṇya*).

The doctrine of the self-luminous nature of knowledge (*svaprakāśa*) has been the basic tenet of Buddhist epistemology and explainable on the basis of the theory of momentariness. If a cognition is just a momentary state of existence ceasing to exist the next moment, then either we can have a cognition of that cognition in the very moment of its origin or we shall have to deny the very possibility of the cognition of the cognition because next moment that cognition will no longer be there to be cognized by the subsequent cognition. Cognition of a cognition is a fact given in our experience. Thus, when a man has the cognition of something blue he has at the same time the awareness of the cognition of something blue. Consistent with the theory of momentariness the only position available to the Buddhists would be to advocate the theory of the self-luminous nature of knowledge (*svaprakāśa*), which would mean that at the very moment of the cognition's cognizing an object it also cognizes itself, just as light illuminates itself while illuminating an object.

The doctrine of accord

As pointed out earlier, *pramāṇa* consists in knowledge having accord, or being free from discordance, with its object. It is the object which gives rise to and thus determines the cognition. The object is regarded as the very ground upon which the cognition is based (*ālambana pratyaya*). In fact, the object not only serves to give rise to the cognition but also differentiates it from another cognition. Though from the transcendental point of view, according to the Yogācāra or Vijñānavāda school, every phenomenon is consciousness only (*vijñaptimātra*), at the empirical level a triple division of consciousness (*vijñāna*) is drawn into the form which is cognized (*grāhyākāra*), the cognition (*grāhaka*) and self-cognition (*svasaṃvṛitti*). It is the cognized form which serves as a differentiating factor between one cognition and another and also accounts for the truth of that cognition. Since every cognition is determined by the object, this determination should be understood as the cognition having the form of the object. Thus, if the object is a pen the corresponding cognition should have the form of the pen. Only then can it be said to be determined by the object and be a true presentation of the object. If a cognition is at variance with the object it will not then be determined by the object, and this will amount to its falsity. In order that a cognition should be true it has to reflect or represent the object in its real form. This will be possible only when the cognition is arising in the form of the object. The truth of a cognition, therefore, consists in this sameness of form with the object. This is what is maintained in the doctrine of accord (*sārūpya*). Dignāga illustrates it by saying that whatever form of the thing appears in the cognition, for example as something white or non-white, it is an object in that form which is cognized.

The function of knowledge is to apprehend an object. In so doing it possesses the form of the object. It is not that knowledge is formless (*nirākāra*). If cognition is held to be formless while the object had a form, then the cognition itself as distinguished from the object will remain the same whether it cognizes something blue or yellow or anything else. Therefore the cognition as an apprehension of an object must be admitted to have the form of the object (*sākāra*). Cognition is thus understood to possess the function of assuming the form of the object.

It seems that the only reason for the Buddhist thinkers to advocate the theory that cognition assumes the form of the object is to provide for the determination of the cognition by its respective object. Every cognition has to refer to an object in so far as it is produced by an object. Thus, there is no formless cognition, because in the very process of being produced by the object it gets the form of the object. It may be that the form of a cognition does not accord with the specific object given in a particular epistemic situation and may accord with some other object which is not given but only hypostatized. This will then be a case of error.

OBJECTS OF KNOWLEDGE

According to the Buddhists there are only two kinds of objects of knowledge, namely the real, objective, unique particular (*svalakṣaṇa*) and the generalized concept or image (*sāmānyalakṣaṇa*). This is because the thing to be cognized has the above two aspects. The objective real in the form of unique particular has no extension in space and no duration in time. It is devoid of all form, attributes, determinations and relations. It is just a point instant or a moment in the incessant movement of a series of reals. It is a unique particular in the sense that it is neither identical with nor similar to any other object. It is a distinct existence dissimilar to and non-comparable with any other real. It is instantaneous because it never endures for the next moment. It is discrete in the sense that it is an isolated existence not at all related to any other existence. So no relation exists between any two unique particulars, all relations being subjective mental constructions. Such an object alone is objectively real. This is a very distinct and unique view held by the Buddhists with regard to the nature of reality. Reality is essentially momentary and dynamic. It is a process in which each moment depends for its existence on the previous moment. Therefore each moment is in itself unique but causally determined by the previous moment. Since it is momentary, we cannot assign any name to this reality because the act of giving a name implies that (1) the real has to exist for more than one moment in order that a name could be recalled and associated with it and (2) since the function of naming requires the possibility of identifying a thing whenever its name is uttered, a momentary real cannot be named and whatever is named is not the reality proper. Therefore, there is one aspect of reality in itself and there is another aspect of reality which is conceptualized and talked about in general terms.

Thus distinct from the unique particular is another type of object of knowledge, known as *sāmānyalakṣaṇa*, which is a construction of our mind and which is in the form of a generalized image. The generalized image is a form imposed by our mind on the objective reality. A generalized image, also known as concept (*vikalpa*), can broadly speaking be of five types, namely pertaining to substantivality (*dravya*), adjectivality (*guṇa*), relations and spatio-temporal locations (*karma*), class character (*jāti*) and linguistic determination (*nāma*). A generalized image is a mental construction (*kalpanā*) having no objective existence. Comprehension of objects as having extension in space and duration in time is nothing but generalization, which is only subjective or inter-subjective and has no counterpart in the objective world. Similarly all attributes, relations, etc. are nothing but generalizations.

KINDS OF KNOWLEDGE

On the basis of the above ontological analysis Dignāga enunciates the theory that since there are only two kinds of objects of knowledge, there are only two kinds of knowledge. Corresponding to the unique particular (*svalakṣaṇa*) we have perceptual knowledge (*pratyakṣa*), and corresponding to the generalized image we have inferential knowledge (*anumāna*). Knowledge is either perceptual or inferential, and there is no knowledge which is beyond the purview of these two. Thus the entire Buddhist epistemology is based on the foundations of the theory of twofold knowledge. Perception (*pratyakṣa*) is pure sensation, a direct sense-apprehension of the unique particular. Inference (*anumāna*) is a mental construction in the form of generalized images. Of course, perceptual knowledge is immediately followed by the inferential one; the former is not at all judgemental or determinate.

The Buddhist thinkers emphatically maintain that the unique particular is knowable in perception only and the generalized image is known only through inference. By implication the unique particular can never be known in inference, and likewise the generalized image can never be known in perception. What is known in perception cannot be known in inference and vice versa. Such a radical dichotomy between mutually exclusive modes of knowing is known as *pramāṇavyavasthā*, which means that each of the two modes of knowing has its own separate and distinct sphere of operation. There is no intermingling in the respective objects of the two. As the unique particular alone is objectively real, while the generalized image is a mental construct, and the one is radically different from the other, there cannot be any cognition which comprehends both at the same time.

Though perception is the foundational type of knowledge in the sense that inference invariably follows it and depends upon it, the two are of equal value in so far as both are knowledge. No doubt perception alone gives us the knowledge of the objective reality and inference is inevitably confined to the conceived reality; however, the latter is also connected with reality in so far as it invariably follows immediately in the wake of the former. Both present the real to us in different ways and hence the two are of equal value. The mere dependence of inference on perception does not deprive it of its epistemic worth.

EARLY BUDDHIST THEORY OF PERCEPTION

Having pointed out that there are two types of discursive knowledge Dignāga and Dharmakīrti proceed to give an analysis of the nature of perception. Before we discuss here their exposition of the theory of perception, it would be helpful first to give a brief survey of the Buddhist theory of perception present in the early Buddhist literature. The theory of perception has been propounded here in very simple terms. According to *Kathāvatthu* every act of perception involves participation by an object, a cognitive sense and a consciousness. This implies the rejection of the view of grasping by an agent, an anthropomorphic view, as it does not fit in with the Buddhistic theory of no-soul (*anattā*). Against the background of the theory of momentariness the possibility of perception poses a problem. In order that perception of an object is possible, the two have to be simultaneous. But the object cannot endure till the time of the occurrence of its cognition. Thus when there is an object there is no cognition of it and when there is a cognition, there is no object corresponding to it. So either the theory of momentariness is to be rejected or the possibility of perception is to be denied. Being faced with this difficulty the Theravādins partially abandon the theory of momentariness by maintaining that material element (*rūpa*) is seventeen times more enduring than mental element (*citta*). That is to say, one matter-moment is equal to seventeen mind-moments. Hence the perceptual cognition of a material object becomes possible. But some other Buddhist thinkers have objected to this double standard because all moments, whether material or mental, should be of equal endurance.

The Vaibhāṣikas solve this difficulty by postulating the idea of the simultaneous rise of all causal factors (*sahabhū-hetu*), i.e. the cognized object, the cognitive sense and the cognizing consciousness all arise simultaneously. They further argue that temporal sequence is not necessary for causal relation. The only necessary and sufficient condition for this is invariable concomitance and not succession, for example a lamp is a cause of light, but both of them are simultaneous. Accordingly perception of an object is possible because it is present along with its cognition.

The Sautrāntikas criticize the Vaibhāṣika view. If object and cognition are present together, they must be co-effects of something else. According to them, perception of an object arises when the object has already disappeared. Then how could it be called perception of *that* object? To answer this they put forward the theory of sameness of form (*sārūpya*). They hold that the object leaves its impression on consciousness through the cognitive sense. The impression has sameness of form (*sārūpya*) with the object, and through this impression we perceive the object in the second moment.

Vasubandhu on perception

On the basis of the information available to us, Vasubandhu (about AD 410) can be regarded as the first systematic epistemological thinker in the tradition followed by Dignāga and Dharmakīrti. In *Vādavidhi*, generally ascribed to him, perception (*pratyakṣa*) is defined as *tato'rthādvijñaṃ pratyakṣam*, i.e. 'perception is a cognition produced from *that* object'. In this definition he maintains that perception is that cognition which is exclusively caused by the object (*ālambana pratyaya*) as distinct from inference, which is a mental construction in the form of conceptualization. The differential character of perception consists in being the opposite of inference. This has been expressed by Vasubandhu with the help of the phrase *tato'rthād*, which by implication means the same as 'free from conceptualization'. Though he does not actually say that a perceptual cognition has no conceptual and verbal elements, this is what he seems to mean when he says that it is exclusively coming from the object. Thus for him perception stands for the bare awareness which is wholly and solely caused by the object and which has no intermingling of conceptual elements whatsoever.

Dignāga on perception

Instead of defining perception in terms of 'object-generated cognition', Dignāga defines it in terms of 'free from mental construction' (*kalpanāpoḍham*), perhaps because the idea of perception being the 'opposite of inference' can be better expressed by the latter term than by the former. It is to the credit of Dignāga that he clearly proposes definitions of philosophical terms in as sharp and clear-cut a way as possible, and he also uses a specific method of definition with the help of the technique of double negation (*apoha* or *atad-vyāvṛtti*), which is radically different from the Nyāya technique of defining things in terms of their essence. He points out that the unique particular (*svalakṣaṇa*) is by nature indefinable. However, our conception of it is definable, and the characteristic feature of all our conceptual knowledge, and of language, is that it is dialectical. Every conception is a negative correlate of its counterpart, and in a definition this is all that can be stated. So a definition is only a negative characterization (*vyāvṛtti*). Perception can, therefore, be defined in terms of its distinction from inference. For the Buddhists all knowledge is either perceptual (*pratyakṣa*) or inferential (*anumāna*), there being no third variety. Thus perception is not inference, and inference is not perception. From this it follows that perception can be understood and defined as the 'opposite of inference'.

Dignāga seems to have two objectives in mind when he proceeds to define perception, namely to distinguish the Buddhist view from the views of the other schools and to distinguish it from inference. The usual definition of perception given by Nyāya–Mīmāṁsā and other non-Buddhist traditions in terms of sense–object contact has been rejected by Dignāga mainly because it takes no notice of the basic feature of perception, which consists in its being a fresh and vivid cognition. Such a cognition can only be in the form of sensation, which is the first moment of every cognition. In the following moments when the conceptualization occurs, it is pure sensation no longer. The Nyāya–Mīmāṁsā definition also contains a confusion between the proper function of the senses and that of the mind. A sense has its own object and its own function. Its object is the unique particular (*svalakṣaṇa*) which alone being real and efficient can produce sensation. Its function is to make the object present to the consciousness. Thus perception consists in an awareness of the presence of an object, its mere presence and nothing more. This is known as sensation (*pratibhāsa*). To construct the image of an object whose presence has thus been sensed is another function which follows in the wake of the first. This is known as mental construction (*pratibhāsa pratīti*), which is the function of the mind.

As pointed out above, Dignāga also disagrees with Vasubandhu's definition of perception, mainly because it suffers from ambiguity. The assertion that a perceptual cognition is that which is caused by a specific object does not specify whether or not this forbids the involvement of conceptualization. Dignāga makes this point quite explicitly by defining perception as free from mental construction (*kalpanāpoḍham*), which emphasizes that it is not in any way constructed by the mind. Perception is a cognition which is not at all determined and conceived in terms of the concepts (*vikalpa*) of substance, quality, relation and class character and language. What is perceived by us is the unique particular which is bare existence devoid of all characterizations and which does not admit of any description in terms of concepts and words. It is just what is immediately and directly given to us in sensation. Concepts and words are common (*sāmānya lakṣaṇa*) to several objects; they are not unique. Perceptual cognition is only the immediately given sensum in complete isolation from all conceptual determinations.

Dignāga's second objective in defining perception has been to distinguish in clear terms perceptual cognition from erroneous cognition, inference, etc., which are not perceptual because they do not have vividness and immediacy as they are vitiated by obscurity. Explaining this Dignāga writes in the *Svavṛtti* of *Pramāṇa-samuccaya* that erroneous cognition is not perception because it arises through conceptual construction. Cognition of empirical reality is also not perception because it superimposes something extraneous upon things which are only empirically true and thus it functions through the conceptualization of forms. Inference is also not perception because it arises through the conceptualization of what has been formerly perceived.

While concluding Dignāga's account of perception it can be stated that he was the first systematic exponent of the theory that perception strictly excludes conceptualization and verbalization. Further, for him, perception is non-erroneous since all errors are due to mental construction only. At the level of sensations there is no possibility of error as they are wholly given by the object. Error arises only when the mental faculty comes to work upon the contents of sensation.

Dharmakīrti on perception

Dharmakīrti following Dignāga defines perception as 'free from conceptualization' (*kalpanāpoḍham*), but adds the qualification that it is non-erroneous (*abhrāntam*). According to him perception consists in the apprehension of an object in its own specific character (*svalakṣaṇa*) which has nothing in common with other objects. The object of perception is thus the particular real which is directly given to consciousness and not an object which is a mental construction (*vikalpa*) in the form of substance, quality, relation, class character or language.

Dharmakīrti defines mental construction as conceptualization which is capable of verbalization. In this definition two aspects of mental construction are pointed out. First, every mental construction is a determinate or judgemental cognition (*pratibhāsa pratīti*) and not just pure sensation (*pratibhāsa*). To be aware of the mere existence of an object is sensation (*pratibhāsa*), but to identify that object as a particular object is judgemental cognition (*pratibhāsa pratīti*). The object is capable of giving rise to sensation (*pratibhāsa*) only. It cannot produce the determinations in the form of recognition that 'it is such and such'. Determination is a function of the cognizing mind, and as such it cannot be regarded as a part of perceptual cognition. Sensation (*pratibhāsa*) alone is genuine perception, and not judgemental cognition (*pratibhāsa pratīti*), which follows in the wake of sensations.

The other aspect of mental construction (*kalpanā*) is potential verbalization (*abhilāpasamsargayogyatā*). Sensation (*pratibhāsa*) is incapable of verbalization. It is pure awareness, which can only be experienced but never expressed. It is bereft of all conceptual elements in the absence of which no verbalization can take place. So only a judgemental cognition can be expressed in language. However, Dharmakīrti makes it clear that though it is necessary that there cannot be verbalization without there being conceptualization, the reverse is not the case. That is to say, it is not necessary that where there is conceptualization there must be verbalization. Concepts are expressible, but they need not necessarily be *couched* in words. That is why while defining *kalpanā* he puts the word *yogya* (capable) in the phrase *abhilāpasamsargayogya*. Commenting on this, Dharmottara writes that we may also have conceptualization which, although not accompanied by corresponding words, is capable of being accompanied, for example the conceptualization of baby which has not been verbalized. Thus, according to Dharmakīrti, verbalization is not incompatible with conceptualization as it is incompatible with perceptual cognition, but it is at the same time not a necessary accompaniment to or a part of conceptualization. Every concept is capable of being verbalized, but it may or may not be actually verbalized.

Besides being free from mental constructions a perceptual cognition has also to be free from error (*abhrānta*). While explaining the term 'free from error' (*abhrānta*), Dharmakīrti mentions different instances of error caused by colour-blindness, rapid movement, travel by boat, mental illness, etc. Commenting on it Dharmottara points out that these four different illustrations represent four types of causes of illusion.

The cause of colour-blindness is located in the sense-organ (*indriyagata*). The cause of the cognition of fiery circle due to rapid movement is located in the object (*viṣayagata*). The cause of the cognition of moving trees while travelling by boat is located in the external circumstances which condition the perceived object (*bāhyāśraya sthita*). Lastly, the cause of hallucinatory experience is located in the internal circumstances (*ābhyantaragata*) like the mental state of a perceiver. All these causes, whether they be located in the cognitive sense or in the object, whether external or internal, affect the cognitive sense and result in illusory sensations. Perception is such a sense-cognition which is distinct from such illusory sensations.

Both Dignāga and Dharmakīrti point out that perception is one of the two modes of knowing. However, in the context of their insistence on the non-conceptuality of perception it can be asked whether they can justifiably regard it as *knowledge*. Dharmottara is aware of this difficulty and tries hard, though not very convincingly, to argue that though perception becomes knowledge only when it has elicited a judgement, it is perception alone which has brought us to this stage and is therefore knowledge.

However, it can certainly be enquired whether perception, as it is understood in the Dignāga–Dharmakīrti tradition, can be knowledge. An answer to this will depend upon our understanding of the term 'knowledge'. If by 'knowledge' we mean just the presence of conformity in the cognition with its object without there being any awareness or confirmation of it, then perception can be regarded as knowledge. But if knowledge is understood as a cognition which is indubitably true, then certainly it cannot be regarded as knowledge because indubitability is something which is dependent on confirmation on the basis of some invincible grounds.

KINDS OF PERCEPTION

Having stated that all perceptual cognitions are alike in so far as they are free from conceptual constructions, Dignāga points out that they can be classified into sense-perception (*indriya pratyakṣa*), mental perception (*mānasa pratyakṣa*), self-perception (*svasaṃvedana pratyakṣa*) and mystical perception (*yogi pratyakṣa*). Sense-perception is caused by an external object. Mental perception consists in the mental awareness of an object which is a derivative from the object of the immediately preceding sense-perception. Self-perception is internal awareness of all mental phenomena like knowledge, desire, etc. This is also free from conceptual constructions and is a variety of perception. The concept of self-perception has been one of the most significant contributions of Dignāga. Its scope has been enlarged by him to include the awareness of conceptual constructions also. According to him each cognition cognizes itself while cognizing an object. Whether it is perception or inference the essential nature of cognition is the same, i.e. it is self-cognizing (*svaprakāśaka*). However, he makes it clear that in being internal awareness and also in not being dependent upon the cognitive senses, self-perception is also characterized as mental (*mānasa*), but this does not mean that it is to be reduced to mental perception. The intuitions apprehended by the *yogi* are non-conceptual direct awareness and hence are to be placed under perception. Here he draws a distinction between mystical perception (*yogi jñāna*) and knowledge derived from the scriptures (*āgama jñāna*), the latter being mental construction (*kalpanā.*)

In Dharmakīrti we find a detailed analysis of these four types of perception. According to him sense-perception consists of the presentation of objects to consciousness through the medium of senses. The senses are only a medium and not an agent. Their function consists only in creating a sort of link between the individual consciousness and the external objective reality. This function is over when the object is presented to consciousness.

Mental perception immediately follows sense-perception. It is in fact the element of attention when a sense-perception arises. That is why Dharmakīrti defines it as mental perception which follows sense-perception which is its immediately preceding homogeneous cause.

The third type of perception is self-perception (*svasaṃvedana* or *ātmasaṃvedana*). Dharmakīrti maintains that consciousness is self-cognizing. The differential character of consciousness as opposed to matter is its self-awareness. Matter is always to be known through consciousness, but consciousness can be known by itself only.

The fourth variety of perception is mystical perception (*yogi jñāna*). It is a mystical intuition of a saint which is produced from a state of deep meditation on the ultimate reality. The Buddhists, like adherents of other mystical traditions, believe in intuitive realizations available to some gifted persons.

A BRIEF HISTORICAL ACCOUNT OF THE BUDDHIST THEORY OF INFERENCE

The other mode of knowing accepted in the Buddhist theory of knowledge is inference (*anumāna*). It is both a mode of knowing and a way of reasoning. Thus it has epistemic and logical aspects inseparably coalesced in one. The earliest formulation of the Buddhist theory of inference is available in the *Yogācārabhūmiśāstra* of Maitreya (about

AD 400) and *Prakaraṇāryavācaśāstra* of Āsanga, though in *Kathāvatthu*, an early Pali text, we come across several terms which are used in the theory of reasoning (*Vāda śāstra*) and logic. A systematic study of the theory of inference is introduced by Vasubandhu. The doctrine of the three-featured logical mark (*trairūpya liṅga*) and the theory of necessary connection (*avinābhāva*) between middle and major terms seem to be his contribution. In Dignāga, however, we find a new direction and impetus to the study of logic in the Buddhist tradition. Both in subject matter and in form his works mark a distinct departure from those of his predecessors. His analysis of inference is so strikingly original that Nyāya circles also had to take cognizance of it. A distinctive contribution of Dignāga has been to draw a distinction between inference as a pure thought process and its linguistic expression (*ākhyāna*). The former is purely propositional and the latter is sentential. The other innovation of Dignāga is advocacy of one variety of inference which may be called analytical entailment (*svabhāvānumāna*), in which one concept is so connected with another concept that the former can be inferred from the latter. For example, the concept of flower is so connected with the concept of rose that the former can be inferred from the latter. This is because if anything is a rose it must be a flower. There is an analytic deduction of flower from rose. The most innovative contribution of Dignāga is the presentation of a formal scheme of different relations of the middle term with the major term (*hetucakra*) and the pointing out of the conditions of validity of inference on that ground. This is an attempt to construct a formal system of logic. Dignāga's theory of inference is further explicated and elaborated by Dharmakīrti. It was Dharmakīrti's achievement to give a systematic formulation of the negative entailment relation (*anupalabdhi*), with its eleven varieties.

Definition of inference

The term *anumāna* (inference) literally means knowledge which follows from some other knowledge. This implies that the inferential knowledge is necessarily one which is preceded by some other knowledge. In other words, the process of inference is a complex consisting of two elements, the premiss and the conclusion. However, it is not the case that any knowledge can be a premiss leading to any other knowledge as a conclusion. The two must have an implier–implied relationship (*gamaka-gamya-bhāva*) which is technically known as entailment (*avinābhāva*). This entailment relation is due to an existential tie (*svabhāva pratibandha*) which is a necessary relation between a logical mark (*liṅga*) and the object of which it is a mark (*liṅgin*). In the Buddhist tradition the logical mark and the object of which it is a mark are concepts only, and not things or events or metaphysical reals.

Inferential knowledge contrasted with perceptual

Inferential knowledge is by its very nature mediate or indirect. Since the object here is not directly apprehended by the cognitive senses (*grāhya*) but only conceived (*adhyavaseya*) on the basis of its logical mark, this implies that inferential knowledge is non-presentative as opposed to perceptual knowledge, which is essentially presentative. Again, in contrast to perceptual knowledge, which is devoid of all conceptualizations, inferential knowledge is essentially judgemental and relational. Lastly, perceptual knowledge is non-verbalizable, but inferential knowledge can be verbalized. Only when it is verbalized its valid or fallacious character is known.

Constituents of inference

The process of inference involves three basic terms and their interrelations. The three terms are minor (*pakṣa*), middle (*hetu* or *liṅga*) and major (*sādhya* or *liṅgin*). There are two types of relations among them which constitute the premisses. The relation of the middle term to the minor term constitutes the minor premiss (*pakṣadharmatva*). The relation of the middle term to the major term constitutes the major premiss (*vyāpti*).

The minor term (*pakṣa*) is the subject under consideration in inferential reasoning. Every inference pertains to some individual or class of individuals about which we want to prove something. This subject of inference has also been regarded as a substratum (*dharmin*) to which the middle and major terms belong as properties. The middle term (*hetu* or *liṅga*) is the pivotal element in the process of inference. It is a necessary mark of the major term and therefore becomes a ground or reason for its inference. In order to serve this function it has to satisfy three formal requirements which I shall analyse later. Only after meeting with these requirements does it become a valid middle term (*sadhetu*) and render the inferential reasoning valid. The middle term is a property of the minor term. Dignāga defines it as that apprehended property of the minor term or subject which is pervaded by the major term. The major term (*sādhya* or *liṅgin*) is that property of the minor term which is to be proved or inferred. The object of inferential reasoning, therefore, is not the major term alone but the major term as being a property of the minor term. What precisely is the object of inferential reasoning (*anumeya*) has been a debatable issue. In the example where knowledge of the presence of smoke on the hill leads to knowledge of the presence of fire on the hill, it may be argued that the presence of fire is the object of inferential enquiry. It may also be argued that it is not fire but the connection between fire and hill which is the object of enquiry. Dignāga rejects both these views. If fire were to be inferred from smoke, it would not give us new knowledge as it is already known that smoke is inseparably connected with fire. If the connection implies knowledge of the things connected, in this case only hill is known and fire is yet to be known. So we cannot infer connection. What we really infer is the fiery hill, i.e. hill having fire as its property.

There are two more terms which occur in the process of inference. They are homologue (*sapakṣa*) and heterologue (*vipakṣa* or *asapakṣa*). Homologue is similar to the minor term in so far as it possesses the major term as its property. In other words, all those objects which possess the property to be inferred are known as homologue. For example, if fire is the property to be inferred in relation to a hill, then all those instances like kitchen etc. where fire is known to be a property constitute homologue. A homologue is similar to the minor term only in the respect that both of them comprehend a similar property. Dissimilar to homologue and the minor term is the heterologue. In other words, heterologue is that which is never a possessor of the property possessed by the subject and the homologue.

The relation of necessary connection (*avinābhāva*)

The inferential process is based mainly on the relation of necessary connection (*avinābhāva* or *vyāpti*) between middle and major terms. This connection is a necessary bond in the form of existential dependence (*svabhāva pratibandha*). Existential dependence means dependent existence of one on another. This may be in the form of causal relation or analytical entailment. For example, dependence of effect on its cause enables us to infer the cause the moment the effect is known to us. Similarly, an analytically deduced object by its very essence depends upon the object from which it is deduced. An example of the former type is the relation between smoke and fire, and of the latter, the relation between rose and flower. We can deduce one thing from another only if there is existential dependence. The possibility of deducing one object from another depends upon a necessary connection which precludes the existence of one in the absence of the other, and therefore from the presence of one follows the presence of the other.

The theory of the three-featured middle term

The concept of the middle term plays a pivotal role in the process of inference. It is the most basic element in the premisses. The Buddhist logicians formulate the law of extension of the middle term in relation to its minor and major terms. This law has three aspects, and that is why a middle term which abides by it is known as the three-featured middle term (*trairūpya liṅga*). Every middle term must possess all three features simultaneously. Only then can it be regarded as valid and provide a valid inference.

It is believed that the first systematic formulation of this theory of three-featured middle term was done by Dignāga. Stcherbatsky (1962 : 244) has put it in English as follows:

1 its presence in the subject of inference;
2 its presence in similar instances;
3 its absence in dissimilar instances.

Dharmakīrti further regulated the formulation of these three features in order to remove ambiguity. He did so by adding and emphasizing the word 'only' to each of the three features and by qualifying the entire formulation by the term 'necessary'. In the modified form it is as follows:

1 the necessary presence of the middle term in the subject's totality;
2 its necessary presence in similars only, although not in their totality;
3 its necessary absence from dissimilars in their totality.

Chi in *Buddhist Formal Logic* (1969: 41) has given a more succinct formulation as follows:

1 the pervasive presence of the *hetu* (middle term) in the subject;
2 the necessary presence of the *hetu* (middle term) in some similar instances;
3 the pervasive absence of the *hetu* (middle term) from dissimilar instances.

The notion of 'pervasive presence' is defined by Chi as follows:

> 'Pervasive presence of *b* in *a*'
> = '*b* is present in every *a*'
> = 'every *a* is *b*'.

The notion of 'pervasive absence' is defined by him thus:

> 'Pervasive absence of *b* from *a*'
> = '*b* is absent from every *a*'
> = 'every *a* is *non-b*'
> = 'no *a* is *b*'.

The notion of 'necessary presence' is defined by him as follows:

> 'Necessary presence of *b* in *a*'
> = '*b* is present in at least one *a*, at most in every *a*'
> = 'at least one *a*, at most every *a*, is *b*'.

Hetucakraḍamaru of Dignāga

In *Hetucakraḍamaru*, Dignāga analyses nine possible relations between the middle and major terms. It is possible to conceive of nine locations of middle term in terms of presence or absence in respect of homologues or heterologues, wholly or partly. He points out that the middle terms which are wholly or partly present in the homologues but wholly absent from the heterologues are valid. Their opposites are contradictory and the rest are uncertain. Only valid ones conform to the three features referred to above. This analysis of nine possible relations presents a formal schema of the validity and invalidity of a middle term and hence of an argument.

Three types of inferences

According to Buddhist logicians there are three types of middle term. A middle term can be affirmative or negative. If affirmative, it can be of two types. If it has a necessary connection with the major term and is coexistent with it, it is known as a middle term having analytic identity (*svabhāva liṅga*). If it has a necessary connection with the major term in the relation of succession, it is known as effect (*kārya*). The analytic identity is defined as that whose mere existence is sufficient for the deduction of the major term. For example, 'rose' has analytic identity with 'flower' such that whatever is a rose is also a flower. To be a rose is sufficient reason to be deduced as flower. Here the terms 'rose' and 'flower' have one and the same object of existential reference though they have different meanings. It is this sameness of reference which is known as analytic identity (*tādātmya*). The middle term which is in the form of an effect necessarily presupposes its cause, which becomes its major term. For example, smoke serves as a middle term in relation to fire, which becomes its major term. The negative middle term (*anupalabdhi liṅga*) is defined as non-cognition of an object which otherwise fulfils the conditions of cognizability. For example, a pen is an object which fulfils the conditions of cognizability. If on a particular table there is no cognition of a pen, this enables us to infer its non-existence. So here non-cognition of a pen is the middle term of which non-existence of that pen is the major term. The non-cognition here is a sufficient reason for inferring non-existence on the ground that if the pen were present it would necessarily have been perceived when all other conditions of perceptibility are fulfilled.

On the basis of three types of middle term there are three types of inference. The inference corresponding to analytic identity is in the form 'It is a flower because it is a rose.' The causal inference is in the form 'There is fire on the hill because there is smoke there.' The negative inference has been classified by Dharmakīrti into eleven types. It is a transition from non-cognition to non-existence. It is in the form 'There is no pen on the table because it is not cognized there.'

THE BUDDHIST THEORY OF LANGUAGE

In the Buddhist system language is a part of logic in so far as it is a means of communicating inferential knowledge. Language is not a separate source of knowledge, nor does it describe reality. For the realist systems like Nyāya-Vaiśeṣika and Mīmaṁsā conceptual knowledge and language deal directly with reality. But for the Buddhist the real is momentary and fleeting, and hence it can only be given in the first moment of sense-stimulus. It can only be perceived, and the perceptual knowledge is inexpressible in language. Only conceptual knowledge is expressible in language, and what is conceptualized by the intellect is not the real but a mental construct of it. Language is a result of mental conceptualization and hence it refers to mental concepts only. It cannot be directly associated with the real. The meaning of a word denotes a referend as distinct from a referent. This referend is a universal which is only a logical construction and not an independent real.

The meaning of a word stands for the relation of word and concept. In a verse attributed to Dignāga it is stated that words originate in concepts and concepts originate in words. The two are interdependent and interspersed. The nature and function of concepts and words are similar. A concept is a mental construct, a universal. It is an exclusion or differentiation of one mental construct from all other mental constructs. By its very essence it is the exclusion of the other. It is the negation of all supposed possibilities other than itself. Likewise, a word, which is the linguistic expression of a concept, conveys its meaning by negating its discrepant meaning. It is the affirmation of its own meaning necessarily through the negation of its opposite meaning.

> The word 'white' does not communicate the cognition of all white objects. They are infinite and no one knows them all. Neither does it communicate cognition of a universal form of 'whiteness' as an external *Ens* cognised by the senses. But it refers to a line of demarcation between white and non-white, which is cognised in every individual case of the white. The white is cognised through the non-white and the non-white is cognised through the white. Just so is the cow or cow-ness. It is cognised through a contrast with the non-cow.
>
> (Stcherbatsky 1962: 460)

A word expresses its meaning *per differentiam*. Without negation it expresses nothing. There is nothing beside the negation of the contradiction that it expresses. All that the word 'cow', for instance, communicates is the exclusion of 'non-cow'. The meanings of the words 'cow' and 'non-cow' consist in the negation of each other. It is a sort of *a priori* judgement in the form of differentiation of A from all that is not A. It is an affirmation qualified by the negation of its contradictory or a complement of its complement. All knowledge expressible in words is differentiation. It posits a mental fiction which is negative in function. It is to be made clear that only the contradictory words are to be negated. Non-contradictory words need not be negated. Thus, we can apply 'cow' and 'white' to what we call 'white cow', but cannot apply 'cow' and 'non-cow' together.

Coming back to the question of the relation between language and reality, it can be asked how language performs its function of reference to reality. Dignāga and his followers developed a theory of dual object of each type of knowledge, perceptual and conceptual. The object, say a cow, is directly grasped or sensed in perceptual knowledge, whereas the object in conceptual awareness is determined as 'cow-hood' or 'cow-form'. In the knowledge arising from the utterance of the word 'cow' what we determine is an object 'out there' on which we superimpose cow-hood or cow-form. This cow-form is to be interpreted as exclusion of non-cows. Here the determination is in the form 'It is not a non-cow': it excludes our non-cow supposition. On hearing the word 'cow' we not only apprehend cow-hood but also determine an external object as being excluded from non-cows. The direct object of conceptual knowledge is the mental image as the universal. But the objective real, which is the unique particular, is indirectly determined and acted upon by conceptual knowledge. So upon hearing the word 'cow' we have a mental image of a cow in general which takes the form of something excluded from non-cows. But the object of our practical activity induced by that verbal knowledge is a particular and real object which is characterized by being excluded from non-cows.

Buddhists have debated how affirmation and negation are related in time. The question is: do they have a temporal sequence or they are simultaneous? If they have temporal sequence, does the affirmation of A follow from the negation of not-A or vice versa? Ratnakīrti (about AD 940) discusses two conflicting views in *Apoha siddhi* and rejects them as extreme. One view is that affirmation is primary and negation is secondary, because the latter follows from the former. Every negation presupposes affirmation. The other view is that affirmation is secondary, for it is arrived at by negation of not-A. It is only by knowing what a thing is not that we can cognize what a thing is. Thus, according to this interpretation, negation is primary and is followed by the positive meaning. Ratnakīrti maintains that both affirmation and negation are dialectically so related that the two have to be simultaneous. They are inseparably related in time, and the negative has an attributive relation to the affirmative.

To conclude, for the Buddhist all concepts and words express their meaning negatively through the exclusion of the contradictory. This is technically known as the theory of *apoha*. Etymologically the word *apoha* means exclusion, separation, differentiation, etc. It is commonly taken as an abridged form of a compound phrase '*anya* + *apoha*' (i.e. other + exclusion). There have been three successive stages in the development of the theory of *apoha*. The basic idea is that words signify concepts and not real entities and that they do so by the exclusion of the opposite. Dignāga and Dharmakīrti emphasize the negative aspect of the meaning of words, which consists in 'negation of the opposite'; of course, this does not mean that they reject the positive nature of the meaning of words. Śāntarakṣita (about AD 750) distinguishes between direct and indirect meanings of words. The direct meaning is positive and the indirect is negative. The latter follows from the former by implication. Jñānaśrī and Ratnakīrti further modified this theory by holding that both positive and negative meanings are simultaneous and not successive, the negative having an attributive relation to the positive.

FURTHER READING

Primary sources

Dharmakīrti (1889) *Nyāya bindu* with Dharmottara's Ṭīkā, ed. P. Peterson, Bibliotheca Indica Series, Calcutta: Royal Asiatic Society.
—— (1949) *Hetu-bindu* ed. Sukhalal Sanghavi, Gaekwad Oriental Series, Baroda.
—— (1968) *Pramāṇa-vārtika*, ed. Dwarikadas Shastri, Varanasi: Bauddha Bharati.
Dignāga (1968a) *Nyāya-praveśa*, Gaekwad Oriental Series, Baroda.
—— (1968b) *Pramāṇa-samuccaya* (*pratyakṣa pariccheda*), trans. M. Hattori, Cambridge, Mass.: Harvard University Press.
Ratnakīrti (1971) *Apoha-siddhi*, ed. G. C. Pande, Jaipur: Darsana Pratisthana.
Śāntarakṣita (1968) *Tattva-saṃgraha* with *Pañjikā* of Kamalaśīla, ed. Divarikadas Shastri, Varanasi: Bauddha Bharati, trans. Ganganath Jha, Delhi: Motilal Banarsidass, (1986) reprint.

Secondary sources

Bhatt, S. R. (1984) 'Buddhist theory of inference', in Mahesh Tiwary (ed.) *Bodhi-raśmi*, New Delhi: Indian Council of Philosophical Research.
Chi, R. S. Y. (1969) *Buddhist Formal Logic*, Delhi: Motilal Banarsidass.
Dravida, R. R. (1972) *The Problem of Universals in Indian Philosophy*, Delhi: Motilal Banarsidass.
Jayatilleke, K. N. (1986) *Early Buddhist Theory of Knowledge*, Delhi: Motilal Banarsidass. Reprint.
Mookerjee, S. (1975) *The Buddhist Philosophy of Universal Flux*, Delhi: Motilal Banarsidass. Reprint.
Randle, H. N. (1976) *Indian Logic in the Early Schools*, Delhi: Munshiram Manoharlal. Reprint.
—— (1981) *Fragments from Dignāga*, Delhi: Motilal Banarsidass. Reprint.
Shastri, D. N. (1980) *Critique of Indian Realism*, Delhi: Bharatiya Vidya Prakasana. Reprint.
Stcherbatsky, T. (1962) *Buddhist Logic*, vol. I, New York: Dover Publications.
Vidyabhusana, S. C. (1978) *A History of Indian Logic*, Delhi: Motilal Banarsidass. Reprint.

22

KNOWLEDGE AND REALITY IN BUDDHISM

Hajime Nakamura

KNOWLEDGE IN EARLY BUDDHISM

The English term 'knowledge' has many equivalents in Indian languages: scholars mention more than seventy Sanskrit words.[1] We feel almost lost. But the word which was most frequently used seems to be *jñāna* (*ñāna* in Pali). When Indian Buddhists meant knowledge acquired by perception, they used the term *upalabdhi*; empirical or scientific knowledge is meant by the term *vijñāna*. The demarcation among these terms, however, was not so clear. The knowledge discussed by Indian Buddhists was not logical or scholarly, but rather practical and religious.

Buddhism did not aim at setting forth a system of empirical knowledge. Man has been the central problem of Buddhist philosophy. Metaphysical speculation concerning problems not related to human activities and the attainment of enlightenment – such as whether the world is infinite or finite, whether the soul and the body are identical or different from each other, or whether a perfect person exists after his or her death – is discouraged.

According to the Buddhist assumption, all metaphysical views are only partial apprehensions of the whole truth, which lies beyond rational analysis. Only a buddha can apprehend the whole truth. In Buddhist scriptures we find the parable of many blind men touching an elephant to know what an elephant looks like. Various metaphysical views are compared to the opinions of many blind men, and the whole truth is compared to the elephant. Buddhists assume that rational analysis is useful in making clear the limitations of rationality, but it is by detaching oneself from philosophical oppositions that one is able to grasp the truth. Thus, the doctrine of the Buddha is not a system of philosophy in the western sense, but rather a path. A buddha is simply one who has walked this path and can report to others on what he or she has found. He or she is not a scientist who endeavours to increase empirical knowledge: his or her standpoint is practical. The Buddha's doctrine is called a vehicle in the sense that it is like a ferryboat. One enters the Buddhist vehicle to cross the river of life from the shore of worldly experience, spiritual ignorance, desire and suffering, to the other shore of transcendental wisdom, which is liberation from bondage and suffering. If a man builds a raft and by this means succeeds in attaining the other shore, then he should abandon the raft. In the same way the vehicle of the doctrine is to be cast away and forsaken once the other shore of enlightenment has been attained.

Religious dogmas are nothing but experiences leading one to the ideal state. At the end religious dogmas should be forsaken. This attitude can already be seen in the early Buddhism and Mahāyāna of India but it has been most emphatically stressed by Zen Buddhism. Just as the difference in shape, weight and material among rafts does not matter, differences in teachings do not matter. Even contradictory sayings are, virtually and practically, not contradictory. They all aim at the same end. This point of view is set forth both in conservative Buddhism (Theravāda and so forth) and in Mahāyāna, the two major divisions of Buddhism.

In the Buddhist world, scriptures were not necessarily the absolute authority of knowledge. Throughout the Buddhist world, the community has never been organized around a central authority. Buddhists of all types in various countries have been comparatively individualistic and unwilling to submit to a rigid outer authority. Even scriptures were not rigid. They were susceptible of undergoing alteration, modification and enlargement. Agreement about the doctrines to be held and the practices to be followed has been reached by discussion within the community, guided by scriptures accepted as a basis for faith. Only in Japan are there marked sectarian differences, but the authorities of the extant sects are not coercive. Buddhist sects in Japan have been willing to collaborate with each other.

In Buddhism faith is indispensable, but it is only a preliminary requirement for practising the Way, an introductory means to the attainment of truth, not an acceptance of definite dogmas. For the Buddhist, faith should not be in contradiction to reason; when unexamined by reason it becomes superstition. Buddhists have accepted two standards for the truth (veracity) of a statement: 'proof by scriptures' and 'proof by reason'. A true statement must be in accordance with the Buddhist canonical scriptures, and it must be proved true by reasoning. No Buddhist is expected to believe anything that does not meet these two tests. When one takes refuge in the Three Jewels (the Buddha, the teaching and the order), it is a partial turning away from the visible to the invisible. Faith does not necessarily mean the realization of truth itself; it is important only in so far as it opens the door of the ideal state to practitioners.

Throughout Buddhist history there have been two currents, the devotional approach and the approach through inner knowledge or intuitive insight. The latter has always been regarded as the truer one, while the devotional approach has been more or less considered a lesser means for the common people. The only outstanding exceptions to this have been Pure Land Buddhism (a Chinese and Japanese sect stressing worship of Amitābha Buddha – the Buddha of infinite life and splendour) and the Nichiren sect (followers of the thirteenth-century nationalist saint Nichiren). For them, faith is made supreme and is essential to deliverance. In Pure Land Buddhism the emphasis upon faith culminated in Shinran, the founder of the Jōdo Shinshū sect in Japan.

Buddhism presupposes universal laws called *dharma*, which govern human existence and may be known by reason. Personal relations should be brought into harmony with the universal norms, which apply to all existence, regardless of time and space. Theoretically it is supposed that they apply not only to human existence but also to all other living beings. Buddhism claims to have made evident these *dharmas*, which are valid in different periods and among various peoples, regardless of the difference of race.

REALITY IN EARLY BUDDHISM

Early Buddhists emphasized the impermanence of all things. There is no Being; there is only a becoming. All matter is effectuation of force; all substance is nothing but motion. The state of every individual is unstable and temporary, sure to vanish. Even form and other material qualities in things we find are impermanent and perishing. There is no substance which abides for ever. There is only becoming, change, passing away. Suffering is virtually one with transiency. According to this view, craving causes suffering, since what we crave is impermanent, changing and perishing. It is the impermanence of the object of our craving that causes disappointment and sorrow. All pleasures vanish eventually.

These cravings are caused by ignorance, according to the Buddhist assumption. We are ignorant concerning the true nature of our existence and of the universe in which we live. And we may be freed from our ignorance by following the Right Path which was taught by the Buddha. The Buddhist beatitude lies in our realization that all things are transient and that we should not cling to them with the attitude of craving. The Buddha stressed the fluidity and transitoriness of everything. From this standpoint, there is no 'reality'.

Admitting the transitoriness of everything, the Buddha did not want to assume the existence of any metaphysical substance. This attitude was logically derived from his fundamental standpoint. The Buddha reduced things, substances and souls to forces, movements, functions and processes, and adopted a dynamic conception of reality. Life is nothing but a series of manifestations of generation and extinction. It is a stream of becoming and change. He repudiated the existence of the individual ego. According to him, the concept of the individual ego as a substance is a popular delusion. The objects with which we identify ourselves are not the true self. Our fortune, our social position, our family, our body and even our mind are not our true self. All the current theories about 'souls' are discussed and rejected in the scriptures (*Dīgha-Nikāya* (*DN*) I).[2]

The 'ego' or 'soul' is the English translation of the Pali *attan* or Sanskrit *ātman*; it is more literally rendered 'self'. But occasionally, I should like to use the word 'ego' in order to distinguish it from the 'true self' which is stressed even in early Buddhism. There is nothing permanent, and if only the permanent deserves to be called the self or *ātman*, then nothing on earth is self. Everything is non-self or *anattā* (the theory of *nairātmya*). Everything is impermanent: body, feeling, perception, dispositions and consciousness; all these are suffering. They are all 'non-self'. Nothing of them is substantial. They are all appearances empty of substantiality or reality. There can be no individuality without putting together components. And this is always a process of becoming: there can be no becoming different without a dissolution, a passing away or decay, which will inevitably come about sooner or later.

In the Buddha's sermon, the non-perceptibility of the soul was set forth:

> The body is not the eternal soul, for it is subject to destruction. Neither feeling nor ideation nor dispositions nor consciousness together or apart constitute the eternal soul, for were it so, feeling etc. would not likewise be subject to destruction. . . . Our physical form, feeling, ideation, dispositions and consciousness are all transitory, and therefore suffering, and not permanent and good. That which is transitory, suffering and liable to change is not the eternal soul. So it must be said of all physical forms whatever, past, present or to be, subjective or objective, far or near, high or low: this is not mine, this I am not, this is not my eternal 'soul'. (*Mahāvagga* I, 6, 38f., PTS edition, vol. I, pp. 13f.; cf. *Saṇgutta-Nikāya* (*SN*) XXII, 59f.)

And the same assertion can also be made of feeling, ideation, dispositions and consciousness. Early Buddhists divided our human existence, the totality of our mind and body, into five parts or components:

Components (constitutents, aggregates)	*Fiction*
Physical form (pertaining to the body) Feeling (pleasant, unpleasant, neutral) Ideation Dispositions (latent, formative force) Consciousness	} Ego

Our human existence is only a composite of the five aggregates (*skandhas*). Buddhism thus swept away the traditional concept of a substance called 'soul' or 'ego', which had up to that time dominated the minds of the superstitious and the intellectuals alike. Instead the teaching of *anattā*, non-self, has been followed throughout Buddhism.

The Buddha neither affirmed nor denied the existence of *ātman*. He exhorted us to be philosophical enough to recognize the limits of ratiocination. Just as 'body' is a name for a system of some functions, so 'soul' is a name for the sum of the mental states which constitute our mind. Without functions no soul can be admitted.

A highly sophisticated form of creation myth was also developed in the later phases of early Buddhism and is set forth in a Buddhist *sūtra* (*DN* XXVII, *Aggañña Suttanta*, § II):

> Now at that time, all had become one world of water, dark, and of darkness that causes blindness. No moon or sun appeared, no stars were seen, or constellations, neither night

> nor day appeared, neither months nor half months, neither years nor seasons, neither female nor male. All creatures were regarded as created things only. And to these creatures, sooner or later after a long time, earth with its savour was spread out in the waters. Even as a scum forms on the surface of boiled milky rice that is cooling, so did the earth appear.

The process of genesis is set forth in full detail (*DN*, vol. III, pp. 85f.).

Towards the natural world the monks of early Buddhism strictly observed the attitude of non-attachment. Their casual reference to the structure of the natural world was rather exceptional and crude.

THE UNIVERSE IN EARLY BUDDHISM

Buddhist beliefs concerning the nature of the universe were shaped by belief in *karma* and rebirth. By adhering to the doctrines of transmigration and *karma*, Buddhists were led to the assumption of good and bad places in which people could be born according to their deeds. So heavens and hells were assumed. Good people can be born in heavens, and bad ones in hells or the like. The Buddha did not deny the existence of divine beings and their realm.

But the state of the perfect man (arhatship) is better than heaven, and the *arhats* are superior to all gods. But still, those who cannot understand that should at least understand that the only way to heaven is not ritual, but righteousness. To the good person, then, the hope of a temporary life in heaven is really held out. And in the same way the fear of purgatory, of a temporary fall into hell, is used as an argument in Buddhism to turn ordinary people from evil.

According to Buddhist theology, there are three spheres, or planes, where living beings dwell:

1. The immaterial plane (sphere) of existence (*arūpadhātu*), where pure spirits without a material body live. They have no place specific to them. This is the uppermost sphere in the world.
2. The material plane of existence (*rūpadhātu*), where ethereal living beings live. They are made of a subtle material. They are beings with subtle bodies. This plane is the higher part of the natural world.
3. The plane of desire (*kāmadhātu*), where living beings of gross matter live. They are concupiscent and subject to sensual and especially sexual desire. This plane is the lower part of the natural world. Roughly speaking, it corresponds to our natural world.

This theory seems to have been thought of in the course of the development of Buddhist dogmatics. The belief in the three planes of existence has been held throughout the Buddhist world, although Zen Buddhism in China and Japan has been rather indifferent to it. It is still widely held, at least nominally, in Buddhist dogmatics, but many present-day Buddhist intellectuals who have been educated in modern sciences, however devout they may be, do not believe in this traditional Buddhist cosmology. In any case, the ways of nature do not matter to the Buddhist. The Buddha dealt only with matters of human conduct.

The world in which human beings live, the plane of desire, is made up of four elements – earth, water, heat and wind – according to the scriptures of both Theravāda and Mahāyāna. The theories of Vajrayāna add space and intelligence to the list of elements, making six of them. Buddhists in Japan, where there is no illiteracy, do not accept literally the concept of the planes of existence and the four or six elements; they accept modern scientific theories concerning the natural world. They think that the theories concerning the planes of existence and the elements are not essential to Buddhism. Theravāda Buddhists also have not been so outspoken on these matters.

Living beings in the plane of desire are divided into five categories, two good and three bad, called 'kinds of existence' (*gati*). They are (1) heavenly beings (gods), (2) men, (3) spirits (*preta*), (4) animals (beasts), (5) the damned (hellish beings, depraved men), who live in hells. Sometimes another kind of existence, *asura* (demons, warlike fighting spirits), is placed between men and spirits. The 'hells' are numerous, and usually divided into hot hells and cold hells. Since life in hell comes to an end someday, they are more like the purgatory of the Catholic Church than the hell of non-Catholic Christianity.

These beings belong to the sphere of transmigration. The notion of five categories was more prevalent in India and south Asian (Theravāda) countries, whereas in China and Japan the notion of six categories was popular among the common people. But whether five or six, they have been popular among the common people throughout the Buddhist world. The gods belong to the mundane world – a feature strongly emphasized by the Buddhists.

One result of this Buddhist theory of the world is the attitude towards animals in Buddhist countries, which is one of kindness to a fellow-being. In some countries, people visiting temples will release birds or fish which have been captured. There have always been many vegetarian Buddhists.

DEPENDENT ORIGINATION (CAUSE AND EFFECT)

Buddhism declared that everything has causes, that there is no permanent substratum of existence. There is general agreement that the only true method for explaining any existing thing is to trace one cause back to the next, and so on, without the hope, or even the possibility, of explaining the ultimate cause of all things. The universe is governed by causality. There is no chaotic anarchy and no capricious interference.

> Of all the phenomena sprung from causes
> The Buddha the causes hath told,

And he tells too how each shall come to its end,
Such alone is the word of the Sage.

In the first place, unconscious wishes and expectations too avidly anticipate the future, and are themselves determined from the past. The suffering and afflictions we get ourselves involved in develop spontaneously from our condition of non-knowing. If we reflect upon ourselves, we see that we are moving in a world of mere conventions and that our feelings, thoughts and acts are determined by these. We are bound by them as by the mesh of a net. They are rooted in our own existence, and we adhere to them, thinking that they are something real. Our craving arises out of this fallacious understanding or nescience of our existence. This false assumption about the true essence of reality is the cause of all the sufferings that affect our lives; ignorance is the main cause from which false desire springs.

Ignorance and false desires are the theoretical and the practical side of human existence. The false intellectual side of wrong desire is ignorance; the concrete realization of ignorance is desire. In actual life the two are one. To the Buddhist, as to Indian thinkers in general, knowledge and will are so closely related that no sharp distinction is drawn between them. The same word, *cetanā*, is used to signify both thinking and willing. So when knowledge is attained, suffering comes to an end. The term 'buddha' means 'Enlightened One', and signifies a person who has attained the truth of existence, and has discovered the doctrine for the cessation of suffering. It was by the attainment of this supreme 'enlightenment' or 'wisdom' that Gautama became a buddha. Here we might say that virtue (*kuśala*) was based upon knowledge (*jñāna*, *vidyā*).

The Buddha contemplated the way to deliverance from suffering and found that the cause of suffering is ignorance, and that by extinguishing ignorance one extinguishes suffering. What, then, is this ignorance (*avijjā*)? The term means 'lack of right knowledge'. It virtually amounts to a lack of the right intuition. Intuition of what? The scriptures are silent on this point. This became the issue for the development of the concept of the dependent origination later. At the outset, probably, the law of impermanence or non-self must have been meant.

At a later time there emerged the explanation of the concept of dependent origination as the interdependence of all causes. Scholars of conservative Buddhism and Mahāyāna Buddhism used the term for anything they wanted to explain. The definition of the term widely accepted in conservative Buddhism, especially in the Sarvāstivāda, is the 'interconnection according to causal laws of all the elements cooperating in the formation of individual life'. The consciousness only school of Buddhist idealism (*vijñaptimātratā*) occasionally took it to mean 'the process of the appearing of all phenomena out of the fundamental consciousness (*ālayavijñana*)'. In Mahāyāna, especially in the Mādhyamika school and the Kegon (Hua-yen [Huayan]) school in China and Japan, dependent origination meant 'interdependence of all phenomena in the universe throughout the past, the present and the future' or 'relationality of things and ideas'.

REALITY IN CONSERVATIVE BUDDHISM (HĪNAYĀNA)

This theory of non-self was subsequently modified. Hīnayāna teachers explained the theory as follows: things are names. 'Chariot' is a name as much as Nāgasena (the name of a Buddhist elder). There is nothing more real beneath the properties or the events. The immediate data of consciousness do not argue the existence of any unity which we can imagine. Using a similar argument, from the silence of the Buddha on the question of the 'soul', the Buddhist philosopher Nāgasena drew the negative inference that there was no soul. This opinion became the orthodox teaching of Hīnayāna Buddhism.

The original teaching of the Buddha seems to have been slightly different, as has been discussed above. From investigations done so far, it is clear that the assertion of no-ego appeared in a later period and that the Buddha did not necessarily deny the soul, but was silent concerning it. Moreover, he seems to have acknowledged the true self in our existence which is to appear in our moral conduct, which conforms to universal norms. The theory of non-self does not mean that the Buddha completely denied the significance of the self. He always admitted the significance of the self as the subject of actions in the moral sense. According to him, the self cannot be identified with anything existing in the outside. We cannot grasp the self as something concrete or existing in the outer world. The self can be realized only when we act according to universal norms of human existence. When we act morally, the true self becomes manifest. In this connection, the self of Buddhism was not a metaphysical entity, but a practical postulate.

In traditional, conservative Buddhism (which is often called Hīnayāna), the existence of many realities was assumed. They were described by the term *dharma* (elements). Various *dharmas* are constituents of the individual (*pudgala*). According to the teachings of various schools, especially those of the Sarvāstivādins, everything in the phenomenal world is changing, perishable and unreal. But *dharmas* are ever-existing, not perishable; they are real, and can be called 'realities'.

THE ANALYSIS OF THE INDIVIDUAL BY THE SARVĀSTIVĀDINS – THE PLURALISTIC CONCEPT OF BEING

The psychological analysis of one's own existence was not yet systematized in early scriptures. It was through the efforts of *abhidharma* teachers that various aspects of human existence were analysed and schematized very elaborately.

The school which was most influential and powerful among the schools of conservative Buddhism (Hīnayāna) was the Sarvāstivādins (literally 'the school which asserts that all *dharmas* exist'). This school was founded by a scholar named Kātyāyanīputra (second century BC), who wrote the *Abhidharmajñānaprasthānaśāstra*, the fundamental text of the school. It maintained the theory that all *dharmas* which constitute a human existence, such as the five aggregates (*skandhas*), the twelve regions (*āyatanas*) and the eighteen elements (*dhātus*), i.e. systems of *dharmas* in their respective viewpoints, do really exist.[3] In this school the term *dharma* meant something like an essence (*Wesen* in German). According to the Sarvāstivādins, these *dharmas exist as substances* (*dravataḥ sat*),[4] or *exist essentially (svalakṣaṇataḥ sat)*.[5] ('Reality' is expressed by the Sanskrit term *vastu* or *dravya*.)

The theory of the five *skandhas* is as follows. The totality of our existence, our mind and body, is composed of the following parts or components:

1 physical form (pertaining to the body) (*rūpa*);[6]
2 feeling (pleasant, unpleasant, neutral) (*vedanā*);
3 ideation (*saṃjñā*);
4 dispositions (latent, formative force) (*saṁskārā*);[7]
5 consciousness (*vijñāna*).

Our human existence is only a composite of these five aggregates (*skandhas*). Buddhism swept away the traditional conception of a substance called 'soul' or 'ego', which had heretofore dominated the minds of the superstitious and the intellectual alike. Instead, Buddhism admitted these *skandhas*, which were also called *dharmas*. The Sarvāstivādins maintained that, although things in the phenomenal world may vanish, these *dharmas* do actually exist (compare Husserl's phenomenology in this respect).

Another theory of Buddhism is as follows. Our individual existence consists of the six sensitive regions and the six regions of objects corresponding to them. The six sensitive regions are: (1) the visual function, (2) the function of hearing, (3) the function of smell, (4) the function of taste, (5) the function of touch and (6) the function of mind. The regions of objects are: (1) visual forms, (2) sounds, (3) odours, (4) tastes, (5) things to be touched and (6) things to be thought. These are the twelve regions (*āyatanas*). When we add the six kinds of cognition (*vijñāna*) corresponding to each of the former functions to these twelve, the system of the eighteen elements (*dhātus*) is formed. According to the Sarvāstivādins, these twelve regions or eighteen elements do exist as *substances* essentially and individually, although human existences and phenomenal things are impermanent, i.e. perishing instantaneously.

It was the Sarvāstivāda school in particular which developed an elaborate system of psychological analysis, according to which seventy-five constituent elements of human existence were identified. These seventy-five are divided into two major groups: (1) *saṃskṛta*: cooperating, impermanent elements, and (2) *asaṃskṛta*: non-cooperating, immutable elements. The former are divided into four major groups.

A Material elements (*rūpa*)
1 *cakṣur indriya*: visual organ;
2 *śrotra indriya*: auditory organ;
3 *ghrāṇa indriya*: olfactory organ;

4 *jihvā indriya*: taste organ;
5 *kāya indriya*: tactile organ;
6 *rūpa viṣaya*: sense-data;
7 *śabda viṣaya*: auditory sense-data;
8 *gandha viṣaya*: olfactory sense-data;
9 *rasa viṣaya*: taste sense-data;
10 *spraṣṭavya viṣaya*: tactile sense-data;
11 *avijñapti rūpa*: unmanifested matter which is the vehicle of moral qualities.

B Mind (*citta*)
This is pure consciousness without content.

C The forty-six mental elements (*caitta-dharma*) or faculties intimately combining with the element of consciousness (*citta-saprayukta-saṃskāra*). These are divided into six groups as follows:

1 Ten 'general functions', i.e. general mental faculties present in every moment of consciousness (*citta-mahābhūmikāḥ dharmāḥ*):
  (a) *vedanā*: faculty of feeling (pleasant, unpleasant and indifferent)
  (b) *saṃjñā*: faculty of ideation
  (c) *cetanā*: faculty of will, causing action of mind
  (d) *sparśa*: sensation, caused by 'contact' among object, sense-organ and consciousness
  (e) *chanda*: faculty of desire
  (f) *prajñā* (or *mati*): faculty of intelligence (discriminative knowledge of *dharmas*)
  (g) *smṛti*: faculty of conscious memory
  (h) *manasikāra*: faculty of attention
  (i) *adhimokṣa*: faculty of ascertainment (or decisive knowledge)
  (j) *samādhi*: faculty of concentration[8]
2 Ten 'general good functions', i.e. universally 'good' moral faculties, present in every good moment of consciousness (*kuśalamahābhūmikāḥ dharmāḥ*):
  (a) *śraddhā*: faculty of belief, causing mind to be pure and joyful
  (b) *vīrya*: faculty of courageousness in good actions
  (c) *upekṣā*: faculty of equanimity or indifference[9]
  (d) *hrī*: faculty of modesty, being respectful to virtuous persons.[10] (According to some teachers: faculty of modesty, being ashamed with reference to oneself.)[11]
  (e) *apatrāpya* (or *apatrapā*): faculty of awfulness with regard to sins. (According to some teachers: faculty of feeling disgust with reference to other people's objectionable actions.)[12]
  (f) *alobha*: faculty of non-greediness.
  (g) *adveṣa*: faculty of non-malevolence.
  (h) *ahiṃsā*: faculty of causing no injury.

(i) *praśrabdhi*: faculty of mental dexterity or mental suitability for any action.
(j) *apramāda*: faculty of making endeavour to acquire good virtues.[13]

3 Six 'general functions of defilement', i.e. universally 'defiled' elements present in every unfavourable moment of consciousness (*kleśa-mahābhūmikāḥ dharmāḥ*).
(a) *moha* (or *avidyā*): faculty of infatuation or ignorance.
(b) *pramāda*: faculty of laziness (i.e. no practice of good virtues).
(c) *kausīdya*: faculty of mental indolence.
(d) *āśraddhya*: faculty of non-believing.
(e) *styāna*: faculty of sloth or indolence, inactive temperament.
(f) *auddhatya*: faculty of being agitated and disturbed of mind.[14]
These six faculties are not always absolutely bad; they may sometimes be indifferent to spiritual progress, but they nevertheless always function with a selfish tendency.

4 Two 'general functions of evil', i.e. universally 'bad' elements present in every bad moment of consciousness (*akuśala-mahābhūmikau dharmau*).[15]
(a) *āhrīkya*: faculty of irreverence, lack of modesty. (According to the orthodox teaching: not being respectful to virtuous persons. According to some teachers: not being ashamed with reference to oneself.)
(b) *anapatrāpya* (or *anapatrapā*): faculty of not feeling awful with regard to sins. (According to some teachers: faculty of not feeling disgust at offences committed by others.)

5 Ten 'minor functions of defilement', i.e. vicious elements of limited occurrence (*parītta-būmikā upakleśaḥ*).[16] They occur occasionally.
(a) *krodha*: faculty of anger.
(b) *mrakṣa*: faculty of hypocrisy (concealing one's own sins).
(c) *mātsarya*: faculty of stinginess.
(d) *īrṣyā*: faculty of jealousy.[17]
(e) *pradāśa*: faculty of insisting on objectionable things.
(f) *vihiṃsā*: faculty of causing injury.
(g) *upanāha*: faculty of resentment.[18]
(h) *māyā*: faculty of deceit.[19]
(i) *śāṭhya*: faculty of fraudulence.[20]
(j) *mada*: faculty of complacency, self-satisfaction.[21]

6 Eight 'indeterminate functions', i.e. elements[22] not having any definite place in the above system, but capable of entering into various combinations (*aniyatā bhūmiḥ*).[23]
(a) *kaukṛtya*: faculty of repenting.[24]
(b) *middha*: faculty of drowsiness.[25]
(c) *vitarka*: faculty of reflection.[26]
(d) *vicāra*: faculty of subtle investigation.[27]
(e) *rāga*: faculty of attachment by mind.
(f) *pratigha*: faculty of hatred.[28]

(g) *māna*: faculty of arrogance.[29]
(h) *vicikitsā*: faculty of doubting.[30]

D Forces which can be included among neither material nor spiritual elements (*citta-viprayuktāḥ saṃskārāḥ*).[31]

1 *prāpti*: 'acquisition', a force which effects the acquisition of the elements in an individual existence.[32]
2 *aprāpti*: 'non-acquisition', a force which occasionally keeps some elements in abeyance in an individual existence.[33]
3 *nikāya-sabhāgatā*: 'similarity of existence', a force producing generality or homogeneity of existences.[34]
4 *āsaṃjñika*: a force which transfers an individual into the realm of the unconscious trance.
5 *āsaṃjñi-samāpatti*: a force stopping consciousness and producing the annihilation trance.
6 *nirodha-samāpatti*: a force stopping consciousness and producing the annihilation trance (the highest trance).[35]
7 *jīvita*: the force of life-duration.[36]
8 *jāti*: the force of origination.
9 *sthiti*: the force of subsistence.
10 *jarā*: the force of decay.
11 *anityatā*: the force of extinction.[37]
12 *nāma-kāya*: the force imparting significance to words.
13 *pada-kāya*: the force imparting significance to sentences.
14 *vyañjāna-kāya*: the force imparting significance to articulate sounds.[38]

E Immutable elements (*asaṁskṛta-dharma*)

1 *ākāśa*: space for all *dharmas*.[39]
2 *pratisaṅkhyā-nirodha*: the extinction of the manifestations of elements through the action of discriminative knowledge.
3 *apratisaṅkhyā-nirodha*: the extinction of the manifestations of elements through lack of productive causes, not through the action of discriminative knowledge.[40]

These seventy-five elements, though separate from one another, cooperate with one another because of causal relations, and actually exist.

To exist actually or to exist as a substance can be said only of *dharmas* (which constitute a human existence as explained above). This kind of being should be distinguished from the following four:

(1) Provisional being (*prajñaptisat*). Men, women, jars, clothes, chariots, armies, forests, houses, etc. are entities in the natural world. They consist of parts, which are transitory, so they exist provisionally.

(2) Relative being (*parasparāpekṣātaḥ sat*) or dependent being. 'Long' and 'short', 'this' and 'that' exist in dependence upon each other.

(3) Nominal being. Such things as 'hairs of tortoises', 'horns of hares' or 'a child of a barren woman' exist only nominally as concepts, in terms of name. They are ideas which comprise contradictions, and cannot find their actual instances in the natural world.

(4) Aggregational being. Its typical example is the existence of the individual person (*pudgala*). It is the subject of transmigration. The translation of the corresponding Chinese term is 'the subject which undergoes transmigration repeatedly'. The individual existence (*pudgala*) is nothing but an aggregate of many constituent elements (*dharmas*), and the individual person itself does not exist in the ultimate sense, when viewed from the highest viewpoint.[41]

These four kinds of being cannot be associated with the *dharmas*, which are real existences.[42] In the philosophical system of this school, all the *dharmas* are classified in the seventy-five categories, as explained above. They do not depend on each other, maintaining their respective, independent existence. Each *dharma* comes to appear, and then vanishes in our consciousness, but a *dharma* preserves its own self-identity throughout the past, the present and the future. This theory was called the theory of 'the permanent existence of the essence (entity) of each *dharma*'[43] or 'the theory of the existence of a *dharma* as a substance throughout the three divisions of time, *i.e.*, the past, the present and the future'.[44]

The common features which the Sarvāstivādin theory shares with the Platonic theory of ideas was already pointed out by such Russian scholars as Otto Rosenberg and Th. Stcherbatsky.[45] The concept of 'normal being' finds its western counterpart in the philosophy (*Wissenschaftslehre*) of Bolzano, a forerunner of Husserl's phenomenology, who discussed such ideas as 'a round triangular form' or 'green virtue'.

The above-mentioned scheme of seventy-five elements was developed and enlarged to a scheme of a hundred elements by some Yogācāra idealists.

KNOWLEDGE AND REALITY IN MAHĀYĀNA PHILOSOPHY

The Mahāyāna schools, both Mādhyamika and Yogācāra (Vijñānavādin), assume the fundamental or ultimate principle of 'emptiness' (*śūnyatā*): everything is void (empty, *śūnya*). Although they admit the reality of *dharmas* which constitute the individual existence in the conventional sense of the word, they say that all these *dharmas* are not real. There is nothing which can be called reality. If we look forward to reality, emptiness (*śūnyatā = tathatā*) can be called the ultimate principle (*paramārthasat*). To realize the emptiness of all things is the absolute knowledge. This is the ultimate goal of religious practice.

If we use the western term 'reality', emptiness (*śūnyatā*) itself can be regarded as 'reality'. The definition of reality (*tattva*) by Nāgārjuna is as follows:

> uncognizable from without (*aparapratyaya*), quiescent (*śānta*), undifferentiated in statements (*prapañcair aprapañcita*), unrealizable in conceptualization (*nirvikalpa*), non-plural (*anānārtha*) – this is the essence of reality (*tattvasya lakṣaṇa*).
>
> (*Madhyamaka-Kārikā* Bibliotheca Buddhica edition, XVIII, 9)

> An existence dependent on something else is no real existence, just as borrowed money is no real wealth.
>
> (*Prasannapadā*, Bibliotheca Buddhica edition, p. 263, line 3)

The thought that emptiness is the ultimate principle is set forth in the *Prajñāpāramitā-sūtras* (Wisdom *sūtras*) and other Mahāyāna *sūtras*.

Inheriting the idea of emptiness, the *Buddha-Avataṃsaka-sūtra* (including the *Daśabhūmika* and the *Gaṇḍavyūha*) advocated the theory of interdependence or interpenetration of all things in the universe. It says that there exists nothing isolated from other existences. This idea is systematically explained by the Hua-yen [Huayan] school of China and Korea, and by the Kegon sect of Japan.

The Yogācāra school advocated the theory of the eightfold consciousness: visual consciousness, auditory consciousness, odour consciousness, taste consciousness, touch consciousness, the conscious mind, the subconscious mind (the substrate of self-consciousness) and the 'store-consciousness (*ālaya vijñāna*)', which is the fundamental consciousness.

According to the orthodox thought of the sixth-century Indian monk Dharmapāla, conveyed by the seventh-century Chinese pilgrim Hsüan-tsang [Xuanzang] to China and Japan, where it became known as the Fa-hsiang [Faxiang] (Japanese Hossō) school, these are separate consciousness, existing as different entities, and the first seven are collectively termed the transformed consciousness. The She-lun [Shelun] school of China (now merged with Hossō) school regarded the store-consciousness that has become pure and taintless as thusness (*tathatā*) and gave it a special name, 'taintless consciousness', designated as the ninth consciousness. Generally speaking, Buddhist psychology is highly coloured with ethical and soteriological evaluations.

THE BUDDHIST LOGICIANS' THEORY OF KNOWLEDGE AND REALITY

Buddhist logic in its incipient stage can be observed in fourth-century texts such as Maitreya's *Yogācārabhūmi-śāstra* (*The Science of the Stages of Yoga Practice*), Asaṅga's *Abhidharma-samuccaya* (a summary of *abhidharma*, or scholastic doctrine) and Vasubandhu's *Vādavidhi* (*Method of Dispute*), and *Vādavidhāna* (*Rule of Dispute*).

The founder of the Buddhist new logic, as against the old logic set forth in the Nyāya school, was Dignāga (*c*.400–85). He established the three-proposition syllogism, replacing the five-proposition syllogism prevalent before his time. The older five-proposition formula consists of: (1) proposition (*pratijñā*) – for example sound is impermanent; (2) reason (*hetu*) – because it is produced by causes; (3) example (*dṛṣṭānta*) – it is like pots; (4) application (*upanaya*) – pots are produced by causes and are impermanent in the same way as sound; and (5) conclusion (*nigamana*) – therefore, sound is impermanent.

In the threefold formula devised by Dignāga, propositions (4) and (5) are omitted. The whole scheme of the syllogism is deductive, but in (3) the inductive method is also implied. The theory of the nine reasons or types of argument was also set forth by Dignāga. *Nyāyapraveśaka*, by the south Indian Śaṅkarasvāmin, is a brief introduction to Dignāga's logic. In China and Japan this work was regarded as almost the only authority and was studied in great detail by traditional scholars of Buddhist logic.

The logic and epistemology (really fused together) of Dignāga was elaborated upon in the seventh century by the Indian Buddhist logician Dharmakīrti. Among Indian and Tibetan thinkers he was regarded as the representative Buddhist philosopher. He admitted only two kinds of valid knowledge: direct perception and inference. He asserted that in the function of mind, cognition and the cognized belong to different moments.

Dharmakīrti denied the authority of scriptures but admitted Buddha as the source of all knowledge in another way. According to him, every being is transitory (*kṣaṇika*), and each person assumes the continuous existence of an individual, who is nothing but a continuation of moments (*kṣaṇa*) and who is constructed by imaginative and discriminative thinking. Objects of inference are universals, which are attained by way of conceptualization, whereas objects of perception are particulars, which are nothing but moments. He distinguished between analytic inference and synthetic inference. An example of the former is 'This must be a tree, because this is a *śimsapā* tree.' An example of the latter is 'There must be fire on the mountain, because there is smoke.' Non-conceptualization was limited to purely epistemological significance; relation between subject and object in cognition was a secondary one.

According the the school of Buddhist logic, beginning with Dignāga, everything is fictitious, the outcome of our human intellect. What can be called 'reality' is just a moment (*kṣaṇa*) which is nothing but the thing-in-itself (*svalakṣaṇa*). This is the thing corresponding to pure sensation, contra the unreality (ideality) of all constructions of imagination or conceptualization.

In Japan the traditional scholarship of Buddhist logic as conveyed by the Buddhist pilgrim Hsüan-tsang [Xuanzang] to China in the seventh century has been preserved, especially in the old capital of Nara. Zen took exactly the opposite standpoint to the formal logic of Buddhist logicians. In the Rinzai school of Zen, meditation on paradoxes (*kōan*) is used to awaken intuitive insight into what transcends logical distinctions. In popular Japanese speech, *Zen-mondō* (Zen dialogue) is almost equivalent to what is not understandable or what is illogical.

CONCLUSION

Throughout all these schools, external reality, which is admitted in the worldly life of ordinary people, should not be regarded as real. It does exist when viewed from the worldly standpoint (*saṃvṛti satya*), but it does not exist in the same form as we perceive it when viewed from the ultimate standpoint (*paramārthasatya*).

NOTES

1 Monier Williams, *A Dictionary, English and Sanskrit*, 4th Indian edn (Delhi, 1976), p. 429; cf. Vasudev Govind Apte, *The Handy and Up-to-date English–Sanskrit Dictionary* (Bombay: Gopal Narayen, 1914), p. 191.

2 *The Dīgha Nikāya*, ed. T. W. Rhys Davids and J. Estlin Carpenter, 3 vols (London: Luzac for the Pali Text Society, 1949).

3 Hsüan-tsang's Chinese version of Vasubandhu's *Abhidharmakośaśāstra*, vol. XXIX, p. 15a; vol. XX, p. 9; *Abhidharmasamayānusāraśāstra*, vol. XXVI (*Taishō Tripitaka*, vol. XXIX, p. 901c). *Manorathapūraṇī* (cited in W. Geiger's *Pāli Dhamma*, p. 87); *Mahāniddesa* (ed. by the Pali Text Society, London), p. 133. Nāgārjuna's *Mahāprajñāpāramitā-upadeśa-śāstra*, vol. I (*Taishō Tripiṭaka*, vol. XXV, p. 61a). Kenei Koyama, *Remarks on the Commentary on the Samayabhedacakra-śāstra*, vol. III, p. 11.

4 Yaśomitra's *Abhidharmakośa-vyākyā*, ed. Unrai Wogihara (Tokyo: Taishō University), p. 524, lines 29–30.

5 Th. Stcherbatsky, *The Central Conception of Buddhism and the Meaning of the Word 'Dharma'* (London: Royal Academy, 1923), p. 26 n. 1.

6 *Abhidharmakośa* I, 9.

7 For (4) and (5) see *Abhidharmā-Koshabhāṣya of Vasubandhu*, ed. P. Pradhan (Patna: K. P. Jayaswal, Research Institute, 1967) (*AKBh*), pp. 60–1.

8 For the ten general functions see *AKBh*, p. 54; Hsüan-tsang's Chinese translation, vol. IV; *Taishō Tripiṭaka*, vol. XXIX, p. 19a.

9 For (a) and (c) see *AKBh*, p. 55; Chinese trans., p. 19b.

10 *AKBh*, pp. 59, 60.

11 '*Hiri* (fem.) – modesty, self-respect, conscience'. Warder *Introduction to Pāli*, p. 320.

12 *AKBh*, pp. 59–60.

13 For (f), (g), (h), (i) and (j) see *AKBh*, p. 55.

14 For the six general functions of defilement see *AKBh*, p. 56; Chinese trans., p. 19c.

15 *Abhidharmakośa* II, 26.

16 *Paritta-kleśa-bhūmikāḥ, Abhidharmakośa* II, 27; *upakleśāḥ, AKBh*, p. 58.

17 For (a)–(d) see *AKBh*, p. 312; Chinese trans., p. 109b.

18 For (e)–(g) see *AKBh*, p. 313; Chinese trans., p. 109c.

19 *Abhidharmakośa* V, 50. In the Sanskrit text of the *Abhidharmakośabhāṣya* there is no explanation of the term *māyā*, but the Chinese translation by Hsüan-tsang (p. 109c) says: '*māyā* means "to deceive others" '.

20 *AKBh*, p. 313, lines 13–14; Chinese trans., p. 109c. Cf. *Abhidharmakośa* V, 51.

21 *AKBh*, p. 60, lines 16–17; Chinese trans., p. 21c. Cf. *Abhidharmakośa* V, 50.

22 *Aniyatāḥ, AKBh ad* II, 27; p. 57, line 8; *Sphutārthā Abhidharmakośavyākhyā, The Works of Yaśomitra*, ed. U. Wogihara (Tokyo: The Publishing Association of Abhidharmakośavyākhyā, 1932–6), p. 132.

23 It is likely that various sorts of defilements were common to Buddhism and Jainism. *Uttrajjhāyā* 28, 20 states: 'He who has got rid of love, hate, delusion and ignorance, and

believes because he is told to do so believes by command.' This verse stresses getting rid of the *kṣāyas* and of ignorance.

24 Cf. *Abhidharmakośa* II, 28.
25 *AKBh*, p. 312, line 17; Chinese trans., p. 109b. Cf. *Abhidharmakośa* V, 47.
26 *AKBh*, p. 60, line 22; Chinese trans., p. 21b. Cf. *Abhidharmakośa* II, 33.
27 See n. 17 above.
28 For (e) and (f) see *AKBh*, p. 39; Chinese trans., p. 14a.
29 *AKBh*, p. 60, line 16; Chinese trans., p. 21c. Cf. *Abhidharmakośa* II, 33.
30 Cf. *AKBh*, pp. 277, 279, 307.
31 *AKBh*, p. 62, line 14; Chinese trans., p. 22a.
32 There are two kinds of *prāpti*: (1) *lābha* and (2) *samanvaya* (*Abhidharmakośa* II, 36). *AKBh*, p. 62, lines 16–23; Chinese trans., p. 22a.
33 See n. 24 above.
34 *AKBh*, p. 67, lines 12–13; Chinese trans., p. 24a.
35 For (4)–(6) see *AKBh*, p. 69; Chinese trans., p. 24c.
36 *Abhidharmakośa* II, 45, p. 73; Chinese trans., p. 26a.
37 *AKBh*, p. 75, line 19; Chinese trans., p. 27a.
38 For (12)–(14) see *AKBh*, p. 80; Chinese trans., p. 29a.
39 *AKBh*, p. 3; Chinese trans., p. 1c.
40 For (2) and (3) see *AKBh*, p. 4; Chinese trans., p. 1c.
41 Hsüan – tsang's Chinese version of Vasubandhu's *Abhidharmakośa-śāstra*, vol. I, p. 13b. Nāgārjuna's *Madhyamaka – śāstra*, XV, 2; *Madhyamaka-vṛtti*, ed. L. Poussin, p. 453, line 4.
42 Hsüan-tsang's Chinese version of the *Abhidharma-mahāvibhāṣā-śāstra*, vol. IX (*Taishō Tripiṭaka*, vol. XXVII, p. 42ab); *Abhidharmanyāyānusāra-śāstra*, vol. L (*Taishō Tripiṭaka*, vol. XXIX, pp. 621c–622a); *Abhidharsamayānusāra-śāstra*, vol. XXVI (*Taisho Tripiṭaka*, vol. XXIX, p. 900c).
43 *Svabhāvaḥ sarvadā cāsti* (*Abhidharmakośavyākhyā*, p. 472, line 25).
44 *Traiyadhvika* (= *sarve saṃskṛtā dharmāḥ*).
45 Otto Rosenberg, *Probleme der Buddhistischen Philosophie* (1918); translated into German (Heidelberg, 1924); Stcherbatsky, op. cit.

FURTHER READING

Jayatilleke, K. N. (1963) *Early Buddhist Theory of Knowledge*, London: George Allen & Unwin.
Nakamura, Hajime (1986) *Buddhism in Comparative Light*, Delhi: Motilal Banarsidass.
Radhakrishnan, S. (1929) *Indian Philosophy*, vol. I, London: George Allen & Unwin.
Stcherbatsky, Th. I. (1923) *The Central Conception of Buddhism and the Meaning of the Word 'Dharma'*, London: Royal Asiatic Society.
—— (1927) *The Conception of Buddhist Nirvāna*, Leningrad: Publications Office of the Academy of Sciences of the USSR.

23

MORALS AND SOCIETY IN BUDDHISM

Stewart McFarlane

Soteriology, its teaching and practice are the central concerns of Buddhist traditions. Although questions of knowledge and reality are formally separated from questions of morals and society for the purpose of this volume, their interrelatedness should not be ignored.

A further difficulty in addressing all these issues is that the terms and concepts which are used to describe and interpret them are derived from language, assumptions and distinctions which are foreign to the Buddhist tradition. Therefore the dangers of distortion and misrepresentation are considerable. Buddhism does not have a developed tradition of moral philosophy, by which I mean the systematic, rational analysis of moral arguments and their underlying terminology and assumptions. Even the more abstract reflections of traditional Buddhists such as those found in the *abhidharma* texts maintain a grounding in and reference to meditational experience and practice on the path.[1] In Buddhism the capacity for abstract rational analysis and discrimination, though awarded some provisional value, is subordinated to the capacity for attentive mindfulness (*smṛti/sati*),[2] which leads to liberating wisdom (*prajñā/paññā*). Many textbooks on Buddhism describe the common division of the path into liberating wisdom (*prajñā/paññā*), moral conduct or precept (*śīla/sīla*), and meditation (*samādhi*), but overlook the extent to which these factors are mutually supportive.

Another difficulty for westerners in gaining an understanding of Buddhist ethical teaching also relates to the soteriological and practical orientation of Buddhism. Buddhist texts and authorities from all schools and traditions accept models of spiritual understanding and moral attainment which are both developmental and hierarchical. Such models are implicit in the notion of 'path' itself. This means that beings at different levels of understanding and attainment are taught in ways and at levels appropriate to their understanding and attainment. The Buddha's skill in teaching, like that of any enlightened teacher, consists in the capacity to identify and adapt to the level of those being taught. This explains why the Buddha's response to what appear to be the same questions could vary according to the situation and understanding of the questioner. For example, on one occasion the Buddha is described as refusing to answer the wandering philosopher Vaccagotta's question, 'Is there a self?' Later, he explains to Ānanda that he was silent because Vaccagotta was already confused about the issue (trans in Rhys Davids and Woodward 1956: 281). On another occasion, when the wanderer Potthapada raises the same issue, the Buddha gives a detailed reply (trans. in Rhys Davids and Rhys Davids 1969: 252–4). The way of articulating this kind of differentiation is through the concepts of conventional truth (*saṃvṛti satya*) and ultimate truth (*paramārtha satya*). This distinction is usually associated with Mahāyāna Buddhism, particularly the philosophical tradition of Mādhyamika. Steven Collins has shown how it is equally appropriate to the Pali texts and the Theravāda tradition. He applies it specifically to the various levels and types of discourse developed around the notions of person (*pudgala/puggala*) and no-self (*anātman/anattā*), and relates these levels to the social categories in Theravāda Buddhist Societies and to the distinction between 'Kammatic Buddhism' and 'Nibbanic Buddhism' (Collins 1982:ch. 5).[3] Given the variety of levels of discourse and the process of accommodation to different levels of attainment which are evident in Buddhist texts and teachings, it is apparent that definitive statements and generalizations about the nature of Buddhist ethics are extremely problematic. The tendency to formulate generalized statements about Buddhist ethics, according to the standards of western ethical theories and assumptions, is one which should be resisted.

One of the clearest indications of the hierarchical and developmental nature of Buddhist teachings is the use of the formula which occurs over twenty times in the Pali canon and in other early canonical collections preserved in Chinese. A significant part of the content of this formula applies the Buddhist understanding of action (*karma/kamma*) to the practical implications of ethics, cosmology and spiritual attainment. It has the value of identifying Buddhist ethical teachings in ways which are integrated with Buddhist theory and practice, rather than isolated in the formal lists which often appear in textbooks and secondary accounts. Some attention will therefore be given to discussing the detailed content of the formula. It takes the following form:

> 1. Step-by-step discourse: (a) first part: giving (*dāna*), precepts (*sīla*) and the heavens; (b) second part: the defects of sensuality and positive gain in freedom from it.
> 2. The particular teaching, i.e. the Four Noble Truths: suffering; its arising; its cessation; and the path to its cessation.
>
> Cousins 1984: 300)

The detailed content of this formula was adapted according to the circumstances in which it was delivered. In some texts it is referred to in little more than the above summary form; elsewhere extensive explanation is given. As Lance Cousins points out, the delivery of this teaching by the Buddha often resulted in the listener gaining a direct perception of *dharma*. The Pali term for this perception is *dhammacakkhu* (*dharma* eye or spiritual vision). It marks that person's entry on to the supermundane (*lokuttara*) path, and their status as noble (*ārya*) in Buddhist terms.

It is clear that in the first part of the step-by-step discourse the main emphasis is on the external features of moral conduct; in the second part there is a move to the more psychological features of ethical teaching. These two parts of the step-by-step discourse provide a platform of moral behaviour and stability so that the follower is ready to achieve an understanding of the teaching of the Four Noble Truths. Although the moral teachings in the first part of the step-by-step discourse are not unique or specific to Buddhism, they are placed in a specifically Buddhist context and given a Buddhist interpretation. In themselves they are part of the preparation for receiving the Four Noble Truths.

The first part of the step-by-step discourse begins with giving (*dāna*). This is understood as a formal religious act rather than a generalized act of charity. It is directed specifically to a monk or spiritually developed person. Its ethical and religious significance is often ignored in doctrinally orientated western accounts of Buddhism. As Lance Cousins points out, *dāna* was taught as a non-violent replacement for the Brahmanical sacrifice. It has the effect of purifying and transforming the mind of the giver (Cousins 1984 : 301).

> The inner intention of the giver is reflected in the care, attention and joy with which the giving is performed. The higher the state of mind the more powerful the action (*kamma*). Important too is the state of mind of the recipient, made infectious as it were by the special nature of the act of giving. Either of these is sufficient to make the act effective. The two together are even more powerful.
>
> (Cousins 1984: 301)

The emphasis on the intention and attitude underlying the act is characteristic of Buddhist ethical teaching and practice. The popular understanding of the merit (*puñña*) which results from the practice of *dāna* is an important feature of lay Buddhist practice in all Buddhist countries (see Gombrich 1988 : 124–7). For those aspiring to systematic practice and attainment on the path, *dāna* helps the preliminary settling of the mind, reduces selfishness, and provides a natural preparation for undertaking the precepts (*sīla*). (This word is commonly translated as precepts, though 'training rule' may be a better translation.) For the laity there are normally five precepts. Again the formal undertaking of the precepts, which usually follows the 'going for refuge' to Buddha, *dharma* and *sangha*, constitutes a religious act which brings about benefits and merit. The refuges and precepts are therefore chanted at the outset of most formal Buddhist activities. The wording of the precepts is significant; it translates as follows:

> I undertake the training rule of refraining from:
> destroying life;
> taking what is not given;
> wrong behaviour in regard to sense pleasure;
> untrue speech;
> causes of intoxication.

The precepts are formulated not as imperatives or commandments, but as training rules voluntarily undertaken to facilitate practice. For laity there are no externally imposed sanctions for transgression of the precepts. According to Buddhist action theory, unwholesome acts will result in unpleasant tendencies and results.

Although it does not, strictly speaking, fall within the category of the step-by-step discourse, the issue of the training rules (*prātimokṣa/pātimokkha*) of the monastic order (*sangha*) will be dealt with here, as it does naturally relate to the general concept of *sīla* (moral conduct) in Buddhist practice. The training rules constitute the core of the *vinaya piṭaka* (discipline collection) section of the Buddhist canon. They are a list of offences recited regularly at the confession ceremony known as *uposatha*, which occurs on the days of the new moon and the full moon. The early form of this ceremony involved the confession of any transgression before the whole community (*sangha*). Gombrich notes that the developed procedure involves the confession of offences in pairs, followed by the communal recitation by all the monks present (Gombrich 1988:109). It nevertheless remains true that the formal and public dimensions of this ritual are central to the maintenance of the *sangha*. It is important to note that a monk's transgressions can be officially acknowledged only if they are confessed voluntarily by the monk himself. Many offences are concerned with details of deportment and decorum, and the simple confession of them incurs no further consequences. Gombrich notes that 75 of the 227 offences in the *pātimokkha* code of the Theravāda tradition are of this nature (1988: 108). Only four types of offence result in permanent exclusion from the *sangha*. These are: killing a person, engaging in sexual intercourse, theft, and the false claiming of higher knowledge and powers. Lesser offences may result in temporary exclusion. Bechert and Gombrich have rightly indicated the importance of the fortnightly confessions of offences and communal recitation of the *pātimokkha* in Buddhist history (Bechert 1982: 61–8; Gombrich 1988: 106–14).

It is clear that it is the sharing of a common *pātimokkha* which is crucial in determining an ordination tradition, and it is the common *pātimokkha* and ordination tradition which defines and determines a sect (*nikāya*). Although to an outsider the differences between the *pātimokkha* of the different sects seem to be inconsequential, it is the preserving of the integrity of these lists of offences in detail which gives the sect its continuity and ensures that lineage's identity. As Gombrich observes, the formation and definition of a sect (*nikāya*) in traditional Buddhism is much more a question of observance and corporate ritual identity than a matter of doctrinal agreement (Gombrich 1988: 110–14).

For the issue of Buddhist morals and society, what is of equal importance is how the personal practice of the individual monk interweaves with the communal and institutional dimensions of the *sangha*. Gombrich has described early Buddhism and the Theravāda tradition as representing a form of religious individualism (1988: 72). Early Buddhist texts describe the Buddha identifying the path by his own example and providing the means for beings to find liberation. It is up to self-reliant individuals to employ these means and follow the path through their own efforts. Buddhist traditions have been virtually unanimous throughout Buddhist history that the most effective and reliable way of following the path is within the community of the *sangha*. This necessarily involves engaging with the social dimensions of the *sangha*, which is best seen as a communal institution with a soteriological orientation, in Gombrich's words, 'an association of self reliant individuals' (1988 : 89). This dual nature of the *sangha* and its effective embracing of individual spiritual concerns and communal institutional concerns has given rise to considerable discussion by western scholars and commentators. It has often been at the heart of some of the more obvious conflicting characterizations of Buddhism in scholarly accounts. One dimension of the *sangha* has often been emphasized at the expense of the other. This is further complicated by the widely divergent perspectives on the issue of the relationship between the *sangha* and wider society, between monk/nun and lay person. It is complicated yet again by the failure to establish whether these issues are being addressed in the context of Buddhist textual or commentarial traditions, or in the context of historical developments and practices within institutions, or at the interface between them.

One example of a difference in emphasis in modern scholarship which relates to the above issues is to be found in the differences between T. O. Ling and R. F. Gombrich. Ling sees early Buddhism as a psycho-social philosophy which incorporates 'a theory of existence consisting of a diagnosis (of the human malaise) and the prescription for a cure' (1973: 120). He rightly takes the teaching of no-self as central to Buddhism, but interprets it specifically as a teaching designed to overcome the 'disease of individualism' (1973: 124). He sees the communal life of the *sangha* as providing the context and environment where individualism can be most effectively broken down. On the issue of the relationship between *sangha* and lay society Ling maintains that the Buddha consciously modelled the *sangha*'s constitution and organization on the methods of government of the tribal republics of north India, and that these principles were ideally seen as a model for government for society in general. His case for the latter largely rests on his interpretation of the 'conditions of welfare' passage in the *Mahāparinibbāna sutta*, in which the survival of the Vajjian confederacy is said to depend on maintaining its regular process of collective decision-making and upholding its established traditions and institutions. In the text the Buddha compares this with the *sangha*'s survival, which also depends on its observance of collective decision-making and upholding its traditions (Ling 1973 : 128–33; Ling 1981:144–52; McFarlane 1986: 98–9). Ling concedes that in practice the early *sangha* had to come to terms with the reality of increasingly powerful centralized and expansionist monarchies in north India in the fifth and fourth centuries BC. But the issue of the *sangha* and kingship will be addressed later in this chapter. It would appear that the characterization of early Buddhism offered by Gombrich reflects a radically different perspective. He sees Buddhism as an early form of religious individualism with a theory of effective individual action which appealed to an increasingly important mercantile class (Gombrich 1988: 72–81).

Despite the apparent differences between Ling and Gombrich in their characterizations of early Indian Buddhism, it is possible to reconcile significant aspects of their positions. One could argue that a soteriological religion of self-help and individual responsibility, with its ethic of merit at a popular level and spiritual endeavour at the élite level (Gombrich), would be forced to confront the psychologically and spiritually damaging implications of its own individualism. Taking this process further, efforts of an individual and inherently 'self-authenticating' kind must be made in order to overcome or uproot the notion of individualism and its attendant excesses. One can of course interpret this as paradoxical vicious circle, or one can assume the Mahāyāna Buddhist perspective of skilful means and see it as using a thorn to take out a thorn.

Returning to the structure of the step-by-step discourse, the first part concludes with an account of the lower heavens. As Lance Cousins points out, the cultivation of giving (*dāna*) and moral conduct (*sīla*) will themselves refine consciousness to such a level that rebirth in one of the lower heavens is likely if further practice and entry on the path are not developed (Cousins 1984: 304). It should be underlined that there is nothing improper or un-Buddhist about limiting one's aims to this level of attainment.

The second part of the step-by-step discourse moves on to address the dangers of attachment to sensory experience. These dangers include the distortion of mental clarity, partiality, selfishness, craving, grasping, violence, dishonesty and theft. The most direct and positive antidote to these states is the cultivation in meditation of the four *Brahmaviharā* or sublime states, of loving kindness (*mettā*), compassion (*karuṇā*), sympathetic joy (*muditā*) and equanimity (*upekkhā*). It has been convincingly demonstrated that these states are meditational achievements and concerned with attitudes rather than practice or providing the direct motivation to social or ethical action (Aronson 1980a: ch. 5, and Narain 1980:1–12). Aronson distinguishes these states from the more general socially motivating qualities of 'simple compassion' (*kāruñña*) and 'sympathy' (*anukampā*) which are available to all Buddhists, whether they are proceeding to an advanced level of practice on the path, or are ordinary householders. He points out that it was this primary motive of sympathy which caused the Buddha to arise and teach in the first place (1980: 4–6).

The sublime states cultivated in meditation will produce a refining of consciousness to such a level that rebirth in a less corporeal realm of existence will be possible. Alternatively, the meditator may choose to follow the path to a higher level of attainment, cultivate their meditational practice and so move on to the level referred to in the 'particular teaching', which is concerned with an understanding of the Four Noble Truths and the advanced levels of meditation practice (see Cousins 1984: 305–9).

It is clear that underpinning and pervading the whole of the Buddhist teaching on the path, at both ordinary (*lokiya*) and supermundane (*lokuttara*) levels, is the notion of *karma*. Because a general knowledge of Buddhist teaching about *karma* is now quite common in the East and West, it is easy to underestimate the impact of the Buddha's innovative reworking of a traditional Brahmanic concept. This impact is dramatically described in early texts dealing with the Buddha's final stages of attainment and his enlightenment. In these accounts the fourth higher knowledge (*abhiññā*) gained by the Buddha is knowledge of his own previous lives, and of how his wholesome actions gave rise to beneficial consequences. This is followed by the fifth higher knowledge, which is the ability to observe the previous lives of all living beings, giving a vivid and direct understanding of the nature of their actions and the attendant consequences (*karmavipāka*). The sixth super knowledge consists in the knowledge of the destruction of the influxes (*āsava*), unwholesome tendencies and mental states, followed by the Buddha's direct experience of the nature of the human condition as suffering or imperfection, its cause, its cessation and the path to its cessation, i.e. the Four Noble Truths (Robinson and Johnson 1977: 28–30).

The Buddha's important contribution to the theory and concept of *karma* has been to give an ethical and psychological orientation to the Brahmanic notion of *karma*, which referred to effective ritual action. The emphasis in Buddhism is on the determining or volitional intention behind the action, and it is this which produces the seeds and tendencies which effect or determine future states and conditions. In the Buddhist context the meaning of *karma* has shifted from ritual act to volitional act or intention. 'It is choice or intention that I call karma – mental work –, for having chosen, a man acts by body, speech and mind' (*Anguttara Nikāya*, quoted in Carrithers 1983: 67). This is reflected in the traditional Buddhist emphasis on the need for controlling and understanding the mind if moral practice and spiritual training are to be cultivated to their higher levels. The emphasis on the psychology of intentions in traditional Buddhist ethical teaching and spiritual practice should not lead to the undermining of the importance of physical behaviour and actual consequences. It would be incorrect to say that the intention or will to perform an unwholesome act which was not actually carried out would produce the same effect as the actual performance of such an act. The subtlety of levels of intention and the relationship between intention and behaviour is acknowledged. For example, the casual thought 'I wish X were dead' is certainly unwholesome, and will produce some unfortunate result. But the results would be much more serious in the case of someone who wished X dead and made detailed plans for murder. The results would be even more grave in the case of someone who raised the initial thought, planned and then actually carried out the murder. The degree of intention or volitional energies (*saṃskāra/saṅkhāra*) involved in the final scenario is clearly greater than those involved in the first two.

It is clear that the notion of *karma* permeates all levels of Buddhist teaching and practice. A generalized 'knowledge of the ownership of deeds' greatly facilitates cultivation of giving and moral conduct. It is also clear that a full understanding of the detailed operation of *karma* and its implications is available only at the highest levels of attainment and practice. It is interesting to note that it is only at this level of practice and attainment, when intentional acts producing harmful consequences are no longer performed, that a full understanding of the nature of that action and its results is achieved (Robinson and Johnson 1977: 38–9). This does not mean that beings at this advanced level no longer act. The teaching career and activities of the Buddha and the *arhats* (worthy/enlightened ones) disprove this. It simply means that their acts are of such a quality that they no longer generate fresh tendencies and consequences.

Much discussion of Buddhism in the context of social and political issues has been concerned with Buddhist attitudes to and interactions with kingship. The textual and historical complexities of these issues cannot be addressed adequately in this brief chapter. I shall try to illuminate some of the main issues by referring to recent discussions. Many scholars have noted an early Buddhist ambivalence towards the realities of kingship, coupled with an acceptance of the need to accommodate to the realities of political power and polity (Gokhale 1969: 731–7; Ling 1973: 140–7; Chakravarti 1987:ch. 6; Gombrich 1988 : 81–6). Chakravarti accepts that early texts reveal a separation between the social world, the concerns of kings and politicians, and the asocial world of the *sangha*. He acknowledges that some texts reflect the Buddha's taking an interest in how kings exercise their power. He argues that this led to the concepts of the righteous universal ruler (*cakkavatti dhammiko dhammarāja*), which appear in early texts to articulate a particular Buddhist notion of normative kingship. This ideal contrasts with and implicitly criticizes the real despotic kings who ruled in north India at the time (Chakravarti 1987: 168–70). Gombrich deals with many of the same texts and concepts but interprets them differently.[4] He questions how 'normative' these references were intended to be, and draws a distinction between passages dealing with 'real kings' and 'fantasy kings'. He sees the material dealing with the latter as largely designed to criticize and undermine established Brahmanic practices and orthodoxies, points out that none of the discourse dealing with 'fantasy' kings is actually addressed to real kings, and questions whether such texts were ever intended to have an effect on policy. The texts in question describe social and economic policies and practices which would seem radical, if not outrageous, to kings and political leaders at the time: policies such as generous financial support for the poor, financing agriculture and commerce, and the abolition of violent legal punishment (Gombrich 1988: 82–4). The radical nature of such ideas would make it inappropriate, tactically and diplomatically, to address them directly to kings and ministers. The fact that they are articulated in the texts at all is not insignificant. It is possible that an indirect effect on sympathetic kings is intended, as well as an implicit criticism of despotic ones. In situations where Buddha, *dharma* and *sangha* were dependent on the goodwill of the ruler, it may have been tactically necessary to couch such radical ideas in the context of myth, fantasy or utopian accounts.

Gombrich does accept that the concept of the idealized, or wheel-turning king (*cakravartin/cakkavati*) described in early texts influenced the policies of the Emperor

Aśoka, and not, as some have suggested, the other way round (1988: 82,130). Despite his remarkable achievements as ruler, and the application of Buddhist ethical values to his policies and his own life, Aśoka nowhere explicitly claims to be a *cakravartin* (Basham 1982:135). Later Buddhist history has simply assumed that Aśoka was a *cakravartin* and that his edicts said as much. Ironically, kings in later Asian history automatically assumed titles such as *cakravartin* and *bodhisattva*, often with far less ethical justification than the claims made for Aśoka (Greenwald 1978: 13–31; Tambiah 1976:81). In China the first ruler to claim such titles explicitly was Emperor Wu of Liang, a great Buddhist patron (Wright 1959:51). Another was Yang Chien (reign title Wen Ti), founder of the Sui Dynasty. He came to power in AD 581 and completed the reunification of China in AD 589. He was raised as a Buddhist and attempted to employ Buddhist concepts and values in the formulation of a new ideology to support his programme of unification. He issued the following proclamation in AD 581:

> With the armed might of a Cakravartin king, We spread the ideals of the ultimately enlightened one. With a hundred victories in a hundred battles, We promote the practice of the ten Buddhist virtues. Therefore we regard the weapons of war as having become like the offerings of incense and flowers presented to Buddha, and the fields of this world as becoming forever identical with the Buddhaland.
>
> (Wright 1959: 67)

An even more famous Chinese ruler to claim such exalted status was Empress Wu, who after effecting various intrigues and untimely deaths officially came to power in AD 684 and ruled China until AD 705. She was an active supporter of Buddhism, and attempted to establish it as the state religion. As part of her own rise to power and pursuit of this policy her monastic supporters discovered textual and commentarial justification for her claim to rule, which incorporated claims to establish her status as a *cakravartin*, and to be an embodiment of the *bodhisattva* Maitreya, the future buddha (Weinstein 1987: 37–40; Paul 1980:ch. 12). It is significant that the figure of Maitreya has served as a focus of popular eschatological hopes and sometimes for dissent, protest and even rebellion in Chinese history. Groups and sects, often identified by the rather vague title 'White Lotus' in official sources, proliferated from the twelfth century onwards. Initially many were peaceful, vegetarian, devotional sects focusing on Amitābha and Maitreya. Later, under the period of Mongol rule in China (1280–1368), many groups became militant and rebellious. It appears that militarized offshoots of White Lotus groups were instrumental in overthrowing Mongol rule (Overmyer 1976:ch. 5). Both peaceful and militant Maitreya-based sects and associations continued to attract popular support throughout the Ming (1368–1644) and Ch'ing [Qing] (1644–1911) Dynasties, despite official disapproval and persecution (Overmyer 1988: 110–14).

One feature of Buddhist ethics in practice which is often overlooked is the role of sanctions revolving around shame rather than concepts of sin and guilt. The shame sanction in Buddhist ethics and Buddhist social attitudes is important both for monks and lay people. It has already been noted that a full understanding of *karma* and its implications is available only to the spiritually more advanced. For ordinary beings and less advanced followers of the path it is clear that other sanctions or supports for wholesome attitudes and conduct become necessary. For the *sangha* this is evident in the ancient practice of communal confession of offences on *uposatha* days. At the level of lay life and practice the motif of shame is evident in the downgrading of certain activities and trades which do not conform to the traditional understanding of Right Livelihood on the Eightfold Path. These would include animal slaughter and hunting and dealing in arms, intoxicants and poisons (Saddhatissa 1970: 72). In practice, rather than prohibiting such activities and trades, Buddhist societies tended to downgrade socially those who pursued them (Conze 1975: 7). This implicit shame sanction is evident in many early texts concerned with ethics and social issues, as well as in a number of Aśoka's edicts, and in Mahāyāna passages dealing with the same themes (Ling 1973: 137–74; De Bary 1958: 142–50, 169, 181–4). In China, where certain Mahāyāna ethical ideas exerted an influence, the shame sanction was particularly invoked to discourage meat eating (De Groot 1980: 102–3; Ch'en 1973: 276–81).

The ethical and social teaching of Mahāyāna Buddhism will now be considered in more detail. Although not exclusive to the Mahāyāna traditions, it was amongst these that the concept of the *bodhisattva* was refined and developed into an ethical and spiritual practice and ideal in its own right. It is impossible to treat Mahāyāna Buddhism as a single unified entity (Williams 1989:ch. 1), but the *bodhisattva* as the embodiment and exemplar of supreme wisdom (*mahāprajñā*) and supreme compassion (*mahākaruṇā*) does provide the nearest thing to a core concept for all the diverse traditions and practices of the Mahāyāna. Many of the familiar virtues and meditational states exemplified in traditional Buddhism reappear in the qualities and practices of the *bodhisattva*, known as the perfections (*pāramitā*). These are giving (*dāna*), moral conduct (*śīla*), patience (*kṣānti*), energy (*vīrya*), absorptive meditation (*dhyāna*) and wisdom (*prajñā*). Some later texts add skilful means (*upāyakauśalya*), resolution (*praṇidhāna*), strength (*bala*) and knowledge (*jñāna*).

A feature evident in this combination of perfections and in many Mahāyāna texts is the tendency to universalize or generalize central concepts and values. In this way, ideas and norms which for earlier traditional forms of Buddhism would have been restricted to the spiritual élite within the *sangha* are extended or made available to the laity as well. Frank Reynolds and Robert Campany have noted this tendency and have identified the concept of the *bodhisattva* as 'an ideal that combined the social virtues of a righteous householder with the ascetic ideals of a meditating monk, bridging what was perceived by its proponents as a gap between monastic and popular Buddhism' (1985, vol. II:501). One feature of this universalizing process is the replacing of the supposedly narrow and 'self-regarding' goal of *nirvāṇa* as achieved by the *arhat* or *śrāvaka* with the universal goal of Supreme Enlightenment (*sambodhi*) for all beings as exemplified by the buddha and *bodhisattvas*. In theory, the *bodhisattva* path is open to all whether monk or lay person, man or woman. In practice, its higher stages are more likely to be achieved within the context of the *sangha*.

Further evidence for the process of universalizing or generalizing at the level of values and norms can be found in texts which take ethical requirements previously confined to the *sangha* and teach them as norms for the laity. For example, the Chinese Mahāyāna version of the *Brahmajāla Sūtra* requires both monks and lay people to abstain from violence and involvement with military affairs (De Groot 1980: 46–7). In the Pali version such requirements are clearly limited to members of the *sangha* (Rhys Davids and Rhys Davids 1969: 4, 5, 13). Similarly, not killing animals and showing compassion to them, which are *encouraged* in early Buddhism (Horner 1967:*passim*), become *requirements* in the Mahāyāna; hence the arguments for vegetarianism noted above.

This process is also evident in doctrinal matters. One of the great heroes of the Mahāyāna is the *bodhisattva* Vimalakīrti, a wealthy householder with a family and many concubines, who teaches the senior monks and whose wisdom and skill equal those of *Mañjuśrī* (Lamotte (1976:ch. 8). A number of other Mahāyāna texts give prominence to advanced lay teachers of *Dharma* (see Williams 1989: 21, 125, 129, 154). I agree with Williams that it would be incorrect to conclude from such texts that the Mahāyāna represents a product of innovations developed by lay Buddhists (1989: 22–6). With the exception of the modern Japanese lay Buddhist movements such as the Soka Gakkai the *sangha* has always remained at the centre of Mahāyāna religious life and doctrinal development. It is almost certain that these spiritually egalitarian *sūtras* were inspired and transmitted by monks.

One of the problems with the arguments that the Mahāyāna had its origins as a lay movement stems, I think, from the tendency to read statements from the standpoint of higher truth (*paramārthasatya*) as both normative and reflective of actual socio-historical realities. From the standpoint of higher truth the capacity for understanding *Dharma* and achieving enlightenment is the same for a lay person as for a monk. Dōgen, the thirteenth-century transmitter of Sōtō Zen to Japan, clearly admits that in theory, practice and enlightenment are attainable by lay men and women (Masunaga 1972: 49; Yokoi 1976: 69). He goes on to qualify this by pointing out the difficulties in doing so for a lay person, and in practice Dōgen devoted much of his time and energy to organizing teaching and regulating the practice of Zen in the monastic setting (Kim 1975:ch. 5). Similarly, there is substantial evidence in early texts that the Buddha acknowledges the spiritual potential of lay people, and even confirms the advanced attainment of a small number of exceptional householders (Saddhatissa 1970: 118–22). On one occasion the Buddha refuses to generalize about the differences between monks and householders from a moral or spiritual point of view (Gombrich 1988: 80). Like Dōgen the early texts do make spiritually egalitarian statements which undermine the monk/householder distinction (Saddhatissa 1970: 121–2). However, the Buddha, like Dōgen, is described as devoting most of his energies to establishing and teaching the *sangha*, predominantly conceived as a community of monks and nuns (*bhikkhu, bhikkhunī*).

There are philosophical or doctrinal reasons behind the Mahāyāna tendency to universalize across the *sangha*/householder distinction. One of the fundamental insights of the Mahāyāna is the non-differentiation of the round of craving, grasping, suffering, rebirth (*saṃsāra*) and the cessation of suffering in the liberated state (*nirvāṇa*). The non-differentiation of *saṃsāra* and *nirvāṇa* was articulated by Nāgārjuna and developed in relation to Mahāyāna thought and practice in the 'Perfection of Wisdom' literature and all later Mahāyāna systems (Williams 1989:ch. 3). Such an undifferentiated insight tends to facilitate a kind of spiritual egalitarianism which sees no ultimate distinction between monk and householder, ordinary being and Buddha. However, Mahāyāna texts and teachers accept that it is at the level of delusion and differentiation that beings need to be taught and guided. So the methods and teachings must be carefully moderated and adapted to the level of understanding appropriate to such beings. The crucial importance of teaching at the conventional level of truth should not be underestimated. In articulating the distinction between ultimate truth (*paramārthasatya*) and provisional/ordinary truth (*saṃvṛtisatya*) Nāgārjuna makes it clear that it is only by recourse to the conventional that the ultimate can be attained (trans. in Williams 1989: 69).

One aspect of the skilful means (*upāyakauśalya*) of buddhas and *bodhisattvas* is their ability to know which expressions of conventional truth to employ in order to bring beings to the path to liberation most effectively. The Mahāyāna identification of levels of truth means that there is no real tension between the spiritual egalitarianism expressed in some Mahāyāna texts and the more traditional Buddhist acknowledgement of a spiritual and moral hierarchy. The problem for commentators is that different levels of truth and different means (*upāya*) interweave in the same passages and texts. This is perfectly illustrated in the context of Mahāyāna ethics, psychology and soteriology in the account of Mañjuśrī's 'attempt' to kill the Buddha, in a text extant in the Chinese Mahāratnakūta collection (trans. in Chang 1983: 66–9). The whole incident is a skilful means devised by the Buddha in order to rid 500 *bodhisattvas* of the spiritually debilitating knowledge of their heinous offences in past lives. The Buddha causes Mañjuśrī to attack him with a sword, then instructs Mañjuśrī that the real way to kill him is to see the Buddha (or any being) as possessing self or person. In reality the Buddha, all beings and all *dharmas* are empty of self; to see them otherwise is actually to 'kill' them. Inasmuch as they are ultimately without self, form or person, killing them is an impossibility. On realizing the emptiness of all *dharmas* the 500 *bodhisattvas* abandon their remorse over past crimes and continue their practice. One of the interesting features of this account is that in creating this skilful means, the Buddha ensures that all the novice *bodhisattvas* of lesser understanding simply do not see the incident or hear the resulting discussion on emptiness and *karma*. This clearly demonstrates the principle of accommodation to different levels of ability and understanding, which is central to the concept of skilful means.

It is clear from a wide range of Mahāyāna texts and teachings that the compassion and skilfulness of buddhas and *bodhisattvas* may permit or even require them to set aside traditional moral or doctrinal norms. The *Lotus Sūtra* (*Saddharmapuṇḍarīka Sūtra/Myōhō-renge-kyō*), which exerted such an influence in East Asian Buddhist teaching and practice, contains many such examples. In chapter 8 the Buddha declares that *bodhisattvas* may appear to adopt deluded and heretical views in order to gain the confidence of beings and lead them to liberation (trans. Hurvitz 1976 : 160). The most famous case of skilful means occurs in the third chapter of the *Lotus Sūtra*, where a father's (the Buddha) deception in promising toys (traditional goals of Buddhist practice) that he does not have to his sons is justified because the promise tempts them out of a burning house (*saṃsāra*). The underlying principles of skilful means are apparent in early Buddhist texts, even though the technical vocabulary and detailed theory are lacking. One striking example is where the Buddha shows the lovesick monk Nanda, the beauty of the nymphs in a heavenly realm to break his attachment, and so causes Nanda to renew his efforts in meditation, in order to be reborn there. In fact, Nanda progresses to become an *arhant* and forgets all about his desires for either human or heavenly maidens (Pye 1978 : 122).

Texts dealing with skilful means, non-duality, emptiness and other central Mahāyāna concepts frequently resort to extreme rhetorical exaggerations to make their point. There is a clear intention to shock conventional Buddhist hearers or readers out of their prosaic assumptions. These considerations are evident when *bodhisattvas* are described as changing their sex at will (Paul 1985:ch. 5), or when the Buddha, in a previous life, breaks a vow of celibacy and lives with a woman for twelve years to prevent her death (Chang 1983 : 433), or in another life, kills a bandit with a spear to save 500 traders, who are really *bodhisattvas*, and to save the man from the consequences of his intended actions (Chang 1983 : 456–7). It is clear from the circumstances of these and similar accounts, and from the high spiritual status of the performers of these deeds, that they are not intended to be employed as blanket justifications of moral transgressions in ordinary situations, outside the context of spiritual training and practice (McFarlane 1986, vol. I:101–2). In scholarly treatises associated with Asaṅga such as the *Bodhisattvabūmi* and the *Mahāyānasaṃgraha*, there is evidence of attempts to formulate general guidelines about the appropriateness of such transgressions (De La Vallée Poussin 1929 : 210–17; Lamotte 1976 : 292–6; Dayal 1932 : 207–9).

The use of the concept of skilful means to justify or rationalize historical cases of moral transgressions is actually quite rare.[5] One notable exception is the celebrated assassination of the Tibetan king gLang dar ma, by the monk dPal gyi rdo rje, in AD 842. The king was violently persecuting the *sangha* and the monk acted to save the *Dharma* and save the king from perpetuating his own wicked acts and their consequences (Williams 1989 : 190). It is significant that even though the Mahāyāna ethic of skilful means theoretically justified the act, the offending monk admitted his offence and excluded himself from ordination ceremonies (Conze 1967 : 74). In another supposedly historical incident, which is typical of the kind of rhetorical extremes already mentioned, the great Mādhyamika teacher Āryadeva invokes the notions of emptiness and non-duality and the illusoriness of the victim and perpetrator of murder. He does this not to justify an act of killing on his part, but rather when he has just been fatally stabbed by an assassin; he proceeds to teach the assassin the above *Dharma*, and to provide him with the means of his escape (Khantipalo 1964 : 174–5).

Buddhist traditions demonstrate depth, diversity and richness in their ethical and social teachings. The flexible and non-absolutist nature of Buddhist teachings has allowed them to be adapted and accommodated to a wide range of different Asian political and social systems. This process of accommodation seems set to continue as Buddhist teachings and practices gain an increasing influence in the West.

NOTES

1 For further information on *abhidharma/abhidhamma* see Cousins 1984 : 289.
2 Where appropriate, Sanskrit terms will be followed by their Pali equivalents.
3 For a critique of this distinction as employed by M. E. Spiro and W. L. King, see Aronson 1979 : 28–36.
4 Chakravarti 1987 and Gombrich 1988 appear to have been in preparation at roughly the same time; therefore neither work directly refers to the other.
5 See McFarlane 1986, vol. I:102. Gombrich makes a similar point on the disquiet evident in relation to historical transgressions of Buddhist ethics (1988 : 70). There does seem to be a reluctance on the part of Buddhists to seek moral justifications for such acts.

REFERENCES

Aronson, H. B. (1979) 'The relationship of the karmic to the nirvanic in Theravāda Buddhism', *Journal of Religious Ethics* 7(1): 28–36.
—— (1980a) *Love and Sympathy in Theravāda Buddhism*, Delhi: Motilal Banarsidass.
—— (1980b) 'Motivations to social action in Theravāda Buddhism', in A. K. Narain (ed.) *Studies in the History of Buddhism*, Delhi: B.R. Publishing Corporation.
Basham, A. L. (1982) 'Aśoka and Buddhism: a reexamination', *Journal of the International Association of Buddhist Studies* 5(1): 131–43.
Bechert, H. (1982) 'The importance of Aśoka's so-called schism edict', in L. A. Hercus *et al.* (eds) *Indological and Buddhist Studies*, Canberra: Australian National University, Faculty of Asian Studies.
Carrithers, M. (1983) *The Buddha*, Oxford: Oxford University Press.
Chakravarti, U. (1987) *The Social Dimensions of Early Buddhism*, Delhi: Oxford University Press.
Chang, Garma C. C. (ed.) (1983) *A Treasury of Mahāyāna Sūtras*, University Park: Pennsylvania State University Press.

Ch'en, K. S. (1973) *The Chinese Transformation of Buddhism*, Princeton, N.J.: Princeton University Press.
Collins, S. (1982) *Selfless Persons*, Cambridge University Press.
Conze, E. (1967) *Thirty Years of Buddhist Studies*, Oxford: Bruno Cassirer.
—— (1975) *Further Buddhist Studies*, Oxford: Bruno Cassirer.
Cousins, L. S. (1984) 'Buddhism', in J. R. Hinnells (ed.) *A Handbook of Living Religions*, London: Penguin.
Dayal, H. (1932) *The Bodhisattva Doctrine in Buddhist Sanskrit Literature*, London: Kegan Paul, Trench, Trubner.
De Bary, W. T. (ed.) (1958) *Sources of Indian Tradition*, New York: Columbia University Press.
De Groot, J. J. M. (1980) *Le Code du Mahāyāna en Chine*, New York: Garland Publishing.
De La Vallée Poussin, L. (1929) 'Notes bouddhiques VII, Le Vinaya et la pureté d'intention', *Bulletin de la Classe des Lettres*, Académie Royale de Belgique, Bruxelles, 15(5): 201–17.
Eliade, M. (1985) *The Encyclopedia of Religion*, New York: Macmillan.
Gokhale, B. G. (1969) 'The early Buddhist view of the state', *Journal of the American Oriental Society* 89(4): 731–7.
Gombrich, R. F. (1988) *Theravada Buddhism*, London: Routledge & Kegan Paul.
Greenwald, A. (1978) 'The relic on the spear historiography and the saga of Duṭṭhagāmaṇī', in B. L. Smith (ed.) *Religion and the Legitimation of Power in Sri Lanka*, Chambersburg, Pa.: Anima Books.
Horner, I. B. (1967) *Early Buddhism and the Taking of Life*, The Wheel Publication no. 104, Kandy, Sri Lanka: Buddhist Publication Society.
Hurvitz, L. (1976) *Scripture of the Lotus Blossom of the Fine Dharma*, New York: Columbia University Press.
Khantipalo, P. (1964) *Tolerance: A Study from Buddhist Sources*, London: Rider.
Kim, H. J. (1975) *Dōgen Kigen – Mystical Realist*, Tucson: University of Arizona Press.
Lamotte, E. (1976) *The Teaching of Vimalakīrti*, trans. S. Boin, London: Pali Text Society.
Ling, T. O. (1973) *The Buddha*, London: Temple Smith.
—— (ed.) (1981) *The Buddha's Philosophy of Man*, London: Dent.
McFarlane, S. (1986) 'Buddhism', in L. Pauling (ed.) *World Encyclopedia of Peace*, vol. I, Oxford: Pergamon.
Masunaga, R. (trans.) (1972) *A Primer of Sōtō Zen*, London: Routledge & Kegan Paul.
Narain, A. (ed.) (1980) *Studies in the History of Buddhism*, Delhi: BR Corporation.
Overmyer, D. L. (1976) *Folk Buddhist Religion*, Cambridge, Mass: Harvard University Press.
—— (1978) 'Messenger, savior, and revolutionary: Maitreya in Chinese popular religious literature of the sixteenth and seventeenth centuries', in A. Sponberg and H. Hardacre (eds) *Maitreya, the Future Buddha*, Cambridge: Cambridge University Press.
Paul, D. (1980) 'Empress Wu and the historians: a tyrant and saint of Classical China', in N. A. Falk and R. M. Cross (eds) *Unspoken Worlds*, San Francisco: Harper & Row.
Paul, D. Y. (1985) *Women in Buddhism*, London: University of California Press.
Pye, M. (1978) *Skilful Means*, London: Duckworth.
Reynolds, F. E. and Campany, R. (1985) 'Buddhist ethics', in M. Eliade (ed.) *The Encyclopedia of Religion*, vol. II, New York: Macmillan, pp. 498–504.
Rhys Davids, C. A. F. and Woodward, F. L. (1956) *The Book of Kindred Sayings* (Samyutta Nikaya), part 4, London: Pali Text Society.
Rhys Davids, T. W. and Rhys Davids, C. A. F. (1969) *Dialogues of the Buddha* (Digha Nikaya), part 1, London: Pali Text Society.
Robinson, R. H. and Johnson, W. L. (1977) *The Buddhist Religion*, Belmont, Calif.: Dickenson.
Saddhatissa, H. (1970) *Buddhist Ethics*, London: Allen & Unwin.
Tambiah, S. J. (1976) *World Conqueror and World Renouncer*, Cambridge: Cambridge University Press.
Weinstein, S. (1987) *Buddhism Under the T'ang*, Cambridge: Cambridge University Press.
Williams, P. (1989) *Mahāyāna Buddhism*, London: Routledge.

Wright, A. F. (1959) *Buddhism in Chinese History*, Stanford, Calif.: Stanford University Press.
Yokoi, Y. (1976) *Zen Master Dōgen*, New York: Weatherhill.

FURTHER READING

Aung Thuin, M. (1985) 'Kingship in southeast Asia', in M. Eliade (ed.) *The Encyclopedia of Religion*, vol. VIII, New York: Macmillan, pp. 333–6.
Bechert, H. and Gombrich, R. F. (1984) *The World of Buddhism*, London: Thames & Hudson.
Demiéville, P. (1957, 1973 reprint) 'Le Bouddhisme et la guerre', in *Choix d'études bouddhiques (1929–1970)*, Leiden: E. J. Brill.
Gokhale, B. G. (1966) 'Early Buddhist kingship', *Journal of Asian Studies* 26(1): 15–22.
Gombrich, R. F. (1971) *Precept and Practice*, Oxford: Clarendon Press.
Gomez, L. (1985) 'Buddhist literature: exegesis and hermeneutics', in M. Eliade (ed.) *The Encyclopedia of Religion*, vol. II, New York: Macmillan, pp. 529–39.
Hazra, K. L. (1984) *Royal Patronage of Buddhism in Ancient India*, Delhi: DK Publications.
Ishii, Y. (1986) *Sangha, State, and Society: Thai Buddhism in History*, Honolulu: University of Hawaii Press.
King, W. L. (1964) *In the Hope of Nibbana*, La Salle, Illinois: Open Court.
Ling, T. O. (1983) 'Kingship and nationalism in Pali Buddhism', in P. Denwood and A. Piatigorsky (eds) *Buddhist Studies Ancient and Modern*, Collected Papers on South Asia no. 4, London: Curzon Press.
Macy, J. (1985) *Dharma and Development*, West Hartford, Conn.: Kumarian Press.
Pye, M. (1985) 'Upāya', in M. Eliade (ed.) *The Encyclopedia of Religion*, vol. XV, New York: Macmillan, pp. 152–5.
Rahula, W. (1956) *History of Buddhism in Ceylon*, Colombo, Sri Lanka: M. D. Gunasena.
—— (1974) *The Heritage of the Bhikkhu*, New York: Grove Press.
Seneviratne, H. L. (1985) 'Saṃgha and society', in M. Eliade (ed.) *The Encyclopedia of Religion*, vol. XIII, New York: Macmillan, pp. 40–7.
Smith, B. L. (ed.) (1976) *Religion and Social Conflict in South Asia*, Leiden: E. J. Brill.
—— (ed.) (1978) *Religion and Legitimation of Power in Thailand, Laos, and Burma*, Chambersburg, Pa.: Anima Books.
Spiro, M. E. (1971) *Buddhism and Society: A Great Tradition and its Burmese Vicissitudes*, London: Allen & Unwin.
Zurcher, E. (1972) *The Buddhist Conquest of China*, Leiden: E. J. Brill.

24

CONTEMPORARY BUDDHIST PHILOSOPHY

Frank J. Hoffman

DEFINITION OF SCOPE

Each word in the phrase 'contemporary Buddhist philosophy' is subject to philosophical scrutiny. In this chapter 'contemporary' is construed (with minor exceptions) as 'post Second World War', but emphasis is placed on writing in the last two decades. 'Buddhist' ideas are philosophical and/or religious ideas held by Buddhist men and women. For the purposes of this chapter, 'philosophy' is a comprehensive world-view which has existential force and purports to describe the world in such a way as to give a meaning to life for the adherents of the philosophy.

This chapter focuses upon the thought of Buddhists and scholars of Buddhism in the latter half of the twentieth century in so far as such thought has philosophical implications. But several caveats are in order. First, there is a certain oddness involved in attempting to introduce Buddhist thought to western philosophers at all, since the categories of western philosophy do not closely mesh with those of eastern philosophy. It should be recognized at the outset that from Asian perspectives it is somewhat artificial to pigeon-hole Buddhist philosophy in western categories (such as branches of philosophy and schools of philosophy). It is, however, in the nature of reference works to use categories, and encyclopedias generally employ categories useful to their readers.

My justification of the major rubrics employed is in terms of ease of use for reference. Since the readership is, in this case, English-speaking philosophers and students of philosophy, it is appropriate to use categories convenient for them. This is a pragmatic strategy and carries no implication of cultural imperialism whatsoever. It would be entirely useless to employ as rubrics categories unknown to western philosophers, no matter how internally faithful these are to Asian traditions from a contextual point of view. Consequently no apology is in order for the use of the categories which follow, just a word of caution that one must not confuse the finger pointing at the moon for the moon itself.

Second, it should also be recognized at the outset that there is a certain oddness in writing a separate chapter on 'contemporary Buddhist philosophy' in view of the fact that there are also chapters on contemporary Indian, Chinese and Japanese philosophies. 'What remains after these other chapters have been written?', it might be asked. Is contemporary Buddhist philosophy some ethereal, ghostly penumbra hovering over particular cultures? Certainly not. It is as if Buddhism were a peculiar sort of elastic glue holding together these disparate countries in dynamic tension. Indeed, contemporary Buddhist philosophy is a pan-Asian phenomenon which contributes somewhat to Asian solidarity.

To the extent that there has been a contemporary Buddhist philosophy across geographical lines in the twentieth century, that is due to the interaction of traditional Buddhist modes of thought with western ones. Issues such as the environment, animal rights and feminism compete for space in the publisher's market of learned books and journals with more traditional topics such as the mind–body problem in philosophy and Buddhist–Christian dialogue. Neither the traditional nor the trendy can be ignored if one aspires to a holistic vision of contemporary Buddhist philosophy. Consequently this chapter includes reference to ethical issues in connection with Buddhism: sexuality and gender issues, rights of non-human animals, issues of race, class and power, vegetarianism, environmental ethics, and inter-religious dialogue. For the convenience of philosophers and their students using this reference work these topics are subsumed under the traditional branches of philosophy.

BUDDHISM AND THE BRANCHES OF PHILOSOPHY

Buddhism and logic

Logic is sometimes said to be the backbone of philosophy, but in Buddhist thought that backbone is particularly supple. Especially in east Asian Mahāyāna one finds a tendency to inclusive patterns of thinking ('both/and') emphasized by Matsuo rather than exclusive ones ('either/or').

Hosaku Matsuo (1987) argues in favour of a view of logic as a unified cognitive process, mind as intuitive and holistic, the interrelatedness of metaphysics and epistemology, and the primacy of synthetic over analytic reasoning in philosophy. Drawing upon *Prajñāparamitrā* tradition and emphasizing the *śūnyata* ('emptiness') doctrine construed as the primordial source of creative potentiality rather than as non-being, Matsuo challenges the familiar western dichotomies of subject/object, mind/body and internal world/external world. Although rooted in the Kyoto school, Matsuo also at once underscores the importance of Kant and a philosophy related to existence.

All too often the term 'Buddhist philosophy' is *identified* with the mystical and non-argumentative. Indeed, a corrective to an overly general and stereotypical view of Buddhist thought is found in the detailed and philosophically perspicuous work (1986) of the late B. K. Matilal.

Another commonly found feature of logic in contemporary Buddhist thought is its close connection with ontology. Rather than understanding logic as only a matter of abstract problems connected with semantics and analytic truth, Buddhist logic is pragmatically grounded in a view of the way things are.

Since there is a long tradition of debate in Buddhist monasteries, it is not surprising that Buddhist logic is fundamentally applied logic, which makes a difference to how debates should be conducted. Although parallels to formal logical principles may be found, Buddhist logic is basically concerned with rules for discussion in order to determine what is true.

Sometimes mythological elements enter into discussions of Buddhist logic, as when it is said that a thunder-bolt-bearing *yakkha* (ghostly being of light) will shatter one's skull into a thousand pieces for a self-contradictory utterance – so greatly is logical consistency valued in Buddhist thought!

Buddhism and epistemology

The importance of a sort of knowing which is also a seeing is evident in Buddhist thought. Buddhist thought has not thus far proven reducible to philosophy without a residual religious remainder, and *a fortiori* is not reducible to a single branch of philosophy such as epistemology.

In the 1990s contemporary Buddhists are not as much exercised by problems of epistemology and philosophical psychology as were those in the times of K. N. Jayatilleke and C. A. F. and T. W. Rhys Davids. For the most part, Buddhist concern with 'survival' in the psychological sense has been replaced by 'survival' in the ecological sense. Instead of how we could *know* that a stream-of-consciousness is neither exactly the same nor entirely different across lives, or even what would it *mean* to say 'neither the same nor different' in this case, contemporary focus is upon how can we *act* so as to promote a harmony with nature.

This change of emphasis is the result of many factors, including the successive move away from both epistemology and linguistic philosophy as orthodoxies in western philosophy towards a more pluralistic understanding of philosophical discourse.

Buddhism and ethics

Sexuality and gender issues

Very broadly speaking there are three attitudes towards sexuality which have found sanctioned expression in the three Buddhist vehicles: repression or denial of sexuality in Theravāda, accommodation of sexuality in Mahāyāna, and overcoming of sexuality by ritual use in Tantrayāna.

'Likes and dislikes' are to be set aside by the even-minded Buddhist adept according to Pali scripture. In Theravāda this applies even to sexual proclivities. Hence it is obvious that Theravāda offers no doctrinal support for homosexual or lesbian behaviour, for these behaviours would themselves be just other sorts of attachment. However, there is no basis provided for discrimination against those of alternative sexual orientation. All beings have 'Buddha-nature' and a chance for enlightenment, making Buddhism a progressive religious force. Robert Aitken (1984: 42) writes:

> My feeling is that with the encouragement of teacher and sangha, the individual member has a chance for personal realization through Zen practice, whether he or she is heterosexual or homosexual. Buddha nature is not either one and it is both.[1]

On south and east Asian Buddhism respectively, I. B. Horner (1975) and Diana Paul (1979) offer important perspectives on women in Buddhism. Important to those who, like Rita Gross (1993), seek a synthesis of feminism and Buddhism is K. R. Norman's (1990) revised edition of C. A. F. Rhys Davids's *Therigatha*.

William R. LaFleur (1992) explores both the ethics and the sociology of abortion in Japan. He calls attention to the Buddhist *mizuko kuyō* (funeral rites for aborted foetuses) and to the curious role Buddhism came to play in a Japan where ritual purification in Shinto shunned death and funerals as polluting. Since contemporary Buddhists sense the unity of all life and the continuities between lives and life-forms, it is self-consistent consistent that they cherish even foetal life. To expiate guilt and to keep the next birth from being that of 'hungry ghost' (Japanese *gaki*, Pali *peta*), the Japanese Buddhists have the funerary ritual for aborted foetuses and stillborn children. A contemporary ritual of this sort is given in the Diamond Sangha, a Zen meditation group in Hawaii. The text for this *mizuko kuyō* ('water child memorial service') is reproduced in Roshi Robert Aitken's (1988) work.[2]

Vegetarianism and animal rights

It should be noticed at the outset that the conceptual underpinnings of the western concern with animal well-being have to do with moral and legal rights in contradistinction to the Buddhist underpinnings of *paṭiccasamuppāda* ('causality') and *kamma* ('action'). Nevertheless some western ethical theorists argue in ways quite consistent with Buddhism.[3]

Robert Thurman's translation of Rock Edict I shows Aśoka as an ancient leader in the concern for the suffering of animals in that he was willing to reduce the numbers of animals used in the cooking in the royal kitchen with a view to eventually eliminating animal slaughter (in Eppsteimer 1988: 113).

Rafe Martin observes: 'After entering the world of the *Jatakas*, it becomes impossible not to feel more deeply for animals.' . . . Was not the Buddha a hare? a quail? a monkey, lion, deer or ox?' (in Eppsteimer 1988 : 100). Since large numbers of Buddhists are vegetarians, many contemporary Buddhists are sympathetic to one strand of ethics started by Peter Singer and Tom Regan.[4] It is a philosophically interesting question how far and in what ways loving kindness should extend in the order of being.

Explicating Pali Buddhism, I. B. Horner (1967 : 2) states that 'according to the Indian way of thinking, a certain form of life called "one facultied", *ekindriya jīva*, inhabits trees, plants, and the soil, and even water may have creatures or breathers (*sappāṇaka udaka*), in it'. While falling short of affirming a plant-life rebirth station, this idea appears to be a bridge between south Asian and east Asian Buddhism. In east Asian Mahāyāna Buddhism at least by the time of the *Lotus Sūtra* there is the emergence of an additional rebirth station, that of plant life. Itō Jakuchu, in apparent disregard of the Pali canonical injunction that to achieve final *nirvāṇa* one must return to the human state, depicts 'Vegetable *Parinirvāṇa*' (Hickman and Sato 1989:164–5). In his research on Itō Jakuchu, Yoshiaki Shimizu observes that Jakuchu's 'Vegetable *Parinirvāṇa*' reflects the traditional Buddhist idea of 'Buddha-nature' as being in all things, including trees and plants (Hickman and Sato 1989 : 164).

The emergence of a plant-life rebirth station in at least some Buddhist texts such as the *Lotus Sūtra* gives rise to the philosophical issue of just why meat eating is prohibited by some Buddhist groups who think nothing of eating plants. One answer is that doing the minimal harm possible to other beings is all that one can do; eating salad is preferable to eating both steak and salad, even if thereby one is not entirely blameless. Whether some Buddhists will regard it as morally obligatory to eat synthetic food should an appropriate technology for producing it become widely available remains to be seen.

There seems to be no *necessary* connection between being a Buddhist and being a vegetarian. It may even have been fortunate for Buddhism's development from south Asian forms to east Asian forms that it was not inflexible on the point of meat eating. Otherwise Buddhism would undoubtedly have met with stiff resistance from the Chinese, accustomed as they are to a highly developed meat-eating culinary tradition.

In a careful and textually based study, Horner (1967) asserts what is an appropriate conclusion for this section:

> The early Buddhist attitude to warfare, agriculture, and meat-eating was more mixed than its attitude to blood sacrifices. It made no wholehearted condemnation of these practices although they all entail the taking of life. But it did what it could to lessen their incidence and popularity. (1967 : 12)

Horner goes on to observe that there are two crucial distinctions with regard to taking life for Buddhism, that between intentional and unintentional behaviour and that between human and animal life. Unintentional taking of life is not regarded as an offence. Intentional taking of life in the case of either human or animal victims is regarded as an offence, although the penalty is less in the case of animal victims (1967 : 18–19).

War, peace and non-violence

As Thurman points out in his translation of Rock Edict IV, non-violence to animals and humans is linked in King Priyadarsi's 'abstention from killing animals and from cruelty to living beings' (Eppstemier 1988 : 113). Contemporary Buddhists are, for the most part, pacifists in that they oppose both physical violence and warfare. The connection between Zen and *bushidō*, however, would suggest that Buddhists are skilful in defending their own turf when necessary. Despite the fact that there have been wars and conflicts in which Buddhist monks played roles, there is a marked anti-war mentality amongst Buddhists today.

Since the Vietnam War occurred in a Buddhist country, Vietnamese Buddhists have been especially mindful of war's negative effects. The self-immolation of a Buddhist nun, Chi Mai, related by Cao Ngoc Phuong, serves as an important reminder of the strength of Buddhist commitments (Eppsteimer 1988 : 155–69).

A Vietnamese Buddhist monk of considerable popular influence is Thich Nhat Hahn, author of several mainly aphoristic works. Nhat Hahn is well known for his activities as chairman of the Vietnamese Buddhist Peace delegation during the Vietnam War.

Race, class and power

Many American Buddhists have become sufficiently self-aware to agree with the sentiment of Gary Snyder (Eppsteimer 1988) that institutional Buddhism has been all too ready to accept or ignore the inequalities and tyrannies of various political systems in which Buddhism has found itself. Some, like Robert Aitken (Eppsteimer 1988), think that the example of Shaku Soen's support for Japanese militarists reveals the danger of letting Buddhism be co-opted by fascist ideology. There is, as Nelson Foster observes, a reticence to engage in social action that characterizes the more reclusive, less activist strand of contemporary Buddhism. Exceptions among some Asian exemplars of Buddhism who have been both selfless and socially active, such as the self-immolating Buddhist nun Chi Mai, should be noted.

George P. Malalasekera (1958/1978) speaks to this important issue, which divides Sinhalese from Tamils and blacks from whites. Sallie King (1991) emphasizes an important strand of Mahāyāna Buddhist philosophy which leaves no room for racism of any kind. For if the 'Buddha-nature' is inherent in all beings, then all beings are in one important sense equal. In the Chinese Buddhist view 'the belief in the *icchantika*, the one forever incapable of attaining Buddhahood, is expressly rejected. At its basis, then, the Buddha-nature concept is an optimistic and encouraging doctrine' (1991 : 1).

Environmental ethics

Contemporary Buddhists generally emphasize the doctrine of dependent co-arising (*paṭiccasamuppāda*), and take a 'seamless web' view of the universe. Accordingly they are very sensitive to the impact of destructive forces on the ecosystem. Buddhist ecological ethics are explored in Callicott and Ames (1989). In A. H. Badiner's *Dharma Gaia*, Wm R. LaFleur discusses the possibility that plants and trees may be enlightened (1990).

According to Buddhist thought everything is intimately connected to everything else in the flux of process. A corollary of this view is that what impacts upon a situation far away may very well impact upon one's own situation.

At this point the philosophical issue arises as to whether the relative distance or proximity of a subject to a situation affects moral responsibility.[5] If (as the nexus of *paṭiccasamuppāda* or 'causality' would indicate to Buddhists) everything is connected to everything else, then distance does not diminish moral responsibility. On such a view, it is not a fact isolated from one's own situation that others are starving, regardless of whether they be far away or nearby.

In this section of the chapter the themes treated are indeed on the 'cutting edge' of Mañjuśrī's swift sword today. But if Nan-ch'uan [Nanchuan] can be hailed now for his legendary act of cutting the cat in two (ostensibly in order to dissolve a monastic dispute over possession of the cat), it is unlikely that contemporary Buddhism can be reduced to the 'politically correct' on issues such as animal rights.[6]

Despite the trendiness of some popular writing on Buddhism today, there remains a fundamental conservatism which especially obtains to expatriate Buddhism. Writers such as Nelson Foster and Gary Snyder emphasize the importance of vigilance against an unduly conservative posture in expatriate Buddhism. As Snyder points out, institutional Buddhism has been all too ready to accept or ignore the inequalities and tyrannies of the political systems it found itself under: 'This can be death to Buddhism, because it is death to any meaningful function of compassion' (Eppsteimer 1988 : 83).

Economic well-being and ethics

Rahula observes that to eradicate crime, the economic condition of the people should be improved. In the same work, Thurman explores the role of Aśoka, suggesting that Aśoka may be a model for the Buddhist social activist (Eppsteimer 1988 : 116–17).

One view about the relationship between economics and Buddhist ethics is that the ideal form of government is the same for both Marx and Buddha. This view is argued for by Piyasena Dissanayake (1977). Dissanayake presents Pali textual exegesis of the Buddhist view of politics and economics, emphasizing such themes as the elimination of poverty, the eradication of private property, and the establishment of a selfless society.

Another view is that one faces a forced option between Buddhism and Communism. Dissanayake's inclusivist view of the relations between Marxism and Buddhism contrasts markedly with the exclusivist view of Ernst Benz (1965). Whilst noticing similarities on some points between Buddhism and Marxism, Benz concludes his study by warning of 'the danger that Buddhists will confound their own variety of Communism with the Marxist brand' (1965: 234).

In the wake of the crumbling of the Berlin wall and talk of openness and restructuring in the former Soviet Union, it is difficult to subscribe entirely to such one-sided views as incline towards either nationalistic Communism or Communist phobia. An attempt at attaining a more balanced picture which emphasizes both the strengths and the weaknesses of Marx's view is articulated by N. V. Banerjee (1978).

Ninian Smart has recently commented on the danger of making Buddhism itself serve the nationalistic sentiments of some Sri Lankans for political ends. Perhaps the south Asians may learn from the experience of their east Asian Buddhist brothers and sisters, and take a lesson from the case of Shaku Soen so as not to see Buddhism once more defiled by militarists.[7]

Buddhism, metaphysics and ontology

It is arguable that metaphysical presuppositions are inherent in world-view formation, such that a sharp wedge between Buddhism of even the earliest sort and metaphysics cannot be validly driven. Although one usually thinks of metaphysics as a self-conscious enterprise, metaphysical commitments can obtain even if one is not aware of them, buried, as it were, beneath the surface of language. The terms of a particular language demarcate the real from the unreal for a user of that language. On this view a metaphysical system is a working out of the implications of linguistic structures (for example the subject–object and substance–attribute distinctions). One may not care to construct a metaphysical system, but metaphysical implications cannot be absent from one's thought in so far as one employs language. Buddhists, for example, think of suffering as a *real* feature of existence, recognition of which is basic.

But Nāgārjuna may be interpreted (along with deconstructionists) as opting for a provisional use of language such that one is not led into metaphysical commitments at all. Even the Buddha's own language use to convey the *Dharma* is sometimes characterized as provisional. Is the best 'philosophy' then no philosophy at all?

So there is controversy in interpreting whether, and if so how, metaphysics plays a role in Buddhism. Proponents of the thesis that Buddhism is a form of empiricism (the early Kalupahana) have often rejected the idea that metaphysics can be found in Buddhism.[8] It may be more correct to say that it is speculation that is eschewed in early Buddhism, rather than that Buddhism holds no metaphysical implications.

Buddhism and the philosophy of religion

General works on the philosophy of religion which include Buddhism are few and far between.[9] Historically it is interesting to note that, although Aśoka was himself a Buddhist lay disciple (*upāsaka*), he did not make Buddhism the state religion (Thurman in Eppsteimer 1988 : 114–16). This shows an exemplary tolerance towards other religions on the part of one of the earliest Buddhist patrons.

Despite Dharmasiri (1974), who shows in detail why Christian concepts of the creator God have no application in early (south Asian) Buddhism, comparative Buddhist–Christian work in journals such as *Buddhist–Christian Studies* (Honolulu) flourishes. It is written mainly from east Asian perspectives compatible with Whitehead's process philosophy and the work of John Cobb.

Arthur L. Herman (1976/1990) is worth consulting as an example of philosophically stimulating work on parallel problems in East and West of interest to philosophers of religion. He is a persistent enquirer who is inclined to probe in true Socratic fashion what many take as obvious.

From east Asian perspectives, the Buddhist–Christian dialogue may be viewed as the greatest opportunity for Buddhists to discover more about their own positions since the days of the Silk Road trade. Much of this dialogue, however, is still emergent.

As William LaFleur observes, the philosophy of Nishida Kitarō and that of the Kyoto school which he spawned came over the decades to be preoccupied with questions of the relationship between Buddhism and philosophical discourse. In the beginning, however, some of Nishida's students, such as (the Marxist) Tosaka Jun, had no interest in Buddhism. After Nishida's death in 1945 the Kyoto school was strongly influenced by existentialism, especially through the work of Nishitani and Hisamatsu Shin'ichi. For these thinkers one main problem was how to be religious without recourse to deity, and Buddhist tradition was studied with a view to finding a solution from within. Shin'ichi Hisamatsu's article 'Characteristics of oriental nothingness' in *Philosophical Studies of Japan* (1960) is one such attempt. Another is represented by Watsuji Tetsuro, who followed his studies of Nietzsche and Kierkegaard with *The Practical Philosophy of Early Buddhism* (*Genshi Bukkyo no Jissen Tetsugaku* (1927), briefly discussed by Yuasa (1987 : 86).[10]

The influence of analytic philosophy on contemporary Buddhist philosophy in Japan is minuscule compared to that of existentialism and German philosophy. Schopenhauer, for example, is much more important in Japanese philosophical circles than in Anglo-American ones. Their earlier and continuing affinity with German developments occupied the Japanese at a time when the analytic tradition was developing in the Anglo-American world. For the most part, the Kyoto school regards analytic philosophers as insufficiently attentive to the core problems of human existence, especially that of death. The massive amount of death and suffering at Hiroshima and Nagasaki could not be far from the minds of intellectuals in Japan immediately after the Second World War.

Instead of viewing analytic techniques as useful for clarifying problems in the philosophy of religion, Kyoto school thinkers tend to regard philosophical analysis as a distraction from the more fundamental problems of human existence. Influenced by Martin Heidegger, Nishitani addresses himself to the problem of nihilism, arguing that the problem of modern nihilism is more easily dealt with by Buddhists than by Christians.

Just as they are comparatively unmoved by the niceties of analytic philosophy, so too the 'God is dead' movement is irrelevant to the members of the Kyoto school. Both Keiji Nishitani and Watsuji Tetsuro held that since the problem of the existence of God does not arise in Buddhism, the philosophical-cultural 'reaction' of the 'God is dead' movement is irrelevant in the Kyoto school context.

Masao Abe (1985) contributes to a deep understanding of what it means to be a Buddhist philosopher in our time and illuminates some of the hidden presuppositions of western tradition. Overall Abe's emphasis is on our common humanity.

Buddhism and aesthetics

One of the best ways to cultivate an appreciation of Buddhism is by understanding Buddhist art and its interplay with nature. If the etymological meaning of *aesthetikos* as a type of perception is emphasized rather than problems in analytic aesthetics, then aesthetics can provide a fruitful introduction to Buddhism. Exposure to images and patterns in nature and in art is essential.[11]

Eliot Deutsch in an exemplary monograph (1975) makes the problems of aesthetics emerge from a consideration of particular works of art in India, China and Japan. Hisamatsu Shin'ichi (1982) articulates an important and accessible work on aesthetics. William R. LaFleur (1988) is a well-written work of special interest for its perspective on Japanese aesthetics.

Buddhism and the philosophy of mind

Here the work of Paul J. Griffiths looms large. Griffiths 1986 is a major contribution to the field, having as it does the twin virtues of Sanskritic detail and serious attention to philosophical arguments. A prolific writer, Griffiths is amongst the very best of the younger generation of Buddhologists.

Steven Collins's work (1982) presents an important study of Theravāda Buddhism from a perspective that will especially interest those trained in the humanities. A note-worthy feature of this work is attention to various kinds of imagery in Buddhist thought, such as vegetation imagery.

A synthesis of Pali Buddhism and contemporary philosophy of religion is presented in Hoffman (1987). He argues against charges that early Buddhism is unintelligible and pessimistic. Mind plays a crucial role in early Buddhism, particularly in connection with the doctrine of rebirth, a view which fits snugly into the conception background of early Buddhism but which may be questioned by philosophically inclined outsiders. The thesis that Buddhism is a form of empiricism is rejected in favour of a view of meaning that does not require falsification. Eternal life is understood as 'not mortal' (*amata*), not limited by birth and death. Throughout, Hoffman advocates and exemplifies a philosophical approach to Pali Buddhist texts.

One problem that needs to be addressed directly by philosophers of mind who draw parallels with eastern thought is the charge of reductionism. Nathan Katz's (1982) anthology presents several contributors (for example Trugpa, Katz and Guenther) who demonstrate awareness of the problem of reductionism, and some (Trungpa and Katz) who point specifically to a problem of reducing eastern thought to fit western categories. But reductionism can take various forms, and although it is doubtful whether Buddhism can be reduced to any western psychological or philosophical school without distortion, it is equally doubtful whether Buddhism can be reduced to western therapeutic training without remainder. One important question which Katz (1982) gives rise to is: to what extent is a psychological interpretation of Buddhism in terms of western categories possible, so that Buddhism is 'explained' without being 'explained away'? A reflective answer to this question would take into account that Buddhism is not merely a matter of technique, but a matter of religious and philosophical commitment as well.

On the east Asian side, a detailed, philosophically interesting yet interdisciplinary study of mind–body is presented in Yuasa (1987). Continuing the tradition of Watsuji Tetsuro and in contradistinction to western views such as that of Descartes, Yuasa emphasizes that mind–body unity is an achievement rather than an essential given. In this he calls attention to the Japanese Buddhist concern with deepening integration between mind and body in contrast to the European concern with how this interaction takes place. Yuasa focuses upon variation in mind instead of on what the mind–body is essentially. The interface between science and religion is opened up in this comparative work, and attention is paid to Japanese thinkers such as Watsuji, Nishida, Dōgen and Kukai. Erudite and stimulating, Yuasa's work is worthy of careful consideration, and the translators Thomas Kasulis and Shigenori Nagatomo are to be commended for introducing his work in the West.

Buddhism and the philosophy of science

Puligandla (1981) and Capra (1983) explore parallels between modern physics and eastern mysticism in south and east Asian contexts respectively, and have called attention to the experientialist orientation of Asian philosophies and their affinity with physics. Whether, and if so in what sense, Asian philosophies may be rightly called 'empirical', however, is a moot question.[12]

Turning to the Japan of the early twentieth century, one finds Inoue and Murakami working to reconcile ideas of karmic causality with modern western causality views. They also compare Buddhism with science and Christianity, but usually more closely with science than with Christianity.

In one way J. E. Lovelock's 'Gaia hypothesis' (roughly, that the earth is a self-regulative system) coheres with Buddhist ideas about causality and interconnectedness (1979/1990: xii, 11). In another way, however, the insistence that it is a faulty assumption that people bear a special relation to the planet as 'owners' or at least 'tenants' in contrast to other sorts of beings militates against Buddhist ecologically aware social activism and suggests a *laissez-faire* attitude to the planet (1979/1990: 145). It will survive, no matter what humankind does, Gaia suggests. A rhetorical Buddhist rejoinder might be: without ecological good sense, will the earth survive in a form permitting the existence of beings capable of meditation?[13] If not, is not that a good reason for humankind to intervene in natural processes in potentially salutary ways?[14]

BUDDHISM AND THE SCHOOLS OF PHILOSOPHY

Analytic philosophy

Comparisons between analytic philosophy and Buddhist thought often cut both ways. First, certainly Buddhist suspicion of substantialist sorts of metaphysics, God and soul, is in keeping with the tenor of mainstream twentieth-century philosophy. But second, equally salient is Buddhist commitment to a path of salvation, in contrast to mainstream twentieth-century philosophy. As a consequence of the second point, it is sometimes erroneously thought that western analytic philosophy and Asian philosophy are simply incommensurable, such that comparisons between them are jejune and unacceptable. The inadequacy of this view was shown by the work of Chris Gudmunsen (1977), and, in a more introductory way, by Jacobson (1970).

More recently Paul Griffiths (1986), although working in theology departments, has called attention to the logic of the Buddhist tradition in such a way as to do a real service to analytic philosophy in the broad sense.[15] Griffiths's (1994) exposition of the idea of buddhahood has the merits of being classificatory, substantive and inclusive of extra-systematic criticism.

Pragmatism

The Buddhist soteriological method is often styled 'pragmatic' in view of the importance attached to 'skillful means' (Pye 1978). Views of Buddhist pragmatism are developed by Upadhyaya (1971) and by Kalupahana (1987).

As Kenneth K. Inada and Nolan P. Jacobson (1984) show in their introduction, there is ample ground for discussion on the interface between Buddhology and philosophy by way of Alfred N. Whitehead and C. S. Peirce. However, the editors do not uncritically exhalt Whitehead in so far as the interpretation of Buddhism is concerned. Although the contributors to the anthology are virtually united in their rejection of substance–attribute metaphysics and subject–object epistemology, beyond this point each uses the occasion as an opportunity for developing their own thoughts in diverse directions.

Existentialism

With its emphasis on the anxiety of the human condition (compare and contrast with *dukkha* or suffering), the importance of choice, thrownness, etc., existentialism is a fertile ground for comparisons with Buddhist thought. Padmasiri de Silva (1974) is one of those to emphasize this point. Elsewhere Padmasiri de Silva (1973) specifically forges links between Buddhism and Freud. If Schopenhauer is an existentialist, then it is arguable that one of the school's leading representatives is sympathetic to Buddhism.[16]

Phenomenology

Ramakrishna Puligandla has emphasized the use of the term 'phenomenology' as applied to Buddhist and Hindu thought and experience. Puligandla (1985) shows the application of phenomenology to 'the way of knowledge' in Hinduism, but *mutatis mutandis* some of what he says there may be applied to Buddhism as well. Puligandla 1981 is a blistering attack on what he regards as the sterility and inanity of contemporary Anglo-American analytic philosophy. Puligandla argues for a view of the self (not soul or ego) as awareness, opposes reductionism, and favours a view of philosophy as concerned with understanding the nature of man and world. Puligandla's philosophical approach throughout is admirable.

Deconstruction and hermeneutics

The recent trend in western philosophy called 'deconstruction' also appears to have some parallels in Asian philosophy. Nāgārjuna, for example, may be regarded as offering a deconstruction of standard Buddhist doctrines while nevertheless saluting the Buddha. Through the efforts of western scholars such as Wm LaFleur one hears of Japanese works in a deconstructionist vein.[17] An interest in 'hermeneutics', variously interpreted, occurs in recent works such as Lopez 1988 and Timm 1992.

Comparative philosophy

'Comparative philosophy' is a label for a very loosely unified movement of philosophers who regard attention to oriental thought as significant for their philosophical work. Paul Masson-Oursel (1926) has numerous references to Buddhism throughout his work. His favoured approach is 'positivity in philosophy' with special emphasis on logic, metaphysics and psychology which works towards the goal of scientific progress and an appreciation of the history of ideas.

Many comparativists are members of the Society for Asian and Comparative Philosophy, begun by Charles A. Moore[18] at the University of Hawaii just after the Second World War.

It is difficult to generalize accurately about comparative philosophy. Some of these philosophers believe that there are philosophical problems which are 'the same' or at least 'similar' when East and West meet and that the main job of philosophy is to focus on philosophical problems; others are interested in a 'descriptive science' of philosophy which would be incomplete without the inclusion of Asian material. Some have an agenda (hidden or not) of championing what they regard as the superiority of selected Asian thinkers or traditions; others have no such *a priori* agenda (although in practice it often turns out in their work that Asian thinkers or traditions are vindicated in the face of criticism). Some take an ontological approach and suffuse their philosophizing with religious overtones; others take the logician's approach and let the chips fall where they may. With such plurality even within 'comparative philosophy', the term is probably more useful to library cataloguers than to philosophers themselves. In this chapter its importance is that Buddhism is often treated by philosophers who consider themselves comparativists.

Almost by default, the Japanese have been much more enterprising in working in cross-cultural philosophy than either the Koreans or the Chinese.[19] Even D. T. Suzuki (1968), who is not usually thought of as a comparative philosopher but as a Zen thinker, has a comparative essay on Meister Eckhart.

Hajime Nakamura, in *Kindai Nihon Tetsugaku Shisōka Jiten*, has dictionary entries on both Enryo Inoue (1858–1919) and Sensho Murakami (1851–1929). These pioneering figures in early twentieth-century Japan attempt to defend Buddhism in view of the impact of western philosophy, for example by considering the concept of *karma* in relation to western ideas of causality.[20]

Masao Abe (1985) deals with western thinkers such as Nietzsche and Tillich, while relating his thought to main trends in interpreting religion and science in culture. Throughout the Zen perspective is evident.

CONTEMPORARY BUDDHIST PHILOSOPHY IN THE 1990s AND BEYOND

In a chapter of this kind the reader may justifiably hope for some sense of 'what's happening now'. Even as this sentence is typed the 'now' recedes into the past and the present slides onward towards the publication date. I shall venture a few remarks without the aid of any New Age crystal ball.

First, from the economic point of view, one notices a movement of research, grants and grant-related activities towards, on the one hand, east Asia (especially Japan) and on the other hand towards Tibet. Even scholars with training in south Asia appear to be shifting somewhat to accommodate east Asian Mahāyāna perspectives on their work. And then there are the many untranslated Tibetan manuscripts (in the Harvard Yen-Ching Institute, for example). There are doubtless political and economic realities behind these current emphases.

Second, from the social points of view, there is the rise of numerous meditation institutes as listed in the useful reference work by Don Morreale (1988) and also in the *International Buddhist Directory* (Boston: Wisdom Publications, 1985). Rick Fields (1981) tells how the lotus unfolds in America, as Russell Webb (1989) does, albeit with a more scholarly focus, for Europe.

There is even the rise of a new type of meta-level institute exemplified by the Buddhist leader, Havanpola Ratanasara, who organizes Buddhists from several cultures in his work in Los Angeles through programmes of the College of Buddhist Studies, and is active in dialogue with other religions as well. Buddhist groups in the United States easily become isolated linguistic and cultural enclaves. Yet some have seen the need to increase cooperation between these enclaves and between Buddhists altogether and the mainstream (predominately Christian) culture. Whereas Ratanasara's enterprise would be a difficult undertaking in any specific Asian country, western countries such as the United States are in a good position to facilitate the emergence of these meta-institutes which attempt to transcend ethnic enclaves, oppose cultural tribalism, and make for mutual understanding among Buddhists in the contemporary world.

As for social and academic opportunities, the meeting of college professors through the National Endowment for the Humanities Summer Institutes and Summer Seminars which pertain to Asia function effectively to promote knowledge of Asian culture, of which Buddhism is one element. In addition, the Summer Seminars on the Sutras (sponsored by Jemez Bodhi Mandala, New Mexico) combine meditation practice with scholarly endeavour. Honourable mention should be made of the Kuroda Institute for extending substantial scholarly support for publications.

Third, there is the development of political activism which is explicitly Buddhistic in its vegetarian, feminist, and animal rights orientation in ways that cut across sectarian lines. Directories such as those mentioned above facilitate contacts among those activists interested in Buddhism. On the European international scene, the events contributing towards a more unified European alliance and those conditioning a decline in the heretofore monolithic Soviet domination of minorities together set the stage for the emergence of more east European publications sympathetic to Buddhistic thinking. A prominent example is Yugoslavia's quarterly, *Kulture Istoka* or *Eastern Culture*, edited by Dusan Paijin in Novi Beograd, Yugoslavia.

Fourth, the development of communications media such as computers, specifically the use of computers for day-to-day on-line communications (such as Indology, Buddha-l and Buddhist lists and text transmission work (such as the Pali Text Society's Pali Canon CD-ROM Project), facilitates interaction amongst scholars of Buddhism. Various newsletters and magazines, such as *Tricycle*, *The Inquiring Mind* (Barre, Massachusetts), *Southern Dharma* (Hot Springs, North Carolina) and *Dharma Voice* (Los Angeles), facilitate communication for the meditation-minded. These media also play an important role in communicating with those who are neither Buddhist scholars nor meditators by providing information.

Factors such as the foregoing contribute towards a concrescence of Buddhistic feeling, what Nolan Pliny Jacobson called 'thinking from the soft underside of the mind'. It is hoped that one result will be a sympathetic attunement amongst diverse Buddhist groups such that they seek points of cooperation where there are sectarian divisions.

The construction of a deep theoretical basis for Buddhist ethics taking into account the work of Saddhatissa and others which provides a unifying framework of intra-Buddhistic cooperation is one possibility. Another challenging task would be the construction of a 'philosophy of Buddhist religion' (distinct from both the entirely *emic* (or internal) 'Buddhist philosophy' and the entirely *etic* (or external) 'philosophy of Christian religion') which would highlight conceptual problems of interest specifically to philosophers.

As Buddhism becomes more and more an established religion in western countries one expects to see more instances of transformation and not just instances of Buddhist–Christian dialogue. For philosophers without a personal stake in Buddhism one expects that the approach of 'analytical rigour tempered with intellectual openness' exemplified so very well by the late B. K. Matilal will also continue.[21]

CONCLUSION

In this contemporary issue-orientated chapter, the links between contemporary Buddhists and concern with pacifism, ecology, animal rights, women's rights and gender issues have been apparent. This pattern gives rise to the philosophical question whether there is any necessary connection between being a Buddhist and being committed to such social agendas as these.

Suppose that tomorrow a new Buddhist sect was founded, producing new Buddhist scripture, new rituals, etc., but it was opposed to one or more of the social agendas just mentioned. Would one rightly say, 'that's impossible – they can't be Buddhists!'?

This thought experiment suggests that the connection between Buddhism and such social agendas is purely a contingent, historical one. The possibility of these connections owes much to the vitality of the ongoing scriptural tradition and to the processes of interpretation and commentary. Although it just happens to be the case in contemporary Buddhist thought that there are such links, *that* there are is a very important fact about the present subject.

What counts as being a Buddhist is not something that can be predicted in advance of the development of Buddhist tradition. Consequently the concepts of 'Buddhist' and 'Buddhism' are analogous to other such 'open-textured' concepts as 'artwork', 'religion' and 'scripture'.

NOTES

Special thanks go to NEH for funding its Summer Seminar on Buddhism and Culture at UCLA in 1989. There William LaFleur, Steven Teiser and several seminar participants offered information, criticism and advice on writing this chapter. The Greater Philadelphia Philosophy Consortium programme of inter-library cooperation opened up access to many important materials for writing this chapter. Specifically, I am grateful for the help of South Asia Bibliographer Kanta Bhatia, who facilitated my library research on this project at the University of Pennsylvania's Charles Patterson Van Pelt Library with characteristic kindness and technical expertise.

1 In 1977 Judge King-Hamilton sentenced poet James Kirkup for blasphemous libel in what became known as 'The *Gay News* trial'. This provided the context for Bhikkhu Sangharakshita's pamphlet *Buddhism and Blasphemy* (London: Windhorse Press), and for subsequent philosophical discussions by Frank J. Hoffman, 'Remarks on blasphemy', *Scottish Journal of Religious Studies* 4(2) (1983) and Roy Perrett, 'Blasphemy', *Sophia* 26(2) (1987), and Hoffman's rejoinder, 'More on blasphemy', *Sophia* 28(2) (1989).

2 *Kuyō* is found in *Japanese–English Buddhist Dictionary* (Tokyo: Daito Shuppansha, 1984), p. 189, but both *mikuko* and *mizuko kuyō* are conspicuous by their absence. Does the oversight suggest scholarly embarrassment about watery worlds and women's concerns? or is it rather that to list one such *kuyō* would open up a lexicographer's Pandora's Box of considerations about needles of seamstresses and other objects, animate as well as inanimate, for which there are *kuyō*?

3 In the popular textbook *Elements of Moral Philosophy* (Philadelphia: Temple University Press, 1986), James Rachels argues that it is simply because animals *suffer* that inflicting unnecessary cruelty upon them is morally wrong.

4 See Peter Singer, *Animal Liberation* (New York: Random House, 1990) and the article by Christoper Chapple in Tom Regan (ed.), *Animal Sacrifices* (Philadelphia: Temple University Press, 1986) for instances of socially orientated literature sympathetic to Buddhist ethics.

5 In *Elements of Moral Philosophy*, James Rachels raises precisely this issue of whether distance can affect moral responsibility.

6 Case 63, 'Nan-ch'uan cuts the cat in two', in Katsuki Sekida (trans.), *Two Zen Classics: Mumonkan and Heikiganroko* (New York: Weatherhill, 1977), pp. 319–20.

7 See Aitken on Shaku Sōen in Eppsteimer 1988.
8 For treatments of the Buddhism empiricism thesis see Kalansuriya 1987 and Hoffman 1987.
9 General philosophical works especially worth reading for their openness to Buddhist perspectives are William H. Capitan, *Philosophy of Religion* (Indianapolis: Pegasus, 1972), John H. Hick, *Philosophy of Religion*, 3rd edn (Englewood Cliffs: Prentice-Hall, 1983) and Paul Knitter and John H. Hick, *The Myth of Christian Uniqueness* (Maryknoll: Orbis Books, 1988).
10 William R. LaFleur *et al.* have a translation of some of Watsuji Tetsuro (1889–1960) underway with the cooperation of Princeton University Press.
11 For a south Asian perspective Ananda K. Coomaraswamy, *The Dance of Shiva* (New York: Dover, 1985), provides a valuable point of departure, as does Kakuzo Okakura, *The Book of Tea* (New York: Dover, 1964) on the east Asian side. Philosophers interested in Asian aesthetics and Buddhism would do well to read Arthur Waley (trans.), *The Nō Plays of Japan* (New York: Grove Press, 1957) and savor the Buddhistic undercurrents.
12 Conceptually, the 'empirical' must be distinguished from the 'experiental', for not everything that is experiential is empirical. Textually, the *Jatakas* and other Buddhist texts do not always deal with putative empirical truths. As Per K. Sorensen's translation of Candrakirti's *Trisaranasaptati* states, 'the *modus operandi* of a Wish-Granting-Gem is beyond the scope of empirical verification' (Vienna: University of Vienna, 1986).
13 For a stimulating critique of Buddhist ecology see Ian Harris, 'How environmentalist is Buddhism?', *Religion* 21 (April 1991), 101–14. Against Kalupahana and Inada, Harris argues: 'If nature is the realm of complex and mutually conditioning interconnectedness represented by the term, *pratityasamutpada*, unilateral actions by human agents can have, at best, unpredictable results' (p. 104). This assumes an ordinary human agent, however, not one with Buddhist *abhiññā* (psychic powers) who can in some sense 'see causality'.
14 As for socio-political thought, Buddhism has no necessary identification with either nationalist right-wing elements or left-wing elements. Sri Lankan Walpola Rahula, Japan's Shaku Soen and others have exhibited nationalistic consciousness. Not without its champions, such as the young David who slew the Goliath Christian missionary in public debate during the heated *Panadura* controversy in Sri Lanka, Buddhism can indeed be a potent social force. Gombrich 1988 concludes with a chapter on 'Current trends, new problems'.
15 A prolific writer of detailed scholarly articles, Griffiths has recently produced (with Noriaki Hakamaya) *The Realm of Awakening: Chapter Ten of Asanga's Mahayanasamgraha* (Oxford: Oxford University Press, 1989). Introduction by John P. Keenan.
16 In this connection see Bryan Magee, *The Philosophy of Schopenhauer* (Oxford: Oxford University Press, 1983) and Bhikkhu Nanajivako's monograph, *Schopenhauer and Buddhism* (Kandy: Buddhist Publication Society).
17 For example, Nakamura Yūjirō, *Nishida Tetsugaku no Datsu Kōchiku* (*Deconstructing Nishida's Philosophy*) (Tokyo: Iwanarni Shoten 1987).
18 Charles A. Moore, *Philosophy: East and West* (Salem: Ayer Co., 1944); *Philosophy and Culture, East and West: East–West Philosophy in Practical Perspective* (Honolulu: University of Hawaii Press, 1962). Charles Moore's edited works, *The Chinese Mind* (Honolulu: University of Hawaii Press, 1967) and *The Japanese Mind* (Honolulu: University of Hawaii Press, 1967) show the very sympathetic but not carefully critical treatment of oriental thought characteristic of the opening phase of comparative philosophy.
19 Exceptions to this general pattern may be found in works by the Korean Choi, Min-hong, and by the Chinese Chang, Chung-yuan.
20 For additional details and translations see Kathleen Stagg's articles in *Monumenta Nipponica*.
21 *Times of India*, 11 June 1991.

REFERENCES

Abe, Masao (1985) *Zen and Western Thought*, ed. Wm LaFleur with foreword by J. Hick, Honolulu: University of Hawaii Press.
Abe, Masao and Ives, Christoper (trans.) (1990) *An Inquiry into the Good* by Kitaro Nishida, New Haven: Yale University Press.
Aitken, Robert (1984) *The Mind of Clover*, San Francisco: North Point Press.
Ames, Roger T. and Callicott, J. Baird (1989) *Nature in Asian Traditions of Thought*, Albany: SUNY Press.
Aoyama, Shundo (1990) *Zen Seeds: Reflections of a Female Priest*, trans. P. Dai-en Bennage, Tokyo: Kosei.
Aronson, Harvey B. (1980) *Love and Sympathy in Theravada Buddhism*, Delhi: Motilal Banarsidass.
Badiner, Allan Hunt (ed.) (1990) *Dharma Gaia: A Harvest of Essays in Buddhism and Ecology*. Berkeley: Parallax Press.
Banerjee, N. V. (1978) *Buddhism and Marxism: A Study in Humanism*, New Delhi: Orient Longmans.
Benz, Ernst (1965) *Buddhism or Communism: Which Holds the Future of Asia?*, New York: Doubleday.
Capra, Fritzoff (1983) *The Tao of Physics: An Exploration of Parallels between Modern Physics and Eastern Mysticism*, Boulder: Shambala.
Chang, Chun-yuan (trans.) (1969) *Original Teachings of Ch'an Buddhism*, New York: Pantheon Books.
Collins, Steven (1982) *Selfless Persons*, Cambridge: Cambridge University Press.
Deutsch, Eliot (1975) *Comparative Aesthetics*, Honolulu: University of Hawaii Press.
Dharmasiri, Gunapala (1974) *Buddhist Critique of the Christian Concept of God*, Colombo: Lake House.
Dissanayake, Piyasena (1977) *Political Thoughts of the Buddha*, Colombo: Dept of Cultural Affairs and Ratnakara Press.
Eppsteimer, Fred (1988) *The Path to Compassion: Writings on Socially Engaged Buddhism*, Berkeley: Parallax Press.
Ergardt, Jan T. (1977) *Faith and Knowledge in Early Buddhism*, Leiden: E. J. Brill.
Fields, Rick (1981) *Why the Swans Came to the Lake*, London/Boston: Shambala.
Gombrich, Richard F. (1971) *Precept and Practice*, Oxford: Oxford University Press.
—— (1988) *Theravada Buddhism*, London: Routledge & Kegan Paul.
Griffiths, Paul J. (1986) *On Being Mindless: Buddhist Meditation and the Mind–body Problem*, LaSalle, Ill.: Open Court.
—— (1994) *On Being Buddha: The Classical Doctrine of Buddhàhood*. Albany: SUNY Press.
Gross, Rita (1993) *Buddhism After Patriarchy*, Albany: SUNY Press.
Gudmunsen, Chris (1977) *Wittgenstein and Buddhism*, London: Macmillan.
Halbfass, Wilhelm (1988) *India and Europe*, Albany: SUNY Press.
—— (1991) *Tradition and Reflection*, Albany: SUNY Press.
Herman, Arthur (1976/1990) *The Problem of Evil and Indian Thought*, Delhi: Motilal Banarsidass.
Hickman, Money L. and Sato, Y. (1989) *the Paintings of Jakuchu*, New York: Abrams/Asia Society.
Hisamatsu, Shin'ichi (1971/1982) *Zen and the Fine Arts*, Tokyo: Kodansha.
Hoffman, Frank J. (1987) *Rationality and Mind in Early Buddhism*, Delhi: Motilal Banarsidass.
Hopkins, Jeffrey (ed.) (1988) *The Dalai Lama at Harvard: Lectures on the Buddhist Path to Peace*, Ithaca, N.Y.: Snow Lion.
Horner, Isaline Blew (1950) *The Basic Position of Sila*, Colombo: Buddha Sahitya Sabha/Lake House.

—— (1967) *Early Buddhism and the Taking of Life*, The Wheel 104, Colombo: Buddhist Publication Society. Originally published in 1945.

Horner, Isaline Blew (1975) *Women Under Primitive Buddhism: Laywomen and Almswomen*, Flushing: Asia Book Corporation.

Inada, Kenneth K. and Jacobson, Nolan P. (eds) (1984) *Buddhism and American Thinkers*, Albany: SUNY Press.

Jacobson, Nolan Pliny (1970) *Buddhism: The Religion of Analysis*, Carbondale: SIU Press.

—— (1983) *Buddhism and the Contemporary World*, Carbondale: SIU Press.

Jayatilleke, K. N. (1963) *Early Buddhist Theory of Knowledge*, London: Allen & Unwin.

Jayawickrama, N. A. (ed.) (1984) *Seminar on Buddhism's Contribution to World Culture and Peace*, Colombo: s.n.

Kalansuriya, A. D. P. (1987) *A Philosophical Analysis of Buddhist Notions: the Buddha and Wittgenstein*, Delhi: Sri Satguru Publications.

Kalupahana, David J. (1975) *Buddhist Philosophy*, Honolulu: University of Hawaii Press.

—— (1987) *The Principles of Buddhist Psychology*, Albany: SUNY Press.

—— (1992) *A History of Buddhist Philosophy*, Honolulu: University of Hawaii Press.

Kapleau, Philip (1967) *Three Pillars of Zen*, foreword by Huston Smith, Boston: Beacon Press.

—— (1981) *To Cherish All Life*. Rochester: The Zen Center.

Kasulis, Thomas P. (1981) *Zen Action/Zen Person*, Honolulu: University of Hawaii Press.

Katz, Nathan (1982) *Buddhist Images of Human Perfection*, Delhi: Motilal Banarsidass.

King, Sallie (1991) *Buddha Nature*, Albany: SUNY Press.

LaFleur, William R. (1988) *The Karma of Words*, Berkeley/Los Angeles: University of California Press.

—— (1992) *Liquid Life: Abortion and Buddhism in Japan*, Princeton: Princeton University Press.

Layman, Emma McCloy (1976) *Buddhism in America*, Chicago: Nelson Haal.

Lopez, Donald (ed.) (1988) *Buddhist Hermeneutics*, Honolulu: University of Hawaii Press.

Lovelock, J. E. (1979/1990) *Gaia: A New Look at Life on Earth*, Oxford: Oxford University Press.

McRae, John (1986) *The Northern School and the Foundation of Early Ch'an Buddhism*, Honolulu: University of Hawaii Press.

Malalasekera, George P. (1958/1978) *Buddhism and the Race Question*, Westport: Greenwood.

Masson-Oursel, Paul (1926) *Comparative Philosophy*, London: Kegan Paul.

Matilal, B. K. (1986) *Buddhist Logic and Epistemology*, Boston/Dordrecht: D. Reidel.

Matsuo, Hosaku (1987) *The Logic of Unity*, trans. and intro. by Kenneth Inada, Albany: SUNY Press.

Morreale, Don (1988) *Buddhist America: Centers, Retreats, Practices*, Santa Fe: John Muir.

Nagatomi, Masatoshi (ed.) (1980) *Essays in Honor of Daniel H. H. Ingalls*, Dordrecht/Boston: D. Reidel/Kluwer.

Nakamura, Hajime (1975) *Buddhism in Comparative Light*, New Delhi: Islam and the Modern Age Society.

Nhat hanh, Thich (1987) *Being Peace*, ed. Arnold Kotler, Berkeley: Parallax Press.

Norman, K. R. (1983) *Pali Literature*, Wiesbaden: O. Harrassowitz. Vol. VII, fasc. 2 of Jan Gonda's series, *A History of Indian Literature*.

Norman, K. R. and Rhys Davids, C. A. F. (1990) *Songs of the Early Buddhist Nuns*, Oxford: Pali Text Society/Wisdom.

Nyanaponika (Thera) (1976) *The Power of Mindfulness*, The Wheel 121/122, Kandy: Buddhist Publication Society.

Paul, Diana (1979/1985) *Women in Buddhism: Images of the Feminine in Mahayana Tradition*, Berkeley: University of California Press.

Potter, Karl (1963) *Presuppositions of India's Philosophies*, Englewood Cliffs, N.J.: Prentice-Hall.

—— (1983) *Encyclopedia of Indian Philosophies*, Delhi: Motilal Banarsidass.

Puligandla, Ramakrishna (1981) *An Encounter with Awareness*, Madras: Theosophical Publishing House.

—— (1985) *Jnana-yoga, the Way of Knowledge: An Analytical Interpretation*, Lanham, Md.: University Press of America.

Pye, Michael (1978) *Skillful Means*, London: Duckworth.

Rahula, Walpola (1974) *The Heritage of the Bhikkhu*, New York: Grove Press.

Ratnayaka, Shanta (1978) *Two Ways of Perfection: Buddhist and Christian*, Colombo: Lake House.

Regan, Tom (ed.) (1986) *Animal Sacrifices: Religious Perspectives on the Use of Animals in Science*, Philadelphia: Temple University Press.

Rouner, Leroy (ed.) (1990) *Celebrating Peace*, Notre Dame: University of Notre Dame Press.

Saddhatissa (1970) *Buddhist Ethics*, London: Allen & Unwin.

Silva, Padmasiri de (1973) *Buddhist and Freudian Psychology*, Colombo: Lake House.

—— (1974) *Tangles and Webs: Comparative Studies in Existentialism, Psychoanalysis and Buddhism*, foreword by Ninian Smart, Colombo: Lake House.

Smart, Ninian (1964) *Doctrine and Argument in Indian Philosophy*, London: Allen & Unwin.

—— (1981) *Beyond Ideology*, Gifford Lectures, University of Edinburgh, 1979–80, San Francisco: Harper & Row.

—— (1983) *Worldviews*, New York: Scribner's.

Suzuki, D. T. (1968) *On Indian Mahayana Buddhism*, New York: Harper & Row.

Tachibana, S. (1926) *The Ethics of Buddhism*, London: Oxford University Press.

Timm, Jeffrey (1992) *Traditional Hermeneutics*, Albany: SUNY Press.

Upadhyaya, K. N. (1971) *Early Buddhism and the Bhagavadgita*, Delhi: Motilal Banarsidass.

Yuasa, Yasuo (1987) *The Body*, Albany: SUNY Press.

Webb, Russell (1989) 'Contemporary European scholarship on Buddhism', in Tadeusz Skorupski (ed.) *Buddhica Brittanica*, series continua. Tring: Institute of Buddhist Studies.

Wiebe, Donald (ed.) (1986) *Concept and Empathy*, New York: NYU Press. Essays in the study of religion by Ninian Smart.

Wijesekera, O. H. de A., Jayatilleke, K. N. and Burtt, E. A. (1977) *Knowledge and Conduct*, The Wheel 50 a/b, Kandy: Buddhist Publication Society.

Part IV

CHINESE PHILOSOPHY

INTRODUCTION

Chinese philosophy has had a very long and complex history. In feudal pre-Qin Dynasty China (that is, before about 200 BC) some towering intellectual figures had already laid the foundation stones of the major philosophical schools of thought, well before the arrival of Buddhism from India. Of these philosophical schools perhaps the best known are Confucianism, Mohism, Daoism and Legalism.

Confucius (551–479 BC) in many ways epitomizes Chinese philosophy. A scholar of the highest order, he was also a teacher and a political adviser. Philosophy for him was centred on issues of political and personal merit, and was therefore a form of enquiry with great practical implications. His ideas concerning the nature of humanity, propriety, loyalty and so forth can be said to have set the agenda very much for later philosophers in the Chinese tradition, up to and including those in contemporary China. Not that they necessarily agreed with him, of course – rather that philosophical progress so frequently involved movement away from Confucius' position.

Mozi, the leading figure of Mohism, argued for a universal love of mankind, against the Confucian emphasis on the claims of kinship and social hierarchy. The parallel, in India, with the Buddha's rejection of traditional Vedic hierarchical social and individual morality is quite striking. Legalism, on the other hand, put the emphasis on the requirements for an orderly social structure in the Warring States Period of Chinese history, subordinating the individual interests of the person to the interests of the state. And in stark contrast to the Legalists, the Daoists encouraged a morality centered on a withdrawal from the trials and tribulations of the political agenda.

After the introduction of Buddhism, with the translation of Buddhist texts which began in the second century AD, its ideas became amalgamated to a greater or lesser extent with the indigenous philosophies and produced a second great wave of original thinkers in medieval China, in the Song and Ming Dynasties. The Confucianism – better called Neo-Confucianism – of this time established itself as the leading socio-political influence, a position in which it remained up to the early twentieth century.

If there is one central emphasis of Chinese philosophy, it is on moral, political and social questions, an emphasis found even now in contemporary Chinese thought. Metaphysical and epistemological questions tend to be addressed from this angle, for example the question of the nature of the universe and of man and his place within it. The source of the physical and social world is of interest primarily because of the implications it has for personal moral rules, for social structure and for principles of good government. This emphasis is found undoubtedly in the writings of Mao Zedong, as it is in those of other prominent thinkers behind the present culture of modern, post-revolutionary China.

This is not to say that Chinese philosophy has ignored issues outside moral and political philosophy. Far from it. As the chapters below will demonstrate, an interest in the nature of argument and the functioning of language was established very early on in Chinese philosophical history; metaphysical questions were paramount in early Daoism and in later Neo-Confucianism alike; and the nature of knowledge and its relation to practice was well and thoroughly explored.

B. C. and I. M.

25

THE ORIGINS OF CHINESE PHILOSOPHY

Chung-ying Cheng

THREE ASPECTS OF ORIGINS

To speak of the origins of Chinese philosophy, we need to take into consideration how the origins of any philosophy are to be decided. There are three such considerations. First, in so far as philosophy is a conscious effort to formulate views and values as expressions of the fundamental beliefs of a people, philosophy cannot be separated from the cultural background and cultural tradition of a people. By culture we mean the cluster of beliefs and behaviour patterns involving such activities as language, art, literature and religion. In this sense philosophy serves an expressive function of its underlying culture *par excellence*. Thus, one may have to trace a philosophy to the beginning of a culture and find its determinants in the cultural experiences, activities and proclivities of a people.

Since there is no complete axiomatization of a culture, there is no complete axiomatic formulation of its philosophy. We cannot completely articulate a culture and its potential in a closed system of principles, and philosophy exists primarily as a form of creative exploration of life and reality, even though it is based on and draws its lifeblood from a cultural fountainhead. Hence to identify the origins of a philosophy one needs to examine the very core of a culture. We can generally identify this core in terms of the ideals and goals of life which are thought worthy of pursuit and which can be used as standards of value judgements for the larger portion of the society. One may even suggest that philosophy is developed primarily to conceptualize the ideal aspirations of a people at a certain stage or under certain specific circumstances of cultural development.

Second, philosophy as continuing activity must be seen as evolving and emerging from that practical activity of life which is centred on solving problems of correct knowledge, genuine understanding, and a fair appraisal of matters important to life, whether individual or social. At the social level, problems of the distribution of resources, the organization of power and the regulation of interpersonal behaviour are essential and vital concerns of a people. Hence, ways of thinking, perceiving and understanding are essential and central to any philosophical enquiry, which involves searching for as well as suggesting issues and problems and their critical solutions. Consequently, in order to understand the beginnings of a philosophy, one needs to enquire into the essential ways of thinking, perceiving and understanding which pervade the spectrum of human activities. This can be done either by examining various activities of a people over a period of time as in Foucault's archaeological approach to knowledge, or by looking for an originative system of thinking which both conscientiously reflects and normatively guides the process of thought.

The third consideration concerns the theoretical constructions resulting from the philosophical thinking or cultural activities of a people. Philosophy in this context does not exist as the cultural pre-understanding of a people or as a hidden form of thinking guiding the problem-solving and evaluating mind of a people. It becomes instead a clearly stated or articulated idea or system of ideas in the form of explicit language. The philosophical idea may be simply stated or may be developed as a system of discourse-forming general propositions. In either case it is addressed to some fundamental issues or ideals of life as well as to some basic views of reality. Life and reality have come to be fully encountered as basic problems, and all other problems are to be related and reduced to them. In this the subject of philosophical thinking also stands out as a specific historical person and thus acts as a human being who philosophizes and hence as a *philosopher*. One has, however, to investigate a historically given view on life and reality as the beginning of a conscious philosophy. The criterion for such a philosophizing activity is rationality in the form of propositional language or discourse. But one has to understand and thus to interpret the language and discourse as an assertion and expression of philosophical thinking in maturity.

In the above I have identified three senses or three aspects of the origins of a philosophy: origins as historicity and cultural experience; origins as hidden methodology and underlying views of reality and life; and finally origins as conscious assertions of ideas and ideals. When we use the term 'origins', we have in mind a multi-dimensional view of origins which must be pluralistically conceived. In fact, in order to understand the origins of a philosophy or a philosophical tradition effectively, we have to face the following questions: What are the fundamental concepts or categories of that philosophical tradition? In which theoretical contexts are they asserted or presented? What is the underlying view of reality which leads to or is presupposed in the philosophical understanding or assertion? What is the guiding methodology or way of thinking for the philosophical idea or ideas? Finally, what kind of cultural experiences or ideals define or give rise to this way of thinking or this way of forming a view? These questions define our three senses of 'origins' in a reverse order, namely historicity, practicality and theoreticity. The three senses of 'origins' form a unity in that each requires the other two in making the notion of origins interesting and relevant. If one speaks of origins only in one sense or with regard to one dimension, one will not be able to answer every question about origins. It should be further noted that these senses of 'origins' could apply to the problem of the origins of any philosophy as a human activity, in so far as this activity cannot be reduced to a single act or view but must assume many dimensions which are essential to the rich meaning of 'origins'.

In my description of the three dimensions of the origins of a philosophy, it is intended that historicity and cultural experience provide the context for the emergence of methodology and cosmology, which in their turn provide the context for the emergence of the language and construction of a philosophy. I use the term 'emergence' to indicate the natural arising or origination of a level of reality from a given background condition. This emergent level need not be considered a result of linear causation or full determination by a basic element. The fact is that there are both causality and creativity in the origination of thinking, perception and understanding in so far as we may understand mental activities as presenting a centre of creativity just as we may understand the cosmos or universe as a self-determining centre of creativity. Philosophically, we must see that creativity in any useful sense must be creative of itself, namely creative of creativity. This is how life can be regarded as creative: life is a result of creative emergence of the universe, and then it becomes creative in its own way and thus participates in the creative process of the world.

To go back to our point about the relation between one dimension of origins and another dimension of origins, this relation is to be aptly described as that of partial determination and partial creativity, which implies partial indetermination and partial non-creativity. This means that philosophy as it arises from a cultural experience and its primary methodological/metaphysical self-reflection can assume many forms and can take many routes of development. This is how philosophy has been developed, and there is always the prospect of the creative development of philosophy, particularly if we realize that philosophy is itself an exploration of the creativity of the universe and the creativity of life and mind in response to the creativity of the universe. This also underlines the fact that philosophy is an unending pursuit requiring a universe of infinite possibilities. Because there is no conceivable ending to a creative universe and a creative mind which arises from the creative universe, there is always enough indetermination and thus creativity inherent in any given formulation of philosophical thinking or understanding.

Another relevant point is that philosophy can make an impact on the social and cultural development of a people. While philosophy arises from a cultural tradition, it also gives rise to new forms and new directions of the cultural activities of a people. It is in this sense that philosophy is the best index or indication of the cultural state of a people and thus forms an organic unity with the continuing development or growth of a culture. Philosophy may thus be regarded as a self-refining, self-criticizing and even self-fulfilling process of a cultural tradition, albeit combined with creativity drawn from the individual or collective mind of a people.

THREE STRAINS OF THINKING IN THE ORIGINATION OF CHINESE PHILOSOPHY

In the light of what we have said about the origins of a philosophy, we can now identify three strains of thinking in the primary cultural experience of the Chinese people as the beginnings of Chinese philosophy. These three strains of thinking present the fundamental orientations and directions of Chinese philosophy as well as setting the stage for Chinese philosophy. They are inherent in the primary cultural experience of the Chinese and form the earliest core of Chinese cultural and intellectual life. But they themselves are interrelated in terms of the succeeding stages of ontogenesis and interanimation. In other words, one stage of thinking gives rise to another without cancelling out the first stage. Hence, each later stage is founded on an earlier stage, and one should consider a later stage as arising from the context of an earlier stage or stages.

What, then, are the three strains of thinking in early Chinese culture which constitute a paradigm model for the origination and inspiration of Chinese philosophy? They are (1) an intrinsic reverence for heaven and ancestral spirits, which provide the source of meaning for the ethical, social and political life of the Chinese people; (2) a dialectical bipolar onto-cosmological reflection which provides the backbone of a methodology implicitly guiding and conditioning the way of perception and thinking in Chinese philosophy; and (3) a timely awakening to the potentiality and creativity of the human subject, which provides the basis for a cosmic naturalism and an intrinsic humanism, whether collective or individual, political or moral, in the formation of the early schools of Chinese philosophy.

In this chapter I shall discuss these beginnings of Chinese philosophy and their interrelations in the given order.

INITIAL TRUST AND PRIMAL ORDER: ANCESTRAL SPIRITS AND THE MANDATE OF HEAVEN

According to recent archaeological finds,[1] the ancient Chinese had settled before the Neolithic period (around 5000 BC) in both north-eastern and north-western China, centring their tribal community life in ancestral gods (ancestral spirits) and natural gods (natural spirits). In this period, known as Yangshao Culture, Dawenko Culture, Liangche Culture or Hungshan Culture, sacred objects and sites of worship (temples) and burials consistent with the practice of ancestral worship are commonly found. One may regard this time as marking the specific era in the prehistory of China which can aptly be called the Period of Jade, which lasted at least another two millennia.

From the time of Lungshan Culture (2600–2100 BC), when sage-kings of Yao and Shun are said to have reigned, Chinese culture centring on sacrifices to natural and ancestral spirits spread further south to Henan, Shandong and Hubei, and a natural process of integration of scattered communities gathered momentum on the eve of the formation of a unified political state, the Xia.[2]

Two observations can be made concerning the formation of early Chinese culture as described above. First, it leaves no doubt that the practice of *li* (ritual/rite) found its beginning in ancestral worship as early as the Period of Jade. In fact part of the word *li* refers to the offering of patterned jade for sacrificial ritual. Though there has been no philosophical discussion of the practice of *li*, the sacrificial practice dating back to the Period of Jade gives us an insight into how *li* arose in connection with ancestral worship and worship of natural spirits. There is no doubt that clans and tribal communities based on family lineage had been firmly established at the time of the Red Emperor (Shenlung) and the Yellow Emperor (Xianyuan), which should fall within the Period of Jade. What makes the family system possible is not only the benefits of care and security yielded by families but the sense of stability, order, peace and solidarity provided by families conceived as rooted in the same ancestral spirits. It is through the recognition of and reverence for the ancestral spirits that the unknown in the past becomes familiar and the fear of the unknown in the past is overcome. This is metaphysically equivalent to finding stability and security in consanguinity and the continuity of time.[3]

A second important element relevant to the establishment of *li* in ancestral worship is the experience of an order of the higher and the lower, the senior and the junior. To be higher and senior, however, does not mean that the higher and the senior should merely dominate the lower and the junior. On the contrary, the higher and the senior should protect the lower and the junior, whereas the lower and the junior should respect the higher and the senior for the benefit of maintaining a holistic totality of order in which the higher and the lower, the senior and the junior, will have their respective places and roles. With regard to this holistic totality, all individual parties are mutually dependent and complementary to one another. Besides, the higher and the senior basically correspond to the earlier and the later, and therefore in the course of time the lower and the junior can in turn become the higher and the senior just as the latter had been the lower and the junior in the past.

In this deep experience of ancestral temporality, one can detect elements of totality, mutual placement, mutual support, interdependence and a natural process of transformation and return. This in fact suggests the initial and inceptive experience of the *dao*, which leads to the formation of the philosophy of the *yi* (change and transformation) and the philosophy of *jing* (reverence and piety). The key point for this experience is the experience of time in the act of reverence for the ancestral spirits as related to us. This experience can also be called reverence for existence in the passage of time. 'Reverence' (*jing*) in this context is an intentional/existential state of piety, solemnity and carefulness of a person towards a situation being conceived or experienced to be an ideal object of emulation and identification. What needs to be stressed in this experience of *jing* is that even though there is a distance between the higher and the lower, there is also at the same time a closeness and attraction between the ideal and the actual.[4] In the experience of reverence one reveals one's subjective existence by facing the limitedness of oneself on the one hand and the consequent acknowledgement of an ideal being beyond oneself on the other. It is in both limiting and stretching oneself that the essential meaning of *li* is formed.

Concerning the reverence for the natural spirits, the ancient Chinese, like any other ancient people, wondered about natural events and phenomena in their environment and were in a situation to respond to, explain and understand them. But instead of developing a full-scale mythology or organized primitive religion, they responded to the natural processes of nature by accepting the natural world without excessive mythological personification. There is a general awareness of life and living in nature as a whole as nature is seen to be full of life. In fact, both heaven and earth have long been regarded as implicit principles of potential vitality and life-giving powers.

Even though there is a general tendency to attribute magical power (*mo*) and personality to natural objects such as mountains and rivers, this is because they appear to have life and the power to provide life. If a power is found to destroy life without giving life or bringing order to life, it is to be eliminated from consideration as a spirit (*sheng*) via a more powerful human intervention. The myth of Hou Yi's shooting the harmful nine extra suns is telling. We might suggest that, in the life-world of the ancient Chinese, what is important is life in the totality of nature and an entity is not worthy of reverence if it does not benefit life and specifically human life as a whole.

In fact, the term *sheng* suggests the power of extending or stretching life. Without this power of extending or stretching life a spirit cannot be an object of reverence given the above sense of 'reverence'. The term *gui* is also used to denote a spirit linked to the past. Like *sheng*, it is to be revered for being capable of benign and beneficial influence on life in general. The difference between *sheng* and *gui* is that the former is spirit considered generally without reference to a past existing history, whereas the latter is referred to in the light of a past existing history, i.e. the *gui* has its trace in the past and came as a trace from the past. When the ancestral spirits are considered as *sheng* and not as merely *gui*, it is their life-preserving and life-protecting power which is focused on.

To go back to ancestral worship, it is not only that *li* was first introduced as a rule governing the required attitudes and the required making of sacrifices to the ancient spirits; the notion of *sheng* was also clearly conceived by way of the experience of the presence of a benign power of life-protection and life-preservation.

It is also to be noted that, when the family relationship extends by way of marriage and the rise of new generations, the common source of the family becomes the revered centring origin of all the life in the family. In this sense the common source which is worthy of reverence is the supreme divinity *shangdi* ('source on the high'). This notion of *shangdi* was known to the Xia and Yin peoples. In fact, we have good reason to believe that it is through the fusion of the communities of different peoples under the reigns of the Xia and the Yin that the supreme divinity of *shangdi* was born. Now if we consider all the lives in nature, then there should be a common source of life and thus a common source of all things in the world. If we try to reach for an ultimate common source for all natural lives in the form of natural spirits, then we can see how the notion of heaven (*tian*) as life-generating and life-preserving power is formed. This notion of *tian* took shape relatively late and did not become well established until the beginning of the Zhou in the twelfth century BC.

Since the Zhou people had integrated all other peoples within an even larger kinship scope than their predecessors the Xia and the Yin, the notion of *tian* as a comprehensive notion absorbs as well as replaces the notion of *shangdi*. Together with this, of course, the *li* system also became more complete and more comprehensive in the classification of all things in the life-world of the Zhou people. This system of *li*, of course, has the *li* to heaven superimposed on it. The symbolic meaning of this development is that the Chinese people had become more unified and more integrated, to the extent that a comprehensive unification and integration of social and political life had taken place. We may now conclude that there is an intrinsic organic interrelation between the rise of beliefs in *shangdi* and *tian*, the institutionalization of *li* as a system of social ordering and the formation of a unified social-political economy based on agriculture.

The spirit of this development is the sense of non-separation between an individual man and his family, his community, his state and nature as a whole. There is a deeply rooted sense of affective accord and consanguine harmony among all these entities, and this is expressed by the notion of *jing*: a sincere acknowledgement of the differences of things and their positions in a totality of reality which brings out their differences and at the same time preserves their equally genuine identities. It is in this sense that the fundamental values of comprehensive harmony (*ho*) and comprehensive transformation (*hua*) in Chinese culture came into being, even though they may not have become fully articulated until the seventh century BC. Given this background of *jing* for understanding *li*, it is clear that *li* does not simply mark out a principle of difference and discrimination but also implies a principle of totality and comprehension which engenders and preserves the difference. But above all *li* implies an existential communicability and required mutual acknowledgement between two different entities in a framework of totality. It is on this basis that the Chinese mode of thinking and the Chinese notion of humanity were to be systematically developed.

As a partial explanation of the rise of *li* together with its inner dimension of *jing* in the sense described above, we may point to the influence of concrete time and concrete space, namely the geological and climatological environment in which the ancient Chinese had found themselves. In this temperate space-time zone, the changes of season and the blending of mountains and rivers in the fold of heaven and earth impressed the ancient Chinese as always generating varied life-forms and forming an inseparable unity. If we compare this environment with those in which the ancient Greeks, the ancient Hebrews and the ancient Indians respectively found themselves, we cannot but see that each culture reflects as well as embodies some dominating qualities of its environment. These qualities bespeak not only the economic, political and social institutions of each people, but their primary life style, their way of thinking as well as their mode of idealization. There is no doubt that their basic orientations in life and their ultimate values in life, whether individual or collective, are also influenced by the overall respective influences from their environments.[5]

Of course, it is to be remarked that human factors also form an integral part of the environment. The sense of cohesion and harmony prevails when there is no essential need for or stress on competition, conquest or conflict in history. The Chinese people as a whole experienced a sense of centrality and totality and thus seemed to strive for more integration and cohesion in history than any other people. This no doubt contributed to the philosophical awareness of harmony as an underlying strain of both cosmos and society in the sphere of Chinese culture.

In connection with the notion of heaven, the notion of the 'mandate of heaven' (*tianming*) arises as a consequence of the defeat of the Shang by the Zhou. As heaven assumes the central and overarching position of power, all major changes such as the change-over of political authority must be derived from the influence and determination of the will of heaven, hence the notion of the *tianming*. The appearance of the 'mandate of heaven' underlines both the universalization and the centralization of the power of a supreme being, because the notion of *ming* was basically a matter of originating and commanding action via one's free will and free choice. In fact the term *ling* ('command'), a cognate of *ming*, was used extensively in the oracle inscriptions (*puci*). In this sense of *ling*, all natural events are conceived as results of the *ling* of the *shangdi* or *tian*. Whereas *ling* expresses the will and command in a gesture, *ming* indicates specifically the verbalization of the *ling*.

In the fall of the dynasty of the Yin, the Zhou founders read the message that the *ming* of *shangdi* is not fixed and instead will change according to the virtues (*de*) of the rulers in their exercise of power over the people. It was clear to the Zhou rulers that it was the support of the people which was crucial for the defeat of the Yin and the rise of the Zhou. Therefore, at a time when the mandate of heaven was conceived to be the basis of political change, an awakening to the importance of winning the support of the people was also taking place. This led to reflection on the doings, abilities and intentions of the rulers. This is the origin of the notion of *de* or virtue. *De* is the power of securing the support of the people, and nothing will secure the following of the people except one's ability and intention to protect them by a ruler's restraining and controlling his desires and arbitrariness. That *de* eventually becomes a moral notion governing individual development and self-cultivation as well as social acceptance and approval is no doubt based on this historical reflection on change of power and is intimately linked to the notion of the *tianming*.

The more the inconstancy of the *tianming* is experienced, through the failures of a ruler's lack of *de*, the more urgent the importance of cultivating oneself becomes. In this process the authority of heaven will be diminished and a moral humanism will take its place, even to the point at which the mandate of heaven is to be internalized and identified with nature (namely the capacity and potentiality of *de* in a person) in the *Zhong Yong*. This is evidently one source of Confucianism. It need not be pointed out that the meaning of *ming* has gradually changed too: as the mandate of heaven is conceived to cause life and determine people's status in life, what life is and the status and fortunes bestowed in people's lives are therefore regarded as a matter of *tianming*. But when people lose sight of heaven because of the perceived weakening of the power of heaven, the *ming* naturally becomes an autonomous power conceived as responsible for the what and how of life, hence the notion of *ming* as fate or 'already determined'. Moreover, the *ming* as the determining power is not only transformed into a determined state but becomes a pre-determined state, as testified by popular beliefs. It is against this transformed notion of *ming* in popular beliefs, which may exist even in Confucian thinking, that Mozi directed his critique at the end of the fifth century BC.

THE EMERGENCE OF INTEGRATIVE WISDOM: DIALECTICS AND COSMOLOGY IN UNION

In separating reality from appearance, objectivity from subjectivity, the ancient Greeks sought the immutable and unmoved as the essence of the real and the objective. In contrast, the ancient Chinese from the very beginning recognized and accepted change and transformation as irreducible attributes of the world, including both things and human selves.[6] In fact, when we now look at the main differences between western and Chinese philosophy, we have to point to this fundamental divergence. The Chinese stress on and grasp of the changing, the becoming, time and temporality not only distinguish Chinese metaphysics of reality and nature from the main trend of western philosophical traditions, but also set the Chinese apart from the orientations of Indian philosophy.

For the Chinese philosophers, the experience of changes in the world, in the seasons and in one's life is not a reason for getting away from changes or for denying their ultimate reality. On the contrary, these experiences lend Chinese thinkers insight into the true nature of things and human self: there is opportunity for development, transformation, interaction and integration in nature and in the human self. This also suggests to them the organic wholeness of the world in which the changing and the unchanging, the objective and the subjective, merge and form a continuum because of the pervasiveness of change. To the ancient Chinese, this way of understanding reality is naturally simple and authentic, as evidenced by the experience of changes alone.

It is in the tradition of the *Zhou Yi* that the experience of changes in nature by the ancient Chinese becomes consciously organized and articulated into a system of thinking about and describing reality. This organization and articulation not only provide a cosmological picture of the world in which man can find his proper place and proper role, but develop a way of thinking towards integrating the world and the self, generating meanings from facts and determining values from understanding. In fact, we may regard the cosmological picture of the world in the *Zhou Yi* as an unfolding of the dialectical thinking inherent in the *Zhou Yi,* whereas we may see the dialectical thinking inherent in the *Zhou Yi* as a natural reflection on the cosmological process of nature in its generative and transformative activities. As nature is seen as dynamically moving and changing, the dialectical way of thinking as embodying natural forces of changing can be said to truly capture the nature of reality. It is in this sense that focusing on changes gives us the simplest and most direct way of understanding reality: it is to 'map' the reality of changes as changes of reality without mediation and without distortion. In this direct and simple way of thinking, one may see that the reality of changes becomes reflexively conscious of itself by way of incorporating the self-conscious mind into the world of changes.

This is the philosophical way to understand the meaning of *jianyi* when the term is used to convey the meaning of changes in the term *yi*. But then it is through the way or method of *jianyi* (direct presentation of changes) that the reality of changes becomes represented, which reveals itself to include changes (*bianyi*) and constancies (*buyi*) as well as combinations of changes and constancies.

The influence of the *Zhou Yi* as a way of thinking in Chinese philosophy cannot be understated. Not only did it introduce a method of organizing thoughts about any matter of importance, but it also served as a way of revealing or discovering features of reality. More important than this, the *Zhou Yi* provided a way of achieving balance, centrality, harmony and comprehension as well as a transformative development and return of things to their ultimate source. The reason why it had this capacity is that it itself is a revelation of reality as reality is and becomes and yet is expressed in the symbolic form of the simplest processes and states of the change-reality. It is thus capable of revealing the open structure or trace of a transforming reality as well as applying to any single aspect or item of reality experienced by man.

Because of the intended completeness of the *Zhou Yi* understanding of reality, it finally but not least importantly provided a way of understanding, controlling and deciding about the future yet unknown to man. In this latter function, the *Zhou Yi* served to integrate the present, the past and the future into a whole in which man could play an active role and make a positive contribution. In the following, I shall elaborate below on important aspects of the *Zhou Yi* as a way of thinking and the impact it has made on Chinese philosophy.

(1) The *Zhou Yi* focused on the totality of reality and thus developed a complete system of reality. The completeness starts from the basic observation of complementary opposites or polarities as defining a whole. The simplest complementary opposites are *yin* (shady) and *yang* (bright) on mountainsides and riverbanks. The *yin* signifies the absence of light, whereas the *yang* signifies the presence of light. *Yin* and *yang* make a difference to things, as things can be regarded as *yin* or *yang* according to the lack or presence of illumination or light. As it is natural to see light as energy, motion and penetrating power, the *yang* acquires characteristics suggestive of creating life and sustaining reality. On the opposite side, the *yin* is naturally associated with characteristics suggestive of hiddenness, passivity, receptivity and comprehension. What is important to note is that if change is possible at all as it is, the simplest way to experience or closely monitor change as real is to see it as going from the stable, the hidden, the possible to the dynamic, the disclosed and the actual, and vice versa. In this simple process one experiences the basic unit of *yin–yang* transformation, which defines a unity and a totality. In it one also sees the complementarity of opposites and the potentiality of progressive return and reversion. Of course, the *yin–yang* relationship of contrast, interdependence and unity can be realized in an apparently non-transformative spatial context: there is the soft and there is the firm existing side by side. But then in so far as there is a unity and whole to contain and present this contrast, this contrast is a harmony and balance which provides a richer experience of changes.

What is important in understanding the totality and unity of *yin–yang* is that the *yin* and the *yang* have to be recognized as opposite qualities in the primary context of the dark and the bright, which when seen as absence and presence of light suggest the absence and presence of being and thus non-being and being. Laozi was the first philosopher to see this and refer to it as the fact that 'The being and non-being mutually generate each other.' He also referred to the latter relationship as the fact that 'The high and the low mutually lean on each other.'

How does one see the *yin* and the *yang* as a universal feature for all unities of things? This may require one to see the wholeness and hence the unity of things in the first place. Not only can *yin* and *yang* not be separated from each other, but they must not be separated from a totality of things to be seen. The seeing of the totality of things is a phenomenal understanding which sometimes depends on the intuitive, comprehensive and detail-discerning opening-up of the mind of the person. In the *Xi Ci*, the description of the inventive activities of the sage-king Fu Xi gives us a retrospective insight into his formation of the initial symbolic system of the *Yi*, the eight trigrams (*bagua*): Fu Xi has to look up to the heavens and to enquire into the earth; he has to look carefully on things far from him and to do the same on things close to him, namely his own person. It is through a scrupulous and meticulous observation and enquiry that he comes to the configuration of the *ba-gua* system, which signifies a totality of things, namely nature as a whole, and which presents the phenomenally most outstanding constituent forces and processes of nature to be understood as a set of *yin–yang* relationships.

It is not until the *Xi Ci* that this *bagua* system is again seen as arising from a process of onto-cosmological thinking: the original ultimate unity called *daiji* gives rise to the norm-setting *yin–yang*, which in turn gives rise to four natural forms, which in their turn again generate the *bagua*. This is no doubt a later articulation of the dialectical thinking underlying the understanding of the totality and dynamics of nature. This dialectical thinking leads on the one hand to the formation of an onto-cosmology of fundamental forces and principles referred to as *jian / kun / kan / li / dui / gen / xun / zhen*, and on the other hand to the formation of a realistic cosmology of natural forms and events referred to as *heaven / earth / water / fire / lake / hill / wind / thunder*. What this development suggests is that the dialectical way of thinking in the *Zhou Yi* requires a process of comprehensive observation and enquiry, analysis and synthesis or integration. The integrative aspect of this way of thinking is twofold: it integrates all elements of observation into a structure of relationships and it allows the relationships to be an open system so that it can extend to other things not yet specifically covered. The latter point pertains to the symbolic nature of the structure and the allowance for interpretation in the dialectical way of thinking.

In this process one sees not only the openness of the system, but that *yin–yang* exists as a pervasive feature of reality on many levels of complexity and relative to many dimensions of structure from many points of view for many different purposes if we allow the subjective and evaluative capacity of mind to play a role. This also suggests that the onto-cosmological reality generated by *Zhou Yi* thinking is an open world of infinite possibilities in which new relationships can be discovered and realized and there is no end to differentiation and integration as there is no end to a process of continuous observation and enquiry, analysis, synthesis and interpretation.

It is by way of this potentiality of the *Zhou Yi* that it has influenced the development of Chinese philosophy in both its form and its substance, pertaining to both the way of thinking in the *Zhou Yi* and the creative onto-cosmology generated by this method of thinking.

I have specifically pinpointed the *Zhou Yi* way of thinking and organization as 'comprehensive observation', which consists of macro-observation of the large features of nature as well as micro-observation of the small features of nature. In regard to the latter, the *Zhou Yi* sees that things and events have their beginnings in a stage consisting of minute and almost imperceptible movements of forces. To see the large trends of things one has to perceive the smallest beginnings and to make changes accordingly relative to a given purpose. This view underlines the importance not only of micro-observation but of participatory agency for a human subject.

Given the above description, we may now formulate the dialectical way of thinking in the *Zhou Yi* as follows:

> Seeing unities – seeing differentiation of a unity into *yin* and *yang* – seeing opposition – seeing transformation – seeing organic dependencies formed – seeing creativity at work – seeing new unities.

(2) The *Zhou Yi* focused on harmony as the inceptive state for creativity (*sheng*) and on harmonization as the natural end state of reality in a process of change and transformation. To explain the variety of things and the vitality of the myriad of life-forms in nature on the basis of the simplest unity of *yin–yang*, creativity has to be assumed. 'Creativity' here means a natural differentiation of life-forms derived from the original unity of reality and the development of life and life activity in nature, which culminates in the formation of human beings as a species. The original unity of reality is called the *daiji* (the great ultimate) in the *Xi Ci* commentary on the underlying cosmology of the *Zhou Yi*.

Cosmologically, one can say that the *daiji* has *yin–yang* activated in the sense of initiating the reality of the world in terms of activity and transformation. When this activity and transformation continue, the maintenance of the creativity of reality amidst change and transformation requires *yin–yang* complementarity, not just their opposition. When this occurs, there is harmony. But this may not happen at any time in the process of creative change and differentiation of things, because there could be opposition without complementarity at any stage in the process of change. Yet the initial creative impulse of the unity of reality is for continuous continuation of the creative, and hence the creation of reality for creativity. In this sense the process of change is therefore a process of harmonization related to an ideal state of harmony as the end state which, of course, is another inception for creativity. The *Zhou Yi* implicitly assumes this onto-cosmological point of view when it sees the combination of water and fire as a harmony and calls it 'completion' (*jiji*), which from a reverse point of view becomes 'incompletion' (*weiji*), the starting point for creative transformation towards harmony.

(3) This cosmological point of view enables us to see the world as ceaseless activity towards the realization of harmony and at the same time as harmony on some level prepared for further creative development. On this understanding, the world is given a meaning in terms of which man not only justifies his position in the world but sees a role for himself in furthering the harmonization of the world and elevating the world to a higher level of creativity. It is in this sense that harmony becomes a central value for both cosmological and human activities. It is also in this sense that human beings are considered as capable of participating in the cosmological/cosmogonic activities of reality. Man can be said to embody the nature of the ultimate reality, which is essentially the inceptive unity of reality for creative change. This also leads to the later Confucian view that the nature (*xing*) of man is what heaven has endowed him with (*ming*). In substance this means that man is endowed with the nature of ultimate reality which is heaven, and thus is capable of creative advance and participation in the cosmological process of creativity. For the Confucianist it is important for the human being to make this a moral self-understanding and a moral duty.

Given consciousness of the human heart-mind, it is consistent also to assume that any inceptive state of existence is a basis for creativity which leads to harmony or a state requiring harmony. Heart-mind activity specifically can be said to demonstrate this view, because any such activity changes a state of existence as well as a view of reality. This point is actually made later in the Confucian philosophy of the *Zhong Yong*. In the light of this point the inceptive state of harmony of mind is called 'centrality' (*zhong*) rather than 'harmony' (*ho*), whereas the end state of harmony is called harmony. But it is worth pointing out that as heart-mind is founded on the same onto-cosmological principle of the *daiji* or unity of the *yin–yang*, and is thus cosmo-spiritually identical, the centrality (*zhong*) as the original state of heart-mind is also a harmony which harbours creativity as its nature. It is not a state of voidness, inactivity or emptiness as is sometimes assumed. The difference between centrality and harmony is a not a matter of substance, but a matter of differentiation and integration of feelings in response to the impact and activation of things from outside the heart-mind. This is no doubt a form of participation in the changes of the world as this leads to the repositioning of the human self in the world and the transformation of the human self.

(4) Given the above understanding of the onto-cosmological philosophy of the *Zhou Yi* and its implications for understanding human existence and human heart-mind or nature, we are in a position to see how this philosophy can turn out to be practical in guiding the decisions and actions of man. One most important practical task for human decisions and actions is to know and master the future. But the problem is that as the future is not yet formed, how could we ever hope to know it? The insight of the *Zhou Yi* is that we may configure the future in terms of the onto-cosmological model of understanding based on the totality of *yin–yang* and its creative tendency towards harmonization and harmony. Another factor which should not be lost sight of is human participation in the cosmological process and thus the ability of the human to define and shape the onto-cosmological order.

Keeping this in mind, we are able to understand how the *Zhou Yi* can be thought of as a book of divination or perhaps could even have first been developed explicitly as a book of divination. It is important to see divination (*pu* and *shi*) as a practical art of knowing and mastering the future to be practised on occasions of momentous importance. But then the knowing and mastering must be correctly understood as just suggested. If we do not have a clear understanding of the onto-cosmological insights of the *Zhou Yi*, if we do not see the working of such an onto-cosmology behind the form of divinatory practice, and if we do not consider the whole system of forms (*gua*) as presenting or hiding such an onto-cosmological way of thinking, we are not in a position to understand the working of the divination, not to mention the inner logic of divination.

Given a proper understanding of the dialectics and onto-cosmology of the *Zhou Yi*, we can now recognize several relevant philosophical aspects of divination which reflect some major features of Chinese philosophy in general. First, divination provides a linking between onto-cosmological thinking and spiritual thinking in the ancient

Chinese tradition. As there are natural spirits in the world and as there is the supreme authority of heaven as an overseeing spirit, the future can be incorporated into the totality of the world and human existence and thus the future and the present can be integrated as a whole. In this regard, to divine is to consult the natural spirits and heaven regarding future events, particularly concerning matters of importance to life and state. This attitude towards divination is actually assumed in the chapter of the *Shang Shu* entitled 'Hung Fan', and the official diviners are regarded as capable of communicating with spirits.

Second, in divination the future is projected into the present on the basis of the cosmology of the *Zhou Yi* as the whole system of the *gua* must be presupposed as a background body of judgements to be drawn out for consultation concerning the future. Although it is not clear how early the system of the *gua* was formed, it can be safely assumed on the basis of historical and archaeological evidence that the text of the sixty-four *guas* in the *Zhou Yi* was formed at the beginning of the Zhou. Earlier systems of the sixty-four *guas* may have existed, but it can also be imagined that the system of sixty-four *guas* arose from accumulation of inspired judgements of divination. In this sense divination may have existed as a simple appeal to the natural spirits on each occasion of divination, and it was through a long process of experiment and trial, matching and collation, comparing and verification, that a systematization of the *guas* and their judgements was finally settled. But this again must assume that an onto-cosmological model of understanding the world and the self emerged at the same time, because without this there is no basis or standard for making the collation and matching of the *guas* with experience.

It is thus reasonable to assume that the systematization of the *guas* was achieved by King Wen of Zhou. By that time heaven had become a dominating and unifying spirit in the world, and divination would then be an implicit appeal to heaven rather than to any other spirit. The unity of spiritual reality and the unity of political reality go hand in hand, and these in turn are accompanied by the systematization and ordering of the *guas*, and thus the appearance of the *Zhou Yi*, which hides a cosmological philosophy of reality and a dialectical way of thinking in the guise of divinatory practice.

It is necessary to point out that in actual divination the future is configured on the basis of the existing onto-cosmology and is interpreted in the light of the dialectical and onto-cosmological meanings of the underlying philosophy. This means that the future is structured in accordance with the principle of creative transformation and that human participation is required for determining the outcome of the transformation. There is not a single trace of fatalism or determinism. Divination provides an opportunity for individuals to participate in the development of the world as well as that of their future. Divination thus provides a way of integrating the future and the past of an individual in the present and so calls for the creativity of the individual for self-realization in the divinatory situation. One may even simply regard divination as a practical way in which the self participates in the transformation of the world. In this regard it is easy to see that divination is an integral part of the dialectical way of thinking in the *Zhou Yi*. This leads directly to the unity of theory and practice or knowledge and action which, in the light of our understanding of the *Zhou Yi* tradition, is evidently profoundly onto-cosmological in nature.

A final point about the divinatory nature of the *Zhou Yi* is that divination is not forecasting but a decision-making process calling for will-power, courage, wisdom, patience and cosmological insight on the part of the individual involved. Thus we may see the divinatory practice of the *Zhou Yi* as providing a process of self-control and self-cultivation and hence a morality of self-understanding and self-transformation which was to receive greater emphasis in Confucianism.

We have seen above how the *Zhou Yi* could be understood as a way of dialectical thinking and as a cosmological modelling at the same time. We can also see how the *Zhou Yi* wielded influence in the development of Chinese philosophy, because, as we shall see, all the major classical schools of Chinese philosophy can be related to it and their way of thinking in general can be traced to it. This is not to reduce all Chinese philosophy to the philosophy of the *Zhou Yi*, but to show how it can be regarded as a starting point and matrix for Chinese philosophy, especially if we take philosophy as a cosmological enterprise. Again this is not to make an analogy between early Chinese and early Greek philosophy, because there is an essential difference between the two: the *Zhou Yi* is both cosmological-dialectical and practical-participatory, whereas early Greek cosmology remains only cosmological-dialectical. In this comparison one sees that Chinese philosophy actually starts as a combination of intellectual and practical interests.

At the practical level, there is common ground between the *Zhou Yi* and the *Li Ji*, which describe the origins of *li*, as we have discussed in the third section of this chapter: both are to guide human life in harmony and unity as harmony and unity are experienced in life in its primary stage. But the origin of *li* is the sources of feelings representing the affective aspect of human life, whereas the origins of understanding (*ming*) are in the domain of intellectual observation and reflection as well as in the domain of hermeneutical interpretation. The former gives rise to a moral and religious order and thus an enrichment and growth of society and state, whereas the latter gives rise to an intellectual and rational order and thus presents an onto-cosmological understanding and thinking in the individual human self. In a certain sense the dialectical way of thinking of the *Zhou Yi* becomes self-fulfilling, for between *li* and *ming* there are opposition and complementarity, and thus there is harmony from beginning to end. This harmony is the basis for the inspiring development of the classical schools of Chinese philosophy in the 'axial age' beginning with the eighth century BC. (*Yi* began as a way of thinking as early as before the Xia Dynasty in the sixteenth century BC.)

CREATIVE INTEGRATION: HUMANISTIC AWAKENING AND NATURALISTIC UNDERSTANDING

In the above discussion the indigenous beginnings of ancient Chinese culture have been presented and analysed in terms of two main traditions, which are rooted in the basic human experiences of life and nature undistorted and uninterrupted by any major human trauma. These two traditions are the tradition of *li* and the tradition of *zhi*. The former is affective in nature and represents the natural human feelings towards the vicissitudes of life, whereas the latter is cognitive in nature and represents human knowledge of changes in nature. The development of the former culminated in the institution of *li* and the formation of belief in *tian* and *tianming*, whereas the development of the latter culminated in the construction of the symbolic system of the *Yi Jing* in which the onto-cosmology of nature and its dialectics dominate, not heaven or the mandate of heaven.

We may now see the birth of Chinese philosophy as resulting from *a creative integration of the affective tradition of* li *and the intellectual tradition of* zhi *in the form of a response to the socio-economic changes and the consequent disintegration of the Eastern Zhou*. The birth of Chinese philosophy actually took the form of the emergence of humanism and naturalism during the eighth to the fifth century BC (770–476 BC, historically referred to as the Period of Chun-Jiu or Spring and Autumn), which led to the rise of Confucianism and Daoism in the personages of Confucius and Lao Zi. But then the crucial questions are: How did the affective tradition and the cognitive tradition merge to give rise to humanism and naturalism? On what condition or conditions or against what kind of background did this merger occur? What kind of transformation took place? When we have answered these questions, we have answered the question of how Chinese philosophy began. In this sense the origins of Chinese philosophy are to be seen in both the shaping of the cultural forces leading to the formation of the classical schools of Chinese philosophy and the actual formation of those schools.

Although this is not the place to reflect on the causes of the disintegration of the Zhou political order in the late seventh century BC, it is relevant to point out that the well-ordered Zhou political and social structures in institutionalized *li* had been increasingly outgrown by economic, demographic, social and political changes from the eighth century BC on. The existing order simply could not cope with the conflicts and contradictions between central authority and local feudal powers, between competing feudal lords, between political title-holders and newly arising groups of economic influences. Both natural and human factors contributed to this large-scale change. A growing population demanding better organization of productivity was a natural factor. But a major source of change certainly came from the very socio-economic and political structures of the Zhou: on the one hand, the peace and stability of the system produced the potentiality for substantial change and a need for substantial change; on the other, the political form of the system was not open or flexible to accommodate this substantial change.[7] Thus one may say that the disintegration of the Zhou ensued from the rise of the new economic and political powers and was not simply the demise of the past and tradition. This explains why the Chun-Jiu Period was politically chaotic but economically, socially and culturally very lively. It was a period awakened to a need for a new political order based on its social and economic development and hence a period in search of a new political order which would be commensurate with the economic and social vitality of the time.

This understanding enables us to see how various schools of philosophy arose and had their beginnings in the Period of Chun-Jiu and continued to develop and blossom in the succeeding Period of Zhan-Guo or Warring States (475–221 BC) before China was unified under the reign of Qin. Each school began with a conscious awakening to the need for a new world order and continued with engagement in a more or less theoretical or practical search for such an order. Each school could therefore be regarded as a response to the fading and break-up of the Zhou system of *li* by way of a new vision of the larger world, a new vision of a more reflective humanity, and a new interpretation or new definition of the past and tradition. It was in this light that each later school developed its own outlook of the world, nature and man and their relationships, some conservative, some liberal, some more or less transcendent, some more or less immanent. But they all centred on the place of man in a new world order. Humanism and naturalism were two main trends which arose to function as a fountainhead for all major schools of philosophy in the classical China of the Chun-Jiu and Zhan-Guo Periods.

It is in this light that we can see that the conservative humanism of Confucius and the liberal naturalism of Laozi may still have something in common, namely the cosmic understanding based on the *qi*-orientated way of thinking in the *Zhou Yi*, because the latter served to liberate human thought from the tradition of the personalized *tian*. They differ in their attitudes towards preserving or casting off the tradition of *li*. Even though Confucius is generally regarded as conservative in his ethical and political thinking, he nevertheless showed innovation by giving new meanings to old terms such as *junzi*, *li* and *ren*. No doubt Confucius did not take note of the importance of economy, society and politics in his time, and this explains why his philosophy was not accepted or even appreciated by influential people of his day. His philosophy would not find a home until a social and political order had already been established, such as in the second century BC. Similarly, the above view explains why it was the Legalist philosophy which captured the attention of the political rulers of the time because it revealed the vitality of forces working towards the formation of a new political, economic and social order.

How did humanism and naturalism arise in the circumstances described above? If we take humanism as the awakening to and advocacy of the importance and centrality of human beings in the acquisition of knowledge, the definition of reality and the construction of values, then any breakdown of an old world order implies and presupposes the self-awakening of humanity in terms of its creativity and importance. Hence, with the disintegration of the Zhou *li*, it is natural to see the stirrings of the humanistic spirit at various levels. In the first place, natural spirits lost their appeal and intelligent people came to see that it was human beings, not spirits, who determined or affected the rise or decline of social and individual life. In the *Zo Juan* there are many passages indicating the superior value of people to spirits. Thus one Ciliang said that 'People are the center (*zu*) of spirits; hence sage-kings take care of people first and then devote time to spirits' (*Zho Zhuan*, Huan Gong 6th Year). There was also one Shiyin, who commented on his ruler's superstition regarding spirits: 'If a nation is to prosper, the ruler is to listen to people; if a nation is to fall, he is to listen to spirits' (*Zho Zhuan*, Zuang Gong 32nd Year).

Alongside this denial of the importance of spirits, there was the reinforcement of belief in self-cultivation and self-responsibility for human action and hence the disclaiming of relevance of a pre-determining fate. Hence even in regard to the use of divination, what is revealed is seen in a human context and evaluated in the light of a person's abilities and virtues. It is not seen as the working of the *tian-ming* or spirits or fate (*xu*). Divination only provides an occasion for configuring and organizing a background knowledge for one's judgement on human actions. Thus, considerations of the human factor always weigh heavily in one's judgement. This indicates a vague recognition of the powers of human self-determination, which we can see even in the 'Hung Fan' chapter of the *Shang Shu*. One Zhou official, Xuxing, answering a query about the fall of a meteorite to earth, asserted that 'Fortune and misfortune are determined by the human person' (*Zho Zhuan*, Xi Gong 16th Year). As early as the 'Hung Fan' chapter of the *Shang Shu* it is said that 'If you have great doubt, consult your mind, consult your assistants, consult your subjects, and consult divination by oracle bones and milfoil stalks.' A ruler has to use his intelligence and wisdom to make decisions and is not expected to depend exclusively upon divination for decision-making.

One important feature of the humanistic awakening in the Spring–Autumn Period was that the human agency was fundamentally located either in people *en masse* or in the single person of a ruler. It was recognized that people in a state, not spirits, nor even *tian-ming*, make a difference to the state and that the ruler must have virtues in order to govern a state well. We may thus see this humanistic awakening as consisting of the discovery of human autonomy and human self-importance in the care and control of people by the ruler, who should rely on his own abilities and virtues in making the care and control of people possible. In a sense it is a political humanism or a collective humanism, a humanism which distances itself from the belief in *tian-ming* and which focuses on the human agency of government in the exemplary and caring functions of a ruler. However, it is this political humanism which provides a basis for developing the universal individual-centred moral humanistic philosophy of Confucius.

The core of naturalistic understanding is the recognition of the importance and centrality of natural factors for the explanation of things in the world. In regard to the rise of naturalism, perhaps the most noteworthy fact is the widespread recognition of nature and the world as resultant states and activities of fundamental forces identified as metal, wood, water, fire and earth. This is the five powers (*wuxing*) theory of nature, which had its origins at the very beginning of the Zhou. Again in the 'Hung Fan' chapter of the *Shang Shu*, the five powers are described in terms of their respective natural qualities: water has the quality of flowing down, fire the quality of flaming up, wood the quality of growing bent or straight, metal the quality of alteration, earth the quality of allowing cultivation. Although this way of describing the five powers is not purely naturalistic, it has specified certain capacities or potentialities of the five powers and hence five types of natural processes in relation to human actions in an objectively experienced way. This suggests that the five powers are recognized in the contexts of the interaction between nature and man where nature is cultivated or husbanded in order to maintain human life. We may regard this as a naturalistic-pragmatic conceptualization of nature. But the development of the 'five powers theory' is such that identifying qualities or relations of the five powers have expanded by association or correlation with other concrete things in nature or human experience. That this is possible is due to certain objective similarities of qualities present in things in the world and/or certain similarities of response-feelings on the part of human subjects. From a transcendental deductive point of view, the human mind seems to have the capacity to identify the natural processes of human experiences and their relationships in a coherent and yet relevant way. But from a metaphysical point of view, the associative-correlative way of thinking in terms of five powers represents a pervading unity and mutuality of order in the world, which perhaps can best be expressed by Whitehead's notion of 'unity of feeling'.

In fact, if this 'unity of feeling' is to be objectively as well as subjectively understood, the five powers become natural symbols referring to some underlying real processes and forces in nature which bind to human experiences in a vast network of interlocking and interweaving relationships. This is a process which may be described by the Whiteheadian term 'symbolic reference'. Given this understanding, the naturalism in the Chun-Jiu Period is one of organicism, not that of mechanism as modern science would have it. In fact, when we take into consideration the generative-destructive order and relations among the five powers, we can see these as natural organic processes taking place under appropriate conditions. There is no absolute causality in these, nor is there a linear functional variability among them. The world is conceived in a circle of mutual circulation and mutual give-and-take, and hence the generation and destruction among the five powers indicate a dynamic structure of harmonization and thus reflect a state of nature in organic interdependence and harmonious balance.

It is clear that this naturalism of five powers is easily linked to the philosophy of change, namely the *Yi Jing* tradition. On the one hand, the *yin–yang* distinction is enriched by the five powers in terms of their mutual support and mutual balance; on the other, the five powers theory is enriched by the organic structure of interdependence of the eight trigrams. In fact, we can see that the so-called post-heaven (*houtian*) diagram of the trigrams reflects, or perhaps is suggested by, the generative/destructive order in the theory of the five powers. Apart from the distinction between the image-orientated representation of the eight trigrams and the stuff-orientated representation of the five powers, these two theories could naturally merge to form an onto-cosmology of nature and world, which later became actually systematized by Dung Zhongxu in the second century BC. This would be the acme of the organic naturalism beginning with the Chun-Jiu Period and dating in turn to the very beginning of the *Yi Jing* and the 'five powers theory' in the 'Hung Fan' chapter of the *Shang Shu*.

In this period, a vivid picture of nature in terms of the activities of *qi* was formed. In the first place, there was the conception of *yin* and *yang* as two *qi* based on observation of the upward movement of growth as *yang* and the downward movement of decline as *yin*. As early as the period of King Yu in Zhou, Pei Yang-fu explained an earthquake thus: 'The *yang* crouching cannot get out and the *yin* suppressing cannot evaporate' (*Guoyu*, *Zhouyu* first part). There are also the so-called *liuqi* (six vapours), referring to the natural events of darkening (*yin*), brightening (*yang*), wind, rain, night and day, which are said to give rise to five tastes, five colours and five sounds (see *Zho Zhuan*, Shao Gong 1st Year and 20th Year). A medical doctor named Ho used this theory to explain various diseases in terms of various excesses of these *qiu*, which points to the beginnings of a medical philosophy on the basis of naturalistic understanding to be built on in the later Nei Jing of the Zhan-Guo Period. From many instances like this, we can see how organic naturalistic beliefs developed and were applied in understanding both natural and human phenomena or incidents which would otherwise have been interpreted in terms of spirits and fate or the mandate of heaven.

This is indeed a rich tradition, which was developed very early and developed very well with good results. What is important to note is that this organic naturalistic understanding is a result of the 'organic and pragmatic attitude' developed from a desire to see a meaning and relevance for human affairs in nature. But a result of this attitude is a methodology of 'comprehensive observation' (*quan*) which leads to detailed and ordered description of natural events and human experiences in correlation. This perhaps explains the very beginning of the *Yi Jing*. But as the development of the *Yi Jing* shows, there comes from this a consciousness of the self-sufficiency of explanation of things and events in naturalistic terms without resort to spirits or heaven. This naturally contributes to the general gradual replacement of the conception of *tian* (heaven) by the conception of the *dao* (way) as the ultimate source and ground of explanation of things and happenings in nature and man. Thus as early as the seventh century BC Zi Chan remarked that 'The way of heaven is far and the way of man is near' (*Zho Zhuan*, Shao Gong 18th Year). Combining this organic naturalistic understanding and the pragmatic collective humanistic spirit, a life philosophy of 'rectifying one's virtues (*chende*), developing utilities (*liyong*) and improving life (*housheng*)' has been suggested (*Zho Zhuan*, Wen Gong 7th Year), which harks back to the early period of the agricultural society of the Xia.

In the above account I have delineated the two main trends of thinking arising from the historical development of early Chinese culture, which I have characterized as the tradition of *li* and the tradition of *zhi*. The tradition of *li* is inner-orientated and society-centred, and opens an order of social interdependencies and human intersubjectivity, a life-world of human values and telos, which culminates in the belief in and awareness of heaven and its mandate. On the other hand, the tradition of *zhi* is outer-orientated and nature-centred, and opens an order of natural forces and event interobjectivity. This is also a life-world on a different level, which presents the large world of things from a comprehensive natural point of view detached from human interest as embodied in the *Yi Jing* organization of the eight trigrams. These two traditions are not really separate or separable, for they arose together from the cultural experience and consciousness of a totality of ordered beings in which human beings formed an integral part and which thus constituted a totality of inherent balance and harmony to be developed in philosophy as methodology or as ontology when circumstances created appropriate occasions for such development.

In this sense, the breakdown of the *Zhou Li* was crucial for the philosophical awakening in classical Chinese philosophy, for it released the potential for development by weakening the holding and restraining powers of the political and social institutions in the *Zhou Li*. This new development was creative and integrative in the sense that the inner resources of *li* and the outer resources of *zhi* could be combined to give rise to new forms of thinking which could be centred in different directions. In the case of political humanism, it is clear that the belief in *tian-ming* was lost and a new confidence and awareness of human autonomy and self-responsibility set in. Philosophically, this indicates a replacement of the mandate of heaven by the mandate of the people (the term was not used by the Confucianists until Mencius in his quotation from the *Shangxu*): a state could not rely on spirits or heaven for its existence, but had to survive and thrive on the basis of the support of the people inspired and encouraged by the virtues and wisdom of the ruler. This was indeed an awakening of the human spirit in a collective sense.

To enhance the understanding of human existence and its value in terms of this understanding became the central task of Confucius and his school. It needs to be pointed out that it requires a human ability to see and recognize the moral autonomy of the state independently of the tradition and thus represents an outer-orientated mentality revealed in the *zhi* tradition. In fact, we may even say that it was the development of the *zhi* tradition which made the humanistic awakening possible and in actuality caused it and strengthened it as well. Thus we can say that the rise of political humanism shows how the two traditions came to merge and how this merging took place via the interaction between the two traditions.

Similarly to the way in which the tradition of *zhi* prompted the tradition of *li* to develop into political humanism, the tradition of *li* stimulated the tradition of *zhi* to develop into organic naturalism. The natural world was given an organic coherence by the internal sense of linkage and relevance informed by the world of *li* and social intersubjectivity. In particular, when the spell of heaven was removed, the world of nature was revealed as nature *qua* nature and thus seen as having its own autonomy. This natural autonomy eventually led to the conception of the *dao* as the ultimate originating source and the sustaining process of things in the world. But as in the case of political humanism, the human is not separate from the world, so that the human as part of the world is not separate from the *dao*, and the natural forces and processes are regarded similarly as parts of the *dao*. When society is seen as incapable of fulfilling the aspirations of the human mind, the return to the *dao* by transcending the social and political becomes the natural consequence of the organic naturalism which is, of course, the Daoist creed. At this point it is clear that organic naturalism is also a result of the creative integration of the two ancient traditions biased towards nature, instead of man, as in the case of political humanism.

An illuminating case of the creative integration of the two traditions is Zi Dashu's reinterpretation of *li* in terms of imitation of nature. Zi Dashu quoted Zi Zhan as saying: '*Li* is the canon of heaven, the norm of earth, and the principle which people follow in their action' and then suggested that all the rules of *li* which govern human relationships and behaviours are introduced to match, symbolize, follow and accord with natural events, natural phenomena, and natural processes and thus to control or balance and edify human emotions and actions and consequently to harmonize with the nature of heaven and earth, and to endure (*Zho Zhuan*, Shao Gong 25th Year). This view led to the reformulation of *li* as embodying and reflecting patterns (*li*) of nature or heaven and earth in the *Li Ji* and the *Guan Zi* ('Neiye' chapter).

AXIAL THINKERS AND THE FORMATION OF PHILOSOPHICAL SCHOOLS

In general, we may regard the development of Chinese philosophy in the classical period from 475 to 221 BC as a creative process in which the two ancient traditions of culture came to interplay in response to the social and political changes of the time. The political humanism and organic naturalism described above were the natural consequences of this creative process. But they were not philosophical schools; rather they were the dominating trends which led to the formation of the philosophical schools. They provided the atmosphere, the incentives and the cues for the coming period of philosophical blossoming, the blossoming of 'a hundred flowers' and the flourishing of 'a hundred schools'. In a sense all the philosophical schools were critical responses to the breakdown of the political and social system of the time by drawing inspiration from the resources of political humanism and organic naturalism. This, of course, does not mean that all philosophical schools were variations of political humanism or organic naturalism or their combinations.

In fact, while we may see political humanism and organic naturalism as two typical positions as well exemplified and further developed by Confucianism and Daoism, they may not exhaust all the possible developments of philosophical positions. We may see them as ways of thinking in which man and nature are made the centres of thinking, and political order and natural harmony are made the goals of human striving. That these ways of thinking may be adopted does not guarantee that they may not produce philosophical positions which modify or even deviate from these positions. In fact, while these two positions may serve as starting points for thinking, they may be transformed into something quite different and even totally opposite. This is allowed by the dialectics of the *Yi Jing* onto-cosmological way of thinking which underlies the organic naturalistic position. Furthermore, the most important factor which could determine the formation of a philosophical position is the experience and insight a thinker has in regard to the impacting problems of political reality. This must be granted: the political reality of the disintegration of the *li* order of Zhou and the consequent struggle and competition for political control towards stability was a deep and profound experience no thinker could ignore or lay aside, even though different thinkers may have resorted to different ways of expression with different focuses.

Mencius identified the central problem of the time as political and social stability (*ding*). His perception and insight into this problem were that the world would be 'stabilized by being unified' (*ding-yu-yi*). Hence the central problem of the time was how the world is to be unified and ordered according to a system of principles such as exemplified by the Zhou order of *li*. If one wanted to enjoy stability and order as in the Zhou, one had to face the problem of unifying different states during that time. This seems to be the underlying wish and assumption of all the philosophical schools, for all their thinkers were confronted with this problem as a pressing life-issue. The problem became increasingly acute and pressing as time went by. Thus by the fourth century BC the focus of political and philosophical thinking had become very much centred around the task of unification as an ideal state of social well-being. This is how Legalism arose and gradually assumed a dominating role in approaching the problem of unification.

Legalism developed from combining and comparing various earlier schools of philosophy such as Confucianism, Mohism and Daoism. It absorbed different ideas from these various schools: from Confucianism, centring on controlling the mass by authority and the doctrine of the evil nature of man (Hsun Tzu); from Mohism the principle of equality and utilitarianism; from Daoism the principle of non-action (*wu-wei*). Yet the most important factor determining the orientation and substance of Legalist thinking was consideration of the urgent need for a centralized and unified government. Hence the Legalist position became realistic, utilitarian, non-humanistic, and perhaps even non-naturalistic. Yet one still can see how it is related to the two main resources of cultural consciousness.

Legalism was not the only school which was transformed into something new from the past. Mohism had earlier learned a good deal from Confucianism, but it became a new type of social and political philosophy which in one sense was ultra-conservative because of the Mohist belief in the *tianzi* (will of heaven) and yet in another sense was very forward-looking and realistic, which is partly compatible with both the humanistic outlook and the organic-naturalistic way of thinking and partly not so compatible.

Apart from the four major schools mentioned above, the Chinese classical period also saw the emergence of the Name School (*Ming Jia*), the Yin–Yang Wu-Xing School, the Military Strategy School (*Bing Jia*), the Agronomy School (*Nung Jia*) and the Diplomatic School (*Zong Heng Jia*), which constitute together with Daoism, Confucianism, Mohism and Legalism the nine schools of thought in the classical period. It is clear that the Military Strategy School and the Diplomatic School were realist and applied schools of practical thought. Even though there were theoretical components in these schools, the schools applied fundamental principles of the *Yi Jing* to practical matters for the purpose of finding a solution to a real issue or problem. The Agronomy School represented a political and social philosophy which dates back to the ancient practice of non-separation of labour. Its purpose was to solve the problem of how to reconstruct or construct a political form of government control. This leaves the Yin–Yang Wu-Xing School and the Name School to be explained.

It is clear that the Yin–Yang Wu-Xing School as headed by Zhou Yen was a natural product of interest in applying the empirical theory of five powers and the cosmic philosophy of the *yin–yang* developed by the *Yi Jing*. It was basically a cosmological theory and a philosophy of history, which was quite compatible with political humanism and organic naturalism, and may actually have been encouraged by ideas and views of political humanism and organic naturalism.

As to the Name School, it may be said that the school originated from the issue of the relation of name (*ming*) to actuality (*shi*) which became a central problem for philosophical schools, because this problem became closely related to the problem of reconstructing name and/or actuality to accommodate the disintegrated Zhou order of *li*, which originally embodied the unity and correspondence of *ming* with *shi*. It is also clear that the Name School as represented by Gungsun Lung did not face up to the challenges of political humanism and organic naturalism, but can be seen as a direct or indirect response to the disintegration of the social and political reality of the time.

We may now organize these philosophical schools in terms of their positions and points of view in relation to solutions to problems bearing upon society and government. It needs to be pointed out first that for each philosophical school we must pay attention to the founding person who presented perceptive views on human nature, human destiny, history, society, government and the world. In these views we can also glimpse his understanding and experience of the material, personal, social and political reality of his time. Although there is an intimate relation between his self-reflection, convictions, aspirations and evaluations of the real world of his time and the theoretical thoughts of his philosophy, this relation creating a unity of his thoughts and the whole person, there is no clear causal link between the thinker's social, political or even economic situation and his self-understanding and theoretical thinking. As a thinker he should reflect the whole age and whole world in which he finds himself, and at the same time he should also think and speak for the whole age and the whole world to which he belongs. In such thinking and speaking he presents the underlying humanity in the universal forms of ideas and principles, which go beyond his age and his world and yet mould and shape his age and his world or the age and the world to come.

In their times and relative to their backgrounds all these founding thinkers became what they were, whether Daoist, Confucianist, Mohist or Legalist, and had specially lent themselves to such moulding and shaping influences because they were 'reality in the making', be it social, political or spiritual. There is a special fluidity and a special transformability which allow different approaches to thinking through the problems and issues presented by a particular time and world. These are the age and the world, as already mentioned, in which the disintegration of the social order and the emancipation of energy take place at the same time. These are the age and the world which have presented a point of epochal inflection which could go down the drain, or which could reach up to the sky. Which thought or idea or view captures the most plausible and most needed depends upon both the times and the world as well as the nature of human thinking.

It is clear that both the classical age and the classical thinker who founded a school of philosophy warranted special distinction for effecting a transformation of values and a reconstruction of tradition or for the creation of new standards and new paradigms. Karl Jaspers called the age of this type the 'axial age' for mankind. In the same vein, we may call the thinker of that age the 'axial thinker'. We may thus see that all the philosophers, especially the noted and influential ones, in this classical period of Chinese history were 'axial thinkers', who responded critically to their age and the world of their time, and who developed directions and visions on a transformation of values for the whole of humanity. They did so on the basis of what I have described as the creative integration of the *li* and *zhi* traditions. What is creative in their insights and convictions is derived from their existential involvement with the world and humanity. They are critically responding to a pervasive crisis of social, political and human disintegration, opening up to all possibilities which call for the evaluation and transformation of reality.

Whether an 'axial thinker' must reflect a social class or a social background in a causal manner cannot be determined absolutely. There is no reason why or conclusive evidence that an 'axial thinker' is confined to the interests and feelings of the social class to which he belongs. He is a member of the world, a member of a whole society, a member of a social class, a resident of a special locality and an individual person at the same time. To call him an 'axial thinker' is to underline the fact that he thinks for the world, a whole society, a social class, a special locality and himself at once. We need not see the philosopher as being merely engaged in the ideological struggle for his class in the social and political reality of his time. We must see particularity in universality and vice versa, otherwise we cannot understand the nature of 'axial thinking' and the nature of an 'axial thinker'. In other words, we do not have to subscribe to the Marxist interpretation of philosophical thinking in the Chinese classical period. But on the other hand, there is no harm in acknowledging the existential links of theoretical views and insights of the philosophical schools with the 'axial thinker's' self-understanding and evaluation of his age and his world as well as the social and political reality of his age in voicing his views and insights as a critical response to the social and political reality of his age. For the social and political reality did provide an occasion and incentive for his theoretical views and insights with a hidden dimension of self-understanding and evaluation of his age.

Another characteristic of the 'axial thinker' is that he is able to exercise influence on his generation and succeeding generations in a natural and spontaneous way. There is no political manoeuvring of his thinking to influence people, because it is not ideology, nor is it created as ideology. It is a creation at the social and cultural level, not at the political level. The philosophical influence it exercises comes out through social and cultural channels such as teaching, lecturing and conversation or dialogue in a basically academic or intellectual environment. It is in this natural and open communication with society and culture and even humanity at large that a seminal philosophical idea may capture the imagination of and stimulate thinking in others, particularly the younger generation, and hence the philosophical school would be formed as a natural consequence. In fact, when we speak of the philosophical school (*jia*) in the Chinese classical period, we are able to do so only retrospectively. For the 'axial thinker' did not normally perceive himself as forming a school, particularly in the early stages of the formation of the school. In fact, it was at the time of Mencius, and even later, at the time of Xunzi and Zhuangzi, that we come to see the term *jia* being used. There is no reference to the *jia* in the time of Lao Zi and Confucius. The conclusion to be drawn from this observation is that Chinese philosophical schools were formed from the natural dissemination of ideas which reflected both the social and cultural trends of the time and the appeal of the ideals and ideas of the 'axial thinkers' as founders of the schools.

Given the above understanding of 'axial thinking' and the formation of philosophical schools in the Late Chun-Jiu to the Warring States Period, we may now see how major Chinese philosophers as 'axial thinkers' emerged and how their philosophies as 'axial thinking' were developed as critical responses to the social and political reality of their times on the one hand, and as disclosures of human values based on underlying human potentialities on the other. We may in fact distinguish three types of critical responses among these philosophers, each of which represents an attitude of critique and evaluation of the confronted or given social and political reality of the time as well as an effort towards its replacement or reform. We may indeed also regard each type as indicating a historical stage in the evolution of the social and political reality of the time and thus representing a typical critical response to that historical period. .

The first type of critical response is to abandon the social and political reality of the time and thus in this sense to transcend the social and political reality in a quest for something totally remote or absolutely utopian. This also implies a thorough critique and rejection of the status quo, whether political, social or cultural, from a point of view which makes this critique and rejection meaningful, not just possible. This means that this rejection and abandoning are of the social and political reality *per se* and so presuppose or reveal a deeper reality, the reality of nature or the *dao* (way). One may also say that the social and political crisis of the period prompted the philosopher's insight into reality on the level of nature and thus led to a radical criticism of culture, knowledge, humanity and society at the time. This is the position of Daoism as initiated and represented by the *Dao De Jing* of Laozi in the sixth century BC.

In the *Dao De Jing*, there are two main themes: first, the deconstruction and critique of human knowledge and cultural artificiality and their consequential desire-ridden struggles and strife; second, the disclosure or presentation of an onto-cosmological point of view which shows the selfless, desireless, speechless, ceaseless creativity of life and truth. The former theme leads to the idealization of a government of non-interference or non-government or non-action; the latter theme leads to a full-scale philosophy or metaphysics of the *dao*. In the long run the *dao*-metaphysics had profound impact and influence. It set the stage for the development of a more systematic thought about reality at large and in the ultimate, which gave new meaning to life and death and transformed philosophies such as Buddhism and Neo-Confucianism. Of course, the philosophy of the *dao* does not arise in an arbitrary way. It arises as a continous expansion and elaboration of the organic naturalism I mentioned above. It is in the *dao* concept that all things in the world become thoroughly integrated.

It is clear that all things can be understood as co-ordinated and interacting in a certain way. Like an *n*-body problem in modern physics, the problem of co-ordinating all things in the world requires a force and a process far greater than any known single principle to be observed among things. Yet the insight into the *dao* is to see the totality of things in co-ordination as well as the co-ordination of all things and anything. The co-ordinating force is conceived in terms of polarities of the *yin* and *yang* and the transformation of polarities in things. As a whole the process of the *dao* exhibits dialectical interaction, reversion, regeneration, and boundless harmonization and balance. However, to see all these and to grasp their meanings and usefulness requires insights into the invisible hidden sides of things, their inceptive movements as well as their infinite involvements with one another. It is to see things of being (*you*) as being of things which is generated from the void (*wu*) or non-being without forms or substances, for the *dao* as the co-ordination of things and as source of movements of things cannot be said to be being in any substantial sense. Thus, in general, Laozi proclaims: 'The *dao* which can be spoken is not the constant *dao*; the name which can be named is not the constant name' (*Dao De Jing*, ch. 1). Speaking and naming change the nature of things, and there is a stage where there is no name and no speaking and hence no-thing.

It is important to note that the *dao* of Laozi finally replaced the notion of heaven (*tian*) as the ultimate reality for philosophy and to a large extent for society as a whole. The process of depersonalization of the *tian* in organic naturalism reached its height in the philosophy of the *dao*. From this it is also noted that the *dao*-metaphysics continued the tradition of, and was nurtured by, the philosophy of the *Yi Jing* and in its turn enriched and nourished the philosophy of the *Yi Jing*.

Since the philosophy of the *dao* in Laozi deconstructed and withdrew from the social and political reality of the time, it can be plausibly said to be the earlier or first response to the disintegration and collapse of the *li* order of the Zhou. The despair at and the distrust in the social and political bespeak a stage in which the crisis of a collapse of the long-term and whole fabric of stability caused deep reflection in a trusting and sensitive mind. In this sense we may call Laozi the first 'axial thinker' of the period. The project of Laozi's 'axial thinking' can be said to be deconstructive, reclusive (or hermitic) and transcendental. His critical response to the social and political can be described in the same way. Zhuangzi followed Laozi, as Zhuangzi himself acknowledged. But Zhuangzi took a more sophisticated attitude towards the social and political world. He could accept reality at face value, but relativized it to the world of the *dao* and thus enjoyed roaming and wandering in it without attachment and anxiety. He was even able to discover infinitely many relativist worlds in the world of the *dao* and thus reached a spiritual freedom which had no counterpart in the realist world of society and politics.

Now we come to the second type of critical response to the social and political reality of the time. This is the Confucian response of *reconstruction*. Instead of deconstructing, abandoning or rejecting the social and political reality, Confucius, on the basis of his cultural experience and historical reflection, came to see the redeeming values of the tradition of *li*. Even though the Zhou *li* of the past could not be fully restored, for Confucius it was important to develop and cultivate the spirit of *li* in order to direct society and politics correctly. Confucius also discovered the existence and power of *ren*, namely the power of the moral transformation of the human individual in his or her relation and transaction with other people. The Confucian faith is that if each individual is able to develop this *ren* quality, he or she is able to restore and reformulate *li* on a social and cultural level and therefore to reconstruct the world of human harmony and human values in which each has a place of worth and an environment for self-realization and self-fulfilment.

What is *ren* in Confucian philosophy? It is the defining quality of humanity which has the power of expanding humanity from the centre of an individual to a community of well-ordered human relationships and harmonious fellowship, in which each individual will be better developed and each life better fulfilled. In anguish at the collapse of the social order of *li*, Confucius searched for a foundation and a source of *li*, which he felt was needed for its re-establishment and the reconstruction of the integrity of society and government. He found *ren* in the sensibility, feeling and power of human care for others as well as for the total benefit of society. He appropriated this concept from the affective tradition of political humanism in which the ruler is to act benevolently towards his people so that his rule can be justified and safeguarded. But in contrast to the political humanist attitude, Confucius transformed this political *ren* into a moral and human *ren*.

There are three points to be made about this transformation. First, compassion and benevolence towards people in general are now enlarged to include feeling and action towards individual persons in society and thus are not confined to the performance of the ruler alone. Second, it is not the ruler alone who is capable of practising *ren* or should practise *ren*. All human persons are capable of practising *ren* and should do so in order to be more human and more humanized. This means that the humanity and goodness of an individual are invested in the common good and goodness or well-being of society and other persons. *Ren* therefore enables an individual to be a ruler of his or her own and a moral ruler in setting examples and standards of good and right. Third, *ren* is seen to be the internal power of a human person, which can be exercised at will and which requires constant care and attention to grow into a perfection which pertains to the growth of the human person. In this way a new concept of human person is introduced: a human person is capable of moral and spiritual growth or perfectibility apart from his or her physical growth. Whereas there is a limit to the physical growth of a person, there is no limit to his or her moral or spiritual growth, which has its asymptomatic convergence towards the ideal person called the sage (*shengren*).

What matters most for a person is his or her continuous and never-to-be-forgotten effort to achieve *ren* in his or her life, and in making this effort he or she is called the 'morally ruling person' (*junzi*).[8] On the other hand, if a person fails to pay attention to the cultivation of *ren*, the quality or power in him or her which makes him or her care for society or a community of people, and if instead he or she cares only about his or her immediate personal profits and material well-being, he or she is called the 'small person' (*xiaoren*).

It is Confucius' perceptive discovery that all human persons have *ren*. It is no less important a discovery that *ren* is the basis and foundation for *li*. Confucius did not discuss how *li* as prevailing in his time reveals *ren*. But he nevertheless came to see that *ren* is a road towards the practice of *li*. In this sense of *li*, *li* is not necessarily any given set of prescribed rules or institutions of a social order; it is the morally and culturally needed or required norm for the harmonization of human relationships in society as well as the social order embodied in formal institutions, which enables human persons to avoid uncivilized fights and conflicts and which provides nourishment and moral space for the moral and spiritual growth of each person. It is in this sense that Confucius spoke of *ren* as 'overcoming the self and practising the *li*'. To overcome the self is to discipline and control the self lest it acts from self-interest alone or acts from personal desire in social relationships. This requires the person always to moderate self-interest for the benefit of others and society. Thus one will be able to care for others and do things which benefit others. This means leaving space for and giving respect to others. Allowing space for and giving respect to others precisely constitute the spirit of *li*.

To find the proper rule or proper form of this *li*-spirit requires understanding of history, culture, convention and custom, and thus requires respect for history and culture in general. But in this sense of establishing *li*, not only will tradition and history have had their importance and their places in society restored to them, but the creativity and wisdom of the individual will also come to play a useful role. This is how *li* can be restored and reconstructed or even revised, modified or added to for the benefit and consequently for the goodness and well-being of society.

There are other meanings of *ren* which make it the foremost and constant virtue to be cultivated, not only for an unmediated bearing on human actions but for mediated relevance to all social, moral and political norms. In other words, although *ren* is manifested in loving all human persons (*airen*) and doing things for the benefit of others and not doing things which would hurt others, the intended effect of *ren* in terms of social harmony and preservation of culture is preserved or made possible via other virtues such as *li*, *yi*, *zhong* and *xiao*. In this sense *ren* should be the source and basis for other virtues and should also be the completion and perfection of all virtues. In analyzing the relation of *ren* to *li*, we have seen that *ren* provides the impetus for *li* reform in that *ren* would create and found new *li*. It is in the same vein that *ren* can be said to create and found other virtues is so far as it is the ultimate source and ultimate justification of other virtues. We may regard *ren* as the formless and most centralized or most interiorized virtue, which always requires expression and exteriorization by way of other virtues; to put it the other way round, the articulation of *ren* in any form calls forth consideration of or creation of another virtue. Thus, for the externalized form of an action we have *li*. But before one embarks on a course of action, one has to determine the right or proper way of acting towards a person, even though one has the motive and objective of benefiting the person and/or the society. The right and proper way of acting calls for a close analysis, knowledge and understanding of the circumstances of action and the person to whom the action is directed.

It calls for an objective assessment of the situation as well as a volitional commitment to one's judgement so that one's action will be consistent with the total understanding and perception of the total order of things. This is then the spirit of *yi* as *a virtue in the sense of rightness or propriety on the objective side and justice and righteousness on the subjective side*. In this sense *yi* substantiates *li* and manifests *ren*.

Relative to *li* (practise), *yi* is the essence of *li*-action, just as relative to *yi*, *li* is the realization of *yi*-perception/thought. But relative to *ren*, *yi* is the objectification of *ren*, just as relative to *yi*, *ren* is the motivating force of *yi*. One thus sees the graduated relation towards externalization in *ren* → *yi* → *li* and the graduated relation towards interiorization in *li* ← *yi* ← *ren*. Since *li* is ultimately rooted in *ren*, an accepted or received *li* can be seen to point to a judgement of propriety or properness in *yi* as a mediation. *Yi* is the mediation between *li* and *ren* just as *li* is the consummation of *ren* and *yi* and *ren* is the motivation and integration of *li* and *yi*. These relations form a mutually enriching and complementary circularity and trinity among the three virtues once they are formed and demarcated in relation to one another, even though we have also to recognize at the same time the originative and perfective unity of the three in *ren*.

In understanding this, two further remarks can be made. First, in distinguishing between *li* and *yi*, one also needs to point out that whereas *li* is role- and status-orientated in the light of societal order, *yi* is reason- and thinking-orientated in the light of a reflection on the meaning of the social structure or social order by a person. Second, *ren* can be seen to be the core and the beginning for *li* and *yi* and by the same token for all other virtues, and thus can be seen as the defining nature of a human person. It is through Mencius that this defining of the nature of a human person is expressed in direct intuition and experience of fundamental moral feelings, whereas this defining is seen in the *Zhong Yong* as metaphysically derived and based on the original or originating creativity of the ultimate reality called heaven to be entitled the 'mandate of heaven'. In any case, *ren* eventually becomes the ultimate potential and sustaining nature of a human person. It is by way of this retracing that one can see how *ren* can be metaphysically or onto-cosmologically conceived as the onto-cosmic nature of the *dao* of heaven and thus the principle and way of life-creativity.

As *ren* can be seen as a process of concretely realizing and expanding the nature of a person in external and actual form and substance, *ren* is conceived as ultimately articulated in the concrete personal form of the sage (*shengren*). In this sense *ren* is the most concrete and most perfect 'form' of all virtues and thus the final embodiment and integration of all virtues.

Without going into too much detail, one can see how *zhi* (intelligence and wisdom) and *xing* (integrity and faithfulness) become the other two vital virtues in the Confucian system of personal, social and cosmic ethics. In order to make correct judgements about action towards *yi* and *li*, one needs *zhi* to work with. *Zhi* is the resource and thinking power for correctly determining the values of things and for correctly seeing the truth of affairs. Thus it can be seen as the first and primary power of objectification in distinction from the primary power of subjectification in *ren* even though *ren* is still the root-nature of a person. Thus we can see *zhi* as intermediate between *ren* and *yi*.

Finally, *xing* is the self-reflection of self-sufficiency of *ren* as a virtue ultimately rooted in the nature of man and heaven. It is the faith bridging the subjective and the objective which makes judgement and knowledge, decision-making and action possible. It is thus the initiating state as well as the final state of existence for all virtues as actualities. In fact, it is the sustaining base for the realization of all virtues which is inherently embodied or present in all virtues. It is specifically an integral part of *ren* which entitles *ren* to social self-justification and social self-expression. Hence *xing* can be called the hidden virtue-making virtue which expresses itself in all spontaneous human action as well as in all accomplishments of virtues in a society. In this way we can regard *xing* as another name for the initiation and integration of virtues as the realization of a social order.

Confucius paid attention to *zhi* and *xing*, but not at great length, yet their importance and their final incorporation into the core system of Confucian ethics via later Confucianists' thinking leave no doubt that they deserve mention in the ontogenetic analysis of Confucian philosophy.[9]

I have described the Confucian position in terms of Confucian ethics at some length. The significance of this effort is to accentuate the social and political orientation of the Confucian position in contrast with the Daoist. Unlike Laozi, Confucius did not wish to give up or bypass society and government as a way of solving social and political problems for a time or once and for all. Although he did not deny the relevance of the natural and the transcendent, he saw the necessary redeeming value of a social and political system for the fulfilment and realization of the value of a human person. In fact, he saw society and government as necessary instruments for such a realization. But unlike the political humanist, Confucius wanted to base the social and political on the moral perfection or moral cultivation towards perfection of individual persons. In doing so he would give society and government a human and moral foundation and motivation. And in so doing he was also able to retrieve *li* from the past for the use of the present as well as to deliver *li* from a foundational source of the humanity of individual persons. This last point serves to mark out Confucius as a philosopher who was engaged in the enterprise of *reconstructing* the social and the political on the basis of the human and the moral.

There are two senses of this reconstruction. First, Confucius wished to reconstruct the *li* of the social and political from the humanity of *ren*. Second, he wished to reconstruct the *li* of the social and political from existing culture and history, in combination with the creative force of *ren* of the individual. In both these senses Confucius vindicated himself as a reconstructionist or retrievalist in his approach to the problem of his times. His philosophy was both an answer to the urgent issue of his times and an answer to the perennial problem of relating the individual to society and government on the one hand and to culture and tradition or history on the other.

Since his reconstructionist or reformist position linked the present with the past, the mundane with the ideal, Confucius was seen as a conservative from the point of view of progressive-minded and only-forward-looking philosophers such as the Legalists, but as a utopian enthusiast from an anarchist-transcendentalist position like the Daoist. In reality, the Confucian position has its traditional elements and its innovative force. But Confucius was not ready to meet the tensions and the needs of the time fully and thus ended up disappointed and frustrated over his failure to secure political implementation. But he succeeded in awakening and inspiring posterity to the way of the mean and the way of harmonizing and integration of stability and creativity, the form and content for a full realization of humanity at both a social and a human level.

After Confucius, Mencius fully developed the philosophy of *yi* and the philosophy of the nature of humanity. He stressed the inner creative force of the nature of humanity (*xing*), which is equivalent to *ren* in a broad sense. But in doing so he stressed the inner world at the expense of the outer as represented by Confucius' consideration of learning (*xue*) and *li*. It was not until Xunzi that such elements as learning and *li* were paid close attention and received significant emphasis. Xunzi developed a full social and political philosophy founded on his philosophy of *xue* (learning) and *li*. In constructing his full philosophy he also came to see the importance of *zhi* and rationality of mind. Thus we can regard Xunzi as a rationalist humanist, in distinction from Mencius as an idealist humanist. It is quite possible that in stressing the social elements of conditioning Xunzi may have failed to give proper account of the creative force of the nature of man and thus opened the way towards the full constructionist view of human nature and human society in the Legalist philosophy.

Before we examine the Legalist view, we should also note that in the Confucian book *Li Ji* endeavoured to develop a full theory of society and political reconstruction on the basis of self-cultivation of persons (via the chapter entitled 'Da Xue') and to explore the metaphysical foundation of human nature and its onto-cosmological source and expression (via the chapter entitled 'Zhong Yong'), perhaps in conjunction with the writing of the commentaries on the *Yi Jing*. The significance of such efforts will not be investigated here: I merely indicate how the Confucian reconstructionist position initiated and inspired a large school of philosophical and cultural thinking which had an impact and influence beyond Confucius' own generation.

Next to Confucianism, we may mention Mohism as representing a variation of the reconstructionist point of view. Mozi learned Confucianism in his early years, but seeing the ineptitude and complacency of many Confucians of his time, he formulated his own social philosophy of universal love (*jianai*) and mutual benefit, and his political philosophy of heavenly will (*tianzi*) and wilful conformity (*xiangdong*) in his zest to reform and save society. He was not only a thinker but a person of action, for he tried to implement what he believed and thus founded the Mohist community, which was economically self-sufficient, craftmanship-orientated, and militarily prepared for just wars.

This utilitarian, practical attitude combined with a rational mentality, suited to persuasion and defensive argumentation, eventually transformed the Mohists into Neo-Mohists, who became the pioneers in logic and science in early China. The reason why we characterize Mozi as a reconstructionist is that he redeemed the ancient belief in *tian-ming* and stressed the importance of society and government, but introduced new methods of thinking and judgement for reconstructing society.

We now come to the *constructionist* position of Legalism. By constructionism I mean the efforts to conscientiously construct laws, methods, skills and conditions for the ordering of society and rule of a people after a thorough critique and rejection of the relevancies of history and culture. To construct requires systematic rationality on the one hand and will-power on the other. Both presuppose a clear determination regarding the objectives of state and society. In the classical period of Chinese history, the rise of Legalist constructionism was not accidental. It began with Shang Yang's doctrine of rule by *fa* (law). *Fa* is not law legislated by people or people's representatives in modern democracies. It consists of commands and regulations which dictate what is to be done and what is not to be done in the interests of the objectives of the state and the ruler. Hence *fa* is basically regulatory and pertains to matters of punishment and reward. In a wider sense it embraces institutions which organize resources and people for the strengthening and enrichment of the state and the ruler. Hence farming and warfare become the two major areas covered by *fa*.

In short, the essence of *fa* is found in the central control of people and society by the state or the ruler in terms of organization, regulations and rules of action and means of publishment and reward. It is based on the social psychology of conditioning and the egoistic ethics of self-interest and fear. *Fa* is efficacious in so far as it is under the control of the state and the state has the power to enforce it. Thus it is through rule by *fa* that an objective of the state can be efficiently attained. We may call this constructive attitude in society and politics 'political realism', which is a flat denial of humanism, whether political or moral.

The doctrine of *fa* proved successful in the state of Qin and others. By the time of Han Fei, it was widely perceived that *fa* was the most powerful tool for achieving a state goal, and the use of *fa* created a powerful machine of control in the state of Qin. In response to the needs of the time, it is clear that the old *li* disintegrated so much that there was no way of recovering it, certainly not by the reconstructive programmes of education and moral cultivation of the Confucian school, or by the altruistic and chivalrous efforts of the community-orientated Mohists. What was needed was a powerful state with the authority and means to implement a social order which guaranteed stability and peaceful living. It is apparent that in envisioning the need for unification of the whole of China and the means for unification by *fa*, the Legalists realistically responded to the issue of the time. It is the reason why Han Fei attracted the attention of the first emperor of Qin. In saying this we may see Legalism as the product of the most realistic historical forces of the time, while it denied the relevance of history to the present. In tracing the historical development of rule by *fa*, I wish to show the historical trends and background for the dialectical formation of schools from Laozi to Han Fei. I shall say more on this point below.

Apart from promotion of *fa*, the Legalists saw the importance of *shu* (skills of control and management) and *shi* (position and situation) for exercising efficient control of ministers and subjects in pursuing state objectives. Shen Buhai stressed the importance of *shu* primarily to enable the ruler to discriminate between the goodness and badness, ability or lack of ability of his ministers. Shen Dao, on the other hand, pointed to the importance of the position a ruling person occupies. A position entails a certain power to coerce and persuade. But the power of coercion and persuasion comes from other factors such as titles, trust and the influences one may have over certain people or people in general. All these pertain to the idea of *shi*, a power position whether one recognizes it or not. But both Shen Buhai and Shen Dao were also strongly in favour of rule by *fa*. It is evident that for them *fa* is primary and *shu* and *shi* are vital elements needed for successful rule by *fa*, because they pertain to effective control by *fa*. In Han Fei, *fa* is primary, but one needs *shi* to enact *fa* and implement *fa* or make *fa* a tool of rule. How to apply *fa* in a given situation for a certain goal is a matter of *shu*. In this way the three are combined to establish the Legalist philosophy of control and leadership, which for Han Fei and other Legalists should suffice to reach the realist goals and change the present order of society under the pressure of the present order of things.

Certain things need to be said about Legalism. First, all Legalists rejected the institutions of the past and appealed to new ways of governing and control. Specifically, they rejected the Confucian ethics of befriending relatives and respecting the highly placed. This means that they rejected *li*, which is based on human emotion. *Fa* is based on utility and rationality, which take no account of emotion and human relations. This is the constructive side of this arrangement. Second, Legalists looked to the future and explained the past in terms of evolution. In this sense, history, tradition and culture would play little role in the construction of social and political reality. Third, Han Fei had the insight that man is basically for himself (*ziwei*) and thus can be motivated and moulded by considerations of self-interest, fear and desire under conditions of *fa*. This is a behaviourist approach to human nature which is not considered either good or bad in any metaphysical sense. Fourth, given the constructive view of history and society, Han Fei criticized other schools, specifically Confucianism and Mohism, as 'foolish and false learning' and as 'useless disputes'. His approach was to scrutinize many facts in order to see whether names match them (*canyen*). It was apparent to him that the social and political reality of his time did not match or warrant either the Confucian or the Mohist programme of reconstruction. Tradition, no matter how we reconstruct it, would not generate the needed power or drive for social progress and political control.

Although Han Fei developed a highly constructive view of society and government, he was not a positivist and remained interested in the nature of the world. In fact, his philosophy included an important element of metaphysics and dialectics. Perhaps, under the indirect influence of the *Yi Jing* and the direct influence of Laozi, Han Fei came to develop a dialectics on three levels.

At the first level, the level of nature, there are coexisting polarities such as large and small and square and circle, which Han Fei called the 'pattern' (*li*). They are opposites which form a unity or continuum to which individual things belong and in terms of which individual things find their natural positions. But nothing is determined on a fixed point, and everything will change according to dialectical laws of transformation from opposite to opposite under relevant conditions. This implies that it is in the nature of things to change and that change takes place when things have reached their utmost development or when other external conditions for change obtain. This point is nowhere clearer than at the human level.

At the human level, it is plain that there is no absolute perfection, for every person has his or her limitations and weaknesses. Han Fei said: 'There is a point where wisdom cannot help; there is a point where force cannot raise, and there is a point where the strong cannot win' (see the chapter entitled 'Guanxing' in *Han Fei Zi*). It is also evident that opposites will naturally transform towards each other. For Han Fei the Laozi statement 'Misfortune is where good fortune resides and good fortune is where misfortune hides' meant that unless one is in control of oneself and watches oneself carefully, the transformation will take place because the conditions for transformation will naturally obtain. Human persons are easily prone to go to extremes, and when this happens the weaknesses come in. This is the principle that 'things will reverse when developed to extremes.'

At the third level, the level of prudence and wisdom, a person should be aware of the dialectical principles of transformation from opposite to opposite, and make efforts to apply them to his or her actions and to human affairs in general. This means that a person should come to know the specific conditions of transformation for each human action and human affair, and in doing so come to follow the *dao* and obey the objective order of things (*li*) (see the chapter entitled 'Jie Lao' in *Han Fei Zi*). Han Fei stressed the importance of planning and design for the purpose of control in the light of knowledge of things and their potentiality for change. This utilitarian and constructivist attitude towards control marks out the way he differs from the Daoist position on spontaneity and natural conformity.

Han Fei basically followed Laozi in accepting the metaphysics of the *dao*. It is natural to understand why Han Fei the great Legalist came to absorb Daoism into his philosophy. Not only did he need a justification for his philosophy of *fa*, but he needed an ultimate principle for the practical application of *fa*. *Dao*, as the source of everything with its dialectical principles of transformation, served this purpose. The grounding of *fa* on the *dao* and the grounding of the application of *fa* on the *dao* were absolutely and logically required. In fact, the idea of 'doing everything by doing nothing' (*wu-wei-er-wu-pu-wei*) gave rise to the ideal of an invisible ruler in perfect and absolute control without any effort. Yet natural as this ideal seems, it cannot really be attained, because rulers, unlike the *dao*, are not totally free from their desires and feelings, and thus cannot achieve the state of non-action either in the formation of *fa* or in the application of their *fa* by means of *shu* or *shi*. In this sense the Legalist attitude contradicts the Daoist position. It should be noted that Han Fei, unlike Laozi, stressed the contrariness of some opposites, which requires a solution in terms of struggle and overcoming. Which of the two will succeed will be seen in time. But in Han Fei's effort to reinterpret Laozi one sees Han Fei's wish to resolve this contradiction to his advantage.

It is interesting, however, to see how Han Fei strived to absorb the Daoist metaphysics and its *deconstructive* wisdom into his *constructive* philosophy of social and political control. For this purpose he introduced the notion of the objective principle of things in their natural and specific contexts, namely the notion of *li* (pattern, order, reason). Although the term *li* was used earlier in Shang Yang's writings, it is Han Fei who raises *li* to the level of metaphysical understanding. For him *li* is the pattern whereby a thing becomes a thing (see the chapter entitled 'Jie Lao' in *Han Fei Zi*) and ten thousand things all have their different *li* simply because they are different things. What, then, is the relation between the *dao* and *li*? The answer is that the *dao* is the totality and receptacle of *li* to which *li* belongs and on which *li* depends (same chapter). Whereas *li* is more or less fixed, though changing according to the change of things, the *dao* is always changing in time and in fact should form the motive force for the change of things. Thus the *dao* and *li* are related in terms of patterns emerging from changing things, for particularity rises and resides in universality.

With this understanding of *li*, Han Fei came to found his philosophy of social and political control on the methodology of 'understand/embody the *dao*' (*didao*), 'follow the *li*' (*luli*), 'deepen one's wisdom' (*zhisheng*), 'reach for a strategy or plan' (*jide*), and finally 'become capable of controlling all things' (*neng-yu-wan-wu*). If one is able to control everything, one will win out against one's enemies (see the 'Jie Lao' chapter in *Han Fei Zi*). It is clear that the highest goal of Han Fei in constructive philosophy is to use the *dao* constructively for the purpose of implementing *fa* towards successful control.

It is interesting to note that Legalism as the last major response to the reality of the time exhibited a return to Daoism, albeit a return for the incorporation of Daoism for political use. This shows a defeat of the original purpose of deconstruction, emancipation and abandonment in Daoism. The deconstructive was constructed or in a sense reconstructed, but not in the Confucian sense of appropriating the tradition of *li*. This suggests a practical ending of the classical period of philosophical thought as a critical response to the world of the time. In this ending culture and history were temporarily suspended or *aufheben* in the interests of realist social and political construction. Philosophy became a matter of forming social and political policies.

The state of Qin succeeded in unifying China in 221 BC and so answered the urgent issue of the time. However, when that purpose was served, an opposite movement began. What was suppressed for the supreme political construction now came back to play its proper role, for there were far more abundant forces of change and needs in social and individual entities, which were beyond the scope of Legalist constructionism. Hence, the Legalist construction finally ran its course and a new age of deconstruction and reconstruction set in. This was the come-back of the *dao* and *li* as well as the setting of the stage for the grand reconstructive enterprise of Han Confucianism.

CONCLUDING REMARKS

In this chapter we have analysed and discussed the rise of Daoism, Confucianism, Mohism and Legalism as four major schools of philosophy arising from the matrix of the early Zhou culture consisting of the tradition of *li* and the tradition of *zhi* as well as from a critical response to this cultural matrix. Different times and different social and political awarenesses have differentiated these positions, and yet there was an abundance of innovative creativity, which suggests the work of the *dao*. There is also inner logic in the web of schools which followed and embodied the dialectical principles of transformation. The whole story of origination suggests the creative development of a cultural *daiji* into opposite and complementary forms of difference. But in a historical course of development these complementary forms also appear to be contradictory and competitive. Which form will dominate at which time and under what conditions is for the contingency of history to determine. What is clear is that there is no historical determinism of everything; rather, there are always co-determining forces, which include human participation and human self-determination. In this sense the origins of Chinese philosophy consist of creative efforts to reach totality, stability, balance and harmony in an ever-fluid context of social, political and moral and historical developments.

There are many other schools which we did not discuss. But it suffices to say that they all fell under the same spell of historical and political co-determination. Even the School of Names (*Ming Jia*) cannot be understood without this backdrop. This means that in Chinese philosophy there is the uncut umbilical cord from which all philosophical ideas and categories derive their nourishment and to which there is always a dynamic feedback which would change the settings and focuses of philosophical thought. The deconstructive, the reconstructive and the constructive attitudes respectively represented by Daoism, Confucianism (and Mohism) and Legalism can be said to capture the three modes or moods of the philosophical mentality: to transcend, to integrate, and to construct, in regard to history, culture, society and politics. It may be noted that transcendence in Chinese Daoism has not reached its extreme limit, namely to isolate and identify a transcendent 'something' as in Christianity or to point to a transcendent 'no-thing' as in Buddhism. But this is precisely the characteristic wisdom of Chinese philosophy: to reach to the centre and respond to an infinity of possibilities. In a sense, the three modes are not only independent guiding lights on a circle; they also interact and mix to the point of being capable of forming a permanent dynamic harmony and unity in a theoretical perspective.

It is from this source, a higher level of consciousness and achievement than the pre-Daoist and pre-Confucianist Zhou culture, that all later philosophical inspiration and ways of thinking came and thrived. This no doubt transforms an incoming philosophy such as Buddhism and leads to new forms of presentation and articulation in reponse to outside stimulation. It is in this light that not only Chinese Buddhism and Neo-Confucianism are to be understood, but even modern and contemporary Chinese philosophy such as Maoism. In this sense, to explore the origins of Chinese philosophy makes it possible to illuminate and unravel the philosophical understanding of Chinese philosophy in general and present-day Chinese philosophy in particular.

We may summarize four major issues across all Chinese philosophical schools in the 'axial age' of their co-origination. They are the problem of the relation between heaven (*tian*) and man (*ren*), the problem of the relation between name (*ming*) and reality (*shi*), the problem of the relation between knowledge (*zhi*) and practice (*xing*), and finally the problem of the relation between substance (*di*) and function (*yong*). These problems are problems because they have been transformed from a stage of no problems. As we have seen above, the earliest development of Chinese culture and pre-philosophy led from succeeding primary states of unity and distinction between subjectivity and objectivity to the achieved state of conscious unifications between heaven and man, name and reality, knowledge and action, and substance and function after distinctions are properly made, related and integrated. These unifications represent the high mark of the Zhou culture, with its tradition of *li* and tradition of *zhi*.

When the Zhou culture fell into disarray, we enter the third stage of origination of Chinese philosophy, namely the stage where all these unities were called into question and thus all required conscious and rational examination. The three major philosophical mentalities were the three modes of self-reflection and critical responses to this crisis and need. They became the discourses in which both question and answer were articulated. It is clear that the Daoist wished to transcend these unifications or to stress one side at the expense of the other; the Confucianist wished to maintain these unifications from an internal and humanist point of view; the Legalist, on the other hand, wanted to deny these unifications and wished to construct a new scheme of distinctions which required the mediation of knowledge and criticism of all possible unities. With this understanding, we can indeed see that all Chinese philosophical categories thus generated were germinated in this age of co-origination, pregnant with rich meanings and references at various levels of human and cosmic existence.

NOTES

1 See *Wen-wu-Zazhi*, vol. II, no. 8 (1986).
2 See Kaogu Xuebao, vol. VII (Wen-wu Publishers, 1954); *Xinghongguo de kaogufaxian yu yenxiu* (Wen-wu Publishers, 1984).
3 We see here the continuity from past to present, and we shall see how continuity can be established from present to future in the formation of the onto-cosmology of the *Yi Jing* tradition.
4 This is because the ideal is often founded on a critical awareness of the limitations and shortcomings of the present and the actual.
5 We may indeed speak of the Greeks as rationally orientated and as having developed abstract reason because their ocean environment challenged them to overcome hardship, whereas the Hebrews had to survive a drastically unfriendly desert environment by way of a faith born out of desperation and despair, and the Indians had to search for a state of total peace and tranquillity of mind under the spell of tropical sun and forest. In all these three cases, the affective ties with nature are basically cut or transcended and man has to face his 'true' self or another transcendent world of value, be it *Eidos*, God or Brahma. For a theory of primary orientations for major historical cultural traditions in the world, I have to wait for another occasion to elaborate.
6 See chapter entitled 'Chinese metaphysics as non-metaphysics: Confucian and Daoist insights into the nature of reality', in Robert Allinson (ed.), *Understanding the Chinese Mind* (Cambridge: Cambridge University Press, 1989), pp. 167–208.
7 We must grant that no political form or system is able to contain or control social and economic changes. Hence the survivability of a political order depends on how open and how flexible the political order is. Perhaps it is in this light that democracy, which allows smooth non-violent self-transformation, may be said to be the best survivable system of political control. But even democracy may lead to disorder if a stable social and economic order is not maintained and education toward independent thinking is not developed.
8 I introduce this new interpretation of *junzi* in order to capture the vividly felt but generally academically neglected or overlooked substance of the notion of *junzi*.
9 One can finally see the five virtues of the Confucian philosophy as forming a unity and circle of *ren-xing-zhi-yi-li-ren* or *xing-ren-zhi-yi-li-xing*. The pervasive quality of *xing* was particularly noted by Zhu Xi.

REFERENCES

The following are available in Standard Chinese editions:

Wen-wu-Zazhi, *Kaogu Xuebao*, *Yi Jing*, *Shang Shu*, *Shu Jing*, *Chun Jiu*, *Guo Yu*, *Zho Zhuan*, *Li Ji*, *Lun Yu*, *Men Zi*, *Xun Zi*, *Guan Zi*, *Dao De Jing*, *Zhuang Zi*, *Shang Jun Shu*, *Shen Bu-hai*, *Shen Dao*, *Han Fei Zi*.

FURTHER READING

Chan, Wing-tsit (1963) *A Source Book in Chinese Philosophy*, Princeton: Princeton University Press.

Creel, H. G. (1953) *Chinese Thought: From Confucius to Mao Tse-tung*, Chicago, University of Chicago Press.

Fung Yu-lan (1952–3) *A History of Chinese Philosophy*, trans. by Derek Bodde, 2 vols., Princeton: Princeton University Press.

—— (1948) *A Short History of Chinese Philosophy*, New York: Macmillan.

Hu, Sheng (1987) *The Great Encyclopaedia of China: Philosophy*, Beijing: The Great Encyclopaedia of China Publishing House.

Ren, Jiyn (1983) *The History of Development of Chinese Philosophy*, Beijing: People's Publishing House.

Waley, Arthur (1939) *Three Ways of Thought in Ancient China*, London: Allen & Unwin.

26

CONFUCIUS AND CONFUCIANISM

Huang Nansen

Confucius, the philosopher, thinker, educationalist and statesman, and the Confucian school which he founded, have influenced Chinese history for two thousand years. Confucianism has formed the kernel of Chinese traditional civilization and extends its influence to many countries all over the world, especially in Asia. Is it possible for Confucian teachings to exert some influence in eliminating the evils which are produced in the single-minded pursuit of material pleasure in a utilitarian age? This problem currently attracts wide attention in international theoretical circles.

CONFUCIUS AND HIS THOUGHT

'Confucius' ('Master Kong', 551–479 BC) was a respectful form of address. His given name was Kongqiu; his literary name was Zhongni. He was born in Lu (Qufu, Shandong province) in the Spring and Autumn Period of the history of China. His ancestors were nobles of Song, but the status of their descendants gradually declined. His father Shulianghe was a minor official – the head of Zou county in Lu. His father died when he was 3 years old, leaving Confucius and his mother in extremely poor financial circumstances. Confucius was principally engaged throughout his life in education, political activities, travelling and persuading princes of his political views, and searching for and revising Chinese classical writings. He expressed his various ideas and opinions during these activities. His life after the age of 15 may be divided into four periods.

Learning period (15–30 years old)

Confucius said: 'At fifteen I was bent on study; at thirty my mind was firmly established' (*Analects of Confucius* or *Lun-yu*, ch. 2). He had studied six skills (ceremonies, music, archery, driving carriages, calligraphy and calculation) and the six classics – *The Book of Songs*, *The Book of History*, *The Book of Rites*, *The Book of Music*, *The Book of Changes* and *The Spring and Autumn Annals* – which he was later to revise. These studies laid a firm foundation for his later educational and political activities. His mother died when he was 17, and he was obliged to earn his own living by doing various kinds of physical labour. He was, however, appointed as a master of ceremonies and a minor official superintending grain, cattle and so on.

Period of teaching and engaging in political activities (30–55 years old)

Confucius set up a private school at about the age of 30, the earliest in Chinese history. Meanwhile he engaged in various political activities, wishing to rank among the nobles of the ruling class of Lu, and at the age of 51 he was appointed as the head of Zhongdu county in Lu. Afterwards he was promoted to Minister of Industry, Minister of Public Security and acting Prime Minister of Lu. Because he had offended Ji Huanzi, the most powerful and influential noble of Lu, he was obliged to leave Lu at the age of 55 and began to journey through the states of princes and dukes.

Travelling period (55–68 years old)

Confucius' aim in his travels was to seek the support of these princes and dukes in putting his political views into practice. During this period he visited the six states Wei, Chen, Cao, Song, Zheng and Cai, and was accompanied by a group of disciples. He was welcomed and respected everywhere, yet he gained no real power or higher appointment. Sometimes he was treated coldly, even besieged by ruffians on the way, and suffered from hunger.

Period of revision (68–72 years old)

Confucius was invited to return home by Ji Kangzi, the Prime Minister of Lu, but though he was treated well the Prince of Lu did not accept his doctrines. Confucius concentrated his energy on revising the classics and on teaching. It was said that he had three thousand students, among whom seventy-two were outstanding. These gradually formed the Confucian school around him, and he became the greatest educationalist in ancient China. The revised classics were not his original writings, though they became regarded as such through his revisions. His work was undoubtedly a great contribution towards preserving and researching these classics.

Confucius did not write any treatise which systemically expounded his thoughts, but elaborated them in these educational and political activities. His disciples recorded his practices and statements with extreme conciseness, compiling them in the book which became known as the *Lun-yu* (the *Analects*). It became the most widely known and most influential book among Chinese classics, and was regarded as the bible of Confucianism. In addition, in other books there were reliable records of Confucius' activities and sayings.

Confucius' thoughts involved various fields of knowledge, especially philosophy, ethics, politics and education. The following paragraphs are concise introductions to these thoughts.

Philosophical thoughts

According to ancient Chinese ideas, 'heaven' or 'heaven–earth' in fact referred to nature, but nature was also deified and natural laws were seen as God's will. Confucius inherited this primitive theism, and made no attempt to study the nature of this universe and its natural laws. His attitude to the gods was rather cold. 'To revere the Gods, and keep at a due distance from them, may be called knowledge', he said (*Analects*, ch. 6). 'You cannot yet serve men, how can you serve the Gods?' (ch. 11).

The fundamental part of Confucius' philosophy was the philosophy of society and of man. What is the kernel of his philosophy? Is it benevolence (*ren*) or propriety (*li*)? Views on this question are quite varied. In most scholars' opinions, the kernel of Confucius' philosophy is the unity of benevolence and propriety, namely a doctrine of social order or system which is penetrated with the spirit of benevolence. Confucius did not define his categories and principles precisely, and did not metaphysically prove or justify his doctrine.

His understanding of propriety (*li*) was distinctive: it meant for him the society of the Zhou Dynasty in its great prosperity, whose economy, politics and culture he idealized. Chinese scholars have different views about the quality of the society of the Zhou Dynasty, but in the mind of Confucius it was definitely not a slave society, but a feudal one. According to his description of it, it was an ideal society in which the population was flourishing: living standards were high, with people living and working in peace and contentment; the king, princes and dukes carried out their functions perfectly in accordance with their ranks; ceremonies and music were flourishing; robbers and thieves disappeared, and the social order was stable and harmonious; people had high moral standards, setting strict demands on themselves and loving one another.

What was benevolence (*ren*)? Its fundamental meaning was the love of mankind, and Confucius therefore paid great attention to the harmony of social relations. Youzi said: 'In the practice of propriety, harmony is valuable' (ch. 1). Confucius called this condition the golden mean and said: 'The due medium is virtue. This is the highest attainment' (ch. 6). Therefore in one's activities 'to go too far, is as bad as not to go far enough' (ch. 20). One ought to 'faithfully hold fast to the due medium' (ch. 11).

Why did Confucius regard benevolence as the fundamental spirit of his society? He seems to have interpreted this view in connection with the doctrine of the good nature of man and said: 'By nature we are nearly equal, but by education very different' (ch. 17). But he did not develop this view. Confucius was dissatisfied with the society in which he lived, because it had fallen into anarchy and disorder, the lower strata rebelling against the upper. He resolved to recover or establish a benevolent society and advocated his ethical, political and educational thoughts towards this goal.

Ethical thoughts

Confucius paid great attention to moral self-cultivation and considered the benevolent or superior man as the ideal personality. The so-called benevolent or superior man was a person in the ruling class, but there was a certain universal significance in his ethical thoughts which can be summarized as follows:

1 One must act as strictly as one's social status demands ('Let the prince act the prince, the minister the minister, the father the father, the son the son' (ch. 12)), which Confucius called 'establishing one's character' (ch. 13).
2 One must love all men. In his view this love was no doubt different with different strata and different relatives, but he consented also to a broad love ('to show universal benevolence' (ch. 1); 'to manifest general benevolence to the people and promote the happiness of all men' (ch. 6).
3 One must treat other people as one treats oneself. 'The virtuous man wishes to be established himself, and to establish others – he wishes to possess perfect intelligence himself, and lead others to perfect knowledge' (ch. 6). 'What you do not wish others to do to you, do not to them' (ch. 12).
4 One must think highly of justice and despise benefit. 'The superior man is influenced by the love of rectitude, the mean man by the love of gain' (ch. 4). He esteemed that man a perfect man 'who, when he sees an opportunity of getting gain, thinks of justice' (ch. 14), who 'seeks not the preservation of life nor the injury of virtue, but will give up life in order to complete his virtue' (ch. 15).

Confucius created around the notions of benevolence and justice a series of moral categories: filial piety, fraternal affection, faithfulness, forbearance, intelligence, bravery and so on.

Political thoughts

Applying the notion of benevolence to politics, Confucius emphasized benevolent government and virtuous rule, and opposed government which depended only on administrative decrees and punishment. The major proposition of his political thoughts was to maintain and consolidate the feudal hierarchy, and he therefore demanded that the ruling strata 'conquer the self and return to propriety' (ch. 12), 'serve their prince with fidelity' (ch. 3), and especially be loyal to the King of Zhou. As for the people, he advocated that the ruler 'lead them by virtue, and regulate them by propriety' (ch. 2), practise a policy of valuing education and culture, lightening penalties and punishment, and reducing taxes and corvée. In this condition the people could live and work in peace and contentment, and public order could be stable.

This was Confucius' benevolent governing and virtuous ruling, to be put into effect by men of virtue and talent. He did not oppose the hereditary privileges of feudal nobles, but because of his own origin and long educational experience, he emphasized the promotion of men of virtue and talent, that is, the choice of ministers from the common people (ch. 13). He considered the best governor to be the superior man, the man of various excellent virtues and talents.

Confucius unified his ethical and political thoughts into a systematic doctrine, which was afterwards generalized in the *Great Learning* as follows: thoroughly investigating the nature of things, perfecting knowledge, purifying one's motives, rectifying one's inclinations, adorning one's person with virtues, regulating one's family, establishing order in the state of the prince, making the world of the king enjoy peace and plenty – the unity of inner sage and outer king.

Educational thoughts

Confucius' educational thoughts, which were formed during his long teaching experience, were penetrated by his philosophy and served his political ideals. Many of these ideas are highly praised to the present day. Although Confucius admitted that in theory some people were born with knowledge, he said that he was not a man of the highest intelligence but a man who loved the ancients and studied them with diligence. In his opinion people of the highest intelligence were very scarce, so he paid much attention to studying and teaching, and said that he 'learned without satiety and taught without being wearied' (ch. 7). The aim of his educational activities was to train his disciples to be men who could realize his political ideal. He advocated that self-cultivation was for governing the state ('he cultivates personal virtue that he may give happiness to all the people' (ch. 14)). 'Learning', he said, 'has its reward in itself. The superior man is grieved that right principles are not practised, but feels no concern about poverty' (ch. 15).

In order to train qualified personnel, Confucius broke away from the monopolization of study and education by nobles, and insisted on 'teaching all without regard to what class they belong' (ch. 15). He completely opened the school gate for common men, and in consequence most of his disciples were of that status. His teaching included not only theory but also practical exercises; he was not simply passing on knowledge, but also cultivating virtues – 'Confucius taught four things: literature, virtuous practice, faithfulness and sincerity' (ch. 7). His many teaching methods were scientific, and are of great value for the present day. For example, 'if you read and do not reflect, you will lose what you learn; if you think and do not study, you are uneasy and in danger' (ch. 2). 'Learn and constantly digest' (ch. 1); 'make yourself completely the master of what you know and constantly learn new ideas' (ch. 2); teach students in accordance with their aptitude; and so forth.

Generally speaking, Confucius' thoughts had the following characteristics:

(1) He valued human society highly, but neglected the world of nature; he emphasized the applied sciences, but neglected the pure sciences. This brought about the practical bias of Chinese culture, but at the same time made the systematization of Chinese natural sciences lag behind that of the West.

(2) He praised stability, harmony and unity, pursuing long-term peace, good order and prosperity and opposing disorder and rebellion. These thoughts were highly praised by the rulers of all dynasties, because they were advantageous to the consolidation of the established social order, but rebels and revolutionaries in Chinese history have always disliked and criticized them.

(3) He emphasized personal spiritual needs and insisted on promoting the cultivation of an individual's virtue, neglecting his or her material needs. This point of view is now appreciated by many Asian countries, which consider it to be a restraint on excessive material desires.

(4) There was abundant experience of life in his thoughts. His many sayings have become Chinese traditional idioms, maxims, aphorisms and public morality, and continue to have universal value. 'What you are acquainted with, consider that you know it, what you do not understand consider that you do not know it; this is knowledge' (ch. 2). 'Government is rectitude. If you, Sir, lead by rectitude, who will dare to act contrary to rectitude!' (ch. 12). 'The general of a large army may be seized, but the will of a common man cannot be forced' (ch. 9). 'If in the morning you hear divine truth, in the evening you may die' (ch. 4). 'When I hear a man speak, I must also see him act' (ch. 5). 'If your own conduct be correct, although you do not command, men will do their duty. But if your own conduct be incorrect, although you command, the people will not obey' (ch. 13). 'If you are in haste, you will not succeed' (ch. 13).

THE FOUNDING AND DEVELOPMENT OF THE CONFUCIANIST SCHOOL

Confucius and his disciples formed during his lifetime a school of Confucianists, or the 'School of Ru'. A *ru* was generally known as a learned man in ancient times who was well versed in the *Books of Songs*, *History*, *Rites* and *Music*, and was engaged in activities such as the practice of witchcraft, writing history and performing divination. The young Confucius was a master of ceremonies by profession, i.e. a *ru*. Afterwards he did not get an official position for a long time, but was engaged in teaching students all his life. He was a typical *ru*.

Confucius' thoughts and speeches did not always follow strict logic, which in consequence allowed of various interpretations, and Confucianists were divided in the Spring and Autumn Period and the Warring States Period into a number of minor schools. Eight schools of Confucianists at that time were identified by the Legalist Han Fei as those led by Zi Zhang, Zi Si, Yan Shi, Mencius, Qi Diaoshi, Zhong Liangshi, Xun Zi and Yue Shengshi. Confucianists led by Mencius and by Xun Zi were the two largest schools in the Warring States Period and exerted tremendous influence on later generations. They formed the first peak in the development of Confucianism after Confucius' death.

However, Qin Shihuang, the first Emperor of the Qin dynasty, burned Confucian books in 221 BC and had some Confucianists put to death, and the emperors of the earlier Han Dynasty (following Huang Di and Lao Zi instead) turned away from Confucian ideas. But on account of Dong Zhongshu's propaganda, Han Wudi recognized in 134 BC the efficacy of Confucianism for consolidating his rule, and held only Confucianism in the greatest esteem and rejected all other schools. This was the second peak in the history of Confucianism, and its domination in the ideology of Chinese feudal society was established from that time until the Chinese 1911 revolution. During the years from the Han Dynasty to the Tang Dynasty, after Buddhism's propagation and development in China, a fierce conflict developed between Confucianism and Buddhism. Sometimes Confucianism defeated Buddhism, and sometimes the other way round, but the rule of Confucianism over social ideology was firm all along.

Confucius was always respected and worshipped by almost all dynasties' emperors. Lixue (the School of Laws or Principles) of the Song and Ming Dynasties assimilated the thoughts of Buddhism and the Daoist School and formed the third peak in the history of Confucianism. On account of its great theoretical accomplishments, Lixue of the Song and Ming Dynasties was called Neo-Confucianism. The three peaks of the history of Confucianism will be introduced briefly as follows:

Confucianism in the Warring States Period

The most important and influential Confucianists in this period were Mencius and Xun Zi. Mencius (approximately 372–289 BC) was born in Zou (Zouxian, Shandong province). He was a disciple of a disciple of Zi Si – the grandson of Confucius. He travelled around the states in order to persuade the kings to put his political doctrines into practice, and was respected and well treated by them, but no one really put his opinions into effect. He engaged in teaching all his life and disseminated and developed

Confucianism. He and his disciples collected and arranged the records of his activities and dialogues, and edited them as the *Book of Mencius*. This is more systematically argued than the *Lun-yu* of Confucius. Later generations respectfully called him the second Sage.

Mencius principally developed Confucius' thoughts on heaven's will, human nature, benevolence, justice and the kingly way. Mencius sought from heaven's will (*tianzi*) the metaphysical ground of the history of society, human nature and ethical principles. He said, 'When that which man cannot do is done, it is Heaven which accomplishes it, and when that which man brings not comes, it is decreed' (*Mencius*, ch. 9). For Mencius, human nature was innate, common and good; specifically, 'all men have compassionate hearts – all men have hearts which feel ashamed of vice – all men have hearts disposed to show reverence and respect – all men have hearts which discriminate between right and wrong' (ch. 11). These virtues were benevolence, rectitude, propriety and wisdom. But he did not approve of fatalism. He thought that these good virtues existed at first as seeds in the mind of everyone, and it was necessary for a man who wished to become a sage to cultivate and temper himself in social life. Therefore for Mencius, conscious exertion was very important, and anyone who fully developed his latent virtues could become a sage.

Why ought a man to become a sage? Mencius answered that it was for the purpose of carrying out the policy of benevolence and the kingly way. The goal of Mencius' political views was no doubt to maintain and consolidate the kings' rule, but how could it be achieved? He objected to tyranny and rule by force, and regarded it as the foundation of stability of political rule that people could live and work in peace, contentment and richness. He deduced from this view the conclusion that 'the people are of the first importance; the local deities and gods of grain next, and the Prince least of all' (ch. 13). He maintained that a king ought to do his best to win people's support, and said: 'When the ruler rejoices in the joy of his people, they likewise rejoice in his joy, and when he sympathises with the sorrows of his people, they also sympathise with his sorrows. It has never been the case, that he who rejoiced with the whole Empire, and grieved with the whole Empire, could not act the true sovereign' (ch. 2). He even became so radical that he thought that people might punish tyrants and corrupt officials, and said, concerning the famous tyrant Zhou: 'I have heard that the private man Zhou was put to death, but have not heard that the Prince Zhou was assassinated' (ch. 2). These words of Mencius were said, of course, from the rulers' standpoint, but also expressed to a certain degree the people's hopes.

Xun Zi (approximately 325–238 BC) or Xun Kuang was born in Zhao (the southern part of Shanxi province). He regarded himself as a disciple of Confucius and of Confucius' disciple Zhong Gong. Xun Zi had been an educational official of Qi (Shandong province) and the head of Lanlin county of Cu (Hubei). He engaged himself during most of his life in teaching and research. His principal writings were collected in the *Xun Zi*, which also included his disciples' records.

Xun Zi and Mencius enjoyed equal popularity at that time as the principal representatives of the Confucianists, but they had opposing points of view on many problems. Xun Zi's thoughts in fact contained the ideological achievements of Lao Zi, Zhuang Zi and the Legalists. He talked about heaven too, and even called it God, but his heaven was the world of nature in reality, and his heaven's will was objective laws of nature. He said: 'There is frequency in Heaven's motion. It does not come into being for the good king or perish for the bad king' (*Xun Zi*: 'On heaven'). He put stress on understanding and applying natural laws in order to serve human beings, and said: 'It is better for us to conquer heaven than to overestimate it. It is better for us to control and use heaven's will than to praise it' ('On heaven'). He regarded human nature as man's biological instincts and said: 'Nature is bad. Its goodness is artificial' ('Badness of human nature'). He thought that a person's moral concepts were acquired after birth, in opposition to Mencius' theory of innate goodness.

He did not deny the value of benevolence and justice, but placed more value on the significance of propriety and music for maintaining and strengthening the king's rule. He thought that 'One cannot be brought up without propriety, a business cannot be done without propriety, and a state cannot maintain peace without propriety' ('Bold strategy'). He also valued highly the function of music and thought that it could mould a person's temperament and assist a king to practise propriety. Propriety for Xunzi was not the propriety of the Zhou Dynasty but of the feudal rules and regulations which were conceived by him as including the laws of a state. He proposed the slogan: 'Take as a model the later kings' instead of Confucius' and Mencius' slogan 'Take as a model the earlier kings.' The famous Legalists Li Si and Han Fei were his disciples, and applied his thoughts to assisting the emperors of Qin in governing the country and unifying all China at last.

The establishment of Confucianism's ideological rule

The ruling position of Confucianism was established in the period of Wudi of the Han Dynasty. Its representative was Dong Zhongshu, who not only developed Confucianism, but also raised it to the position of national philosophy in the Chinese feudal epoch by means of political power.

Dong Zhongshu (179–104 BC) was a scholar of Confucian classics, a tradition which began in the Han Dynasty and continued until the Tang Dynasty, taking the annotations and explanations of Confucian classics as its principal assignment. Dong Zhongshu was a specialist in the Gongyang's *Spring and Autumn Annals* and a doctor. In the year 134 BC he submitted a written statement to Wudi of the Han Dynasty proposing 'to pay the greatest esteem only to Confucianism and reject all other schools'. Han Wudi accepted his proposal, and he was twice appointed prime minister of princes of the Han Dynasty and earned Han Wudi's confidence and respect. Han Wudi often sought advice about national affairs from him. His principal work was the *Chunqiu Fanlu*. He developed Confucianism to a new level and steadily established Confucianism's ruling position in ancient Chinese ideology.

Dong Zhongshu carried forward the Confucian requirement of loyalty to the king, but rejected the requirement to love people, and sought a metaphysical foundation for it. His teachings formed a well-organized ideological system. He founded a theory of three cardinal guides, that is, that the ruler guides the subject, the father guides the son, and the husband guides the wife. He maintained that the subject must be absolutely loyal to the ruler. 'All virtues belong to the ruler; all evils belong to the subjects' (*Chunqiu Fanlu*). Why? Because it was heaven's will. If it was not so obvious to Confucius that heaven should be regarded as a personified god, heaven for Dong Zhongshu was completely identified with God. He thought that all affairs on earth were determined by heaven and that rulers were the sons of heaven. In addition, he thought that heaven always closely supervised activities on earth, and that various natural disasters were heaven's warning to rulers on earth. There were interactions between heaven and human beings. He saw an interaction between nature and human beings in the forms of theology and superstition. He approved of benevolent rule and opposed penalties, as Confucius and Mencius had done. Synthesizing the doctrines of human nature of Mencius and Xunzi, he founded the doctrine of three human natures: the sage's nature was good, and the villain's nature was bad; but they were in the minority, and the majority belonged to the intermediate state, that is, to a mixture of goodness and badness. The majority must therefore be educated to become good people.

Neo-Confucianism

Neo-Confucianism, namely the Lixue of the Song and Ming Dynasties, was the third peak in Confucianism's development. The study of the Confucian classics of the Han Dynasty had gradually declined since the Three Kingdoms Period. The thoughts of Lao Zi and Zhuang Zi advanced little by little in the Wei and Jin Dynasties, and Buddhism flourished from the Northern and Southern Dynasties to the Sui and Tang Dynasties. But Confucianism did not entirely lose its pre-eminence in ancient Chinese ideology. It still enjoyed the emperors' respect and clearly influenced the metaphysics of the Wei and Jin Dynasties and the Buddhism of the Northern and Southern Dynasties. Lixue of the Song and Ming Dynasties raised Confucianism to new heights both on a theoretical level and in its political standing. Hanyu and Liao in the Tang Dynasty were forerunners of the Lixue of the Song and Ming Dynasties. Hanyu's doctrine of Confucian orthodoxy exerted a great influence on the Lixue of the Song and Ming Dynasties. Lixue included various schools and a great number of philosophers, among whom were Fan Zhongyan, Ouyangxiu, Zhou Dunyi, Zhangzai,

Cheng Hao, Cheng Yi, Sima Guang and Zhuxi. Lu Jiuyuan in the Song Dynasty and Wang Shouren in the Ming Dynasty were a special school of Lixue, which went under the name of Xinxue.

Lixue of the Song and Ming Dynasties as a new period of Confucianism had the following characteristics: a. It formed the most accurate and complete ideological system in the history of Confucianism. The principal component of Confucianism was political and moral philosophy. The contribution of Lixue of the Song and Ming Dynasties was to investigate its metaphysical roots and to found as a result a Confucian ontology and epistemology, in which Confucianism rose to a higher theoretical level. b. Lixue was produced in the process of criticizing Buddhism and Daoism; therefore it not only answered their interrogations, thus developing Confucianism, but also absorbed certain of their thoughts from the standpoint of Confucianism, thus enriching its own doctrines. c. The worship and respect of the emperors of the Song, Yuan and Ming Dynasties greatly enhanced and strengthened Lixue, and Lixue supplied feudal autocratic monarchy with more valuable support. For example, Zhuxi picked out *Lun-yu*, *Mencius*, the *Great Learning* and the *Doctrine of the Mean* from Confucian classics, the so-called Four Books, and himself wrote annotations for them. By imperial order they became the prescribed texts for the feudal imperial examinations.

The representatives of the three important schools of Lixue of the Song and Ming Dynasties were as follows.

(1) Zhangzai (1020–77), a materialist representative in the Song Dynasty, had been appointed to several government posts, but his principal activities were always teaching and research. He believed in and propagated Confucian ethical teaching, in order to maintain the feudal social system. He criticized the idealism of Buddhism and Daoism, which denounced the world and did nothing. He considered gas-monism to be the ontological basis of his political and ethical thought. He thought that the essence of the world was the great void, that is, gas. Gas condensed into manifold objects, and manifold objects dispersed into gas. Human beings were made by the condensation of gas just like other objects. The embodiment of gas in human bodies was human nature. There were two kinds of human nature: the nature of heaven and earth and the nature of temperament. The former was the primitive state of heaven and earth, namely reason, which was pure and good. The latter was mingled with desires and feelings and was impure and evil. Therefore a person ought to restrain the nature of temperament and recover the nature of heaven and earth by means of self-cultivation. He regarded feudal society as an enormous family which contained heaven, earth and human beings, and said: 'Heaven is my father, earth is my mother; I, tiny and slight, live simple-mindedly between them. . . . The emperor is the eldest son of my parents; his ministers are his family officials' ('The Western Motto'). He thought that he had proved the eternity and absoluteness of feudal society by this argument. Zhangzai's social-ethical thoughts were inherited by Cheng Hao, Cheng Yi and Zhuxi; his materialism greatly influenced Wang Tingxiang and Wang Fuzhi in the Ming Dynasty.

(2) The two Chengs and Zhuxi were the principal exponents of idea-monism, which was the mainstream system of the Song and Ming Dynasties. Lixue in the strict sense was the Lixue of the two Chengs and Zhuxi. The brothers Cheng Hao (1032–85) and Cheng Yi (1033–1107) were founders of idea-monism, and Zhuxi (1130–1200) was its greatest exponent. Zhuxi thought that Confucian orthodoxy had lapsed after Mencius for more than one thousand years, but the two Chengs had established a continuity and he followed them. They had both been appointed to government posts, but their principal activities were teaching and research.

The Lixue of the two Chengs and of Zhuxi was a kind of objective idealism, but Cheng Hao was inclined to subjective idealism. They inherited Confucian political and ethical thought, but in arguing with Buddhism and Daoism absorbed some of their beliefs too. They thus regarded idea (*li* in Chinese) as the essence of the world, and so followed traditional Confucian thoughts more closely. Idea was the universal or law for them, which made a thing what it was. Cheng Yi said: 'All things in the world are controlled by idea. A thing must have its principle. A thing must have its idea' (*Posthumous Papers* V.18). They distinguished the metaphysical from the phenomenal. Idea was metaphysical. Gas was phenomenal. Idea was more fundamental than gas. Zhuxi developed this point of view, advancing the new judgement: 'Idea goes before matter.' Material things were gas. Zhuxi said that in terms of time, 'none of idea and matter is earlier or later, but if we must trace its source, it is only possible for idea to be first' (*Analects* V.1). That is, the relation between idea and matter was logical, as between premiss and conclusion. 'Idea exists before matter comes into being. For example, the ideas of ruler and subject exist before ruler and subject come into being. The ideas of father and son exist before father and son come into being' (*Analects* V.94). In their opinion, idea was not disorderly and unsystematic, but unified. Idea was only one, that is to say, 'idea is one, but its appearances are manifold' (*Analects* V.94). Cheng Hao considered this unified idea to be mind, Cheng Yi considered it to be heaven's idea, and Zhuxi called it the absolutely utmost. Zhuxi said:

> The absolutely utmost is nothing but the finest and extremely good principle . . . and the highly good and infinitely fine virtues of Heaven, earth and human beings . . . which contain all ideas. There are four greatest virtues, namely benevolence, justice, propriety and wisdom:
> (*Selected Works*)

Thus, Zhuxi endowed feudal moral categories with absolute, infinite, metaphysical significance.

The Lixue of the two Chengs and of Zhuxi derived its doctrines concerning human nature and its political and ethical views from idea-monism. The two Chengs divided human nature into the nature of heaven's will and the nature of human life. Zhuxi divided human nature into the nature of heaven's will and the nature of temperament. In their opinion, the former came from idea, the latter from gas; the former was good, and the latter was good or evil according to whether it was controlled by heavenly principles or not. For example, 'eating and drinking were heavenly principle, eating delicious food was human desire' (*Analects* V.13). They further advocated asceticism. Zhuxi maintained that one should clear away all human desires and recover all heavenly principles. Cheng Hao said: 'It is extremely insignificant for a woman to be starved to death, but extremely significant to lose her chastity' (*Posthumous Papers* V.22). From these words it is not difficult to find the influence of Buddhist asceticism. The two Chengs and Zhuxi thought that one who could persist in recovering heavenly principles and clear away human desires was a virtuous person; if everyone could do the same, then rulers, subjects, fathers and sons could fulfil their duties and a harmonious and peaceful social system could be maintained for a long time.

Their epistemology was a sort of rationalist apriorism, founded on idea-monism. Cheng Yi said: 'Knowledge is innate in my mind, but if I do not pursue it I cannot get it. There must be a way of pursuing knowledge, which is researching objects' (*Posthumous Papers* V.25). They considered this process of acquiring knowledge as 'making a thorough enquiry of ideas through researching objects.' Zhuxi further developed this doctrine, saying: 'If I have exerted myself in pursuing knowledge for a long time, then I can suddenly see the whole matter in a clear light, thus knowing its surface and kernel, its dross and essence, and understanding the substance and function of my mind' (*Analects* V.15). Thus one recognized ideas innate in one's mind, and became a virtuous person. It is obvious that their epistemology served their political and ethical thoughts well.

(3) Lu Jiuyuan and Wang Shouren were the principal representatives of mind-monism; their doctrine was called also Xinxue (the doctrine of mind). Lu Jinyuan (1139–93), a local government official, agreed with Cheng Hao's subjective idealism, which regarded idea as mind, and provoked a heated debate with Zhuxi. Wang Shouren (1427–1528), a senior government official in the Ming Dynasty, further developed Lu Jiuyuan's thoughts, holding subjective idealist views, such as 'There is no idea out of my mind' and 'There is not anything outside of my mind' (*Complete Works* V.1). Their political and ethical thoughts were the same as Zhuxi's, but the philosophical foundations and modes of argument were different. They opposed Zhuxi's distinction between idea and mind. Lu Juiyuan said: 'The universe is my mind, my mind is the universe' (*Complete Works* V.22). Once Wang Shouren's disciples asked him: 'If there is nothing outside of my mind, then when this flowery tree blossoms and shades by itself in high mountains, what has this to do with my mind?' Wang Shouren replied: 'When you do not see this flower, it and your mind are nothing at all; but when you see this flower, it suddenly becomes bright and clear. Therefore we know that this flower is not outside of your mind' (*Complete Works* V.3). The influence of the Chan sect of Buddhism is obvious here.

For Lu Jiuyuan, ideas in the mind were benevolence, justice, propriety and wisdom, which he called 'the original mind'. It was pure and good. It was only with pollution by natural desires that there appeared errors, crimes and unorthodox opinions. He therefore regarded Zhuxi's method of recognizing them as cumbersome and unnecessary. These ideas could be known only by self-reflection. Self-cultivation did not mean the addition of virtues, but clearing away pollution from outside. Wang Shouren called the 'original mind' 'intuitive knowledge', which could be obtained by means of self-reflection. From this he deduced the doctrine of 'identity of knowing and doing'. According to him, intuitive knowledge was moral standards, whose most fundamental character was practice, and thus he paid great attention to practice. He said: 'Knowledge is the aim of practice; practice is the work of knowledge. Knowledge is the beginning of practice; practice is the completion of knowledge' (*Complete Works* V.1). Although Wang Shouren confused unity with identity, he was the first of the philosophers to study systemically and demonstrate the relation between knowledge and practice.

CONFUCIANISM AND MODERN CULTURE

The Lixue of the Song and Ming Dynasties gradually declined at the end of the Ming Dynasty. It was subjected to the criticism of many thinkers, such as Wang Tingxiang, Wang Fuzhi, Gu Yanwu and Huang Zongxi, who advocated replacing empty scholastic Lixue by real learning. Lizhi even opposed Confucius. But the rule of Confucianism in ideology was still firm. At the end of the nineteenth century, when the feudal social system was faced with the fate of being overthrown, the rule of Confucianism began to decline seriously. After the final dynasty, the Qing, had been abolished, the rule of Confucianism lost its political basis, and began to collapse entirely.

The 'Down with Confucius' and 'Critique of Confucius' movement aroused by the 4 May movement of 1919

In recent times the leaders of the Taiping Heavenly Kingdom were the first to stand up against Confucianism. The reformist Kang Youwei attempted to transform Confucius into a modern sage, thus in reality substituting democracy for Confucianism. The democratic revolutionaries Sun Yatsen and Zhang Taiyan were anti-Confucianists too. Yuan Shikai attempted to rebuild autocratic monarchy, thus making Confucianism the national religion by imperial order. The 4 May movement of 1919 was a political movement against imperialism and feudalism and a new cultural movement for democracy and science; 'Down with the Confucian shop!' therefore became its principal slogan. As the new cultural movement developed and grew, Confucianism was systematically and thoroughly criticized. The 4 May movement declared the end of Confucianism's rule in ideology.

The leaders of the 4 May cultural movement – Chen Duxiu, Li Dazhao and so on – completely rejected Confucianism. Chen Duxiu called on young people to rise up against Chinese feudal systems and ideology supported by Confucianism, and said: 'If we cannot overturn Confucianism, the national strength cannot be recovered, and our society must be lost in anarchy' (*New Youth*, first issue). Wu Yu was called 'old hero overthrowing Confucius' shop', and thought that Confucius' ideas of loyalty and filial piety were instruments for consolidating Chinese monarchy and the patriarchal clan system. It was inevitable that Confucius and Confucianist thoughts, as the ruling ideology of Chinese feudal society, were furiously attacked and thoroughly criticized in the anti-feudal revolutionary movement.

But, even amid this anti-Confucianist feeling, some leaders of the 4 May cultural movement tried to make a scientific evaluation of the historical position of Confucius. Li Dazhao emphasized the difference between Confucius himself and the Confucius moulded by rulers of feudal dynasties in order to suit their political needs. Hu Shi examined Confucius' speeches and activities in the context of Confucius' own times in his *Outline of Chinese History of Philosophy*. Hu Shi thought that the Spring and Autumn Period was a period of great transformation, in which Confucius always strived to turn a chaotic situation into peace and prosperity, and that his speeches and activities simply advocated self-cultivation. No matter how accurate Hu Shi's analysis and valuation are, it is always necessary to regard Confucius as a historical personage and Confucianism as a historical phenomenon. Mao Zedong also maintained that for the sake of advancing modern Chinese culture we could neither blindly imitate nor completely reject Chinese cultural heritage including Confucianism: 'We should sum up our history from Confucius to Sun Yatsen and take over this valuable legacy' ('The Role of the Chinese Communist Party in the National War').

The rise of modern Neo-Confucianism

The end of Confucianist ideological supremacy does not mean the end of the Confucianist school, or the end of Confucianist influence. After the 4 May movement, not only were there surviving adherents of the Qing Dynasty who regarded themselves as Confucianists, but scholars were emerging who had modern cultural accomplishments and approved of modern sciences and democracy. They sought to update Confucianism and direct the modernization of China with such an updated Confucianism. They strived to form modern Chinese culture on the foundation of Confucianism. They are called modern Neo-Confucianists.

Many scholars divide modern Neo-Confucianists into three generations. The first generation worked between the 1920s and the 1940s; the second, between the 1950s and the 1970s; the third, in the 1980s. The first generation included Liang Shuming, Zhang Junmai, Xiong Shili, Qian Mu, Feng Youlan and He Lin, who strived to combine Confucianism with modern Western philosophies in order to form a type of Neo-Confucianism. For example, Feng Youlan combined neo-realism with the Lixue of the Song and Ming Dynasties, and called his philosophy neo-Lixue. After the founding of the People's Republic of China, Zhang Junmai, Qian Mu and some other followers of Confucianism went to Hong Kong and Taiwan and continued their rejuvenation of Confucianism. Those who remained in China abandoned their original views of Confucianism.

The second generation worked mainly in Taiwan and Hong Kong. Examples of its younger representatives are Fang Dongmei, Tang Junyi, Mou Zongsan and Xu Fuguan besides the veterans Zhang Junmai and Qian Mu. They launched a series of activities to carry forward Confucianism, which exerted such a great influence on the development of traditional Chinese culture.

Most members of the third generation are middle-aged, and have a distinctly modern consciousness. In recent years, Western countries have secured great economic advantages and their inhabitants are enjoying a very high standard of living, but their spiritual culture lags behind. Social problems such as drug taking, prostitution, rape, robbery and pollution of the environment proliferate. Similar things are happening in Asian countries or territories such as Japan, South Korea, Taiwan, Hong Kong and Singapore, which are influenced to a certain degree by Confucianist ideology. In this context some scholars and even politicians have thought that Confucianism may avert and remedy these corrupt practices. In October 1982, a meeting on the theme 'Neo-Confucianism and the modernization of China' was held in Taipei, Taiwan, and various issues about Confucianism were discussed. The participants Yu Yingshi, Liu Shuxian, Zhang Hao, Lin Yusheng and non-participants such as Du Weiming and Lao Siguang are regarded as representatives of the third generation of modern Neo-Confucianists. This generation and their activities have secured the attention of academics in China and internationally.

In brief, modern Neo-Confucianists have the following characteristics: a) They are not a political party, though they have their political views. They are a school, or strictly speaking a cultural trend of thought including many schools; b) They are patriotic and hope that China can become prosperous and powerful. They value traditional Chinese culture highly, but do not wish to return to the feudal system and monarchy; c) They have a good understanding of Western culture, but do not favour a wholesale Westernization of China; d) They try to enhance Confucianism, especially the Lixue of the Song and Ming Dynasties, and combine it with Western culture in order to form a modern Chinese culture with Confucianism as its core; e) There are many Confucianist schools, but they have some common moral ideas such as humanism, peace, fraternity and so on.

The study of Confucius and Confucianism in China since the 1950s

Since the founding of the People's Republic of China, Marxism has become the guiding ideology in national life as a whole. Confucius and Confucianists began to be studied and evaluated as historical personages. Estimations of their worth varied, but all Chinese scholars generally affirmed their important standing in traditional Chinese culture, and regarded Confucianism as a part of a superior Chinese cultural tradition. The Chinese Cultural Revolution started another movement criticizing Confucius and negating Confucianist thoughts, but this critique was different from that of the 4 May movement, because it was deliberately provoked by ambitious individuals to suit their political aims. But this critique was negated after the end of the 'Cultural Revolution'. Moreover, with the development of 'reformation and opening', along with the carrying out of the 'Double Hundred' policy, academic research into Confucianism became more thorough than ever.

The academic activities of Confucianism in recent years may be summarized as follows. A great number of academic institutes and societies engaged in the research of Confucianism were founded. Many scientific conferences and symposia on Confucianism were held, including some international meetings. The largest-scale international symposium was at the time of the 2,540th anniversary of the birth of Confucius; the Academic Symposium was held in October 1989, earlier in Beijing and later in Qufu, Shandong province. There were about 300 specialists and scholars taking part in the symposium, including contributors from Taiwan, Hong Kong and more than twenty countries and territories; 300 articles were contributed to the symposium. A great quantity of articles and books researching Confucianism were published. According to incomplete statistics, 400 articles and 30 books had been published up to 1988. The quarterly *Researches in Confucius*, sponsored by the Confucius Foundation in 1986, is a journal devoted to the study of Confucianism. Shandong province is publishing the *Confucius' Cultural Encyclopedia*, which systematically collects, explores and sorts out all materials relating to Confucianism over more than two thousand years. Many problems about Confucianism have been discussed and resolved. There were many differences of opinion on Confucius and Confucianism ten years previously, but through discussion scholars have reached a consensus of opinion on some matters. For example, most scholars now agree that we should neither worship Confucius as God nor regard him as a criminal who was responsible for the backwardness of China; he was a historical personage. Most scholars also agree that it is correct to adopt a historical, analytical attitude for evaluating traditional Chinese culture with Confucianism as its core. As for the fundamental characteristics of Confucianism, most scholars are of the same opinion. At present the central issue in academic research in China is the problem of the relation between Confucianism and modern society, most scholars affirming its value in modern social life. They maintain that though ancient society is quite different from modern society, they have some elements in common, so that a number of norms concerning ancient social life are significant for modern social life. For example, Confucius' teaching of 'benevolence', if its connection with social strata is disregarded, is similar to the modern virtues of self-reliance, justice, equality and harmony. But scholars have different views regarding the value of Confucianism in the present day, and whether it can be updated into a modern ideological system as modern Neo-Confucianists think. Research on Confucius and Confucianism will undoubtedly continue to gather strength in China and the rest of the world.

FURTHER READING

Collie, David (trans.) (1970) *The Four Books*, Gainesville, Fla.: Scholars' Facsimiles and Reprints.

Eber, Irene (ed.) (1986) *Confucianism – The Dynamics of Tradition*, New York: Macmillan.

Fang Keli (ed.) (1989) *A Collection on Modern Neo-Confucianism*, Beijing: Chinese Social Sciences Publishing House.

Hu Sheng (1987) *The Great Encyclopedia of China, Philosophy*, Beijing: The Great Encyclopedia of China Publishing House.

Kuang Yaming (1985) *Critical Biography of Confucius*, Shandong: Qi-Lu Publishing.

Ren Jiyu (1983) *The History of Development of Chinese Philosophy*, Beijing: People's Publishing House.

Researches in Confucius (1986–90) (Quarterly), Chinese Confucius Foundation.

A Special Issue at the 2540th Anniversary of the Birth of Confucius (1989) *Openings* (two-monthly).

Summary of Academic Papers of the 2540th Anniversary of the Birth of Confucius and the Academic Symposium (1989) Beijing: Preparatory Office.

27

DAOISM IN CHINESE PHILOSOPHY

Charles Wei-hsun Fu

Taken together, Daoism and Confucianism share the distinction of being the philosophical grounding forces of Chinese culture. In a sense they may be considered respectively as the *yin* and *yang* of Chinese thought – Daoism being primarily concerned with helping us to accommodate the Way of Humanity to the Way of Nature, while Confucianism's focus emphasizes the cultivation of the Way of Human Morality. Hence, although many in the West tend to assume that the two schools are ideological rivals, their division of philosophical territory makes them complementary more often than competitive. For more than two thousand years the traditional Chinese have managed to perform a delicate balancing act that allows them to be simultaneously Confucian and Daoist (with the later addition of Buddhist thought) as appropriate to changing situations.

The *Zhuangzi* text illustrates the complex relationships between these schools of thought. In its chapters are found two apparently contradictory depictions of Confucius as a character in Zhuangzi's philosophical fables. Sometimes Confucius is presented as pretentious and hopelessly inept, a comic figure used to argue against a Daoist point. On other occasions, however, the character of Confucius is that of a Daoist *par excellence*, pouring forth appropriate gems of wisdom.[1] The author or authors of the text did not feel compelled to acknowledge, much less explain, the apparent inconsistency.

Primal Daoism is said to have originated in the same crucible of social upheaval that gave birth to Confucianism, the declining years of the Zhou Dynasty. More specifically, the 'founder' of philosophical Daoism is the quasi-legendary Laodan, more commonly known as Laozi (Old Master). According to tradition he was an older contemporary of Confucius, with dates ranging from 580 to 480 BC. Zhuangzi, the next important figure in the development of Daoist thought, has a more solid historical status (369–286 BC). He stands in relation to Laozi as his contemporary Mencius does to Confucius, both a follower of the original master and a creative interpreter of the philosophical heritage.

I shall attempt to provide a modern reconstruction of Laozi's philosophy, along with its ethical and socio-political implications. Then I shall consider how Zhuangzi advanced the philosophical and social political thought of Laozi, completing the classical Daoist Way through an exploration of new dimensions and new emphases.

THE NATURAL WAY OF LAOZI

As Chinese tradition has it, we are indebted to a border guard with philosophical proclivities for the existence of the key Daoist text, the *Dao De Jing* (*Classic of the Way and its Virtue*), also known under the name of its reputed author, Laozi. The story states that Laozi, after long service as imperial librarian to the Zhou Dynasty in 'the dusty world', decided to live as a recluse. He mounted his ox and set out for the misty mountain recesses so well suited to the Daoist temperament. Chinese art provides numerous depictions of the scene in which Laozi is confronted by an earnest guardian of the mountain pass. After nearly exhausting his powers of persuasion, the guard finally elicited a reluctant agreement from Laozi to leave behind him some testament to his wisdom, and penned the very brief (some 5,000 characters in Chinese), yet profoundly rich, poetic lines of the *Dao De Jing*. Since that time, many have engaged themselves in the task of bringing forth the infinite variety of meanings from this inexhaustible source of wisdom.

The text itself is problematic from a scholarly point of view. A number of passages are corrupted, and some are so abstruse as to be incomprehensible. None the less it continues to attract attention and is said to have been translated more often than any other book except the Bible. There are no fewer than eighty translations in English alone, each with its own creative reinterpretation of the cryptic contents.

As reflected in the title, the text consists of two parts – the *Dao Jing* (*Classic of Dao*) and the *De Jing* (*Classic of Virtue*). The oldest known copy, the Silk Manuscript, was found in mainland China in 1973. Its discovery has served to fuel the fires of controversy since it reverses the order of chapters found in what has long been considered the standard edition, divided into eighty-one chapters with commentary by the Neo-Daoist Wangbi in the third century AD. Thus, the Silk Manuscript begins with the socio-political and military chapters of the *De Jing*, and then moves on to the metaphysical concerns of the *Dao Jing* that open the standard edition. On the basis of this reversal of emphasis, current speculation tends to interpret the text as essentially political in orientation, perhaps even closely tied to the Legalist school so influential in the Qin Dynasty. On this interpretation, Daoist metaphysics becomes an afterthought to, rather than the focal point of, the text.

Despite the charming legend of Laozi and his ox, the questions of both the authorship of the text and the origins of the Daoist school, or school of Dao (*Dao Jia*), remain open to debate. (The following discussion adopts the convention that Laozi is indeed the author of the text.) It is generally assumed that Laozi and others like him were contemporaries of Confucius. Mention is made in the *Analects* of certain recluses who seemed to take great delight in taunting both the Master and his disciples. The response from Confucius was a reassertion of his humanistic orientation, as he dismissed his opponents for indiscriminately associating with birds and beasts.

However, it would be a mistake to conclude from the Confucian account that all of these recluses were disillusioned, selfish intellectuals who, as Mencius claimed, were unwilling to sacrifice a single hair for the sake of the world. While some were indeed seeking to escape from the turmoil of their times, others were more constructively in search of a philosophically valid return to the natural Way (*Dao*) rooted in primeval Chinese culture. That this is the goal of the author of the *Dao De Jing* is demonstrated by repeated references to 'the *Dao* of old' (chapter 14) and 'ancient ones adept in the practice of *Dao*' (chapters 15 and 39).[2]

Laozi's metaphysics of *Dao*

The concept of *Dao* is a multi-dimensional one. As noted above, the most common rendering of the Chinese term is 'Way', which most closely approximates the original. *Dao* is the 'way' in both the concrete sense of a road travelled and the more abstract sense of the natural course or route to be followed. *Dao* is the Way things are, the Way of process and reality, and Way of being in the world.

Some have sought to reduce *Dao* to some more familiar Western concepts, such as 'God' or 'Logos', thinking thereby to smooth the path to comprehension. However, such attempts both misunderstand and distort the actual meaning (or complexity of meanings) of the original term. *Dao* cannot be identified with the Western sense of godhead inasmuch as God is commonly conceived of as transcending nature. *Dao*, on the other hand, is both immanent and transcendent, inherent in nature yet extending beyond, or more precisely, beneath it. Thus *Dao* is said to emulate nature's spontaneity (25), while its mystery remains hidden in profound darkness (1). *Dao* is also creative or more precisely procreative, but not predominantly a creator in the sense that the Western deity is. *Dao* engages in spontaneous procreativity rather than the *ex nihilo* act of creation ascribed to God in Genesis.

Similarly, to equate *Dao* with Logos mistakenly assumes that it represents a rational core to reality, as conceived of by the early Greeks. But the analytic differentiation of reason ill fits the holistic non-duality of Dao. Nor does its abstractness accord with *Dao*'s concrete manifestations. *Dao* is, in fact, trans-rational, the paradoxical 'No-thingness' that gives rise to the world and its infinite wonders, surpassing in reality even the Being or Substance which Western philosophers exalt.

Thus far we have discussed only what *Dao* is not. What, then, is *Dao*? In the *Dao De Jing*, *Dao* is referred to in at least six different ways. The first five represent attempts to define or characterize *Dao* in terms of its multi-dimensional manifestations: as Origin or Mother of the Ten Thousand Things (a stock phrase in Chinese referring to the sum total of existence), as Principle, as Function, as Virtue, and as Technique. Each of these constitutes one expression of 'Named' *Dao*, that is, *Dao* as it has been delineated within the confines of philosophical speculation and metaphorical imagination. Such names satisfy our need to circumscribe reality and foster the illusion of artificial control ('knowledge is power').

Beyond these restrictions lies the primordial – but humanly inconceivable – reality that can only be referred to as 'unnamed' or 'name-less' *Dao*. In order to avoid confusing it with any specific thing, it is also referred to as 'No-thingness' (*wu*). Thus it is rightly said to be 'Profoundly dark and ever profoundly dark,/The gateway to infinite wonders' (1). Only this *Dao* of no name is the 'enduring *Dao*', which is trans-metaphysically non-dual and paradoxical.

Dao's names do have a heuristic value, but ought not to be taken too seriously, as is made clear in the opening chapter:

> Thus, always in terms of No-thingness,
> One contemplates its [hidden] wonders;
> Always in terms of Being,
> One contemplates its [manifest] forms.
> These two spring forth from the same [source],
> And yet they differ in name.[3]

Like *yin* and *yang*, No-thingness and Being are mutually complementary terms that serve an important function in satisfying our metaphysical aspirations. Like Buddhist *śūnyatā*, No-thingness attempts to transcend the unavoidable dualism of language, taking us beyond reality/unreality, substance/function, existence/non-existence, subject/object. To borrow a metaphor from Mahāyāna Buddhism, No-thingness or name-less *Dao* may be likened to the unlimited ocean and Being or named *Dao* to its waves. There is, in fact, no referential difference between the ocean and the waves; the existence of each is dependent upon the other. It is merely a matter of human perspective whether one sees the ocean or the waves, the forest or the trees. The distinction is, provisionally speaking, only a functional one.

Laozi describes our metaphysical dilemma as follows:

> We look but see it not;
> It is named 'the Invisible'.
> We listen but hear it not;
> It is named 'the Inaudible'.
> We try to seize it but find it not;
> It is named 'the Intangible'.
> These three elude our scrutiny,
> And thus are intermingled into One.
>
> (14)

It is we who are unable to see, hear, or seize reality, and thus decide that it is invisible (*yi*), inaudible (*xi*), and intangible (*wei*).[4] The fault lies not in *Dao*, but in the limits and limitations of our metaphysical vision and the inadequacy of our language.

It can only be referred to as a 'something', which provisionally may be termed 'Great' or *Dao* (25).

Always keeping in mind the intellectual pretence involved in attempting to divide the one *Dao*, we can return to the first five 'names' assigned to *Dao* in the text. Let us consider each name in turn as a means to unveiling at least a portion of the profoundly dark mystery that is *Dao*. Origin, Principle and Function can be seen as *Dao's* intertwined metaphysical manifestations, while Virtue and Technique constitute the ethical and socio-political means for human implementation (Inner Sagehood and Outer Kingliness). The same currents will be seen to run through each of these five, differing only in terms of our own limited perspective.

Dao *as Origin*

Dao is the primordial source of all that exists and 'comes before Heaven and Earth./Silent, boundless, standing alone, and changeless' (25). The procreative process of the Mother of the Ten Thousand Things is detailed in chapter 42:

> *Dao* gives birth to the One;
> The One gives birth to the Two;
> The Two give birth to the Three;
> The Three give birth to the Ten Thousand Things.
> The Ten Thousand Things carry *Yin* and embrace *Yang*,
> Infusing these two vital forces to realize harmony.

This passage prompts several important questions. First, what are the referents that correspond to the One, the Two and the Three? Much scholarly debate has been stimulated over the various answers proposed to this question. Fung Yu-lan, for example, contended in the 1930s that the One refers to being, the Two refers to heaven and earth, and the Three to *yin*, *yang*, and the blending of these two vital forces (*qi*). Later, in 1962, he offered a radically different interpretation, influenced by Marxist-Leninist dialectics:

> What is first differentiated from *Dao* is called One. From One are differentiated the opposites (thesis and antithesis); this is (the meaning of) 'One produces Two.' The synthesis of the opposites and the original opposites become Three; this is (the meaning of) 'Two produces Three.' The following sentence, 'All things carry *yin* and embrace *yang*, and attain their harmony through the proper blending of *ch'i* [*qi*]', is an example to illustrate the above point. *Yin* and *yang* are opposite to each other; and 'the blending of *ch'i*' is the synthesis of the vital forces of *yin* and *yang*.
>
> (Fung 1962: 261)

Other scholars view Laozi's words as a commentary on the following passage from the *Great Treatise on Yijing*: 'In the system of *Yi* (Changes) there is the Supreme Ultimate, which generates (*sheng*) Two modes (*yin* and *yang*); the Two Modes generate

Four Forms, and the Four Forms generate Eight Trigrams.' Given the uncertainty of both the date and authorship of this treatise, there is insufficient proof for assuming that it may have influenced Laozi's thought. A more plausible explanation comes from Wing-tsit Chan:

> The similarity of this process to that of the Book of Changes, in which the Great Ultimate produces the Two Forces (*yin* and *yang*) and then the myriad things, is amazing. The important point, however, is not the specific similarities, but the evolution from the simple to the complex.
>
> (Chan 1963 : 176)

Chan continues by describing the mode of production (*sheng*) here as 'not personal creation or purposeful origination, but natural causation.' However, he does not provide any further explanation of either natural causation or the evolution from simplicity to complexity. This leads, then, to the second question raised by chapter 42 – in what sense can *Dao* be said to 'give birth'? There seem to be two possible interpretations. Most translators use the past tense in their English rendering of the word *sheng*, thereby imputing a sense of temporal priority to *Dao* as first cause (see, for example, the translations of R. B. Blakney, John Wu, James Legge, and Wing-tsit Chan). Unfortunately such an interpretation overlooks Laozi's use of figurative language throughout the text and in fact leads to an inconsistency in the text. If *sheng* is taken in a literal sense as an actual process of natural causation or evolution, a conflict arises with Laozi's statement in chapter 41 that *Dao* is 'hidden and nameless'. How, then, could it be construed as prime mover, begetting the One, Two, Three, and Ten Thousand Things? Furthermore, since *Dao* is said to be non-assertive and non-interfering ('*Dao* is always *wu-wei*', 37), emulating the spontaneity of nature (25), it cannot be conceived of as exerting itself in the effort of actual creation (except, perhaps, in the sense of natural procreation).

The second, less literal, interpretation here is philosophically far sounder: *sheng* is intended to indicate an ontological, rather than a temporal, priority, without regard to the question of an actual beginning or production. The passage should then be understood as stating that the enduring *Dao* as name-less has metaphysical priority over the named *Dao* manifested by the One, the Two, etc. In other words, before *Dao* can be daoed or named, it must first be name-less and defy metaphysical designations. To paraphrase chapter 25, what is non-differentially all-complete ('nebulously complete in and by itself'), that is, the undaoable *Dao*, must be metaphysically or more precisely trans-metaphysically prior to the beingness of heaven and earth, which discloses nameable *Dao*. The originating aspect of *Dao* also emerges in chapter 40: 'The Ten Thousand Things in the world originate in Being;/Being originates in No-thingness.' Being here corresponds to named *Dao* and No-thingness to the *Dao* that remains name-less, although No-thingness and Being, or the name-less and the named, are ultimately and paradoxically non-dual.

Dao *as Principle*

Dao as Origin cannot be understood properly without reference to *Dao* as Principle,[5] which is the key metaphysical dimension of *Dao*. Laozi notes that 'Being and Non-Being give birth to each other' (2), meaning that, although metaphysically different, Being and Non-Being are mutually complementary ways of revealing the inexhaustible richness of the enduring *Dao*. From the perspective of Non-Being, emphasis is placed upon the unnamed and hidden aspect of *Dao* defying definition. From the perspective of Being, emphasis is placed upon the nameable manifestations of *Dao*. Taken together, Non-Being and Being demonstrate the perpetual interplay that constitutes reality and stimulates our ultimately inadequate metaphysical flights.

Following the same pattern as this primal interplay of Non-Being and Being, Laozi recognizes the perpetual interplay of all pairs of seeming opposites, governed by the Principle of Reversion. *Yin* and *yang*, birth and death, spring/summer and autumn/winter: each reverts or returns to its opposite once it has peaked and exhausted its own essence:

> A whirlwind lasts not a whole morning,
> Nor does a rainstorm last a whole day.
> Who makes these happen?
> Heaven and Earth.
> Even Heaven and Earth cannot [make them] last long.
> How much less so can human beings?
>
> (23)

It is here that the nameable aspect of *Dao* as Principle is revealed.

Laozi conveys the invariable principle of cyclical reversion in many ways, often expressing himself in highly figurative language: 'The *Dao* of Heaven reduces what is excessive,/Supplements what is deficient' (77); 'Heaven and Earth are impartial (*bu ren*),/And treat the Ten Thousand Things as if they were straw-dogs' (5; see also 79). Yet, paradoxically, all things change and become agents of their own transformation of their own accord because of the spontaneously natural working of *Dao* as Principle: '*Dao* is always *wu-wei*,/And yet nothing is left uncared-for' (37).

The Legalist Han Fei Zi (d. 233 BC), author of the oldest extant commentary on the *Dao De Jing*, attempts his own clarification of *Dao* as Principle or Reason (*li*):

> *Tao* is that by which all things become what they are. It is that with which all principles are commensurable. Principles are patterns (*wen*) according to which all things come into being. Therefore it is said that *Tao* puts things in order (*li*). Things have their respective principles and cannot interfere with each other. Since things have their respective principles and cannot interfere with each other, therefore principles are controlling factors in things. Everything has its own principles different from that of others, and *Tao* is commensurate with all of them [as one]. Consequently, everything has to go through the process of transformation . . . it has no fixed mode of life . . . its life and death depend on the endowment of material force (*ch'i*) [by *Tao*]. . . . Only that which exists from the very beginning of the

> universe and neither dies nor declines until heaven and earth disintegrate can be called eternal. What is eternal has neither change nor any definite particular principle itself. . . . This is why [it is said in the *Lao Tzu*] that it cannot be told.
>
> (*Han Feizi*, ch. 20)[6]

Han Fei's use of the term 'Reason' should not be assumed to be equivalent to the common Western sense of the term as an abstract, purely intellectual entity related to the concept of Logos. The original Chinese character, variously translated as 'principle' or 'reason', derives from the concept of the patterns of nature, such as the grain in a piece of wood or the stratification in a stone.

From the standpoint of Being as manifestations of *Dao*, all things are governed by different specific principles or patterns by means of which they spontaneously change and transform themselves. These principles, which undergo constant change and transformation, may be considered the substratum of the laws of nature. However, there is something that endures behind these changes, functioning as the ultimate principle of natural spontaneity. This changeless principle of change is what we may refer to as *Dao* as Principle.

What interested Laozi about this aspect of *Dao* is not its abstract 'scientific' basis, but rather the possible implications for ethical and socio-political practice:

> Crookedness prefigures perfection;
> Bending prefigures straightness;
> Hollowness prefigures fullness;
> Wearing out prefigures renewal;
> Deficit prefigures gain;
> Plenitude prefigures perplexity.
>
> (22)

The Western scientific mindset has sought to uncover the laws of nature as a means to the end of controlling, manipulating and even conquering nature, guided by the Baconian conviction that knowledge is power. In contrast, the Daoist seeks to know those laws not to exploit them for personal aggrandizement, but to have them serve as a natural standard to which we accommodate ourselves.

Just as *Dao* as Principle points out the Way of Nature, *Dao* as Virtue and Technique represents the Way of Humanity (as will be seen below). The unity of nature and humanity is demonstrated by the continuity that exists between their respective ways. Those who recognize the Principle of Reversion (*fan*) are said to be enlightened (*ming*):

> In order to shrink one must first allow for expansion;
> In order to weaken one must first allow for strengthening;
> In order to abolish one must first allow for advancement;
> In order to take one must first allow for giving–
> This is called 'subtle enlightenment'.
>
> (36)

By the returning (*fu*) 'to the root' we realize a state that brings us into harmony with that of *Dao* itself, becoming receptive to the facticity of human life and death:

The Ten Thousand Things all come into being,
And I thereby contemplate their return.
All things flourish,
Each returning to its own root.
Returning to the root is called 'tranquillity';
This is called 'returning to [natural] destiny';
'Returning to destiny' is called 'the enduring' [*Dao*].
To know the enduring is called 'enlightenment';
Not to know the enduring is to blindly invite disaster.
To know the enduring is to be all-encompassing;
To be all-encompassing is to be none other than impartial;
To be impartial is to be none other than complete;
To be complete is to be none other than natural;
To be natural is to be none other than *Dao*;
To be *Dao* is to be none other than everlasting–
Free from danger throughout one's life.

(16; see also 22,24,27,33,52,55,65)

Dao *as Function*

The functionality or usefulness of comprehending the working of *Dao* in the world is revealed through the dimension of *Dao* as Function, by means of which human beings can implement the 'infinite wonders' (1) of No-thingness in their own lives. Parallels are drawn between the functionality of No-thingness and several concrete instances of the usefulness of what is not: the empty space between the spokes of a wheel, the hollowness of a moulded vessel, and the empty space that constitutes a window: 'Therefore, benefits are derived from Being (what-is),/While the function lies in Non-Beingness (what-is-not)' (11). This lesson of the usefulness of the seemingly useless is a favourite subject of Zhuangzi, who devoted many passages to it (see, for example, chapter 1).

A key Daoist concept helps to account for this metaphysical truth, *Dao*'s methodology of *wei wu-wei*. Though often rendered into English as 'action by non-action', *wei wu-wei* is not passivity or the absence of action, but rather an avoidance of forced or unnatural action motivated by gain or striving, eschewing all artifice. The problem lies not so much in *what* we do, as in the *attitude* with which we undertake it. Phrased in more positive terms, *wei wu-wei* denotes effortlessness and spontaneity, characteristics of the working of *Dao* itself (37,48,57,64).

Another significant aspect of *wei wu-wei* is egoless non-possessiveness: the ability to accomplish the task and then let it go. *Dao* is once again a model for us:

[*Dao*] gives life to [the Ten Thousand Things],
[Its virtue] fosters them.
To give them life, and yet not be possessive of them;
To succour them, and yet expect no gratitude;

To rear them, and yet not claim mastery over them–
This is called 'profoundly dark virtue'.

(10; see also 2,51,64)

The success of *wei wu-wei* follows from the Principle of Reversion, inasmuch as things revert to their opposites. Hence, hardness must eventually give way to softness, striving to non-striving, and so on:

In the world, nothing is more supple and soft than water,
Yet for attacking the hard and strong nothing can match it.
Hence, there is no substitute for it.
That the supple overcomes the strong,
And that the soft overcomes the hard–
None in the world does not know [this],
Yet none can put it into practice.

(78; see also 36,43)

Appearances, then, can be deceptive:

The greatest perfection seems imperfect,
Yet its function remains intact;
The greatest fullness seems empty,
Yet its function remains inexhaustible.
The greatest straightness seems crooked;
The greatest skill seems inept;
The greatest eloquence seems to stammer.
Tranquillity overcomes the impulsive.
Coldness overcomes heat.

(45; see also 41)

This method of going with the natural flow, taking the line of least resistance, also accounts for the functional inexhaustibility of *Dao* (6,35).

Inner sagehood and outer kingliness

The remaining two names of *Dao* encompass the core of Laozi's ethical thought and socio-political philosophy.

Dao *as Virtue*

Each of us as an individual is fostered by *Dao* as Virtue (or power, in the sense of potentiality), giving us the wherewithal to survive. The life of each and every being is formed through the spontaneously effortless change and transformation of nature. The natural being of each individual is completed through the blending of *yin* and *yang*. All things grow, flourish, decay and perish, without any interference. The primordial nature (*Dao* as Virtue) of all things is not governed or controlled by any unnatural force. Life and death naturally follow the invariable Principle of Reversion (51).

Reliance upon this Virtue is itself a kind of returning to the primal state, symbolized by the infant:

One whose virtue is deep can be compared to an infant.
Poisonous insects will not sting it;
Fierce beasts will not pounce upon it;
Birds of prey will not feed upon it;
Its bones are soft, its sinews supple,
And yet its grip is firm;
It does not know the union of male and female,
And yet its member is erect–
Its vital essence remains at its peak.
It cries all day long, and yet never becomes hoarse–
Its harmony remains at its peak.

(55)

Virtue in its highest expression 'is to follow nothing but *Dao*' (21). Participation in *Dao*'s Virtue is predicated upon the metaphysical assumption of a pre-existing oneness with *Dao*. It is this to which the Daoist sage seeks to return:

Whoever engages in [*Dao*'s] virtue,
Is identified with virtue;
Whoever abandons [*Dao*],
Is identified with abandonment [of *Dao*];
Whoever is identified with *Dao*,
Dao is also happy to have them;
Whoever is identified with virtue,
Virtue is also happy to have them;
Whoever is identified with abandonment,
Abandonment is also happy to abandon them.

(23; see also 28,54,59,65,79)

Elsewhere we are told that partaking of the One or *Dao* makes heaven clear, puts earth to rest, empowers the spirits, fills the valleys, allows the Ten Thousand Things to flourish, and stabilizes the world through rulers (39).

The virtues with which we are to identify include non-action, non-affairs, non-acquiring, non-striving, impartiality, non-desire, non-knowledge, non-self, teaching by no-words, receptivity, vacuity, tranquillity, yielding, simplicity, and so on. They tend to be expressed in negative terms, as with *Dao*'s characterization as 'No-thing-ness' or 'name-less'. This characterization is a negativity induced by the limitations of language. Each virtue poses a challenge to the artifice and distortion of natural spontaneity engaged in by the worldlings. It is not surprising, then, that the sage strikes most people as a dull-witted aberration:

Worldings make merry,
As if enjoying sacrificial banquets,
As if climbing the terrace in spring;

I alone remain detached,
Like an infant who has yet to smile,
Listless, like one with nowhere to return.
The worldlings have more than enough,
While I alone look as if left out.
Oh, mine is a fool's mind,
So muddled and ignorant!
The vulgar are pompous and flashy,
I alone look dull and dense;
The vulgar are clever and showy,
I alone am nebulous and in the dark–
Tranquil as the sea,
Gliding, as if without purpose!
The worldlings all have a purpose,
While I alone appear stubborn and uncouth;
I alone differ from the others,
And value the suckling mother.

(20)

Note the sage's self-comparison to the infant, cited above as an example of the virtue that is pure and intact, prior to being corrupted by spurious social conventions.

The means to the end of recovering our natural virtue is likewise expressed in negative terms, consistent with the need to remove the layers of artifice acquired by living in the self- and *Dao*-alienating human world. What remains for us is to undo the damage done by living in the mundane world, to recover the true self naturally in tune with *Dao*, to become again 'Like an infant who has yet to smile' (20). Thus, a contrast is drawn with the moral rigours of Confucian self-cultivation: 'Learning is a matter of daily increase;/Practising *Dao* is a matter of daily diminution' (48).

Also revealed by this process of unlearning is the inherent hypocrisy of what is commonly considered virtue. People speak of morality only when it is the exception rather than the rule; they promote the value of 'filial piety' and 'parental affection' only when social order has disintegrated (18). In other words, we concern ourselves with such topics only when they cease to be viable options:

Accordingly, when *Dao* is lost, virtue arises;
When virtue is lost, humanity arises;
When humanity is lost, morality arises;
When morality is lost, propriety arises.
Now propriety is the thinning-out of loyalty and trust,
And the beginning of disorder.

(38)

The sage thus holds to 'the fruit' or reality, rather than 'the flower' of appearance – 'prefers the one and avoids the other' (38; see also 81).

The intimate connection between Daoist philosophy and the aesthetic tradition of China grows out of the realization of 'profoundly dark virtue' (51) within oneself. The person who achieves this is able to become co-creative with *Dao*, to create along with nature in his/her artistic endeavours. Nowhere is this more evident than in

China's exceptional tradition of landscape painting and image-laden nature poetry. These works represent not copies of nature, but creative expressions stimulated by natural beauty, which in turn invite the viewer/reader to ever more creative expressions. Speaking of such art, Chang Chung-yuan observes:

> There is something in these works that leads us to the ultimate that man shares with the universe. There is in them a dynamic process that interfuses with a higher grade of reality. They draw us into a spontaneous and even unintentional unity which, as the Daoist sees it, refers back to *Dao* itself, the primordial course of creativity. Only *Dao*, the mother of all things, is invisible and unfathomable, but it is through her manifestations, nevertheless, that all things are produced.
>
> (Chang 1963: 55–6)

For this reason, some of the most apt expressions of *Dao* are found not in heavy tomes of philosophy, but rather on brush-washed silk and in volumes of poetry. A particularly fine example of the latter comes from an autobiographical piece by T'ao Yüan-ming (365–427), entitled 'Rural living', which begins:

> As a lad I was ill attuned to the loud, vulgar world,
> My dispositions being prepossessed by the still, silent hills.
> Caught unawares in the net of pomps and vanities,
> After thirty long years I have set myself free.
> The migrant bird seeks out the woods that were its shelter;
> The fish in the pond remember thriving in deeper waters.
> To my farm on the edge of the southern wastes,
> I, creature of instinct not reason, have returned.
>
> (Chang 1977: 30–1)

Another example comes from the Tang Dynasty master, Wang Wei, who was proficient as both poet and painter. Su Shih said of Wang that 'in his poetry there is painting and in his painting there is poetry.'

> Magnolia bank
> Like the lotus flower grown on a tree,
> The pink magnolias sprinkle the hill-side;
> Hidden in a gorge, unnoticed,
> A thousand buds flower, then wither and die.
>
> (Chang 1977: 76)

Chan Buddhism and Japanese Zen were profoundly influenced on this point, giving rise to a diversity of creative expressions for enlightenment. A wide range of 'ways' (Chinese *dao*; Japanese *dō*) emerged – the tea way (*chanoyu*), the flower way (*kado*), and even the way of the warrior (*bushidō*). As a person of practical wisdom, Laozi would certainly have approved heartily of this proliferation of 'ways' in the world as reflective of the one, inexhaustible Way. The very structure of his text confirms his recognition of the impossibility of fully communicating *Dao* by mere verbal means, and we have seen how he availed himself of many evocative poetic images in his own attempts at communication.

Dao *as Technique*

The artistic practice of *Dao*'s virtue shades imperceptibly into our next dimension of *Dao*, *Dao* as Technique or the Daoist art of rulership. The focus of attention here is not an aesthetic application but implementation in the ordering of society. The Daoist sage emerges as simultaneously enlightened leader of the people. For some interpreters of Daoism, such as Arthur Waley, this aspect constitutes the main thrust of the text as a response to the Realist school of political philosophy.

The sage/ruler is one who emulates *Dao* in relating to the masses, even in the sense of the parent/child bond:

> Having no fixated mind,
> The Sage takes on the mind of the people as his own:
> 'Those who are good, I treat well,
> Those who are not good, I treat equally well.
> [In this way] goodness is realized;
> To those who are truthful, I am truthful,
> To those who are untruthful, I am equally truthful,
> [In this way] truthfulness is realized.'
> Living in the world,
> The Sage is unpretentious and unbiased,
> In handling worldly affairs,
> His mind is simplified and nebulous.
> The subjects all strain their ears and eyes,
> While the Sage treats all as his own children.
>
> (49)

It is the ruler's responsibility to provide an environment for the people devoid of contention and avarice, 'by emptying their hearts/minds,/Filling their stomachs,/Weakening their ambitions,/And strengthening their bones' (3). In this way their essential needs, represented by the stomach, are met without stirring up unnatural desires, associated with the more superficial yearnings of the human heart/mind (see also 12). Such a ruler exemplifies *wei wu-wei* by being non-interfering and allowing the subjects to act on their own behalf:

> The best (rulers) are those whose subjects know [only] of their existence;
> The next best are those who are loved and praised;
> The next are feared;
> And finally are those who are despised.
> Because of a lack of trust, distrust arises;
> Self-effacingly [the Sage] values [truthful] words.
> When the task is accomplished and the work completed,
> The subjects all say: 'We have done it ourselves – so naturally!'
>
> (17; see also 57)

A revealing analogy used by Laozi compares ruling an empire to frying small fish (60) – both tasks require consummate self-control and the ability to overcome the temptation to interfere with the natural process. The world is also compared to a 'sacred vessel' that ought not to be either mishandled or coveted (29). The efficacy of rulers is judged in direct proportion to their degree of inconspicuousness (17).

As a practical thinker, Laozi does not omit reference to the inevitable question of armed conflict in defence of the state. To the Daoist, even the victorious general has occasion for regret. Although Daoists are not pacifists in the strict sense of the term, they certainly cannot be classified as seekers of military glory:

> Weapons and armaments are tools of ill-omen,
> Things detested by all.
> Therefore, whoever has *Dao* turns away from them.
> The noble when at home honor the left (the place of good omens);
> When at war, they honor the right (the place of bad omens).
> Weapons and armaments are tools of ill-omen,
> Not tools of the noble.
> If using them is unavoidable,
> The best policy is calm restraint.
> Victory is not worthy of being glorified,
> So whoever glorifies it takes pleasure in slaughter.
> If one takes pleasure in slaughter,
> One may not have one's ambitions fulfilled in the world.
> Auspicious affairs honor the left;
> Inauspicious affairs honor the right.
> The lieutenant general occupies the left;
> The commanding general occupies the right.
> That is to say, war is to be treated as a funeral rite.
> After multitudes have been slaughtered,
> Weep with sorrowful grief;
> After the victory,
> Observe the occasion with funeral rites.
>
> (31; see also 46,57)

The purpose is to be achieved without domination, bragging, boasting or arrogance, and with the understanding that it is 'unavoidable and regrettable' (30).

Sunzi's *Art of War* evidences obvious Daoist influence with regard to its position on war. Although we cannot classify the author as a genuine Daoist, his recommendations coincide with Laozi's advice: 'To win every battle by actual fighting before a war is won, it is not the most desirable. To conquer the enemy without resorting to war is the most desirable' (Sunzi 1966: 26); 'to be able to conquer the whole Empire because of the skill in killing does not deserve the highest praise' (34). There are obvious comparisons here with Laozi's thoughts on military strategy (69).

In sharp contrast to these bleak depictions of war, Laozi provides us with his own utopian vision of the ideal Daoist community in chapter 80. The inhabitants are few, and they are distinguished by their contentment with their own situation, lacking any curiosity about immediate neighbours. Technology for both military prowess and transportation is available, but of no interest whatever. Instead, people concern themselves with the primal, simple pleasures of food, clothing and shelter. Even a written language is dispensed with – as is appropriate to one who realizes the inherent limitations of language for communicating ultimate reality.

Finally, Daoist principles are recommended in the field of international relations. Like *Dao*, the large state should assume a lowly position so that, as with the delta of a river, smaller flows will flow towards it of their own accord. When each assumes its appropriate role, their mutual expectations can spontaneously be met (61; see also 66). In modern terminology, Laozi's advice to the large state is to maintain a low profile, resisting the temptation to flaunt its obvious power. This is but another instance of two gems of Daoist wisdom: 'Whoever knows does not speak;/Whoever speaks does not know' (56) and 'to know that enough is enough is always to have enough' (46).

Images of Dao

In addition to the names provisionally bestowed upon *Dao*, Laozi employs a wealth of poetic images in the text to reveal further the *Dao*'s infinite dimensions and wonders. The Mother of the Ten Thousand Things (1,52), mentioned above in the context of *Dao* as Origin, also signifies the *yin*/feminine aspect of *Dao*. In a similar vein, reference is made to 'the profoundly dark female':

> The gateway of the profoundly dark female–
> This is called the root of Heaven and Earth.
> Continuous and ceaseless,
> It looks as if it were ever-present;
> Its function never wears out.
>
> (6)

Later we are told to 'know the male' yet 'hold fast to the female' as the means to return to the primal virtue (28; see also 61).

The value of emptiness or No-thingness is reinforced through the several images. In addition to the natural functionality of emptiness in a bowl (4) and a window (11), multiple references are made to the valley, whose essence consists in what it is not (6,15,28,39,40). The working of *Dao* is compared to a bellows: 'Vacuous and yet inexhaustible,/The more it is worked, the more it brings forth' (5). In a similar vein, we are cautioned to avoid becoming filled to overflowing, so that one may become, like *Dao*, 'beyond exhaustion and renewal' (15).

Water is a characteristically Daoist image that teaches the lesson of the value of the lowly position. It benefits the world, but being pliant never competes (8; see also 61). None the less, in this pliancy there is strength to overcome the unyielding (78). The encompassing character of water, as exemplified in the sea, also reflects *Dao*, which both nourishes things and invites them to flow into it without claiming credit or dominance (32,34).

The wholeness of *Dao* is represented by the Uncarved Block (*pu*), that is, a piece of wood in its primordially natural state. Unlike the carved product of artifice, the

Uncarved Block remains name-less (32,37). Its solidity is praised (15) and its simplicity is to be embraced (19). To attempt to partition it is a violation of its integrity and invites disintegration (28).

Dao is also the sanctuary of the Ten Thousand Things, and a treasure for both the good and the not good (62). Like an outstretched bow, its flexibility matches concrete circumstances as it 'reduces what is excessive,/Supplements what is deficient' (77).

To summarize, Laozi merges metaphysics, ethics and socio-political thought as well as military strategy in his terse, often cryptic, poetic exposition of Daoist philosophy. Beginning with a qualification as to the ultimate inadequacy of language for conveying reality, he goes on to evoke meanings through images and concrete analogies. The named *Dao* with which he presents us is admittedly incomplete, but suggestive of the 'profoundly dark' *Dao* that shall ever remain name-less and unnameable.

ZHUANGZI'S COMPLETION OF DAOIST PHILOSOPHY

Given the numerous references to Laozi and his work in the *Zhuangzi*, it is in part accurate to describe Zhuangzi as the most important of Laozi's commentators. The philosophical thought of these two shows great affinity, and a commonality is found in even their Daoist modes of expression. However, subtle but significant differences exist in terms of their respective explorations of *Dao* and its multi-dimensional manifestations. These differences include variations in literary style and philosophical emphasis.

The most obvious difference is in their style of exposition. In contrast to the suggestive poetic reveries of the *Dao De Jing*, the *Zhuangzi* provokes the reader with a continual critique of the world and its follies. Zhuangzi marshals myriad satirical allegories, fables, metaphors and analogies to expose the metaphysical myopia of his fellow human beings. His ingenious employment of the language of *Dao* makes the text a masterpiece of world literature, which combined with his philosophical depth and profundity prompted Kuang-ming Wu to dub Zhuangzi 'World Philosopher at Play' (1982). This is reflected from the opening chapter, suitably entitled 'Leisurely strolling'.

Rather than relying upon the force of analogical thinking, as does Laozi, Zhuangzi provides a philosophical justification of his views. Moreover, Zhuangzi shifts the focus from the known truth of *Dao* to the individual knower, stating that 'There must be True Personhood before there can be True Knowledge.' Hence, that knowledge is validated through, and only through, one's own authentic existence. Zhuangzi's metaphysics is much more radical than that of Laozi, and indeed may be termed trans-metaphysical, as he points out our bondage to our own narrow human perspectives. The huge bird, P'eng, introduced in his first chapter, illustrates this point. When told of its long flights the cicada and dove laugh in disbelief, bound as they are by the natural limitations of their own experiences.

Rather than relying upon the force of analogical thinking, as does Laozi, Zhuangzi provides a philosophical justification of his views. Moreover, Zhuangzi shifts the focus from knowledge or truth (in its theoretical formulation) of *Dao* to the Daoist practitioner's spiritual self-realization. That is to say, the knowledge or truth of *Dao* can be validated only if it provisionally functions as a philosophical guide for one's ultimate liberation or enlightenment. As soon as one attains ultimate enlightenment and undergoes spiritual transformation into what Zhuangzi calls 'the magnificant True Person', this very knowledge or truth has to be left behind, if not totally abandoned. It can be said that Zhuangzi's philosophy is trans-metaphysically more radical than Laozi's for the simple reason that all the metaphysical speculations, including Daoist ones, must ultimately be put into what may be trans-metaphysically transcended.

Accordingly, Zhuangzi lays great emphasis upon individual enlightenment, and much less emphasis upon the broader socio-political applications dealt with by Laozi. Chapter 17 gives some insight into Zhuangzi's own life in the story of his rejection of a royal summons. He enquires of the messengers as to the status of the sacred tortoise kept by the king, asking whether it would not rather be alive to drag its tail in the mud than honoured as dead bones. The answer obviously being the former, Zhuangzi curtly orders them away so that he may continue to drag *his* tail in the mud.

As for the process of spiritual growth, while Laozi counsels mental vacuity in emulation of *Dao*, Zhuangzi speaks more specifically of the methods of self-forgetting, mind fasting, no-thought, and so on. Because of a common interest in spiritual cultivation, he exerted a great influence upon the development of Chan Buddhism. For example, the opening passage of the second chapter even seems to refer to meditational practice, which was subsequently characterized as *wu-xin* (no-mind) in Chan Buddhism.

Zhuangzi also expands upon Laozi's concept of *Dao* as unnameable. He coins terms like 'Supreme Nothingness' and 'Nothingness-Nothingness' to reinforce the nameless *Dao*'s trans-metaphysical transcendence of the duality of Being and Non-Being. This boundless *Dao*, Zhuangzi argues, ought not to be subject to metaphysical fragmentation: '*Dao* is concealed in small accomplishments; the language (of *Dao*) is concealed in pompous words.' Like Laozi's oceanic *Dao*, his *Dao* is 'all-complete', 'all-pervading', 'all-encompassing':

> I go nowhere and don't know how far I've gotten. I go and come and don't know where to stop. I've already been there and back, and I don't know that my journey is done. I ramble and relax in unbordered vastness; Great Knowledge enters in, and I don't know where it will ever end.
>
> (Watson 1968: 241)

The language of *Dao*

Echoing Laozi's concern with the inability of language to convey the functional multidimensionality of name-less *Dao*, Zhuangzi takes a somewhat different approach to this perennial problem. For he sees in language, as in all futile human attempts to reduce reality to humanly comprehensible terms, the major stumbling block to realization of the mind of *Dao*. In contrast to the dualistic 'calculative mind' of deluded humans, Zhuangzi advocates the 'no-mind' of spontaneous self-forgetfulness. We must disabuse ourselves of the assumption that logical wrangling can come to any satisfying conclusion reflective of reality (see chapter 2).

Eschewing futile metaphysical speculations, Zhuangzi asserts that it is through our experience of profound unity with *Dao* that *Dao* can come to be realized, if not intellectually conceived. The following passage may serve as Zhuangzi's commentary on the *Dao De Jing*'s statement that '*Dao* gives birth to the One;/The One gives birth to the Two;/The Two give birth to the Three;/The Three give birth to the Ten Thousand Things' (42):

> Heaven and Earth were born at the same time I was, and the ten thousand things are one with me. We have already become one, so how can I say anything? But I have just *said* that we are one, so how can I not be saying something? The one and what I have said about it make two, and two and the original one make three. If we go on this way, (differentiating in thought and language) then even the cleverest mathematician can't tell where we'll end, much less an ordinary man. If by moving from nonbeing to being we get to three, how far will we get if we move from being to being? Better not to move, but to let things be!
>
> (Watson 1968 : 43)

Hence, the dimension of *Dao* as Origin is deconstructed, while greater stress is placed upon *Dao* as Principle. The term 'principle' (*li*) often appears in Zhuangzi's text, and he in fact observes that '*Dao* is none other than Principle', and more specifically the principle of the perpetual 'transformation of things' (*wu-hua*):

> The life of things is a gallop, a headlong dash – with every movement they alter, with every moment they shift. What should you do and what should you not do? Everything will change of itself, that is certain!
>
> (Watson 1968 : 182)

What remains for Zhuangzi, then, is the self-imposed task of creating a language able to advance his trans-metaphysical philosophy of ultimate liberation or awakening, prefigured by Laozi's 'teaching of no-words' (43): 'With words that are no-words, you may speak all your life long and you will never have said anything. Or you may go through your whole life *without* speaking them, in which case you will never have stopped speaking' (chapter 27; Watson 1968: 304). He also refers to such words as 'goblet words' (*zhi-yen*), explained by Burton Watson as 'words that are like a goblet that tips when full and rights itself when empty, i.e., that adapt to and follow along with the fluctuating nature of the world and thus achieve a state of harmony' (Watson 1968: 303). Hence, the Daoist of the metaphysical language game must be adept at both verbal eloquence and an eloquent, trans-metaphysical silence in a dialectical interplay of *Dao* as named and name-less. 'Neither words nor silence can exhaust the ultimate nature of *Dao* and things. Not to talk, not to be silent: human discourse reaches its limit here' (my translation, chapter 25).

Language thus becomes recognized as a humanly indispensable means to the end of approximating *Dao* – but it ought not to be taken too seriously, nor should we allow ourselves to become dependent upon language:

> The fish trap exists because of the fish; once you've gotten the fish, you can forget the trap. The rabbit snare exists because of the rabbit; once you've gotten the rabbit you can forget the snare. Words exist because of meaning; once you've gotten the meaning, you can forget the words. Where can I find a man who has forgotten words so that I can have a word with him?
>
> (Watson 1968 : 302)

The art of living

To be a great artist in the skilful employment of the language of *Dao* is in a deeper sense to be an artist of everyday living. Accordingly, an appreciation of the creative and artistic aspect of *Dao* pervades Zhuangzi's text. Above all else, this art requires the Daoist ability to equalize or harmonize all things (chapter 2), by overcoming artificial human distinctions. In effect, this requires that we assume the transcendental perspective of the enduring and impartial *Dao*.

Transcendental harmony comes about through the practice of *wei wu-wei*. The fatal consequences of failing to apply this approach are illustrated in the story of Hun-tun (Chaos), whose friends Shu (Brief) and Hu (Sudden) seek to repay his kindnesses by providing him with seven openings to compensate for his natural lack of any openings (7). However, like trying to carve the Uncarved Block, such an enterprise, which is contrary to *wei wu-wei*, cannot but end in disaster, and so the hapless Hun-tun is literally killed by the 'kindness' of his friends.

The most existentially significant point in Zhuangzi's art of living has to do with his Daoist attitude towards death and dying. *Wei wu-wei* allows for total liberation from the nearly universal human fear of death. It is a liberation that is due not to some hope of a life after death or faith in some saving deity, but relies instead upon the natural course (*zi-ran*) of the life/death cycle. Hence:

> With the Sage, his life is the working of Heaven, his death the transformation of things. . . . He discards knowledge and purpose and follows along with the reasonableness of Heaven. Therefore he incurs no disaster from Heaven, no entanglement from things, no opposition from man, no blame from the spirits. His life is a floating, his death a rest.
>
> (Watson 1968 : 168)

That Zhuangzi lived by his own advice is seen in the story of his reaction to his wife's death, as told in chapter 18. Although he admits to feelings of grief, he soon regains his composure through contemplating her death as part of the natural cycle of things in the world. As for his own death, the following remarks to his disciples are recorded, as he seeks to convince them to avoid an elaborate funeral:

> I will have heaven and earth for my coffin and coffin shell, the sun and moon for my pair of jade discs, the stars and constellations for my pearls and beads, and the ten thousand things for my parting gifts. The furnishings for my funeral are already provided – what is there to add?. . . . Above ground I'll be eaten by crows and kites, below ground I'll be eaten by mole crickets and ants. Wouldn't it be rather bigoted to deprive one group in order to supply the other? . . . the fool trusts to what he can see and immerses himself in the human. All his accomplishments are beside the point – pitiful, isn't it?
>
> (Watson 1968 : 361)

To Zhuangzi's list of natural riches we may add his own words, which stand as his parting gift to readers for ages to come, as well as a testament to his own skill in the art of living.

NOTES

1 In chapter 4 the character of Confucius offers very Daoistic advice to Yen Hui, who is enthusiastically about to set out to reform the ruler of Wei. Confucius warns him of the consequences of trying to force a situation, to convert people to virtue:

> Virtue is destroyed by fame, and wisdom comes out of wrangling. Fame is something to beat people down with and wisdom is a device for wrangling. . . . Though your virtue may be great and your good faith unassailable, if you do not understand men's spirits, though your fame may be wide and you do not strive with others, if you do not understand men's minds . . . this is simply using other men's bad points to parade your own excellence.
>
> (Watson 1968 : 55–7)

As an alternative approach he recommends 'fasting of the mind'.

2 All quotations from the *Dao De Jing* are taken from the translation by Charles Wei-hsun Fu and Sandra A. Wawrytko, soon to be published. Chapter numbers are noted parenthetically after each reference.

3 My punctuation here, based on some other texts, differs from both Wang Bi's standard edition and that of the Silk Manuscript.

4 Lin Yutang notes a parallel between these sounds and Hebrew tradition: 'Jesuit scholars consider these three words (in ancient Chinese pronounced like *i-hi-vei*) an interesting [linguistic] coincidence with the Hebrew word "*Jahve*"' (Lin 1948: 101).

5 As Origin, *Dao* is 'No-thingness', while as Principle it is 'Non-Being' and 'Being' in their metaphysical interplay, although ultimately these two are one and the same (as Lao Zi emphasizes in the opening chapter of the *Dao De Jing*).

6 Wing-tsit Chan, *A Source Book in Chinese Philosophy* (Princeton: Princeton University Press, 1963), pp. 260–1.

REFERENCES

Chan, Wing-tsit (1963) *The Way of Lao Tzu*, New York: Bobbs-Merrill.

Chang, Chung-yuan (1963) *Creativity and Taoism: A Study of Chinese Philosophy, Art, and Poetry*, New York: Harper & Row.

Chang, H. C. (1977) *Nature Poetry*, Chinese Literature 2, New York: Columbia University Press.
Fung, Yu-Lan (1962) *A New History of Chinese Philosophy* (in Chinese), vol. I, Beijing: People's Publishing House.
Lin, Yutang (1948) *The Wisdom of Laotse*, New York: Random House.
Sunzi, trans. Cheng Lin (1966) *The Art of War*, Taipei: Confucius Publishing Company.
Watson, Burton (1968) *The Complete Works of Chuang Tzu*, New York: Columbia University Press.
Wu, Kuang-ming (1982) *Chuang Tzu: World Philosopher at Play*, New York: Scholars Press.

FURTHER READING

Allinson, Robert (1989) *Chuang Tzu for Spiritual Transformation*, Albany, N.Y. SUNY Press.
Chang, Chung-yuan (1975) *Tao: A New Way of Thinking*, New York: Harper & Row.
Creel, H. G. (1970) *What is Taoism?*, Chicago: University of Chicago Press.
Fung, Yu-lan (1964) *Chuang Tzu*, New York: Paragon Books, repr.
Graham, A. C. (1981) *Chuang Tzu: The Inner Chapters*, London: George Allen & Unwin.
—— (1989) *Disputers of the Tao*, La Salle, Ill.: Open Court.
Lau, D. C. (1963) *Lao Tzu*, Baltimore, Md.: Penguin Books.
Merton, Thomas (1969) *The Way of Chuang Tzu*, New York: New Directions.
Waley, Arthur (1958) *The Way and its Power: A Study of the Tao Te Ching and its Place in Chinese Thought*, New York: Grove Press.
Wu, John (1963) *Lao Tzu*, New York: St John's University Press.

28

BUDDHISM IN CHINESE PHILOSOPHY

Whalen Lai

INTRODUCTION: BUDDHIST MIND AND BUDDHIST REALITY

Within the larger context of the history of Chinese philosophy, the major contribution of Chinese Buddhism can be said to be its insight into the working of the human psyche and the structure of ultimate reality, in short, psychology and metaphysics. Chinese understanding of these two areas has not been the same since the medieval Buddhist period. As the Qing scholars charged, the Neo-Confucian philosophers of the Song and Ming period (which came after the Buddhist era) had been so heavily influenced by Buddhism in their inner cultivation and in their metaphysics as to be crypto-Buddhists.

Before Buddhism came to China, the two dominant traditions were Confucianism and Daoism. In Confucianism, man sees himself as a social being tied from birth to family and state; to be human is to be son of one's father and subject to one's lord and king. In Daoism, man sees himself as part of nature; to be true to nature, it is sometimes necessary to renounce the artificiality of human culture, even to reject society and return to the hills. In the Han Confucian synthesis of these two traditions under the rubric of so-called Yin–Yang Confucianism, the ideal was to integrate man into the family, the family into the state, and the state into the cosmos under the guidance of the emperor, the Son of Heaven who binds heaven, earth and man together. There was no need then to look for a very subtle self like the Chan (Japanese Zen) idea of 'your original face before you were born' or to seek an escape from both society and nature to some acosmic Beyond higher than the limit of heaven itself.

It is Buddhism that led the Chinese to scrutinize the innermost reaches of their psyche while promising a personal deliverance to a transcendental realm beyond the natural cosmos. Not only that: it is in the nature of this medieval philosophy that this depth psychology is a reflection of the new heights reached by the new metaphysics. The classic Buddhist universe organized around Mount Sumeru and divided into the *triloka* (the three realms of desires, form and formlessness) is in fact a psychic universe. Mind and reality correlate. As a salvific or liberating religion, Buddhism had its leading practitioners, the monks, turning their attention away from the social and natural definition of man towards discovering the pneumatic mind and some acosmic Beyond. It is no accident that the Chinese word for 'transcendence', like the English one, came into philosophical usage largely from this period on. Just as the Buddhists would introduce into Chinese many more senses of 'mind' than it had words for before, they would also give to it the idea of 'transcendence' based on the verbs 'to leave, to go above, to shed, to be released from'. It is this medieval flight of the spirit in philosophical expression that this chapter will describe.

THE NEW PARAMETERS OF DISCOURSE

To accomplish this explication of the inner reality and its lofty end, Chinese Buddhist philosophy, while building on the wisdom of the Buddhist tradition that went before, transformed Chinese thought in the following three crucial areas:

1 Understanding Mahāyāna Emptiness as a more profound wisdom-reality than the naïve realism of the Confucian world of Being as well as the nihilism of the Daoist Non-Being or Nothingness.
2 Uncovering a corresponding non-self (*anātman*) through an emptying of the empirical self or selfhood as such . . . until this dual approach, still predicated upon a negative rhetoric, reverses itself during . . .
3 The final Mahāyāna transvaluation of the same into a positive, direct and immediate identity between the Buddha-nature self and the Suchness nature of reality.

Using the above as a framework, this chapter will recapitulate the major developments of Chinese Buddhist philosophy, namely: the maturation of the insight into Emptiness from the early Prajñāists to Sengzhao (AD 384–414?); the development of the Nirvāṇa School from Daosheng (AD 355–434) to Jizang (AD 549–623); and the flowering of Sinitic Mahāyāna from Tiantai to Huayan, i.e. from Zhiyi (AD 538–97) to Fazang (AD 643–712).

The discovery of Emptiness as transcendental

The Buddhist teaching of cessation of the passions and of life's sufferings had initially defined *nirvāṇa* negatively as 'extinction'. This negativism had, however, the positive function of eroding the reality of this world of rebirth (*saṃsāra*) and opening up a dimension of the 'other shore' (*nirvāṇa*). This set up in Hīnayāna a dualism of *saṃsāra* and *nirvāṇa*. But the rise of Mahāyāna with the Wisdom Sūtras (*Prajñāpāramitā Sūtras*) challenged that dualism with the new wisdom of Emptiness.

Emptiness denies the duality. It negates the opposition of *saṃsāra* and *nirvāṇa*, Form and Emptiness, or, in Chinese shorthand, Being and Non-Being. Both *saṃsāra* and *nirvāṇa* are empty; both Being and Non-Being are relative. Emptiness even empties itself to guard against those who cling on to it as another, real absolute. This is because true freedom is freedom from the fixities of mind, from habits of thought, and mental defilements that created those distinctions in the first place. In more positive terms, it is freedom to realize the interdependence of all things, to see the non-dual, the nature of what truly is. This Emptiness philosophy (*śūnyavāda*) is therefore not nihilistic. It just happened to retain the negative rhetoric associated with early Buddhism.

These Wisdom or Emptiness Sūtras reached China in the late second century AD. By the third century, they struck a chord among those Chinese philosophers, the Neo-Daoists, who were then interested in the mysteries of the *Yijing*, the *Laozi* and the *Zhuangzi*. At first, 'Emptiness' was mistaken for just another word to express the Daoist idea of Nothingness or Non-Being. In fact, it was translated as such.

Before the rise of Neo-Daoism, though, Non-Being was not a central concept in Chinese thought. During the Han Dynasty (206 BC – AD 220), it was assumed that beings with forms and shapes somehow arose from some formless Non-Being. But then Non-being meant not absolute Nothingness but rather some nebulous 'stuff', some *materia potentia*. It was the Neo-Daoist Wangbi (226–49) who discovered the importance of Nothingness.

Wangbi made much of chapter 40 of the *Laozi*, which says 'and Being comes from Non-Being'. Whether he knew the Emptiness Sūtras or not we cannot be certain. (The word *śūnya* in Sanskrit does denote the mathematical zero.) Wangbi made Non-Being the ground and substance of all beings. When it became fashionable to read Buddhism by matching its concepts with the Daoist ones (*geyi*), most assumed that the teaching of universal Emptiness also reduced all things to some primal void. Even Dao'an (312–85) did not entirely avoid that error.

The mistake was not corrected until the early fifth century by Kumārajīva (344–413), who not only translated more Emptiness Sūtras but also introduced the *śāstra* commentaries of Nāgārjuna. With his guidance, Sengzhao came to the first proper reading of Emptiness. Emptiness is not Non-Being; it is not a conceptual device for 'reducing Being to Nothingness'. If it were, it would have committed two fallacies: (a) the retention of a dualism of Being and Non-Being and (b) a confusion of an epistemic wisdom with an ontic faith in some nihilistic reality.

The proper understanding is that Being and Non-Being – conceived of as self-sufficient entities – are equally empty; that the goal of philosophy is to expose the antinomies of reason; and that by such destructive dialectics, one attains freedom from all misconceptions and misrepresentations of the real. With this, Sengzhao exposed the limits of Neo-Daoism. Wisdom is not something known (*gnosis*); it is more a way of knowing (*gnoma*). It is realizing that all positions staked out as absolute are ultimately false, delimiting and biased. The true position is a positionless position.

Sengzhao offered his own reading of Emptiness in the essay 'The Emptiness of the Unreal': Being is empty because this (claim to a self-nature of) Being turns out to be Unreal. Sengzhao also demolished three current schools of or opinions on Emptiness. He censured the School of No Mind by charging it with a subjective bias. The school would empty only mind and not the physical reality. He then faulted the School of Abiding with Form for trying to sit astride two worlds. This school proposed that a person should abide physically in form while roving psychically in Emptiness. He then criticized the School of Original Nothingness, noting how it prized Non-Being at the expense of Being. This amounts to missing the Middle Path.

The issues behind this exchange are actually more complicated than this. The School of Original Nothingness appeared first. It was indeed guilty as charged. But the School of No Mind had already disputed that school's ontological nihilism. Arguing rightly that the *sūtras* never asked one to annihilate reality, it went on to propose that what one should do – and what one can only do in the circumstances – is to empty the (wrong) concepts (about the real) in the mind. Reality is not changed, but our perception of it should be. Reality now appears empty as the mind is emptied. The School of Abiding with Form in turn tried to improve on this view. It agreed that one should not reduce Being to Non-Being, i.e. one should remove the distinction Being versus Non-Being created by the mind. So doing, one can abide physically in the world of forms while mentally roving in the mysteries. One proponent of this school, Zhidun (314–66), however, believed that the mystery involved a higher self, a spirit. It is this refined spirit that roves in the vacuous. In this, Zhidun believed, as even did Dao'an, that Buddhism accepted the existence of a soul that transmigrates from rebirth to rebirth. Only the School of No Mind dared to imagine the possibility of no-mind, i.e. no-soul, *anātman*. For that, it became the most maligned and misunderstood of the early Prajñā schools.

When we examine the evolution of these three schools, we see that Sengzhao's dialectical negation of them was simply an extension of their tradition of internal criticism. After Sengzhao, the same dialectics would unfold, almost always keeping to the triadic structure of thesis, antithesis and synthesis.

The early Emptiness spokesmen were, however, better at applying Emptiness to reality than to mind. Even Sengzhao's description of the mind drew more on the native Daoist ideas of the psyche. The mind should be emptied of thought so that it can mirror all things impartially. By coincidence the metaphor also appeared later in Yogācāra psychology.

The discovery of the transcendental Buddha-nature

One reason why the Chinese were not very well informed about Buddhist psychology is that they were not exposed to the Indian reflections on the mind until relatively late. It was Saṇghadeva who first really introduced the Abhidharmic literature in the last decade of the fifth century. Soon Kumārajīva taught Mādhyamika and discredited the Hānayāna scholarship of Saṇghadeva. But Kumārajīva did not anticipate that soon after he died, the *Mahāparinirvāṇa Sūtra* would arrive and introduce the still higher notion of a Buddha-nature in man. In a short space of time, the Chinese had to adjust to doctrines of soul, no-soul, universal Emptiness, and universal Buddha-nature.

Daosheng (355–434) tried to reconcile these various notions of the psyche. Armed with the still incomplete translation of the *Mahāparinirvāṇa Sūtra*, Daosheng foresaw its final teaching concerning the presence of a seed of enlightenment in all sentient beings. But what is this Buddha-nature? Although the *sūtra* called it *ātman* (permanent self), it also specified that it is not the *ātman* of the Hindu *Upaniṣads* and that it is not other than wisdom or Emptiness. And indeed, Buddha-nature is not the Hindu *ātman*. It retains that traditional Buddhist criticism of atmanic self-sufficiency and endorses the self only in the context of the interdependence of all realities.

It is well to review briefly the history of the Buddhist understanding of the self. The Buddha had taught *anātman* and dependent co-origination, in opposition to the *Upaniṣads*. Then the Hīnayāna Abhidharmist tried to give rational support to this teaching by breaking down the self and the elements of causation, by arguing that there is not the whole called the self; there are only these elements or *dharmas*. Mahāyāna came along and its Emptiness philosophy criticized even that, noting that there is no reason to deny the reality of the whole while believing in the *svabhāva* or self-sufficiency of the parts. Both *dharma* and *ātman*, part and whole, are empty. For a time, that seemed to be the last word on the matter.

To see how the Buddha-nature concept arose, it is necessary to remember its source. All the talk about the psyche mentioned above emerged from Buddhist reflection on the *Dharma* (Reality, Truth). The Wisdom Sūtras were *Dharma*-centric in that regard. But there is a different strand in Mahāyāna, the one that focused not so much on the *Dharma* Jewel as on the Buddha Jewel. Mahāyāna had idealized the Buddha into a transcendental (*lokottara*) reality and showered him with infinite, real attributes. Given the Buddha's omniscience and omnipresence (a boundless body), it was only natural that speculation about the presence of his wisdom in all sentient beings would arise. And indeed it did, in *sūtras* that are more Buddha-centric than *Dharma*-centric. A subgroup of these *sūtras* is now recognized as the Tathāgatagarbha (Buddha-nature, womb of the Buddha) corpus. The *Mahāparinirvāṇa Sūtra* is one of those. It pictured the presence of the transcendental wisdom in man as a *buddha*-seed (*buddhagotra*). So stated, this positive doctrine would in time reverse the negative vocabulary about the self as *anātman* in early Buddhism. Now we may return to Daosheng.

Daosheng, who discovered this doctrine of a universal Buddha-nature, noted that there is in man not the self of the eternal soul (*ātman*), but this Buddha-nature. This true self is expressive of the omnipresence of wisdom. It appears as seminal enlightenment in all sentient beings. What this means, in the later Chan-inspired appreciation of Daosheng, is that it removes any need of mediation between the innermost Self and the highest Good. Such a one-step identity of the two is more radical than anything in classical China – more than the moral metaphysics of Mencius or the oceanic self-loss in Zhuangzi. Thus to Daosheng is attributed the first theory of 'sudden enlightenment' based on his having 'seen into the Buddha-nature'. Later Chan (Zen) would do the same.

This Chan-inspired reading of Daosheng has to be qualified, however, for there are actually some important differences:

1 Unlike Chan, Daosheng never said that there is a full-grown Buddha-nature. Buddha-nature is only the seed, the beginning, of an eventual perfection of wisdom.
2 It follows then that his 'sudden enlightenment' was predicated upon gradual cultivation. Sudden or total insight refers only to the final break with *saṃsāra*.
3 Daosheng still analysed the issue from the side of man more than seeing it from the side of the Buddha. His is a relative instead of an absolute perspective.

Finally, despite all caution, the Nirvāṇa (Sūtra) School that Daosheng brought into being often lapsed back into confusing self, soul, *anātman*, Emptiness, and Buddha-nature. Thus a common assumption then was that Buddha-nature was still some ontic entity located within man. At its worst, as in the writing of Emperor Wu of the Liang Dynasty (502–56), it was confused with the immortal soul that transmigrates. However, it is the third point above that is definitive. In simple terms, a mature understanding of Buddha-nature is not just that man possesses it in himself; it is rather that all humanity is 'possessed' by it. We 'store' the *tathāgatagarbha* in us, but we are also 'stored' in that cosmic womb of the One Thus Come. This Buddha-centric reading did not mature in China until the sixth century, however.

The first volley of fire against the shortcomings of the Nirvāṇa School of Daosheng came, however, from Jizang (540–623). Heading a Sanlun (Mādhyamika) revival, he looked like a latter-day Sengzhao. Jizang criticized the mistaken reading of an ontic Buddha-nature. Buddha-nature, he said, is not an entity; it is a state of mind free from all definition of the self or no-self. It is the wisdom of Emptiness. In this way, Jizang brought the understanding of Buddha-nature squarely back into the fold of Mādhyamika. Unlike Sengzhao, though, he had a better grasp of the One Vehicle.

'Ekayāna', or 'One Vehicle', was introduced as a synonym for 'Mahāyāna' in the *Lotus Sūtra*. When the Emptiness Sūtras first declared the path of the *bodhisattva* to be Mahāyāna, they set Mahāyāna apart from the Two Vehicles of the *śrāvaka* and the *pratyekabuddha*, which were Hīnayāna. Later, though, the *Lotus Sūtra* – the earliest of the Buddha-centric corpus – came up with an 'inclusive Mahāyāna' idea. It subsumed all three Vehicles under the one, inclusive Ekayāna. Sengzhao failed to see this. In a 410 essay entitled 'Nirvāṇa is Nameless', now reauthenticated as his, Sengzhao defended the discreteness of the Three Vehicles against the Ekayāna thesis of Daosheng. He was using Triyāna (Three Vehicles) to support gradual enlightenment as Daosheng was using Ekayāna to support sudden enlightenment. That failure to recognize Ekayāna is probably the reason why Sengzhao was not counted by Jizang as belonging to the true lineage of the Sanlun masters.

Beyond the Two Truths towards the One Vehicle

The impulse towards an Ekayāna, 'monistic' philosophy in the late sixth century would lead to Zhiyi (538–97) of the Tiantai or Lotus Sūtra School. But Jizang, a defender of Mādhyamika, non-dual Emptiness, did not go that far. Nevertheless, he was instrumental in criticizing current readings of the Two Truths theory by Nirvāṇa School thinkers, who were then sidetracked into following a reading in the treatise called 'To establish the real truth' or *Satyasiddhi*.

The Two Truths theory originated in Nāgārjuna. He had noted how the Buddha taught the *Dharma* with recourse to the Two Truths: the Mundane Truth for living in the mundane world and the Highest Truth for gaining *nirvāṇa*. The former grants the world a nominal ontic reality; the latter finds it truly empty. In this original form, the 'two' does not refer to two realities. There is only one reality. The 'two' are just two ways of looking at it. The Chinese Buddhists were new to such theories of knowledge and were not able to keep the ontic and the epistemic apart. They sometimes naïvely thought that the Mundane Truth was *saṃsāra*; the Highest Truth was *nirvāṇa*. If so, since there is wisdom insight into how '*nirvāṇa* is none other than *saṃṣāra*', should not the Two Truths meet in that higher union of *saṃsāra* and *nirvāṇa*? If so, should there not be a Third Truth?

The Chinese also tended to apply the 'substance–function' relationship to analysing the Two Truths. Substance and function are categories that Wangbi brought to his analysis of Non-Being and Being. Non-Being is said to be the substance of Being and Being is seen as the function of Non-Being. Previously, during the Han Dynasty, Non-Being was origin, and Being was end. In this old origin/end model, Non-Being temporally preceded Being. In the new substance/function model, Non-Being is the eternal ground of Being. Applying this to the Two Truths, the Chinese Buddhists misconstrued Emptiness as some actual substance supporting mundane forms which act as its function. Since function is other than but not exactly separate from substance, this also led these Chinese Buddhists to assume that substance/function well described the non-duality nature of *saṃsāra* and *nirvāṇa*.

Closer scrutiny reveals that this is not exactly what Nāgārjuna meant. The non-dual in Nāgārjuna is the Neither/Nor of the two extremes; it is synonymous with the Middle Path. But in the substance/function model, substance subsumes function under itself. (It is closer to the Hindu *bhedābheda* than to Buddhist *advyava*.) Being asymmetrical, substance/function does not offer two real extremes for the Middle (Path) to avoid. This subtle difference between Indian and Sinitic non-duality was noticed by Jizang, who launched a sharp critique of the Two Truths theories then current.

Jizang first noted how the Two Truths are not supposed to describe reality. They pertain only to two ways of discourse on reality. Since they are a didactic device with no ontic substance of its own, there is no reason to dream up a Third Truth to unite the Two Truths. Then Jizang corrected the misperception of the Higher Truth as the substance of the Lower Truth. If indeed something has to be designated as 'substance' upon which everything else hangs, it would be the Middle itself.

No dialectician, however, could ignore the structure of thought already in place. So, since his Chinese contemporaries had already piled up, like steps in a pyramid, higher and higher unions of Two Truths, Jizang countered with his own Threefold and Fourfold Two Truths. The purpose there was not to build more castles in the air. It was to undercut the assumptions of his opponents. Jizang's pyramids did not 'build up'; they just 'undercut'. The so-called Ultimate Emptiness topping his system serves only to bring the whole scaffold down. In it, one realizes that 'there is nothing (definite or absolute) to be gained'.

So destructive is Jizang's dialectics (*prāsaṅgika*) that it is sometimes said that his school could not have survived in China for that reason. China knew negations before. Zhuangzi and Wangbi had known how words cannot exhaust reality. There is a silence beyond words. But the Mādhyamika art of 'using words against words' – demolishing words not by silence but by the words themselves – is arguably something new. Even now, reading Jizang, most of us would find it unnecessarily mind-bending. Jizang keeps pulling the rug from underneath us just when we think we know what he is talking about. That, however, is his intention: to bend minds that have become too comfortable.

Jizang's school did not last, but recent scholarship has shown that the cutting edge of his razor-sharp intelligence actually persisted in the Ox-head branch of early Chan. Led by Fayong (599–657), this school disseminated the art of saying an Eternal Nay into all surviving Chan sects. The spirit of that resolute 'No!' is still captured in the *Wumenguan* (Japanese *Mumonkan*) headed by the *Gong'an* (*koan*) of Master Zhaozhou: 'Does a dog have Buddha-nature?' 'No!'

A different symmetry of mind and reality

In the late sixth century, there was more than one way to react to the Nirvāṇa School and its Two Truths theory. Besides Jizang, there was Zhiyi. Regarding Emptiness as the Middle Path, Jizang would not take Ekayāna as implying monism. Critical of the self-sufficiency of mind, he would not make mind absolute either. Zhiyi felt differently. He came up with the first theory of a symmetry between the structure of one Mind (with three yogic stances) and the structure of one Reality (with its own three truth aspects).

In this, Zhiyi took in more of the Nirvāṇa School's teaching than Jizang would. His Lotus [Sūtra] School absorbed the Nirvāṇa [Sūtra] School. The Nirvāṇa School had been speculating on the whereabouts of the Buddha-nature. Since the *sūtra* said that all sentient beings have Buddha-nature, and since sentience (*sattva*) meant having consciousness or mind, the Nirvāṇa School generally located Buddha-nature in the mind, above all, of men. Zhiyi, who was a yogin cognizant of the need to cleanse the mind, inherited this reading of the Mind as the locus of enlightenment.

Building on *abhidharma*, Zhiyi also accepted a correlation of subject mind and object-realm. To this, he added his own Mādhyamika reading of the Three Aspects of One Reality being correlated to the Three Meditative Stances of One Mind. (On the triads, see the next section.) This symmetry of Mind and Reality gave his Tiantai school a stability that Jizang scrupulously shunned in his. Symmetry is not identity. *Rūpa* and *citta* (form and mind) are two, perceived and perceiver. The goal of wisdom is to capture the whole of the universe (the trilocosm) in the unity of the mind (as one); it is not to absorb matter into mind or reduce mind to matter. Those two extremes of idealism and materialism Zhiyi considered to be contrary to the Middle Path. In this, he continued the Indian Mādhyamika criticism of Yogācāra.

It should be remembered that Yogācāra – the second major Mahāyāna philosophy, which traces all representations of reality to the storehouse consciousness (*ālayavijñāna*) – originated later than Mādhyamika. It also arrived in China late, i.e. a century after Kumārajīva. Committed to Mādhyamika and suspicious of the recent arrival, Jizang and Zhiyi would not include the latter's idealist tendency in their own systems. That was left to the later schools of Huayan and Chan: under Fazang (594–657) and Daoxin (580–651), the symmetry of Mind and Reality ended not just in correlation but in identity. Reality is Mind Only; Mind is the True Suchness.

The Mind as Suchness in the *Awakening of Faith*

That equation of Mind with Suchness (*tathatā*, the ultimate reality and nature of all things) was not spelled out as much in Indian Yogācāra as it was in a text compiled in China called the *Mahāyāna Awakening of Faith*. Appearing around AD 550, it stated in no uncertain terms how all of Reality is One Mind. (The formula was taken freely from the *Huayan* (*Avataṃsaka*) *Sūtra*, where the *triloka* (three realms) are said to be of One Mind.) Suchness and Mind are One. That being the case, there is an *a priori* identity of the mind of sentient beings and the truth of Suchness, such that we are all *de facto* enlightened. That we do not see this simple fact is due to an accidental, deluded thought. With this, the text overcame the limitations of Daosheng's understanding of Buddha-nature and sudden enlightenment noted earlier. Now (a) the essence of *a priori* enlightenment in man is total, not seminal; such that (b) gradual cultivation is now predicated upon sudden enlightenment, not just leading up to it; and (c) the mode of discourse is no longer anthropocentric but rather Buddha-centric, i.e. not from the side of mundane cause but from the side of transmundane effect.

Thereupon, this philosophy permits the telescoping of all Reality into the One Mind. Mind here is no longer just a human faculty, the perceiver of the perceived, but is rather the Suchness Mind manifested as the *tathāgatagarbha* (Buddha-nature) in us. This *tathāgatagarbha* is empty (*śūnya*) in terms of mundane self-natures, but it is not empty (*aśūnya*) in that it is endowed with transmundane powers to liberate itself from bondage. This formula came from the *Śrīmālādevi Sūtra* and is indicative of the higher awareness that it is not man possessing the Buddha-nature but the Womb (*garbha*) of the Buddha (*tathāgata*) possessing all men. On this note, Mahāyāna reversed the premiss of early Buddhism, where life is suffering and *nirvāṇa* is a Beyond. Now, to put it simply, suffering is an illusion and *bodhi* is here and now.

This radical idealism of the *Awakening of Faith* did not catch on immediately. Zhiyi and Jizang avoided it. The work was even suspected by some to be a forgery because it contradicted other Sanskrit Yogācāra texts in translation. The pilgrim Xuanzang (602–64) even went to India in the hope of finding a judgement for or against. In 645, he brought back from Nālandā the Yogācāra of Dharmapāla, which contradicted the *Awakening of Faith*'s teachings. His Weishi (Consciousness Only, Vipñaptimātratā) School won the day.

But then, as another ideological legend has it, Fazang (643–712) was working on Xuanzang's monumental translation project when he broke away because of a disagreement, and that led to his formulating the Huayan philosophy. Fazang's basic charge is that Xuanzang's Yogācāra idealism was fixated with a deluded *ālayavijñāna* (storehouse consciousness) tied to phenomenal reality. It is one grade lower than the Pure Mind immediately identical with the noumenal Suchness. Weishi's *ālayavijñāna* itself is a devolution of this Suchness Mind; it represents the *tathāgatagarbha*-in-bondage (to the world). So successful was Fazang's campaign against Xuanzang that we now have a distinction made only in Chinese Buddhism between the higher philosophy of 'Mind Only' (meaning Huayan and Chan) and the lesser philosophy of 'Consciousness Only' (Xuanzang's Weishi).

In the process Fazang also uncovered in Indian Mahāyāna a separate *tathāgatagarbha* corpus. The Huayan School then claimed for itself a knowledge of *Dharmatā* (*Dharma* essence) and berated Xuanzang's expertise in knowing only *Dharma-lakṣaṇa* (*Dharma* phenomena or *Faxiang*). Hence *Faxiang* was used pejoratively to describe this 'crypto-Hīnayāna' school of Weishi. Many buddhologists still labour to prove that Fazang was right, but to date no one has found even a Sanskrit or Tibetan reference to the *Awakening of Faith* or a theory of Mind and Reality in India or Tibet that is anything like the one Fazang developed.

The *Awakening of Faith* also had an impact on the two other Sinitic Mahāyāna schools: Chan and Pure Land. The historical (as distinct from the mythical) beginning of Chan came with Daoxin (580–651), now counted as the Fourth Patriarch. He had apparently popularized his meditative practice using the philosophy of this text. But with Xuanzang back and the authenticity of this text in question – plus the fact that it is only a *śāstra* and not a *sūtra* – it seems that his circle eventually came up with a more respectable name for his emerging school. It called itself the lineage of the Masters of the *Laṅkāvatāra Sūtra*. This is the *sūtra* considered in China to be the inspiration behind the *śāstra* that is the *Awakening of Faith*. The proclamation of this lineage is the first indication of a Chan movement.

The *Awakening of Faith*'s impact on the Pure Land School is more indirect. The final section of this text encouraged a meditation on Amitābha Buddha as the most expedient means of realizing the Suchness Mind for most people. One meditates here on the *Dharmakāya* manifested through this Buddha's icon. I shall conclude this section with a problem which the *Awakening of Faith* left for them. If the Mind is indeed Suchness, how did illusion, suffering and *saṃsāra* arise in the first place? The answer offered by the text creates more problems than it solves. It says: 'Suddenly, a deluded thought arose' – and there was the illusion of *saṃsāra*. This is the beginningless Ignorance. But since Suchness or enlightenment is also beginningless, are we now left with two irreducible and opposing principles? If so, how can one speak of there being just One Mind? In AD 681, a treatise by the monk Fuli asked even more pointedly: did not the Buddha himself teach that all things have causes? Only things with causes and conditions can be brought to a cessation. If indeed ignorance is beginningless (causeless), how can we ever effect its cessation so as to achieve enlightenment?

The character of the Sinitic Mahāyāna schools

By the ninth century, the Buddhist schools in China with obvious Indian antecedents had disappeared as distinct entities. Weishi Yogācāra had been discredited by Fazang. Jizang's Mādhyamika had disappeared into Ox-head Chan. Except for popular rituals, Tantrayāna never reached beyond the initiated few either – though it did claim the thinker Yixing (673–727). The Sinitic Mahāyāna schools with no known Indian forerunners were the ones that counted. Though all of them espoused theory (philosophy) and practice (path), tradition associates theory with Huayan and Tiantai and practice with Chan and Pure Land. By association, Pure Land feeds off Tiantai, which has more of a faith component, as Chan draws on Huayan, which has more of a wisdom bias. The Pure Land School knew of eschatological anxiety and the paradox of finding grace in the midst of despair, but it had more impact on popular piety than on rational philosophy as such.

The comprehensiveness of Tiantai

Of the remaining and more philosophical three, Tiantai, the earliest, developed a unique philosophy of the Round or in the Round. 'Round' refers to the circle; the closest English translation of this *yuan* ideal is perhaps 'comprehensiveness'. (I avoid the term 'Holism', for that is also a characteristic of Huayan.) Metaphorically, nothing escapes this circle; everything is included in it. The root-metaphor may be Chinese; it is the old harmony of *yin–yang*. But instead of the simple complement of *yin* and *yang*, we have a much more subtle trinity of One-in-Three and Three-in-One.

The *Lotus Sūtra*'s idea of the Three Vehicles being in the end just One provided the scriptural norm here, but it is Nāgārjuna's *Mādhyamika-kārika* that was credited with working out this Three/One dialectics. Nāgārjuna spoke of only Two Truths, but, as we noted earlier, the Chinese came up with the idea that if there are (1) *saṃsāra* and (2) *nirvāṇa* and then (3) *saṃsāra* is none other than *nirvāṇa*, there should be correspondingly the Three Truths of the Real, the Empty and the Middle. Among the Nirvāṇa/Satyasiddhi masters, this had led to the idea of a Third Truth that is the Unity of the Two Truths. Zhiyi only inherited this triadic format. Instead of deconstructing the trio as Jizang had done, he rearranged the pyramidal Three Truths into a circular triad in the Round. The circle represents the One of Ekayāna, of Reality as well as of Mind. The circle knowing no beginning and no end represents a timeless perfection. (Tiantai traditionally disputed causation and favoured a non-causative whole.)

It is in that sense that the Round is more than the old Harmony of complementary *yin* and *yang*. Yin–yang philosophy still distinguishes *yin* from *yang*; though they mix (quantitatively), their quality (passive versus active) remains distinct. In Tiantai philosophy, the Three Truths collide only to be fused, so that everything is at once Empty, Real, Middle. Furthermore, the *yin–yang* philosophy admits of a Unity (the Great Ultimate) prior to the emergence of the Two (*yin* and *yang*), but this is based on the classic 'origin-and-end' sequence. In Tiantai, the Empty, the Real and the Middle blend timelessly 'in the Round (One)'. The One is present in the Three, though. The catchy Tiantai dictum – 'Every form (colour) or smell (odour) is the Middle Path' – denotes that omnipresence of the One in every phenomenon. When later the Neo-Confucians talked about finding the Great Ultimate in every object in the world, they did so after the manner of Zhiyi, not after the manner of the Han Confucians. In Han thought (religious Daoism excepted), the preservation of the origin (One) intact in the subsequent (Many) is not possible.

What does that mean in real life? Let us take a common problem in philosophy to illustrate the efficacy of this dialectics. Whether we are sinners or images of God, whether human nature is evil or good, cannot be answered one way or the other. There is no lack of trying, though: thinkers, East and West, down the centuries have argued for man being evil, not evil, both or neither. These positive, negative and in-between answers are manifestations of the Three Truths of the Empty, the Real and the Middle. But every one of those positions is incomplete and biased. None is absolutely right, for otherwise the question would have been solved long ago. The answers contradict one another endlessly; they just drive us around 'in circles'.

The only resolution is to accept the whole. Truth, as Hegel says, is the Whole. Freedom is learning to stop momentarily before the Mystery. There, 'beyond the reach of words and speech,' says Tiantai, 'the *karma* of the mind is simply cut off.'

This is the Tiantai dialectics, a Hegelian 'Whole of the Wholes' without further progress. This is Nāgārjuna's 'Non-dual Emptiness' given a Harmonic twist. In this *Dharmatā* seen as the 'various phenomena's true form', there is no essence/phenomena divide. The Truth of Emptiness is in the Whole of the Real. And that holism can be found in any 'colour' or 'aroma'. The Whole is so important to Tiantai that this school would not throw out any part of it, however negative. Thus in a unique phrasing of the interdependence of all things, Tiantai would say 'There is the Devil in heaven; there is God in hell.' Even the Buddha has an essential evil in him. His goodness is acquired. (That sounds almost like Xunzi!) Perfectly enlightened, the Buddha retains that innate evil in order to be present in all Ten Realms. In this philosophy one learns to affirm, deny, transcend; transcend, deny, affirm everything; *ad infinitum*. We who live in an imperfect world might aspire to a perfection beyond, but real redemption comes when the *bodhisattva* accepts his present lot as 'perfectly imperfect' in the only 'imperfectly perfect' world there is. This is the genius of Tiantai Comprehensiveness.

The world of infinity in Huayan

If Tiantai cultivates the perception of the Whole, it still does so in a circle. A circle has clear boundaries. Tiantai might traffic in astrological numbers ('3,000 worlds in a split second of thought'), but its favourites are the prime numbers three and one. Huayan alone truly looked into the face of infinity itself. Only it could toy with the Mystery of the Ten – ten is a full number that is the sum of all numbers – and talk of 'millions and millions' of Buddha-worlds as if they were everyday realities. Although it has been pointed out by the leading Tiantai scholar in Japan (Andō Toshio) that in the later writings of Zhiyi, there were already intimations of such Totalistic extravagance, in the end, its *Lotus Ekayāna* stopped far short of the grandiose world of the *Avataṃsaka Sūtra*.

Details aside, the catch-phrase of Huayan philosophy is 'One is All; All is One.' What that claims is that in every tiny speck of the universe the whole of the universe is present and that everything in the universe is somehow coextensive with every other thing there is. Imagine stepping into a realm of light, where every light lights up every other light, and each point of light is so free of substance as to be transparent to all other points of light. This is the hall of mirrors that Fazang once used to illustrate his point to his patron, the Zhou Empress Wu. This is Sudhana's 'entry into the boundless *dharmadhātu* (realm of reality)' only to find the seer becoming the seen and the pilgrim disappearing into and becoming the Buddha.

Once again, though one can trace some precedence for this philosophy in the Chinese tradition in the likes of Zhuangzi or Huishi, there is a difference. The *Dao* 'found in a piece of dust' is a certain principle; it is not the physical sum of all things. 'The ten thousand things in one finger (pointing, category)' is not yet 'millions and millions of worlds in a speck of dust'. This is because generally speaking, classical philosophy knew only a finite universe. Heaven had its edge; earth had its limit. But there is, in medieval cultures, an explosion of the universe and an expansion of consciousness, although the parties did not then have the vocabulary to account for the difference that we now have. The simple fact is this. Mathematically speaking, a part can be immediately the whole – as Huayan's One-is-All equation claims – only when we are dealing with the infinite. Any part of infinity is still infinity. That sense of the infinite, not there in Tiantai yet, is the mark of Huayan.

An aside: answers to 'Whence ignorance?'

Huayan philosophy is more than that. There is a dynamic and optimistic side to it that is not in Tiantai. Scholars are divided on which is the higher philosophy. Tradition grants Huayan superiority because Tiantai still accepts the presence of delusion in the mind. Huayan knows only a totally pure mind. But then it is in the nature of Tiantai Comprehensiveness not to dismiss evil, while it is the *Awakening of Faith* (which Zhiyi rejected) that led Huayan to imagine a radical idealism based on the Suchness Mind. Yet as we queried above in the case of the *Awakening of Faith*: whence then comes delusion? It is in struggling with this question that Fazang arrived at new answers.

The simplest answer, one found in the *tathāgatagarbha* corpus, is to leave it unanswered. The defilements are simply accidental and inconceivable – but they are there. But as Ignorance (*avidyā*) is privation of wisdom with no ontological reality of its own, it can be removed by wisdom. This is the logical Indian answer.

The *Awakening of Faith*, however, has suggested a Chinese answer. This work has taken in the 'substance and function' paradigm that Wangbi pioneered. Calling Suchness substance, it compares it to a body of water. Ignorance is presented as the wind. The text then has the wind of Ignorance ruffling up the water of Suchness into the waves of *saṃsāra*. With the waves being the function that is not 'separate from' the substance of the water, the text came up with a pseudo-Mādhyamika reading of their non-dual relationship: *saṃsāra* (waves) generated out of Suchness (water) remains 'not other than' *nirvāṇa*, because waves are still wet as water. The text used this to explain the canonical teaching about how the pure *tathāgatagarbha* could somehow possess the impure world (both *saṃsāra* and *nirvāṇa*) within its womb.

Fazang, however, took the intent of the metaphor one step further. Since it was the interaction between water and wave that created *saṃsāra*, he inferred that it was the coming together of Suchness and Ignorance that created the world. In his commentary on the *Awakening of Faith*, he treated Suchness and Ignorance as if they were *yang* and *yin*. He mapped out, implicitly, a genesis of the phenomenal world according to the logic of the broken and unbroken lines in the hexagrams of the *Yijing*. He called this elsewhere the 'Causation [of reality out] of the *tathāgatagarbha*' and ranked it above the causation due to the *ālayavijñāna*. The latter is a lower manifestation of the former.

Making the wind and the water co-creators of *saṃsāra* (waves) has the unintended consequence of making light of Ignorance. This is because since the waves (*saṃsāra*) are no less water (*nirvāṇa*), a person should realize the presence of Ignorance, but there is not really the need to remove it (wind). This is not how the original 'water–wave metaphor' in the *Laṅkāvatāra Sūtra* intends it to be. In the original metaphor, *saṃsāra* as object-realm is the wind; and the waves represent the agitated, object-clinging consciousness. Ridding the wind of object-forms so as to calm the waves of turbulent, subjective mentation would be imperative. This describes more faithfully the Yogācāra psychology.

In the redacted metaphor of the *Awakening of Faith*, Ignorance as wind and *saṃsāra* as waves were given more positive value. But as if that were not enough, Fazang came up with a still higher theory known as *Dharmadhātu* causation. In this theory, *Dharmatā* as essence (water) could generate all phenomenal realities (waves) from itself without even the help of Ignorance (wind) serving as condition (*pratyaya*) that brought the world into being. The elements of the whole universe, one and all, simply generate themselves by themselves. This 'conditionless' co-arising (*samutpāda*) happens from second to second, non-stop, from every point in the universe. This provided the dynamic side to the 'One is All; All is One' formula that Huayan has and that Tiantai never knew and, content with the Round, never cared to acquire. But with this totalistic world-view, Fazang also removed the last trace of evil from the world. But if so, whence Ignorance?

The subitism of Chan

Chan did not indulge in the same speculations as Huayan, but rather confronted the question 'Whence Ignorance?' head on. To the question 'If we are in fact already *buddhas*, why do we not feel enlightened?' it offered no ready-made answer. No such answer exists. Everyone must face that paradox of life itself. Later Chan would even intentionally precipitate this sense of crisis, this Great Doubt – why am I not enlightened when the truth is that I am? – that when resolved would effect the Great Enlightenment. Just as 'suddenly a deluded thought arose to cloud the Suchness Mind', as suddenly would the *a priori* enlightenment break through. That is the subitism of Chan.

The basic teachings of Chan are often expressed thus: 'No reliance on words; transmission outside the teachings; point directly at the minds of men; see your Buddha-nature and become enlightened.' Those teachings really belonged to Mazu Daoyi (709–88), but legend would attribute them to Bodhidharma in the early sixth century. But perhaps the best-known Chan story concerns the Sixth Patriarch Huineng (538–713). One generation removed from Daoxin (580–651), Huineng supposedly succeeded Hongren (602–75) by defeating Shenxiu (d. 706) of the so-called Northern School.

The episode of their exchange of Mind Verses told in the *Platform Sūtra* is now recognized by critical scholars as mere fiction. The story has it that Huineng, an illiterate youth from the barbaric South, upstaged Shenxiu by answering his Mind Verse:

> The body is the *Bodhi* Tree
> The mind is a mirror bright
> Daily with diligence (the
>   mirror) to clean
> Let no dust upon it adhere.
>
> (Shenxiu)

> *Bodhi* is not some tree
> Nor needs mirror a stand
> Originally there being
>   not a thing
> Whence the dust to adhere.
>
> (Huineng)

These poems about the Mind are not ground-breaking. There is nothing in them that cannot be traced back to the basics of Mahāyāna. If Shenxiu only described the basic technique of removing the mental defilements (*kleśa*), then Huineng only reiterated the Emptiness dictum to deny that last duality of the pure and the impure. What is new here is not the content. What is new is the form. The story is historically unique.

This story has encapsulated volumes of Mahāyāna wisdom in very few words concerning a fabled life. The form of the exchange recalls the *Analects* of Confucius; the aphorism of the *Laozi*; the Mencian interest in human nature; and the anecdotes of Zhuangzi. The folklore transferred wisdom from the centre of learning to the countryside. The young, illiterate, barbaric Huineng had exposed the folly of age, learning and high culture. *Bodhi* is no longer for the few. Sagehood is now within the reach of everyone.

By the mid-ninth century, when this tale gained currency, however, Buddhism was ready to bow out to a Confucian revival. The symmetry of Mind and Reality – body/mind and *bodhi*/mirror – is now set out by Zongmi (780–841), who belonged both to the Huayan and the Chan lineage, in his *Essay on Man*. By making man – instead of buddhahood or general sentience – the topic and by including Confucianism and Daoism as legitimate, non-Buddhist, paths to the same *Dharma*, Zongmi paved the way for the transition. He might believe the Suchness Mind to be the most profound of anthropologies, yet he helped the Neo-Confucians to file their counter-claim.

Figure 28.1 The later *yin–yang* circle

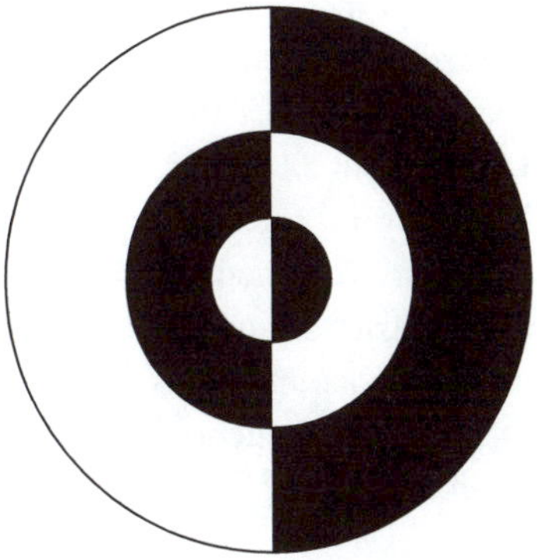

Figure 28.2 The *Li Kan* circle

Zongmi also capitalized on Fazang's alignment of Huayan and the *Yijing* philosophy. He produced a diagram for the *ālayavijñāna* based on the *Li Kan* hexagram, which, when modified in the twelfth century, would become the well-known *yin–yang* circle (see Figures 28.1, 28.2). All that affected Neo-Confucian metaphysics. After Zongmi, the only real thinker was the Tiantai master Siming Zhili (960–1028). Hence, Chinese Buddhism generally gave up on speculative reason even as Neo-Confucians acquired it.

The legacy of Buddhist psycho-metaphysics

Han Confucianism knew how to integrate man into society and cosmos. Buddhism knew how to fathom the depths of the psyche to reach acosmic heights – but usually by bypassing family and state. Although by the high medieval era (AD 600–800), Sinitic Mahāyāna had already renounced renunciation and reaffirmed the goodness of the world, there was a limit to that secularization. It was left to the Neo-Confucians to emulate the monk's pneumatic (spiritual) independence but to redirect it to the ends of family and state. They took over the Buddhist interest in mind and metaphysics, but looking now to Mencius, they mapped the vocation of moral man in a moral universe. In this, they changed the basic definitions of man and the world.

The Chan Buddhists still looked for 'their original face before they were born', something aligned with a Suchness Principle that is universally self-same. For the Neo-Confucians, that 'original face' is so pre-natal as to be asocial and pre-moral; and that self-same principle too uniform to take into account the differentiation in the world. Accordingly, the Neo-Confucians modified Buddhist psychology and metaphysics. The early Song masters would practise 'quiet sitting', but they meditated not on some 'faceless (Buddha) face', but on the mind at its moral inception – the moment when it can freely follow the good or else let the emotions and inclinations draw it towards selfish ends. Mystical meditation, in short, had been remade into moral introspection. Likewise the Neo-Confucians, while accepting the presence of the One (Great Ultimate) in all things, insisted that the same principle would and did underwrite the hierarchy of ruler/minister, father/son and husband/wife. In the end, these neo-classicists returned their fellow Chinese to the more rational, if limited and more Sinocentric, cosmos of the Han. But they kept a gift from the Buddhists. Very few men ever became sages in ancient Han, but in late medieval Song, all men had a duty to realize this sagehood in them. This was the Confucianization of the Buddhist idea of an *a priori*, *in toto*, Buddha-nature in all men.

FURTHER READING

Chen, Kenneth (1964) *Buddhism in China*, Princeton: Princeton University Press.
Cook, Francis H. (1977) *Hua-yen Buddhism: The Jewel Net of Indra*, University Park/London: Pennsylvania State University Press.
Hakeda, Yoshito (trans.) (1967) *The Awakening of Faith*, New York: Columbia University Press.
Hurvitz, Leon (1960–2) 'Chin-i (538–597): an introduction to the life and ideas of a Chinese monk', *Mélanges chinois et buddhiques* 12.
Liebenthal, Walter (1968) *The Treatise of Seng-chao*, 2nd edn, Hong Kong: Hong Kong University Press.
McRae, John (1986) *The Northern School and the Formation of Early Ch'an Buddhism*, Honolulu: University of Hawaii Press.
Robinson, Richard (1967) *Early Mādhyamika in India and China*, Madison: University of Wisconsin Press.
Swanson, Paul (1989) *Foundations of T'ien-t'ai Philosophy*, Berkeley: Asian Humanities Press.
Takakusu, Junjiro (1947) *The Essentials of Buddhist Philosophy*, Honolulu: University of Hawaii Press.
Zürcher, Erik (1959) *The Buddhist Conquest of China*, 2 vols, Leiden: Brill.

29

MAO ZEDONG AND 'CHINESE MARXISM'

Arif Dirlik

The thought of Mao Zedong (1893–1976) stands at the intersection of two histories: a global history that, beginning in the late nineteenth century, intruded with increasing forcefulness on Chinese thinking, and provided a new frame of reference for thinking about the past, present and future of Chinese society; and a Chinese history the autonomy of which appeared as an issue as the new world impressed itself on Chinese consciousness. As 'Mao Zedong Thought'[1] took shape in the course of the Communist Revolution in the 1930s it drew upon a foreign ideological import – Marxism – for its constituent elements; but it was the crucible of that revolution – Chinese society, with its social formations and quotidian culture – that gave it its form. At the heart of Mao's philosophical formation lies an account of a Third-World revolutionary consciousness seeking to remake itself into an autonomous subject of this new world against the immanent threat of degradation into its marginalized object. The contradictions in Mao Zedong Thought, no less than its contributions, are located in this account.

Mao's philosophy is the articulation of a 'Chinese Marxism', at once Marxist *and* Chinese. It is Marxist not only because Mao himself (and Maoism) has placed his thought unambiguously within a Marxist tradition, but more importantly because the categories of his philosophy are derivative of Marxism; indeed, we might suggest that there is no constituent conceptual element of Mao's thought that is not traceable to Marxism. At the same time, there is something ineluctably Chinese about Mao's Marxism. Mao did not just read Marxism in accordance with a Chinese historical experience, as is commonly recognized, but insistently read the Chinese historical experience into Marxism, in the process 're-creating' Marxism.[2] Universally Marxist in its conceptualization of the world, Mao's Marxism is particularly Chinese in expression. One of Mao's greatest strengths as a leader was his ability to translate Marxist concepts into a Chinese idiom; and it was at the level of language (which to Marx represented 'practical consciousness') that he read the Chinese historical experience into Marxism. Even at the most abstract exposition of his philosophical ideas, Mao drew his references from Chinese history, past and present, which placed his Marxism within a Chinese world of discourse that in its vocabulary is not readily accessible to the outsider, no matter how thoroughly armed with Marxist concepts.

Three caveats are necessary by way of introduction. First, while it is possible (and necessary) to speak of Mao's philosophy, this should not be taken to suggest that Mao may, or should, be viewed primarily as a philosopher, if by philosophy we understand the pursuit of abstract questions. Mao, who described himself on one occasion as a 'graduate of the university of the greenwoods', observed of the pursuit of abstractions: 'The way they go about it in the universities at present is no good, going from book to book, from concept to concept. How can philosophy come from books?'[3] First and foremost a practical revolutionary, Mao even at his most abstract had as his goal not to interpret but to change the world. This is not to say that he did not seek to ground practical problems of revolution in abstract principles, or that we may not extract such principles from his discussion of practical problems; but it is important to keep in mind that for Mao the criterion of validity even for abstractions was not their inner logic but whether or not they withstood the test of practice. Mao's was a philosophy of revolutionary practice. All Marxism may be viewed as a philosophy of *praxis* (or practice intended to change the world), as it was Karl Marx himself who stated that the goal of philosophy was not just to interpret but to change the world; but Mao was much more practice-orientated than Marx, and less constrained even than his immediate inspiration, Lenin, by the demands of abstract theory. Philosophy was of value to Mao only to the extent that it was 'any good for making revolution'.[4]

Second, the focus below on Mao's Marxism as he articulated it in the late 1930s does not imply that Mao had always been a Marxist, or that his thinking remained the same over the years. Mao's thought had a history. Mao was already a mature adult of 27 when he participated in the founding of the Communist Party in 1920–1, and he did not have any serious familiarity with the basic texts of Marxism until the 1930s, when those texts became available in Chinese. F. Wakeman has provided a catalogue of the diverse sources that went into the making of Mao's thinking ('confused', by Mao's own admission) in his pre-Marxist years.[5] This calls for a distinction between the pre- and post-Marxist phases of Mao's thinking. Moreover, while it is not clear if and how these pre-Marxist sources entered Mao's later reading of Marxism, it seems plausible that his pre-Marxist disposition to a populist approach to the relationship between the leaders and the led, to an anarchist suspicion of centralized power as well as anarchist conceptions of social organization, and even a basic emphasis on the unity of thought and action (theory and practice),[6] played a formative part in his thinking as well as his vision of revolutionary society, predisposed him to one reading of Marxism over other possible readings, and even introduced lasting (and dynamic) contradictions into his Marxism. In later years, too, Mao's thinking went through change, or at least elaborations, with regard to the practice of revolution in post-revolutionary society; especially controversial is the reasoning that was to culminate in the Cultural Revolution of the 1960s.

The analysis offered below is formal, rather than historical. While it is not intended to imply that Mao's thought remained changeless, it does suggest that the mature Mao's articulation of Marxism is representative of his philosophy in its most comprehensive statement, and reveals the characteristic tenor of his thinking as a practising Marxist revolutionary. The crystallization of the intellectual and experiential sources of his thinking, Mao's articulation of his Marxism in the late 1930s was also to provide the source for the changing (and conflicting) claims to be made on 'Maoism' in later years.

Finally, it is important while discussing Mao's philosophy to remember that this philosophy owed much to the contributions of others. The question of whether or not Mao's philosophy was a product of individual creativity or of the collective wisdom of the Party leadership, acquired over the course of revolutionary struggle, is a problematic one; but there is sufficient evidence to indicate that others participated in casting Mao's ideas in philosophical formulations, if not in their evolution in the first place. Those writings of Mao which offer the most systematic exposition of his philosophy are available only in their officially revised form. R. Wylie has suggested that in their origins also these writings owed much to contributions from young revolutionary scholars who served Mao as an unofficial 'think-tank'.[7]

The discussion below is divided into three parts: the relationship of Mao's Marxism to Marxism in general, especially an elucidation of his 'sinification' of Marxism in relationship to the circumstances of the Chinese Revolution, which it sought to illuminate and to guide; a formal discussion of the philosophical premisses of Mao's thought as they were articulated during the Yan'an Period (1937–45) of the Chinese Revolution, especially in the two essays 'On contradiction' and 'On practice', which are commonly recognized as the most important efforts on Mao's part to formulate systematically the abstract principles underlying his revolutionary practice; and an evaluation of these principles with reference to Marxist theory, with particular attention to the contradictions they were to bequeath to revolutionary thinking in China – and to the unfolding of Marxism.

'MAKING MARXISM CHINESE'

Of all the innovations that have been claimed for Mao's Marxism, none is as fundamental, or as far-reaching in its implications, as its 'sinification of Marxism' or, more appropriately, 'making Marxism Chinese' (*Makesi zhuyide Zhongguohua*). In its articulation of national to socialist goals, Mao's Marxism represented the epitome of a 'Chinese Marxism' (or, even more broadly, a 'Chinese socialism'), at once Chinese *and* Marxist. The same procedure lay at the root of Mao's restructuring of Marxism, by demanding a Chinese voice in a global Marxism, which would have far-reaching implications not just for the Chinese Revolution, but for Marxism globally.

Following Mao, Chinese students of Mao have conventionally described the 'sinification of Marxism' as 'the integration of the universal principles of Marxism with the concrete practice of the Chinese Revolution'.[8] This seemingly straightforward formulation conceals the complexity of, not to say the contradictions presented by, the procedures of integrating universal principles (or theory) with revolutionary practice under particular circumstances. Stuart Schram has described 'sinification' as 'a complex and ambiguous' idea,[9] which is evident in the conflicting interpretations to which 'sinification' has been subject. At the one extreme 'sinification' appears simply as the 'application' (*yunyong*) of Marxism to the revolution in China, with no further implications for theory, or even as the ultimate fulfilment of the fundamental practice orientation of Marxism. At the other extreme it represents the absorption of Marxism into a Chinese national or cultural space, irrevocably alienated from its origins in Europe. In between are a variety of interpretations which hold that while 'sinification' left Marxism untouched in its basics, it brought to Marxism a Chinese 'air' or 'style'.[10]

It is arguable that Mao's Marxism accommodated all these different sense of 'sinification' (without a sense, however, that a Chinese Marxism thus defined represented an alienation or deviation from Marxism). Sinification was the articulation of Marxism to a historical situation of which Chinese society was the terrain, but a terrain in the process of transformation by global forces. Mao's Marxism was successful politically because it was able to speak to the multi-faceted demands of an overdetermined historical situation. And it is of long-term historical significance not because of any profound theoretical contribution Mao made to Marxism, but because it articulated in its structure the problematic of this historical situation, which was to recast Marxism in a global perspective with consequences that were not just political but theoretical as well. As a Chinese *and* a Marxist, Mao sought at once to transform China through the general principles of Marxism, and to transform Marxism to meet the demands of China's specific historical circumstances; the sinification of Marxism presupposed both of these procedures. It is possible to read Mao's Marxism in different, even contradictory, ways because it was structured by these countervailing procedures. For the same reason, those interpretations of Mao that opt for one or another of the above readings, and ignore the contradictions that are built into the very structure of his Marxism (and the contradictions the latter presents to Marxism in general), are likely to fall into an arbitrary reductionism both in their readings of Mao and in their restriction of Marxism to some essence or other against which to evaluate the authenticity of Mao's Marxism.

Mao's Marxism, I should like to suggest here, forces us to rethink Marxism as a global/universal discourse. The tendency often is to think of Mao's Marxism in terms of an original Marxism; it is also possible, however, to rethink Marxism in terms of Mao's Marxism. I shall argue here that Mao's Marxism represents a local (or vernacular) version of a universal Marxism. Mao's Marxism was very much a product of the globalization of Marxism outside Europe (through the agency of the Russian

Revolution, and Lenin). While this globalization of Marxism may also be taken as the universalization of a Marxist discourse, it also represents a dispersion of the discourse. Mao (like Lenin) was not a passive recipient of this discourse, but was to rephrase it in a Chinese vernacular. His Marxism, while very much a product of the globalization of Marxist discourse, introduced disruptive contradictions into the discourse in this very process. Mao's Marxism is most significant in the development of Marxism as the first fully articulated Third-World instance. In its insistence on the vernacular, it also represents the first significant challenge to a Marxist hegemony. Perhaps most significantly, it points to a new kind of non-hegemonic universality, in which a genuinely universal Marxist discourse is to be constituted out of various vernacular Marxisms.

Such a perspective becomes evident if we view Mao's Marxism in terms of the historical situation from which it springs. The contradictions in Mao's Marxism are found upon close examination to be implicit in the historical situation in which Chinese society was placed in the twentieth century. It was this situation that rendered Marxism attractive to Chinese revolutionaries. In their efforts to find Marxist resolutions to China's problems, revolutionaries were to restructure Marxism to accommodate the questions thrown up by this multidimensional historical situation. The identity of Mao's Marxism (and of Chinese Marxism), as well as its discursive structure, rests not upon some abstract notion of China conceived in isolation from its historical context, but upon this historical situation which appears with the location within Chinese social structure and consciousness of unprecedented historical forces that displaced Chinese society from its earlier historical context, and relocated it irretrievably within a new global economic, political and ideological process.

There are three strategic dimensions of China's historical situation in the twentieth century that have been crucial in structuring Chinese Marxism. The first is the global dimension. Beginning in the nineteenth century, China was drawn inexorably into a global history of which the dominant motive force was capitalism. Whether or not China was completely incorporated into a capitalist world-system or became capitalist in the process are moot questions; indeed, a basic goal of most socialists in China was to counteract such incorporation.

The second is the 'Third-World' dimension. The Chinese, unlike western European or North American societies but like most Asian and African (and to some extent South American) societies, experienced the globalization of history and its motive force, capitalism, not as an internal development but as alien hegemony. While Chinese history was conjoined to global history, in other words, the Chinese experienced the process as one of subjugation, as a Third-World society. Under the circumstances, socialism was not merely an alternative to capitalism, but an alternative that promised national liberation from capitalist hegemony, and the possibility of entering global history not as its object but as an independent subject.

The third dimension is the national dimension: Chinese society itself, which, in spite of its Third-World status in a capitalist world, remained the locus of its own history. The conjoining of China to a global history did not mean the dissolution of Chinese society into a global pool, any more than its identification as a Third-World society implies its reduction to some homogeneous Third-World configuration. The national dimension, while seemingly transparent, is in actuality quite opaque. In a historical situation where the very conception of China is overdetermined by the incorporation of Chinese society into a global structure, it is difficult to distinguish what is pristinely Chinese (which, as an idea, was itself a product of the historical situation, since the Chinese did not think of China as a nation among others before this situation came into existence) from what is insistently Chinese in response to global pressures for transformation. The historical situation, in other words, is characterized by mutual incorporation (and contradiction): the incorporation of China into a global structure, and the incorporation into Chinese society of new global forces. It is in the structure of this mutual incorporation that we may discover the multiple dimensions of the historical situation. Our conception of China (as well as the Chinese conception of self), correspondingly, is of necessity overdetermined, a product of the moments in the conjuncture of historical forces that relocated China in a new world situation. Marxism, in its anti-capitalism, also promised the possibility of national self-discovery for a society that a capitalist world threatened to consume. In order for the promise to be fulfilled, however, Marxism itself had to be rephrased in a national voice, for a Marxism that could not account for a specifically national experience abdicated its claims to universality; worse, under the guise of universalism, it replicated in a different form the hegemonism of capitalism, of which it was historically a product.

These three dimensions were also the structuring moments of Chinese Marxism, which would find its most comprehensive articulation in Mao's 'sinification of Marxism'. Mao's Marxism is most properly conceived as a reflection upon this historical situation (which must be distinguished from reflection *of* the situation) if we are to grasp it in its structural complexity. As a discourse, Mao's Marxism bears upon its discursive structure the imprint of the multidimensional historical situation from which it derived its problematic. It is at once a reflection upon Chinese society from a universalist Marxist perspective and a reflection upon Marxism from the perspective of China as a Third-World society and a nation. The two procedures, while coextensive, are also contradictory. Nevertheless, they have with all their contradictions structured the discourse that we may call Chinese Marxism.

That this historical situation served as the point of departure in the formulation of a Chinese Marxism is in evidence everywhere in the texts (authored by Mao or his close associates) associated with the 'sinification of Marxism', of which the culmination was Mao's January 1940 essay 'On New Democracy', which stands as the classic formulation of the premisses of Chinese Marxism.[11] 'New Democracy' referred to an economic and political formation (a mixed economy to facilitate economic development, and an alliance across classes – under Communist leadership – in the pursuit of national liberation) suitable to China's immediate needs; but more significantly it also represented the insertion of a new stage in historical progress appropriate to all societies placed similarly to China in the world. Its premisses were: (a) that the Chinese Revolution is part of a global revolution against capitalism; (b) that it is, however, a revolution against capitalism in a 'semi-feudal semi-colonial' society to which national liberation is a crucial task; and (c) that it is also a national revolution, a revolution to create a new nation – and a new culture which would be radically different from both the culture inherited from the past and the culture imported from abroad. The latter, significantly, included Marxism:

> in applying Marxism to China, Chinese communists must fully and properly integrate the universal truth of Marxism with the concrete practice of the Chinese revolution or, in other words, the universal truth of Marxism must be combined with specific national characteristics and acquire a definite national form.[12]

In the end, the 'sinification of Marxism' did not achieve an 'integration of the universal truth of Marxism with the concrete practice of the Chinese revolution', if by that we understand a seamless synthesis which dissolved Marxism into China's circumstances, or integrated China's peculiarities into the existing conceptual framework of Marxist theory. Mao's Marxism did not consist of merely applying Marxism to China's circumstances (which suggests too passive a role for what is Chinese in it, that is, contrary to his insistence on the project of sinification in the first place), or of just developing it (which, while arguable, is misleading to the extent that it suggests the absence of any disjuncture between Mao's Marxism and Marxism in general). The very tortured way in which Mao presented the project of 'sinification' may offer the most persuasive clue that the 'sinification of Marxism' entailed an effort to 'integrate' what might not be integrable in the above sense of the term. It is worth quoting at some length the passage in which Mao used the term 'sinification' for the first time (and is also one of his fullest descriptions of what he means by it) to convey a sense of the reasoning that, rather than argue out the logic of the project it proposes, seeks instead to suppress the contradictoriness of the project by the force of its metaphors:

> Another task of study is to study our historical legacy, and to evaluate it critically using Marxist methods. A great nation such as ours with several thousand years of history has its own developmental laws, its own national characteristics, its own precious things. . . . The China of today is a development out of historical China. We are Marxist historicists; we may not chop up history. We must evaluate it from Confucius to Sun Zhongshan, assume this precious legacy, and derive from it a method to guide the present movement. . . . Communists are Marxist internationalists, but Marxism must be realized through national forms. There is no such thing as abstract Marxism, there is only concrete Marxism. The so-called concrete Marxism is Marxism that has taken national form; we need to apply Marxism to concrete struggle in the concrete environment of China, we should not employ it in the abstract. Communists who are part of the great Chinese nation, and are to this nation as flesh and blood, are only abstract and empty Marxists if they talk about Marxism apart from China's special characteristics. Hence the sinification of Marxism, imbuing every manifestation of Marxism with China's special characteristics, that is to say applying it in

> accordance with Chinese characteristics, is something every Party member must seek to understand and resolve. We must discard foreign eight-legged essays, we must stop singing abstract and empty tunes, we must give rest to dogmatism, and substitute in their place Chinese airs that the common people love to see and hear. To separate internationalist content and national form only reveals a total lack of understanding of internationalism.[13]

Rather than resolve the contradiction between 'internationalist content and national form', the sinification of Marxism was to produce an ideological construct of which Marxism was a determining moment, but which in turn rephrased Marxism in its own particular grammar. Marxism helped define Mao's vision of a new China; but the vision is not therefore reducible to Marxism, for it retained its fundamental sources outside Marxism. Likewise, a deep awareness of China's national needs conditioned Mao's understanding of Marxism, but did not therefore dissolve Marxism into Chinese nationalism. This *irreducibility* of the moments that went into the making of Mao's Marxism invites its conceptualization in structural terms: structure in Louis Althusser's sense, that is, visible in the interaction of the moments constituting it; which, although mutually transformative, are not reducible into one another or dissolvable into the structure, and in their irreducibility retain their contradictory relationship within a context of structural unity.[14] It is just such a structure that the sinification of Marxism produced; and it is this structure that is Mao's Marxism (or Chinese Marxism, as understood here). It is Marxist because Marxism was present in it as a determinant moment; it also broke with the Marxism that informed it because it rendered Marxism into one moment of a structure that had multiple sources in its construction.

The consequences of this new structural context for Marxist theory will be discussed below. Suffice it to say here that Mao's Marxism appears differently depending on the perspective provided by the different moments that constituted it. In their conjuncture these alternative perspectives yield a comprehensive appreciation of its structural complexity.

In its relationship to Marxism world-wide, Mao's Marxism is universal/global, for there is little in its formal-theoretical articulation that is not derivative of European Marxism. The new structural context would have the consequence of opening up ('deconstructing') Marxist theoretical formulations, but neither its political premisses nor its theoretical concepts suffice to distinguish Mao's Marxism from Marxism elsewhere. Basic to it was the equation of Marxism with a 'social revolution' to which the transformation of class relations was central. As a political discourse, it is also global in compass because, both in its origins and in its unfolding, it has been part of a global discourse on Marxism; in other words, it was global currents in Marxism that nourished it, and Mao's Marxism at all times spoke to issues raised by Marxism globally.[15] It is difficult to identify elements in Mao's theoretical formulations that render his Marxism any the less Marxist than any other. In its global guise, his Marxism appears as a transformative idea, as a reflection in Marxist language upon

Chinese society that sought to reshape the terrain upon which it reflected in accordance with universal Marxist aspirations. Mao was even capable of referring to China as a 'blank sheet of paper' upon which Marxism could write its agenda!

Within this global discourse, however, Mao's Marxism appears in the guise of a Third-World Marxism that reflects upon socialism from a Third-World perspective. For reasons that should be apparent from China's relationship to capitalism as a Third-World society, socialism in China appears throughout its history as part of a national project; in other words, the socialist struggle for a social revolution against capitalism as well as against the legacy of the past has been obsessively involved with the struggle for national liberation and development: as capitalism appeared in China in the guise of imperialism, the struggle against capitalism likewise has been indistinguishable from the struggle for liberation from imperialist hegemony. This qualification compels us to modify the universality of Mao's Marxism; not only because the commitment to national liberation rendered problematic the theoretical assumption of social change through class struggle (divisive of necessity), but also because socialism as he conceived it had to assume burdens which were of slight concern to socialism in its origins in capitalist Europe: state-building to render China into a viable nation (which ultimately had to face the problem of creating a 'civil society' as well), economic development to withstand imperialist hegemony as well as to create a basis for socialism, and not least cultural reconstruction. These burdens, commonly shared by the socialism of Third-World societies, have had far-reaching consequences for socialism in these societies and, by implication, the unfolding of socialism globally. Mao, quite aware of this commonality, explicitly conceived of Marxism in relationship to the problems of such societies.

Mao's Marxism, finally, is a Chinese reflection upon global socialism, spoken in a vernacular voice by a Chinese subject who expressed through Marxism local, specifically Chinese, concerns. From a Chinese perspective, socialism too appears as an alien idea and, in its claims to universality, a hegemonic one; hence the urge to rephrase it in a Chinese vernacular, to assimilate it to a quotidian Chinese consciousness or 'structure of sentiment',[16] in order to guarantee a Chinese voice in a universal socialist language. What is involved here is more than a Third-World assimilation of socialism to a national project. The vernacularization of socialism by Mao does not consist merely of making the national good, or national considerations of wealth and power, into the measure of the relevance of socialism, or the validity of its claims; rather, it represents an authentic nationalization of socialism, bringing into it the voices of its local social and cultural environment. If the one is political and economic in its appreciation of socialism, the other is insistently social and cultural. It seeks to domesticate socialism by endowing its language with the phraseology and nuances of a specifically Chinese historical experience. Vernacular socialism represents the absorption of socialism into a Chinese terrain, the re-presentation of its universal aspirations in the language of native ideals. In Mao's Marxism, this is evident not only in his formal calls for making Marxism Chinese, but more eloquently in the very language in which he presented Marxism to his Chinese audiences, in which Chinese history past and present served as the medium for communicating Marxist abstractions.[17]

These three perspectives, in their conjuncture, are essential to appreciating Mao's Marxism in its structural complexity, and contradictions. The problems which Mao's Marxism present are largely a consequence of the fact that it is at once locally Chinese and universally Marxist, the one as compellingly significant as the other. The grounding of Mao's Marxism in its historical situation may not resolve the questions it raises, but it allows us to reformulate its *problematic* as a discourse without reductionism, in such a way as to accommodate the contradictions that it presents. As a reflection on China's historical situation, Mao's Marxism is best read as what Jurgen Habermas has described as a 'practical discourse'.[18] A practical discourse is to be distinguished, on the one hand, from a theoretical discourse that is divorced from practice (and, therefore, its concrete premisses) and, on the other hand, from practice (understood as practical activity to change the world) that takes its theoretical premisses for granted. This distinction is significantly different from the formal distinction Chinese Marxists (beginning with Mao) have drawn over the years between theory and practice. The latter objectifies Chinese society as a 'target' for the 'arrow' of theory, or a 'blank sheet' upon which Marxism may write its agenda (both, by the way, Mao's metaphors), which privileges theory as a universal over its application in practice, even if in actuality the reverse may have been the case more often than not. The notion of practical discourse recognizes Mao (and Chinese practitioners of socialism) as the subjects who reflect on Marxism; their relationship to a global Marxism appears, therefore, not as a subject–object relationship but as an intersubjective one. It allows, in other words, a genuine Chinese national participation in a global socialist discourse. It is the irreducibility of the national and the global in this practical discourse, and the centrality to resolving its contradictions of the reflecting subject, that lay at the core of Mao's philosophical restatement of Marxism.

CONTRADICTION AND PRACTICE

Mao articulated the philosophical premisses of his Marxism in the process – and as an integral part – of the sinification of Marxism. His two essays 'On practice' and 'On contradiction' were delivered as speeches in July and August 1937 respectively, coinciding with his call for a shift in Communist revolutionary strategy in response to Japan's full-scale invasion of China in July 1937. As its most fundamental level of vernacularization, the sinification of Marxism was a product of revolutionary problems (especially the problem of a Marxist revolution in agrarian China, which theory was ill-prepared to contain); some of the key ingredients that were to go into the making of a 'sinified' Marxism had been enunciated earlier in response to these problems, which were quite independent of the national problem.[19] The national problem as a problem in Marxism was also a subject for intensive discussion in Chinese intellectual circles as early as 1936.[20] Nevertheless, the project of sinification was clearly formulated and realized only between 1937 and 1940: there was a direct line connecting the theoretical formulations of Mao's philosophy in these two essays and the reasoning underlying the sinified Marxist strategy that Mao was to enunciate in his 'On New Democracy' in 1940. Eminently practical and tactical in intention, the two essays nevertheless sought to ground the problems of the Chinese Revolution within Marxist theory, in the process offering Mao's fullest and most comprehensive statement on the philosophical considerations underlying his reformulation of Marxist theory. What Mao wrote in later years of a philosophical nature represented primarily an application and extension of ideas first enunciated in these essays.

There is a further, possibly more intrinsic, connection between the practical project of sinification and Mao's theoretical formulations in these essays. Central to Mao's Marxism as presented in the essays is the concept of contradiction. Norman Levine has suggested that while the concept of contradiction originated in Hegel, and was used extensively by Lenin, it acquired an unprecedented significance and elaboration in Mao's Marxism.[21] I suggested above that sinification produced an explicitly structural reading of Marxism by its very effort to reconcile contradictory demands, which in turn rested upon the irreducibility of the moments that went into its constitution. The centrality of the concept of 'contradiction' in Mao's Marxism, I should like to suggest, was a direct product of his reformulation of Marxism to account for China's historical situation, which was defined structurally by the contradictoriness of its various moments, and the articulation of this contradictoriness as a contradiction between theory and practice. We must underline here that while the contradiction between national and social revolutionary needs is the most obvious, the problem went deeper into the very practice of revolution in a social situation that was not anticipated in theory: an agrarian society in which a socialist revolution had to be engineered out of components that theory did not account for; in which the revolutionaries themselves were outsiders to the social situation (and, therefore, in contradiction to it), and had to manoeuvre with great care in order not to antagonize the population and jeopardize their own existence; and, therefore, could not translate the multi-faceted conflicts they encountered readily into *their* theoretical categories, but rather had to recognize them as *irreducible* features of the social situation into which to articulate theory. This is what raised the question of the language of revolution at the most fundamental level. And ultimately, beyond the level of the national struggle, it was this social situation that made the 'sinification' of Marxism into a total theoretical project, and called for the reformulation of theory in terms of the multitude of contradictions that revolution faced at the level of practice. This is evident, I think, in the intrinsic relationship Mao establishes in the two essays between a social analysis based on contradictions and the activist epistemology that he sets forth in his analysis of practice.

'The law of contradiction in things, that is the law of the unity of opposites, is the basic law of materialist dialectics.'[22] Thus began Mao's discussion of 'Contradiction'. He continued:

> As opposed to the metaphysical world outlook of materialist-dialectics holds that in order to understand the development of a thing we should study it internally and its relations with other things; in other words, the development of things should be seen as their internal and necessary self-movement, while each thing in its movement is interrelated with and interacts on the things around it.
>
> (p. 313)

'On contradiction' depicts a world (and a mode of grasping it) in which not 'things' but relationships are the central data. Such relationships are relationships of mutual opposition as well as transformation (difference as well as identity). These relationships do not coexist haphazardly, moreover, but constitute a totality structured by their many interactions, a totality that is nevertheless in a constant state of transformation because the relationships between the whole and the parts that constitute it, no less than the relationships between the parts, are not merely functional but also (and more importantly) oppositional. The idea of 'contradiction', as a dialectical idea, encompasses both functionality and opposition ('unity of opposites'); 'contradiction' as a constitutive principle of the world (and the cosmos) produces a totality where everything (the parts no less than the whole) contains everything else, and yet nothing is therefore reducible to anything else. As Mao puts it later on in the essay:

> Since the particular is united with the universal and since the universality as well as the particularity of contradiction is inherent in everything, universality residing in particularity, we should, when studying an object, try to discover both the particular and the universal and their interconnection, to discover both particularity and universality and also their interconnections of this object with the many objects outside it.
>
> (p. 329)

As a philosophical essay, 'On contradiction' is devoted to an elaboration of the characteristics of 'contradictions' in which these general ideas are embedded. These characteristics may be summarized (using Mao's own wording) as follows:

1 Contradiction is universal:

> The universality or absoluteness of contradiction has a twofold meaning. One is that contradiction exists in the process of development of all things, and the other is that in the process of development of each thing a movement of opposites exists from beginning to end. . . . There is nothing that does not contain contradiction; without contradiction nothing would exist.
>
> (p. 316)

2 Contradiction is also particular:

> Every form of motion contains within itself its own particular contradiction. This particular contradiction constitutes the particular essence which distinguishes one thing from another (p. 320) . . . there is always a gradual growth from the knowledge of individual and particular

things to the knowledge of things in general. Only after man knows the particular essence of many different things can he proceed to generalization and know the common essence of things. When man attains the knowledge of this common essence, he uses it as a guide and proceeds to study various concrete things which have not yet been studied, or studied thoroughly, and to discover the particular essence of each; only thus is he able to supplement, enrich and develop his knowledge of their common essence. . . . These are the two processes of cognition: one, from the particular to the general, and the other, from the general to the particular (pp. 320–1) . . . Qualitatively different contradictions can only be resolved by qualitatively different methods (p. 321) . . . contradictions [in Chinese society] cannot be treated in the same way since each has its own particularity; moreover, the two aspects of each contradiction cannot be treated in the same way since each has its own characteristics. We who are engaged in the Chinese revolution should not only understand the particularity of these contradictions in their totality, that is, in their interconnectedness, but should also study the two aspects of each contradiction as the only means of understanding the totality.

(pp. 322–3)

3 Principal contradiction and the principal aspect of a contradiction:

There are many contradictions in the process of development of a complex thing, and one of them is necessarily the principal contradiction whose existence and development determine or influence the existence and development of the other contradictions (p. 331) . . . In any contradiction the development of the contradictory aspects is uneven (p. 333) . . . The nature of a thing is determined mainly by the principal aspect of a contradiction, the aspect which has gained the dominant position. But this situation is not static; the principal and the non-principal aspects of a contradiction transform themselves into each other and the nature of things changes accordingly (p. 333). . . . At certain times in the revolutionary struggle, the difficulties outweigh the favourable conditions and so constitute the principal aspect of the contradiction and the favourable conditions constitute the secondary aspect. But through their efforts the revolutionaries can overcome the difficulties step by step and open up a new favourable situation.

(p. 355)

4 Identity and struggle of the aspects of a contradiction:

Identity, unity, coincidence, interpenetration, interpermeation, interdependence (or mutual dependence for existence), interconnection or mutual cooperation – all these different terms mean the same thing and refer to the following two points: first, the existence of each of the two aspects of a contradiction in the process of development of a thing presupposes the existence of the other aspect, and both aspects coexist in a single entity; second, in given conditions, each of the contradictory aspects transforms itself into its opposite (p. 337) . . . How then can one speak of identity or unity? The fact is that no contradictory aspect can exist in isolation. Without its opposite aspect, each loses the condition for its existence (p. 338) . . . the unity of opposites is conditional, temporary and relative, while the struggle of mutually exclusive opposites is absolute.

(p. 342)

5 Antagonism in contradiction:

Antagonism is one form, but not the only form, of a struggle of opposites. In human history, antagonism between classes exists as a particular manifestation of the struggle of opposites

> (p. 343) . . . Contradiction and struggle are universal and absolute, but the methods of resolving contradictions, that is, the forms of struggle, differ according to the differences in the nature of contradictions. Some contradictions are characterized by open antagonism, others are not.
>
> (p. 344)

'On contradiction' is a revolutionary hermeneutics; an interpretative strategy, in other words, the premiss of which is 'making revolution'. While it is revealing of a life outlook that may include native philosophical elements in addition to Marxism (of this more below), all these elements are subsumed under, and refracted through, this basic problem.

At one level, it is possible to read the essay simply as a statement in the abstract of specific problems of revolution in the immediate circumstances of Chinese society in 1937. The statements above are interspersed with observations on contemporary developments in China's historical situation that are used in illustration of Mao's various abstractions. It is difficult to say which came first, the abstractions or the illustrations, but there is little question that the historical situation depicted in the illustrations had priority in Mao's thinking.[23] A fundamental goal of Mao in the essay is to provide a theoretical justification for the change in the Party's revolutionary policy in response to the Japanese invasion of China (which shifted the 'primary' contradiction from class struggle to national struggle). This also explains why the major part of the essay is devoted to discussion of the 'particularity' of contradiction (which includes discussion of primary/secondary contradictions, as well as the discussion of its primary/secondary aspects). It is in the process of this legitimation of change in policy that Mao articulates the priority of practice to theory. As he put it:

> The dogmatists . . . do not understand that conditions differ in different kinds of revolution and so do not understand that different methods should be used to resolve different contradictions; on the contrary, they invariably adopt what they imagine to be an unalterable formula and arbitrarily apply it everywhere, which only causes setbacks to the revolution or makes a sorry mess of what was originally well done.
>
> (p. 322)

In spite of the priority of practical questions in Mao's thinking, however, it would be reductionist to read the essay simply as a discussion of practical questions, and ignore the consequences for theory of Mao's theoretical justification of practice. Louis Althusser grasped the significance of this problem when he wrote of 'On contradiction':

> Mao's essay, inspired by his struggle against dogmatism in the Chinese Party, remains generally *descriptive*, and in consequence it is in certain respects *abstract*. Descriptive: his concepts correspond to concrete experiences. In part abstract: the concepts, though new and rich in promise, are represented as *specifications* of the *dialectic* in general rather than as *necessary implications* of the Marxist conception of society and history.[24]
>
> (italics in the original)

What Althusser tells us is that while Mao's theoretical formulations remain incompletely theorized, they are nevertheless pathbreaking and significant (and are not therefore reducible to descriptive abstractions). The former is evident. While Mao sought in the essay to theorize the particularity of revolutionary practice, he consciously demoted theory: 'in the contradiction between theory and practice, practice is the principal aspect' (p. 335). This demotion of theory was also to lead to a restatement of the role of theory: Mao conceived of theory primarily as an abstraction of concrete revolutionary practice, and only secondarily as an abstract formulation of 'laws' of social movement. Mao did not repudiate theory, or the necessity of understanding it. On one occasion, responding to an imaginary audience which held that those who were 'instinctively' dialectical in their activity did not need to read books to understand theory, he reaffirmed the importance of studying theory because, without such study, there was no possibility of synthesizing the multi-faceted phenomena that the revolutionary faced.[25] 'Without revolutionary theory', he believed with Lenin, 'there can be no revolutionary movement.'[26] Indeed, given his revolutionary hermeneutics, theory was to reappear in Mao's thinking as an essential guide to the revolutionary in determining the direction of revolution.

It was another matter, however, with the practice of revolution. The priority that Mao assigned to practice meant that, unlike Althusser, he was only marginally interested in theorizing his abstract formulations; it is even possible to suggest that 'On contradiction' was only 'in part abstract' because Mao's historicism (by which I mean his emphasis on concreteness and particularity) did not allow theorization beyond a certain point. What it did produce was a hermeneutics: revolutionary practice was no longer predictable from theory; rather, the latter became a guide to 'reading' historical situations in the activity of making revolution. Mao's appreciation of theory was itself 'contradictory' in the double meaning he assigned to it as at once guide and instrument: 'guide' in the long-term direction of revolution, 'instrument' in immediate analysis. Theory, in other words, was part of the very contradictions that it was intended to unravel and to resolve. This was the key to Mao's restructuring of theory.

The world of 'On contradiction' is a world of ceaseless and endless confrontation and conflict, where unity itself may be understood only in terms of the contradictoriness of its moments, where no entity is a constant because it has no existence outside its contradictions or a place of its own other than in its relationship to other contradictions. It may be that all Marxism is a conflict-based conceptualization of the world. But how ever differently Marxists may have structured conflict or organized the structure of society, conflict in most interpretations of Marxism is conceived of in terms of a limited number of social categories (production, relations of production, politics, ideology, etc.), and there has been an urge to hierarchize these categories in terms of their effectivity in the social structure. Mao's multitude of contradictions resist such hierarchization and, more significantly, reduction to a limited number of categories. Some contradictions are obviously more significant than others in determining social structure or historical direction, but Mao refuses to deny a role in social dynamics to what seem to be the most trivial contradictions (and, therefore, to dissolve them into broader categories) or to hierarchize them except on a temporary basis, for in their interactions they are in a constant state of flux as regards their place in the structure. What he says of the primary categories of Marxist theory is revealing:

> For instance, in the contradiction between the productive forces and the relations of production, the productive forces are the principal aspect; in the contradiction between theory and practice, practice is the principal aspect; in the contradiction between the economic base and the superstructure, the economic base is the principal aspect; and there is no change in their respective positions. This is the mechanical materialist concept, not the dialectical materialist conception. True, the productive forces, practice and the economic base generally play the principal and decisive role; whoever denies this is not a materialist. But it must also be admitted that in certain conditions, such aspects as the relations of production, theory and the superstructure in turn manifest themselves in the principal and decisive role. (pp. 335–6)

This, I think, yields a conception of causation that may best be described in terms of Althusser's notion of 'structural effectivity' (or causation); that is, a notion of causation without hierarchy, where the structure is visible only in the interaction of its constitutive moments, which are mutually determinant through the intermediation of the structure as 'absent cause'. (It is no coincidence that Althusser finds in Mao's idea of contradiction a point of departure for his own reflection on causation.[27]) Causation here is conjunctural and overdetermined: social and historical events are products of the conjuncture of multiple contradictions. Mao's difference from Althusser may be that he conceived of conjunctures in more contingent (and historical) terms than Althusser was willing to do. His notion of causation, therefore, remains less theorized than Althusser's. More importantly, essential to Mao's idea of contradiction was the role of the revolutionary subject. In the first place, an 'overdetermined conjuncture' points to a revolutionary alternative as one possibility among others, because such a situation is of its very nature open-ended; in other words, open to interpretation. It is up to the revolutionary to interpret it in accordance with revolutionary goals. This is also where the importance of abstract theory as guide to action comes in; because without the aid of theory, the revolutionary will be at a loss to make choices consistent with long-term goals. Second, while itself a product of contradictions, revolutionary practice is part of the structure of contradictions, and effective in aligning the contradictions in a manner most consistent with revolutionary goals. The role of revolutionary struggle in converting an unfavourable to a favourable situation was part of Mao's analysis of contradiction (see above); it appears most prominently in other places in the context of his discussions of the military strategy of revolutionary struggle.[28]

Mao's companion essay, 'On practice' offers in epistemological form a more direct statement on interpretation as an essential component of revolutionary activity (or, if I may overstate the point, on revolutionary activity *as* interpretative activity). On the surface, the epistemology which 'On practice' offers is an empiricist one. As he presents it, cognition begins with perceptual cognition, which is 'the stage' of sense perceptions and impressions'.[29] As sense perceptions are repeated and accumulate, 'a sudden change (leap) takes place in the brain in the process of cognition, and concepts are formed. Concepts are no longer phenomena, the separate aspects and the external relations of things; they grasp the essence, the totality and the internal relations of things' (p. 298). (Mao also describes this as 'the stage of rational knowledge'.) The knowledge thus acquired is then tested for its validity in actual practice, which leads to further perceptions, conceptual modifications, back to practice in an ongoing cycle of perception–conception–practice–perception.

If Mao's epistemology is empiricist, however, it is the empiricism of an activist who constructs knowledge in the process of reconstructing the world with revolutionary goals. While there is one illustration in the essay which suggests that cognition may be a passive process of the accumulation of perceptions, the essay in its totality points to an activist epistemology. Mao believes that cognition has a class character, and he clearly elevates dialectical materialism over other possible methods in understanding the world (p. 305). Mao begins his discussion of cognition at the stage of perception, but this does not imply that the mind is a blank sheet of paper upon which perceptions rewrite themselves into conceptions, because the mind already has a conceptual apparatus for organizing perceptions (implicit in the class character of knowledge), and a theoretical apparatus (dialectical materialism) for articulating them. His epistemology, furthermore, elevates certain activities over others in the acquisition of knowledge (the struggle for production and class struggle) (pp. 296, 300), and knowledge has a clear goal: 'making revolution'. Most important is the place of practice (which Mao consistently uses in the sense of *praxis*, activity to change the world in cognition). While in his discussion of cognition Mao represents 'practice' as one stage of the process, 'practice' clearly plays a much more important part in his thinking. It is practice, rather than perception, that stands at the beginning of the process of cognition (since different practices lead to different understanding of the world, and Mao elevates those perceptions that arise from the struggle for production and class above all others). Practice also intermediates the transformation of perceptions into conceptions: 'The perceptual and the rational are qualitatively different, but are not divorced from each other; they are unified on the basis of practice' (p. 299). The goal of 'On practice' is not to argue for a vulgar empiricism ('seeking truth from facts'), but to assert the priority of practice in cognition against a theoretical dogmatism oblivious to concrete circumstances of revolution. Quoting Stalin, Mao observes: 'Theory becomes purposeless if it is not connected with revolutionary practice; just as practice gropes in the dark if its path is not illumined by revolutionary theory' (p. 305).

'On practice' may be viewed as a call for the revolutionary hermeneutic which Mao would elaborate a month later in 'On contradiction'. Composed as parts of a single project, the two discussions illuminate each other in their intertextuality. Mao's understanding of knowledge as interpretation, as well as his unwillingness to view it *just* as interpretation, is expressed in the following statement:

> Fully to reflect a thing in its totality, to reflect its essence, to reflect its inherent laws, it is necessary through the exercise of thought to reconstruct the rich data of sense perception, discarding the dross and selecting the essential, eliminating the false and retaining the true, proceeding from the one to the other and from the outside to the inside, in order to form a system of concepts and theories – it is necessary to make a leap from perceptual to rational knowledge. Such reconstructed knowledge is not more empty or more unreliable [than empiricism]; on the contrary, whatever has been scientifically reconstructed in the process of cognition, on the basis of practice, reflects objective reality.
>
> (p. 303)

There is a profound contradiction in Mao's thinking. As a Marxist materialist, Mao believes that there is an 'objective reality' against which to judge the validity of competing forms of knowledge; hence his repeated references to cognition as a 'reflection' of the world in the mind. At the same time, as the essay 'On contradiction' leaves little doubt, Mao views objective reality (or the context of thought) itself to be a product of contradictions; which renders it into an object of interpretation and 'reconstruction'. His foray into the discussion of 'truth' is revealing of this contradiction in its simultaneous assertion of the 'relativity' of truth, even of revolutionary truth, and his conviction of the possibility of an 'absolute truth':

> Marxists recognize that in the absolute and general process of development in the universe, the development of each particular process is relative, and that hence, in the endless flow of absolute truth, man's knowledge of a particular process at any given stage of development is only relative truth. The sum total of innumerable relative truths constitutes absolute truth. . . . Marxism-Leninism has in no way exhausted truth but ceaselessly opens up roads to the knowledge of truth in the course of practice.
>
> (pp. 307–8)

The contradiction between absolute and relative truth presents Mao with an unresolvable contradiction, which he seeks to overcome by resorting to practice as 'the criterion of truth' (p. 305). Practice as activity to change the world is bound up in Mao's thinking with the notion of contradiction: that is, changing the world is a process of resolving contradictions, which leads to new contradictions, which leads to new practices and so on in an endless process. This itself is problematic, however, because, as the discussion of 'contradiction' tells us, practice in and of itself does not provide a direction to history unless guided by some notion of 'truth' (Mao is quite disingenuous in his representation of 'absolute truth' as the 'sum total of relative truths', since he obviously does not recognize the truthfulness of all relative truths), or any judgement of validity other than 'what works, works'. The assumption of an 'absolute truth', in other words, serves as an ideological closure upon a fluid reality that is hardly an 'objective reality', but is itself the product of human activity, which constructs its understanding of the world in the process of reconstructing the world:

> The struggle of the proletariat and the revolutionary people to change the world comprises the fulfillment of the following tasks: to change the objective world and, at the same time, their own subjective world to change their cognitive ability and change the relations between the subjective and the objective world.
>
> (p. 308)

This very representation of the world as ongoing revolutionary interpretation and construction, on the other hand, is disruptive of the ideological closure, and exposes the latter as a contradiction between theory and practice, absolute and relative truth, which, in its open-endedness, may be resolved only through the intervention of an omniscient will. For all its effectiveness in practice as a revolutionary hermeneutic, or perhaps because of it, Mao's Marxism could in the end restore a direction to history only through revolutionary will.

GUERRILLA SOCIALISM/VERNACULAR MARXISM

Mao did not come to Marxism as a 'blank sheet of paper', and there are tantalizing traces in his philosophy of various traditions in Chinese thought. There is, for instance, a parallel between his emphasis on 'practice' and the practical orientation of Confucian philosophy; Frederick Wakeman, Jr has pointed to parallels between Mao's thought and the emphasis on the 'unity of thought and action' in the Wang Yangming school of Confucianism in which Mao was interested as a young radical.[30] Thomas Metzger suggests, even more directly, that 'The Sinification of Marxism . . . came to express and implement the traditional ethos of interdependence.'[31] Benjamin Schwartz has observed a continuity with Confucian tradition in Mao's preoccupation with morality in politics.[32] At a more obscure level, it may be possible to perceive in Mao's assertion of the ceaselessness of change traces of more esoteric currents in Chinese thought going back to the *Yi Jing* (*Book of Changes*) and *yin–yang* naturalism which held that change was the only constant in the universe.[33] Even Mao's dialectic, with its insistence on everything containing everything else, is at times reminiscent more of certain currents in a Buddhist dialectic than the dialectic of Hegel and Marx. These ideas or their traces were part of the political and cultural discourse in Mao's environment, and the possibility of their presence in Mao's discourse on Marxism is not to be denied. It is important nevertheless that such presence, if possible, is informal (that is, Mao made no formal effort to integrate his Marxism with any of these traditions); and any parallels drawn between his Marxism and native traditions is of necessity speculative.

More importantly, if Mao's thinking indeed contained traces of these intellectual traditions, these were mediated by and refracted through the problematic of revolutionary practice.

There is little ambiguity in the direct relationship between Mao's Marxism and the immediate experience of the Chinese Revolution. The above analysis has stressed

Mao's vernacularization of Marxism, which may be viewed at two levels. First the national level; that is, his effort to render Marxism relevant to China as a nation, with a problematic identity in a new historical situation. While this already implies a localization of Marxism, what made Mao's Marxism authentically radical (and not just an excuse for nationalism) was his insistence on integrating Marxism into the language of the masses, which he believed should reconstitute China as a nation; in other words, localizing it *within* the nation at the level of everyday life. (This is the major difference between Mao's Marxism and the post-Mao 'socialism with Chinese characteristics'.) Mao's vernacularization of Marxism was bound up at its most profound (and comprehensive) level with the experience of revolution in China as guerrilla warfare; it is not surprising that the first calls for translating Marxism into the language of the masses coincided with the appearance of a guerrilla strategy of revolution (and not by Mao, but others in the Party).

As the hermeneutic of a guerrilla strategy of revolution, Mao's philosophical abstractions bore the imprint of this historical situation both in its basic concepts and in his mode of presentation. The oppositions in the historical situation, whether at the national level (between China and a hegemonic European culture, including a universalized European Marxism) or at the social level (where the oppositions were much more multi-faceted and complex than class oppositions), were irreducible to one another, or the theoretical categories of Marxism – to the point where the relationship between theory and practice itself appeared as an oppositional relationship. The concept of 'contradiction' (conceived dialectically as the 'unity of opposites') provided Mao with an intellectual instrument for integrating within a structural totality these oppositions between the whole and the parts (including theory and practice), as well as the numerous parts (themselves conceived as contradictory 'pairs') that constituted the historical situation that guerrilla struggle sought to transform. Mao's insistence on practice as the ultimate test of validity was also a product of the conjunctural and, therefore, contingent nature of causation in such a situation, which could not be based on predictions from theory but called for interpretation at every step.

Mao's mode of presentation of his ideas was an elaboration of the simultaneously integrative and dispersive implications of relationships characterized by contradiction. Integrative: because everything depends for its existence on everything else and is, therefore, in a state of identity. Dispersive: because everything has its own irreducible particularity and is, therefore, in a state of difference and opposition. Analysis, including the analysis of the relationship between universal Marxist theory and the practice of revolution in China, must at all points remain cognizant of this basic relationship. The relationship, moreover, is not extrinsic but intrinsic: both identity and difference are intrinsic qualities of things that at once exclude and include one another. The whole and the parts, as well as the parts and the parts, may not be reducible to one another. As Althusser suggests, it is possible at one level to read these abstractions as a description of guerrilla warfare: guerrilla struggle, for its success, demands that guerrillas remain part of a unity even as they disperse into different terrains as they respond to local conditions. The vernacularization of Marxism appears here as the abstraction to a paradigmatic level of a guerrilla socialism. At its most comprehensive level, this was the significance of the 'sinification' of Marxism.

What are the implications of this procedure for the relationship between Marxism and Mao's Marxism? Mao did not reduce Marxism to a Chinese version of it, or view China merely as another illustration of universal Marxist principles. In its rhetorical trope, his exposition of the relationship is at once metonymic (reducing the Chinese Revolution to 'the status of an aspect or function' of Marxism in general, from which it differs nevertheless in a relationship that is extrinsic) and synecdochic (in construing the relationship 'in the manner of an *intrinsic* relationship of shared *qualities*').[34] The result was a conception of the relationship that insisted on China's *difference*, and yet represented Chinese Marxism as an embodiment of Marxism. Ai Siqi, one of Mao's close collaborators in the project of 'sinification', put it as follows (in an essay that followed Mao's 'On New Democracy', in the journal *Chinese Culture*, which started publication in January 1940 as an organ of a 'sinified' Marxism):

> Marxism is a universal truth (*yibande zhengquexing*) not only because it is a scientific theory and method, but because it is the compass of the revolutionary struggle of the proletariat. . . . That is to say, every country or nation that has a proletariat or a proletarian movement has the possibility (*keneng xing*) and necessity (*biran xing*) of giving rise to and developing Marxism. Marxism can be sinified (*Zhongguohua*) because China has produced a Marxist movement in actuality (*shiji*); Chinese Marxism has a foundation in the internal development of Chinese economy and society, has internal sources, it is not a surface phenomenon. . . . The Chinese proletariat has a high level of organization and awareness, has its own strong Party, has twenty years of experience in struggle, has model achievements in the national and democratic struggle. Hence there is Chinese Marxism. If Marxism is a foreign import, our answer is that Marxism gives practice (*shijian*) the primary place. If people wonder whether or not China has its own Marxism, we must first ask whether or not the Chinese proletariat and its Party have moved the heavens and shaken the earth, impelled the masses of the Chinese nation to progressive undertakings. The Chinese proletariat has accomplished this. Moreover, it has on this basis of practice developed Marxist theory. Hence it has its own Marxism. These are the real writings of Chinese Marxism, the texts (*shujue*) of Chinese Marxism. . . . Marxism cannot but assume different forms depending on the different conditions of development of each nation; it cannot assume an international form globally. Presently, 'Marxism must be realized through national forms (*minzu xingshi*). There is no such thing as abstract Marxism, there is only concrete Marxism. The so-called concrete Marxism is Marxism that has taken national form.'[35]

The Marxism (Marxism-Leninism) that Chinese Communists inherited was a Marxism that had already been 'deterritorialized' from its original terrain in European history. Ai's statement metonymically recognizes the difference of Chinese Marxism from an international Marxism, but in the process also restates the relationship between Chinese and European (or any other) Marxism as a part–part relationship within a Marxism that as a whole has now been removed from any territorial associations.

Synecdochically, he 'reterritorializes' Marxism upon a Chinese terrain, by asserting that Chinese Marxism is 'intrinsically' as representative of a whole Marxism as any other.[36] In this simultaneous recognition of a global Marxist discourse as a pervasive unity and the discursive appropriation of Marxism in a Chinese terrain is expressed the fundamental essence and the contradictoriness of the structure of Mao's Marxism, and the procedure of sinification of which it was the product.

CONCLUSION: IN HINDSIGHT

I have discussed above Mao's philosophy, not his politics. In the light of what Mao's politics after 1949 has done to the memory of his philosophy, however, a few words may be in order here concerning the relationship of his philosophy to his politics that may further illuminate his philosophical formulations, as well as the contradictions embedded therein.

Mao's philosophy was a product of the years we have focused upon above. His 'philosophical' essays after 1949 added little of a philosophical nature to his earlier statements, and mainly represent applications in a new situation (with the Communist Party having moved from the 'greenwoods' into state power) of these earlier formulations.[37] Mao's use of his ideas may have changed after the mid-1950s, but there is little basis for arguing that his philosophical premisses or revolutionary assumptions had also changed in the process.

The point at which Mao began to diverge from his colleagues in the Communist Party is revealing also from a philosophical perspective, however. In hindsight the divisions that were to culminate in the Cultural Revolution of the 1960s first appeared in the Eighth Party Congress of 1956, when the Communist Party declared that China had achieved the transition to socialism (from New Democracy), and charted the course for future development to Communism. This Congress also formulated the 'primary contradiction' of the present stage of the Chinese Revolution as the contradiction between highly advanced relations of production (socialism) and backward forces of production. This agreement on the identification of the 'primary contradiction', however, was not accompanied by an agreement on how to resolve the contradiction. The contradiction was interpreted differently by different factions. Mao was to place a revolutionary interpretation on it, and seek its resolution in a renewed revolutionization of society through further transformation of the relations of production, while others sought to develop the forces of production to align them with relations of production that had already advanced beyond the ability of production to sustain them. For the next twenty years, radical Maoists had their way. Since Mao's death in 1976, the Party has opted for the alternative interpretation, and shifted its emphasis to production, even backtracking from the relations of production that had come into existence by 1956.

I am not concerned here with these developments, but with what they reveal about Mao's philosophical assumptions. The availability of alternative choices in the resolution of a commonly recognized contradiction underlines the interpretative problems raised by an analysis based on contradictions. Such an analysis, in other words, does not automatically point to a single resolution, but merely raises alternative possibilities, where the choice of one resolution over an alternative one depends on considerations exterior to the contradiction, or some long-term ideal of 'absolute truth'. Mao, in spite of his recognition in theory of the 'relativity' of the truths yielded by such analysis, was prepared when it actually came to disagreement to assert the 'absoluteness' of his 'relative truth' against others. Depending on our own political proclivity, we may describe this as absolutism or the assertion of 'revolutionary will', but the point here is that the very existence of choice is indicative of a basic problem (or 'contradiction') in Mao's philosophical formulations, and reveals *their* contingency.

Much the same may be said of the relationship of Mao's Marxism to Marxism, which lay at the heart of those formulations. The Cultural Revolution is itself quite revealing in this regard, because at the height of the Cultural Revolution an unprecedented national chauvinism coincided with unprecedented claims on the authenticity of Chinese Marxism to the exclusion of all other Marxisms. In its very extremeness, the national appropriation of Marxism during the Cultural Revolution is revealing of the contradictions created by Mao's Marxism within Marxism in general. The introduction of a Chinese national voice into a global Marxism represented a major contribution to Marxism. It forced an opening up of Marxist categories to reveal a complexity to revolutionary practice that rendered Marxism a more effective instrument of revolution in diverse terrains. Politically, it pointed the way to the possibility of a genuinely universal Marxism in its insistence that a Marxism that refused to incorporate local voices into its structure reintroduced in a radical form the Eurocentric hegemony that was built into it in its historical origins.

At the same time, however, this insistence on the national voice, if divorced from its dialectical structure, promised the dissipation of Marxism into many local contexts, losing all coherence as a theory either of social development or social revolution. This is what happened during the Cultural Revolution. And it may be the historical fate of Marxism (as it would now appear) unless Marxists are able to formulate a new, universal Marxism out of the intertextuality of many national experiences.

In the long run, and in spite of the negation of his own philosophical premisses that he may have orchestrated after 1949, Mao's significance as a philosopher of Marxism rests upon his recognition of a problem that was not just a Chinese problem but would emerge in later years as a global problem of Marxism, and his articulation of it in a philosophical formulation which remains one of the most comprehensive statements of it in the abstract. Whether or not this formulation retains its significance beyond that of the merely historical will depend on the future of Marxism in the contemporary world.

NOTES

1 'Mao Zedong Thought' is the official designation for Mao's Marxism. As such, it is an abstraction, and needs to be distinguished from 'Mao's Marxism', because it refers to a body of thought that was the product of collective effort while the latter refers to the thought of Mao the individual. Thus it is possible for the Communist Party to reject Mao's Marxism while upholding Mao Zedong Thought. While recognizing this distinction, I use the two terms interchangeably here because such a distinction did not become necessary until the 1950s, when (at least officially) consensus broke down over the meaning of the revolution.

2 Norman Levine, *Dialogue Within the Dialectic* (London: George Allen & Unwin, 1984), p. 332.

3 'Talk on questions of philosophy' (1964), in Stuart Schram (ed.), *Chairman Mao Talks to the People* (New York: Pantheon Books, 1974), pp. 212–30, p. 213.

4 ibid., p. 214.

5 Frederic Wakeman, Jr, *History and Will: Philosophical Perspectives of Mao Tse-tung's Thought* (Berkeley: University of California Press, 1975). For Mao's 'confusion', see Edgar Snow, *Red Star Over China* (New York: Grove Press, 1961), pp. 147–8.

6 For Mao's 'populism', see Maurice Meisner, 'Leninism and Maoism: some populist perspectives on Marxism-Leninism in China', *China Quarterly* 45 (1971), 2–36: for 'anarchism', see Robert A. Scalapino, 'The evolution of a young revolutionary: Mao Zedong in 1919–1920', *Journal of Asian Studies* 42 (November 1982), 29–61; for 'thought and action', see Wakeman, op. cit., especially pp. 238–58.

7 Raymond Wylie, *The Emergence of Maoism: Mao Tse-tung, Ch'en Po-ta and the Search for Chinese Theory, 1935–1945* (Stanford, Calif.: Stanford University Press, 1980). See also Thomas Kampen, 'Wang Jiaxiang, Mao Zedong and the "triumph of Mao Zedong Thought" (1935–1945)', *Modern Asian Studies* 23(4) (October 1989), 705–27.

8 Shu Riping, 'Shinian lai Mao Zedong zhexue sixiang yanjiu shuping' ('An account of research on Mao Zedong's philosophy over the last ten years'), *Mao Zedong zhexue sixiang yanjiu* (*Research in Mao Zedong's Philosophical Thought*), no. 5 (1989), 4–10, p. 6. This article also offers a useful survey of discussions of Mao's thought over the preceding ten years; such discussions achieved an unprecedented intensity in the early 1980s but have declined in recent years.

9 Stuarr S. Schram, *The Political Thought of Mao Tse-tung* (revised and enlarged edn, New York: Praeger Publishers, 1971), p. 112.

10 For differences among Chinese interpretations, see Shu, op. cit., p. 6. For different interpretations among Euro-American analysts, see 'Symposium on Mao and Marx', *Modern China*, 2(3), 3(1), 2 (October 1976–7 April 1977).

11 Published originally as 'Xin minzhu zhuyide zhengzhi yu xin minzhu zhuyide wenhua' ('The politics and culture of New Democracy'), *Zhongguo wenhua* (*Chinese Culture*) 1 (January 1940). An English translation is available in *Selected Works of Mao Tse-tung* (hereafter *SWMTT*) (4 vols, Beijing: Foreign Languages Press, 1965–7), vol. II, pp. 339–84.

12 ibid., pp. 380–1.

13 Mao Zedong, 'Lun xin jieduan' ('On the new stage'). Speech to the Enlarged Plenary Session of the Sixty Central Committee (12–14 October 1938). In Takeuchi Minoru (ed.), *Mao Zedong ji* (*Collected Works of Mao Zedong*, hereafter *MZDJ*) (10 vols, Hong Kong: Po Wen Book Co., 1976), vol. VI, pp. 163–263, pp. 260–1.

14 For Althusser's statement on structural effectivity (or causality) and an illuminating discussion of the idea, see Fredric Jameson, *The Political Unconscious: Narrative as a Socially Symbolic Act* (Ithaca, N.Y.: Cornell University Press, 1981), pp. 23–8.

15 For an excellent discussion of Mao's global relevance, see Rossana Rossanda, 'Mao's Marxism', *The Socialist Register*, eds Ralph Millibrand and John Savill (London: The

Merlin Press, 1971), pp. 53–80. See also Arif Dirlik, 'The predicament of Marxist revolutionary consciousness: Mao Zedong, Antonio Gramsci and the reformulation of Marxist revolutionary theory', *Modern China* 9(2) (April 1983), 182–211.

16 For this concept, see Raymond Williams, *Marxism and Literature* (London: Oxford University Press, 1977), pp. 128–35. The term is especially appropriate to the discussion of 'sinification', which its authors conceived as a problem not just of material conditions and ideology, but in terms of a Chinese 'air' or 'style'. *Guoqing*, the term used to describe this, ranges in meaning from 'national circumstances' to 'national sentiment'. Whether or not Marxism was consistent with a Chinese *guoqing* was a matter of intense debate during this period. For a statement by one of Mao's close collaborators in 'sinification', see Ai Siqi, 'Lun Zhongguode teshuxing' ('On China's special nature'), *Zhongguo wenhua* (*Chinese Culture*) 1 (January 1940), 26–8.

17 Schram has recognized the importance of the issue of language in Mao's Marxism: op. cit., p. 113. Nick Knight offers a careful analysis of Mao's use of native sources and language even in an abstract essay such as 'On contradiction' in his important textual analysis of Mao's philosophical texts, 'Mao Zedong's On contradiction and On practice: pre-liberation texts', *China Quarterly* 84 (December 1980), 641–68, pp. 658–9. Knight has recently published his textual studies (including, in addition to these two essays, the 'Lecture notes on dialectical materialism') in Nick Knight (ed.), *Mao Zedong on Dialectical Materialism* (Armonk, N.Y.: M. E. Sharpe, 1990). His translations and annotations of Mao's philosophical writings from this period, supplemented with an excellent introduction on the sources of Mao's writings, provide the most up-to-date textual analysis of Mao's philosophical writings.

18 Jurgen Habermas, *Theory and Practice*, trans. John Vierted (Boston, Mass: Beacon Press, 1973), pp. 2, 10–16.

19 Indeed, some of the earliest and most important discussions on the need to translate Marxism into the language of the masses were provided not by Mao, or Maoists, but by Qu Qiubai, an earlier secretary of the party and a literary theorist. For a discussion of his ideas, see Paul Pickowicz, *Marxist Literary Thought in China: The Influence of Ch'u Ch'iu-pai* (Berkeley: University of California Press, 1981). A more direct discussion of Qu's (and the party's) efforts to accomplish this through literary means in the early part of the agrarian revolution is to be found in Ellen Judd, 'Revolutionary drama and song in the Jiangxi Soviet', *Modern China* 9(1) (January 1983), 127–60. Mao's own early practice is most readily (and comprehensively) apparent in a recently (1982) published account of a local investigation he conducted in 1930, which has just become available in English. See Mao Zedong, *Report from Xunwu*, ed. with an Introduction by Roger R. Thompson (Stanford, Calif.: Stanford University Press, 1990). This essay has justified some Chinese authors in carrying Mao's 'sinification' of Marxism past the war years back to 1930. See Shu, op. cit.

20 These discussions were published under the title of *Xian jieduande Zhongguo sixiang yundong* (*The Chinese Thought Movement of the Present*) (Shanghai: Yiban shudian, 1937).

21 See Levine, op. cit., pp. 317–47, 363–91, for the debt Mao owed to 'Hegelianized Leninism' for his ideas as well as the ways in which he moved beyond it. Levine does an illuminating job of placing Mao within Marxist discussions of the dialectic. For a contrary view, which stresses the significance of 'contradiction' as a *Marxist* break with the Hegelian dialectic, see Louis Althusser, 'Contradiction and overdetermination', in L. Althusser, *For Marx* (New York: Vintage Books, 1970), pp. 89–128, especially pp. 90–4.

22 *SWMTT*, vol. I, p. 311. The parenthetical references in the text will all be to this translation, pp. 311–47. Nick Knight has demonstrated that this text is an edited version of the pre-Liberation text of 'On contradiction' (which contained additional passages which were edited out after 1949), but has not otherwise questioned what is given in this translation.

23 Textual analyses by Schram and Knight in the works cited above have revealed (contrary to earlier opinions) that 'On contradiction' and 'On practice', along with 'Lecture notes

on dialectical materialism', were composed in 1936–37, and together represented 'a single intellectual enterprise'. Mao's philosophical effort at the time was part of the struggles for leadership within the Communist Party, as an endeavour to demonstrate his qualification for leadership against theoretically much better-informed opponents. Indeed, Wylie has argued that the 'sinification of Marxism' was a product of organizational struggles against 'dogmatists' within the party. While this view has much virtue, it needs to be placed within the broader context of the problem of revolution. I focus on the first two essays, because unlike the 'Lecture notes on dialectical materialism', which were mainly copied from other sources, 'On contradiction' and 'On practice' represent original contributions by Mao. While these essays were part of an ongoing philosophical effort that preceded Japan's invasion of China, moreover, they were still rooted in practical considerations, and the texts we have are explicitly devoted to the legitimation of change in political policy in response to the 'new situation'.

24 Althusser, op. cit., p. 94n.

25 Mao, 'Bianzhengfa weiwulun' ('Dialectical materialism'), in *MZDJ*, vol. VI, pp. 265–305, pp. 302–3.

26 Mao quotes Lenin in both essays. See *SWMTT*, vol. I, pp. 304, 336.

27 Althusser, op. cit.

28 See, for instance, 'On tactics against Japanese imperialism' (1935), in *SWMTT*, vol. I, pp. 152–254.

29 *SWMTT*, vol. I, p. 297. References in the text will be to this translation, pp. 295–309.

30 Wakeman, op. cit., pp. 238–58.

31 Thomas A. Metzger, *Escape from Predicament: Neo-Confucianism and China's Evolving Political Culture* (New York: Columbia University Press, 1977), p. 233.

32 Benjamin I. Schwartz, 'The reign of virtue – some broad perspectives on leader and party in the Cultural Revolution', *China Quarterly* 35 (1968), 1–17.

33 Joseph Liu, 'Mao's "On contradiction"', *Studies in Soviet Thought* 11 (June 1971), 71–89, especially pp. 78–81.

34 For a discussion of these rhetorical tropes, see Hayden White, *Metahistory: The Historical Imagination in Nineteenth-Century Europe* (Baltimore, Md.: The Johns Hopkins University Press, 1973), pp. 31–8.

35 Ai, op. cit., pp. 31–2.

36 For 'deterritorialization' and 'reterritorialization', see Gilles Deleuze and Felix Guattari, 'What is a minor literature?', *Mississippi Review* 11(3) (1983), 13–33.

37 I am referring here to such essays as 'On the ten great relationships' (1956) and 'On the correct handling of contradictions among the people' (1975), and his discussions of 'permanent' or 'uninterrupted' revolution in 1958.

FURTHER READING

Biography

Ch'en, Jerome (1970) *Mao and the Chinese Revolution*, New York: Oxford University Press.

Li Jui (1977) *The Early Revolutionary Activities of Comrade Mao Tse-tung*, trans. Anthony W. Sariti, White Plains, N.Y.: M. E. Sharpe.

Schram, Stuart R. (1966) *Mao Tse-tung*, Baltimore, Md.: Penguin.

—— (1988) *Mao Zedong: A Preliminary Reassessment*, Hong Kong: Chinese University Press.

Thought

Chin, Steve S. K. (1979) *The Thought of Mao Tse-tung: Form and Content*, trans. Alfred H. Y. Lin, Hong Kong: Centre for Asian Studies Papers and Monographs.
Dirlik, Arif, Healy, Paul and Knight, Nick (eds) (forthcoming) *Critical Perspectives on Mao Zedong Thought* (Humanities Press).
Schram, Stuart R. (1969) *The Political Thought of Mao Tse-tung*, revised edn, Harmondsworth: Penguin.
—— (1989) *The Thought of Mao Tse-tung*, New York: Cambridge University Press.
Soo, Francis (1981) *Mao Tse-tung's Theory of Dialectic*, Dordrecht: Reidel.
Wilson, Dick (ed.) (1977) *Mao Tse-tung in the Scales of History*, New York: Cambridge University Press.
Womack, Brantly (1982) *The Foundations of Mao Zedong's Political Thought*, Honolulu: University Press of Hawaii.

For interesting comparisons between Mao's thought and those of other Marxist and non-Marxist thinkers, see

Brugger, Bill (1989) 'Mao, science, technology, and humanity', in Arif Dirlik and Maurice Meisner (eds) *Marxism and the Chinese Experience*, Armonk, N.Y.: M. E. Sharpe.
Friedman, Edward (1983) 'Einstein and Mao: metaphors of revolution', *China Quarterly* 93:51–75.
Jung, Hwa Yol and Jung, Petee (1977) 'Revolutionary dialectics: Mao Tse-tung and Maurice Merleau-Ponty', *Dialectical Anthropology* 2 (1) (February), 33–56.
Meisner, Maurice (1982) *Marxism, Maoism and Utopianism: Eight Essays*, Madison: University of Wisconsin Press.

30

LOGIC AND LANGUAGE IN CHINESE PHILOSOPHY

Zhang Chunpo and Zhang Jialong

There is a short section, 'Chinese logic', in the entry 'History of logic' in the *Encyclopaedia Britannica* (15th edition):

> for the most part, Chinese philosophy is concerned with practical and moral problems on the one hand and with mystical interpretations of life on the other. It has little room for the study of logic which has remained neglected since the establishment of Neo-Confucianism in the eleventh century AD. In developing logic, the Chinese thinkers did not advance beyond the stage of preliminaries, a stage that was reached in Greece by the Sophists in the fifth century BC.

We cannot agree with this viewpoint. We think that Chinese logic has its own characteristics, and that Chinese logicians have achieved great success in the investigation of logical and linguistic problems.

CONFUCIUS' THEORY OF THE RECTIFICATION OF NAMES

First of all, let us discuss Confucius' logical thought. Confucius (551–479 BC), the founder of Confucianism, was born in the state of Lu, the present Qufu in Shandong province. His doctrine is to be found in the *Lunyu* (*Analects*), a collection of sayings by Confucius and some of his disciples. In the age of Confucius China was in transition from a slave to a feudal society, but Confucius was a conservative and proposed the theory of the rectification of names. The *Lunyu* says:

> Zi Lu [a disciple] said: 'The prince of Wei is awaiting you, Sir, to take control of his administration. What will you undertake first, Sir?' The Master replied: 'The one thing needed is the rectification of names. . . . If names be incorrect, speech will not follow its natural sequence. If speech does not follow its natural sequence, nothing can be established. If nothing can be established, no rules of conduct or music will prevail, laws and punishments will not be just. When laws and punishments are not just, the people will not know where to place their hands and feet.'

The signification of the rectification of names is 'Let the ruler be ruler, the minister minister; let the father be father, and the son son.'

Thus it can be seen that Confucius' rectification of names is a political matter, but also has a logical aspect. He thought that the changing society of his times reflecting feudal changes did not accord with the ceremonials and institutions of the Western Zhou Dynasty (a slave society), according to which the ruler, the minister, the father and the son should all keep to their places in the hierarchy and not exceed the limits which had been set. However, the actual situation at the time was that 'the ruler is not ruler, the minister not minister, the father not father, and the son not son.' The rulers lost the authority regulated by the ceremonials of Zhou, and existed only in name but not in reality. On the other hand, the ministers did not abide by the law, and usually went against their superiors. Confucius thought that this situation resulted from the confusion of name and reality. He maintained that the name came first and the reality second epistemologically. He tried to rectify reality by means of names. Logically a 'name', so called by Chinese philosophers, is a term or concept. Confucius realized that names ought to have definiteness; a name refers to one thing, and cannot refer to another at the same time. That is to say, names must follow the law of identity. Confucius' theory of rectification of names has had great influence on Chinese logic and language.

After Confucius, most philosophical schools in ancient China referred to logic. Huishi, Gongsun Long, the later Mohists, Xunzi and Han Fei were very famous representatives of them.

HUISHI'S ANTINOMIES

Huishi (*c.* 370–310 BC) was a dialectician, and a leader of the Name school (*Ming Jia*). He and Zhuangzi, who was a leader of the Daoist school (*Dao Jia*), were on friendly terms. The Name school consisted of dialecticians in the Warring States Period (475–221 BC). This school was divided into two sections, the Huishi section and the Gongsun Long section. Huishi proposed ten antinomies; the main ones were: (1) 'The greatest has nothing beyond itself, and is called the Great Unit (*Da Yi*); the smallest has nothing within itself, and is called the Little Unit (*Xiao Yi*).' (All quotations are from *Zhuangzhi*, ch. 33.) Viewed as a whole, a space is 'the Great Unit' having nothing beyond itself; viewed as a small bit, a space is 'the little unit' having nothing within itself. The greatest and smallest are relative, oppose each other and yet complement each other. (2) 'That which has no thickness, yet in extent it may cover a thousand miles': the plane in geometry has no thickness. What is without thickness cannot have volume, but has area, therefore 'in extent it may cover a thousand miles.' That is to say, the size of a space is relative. (3) 'The heavens are as low as the earth; mountains are on the same level as marshes.' The average person thinks that the heavens are high and earth is low; when one looks towards a distant place, it seems that the heavens link up with the earth. So we can say: 'The heavens are as low as the earth.' The average person thinks that mountains are high and marshes low; however, the marshes at a place of a higher elevation are almost on the same level as mountains at a place of a lower elevation. So we can say: 'mountains are on the same level as marshes.' This shows that height is relative. (4) 'The sun at noon is the sun declining; the creature born is the creature dying.' When the sun rises to the meridian, it is beginning to decline; when a creature is born, it is beginning to die. This antinomy shows that Huishi recognized the absolute motion of things, but he negated the relative stability of things. (5) 'A great similarity differs from a little similarity. This is called the little similarity-and-difference (*Xiao Tong Yi*). All things are in one way all similar, in another way all different. This is called the great similarity-and-difference (*Da Tong Yi*).' Every great class of things has a common property; this is a 'great similarity'. Every different genus or species of a class also has common properties respectively; this is a 'little similarity'. The great similarity is different from the little similarity; this is a kind of similarity and difference, investigated from the relation between genera or species and called 'the little similarity-and-difference'. So far as the generality is concerned, all things are things, therefore they are all similar; so far as the individuality is concerned, all things have their properties, therefore they are all different, investigated from generality and individuality and called 'the great similarity-and-difference'. This antinomy shows us that similarity and difference are relative, and can transform each other.

GONGSUN LONG'S ANTINOMIES

Gongsun Long (*c.* 325–250 BC), who shared equal popularity with Huishi, was a leader of another group of dialecticians. His doctrine is preserved in *Gongsun Long Zi*, a small book bearing his name.

Gongsun Long's most famous thesis is 'a white horse is not a horse' ('Bai ma fei ma'). His arguments were as follows: (1) 'The word "horse" denotes a shape; "white" denotes a colour. What denotes colour does not denote shape' (All quotations are from (*Gongsun Long Zi.*) That is to say, the word 'horse' refers to a shape, 'white' to a colour, and 'white horse' to both a shape and a colour, therefore their intensions are different. Thus, a white horse is not a horse. (2) 'When a horse is required, yellow and black ones may all be brought forward, but when one requires a white horse, a yellow or black horse cannot be brought forward. These can meet the requirement of a horse, but not the requirement of a white horse.' So far as the extension is concerned, the word 'horse' refers to all horses, and the word 'white horse' to a part of the extension of 'horse'. The word 'horse' neither excludes nor includes any colour. Therefore, when a horse is required, yellow and black ones may all respond to it. But the word 'white horse' excludes and includes colour. When one requires a white horse, yellow and black horses are all excluded owing to their colour. Therefore it is only a 'white horse' that will correspond. That from which nothing is excluded is not that from which something is excluded. Therefore, a white horse is not a horse. (3) 'Horses certainly have colour. Therefore, there exist white horses. Suppose there is a horse without colour, then there is only the horse as such. But how can we get white horses? Therefore, "white" is not "horse". A white horse is "horse" together with "white", "white" together with "horse". Therefore, I say that a white horse is not a horse.' In Chinese, 'horse' and 'white', etc. are used to designate both the concrete particular and the abstract universal; 'horse' is a universal in which there is no quality of colour; 'white horse' is a universal of horse together with whiteness. According to Gongsun Long, 'horse', 'white' and 'white horse' are all separate and independent universals. Therefore, a white horse is not a horse. We can formulate Gongsun Long's thesis as follows:

$$WH \neq H.$$

Obviously this is not a sophism, as some Chinese scholars think.

The dialecticians of the Gongsun Long group proposed some antinomies. For example: (1) 'There are times when a flying arrow is neither in motion nor at rest' (*Zhuangzi*, ch. 33). This antinomy is similar to Zeno's paradox 'the flying arrow never moves'. (2) 'If a rod of one foot in length is cut short every day by one-half of its length, it will still have something let even after ten thousand generations' (*Zhuangzi*, ch. 33). This antinomy is similar to Zeno's dichotomy paradox.

THE LOGIC OF THE MOHIST CANONS

The Mohist Canons (*Mo Jing*) represented the peak of logic in ancient China. It was written by the later Mohists in the third century BC. It consisted of Canons I and II, Expositions I and II, Major Illustration and Minor Illustration.

Mohist logic is about dialectic. What is dialectic (*bian*)? There are two kinds of dialectic, dialectic in the narrow sense and dialectic in the broad sense.

Dialectic in the narrow sense is 'conflict over something. In dialectic, the one who wins is right' (Canon I). 'In dialectic, one says something is an ox, and the other says it is not. This is conflict over something. They cannot both be right, and not being both right, there must be one who is wrong, as, for example, if it is a dog' (Exp. I). 'To say that in dialectic there is no winner is incorrect' (Canon II). 'Dialectic is that in which one person says a thing is so, and another says it is not so. The one who is right will win' (Exp. II).

This dialectic is just an argument between two parties. They have contradictory opinions on the same object: one says a thing is so, another says it is not so, and therefore there is a conflict or argument between them. For example, if one says something is an ox, while the other says it is not, and if the latter is right, then the latter will win.

In this kind of dialectic, two parties have to follow two laws of thinking. 'They cannot both be right: there must be one who is wrong.' 'This is the law of non-contradiction: $\neg (P \wedge \neg P)$. 'To say that in dialectic there is no winner is incorrect'; 'The one who is right will win', that is to say, two contradictory propositions cannot both be false: there must be one that is true. This is the law of excluded middle: $P \vee \neg P$.

Mohist logic is dialectic in the wide sense:

> Dialectic serves to make clear the distinction between right and wrong, to discriminate between good and disordered government, to make evident the points of similarity and difference, to examine the principles of names and actualities, to differentiate between what is beneficial and what is harmful, and determine what is uncertain. It describes the forms of all things, and in discussions seeks to compare the various speeches. It uses names to imitate actualities, propositions to express ideas, argumentation to set forth causes, taking and giving according to classes. What one oneself has, one should not blame another for having, and what one is oneself without, one should not blame another for not having.
>
> (Minor Illustrations)

The functions of this kind of dialectic are:

1. 'To make clear the distinction between right and wrong.' This concerns people's knowledge.
2. 'To discriminate between good and disordered government.' This is to apply dialectic to society.
3. 'To make evident the points of similarity and difference.' This concerns the objects of dialectic.
4. 'To examine the principles of names and actualities.' This is the means to the end of dialectic.
5. 'To differentiate between what is beneficial and what is harmful.'
6. To determine what is to be undertaken.'

The last two functions apply dialectic to practice. 'Using names to imitate actualities, propositions to express ideas, argumentation to set forth causes, taking and giving according to classes' are the methods of dialectic. The forms of dialectic include imitation (*xiao*), comparison (*pi*), parallel (*mou*), analogy (*yuan*) and extension (*tui*).

Imitation (*xiao*)

'Imitation consists in taking a model.' 'A model is that according to which something becomes' (Canon I). 'Model: either the concept [of a circle] or the compasses or a finished circle may be used as the model [for making a circle]'. (Exp. I). 'The mutual sameness of things of one model extends to all things in that class. Thus squares are the same, one to another. The reason is given under "square"' (Canon II). 'All things which are squares have the same model, though [themselves] different, some being of wood, some of stone. This does not prevent their squares mutually corresponding to one another. They are all of the same kind, being all squares. Things are all like this' (Exp. II).

To sum up, a model is just a pattern of all things in the same class, which is applicable to any individual of this class. A model may be the concept of the thing, or the instrumentality with which it is made, or a typical member of the class to which the thing belongs. The square is a model of all square things, which belong to the one class, of which square wood and square stone are members.

Imitation consists in taking a model. What is imitated is what is taken for a model. Whatever imitates the model of circle (or square) becomes a circle (or square). 'If the cause is in agreement with the imitation, it is correct. Otherwise it is not correct.' That is to say, if a cause is a model in forming a conclusion, then the form of inference is valid; otherwise invalid. It can be seen from this that the inference of imitation is a deductive one. For example, 'This geometric figure has equidistant radii from the centre, therefore it is a circle.' This is a valid inference because 'this geometric figure has equidistant radii from the center' is a cause or model of the conclusion 'it is a circle', which is in agreement with imitation.

Comparison (*pi*)

'The method of comparison consists in using one thing to explain another.' This method is not one which discovers new truths, and is only used to explain one thing by means of something else which belongs to the same class. It includes metaphors, similes and comparisons. For example, 'Knowing is a faculty. This knowing is that by means of which one knows, but which of itself does not necessarily know, as in the case of light.' 'As in the case of light' is an illustration of the use of the method of comparison.

Parallel (*mou*)

'The method of parallel reasoning consists in comparing two propositions consistently throughout.'

'A white horse is a horse. To ride a white horse is to ride a horse. A black horse is horse. To ride a black horse is to ride a horse. Huo is a man. To love Huo is to love a man. Zhang is a man. To love Zhang is to love a man' (Minor III).

These parallel inferences can be formulated as:

S is P
∴ RS is RP (where 'R' represents a relation) or in detail as:

$\forall x(Sx \rightarrow Px)$
$\therefore \forall x[(Mx \rightarrow \exists y\,(Sy \wedge R(x, y))) \rightarrow (Mx \rightarrow \exists y\,(Py \wedge R(x, y)))]$.

Here S represents '— is white horse', P '— is a horse', M '— is a man', and R 'to ride'. ∀ is the universal quantifier, ∃ the existential one, ∧ the symbol of conjunction, and → the symbol of implication.

There is also a negative form of parallel inference: 'The premiss is negative, and the conclusion is also negative' (Major III), for example 'The souls of the men are not men; to offer sacrifices to the souls of men is not to offer sacrifices to men' (Minor III).

Its form is:

S is not P
∴ RS is not RP.

Analogy (*yuan*)

'The method of analogy says: "You are so. Why should I alone not be so?"' This is an example of 'taking according to class', the form of which is as follows:

Let *u* and *v* be analogous.

You accept *u*
∴ I accept *v*.
You do not accept *u*
∴ I do not accept *v*.

Extension (*tui*)

'In the method of extension, when what has not been accepted is the same as what has been accepted, it is permissible to make a general affirmation. For example, when it is said that the others are the same, how can I say that they are different?'

Obviously this is induction, which is a method of inferring from what has been accepted to what has not been accepted. *Mo Jing* claims that the basis of induction is 'to make evident the points of similarity and difference', and 'giving according to classes.' *Mo Jing* says: 'When similarity and difference are jointly considered, what is present and what is absent can be set forth' (Canon I). For example,

> A cow differs from a horse. But to prove their difference by saying 'Because a cow has teeth and a horse has tail' is not permissible. These things are possessed by both. Neither the one attribute nor the other is present in the one instance and absent in the other. Say rather: 'A horse differs from a cow because the latter has horns whereas the former has none.' That is the differentia of the two species.
>
> (Exp. II)

This is an induction based on the joint use of the methods of similarity and difference.

This method is similar to J. S. Mill's joint method of agreement and difference. Its schema is as follows:

Every element of the class K has attribute P
Every element of the class L does not have attribute P
∴ K is not the same as L.

Drawing out (*zhuo*)

'The drawing out (*zhuo*) is an inference where there is no doubt' (Canon II). 'In a case of *zhuo*, there is no reason for doubt. Zhang dies of an acute disease; Zhun is affected with this disease; hence we may conclude that Zhun will also die' (Exp. II).

Zhuo is a form of induction based on the typical instance. From the fact that Zhang dies of an acute disease we infer that all who are affected with this disease will die; Zhun is affected by this disease; therefore Zhun will die.

The method of refutation (*zhi*)

Mo Jing says: 'If a man thinks that this is so and says that all these are so, I may show that that is not so, and thereby disprove the generalization that all these are so' (Exp. II).

That all S is P, a conclusion following from induction by simple enumeration, is not necessarily true, and is disproved by that S_1 which is not P which is a singular negative proposition. *Mo Jing* says again:

> To refute 'all men are black' because there are black and not-black men, or to refute 'all men are loved by men' because some men are loved and some are not loved. . . . If someone mentions those instances that are so and concludes that all instances are so, then I show him those cases that are not so.
>
> (Exp. I)

That is to say, in order to refute a universal affirmative proposition that follows from some instances that are so, we can use a particular negative proposition. To refute 'all men are black', we use 'some men are not black'.

In short, to refute 'all S is P', we can use either 'S_1 is not P' or 'some S is not P'.

Mo Jing examined the causes of fallacies. In the method of comparison, 'there are ways in which things may be similar, without being similar throughout.' 'The method of parallel reasoning between propositions comes to a point where it stops.' In the method of analogy, 'things are so, and there is a reason why they are so. They may be the same in what they are, while at the same time the reason why they are so may not be the same.' In the method of extension, 'Things are accepted, and there is a reason why they are accepted. They may be the same inasmuch as they are accepted, whereas the reason why they are accepted need not be the same.' Hence,

> the methods of comparison, parallel, analogy and extension, when they are used, may lead to differences and turn into difficulty; and when they are carried far, may lead to error. They may became loose and detached from their bases, and so cannot but be examined, and cannot always be used. Hence in speech there are many aspects, various classes and different causes, so that one cannot be one-sided.
>
> (Minor III)

To sum up, 'in speech there are many aspects, various classes and different causes' of fallacies.

Mo Jing discussed two kinds of fallacies in the method of parallel reasoning:

(1) 'The premiss is true, but the conclusion is false.'

Examples are as follows:

> Huo's parents are men. Yet when Huo serves his parents, he is not serving men. His younger sister is a beautiful woman. But to love his younger sister is not to love a beautiful woman. A cart is wood, but to ride a cart is not to ride wood. A boat is wood, but to enter a boat is not to enter wood. A robber is a man, but many robbers are not many men; and that there are no robbers does not mean that there are no men . . . to hate the existence of many robbers is not to hate the existence of many men, and to wish that there were no robbers is not to wish that there were no men. . . . Although a robber is a man, to love robbers is not to love men. Likewise to kill a robber is not to kill a man.
>
> (Minor III)

How are these explained? 'Serving men' means working as a servant, which is different from serving parents. That is to say, 'to serve' and 'serving' have different senses. Therefore:

(a) 'Huo's parents are men' is true
(b) 'Huo, who serves his parents, is serving men' is false.

That is to say, Huo serving his parents is not serving men.

'To ride wood' means to ride a board which is not chiselled, and so 'a cart is wood, but to ride a cart is not to ride wood.' 'To ride' has different senses. 'To enter wood' in Chinese means 'to enter a coffin', i.e. 'to die', and so 'to enter a boat is not to enter wood.'

Huo's sister is a beautiful woman, but Huo loves his sister because they are full brother and sister, not because she is a beautiful woman. So 'to love his younger sister is not to love a beautiful woman.' Here 'to love' has different meanings. 'To love man' means to love all men but robbers; therefore, from 'a robber is a man' we cannot conclude 'to love robbers is to love men.'

The standard by which to judge quantities of robbers is different from that for quantities of men, therefore 'a robber is a man, but many robbers are not many men; that there are no robbers does not mean that there are no men; to hate the existence of many robbers is not to hate the existence of many men; to wish that there were no robbers is not to wish that there were no men.'

'To kill a man' means to commit the crime of killing a man; 'to kill a robber' means to kill a robber in self-defence. 'To kill' has different meanings. So 'to kill a robber is not to kill a man.' The above examples can be formulated as A is B; but R_1A is not R_2B, i.e. that R_1A is R_2B is wrong ('R_1' and 'R_2' are expressed by the same word but actually represent two relations).

(2) 'The premiss is false, but the conclusion is true.'
Examples are as follows:

> Reading a book is not a book; to love reading a book is to love a book. To fight a cock is not a cock; to like to fight a cock is to like a cock. To be about to fall into the well is not to fall into the well; to stop being about to fall into the well is to stop falling into the well. To be about to go out is to not to go out; to stop being about to go out is to stop going out.
>
> (Minor III)

'Reading a book' is an action, and of course not a book. 'To love reading a book' implies 'to love a book', because 'to love reading' is a compound relation which implies 'to love'. Let 'r' represent 'to read', 'R' 'to love' and 'B' 'book'. 'Reading a book is not a book; to love reading a book is to love a book' can then be formulated as:

Not rB is B
But RrB is RB.

The other example is similar.
Further, *Mo Jing* proposed two fallacies which occurred in the other inferences:

(3) 'One concept is sometimes distributable and sometimes indistributable.' For example, 'To ride a horse does not involve distributing riding a horse; riding a horse means to ride some horse (or horses). Not to ride a horse means to distribute not riding a horse' (Minor III).

That is to say, to ride a horse does not mean to ride all horses, only some horses, Not to ride a horse means not to ride any horse. Confusing the two produces error.

Mo Jing proposed the use of quantifiers in relative propositions. In 'to ride a white horse is to ride a horse', 'to ride a white horse' or 'to ride a horse' is not distributed, and so we should use an existential quantifier before them:

$$\forall x[(Mx \rightarrow \exists y\ (Wy \wedge R(x, y))) \rightarrow (Mx \rightarrow \exists y\ (Hy \wedge R\ (x, y)))].$$

From 'to ride a white horse is to ride a horse', 'not to ride a horse is not to ride a white horse' can follow. 'Not to ride a horse' or 'not to ride a white horse' is distributed, and we should use a universal quantifier before them:

$$\forall x\ [(Mx \rightarrow \forall y\ (Wy \rightarrow \neg\ R(x, y))) \rightarrow (Mx \rightarrow \forall y\ (Hy \rightarrow \neg\ R(x, y)))].$$

(4) 'One proposition is right, but another is wrong.'

For example, 'A fruit of the peach is a peach; a fruit of the thorn is not a thorn. To ask after a man's disease is to ask after the man; to dislike a man's disease is not to dislike the man' (Minor III).

That is to say, $f(A) = g(A)$, but $f(B) \neq g(B)$. In general, that $f(A)$ and $g(A)$ are synonymous is based on some conditions, but if we substitute B for A in $f(A) = g(A)$, then $f(B) \neq g(B)$ because of changing conditions.

In (1), (2) and (4), *Mo Jing* actually proposed that the extensional viewpoint is not applicable to the intensional words, such as 'to kill', 'to love', 'a fruit of', etc.

Mo Jing formulated another famous paradox: 'To hold that all speech is perverse, is perverse. The reason is given under "his speech"' (Canon II). 'To hold that all speech is perverse is not permissible. If the speech of this man [who holds this doctrine] is correct and not perverse, then at least it is correct. But if this man's speech is not permissible, then it is wrong to take it as being correct' (Exp. II).

We can see that this is an incomplete liar paradox like Epimenides' paradox ('A Cretan says: "All Cretans lie"').

If this man's speech 'all speech is perverse' is true, then it, at least, is not perverse, which means that it is false to say that 'all speech is perverse'. If such speech is false, then some speech is not perverse, i.e. some speech is true, but the true speech is not necessarily this man's.

In fact, *Mo Jing* pointed out a vicious circle as the origin of the liar paradox, and solved the paradox 'all speech is perverse' by prohibiting vicious circles.

XUNZI

Xunzi (*c.* 325–238 BC), the Master Xun, whose first name was Kuang, was a great philosopher as well as a great logician. He is the last representative of Confucianism during the Warring States Period. His famous work is *Xunzi*, in which there is a chapter entitled *Zheng Ming* (*The Rectification of Names*) that specializes in logic. The quotations below are from *Zheng Ming*.

Why should there be names? Xunzi says:

> Names were made in order to denote actualities, on the one hand so as to make evident the noble and base, and on the other distinguish similarities and differences. When the distinction between the noble and base is evident and similarities and differences are distinguished, under these circumstances a man's mind will not suffer from the misfortune of being misunderstood, and affairs will not suffer from the calamity of being hindered or wasted. This is the reason for having names.

Confucius' rectification of names is mainly political and moral; Xunzi extended it to the logical domain. The function of names is not only 'to make evident the noble and base' but 'to distinguish similarities and differences' as well. 'To distinguish similarities and differences' is a rectification of names in the logical sense.

Of the relation between names and actualities, Xunzi says: 'Names were made in order to denote actualities.' That is to say, actualities are primary and names secondary, which is a materialist viewpoint. Xunzi pointed out that different actualities have different names, and therefore one never refers to different actualities except by different names; likewise one who refers to the same actuality should always use the same name. Xunzi says:

> For although all things are innumerable, there are times when we wish to speak of them all in general, so we call them 'things'. 'Things' is the most general name. We press on and generalize; we generalize and generalize still more, until there is nothing more general. Only then do we stop. There are times when we wish to speak of one aspect, so we say 'birds and beasts'. 'Birds and beasts' is the great classifying name. We press on and classify. We classify and classify still more, until there is no more classification to be made, and then we stop.

According to Xunzi, names are divided into general names and classifying names based on the extension of those names. A general name is that of a class of things; a classifying name is that of a part of a class of things. They have different ranks. A general name is also a classifying name relating to a general name above it and it is different from that of an individual, which is called the great classifying name. The most general name has the most extension, such as 'things'. The name which allows no further classification is the name of an individual. So for Xunzi's defining 'birds and beasts' as the great classifying name is incorrect. Xunzi refuted three fallacies arising from using names.

(1) Using names to confuse names:

'It is no disgrace to be insulted', which is a viewpoint of a philosopher, is an example of this fallacy: the intension of 'to be insulted' includes the sense of disgrace.

Xunzi considered also the Mohist proposition 'to kill a robber is not to kill a man' as using names to confuse names. We think that this is not correct, because 'to kill a robber is not to commit the crime of killing a man.' How can this fallacy be escaped? Xunzi says: 'Investigate the reason for having names, observe of what sort the names are, and then you will be able to stop this confusion.'

(2) Using actualities to confuse names:

Xunzi's example is 'mountains are on the same level as marshes', which is Huishi's opinion. Although sometimes mountains at a place which has lower elevation are on the same level as marshes at a place which has higher elevation, in general mountains are higher than marshes. Xunzi thought that one cannot negate the general law by means of the particular case.

This fallacy can be escaped as follows: 'Investigate the means through which similarities and differences are found, and see what fits the actuality, and then you will be able to stop this confusion.'

(3) Using names to confuse actualities:

Xunzi's example is 'an ox-horse is not a horse', which is the Mohist viewpoint, and is right. This is not using names to confuse actualities. We offer a similar example, 'a fruit of a peach is not a peach', which is a case of using names to confuse actualities.

How can we stop this confusion? 'Investigate the agreement about names; take what these agreements accept, reject what they refuse to countenance; then you will be able to stop this confusion.'

Another problem discussed by Xunzi is on dialectic. There are a variety of things in the world, which are various actualities.

> Names are that whereby we define various actualities. Propositions are the combination of names of different actualities wherewith to discuss one idea. Dialectic and explanation take one actuality and its name under discussion, so as to understand their different aspects. Designation and naming are the object of dialectic.

According to Xunzi, dialectic has to meet the following conditions:

1. A person's mind accords with the objective law.
2. His dialectic accords with his mind.
3. His propositions accord with his dialectic.
4. Names are founded on actualities and are understood.
5. He discriminates differences without making mistakes.
6. He infers a class of things from another without error, and estimates a class by means of another.
7. He can listen to discussions and tell if they are in accord with a cultivated style.
8. He can argue and exhaust all possible causes.
9. By the objective law he can distinguish wickedness.
10. When things are alike, they are named alike; when different, they are named differently. One who thought the right is the right and the wrong is the wrong is wise; one who thought the right is the wrong and the wrong is the right is foolish. This is the law of identity.
11. There cannot be two reasons in the same class of things, and so a wise man selects only one. This is the law of contradiction.
12. In any doctrine something is either right or wrong. This is the law of excluded middle.

HAN FEI

Han Fei (*c.* 280–233 BC) was a disciple of Xunzi. He was a representative of the Legalists (Fa Jia) during the Warring States Period. His writings are collected in *Han Feizi* (quoted below):

> In using the method of maintaining uniformity, names are of primary importance. When names have been rectified, things will be fixed. When names have not been rectified, things undergo change. . . . When the name is unknown, the actuality is investigated. When the actuality and name are seen to be in agreement, what comes forth from them is utilized.

That is to say, the most important matter in the rectification of names is correspondence between actualities and names. Han Fei's words expounded the relation between the name and the actuality logically. However, the Legalists advocated the rectification of names as a means by which the ruler might dominate his subjects. Han Fei as a Legalist applied the theory of the rectification of names to political affairs. He said: 'The ruler holds the names in hand, and his subjects model their actualities after the names. When actualities and names are in agreement, superior and inferior are in harmony with one another.'

Han Fei told a famous fable:

> There is a Chu man who sells the lance as well as the shield. He praises his shield and says: 'Nothing can pierce my hardshield.' At the same time, he praises his lance and says: 'My sharp lance can pierce anything.' Someone asks him: 'What will happen if someone tries to pierce your shield with your lance?' He cannot answer. The shield which cannot be pierced and the lance which can pierce anything must not hold true at the same time.

Let 'a' represent the lance, 'b' the shield and 'R' the relation 'pierce'.

'Nothing can pierce my hard shield' can be symbolized as

(1) $\forall x \neg R(x, b)$.

'My sharp lance can pierce anything' can be symbolized as

(2) $\forall x R(a, x)$.

We infer from (1) according to the law of universal instantiation:

(3) $\neg R(a, b)$.

We infer from (2):

(4) $R(a, b)$.

Propositions (1) and (2) are a pair of opposite propositions; they cannot be true at the same time, but can both be false; (3) and (4) are a pair of contradictory propositions; they cannot be true at the same time, and one of them must be false. Propositions (1) and (2) imply (3) and (4). Han Fei knew that because he said: 'Someone asks him: "What will happen if someone tries to pierce your shield with your lance?" He cannot answer.'

Therefore Han Fei's story of the lance and the shield illustrates the law of contradiction, that a pair of contradictory propositions cannot be true at the same time, and one of them must be false. The word *maodun* in Chinese is derived from *mao* (lance) and *dun* (shield), and it means contradiction.

To sum up, logical investigations in ancient China achieved excellent results. Chinese logic runs parallel to Greek and to Indian logic, and so is one of the three great traditions of logic in the world. On the other hand, we must recognize that Chinese logic did not develop after the Warring States Period. *Hetuvidyā* (Indian syllogistic logic) spread to China in the sixth century, but research in *hetuvidyā* declined before long. The underlying causes of the lack of development of Chinese logic were that the feudal rulers enjoyed cultural autocracy, which strangled the development of logic, and that the Chinese written character is not alphabetic so it is difficult to introduce logical variables in Chinese. Classical logic spread to China in the seventeenth century, and modern logic in 1920. Now there is a contingent of modern logicians in China.

FURTHER READING

Fung Yu-Lan (1937) *A History of Chinese Philosophy*, Peiping: Henri Vetch.
Graham, A. C. (1978) *Later Mohist Logic, Ethics and Science*, Hong Kong: The Chinese University Press; London: School of Oriental and African Studies.
Han Fei (1939, 1960) *The Complete Works of Han Fei Tzu*, trans. by W. K. Liao, 2 vols., London: Probsthain.
Hansen, Chad (1983) *Language and Logic in Ancient China*, Ann Arbor: University of Michigan Press.
Hu Shih (1922) *The Development of the Logical Method in Ancient China*, Shanghai: The Oriental Book Company.
Knoblock, John (1988) *Xunzi: A Translation and Study of the Complete Works*, vol. 1, Stanford: Stanford University Press.
Mei, Y. P. (1953) 'The Kung-sun Lung Tzu, with a Translation into English', *Harvard Journal of Asiatic Studies*, vol. 16, 404–437.
Society for the History of Chinese Logic (ed.) (1985) *Source Book of Chinese Logic*, Langhou: Gansu People's Publishing House.
Zhuangzi (1933) *Chuang Tyu, A New Translation with an Exposition of the Philosophy of Kuo Hsiang*, trans. by Yu-Lan Fung, Shanghai: Commercial Press.

31

KNOWLEDGE AND REALITY IN CHINESE PHILOSOPHY

Zhang Chunpo and Li Xi

Knowledge and reality are two basic categories in epistemology; they are called the relation of 'knowing' and 'doing' in the history of Chinese philosophy. The approach to the problem of knowledge and reality was of great practical significance. By the end of the Spring and Autumn Period (770–476 BC), philosophers of different schools in Chinese philosophy had been raising and debating it constantly. Their subsequent controversies can be summarized as falling into three periods. The first, from the end of the Spring and Autumn Period to the end of the Warring States Period (*c.* 540–220 BC), was a revolutionary period of the new rising landlord class; and also the time when the foundations of Chinese culture and philosophy were laid. It was then that questions involving every aspect of the relation of knowing and doing came in for wide and deep discussion, with positive results. The second was from the Song to the Ming Dynasty (AD 960–1644), a period which saw capitalism germinating twice: the first time following the middle period of the Northern Song Dynasty (*c.* AD 1043), and the second time following the middle period of the Ming Dynasty (*c.* AD 1490). The buds of capitalism gave rise to large changes in man's mentality, and thus the problem of knowing and doing again became prominent in philosophical circles, and was studied in accordance with the needs of the times. The third was the period of the democratic revolution, which can be divided into two stages. One was the stage of the old democratic revolution, when bourgeois thinkers and politicians generally copied the cultural model of the West. Sun Yatsen, however, continued to reflect on the failure of the 1911 revolution in the latter half of his lifetime. He laid stress upon a psychological reconstruction, contributing much originality in philosophy generally as well as in the relation of knowing and doing. The other stage was the period of the new democratic revolution, during which the leader of the working class, Mao Zedong, who directed the new democratic revolution under the guidance of Marxism and Leninism, carried the discussion of the problem of knowing and doing to a higher level of 'integrating theory with practice'. He opened a new era of Chinese philosophy with his famous work *On Practice*, making a contribution of epoch-making significance in Marxist-Leninist epistemology.

As the problem of the nature of the relation between knowing and doing is essentially an epistemological one the answer to it and related aspects could be given either from the standpoint of materialism or from that of idealism. The discussion and controversy over it in the history of Chinese philosophy has finally given expression to materialism in opposition to idealism.

So far as Chinese philosophy is concerned, the main points discussed and debated concerning knowing and doing are as follows: (1) Is knowing divorced or derived from doing? (2) Is it easy to know and hard to do, or the reverse? (3) How can a criterion be worked out by which to judge if 'knowledge' is true or false? (4) Should knowing or doing be given priority; and should the two be combined or unified?

IS KNOWING DIVORCED OR DERIVED FROM DOING?

In the history of Chinese philosophy, the first person who posed and discussed the problem of the relation between knowing and doing was Laozi (*c.* 570 BC), the philosopher of objective idealism. He formulated *Dao* as the basic category of his philosophical system. *Dao* was assumed to be the very source from which came into being the absolute soul of the material world, i.e. the spirit that was separated from the human brain and existed in itself independently. Thus, in his view, if one attains *Dao*, one can, by means of *Dao*, understand the universe without resorting to any action which would prevent one from understanding. Laozi said,

> Without going out of doors, one can know all that happens in the world; without looking out of one's window, one can grasp the law of heaven. The further one goes out from one's gate, the less one knows about. Therefore, a divine sage sees all he needs to see without action, understands all he wants to understand without looking elsewhere, and accomplishes his object without exertion.[1]

This is a typical idealist view that severs the connection between the human mind and the external world. He said elsewhere, 'Shutting up one's sense-organs of ears, eyes, nose and mouth, one would commit no mistake throughout one's life; and, if one let loose one's sense-organs to engage in external affairs, that would be a danger.'[2] Such a view separating knowing from doing can be reckoned as an extreme one – knowing has nothing to do with doing, while doing prevents one from knowing. This reflects Laozi's conservative defence of the slave-owning system, which was on the verge of disintegration and abolition. Towards the end of the Spring and Autumn Period, great changes took place in society, and any action effectively touching social reality was indeed an impediment to traditional ideas. Nevertheless, Laozi's contribution to philosophy deserves respect. In the history of Chinese philosophy, Laozi was the first philosopher who worked out a philosophical system with epistemology, and also the first philosopher who posed the question of the relation between knowing and doing. Though his answer to it is wrong, it played a significant role in the development of epistemology in Chinese philosophy.

Han Fei (*c.* 280–233 BC) of the Legalist school, a representative of the new rising landlord class, appeared at the close of the Warring States Period. He advanced a materialist theory of knowing and doing in the process of elucidating Laozi's philosophy. He did so first in his two works *Jie Lao* (*Explanation of Laozi's Philosophy*) and *Yu Lao* (*Laozi's Philosophy in Illustrative Analogy*). The book of Laozi has many passages dedicated to the derivation of the material world from *Dao*. But in his commentaries Han Fei bypassed the issue by not quoting and elucidating even a sentence from Laozi. This is just like cutting off the head of Laozi's objective idealism, and so turning his philosophy into a form of materialism. This was the chief method Han Fei adopted in interpreting Laozi's theory. As for Laozi's important propositions like 'the further one goes away, the less one knows', 'knowing without doing' and 'understanding without looking', Han Fei gave his own explanation of them. For instance, he said,

> A divine sage has no fixed rule for his action. He can know things either close to or far from him. To quote Laozi's words, it is 'knowing without doing'. He is also able to discern the obverse phase or the reverse of a thing; this is, in Laozi's words, called 'understanding without seeing'. The sage also possesses the capacity of engaging in all affairs in concordance with the trend of times, of performing meritorious feats in accordance with the circumstances concerned, of winning victory by grasping the inherent nature of all things on earth. This is what Laozi calls 'accomplishment without exertion'.[3]

Obviously, this explanation by Han Fei of Laozi is a misinterpretation. However, his interpretation is still considered a very great contribution as far as the development of philosophy is concerned. Han Fei affirms the idea of knowing derived from doing, and doing being a foundation of knowing; and he advocates the viewpoint of all-sidedness in, and of preventing one-sidedness from, any observation.

In the pre-Qin Dynasty (i.e. before 221 BC), no definite opinion about the relation of knowing and doing was expressed by the Confucian school; and it was unsympathetic towards Laozi's philosophy in general. Confucius said, 'The knowledge one obtains immediately after one's birth is superior, while that which one derives from learning is inferior.'[4] The latter, so-called 'learning', is derived from books, not from practice. This is, in effect, also a 'knowing without doing' view. Mencius (*c.* 372–289 BC) carried the point to extremes by forming the theory of 'intuitive ability' and 'intuitive knowledge'; by the former he meant 'ability without learning', and by the latter 'knowledge without reflecting'.

In the Song Dynasty, the Confucian school of idealist philosophy founded by Cheng Hao (AD 1032–85) and Zhuxi (1230–1300) started a wide-ranging discussion over the problem of the relation between knowing and doing. They stated in unequivocal terms their belief in 'knowing first and doing next', which is, of course, again a belief in 'knowing without doing'. Cheng Hao, however, coining a new idea, said:

> The knowledge derived from hearing and seeing with ears and eyes is not in common with that which is inborn; the former is obtained through the intercourse between the internal subject and the external object, and not a knowledge innately endowed in the subject itself.

> Today, the so-called knowledge that enables man to understand all phenomena of nature, and to acquire many a skill and talent is confined in this category.[5]

Such knowledge, in Cheng Hao's view, is not inborn with a person's brain; it is acquired by contact between sense-organs and external objects, that is, it comes from hearing and seeing. This view is directly opposed to that of Laozi – 'Without going out of doors, one can know all that happens in the world; without looking elsewhere, one can understand what one wants to understand'; it also differs greatly from the traditional ideas of the Confucian school. Still, he accepted a 'knowledge of morality' which mainly refers to feudal ethics and morality. He spoke of this kind of 'knowledge' as 'being acquired not by means of learning'; it is innate in one's nature, and can be enhanced and developed to a full degree through one's subjective cultivation or refinement. Cheng Hao's philosophy is a kind of monistic objective idealism, but this view does show a dualistic inclination.

Wang Fuzhi (1619–92), living between the end of the Ming Dynasty and the beginning of the Qing Dynasty, brought his philosophy to maturity in the early Qing era; but, as viewed from the developmental perspective of philosophical history, it ought to be considered as pertaining to a philosophy of the Ming Dynasty. His thought reflected the demands of the early stages of capitalism. He suggested that the ruling class should have resort to heavy taxation as a measure by which to launch an economic attack on land-leasing landlords on the one hand, and to give encouragement to land-holding peasants on the other; the latter included land-managing landlords (employing both short and long-term labour), who also represented a tendency towards the beginnings of capitalism. Wang Fuzhi, in the drama *Dragon-boat Meet*, written in the later years of his life, consciously broke with the feudal ethical code. It was by this social background that he was encouraged to make a major contribution to promoting philosophy to a high peak in feudal times. In the history of Chinese philosophy, Wang was the first philosopher to formulate the thought 'knowing first and doing next; doing is the source and foundation of knowing', though he had not come to understand the social significance of practice, and was not in a position to explain the developmental course of moral nature correctly; hence some idealist impurities in his thought remained. Generally speaking, his view of the relation of knowing and doing falls into the category of materialism. He said, 'A gentleman can never have his scholarship separated from his action.'[6] This thinking is of great help to Chinese philosophers in a new age in developing a Marxist-Leninist epistemology.

IS IT EASY TO KNOW AND HARD TO DO, OR THE REVERSE?

Shang Shu: Shuo Ming,[7] which according to tradition is a historical document of the ancient Yin Dynasty, records an old proposition: 'It is not difficult to know, but to do.' This aphorism has since played an influential role in the political and intellectual life of China. Yan Ruoqu (1636–1704), a famous scholar of the Qing Dynasty, wrote a commentary on the legendary classic called *Gu Wen Shang Shu Shu Zheng* (*A Textual Investigation of the Ancient Shang Shu*), in which he proved that the existing text of *Shang Shu*, including the three chapters of *Shuo Ming*, was a forgery by someone from the Jin Dynasty (AD 265–420), because the original *Shang Shu* discovered in the Han Dynasty (206 BC – AD 23) had been lost long ago. The forgery is, however, not sheer fabrication by the forger: he based his creation on materials (such as certain sentences and passages and their sense) which he collected from historical records and Confucian literature of the Han Dynasty and pre-Jin Dynasty, and put together in a logical order. Regarding the old proposition 'It is not difficult to know, but to do', some similar records are also seen in *Zuo Zhuan* (*A Critical History*), written by Zuo Qiuming at the beginning of the Spring and Autumn Period. By the close of the same period, the theory of 'easy to know and hard to act' had already been put forward by certain scholars, probably contemporaries of Laozi. This was also a reflection of a new era taking the place of an old one, i.e. of a time when a new thought was in vogue: to have knowledge already gained is not difficult, but to act upon it is difficult. And that was the very age in which the old knowledge was colliding with the new reality. Therefore, those who clung to the old spoke of 'easy to know and hard to do', laying stress upon 'hard to do'. From a philosophical perspective, though the position is wrong as a whole, it contains a useful insight, namely that to have knowledge (mainly book-learning) already gained by predecessors is much easier than to act upon it. So, often '(people) talk about war on paper' and 'they have knowledge, yet cannot put it into practice.' Knowledge like this is, of course, incomplete. To make book-learning become one's own knowledge in reality, one has still to combine it with practice.

The question of 'easy to know and hard to do' had attracted much attention from learned circles in the pre-Qin period. Then, from the Jin Dynasty onwards, the ancient *Shang Shu* served as an authoritative scripture of successive imperial dynasties; and 'It is not difficult to know, but to do' became holy dogma, having much effect on people's ideology, right up to the Northern Song Period (AD 960–1127), when the idealist philosopher Cheng Hao asserted that 'to do is difficult and to know is also the same'. He said,

> Before taking an action, one must have knowledge of that action beforehand. Therefore, it is not only difficult to act, but also to have knowledge that guides one's action. A person who wants to go to the capital has to know beforehand which gate to go out of and which road to take, and then he acts on what he knows. If he has no knowledge of the gate and road, how can he take action in spite of his having subjectively in mind a desire to go.[8]

In the Song Period, emerging capitalism was pounding at the gates of the feudal system and the feudal ideology; and in order to maintain and strengthen its feudal reign, the ruling class required a new theory at its service. This was the historical background to Cheng Hao's dedicating himself to establishing his philosophical system of subjective idealism. Cheng Hao's 'to know is also difficult' was indeed uttered with real feeling. What he meant by 'to know is also difficult' was the difficulty of creating and attaining new knowledge. This view contains an epistemological rationality in itself. From then on, political and intellectual circles generally held that 'to know is as difficult as to act', until Sun Yatsen unequivocally put forward his objection against the theory.

Regarding Sun Yatsen's philosophy, it is still uncertain whether it is basically a form of dualism, as interpreted by some, or a form of materialism, as understood by others. In respect to the relation between knowing and doing, he held the view 'difficult to know and easy to do.' On account of the failure of the 1911 revolution, he felt keenly the necessity for an intensification of studies in theory. In the winter of 1918 he wrote a philosophical work – his famous book *Psychological Reconstruction* (also known as *Sun Wen's Doctrine*) – dealing especially with the problem of knowing and doing. He considered the view 'It is difficult to know and to do' as harmful, saying that the might of this idea was ten thousand times that of the feudal rule of the Qing Dynasty. And then he subjected the view that it is 'easy to know and hard to do' to merciless criticism. He said, 'The source of anxiety for us is our inability to know all things on earth; and if we can seek and obtain true knowledge by virtue of scientific principles, we shall encounter no difficulty whatsoever in practicing them.' Lenin had also said, 'Without revolutionary theory there can be no revolutionary movement.'[9] Such was the period in which Sun Yatsen was living after the failure of the 1911 revolution. He wrote *Psychological Reconstruction* in order to reinterpret 'the Three People's Principles' (i.e. Nationalism, Democracy and the People's Livelihood); and also worked out 'The National Plan', by which to develop the old democracy into a new 'Three People's Principles', including a policy of entering into alliance with the Soviet Union and the Chinese Communist Party, giving support to workers and peasants, equalizing land ownership and regulating capital. Though the theory of 'difficult to know and easy to do' as advanced by Sun Yatsen was not a scientific solution of the problem of the relation between knowing and doing, it did make a contribution epistemologically; and it did also play an important role at the time in heightening the people's revolutionary spirit and removing their fear of setbacks.

Mao Zedong, guided by Marxism, transcended the formulae 'easy to know and difficult to do' or 'difficult to know and easy to do.' He attached importance to practice on the one hand, and laid stress upon the motto 'Without revolutionary theory there can be no revolutionary movement' on the other. He advocated the combination of theory and practice, and thus addressed and solved the problem of the difficulty and easiness of knowing and doing.

HOW CAN A CRITERION BE WORKED OUT BY WHICH TO JUDGE IF 'KNOWLEDGE' IS TRUE OR FALSE?

In the Warring States Period, Mozi (468–376 BC), together with his Mohist school, had rendered a service of no less importance to the development of Chinese epistemology. This was a philosophical school and a political group representing the interest of small producers. They advocated social reform to be realized by supporting the demands of small producers. Mozi himself laid emphasis on practice and experience as well, and his unique contribution to philosophy was the so-called *San Biao* (three criteria) for how to judge a belief as correct or not. Mozi said,

> There are three criteria for judging utterance to be correct or not. What are these three criteria? Tracing its source, examining its situation and testing its practicality. Whence does one trace its source? By looking upwards, that is, by looking for historical events of emperors of past successive dynasties. How does one examine its situation? By looking downwards, that is, by minutely acquainting oneself with what the common people hear with their ears and see with their eyes. How does one test its practicality? This means that one has to apply one's own theory to state affairs such as criminal law and politics so as to see if it is in conformity with the interests of the nation and the people. These are the three criteria of speech, also called *San Biao*.

So, any utterance that corresponds to these three principles is regarded as correct; otherwise, as incorrect. Obviously, these three criteria are strongly tinged with empiricism.

The empirical tendency in Mozi's doctrine is greatly reduced in the later Mohist school. They posited, for the first time in the history of Chinese philosophy, distinctions between perceptual knowledge and rational knowledge, and founded a theory of reflection as well as a comparatively good cognitive theory of naïve materialism.[10] As to the question of a criterion used to judge a belief as being correct or not, the Mohist school worked out four concepts, *ming* (name), *shi* (fact), *he* (correspondence) and *wei* (action), and their relationships. *Ming* is a name used to demonstrate a thing; *shi* is the thing described by that name; *he* means conformity, i.e. the name conforming to that thing; *wei* means a decision to act upon it. Again, *ming* is a conception and knowledge of something, and so the phrase *ming shi ou* means a name corresponding to a thing. How can we judge that a name corresponds to a thing? That will be decided according to what would result from an action. This is a kind of naïve approach to putting a cognition to the test in practice, getting rid of the empirical view of 'minutely acquainting oneself with what the common people hear with their ears and see with their eyes.' It has not, of course, solved or even referred to the problem of the contradiction between a short-term result and a long-term result or a partial result and an overall result, and hence it cannot avoid empiricism completely.

After the founding of the great feudal empire by Qin Shi Huang (the first emperor of the Qin Dynasty, 206 BC – AD 23), Mozi's philosophy was almost buried in oblivion, and no longer taught; and thereafter no discussion was resumed over the question of setting up a criterion for judging whether a belief is right or not. It was not until the arrival of the new age that Mao Zedong solved the problem in his work *On Practice*, written in accordance with Marxist principles. The book of *Mozi* as handed down to us had many bamboo slips (pages) misplaced and words written incorrectly; in particular, the section *Mo Jing* is simply unintelligible. The effort to collate and edit *Mozi*, initiated by the scholars of the Qian Jia school (1736–96) in the Qing Dynasty and continued for several generations, succeeded in making even the difficult *Mo Jing* comparatively readable. In recent decades, the study of the latter carried out by Chinese scholars has yielded good results, and it will play a positive role in encouraging studies in the subject of epistemological development.

SHOULD KNOWING OR DOING BE GIVEN PRIORITY; AND SHOULD THE TWO BE COMBINED OR UNIFIED?

According to universal logic, a materialist philosopher taking 'doing' as the basis of knowledge must set great store by 'doing'; while, conventionally speaking, an idealist philosopher advocating the divorce of 'knowing' from 'doing' ought to respect 'knowing' and despise 'doing'. Nevertheless, the latter case turns out to be rather complicated. For instance, Cheng Hao of the Northern Song Period, whose epistemology was on the whole idealist, respected knowing and despised doing. Zhuxi of the Southern Song Period, who was also an idealist, believed in 'knowing first, and doing next'; and at the same time he also asserted with certainty that 'doing is of most importance'. He said, 'Erudition alone is not as valuable as useful knowledge; merely possessing useful knowledge is not better than putting into action knowledge already obtained; 'True, reading is compulsory, yet it is secondary when compared with action', and 'Exertion dedicated to learning lies in one's practice' and 'lies in trying one's best to act upon the knowledge already gained.'[11] The respect Zhuxi had for 'doing' is not inconsistent with his 'knowing first and doing next'; and, in essence, there is no discrepancy between it and Cheng Hao's 'to respect knowing and to despise doing'; the latter is said simply from an epistemological viewpoint, i.e. to mean that the most important 'knowledge of a moral nature' does not come from practice, and so 'doing' is not important for 'knowing'. Zhuxi's 'respect for doing' does not embrace any important role that it plays in the course of forming an epistemology; it means only his emphasis upon action after having knowledge. The real aim of his theory was still 'to preserve heaven's law and to quench man's desire' so that people would put the knowledge of feudal morality into action. This was the background of his statement: 'The more forcible the practice, the more progressive the knowledge; the solider the action, the wiser the awareness.'[12] Though what he meant here by 'knowledge' was feudal morality, and by 'action', acting upon that feudal morality, if we were to discard the content or subject matter of the statement and draw a general meaning from it, then it would be very conducive to developing a dialectic of knowing and doing.

Wang Yangming (1472–1528), whose idealist philosophy was called 'the science of mind', set out a theory of 'combining knowing and doing into one.' He was opposed to Zhuxi, who made knowing and doing two different entities. He said, 'Knowing is the origin of doing, while doing is the realization of knowing.' But what he meant by 'doing' was not action directed to changing the objective world, but an emotional activity. He proceeded to illustrate his assertion with an example: when a person sees a good colour with his eyes, his seeing is called 'knowing'; and as soon as he has a liking for the colour, his liking is called 'doing'. This as described by him is such a state: 'When knowledge directly reaches the truth and reality, it becomes an action.' Here 'truth and reality' means a mentality completely devoid of man's selfish desire. His so-called 'doing' is hence actually no less than an endeavour for moral cultivation or refinement, and what he meant by 'combining knowing and doing in one' is in essence trying to attain to the object – 'To preserve heaven's law and to quench man's desire.' Philosophically speaking, he retreats from true 'doing' by his theory. This is wrong, of course. Be that as it may, his criticism of 'knowing first and doing next' and of the view that 'doing should be respected while knowing should be despised' still holds good for the theory of knowing and doing to be developed correctly.

Wang Fuzhi, having criticized Wang Yangming's 'combination of knowing and doing into one', proposed a preliminary view of the 'unity of knowing and doing'. As to the theory of 'doing first and knowing next', he held that 'doing' was a basis of 'knowing', and accepted 'knowing' as being formed on the basis of 'doing'. To this he added a new theory: 'Knowing and doing complement each other by their respective functions.' As knowing and doing have their respective functional effects, he considered a cognition to be an endless process beginning from doing to knowing and again from knowing to doing. This is a simple view of the unity of knowing and doing conforming to a process of dialectical cognition. Of course, he did not, and also could not, have a view of historical materialism as the basis of his theory; he failed to characterize 'doing' as a social practice, and also failed to apply this view of the 'unity of knowing and doing' to explaining the formation and function of man's moral notions.

In the new era, namely in the period of the new democratic revolution, Mao Zedong, guided by Marxist philosophy, summed up the discussion on knowing and doing in Chinese history, especially the practical experience of the Chinese revolutionary movement; and hence successfully formulated a scientific theory of the unity of knowing and doing:

> Discover the truth through practice, and again through practice verify and develop the truth. Start from perceptual knowledge and actively develop it into rational knowledge; then start from rational knowledge and actively guide revolutionary practice to change both the subjective and the objective world. Practice, knowledge, again practice, and again knowledge. This form repeats itself in endless cycles, and with each cycle the content of practice and knowledge rises to a higher level. Such is the whole of the dialectical-materialist theory of knowledge, and such is the dialectical-materialist theory of the unity of knowing and doing.[13]

NOTES

1 *Laozi*, ch. 47.
2 ibid., ch. 52.
3 *Han Feizi Yu Lao.*
4 *Lun Yu Ji Shi.*
5 *Er Cheng Ti Shu.*
6 *Zhangzi Zheng Meng Zhu.*
7 *Shang Shu* (*An Ancient Collection of Historical Records*) is said to have been written in the Yin Dynasty (*c.* 1324 – *c.* 1066 BC). *Shuo Ming* (*On Life*) is one part of the records.
8 *Er Cheng Yi Shu.*
9 See V. I. Lenin, *Conspectus of Hegel's The Science of Logic* (September-December 1914), *Collected Works* (Moscow, 1958), vol. XXXVIII, p. 203.
10 *Mozi Fei Ming.*
11 *Zhuzi Wen Ji.*
12 ibid.
13 *On Practice*, in *Mao Tse-tung's Selected Works* (Beijing: People's Publishing House, 1966), p. 285. For an English version, see Mao Tse-tung, *Four Essays On Philosophy* (Beijing: Foreign Languages Press, 1966), p. 20.

FURTHER READING

Chan, Wing-tsit (1963) *A Source Book in Chinese Philosophy*, Princeton: Princeton University Press.

Creel, H. G. (1953) *Chinese Thought: From Confucius to Mao Tse-tung*, Chicago: University of Chicago Press.

Fung, Yu-lan (1937) *A History of Chinese Philosophy*, Peiping: Henri Vetch.

—— (1948) *A Short History of Chinese Philosophy*, New York: Macmillan.

Graham, A. C., (1978) *Later Mohist Logic, Ethics and Science*, Hong Kong: The Chinese University Press; London: School of Oriental and African Studies.

—— (1992) *Two Chinese Philosophers: The Metaphysics of the Brothers Ch'eng*, La Salle, Illinois: Open Court.

Lao Tzu (1935) *The Way and its Power*, trans. by Arthur Waley, London: Allen & Unwin.

Sun Yatsen (1936) *The Three Principles of the People*, trans. by Frank W. Price, Shanghai: Commercial Press.

Wang Yangming (1963) *Instructions for Practical Living, and Other Neo-Confucian Writings of Wang Yang-ming*, trans. by Wing-tsit Chan, New York: Colombia University Press.

Zhuxi (1922) *The Philosophy of Human Nature, by Chiu Hsi*, trans. by J. Percy Bruce, London: Probsthain.

32

MORALS AND SOCIETY IN CHINESE PHILOSOPHY

Wang Rui Sheng

From its beginnings, morality has always been the focal point of Chinese traditional philosophical study. Chinese philosophy merges morality, epistemology and metaphysics into a single whole. The fact that morality and socio-political issues were treated together has its roots in the following factors: first, the long-standing existence of a patriarchal clan system linked to consanguinity; and second, an autocratic monarchy which was highly centralized and formed on the basis of a scattered natural economy.

The relation of morals and society in Chinese philosophy can be traced back to Zhou *li* (the norms of social activity in the Zhou Dynasty) and to Zhou music. Zhougong was the first ethicist in Chinese history, and laid the foundation of an ethics of a slave society. But an integrated theory of ethics can be found only in the Spring and Autumn Period (770–476 BC) and the Warring States Period (475–221 BC).

MORALS AND SOCIETY IN THE PRE-QIN DYNASTY

In Chinese history, this period is one of transition from a slave to a feudal system. The major social changes and the formation of various philosophical theories provided the necessary conditions for the genesis of ethical theories. There are four schools of ethical thought in this period: Confucianism, Mohism, Daoism and Legalism. Confucianists and Mohists advocate moral education and ruling by means of *ren* (humanity) and *yi* (righteousness). They are therefore the advocates of rule by virtue. The Legalists, on the other hand, deny the effectiveness of moral education and emphasize the rule of law alone. The Daoist school aims at the individual's tranquillity, some Daoists even completely separating themselves from social existence. These four schools of thought dispute with each other on the following problems; first, egoism and altruism; second, utilitarianism and anti-utilitarianism; third, consequentialism and the nature of motivation.

Confucianism

The central idea of Confucianism is to see morality, as in humanity and righteousness (*ren* and *yi*), as the standard for human activity. Characteristic of Confucianists' ethics, too, is the dominion of morality over every other field.

There are two sides to the relation of morals and society in Confucius' works. One is that morality is merged with social and political issues. Confucius assumes that moral activity should be divided into two aspects: *dao* and *de*. In his ethics, the meaning of *dao* is objective social norms. One of the necessary conditions of moral activity is the observation of these social norms, such as *li* (the propriety of one's social activity), *zhong* (loyalty), *xiao* (filial piety), *yi* (righteousness) and *xin* (confidence). *De* is the inner life of man, his passions and beliefs. The other necessary condition of moral activity is that a man do his best so to cultivate himself as to observe consciously these social norms. In consequence he can become a man of moral integrity and can then be a good ruler.

Those social norms which embody Confucius' *dao* are ethical as well as socio-political. They reflect not only the social hierarchy of his times, but also the ethical ideas with which Confucius underpinned this hierarchy. For instance, the thesis that 'humanity means self-mastery and the return to ritual'[1] is a moral principle and a political directive as well. According to this moral principle, humanity cannot be in contradiction with *li*, the hierarchy which separates the noble from the base. That is to say, individuals' ethical activity cannot go beyond the scope which their positions in the hierarchy have already defined.

Another side of the relationship between morals and society in Confucius' philosophy is that morality is prior to all other things. In Confucianism, moral education is a preparation for governing and politics itself 'means correcting one's activity'.[2] Morality is much more important than economics. Fan Chi, a student of Confucius, applied himself to planting, but he was reproached by his teacher, for planting is not what a gentleman should do.[3] When Zi Kong, another student, asked a question about politics, Confucius replied that given the choice between an army, a means of subsistence and morality, he preferred the latter.[4] In Confucianism, morality is the end of education. Studying morals is prior to other knowledge, because a learned man without virtue is not worthy of praise. Such is Confucius' standard for evaluating men: he bestowed praise on his student Yan Hui not for his knowledge but for his high character.[5]

After Confucius himself the most important Confucianists in the ethics of the Pre-Qin Dynasty are Mencius and Xunzi. If the special characteristic of Confucius' own ethics is the combination of *li* (propriety) and *ren* (humanity), Mencius and Xunzi each developed one of the two. Mencius emphasized humanity and combined it with *yi* (righteousness), these two virtues being taken to be prior to all others. Xunzi emphasized propriety and took it to be the highest standard of human activity. Mencius thereby emphasized mental self-cultivation, and Xunzi the role of objective social and moral norms.

Confucianism objects to the self-seeking theme of Legalism, assuming instead that people with high ideals will be self-sacrificing and, if need be, will die a glorious death for righteousness. Such a concept of righteousness and interest is anti-utilitarian and emphasizes motive rather than effect.

The reason why the ethics of Confucianism has this characteristic is simply that China was torn apart by rival principalities. Confucianists therefore opposed violence, which caused great suffering for the masses. They persuaded the nobles or householders not to indulge in slaughter and opposed the new rising force seizing power by violent means.

Mohism

Advocating humanity (*ren*) and righteousness (*yi*), taking them as the standard of human activity and assuming that these virtues are not only characteristics of the sage, but also the most important principles of governing a state – these are common to Confucianism and Mohism. Nevertheless, Mohism has its own account of a series of moral norms.

Mozi explained *ren* as *jianai* (universal love).[6] This word has three senses. First, love without grades: a sense far removed from that which Confucius had given it. To be sure, in Confucius' works *ren* means humanity, but still it is a graded love giving preference to the claims of kinship. Not only that, but Mozi assumed that Confucianists spoke of benevolence only because they needed the means of subsistence offered by the masses. That would amount to loving the labouring masses as if they were cattle. Mozi said that *jianai* means love for others as much as love for oneself. There are no grades in love. One loves another not for the sake of making use of him, for loving men is not the same as loving horses. Second, advocating *jian* instead of *bie* (separation),[7] Mozi assumed that people opposing one another is the root of social confusion. Therefore he was against *bie*, that is, he sought to eliminate the insult and humiliation which originated from hierarchical discrimination. *Jianai* is the means to attain this goal. Third, you must love others so that they will reciprocate that love.

Jianai originated from Mozi's concept of the universe. According to his works, the universe is a whole (*jian*) from which parts and individuals can be separated though the latter still exist inside the former.[8] From his concept of the universe Mozi deduced the social concept which assumes that society is a whole. So people should not strive against each other but love each other and benefit each other accordingly.

Jianai is a moral and also a political principle. In accordance with it, Mozi opposed warfare and proposed *jianai* as a guiding principle of political affairs. This is called 'the politics of righteousness'. In this political life, there is a harmonious relation between the big and the small, the many and the few, the strong and the weak, the noble and the base, the rich and the poor. In contrast to this, the politics guided by the principle of *bei* is called 'the politics of power'.[9]

Jianai does not mean eliminating the line between the noble and the base, but is a morality of improving or adjusting the relationship between them. One should not discriminate against the other. Therefore Mozi assumed that *li* only meant 'respect'. If one can practise *jianai*, one can benefit others. *Jianai* can be explained as mutual benefit, so *jianai* reflects the utilitarianism of Mohism.

Righteousness (*yi*) in Mozi differs from that in Confucius. There, *yi* meant that one's acts and ideas must conform to the hierarchical order. In contrast, Mozi explicates *yi* in terms of interests: for him, *yi* means that one does not infringe upon another's interests and the fruits of that person's labour.

As a moral category, *yi* is also a political standard for selecting officials. Mozi said that those who are able to benefit the masses should be on intimate terms with them and should be elevated to a high rank. Such a principle is quite contrary to that of Confucius, who thought that those of a high rank should be senior officials and that they should be on intimate terms only with their equals. The results of practising these two principles are quite different. In the former case, the result will be that officials cannot hold posts for ever, and the common people will not always live a hard life. A senior post depends upon one's abilities. In the latter case, rewards are not meted out to an able and virtuous person and punishments are not for the vicious person.

In Mozi's ethics, frugality is a major virtue. It involves a simple standard of living, economical funeral rites, and the rejection of musical entertainment. This point of view has been criticized as lacking an aesthetic dimension and as hostile to culture. In fact, Mozi did not say that listening to good music does not bring mental enjoyment, that living in the magnificent palace is not a comfort and that eating delicious food is not a delightful thing. He assumed this austere attitude to music only because providing music causes poverty. For instance, ten thousand musicians were kept by Qi Kang Gong (the monarch of Qi state, 404 BC). In order to maintain his musical enjoyment, his subjects had to lead a poor life. Mozi's proposed three days funeral rites instead of three years is also based on a concern for the poor. Confucius also talked about living frugally, but, according to his beliefs, a noble way of life is not luxurious if enjoyment does not exceed what the feudal ritual allows. Mozi firmly opposed this way of life, because it wastes a great deal of society's property.

A utopian characteristic is prominent in Mozi's concept of morality; therefore a superhuman or celestial power is needed to guarantee its realization. So the will of heaven (*tianzi*) is the standard for evaluating the activity of the human race – whether it is virtue or vice. And *Jianai* and *yi* (humanity and righteousness) are to be regarded as the intention of heaven. The fact that Tian Zi and Ming Gui (the understanding ghost) are the corner-stones of *jian* and *yi* is consistent with the social psychology of the small producers whom Mohists represent, a psychology dominated by a traditional sense of religion.

In the later period of Mohism, *jianai* is developed into altruism and the moral principle of Mozi's utilitarianism is developed into the principle of activity that follows interests and avoids harm, that selects the largest profit possible and chooses the smallest harm. But this does not mean that moral activity should be based on personal pleasure and pain. On the contrary, Mohists still insist that the largest interest is the interest of all the people.

Legalism

Legalists advocated the rule of law, that is, the principle of conforming the subject's activity to the law and of rewarding or punishing the subject in accordance with the law. Legalists opposed the institution of propriety (*li*) of a slave society, and trying to rule by means of moral education. One of the earliest Legalists was Quan Zhong (?-645 BC), and in the Warring States Period major Legalists included Shang Yang (390–338 BC) and Han Fei (280–233 BC).

The rise of Legalism in the Warring States Period is the product of political reform. The new landlord class opposed the hereditary hierarchy and advocated establishing a new hierarchy according to a warrior's prowess. As to the masses, what Legalists requested of them was cultivation and fighting. This policy was to meet the need of annexing wars between dukes and princes. And these reform measures were to be sustained by law, not by virtue. Their logic was that if you wanted to win a battle you could not depend upon morality. Therefore the dispute between Confucianists and Legalists was not whether we should have morality, but that in the matter of governing a state Legalists preferred to rule by law rather than by morality.

The early Legalist Shang Yang assumed that if you really wanted to attain morality, first of all you must depend on punishment. This point of view is based on taking the nature of human beings as vicious, on seeing men as afraid of death and selfish. Therefore you could not cultivate the masses or bring them to fight except by punishment. And the prerequisites of *zhong* (loyalty of subjects to the ruler) and *xiao* (filial piety) are cultivation and fighting. So in essence, to rule over the masses with punishment is to take care of them and get them back to righteousness. To please the masses with what they like, as the Confucianist assumed, would on the contrary lead them to pursue injustice.

This overestimation of rule by law led the early Legalists to praise violence. Han Fei (the late Legalist) rejected moral education as well. Nevertheless, the Legalists of Qi state, for example Quan Zhong, advocated the incorporation of law and virtue. In this, he absorbed something of the Confucian view. Quan Zhong assumed that propriety is in essence making rules governing people's activity so that they conform to the hierarchy. And the function of law is to proclaim the hierarchy in ordinances, which demand the submission of everyone without regard to their will, that is, to unify the thoughts and activities of the people by means of punishment. So morals and law are unified on the basis of upholding the feudal hierarchy. Quan Zhong proposed that *li*, *yi*, *lian*, *chi* (propriety, righteousness, honesty, sense of shame) are the four guarding principles of the existence and development of the state, which emphasizes the social role of morals at the level of consolidating the regime. Since the viewpoints of the Legalists of Qi state synthesize the theories of Shang Yang and the Confucianists, they could promote a more comprehensive and reasonable policy and uphold the new hierarchy.

The essence of the Legalists' morality is anti-egoism. Unlike the Confucianists, whose anti-egoism argument is based on patriarchal morals, the Legalists base their argument on human nature. That is to say, in nature man follows his interests and avoids harm. And from this the Legalists draw the conclusion that giving up selfishness and adopting a public morality provides a standard of evaluating the individual's activity, of judging whether it is virtuous or vicious. Here, 'public' means the interests of the centralized feudal and autocratic state. A state's interests are equal to the interests of the monarch, for politically he is the general representative of the landlord class. The personal interest of the subject is reasonable only when it conforms to that of the monarch. If it conflicts with that of the monarch, that is 'selfishness', which is the root of all vices. The submission of the individual to the state is applicable to the monarch as well, for he is not allowed to put the state in danger by his selfishness or his patriarchal love.

The Legalists had a deep grasp of the relationship between morality and society. Shang Yang noted that if the land was wasted and the granary was empty, people would not observe the proprieties and there could not be filial piety.[10] Quang Zhong also noted that if the granary was full, then people would comprehend the rituals.[11] From these observations the Legalists generalized a dialectical concept of history, one which identified the root of social norms of morality and political institutions in the living conditions of an epoch.

Daoism

The major representatives of Daoism are Laozi and Zhuangzi.[12] Concerning the problems of morals and society, the general trend of the Daoist school is one of detachment from secular life and mere survival – that is the highest moral principle of Daoism.

The philosophical meaning of *dao* in the Daoist school is the origin of the world, and its meaning in ethics is the common norm of human activity. Laozi said '*Dao* models itself on nature.'[13] Since the understanding Daoists have of nature is the opposite of artificiality (*ren wei*) and efficiency or intervention (*youwei*), the word 'nature' here means natural in its true colours, and a non-intervention (*wuwei*) or desireless condition (*wuyu*) as well.[14] *Dao* as the highest standard of human activity means taking non-intervention as the highest virtue of man. On the basis of this moral concept, Laozi criticized the Confucianists, asserting that their morality was the result of giving up the 'great *dao*'. *Ren* and *yi*, the moral concepts of Confucius, are in contradiction with the nature of non-intervention. Laozi said 'The sage is far from *ren* (humanity); he takes people as *chou gou*' (a dog made up of straw).[15] This metaphor tells us that the concept of *ren* and *yi* in Confucianism is not the real morality, because it ignores the principle of non-intervention. A true sage does not talk about humanity and bestow favours on the masses, for that will merely enlarge their desires. A man of real morality would never perceive himself as being moral and he would not pursue anything either, including morality itself.[16] Of course, Laozi still has a kind of morality, a morality of anti-utilitarianism. The virtues which Laozi praised highly are: the greatest esteem for weakness, an acceptance of things as they are, never being the first, never contending for anything. (One should simply esteem oneself far more important than the whole world.)[17] Laozi's concept of morality is based on a concept of human nature in which man is ignorant and in a desireless condition by nature. Its characteristic aim is to make for a complete serene life. And the mental serenity of the individual is the highest virtue and the greatest happiness. The aim of Laozi's concept of morality is not to adjust the relationship between men, but to request individuals to part from the social relations in which they are situated.

Zhuangzi drew a form of nihilism from Laozi's moral concept of non-intervention. Like Laozi, Zhuangzi criticized human life from the viewpoint of *dao*. In Laozi, *dao* was a kind of general substance with neither figure nor name. And from it originated Zhuangzi's *dao*. He bestowed indifference on Laozi's *dao*, that is to say, *dao* is in a state where no disparity of things can be discerned. There is no difference between right and wrong. Zhuangzi assumed that originally *dao* was a state of indifference, and later on it suffered losses. And then there emerged the difference between left and right, matters of morality, settlements of disputes, and competition. In the state of the sage there is no need to pursue and dispute the differences and opposites. Therefore, in social life, it is not worth valuing moral relations and hierarchal differentiation between senior and junior, elite and lowly, monarch and subject, father and son, husband and wife, because they are the losses in *dao*. In Laozi there is still a kind of morality of pursuing social withdrawal, but in Zhuangzi there is no moral life at all. In Laozi, there is a kind of simple, plain and virtuous nature in the human race, but in Zhuangzi there is no need to differentiate between virtue and vice. To him, the only good character is one who keeps his heart in a state of indifference. The ideal personality which Zhuangzi pursued is the sage, the real man, the supreme man, and the divine man who detaches himself from secular life, restrains his feelings, gives up any human effort, and lets things go their own natural way.

MORALS AND SOCIETY FROM THE QIN TO THE TAN DYNASTIES (221 BC – AD 907)

The rise of the unified great empires of the Qin (221–207 BC) and Han (206 BC – AD 220) Dynasties terminated the state of a hundred schools of thought in the Warring States Period. The political unification required a mental unification. In this process, Mohism gradually declined, and Confucianism steadily assimilated Daoism and Legalism and came to occupy a dominant position in the ideological field. This synthesizing trend resulted in the policy of banning the contending of a hundred schools of thought and establishing the sole dominion of Confucianism, which was suggested by Dong Zhongshu (179–104 BC) and accepted by the Emperor Han Wu (140–87 BC).

In Dong Zhongshu's Confucianism, ethics merges with politics to a greater extent than ever on the basis of combining heaven and man into one, and emphasizing the interaction between them. According to Dong's ethics, moral norms and moral institutions originated directly from the will of heaven. Dong assumed that heaven was a mental substance endowed with purpose, will, and the moral character of humanity, which denounces the mistakes of the monarch through catastrophes so as to show its kindness. He also bestowed a moral character on the phenomena of nature in order to draw a social principle of morality from it. That is to say, secular human relations, moral norms, human morality, feelings and desires are all copies of heaven. The way of heaven is that supremacy belongs to *yang* (the positive principle), and *yin* (the negative principle) subordinates itself to *yang*, because *yin* is inferior. In secular life, monarch, father and husband belong to *yang* and subject, son and wife belong to *yin*. So monarch guides subject, father guides son, and husband guides wife. These are the so-called three cardinal guides, which represent three fundamental social relations or three social powers in Chinese feudal society. And they originate from heaven. Therefore the origin of morals in Dong's ethics has the characteristic of a theological teleology. Dong merged the three cardinal guides with five constant virtues (benevolence, righteousness, propriety, wisdom and fidelity) so as to construct a complete system of moral norms for feudal society. This system of morality pushed forward early Confucianists' moral determinism, representing a trend of anti-utilitarianism. Besides, it put undue emphasis on motive rather than effect. Dong's famous exhortation: 'uphold justice instead of working for your own interests; understand truth instead of counting achievement'[18] illustrates the dominant concept in Chinese feudal society.

In the eastern Han Dynasty, both Daoism and Buddhism were followed. Although Daoism as a religion has some historical relation with Laozi, it is still a mass religion. The creeds and doctrines of Daoism include some philosophical thought and ethical concepts. And yet, at the theoretical level, Daoism as a religion has not had an important effect on Chinese philosophy and ethics. Buddhism is quite different. The origin of Buddhism is in India, and it spread to China in the Han Dynasty. It is also a mass religion, but there is theoretical and speculative content in its scriptures which had a deep impact on Chinese philosophy, morality, culture and art. In the Sui (AD 581–618) and Tan (AD 618–907) Dynasties the spread of Buddhism in China took place in a period of great prosperity, and a series of religious factions which suited Chinese feudal society were formed. Later on, in the Song Dynasty, the theoretical viewpoints of these Buddhist factions were absorbed by Confucianism, and merged with it.

The discussion of morals and society in the Xuanxue of the Wei (AD 220–65) and Jin (AD 265–420) Dynasties reflects a new philosophical period of combination of Confucianism and Daoism. The word *Xuan* originated from Laozi,[19] and *Xuan-Xue* means a theory of studying subtle and obscure matters. The aim of this study is to solve the problem of the relation between nature and *mingjiao* (feudal propriety education and moral norms, the role of which is to confirm a person's status and to fix who is superior and who inferior).[20] Xuanxue originated in the work of Laozi and Zhuangzi, but is quite distinct. In Laozi and Zhuangzi, its fundamental feature was advocating nature and opposing the propriety education of Confucianism. In Xuanxue, the main purpose of most scholars is to reconcile the Daoist school and Confucianism, bringing them into harmony. But there is an exception. Ruan Ji (AD 210–63) and Ji Kong (AD 223–62) opposed this trend. Ji Kong proposed: 'Go beyond the propriety education and let things take their own course.' He criticized Zhou Kong (the sage of Confucianism) and Confucius. Meanwhile they also recognized that the propriety education of Confucianism can play the role of changing prevailing habits and customs. The reason for this paradoxical attitude is that their real purpose was to oppose the hypocritical propriety education of Confucianism which was propagated by the clique of Si Ma (ruler during the Jin Dynasty).

MORALS AND SOCIETY IN THE SONG, MING AND QING DYNASTIES (AD 907–1912)

In late Chinese feudal society, Confucianism absorbed the theoretical fruits of the Buddhist and Daoist schools and established itself as a new form of Confucianism, that is, Lixue in the Song (960–1279) and Ming (1368–1644) Dynasties. The effect of Buddhism on Lixue is worthy of mention here. The philosophical and ethical thoughts of many famous scholars in late Chinese feudal society are deeply affected by Buddhism, especially by Chan Buddhism (Chan Zong).[21] In Zhuxi (1130–1200) the theory of 'attaining knowledge through investigating matter' originated from Chan Buddhism's thesis of 'suddenly realizing the truth' (*dunwu*). In Wang Shouren (1472–1529) the thesis that 'nothing can exist outside one's heart' echoes Chan Buddhism's thought that 'the whole world originated from one's heart'.

The core of the system of Lixue is the theory of human nature. Therefore ethics is its noumenon, and its end as well. The essence of this theory is to confirm the general necessity of feudalism. In order to justify this, Lixue emphasized that *tianli* (the law of the universe) exists in *ren dao* (ethical principles), that is to say, the consciousness endowed with objective *li* is moral consciousness itself. As a matter of fact, the scholars of Lixue took these principles, and the laws of their specific society (that is, the late feudal society in China), as the law which dominated the universe. These social principles are what these scholars called *tianli*. Thus morality is more subordinated to social politics than ever before. The expression of *tianli* in human moral life is the three cardinal guides and the five constant virtues. Since secular principles and the norms of activity originated from *tianli*, they have nothing to do with utility, happiness and sensual pleasure. Therefore personal sensual desires which are unfit for feudal relationships are to be condemned as contradicting *tianli*. 'Deeply research *tianli* and suppress selfish desire';[22] 'Prefer to be starved to death rather than lose a woman's chastity';[23] 'The opposition of righteousness and interests'[24] – these claims reflect the fact that Lixue as a whole emphasized the determinative role of abstract noumenal *li* in feudal principles.

In the late Ming Dynasty, some seeds of capitalism sprouted in certain areas of China. Rifts can be found in the social relations of feudalism. Accordingly, a series of scholars broke away from traditional Confucianism. They included Huang Zongxi (1610–95), Gu Yanwu (1613–82), Wang Fuzi (1619–92), Yan Yuan (1635–1704) and Dai Zhen (1724–77), who were critical of the idle and abstract talk of Lixue, especially in the field of ethics and politics. Huang Zongxi said: 'Autocracy means that the subject only belongs to the monarch, and the object is the whole world.' 'The law of the world should be that supremacy does not belong to the imperial court, and inferiority does not belong to the masses.'[25] As to the concepts of righteousness and interests, these scholars of the enlightenment assumed that one should advocate the interests fitted to righteousness.[26] Wang Fuzi, one of the Lixue scholars in the early Qing Dynasty, protested against the negation of human sensual desires. He assumed that *tianli* is within human sensual desires: once you suppress the desire, you do the same to *tianli*.[27]

In modern times, the philosophy of morals and society has undergone a fundamental change. Traditional Confucianism emphasized moral education, persuading people to be sages, and being a sage meant submitting oneself to propriety education and neglecting personal freedom. That is completely unadapted to the new age. Starting from the middle of the nineteenth century, philosophy in modern times preserves the heredity of the enlightenment, all the more emphasizing the will, freedom and liberty of the individual. From the viewpoint of ethics, the 4 May Movement of 1919 was a great democratic movement protesting against feudal morality and striving for the liberation of the individual.

NOTES

1 *The Analects of Confucius* (*Lun-yu*) (Shanghai: Gu Ji Press, 1958), p. 130.
2 ibid., p. 136.
3 ibid., p. 142.
4 ibid., p. 133.
5 ibid., pp. 61, 63.
6 Mozi, *Mojing, Jing Shuo*, part 1, quoted from Tan Jie Fu, *Mo Bian Fa Wei* (Beijing: Zhong Hua Shu Ju, 1964), p. 83.
7 Mozi, *Tian Zhi* 2, quoted from Jiang Jen Feng, *Philosophy and Science of Mo Zi* (Beijing: Ren Min Press, 1981), p. 68.
8 Mozi, *Mojing, Jing Shuo* 1, op. cit.
9 ibid.
10 Shang Yang, *section 3. Shang Jun Shu* (Beijing: Zhong Hua Shu Ju, 1974), p. 80.
11 Quan Zhong, *Guan Zi Ji Xiao* (Beijing: Science Press, 1956).
12 There is a difference between the Daoist school (Daojia) and Daoism (Daojiao): the former is one of the major schools of ancient Chinese philosophy, and the latter is a kind of traditional Chinese religion which did not appear until the Eastern Han Dynasty. Daoism originated from ancient sorcery, and its predecessors were necromancy and alchemy in the Qin and Han Dynasties.
13 Laozi, *Dao De Jing*, ch. 25, quoted from *Lao Zi Zheng Gu* (Beijing: Gu Ji Press, 1956), p. 61.
14 ibid., ch. 3, p. 10.
15 ibid., ch. 5, p. 12. *Chuo gou* is a sacrifice made of straw and offered ceremonially to the god, after which it is taken away and trodden on or burned. 'Taking people as *chou gou*' here means non-interference with them.
16 ibid., ch. 38, p. 85.
17 ibid., chs 8, 46, 67, 76, pp. 21, 102, 136, 144.
18 Ban Gu, *Han Shu, Biography of Dong Zhongshu* (Beijing: Zhong Hua Shu Ju, 1962).
19 Laozi, *Dao De Jing* (He Nan: He Nan Ren Min Press, 1980), ch. 1, p. 21.
20 *Mingjiao* and nature are categories of Xuanxue, originating from the philosophies of Confucius and Lao Zi in the pre-Qin Dynasty. The proper interpretation of these categories has a very long history.
21 Chan Buddhism is a type of Chinese Buddhism. Its fundamental idea emphasizes mental understanding. Since everybody can reach the Buddha without long religious practice, the key to moving from the secular to the Buddha lies in leaving perplexity behind and reaching the Buddha by sudden realization. This constitutes a great reform in the history of Buddhism.
22 Zhuxi, *Zhuzi Yulei*, vol. 13, quoted from Zhang Dai Lian, *Outline of Chinese Philosophy* (Beijing: Chinese Social Science Press, 1982), p. 457.
23 Cheng Yi, *Yishi*, vol. 22, quoted from Ren Ji Yu, *History of Chinese Philosophy* (Beijing: Ren Min Press, 1966), para 3, p. 229.
24 Cheng Hao, *Yulu*, vol. 11, quoted from Zhang Dai Lian, op. cit., p. 339.
25 Huang Zongxi, *Mingyidaifenlu* (Beijing: Gu Ji Press, 1955).
26 Yan Yuan said that Mencius' criticism of interests was really only aimed at exploitation by the feudal ruler. 'In fact, interest included in justice is required of a gentleman. The later Confucianists are mistaken when they say "Uphold righteousness instead of interest."' In order to correct this mistake, he proposed the new principle: 'Uphold righteousness for its interest; understand truth for its achievement' (Yan Yuan, *Sishi zhengwo*, quoted from Zhang Dai Lian, op. cit., p. 398.
27 Wang Fuzi, *Zhouyi Waizhuan* 4 (Beijing: Zhong Hua Shu Ju, 1977).

FURTHER READING

Dong Zhongshu (1975) *Chung Qiu Fan Lu*, Beijing: Zhong Hua Shu Ju.
Guo Moruo (1954) *Shipipanshu*, Beijing: Ren Min Press.
Huang Zongsi (1955) *Ming Yi Dai Fan Lu*, Beijing: Gu Ji Press.
Hu Shi (1919) *Outline of History of Chinese Philosophy*, Shanghai: Shang Wu Yin Shu Guan.
Kang You Wei (1956) *Da Tong Shu*, Beijing: Gu Ji Press.
Laozi (1980) *Laozi Daodejing*, He Nan: Ren Min Press.
Mencius (1962) *Meng Zi*, Beijing: Zhong Hua Shu Ju.
Mozi (1986) *Mozi Xian Gu*, Beijing: Zhong Hua Shu Ju.
Ren Jiyu (1981) *Analects on Han Tang Buddhist Thoughts*, Beijing: Ren Min Press.
Ruan Ji (1958) *Daren Xiansheng Zhuan*, included in *Quan San Guo Wen*, Beijing: Zhong Hua Shu Ju.
Tang Yongtong (1962) *Wei-Jin Xuan-xue Lunguo*, Beijing: Zhong Hua Shu Ju.
Wang Fuzi (1977) *Zhouyi Waizhuan*, Beijing: Zhong Hua Shu Ju.
Xunzi (1974) Shanghai: Shanghai Ren Min Press.
Zhang Dainian (1987) *History of Chinese Philosophy*, Chinese Encyclopedia Press.
Zhuong Zhou (1961) *Zhong Zi Ji Xi*, Beijing: Zhong Hua Shu Ju.
Zhuxi (1957) *Si Shu Ji Xhu*, Beijing: Zhong Hua Shu Ju.
Zi Si (1936) *Zhongyong*, included in *Si Shu Wu Jing*, part 1, Shanghai: Shi Jie Shu Ju.

33

CONTEMPORARY CHINESE PHILOSOPHY

Francis Soo

The scope of 'contemporary Chinese philosophy' in this chapter is philosophies of the past hundred years or so. Two questions immediately arise: (1), what is the precise meaning of the term 'contemporary Chinese philosophy'? and (2), how does one approach it? First, there is, strictly speaking, no 'contemporary Chinese philosophy' which serves as an official philosophy, or a universally accepted Chinese philosophy, even though individual Chinese philosophers have emerged during this century. Second, there are perhaps as many approaches to studying contemporary Chinese philosophy as there are writers. Some may choose a historical approach by studying different historical periods; others may choose a topical approach; still others may choose to study individual Chinese philosophers.

The approach chosen here is twofold. First, I shall divide the ideas of various Chinese philosophers into three main philosophical orientations: neo-traditional Chinese philosophy, Sino-Western philosophy, and Chinese Marxism. Then within each of these three main philosophical groups, I shall discuss individual Chinese philosophers and their ideas.

HISTORICAL CONTEXT

However, in order to achieve a better understanding of contemporary Chinese philosophy, I should like to digress briefly to place it in historical context. No philosophy can develop in a historical and cultural vacuum; contemporary Chinese philosophy is no exception.

While the detailed history of contemporary China is extremely complex and contentious, there are three general factors that seem to be related to the development of contemporary Chinese philosophy.

1. If we had to use one phrase to characterize the history of contemporary China (ever since 1840), the title of one of John K. Fairbank's books, *The Great Chinese Revolution: 1800–1985* would be the best description.[1] The history of modern and

contemporary China has been a continuous process of revolution: the Opium War, uprisings, the revolution of 1911, wars among warlords, the Sino-Japanese War, the civil war between the Nationalists and the Communists, the revolution of 1949, and the Cultural Revolution, to name just a few. For China and her people, there has never been a peace which lasted long enough to bring about any change in her political, economic or educational institutions.

2. While the causes of the crisis of modern China (before 1911) were multiple and complex, one primary factor seemed to stand out: the impact of the encroachment of Western powers. For centuries prior to the Opium War, China had lived in isolation, peaceful and content, but convinced of her cultural superiority on the basis of Confucianist political philosophy. Then, China was defeated and humiliated militarily and economically, as well as politically and culturally. All this had a devastating impact on the consciousness of a generation of Chinese leaders and intellectuals. Consequently, it played a challenging role in most, if not all, philosophical discussions and reflections upon contemporary China.

3. The central focus of (modern and) contemporary China was the 'China problem', a rallying phrase for Chinese intellectuals. In retrospect, the China problem had two sides to it. The first was that some Chinese intellectuals considered it as a problem of 'poverty and weakness'.[2] That is, since China was (militarily) weak and (economically) poor, the solution was to make China strong and rich. The second was felt by other Chinese intellectuals to be much deeper than that. As Tang Jun-yi put it in the 1960s, it was a cultural problem caused by the loss of Confucianism, the very basis of the cultivation of one's moral self.[3]

Within this historical context, Chinese leaders and intellectuals have tried first to understand and reflect on the China problem, and then to save and reconstruct China. These efforts have resulted in many political programmes and theories as well as philosophies. Against this background we can understand why many, if not all, Chinese philosophies in the twentieth century have been political philosophies.

NEO-TRADITIONAL CHINESE PHILOSOPHY

During the last hundred years or so, in the midst of 'one hundred schools competing', one philosophical movement seemed to stand out: that of reviving traditional Chinese philosophy, especially Confucianism (and Neo-Confucianism). This was not easy or popular given the revolutionary mood sweeping through China at the turn of the nineteenth century. In some cases it meant political persecution. And yet, some Chinese philosophers were deeply convinced of the transcendental values of Chinese culture and traditional philosophy. At the same time, however, they also realized, through studying Western philosophy, that traditional Chinese philosophy needed reinterpretation and even rejuvenation. In this section, I shall present the philosophies of five such philosophers: Kang Youwei, Xiong Shili, Tang Junyi, Liang Shuming and Feng You-lan.

Kang Youwei (1858–1927)

Kang is commonly considered the last of the great traditional Confucian scholars. However, like most Confucianists of his time, Kang was also a reformer, attempting to put Confucianism into practice to save China. To achieve this purpose, he had not only to modify his interpretation of Confucius and his teachings, but also to present his own philosophical utopia, the World Commonwealth.

Reformer

As a reformer, Kang was Confucian and also modern. Being a Confucian scholar, he presented Confucius both as a great teacher-sage and as a political reformer for his time.[4] In so doing, he seemed to look to the past authority, Confucius and his teachings, to provide a philosophical foundation for his own political reforms. On the other hand, Kang was also a modern reformer. This is perhaps because his education included not only Confucianism, but also Buddhism and Christianity, as well as many other subjects like history, politics and science from the West. The Hundred-Day Reform (1898), which Kang successfully persuaded the idealistic young Emperor Guang Xu to launch, aimed at modernizing China's political, economic, educational, legal and military systems. Unfortunately, despite the rapid succession of edicts issued within a hundred days, the reform movement failed because of the strong opposition from the ultra-conservative forces led by the Empress Dowager Ci Xi. In the end, Kang had to flee for his life.

Philosopher

While the Hundred-Day Reform came and went quickly, it is Kang's philosophy that proved to be both novel and significant. First, he made a great contribution to the revival of Neo-Confucianism at a critical moment in China's history. Raised in the Confucian tradition, Kang embraced and promoted the idealistic Neo-Confuciansm of Wang Yang-ming (1492–1529), rather than the rationalistic Neo-Confucianism of Zhu Xi (1130–1200). The main difference between these two schools, according to Kang, was that while the latter emphasized abstract and logical speculation, the former emphasized the spirit of purposeful action. In addition, Kang also offered a new interpretation of Confucius, and of the Confucian classics. In his *Study of Confucius' Reform of*

Institutions, he claimed that Confucius actually wrote (not just edited, as was traditionally believed) all the six classics: *The Book of Changes*, *The Book of Poetry*, *The Book of History*, *The Book of Rites*, *The Book of Music* and *The Spring and Autumn Annals*.[5] Later, Kang even went so far as to consider Confucius a supernatural being with a mission to save China and the world, and advocated establishing Confucianism as an organized national religion.

Another important philosophical idea of Kang's was his notion of history and its development. In his commentary on the Confucian classic *The Book of Rites*, Kang explained that history was nothing but an evolutionary process of historical events in three stages or ages: the age of chaos, the age of small peace and the age of great unity.[6] Furthermore, history and historical development seemed to follow their own purposeful direction, moving almost inevitably towards greater and greater realization of humanity: goodness, harmony, equality, universal love, etc. In fact, this theory of three stages or ages provided a philosophical foundation for his proposed political reform, arguing that while China was not ready for the age of great unity, her conditions were certainly ripe for the age of small peace.

Kang's third important philosophical idea was that of a World Commonwealth based on the principles of universal love and equality. Influenced by both Buddhism and Christianity, Kang believed that all people seemed to have a universal and innate compassion in the face of human suffering. In fact, he interpreted 'humanity' in terms of compassion, saying, 'The mind that cannot bear to see the suffering of others is humanity.'[7] Furthermore, in explaining the innumerable and ever-changing suffering of mankind, Kang listed six major kinds of suffering: (1) from physical life, such as birth and death, (2) from natural calamities like famine, (3) from one's situation in life, like widowhood, (4) imposed by governments, for example imprisonment, (5) from human feelings, such as hatred, and (6) from having a position of honour, as might a king.

All these were sufferings of human life, and all people seemed to be troubled by them. What caused such sufferings? How could these causes be eliminated? After a thorough examination of human conditions, laws, institutions and history, Kang concluded that all human suffering could be traced to nine causes, or spheres of distinctions:

> The first is the distinction between states, because it divides the world into territories and tribes. The second is class distinction, because it divides people into the honored and the humble, the pure and the impure. The third is racial distinction, which divides peoples into yellows, whites, browns, and blacks. The fourth is the distinction between physical forms, because it makes the divisions between male and female. The fifth is the distinction between families, because it confines the various affections between father and son, husband and wife, and brothers to those personal relations. The sixth is the distinction between occupations, because it considers the products of farmers, artisans, and merchants as their own. The seventh is the sphere of chaos, because it has systems that are unfair, unreasonable, non-uniform, and unjust. The eighth is the distinction between species, because it divides

> them into human beings, birds, animals, insects, and fish. And the ninth is the sphere of suffering. Suffering gives rise to suffering, and so they pass on without end and in a way that is beyond imagination.[8]

Since these nine spheres of distinction were the sources of all human suffering, Kang called for their total abolition. He envisioned a perfect society or World Commonwealth with no spheres of distinction based on nationality, race, sex, family, occupation, etc. This World Commonwealth would be administered by a world government which would be an administrative, rather than a political, organ. Its sole purpose would be to ensure that all people lived together in harmony, peace and unity. Being all equal, they would treat each other with compassion, respect and universal love. As a result, this World Commonwealth would progress gradually but surely towards the full realization of humanity itself.

Xiong Shili (1883–1968)

Together with Feng, Xiong was one of the two outstanding philosophers in China who not only tried to revive traditional Chinese philosophy, especially Neo-Confucianism, but also were able to develop their own philosophical system. It is interesting to note that while Feng attempted to reconstruct rationalistic Neo-Confucianism, Xiong tried to reconstruct idealistic Neo-Confucianism. Xiong's philosophical orientation is a reflection of the sources of his philosophical ideas. As a young man, Xiong was interested in Western science and politics, perhaps with the practical purpose of saving China. Soon, however, his interest shifted to the study of philosophy. He began with the study of Buddhism, especially the Consciousness-Only school, and Indian philosophy. Later, not totally satisfied with many Buddhist ideas, Xiong returned to the study of traditional Chinese philosophy, especially *The Book of Changes*, as well as the idealistic Neo-Confucianism of Wang Yangming.

He became professor of philosophy at Peking University in 1925, and retired in 1949. He wrote many books and articles, chief among which were *The New Doctrine of Consciousness Only* (1947), *An Inquiry on Confucianism* (1956) and *The Development of the Philosophy of Change* (1961). Through these writings (especially the first), he developed his own philosophical system, which can be considered as a new idealistic Neo-Confucianism.

Reality and change

Influenced also by Daoism (particularly by *The Book of Changes*), Xiong made use of 'change' or 'transformation' as the central concept of his entire philosophy. Reality was the 'original substance' or the 'totality of things or beings', which was nothing but the eternal process of change and transformation, production and reproduction, resulting in ten thousand things.[9] According to Xiong, this ever-changing and dynamic process consisted of two movements: 'closing' and 'opening'. The latter movement tended to differentiate the original substance, resulting in its myriad different manifestations. The former tended to synthesize diverse things into the original substance or Whole.

The original mind and the mind

To explain further the relationship between the original substance and its functions (i.e. between reality and its manifestations, between one and many), Xiong made use of two Buddhist terms: the 'original mind' and the 'mind'.

What was the mind? The 'mind', including will and consciousness, referred to particular, concrete and individual existences. They came into being when the original substance, through a perpetual process of change and transformation, of production and reproduction, was differentiated, and hence resulted in myriad things which were called the 'mind'. Thus, the mind was the manifestation of the original substance; and therefore, it was only a part of, and participating in, the original substance, which was also called the 'original mind'. From this perspective, the original substance, or totality of existences, could be considered as the 'original mind'.

What then, was the 'original mind'? This, according to Xiong, has two connotations. First, it was the original substance, or the totality of all existences, and hence universal and eternal. Second, the original mind was the metaphysical foundation and the universal of morality. As such, it was identical with *ren*, or humanity. To explain this identity or unity between the original mind and humanity, Xiong wrote:

> Humanity (*ren*) is the original mind. It is the original substance common to man . . . and all things. From Confucius and Mencius to teachers of the Song and Ming periods, all directly pointed to humanity, which is the original mind. The substance of humanity is the source of all transformation and the foundation of all things.[10]

Therefore, in the original mind, the totality of existence, the Real, and the totality of moral values, or Humanity, became the Whole. In other words, this view was a new interpretation of the Confucian teaching: 'to be is to be moral!'

Finally, Xiong pointed out that while the original mind and the mind are separate (because they are on two different levels, metaphysical and physical), they also complement one another. To explain such a dialectic relationship, Xiong made use of the analogy of 'water in the big ocean and the many waves'. The water was the original substance; and the waves (which can be considered as a function of the water) were the myriad different manifestations of water. Thus, the water was one; and the waves were many. The water and the waves were different, but they both belonged to the original substance, the water.[11] Through this analogy, Xiong seemed to argue that his philosophy had overcome the question of dualism of Western philosophy by insisting on the unity between substance and function, between the original mind and the mind.

Knowledge

In the light of the distinction between the original mind (noumenal realm) and the mind (phenomenal realm), Xiong went on to describe two corresponding types of knowledge: scientific knowledge and philosophical (metaphysical) knowledge. Science dealt with concrete existences or things, and hence appealed to the experimental methods of analysis to arrive at scientific knowledge of things investigated. Metaphysics, on the other hand, dealt with the original substance, or metaphysical structures of a totality of beings, and hence relied on the philosophical methods of logic and inner enlightenment (obviously a Buddhist influence) to arrive at ontological truth. Furthermore, scientific knowledge could yield only relative validity, or probability in the phenomenal realm, which could not be compared with certainty in the noumenal realm.

From all this, it is clear that Xiong's own philosophical system, while influenced by many sources, was still essentially a part or continuation of traditional Chinese philosophy. The central concept of *Dao* as a perpetual process of change and transformation, production and reproduction was derived from *The Book of Changes* and Daoism. His use of the concepts of the original mind and the mind came from the Consciousness-Only school and the idealistic Neo-Confuciansm of Wang Yangming. Finally, it is worth noting that, often challenged by Chinese Marxism after 1949, Xiong steadfastly maintained his own independent philosophical thinking. Thus it is understandable why Xiong and his philosophy have already influenced many Chinese thinkers, and will surely continue to inspire the revival of traditional Chinese philosophy which China sorely needs today and into the next century.

Tang Jun-yi (1908–78)

While being perhaps less known and less studied, Tang was one of the great twentieth-century Confucian philosophers. Well trained in Chinese classics under Fang Dongmei (1897–1966), he taught in many universities such as the National University in Nanking, the South-West University, and the Overseas University of Guangzhou in China. Exiled in Hong Kong after the People's Republic of China was established, Tang, with other Confucian scholars, established the New Asia College, which became part of the Chinese University of Hong Kong in 1963. He taught philosophy there until he died in 1978.

While living outside China, Tang was also influenced by Western philosophy, especially Hegelianism. He wrote many philosophical works, but unfortunately his style and turn of phrase made them difficult to understand. The most important among his writings are *The Origins and Development of Chinese Philosophy* (6 vols, 1966–73) and *The Existence of Life and the Spiritual World* (2 vols, 1977). His philosophy can be divided into two parts: a reconstruction of Chinese philosophy and his own philosophical synthesis.

Reconstruction of Chinese philosophy

From his study of Chinese philosophy, Tang realized that on the one hand traditional Chinese philosophy was rich and profound, and that on the other there were many concepts whose meanings were less precise and clear, because different philosophers in history used these concepts with different connotations. He undertook a systematic study of them, and in his book *The Origins and Development of Chinese Philosophy*, through careful and systematic analysis, Tang reconstructed many important philosophical concepts such as 'principle', 'mind' and *Dao*. For example, 'principle', one of the most important concepts, had five different connotations: metaphysical principle, rite, law, cause (reason why), and nature. 'Mind', another key concept, had at least five connotations: heart, goodness (of human nature), compassion, shame (moral) and intuition. *Dao*, still another important philosophical concept, also had five connotations: substance, form, the way (of life), the (moral) way, and the whole.[12] With this analysis, Tang seemed to be the first philosopher in contemporary China to make a serious and systematic effort to reconstruct some of the most important basic concepts of traditional Chinese philosophy. And then, on the basis of his reconstruction, Tang went a step further to reinterpret the major traditional philosophical schools: Confucianism, Daoism, Moism, Buddhism, etc.[13]

Philosophy of life

In addition to his clarification of the basic concepts of traditional philosophy, Tang also developed his own philosophy as presented in his last important work, *The Existence of Life and the Spiritual World*. Like the Western notion of philosophy, love of wisdom, Tang started his philosophical enquiry with 'wisdom'. To him, wisdom always meant 'human wisdom' derived from experience of life, which consisted not only of intellectual analysis of the 'object' and 'subject' and their relationship, but also living emotional experience.

To explain such a philosophy of life, Tang worked out three related movements.[14] The first was the outward movement in which the subject moved out of himself or herself and interacted with the object. The knowledge of the object, then, was based on empirical experience and hence would give rise to natural science. The second movement was the inward movement in which the subject returned to himself or herself. Such a return would yield subjective experience and hence would give rise to epistemology, logic and morality. The third movement was the transcendental ascent, giving rise to spiritual or religious experience; as a result, there evolved such religions as Confucianism and Buddhism.

Furthermore, in his own philosophy, Tang put great emphasis on the primacy of spirit, and hence on morality. A firm believer in Confucianism, he maintained that the purpose of human life was to establish the moral self. He argued that the development of the moral self began with overcoming human instincts, moved to moral sensitivity, and eventually arrived at transcendental ethics as practised by the Confucian sage. When one had achieved this cultivation of the moral self, one would be able to communicate with others who were on the same moral level. It was only then that the world of spirituality was possible.

Philosophy and culture

Since his notion of philosophy was a philosophy of life in all its dimensions, Tang was very much concerned with China and her existential problems in science and technology and economics and politics, as well as culture. In fact, together with Zhang Jiasen (also known as Carsun Chang), Mou Zongsan and Xu Fuguan, Tang published 'A manifesto for a re-appraisal of Sinology and reconstruction of Chinese culture' (1958),[15] which advocated a return to traditional Chinese culture, especially Confucianism. From his Confucian perspective, Tang considered that culture was the objective experience of the spiritual life of mankind, and that Chinese culture was the Chinese people's expression of their spiritual life. On the surface, China's problems in the first half-century seemed to be those of (economic) poverty and (military) weakness, and failure to keep pace in science and technology, as well as lack of democratic institutions. But upon deeper reflection, Tang claimed that while China's problems were concerned with science and technology and politics and economics, they were primarily problems of culture. China had lost its own source of vitality: its Confucian moral foundations. Therefore, to solve China's problems, it was not enough merely to add science and technology, or to dress her in democratic institutions. Rather, the solution must entail not only material progress through science and technology, but also the return to Confucian self-cultivation of moral values.

Throughout his life, Tang's philosophical interest was always in the question of morality and spirituality. In his book *The Existence of Life and the Spiritual World*, published two years before his death, he seemed to have worked out his own philosophy. By returning to Confucianism, the individual would become a moral self and China would become a moral society. Only then, based on a solid moral foundation, would China be able to develop science and technology, to adopt democratic institutions, and eventually to effect material progress. All this in turn would bring about the possibility of a world in which all people could be united in and through spirituality.

Liang Shuming (1893–1988)

After the successful revolution of 1911, the centuries-old dynastic system was finally overthrown. The Republic of China was established. The Chinese intellectual climate at that time was definitely anti-traditional and pro-Western. The leaders of the new culture movement such as Chen Duxiu and Hu Shi were iconoclasts. Amid this tide of pro-Western sentiment, Liang Shuming emerged as a rare defender of Chinese tradition, especially Confucianism.

However, Liang's philosophical awakening was not that smooth. It went through three stages. First, like many young men of his time, Liang took part in the revolution of 1911, and was very interested in Western political philosophy. Then, frustrated by later political events, he was attracted to the study of Buddhism, a very influential philosophy in China. However, Liang's philosophical interest in action did not fit well with the detachment of Buddhism, which he therefore abandoned. Finally, he turned to the study of traditional Chinese philosophy, especially Neo-Confucianism (in which he did not receive rigorous training). Through a period of intensive and extensive study, Liang became a self-made Confucian scholar, firmly convinced of Confucianism's merits. After his conversion, Liang undertook to give a modern interpretation of Confucianism. In addition to his theoretical defence of Confucianism, he also devoted himself in the next two decades to promoting rural reconstruction according to the Confucian values of cooperation and harmony. But for various reasons, Liang's efforts on this project achieved minimal success.

Liang's philosophy dealt primarily with three important topics: philosophy of culture, the Confucian way of life, and praxis.

Philosophy of culture

Liang's philosophical reflection focused on China's culture, the collective way of life of her people. In his major work, *Eastern and Western Civilizations and their Philosophies* (1922), Liang expounded three different types of cultures or civilizations based on their corresponding tendencies or attitudes towards life.

The first type of civilization was that of the West. Western civilization was forward-looking, actively seeking to gain material things indispensable to its needs. Through competition, it aimed at individual satisfaction, but often at the expense of social harmony and spiritual values.

The second type of civilization was that of the Chinese. It centred on the inner spirit of man. It aimed at achieving a harmonious and cooperative society which could foster happiness through peace and order. To achieve this goal, material gain and enjoyment had to be de-emphasized in favour of the self-cultivation of spiritual values. But the results were mixed. On the one hand, the Chinese had enjoyed inward satisfaction and contentment; on the other, they had lagged behind in science, technology and industry, as well as in democracy.

The third type of civilization was that of the Indians. It was based on a way of life which reflected the spirit of resignation. Since finding happiness in life was impossible, the Indians took the path of getting away from life. Through resignation to life as suffering, they strived for Buddhist wisdom: passivity, patience and transcendence.

Among these three types of civilizations, according to Liang, Chinese civilization had adopted the happy medium and hence was preferable.[16] His confidence was further strengthened by the views of Russell and Dewey, who, during their visits to China in the 1920s, had expressed their appreciation of Chinese culture and suggested a synthesis between East and West.

The Confucian way of life

Since Liang was influenced by both idealistic Neo-Confucianism and Bergson's philosophy of life, he considered 'philosophy' as a 'philosophy of life'. The central concept of his philosophy of life was the 'life force', which was the essence of man as well as culture. In other words, man and culture could be considered as the manifestations and continuation of this life force. For it was through the process of evolution of the life force that myriad things, including man and culture, came into being.

Once human beings emerged, Liang believed, human life was essentially good, endowed with intuitive power and reason orientated towards moral values. To recognize and bring out this innate goodness of man was the goal of Confucianism, which was, unfortunately, ignored by his contemporaries. Liang therefore argued that China's problem was not a political problem, but rather a fundamental problem of culture. In his article 'Culture is the root of politics', he wrote:

> What is our problem? . . . Many think that it is a political problem. . . . But I would like to tell our people that the political problem is only an immediate problem, not the fundamental problem, a problem of culture. . . . (In other words), the political problem is only part of this fundamental problem. . . . Culture is not an abstract concept; it includes politics, economics, all other essential aspects of society.[17]

To counteract this neglect, Liang advocated the return to Chinese tradition, Confucianism and spiritual values; for China's problems of weakness and poverty could not be solved only by science, material progress, or even Western social and political systems. On the contrary, by returning to its own tradition and philosophy, Chinese civilization would be energized and the people would regain their self-confidence. Only then could they create an ethical society based on intuition and reason which would produce material progress on the one hand and maintain their spiritual traditions and heritage on the other.

Praxis

Convinced that China in the 1920s and 1930s was ready for neither the development of democracy and capitalism nor for Communist revolution, Liang turned his attention to a practical solution: rural reconstruction. Since China was predominantly an agricultural society, Liang's solution was to reconstruct a new ethical society based on the traditional spirit of Confucianism. It was only this kind of ethical society which could save China from ruin and restore spiritual values lost to the Chinese people.

Liang's rural reconstruction programme had three objectives.[18] The first was to make China a strong and dynamic agricultural society: self-sufficient, consumption-orientated and having its own industry. In this agricultural society, the spirit of cooperation (not competition), peace and moderation would prevail. The second objective was to promote education as the way to vitalize the rural populace and mobilize it into a powerful social force behind this agricultural society. Intellectuals were therefore encouraged to go to the countryside to lead the fight against ignorance and individual selfishness. Liang stressed the importance of personal contact, not only between students and teachers, but also between leaders and the masses. Through education, the Chinese would obtain both scientific and moral knowledge. As a result, local communities would become havens of Confucian virtues, especially mutual aid and cooperation, which would in turn replace competition and struggle.

Furthermore, the rural reconstruction movement, according to Liang, should be free from government intervention. Such a free movement would eventually become a social force capable of influencing the government and society at large. Liang's experiments in rural reconstruction met with minimal success, and this for three reasons: the conservative peasants did not respond to any intellectual proposals; there were too many groups of rural reconstructionists, both nationalist and Communist, leading to even greater confusion; and with the Japanese invasion of China in 1937, the rural reconstruction movement, for all practical purposes, ended.

Although Liang's rural reconstruction movement did not achieve its intended purposes, he was true to his own philosophy, both in theory and in practice. In theory, he had great confidence in the future of Confucianism or Neo-Confucianism because he believed that Chinese traditional values, not material progress and technology, could save China. And in practice, he tried to create local agricultural communities based on the Confucian spirit of harmony, mutual aid and cooperation.

One final note on Liang's fate after 1949. When the People's Republic of China was established, Liang went to Beijing, hoping to be involved in social reconstruction. He became a member of the Political Consultative Council. But his philosophical thought and political views proved to be too dangerous. After 1953, he was criticized, recriticized and eventually condemned as the reckless exponent of idealistic and feudalistic ideas. Thus, he was silenced until the 1980s, and died in 1988, with his vision unrealized.

Feng Youlan (1895–1990)

There is no doubt that Feng Youlan was one of the best and most original Chinese philosophers in the twentieth century. Educated in traditional Chinese philosophy at Beijing University, he went to the United States in 1919 to study with John Dewey at Columbia University, where pragmatism was predominant at the time. After gaining his Ph.D., he returned to China to teach philosophy at various universities, and eventually returned to Beijing University. During the following two decades, he produced his most scholarly and original works. He is well known for his two-volume *A History of Chinese Philosophy* (1931), *A New Rational Philosophy* (1939) and *The Spirit of Chinese Philosophy* (1947), and, to a lesser degree, a series of other books. Through these works, Feng seems to have achieved two tasks: to organize systematically the history of traditional Chinese philosophy; and to develop his own philosophical system, which he called 'the new rational philosophy'. His ideas were based on the rationalistic Neo-Confucianism of Cheng-Yi (1033–1108) and Zhuxi (1130–1200) with the help of many Western philosophical ideas and methodology.

New rational philosophy

Feng's own ideas are presented in *A New Rational Philosophy*. He attempted to work out a Neo-Confucian metaphysics by using not only the concepts of rationalistic Neo-Confucianism and Daoism (such as principle or *li*, and *Dao* or becoming) but also the concepts of Western philosophy, especially Aristotle's (metaphysical) four causes and logical methodology. In fact, Feng's new rational philosophy was based on four metaphysical concepts designed to explain a concrete existence, or 'thing'.

The first metaphysical concept was 'principle' (*li*), the primary concept of rationalistic Neo-Confucianism. Feng's use of 'principle' was unique, so its exact nature was quite difficult to explain. Generally speaking, its meaning was similar to the combination of Plato's idea or concept (for example of a tree) and Aristotle's formal cause, the form or basic structure (of a tree). As such, principle (*li*) did not need any temporal or spatial existence; it could exist in the abstract. Therefore, principle was universal, eternal, (metaphysically) self-existing. For example, the principle of 'tree' was not this or that particular tree; rather it was the metaphysical principle by which any tree, this one or that one, was actualized.[19]

The second metaphysical concept was 'material force' (*qi*), which was responsible for the material dimension of a thing. That is, if a thing was to exist, in addition to principle there must be the concrete matter in which its existence took place. For example, in order for the concept of 'table' to be actualized, there must be a material force such as wood or metal, by which the concept of table could become a concrete wooden or metal table.

The third metaphysical concept was *Dao*, or the substance of *Dao*, which could be considered as 'becoming' or 'transforming'. In order for anything to exist, principle and material force could not be separate and static; they must be brought together. It was the function of *Dao* to bring about the interaction between principle and material force, producing the actuality of a thing. In other words, all things came into existence through a process of becoming or transforming, which, according to the Daoist tradition, produced one, two, three, and ten thousand things.

The fourth metaphysical concept was the 'Great Whole', which could be considered as a synthesizing or unifying principle of all existents. Influenced by Buddhism, and Neo-Confucianism, Feng explained that all (existents) were one, 'One was All' – together producing unity, or the Great Whole.[20] In this sense, the Great Whole was very similar both to *Dao* in Daoism as unifying all existents, and to Hegel's concept of the 'Absolute' or 'Totality'.

On the basis of these four metaphysical concepts, Feng called his own philosophy a 'new rational tradition', new in two senses. First, he attempted to reinterpret traditional Chinese philosophy by using and adding many Western philosophical ideas, while maintaining 'reason' or 'rationality' as the foundation of his own system. Second, in so doing, he seemed to be able to transform Neo-Confucianism from a philosophy of immanence into a philosophy of transcendence. In this connection, like Aristotle, Feng also made a distinction between philosophy (especially metaphysics) and science. The former dealt with metaphysical concepts and the principles of things or existence (which are universal, formal and logical). The latter dealt with actual, concrete existence and its material structures and activities.

Rationality and ethics

As he developed his new rational philosophy, Feng also reaffirmed rationality as the very foundation of ethics. Deeply rooted in the Chinese ethical tradition, Feng believed that it was reason or rationality which made man different from, and above, things or animals.[21] Furthermore, it was reason or rationality which would provide moral values for man as well as society.

Since morality was so important, Feng also worked out in his book *A New Treatise on the Nature of Man* a theory of four different moral spheres of living. The first was the 'natural sphere'. Living in this sphere, people followed their natural instincts, or social traditions and customs, without any critical examination. In a sense, they lacked moral sensitivity. The second sphere was that of 'utilitarianism'. Living in this sphere, people followed the principle of 'utility': self-interest, profit, or egoism. They tried to be moral as long as their moral behaviour would not conflict with their own interest or profit. The third sphere was that of 'morality'. Living in this sphere, people followed the principle of altruism, the opposite of egoism. They tried to contribute not to the interests of 'small egos', but to the common interests of 'big egos', i.e. the well-being of society as a whole. The fourth sphere was that of 'heaven and earth'. Living in this sphere, people had already achieved moral perfection or sagehood. As a result, they would always do what was morally right. In this sense, they were the citizens of heaven and earth, in tune with *ren* or humanity.[22]

History and society

Affected by the turbulent conditions in early twentieth-century China, Feng's philosophy also reflected a practical dimension. In his article 'China's road to freedom' (1939), he had already tried to reflect on the political and cultural reconstruction of Chinese society. Confronted with the economic backwardness of China, Feng seemed to have accepted a materialistic interpretation of history, for he argued that, at least in theory, socialism was superior to capitalism. The relative superiority of the socialist system, according to Feng, was due precisely to its ability to produce greater social good and harmony for the majority of people.

This perhaps explains why immediately after the establishment of the People's Republic of China in 1949, Feng was so optimistic and enthusiastic about the socialist reconstruction of Chinese society. He turned to a serious study of Marxism-Leninism, hoping to discover a new philosophy which could offer a practical way to transform China. But the political situation soon changed radically, and perhaps not as Feng had hoped. Subsequent events made Feng's philosophical career even more difficult. As early as in 1957, his ideas were widely criticized, prompting him to modify or reinterpret, and even reverse, many of his earlier philosophical views. Before the Cultural Revolution, he was forced to rewrite *A History of Philosophy* in the light of Marxism-Leninism and Maoism.

But, in view of China's political system, it was (and still is) extremely difficult to make a fair and correct judgement about many statements by Feng. When he came to Columbia University in 1982 to receive an honorary degree, he still refused to discuss the last three decades, saying only, 'The present should embrace all the best of the past!' One consolation was that in the 1980s, his standard of living was much better, and he was allowed to do research. He died in 1990.

Regardless of people's opinions of Feng's behaviour under the Communist system, one thing remains clear. His contribution to the history of Chinese philosophy, his own new rational philosophy, and his efforts to revive traditional Chinese philosophy, especially Neo-Confucianism, have all made him one of the very best, if not the best, of the contemporary Chinese philosophers.

SINO-WESTERN PHILOSOPHY

As the revolutionary tempo of late nineteenth-century Qing Dynasty China accelerated, the opposition to Confucianism also grew much stronger. However, when the revolution of 1911 successfully overthrew the Qing Dynasty, the centuries-old Confucian tradition was not immediately wiped out with it. In fact, a prolonged and difficult struggle against Confucianism, a symbol of the old philosophy, the old political ideology, the old morality and the old way of life, was just beginning. It began with the intellectual attack, 'Down with the house of Confucius', and was then reinforced by the literary revolt, and finally a total attack on (Confucian) feudalism under Communist rule. This struggle, though with some moderation, continues in China even today.

Against this historical background, it is understandable that in addition to the first philosophical movement, the revival of traditional Chinese philosophy, there was another philosophical movement: to introduce Western philosophy, science and institutions into China. Many Chinese leaders and intellectuals, led by Yan Fu at the end of the nineteenth century, genuinely believed that both the traditional political system and philosophy were outdated, and therefore advocated adopting various degrees of 'Westernization': from borrowing fragments of Western ideas, to 'partial Westernization', even to 'total Westernization'.

In this section, I shall discuss five Chinese philosophers (Yan Fu, Sun Yatsen, Hu Shi, Zhang Dongsun, and Jin Yuelin) who, in various degrees, have contributed to this philosophical movement. However, because of their different backgrounds, training and philosophical perspectives, their approaches were very diverse, from translating Western thought, adopting Western political systems and introducing Western logic to synthesizing Chinese and Western ideas. But in each case, the emphasis upon Western philosophy and the Western democratic system played a predominant role.

Yan Fu (1854–1921)

While China had some previous contact with Western ideas, primarily through missionaries,[23] it is commonly agreed that Yan Fu was the first to effect a serious and systematic introduction of Western thought in various fields such as political science, sociology, law and philosophy. Through his translation of many important works, especially Huxley's *Evolution and Ethics*, he exerted a great influence on generations of Chinese intellectuals, including Liang Qichao, Hu Shi, and even Mao.

Although he was born into a family of modest means in 1854, Yan received a solid education in Chinese classics and literature. In 1876, he was selected to be among the first group of arsenal students to go to Europe as part of the self-strengthening movement. During his stay at the Royal Naval College in England, Yan not only acquired a new education in natural sciences and navigation, but also learned much about the ideas of great thinkers of the time such as Darwin, Huxley and Spencer.

On his return to China, Yan spent more than twenty years teaching and doing administrative work in various naval schools. Meanwhile, however, he felt frustrated, because he could not make use of his knowledge of Western thought for China's political reforms. As a result, he devoted his energy to writing and translation. During the next two decades, he offered China the first translations of many important Western works including Huxley's *Evolution and Ethics* (1898), Mill's *On Liberty* (1903) and *Logic* (1905), Spencer's *A Study of Sociology* (1902), Adam Smith's *The Wealth of Nations* (1902) and Montesquieu's *The Spirit of the Laws* (1905).

Through these works, Yan introduced Chinese intellectuals to the theories of evolution and capitalism, as well as to social and political ideas: liberty, democracy, legal systems, etc. However, while he was a most prolific translator of Western thought, Yan was not a philosopher himself. He never attempted to develop his own philosophical system; his primary contribution was to enlighten. Among the many Western ideas he introduced, the most important and influential ones were the theories of evolution and of the natural rights of man, and a comparison between Western and Chinese civilizations.

The theory of evolution

While it was true that the idea of evolution had been mentioned by others before Yan, it had always been presented piecemeal, not as a theory. It was Yan who presented Darwin's theory of evolution as a whole to China. The universe was not created by God; rather, it evolved into existence. Therefore, everything was constantly changing. Furthermore, Yan also pointed out that the theory of evolution was very similar to the Daoist view of the universe. According to *The Book of Changes*, the universe was a natural process of evolution in which 'being came from non-being', and being (undifferentiated) in turn was differentiated into myriad beings.[24]

Moreover, Yan explained that the entire process of evolution could be divided into two stages: natural and human. Natural evolution consisted of the development of inanimates, plants and animals. Its guiding principle was natural selection, the survival of the fittest. However, human evolution took place when human beings emerged. The guiding principle of natural selection was replaced by that of ethical values, moral conscience and cooperation.[25] This thinking was obviously influenced not only by Darwin's theory of evolution but also by Spencer's social Darwinism.

Natural rights of man

Another important Western idea which Yan introduced into China was 'natural rights', based on Western natural and liberal traditions. Influenced by Rousseau's ideas, Yan explained that the relation between the people and the state was that the former was sovereign and the latter subordinate. Since the people were endowed with natural, non-transferable rights such as life, property and liberty, the reason they formed the state through social contract was to protect their natural rights. Furthermore, Yan believed that among these natural rights of man, the most important was 'liberty'.[26] Without liberty, man and civilized society could not exist.

But it must be pointed out that Yan's political view (especially after 1911) of revolution and monarchy was just the opposite of the notion of liberty which he had introduced to China. In fact, his own political life towards the end proved to be ironic. While many young Chinese intellectuals were enlightened by his translations, he became more and more reactionary. He opposed the revolution, and even allowed his name to be used by Yuan Shikai in his attempt to restore monarchy to China in 1915. His rationale was that a good emperor could improve China and solve all her problems.

Western logic

By translating Mill's *Logic* (1905) and Jevons's *Logic* (1909), Yan was also the first to introduce Western logical method in a systematic manner to China. In fact, he believed that the source of wealth and power of the West depended on science and technology; and that the development of science and technology in turn depended on scientific methods, especially Western logic.[27] In addition, Yan thought that Western logic was directly related to empiricism, because the former was essentially a method of induction and deduction derived from objective empirical experience as well as subjective reasoning. Against this background, it was understandable why Yan deplored the lack of scientific, logical method in Chinese thinking. The study of the Chinese classics had been based on memorization and intuition. What China needed therefore was to learn Western scientific and logical methodology based on empiricism.

Philosophy of culture

Influenced by Western liberal ideas as well as material progress, Yan tried to discover why China was so poor and weak, and the West so rich and strong. His answer was that there were some basic differences between Chinese and Western civilizations, representing two different ways of life.[28]

Western civilization was action-orientated, dynamic and assertive. It emphasized the importance of the individual with relation to liberty, equality and democracy based on a legal system. In the West, the government had the responsibility of creating conditions that were favourable to channelling individual energies and initiative to effect material progress in a civilized society. As a result, the West became rich and strong. On the other hand, Chinese civilization was stability-orientated, passive and reserved. It emphasized not the individual or the spirit of individualism, but family and the spirit of community through harmony, authority and submission. The government deplored competition and assertiveness, and promoted contentment and cooperation. As a result, China became poor and weak.

Because of these basic differences, Yan believed that the West represented the new culture, and China the old. For China to survive, people had to discard the old way of life and adopt the new. Not everyone agreed with Yan's position. But his clear and critical analysis of Western culture impressed the generation of Chinese intellectuals who later became the leaders of the new culture movement.

Sun Yatsen (1866–1925)

As the 'Father of the Republic of China', Sun has always enjoyed exceptional prestige. Although both as a political leader and as a thinker, he did not accomplish all of his goals, he has been more famous and more revered (even by the Communists) than anyone in twentieth-century China. His influence, especially his political legacy, will certainly continue to have an impact upon the future development of China.

Sun grew up during the most humiliating period of China's modern history. Although he received some training in the Chinese classics, his education was primarily Western, because he joined his brother in Honolulu when he was only 13. His experience of Western democracy and Christianity, his medical studies and his wide travels in Japan and Europe all had a tremendous influence upon his own revolutionary activities and political philosophy.

His most important political activities included the establishment of the Guomindang, or Nationalist Party (evolved from the League of Common Alliance),[29] the successful revolution of 1911, the first presidency, and his final attempt to unify the North and the South of China. In addition to his political activities, Sun also developed his own political philosophy as expounded in his book *The Three Principles of the People* (1924), a practical programme for the reconstruction of China. However, he saw neither the unification of China nor any degree of implementation of his political philosophy (in Taiwan), because he died in 1925 while in Beijing negotiating for unification.

Political philosophy

Just as his life was directly related to the political events of China, Sun's political philosophy also evolved gradually over three decades. Some ideas were conceived as early as the 1890s; others were developed much later; and in its final form, his thought was expounded in *The Three Principles of the People*.

1. The first principle was nationalism. When this principle was originally conceived, its sole purpose was to overthrow the Qing Dynasty. However, after the establishment of the Republic of China in 1911, its goal was extended to oppose Western political and economic imperialism. In addition to these political goals, the principle of nationalism also addressed the much deeper and more difficult question of the Chinese people and culture. For through his personal experience in revolutionary activities, Sun believed that the Chinese people had solidarity and loyalty only towards family and clan; they had no national spirit or allegiance towards the nation. That was why he compared the Chinese people to a heap of loose sand:

> The Chinese people have only family and clan solidarity, but they have no national spirit. Therefore even though there are four hundred million people gathered together in one China, in fact they are just a heap of loose sand. That is why at present we are the poorest and weakest nation in the world, and occupy the lowest position in the international community. . . . If we do not earnestly espouse nationalism and consolidate our four hundred million people into one strong nation, there is danger of China's being lost and our people being eliminated.[30]

To overcome such fragmentation, Sun proposed the principle of nationalism to achieve national unity among all races: the Han race with all other minority races. Only when unified could the Chinese people become one strong nation.

Another goal of the principle of nationalism, according to Sun, was to achieve a true, independent and free status for China. To achieve this goal, China must shake off Western imperialism, not only political control but also economic dominance. Furthermore, Sun also provided the principle of nationalism with a moral foundation, Confucianism. He came to believe, towards the end of his life, that any political philosophy without an ethical basis was like a house built on sand. Thus he wanted to be sure that the principle of nationalism was based on the solid moral foundation of the eight Confucian virtues: loyalty and filial piety, humanity and love, faithfulness and righteousness, and harmony and peace. When these eight Confucian virtues were practised, the people would be bound by a common moral sentiment to produce a unified national spirit: nationalism.

2. The second principle was democracy. Influenced by both his education and his experience of life, Sun proposed that the best political system to replace China's dynastic system was democracy. In elaborating this principle, Sun made a distinction between the sovereign powers of the people and the constitutional powers of the government. The former consisted of the four powers of the people (influenced by the Swiss doctrine):

initiation, referendum, election and recall. Through these four powers, the people would have ultimate control over the government. The latter were the five powers or branches of the government based on the constitution: executive, legislative, judicial, examinatorial and censorial.[31] The last two powers, obviously derived from Chinese traditional institutions, aimed to select the best and ablest persons for the government on the one hand, and to ensure appropriate behaviour in their official positions on the other.

While democracy was designed to achieve a constitutional government based on popular sovereignty, it did not address the issue of the fundamental rights of the individual, especially liberty. Thus, some people even criticized Sun for omitting and opposing individual liberty. This was not entirely fair. In proposing democracy, Sun argued explicitly for the electoral rights of the people, and hence argued at least implicitly for the fundamental rights of the individual. However, as a revolutionary leader, Sun perhaps had to emphasize authority and discipline in a modern party. In times of revolution, he also asked members of his own party, the Guomindang, to sacrifice their individual liberty for the freedom of the nation. All this, however, did not mean that Sun was opposed to individual liberty *per se*; indeed, he intended to protect the liberty of the people as a whole.

3. The third principle was livelihood. It must be pointed out that while the principle of livelihood was just as important as the other two principles of nationalism and democracy, its meaning was less clearly defined. This was so because the Chinese term, *min-sheng*, can yield different interpretations such as 'people's livelihood', 'the life of the masses', 'the nation's economy', or 'society's existence'. As a whole, however, the primary goal of the principle of livelihood was still clear. According to Sun, when China became a free and independent nation, when her government was organized according to democratic principles, it was imperative to attend to the livelihood of the people, that is, to solve all economic problems related to people's lives.

What was the best economic system for China? From the competing economic systems of his time, democratic capitalism, socialism and communism, Sun seems to have chosen socialism. Since China was so large in size and in population, only socialism (even state socialism) would emphasize a community which would foster mutual dependence and cooperation. In addition, mindful of the problems which China faced as an agrarian society, Sun proposed two solutions for them. The first was equalization of land ownership through nationalizing all land and then redistributing it, as equally as possible, among the people. The second was regulation of capital. Since capitalism was not well developed in China, Sun intended to provide a theoretical framework to control future capitalism. He regarded the free enterprise and industrialization aspects of capitalism as desirable; he did not want to see the monopolization of national wealth which capitalism also tended to bring with it. Viewed from this perspective, the principle of livelihood was in a sense socialism or state socialism, which was also in accordance with the perennial desire of the Chinese people to share all national wealth. On this point, many disagreed with Sun, or even accused him of being a 'Marxist'.

Knowledge and action

Another philosophical problem Sun had discussed was the relation between knowledge and action, which had always been a perennial question in traditional Chinese philosophy. The traditional position had always been: 'to know is easy, to act is difficult'. Disappointed by the people's hesitation to act, by joining the revolutionary movement, Sun surmised that their inaction might have been affected by the traditional position, that 'to act is difficult'. To replace this traditional teaching, Sun proposed: 'to act is easy, to know is difficult'. For, throughout different stages of evolution, man always tended to act without clear knowledge, and then after action, to derive knowledge from it. The key to human progress, according to Sun, was action, because 'to act is easier than to know'.

Strong criticism came from Hu Shi, who considered it wrong to separate knowledge from action. For Hu, knowledge and action were one, and hence inseparable, especially knowledge of social science, which was derived from experience, the result of action. In joining this controversy, Feng Youlan made a philosophical distinction between different types of knowledge. He pointed out that knowledge in the sense of cognition was easy, but knowledge in the sense of understanding was difficult. Furthermore, in the realm of morality, to know what one ought to do was easy, but to act upon it required will-power or determination, which was often more difficult. It must be pointed out, however, that the relation between knowledge and action as discussed by Sun had a primarily practical orientation.[32] By proposing that 'to act is easy', he intended to restore the Chinese people's faith in the revolution and in their revolutionary leaders.

To conclude, a comment on Sun and his political philosophy of the three principles of the people is in order. As a political leader, Sun has always been revered in China. His political philosophy, though not original in content, was a creative synthesis of primarily Western ideas with some traditional Chinese thought. That is, through his political philosophy with a practical programme of reconstruction, Sun was the first of his countrymen to propose a comprehensive solution to China's problems, though because of complicated and intriguing circumstances, he did not succeed. When Chinese Marxism flourished in the People's Republic of China after 1949, Sun's political philosophy was implemented in Taiwan, slowly but with considerable success.

Hu Shi (1891–1962)

Since 1917 China's intellectuals have all been deeply influenced by the 'new culture movement' or 'renaissance'. Among its proponents, the one best known to the West was Hu Shi. Hu Shi and Chen Duxiu joined forces and advocated replacing the classical language with the vernacular language, a literary revolution which eventually developed into a comprehensive movement away from China's old culture and towards a new Western one.

Born in Shanghai in 1891, Hu received an early education which was still essentially traditional. In 1910, he went to the United States, first to Cornell University, and then to Columbia University to study philosophy with Dewey. It was during this period that he embraced pragmatism, which became the guiding principle of his life and the foundation of his own philosophy.[33] Upon his return to China, he became the first ardent promoter of pragmatism in China. When Dewey went to China to lecture on American philosophy, Hu acted as his interpreter. Together they generated an overwhelming enthusiasm for pragmatism among Chinese intellectuals. However, with the rapidly changing political events in China, this enthusiasm was short-lived and was eventually replaced by Chinese Marxism.

However, the fact that numerous books and articles were written on American pragmatism, and that after 1949 the Communists launched a fierce campaign against him, shows the tremendous influence of Hu and his philosophy. In the following account, his philosophy will be explained under three headings: a critique of Confucianism, a reconstruction of traditional Chinese philosophy, and pragmatism.

Critique of Confucianism

In launching both the literary revolution and the new culture movement, Hu advocated one clear goal: to reject China's old culture in favour of Western culture. Having studied in the West, Hu was convinced that this was necessary because China's old culture, based on Confucianism, was inferior to Western culture.

> There are (those) who wish you to believe that the old Chinese culture and moral values are superior to all others. There are also fools who, having never been abroad, shouted: 'To the East! to the East! The Western tricks no longer work now.' I want to say to you, don't be fooled. We must admit . . . that we are inferior to others not only in technology and political institutions but also in moral values, knowledge, literature, music, fine arts and body physique.[34]

Thus Hu's attack on Confucianism was uncompromising, because he believed that Confucianism served as the foundation of China's old customs, traditions and values. With its emphasis on submission, and loyalty to family and authority, it was responsible for all of modern China's woes. Therefore, Hu and his followers shouted: 'Down with the house of Confucius!' What China needed was a new culture based on Western values, especially science, democracy and pragmatism.

Reconstruction of Chinese philosophy

While Hu's criticism and attack on Confucianism has always been noted, his contribution to, or reconstruction of, Chinese philosophy has often been neglected. As early as 1919, Hu, by using Western logical methods, was the first to provide Chinese philosophy with a clear and well-defined outline, while eliminating all non-historical, vague or irrelevant material. In addition, he also published many books and articles on Chinese philosophy, notably *The Development of the Logical Method in Ancient China*, *A Book on Huai-nan Zi* (179–122 BC), *A Collection of Works by Monk Shen-hui* (670–762), and *The Philosophy of Tai Tung-yuan* (1723–77).[35] Furthermore, he argued against the popular belief that Chinese philosophy lacked any methodology. He discovered various methods used in different philosophical schools, such as the method of reference in Confucianism, the logical method in the philosophy of Mozi, and the inductive method of Neo-Confucianism. In addition, his research contributed to a new understanding of Buddhism and the demythologization of Daoism, as well as the relationship between Chinese philosophy and its socio-historical environment. All this shows that while Hu opposed Confucianism as 'China's old political ideology', he had no quarrel with 'traditional Chinese philosophy' *per se*. On the contrary, aided by Western philosophy and logical methodology, he devoted a great deal of effort, with some success, to reinterpreting and reconstructing traditional Chinese philosophy.

Pragmatism

Whatever contribution Hu made to traditional Chinese philosophy, he was much better known as the vigorous and tireless promoter of pragmatism, especially Deweyan pragmatism. Reflecting upon his early education in the West, Hu acknowledged, in his 'Introduction to my own thought' (1930), that 'two persons who have influenced my thought most are Huxley and Dewey'.[36] From the former, he acquired a spirit of doubting or scepticism; from the latter, he learned how to think scientifically and logically. It was primarily from these two sources that Hu developed his own philosophy of pragmatism, both as a method and as a philosophy of life.

For Hu, pragmatism was a scientific method, a method developed after Darwin's theory of evolution, and therefore superior to (non-scientific) dialectic, a method developed before Darwin's theory of evolution. This scientific method was based on 'experience', which was a concrete, dynamic and unified whole. As such, it was not to be studied abstractly; on the contrary, it was to be studied empirically or experimentally. This scientific method, according to Hu, consisted of the following five steps. First, one needed to begin with a spirit of doubting, taking no unproved facts or principles for granted. Second, it was important to 'Be bold in proposing hypotheses and cautious in seeking proofs.' Third, in respecting facts and evidence, it was necessary to collect concrete and objective data through experimental methodology. Fourth, the principle of empirical verification was to be followed. Fifth, scientific method was the final criterion for truth.

For Hu, pragmatism was not only a method but also a philosophy of life based on the spirit of science. However, its content was much broader, because it included, in addition to the scientific spirit, individualism, freedom, democracy and gradualism.

Having lived in the West, Hu was convinced that China lacked individualism as the source of vitality and creativity. In urging young people to pay attention to individualism, he wrote:

> All that I expect from you is a kind of true, pure individualism. I want you to feel that in all the world, only matters concerning yourself are the most important. Compared to them, other things mean little.[37]

To be individual, according to Hu, also entailed being free. This was also consistent with his attack on China's old culture, in which conformity and submission to authority (family and state) were the norm. In the new culture which Hu advocated, individuals must be free, free to express their personal views, free to develop their own independent way of life. Without individuality and freedom, China would remain in her old predicament of complacency, inertia and backwardness.

Based on these two Western ideas of individualism and freedom, Hu went beyond these to advocate democracy for China. He believed that democracy was nothing but individualism universalized, for when individuals were free, they could develop their full potential, fulfil their social responsibility and improve the quality of human life in society. To realize all this, Hu proposed another of Dewey's beliefs, that education was one of the most important means of attaining democracy. This was so because education was not only the vehicle to transmit knowledge and values; it could also bring about social, political and cultural change. From this perspective, education was the most effective instrument for social change. In fact, democracy would be impossible without education, because without education, people would remain ignorant and uninformed, unable to participate fully in any democratic process.

Finally, while attacking China's old culture and advocating social change, Hu took a gradual and evolutionary approach. For this reason, he parted with Chen, who took a much more radical road in establishing the Chinese Communist Party. Obviously influenced by Darwin's theory of evolution, Hu believed that since China was such a large country, any large-scale change in her culture must proceed slowly. In finding this prudent course, Hu put great emphasis on 'creative intelligence', man's capacity to sort out complex social forces and problems, to find appropriate solutions, and to establish a new culture and a new China, free and democratic, in which all people could share and participate.

Zhang Dongsun (1886–1962)

While the serious introduction of Western philosophy began with Yan Fu, Zhang was indisputably considered to be one of the most influential interpreters of Western thought. However, he was a self-educated philosopher, whose academic career followed a very unusual route: from newspaper editor to professor at Yanjing University. Although he never went to the West to study (except for a short stay in Japan), he read perhaps more of Western philosophy than any of his contemporaries. He also translated Plato's dialogues and Bergson's *Matter and Memory* and *Creative Evolution*, and other works, into Chinese. He wrote more than a dozen other books, including *Reason and Democracy*, *Democracy and Socialism* and *Thought and Society*.

Moreover, while influenced by a variety of Western thinkers from Plato to Kant, to contemporary philosophers such as Dewey, Russell and Lewis, Zhang seemed to possess an extraordinary ability to assimilate most of Western thought, to organize it into a comprehensive system, and to exert the greatest influence upon Chinese intellectuals in the first few decades of the twentieth century. His philosophy as a whole (especially his theory of knowledge) was based essentially on a modified Kantianism. However, because of many other influences, Zhang considered his own philosophy 'epistemological pluralism' or 'panstructuralism'.[38]

Human knowledge

Zhang believed that starting with sensation, human knowledge was actually the result of a synthetic process of sense-data, form (or in Kantian terms, categories), and various methodological assumptions. The sources of human knowledge were pluralistic, because knowledge came from both 'object' (sense stimuli) and 'subject' (forms), as well as from their interaction. However, unsatisfied with the Kantian dualism in human knowledge, Zhang tried to overcome it by insisting on the unity of knowledge and action, as well as on the unity of substance and function. In his book *Epistemology*, he tried to elaborate on this difficult problem:

> My epistemological pluralism may be said to follow Kant's path generally. But there are important points of difference, and that is that I do not consider form as a subjective construction. Unlike Kant, I do not regard the external world as without order, or regard sense data (merely) as material for knowledge . . .
>
> With regard to the nature of knowledge . . . at the one end is the knower, and at the other end the known. . . . At the end of the knower, there are external things which are absolutely unknowable, but there is also an external world that is relatively knowable. At the end of the known there is the self which is absolutely unknowable but also an internal world which is relatively knowable. . . . Although knowledge cannot be separated from action or even restricted by it, nevertheless knowledge itself is not the product of action, nor does it exist solely as an instrument of action.[39]

All this was designed to bridge the gap between what Kant calls 'noumena' (things-in-themselves) and 'phenomena' (things-as-they-appear).

Moreover, Zhang was also interested in the relationship between knowledge and culture. All our knowledge, such as perceptions, concepts and theories, was not totally a product of individual mental activity, but rather a synthetic product that was socially and culturally conditioned. That is, human knowledge was not only based on external sense stimuli, i.e. reality; it was also formed to meet people's social needs. In his book *Knowledge and Culture*, he wrote:

> What we have been talking about . . . [shows] how social conditions are reflected in ideas. . . . While ideas seem on the surface to be independent and represent laws of logic or the structure of the universe that we talk about, actually they are secretly controlled by social needs.[40]

Finally, Zhang went even further to explain that the criterion for knowledge or truth was also socially conditioned. At times, social needs could make people accept certain things, events or ideas, including religious ones, as true. As Zhang explained, 'When society needs a centripetal force stronger than the centrifugal force, some theory or idea must arise to hold the people together so that they feel in their own minds that it is the truth.'[41]

Reason and society

While Zhang's early interest was primarily metaphysical and epistemological in nature, as he matured he became more interested in society and culture, the praxis of philosophy. This in turn led him to participate actively in political movements.

In discussing philosophical issues of a social and cultural nature, Zhang was obviously influenced by Neo-Confucianism and Kant (and to some extent pragmatism). While recognizing the importance of matter, or material environment, Zhang believed that it was reason that should be both the moral foundation and the guiding principle of social progress. In fact historical development, according to Zhang, followed three discernible stages. (1) The first stage was characterized by the powerful dominance of natural forces in which magic and superstition were abundant. (2) The second stage was characterized by social conflicts between man and man, in which science and technology would predominate. (3) The third stage was characterized by the reign of reason, which would give rise to the establishment of a rational society.[42]

A rational society, according to Zhang, was a final synthesis of a process of historical development; and it was a society guided by the principle of reason or rationality in which equality, liberty and justice could be realized. However, given China's social (and political) situation at the time, Zhang believed that the best concrete form of this rational society would be a socialist democracy. Democracy, according to Zhang, was not just a political (or economic) system, but rather a broad politico-economic and cultural system with a moral attitude towards life. Here Zhang seemed to have synthesized his notion of 'democracy' with the moral values of traditional Chinese philosophy. The term 'socialist' was used to refer to a system which would work towards the common good, general happiness, and the full realization of the general will (an obvious reference to Rousseau) shared by every member of that society.

While Zhang's notion of a rational society was somewhat idealistic, he firmly believed that it was achievable. This might perhaps explain at least in part why, after the Second World War, he embraced Chinese Marxism by becoming a member of the Central Committee of the Communist government after 1949.[43] But historical events did not develop as he had hoped. He retired soon afterwards, and died in 1962, his philosophical idealism unfulfilled.

Jin Yuelin (1895–1988)

Throughout its entire history, Chinese philosophy can be characterized as almost exclusively anthropocentric. While some attention was given to the study of nature, the primary philosophical concern has always been humanistic, focusing on human relationships and moral values. To achieve virtue and wisdom, the primary philosophical method has been meditation, reflection, and especially intuition. As a result, it is understandable that except for some logical discussions and debates among the logicians such as Huishi (*c.* 370–318 BC) and Gongsun Long (*c.* 320–250 BC), logic as a system or scientific method was never developed.

However, when Western thought was introduced to China at the turn of the twentieth century, many Chinese intellectuals were interested in Western logic. As mentioned before, Yan Fu was the first to translate Mill's *Logic* in 1905 and Jevons's *Logic* in 1909. Hu Shi promoted pragmatism both as a philosophy and as a method. Later, there were Russellian or mathematic logic and Hegelian and Marxist logic and dialectic. However, among those and others who were interested in logic, Jin Yuelin seemed to stand out.[44]

He was born in Changsha, Henan province. After completing his studies at Qinghua University, Beijing, he went to Columbia University to study Western philosophy, especially that of Green. He took a doctorate, then went to Europe for another four years. His philosophical thought was thus greatly influenced by British empiricism, especially that of Hume and Russell. Returning to China, he taught in many universities, including Qinghua and Peking. After 1955, he devoted himself mainly to research in philosophy at the Chinese Academy of Social Science.

He wrote many articles such as 'External relationship' and 'On facts', but his major philosophical works were his two famous books *Logic* (1935) and *The Tao* (1940). Through his writing and teaching, Jin worked out his own system, especially in logic and metaphysics.

Logic and knowledge

While abroad, Jin became very interested in Western logic, or logical method, and upon his return he began to develop his own system. In his book *Logic*, and in other writings, he expounded on the importance of clarity of logical concepts such as object, subject, perception and truth, as well as the intrinsic relationship between logic and knowledge.

Jin believed that knowledge was both empirical and experiential. Knowledge had an objective foundation, or 'external object', and a subjective foundation, or 'knowing subject'. This external object must have three characteristics: actual existence, independence, and unity. As such, the object would reveal itself as an objective stimulus to the knowing subject. On the other hand, the knowing subject, through its sense-organs, tried to grasp the self-revelation of the object, and form the 'idea' or 'concept'. This was achieved, however, by 'abstraction', which, in Jin's views, was the most important instrument of the knowing process.[45] In fact, without this process of abstraction there would be no language, no communication, no concept, and no knowledge.

Jin also discussed the problem of causation. On the basis of a modified view of Hume, Jin believed that causation was more than a mere temporal-spatial association. In a cause–effect context, the relation was a necessary one. This necessity between the cause and the effect depended on the environment, those conditions which could be classified as 'necessary' or 'non-necessary' (i.e. 'related' or 'non-related'). When the conditions within any given environment were proved, through empirical verification, to be absolutely regular and predictable, then the necessary connection, i.e. causation, existed.

Finally, influenced by the formal logic of Aristotle, Jin claimed that knowledge was intrinsically related to logic, the law of laws. This was so because both the external object and the knowing subject were guided by the laws of logic, especially its three fundamental principles: the principle of contradiction, the principle of identity and the principle of the middle. All these and other logical rules constituted the basic framework of logic according to which 'thinking' took place. From this perspective, Jin affirmed that without the laws of logic, nothing – no thinking, knowing, or knowledge – would be possible.

Metaphysics of Dao

While logic dealt primarily with particular, actual and concrete existences, their logical relationships, as well as their meanings as grasped by the knowing subject, metaphysics dealt primarily with what were universal, actual-possible, and abstract existences, their metaphysical relations, as well as their meanings as a totality. Jin constructed his system of metaphysics on three fundamental principles: *Dao*, form (or *shi*) and energy (or *neng*).[46]

One of the perennial metaphysical questions has always been: what is the meaning of existence? Why should there be 'being' rather than 'non-being'? What is the meaning of reality? Influenced by traditional Chinese Daoism, Jin's answer was: *Dao*. The *Dao* was the reality, including both all actual existences and all possible existences; it was the totality. To elaborate this further, Jin made use of two other concepts: 'form' and 'energy'. Form, which is similar to the principle (or *li*) of Neo-Confucianism and to Aristotle's notion of 'form', was used to refer to the 'mode of existence' *per se*. As such, the form was universal and absolute. It was a metaphysical principle, embracing both all actual existences and all possible existences. On the other hand, energy, similar to the spirit (or *qi*) of Neo-Confucianism and to Aristotle's notion of matter, was used to refer to the 'mode of activating energy' in all and every actual and concrete existence. In other words, energy could be considered as the activating principle which caused, as it were, the concept of existence (universal, absolute and metaphysical) to become particular, actual and concrete existences. As for their relationship, on the metaphysical level, form and energy were related and complementary to each other, but separable; whereas on the physical level, they were related, complementary and inseparable.

Finally, by using the theory of evolution, Jin worked out a synthesis. Through the process of evolution, when form and energy were united, all things, large and small, actual and possible, came into existence. They were one in *Dao*. The *Dao* was One; the *Dao* was Many; the *Dao* was Totality.[47] The meaning of reality, according to Jin, could be grasped through logic, because both man and reality were logically and metaphysically structured.

CHINESE MARXISM

Around the turn of the twentieth century, socialism caught the attention of Chinese intellectuals. As early as 1902, Liang Qichao already discussed Marx in his *New People's Magazine* published in Japan. Sun's principle of livelihood (first introduced in 1905) was a modified version of socialism. After the revolution of 1911, socialism was openly advocated, and the first Chinese Socialist Party was organized by Jiang Kanghu the same year.[48]

However, when the New Culture Movement began in 1917, and as China's situation became more precarious, it became painfully evident that neither socialism nor democracy would prove to be a viable ideology, strong enough to solve China's problems. It was also during this period that Marxism was introduced by the Comintern into China, and thus the Chinese Communist Party was established in 1921.[49] Ever since then, the development of Chinese Marxism has been directly linked to China's political events during this century to the present day. It took a tortuous route, from its birth, to its struggle and survival, to its eventual triumph with the establishment of the People's Republic of China in 1949.

Their new republic gave the Chinese people a historical opportunity to build China and make her wealthy and powerful, a centuries-old goal that had proved ever elusive. But 'to destroy is easy, to reconstruct is difficult' remained true even under the Chinese

Communist system. Four decades have passed, producing mixed results. After a relatively successful first decade, Chinese Marxism and the government began to experience political and economic difficulties. In addition, international politics, especially the Sino-Soviet split in 1960, made things even worse. 'The ten years of calamity', the Cultural Revolution, proved to be one of the darkest periods in China's entire history.

But China's long history has demonstrated the resilience of her people; the open-door policy of Deng Xiaoping in 1980 seemed to indicate another new beginning. However, during the last decade, the open-door policy produced two paradoxical results: one, economically good for China and her people, and the other, politically bad for China's political system based on one-party control. The Tiananmen Incident of 1989 was only a public manifestation of the intrinsic tensions of the Chinese Communist system. Unless China makes major changes in her political system, her future will continue to be uncertain.

Since Chinese Marxism as a whole has been used primarily as a political ideology, I shall select those theoretical aspects of four thinkers, Chen Duxiu, Li Da, Ai Siqi and Mao Zedong, in so far as they have contributed to the development of Chinese Marxism as a political philosophy. (See also Chapter 29 above, 'Mao Zedong and "Chinese Marxism"'.)

Chen Duxiu (1879–1942)

In the history of Chinese Marxism, the importance of Chen is almost self-evident. He was the founder of the Chinese Communist Party in 1921, and directed it until 1927.[50] He was sometimes called 'the Chinese Lenin'. However, during the next two decades (the 1920s and 1930s), Chinese politics, especially those of the Chinese Communist Party controlled by the Comintern, were extremely complex. Not only did Chen encounter constant opposition; he was also later stripped of his leadership, and eventually expelled from the party he founded.

As for his philosophical background, Chen was trained in the Chinese classics. In 1901, he went to Japan to study, and so was influenced by Western thought. Returning to China, like many young intellectuals Chen became involved in revolutionary activities. Together with Hu Shi, Chen launched a fierce campaign against Confucianism. Being politically radical, he was easily attracted to Marxism and became a convert. But when he tried to implement Marxism in China, he found out that theory and practice were not the same, and even worse, that the world of politics could be a very harsh one.

As a political philosopher, Chen wrote on many subjects such as culture, politics and morality. But without a unified system, his philosophy remained as fragmented and isolated philosophical discussions. These centered around four topics: evolution, science and democracy, morality, and Marxism.

Evolution

Just as the whole generation of Chinese intellectuals at the turn of the century was influenced by the theory of evolution (introduced by Yan Fu), so was Chen. In fact, he became both a believer in and a promoter of evolutionary ideas. 'To evolve is to create', he told Chinese youth; 'to create is to evolve. Continuous evolution means creation; without creation, there would be no evolution.'[51] What Chen found most important in the theory of evolution was its fundamental principle of natural selection: the survival of the fittest. To survive, things must change, compete with other things, and adapt to a new environment. All this, in Chen's view, was exactly what China needed. As on the battlefield of evolution, China must change, fight against the old Confucianism, and adapt the new Western science and democracy.

Science and democracy

Why must China adopt Western science and democracy? The reason was, according to Chen, that science and democracy were two primary forces of social progress in the West. Because of them, people in the West were free and independent; Western civilization was very dynamic and progressive. Chen believed that China should follow the same path to rid itself of feudalism and ignorance. In 'The new youth', Chen repeatedly promoted the same message that 'only Mr. Science and Mr. Democracy could save China and cure all her political, moral, educational and intellectual problems.'[52] In other words, what Chen suggested was in a sense a total Westernization, but based on only two ideas: science and democracy. Mr Science could provide China with a spirit of science, both as a scientific method and as a scientific attitude. By respecting 'facts' and by making use of technology, China could conquer nature and effect great material progress. On the other hand, Mr Democracy could provide China with free, independent and democratic institutions to replace her old, backward, stale system. As a result, the Chinese people, free and independent, would be able to realize their creative potential.

Morality

It should be noted that morality was one of Chen's most important philosophical ideas before his conversion to Marxism. In his campaign against Confucianism, a symbol of China's old system, he pointed out that to save China, political awakening was necessary. However, political awakening alone was not enough; moral awakening was also needed.

Morality, according to Chen, was nothing but man's reaction to his total existence: natural instincts, feelings and emotions. Being organic and unified as a whole, man's morality contained both a 'good side' (a positive force) and a 'bad side' (a negative force). The negative side referred to selfishness, envy, hypocrisy, aggression, dominance. The positive side referred to compassion, mutual aid, love, public conscientiousness, altruism. Moreover, from studying human nature and social phenomena, Chen believed that the primary cause of most social problems and calamities was lack of morality: the correct solution was therefore an emphasis on will-power, discipline and a sense of responsibility.[53] However, Chen later modified this view after his conversion to Marxism, which itself was the foundation of socialist morality.

Marxism

While the distance from radicalism to Marxism was short, actual conversion for Chen was not that easy. The reason was that Marxism as a political ideology was almost totally new and different from Confucianism, or even from Western democracy. However, once converted, Chen became one of its most forceful promoters. As the founder and first leader, Chen vigorously preached some basic Marxist ideas, as interpreted by the Comintern. Socialism was superior to capitalism; but Marxism was scientific socialism, and hence superior to old pre-Marxist socialism. Of course, Marxism was based on the fundamental concepts of class struggle, economic base and its superstructure, historical materialism and dialectical materialism, socialism and Communism.

All these and other Marxist ideas which Chen embraced and promoted were both elementary and fragmented. While they were not philosophically important, they proved to be an effective political ideology, upon which the Chinese Communist movement was developed.

Li Da (1890–1966)

While Chen was one of the earliest Chinese Marxist theoreticians, his writings were only fragmentary. The first systematic interpreter of Marxism was Li Da. Born in the last decade of the nineteenth century, Li Da still received a solid training in the Chinese classics. In 1913, he went to Japan to study politics, economics, sociology and Western thought, including Marxism. As soon as he returned to China in 1918, he began translating Marxist works, including 'Interpretation of dialectic materialism' and 'The economic theory of Marxism'. However, his major philosophical writings are his two books *Essentials of Sociology* (1937) and *Modern Sociology* (1946). Through these two works, Li Da provided China and Chinese intellectuals with the first systematic presentation of Marxism as both a world-view and a method.

Marxism as a world-view

Li Da first identified three wrong approaches to the study of society and history: social contract theory, biological sociology and psychological sociology.[54] Then he explained that Marxism was first and foremost a scientific philosophy based on both dialectical materialism and historical materialism. Together, they constituted a Marxist world-view by which the nature and development of society and history could be explained. Therefore, in studying society, one must begin with its economics: labour, products, technology, etc. The economics of a society constituted its material base, which in turn would create a corresponding superstructure: politics, laws, education, religion, culture. Viewed from this perspective, the relation between the material base and the superstructure was clear. The former determined the latter; social existence determined social consciousness, not vice versa. Furthermore, the primacy of the material base also holds true when studying the historical development of society. Since the economic base was the foundation of society and was always dynamic and ever-changing, social development was always brought about by changes in various forces of the economic base. This is the essence of historical materialism.

Marxism as a method

In addition to the Marxist world-view, Marxism, according to Li Da, offered a dialectic method for knowing society and history: human knowledge. In the process of human knowing, one must begin with practice, concrete and material living experience. For knowledge was nothing but subjective reflection on objective practice. Thus practice or social practice was the key factor to human knowing, and for two reasons: first practice or social practice was the material base from which knowledge was derived; and second it was also the criterion by which the truth or falsehood of any knowledge was judged. For in determining whether particular knowledge was true or not, one had to go back to 'practice', i.e. concrete and material existence.

In addition to the above philosophical ideas, Li Da also discussed many other topics such as sociology, culture, or political events in China. But it was the philosophical part of his writing that contributed to the development of Chinese Marxism.

Ai Siqi (1910–66)

Of all Chinese Marxists, Ai was considered the most effective promoter of Chinese Marxism to the masses. Ai was born into a prominent Mongol family in Yunnan in 1910. Thus he grew up during the most violent period of China's history, and became politically minded at an early age. In 1927, he went to Japan to study Western thought, and at the same time, joined a group studying socialism and Marxism.[55] Already attracted to Marxist ideas, when he returned to China he immediately engaged in political activities and joined the Chinese Communist Party in 1935. After that, his primary work was to promote Marxism to the masses by popularizing its essential points. He wrote many articles and books; his most important philosophical works were *Philosophy for the Masses* (1936), *Philosophy and Life* (1937) and *Readers in Contemporary Philosophy* (1937). Through these writings, he promoted three important topics: the accessibility of philosophy, the relationship between social existence and social consciousness, and science and metaphysics.

Accessibility of philosophy

Ai's primary goal was to convey to the people that philosophy, and hence Marxism, was not difficult but easy. For centuries, the Chinese people had always considered philosophy as abstract, obscure and mysterious. Ai made every effort to overcome this long-time fear of philosophy, and to popularize Marxism, and he succeeded. In *Philosophy for the Masses*, he explained, first of all, the direct relationship between philosophy and everyday life. Since different people had different experiences of life, they had different ways of thinking. For people to know if their thinking was correct, they had to find a correct philosophy that could explain everything to them in an understandable way. This correct philosophy, according to Ai, was none other than Marxism.

What was Marxism? Ai tried to answer this question in a practical way. Marxism was materialism. People needed to eat, to drink, and to use material things. This was the material basis of human life, and hence Marxism was materialism. Again, Ai made use of social conflicts to explain that Marxism was historical materialism. In old China, there were concrete conflicts and injustice in rural areas, especially exploitation by the landlords. Therefore, it was obvious that class struggle was needed to resolve these social problems. This was nothing but historical materialism. By using these and other simple examples taken from everyday life, Ai seemed to be able to popularize Marxism, and make its essential ideas understandable to the people. This was demonstrated by the fact that when *Philosophy for the Masses* was published in 1936, it sold out immediately. In the next decade, it went through thirty-two editions.[56]

Social existence and social consciousness

Another important philosophical issue Ai tried to explain to his people was the relationship between social existence and social consciousness. This was one of the fundamental ideas of dialectical materialism, and had been the subject of one of the classic Marxist debates. Again, Ai made use of Chinese culture to explain this abstract subject. To understand the Chinese people and their culture, their ideas, customs and philosophies, we had to find out how they lived their concrete, material lives, and especially about their economic conditions. Once we knew how the Chinese people lived in their concrete and material conditions, we would be better able to understand other aspects of their culture such as ideas, customs and philosophies. In other words, the way the Chinese people lived determined how they thought.[57] The same was true for understanding China's semi-colonial status. According to Ai, when China was forced into the status of a semi-colony by the Western powers, people became submissive, did not think of themselves as free, and lacked self-confidence. Thus their semi-colonial mentality was determined by their concrete existence in China as a semi-colony.

Science and metaphysics

The debate between 'science' and 'metaphysics' started long before Ai's time. But when Ai tried to popularize Marxism in the 1930s, he also became involved in this debate; and his views were quite enlightening. He of course opposed metaphysics, a coded name for Confucianism, because it was abstract, obscure and mysterious. But he was not in total agreement with the position of science either. He argued that to promote science was good and proper; but it would be inappropriate to make science omnipotent and supreme, because science, especially natural science, could not resolve all social problems. Ai offered Marxism as a synthesis of these two extreme tendencies.

Given his successful and systematic popularization of Marxism, Ai made a great contribution to the spread of the Chinese Communist movement. While his writings were by no means original, they were part of Chinese Marxism. Within this context, Ai should also be considered one of the most important popularizers of Chinese Marxism.

Mao Zedong (1893–1976)

As the 'Father of the People's Republic of China', Mao has always appeared larger than life. His impact on China and the Chinese people (as well as on the world), for better or for worse, has exceeded that of any one person in the history of modern China. But there has been no universal, definitive evaluation of Mao and his thought, and perhaps there never will be. In fact, Mao was, and still is, a 'sign of contradiction'. Throughout the past fifty years or so (especially since 1935, when he took over the leadership of the Chinese Communist Party), some have honoured him as a great leader, a brilliant revolutionary, or even a god; others have regarded him as a cruel dictator, a cunning deceiver, or even the devil incarnate. Even since his death in 1976, China's leaders and people have never agreed on their final judgement of him. His merits and faults will perhaps continue to be the subject of evaluation and re-evaluation for some time to come.[58]

Mao's life in perspective

Because of the significance of Mao's life – controversial, ever-changing, and contradictory and yet crucial to the development of Chinese philosophy in Communist China – I should like to put his entire life into perspective. Without going into too much detail, his life can be summarized in the following five periods:

1. Pre-revolutionary period (1893–1921): The first period of Mao's life was not out of the ordinary. Born into a relatively affluent peasant family in 1893,[59] he received some basic education in the Chinese classics. Like many young intellectuals of his time, Mao was involved in revolutionary activities, and joined one of the study groups devoted to Marxism in Beijing in 1917. Eventually, he became one of the founders of the Chinese Communist Party in 1921.

2. Revolutionary period (1921–35): The second period consisted of Mao's revolutionary activities. However, while Mao was one of the founding members of the Chinese Communist Party, his role in the next decade or so was only secondary; he was not part of the leadership which endorsed the orthodox Soviet interpretation of Marxism. However, Mao's revolutionary activities always reflected the life of the party as it went through its many phases: establishing itself, cooperating with the nationalist party, surviving or fleeing from the continuous campaigns of the nationalists against the Communists. But even as a founding member, Mao did not always agree with official policy,[60] and sometimes, his unorthodox doctrine was barely tolerated.

3. Experimental period (1935–49): The third period was the golden period of the Chinese Communist Party. When the party was almost wiped out during the Long March, it turned to Mao for leadership in 1935.[61] As he took command, Mao made many bold decisions, which led to the breakthrough at Yanan. The next decade proved to be the most successful period for Mao and his ideas: the Yanan experiment of Chinese socialism met with great success. When the Sino-Japanese War broke out, Mao also joined forces with the nationalist government to fight against the Japanese invasion. But after the Second World War, China did not enjoy peace right away because of civil war between the Communists and the nationalists. Eventually, Mao's forces prevailed, and so he declared that 'China stood up!' in 1949.

4. Socialist reconstruction period (1949–60): The fourth period offered great hope and expectations. Having emerged as the 'Father of the People's Republic of China', Mao immediately launched a socialist reconstruction of Chinese society. There were

some initial successes: in restoring social order, land reform, collectivization, and even some degree of success in industrialization. However, while Mao (together with other leaders) continued to apply his previous revolutionary zeal, goodwill, and smart common-sense approach,[62] in retrospect, he did not, and perhaps could not, realize two plain truths. First, Mao and other leaders did not have the knowledge necessary to carry out such an unprecedented, vast and complicated socialist reconstruction for China. Second, Mao and other leaders did not realize that the Chinese Communist one-party system with its built-in tensions was detrimental to China's socialist reconstruction, either in isolation or in cooperation with other free and democratic countries.

5. The final period (1960–76): This period was one of decline, despair and old age, resulting in power struggle, destruction and suffering.[63] Mao's undisputed authority was first seriously challenged in 1958. Moreover, the split between China and the Soviet Union, three years of natural calamities and the struggle for power among the inner circle of the leadership all further precipitated the decline of Mao's complete and undisputed power. After a few years of 'retirement', however, not content with his limited role and the direction of China's course towards capitalism, Mao mounted the Cultural Revolution to regain his power and to redirect China's course towards socialism. He succeeded, but the price was very high: the suffering and death of millions of people, a decade of violence and power struggle, and a ten-year interruption in education. When Mao died in 1976, China was a ruined country and the succession problem remained unresolved.

Mao's philosophy

Before discussing Mao's philosophy, I should like to make a distinction between 'Mao's philosophy' and 'Mao Zedong Thought'. The latter phrase has been used in Communist China in three ways: (1) as a continuation and development of the teachings of Marx, Lenin and Stalin (less important); (2) as the final political authority in Communist China by which to judge everything, both theoretical and practical; and (3) as Chinese Marxism, or better, as the theoretical part of Chinese Marxism.[64] Mao Zedong Thought includes all writings, speeches, directives, poems and even conversations of Mao. The phrase 'Mao's philosophy', used here, refers to the philosophical thought of Mao, which includes the following important writings: *On Practice* (1937), *On Contradiction* (1937), *On New Democracy* (1940), *On the Ten Great Relationships* (1956), *On the Correct Handling of Contradictions among the People* (1957), *Where do Correct Ideas Come from?* (1963) and *Talk on Questions of Philosophy* (1964). Through these and other works, Mao worked out his own philosophy, or rather political philosophy, which included three important topics: theory of contradiction, knowledge, and democracy and culture.

Theory of contradiction To understand Mao's theory of contradiction, we must first understand his notion of 'contradiction'. For Mao, contradiction had a special connotation: contradiction as 'a process of interaction', 'relationship' or 'relationality'. In the light of this, Mao proceeded to explain that reality (which was never static, but complex and ever-changing) was actually 'contradiction'.[65] That is, reality, in Mao's view, was a dynamic process of all sorts of relationships, all interrelated and interacting. Furthermore, in knowing reality, it was imperative to make a distinction between primary and secondary contradictions. The former were those contradictions which were antagonistic in nature, and hence could be resolved only through violent means. The latter were those contradictions which were non-antagonistic in nature, and hence could be resolved through peaceful means.

Once any given contradiction was understood, according to Mao, then it had to be resolved correctly, either peacefully or violently.[66] However, since reality was ever-changing, the nature of a contradiction could also change. As conditions changed, an antagonistic contradiction could be transformed into a non-antagonistic contradiction; and vice versa. This was, in Mao's view, the principle of transformationality.[67] By using this principle of transformationality, Mao's interpretation and handling of the question of contradictions in China showed much more flexibility than that of the orthodox Marxist interpretation.

Knowledge Mao's theory of knowledge was essentially Marxist, or better a Marxist copy-theory based on a continuous process of 'practice–theory–practice' cycles. For human knowledge began with practice or social practice, including all of man's activities related to practical life in society. Social practice could mean any activity dealing with material productivity, scientific research, or social reconstruction. Therefore, it was social practice that gave rise to human knowledge, which involved two movements: perceptual and rational.[68] The process of human knowing began with the perceptual movement, the interaction between the objective world of reality and the subjective sense-organs. This interaction resulted in perceptual knowledge, perception which was the phenomenon. However, if perceptual knowledge i.e. perception, once formed, repeated itself sufficiently, it would be transformed, through a sudden change, or 'leap' into rational knowledge.[69] From this perspective, perceptual knowledge and rational knowledge, though different, were not opposed but complementary, because they were produced and united in the same process of human knowing.

To elaborate further on the process of human knowing, Mao explained that social practice was not only the origin of human knowledge, but also the criterion for testing its validity. In *On Practice*, Mao wrote:

> Man's social practice alone is the criterion of the truth of his knowledge of the external world. What actually happens is that man's knowledge is verified only when he achieves the anticipated results in the process of social practice.[70]

Since social practice was both dynamic and ever-changing, human knowledge was never complete; in fact, Mao believed that the entire process of human knowing was the endless cycles of development. At the conclusion of *On Practice*, he gave a detailed description:

> Discover the truth through practice, and again through practice verify and develop the truth. Start from perceptual knowledge and actively develop it into rational knowledge; then start from rational knowledge and actively guide revolutionary practice to change both the subjective and the objective world. Practice, knowledge, again practice, and again knowledge. This form repeats itself in endless cycles, and with each cycle the content of practice and knowledge rises to a higher level. Such is the whole of the dialectical-materialist theory of knowledge.[71]

In this and other writings, it is interesting to note, Mao seemed to expound on the unity between knowledge and action, one of the perennial questions in all of Chinese philosophy. The key to understanding this unity was again social practice. For, as a criterion of human knowledge, social practice seemed to go through endless cycles of practice, knowledge and practice, which would become closer and closer so as to produce the truth. The resulting truth was nothing but the unity of action (social practice) and knowledge (perceptual and rational).

Culture and democracy Mao's philosophical discussion of culture and democracy was often overlooked. People seemed to think that Mao advocated total Marxization on the one hand, and on the other, a total rejection of China's old culture. This was only partly true. While he embraced Marxism early, Mao's interpretation of Marxism had always been independent. In fact, he insisted on the sinification of Marxism, interpreting it in the Chinese context. On the issue of Chinese culture, Mao called for a critical attitude, both in rejecting the old culture and in adopting a new one. In his *On New Democracy*, Mao explained his view clearly:

> A splendid old culture was created during the long period of Chinese feudal society. To study the development of this old culture, to reject its feudal dross and assimilate its democratic essence is a necessary condition for developing our new national culture and increasing our national self-confidence, but we should never swallow anything and everything uncritically. It is imperative to separate the fine old culture of the people which had a more or less democratic and revolutionary character from all the decadence of the old feudal ruling class. China's present new politics and new economy have developed out of her old politics and old economy, and her present new culture, too, has developed out of her old culture; therefore, we must respect our own history and must not lop it off.[72]

In the same work, Mao insisted repeatedly on this critical attitude, 'never swallow anything and everything uncritically.'

Furthermore, Mao envisioned a new democratic culture for China, with three characteristics.[73] First, the new democratic culture must be national in the sense that China would be a free and independent nation among all other nations. Second, the new democratic culture must be scientific, that is, opposing all feudal and superstitious ideas on the one hand, and on the other, seeking objective truth from facts. Third, the new democratic culture must belong to the broad masses, serving all the people, especially workers and peasants. In other words, when China's new culture became a truly national, scientific and mass culture, according to Mao, a new China both in name and in reality would be within sight.[74]

One final comment on Mao's philosophy and its impact on Chinese philosophy in Communist China. In theory, Mao's philosophy, or better political philosophy, represents his world-view (i.e. reality as contradiction), his epistemology (practice–theory–practice), and his political and philosophical views on many other issues. As such, Mao's philosophy, like the thought of any other Chinese philosopher, should be viewed as part of contemporary Chinese philosophy and hence be judged accordingly. But because of Mao's political authority in Communist China, his philosophy is unique in the context of contemporary Chinese philosophy, especially since 1949. In fact, as part of Mao Zedong Thought, Mao's philosophy had quite a negative impact on Chinese philosophy in Communist China. Except in the early 1950s, Mao's philosophy, as part of Mao Zedong Thought, became *de facto* the supreme, absolute and final authority in Communist China by which anything and everything, theoretical and practical, political and otherwise, was judged. Similarly, all Chinese philosophers during this period were made to study Marxism and Mao Zedong Thought. Any Chinese philosopher who was not in conformity with the official philosophy was criticized, recriticized, or even punished. In short, in Communist China, even today, no independent, original or genuine Chinese philosophy is yet possible.

CONCLUSION

Having presented various twentieth-century Chinese philosophers and their philosophies, I should like to conclude this chapter with three comments.

1. The first concerns the organization or division of the chapter according to the three philosophical orientations: neo-traditional Chinese philosophy, Sino-Western philosophy and Chinese Marxism. These should not be understood or interpreted as rigidly defined philosophical schools. In fact, they were intended only to assist in focusing our discussion of various Chinese philosophers and their diverse philosophies, which are otherwise unrelated and fragmented. Philosophers discussed within each group were chosen according to their main philosophical orientation, though the ideas of some philosophers such as Feng Youlan or Jin Yuelin overlap with more than one philosophical trend.

2. The second is about the paramount concerns of almost all of the philosophers discussed: the 'China problem' and how to save and reconstruct China. Perhaps two reasons can be given for this. The first is that China's situation this century was so

critical and volatile that all Chinese intellectuals and leaders, including philosophers, were affected, and hence wanted to do something, both theoretical and practical, about it. The second and perhaps even more fundamental reason seems to come from the spirit of traditional Chinese philosophy. Traditional Chinese philosophy had always had a practical orientation, practical not in the sense of producing material progress, but in the sense of concerning itself with the well-being of the total human person: the cultivated person, human relationships, and a well-ordered society. This was demonstrated clearly in *The Great Learning*, through the eight steps: investigation of things, extension of knowledge, sincerity of the will, rectification of the mind, cultivation of personal life, regulation of the family, national order, and world peace.[75] In fact, this had always been the practical application of the central Confucian doctrine of humanity. Therefore, from this perspective, the fact that most Chinese philosophers seem to have focused on political philosophy has actually continued to be part of this practical application of traditional Chinese philosophy.

3. The last comment is a regret. Since this chapter is already too long, I have omitted many Chinese philosophers of this century who have also contributed to the development of contemporary Chinese philosophy. I feel obliged at least to recognize this fact.

To begin with, I could mention Tan Sitong (1865–98), who was 'the elaborator and modifier of Kang's basic philosophy of humanity'.[76] Similarly, in discussing Tang Jun-yi, I only mentioned Mou Zongsan, who, influenced by Xiong, his teacher, developed the basic insights of his teacher. Together with Tang, Mou introduced contemporary Neo-Confucianism in Hong Kong, believing that the essential insights of Confucianism and especially Neo-Confucianism needed to be reconstructed and further developed today. Along the same orientation, we can also include Chen Wenjie (Chan Wing-tsit) and Du Weiming in the United States. Having taught Chinese philosophy for many decades, the former has added a new and significant development to Chinese philosophy through his *Source Book in Chinese Philosophy* and numerous other works. While he is knowledgeable in all the philosophical schools of China, his own philosophical orientation seems to be that of Confucianism. The latter, the representative of a younger generation of contemporary Confucian scholars, has been the foremost exponent in the revival of Confucianism. In his *Confucian Thought: Selfhood a Creative Transformation*,[77] he presents his interpretation of Confucian humanism as a living tradition.

There are others again: Fang Dongmei (1897–1976), Yin Haiguang (1919–69) and Hong Qin (1909–). Fang, educated as a philosopher in the United States, taught philosophy for over fifty years in China and especially in Taiwan. Through both teaching and writing, he influenced many younger students. Yin, who was influenced by Dewey and Russell, as well as by Jin Yue-lin (early in China), was known for his interest in logic and analytic philosophy. In China, Hong, who had been one of the founding members of the Vienna Circle, studied with Rudolf Carnap (1891–1970).

Returning to China, he taught logic and analytic philosophy. Recently, he has been doing administrative work, while continuing his research and writing.

Finally, a word on Chinese philosophers who have devoted their efforts to the development of Chinese Buddhism this century, notably Ouyang Jingwu and Master Taixu. However, since Chapter 17 and Chapter 28 of this encyclopedia deal with Indian and Chinese Buddhism, they are not discussed here.

With this, we can summarize that while conditioned and restricted by China's critical and revolutionary situation in this century, contemporary Chinese philosophy as a whole has shown the vitality and creativity of Chinese philosophers of various orientations. But, as events continue to unfold with, we hope, more freedom for Chinese intellectuals, Chinese philosophers will surely continue to reflect on and search for 'wisdom' in contemporary society.

NOTES

1 John K. Fairbank, *The Great Chinese Revolution: 1800–1985* (New York: Harper & Row, 1987).
2 Benjamin Schwartz, *In Search of Wealth and Power* (New York: Harper & Row, 1964), p. 18.
3 Zhang Jiasen (Carsun Chang), *The Development of Neo-Confucian Thought* (2 vols, New York: Bookman Associates, 1962), p. 466.
4 John K. Fairbank, *The United States and China* (Cambridge, Mass.: Harvard University Press, 1979), p. 204.
5 Fung yu-lan (Feng you-lan), *A History of Chinese Philosophy*, 7th edn (2 vols., Princeton, N. J.: Princeton University Press, 1973 (1953)), p. 679.
6 ibid., p. 684.
7 Chan Wingtsit (Chen Wen-jie), *A Source Book in Chinese Philosophy* (Princeton, N. J.: Princeton University Press, 1963), p. 734.
8 ibid., p. 732.
9 Xiong Shili, *The New Doctrine of Consciousness-Only*, in Ji Zhenfu *et al.* (eds), *Selections from the History of Contemporary Chinese Philosophy* (5 vols, Shanghai: Shanghai Academy of Social Sciences, 1986–9), p. 433.
10 Chan Wingtsit, op. cit., p. 769.
11 ibid.
12 Luo Guang, *The History of Chinese Philosophy: Republican Period* (Taipei: Xue sheng shu ju, 1986), pp. 301–8.
13 Tang Junyi, 'The development of ideas of spiritual value in Chinese philosophy', in Charles A. Moore (ed.), *Philosophy and Culture: East and West* (Honolulu: University of Hawaii Press, 1968), pp. 227–43.
14 Luo Guang, op. cit., p. 356.
15 The 'manifesto' was drafted by Tang Junyi, and can be found in Zhang Jiasen, op. cit., pp. 455–83.
16 Feng Qi (ed.), *The History of Contemporary Chinese Philosophy* (2 vols, Shanghai: Shanghai People's Press, 1983), vol. II, p. 825.
17 Cai Shang-si *et al.* (eds), *The History of Contemporary Thought of China* (5 vols, Zhe Jiang, China: Zhe Jiang People's Press, 1983), vol. V, p. 66.
18 Chester C. Tan, *Chinese Political Thought in the Twentieth Century* (Garden City, N. Y.: Doubleday, 1971), pp. 287–9.

19 Chan Wingtsit, op. cit., p. 755.
20 ibid., p. 752.
21 Feng Qi, op. cit., p. 1060.
22 Chan Wingtsit, op. cit., p. 762.
23 Fairbank, *The United States and China*, pp. 147–55.
24 Laozi, *The Natural Way of Lao Tzu*, in Chan Wingtsit, op. cit., p. 139.
25 Schwartz, op. cit., p. 110.
26 ibid., p. 134.
27 ibid., p. 186.
28 Feng Qi, op. cit., p. 286.
29 Fairbank, *The United States and China*, p. 216.
30 Ch'u Chai and Winberg Chai, *The Changing Society of China* (New York: New American Library, 1969), p. 217.
31 Chester C. Tan, op. cit., p. 130.
32 ibid., p. 142.
33 Jerome B. Grieder, *Hu Shih and the Chinese Renaissance* (Cambridge, Mass.: Harvard University Press, 1970), p. 45.
34 Y. C. Wang, *Chinese Intellectuals and the West: 1872–1949* (Chapel Hill: The University of North Carolina Press, 1966), p. 395.
35 Chan Wingtsit, 'Hu Shih and Chinese Philosophy', in his *Neo-Confucianism, etc.: Essays* (Hanover, N. H.: Oriental Society, 1969), p. 285.
36 Feng Qi, op. cit., p. 778.
37 Y. C. Wang, op. cit., p. 400.
38 Chan Wingtsit, *Source Book in Chinese Philosophy* p. 744.
39 ibid., pp. 745–6.
40 ibid., p. 744.
41 ibid., pp. 749–50.
42 Chester. C. Tan, op. cit., p. 272.
43 It is worth noting that Zhang's political activities had a long history. Originally, he was a leader of the Progressive Party in the 1920s; then he formed the Socialist Party in 1931 with Zhang Jiasen. As a result, he opposed both the Nationalist Party and the Chinese Communist Party. After the second World War, he joined the Democratic League. Cf. Tan, op. cit., pp. 266–70; and Chan Wingtsit, *Source Book in Chinese Philosophy*, p. 744.
44 O. Briere, *Fifty Years of Chinese Philosophy: 1898–1949*, trans. Laurence Thompson (New York: Frederick A. Praeger, 1965), p. 87.
45 Feng Qi, op. cit., p. 1019.
46 Jin Yuelin, *The Tao* revised edn (Beijing: Commercial Press, 1987), p. 19.
47 ibid., pp. 218–21.
48 Chester C. Tan, op. cit., p. 66.
49 Jerome Ch'en, *Mao and the Chinese Revolution* (London: Oxford University Press, 1965), p. 80.
50 Hsueh Chuntu (ed.), *Revolutionary Leaders of Modern China* (London: Oxford University Press, 1971), p. 385.
51 Feng Qi, op. cit., p. 700.
52 Briere, op. cit., p. 23.
53 Feng Qi, op. cit., pp. 711–13.
54 ibid., p. 989.
55 Joshua A. Fogel, *Ai Ssu-ch'i's Contribution to the Development of Chinese Marxism* (Cambridge, Mass.: Harvard University Press, 1987), p. 17.
56 Briere, op. cit., p. 78.
57 Feng Qi, op. cit., p. 1008.
58 One of the best works on the re-evaluation of Mao and his thought is Stuart R. Schram's *Mao Zedong: A Preliminary Reassessment* (New York: St Martin's Press, 1983). Schram has been commonly recognized as the leading authority on Mao and his thought.

59 For Mao's biography, cf. Edgar Snow, *Red Star Over China* (New York: Random House, 1971); Stuart R. Schram, *Mao Tse-Tung* (New York: Simon and Schuster, 1966); and Ross Terrill, *Mao: A Biography* (New York: Harper & Row, 1980).
60 Benjamin I. Schwartz, *Chinese Communism and the Rise of Mao* (New York: Harper & Row, 1951), p. 78.
61 Snow, op. cit., p. 158.
62 Schram, *Mao Zedong: A Preliminary Reassessment*, p. 50.
63 Terrill, op. cit., pp. 400–23.
64 Schram, *Mao Zedong: A Preliminary Reassessment*, pp. 89–99; Lu Xichen, *Revised History of Contemporary Chinese Philosophy* (Jilin, China: Jilin People's Press, 1981), pp. 624–33.
65 Francis Soo, *Mao Tse-tung's Theory of Dialectic* (Dordrecht: Reidel, 1981), p. 53.
66 Mao Zedong, *Four Essays on Philosophy* (Beijing: Foreign Languages Press, 1968), p. 80.
67 Soo, op. cit., p. 67.
68 Mao Zedong, *Selected Works of Mao Tse-tung* (4 vols, Beijing: Foreign Languages Press, 1967), vol. I, pp. 297–9.
69 ibid., p. 308.
70 ibid., p. 296.
71 ibid., p. 308.
72 Mao, *Selected Works of Mao Tse-tung*, vol. II, p. 381.
73 ibid., pp. 380–2.
74 ibid., p. 382.
75 Chan Wingtsit, *Source Book in Chinese Philosophy*, p. 87.
76 ibid., p. 737.
77 Tu Weiming, *Confucian Thought: Selfhood as Creative Transformation* (Albany, N. Y.: State University of New York Press, 1985), p. 203.

FURTHER READING

Adelmann, Frederick J. (1982) *Contemporary Chinese Philosophy*, The Hague/Boston: Nijhoff.

Ai Siqi (1936) *Da-zhong zhe-xue* (*Philosophy for the Masses*), Shanghai: Du-shu chu-ban she.

Briere, O. (1965) *Fifty Years of Chinese Philosophy: 1898–1948*, trans. Laurence G. Thompson, New York: Praeger.

Cai Shangsi *et al.* (eds) (1983) *Zhong-guo jin-dai si-xiang shi zi-liao jian bian* (*The History of Contemporary Thought of China*), 5 vols, Zhe Jiang, China: Zhe Jiang People's Press.

Chai, Ch'u and Chai, Winberg (1969) *The Changing Society of China*, New York: New American Library.

—— (1973) *Confucianism*. Woodbury, N.Y.: Barron.

Chan Wingtsit (Chen Wen-jie) (1963) *A Source Book in Chinese Philosophy*, Princeton, N. J.: Princeton University Press.

—— (1969) *Neo-Confucianism, etc.: Essays*, Hanover, N. H.: Oriental Society.

Chan Wingtsit and Fu, Charles W. H. (1978) *Guide to Chinese Philosophy*, Boston, Mass.: G. K. Hall.

Ch'en, Jerome (1965) *Mao and the Chinese Revolution*, London: Oxford University Press.

Chen Duxiu (1933) *Du-xiu wen-cun* (*Collected Essays of Du-xiu*), Shanghai: Ya dong tu shu guan.

Chow Tsetsung (1960) *The May Fourth Movement: Intellectual Revolution in Modern China*, Cambridge, Mass.: Harvard University Press.

Creel, Herrlee G. (1953) *Chinese Thought from Confucius to Mao Tse-tung*, Chicago: University of Chicago Press.

De Barry, William T., Chan Wingtsit and Burton Watson (eds) (1960) *Sources of Chinese Traditions*, New York: Columbia University Press.

Fairbank, John King (1979) *The United States and China*, Cambridge, Mass.: Harvard University Press.
—— (1987) *The Great Chinese Revolution: 1800–1985*, New York: Harper & Row.
Feng Qi (ed.) (1983) *Xhong-guo jin-dai zhe-xue shi* (*The History of Contemporary Chinese Philosophy*), 2 vols, Shanghai: Shanghai People's Press.
Feng Youlan (Fung Yu-lan) (1939) *Xin li xue* (*A New Rational Philosophy*), Changsha: Commercial Press, 1939.
—— (1943) *Xin yuan ren* (*A New Treatise on the Nature of Man*), Chongqing: Commercial Press.
—— (1946) *Xin zhi yan* (*A New Understanding of Words*), Shanghai: Commercial Press.
—— (1947) *The Spirit of Chinese Philosophy*, trans. E. R. Hughes, London: Kegan Paul.
—— (1961) *Xin yuan dao* (*A New Treatise on the Nature of Tao*), revised edn, Xiang gang: Zhong-guo zhe-xue yan jiu hui.
—— (1973) *A History of Chinese Philosophy*, 2 vols, Princeton, N. J.: Princeton University Press.
Fogel, Joshua A. (1987) *Ai Ssu-ch'i's Contribution to the Development of Chinese Marxism*, Cambridge, Mass.: Harvard University Press.
Grieder, Jerome B. (1970) *Hu Shih and the Chinese Renaissance*, Cambridge, Mass.: Harvard University Press.
Guo Kanbo (1935) *Jin wu-shi-nian Zhong-guo si-xiang shi* (*An Intellectual History of China in the Last Fifty Years*), Beijing: Ren-wen shu-dian.
He Lin (1947) *Dang-dai zhong-guo zhe-xue* (*Contemporary Chinese Philosophies*), Nanjing: Sheng-li Publishing Company.
Hou Wailu *et al.* (1978) *Zhong-guo jin-dai zhe-xue shi* (*The History of Contemporary Philosophy of China*), Beijing: People's Press.
Hsu, Immanuel C. Y. (1970) *The Rise of Modern China*, London: Oxford University Press.
Hsueh Chuntu (1971) *Revolutionary Leaders of Modern China*, London: Oxford University Press.
Hu Shi (1953) *Hu Shi wen-cun, 1–4* (*Collected Essays of Hu Shi, Collections 1–4*), Taipei: Yuan dong tu-shu gong si.
Ji Zhenfu *et al.* (eds) (1986–9) *Zhong-guo jin-dai zhe-xue shi zi-liao xuan pian* (*Selections from the History of Contemporary Chinese Philosophy*), 5 vols, Shanghai: Shanghai Academy of Social Sciences.
Jin Yuelin (1935) *Lo ji* (*Logic*), Beijing: Qinghua University Press.
—— (1987) *Lun Dao* (*The Tao*), revised edn, Beijing: Commercial Press.
Kang Youwei (1958) *Ta T'ung Shu* (*The One-World Philosophy*), trans. Laurence G. Thompson, London: George Allen & Unwin.
Koller, John M. (1985) *Oriental Philosophies*, New York: Charles Scribner's Sons.
Kwok, D. W. Y. (1965) *Scientism in Chinese Thought: 1900–1950*, New Haven, Conn.: Yale University Press.
Li Da (1937) *She-hui xue da gang* (*Essentials of Sociology*), Shanghai: Bi geng shu-dian.
Liang Shuming (1925) *Dong-xi wen-hua ji qi zhe-xue* (*Eastern and Western Civilizations and their Philosophies*), Shanghai: Commercial Press.
—— (1972) *Jiao-yu wen zhai* (*Writings on Education*), revised edn, Taipei: Wen Jing Publishing Co.
Luo Guang (1986) *Zhong-guo zhe-xue shi: min-guo pian* (*The History of Chinese Philosophy: Republican Period*), Taipei: Xue sheng shu ju.
Lu Xichen (1981) *Zhong-guo xian-dai zhe-xue shi xin-bian* (*Revised History of Contemporary Chinese Philosophy*, Jilin, China: Jilin People's Press.
Mao Zedong (1967) *Selected Works of Mao Tse-tung*, 4 vols, Beijing: Foreign Languages Press.
—— (1968) *Four Essays on Philosophy*, Beijing: Foreign Languages Press.
Moore, Charles A. (ed.) (1968) *Philosophy and Culture: East and West*, Honolulu: University of Hawaii Press.

Naess, Arne and Hannay, Alastair (eds) (1972) *Invitation to Chinese Philosophy*, Oslo: Universitetsforlaget.
Ren Jiyu (1961–3; 1979) *Zhong-guo zhe-xue shi* (*The History of Chinese Philosophy*), 4 vols, Beijing: People's Press, 1961–3 (vols I–III), 1979 (vol. IV).
Riepe, Dale (ed.) (1981) *Asian Philosophy Today*, New York, Gordon and Breach.
Schram, Stuart R. (1963) *The Political Thought of Mao Tse-tung*, New York: Praeger.
—— (1966) *Mao Tse-tung*, New York: Simon & Schuster.
—— (ed.) (1973) *Chairman Mao Talks to the People*, New York: Random House.
—— (1983). *Mao Zedong: A Preliminary Reassessment*, New York: St Martin's Press.
Schwartz, Benjamin (1951) *Chinese Communism and the Rise of Mao*, New York: Harper & Row.
—— (1964) *In Search of Wealth and Power*, New York: Harper & Row.
Snow, Edgar (1971) *Red China Today*, New York: Random House.
Soo, Francis (1981) *Mao Tse-tung's Theory of Dialectic*, Dordrecht: Reidel.
Sun Yatsen (1936) *San-Min Zhu-Yi* (*The Three Principles of the People*), trans. Frank W. Price, Shanghai: Commercial Press.
—— (1957) *Guo-fu quan-ji* (*Complete Works of Sun Yat-sen*), 6 vols, Taipei: Zhong-yang wen-wu gong-ying she.
Tan, Chester C. (1971) *Chinese Political Thought in the Twentieth Century*, Garden City, N. Y.: Doubleday.
Tang Junyi (1966–73) *Zhong-guo zhe-xue yuan lun* (*The Origins and Development of Basic Concepts in Chinese Philosophy*), 6 vols, Hong Kong: Institute of New Asia College.
—— (1977) *Sheng-ming cun-zai yu xin-ling jing jie* (*The Existence of Life and the Spiritual World*), 2 vols, Hong Kong: Xue sheng shu dian.
Terrill, Ross (1980) *Mao: A Biography*, New York: Harper & Row.
Tu Weiming (Du Wei-ming) (1985) *Confucian Thought: Selfhood as Creative Transformation*, Albany, N.Y.: State University of New York Press.
Xiong Shili (1947) *Xin Wei shi lun* (*The New Doctrine of Consciousness-Only*), Shanghai: Commercial Press.
Wakeman, Frederic (1973). *History and Will*, Berkeley Los Angeles: University of California Press.
Wang, Y. C. (1966) *Chinese Intellectuals and the West: 1872–1949*, Chapel Hill: University of North Carolina Press.
Yan Fu (1902) *Yuan fu* (*The Wealth of Nations*), Shanghai: Commercial Press.
—— (1923) *Jian yan lun* (*On Evolution*), revised edn, Shanghai: Commercial Press.
Zhang Dongsun (1931) *Dao-de zhe-xue* (*Moral Philosophy*), Shanghai: Zhong-hua Publishing Company.
—— (1934a) *Ren-shi lun* (*Epistemology*), Shanghai: Shi-jie shu-ju.
—— (1934b) *Xian-dai zhe-xue* (*Modern Philosophy*), Shanghai: Shi-jie shu-ju.
—— (1946) *Li-xing yu min-zhu* (*Reason and Democracy*), Shanghai: Commercial Press.
Zhang Jiasen (Carsun Chang) (1957, 1962) *The Development of Neo-Confucian Thought*, 2 vols, New York: Bookman Associates.

Part V

JAPANESE PHILOSOPHY

INTRODUCTION

The indigenous religion of Japan, Shintoism, cannot be regarded as a philosophical system in the sense of Buddhism and Confucianism. Without a developed theoretical basis in metaphysics, epistemology or moral philosophy, it stands alone as a religious and ceremonial practice. It has, however, undergone substantial evolution in the context of the changes in Japan's political environment and served as an underpinning of the authority of the ruling powers at various times in Japan's history.

Buddhism and Confucianism were brought to Japan from Korea during the fourth to sixth centuries AD, and were accommodated in various ways to the indigenous religious tradition. Scholars travelled to China to seek the Chinese understanding of the original texts, and attempted to interpret them within the very different social and political context of Japan.

The Tokugawa period (1600–1868) saw a flourishing of Buddhism in particular, though Neo-Confucianism had an important if not so firmly established a place in Japan's intellectual life. This period saw too an awakening of interest in Western thought, called 'Dutch Learning' since it was through trading contacts with Holland that the Western sciences became known.

The Meiji restoration of 1867/8 brought with it an even livelier enthusiasm for Western thought, with authors like Auguste Comte and J. S. Mill being translated into Japanese. A major effort was made to translate and interpret such ideas in Japan's own intellectual vocabulary and to find an accommodation for them within the Buddhist and Confucian systems. In more recent years Japanese philosophers have found inspiration especially from Continental philosophy – phenomenology in particular – which manifests interests and methods more amenable to Buddhism.

Two preoccupations stand out prominently in the history of Japanese philosophy. The first concerns moral and political issues, and here Confucianism has provided a fertile system of ideas to be adapted to the realities of Japanese society. The second, again an abiding preoccupation, is the desire to find an intellectual accommodation between what is seen as the objective, logical and analytic nature of Western philosophy, with its scientific and technological context, and the more subjective and human-centered emphasis of traditional Japanese thought. This latter preoccupation can be seen as a contemporary manifestation of the perennial task of finding a fit between science and religion.

B. C. and I. M.

34

THE ORIGINS OF JAPANESE PHILOSOPHY

Brian Bocking

'Japanese philosophy' can be understood in a narrow sense as intellectual analysis conducted by particular Japanese philosophers, and in a much broader sense as world-views or approaches to life which are characteristic of the Japanese people and which have provided the context and motivation for philosophical and other intellectual endeavours in Japan. Succeeding chapters on Japanese Confucianism, Buddhism, morals and society and contemporary Japanese philosophy demonstrate in more detail the variety of philosophical, ethical and metaphysical standpoints espoused by particular thinkers in Japan from the sixth century to the present day. The purpose of this chapter is to indicate some of the foundations of these ideas and orientations. The European and American origins of the schools of Western philosophy introduced to Japan since the nineteenth century are not covered here.

THE JAPANESE PHILOSOPHICAL TRADITION

Nowadays, Japanese intellectuals are to be found actively involved in every branch of learning, including most schools of Western and Eastern philosophy. Such full involvement in modern international academic life developed rapidly after the Meiji restoration (or coup) of 1867/8, in which the feudal Tokugawa government was overthrown and Japan was opened to international exchange. Since the 1860s Japanese academics have routinely studied abroad, and all kinds of philosophical works published in English, French, German, Russian and other important Western languages, as well as modern Asian writings, have been made available in Japanese translation. Even during the Tokugawa period (1600–1868) a limited number of Western books were studied in Japan in the period of 'Dutch Learning' which followed the introduction of Christianity in the sixteenth century and its suppression in the seventeenth. For a thousand years before that, educated Japanese were able to study, principally through the medium of Chinese (the Latin of Japan), a variety of East Asian arts, philosophies and sciences of foreign origin. As a result, Japanese thinkers have had access – both through primary sources and in their own language – to a range of contrasting philosophical views and sources of inspiration far wider than that normally available within the Eurocentric world of Western philosophy. Japanese thinkers have been able to draw upon a variety of authoritative traditions from different parts of the world (initially Chinese and Indian Buddhism, Confucianism, Daoism and Japanese Shintō, and later Western thought), for in Japan no single religious or intellectual tradition has ever predominated for long. Early on, the plethora of authoritative yet apparently inconsistent sources of knowledge available to the Japanese had the effect of relativizing views about ultimate matters such as the nature of God(s), the origin of the world or the source of evil and suffering, matters which in other cultures have been determined at least in broad outline by reference to a single scriptural source such as the Bible or the Koran.

JAPAN'S INTERNATIONAL PERSPECTIVE

It is tempting to assume – and a number of influential modern Japanese thinkers, the proponents of the so-called *nihonjin-ron* or 'theory of Japaneseness', will encourage such an assumption – that an outward-looking international perspective is a new phenomenon in Japan and that before the hasty introduction of modern Western thought to Japan in the second half of the nineteenth century, Japanese society and Japanese thought had run along traditional and more or less unchanging lines within a traditional and more or less unchanging society, the essentially 'Japanese' elements of which should be protected and preserved for the future. While Japanese society today exhibits a degree of cultural homogeneity and apparent continuity of tradition which contrasts sharply with the experience of multicultural 'melting-pot' societies such as the USA, the explanation for this outward homogeneity is not to be found in an elusive yet unchanging quality of 'Japaneseness', but in modern processes of socialization from childhood which have encouraged behavioural conformity and discouraged individual expression of dissent. Contemporary Japanese social homogeneity is above all a legacy of the overt and extremely thorough programmes of social and political indoctrination practised by the Meiji to early Showa governments during the period of Japan's rapid modernization and economic expansion from 1868 to 1945.

Japanese society is currently undergoing profound changes with the passing of the last generation of parents and legislators to be brought up under the 'old' (i.e. pre-1945) education and social system. The members of the post-war generation now rising to positions of real influence in Japanese society have been brought up in a world very different from that which formed the thoughts and values of their parents and grandparents. Nor is this the first time that Japanese society has undergone radical transformation. The Japanese of the second half of the nineteenth century who witnessed its opening after two and a half centuries of seclusion felt the direct impact of a world beyond the Japanese islands which had been inaccessible to their parents and grandparents. In the seventeenth and eighteenth centuries the Japanese had a narrow view of the world coloured by their country's isolation and inwardness. By contrast, earlier generations living in the sixteenth and seventeenth centuries, before Japan was 'closed', had access to Western religious and philosophical ideas and ways of life through the activities of Christian missionaries and Western traders. Earlier still, Japan's relations with China and Korea fluctuated in degree of intensity and amity over many centuries, so that the influence of philosophical and scientific ideas from the Eurasian continent also waxed and waned. 'Foreign' influence indeed was arguably at its height at the very beginning of Japan's historical existence, from about the fourth to the seventh centuries AD, when Japanese culture was radically transformed by the introduction of Chinese civilization. It is sometimes said that the Japanese took only those aspects of Chinese culture which suited them, and rejected the rest. If so, the net of acceptability had a very large mesh, and was itself partly made in China or Korea. Nothing of any significance in Japanese intellectual and cultural life has completely escaped the influence of China and Korea, from the very notion of Japan as an empire to ideas of the afterlife, from rice to writing, from architecture to beliefs about gender. One should not, therefore, look for the origins of Japanese philosophy only in Japan. Far from being a closed, traditional society only recently opened to the world, Japan on close inspection reveals itself as a country shaped from the very beginning by outside influences. Indeed, a marked and continuing feature of Japanese thought and culture is its openness and readiness to embrace – subject always to political constraints – ideas from outside: an openness amounting almost to a thirst for what is new.

Yet there is something undeniably 'Japanese' about the way Japanese people approach ideas, the art of living, personal relationships and even death. Most scholars, while recognizing that Japan is in various ways different from other cultures, try hard to avoid locating these differences in a concept of 'Japaneseness', as if there is something essential in the difference between Japan and other countries. Yet there is something to be explained. Why is Japan different from China and from Korea, both Confucian/Buddhist cultures like Japan? The answer must lie in the combination of a whole host of factors – political, economic and geographical as well as cultural – which have moulded Japanese minds over the centuries and contributed to the distinctive 'feel' of Japanese culture and thought.

INDIGENOUS JAPANESE INFLUENCES

Although it is possible to trace early Japanese settlements to around 15000 BC, and important archaeological discoveries which enhance or change our understanding of the distant origins of the Japanese are continuing to be made, we can do little more than speculate about the intellectual concerns of prehistoric Japanese people. Archaeologists working with pottery and bronze artefacts have identified themes and motifs which find parallels in ancient China, the Near East, Africa and America, indicating that the ancient peoples of Japan may have had preoccupations about life, time, death and rebirth similar to those of cultures now far distant from modern Japan.

Third-century AD Chinese chronicles concerning the 'Eastern Barbarians' describe the Japanese as 'the people of Wa' and indicate that the Japanese islands contained many separate kingdoms. The main kingdom of Yamatai was ruled by Queen Himiko, who is credited with magical and shamanistic powers. The possibility of women occupying such prominent public roles is a feature of prehistoric Japanese society which did not survive the introduction of Confucian and Buddhist teachings, both of which encouraged the subordination of women. Japanese women have nevertheless retained more freedom and exercised more influence than their Chinese counterparts; they were not, for example, subjected to such forms of ritual repression as foot-binding, and they continued to make a significant impact in areas of public life including religion and the arts, despite the limitations of a patriarchal society.

Reliable knowledge of what the early Japanese thought, as opposed to the artefacts they used, the impression they conveyed to the Chinese or the monuments they left, comes with the introduction of a writing system for Japanese sometime between the fifth and sixth centuries AD. Although brief inscriptions dating from the first century AD have been found on Chinese objects discovered in Japan, the earliest native Japanese inscriptions date from the fifth century AD, by which time large areas of Japan had come under the rule of the Emperor Yūryaku. Chinese writing was probably introduced to Japan by immigrant Korean families who, along with visiting advisers and scholars from Korea and with the encouragement of progressive Japanese clans such as the Soga, were instrumental in transforming Japan from a tribal culture to a centralized bureaucratic state along Korean/Chinese lines by the seventh century. Buddhism had been successfully introduced to Korea in the fourth century AD, and the Japanese chronicles record that Buddhism was officially transmitted to Japan in 538 or 552 by a delegation from the King of Paekche (Korea). Confucianism too was introduced to Korea in the fourth century and may have been transmitted to Japan as early as the fifth century by Korean scholars. Confucian ideals are reflected, along with Buddhist ideas, in the 'Seventeen-Article Constitution', which is not a constitution but a set of moral exhortations to government officials attributed to Prince Shōtoku (d. 622). Confucian influence is also evident in the Taika ('great change') reforms of government of 645–9, which sought to establish the power of central government and to reduce the influence of independent clans (*uji*).

Although the Chinese writing system was adapted to cope with the Japanese spoken language (which is similar to Korean in some respects but radically different from

Chinese), all early Japanese ideas of which we have a written record are Sino-Japanese ideas, at least to the extent that they are Japanese ideas expressed through the medium of Chinese script. The earliest Japanese chronicles cannot be said to represent a pure indigenous stratum of Japanese thought, even though they incorporate native oral traditions. The name 'Nihon' (also pronounced 'Nippon', and meaning '[land of the] sun's origin') indicates a Chinese perspective on Japan, and the eighth-century *Nihongi* (*Chronicle of Japan*) is written in Chinese. Its first sentence reads 'Of old, heaven and earth were not yet separated, and the *yin* and *yang* not yet divided' – sentiments which are unmistakably Chinese. Other early writings, such as the *Kojiki* (*Record of Ancient Matters*) and two famous collections of poetry, the *Kaifūsō* (*Fond Recollections of Poetry*) and the *Man' yōshū* (*Collection of Ten Thousand Leaves*), are permeated by Chinese thought. Clearly the Japanese clans had a rich tradition of oral literature, poetry, myth and legendary history, a proportion of which finds its way into these early written works (the *Man' yōshū* is particularly valued for its 'Japanese' quality), but by the time these writings were produced Chinese culture and philosophy had already become the measure against which the native tradition was being evaluated and amended.

Japan was not conquered by China or by Korea, and in the early period the influence of Chinese thought was restricted to the relatively small circle of nobles, priests and government officials surrounding the imperial court, only gradually permeating the lives of ordinary people. The gulf between the world-view of the few hundred cultured and educated court officials, whose knowledge of Chinese gave them access to the intellectual wealth of a thousand years of Chinese civilization, and the traditional outlook of the three to five million Japanese peasants and artisans at this time was profound. As time went on, Chinese and élite ideas pervaded all classes of society, particularly through the religious institutions of Buddhism and Daoism, which spread popular ideas of morality, *yin–yang* and divination and syncretized with indigenous traditions, loosely described as *Shintō*, 'the Way of the Gods'.

The dimension of Chinese thought which most influenced the Japanese was undoubtedly that of Confucianism, which dealt with day-to-day conduct and ethics against a background of cosmological ideas fundamental to the authority of the imperial court. Confucianism not only provided the content of much Japanese philosophy, but shaped the social and institutional framework within which the enterprise of philosophy was, and to some extent continues to be, conducted.

CONFUCIANISM

Confucianism first entered Japan as part of a package of Chinese thought and culture during the fourth to sixth centuries AD. By the time the first Japanese written records were produced in the eighth century, a cultural revolution had taken place in Japan.

From a background of competing regional clans the Japanese imperial court had emerged, consciously modelled on the Chinese system of centralized government. The earliest capitals adopted all the essential features of a Chinese imperial capital, and when the Nara court, in imitation of Chinese practice, removed to the new capital of Heian-kyo (Kyoto) in 794, the new city was laid out in conformity with the plan of the great Chinese capital Ch'ang-an (now Xian), with streets, walls and even courtly ranks arranged, like Prince Shōtoku's earlier 'Seventeen-Article Constitution', in auspicious combinations of eights and nines to conform to *yinyang* thought.

The syncretism of Confucianism with Daoist *yin–yang* thought and with Buddhism was an enduring feature in China, Korea and Japan, and in practice Confucianism cannot be disunited from the other traditions together with which it has formed the world-view of most of East Asia. However, for purposes of analysis it is helpful to isolate some key features of Confucianism, both to make the contrast with Western (including Indian) thought and to indicate what features originating in Confucianism still permeate Japanese society and culture, including intellectual life.

Confucius was the perfect man. This presupposition of Confucianism identifies Confucian thought as optimistic (human perfection *is* possible in the world), humanistic (perfection is to be achieved within human relationships rather than in an afterlife) and nostalgic (perfection was once achieved at the time and through the personality of Confucius – our task is at best to reconstruct his achievement in today's degenerated conditions). Confucius was no recluse: he conducted himself in an exemplary way in a variety of social roles, and from his example are derived normative rules about social conduct, that is to say, what characterizes the perfect ruler, servant, father, son, spouse, friend, philosopher and so on. Confucians perceive a link between the individual, the social and the cosmic realms, to the extent that selfish (anti-social) behaviour is seen as a cause not only of social upheaval but also of upheaval in the natural world and the cosmic order.

Confucius achieved perfection around the age of 70, after a life of rigorous self-cultivation; continuous education or training leading ultimately to the identification of individual desire with social duty. The Confucian therefore seeks, like Confucius, to integrate two superficially conflicting elements within the self – what one *should* do, and what one *wants* to do. Self-cultivation is not simply the suppression of self for the sake of society, as if a self could exist without its social dimension, but the happy harmonization of the social and individual elements which constitute the concrete individual. On completion of the task of self-cultivation we actively *want* to be what we are *expected* to be, and the apparently intractable contradictions of the human condition are resolved.

The Confucian problem is *how* the integration of individual will and social role or duty is to be achieved, not whether it should be. This raises the question (paralleled in Mahāyāna Buddhism) of whether human perfection is innate, waiting to be revealed, or something external to the self that must be obtained by strenuous and gradual effort, possibly involving suppression of evil tendencies. Self-cultivation is in either case seen as essential, and the enormously high value placed on education and disciplined conduct throughout East Asia today is testament to the power of Confucius' example. In Neo-Confucianism, which developed later in China as a blend of Buddhist and Confucian thought and was introduced to Japan by Zen monks, contemplative and meditational techniques were seen as an effective means to achieve this integration. The various Japanese 'ways' (of tea, of the warrior, of archery, etc.) represent a fusion of Zen and Neo-Confucian ideas applied to practical arts and activities of the nobles, *samurai* and even merchant classes. Such 'ways' involve a degree of application to a particular skill (such as swordsmanship) which takes the practitioner from the stage of conscious effort to a selfless, transcendent mastery of the technique – a mastery which automatically extends to other aspects of life.

Self-cultivation is a maturing process, and the fact that Confucius spent almost the whole of his life engaged in self-cultivation in a successful quest for perfection has deeply coloured Japanese attitudes to age. To the Confucian mind there is inevitably something suspect about a buddha who achieved enlightenment at the raw age of 40, or a Jesus who is said to have completed his mission at 30, while still a youth, especially since both these spiritual leaders appear to have taken their social and family responsibilities lightly. A young Confucian is an incomplete person with incomplete ideas, and typically a long-term apprenticeship within a master–disciple relationship is seen as the only reliable means of ensuring that the accumulated wisdom of maturity and self-cultivation is transmitted from one generation to the next, not dissipated in the wilful and unfettered intellectual passions and enthusiasms of youth. As the saying goes in Japan even today, you should not disagree with your teacher more than 35 per cent! Most importantly, Confucianism presupposes that thought and conduct go hand in hand, so that there can be no such thing as a good (mature) idea from a bad (immature) person, and a bad or immature person is one who does not behave in a way appropriate to his social role. It takes an unlikely effort of imagination for a young Western philosopher (i.e. under the age of 40) to acknowledge that his or her ideas, however brilliant and persuasive, are without value because their author is not yet mature. Within the Confucian world-view, however, this is self-evidently true.

BUDDHISM

Buddhism is one of the mainsprings of Japanese philosophy. Though originating in India, Buddhism spread and adapted to many different cultures, and it is Chinese Buddhism that has most directly influenced Japanese thought. A more detailed account of Japanese Buddhism is found in Chapter 36 below. Buddhism has been seen by most Japanese not as an Indian religion, but simply as one of the 'three religions' of Shintō, Buddhism and Confucianism, corresponding to the three religions of

Confucianism, Daoism and Buddhism in China. There are many schools of Buddhism in Japan, and many ways of categorizing Buddhist thought, including schemes devised by the Chinese and Japanese themselves to account for the diversity of Indian Buddhist teachings which found their way to the Far East along the silk roads. Chinese and Japanese forms of Buddhism are overwhelmingly Mahāyānist in content and approach. They regard the Buddha as a cosmic, eternal entity or principle and adopt as their religious role-model the *bodhisattva* who vows to save all beings before himself entering perfect supreme enlightenment. Of the hundreds of texts which constitute authoritative Buddhist teachings in Japan, some are scriptures believed to represent the words of the Buddha himself, while others are treatises attributed to enlightened commentators spanning the entire history of Buddhism. There is no agreement within Japanese Buddhism on what constitutes the 'essence' of Buddhism or which is its purest form, although the various Buddhist schools each claim to convey the authentic teaching. Factional divisions have been as important as doctrinal or philosophical debates in the development of Buddhist denominations in Japan.

Mahāyāna Buddhist thought developed in India and thereafter in two broad streams or tendencies, Yogācāra and Mādhyamika. Both types of philosophy aim to account for the way things really are, in conformity with the teachings of the Buddha. A brief account of these two fundamental types of Buddhist philosophy, and of Esoteric or Tantric Buddhism, which has been exceptionally important in Japan, will be given in this chapter, since developed Japanese forms of Buddhism such as Tendai, Pure Land, Zen and Nichiren Buddhism are dealt with in detail in Chapter 36.

Yogācāra is a form of Buddhist idealism which presents a *model* of the realms or levels of consciousness to explain why and how Buddhist practice operates as a vehicle of liberation from ignorance, craving and delusion. According to Yogācāra (known in China and Japan as 'Mind-only' philosophy), perfect unconditioned enlightenment is inherent within us, but is obscured by the layers of the unenlightened mind. Enlightenment will manifest spontaneously through all the spheres of consciousness once unenlightened mental impulses are transmuted through Buddhist practice. The Yogācāra interpretation of Buddhism is not dissimilar to Vedāntic idealism in positing a 'light within' model of the mind.

Yogācāra conscientiously preserves the Buddha's psychological approach to the objective world, seeing the 'objective' cosmos as the reflection or projection of consciousness. Yogācāra-type Buddhist philosophies have profoundly influenced Japanese thought, both directly through schools of Buddhist philosophy popular in Japan (Tendai, Pure Land and Zen in particular) and indirectly through the legitimacy this philosophical school bestows on views of the world which emphasize the illusory, subjective and hence transient nature of 'objective' reality. Buddhists have debated whether the process of restraining unenlightened impulses described by Yogācāra takes many lifetimes or can be completed in the twinkling of an eye; the Japanese have leaned, under the influence of Esoteric Buddhism, towards the view that the process can be completed at least in this lifetime, and under the influence of Zen, through philosophers such as Dōgen, to the view that enlightenment can only be obtained in the present moment, since no other time exists.

The Mādhyamika line of approach is somewhat different from Yogācāra in that it identifies unenlightenment with attachment to concepts, however orthodox, exalted and meaningful these concepts may be. Mādhyamika understands the task of Buddhist philosophy to be more than just describing how things are; for the Mādhyamika, language and ideas should be used to subvert themselves. '*Nirvāṇa*', 'Buddha' and 'attaining perfect supreme enlightenment' are merely 'empty' conventional verbal formulations, and enlightenment is brought no closer by understanding intellectually what these terms mean, for grasping a concept intellectually is just another form of grasping or craving, and the Buddha taught that the mind which grasps remains unenlightened. Mādhyamika has inspired a self-subverting strand in Buddhist philosophy in relation to the very doctrinal formulations which are conventionally thought to be essential to Buddhist thought. The distinctive philosophical mood of Mādhyamika is preserved in Japan in Zen Buddhist *kōan* or riddles and the often nonsensical master–pupil dialogues known as *mondō*, although the underlying philosophical basis of Zen owes more to Yogācāra and the notion of innate enlightenment than to Mādhyamika logic. Mādhyamika philosophy was consciously incorporated in Japanese Tendai Buddhism and is formally acknowledged as authoritative in schools derived from Tendai, such as Pure Land Buddhism.

A notable element of Mādhyamika is the 'collapse of distance' or 'collapse of transcendence' implied, for example, between *nirvāṇa* (liberation) and *saṃsāra* (this world, rebirth, bondage), or between the unenlightened being and the Buddha. Since '*nirvāṇa*' and '*saṃsāra*' are just words, there is no difference between them. The same critique is applied to the notion of causality, where causes and effects are said to be 'empty' of any own-being by virtue of their interdependency as terms. Important also in Mādhyamika is the notion of Two Truths, the first or Lower Truth being the accessible, expressible, conventional truth, a necessary precursor to attainment of the second and ungraspable Higher Truth, which can never be expressed in words. Mādhyamika-influenced thinkers who understand the dialectical relationship between these two levels of truth regard that which can be said, written and expressed as a necessary stage in attaining that truth which is beyond speech. Moreover, when Mādhyamika says that there is no difference between *nirvāṇa* and *saṃsāra*, it acknowledges that this assertion, too, belongs in the realm of conventional speech.

Japanese Buddhists have inherited both Yogācāra and Mādhyamika approaches to Buddhist philosophy and commonly regard them as complementary. Yogācāra-type philosophies try to explain how things are, emphasizing that things are not what they seem (nor are they otherwise, adds Zen), while Mādhyamika reminds the philosopher that all such explanations belong in the realm of conventional truth and that not too much importance should be attached to them. The doctrine of two levels of truth casts suspicion on all verbal formulations, since it can be applied to any mental constructs, whether Buddhist or not. While Japanese philosophers have traditionally been, unlike their post-Enlightenment Western counterparts, respectful towards rather than sceptical of received truths, a flavour of wry scepticism about *any* conceptual formulation has pervaded Japanese thought.

A Buddhist text which has had enduring influence in Japan and should receive special mention is the *Lotus Sūtra*. As well as expounding basic Mahāyāna ideas of the eternity and omnipresence of the Buddha, the *Lotus Sūtra* states that the Buddha out of compassion has provided different paths to the same goal of enlightenment to suit living beings of different dispositions. The *sūtra* also offers a number of *darani* or *mantras* which can be used to evoke the power of the Buddha. The *Lotus Sūtra* thereby relativizes once again the 'truths' of Buddhism, and emphasizes the role of magical methods in Buddhist practice, a key feature of Esoteric Buddhism.

ESOTERIC BUDDHISM

Esoteric or Tantric Buddhism was popularized in Japan by Shingon and Tendai teachers from the ninth century, although elements of Esoteric Buddhism had existed in Japan before this time. Esoteric Buddhism is built around the guru–disciple relationship and a secret or private transmission of methods and teachings. It can accommodate exoteric philosophies but is not dependent on them, since it claims to be based on esoteric practical teachings unavailable except to the initiate. Esoteric Buddhism involves the progressive identification of the practitioner with a Buddha, an identification which involves the whole body and not just the mind. It therefore incorporates physical sounds, sacred images and *mudra* or gestures. Esoteric Buddhism has been responsible for much of the Buddhist art in Japan, and its magical view of the world has proved deeply appealing to the Japanese. 'Magical' in this context refers to the transformation of one substance into another by esoteric ritual means. In Tantric Buddhism proper the substance in question is the practitioner's own mind and body, while in teachings such as those of Nichiren (1212–82) the concept becomes that of the country of Japan itself magically transformed by repetition of a powerful mantra into the realm of buddhahood, a notion which later attracted nationalistic interpretations.

DAOISM

Daoism is a collective term for practices and beliefs sometimes subdivided into philosophical, religious and popular Daoism, although it is in practice difficult to separate such strata within Daoism or even distinguish Daoism from Buddhism or

Confucianism in China and Shintō in Japan. Daoist books explaining the complex interactions of *yin* and *yang* were available in Japan from the earliest period of Chinese influence, and elements of Daoism quickly spread throughout the country. Particularly popular in Japan in the Heian period were Daoist-derived forms of divination, dealing with auspicious and inauspicious days, names, years and directions of travel. These kinds of Daoist ideas have remained widespread in Japan, where not only specialist almanacs sold at Shintō shrines but ordinary office diaries indicate lucky and unlucky days, and it is statistically obvious that many parents take care not to have a girl born in the year of the horse, lest she be strong-willed and unmarriageable. The Japanese government established a 'Bureau of *Yin and Yang*' in the seventh century as a kind of spiritual meteorological office to establish the calendar, calculate auspicious days and directions for travel and prescribe the taboos, stratagems and rituals which would avert misfortune. Unlucky directions are linked with the pantheon of Daoist divinities who move around the compass in complex cycles. Some directions, such as the north-east 'Demons' Gate', remain permanently inauspicious. Houses in Japan to this day avoid facing in this dangerous direction.

The key notion of Daoism which unites the refined nature-mysticism of Chinese Daoist hermits with popular Japanese interest in fortune-telling is that of the *Dao* itself, the ordered flow and fluid ordering of events which both constitutes and underlies appearances. The *Dao* is not, it should be noted, governed by eternal regular clockwork laws of the kind often sought by Western science, for divination or intuition of the *Dao* is intended not to discern basic laws once and for all but to map for practical purposes the local operations of the *Dao* and interpret and explain the significance of unusual phenomena. Daoist thought has contributed to Japanese philosophy a view of the world which eschews any kind of mechanical determinism and celebrates the unusual and the particular, while recognizing that there are recurring patterns in nature and human affairs.

Daoist beliefs and practices also reinforce the notion that the objective world is not to be taken for granted, that there is a coherent power behind and within events regulated by the interplay of *yin* and *yang*, a power which can be resisted at our cost or intuited and accepted to our benefit. This power is not normally conceived of as personal; although there are Daoist divinities, their conduct conforms to the *Dao*. To merge with the operation of *Dao* through spiritual practice is to internalize the irresistible tide of nature itself, to achieve immortality through union with the deathless flow of events. At the highest philosophical level, the *Dao* is indistinguishable from the *nirvāṇa* of Buddhism, and the terms were interchangeable in Chinese translations of Buddhist texts. In Japan, practical 'ways' (Chinese *dao*; Japanese *tō* or *dō*), spiritualized techniques and roles including *sadō*, the way of tea, and *bushidō*, the way of the warrior, became popular in the Tokugawa period, where they represented – in a Confucian context – paths to transcendence of self and spiritual perfection within one's narrowly defined social role.

SHINTŌ

Shintō (*Shin-tō*, 'the way of the gods') is the Japanese religious tradition which reflects most obviously the native outlook of the Japanese, but it would be naïve to assume that Shintō constitutes some kind of unchanging substrate within Japanese culture. Shintō has undergone profound changes over its long history, and particularly since the Meiji restoration of 1868. Even a brief examination of Shintō ideas reveals that changes in the political and social sphere have meant changes in the meaning of Shintō itself.

Early Shintō consisted of the imperial family cult and the worship of other local deities (*kami*) attached either to a clan (*uji*) or to a locality, which might be an unusual or impressive feature of the landscape such as a mountain or waterfall. The early eighth-century imperial chronicles which contain the Shintō creation myths are essentially political documents which retail in a way favourable to the Yamato court the story of the descent of the imperial family, the land and the people of Japan from the gods (*kami*). Prominent among these *kami* is the sun goddess Amaterasu ('Heaven-Shining'). A shrine to Amaterasu at Ise in central Japan was, and remains, the private imperial household shrine. Such a clear and close correlation between myth, deity and location of shrine is rather rare in Shintō, whose religious teachings have been well described as 'inherently vague'. The term '*kami*' does not necessarily imply a named deity, since the primary meaning of *kami* is 'sacred' – a numinous, ambivalent and energetic quality which may attach to or inhere in a variety of objects and entities, including on occasion living or dead human beings. Shintō is local and shrine-based, rather than rooted in a doctrinal tradition.

As an inherited oral tradition, strong in ritual and closely enmeshed in Japanese daily life but lacking any sophisticated system of thought, Shintō survived as a strong partner to the new philosophies and imported rituals of Buddhism and Confucianism from the sixth century onwards. In the areas of philosophy, ethics and theology Shintō was virtually eclipsed by the incoming traditions. Throughout Japanese history Shintō has provided ritual and ceremonial support to governments, clans and communities whose ethical ideals and many of whose religious beliefs were actually derived from Confucianism and Buddhism. For example, death, preparation for the afterlife and ideas of salvation became almost entirely the province of Buddhism, while social morality was a Confucian concern. Shintō rites nevertheless punctuated the life cycle and the agricultural calendar and bound together the local community under the protection of its deities. In the minds of ordinary people there was no dividing line between the teachings of Shintō, Buddhism and Confucianism. The three traditions constituted a synthetic unity, on the one hand shading off into folk religious practices and specialized cults such as the Shintō-Buddhist mountain religion of *Shugendō*, and on the other underpinning popular morality, communal festivals and government ceremonial.

Following the Meiji restoration of 1868, a completely new form of Shintō, retrospectively referred to as 'State Shintō', was developed by the Japanese government in a conscious effort to close the door on Japan's feudal past and unite the minds of the Japanese behind an ambitious programme of modernization and industrial expansion in order to catch up with the West. Ruthlessly separated from Buddhism, and incorporating a Confucian-style doctrine of the divine emperor as the head and the ordinary people as the body of the nation, State Shintō was vigorously propagated through schools and public institutions in a programme which nationalized the Shintō shrines and used them as vehicles for the inculcation of patriotic religious ideals and political docility. Eventually, any religious or indeed secular teachings which did not conform to State Shintō were either forced to adapt or were suppressed – a quashing of dissent which finally spread through every area of Japanese life in the immediate pre-war period.

Unusually, then, during the period 1868–1945 'Shintō' embodied very specific teachings. These artificially created teachings were of course almost totally discredited by Japan's military defeat in 1945, and the post-war constitution denationalized the Shintō network and, following the North American model, brought about a complete constitutional separation between religion and government. Part of the 'vagueness' of Shintō these days is actually due to the doctrinal void created by the abrupt demise of pre-war State Shintō and the consequent reticence of Shintō philosophers in the post-war period to articulate a Shintō theology.

'Shintō' is therefore a collective term rather like 'Hinduism'. It refers to a great variety of local cults, attitudes and beliefs changing over time rather than to any centralized religious or philosophical system. Certain ideas characteristic of (but not exclusive to) Shintō have influenced Japanese philosophy; such ideas include the elusive concept of *kami* itself, and a strong emphasis on ritual purification and cyclic renewal. But Shintō has never – except in the case of State Shintō – claimed to be a complete system of thought, and has readily incorporated ethical and metaphysical elements from Confucianism and Buddhism. *Kami*, for instance, can be seen as autochthonous Japanese deities but were traditionally identified as local manifestations of Buddhist divinities, while purification can be interpreted in either a ritual or Confucian ethical sense. The notion of *kami* usually goes hand in hand with a sense of local community, periodically expressed through Shintō festivals, and it is probably the communal aspect of Shintō which has had most influence on Japanese thinkers. Shintō has contributed strongly to the Japanese view that one's identity is defined by the community rather than inhering in the individual. Shintō has also provided the Japanese with a sense of national identity through its myths of creation, and the scholars of 'National Learning' in the eighteenth century drew inspiration from the study of the early Shintō myths, even though these were myths of only one aspect of Shintō, the divine ancestry of the imperial household. It is easy to make too much of the 'nationalistic' aspect of Shintō, however. While conservative patriotism is undeniably bolstered in Japan by Shintō sentiments, 'State

Shintō' drew as much on Confucianism as on traditional Shintō ideas to construct an ethic of subservience to the national entity, and pre-war nationalism was also reinforced by Buddhist, Christian and other Japanese sectarian religious teachings. Nationalism should not be seen as a feature of Shintō *per se*, although support for Shintō is very often a feature of Japanese nationalism.

THE FAMILY SYSTEM

The importance attached to community, to the group of people with whom one interacts daily face-to-face, and in particular to family and ancestral lineage, can be identified as a distinctive (though not unique) feature of Japanese society, and one which has a direct bearing on Japanese ethics. The family or household (Japanese *ie*), whose members were traditionally bound by an ethic of mutual loyalty and the constraints of collective legal responsibility, has traditionally been the basic unit of social organization in Japan. The family was a far more significant unit than the individual, whose personal interests and desires, to the extent that they conflict with family and social duty, are viewed as weaknesses according to Confucian thought. The Japanese have gone further than Confucian thought demands in attributing a religious significance to the family line, and replicating the 'family' or 'household' structure, with its attendant virtues of filial piety, loyalty and reciprocity between family members, in other social groups outside the 'biological' family. The notion of family or *ie* is not in fact rooted in biological heredity, because adoption of an outsider to be the new heir and head of the household has been from the Nara period to the present day a common practice of Japanese families seeking to preserve their 'house', its profession, business, property and ancestors. Perhaps a quarter of rural families still pass on their household to adopted sons, enabling the household head to choose a successor on the basis of competence or social advantage rather than simple heredity. Well-known political and business households succeed by adoption. It is not therefore surprising to find that in several areas of Japanese life including religious, political and academic structures one finds replicated the 'parent–child' relationship in which the superior is responsible for the inferior, and the inferior depends upon his or her superior to a much greater extent than is common in the West. To take an example relevant to academic philosophy, most if not all academic posts in Japan are filled by graduates recommended by their 'parent' professor to a post in a department typically filled by other members of the professor's academic 'family', and advertising of lectureships is virtually unknown, since it suggests that a department is so worthless as to belong to no 'family' at all.

The reality of family life in Japan has approximated rather than conformed to traditional ideals of the family, but the notion that the family or quasi-family group rather than the individual is the basic unit of society has been central to Japanese thought and social institutions up to the present day, despite attempts by various social reformers to encourage people to think in terms of the individual first. The development of a 'modern' (by which is meant no more than 'Western') notion of the individual as the basic unit in society and the development of personalist philosophies did not spread among intellectuals until the Meiji period, following the importation of Western thought. Many aspects of individual identity are still determined by family, including one's religious identity, which, rather like Judaism, is inherited through the family line whether the individual wishes it or not. Thus many Japanese find out what denomination of Buddhism they belong to only when a member of the family dies and the Buddhist priest has to be called in.

DEATH

A discussion of death might seem out of place in an examination of the origins of Japanese philosophy, but attitudes to death have figured significantly in Japanese thought. A pervading agnosticism or indeterminacy about the afterlife (deriving from Confucian concern with social order rather than individual fate) has, paradoxically, led the Japanese to place greater stress on the moment of death and particularly the quality of one's dying than is the case in Western culture. A Confucian culture expects a philosopher to practise what he preaches, and overcoming the weakness of a fear of death is a prerequisite of the exemplary life expected of the 'superior man'. Death and the manner of one's dying preoccupied the *samurai* class, who rose to prominence from the late twelfth century onwards and who fulfilled an exemplary function in Japanese society during the Tokugawa period. The *samurai* developed a code of conduct (*bushidō*, the *Dao* of the warrior) based on an ethic of absolute loyalty to one's lord, defence of personal and family honour and perfection in the martial arts. Central to this ethic, which arose out of legendary tales and ballads of *samurai* heroism, was the notion of overcoming death through the death of 'self', so that no thought of personal gain interfered with devotion to the feudal lord. *Bushidō* was based on Neo-Confucianism and incorporated Confucian ethics and Zen meditational techniques built into martial skills. *Bushidō* became generalized during the Tokugawa period into a social ideal applicable to all classes. Despite the official demise of the feudal system, *bushidō* has represented for a number of twentieth-century Japanese thinkers, from right-wing militarists to the Quaker Nitobe, the epitome of Japanese virtue.

CHRISTIANITY

Christianity in the form of Roman Catholicism was introduced to Japan in 1549 by Jesuit missionaries, and spread through outlying parts of Japan by the conversion of local feudal lords and hence their territories (on the principle of *cuius regio, eius religio*). These 'Christian *daimyō*' had mixed motives for turning to Christianity: some were clearly attracted mainly by trade advantages promised by the Jesuits, while a few remained believers despite later persecution.

Since the Japanese were already well versed in sophisticated theological arguments through their knowledge of much older traditions of Chinese thought and the development of their own Buddhist philosophies, Christian philosophy and theology had little lasting impact on leaders of Japanese opinion. The despot and would-be unifier of Japan, Oda Nobunaga, and his successor Toyotomi Hideyoshi, were interested largely for political reasons in the Christian missionaries, and it was eventually fear of the political and economic influence of foreign missionaries which provoked Ieyasu Tokugawa to proscribe Christianity in 1614, after which missionaries and converts who refused to apostatize were persecuted. Following the 'Christian' Shimabara uprising of 1637–8 all connections with the West were prohibited except for restricted contact with Dutch traders, who were perceived to have no religious motives. Although a few 'hidden Christians' secretly preserved a form of the faith during Japan's seclusion, Christianity effectively disappeared until the second half of the nineteenth century, when, following the opening of Japan, Western missionaries and scholars began again to promote Protestant, Orthodox and Catholic forms of the faith.

The percentage of Christians in Japan during the 'Christian century' was higher than it is today, and there is no doubt that some Japanese were impressed by the missionaries' example and by the novel teachings of Christianity. Christianity had the advantage of being a new and 'foreign' faith at a time of national turmoil, when the native traditions seemed unequal to the task of pacifying the country, but its strangeness was also one of the factors which have remained a stumbling block for Japanese to the present day. Following the expulsion of Christians, well-informed treatises, including those by the apostate Japanese priest Fabian, were published attacking Christianity from a philosophical point of view. The image of Christianity in Japan since the seventeenth century has therefore been profoundly negative. Particularly difficult for cultured Japanese to accept was the Christian insistence that Buddhist ancestral rites were unacceptable, since this struck at the heart of the ethic of filial piety. (But in practice, it is quite common for Japanese Christians today to have a *butsudan* or Buddhist altar for the ancestors in the house.) The 'foreign' image persisted during the return of Christianity in the late nineteenth century, but Christianity has nevertheless had a considerable influence in Japan over the last century, particularly in the areas of education (in particular education for women) and social service.

A central teaching of Christianity, which conflicts completely with the traditional Japanese family-based ethic, is that a human being cannot give unconditional loyalty to any temporal master. Loyalty to Christ, through the agency of the Bible, conscience or the church, will always have priority over social duty. A convert to Christianity is empowered to choose whom he or she will obey – church or state – in a way that Confucianism finds inexplicable and abhorrent, for Confucianism is a 'single-apex' system in which ultimate loyalty is owed solely to one's superior. Attraction to a philosophy like Christianity, which exalts individual conscience, is seen as a weakness by Confucianism because it panders to individual or selfish preference rather than cultivating the mind of the selfless servant of a superior. While there is room for dialogue here, Japanese Christians have in fact found it difficult to reconcile their patriotism and identity as Japanese with the implicit individualism of the Christian faith.

Christianity therefore has an ambiguous status among the origins of Japanese philosophy. Experience of Christianity certainly stimulated the desire of Japan's leaders to keep foreign ideas and institutions out of Japan, and thereby encouraged a degree of xenophobia and assisted the development of 'National Learning', which in turn laid the groundwork for ultra-nationalistic political philosophies in the modern period. At the same time, the experience of Western ideas and technology brought through Christianity aroused curiosity in the minds of the Japanese about European civilization, and despite the label of 'closed country' the Japanese continued to maintain limited trading relations with a small delegation of Dutch traders. Through their agency, what was later known as 'Dutch Learning' (*rangaku*) – a collective term for Western knowledge studied principally through Dutch – was made available to a number of Japanese scholars throughout the Tokugawa period.

'DUTCH LEARNING'

In 1720 the Tokugawa shogun Yoshimune removed the restriction on import of all Western books with the exception of those propagating Christianity, and Dutch Learning proceeded apace from the mid-eighteenth century. Studies were focused on science, particularly medicine, and useful military knowledge, and Western learning had some influence in art. As a result, Japanese scholars became familiar with Western natural philosophy and the foundations of modern science, which prepared them for immediate and successful participation in international technological and scientific endeavours following the Meiji restoration. Studies of Western social philosophy and psychology, however, did not begin until Nishi Amane and Tsuda Mamichi travelled to Holland in 1862, and on their return in 1865 introduced the thought of Comte and John Stuart Mill to Japan.

PHILOSOPHICAL PLURALISM

Japanese philosophy arises out of the problem of the human condition, a problem as acute in Japan as anywhere else in the world, and one which continually presents itself in new forms despite our best attempts to plumb its depths. When we ask about the 'origins' of Japanese philosophy we are really asking why problems about the nature and meaning of human existence have arisen and been answered in particular ways in Japan. Japan is a country, not a school of thought, and Japanese thinkers who based their arguments on a Confucian text, Buddhist scripture, Shintō chronicle or Western treatise were always acutely aware that other different, independent and authoritative sources of knowledge existed. Japanese philosophers have for many centuries been in a situation akin to that of a contemporary Western philosopher of religion trying to resolve the problem of free will in a form posed not just by the Bible but simultaneously by the Koran, Sartre and the *Bhagvadgītā*. The origins of such a pluralistic problematic, which is a fairly new phenomenon in the West, lie not in the traditions concerned (although they play a part), but in the way in which those traditions come together in the mind and culture of the philosopher, who has to make an *a priori* decision about the status of different yet authoritative sources before deciding how to approach an issue.

In such circumstances, several strategies may be adopted to make sense of apparently conflicting truths. Certain sources may be accepted as authoritative and others rejected, which is a political choice; a philosopher may adopt a 'phenomenological' approach, seeking to understand and describe meanings rather than judge what is Truth; or perhaps a synthetic approach, seeking to develop a system of thought which unifies apparently conflicting claims. Japanese philosophers have adopted all of these approaches, so as well as asking what are the distant origins of Japanese philosophy, it is worth indicating some of the different strategies adopted by Japanese philosophers to make sense of the different traditions of authoritative knowledge which constitute their inheritance.

There are Japanese philosophers who have consciously selected one or more sources of knowledge within the Japanese tradition as authoritative and rejected others. Typically, these philosophers reject one or another tradition (such as Buddhism, or Christianity, or Western thought) on the grounds that it is foreign to Japan. Particularly from the 1700s onwards proponents of 'National Learning' such as Hirata Atsutane (1776–1843) adopted such an approach in asserting the primacy of the indigenous Shintō tradition over foreign imports. This approach originates in the notion of Japan as a special place, different in kind from other countries of the world, a view legitimated by Shintō creation myths which concern Japan, the Japanese deities, the imperial family and the Japanese people alone and make no significant reference to the wider world or cosmos within which the islands of Japan exist.

Japanese Buddhists have sometimes claimed that Buddhism is meant specially for Japan; indeed the most striking example of a Japanese thinker who rejects other established traditions out of hand is Nichiren (1222–82), a Buddhist monk who sought to abolish all forms of Buddhism except devotion to the *Lotus Sūtra* on the grounds that they were not suitable for Japan, and that devotion to them had caused the local

Shintō deities to abandon the country. More recently, in the late nineteenth century, the Japanese government sponsored a ruthless repression of Buddhism in order to promote the concept of Shintō as the native religion and moral basis of the Japanese nation (see above), while at the same time encouraging the selective adoption of Western technology and modern science, an approach founded in the writings of some Meiji philosophers attempting to come to terms with rapid modernization. Marxism has had a considerable influence in the twentieth century amongst Japanese academics, often displacing respect for traditional Japanese cosmologies and values which are identified with an earlier social phase. For some, Marxism, like Christianity, provided a platform for rejecting nationalistic Shintō in the pre-war period. With Japan's post-war economic success and the decline of Marxism, contemporary Japanese academics are once again inclined to look within rather than outside the Japanese tradition for worthy insights and values which may be 'unique' to Japan.

Japanese thinkers who have adopted what might be called a 'phenomenological' approach to conflicting truths, an approach which is comfortable with relativism, have typically been influenced by the logic and metaphysics of Mahāyāna Buddhism, which spread through China, Korea and Japan partly by dint of its ability to respect, absorb and syncretize with existing beliefs and practices, offering a reinterpretation of them at one level without denying their value and efficacy at another. Nichiren, referred to above, is an exception to this general rule. The Buddhist attitude to propositional truths is inherently relativistic, for Mahāyāna Buddhists typically see the objective world as a projection of consciousness, and propositions about the objective world are therefore only ever 'true' at a phenomenal level. Even the Buddha's teachings are seen as a temporary device for a particular purpose – the key teaching of non-self, it is widely acknowledged within Buddhism, could be a teaching of self in different circumstances. Special mention should be made of the little-known Tokugawa thinker Tominaga Nakamoto (1715–46), who advanced an original and scientific theory to account for divergences in religious traditions, independently and in advance of similar intellectual developments in the West. His theory started with Buddhist ideas but went beyond any particular viewpoint within Buddhism. The modern Buddhist-inspired philosopher Nishida Kitarō (1870–1945) exemplified a Buddhist approach to epistemology when he set experience above words in the search for truth. Nevertheless to claim, as Buddhists traditionally have done in Japan, that Shintō gods are really local forms of Buddhist *bodhisattvas* and that Confucianism is a valid but lower form of truth than Buddhism implies some hierarchical evaluation of truths if not actual rejection, so that a certain tension remains.

Finally, there are Japanese philosophers who have attempted to unify in a comprehensive synthesis at least the 'three teachings' of Buddhism, Confucianism and Shintō, or more recently Japanese and Western theoretical perspectives. Buddhism and Confucianism arrived in Japan almost simultaneously, and were already enmeshed together in Chinese thought and culture. What is now called 'Shintō' emerged from local and familial cults at about the same time, and blended with Buddhism and Confucianism in the development of the centralized Japanese state from the sixth century onwards. From the beginning, therefore, Shintō, Buddhism and Confucianism constituted a syncretic blend as far as the Japanese were concerned. Theological views – which could easily become divisive – about exactly how the three traditions might be interrelated followed rather than preceded their successful if naïve integration at the level of ritual observance. For example, Shintō shrines were included in the precincts of Buddhist temples throughout Japan from earliest times. Such symbols of the interdependence of Buddhas and Shintō *kami* survived until the unprecedented separation of Buddhism and Shintō by government decree in the late nineteenth century.

Nowadays the majority of Japanese families, though professing a conventional secularism, have a Buddhist altar for the ancestors and a Shintō 'god-shelf' for protection of the home, and visit Shintō shrines or Buddhist temples at least once a year (at New Year, or during the summer festival of the dead). For the ordinary person Buddhism and Shintō are complementary – perhaps a new English term such as 'Shinddhism' should be used to convey this idea. As is well known, the Japanese are commonly married in a Shintō or Christian-style ceremony (both relatively recent innovations for ordinary people in Japan), while funeral and memorial rites are generally performed by Buddhist priests. The instinct of many Japanese is thus to add the merits of different religious observances together, rather than regard different types of religiosity as mutually exclusive; an attitude which can readily be extended to different modern philosophies. While foreign observers have often remarked on the inconstancy of the Japanese in drawing on different traditions at the same time, the Japanese tendency to synthesize a conceptual framework from diverse sources is in principle no different from that of the Western Christian who believes in the power of prayer and relies on modern medicine at the same time.

At the level of ritual observance it is relatively simple to regard all world-views as equally valid. Theories which aim to synthesize diverse traditions, once elaborated, are bound to involve interpreting one tradition through the eyes of another. In the pre-modern period the most famous exponent of the synthetic approach was probably the agrarian reformer and practical philosopher Ninomiya Sontoku (1787–1856), whose recipe for the 'pill' or powder of the three religions was a spoonful of Shintō and a half-spoonful each of Confucianism and Buddhism, mixed together to become indistinguishable from each other. Ninomiya's prescription exemplifies the way in which Shintō and Buddhism were employed to promote Confucian values during the Tokugawa period. This was a result of the government's resolve, following the suppression of Christianity in the early seventeenth century, to outlaw religious dissent for the sake of social harmony – an example of a religious policy very firmly rooted in Confucian priorities. During the Tokugawa period the moral teachings of both Buddhism and Shintō became almost indistinguishable from popular Confucianism.

Efforts to synthesize patriotic and nationalistic sentiments with Western liberalism, Christianity and Buddhism have been made in modern times. In the post-war period, as Japanese intellectual influence has spread in the wake of economic growth, and Westerners have come to appreciate more of the depth and complexity of the Japanese tradition and of East Asian philosophy in general, Japanese philosophers no longer feel defensive about their native traditions, and there are new possibilities for synthesizing the insights of East and West within a range of disciplines.

Since freedom of expression in Japan has been constitutionally protected since 1945, Japanese philosophers are currently well placed to explore and reinterpret philosophical ideas from both East and West. Increasingly, the results of such explorations are becoming available in the West, either through translations of Japanese philosophy into European languages or, as Japanese rapidly emerges at the end of the twentieth century as one of the major modern world languages, through the increasing ability of Western academics to study publications in Japanese.

FURTHER READING

Aston, W. (1956) *Nihongi*, London: Allen & Unwin.
Blacker, Carmen (1975) *The Catalpa Bow: A Study of Shamanistic Practices in Japan*, London: Allen & Unwin.
Bocking, B. (1996) *A Popular Dictionary of Shinto*, London: Curzon.
Boxer, C. R. (1967) *The Christian Century in Japan, 1549–1650*, Berkeley, Calif.: University of California Press.
Earhart, H. B. (1974) *Japanese Religion: Unity and Diversity*, Encino: Dickenson.
Herbert, Jean (1967) *Shintō at the Fountain-head of Japan*, London: George Allen & Unwin.
Hori, I. (ed.) (1972) *Japanese Religion: A Survey by the Agency for Cultural Affairs*, Tokyo: Kodansha.
Hyakudai, Sakamoto (1993) 'Japanese philosophical thought', *Japan Foundation Newsletter* 21 (2):11–16 (September).
Kodansha (1983) *Kodansha Encyclopaedia of Japan*, 8 vols, Tokyo: Kodansha International.
Matsunaga, Alicia (1969) *The Buddhist Philosophy of Assimilation*, Tokyo: Sophia University.
Ono, Sokyo (1962) *Shinto, the Kami Way*, Rutland, Vt.: Tuttle.
Reader, Ian (1991) *Religion in Contemporary Japan*, London: Macmillan.
Tominaga, Nakamoto (1990) *Emerging from Meditation*, trans. Michael Pye, London: Duckworth/Honolulu: University of Hawaii Press.
Tsunoda, R. *et al.* (1958) *Sources of Japanese Tradition*, New York: Columbia University Press.

35

CONFUCIANISM IN JAPAN

B.M. Bodart-Bailey

INTRODUCTION

Tracing the influence and development of Confucianism in Japan is a complex task. Just as the introduction of Christianity brings to a country an elaborate system of cultural values which might or might not have Christian origins, so Confucianism when exported to regions outside China came not just as the moral philosophy of Confucius, but as a total cultural package, as a complete *Weltanschauung*. Moreover, as new schools of Confucian thought arose in China, these again entered the countries on its periphery accompanied by cultural values current in China at the time. Owing to differences in political and social organization, these values were frequently not appropriate for Japan, and acceptance of items from this cultural 'package' was highly eclectic. While those elements that were adopted often left a profound mark on Japanese culture, it is argued below that only those theories and beliefs found wider acceptance for which a precursor or counterpart existed in the native culture. Again, one may ask, for instance, whether one should include under the label of Confucianism theories such as the dualism of the *yin–yang* system expounded in the *Book of Changes*, one of the 'Five Classics of Confucianism', and all its popular appendages, including divination and geomancy. A good case can be made for both sides of the argument, and the outcome plays an important role in determining the degree of penetration of Confucian elements in the native culture. In other words, there is no hard and fast rule determining the influence of Confucianism on Japanese culture. The answer depends on a number of variables and the values assigned to them. Consequently the debate on 'How Confucian was Japan?' or even 'How Confucian is Japan?' continues.

BEGINNINGS

According to Japanese chronicles Confucianism was introduced into Japan in the year AD 285, when an envoy from the Korean court of Paekche presented the Japanese emperor Ōjin with copies of the *Analects* of Confucius (Chinese *Lun-yu*; Japanese *Rongo*) and a Confucian primer, the *Thousand Character Classic* (Chinese *Ch'ien-tzu wen*; Japanese *Senjimon*). However, the accuracy of both the date and the story is doubtful.[1]

While there is a strong possibility that migrants from Korea and south China introduced knowledge of Confucianism into Japan in the fourth century, reliable historical material exists only for the fifth century, when Japanese inscriptions and a reference in the Chinese classics (*The History of the Liu Sung Dynasty* referring to a memorial sent by 'the King of Japan' to the Wei emperor in 478) indicate that Confucian terminology had been absorbed in Japan together with the Chinese writing system.[2]

For centuries to come literacy was attained through a study of Confucian primers, and the relatively small number of people who were literate presumably had a basic knowledge of Confucianism. Politically unsettled conditions on the Korean peninsula and Japan's involvement in this strife resulted in a considerable number of immigrants of Korean and Chinese descent coming to the Japanese islands. From the early seventh century Japanese students began to travel to China to study at the source of what was viewed as a more advanced culture. Foreign migrants and returning students brought with them not only superior knowledge in the field of technology and art, but also scholarly knowledge.[3]

This scholarly knowledge, which is conventionally called Confucian and matured in China during the Han Dynasties, contained much more than the moral philosophy of Confucius. It was a synthesis of various Chinese traditional beliefs and political theories with the sayings attributed to Confucius, furnishing an all-embracing system explaining the universe and man's position in it. It gave legitimacy to the ruler, but also set out his duties towards his subjects and provided detailed regulations on how he must govern the empire in accordance with 'the Will of Heaven'. The Will of Heaven made itself manifest in natural occurrences and phenomena, and consequently a staff of specialists consisting of astronomers, astrologers, geomancers, diviners, etc. was essential for the good government of the country. Of importance in this world order was the *yin–yang* and Five Elements theory (Japanese *in yō go gyō*). In the simplest terms *yin* and *yang* were viewed as the opposing forces of negative and positive, passive and active, dark and light, which by their interaction produce and control events; in order to avoid calamities, both must at all times be kept in harmony. The Five Elements wood, fire, earth, metal, water – not elements in the Greek sense but dynamic concepts – make up the cosmological world order and control the rhythm of life. The schematic representation of *yin* and *yang* and the five elements forms the basis of the eight trigrams and their combinations of sixty-four hexagrams contained in the *Book of Changes* (Chinese *I-ching* [*Yijing*], Japanese *eki kyō*), which was thus a symbolic representation of the world order and used for purposes of divination.[4]

The introduction of the ethical teachings of Confucius into Japan cannot be separated from the adoption of this wider body of theories and beliefs which had become associated with these teachings in China. In fact it was *yin–yang* dualism rather than Confucius' moral doctrine which first entered popular culture and came to shape all aspects of everyday life. Further, the body of knowledge referred to as Confucianism recommended itself less as an ethical philosophy than as a political system, by which the culturally advanced empire of China and the increasingly powerful kingdoms of the Korean peninsula were governed. This is not to say, however, that the moral component of Confucianism was of no importance. On the contrary, it was believed that the individual behaviour of men, and especially those in a high position, had an effect upon the whole natural order and that their misdeeds would show themselves in natural catastrophes. Thus aberration from the moral code, the 'Way', as Confucius defined it, was not merely considered an offence against human law, but an act destabilizing the whole natural order. It was here that the *yin–yang* theory came into play, because harmonizing the two elements was essential to restore the natural balance. Yet right conduct meant more than following a set of moral principles, for it included a complex system of rites that had evolved in China. The adoption of these rites and associated customs deeply influenced the life of the Japanese ruling class during the early period. There remains, however, the question of how far the philosophical premisses underlying these rites and customs were understood or accepted by an élite with a very different cultural background from that of its counterpart in China.

Taking the word 'Confucian' in its broader sense, one may say that Japanese government administration was remodelled in the seventh and eighth centuries along Confucian lines, government edicts were couched in Confucian terms, and the authors of official chronicles attempted to harmonize native lore with Confucian theories of history to trace the beginnings of the ruling house and substantiate its claim to legitimacy. As in China, the functions of the Chancellor of the Empire in eighth-century Japan came to be defined as 'ordering the state and deliberating on the (Confucian) Way' and 'harmonizing Yin and Yang'.[5]

In accordance with the Chinese model, a government university (Japanese *daigaku*) was established in the early eighth century, where the sons of the aristocracy prepared themselves for civil service examinations. In the early period the curriculum consisted mainly of the study of Confucian texts. Twice a year a service in honour of Confucius was conducted, the cost of which was met by government funds. Examinations were held regularly and were difficult; between the years 704 and 937 only sixty-five students attained the first (highest) degree in the scale of five. However, while this Confucian college during its most flourishing period resembled its Chinese counterpart in many aspects, an essential condition guaranteeing the importance it enjoyed in China was lacking in Japan: government appointments were dictated by family background in the first place and by success in examinations only in the second. Also in the latter part of the eight century interest in the Confucian classics declined in favour of Chinese literature, in particular Chinese poetry. The professor of literature came to hold the senior rank, and those students who lacked knowledge of the Confucian classics but could compose well in Chinese were given preferment in government appointments. Especially during the Heian period, being a good poet was considered an important qualification for an official appointment. The Heian novel *The Tale of Genji* provides a glimpse of how this quasi-Confucian scholarship was viewed by the aristocracy. In the chapter 'Otome' the author, Murasaki Shikibu, describes the scene of Genji's son being given a school-name before entering the 'university'. Most of the princes and courtiers attending the ceremony thought the manners and appearance of the professors comic and believed that education of this kind was not necessary for young men of high birth. After Genji's son was successful in the examinations, however, the university began to attract other young men from important families, and soon it became quite usual for men of high office to hold a degree.[6]

This incident illustrates the dual nature of Confucianism in early Japan. While certain elements ranging from the legitimization of the emperor as 'Son of Heaven' to the designation of auspicious days were totally absorbed by Japanese culture, others, such as the rites, manners, and dress of the Confucian scholar, remained alien.

THE INTRODUCTION OF NEO-CONFUCIANISM

The introduction of Neo-Confucian texts in the late thirteenth century generated new interest in Chinese philosophy amongst the Japanese aristocracy. Emperor Godaigo (1288–1339) was especially known for his deep interest in the new 'Sung Learning', as it is known in Japan. But Godaigo failed in his struggle to re-establish the authority of the emperor, and his association with Neo-Confucianism might have done little to recommend it as political philosophy. Over the next centuries Neo-Confucian texts were studied in Zen monasteries. Rinzai monks, such as Chūgan Enketsu (1300–75), went to China for their studies and brought back with them firsthand knowledge and books on Neo-Confucianism.[7] One of the closest confidants of the third Ashikaga *shōgun* Yoshimitsu (1358–1408), the monk Gidō Shūshin (1325–88), encouraged the *shōgun* to study the Neo-Confucian writings and lectured to him on the *Doctrine of the Mean*.[8] At the so-called Ashikaga Academy, founded around 1439, several thousand students, the majority of whom were Zen monks, studied Neo-Confucian teachings.[9] In spite of its popularity amongst the upper classes, Neo-Confucianism did not attain independent status. The experts on the Confucian classics were Zen monks, who held that while Confucian teaching could not contain Buddhism, Buddhism could contain Confucianism.[10]

With the increasing popularity of Zen Buddhism in warrior circles throughout the country, knowledge of Neo-Confucianism spread beyond the aristocratic élite of the capital, Kyoto. For instance, the Rinzai monk Keian Genju (1427–1508), after some six years of study in China, lectured on Neo-Confucianism in various provincial centres in Japan until finally, at the invitation of the *daimyō* Shimazu Tadamasu (1463–1508), he settled in Satsuma. Under Keian's guidance, the first Neo-Confucian work to be printed in Japan was published in Satsuma in 1481.[11]

Neo-Confucianism's association with Zen Buddhism in Japan was no historical accident. In China Neo-Confucian thought had been influenced by Zen Buddhist ideals, and the Japanese Zen monks who went to the continent to study, as well as their Chinese counterparts who came to Japan, transmitted this syncretic learning as they had received it. Moreover, socio-political conditions in Japan differed widely from those discussed in the Confucian texts, and it was mainly those teachings relating to the cultivation of the self, rather than those dealing with political theory, that were of relevance in the Japanese setting at the time.

The development and spread of Neo-Confucianism in Japan during the centuries of its close association with Zen Buddhism have received relatively little scholarly attention in the West, since during this period Confucianism is believed to have played only a subordinate role in the intellectual and religious life of the country. The influx of new Neo-Confucian texts from Korea after Toyotomi Hideyoshi's abortive campaign on the peninsula in the late sixteenth century is often seen as an ingredient in the process that stimulated a break with this tradition and brought about the independent development of Neo-Confucianism in the early Tokugawa period. While the stimulus from Korea was important, one of the pre-conditions for Neo-Confucanism's relative sudden popularity with the beginning of the Tokugawa period was that Neo-Confucian texts had been disseminated throughout the country by the extensive network of the Zen monasteries. Thus a relatively large number of men in search of spiritual and philosophical truth were not only brought in contact with these texts, but also educated to read them. The greater part of first-generation Tokugawa Confucianists started their career as Zen monks, who passed the scholarship they had acquired in the monasteries on to their disciples. On the other hand, the traditional association of Neo-Confucianism with Zen Buddhism became a major obstacle when Confucians attempted to establish themselves as independent scholars and philosophers.

CONFUCIANISM IN THE TOKUGAWA PERIOD

Confucianism reached its widest popularity in Japan during the Tokugawa period (1603–1868). While it has traditionally been held that the Tokugawa government (*bakufu*) from its inception adopted Confucianism as its state ideology, strictly enforcing heterodoxy, this view is no longer tenable.[12]

The tenets of political Confucianism ill fitted conditions in Japan.[13] There was in Japan no almighty 'Son of Heaven', no emperor who held political power, and no class of civil servants with homogeneous Confucian education who were dispatched from the centre to govern the provinces. From the twelfth century on, political power in Japan rested with the warrior class and was localized to varying degrees. The right to govern was obtained not by sitting for examinations in the Confucian classics as in China and Korea, but by virtue of a man's birth in times of peace, and sword skill in times of political turmoil. Even when the first *shōgun* Ieyasu established the Tokugawa hegemony at the beginning of the seventeenth century, he governed as *primus inter pares* rather than as autocrat.

Not only were Japan's socio-political conditions greatly different from those of its Confucian neighbours, but its ruling class also lacked the cultural traditions essential for understanding the Chinese classics. For instance, Confucius' saying that to obtain perfect virtue men must return to performing the rites (*Analects*, book XII) made little sense in the Japanese environment, for these rites were not known, nor was there in most cases room for their introduction. When in the early eighteenth century the Confucian scholar Arai Hakuseki (1657–1725), as adviser to the sixth *shōgun* Ienobu, insisted that the proper rites should be observed at the *shōgunal* court at least on the occasion of the visit of Korean envoys, he met with incomprehension and resistance.[14]

The fulfilment of other duties posed even more fundamental problems and contained the seeds of politically dangerous developments. When loyalty to the 'Son of Heaven' – in China the emperor – was demanded in the classics, was the Japanese Confucian to pay loyalty to the Japanese emperor or the *shōgun*, who had usurped the latter's power?

The discrepancies between the tenets of Confucianism as it had developed in China and Japanese historical realities governed both the history of its socio-political acceptance and the philosophical content of the schools that developed in Japan.

Socio-political acceptance and influence

The first Tokugawa *shōgun* Ieyasu is purported to have announced to his followers that although he had conquered the nation on horseback, Japan could not be governed from a horse, and from that time on he is said to have actively patronized the study of Confucianism.[15] The prospect of conducting government with the help of Confucian-trained, obedient civil servants rather than ambitious warriors might have been a highly attractive one to Ieyasu, but neither during his government nor that of his three successors did Confucian scholars play a significant part in the central administration of the country.

Ieyasu summoned the scholar Fujiwara Seika (1561–1619), who after some thirty years of monastic experience had given up his high-ranking position in a Zen temple and declared himself a Confucian. Fujiwara is known as the first Zen monk to declare his independence from Buddhism and is thus called the 'father' of Japanese Neo-Confucianism or Tokugawa Confucianism. In a rather un-Confucian manner Fujiwara declined to enter into government service and eventually spend the last years of his life in a fashion more appropriate to a Buddhist monk, namely as a semi-recluse.[16]

The position of official Confucian scholar went to his student Hayashi Razan (1583–1657), who, like Fujiwara, had begun his Neo-Confucian studies as a Zen monk. Hayashi's descendants were to occupy this position throughout the Tokugawa period, and their writings, calculated to enhance the importance of their house, are to some extent responsible for the view that from the beginning of the Tokugawa period the official Confucian scholar played an important role in government affairs. Hayashi, however, was treated little differently from the many monks in government employment, and had far less influence than the most important of them, Ieyasu's confidant, the Zen monk Ishin Sūden (1569–1633). It is the latter, rather than the Confucian Hayashi, who is credited with having drafted the final version of foreign diplomatic correspondence and government laws.

Hayashi was not permitted to wear his hair in the fashion of the Confucian scholar, but was ordered to shave his head like a monk and adopt the Buddhist name Dōshun. His request to establish a Confucian temple was initially refused, and it was only under the third *shōgun* Iemitsu that he was granted some land and a modest sum of money to build a Confucian hall. Hayashi himself noted in his correspondence that he led a life unworthy of a Confucian scholar.[17]

The fact that during the early Tokugawa period Confucianism was still considered a philosophy subordinate to Buddhism is also apparent from the government's temple legislation. The laws, which became effective mainly in areas under direct control of the government after 1613 and only later throughout the country, laid down that every citizen should be registered at, as well as patronize, a Buddhist temple, and made no allowance for Confucian. Although these laws were designed to eliminate the last vestiges of Christianity, they were considered as oppressive by Confucians, for whom an association with Buddhism was no longer acceptable. Scholars, such as Arai Hakuseki (1657–1725), bemoaned the fact that on death the body could not be interred in the ground, as demanded by Confucian ritual, but had to be cremated with Buddhist rites.[18] Also the German physician Engelbert Kaempfer, who visited Japan in 1690–2, reported that Confucian scholars felt persecuted by these laws.[19]

The laws were resisted by several domain lords, in particular Ikeda Mitsumasa of Bizen (1609–82), Hoshina Masayuki of Aizu (1611–72) and Tokugawa Mitsukuni of Mito (1628–1700), who were well disposed towards Confucianism and actively patronized Confucian scholars. The fact that these three domain lords who ignored government orders later became known as the Three Wise Lords (*san ken kō*) is symptomatic of the shift that took place in the acceptance of Confucianism.[20]

Under government pressure, Ikeda Mitsumasa was forced to close the Confucian schools he had established in his domain for both *samurai* and commoners. At an earlier stage the *bakufu* had obliged him to release from service the Confucian scholar Kumazawa Banzan (1619–91), to whom Ikeda had accorded a position and salary unusual for a Confucian scholar. Kumazawa was conducting an intensive reform programme after the domain had suffered greatly from floods, and is one of the few Confucian scholars of the early Tokugawa period who, albeit over a brief period, played an active part in local government affairs.[21]

The dismissal of Banzan as well as the punishment of another Confucian, Yamaga Sokō (1622–85), has traditionally been interpreted as indication that Hayashi Razan, as official Confucian scholar, possessed the authority to enforce orthodoxy. More recent research has shown that these Confucians were punished not because their teachings differed from those of the Hayashi house, but because they were believed to be implicated in anti-government plots and Christian activity.[22] Similarly, Mitsumasa was told to close his schools because the gathering of large numbers of people was considered politically dangerous. Other Confucian scholars, such as Itō Jinsai (1627–1705), whose teaching emphasized self-cultivation, were not molested by the government, and this indicates that what was being condemned was not Confucianism *per se*, but teachings considered politically dangerous. Certain Buddhist sects also faced persecution during this period for similar reasons.

A number of early Tokugawa Confucian scholars noted in their writings that in their youth they studied the Chinese texts in secrecy for fear of being ridiculed by their fellow-*samurai* for monkish pursuits. Moreover, the scholar Arai Hakuseki maintained that when he was young, even educated men could not tell the difference between Confucianism and Christianity. He attributed this mainly to the fact that Christians had employed Confucian vocabulary when translating their message.[23]

The status of Confucianism amongst the Japanese warrior élite changed rapidly under the administration of the fifth Tokugawa *shōgun* Tsunayoshi (1680–1709).[24] Tsunayoshi was ordered by his father, the third *shōgun* Iemitsu, to be educated as a scholar so he would not be equipped for the position of *shōgun* and thus not challenge the succession of his elder brothers. But as his elder brothers died either young or childless, Tsunayoshi was installed as *shōgun* with an upbringing very different from that of his predecessors.

Tsunayoshi publicly condemned the military ethic of previous generations and urged the *samurai* to study the Confucian classics. He officially sanctioned the independence of the Confucian scholar by abolishing the obligatory tonsure. A large Confucian temple and academy were built for the Hayashi family, which he honoured with his visits and personal patronage. He summoned Confucian scholars into his presence to lecture on the classics or debate with Buddhist monks. On occasion the *shōgun* himself delivered lectures on the Chinese texts. His patronage rapidly increased the demand for Confucian scholars, since some knowledge of Confucianism began to be considered an important part of the education of the upper classes.

It was during Tsunayoshi's administration that the Tokugawa government for the first time adopted the opinion of a Confucian scholar in a politically difficult situation. When in 1702 the so-called Forty-Seven *Rōnin* (masterless *samurai*) slew a high-ranking official to avenge their former lord, the *bakufu* was at a loss whether to praise them for their loyalty or condemn them for violating the judgement of the court, which had decreed that the official should go unpunished. Public opinion was running high in favour of the loyal warriors, and the view of various Confucian scholars was sought. That of the scholar Ogyū Sorai (1666–1728), which advocated an honourable death by self-immolation for the offenders, was adopted.[25]

Tsunayoshi attempted to overcome the contradictions between the socio-political situation idealized in the Confucian texts and those existing in Japan by altering the latter to accord with the former. His ideal was the government of the mythological sage kings Yao and Shun, autocrats who ruled with the assistance of able advisers. Tsunayoshi's political strategies were motivated by his desire to increase shogunal authority at the expense of the *samurai* and turn the latter into obedient civil servants akin to the Chinese model. The military aristocracy much resented this attack on their traditional status, and Tsunayoshi's government was severely criticized. In tune with this criticism his patronage of Confucianism has often been belittled. Moreover, the fifth *shōgun* was as ardent a Buddhist as he was a Confucian and maintained that the two doctrines were like the two wheels of a cart, and both deserved equal patronage. This view, or a variant which ranked Shintō with Buddhism and Confucianism, had been expressed since Confucianism was first introduced into Japan, and shows that Confucian doctrine alone was not considered totally satisfactory for the Japanese environment.

While Tsunayoshi's successors did not continue his keen, public patronage of Confucianism, the three decades of his rule had secured a place for the Confucian scholar as educator of the *samurai* and government adviser, albeit mostly in fairly lowly capacity. Thus the scholar Arai Hakuseki became tutor to the sixth *shōgun* Ienobu (1663–1712) and his infant son Ietsugu (1709–16), and played a modest role in the central administration of the country.[26] Ogyū Sorai, who had achieved prominence under the fifth *shōgun* as scholar of the latter's senior minister Yanagisawa Yoshiyasu (1658–1714), was consulted by advisers to the eighth *shōgun* Yoshimune (1684–1751) and is believed to have composed his major political writings at their instigation.

The importance accorded to Confucian learning stimulated the establishment of domain schools, of which there were well over two hundred at the time of the Imperial Restoration in 1868. The curriculum taught relied heavily on the Confucian classics, and was designed to create loyal and efficient administrators. Thus Confucianism became a major force in the bureaucratization of *samurai* society.

The closest Japan came to the Chinese ideal of Confucian-trained, high government official was in the person of the reformer Matsudaira Sadanobu (1758–1829).[27] Matsudaira was the grandson of the eighth *shōgun* Yoshimune, and at the age of 29 was entrusted with the important position of head of the Council of Elders (*rōjū*) while the country was beset by economic problems and popular unrest. He instituted the Kansei Reform, which attempted, true to Confucian dogma, a return to earlier, less troubled times. Further he considered Confucian learning and the teaching of the official Confucian scholars, the Hayashi house, to have fallen into decay. He believed that the ideal had existed when the first shogun Ieyasu founded the house, and he tried to restore this ideal with an edict known as 'The Kansei Prohibition of Heterodox Studies' (*Kansei igaku no kin*). The decree banned certain publications and enjoined strict observance of Neo-Confucian doctrine, especially with regard to the curriculum of the official Hayashi school. Scholars vary in their opinion on how far this heterodoxy was enforced and whether this first official insistence on heterodoxy constituted the high point of Confucianism in government affairs or signalled its decline.

As a political system Japan moved closer to the Confucian ideal with the restoration of the imperial house in 1868 and the establishment of a strong central government. With the influx of Western culture and the ensuing reaction from traditional forces, Confucianism in Japan assumed a new image. If during the earlier period Confucianism had been considered to varying degrees as a foreign import, it now came to be seen as a native Asian tradition which distinguished Japan from the West. An important role in this respect was played by Motoda Nagazane (also Eifu, 1818–91), the Confucian tutor and adviser to the Meiji emperor. To counteract what was considered excessive Western influence, the Imperial Rescript on Education was issued in 1890, firmly establishing the teaching of Confucian morals, especially those of loyalty and filial piety, in the school curriculum.[28] In the ensuing period Confucianism was called upon whenever it was felt necessary to present a rational, native alternative to Western religion and ideology, and the role it played in this respect obscured the fact that its adoption had been sporadic and eclectic.

Schools of thought

Unlike in China and Korea, Confucianism in Japan was not closely tied to the central government, and this permitted the more or less free development of a wide range of schools of thought. While these often differed considerably in their approach, they were united in their endeavour to overcome the disparity existing between the Chinese world and the Japanese environment.

The process of adapting Confucianism to Japanese socio-political realities can be well observed in the teachings of Yamaga Sokō (1622–85). Yamaga was the son of a *samurai*, concerned to find moral justification for the *samurai*'s existence in times of peace. Neither his life as a Zen monk nor the study of Neo-Confucian texts could provide the answer. The solution, he decided, lay in ignoring the commentaries and interpretations of later Chinese philosophers and studying solely the earliest Confucian writings. Yamaga is thus classified as an early representative of the so-called School of Ancient Learning (*ko gaku ha*).

The reason why the earliest writings, such as the *Analects* of Confucius and the book of Mencius, had attracted a voluminous amount of commentaries in China was that in their terseness they are frequently ambiguous. By returning to the original texts, Japanese Confucians could dispense with the commentaries written to impart an interpretation within the socio-political conditions of China, and present them in keeping with their own environment. Thus Yamaga Sokō succeeded in combining the ethics of Confucianism with the Japanese warrior tradition and create the 'way of the warrior', *shidō* or *bushidō*: 'Within his heart he keeps to the ways of peace, but without he keeps his weapons ready for use.' It was a philosophy that gave meaning to the life of the warrior in times of peace, a teaching thoroughly appropriate when his military skills were rarely needed and he functioned increasingly as a civil administrator. Yamaga's large following of *samurai*, who under his guidance not only studied the Confucian classics but were also trained in the martial arts and military strategy, as well as his connection with an anti-government plot, resulted in his temporary banishment.[29]

A very different representative of the School of Ancient Learning was Itō Jinsai (1627–1705). In contrast to Yamaga, who stressed the superior qualities of the warrior, Itō, the son of a Kyoto merchant, was concerned with universal human values. The development of the life force within and the cultivation of the virtue of humanity (*jin*) were given the highest importance. According to his interpretation of the Confucian classics, humanity was nothing else than love and human compassion. It was love, not duty, which lay at the base of the five human relationships, an interpretation more congenial to the Japanese mind than the traditional Chinese one. With the assistance of his son Itō Tōgai (1670–1736), he operated a highly successful private school in Kyoto known as Kogi-dō (School for the Study of Ancient Meaning), visited by several thousand students. His writings, such as instructions to his students (*Dōji-mon*, *Boys' Questions*) and explanations of why it was essential to return to the original classics (*Kokon gakuhen*, *Changes in Confucian Teaching Past and Present*), were mostly edited and published by his son Tōgai.[30]

The process of adapting Confucian dogma to Japanese conditions found its most radical expression in the teachings of Ogyū Sorai. Not only did he claim for himself the right to interpret the classic texts at variance with Chinese commentators, but he also insisted that the application of Confucian dogma must differ according to the conditions of the times. For instance, the practice of benevolent government (*jinsei*) might, occasionally, justify the use of cruelty. Moreover, centralization of authority was an important prerequisite for the execution of benevolent government. These tenets have earned for Ogyū the nickname 'the Japanese Machiavelli'.[31] Ogyū's major political writings, such as *Bendō* (*Distinguishing the Way*), *Taiheisaku* (*Proposal for a Great Peace*) and *Seidan* (*Discourse on Government*), were composed during the government of the eighth *shōgun* Yoshimune (1716–45), but reflect the political ideals of the administration of the fifth *shōgun* Tsunayoshi, when Ogyū gained his political experience. Ogyū had a number of distinguished students, such as Dazai Shundai (1680–1747), Hattori Nankaku (1683–1759) and Yamagata Shunan (1687–1752), who added their own interpretations to his philosophy and deserve study in their own right.

An important corollary to the activities of the School of Ancient Learning was scholarly occupation with the language of ancient China, a prerequisite for finding new meaning in the original texts. The study of language as well as principles of logic inherent in Confucian texts in turn prepared the ground for the assimilation of Western learning or *Rangaku* (Dutch Learning), as it was known in Japan. A prominent scholar in this area is another adherent of the School of Ancient Learning, Miura Baien (1723–89), who learned Dutch and incorporated Western ideas on astronomy and economics in his own writings.[32]

A different brand of Confucianism was taught by the man who came to be known as the 'Sage of Ōmi', Nakae Tōju (1608–48). For him filial piety was the most important virtue, and in accordance with his teaching he gave up his official employ to return to his native province of Ōmi to care for his ailing mother. Nakae was influenced by the writings of Wang Yang-ming (Japanese Ōyōmei, 1472–1529), the Chinese Neo-Confucianist, who was the main proponent of the School of Intuition of Mind (*shin*). This school emphasized man's natural moral sense or intuition rather than his intellect and stressed the importance of action. Man did not attain virtue through the performance of rites, or erudition, but by courageous action according to his moral conscience. This moral conscience, or 'Divine Light of Heaven', as Nakae called it, had for him strong theistic overtones, resulting in a Confucianism with deeply religious aspects.[33] But while Nakae's emphasis lay on self-cultivation, these same teachings provided his followers with the moral foundation for political action.

One of Nakae's best-known students in this respect was the reformer Kumazawa Banzan (1619–91). In common with Yamaga Sokō, Kumazawa emphasized practical military training, but rather than cultivating an interest in military science, he focused his attention on economic measures. His outspoken criticism of *bakufu* policies and the suspicion that he was connected with an anti-government plot led to his dismissal as administrator of the daimyo Ikeda Mitsumasa earlier in life and house arrest at a later stage.[34]

Some of Japan's most idealistic and celebrated revolutionaries were followers of the Ōyōmei School of Confucianism. These include men such as Ōshio Heihachirō (1793–1837) and Yoshida Shōin (1830–59) as well as the Meiji statesman and general Saigō Takamori (1827–77), who ended his life as an opponent of the government he had helped to create.

The majority of Confucian scholars saw some affinity between Confucianism and the native religion of Shintō, and some wrote treatises to this effect. The strongest proponent of this theory was Yamazaki Ansai (1618–82), who, like many contemporary scholars, had begun his study of Neo-Confucianism as a Zen monk. He was an ardent proponent of the philosophy of Chu Hsi [Zhu Xi], and like him attached great importance to his responsibilities as a teacher. Yamazaki greatly simplified Chu Hsi's complex system of Neo-Confucian metaphysics and stressed the virtue of 'devotion'. Later in life he came to identify the metaphysical principles of Neo-Confucianism with the Shintō pantheon and Chinese cosmology with Shintō creation legends. Devotion became devotion to the Shintō gods, and especially the emperor as the gods' representative on earth. Yamazaki's combination of Confucianism and Shintō became known as 'Suika Shintō.'[35]

Devotion to the emperor was also an important theme in the Confucianism of the Mito School. The powerful *daimyō* Mito Mitsukuni, a grandson of Ieyasu and member of the so-called 'Three Houses', invited the Chinese refugee scholar Chu Shun-shui (Japanese Shu Shunsui, 1600–82) to his domain.[36] Under the latter's guidance a Confucian temple was built and Confucian rites were observed. Confucian principles were applied in a major rewriting of Japanese history, *The History of Great Japan* (*Dai Nihon Shi*). Owing to Chu Shun-shui's influence, the Confucianism of the Mito School largely adhered to Chinese practices and dogma rather than compromise with the Japanese environment. As a logical outcome of its faithfulness to the Chinese model, its teachings eventually became a major intellectual force in the movement to restore imperial rule.

Another intellectual force behind the Restoration movement was the School of National Learning (*Kokugaku*). While early proponents of this movement displayed strong anti-Confucian sentiments, later scholars, like Hirata Atsutane (1776–1843), incorporated Confucian social and ethical precepts, especially those concerning loyalty, in their teaching.

The scholar Muro Kyūsō (1658–1734), on the other hand, concluded that the 'Son of Heaven' in Japan was not the emperor, but the first *shōgun* Tokugawa Ieyasu, who had obtained the 'Mandate of Heaven' by bringing order to the war-torn country. In this respect his teaching lent ideological support to the cult of Ieyasu. In other respects he adhered firmly to traditional Chinese teaching, convinced that the Chinese Neo-Confucianists were the rightful inheritors and interpreters of the original texts and that the attacks on their teaching by Wang Yang-ming and his own Japanese contemporaries were unjustified.[37]

Many of the above scholars were born as *samurai* and directed their message towards the *samurai*, the ruling class. But Japanese culture was most widely influenced by Confucianism when the commoners, making up about 93 per cent of the population, were addressed. The Confucianism which was popular in this context was designed to increase the fortune and reputation of the family. It was a secular, practical teaching and has therefore been compared with Max Weber's 'Protestant Ethic'.[38]

Nakae Tōju, the sage of Ōmi, believed his message to be of value not only to the common man, but even to women. He agreed with the commonly held opinion that women rarely possessed virtues such as compassion and honesty, but concluded that for this very reason they were in special need of discipline, because 'if a wife's disposition is healthy and pious, obedient, sympathetic and honest, then . . . every member of her family will be at peace and the entire household in perfect order.'[39]

A work specifically directed at women was *Onna Daigaku* (*The Great Learning for Women*), believed to have been written by the Confucian scholar Kaibara Ekken (1630–1714) with the assistance of his wife. Kaibara, the son of a *samurai*, was the author of a scholarly work on the natural history of Japan (*Yamato honzō*), but did not consider it below his dignity to write in simple language for women and children. Especially in the competitive world of the thriving cities, where fortunes were quickly made and lost, advice on how to succeed in life was welcome. The popular writer Ihara Saikaku (1642–93), for instance, lists knowledge of the Confucian teachings of the scholar Utsunomiya Ton'an (1633–1709), together with other skills such as archery and poetry, as one of the desirable accomplishments of a merchant.[40]

A high degree of eclecticism can be observed in the popular teachings of Ishida Baigan (1685–1744). His moral philosophy, which combined elements of Confucianism, Buddhism and Shintō and was known as *Shingaku*, was one of the greatest influences on the moral life of Tokugawa Japan.

The message of these popular philosophers, however varied in its vocabulary, was always a stern one. It demanded adherence to one's station in life, loyalty and subservience to superiors. It extolled hard work and honesty, and condemned waste and frivolity. Many merchant families incorporated these precepts in their house rules, and the conflicts their strict observance might create became the favourite subject of the performing arts and popular novels.

These philosophies advocated conduct close to what the sociologist Max Weber described as 'worldly asceticism', a behaviour pattern frequently considered one of the key factors of economic success. In line with this argument Japan's rapid postwar economic recovery has been attributed to the 'worldly asceticism' that originated in the Tokugawa period. The question remains whether these philosophies and teachings can be described as Confucian, or must be seen as a social ethic which merely found confirmation in and eclectically cited those precepts in the Confucian classics that answered the needs of the people and the times.

CONCLUSION

The Confucian classics have been studied in Japan for a millennium and a half, and their teachings have left a profound mark on Japanese culture. Yet Japan was never a Confucian country in the same sense as China and Korea. The Confucianism that developed was highly eclectic and was shaped to serve the particular needs of the country.

NOTES

1 Wang Jia Hua, *Nicchū jugaku no hikaku* (*Comparison of Japanese and Chinese Confucianism*) (Tokyo, 1988), pp. 50–4.
2 W. T. De Bary (ed.), *Sources of Japanese Tradition* (2 vols, New York, 1964), vol. I, p. 7.
3 G. Sansom, *A History of Japan* (3 vols, Tokyo, 1987) vol. I, p. 53.
4 De Bary, op. cit., vol. I, pp. 57–60.
5 Sansom, op. cit., vol. I, pp. 70–3.
6 Murasaki Shikibu, *The Tale of Genji*, Edward G. Seidensticker, trans., New York, 1977, vol.1, pp. 362–5.
7 Y. Wajima, *Nihon sōgaku shi no kenkyū* (*A Study of the History of Japanese Neo-Confucianism*) (Tokyo, 1988), p. 100.
8 Sansom, op. cit., vol. II, pp. 161–6.
9 For detailed treatment see Wajima, op. cit., pp. 244–74.
10 Y. Wajima, *Chūsei no jugaku* (*Medieval Confucianism*) (Tokyo, 1965), pp. 73–5.
11 Y. Wajima, *Nihon sōgaku shi no kenkyū*, pp. 234–5.
12 H. Ooms, *Tokugawa Ideology* (Princeton, 1985), p. 72.
13 The following discussion of the discrepancies between political Confucianism and conditions in Japan follows Watanabe Hiroshi, *Kinsei Nihon shakai to sōgaku* (*Early Modern Japanese Society and Neo-Confucianism*) (Tokyo, 1987).
14 K. Wildman Nakai, *Shogunal Politics: Arai Hakuseki and the Premises of Tokugawa Rule*, (Cambridge, Mass., 1988), pp. 196–201.
15 Maruyama Masao, *Studies in the Intellectual History of Tokugawa Japan* (Princeton, 1974), p. 15.
16 Ooms, op. cit., pp. 110–14.
17 This topic is discussed in detail by Hori Isao, *Hayashi Razan* (Tokyo, 1963). Ooms, op. cit., pp. 73–80; Sansom, op. cit., vol. III, pp. 7, 39, 73.
18 Arai Hakuseki, *Honsaroku kō* (*Annotations to the Records of Honsa*), in *Arai Hakuseki Zenshū* (Tokyo, 1907), vol. VI, pp. 551–2, translated in B. M. Bodart-Bailey, 'The persecution of Confucianism in early Tokugawa Japan', *Monumenta Nipponica* 48:(3) (Autumn 1993), 300.
19 Bodart-Bailey, op. cit., pp. 293–9.
20 Ikeda ke (ed.), *Ikeda Mitsumasa Kō Den* (*The Biography of Lord Ikeda Mitsumasa*) (2 vols, Tokyo, 1932), vol. I, p. 1; also *meikun* (wise ruler), Watanabe, op. cit., p. 15. See also B. M. Bodart-Bailey, *Kenperu to Tokugawa Tsunayoshi (Kaempfer and Tokugawa Tsunayoshi)* (Tokyo, 1994), pp. 114–26.
21 Shizugatani Gakkō Shi Hensan Iinkai (ed.), *Shizugatani Gakkō shi* (*The History of the Shizugatani School*) (Okayama, 1971), pp. 5–7.
22 Ooms, op. cit., p. 208 n. 36.
23 Bodart-Bailey, 'Persecution', pp. 301–2.
24 On Tsunayoshi's government see: B. M. Bodart-Bailey, 'Tokugawa Tsunayoshi (1646–1709): A Weberian analysis', *Asiatische Studien/Etudes Asiatiques* 43(1) (1989), 5–27.
25 O. Lidin, *The Life of Ogyū Sorai: A Tokugawa Confucian Philosopher* (Lund, 1973), pp. 42, 48–50. Bodart-Bailey, 'Tokugawa Tsunayoshi', p. 24.
26 On Arai Hakuseki's role in government affairs see Nakai, op. cit., (Chicago, 1975).
27 For a detailed study see H. Ooms, *Charismatic Bureaucrat* (Chicago, 1975).
28 De Bary, op. cit., vol. II, pp. 139–40.
29 ibid., vol. I, pp. 385–401.
30 ibid., vol. I, pp. 401–13.

31 Maruyama, op. cit., pp. 82–4.
32 G. K. Goodman, *Japan: The Dutch Experience* (London, 1986), pp. 101–2.
33 De Bary, op. cit., vol. I, pp. 369–75.
34 ibid., vol. I, pp. 375–83.
35 ibid., vol. I, pp. 354–62.
36 See J. Ching, 'Chu Shun-shui, 1600–82, a Chinese Confucian scholar in Tokugawa Japan', *Monumenta Nipponica*, 30(2) (Summer 1975), 177–91.
37 De Bary, op. cit., vol. I, pp. 424–33.
38 This theory is discussed in R. N. Bellah, *Tokugawa Religion: The Cultural Roots of Modern Japan* (1957); repr. New York/London, (1985).
39 De Bary, op. cit., vol. I, p. 372.
40 P. Nosco (ed.), *Confucianism and Tokugawa Culture* (Princeton, 1984), p. 12.

FURTHER READING

Bellah, Robert N. (1957) *Tokugawa Religion: The Cultural Roots of Modern Japan*, Glencoe, Ill.: The Free Press.

Bodart-Bailey, Beatrice M. (1993) 'The persecution of Confucianism in early Tokugawa Japan', *Monumenta Nipponica* 48(3) (Autumn).

Ching, J. (1975) 'Chu Shun-shui, 1600–82, a Chinese Confucian scholar in Tokugawa Japan', *Monumenta Nipponica* 30(2) (Summer).

De Bary, W. T. (1981) *Neo-Confucian Orthodoxy and the Learning of the Mind-and-Heart*, New York: Columbia University Press.

De Bary, W. T. and Bloom, I. (eds) (1979) *Principle and Practicality: Essays in Neo-Confucianism and Practical Learning*, New York: Columbia University Press.

Lidin, O. G. (1973) *The Life of Ogyū Sorai: A Tokugawa Confucian Philosopher*, Scandinavian Institute of Asian Studies Monograph Series 19, Lund: Studentlitteratur.

Maruyama Masao (1980) *Studies in the Intellectual History of Tokugawa Japan*, Princeton: Princeton University Press.

Najita, T. (1987) *Visions of Virtue in Tokugawa Japan: the Kaitokudō Merchant Academy of Osaka*, Chicago: The University of Chicago Press.

Najita, T. and Scheiner, I. (eds) (1978) *Japanese Thought in the Tokugawa Period, Methods and Metaphors*, Chicago: The University of Chicago Press.

Nakai-Wildman, K. (1988) *Arai Hakuseki: Politics and Ideology in the Mid-Tokugawa Bakufu*, Cambridge, Mass: Harvard University Press.

Nosco, P. (1984) (ed.) *Confucianism in Tokugawa Culture*, Princeton: Princeton University Press.

Ogyū Sorai (1970) *Bendō: Distinguishing the Way*, trans. Olof G. Lidin, Tokyo: Sophia University Press.

Ooms, H. (1975) *Charismatic Bureaucrat: A Political Biography of Matsudaira Sadanobu, 1758–1829*, Chicago: Chicago University Press.

—— (1985) *Tokugawa Ideology, Early Constructs, 1570–1680*, Princeton: Princeton University Press.

Tsunoda, R., De Bary, W. T. and Keene, D. (comps) (1964) *Sources of Japanese Tradition*, 2 vols, New York: Columbia University Press.

Tucker, M. E. (1989) *Moral and Spiritual Cultivation in Japanese Neo-Confucianism, The Life and Thought of Kaibara Ekken (1630–1714)*, Albany: State University of New York Press.

36

BUDDHISM IN JAPAN

Masao Abe

THE INTRODUCTION OF BUDDHISM TO JAPAN

Buddhism was introduced into Japan in the sixth century AD. According to the *Nihongi*, one of the oldest records of early Japan, Buddhism was officially introduced into Japan in AD 552 from Korea. At that time the King of Paekche, a kingdom in south-west Korea, sent a mission to the Emperor of Japan with presents consisting of 'an image of Śākyamuni Buddha in gilt bronze, several flags and umbrellas, and a number of sūtras (scriptures)'.[1] But some years earlier Buddhist images and instruments must have been brought to Japan privately.

The message accompanying the presents stated:

> The religion (*Hō*, Sanskrit, *Dharma*) is the most excellent of all teachings, though difficult to master and hard to comprehend; even the sages of China would have found it not easy to grasp. It brings endless and immeasurable blessings and fruit (to its believers), even the attainment of the supreme enlightenment (*bodhi*). Just as the *cintā-maṇi* jewel is said to fulfill every need according to desire, so the treasures of this glorious religion will never cease to respond in full to those who seek for it. Moreover, this religion has come over to Korea from India, and the people (in the countries between the two) are now ardent followers of its teachings, and none are outside its pole.[2]

The Japanese court was much impressed with the presents and their accompanying message from Paekche. The Emperor Kimmei (*r.* 539–71) thought it prudent to consult his ministers as to whether Japan should accept Buddhism or not. Ancient emperors were not only the superintendents of political power, but also the high priests of the native religious tradition, Shintō. Their authority and political power derived from the Shintō *kami* (deity).

In response to the emperor's enquiry, Soga, a leading minister whose clan already had contact with Korea and who was quite progressive, argued that Japan should follow the example of other civilized countries by adopting this new religion, whereas another powerful minister, Mononobe, whose clan both depended on and represented the interests of the imperial family, insisted that the native gods might be offended if such respect were shown to a 'foreign deity'. The issue was disputed, but it was the former party which finally won. Thus the path was open to accept Buddhism.

Ancient Japan, a theocratic state, was based on the unity of religious cult (*matsuri*) and the government administration (*matsuri-goto*). Thus the ethnic religion, Shintō, provided the basis not only for Japanese society, but for its politics as well. The worship of nature is a prominent feature of Shintō, which is also very affirmative of this-worldly realities. However, in the ancient period, Shintō had very little systematic intellectual content; it had no established form of doctrine or religious ritual. For this reason, the acceptance of such a universal religion as Buddhism did not raise serious opposition or conflict with Shintō on a doctrinal level. Instead, Buddhism was accepted as another ethnic and magical religion like Shintō. Thus Buddhist teachings were turned into prayers for promoting good fortune and avoiding misfortune. For example, the ruling classes who were converted to Buddhism would pray to Buddha for the welfare of their own clan in this world and the next. The Buddha was worshipped by them on an equal footing with the Shintō *kami*.

The ancient Japanese view of the other world consisted of four realms: *Takamagahara* (the realm of *kamis* in heaven), *Nenokuni* (the domain of roots or materials), *Tokoyo* (the domain of the wizard of immortality) and *Yominokuni* (the underground domain of the dead). Coming and going between this world and these four domains was considered quite possible. In other words, these domains were understood as the extension of this present world and in continuity with it. In contrast Buddhism speaks of the previous, the present, and future lives, which are separate from each other. Rebirth through the realization of death is necessary because movement between these three lives is impossible in this body. It also teaches that due to *karma* (volitional act) all human beings are subject to transmigration, the unending chain of rebirth, that is, *saṃsāra*. The Buddha saves beings from endless transmigration to attain *nirvāṇa*, the blissful freedom from life and death. Further, Buddhism helped the Japanese for the first time to go beyond a naïvely optimistic view of man and nature and to face the darker side of human reality such as sickness, old age, and death. Buddhist teaching insists that suffering can be dealt with through awakening to the Buddha Dharma. All the same, by accepting Buddhism for the practical and mundane benefits it promised, and by practising Buddhism in the same manner in which native Shintō liturgical prayers were recited, the Soga Clan and other pro-Buddhist families did not properly understand the universal religious nature of Buddhism.

PRINCE SHŌTOKU AND BUDDHISM

Prince Shōtoku (574–622) was the first to appreciate the universal significance of Buddhism. He sought to establish Buddhism as the basis of political and social order and unity which transcended the current clan and political structure in Japan. Shōtoku ascended to the regency under his aunt, the Empress Suiko, and during the thirty years of his reign, he pursued a political and cultural revolution which was marked by a striking advance of Buddhist influence and continental civilization. In 604 Shōtoku proclaimed what is known as the 'Seventeen-Article Constitution'. This was Japan's first legislative step in the direction of a state constitution. However, it bears more of the features of a moral and religious treatise than a legal decree. In the First Article of his constitution, Shōtoku advocated 'harmony' as the chief principle for the regulation of human behaviour. He wrote:

> Harmony is to be valued, and an avoidance of wanton opposition to be honoured. All men are influenced by class-feelings, and there are few who are intelligent. Hence there are some who disobey their lords and fathers or who maintain feuds with neighbouring villages. But when those above and those below are harmonious and friendly, things spontaneously and of themselves harmonize with truth. Then what is there which cannot be accomplished?[3]

The theme of harmony is characteristic of the entire constitution, not only the First Article. Shōtoku's notion of harmony is more Buddhistic than Confucian, because, as Hajime Nakamura states, 'his attitude derived from the Buddhist conception of benevolence, which needs to be distinguished clearly from the Confucian conception of propriety'[4] appropriate to one's status.

In the Second Article Buddhism is clearly advanced as the fundamental principle of harmony:

> Sincerely revere the Three Treasures – Buddha, Dharma, and Sangha, the final refuge of all beings and the supreme object of faith in all countries. Should any age or any people fail to revere this truth? There are few men who are utterly vicious. Everyone will realize truth if duly instructed. Could any weakness be corrected without taking refuge in the Three Treasures?[5]

These statements imply at least the following two ideas: first he advocates Buddhist truth as the most fundamental principle for human life regardless of difference of nation or age; second, few men are thoroughly bad, and even wretched men can realize the truth by being duly instructed, indicating that the idea of eternal damnation was alien to Buddhism.[6] For Shōtoku, everything converges in the one fundamental principle called the *Dharma*.

Some interpreters argue that in the constitution, Shōtoku intended to build a centralized authoritarian state on the absolute authority of the emperor. This position is supported by the following passage in the Third Article:

> When you receive the imperial commands, fail not scrupulously to obey them. The lord is Heaven, the vassal is the Earth. Heaven overspreads, and the Earth upbears. When this is

> so, the four seasons follow their due course, and the powers of nature obtain their efficacy. If the Earth attempts to overspread, Heaven would simply fall in ruin. Therefore is it that when the lord speaks, the vassal listens. When the superior acts, the inferior yields compliance. Consequently, when you receive the imperial commands, fail not to carry them out scrupulously. Let there be a want of care in this matter, and ruin is the natural consequence.[7]

This article certainly demonstrates Confucian influence and emphasizes a single hierarchy of authority which culminates in the emperor. However, as William Theodore de Bary rightly points out, 'sovereignty derives from Heaven, symbolizing the natural moral order. Individual and social morality likewise derive from Heaven.' Thus there is 'a hierarchy of mutual respect based upon the ritual order ordained by Heaven to govern political life and social intercourse.'[8] More importantly we should notice the fact that the exhortation, 'when you receive the imperial commands, fail not scrupulously to obey them' is placed after the command 'sincerely revere the Three Treasures – Buddha, Dharma, and Sangha.' When Shōtoku asks rhetorically, 'could any wickedness be corrected without taking refuge in the Three Treasures?' he intends to establish the political life of the state principally on Buddhism, even implying that the emperor himself in issuing imperial commands must look to the guidance of Buddhism.

Shōtoku probably envisioned the ideal emperor not as one who insists on the absolute authority of his commands, but as one who is able to correct errors in the light of universal religious truth. This model of imperial authority is not Confucian, but Buddhist.[9]

A careful reading of the Seventeen-Article Constitution leads to the conclusion that Shōtoku not only emphasized the importance of Buddhism as a universal teaching, but also urged his countrymen to overcome egocentrism and factionalism through existential self-reflection. We see this point clearly in the Tenth Article:

> Let us cease from wrath and refrain from angry looks. Nor let us be resentful simply because others oppose us. Every person has a mind of his own; each heart has its own leanings. We may regard as wrong what others hold as right; others may regard as wrong what we hold as right. We are not unquestionably sages. Nor are they assuredly fools. Both are simply ordinary men. Who is wise enough to judge which of us is good or bad? For we are all wise and foolish by turns, like a ring that has no end. Therefore, though others may give way to anger, let us on the contrary dread our own faults, and though we may be sure that we are in the right, let us act in harmony with others.[10]

This article shows that Shōtoku is urging both lord and subject, superior and inferior to transform their subjective standpoint by overcoming self-justification and self-attachment and awakening both self and others as 'simply ordinary men'.

Only when the universality of the teaching is realized existentially by individuals and collectively can the universality of the Buddhist teaching be established.[11] In other words, through the transformation of one's subjectivity the universal standpoint of

Buddhism will come to be realized. The Tenth Article suggests the necessity of shifting from an egocentric standpoint to an existential openness by negating the former. Realization of both self and others as 'simply ordinary men' in the light of Buddhist teaching is a crucial point in this existential transformation and indicates the essence of Shōtoku's Buddhism.

Shōtoku, however, adopted Buddhism not as a means of enhancing political power, but as the principle which orientates political power and its employment. While Shōtoku was a pious and devoted Buddhist he was, as Masaharu Anesaki points out,

> not a mere idealist, but a statesman who struggled to build a nation out of a people divided into clans and who carried out numerous practical reforms in government and social work.[12]

Precisely because Shōtoku was a political reformer who was an authentic Buddhist, clearly realizing the universal truth implied in Buddhism when he adopted Buddhism as the basic principle of the Japanese state, he did not subordinate Buddhism to the state, but subordinated the state to Buddhism. Shōtoku's existential acceptance of Buddhist universalism is attested to by his attempts to overcome partisanship by urging his fellow-beings of all classes to change their outlook and realize that all are 'simply ordinary men'.

In addition to the 'Seventeen-Article Constitution' Prince Shōtoku is credited with having lectured and written commentaries on three Mahāyāna scriptures which had a great impact on the character of Japanese Buddhism: (1) the *Lotus Sūtra*, with its affirmation of universal salvation; (2) the *Discourse of Vimalakīrti* (*Yuima-gyō*), a wealthy lay-Buddhist sage and a patron saint for lay Buddhists in China and Japan, and (3) the *Discourse between Buddha and Queen Śūmālā* (*Shōman-gyō*), the paradigm of Buddhist womanhood.[13]

The selection of these three *sūtras* out of the multitude of texts making up the Buddhist canon clearly shows the Japanese way of thinking and the character of Japanese Buddhism. The intention of Shōtoku was to emphasize the importance of realizing Buddhist truth within a concrete human nexus. In his view, human beings should ideally realize unity with the ultimate truth in daily life.

Buddhism originally urged the renunciation of this world and the merits of other-worldliness. Although the laity was included in this Buddhist order of things, monks and nuns, who had freed themselves from their families and any specific human nexus, were its main adherents. Early Buddhism and the Theravāda branch were profoundly shaped by monasticism. When Buddhism was introduced into Japan, Buddhism's other-worldly tendencies were rejected in favour of the more world-affirming Buddhism of the Mahāyāna movement.

Shōtoku, for instance, criticized the other-worldly practice of conservative Buddhists:

> Hīnayāna ascetics, hating the distractive world, escape into mountains and forests to practise careful discipline of mind and body. If one still thinks that various objects exist and cannot

> give up the assumption, how can one rid one's mind of such distractions, even if one stays in mountains and forests? [14]

Throughout the three commentaries Shōtoku seeks absolute significance within each practical act of everyday life. He asserts, 'Reality is no more than today's occurrence of cause and effect.'[15]

However, his emphasis on this-worldliness in Buddhist practice does not indicate a mere affirmation of the given world situation. The following words ascribed to Shōtoku, woven into a tapestry by his princess-consort Tachibana, have been preserved in Shōtoku's Temple, the Hōryūji. 'The world is empty and false; only the Buddha is true.' This statement clearly shows his critical view of the present world and devotion to Buddhist truth, and may be regarded as the first expression of world-negating thought in the intellectual history of Japan.

Shōtoku erected many temples, among which the Hōryūji and Shitennōji are especially important. Hōryūji was the central temple for Buddhist activities, but as its formal name, *Hōryū gakumonji*, or Temple of Learning for the Prospering of the *Dharma*, shows, it is not simply a place of worship but also a sort of university for Buddhist learning. Shitennōji (Four Deva King Temple)

> was laid out in the four main divisions: Kyōden-in, the great central hall or religious sanctuary proper, used for training in Buddhist discipline and in aesthetic and scholarly pursuits; Hiden-in, a hall where the poor could obtain relief; Ryōbyō-in, a hospital or clinic where the sick could receive treatment without charge; and Seyaku-in, a dispensary where medicinal herbs were collected, refined and distributed free of charge.[16]

It seems clear that Shōtoku's adoption of Buddhism as the universal foundation for a centralized Japanese state had important consequences not only for the spread of Buddhism in Japan but also for the social and political welfare of the Japanese people. [17]

BUDDHISM IN THE NARA PERIOD (EIGHTH CENTURY)

After the death of Prince Shōtoku in 622 Buddhism did not develop smoothly. Rather it was involved in serious political struggles and suffered their consequences. It was through the 'Taika Reform' (645–9) that Buddhism became well established in Japanese society. As a result, the Buddhist-inspired political reformation inaugurated by Prince Shōtoku came to fulfilment. This time, however, Buddhism was closely associated with the centralization of government and the codification of legal structures. Thus in bestowing on Buddhism the dignity of a state religion the idea of the superiority of Buddhism over the state was lost. Buddhism was supported by the court and government in return for ensuring the safety of the nation. The most magnificent example of the protection of the nation by Buddhism is the erection of Tōdai-ji Temple in the capital, Nara, during the reign of the Emperor Shōmu

(724–48). Shōmu was a devout Buddhist who tried to establish a centralized government and national unity on Buddhist teachings. Tōdai-ji was built as a national cathedral featuring a giant bronze image of the Buddha Vairocana (it was more than fifty feet in height). This image is taken from the teaching of the *Avatamsaka Sūtra*, the scriptural foundation of the Flower Garland (Kegon) school. The Emperor Shōmu also ordered each province to build a seven-storeyed pagoda, and to establish a Guardian Temple and an Atonement Nunnery for the province. All this can be traced to the fact that the *Avatamsaka Sūtra*

> preached a cosmic harmony presided over by the [Vairocana] Buddha, who sits on a lotus throne of a thousand petals, each of which is a universe containing thousands of worlds like ours. Within the harmony of the Flower Garland all beings are interrelated and interdependent. Religious deliverance is attained through the realization of this fundamental communion of all things in the Buddha. The world is potentially a Buddha-land, providing only that the ruler and his subjects join in making it so. Thus the cosmic harmony becomes the spiritual basis of the universal state as the state becomes the material support of Kegon Buddhism.[18]

In short, the Buddhist ideal of universal spiritual communion centred in the Vairocana Buddha was taken as parallel with the political unity of national life centred in the monarch.

However, this close affinity between state and religion, between the political regime and Buddhism, proved later to be a cause of the corruption of the priesthood. The evil effects of this corruption had become manifest by the latter half of the eight century.

SAICHŌ AND THE LOTUS TEACHING

Saichō (767–822), also known by the posthumous name Dengyō, entered a monastery at an early age, and was ordained at 18. As he was dissatisfied with the decadence of the monasteries of Nara, he left the city to live in solitude on Mount Hiei, near his birthplace. There he built a small monastery, motivated by his belief that only in an entirely different environment could moral renovation and ethical awakening take place. Six years later in 794 the Emperor Kammu moved the capital from Nara to Kyoto. Through the patronage of the Emperor Kammu, Saichō was able to develop his monastic institutions and establish a new centre of Buddhism in co-ordination with the new political centre. Numerous sanctuaries and colleges were built in the area of Mount Hiei, and the whole institution was officially declared to be the 'Centre for the Protection of the Nation'. For Saichō, Buddhism was in the service of the court and the state, not their master, and Saichō constantly expressed his belief that Mahāyāna Buddhism was the great benefactor and protector of Japan.[19]

In 804 he was sent by the emperor to China to discover the best form of Buddhism. He studied the T'ien-t'ai [Tiantai] (Tendai) school at its headquarters, finding it to be the most authentic and profound form of Buddhism. Tendai teaching is based on the *Lotus Sūtra*. He also studied the Shingon and Zen schools. After his return to Japan Saichō was very active in developing a new form of Buddhism different from Buddhism in Nara on the basis of Tendai doctrine.

The most remarkable characteristic of Tendai is its comprehensive and encyclopedic character. It finds a place for all scriptures, regarding these teachings as a progressive revelation, gradually disclosed by the Buddha during his life, as he found that the intelligence of his listeners ripened.[20] This idea was formulated by Chih-i [Zhiyi] (531–97) in the 'Theory of the Five Periods and Eight Kinds of Teachings'. According to this theory the Buddha revealed his teaching gradually in the five periods of his lifetime. The teaching of the *Lotus Sūtra* is to be considered the ultimate. He also classified the teachings of the Buddha into the following forms: sudden, gradual, secret, undetermined, collected, developed, distinguished, and accomplished. The Tendai school held that the Buddha's teaching in its accomplished form should be considered the most perfect.[21]

Unlike the Hossō school, which prevailed in Nara and emphasized hierarchic degrees of spiritual attainment both in theory and practice, implying that the privileges of spiritual awakening were enjoyed only by a select few, the Tendai doctrine adopted by Saichō emphasized the universality of salvation or attainment of buddhahood, embracing even the crude and vicious such as beasts and infernal beings.[22] This approach led to an acrimonious controversy which came to be known as the 'Three Vehicles versus the One Vehicle' controversy. The Three Vehicle (Triyāna) doctrine argues that there are three paths or three Vehicles to attain enlightenment conforming to the nature and ability of sentient beings: *śrāvaka* (hearers, disciplines), *pratyeka-buddha* (self-enlightened, enlightened for oneself) and *bodhisattva* (would-be Buddha). The first two are called Hīnayāna (Small Vehicle) because with these teachings only the élite could attain enlightenment, whereas the third is named Mahāyāna (Great Vehicle), because it holds the possibility of supreme enlightenment for all. The Hossō school is based on the Three Vehicle theory and its discriminative view of humanity. On the other hand the Tendai school insists on One Vehicle (Ekayāna) theory. While it admits the differences between Hīnayāna and Mahāyāna Buddhism, it regards the Hīnayāna as the teaching of the Buddha which is able to lead ignorant people to higher enlightenment. All people will be able to attain the supreme enlightenment. Thus the Ekayāna theory presumes the equality of all humanity.

The mainline of Japanese Buddhism after Saichō has been based on the Ekayāna doctrine. Considering that all the new schools of the Kamakura era derived from the Tendai school and thus were based on the Ekayāna doctrine, Saichō's confrontation with the Hossō school has profoundly influenced the character of Japanese Buddhism after him.

One of the basic doctrines of Tendai Buddhism is contained in the following maxim: a moment of thought is itself the three thousand worlds (that is, the whole universe).

As Junjirō Takakusu properly points out, 'The expression "three thousand" does not indicate a numerical or substantial immensity, but is intended to show the interpermeation of all *dharmas* and the ultimate unity of the whole universe.'[23] According to the *Makashikan*, an important scripture of the Tendai school, one moment of thought has ten realms. They are the realms of the Buddha, *bodhisattva* (a buddha-to-be), *pratyekabuddha* (a buddha for himself, not teaching others), *śrāvaka* (a direct disciple of the Buddha), heavenly beings, *asura* (fighting spirits), human beings, *preta* (hungry spirits), beasts, and hellish beings. These ten realms are mutually immanent and mutually inclusive, each one having in it the remaining nine realms.[24] Again, as Takakusu states,

> For example, the realm of men will include the other nine from Buddha to Hell, and so will any of the ten realms. Even the realm of the Buddha includes the nature of hell and all the rest, because a Buddha, though not hellish himself, intends to save the depraved and hellish beings, and therefore also has hell in his mind. In this sense, the realm of Buddhas, too, includes the other nine realms.[25]

The immanence of each of the ten worlds in all of them accounts for a hundred worlds. Further, each of these realms has ten different features (*ju'nyoze*), and thus we arrive at the doctrine of a thousand realms. Moreover, each realm consists of three divisions: the species of living beings, the species of living-space, and the species of the five *skandhas*. [26] Thus there are three thousand realms which constitute the whole of reality.[27] In short, even in one moment of our present thought three thousand realms of the whole universe are implied. There is no universe apart from this single thought. The Tendai school urges us to realize fully this unity of the mind and the world with our whole existence through the practice of *śamatha-vipaśyanā* (calmness and insight). This theory entails the doctrine of Three Truths: *śūnyatā* (emptiness), the Temporary and the Middle.

All things have no enduring, unchangeable, own-being and therefore are non-substantial and empty, that is, *śūnya*. However, they have temporary existence and particular form. *Śūnyatā* (the emptiness of all things) cannot be realized apart from temporary existence. Emptiness and temporariness are inseparable. Emptiness is realized in temporariness, and temporariness is revealed in emptiness. This is the meaning of the middle. The middle is neither emptiness nor temporariness, and yet includes both. Thus it is an ultimate which by opposing nothing is able to embrace all opposition. Accordingly the middle is called *jissō*, 'true state'. Although the Tendai school interprets the 'true state' as 'no state' or 'no truth', this does not mean that it is false. 'No truth' or 'no state' here means that it is not a truth or a state established by argument or conceived by thought, but that it transcends all speech and thought. Again Tendai interprets it as 'one truth' (*eka-satya*), but 'one' here is not a numerical one: it means 'absolute'. The principle of Tendai doctrine centres on this true state of all elements.[28]

The *Lotus Sūtra* states:

> What the Buddha has accomplished in the *dharma* is foremost, rare and inconceivable. Only the Buddha can realize the true state of all *dharmas*: this is to say, all *dharmas* are thus-formed, thus-natured, thus-substantiated, thus-caused, thus-forced, thus-activated, thus-circumstanced, thus-effected, thus-remunerated, and thus-beginning-ending-completing.[29]

Through these manifestations of 'Thusness' we can see the true state. In fact, these manifestations *are* the true state.

We should not consider the Three Truths, *Śūnyatā*, the Temporary and the Middle, as separate, because these three penetrate each other and are found perfectly harmonized and united with one another. A thing is empty, but is also temporarily existent. It is temporary because it is empty, and the fact that everything is empty and at the same time temporary is the Middle truth.[30]

On the basis of the *Lotus Sūtra* and Tendai doctrine, Saichō strongly emphasized a universal salvation in terms of *Ekayāna* and the realization of ultimate reality in this actual life in terms of 'Thusness'. These two emphases characterized Japanese Buddhism thereafter.

KŪKAI AND ESOTERIC BUDDHISM

Another outstanding Buddhist figure of the Heian period is Kūkai (774–835), popularly known as Kōbō Daishi (Great Teacher Kōbō). Scion of one of the more powerful clans, Kūkai was educated in his youth by his Confucian-scholar uncle in the Confucian and Daoist classics. He later studied Buddhism. Although he appreciated Buddhism the most, he was not satisfied with the forms of Buddhism which were being practised in Japan at that time. His dissatisfaction was due in part to the corruption of the monks and to what he perceived to be an inadequate understanding of Buddhist doctrine and practice by the monks. This discontent led him to China in search of a more authentic and unified Buddhist tradition.

While in China Kūkai met the great esoteric master Hui-kuo (746–805), the celebrated abbot of the Ch'ing-Lung Temple in the capital of Ch'ang-an. Kūkai studied Esoteric Buddhism in Ch'ang-an between 804–806. On his return to Japan Kūkai was well received by the emperor. He founded a great monastery on Mount Kōya which eventually became the centre of Japanese Esoteric Buddhism. In 823, after the death of his rival Saichō, Kūkai was appointed abbot of Tōji, which later became the centre of Esoteric Buddhism in the Japanese capital. Kūkai died on Mount Kōya in 835.

The Buddhism which Kūkai learned in China and transmitted to Japan is called *Shingon*, or 'true word'. *Shingon* is the Japanese pronunciation of the Chinese translation of *mantra*, a Sanskrit expression which refers to a sacred spell or mystic hymn. The expression *Shingon* signifies the importance of speech, one of the three mysteries. The other two are body and mind. Shingon doctrine and practice maintain that through the mystical vitality of these three faculties – speech, body and mind, the practitioner can commune with the body, speech and mind of the Mahāvairocana, the cosmic Buddha. While every human being may possess the mystical vitality of these three faculties, it is through specific ritual developed by the Shingon masters that the practitioner can touch the vital virtues of the Mahāvairocana Buddha and thereby manifest the Buddha's virtues. Any act, speech and thought may invoke the mysterious powers of the Mahāvairocana Buddha when performed in faith and harmony with this Buddha's cosmic-life activities.[31]

Esoteric Buddhism is often regarded as a degenerated and Hinduized form of Buddhism which has been corrupted by magic and occult practices. We should, however, make a distinction between 'Miscellaneous Mystic' and 'Pure Mystic' forms of Esoteric Buddhism. Miscellaneous Mystic is a form of Esoteric Buddhism which developed before the emergence of the *Mahāvairocana Sūtra* and the *Ritasangraha* or *Vajra-sekhara*. In contrast Pure Mystic is that form of Esoteric Buddhism which is based on these two documents. Miscellaneous Mystic was based on texts which 'were charms, cures and other sorts of sorcery, often containing some *mantra* prayers and praises of gods or saints of higher grades, but generally speaking they could not be regarded as expressing a higher aspiration.'[32]

On the other hand, the 'Pure Mystic' is based on a profound understanding of the fundamental beliefs and doctrine of Mahāyāna Buddhism. The *Mahāvairocana Sūtra* depicts the Vairocana Buddha as a cosmic Buddha, whose body is formless and non-substantial, devoid of all marks. Further, the Vairocana Buddha is believed to be the universe, which is represented by six elements: earth, water, fire, air, space and consciousness. Because the universe is believed to be the life and body of the Vairocana Buddha, it is possible to apprehend, when our minds are freed of delusion, the Buddha even in a grain of dust or in the slightest movement of our consciousness.

Pure Mystic Esoteric Buddhism is called *Vajrayāna*, or Diamond Vehicle. Followers of *Vajrayāna* believe that they adhere to a mystic doctrine which transcends all previous Buddhist traditions. Kūkai transmitted this *Vajrayāna* tradition to Japan. Although Pure Mystic Esoteric Buddhism was not fully structured in China, Kūkai skillfully systematized its theory and practice. The result was *Shingon mikkyō*, True Word Esoteric Buddhism.

In essence, Kūkai clarified what he believed to be the distinction between exoteric and esoteric doctrines. He believed Esoteric Buddhism to be superior to exoteric forms of Buddhism. Kūkai also claimed that Shingon represented Esoteric Buddhism. All other Buddhist schools should be considered to be exoteric. Kūkai explained the distinction between Exoteric and Esoteric Buddhism in several ways.

1. Exoteric Buddhism is the teaching preached by the historical Buddha. Because the historical Buddha expounded the *Dharma* in accordance with the limitation of his audience, he could not reveal the full profundity of his enlightenment. On the other hand, Esoteric Buddhism is the teaching preached by the Vairocana Buddha, who

personifies the *dharmakāya* or the spiritual body of the Buddha. However, the Vairocana Buddha is not simply formless, colourless and speechless. The Vairocana Buddha is the cosmos. This Buddha preaches the *dharma* with form, colour and speech throughout the universe as the spiritual body. The speech of the Vairocana Buddha is revealed in the *Mahāvairocana Sūtra* and the *Vajra-sekhara*.

2. In Exoteric Buddhism the cause of buddhahood can be analysed, but the effects of it can in no way be explained. Exoteric Buddhism teaches *upāya* (skilful means) as a means for saving others. On the other hand, in Esoteric Buddhism, *dharmakāya* preaches the essence of his realization in its fullness, and this teaching is voiced for his own enjoyment. In other words, the state of the inexplicable buddhahood has been explained in esoteric teachings.

3. As for the duration of time to attain buddhahood, there is another significant difference between Exoteric and Esoteric Buddhism. Exoteric Buddhism advocates religious practice through countless lives in three long periods (*kalpas*) to attain buddhahood. By contrast, Esoteric Buddhism emphasizes *sokushin jōbutsu* ('becoming a living Buddha in the human body'). We must note that Saichō also uses the phrase *sokushin jōbutsu*. But from Kūkai's point of view Saichō's understanding was not sufficiently developed, because 'even if a man achieves Buddhahood in his lifetime, it was supposed to be the consequence of ascetic practices achieved through many lives so that one could become a Buddha only upon reaching the threshold of true religion'.[33] In Esoteric Buddhism and through the practice of the three mysteries – body, speech and mind – one can attain buddhahood within this corporeal body.

4. A fourth difference has to do with salvation. Even the evil or sinful person, who cannot be saved in Exoteric Buddhism, such as *icchantika*, can be saved and emancipated from *saṃsāra*, that is, life–death transmigration by virtue of reciting *mantras* in Esoteric Buddhism.

A synthesis of divergent philosophical currents developed early in China and Japan because Buddhism's extensive canon of divergent, sometimes contradictory scriptures presented these cultures with the need to reconcile these different teachings. In Japan Saichō established a synthetic system of Esoteric Buddhism, Zen and Vinaya (precept) based on Tendai Buddhism, but it was a system within Buddhism. By contrast Kūkai was more comprehensive and included not only various forms of Buddhism, but also Confucianism and Daoism in his system with the understanding that even non-Buddhist thought can be manifestations of the basic principles of Mahāvairocana Buddha.

Kūkai expounded a doctrine of human spiritual development in his work *Ten Stages of Religious Consciousness* (830) as follows:

1 The first stage is that of 'common people who are like sheep'. Their desire is simply the satisfaction of appetite. They are not capable of differentiating good from evil.
2 The second is that for 'foolish children who practise fasting'. They cautiously observe moral precepts in order to prevent society from falling into disorder.

Among other religious systems Confucianism will be the one which also emphasizes the importance of morality by observing the five relationships. But it gives no indication of liberating people from mundane existence.

3 The third is that of those who practise to become an 'infant who knows no fears'. This idea is illustrated in Daoism. The Shingon sect also accepted Daoist claims for longevity and magic arts, although these were regarded as of lower value.

Stages (4) and (5) are the stages which are represented by Hīnayāna philosophy. The fourth stage pertains to those who realize that there is no ego and that that which is called ego or self is merely a conglomeration of aggregates (*skandhas*). The fifth stage includes those who endeavour to uproot evil *karma* until all passion and trouble ceases.

6 With the sixth stage we rise to the realm of Mahāyāna, as is shown in Buddhist idealism (the Hossō sect). Those who have reached this stage take all phenomena for nothing other than the revelation of the storehouse consciousness or memory and feel an infinite compassion for the salvation of all beings.

7 The seventh stage is that of the philosophers of emptiness. According to these philosophies there is neither becoming nor perishing, neither singularity nor plurality. The idea of undifferentiation of nothingness is a clear characteristic manifested in the Sanron sect both in China and Japan.

8 The eight stage is that of the Tendai school, which teaches 'one way without action'. It means that the ultimate reality is identical with our experience of the phenomenal world, in the assumption that there is no realm of reality apart from the mundane world.

9 The ninth stage is that of the Kegon school. It teaches the truth that there is no separate entity and that truth is realized in the ceaseless functions of the universe.

10 The tenth and highest stage is that of the Shingon. Now the doors to esoteric truth, whose realm is beautifully adorned, are open to the practitioner. Through the performance of the mystic rites of Shingon the adept realizes that man and the universe are Mahāvairocana himself.[34]

This all-comprehensive view of human spiritual development is based not merely on his speculation, but on his spiritual struggle and religious quest for many years. In the Introduction to his work, *Precious Key to the Secret Treasury*, a condensed version of the *Ten Stages of Religious Consciousness*, Kūkai expresses his deep compassion towards all beings involved in the transmigration of births and deaths through his own spiritual struggles in his youth.

> Mad are beings in the three realms of existence,
> And none are aware of his own madness!
> Blind are beings, four in the modes of their birth,
> Yet all unaware of their blindness!

Born, born and reborn without limit,
And still dark as to the origin of birth
Dying, dying, and dying without end,
Yet veiled is the ultimate goal of life.[35]

However, Shingon Buddhism is the key to open the Secret Treasury of salvation.

The healing power of the exoteric doctrine has wiped away all dust;
Now opens the store of the True Word (Shingon),
In which all hidden treasures are brought to light,
And there embodied are all virtues and powers.

The Buddha in the innumerable Buddha-lands
Are naught but the Buddha within our own soul;
The Golden Lotus, as multitudinous as the drops
Of ocean water, is living in our body.
Myriads of figures are contained in every mystic letter;
Every piece of chiselled metal embodies a Deity,
In whom are pregnantly present the realm of entities of Virtue and Merit.
In realizing all this everyone shall attain
The glories of being, even in this corporeal life.[36]

Shingon Buddhism attempted to unify the pantheons of various religions and thus moved from its mystic ritualism to a systematization of its world-view. The result was a curious but ingenious device graphically representing the cosmos in two pictures or diagrams called *maṇḍalas*. These diagrams symbolized two aspects of cosmic life, its being and its vitality, in the ideal or indestructible potential entity and in its dynamic manifestations.[37] The former is depicted in the Vajra or Diamond Maṇḍala, whereas the latter is depicted in the Garbha or Womb Maṇḍala. Both of them emphasize the harmony between unity and diversity. The *maṇḍalas* were used to represent the life and being of Vairocana Buddha, and also served to evoke mysterious powers. As Anesaki discusses,

> The universe thus seen under its two aspects, the potential and the dynamic, is nothing but the life and being of Vairocana Buddha himself, while developments of the world embody the inexhaustible fullness of his wisdom and mercy. This graphic representation of the two cycles in the two Mandalas was partly an outcome of speculation but largely a modification of ritual performance, in which those figures and symbols were arrayed on the ceremonial dais and were used for the purpose of evoking the respective mysterious powers. Each figure and symbol is conceived to contain a certain power which is inherent in every one of us too, and worship means nothing but a realization by acts of ritual performance of the inherent unity. Seen in this way, religion is enlightenment in the truth of essential unity, which means a harmonious union in faith with the 'enfolding power' (Skt. *adhiṣṭhāna*, Jap. *kaji*) of the universal Lord.[38]

Kūkai was not only the founder of the Shingon school, the most important religion of Heian Japan and one of the most popular forms of Buddhism in the subsequent history of Japan. He was also an outstanding sculptor and calligrapher. He founded a private school of arts as an educational centre for the common people at a time when secular education was largely restricted to the ruling classes. Thus we may say with justification that Kūkai himself is a *maṇḍala*.

AMIDA BUDDHA AND PURE LAND BUDDHISM

From the mid-Heian period (794–1192) to the Kamakura period (1185–1333) Pure Land Buddhism became increasingly popular among the court nobles and the general population. Pure Land Buddhism originated in the first or second century AD in India. Its teachings are based on the Larger and Smaller *Sukhāvāti-vyūha Sūtras* and the *Amitayur-dhyāna Sūtra*. These *sūtras* advocate the existence of the Western Paradise or Pure Land (*Sukhāvāti*). Amitābha Buddha presides over the Pure Land. Devotees of the Amitābha faith believe that they will be born in the Pure Land (after death) as a reward for their faith and merits which they have achieved in their life-time.

Pure Land Buddhism and the worship of Amitābha (Japanese Amida) Buddha were introduced to Japan as early as the seventh century along with other forms of Buddhism. However, Pure Land beliefs and practices were relegated to a secondary status in Tendai and Shingon traditions. The pious meditation on Amida Buddha, however, provided an alternative to the mystic ritualism of Esoteric Buddhism. Very few practitioners were capable of attaining deep spiritual insight.

Pure Land Buddhism is uniquely different from other forms of Buddhism. While most other schools of Mahāyāna insist on self-awakening, Pure Land Buddhism teaches sole reliance on the power of Amida Buddha. Followers of Pure Land Buddhism seek buddhahood (enlightenment) through rebirth in Amida's Pure Land. Rebirth in the Pure Land is attained through faith in the Power of the Amida Buddha's Vow to save all beings. According to the *Larger Sukhāvāti Sūtra*, Amida Buddha while still the *bodhisattva* Dharmākara made forty-eight vows which were to be fulfilled before he became a buddha. Dharmākara has since fulfilled his vows and is now the Amida Buddha.

The rise of Pure Land Buddhism was closely related to a belief that the world had entered the period of *mappō*, the era of the degenerate *Dharma* or Law and the existential realization of one's own powerlessness and sinfulness. The awareness of *mappō* is based on a pessimistic view of the fate of Buddhism which was long current among some Mahāyāna Buddhists in India and China. This view of history distinguished three periods in the destiny of the Buddhist religion after the Buddha's death: that is, three periods of *Shōbō* (*saddharma*), *Zōbō* (*saddharma-pratirupaka*), and *Mappō* (*saddharma-vipralopa*).

There are different views as to the duration of these periods. According to a view prevalent during the Heian period, the first period, believed to last a thousand years, is called *shōbō*, the right *dharma*, in which Buddhist doctrine, practice and enlightenment all exist; the second period of a thousand years is the period of *zōbō*, the semblance, or imitative *dharma*, in which doctrine and practice exist without enlightenment; the third and last period of ten thousand years is that of *mappō*, the latter or final *dharma*, in which only doctrine remains, but no practice and no enlightenment. The advent of *mappō* was believed to fall sometimes during late Heian times. Some Buddhists calculated the year 1052 as its commencement. In addition to the degeneration of Esoteric Buddhism as a result of its magical ritualism and close connection with secular power and authority, civil war, natural disaster and famine gave rise to a deep sense of pessimism. Along with this pessimistic realization of time and history, people were also left with an anxious sense of their own incapability of attaining enlightenment through formal practice and a sense of their own helplessness and sinfulness. Such a social and spiritual situation and a radical change of the social order (the uprising of the warrior class with the weakening of the central imperial court) inspired new types of Buddhist schools. Thus Pure Land Buddhism and the practice of meditation on the name of Amida became more and more appealing to the desperate people in the late Heian period.

It was Genshin (942–1017) and Hōnen (1133–1212) who played leading roles in popularizing Pure Land Buddhism. Believing that Pure Land faith is the way for obtaining a salvation open to all, laymen as well as monks, women as well as men, Genshin wrote *Ōjō yōshū*, *Essentials of Salvation*. Bringing together important passages from the great body of Buddhist scriptures describing various aspects of religious life, especially the torments of hell in contrast to the glories of paradise, his work inspired all people with a strong feeling for the horrors of hell, the attractions of the Western Paradise, and the advantages of the *nembutsu*, the invocation to Amida, among various practices for rebirth in the Pure Land.

Hōnen trained as a Tendai priest at Mount Hiei, like many of the new Buddhist leaders of the Kamakura era.

> In the late Heian period the Tendai monastic centre at Mt. Hiei prospered externally but suffered from an internal power struggle among the prince-abbots. . . . In time, he realized that the path of sanctification and enlightenment by means of precepts, meditation, and knowledge was theoretically possible but practically impossible. He came to realize, in reading Genshin's *Essentials of Salvation* (*ōjō yōshū*), that he was to seek not "enlightenment" but "salvation in the Pure Land". Based on this faith, Hōnen wrote the *Senchaku Hongan Nembutsu-shu* (Collections of passages on the original vow of Amida in which the *nembutsu* is chosen above all other ways of achieving rebirth).[39]

In this work, Hōnen made it unmistakably clear that *nembutsu* was superior to all other religious practice. Hōnen thoroughly re-examined all of the Buddhist schools not in terms of superiority or inferiority of doctrine but in terms of their soteriological efficacy. Following the teaching of the Chinese patriarch Tao-ch'o, Dōshaku (*c.* 645), he advanced the critical division of Buddhism into two parts: the path of the sage and the path of the Pure Land. The former involved the practice of severe disciplines leading to enlightenment, and relied for its efficacy upon the personal merits and effort of the aspirant. Accordingly this group is often referred to as the way of self-power and the difficult way. The latter involved only the recitation of the *nembutsu* and complete reliance on the grace of Amida, not upon oneself. Accordingly this group is called the way of other-power and the easy way. Hōnen believed that the path of the sage was beyond the capability of most people to pursue successfully. Their only sure hope of salvation, during the *mappō* period, was to follow the path of Pure Land, since its success was dependent only on the unfailing mercy and power of Amida.[40]

Hōnen's teaching of the exclusive practice of *nembutsu* was very critical of the established forms of Buddhism and sought to overcome the old synthesis in which state and church were closely linked together. His teaching widely opened the way of salvation to all people regardless of class, social status and intellectual ability.

Ichimai Kishōmon, the *One-Page Testament*, written by Hōnen two days before his death, is his final instruction to his disciples and concisely expresses the essence of his faith and teaching:

> The method of final salvation that I have propounded is neither a sort of meditation, such as has been practised by many scholars in China and Japan, nor is it a repetition of the Buddha's name by those who studied and understood the deep meaning of it. It is nothing but the mere repetition of the '*Namu Amida Butsu*',[41] without a doubt of his mercy, whereby one may be born into the Land of Perfect Bliss. The mere repetition with firm faith includes all the practical details, such as the threefold preparation of mind and the four practical rules. If I as an individual had any doctrine more profound than this, I should miss the mercy of the two Honorable Ones, Amida and Shaka, and be let out of the Vow of the Amida Buddha. Those who believe this, though they clearly understand all the teachings Shaka taught throughout his whole life, should behave themselves like simple-minded folk, who know not a single letter, or like ignorant nuns or monks whose faith is implicitly simple. Thus without pedantic airs, they should fervently practice the repetition of the name of Amida, and that alone.[42]

As can be clearly seen from this *Testament*, Hōnen rejected meditation practised as an intellectual pursuit and *nembutsu* uttered in enlightenment through learning. He exclusively emphasized the centrality of single-minded *nembutsu* through faith in Amida's original vow, entirely giving up the demeanour of a wise man and equating oneself with the most ignorant. This new movement provided by Hōnen was accepted enthusiastically by a wide spectrum of Japanese society, but was severely persecuted by the old Buddhist orders. In his later years, he suffered the injustice of condemnation and exile.

When Hōnen was exiled from the capital, several of his disciples were also banished to various places. Shinran (1173–1262), who would later come to be regarded as the founder of the most powerful of all Pure Land sects, Jōdoshinshū, was exiled to the northern province of Echigo because he married in violation of the clerical vows of celibacy. As de Bary states,

> His followers later alleged that Shinran had married this woman at the express request of Hōnen in order to demonstrate that monastic discipline was not essential to salvation and that the family rather than the monastery should be the center of the religious life.[43]

This matter holds within it three points which are characteristic of Shinran. First, Shinran entirely and completely relied upon the instruction of Hōnen. He became a disciple of Hōnen at the age of 29 after a desperate inner struggle in his search for salvation. His encounter with Hōnen was a definitive event which caused a radical conversion in him to the pure and simple faith in *nembutsu*, the recitation of Amida's name. We can clearly see this in his words in *Tannishō*.

> As for myself, Shinran, I simply receive the words of my dear teacher, Hōnen, 'Just say the *nembutsu* and be saved by Amida' and entrust myself to the primal vow. Besides this, there is nothing else. I really do not know whether the *nembutsu* may be the cause for my birth in the Pure Land, or the act that shall condemn me to hell. But I have nothing to regret, even if I should have been deceived by my teacher, and, saying the *nembutsu*, fall into hell.[44]

Second, Shinran's complete reliance on his teacher, Hōnen, however, was not a blind faith rooted merely in the human dimension. It was based rather in a deep devotional trust in the mercy of Amida. He shared with Hōnen an exclusive reliance on the saving power of the Buddha. To Shinran this utter reliance on the power of Amida was enhanced, as seen in his words immediately after the above quotation from *Tannishō*, by his painful realization of his own inability to attain buddhahood by any other religious practice.

> The reason is that if I were capable of realizing Buddhahood by other religious practices and yet fell into hell for saying the *nembutsu*, I might have dire regrets for having been deceived. But since I am absolutely incapable of any religious practice, hell is my only home.[45]

Third, in those days married life for a priest was hardly exceptional, but it had never been justified by doctrine or faith and was regarded as a mere concession. Shinran, on the contrary, regarded celibacy rather as a sign of lack of absolute trust in the Buddha's grace, because no sin was an obstacle to salvation through grace.[46] He believed that if salvation truly depended on nothing but the grace of Amida, celibacy and sobriety were unnecessary standards of conduct that presented no hindrance to salvation but rather indicated continuous reliance on self-power. Thus he had a family in order to 'give living testimony' as his followers say, that the secular life of ordinary people was no obstacle to salvation.[47]

Shinran carried Hōnen's instruction regarding the Amida's grace to its extreme conclusion. In *Tannishō*, section 3, Shinran declared

> Even a good person attains birth in the Pure Land.
> How much more so the evil person.

On this he comments as follows:

> The people of this world constantly say, even the evil person attains birth, how much more so the good person. Although this appears to be sound at first glance, it goes against the intention of the Primal Vow of Other Power. The reason is that since the person of self-power, being conscious of doing good (may be able to save himself by his own merit and thus) lacks the thought of entrusting himself completely to Other Power, he is not the focus of the Primal Vow of Amida. But when he turns over self-power and entrusts himself to Other Power, he attains birth in the land of true fulfillment.
>
> The Primal Vow was established out of deep compassion for us who cannot become freed from the bondage of birth-and-death through any religious practice, due to the abundance of blind passion. Since its basic intention is to effect the enlightenment of such an evil one, the evil person who entrusts himself to Other Power is truly the one who attains birth in the Pure Land. Thus, even the good person attains birth, how much more so the evil person![48]

Shinran himself painfully realized the sinfulness innate in human existence and lamented,

> My evilness is truly difficult to renounce:
> The mind is like serpents and scorpions,
> Even doing virtuous deeds is tainted with poison,
> And so it is called false practice.[49]
>
> Although I have taken refuge in the true teaching
> The mind of truth hardly exists in me.
> Moreover, I am so false hearted and untrue
> That there cannot be any mind of purity.[50]

Accordingly, Shinran changed the meaning of the term *ekō* radically. Traditionally *ekō* signified merit-transference, that is, a practitioner's directing of merit towards one's own and others' attainment of enlightenment. However, because of the keen realization of his own insincerity and wickedness, Shinran could not recognize any possibility of merit-transference from his side. Instead, *fuekō* or 'no-merit-transference from the human-side' was his position. Merit-transference is possible only from the side of Amida Buddha. Accordingly, to Shinran, even faith in Amida, if it is genuine, is not our own act or possession, but exclusively the gift of Amida. The devotional repetition of Amida's name is not a necessary action to be saved by Amida, but an action of gratitude or an expression of thanksgiving for the salvational power of Amida's Primal Vow. This is precisely Shinran's so-called faith in Other Power. To Shinran the deeper the realization of sinfulness becomes, the greater the joy of being saved by Amida becomes.

> Because the power of the Vow is without limits,
> Even our evil karma, so deep and heavy, is not burdensome;
> Because the Buddha's wisdom is without bounds,
> Even the bewildered and wayward are not abandoned.[51]

Passions obstruct my eyes and I cannot see him;
Nevertheless, great compassion is untiring and
Illumines me always.[52]

How shameless and unrepentant a person am I
And without a heart of truth and sincerity;
But because the Name is transferred by Amida,
Its virtue pervades the ten directions.[53]

He expressed the Other Power in the phrase *gi naki o gi to su*. *Gi* usually means reason, meaning, justification, principle, etc. In Shinran, however, *gi* indicates more specifically the mental, emotional and volitional working of unenlightened man (self-power) to fathom Amida's Primal Vow, which surpasses conceptual understanding. Thus *gi* may be translated as 'self-working' and *gi naki o gi tosu* is rendered 'no self working is true working', implying that where no activities of the ego-self exist the true working of Amida's compassion manifests itself.[54]

In the concluding years of his life Shinran talked much about *jinen hōni*, one of the key terms of his religious faith, which is difficult to translate. *Jinen* indicates things-as-they-are or 'suchness'. It is another term for Buddhist ultimate reality, the *Dharma* which is realized only when we are free from human calculation.

Hōni means 'One is made to become so by virtue of the *Dharma*',[55] the same meaning as that of *jinen*. In short, *jinen hōni* indicates that when the practitioner becomes completely free from human calculation, everything throughout the universe manifests itself just as it is in its suchness. Accordingly *jinen hōni* may be rendered 'primordial naturalness by virtue of the *Dharma*'. It is not naturalness as a counter-concept of human artificiality. It is rather the fundamental naturalness as the basis of both the human and nature, or the primordial naturalness prior to the dichotomy of man and nature.

Accordingly *jinen hōni* is not a static state but a dynamic working which makes both human and nature live and work just as they are. *Jinen hōni* is simply another expression of *gi naki o gi tosu*, 'no-self-working is true working'. Through the deep realization of sinfulness innate in human existence, Shinran exclusively relied on Other Power, the power of Amida's Primal Vow. Primordial naturalness is nothing but naturalness as the dynamic working springing from the Other Power. It is the working of Wisdom and Compassion based on the power of Amida.

Shinran's spirituality with its profound, pure faith and simple practice of *nembutsu* appealed a great deal to a wide range of people from the Kamakura period down to the present, and his school, Jōdoshinshū, became one of the most powerful sects in Japan. His teaching critically moves Japanese mentality and profoundly cultivates Japanese religious life.

DŌGEN AND ZEN BUDDHISM

Zen was introduced to Japan several times in earlier centuries. In these cases the propagation was assisted by the court but did not continue for long. It was through the efforts of two great Japanese Zen pioneers that it came to take firm root in Japanese soil. These pioneers were Eisai (1141–1215) and Dōgen (1200–53).

Eisai first studied Tendai Buddhism at Mount Hiei but was not satisfied with the scholastic doctrinalism of that school and visited China twice, pursuing training in Zen, particularly Linchi (Rinzai) Zen, Tendai and Vinaya (precept). On his return, he taught and practised Zen, but only as one important element in the comprehensive Tendai system.[56] He wrote a treatise, *Kōzen Gokokuron* (*Propagation of Zen as the Protection of the Nation*), in which he asserted that the propagation of Zen practice would serve to protect the prosperity of the nation.

It was Dōgen[57] who established Zen in Japan as an independent school without affiliating with other forms of Buddhism and who is far more important in terms of philosophico-religious thought. Of noble birth, Dōgen entered the priesthood at the age of 13, following the death of his parents. According to the traditional account of Dōgen's life, a serious question arose for him in his study of Tendai Buddhism at Mount Hiei:

> Both the exoteric and esoteric Buddhism teach the original Dharma-nature of all sentient beings. If this is the case, why have the Buddhas of past, present, and future awakened the resolve for and sought enlightenment through ascetic practice?[58]

This question concerns the Tendai idea of 'original awakening' as opposed to 'acquired awakening'. Tendai Buddhism emphasizes 'original awakening', the doctrine that everyone is originally awakened or enlightened. It rejects 'acquired awakening' as inauthentic because that doctrine indicates that awakening can be acquired only as a result of sustained practice. Dōgen came to doubt this fundamental standpoint of Tendai Buddhism, and asked, 'Why should people engage in religious practice to overcome delusion if they are originally enlightened?'

An emphasis on 'original awakening' that is *a priori*, fundamental to all sentient beings and eternal is apt to become pantheistic or mystical, neglecting ethical and religious practice. On the other hand, an emphasis on 'acquired awakening', which an unenlightened one can attain *a posteriori* only through various stages of practice, is inclined to become idealistic or teleological, setting enlightenment far afield as the end. The relationship between original and acquired awakening is a dilemma in Mahāyāna Buddhism, particularly in the Tendai school, in which Dogen started his Buddhist studies. It is, however, not a theoretical problem. It is *the* practical problem *par excellence*.

In order to solve this critical question Dōgen sailed to China at the age of 24. In China, he 'visited many leading priests of Liang-che, and learned of the different characteristics of the five Gates'.[59] Dōgen wrote 'ultimately I went to Tai-pai peak and engaged in religious practice under the Zen master Ju-ching until I had resolved the one great matter of Zen practice for my entire life.'[60] The solution which he realized under Ju-ching provided the foundation for his later religious viewpoint and thought.

Dōgen's enlightenment experience left him with the strong conviction that he had attained the authentic *Dharma* that was directly transmitted from buddha to buddha. To him the authentic Buddha *Dharma*, that is, 'right *Dharma*', is universally working regardless of differences in time and space. Thus he rejected the idea of *mappō*, i.e. the last or degenerate *Dharma*, an idea with wide acceptance in the Japanese Buddhism of his day. He also strictly refused to speak of a 'Zen sect', to say nothing of a 'Soto sect', which he was later credited with founding. He said 'Who has used the name, "Zen sect"? No buddha or patriarch ever spoke of a "Zen sect". Those who pronounce a devil's appellation must be confederates of the devil, not children of the Buddha.'[61] And to him among various forms of practice, *Zazen* (seated meditation) is the 'right entrance' to the Buddha *Dharma*.

Accordingly, in Kyoto after his return to Japan, he wrote a treatise named *Fukanzazengi*[62] (*The Universal Promotion of the Principles of Zazen*). In this treatise Dōgen clarified the religious significance of seated meditation and its method, emphasizing the importance of concentrating one's effort singlemindedly regardless of intelligence or lack of it. In the following years in Kyoto and Echizen until his death at the age of 54 in 1253, Dōgen delivered many discourses and sermons and tried to compile them in a one-hundred-volume book entitled *Shōbōgenzō* (*A Treasury of the Right Dharma Eye*). Owing to an untimely illness he could not complete it. Later his descendants compiled the ninety-five-volume *Shōbōgenzō*, which is regarded as the standard version.

His solution attained in China to the doubts of his youth appears here and there in his writings:

> This Dharma is amply present in every person, but unless one practises it is not manifested; unless there is realization, it is not attained.[63]

> To think practice and realization are not one is a heretical view. In the Buddha Dharma, practice and realization are identical. Because one's present practice is practice in realization, one's initial negotiation of the Way in itself is the whole of original realization. Thus, even while one is directed to practice, he is told not to anticipate realization apart from practice, because practice points directly to original realization. As it is already realization in practice, realization is endless; as it is practice in realization, practice is beginingless.[64]

> As for the truth of the Buddha-nature: the Buddha-nature is not incorporated prior to attaining Buddhahood; it is incorporated upon the attainment of Buddhahood. The Buddha-nature is always manifested simultaneously with the attainment of Buddhahood. Thus truth should be deeply, deeply penetrated in concentrated practice. There has to be twenty or thirty years of diligent Zen practice.[65]

> In the Great Way of Buddhas and patriarchs there is continuous practice which is supreme. It is the Way which is circulating ceaselessly. There is not even the slightest gap between resolution, practice, enlightenment, and nirvana. The way of continuous practice is ever circulating.[66]

These statements all show that awakening is not subordinate to practice, attainment to discipline, Buddha-nature to becoming a buddha, or vice versa. Both sides of such contraries are indispensable and dynamically related to each other. Dōgen's expressions such as 'Oneness of practice and attainment', 'the simultaneous realization' of Buddha-nature and the attainment of buddhahood, and 'the unceasing circulation of continuous practice' clearly indicate this dynamic and indispensable relation. Unless one becomes a buddha, the Buddha-nature is not realized as the Buddha-nature, and yet at the same time one can become a buddha only because one is originally endowed with the Buddha-nature. It is at this point that the dynamic truth of the simultaneous realization of the Buddha-nature and its attainment can be seen.

Dōgen thus rejected sheer original awakening as a naturalistic heresy that regards the human mind itself as Buddha by identifying the given human consciousness with true awakening. Accordingly he emphasized the importance and necessity of practice. At the same time, Dōgen also rejected an idea of a mere acquired awakening as an inauthentic Buddhist teaching which distinguishes practice and enlightenment, taking the former as a means to the latter as the end. Instead he strongly emphasized the oneness of practice and attainment. Thus by rejecting both the naturalistic-pantheistic and the idealistic-teleological views of the Buddha-nature, Dōgen broke through the relativity of 'original' and 'acquired' awakenings and opened up a deeper ground that is neither *a priori* nor *a posteriori*. This very ground is the original Awakening in its absolute sense because it is prior to and liberated from any dualistic thought or any discriminatory view.

For Dōgen it is the 'immaculate' Buddha-nature that is realized in *zazen*, seated meditation, which he calls 'the casting off of body-mind' (*shinjin datsuraku*). The original awakening as understood by Dōgen is not an awakening which is looked at and aimed at from the point of view of acquired awakening. Rather Dōgen's 'original awakening' is deeper than both original and acquired awakening in their relative sense, and takes them as aspects of itself. This is the reason Dōgen emphasizes, 'What is to be understood is that one must *practise in realization*'.[67] For Dōgen the Buddha-nature manifests itself regardless of human illusion and enlightenment. Practice and attainment, if immaculate and free from human intention, are not two but one. This realization of oneness of practice and attainment is the basis of Dōgen's philosophy and religion, which is the solution to the dilemma he faced as a youth.

Taking the realization of 'oneness of practice and attainment' as his basis Dōgen expounds three more doctrines: (1) the whole of being is Buddha-nature; (2) impermanence is Buddha-nature; and (3) *uji*, the identity of being and time.

The whole of being is Buddha-nature

In the opening section of the 'Busshō' (Buddha-nature) fascicle of the *Shōbōgenzō*, Dōgen quotes the following passage from the *Nirvāṇa Sūtra* which had traditionally been read as 'All sentient beings without exception *have* the Buddha-nature.' Against this traditional reading Dōgen dares to read the passage as follows: 'All is sentient being, the whole of being *is* the Buddha-nature.'[68] Grammatically speaking this way of reading is unnatural and might even be termed wrong. Dōgen dares to read the passage in this manner because this is the only way for him to express clearly what he believes to be the fundamental standpoint of Mahāyāna Buddhism. It is more important for him to convey the Buddhist truth rightly and correctly than to be grammatically correct.

According to the traditional reading, it is understood that all sentient beings have the Buddha-nature within themselves as the potentiality for becoming a buddha. Naturally this reading implies that, although all sentient beings are at this moment immersed in illusion, they can all be enlightened sometime in the future because of their potential buddhahood. The Buddha-nature is then understood as an object possessed and aimed at to be realized by the subject (sentient beings). In this understanding, dichotomies of subject and object, potentiality and actuality, within and without, present and future, and so on are implied. This results in a serious misunderstanding of the basic standpoint of Buddhism. The traditional understanding of the Buddha-nature not only does not represent the right *Dharma* of Buddhism, which Dōgen mastered and confirmed in himself, but is in fact a violation of it. Thus he rejected the ordinary way of reading this passage with all the above implications, and gave a new reading, even though it meant breaking grammatical rules to clarify the right Buddha *Dharma*. As a result he read it as 'the whole of being *is* the Buddha-nature' instead of 'all sentient beings *have* the Buddha-nature.'

When Dogen emphasizes 'the whole of being' in connection with the Buddha-nature, he definitely implies that a person can be properly and completely emancipated from *saṃsāra*, i.e. the recurring cycle of birth-and-death, not in the 'sentient' dimension, but in the 'being' dimension. Dōgen finds the basis for human liberation in a thoroughly cosmological dimension which is completely trans-anthropocentric.

Since 'the whole of being' and the 'Buddha-nature' are non-dualistic, the Buddha-nature is neither immanent nor transcendent (or both immanent and transcendent) in relation to all beings. Thus, despite frequent misunderstanding to the contrary, one may readily notice that Dōgen is not a pantheist, however pantheistic his words may appear at first glance. Indeed, he is as unpantheistic as he is non-theistic.[69]

Impermanence is Buddha-nature

To make the non-dualistic and dynamic oneness of 'the whole of being' and the 'Buddha-nature' absolutely clear Dōgen goes further by saying that *mujō* (impermanence) is the Buddha-nature. In Buddhism the impermanence of phenomena had been emphasized in contrast with the permanence of the Buddha-nature. And the task of Buddhism is to emancipate oneself from impermanence (*saṃsāra*) and to enter *nirvāṇa* by attaining the Buddha-nature. However, if *nirvāṇa* is sought simply as a state beyond impermanence it is not true *nirvāṇa*, because it stands against impermanence and thereby is still related to and limited by impermanence. True *nirvāṇa* is attained only by emancipating oneself even from *nirvāṇa* as transcendence of impermanence. In other words, it is realized by complete return from *nirvāṇa* to the world of impermanence through liberating oneself from both impermanence and permanence, from *saṃsāra* so-called and *nirvāṇa* so-called. Therefore genuine *nirvāṇa* is nothing but the realization of impermanence just as impermanence. If one remains in '*nirvāṇa*' by transcending *saṃsāra*, one must be said to be still selfish because one loftily abides in one's own enlightenment, apart from the sufferings of other *saṃsāra*-bound sentient beings. True compassion can be realized only by transcending '*nirvāṇa*' to return to and work in the midst of the sufferings of the ever-changing world. This is the characteristic realization of Mahāyāna Buddhism, which emphasizes, 'Do not abide in *saṃsāra* or *nirvāṇa*.' This complete no-abiding is true *nirvāṇa* in the Mahāyāna sense.[70]

In this true and dynamic *nirvāṇa* the realization of impermanence is the realization of Buddha-nature, and vice versa. For Dōgen impermanence itself is preaching impermanence, practising impermanence, and realizing impermanence, and this, as it is, is preaching, practising and realizing the Buddha-nature.

The identity of being and time

Dōgen emphasizes the identity of being and time by saying 'Time, just as it is, is being, and being is all time'.[71]

> Mountains are time and seas are time. If they were not, there would be no mountains and seas. So, you must not say there is no time in the immediate now of mountains and seas. If time is destroyed, mountains and seas are destroyed. If time is indestructible, mountains and seas are indestructible.[72]

Dōgen does not simply identify being and time, however. Their common denominator is mutability or impermanence. For Dōgen all beings without exception are impermanent; for this very reason all beings are the Buddha-nature, for he rejects an immutable Buddha-nature beyond impermanence. Here we have seen a radical reversal of the traditional understanding of the Buddha-nature. Similarly, Dōgen makes a radical change in the common understanding of time. For him, time does not simply flow.

> You should not only learn that flying past is the property inherent in time. If time were to give itself to merely flying past, it would have to have gaps. You fail to experience the passageless passage of being-time and hear the utterance of its truth, because you are learning only that time is something that goes past.[73]

Against the ordinary understanding, for Dōgen, time is flying, yet not flying; flying-*qua*-not flying is time's virtue. That is passageless passage.

> Being-time has the virtue of passageless passage. It makes passageless passage from today to tomorrow, from today to yesterday, from yesterday to today, from today to today, from tomorrow to tomorrow. This is because passageless passage is a virtue of time. . . . As self and other are both times, practice and realization are times; entering the mud, entering the water (compassionate work to lead the unenlightened to salvation) is equally time.[74]

In Dōgen, passageless passage as flying-*qua*-not flying is always the *present* in which the Buddha-nature manifests itself. In other words, the Buddha-nature always manifests itself as time, specifically as present time.

For Dōgen the complete discontinuity of time, that is, the negation of temporality, is not a mere spatialization of time, but rather an essential element for the full realization of time itself. Only by the realization of the complete discontinuity of time and of the independent moment, i.e. only by the negation of temporality, does time become real time. For Dōgen there is no time that is not the fullness of time. If time is already here, the Buddha-nature does not have to come. Therefore, time-being already arrived is in itself the immediate manifestation of the Buddha-nature. There has never yet been a time not arrived. There can be no Buddha-nature that is not Buddha-nature manifested right here.

In Dōgen the impermanence of the universe and the passageless passage of time are inseparable. The mediating point of these is sustained practice and realization. His ideas of the oneness of being and time, and the fullness of time at each and every moment, are based on severe religious practice, especially *zazen*. At the culminating point of religious practice, 'whole being is the Buddha-nature' is fully realized. Through *zazen* all beings in the universe are enlightened and all times in history manifest eternity. Yet this takes place here and now in the absolute present. Apart from the here and now, apart from 'the casting off of body-mind' in the present, this cannot take place. Time elapses from present to present. Things in the universe are mutually interpenetrating, with self and others being undifferentiated yet distinct. This is Dōgen's world of manifestation of the Buddha-nature. To Dōgen, however, this is not merely the goal but the starting point of Buddhist life.[75]

NICHIREN AND THE *LOTUS SŪTRA*

Nichiren was born in 1222, the son of a humble fisherman on the south-eastern coast of Japan. He was ordained a Buddhist priest in the Tendai sect in his sixteenth year.

At that time he prayed for the fulfilment of his wish to become 'the foremost wise man in Japan'. Unlike Hōnen and Dōgen, he was not motivated to enter the priesthood by a realization of the world's transience. There is no darkness about his motivation. He entered the priesthood to live out for himself the true life and to save his fellow-beings. His quest was for a Buddhism as pure and bright as the sun. However, as a young monk he was haunted by the question, 'which, among the various branches of Buddhism then prevailing, was the true doctrine of the Buddha himself?' In 1242, when he was 21, he went to Mount Hiei, where he stayed until 1253. Then he came to be convinced that true Buddhism was nothing but the doctrine of the 'Lotus of Truth' as stated in the *Saddharmapundarika Sūtra*, expounded by Saichō, the founder of Mount Hiei.

In 1253 Nichiren began a prophetic mission, urging the whole nation to return to the teaching of the *Lotus Sūtra*. A series of natural calamities that plagued the nation at that time was a sure sign, in his mind, that the period of *mappō* (the degeneration of the Buddha's Law) had come. In 1260 he presented his trenchant essay, *Risshō Ankoku Ron* (*Establishment of the Legitimate Teaching for the Security of the Nation*), to the authorities, prophesying that Japan would not only suffer from natural calamities but would be invaded by foreign enemies.[76]

In this essay Nichiren denounced the regent Hōjō's regime for countenancing false teachings and strongly urged the suppression of all other Buddhist sects in favour of the *Lotus* in order to maintain national security and ward off grievous calamities including foreign invasion. On the basis of his strong belief that the *Lotus Sūtra* is the final and supreme teaching of Śākyamuni (the historical Buddha), Nichiren condemned all existing Buddhist sects except the Tendai sect. His famous maxim was:

> Those who practise invocation to Amitabha are due to suffer continuous punishment in Hell; the Zen sect is the devil; the Shingon sect is the ruiner of the country; the Ritsu sect is the enemy of the country.[77]

Nichiren's attack on Pure Land Buddhism ('those who practice invocation to Amitābha') was especially severe because he thought that through the perverse influence of Hōnen's *Senchaku Hongan Nembutsu-shu* (*Collection of Passages on the Original Vow of Amida*, in which invocation of the *nembutsu* is chosen above all other ways of achieving rebirth),[78] the people of Japan had come to believe in *nembutsu* at the expense of the scriptures, temples and priests of the other schools. Because of this, divine protectors had left Japan while devils and demons had entered the country, causing various natural and human calamities. From this he concluded that national peace and prosperity could be attained only through the unification of all Buddhism in the doctrine of the *Lotus* of Truth.

Nichiren envisioned Japan as the land in which the true teaching of the Buddha was to be revived and from which it was to spread throughout the world.[79]

> To accomplish this aim Nichiren urged all his followers to imitate the *bodhisattva* ideal of perseverance and self-sacrifice. In an age of utter decadence, everyone must be a man of Superb Action (*viśiṣṭacāritra*), ready to give his life if necessary for the cause. Nichiren himself was sentenced to death for his bold censure of the Hōjō regency in Kamakura, and was saved only by miraculous intervention, according to his followers, when lightning struck the executioner's blade. Banished then to a lonely island (Sado) in the Sea of Japan, Nichiren wrote, 'Birds cry but shed no tears. Nichiren does not cry, but his tears are never dry.'
>
> Even after his narrow escape at the execution ground, Nichiren regarded himself as one who had risen from the dead, who had been reborn in the faith. 'Tatsunokuchi is the place where Nichiren renounced his life. The place is therefore comparable to a paradise, because all has taken place for the sake of the Lotus of Truth. . . . Indeed every place where Nichiren encounters perils is Buddha's land.' In this way Nichiren made of suffering a glorious thing, and set an example for his disciples which did more to confirm their faith in the *Lotus* than volumes of scripture.[80]

All Nichiren's ideas and arguments are founded on the *Lotus Sūtra*, especially its second half, which he called *honmon*, i.e. the 'realm of origin'. Why did he insist that the *Lotus Sūtra*, especially its second half, is the final and supreme teaching of the Truth? The answer lies in his theory of the fivefold contrasts. The first is 'the contrast between the inside and outside', which refers to the superiority of the Buddhist scriptures (the 'inside') over non-Buddhist scriptures (the 'outside'). The second is 'the contrast between the great and small', referring to the superiority of the Mahāyāna Buddhist scriptures over the Hīnayāna scriptures. The third is 'the contrast between the real and the provisional', which indicates the superiority of the *Lotus Sūtra* above all other Mahāyāna scriptures. The fourth is 'the contrast between the original and the trace', referring to the superiority of the second half of the *Lotus Sūtra* (which expands the realm of the activity of the Buddha of the original position) over the first half of the *sūtra* (which relates to the trace-leaving manifestation of the Buddha). The fifth is 'the contrast between teaching and contemplation', referring to the superiority of Buddhism practising the teaching of the *Lotus Sūtra* as opposed to Buddhism merely teaching the theory of the *Lotus Sūtra*.

The last three contrasts need some further clarification. Nichiren believed that among the various Mahāyāna *sūtras* it is the *Lotus Sūtra* that expounds the most authentic teaching of Śākyamuni Buddha. The distinguishing characteristics of the *Lotus Sūtra* are twofold. (1) This *sūtra* proclaims the doctrine of *Ekayāna*, i.e. the One Vehicle. This teaching asserts that there is a universal salvation which includes not only Hīnayāna practioners, but also the laity and the monastics, the sinful and the virtuous. (2) The *Lotus Sūtra* also affirms the doctrine of the eternally enlightened Buddha, meaning that the real Buddha is not the corporeal, historical Buddha, but rather the Buddha of immeasurable ages past, ever present as the Enlightened One. These two points establish for Nichiren the unexcelled superiority of the *Lotus Sūtra* over all other Mahāyāna scriptures.

Further, within the *Lotus Sūtra* the first fourteen sections refer to *shakumon*, the realm of the trace, or trace-manifestation of the real Buddha, while the last fourteen sections relate to *honmon*, the realm of the origin or original position of the real Buddha. In the realm of the trace, Śākyamuni is said to have attained enlightenment at Buddhagaya, but to trace him to his origin, that is, in the realm of the origin, he is the Enlightened One of immeasurable ages past. The overall intent of the *Lotus Sūtra* is to be a revelation of Truth. In the earlier sections the Buddha reveals that what he taught before the *Lotus* was determined expediently by the limited capacities of his disciples, whereas in the later sections he teaches clearly that his 'Truth Body' (*dharmakāya*), being beyond historical existence, is from time immemorial a realization of enlightenment itself.[81] Even during the *mappō* period (when virtue and the observance of the *Dharma* have completely degenerated), the True Buddha is always and everywhere preaching the *Dharma* to save all sentient beings. For this reason Nichiren established his school on the basis of the original *Lotus*, that is, *honmon*.

Furthermore, Nichiren criticized his own Tendai tradition by insisting that the Tendai school has been too much inclined towards the theoretical side of the truth, forgetting its practical side. The Tendai sect from China onwards had taken the standpoint of 'action according to principle'. Nichiren emphasized 'action according to things'.[82] For example, he read the *Lotus Sūtra* 'by the body' and not just with the eyes. He also accepted the Tendai doctrine of *ichinen-sanzen*, i.e. that each moment of thought contains the three thousand spheres of living creatures.[83] But he transformed this doctrine from the realm of principle to the realm of everyday things, from the metaphysical realm to the religious and practical realm. In this way he promoted the practice of *ichinen-sanzen*, which can be practised by anyone. This practice of *ichinen-sanzen* is *daimoku* – uttering the sacred title of the *Lotus Sūtra* in the formula: *Namu myo-horenge-kyo*, which means 'Adoration of the Lotus of Perfect Truth'. As Masaharu Anesaki states:

> It (*daimoku*) was for him not a mere oral utterance but a real embodiment of the truths revealed in that scripture, because the 'Title' was representative of the whole revelation, which was to be realized in the spirit and embodied in the life of all who adored Buddha and his revelation. To utter the 'Sacred Title' was, according to Nichiren, the method of at once elevating oneself to the highest enlightenment of Buddhahood and of identifying self with the cosmic soul. This method he deemed to be the only adequate way available for the degenerate men of the latter days.[84]

In the attainment of enlightenment, whether or not one believes in the *Lotus Sūtra* is crucial. However, it is not enough merely to believe in the *sūtra*. If one truly believes in the *sūtra*, then one must utter the title of the *sūtra*. Faith without utterance is only pseudo-faith. In this respect, we see some influence from Hōnen, who advocated the recitation of the name of Amida Buddha, *Namu amida butsu*, in order to be saved – although Nichiren severely attacked Hōnen's Pure Land teaching.

In the desolate island of Sado, the place of his exile, he experienced severe hardships and troubles. However, when his suffering reached its zenith, so did his religious zeal and theoretical activities. In Sado he wrote several important works including *Kaimoku-sho*, *Opening the Eyes*. At the end of this work, after reviewing various religious and moral systems critically, Nichiren made his famous vow: 'I will be the pillar of Japan; I will be the eyes of Japan; I will be the vessel of Japan. Inviolable shall remain these vows!' Here he became conscious of himself being the *bodhisattva* of Supreme Action to whom Śākyamuni is said to have entrusted the work of protecting the Truth.

Unlike Shinran and Dōgen, Nichiren was deeply concerned with the country of Japan. He was, however, not a nationalist in the usual sense. To him the ideal country is one which is governed by a ruler who defends the Buddha *Dharma*. The throne and government should be subservient to religious authority. At the same time, he believed that Japan is a country with a special destiny linked to the *Lotus* teaching and its promulgation. Nichiren envisioned the establishment of the great Buddha land in Japan as the central seat of the universal truth to be realized throughout the world. Nichiren regarded himself as the man sent by the Buddha to prepare the way for the transformation of the world, as the messenger of Buddhism, the incarnation of the Truth.[85]

After three years of exile in Sado, he was allowed to return to Kamakura in 1274. Despite ardent efforts, the government was not able to secure any compromise or mitigation of Nichiren's teaching. He retired to Minobu, west of Mount Fuji, and lived peacefully. He died at Ikegami near present-day Tokyo in 1282 at the age of 60.[86]

Nichiren has two rather contradictory aspects. While he declared himself to be an incarnation of the *bodhisattva* of Supreme Action, he also confessed that 'my body looks human, but is a brutish body'. At the same time that he was violently aggressive, he was also deeply self-composed and sensitive. In him were harmonized the fervour of a prophet and the sweetness of a saint, the wisdom of a learned doctor and the enthusiasm of an ardent reformer.[87] Out of this paradoxical, chaotic character, a huge figure emerges. He was full of passion; once he became settled in his conviction, he persistently carried out everything to its final end.

There is no one who was more seriously persecuted than Nichiren in the history of Japanese religion. Yet, every time he suffered persecution his conviction about being a *bodhisattva* became stronger. This was in keeping with the teaching of the *Lotus Sūtra*, which predicts the persecution of those who practise it. To him, the more serious persecutions were the strongest evidence of his being an active practitioner since he heard the calling of the Buddha in severe peril. Nichiren tasted religious exaltation even in the midst of harsh persecution.

It is not coincidental that the school was called after the founder's name, because it is Nichiren's personality that constitutes the uniqueness of the school.

BUDDHISM IN THE TOKUGAWA PERIOD

After a century of political and social disintegration Japan was unified by the powerful shogun Tokugawa Ieyasu (1542–1616) in 1603. For roughly two hundred and sixty years, until 1867, when the regime declined, Japan enjoyed a period of relative peace and order. This span of years is called the Tokugawa period. During this period, as Joseph Kitagawa states:

> The Tokugawa shogunate incorporated Buddhist institutions into its political framework. With the prohibition of Catholicism, the Tokugawa regime ordered every Japanese household to affiliate with specific Buddhist temples, thus creating a 'parochial system' (*danka seido*) hitherto unknown in the history of Japanese Buddhism. Government patronage, and the financial security that comes with it, enabled Buddhist schools to develop gigantic ecclesiastical superstructures, but they were robbed of nearly all spiritual freedom, influence, and initiative. While Buddhism left conspicuous imprints on poetry, literature, art, and other areas of aesthetics, the intellectual leadership during the Tokugawa period was in the hands of Neo-Confucian and Shinto (or 'national learning') scholars who were, for the most part, critical of Buddhism both on philosophical and practical grounds.[88]

Nevertheless, we see a number of powerful Buddhist leaders who revived or reformed their own traditions and popularized Buddhism widely among the masses of the people. The feudal society of the Tokugawa period offered little social mobility, but was relatively well ordered. In this peaceful social climate, intellectual and spiritual developments, leading from the medieval towards the modern Japanese world-view, began to appear. They may be enumerated as follows:[89]

Renunciation of charismatic authority and consciousness of self

In the Middle Ages spiritual teachers claimed special authority over their disciples and followers. They assumed the role of superior men and were regarded as higher than common people. This attitude was criticized by Zen masters in the Tokugawa period. Let me offer a few examples. During the Kamakura period Dōgen (1200–53) denounced the 'theory of perceiving one's own nature' intuitively set forth in the *Sūtra of the Sixth Patriarch*. But Tenkei (1648–1735), his spiritual descendant, rejected Dōgen's opinion as 'absurd sheer nonsense'.[90] According to the traditional attitude, 'one's own enlightenment should be conveyed face to face, from master to disciple, and it should be approved by a single master.' It is likely that this attitude reflected the feudal tendency of the Tokugawa period. But Tenkei gave a different interpretation. To him 'master' means 'one's own self'; 'disciple' also means 'one's self'; 'a single master' means 'one's self'. So, the whole phrase means: 'the attainment of one's own or true self by oneself.' We need not practise under the guidance of a single teacher. Even by looking at peach blossoms one can make one's own self clear.[91] Again, interpreting Dōgen's teaching 'learning one's self' Tenkei asserts 'it was nothing but the way of following "the Great Self".'[92]

Suzuki Shōsan (1579–1655), a reformer of Zen Buddhism, denied the authority of the founders and previous masters of various sects. He said, 'Looking into written sayings of previous masters, it does not seem that there have been persons who have practised with zeal.'[93] Advocating lay Buddhism, he discouraged people from taking holy orders and thus forsaking their vocations in the world.

Hakuin (1685–1768), another powerful Zen reformer, rejected formalistic and intellectual Zen and searched for the truth of Zen in his own sincere and extraordinary way. On the one hand, he criticized the traditional form of *kōan* practice and established a unique *kōan* system by completely reorganizing traditional *kōans*. The continuance of present-day Rinzai Zen tradition has been attributed to his *kōan* system. On the other hand, Hakuin gave up his authoritative attitude completely, identified himself with the common people and wrote discourses and letters in colloquial Japanese. He composed popular songs and produced painting and calligraphy to convey the truth of Zen. He combined profound spirituality with a popular evangelistic style.

Similarly in the Tokugawa period we see a critical attitude towards the authority of the scripture. In the medieval period, the absolute sacredness of religious canon was stressed. Scholarship was no more than a deduction from, and the elucidation of, the fundamental dogmas of religions. Learning was, in the main, scholastic. Free thinking was not permitted. In the Tokugawa period, however, Tominaga Nakamoto (1715–46), a merchant-scholar who lived in the commercial town of Osaka, formulated a historical and developmental system of Buddhist philosophy out of the same materials that the tradition-bound Buddhist scholars used to reiterate their scholastic conclusions. His uniqueness lies in his philological method of study. In his philological studies he did not commit himself to any traditional discipline such as Shinto, Buddhism or Confucianism. He was a critical observer who maintained a personal viewpoint. In his book *Shutsujō Kōgō* (*Emerging from Meditation*),[94] Tominaga stated that moral philosophers ought to be considered in the context of climatic and geographical conditions. He proclaimed that no philosophy could overcome circumstantial and ethnic limitations in forming its characteristics. Therefore, in preaching or founding a way, the masters since the Divine Antiquity always made use of the local customs of the places where they were to propagate their views. No matter how sublime a way may be, it cannot escape this principle.[95] With this idea as background, Tominaga developed a 'Mahāyāna non-Buddhist' thesis by saying that the Mahāyāna scriptures are not the record of the *ipsissima verba* of the historical Buddha but were composed by later Buddhists.

Tendency towards this-worldliness

The general tendency of religious thought in the Middle Ages throughout many countries can be described as being other-worldly. The happiness people yearned for in those days was the one which was believed to exist only in the future world after death. Religious life was regarded as noble, secular life as vile and mean. However, during the Tokugawa period a shift from other-worldliness to this-worldliness took place. Some Buddhist reformers tried to change their traditional attitude. For instance, Suzuki Shōsan taught his lay followers that

> To pray for a happy future does not mean to pray for a world after death. It means to be delivered here and now and thus to attain a great comfort. Then, where do you think the afflictions of this world come from? They are originated from your attachment to your own flesh and to the demands of it. To be delivered from this attachment is the way to become a buddha.[96]

As earthly life consists in action, the attitude of this-worldliness tends to emphasize action in social life. He discouraged laymen from practising meditation; instead, he encouraged them in their faithful performance of daily duties. Thus, in the Tokugawa period we witness the increasing prevalence of the idea that anyone pursuing his own secular vocation with his whole heart and soul is in effect a practising Buddhist ascetic.

For instance, Takuan (1573–1645), a Zen priest, taught: 'The Law of the Buddha, well observed, is identical with the Law of mundane existence. The Law of mundane existence, well observed, is identical with the Law of the Buddha.'[97]

This idea was especially stressed by Suzuki Shōsan. In his book *Bammin Tokuyō* (*The Significance of Everyman's Activities*) he discussed the problem of vocational ethics. He found absolute significance in the pursuit of any vocation, whether it be that of a warrior, a farmer, a craftsman, a merchant, a doctor, an actor, a hunter or a priest. He reasoned that to pursue one's own vocation is to obey the Absolute One because the essence of Buddhism consists in reliance upon the original self or upon 'the true buddha of one's own', and every vocation is the function of this 'one buddha'. Thus he preached to farmers: 'Farming is nothing but the doings of a buddha.' To the merchant he taught: 'Renounce desires and pursue profits single-heartedly. But you should never enjoy the fruit of your labour. You should, instead, work for the good of all others.'[98]

It is noteworthy that soon after the death of Calvin, an idea similar to his appeared in Japan. The fact, however, that it never grew into a religious movement of great consequence ought to be studied in relation to the fact that a modern bourgeois society had not really developed in Japan.[99]

A corollary of the new value placed on activity in the world was the denigration of the life of monastics. The worldliness of the Tokugawa period tended to extricate religion from the exclusive possession of the priesthood and to promote a vibrant lay Buddhism. Buddhism in the Tokugawa period, however, did not succeed in effecting any new economic movement.

Equality of man and human dignity

By the end of the eighteenth century, the rigidity of the class system had already begun to show signs of collapse. The new value placed on the human person as such led to the weakening of social distinctions and traditional authority. Already in medieval Japan there are examples of religious leaders advocating a religious egalitarianism. For instance, Shinran would not allow that women were less capable than men of attaining the state of bliss. For Nichiren, some of the appeal of the *Lotus Sūtra* lay in its teaching regarding the equality of the sexes. The esoteric teaching of the Japanese Tendai sect advocated the equality of all humankind. But their recognition of human equality remained within the narrow bounds of religion and did not develop into a social movement.

In the Tokugawa period, Jiun Sonja (1718–1804), a Buddhist scholar with a Shingon background, preached that morality means to follow our natural disposition as human beings. He said, 'What is called man is gifted with the Ten Virtues[100] and at the same time the world of humanity is by nature endowed with Ten Virtues. . . . One should have cognizance of man in contrast to animals.'[101] To him Buddhism is the True Law, and the practical observance of its teachings, the Ten Virtues, enables even ordinary men to regulate themselves and their homes and finally to walk in the path of righteousness.

In accordance with this new trend, Buddhist masters came to reject the former attitude of asceticism. Hakuin said, ' "To cast away oneself" does not mean "ill-treat oneself" or "to disregard diet and health." '[102] With such an emphasis on human dignity and significance, the equality of human existence was advocated. However, human equality was not stressed to the extent that the feudal social system was threatened.

Even brilliant Buddhist leaders such as Jiun Sonja, who was so progressive in other respects, complied with the hierarchical social system of the time. Jiun's own interpretation of the Buddhist teaching of equality is as follows:

> Buddhism approves of distinctions of grade and position. The equality it teaches is not . . . such foolishness as that of breaking down high mountains, filling in deep valleys and making all into a dead level. Buddhism teaches us the way between lord and subjects, father and son, master and disciple.[103]

Although this understanding of human equality includes some truth, it is apt to be used to support the *status quo* of the social order.

Realization of the Buddhist truth in mundane activities entails appreciation of the practical activities of Buddhism within the human social nexus. This may be regarded as one of the causes of Japan's rapid progress in modernization in the last century. There is great danger in the fact that the practical view of religion of the Japanese people easily degenerates into the sheer utilitarianism of profit-seeking activities if sight is lost of the absolute which underlies the productive life of occupations. But, at the same time, credit should be given to the tendency to esteem religiously the human nexus.[104]

BUDDHIST THINKERS IN MODERN JAPAN

The year 1868 marked the beginning of modern Japan. The Tokugawa feudal regime declined internally by losing control over the feudal lords and externally by the pressure of foreign powers urging Japan (which had maintained a national seclusion policy for over two hundred years) to open the doors to trade with the West. With the decline of the Tokugawa regime, imperial rule was restored and sweeping changes were introduced by the new regime. However, the termination of the feudal regime and the beginning of imperial rule in 1868 was not an abrupt change from pre-modern to modern Japan.

> To be sure, in one sense the new imperial Meiji regime (the regime under the Emperor Meiji) eagerly joined the modern world; it welcomed new knowledge from the West. But it soon became evident that the aim of the imperial regime was not only a renovation (*ishin*) that implied forward motion, but also a restoration (*fukko*) or a reversion to the ancient ideal of the emperor-centered religious, political, and national polity. In short, the Meiji regime intended to develop a modern nation-state without losing the traditional Japanese religious and cultural framework.[105]

To cope with this difficult task, the architects of modern Japan tried to reform religion through the rejection of the historical amalgamation of Shinto and Buddhism. In this situation there arose a movement called *haibutsu kishaku* ('extermination of Buddhism'), which constituted a serious threat to established Buddhist institutions. However, some enlightened Buddhist leaders accepted the challenge of the new situation and tried to reform Buddhism from within.[106] Further,

> The enlightened Buddhist leaders were not afraid of the onslaught of Western civilization either. Rather, they sensed the need of appropriating Western philological and philosophical scholarship in order to broaden and enrich the Buddhist tradition in Japan. Realizing that Japanese Buddhists had depended solely on the Chinese translation of the Buddhist scriptures, some able Japanese Buddhist scholars were sent abroad to learn Sanskrit, Pali, and Tibetan. . . . philological scholarship greatly stimulated modern Japanese Buddhist scholars' understanding of the Theravada and Mahayana branches of Buddhism, as well as their reexamination of Japanese Buddhism itself.[107]

For our purpose what is more important is the efforts of Buddhist thinkers in coming to terms with Western philosophical systems. Among this type of thinker probably the most influential is Nishida Kitarō (1870–1945), the founder of the Kyoto school of philosophy. However, before discussing the philosophical thought of Nishida and some leading members of the Kyoto school, it may not be inappropriate to explore the thought and work of D. T. Suzuki (1870–1966).

D. T. Suzuki

In the West as well as in Japan, D. T. Suzuki has often been regarded exclusively as an exponent of Zen in the twentieth century. Especially in the West, Suzuki is remembered as a person who introduced Zen to the Western world. Here we must realize the following two points. First, Suzuki's concern and writings are not limited to Zen, but include Mahāyāna Buddhism as a whole – especially Prajñāpāramitā, Hua-yen and Pure Land Buddhist traditions – as well as Japanese culture. He often compared all of these fields with Christianity, particularly Christian mysticism. Thus, his concerns extended over a wide area, although it is true that he focused on Zen.

Second, Suzuki did not simply introduce Zen to the West, but tried to build

> a bridge to span the gulf between Eastern and Western thought, which are not only different in their traditions, but are even mutually conflicting and contradictory. For there is, in fact, a fundamental difference between East and West concerning the most serious problems of being human – our ultimate problem. For instance, regarding such things as life, death and God, the viewpoints of East and West fundamentally oppose each other.[108]

In the West death is understood as the end of life, and how to live *well*, how to conquer death in order to attain eternal life, is the problem. But in the East, particularly in Buddhism, life and death are understood as being inseparable and non-dual, and how to be emancipated from living–dying in order to attain *nirvāṇa* is the problem. In the West, God is thought of as Absolute Being, while in the East God is often understood as Absolute Nothingness. Again, in the West religious faith transcends the intellect, but in Buddhism that transcendence takes place though *satori*, or Awakening, which is a higher form of intellect.[109]

If we analyse Suzuki's work in terms of how he tried to build a bridge to span the gulf between Eastern and Western thought, we may argue as follows. As a first step, he emphasized the difference between the Eastern and Western ways of thinking in order to clarify the originality of the former – to clarify the basic meaning of authentic Zen experience in the Orient. However, just emphasizing the differences between the two ways of thinking is not sufficient for conveying oriental thought to the West. Thus, as a second step, he liberated Zen experience from the distinctly oriental standpoint and opened up for Zen a universal world-wide basis. In order to do so he grasped Zen experience through a confrontation with Western forms of religious experience – including Christian mysticism. He verbalized and conceptualized Zen experience (which is originally beyond words and conception) through confrontation with Western religious experience. To be more specific, he tried to elucidate the essence of Zen in English by liberating Zen from the traditional bonds of Chinese and Japanese character (this is a more serious work than mere translation) and make it directly confront the Western view of reality. Third, realizing that Zen must be radically renewed and reaffirmed by itself through the encounter with Western thought, he sought to create a new logic which had a universality communicable to

Western people. This entails a challenge to the Western way of thinking and life. Only then may Zen be said to have been introduced to the West. D. T. Suzuki was the first one who tried to take these three steps to open up a new spiritual foundation for the one world to come.

Throughout his life, especially in his mature period, Suzuki was explicitly critical of the dualistic, conceptual and analytical way of thinking so predominant in the Western tradition, and he repeatedly emphasized the importance of returning to the basic experience prior to the dichotomy between subject and object, being and non-being, life and death, good and evil in order to awaken the most concrete basis for life and the world. Suzuki tirelessly expounded Zen simply because he believed that Zen is nothing but this non-dualistic Awakening.[110]

In *Zen and Japanese Culture* (1959) Suzuki wrote:

> If the Greeks taught us how to reason and Christianity what to believe, it is Zen that teaches us to go beyond logic and not to tarry even when we come up against 'the things which are not seen'. For the Zen point of view is to find an absolute point where no dualism in whatever form obtains. Logic starts from the division of subject and object, and belief distinguishes between what is seen and what is not seen. The Western mode of thinking can never do away with this eternal dilemma, this or that, reason or faith, man or God, etc. With Zen, all these are swept aside as something veiling our insight into the nature of life and reality.[111]

Still earlier, in *An Introduction to Zen Buddhism* (1934), Suzuki writes as follows:

> We generally think that 'A is A' is absolute, and that the proposition 'A is not-A' or 'A is B' is unthinkable. We have never been able to break through these conditions of the understanding; they have been too imposing. But now Zen declares that words are words and no more. When words cease to correspond with facts it is time for us to part with words and return to facts. As long as logic has practical value it is to be made use of; but when it fails to work, or when it tries to go beyond its proper limits, we must cry, 'Halt!' Ever since the awakening of consciousness we have endeavored to solve the mysteries of being and to quench our thirst for logic through the dualism of 'A' and 'not-A' . . . but to our great disappointment we have never been able to obtain peace of mind, perfect happiness, and a thorough understanding of life and the world. We have come, as it were, to the end of our wits. No further steps could we take which would lead us to a broader field of reality. The inmost agonies of the soul could not be expressed in words, when lo! light comes over our entire being. This is the beginning of Zen.[112]

Here Zen is presented as the realization of reality which is beyond the dualistic logic of 'A' and 'not-A'. However, in what sense does 'light come over our entire being?' Suzuki continues:

> For we now realize that 'A is not-A' after all, that logic is onesided, that illogicality so-called is not in the last analysis necessarily illogical; what is superficially irrational has after all its own logic, which is in correspondence with the true state of things. . . . The meaning of the proposition 'A is A' is realized only when 'A is not-A.' To be itself is not to be itself – this is the logic of Zen, and satisfies all our aspirations.[113]

Referring to the contrast between *vijñāna* (reason or discursive understanding) and *prajñā* (intuition) in the *Prajñāpāramitā Sūtra*, Suzuki tries to clarify this logic of Zen in his essay 'Reason and intuition in Buddhist philosophy' (1951), now included in *Studies in Zen*.

> *Prajñā* goes beyond *vijñāna*. We make use of *vijñāna* in our world of senses and intellect, which is characterized by dualism in the sense that there is one who sees and there is the other that is seen – the two standing in opposition. In *prajñā* this differentiation does not take place; what is seen and one who sees are identical; the seer is the seen and the seen is the seer. *Prajñā* ceases to be *prajñā* when it is analyzed into two factors as is done in the case of *vijñāna*. . . . *Prajñā* is the self-knowledge of the whole in contrast to *vijñāna*, which busies itself with parts. *Prajñā* is an integrating principle while *vijñāna* always analyses. *Vijñāna* cannot work without having *prajñā* behind it.[114]

He continues to emphasize the nature of *prajñā*:

> *Prajñā* is what makes the law of identity workable, and this law is the foundation of *vijñāna*. *Vijñāna* is not the creator of the logical law, but it works by means of the law. . . . The eye cannot see itself; to do this a mirror is needed, but what it sees is not itself, only its reflection. *Vijñāna* may devise some means to recognize itself, but the recognition turns out to be conceptual, as something postulated.
>
> *Prajñā*, however, is the eye that can turn itself within and see itself, because it is the law of identity itself. It is due to *prajñā* that subject and object become identifiable, and this is done without mediation of any kind. *Vijñāna* always needs mediation as it moves on from one concept to another – this is in the very nature of *vijñāna*. But *prajñā*, being the law of identity itself, demands no transferring from subject to object. Therefore, it swings the staff; sometime it asserts; sometimes it negates and declares that 'A is not-A and therefore A is A.' This is the logic of *prajñā*-intuition.[115]

Suzuki formulated this logic of *prajñā*-intuition also as 'A is A because it is non-A' and called it the logic of '*soku-hi*', which may be translated *sive/non* or is/is not. Here *soku* (*sive*) means the essential inseparability of two entities, and *hi* (*non*) expresses negativity.[116] For the original identity of two entities prior to bifurcation, or dualistic analysis, is realized only through negation of negation, i.e. absolute negation, which is after all absolute affirmation.

To Suzuki, however, the logic of *prajñā*-intuition, the logic of Zen, does not exclude but rather includes dualistic or analytic logic. For mere non-discrimination as the negation of discrimination still stands against and is discriminated from discrimination. True non-discrimination is realized only by negating non-discrimination and transcending the duality of discrimination and non-discrimination. However, this transcendence does not exist apart from the duality but includes it through negation of negation. Thus, in true non-discrimination, discrimination and non-discrimination in the relative sense are *re*-established and *re*-grasped in the light of true non-discriminating wisdom – that is, *prajñā*-intuition. Thus, Suzuki emphasizes 'discrimination of non-discrimination' – i.e. 'discrimination that transcends discrimination' – in order to indicate the truth and logic of Zen. Suzuki tried to build a bridge to span the gulf between Eastern and Western thought with the notion of 'discrimination of non-discrimination' and the logic of *soku-hi* – that is, the logic of *sive/non*, or the dialectic of 'is' and 'is not'.

Nishida Kitarō

Strictly speaking, Nishida Kitarō was not a Buddhist thinker but a philosopher *par excellence*. It is, however, also true that from his youth Nishida was deeply involved in Zen practice and Buddhism, and thus his philosophy was fundamentally influenced and inspired by Buddhism while he extensively studied Western philosophy.

Nishida and Suzuki were friends throughout the long span of their lives. While Suzuki was active internationally writing and lecturing in English, Nishida, never away from Japan, concentrated his philosophical thinking on the problem of the self and the world, to become the most influential philosopher of modern Japan. Throughout his long career, his constant concern was the problem of 'True Reality' and the systematic treatment of philosophical issues on that basis – ontology, epistemology, ethics, religion, etc.

Like Suzuki, Nishida clearly realized the fundamental difference between the Eastern and the Western ways of thinking, and he also tried to build a bridge between them – or perhaps it is better to say that he tried to open up a new and deeper spiritual foundation common to the East and the West. We can see his intention in the following quotation:

> Must we assume Occidental logic to be the only logic, and must the Oriental way of thinking be considered simply a less-developed form [of the same way of thinking]? In order to decide these problems we shall first have to go back and reexamine the underlying sources from which logic emerged into the historical world and the part logic played in history.
>
> Thinking in the last analysis is nothing but an historical event, which acts as the self-formative function of our historical life. Willing as I am to recognize Occidental logic as a magnificent systematic development, and intent as I am on studying it first as one type of world logic, I wonder if even Western logic is anything more than a special feature of the historical life, an aspect of the self-formation of the historical life. Such a thing as formal, abstract logic will remain the same anywhere, but concrete logic as the form of concrete knowledge cannot be independent of the specific features of historical life.[117]

In his first book, *An Inquiry into the Good*, Nishida argued that pure experience prior to subject–object separation is the sole reality, and he tried to explain thinking, will, intellectual intuition, reality, good and religion on that basis. In the West 'experience' and 'the metaphysical' are often separated from and opposed to each other. Metaphysics is established by going beyond the realm of experience, while empiricism denies the metaphysical, strictly adhering to empirical facts. In Western philosophy it was almost inconceivable to establish the transcendent, metaphysical realm without separating it from the realm of empirical facts. Starting from 'experience', as in empiricism, Nishida returned directly to the root-source of experience by going immediately into experience itself more than had been done in empiricism.

Nishida thereby opened a new path to metaphysical reality in a direction completely opposite to that in which Western metaphysics had been established. That is his theory of 'pure experience'. Although Nishida's notion of pure experience was influenced by William James, Wilhelm Wundt and others, he was not satisfied with their psychological philosophy and criticized their grasp of pure experience as not being from within but rather from without, thus missing the true reality of pure experience. The directness of pure experience is realized only from within the actual living reality of experience prior to the separation of subject and object. To grasp pure experience in its strict sense, we must return to the basis of experience that is individual and yet trans-individual and universal. On this horizon of pure experience, a new metaphysics is possible.[118]

After identifying 'True Reality' with 'pure experience' in *An Inquiry into the Good*, Nishida developed it in *Jikaku* (*Self-awakening*) as the common basis of intuition, reflection and 'absolute free will' through the mediation of Fichte's *Tathadlung*, and then he arrived at the idea of *basho* (place, topos or matrix). To Nishida, 'place' is identical with 'absolute Nothingness' because it is completely unobjectifiable and non-substantial, and envelops everything including being and non-being just as it is. True 'place' is not something whatsoever, but nothingness, and true absolute Nothingness is 'place', which makes everything alive and work.

With the notion of 'place', Nishida moved from voluntarism to a sort of intuitionism. He considered intuition as the basis of will and, like Plotinus, stressed that to act is to see. Nishida, however, did not halt his enquiry with this mystical intuition, because he persistently strove to take a philosophical approach to the problem of ultimate reality. He approached ultimate reality by overcoming subjectivism through a confrontation with Greek philosophy – especially Aristotle's realism and his notion of *hypokeimenon*. By inverting Aristotle's definition of the individual as 'the subject that cannot become predicate', Nishida defined the most concrete universal as 'the predicate that cannot become subject' and undertook to establish a logic of unobjectifiable reality. This logical foundation for ultimate reality is formulated in terms of the 'logic of place', or the 'logic of absolute Nothingness', which is not apart from the directness of life and yet is thoroughly metaphysical and logical. It is a logic of oriental *nothingness* (*śūnyatā*), and it is essentially different from Western logic, which Nishida calls 'objective logic'.

After retiring in 1928 from Kyoto University, where he had been professor of philosophy since 1913, Nishida began to write more and publish many books. During these years he advanced unique concepts such as action-intuition, continuity of discontinuity, historical body, the dialectical universal, and absolutely contradictory self-identity.

The notion of 'absolute Nothingness' is most characteristic of Nishida's philosophy. To Nishida the true Reality, or the true absolute, is not absolute Being but absolute

Nothingness. Unlike relative nothingness, which is the negation of being, absolute Nothingness is realized only by negating relative nothingness. Absolute Nothingness is realized through the negation of negation – that is, the negation of both being and nothingness in the relative sense. However, the negation of negation in this realization does not signify a logical development of negation in an objective or external manner, but a self-negation of self-negation in an internal existential sense. Accordingly, the negation of negation is a great affirmation – that is, affirmation in the absolute sense. Thus, we can say that in this existential realization, absolute negation is absolute affirmation and absolute affirmation is absolute negation. This conversion between absolute negation and absolute affirmation takes place in the realization of absolute Nothingness which is dynamically absolute Being. Accordingly, absolute Being is realized only through the realization of absolute Nothingness. Absolute Being realized without the realization of absolute Nothingness is already objectified and conceptualized; therefore, it is not true absolute Being. True absolute Being is properly realized in and through the realization of absolute Nothingness. This is why the notion of absolute Nothingness is so crucial.

Nishida characterized this absolute Nothingness in terms of 'absolutely contradictory self-identity', or 'identity of absolute contradiction'. From this point of view, he grasped the problems of the self, the world, and God as well.

To Nishida the self is an absolute contradictory existence between life and death, good and evil, self and others. The self clearly realizes its individuality when it faces eternal death. Facing one's own death, one realizes the fundamental meaning of one's own existence. 'Only a being that knows its own eternal death truly knows its sheer individuality. Only a true individual, a true person, can achieve this realization of the inherent contradiction of self-existence.'[119] The living self relates to the divine and encounters God only through the eternal death – only in this paradoxical form.

In Nishida, the world is also understood in terms of the identity of absolute contradiction.

> In human consciousness the world is bottomlessly self-determining and creative, a transformational process which has the form of the contradictory identity of space and time. I refer to this self-forming, creative world as the self-determination of the absolute present. I hold that it is only in this dynamic form of contradictory identity that we can truly conceive of something that moves by itself and is self-conscious.[120]

> That I am consciously active means that I determine myself by expressing the world in myself. I am an expressive monad of the world. I transform the world into my own subjectivity. The world that, in its objectivity, opposes me is transformed and grasped symbolically in the forms of my own subjectivity. But this transactional logic of contradictory identity signifies as well that it is the world that is expressing itself in me.[121]

If we express God or the absolute in logical terms, Nishida says, we must speak of God in terms of the identity of absolute contradiction:

> [A] God merely transcendent or self-sufficient would not be a true God. God must always, in St. Paul's words, empty himself. That God is transcendent and at the same time immanent is the paradox of God. This is the true absolute.
>
> If it is said that God creates the world out of love, then God's absolute love must be essential to the creative act as God's own absolute self-negation.[122]

Nishida's standpoint is not pantheism but *panentheism*. Pantheism does not include the realization of God's own absolute self-negation. In this sense, Nishida's standpoint is identical with the *Prajñāpāramitā Sūtra*:

> [The] true absolute must face its own absolute negation within itself. It must absolutely negate, and thereby express, itself within itself. This paradox is articulated in the dialectic of 'is' and 'is not' (*soku-hi*) of the *Prajñāpāramitā Sūtra* schools of thought.[123]

Here we see consonance between D. T. Suzuki and Nishida Kitarō. While the former stressed religious experience and the latter was mainly concerned with philosophical logic, both of them shared the view that ultimate reality can be expressed only in a paradoxical manner. Realizing the characteristics of the Eastern way of thinking, Nishida took absolute Nothingness as ultimate Reality and tried to give it a logical formulation through his confrontation with Western philosophy. Forming his synthesis on the basis of historical life innate in human existence, which is neither Eastern nor Western, he neither established a new Eastern philosophy nor reconstructed Western philosophy, but created a new world philosophy.

Under Nishida's influence, a number of philosophers developed his philosophy in various ways, especially by newly interpreting his notion of absolute Nothingness, and thus came to be known as the Kyoto school of philosophy. The most notable philosopher who developed Nishida's philosophy, through a serious critique of it, was Tanabe Hajime (1885–1962). He criticized Nishida's logic of place as being akin to Plotinus' emanation theory and as lacking a philosophical foundation for ethical practice and historical reality. He advanced his own logic of species and Philosophy of Metanoetics.[124]

Among the many members of the Kyoto school only two leading members can be mentioned here – Hisamatsu Shin'ichi (1889–1980) and Nishitani Keiji (1900–90). Grasping absolute Nothingness as the 'formless self' Hisamatsu elucidated the absolute subjectivity of nothingness and the threefold structure of the Self, World, and History on the basis of the awakening to the formless self.[125]

Radically reinterpreting the Mahāyāna Buddhist notion of *Śūnyatā* (Emptiness), which was to him another term for absolute Nothingness, Nishitani tried to open up a new path to overcome the modern realization of nihility caused by the scientific way of thinking and nihilism. He thus established a philosophy of religion in which the problems of God, personality, being, self, time and history are grasped in the light of *Śūnyatā*.[126]

In short, the philosophy of the Kyoto school initiated by Nishida Kitarō is attempting to establish a world philosophy through the confrontation of Eastern and Western thought.

NOTES

1 *Nihongi: Chronicles of Japan from the Earliest Times to A.D. 697*, trans. W. G. Aston (London: George Allen & Unwin 1896), part II, p. 65.
2 Masaharu Anesaki, *History of Japanese Religion*, (Rutland, Vt., Tokyo: Charles E. Tuttle, 1963), p. 53.
3 *Nihongi*, op. cit., part II, p. 129.
4 Hajime Nakamura, *A History of the Development of Japanese Thought* (2 vols, Tokyo: Kokusai Bunka Shinkokai, 1967), vol. I, p. 5.
5 *Nihongi*, op. cit., part II, p. 128.
6 Nakamura op. cit., p. 7.
7 *The Buddhist Tradition in India, China, and Japan*, ed. William Theodore de Bary, The Modern Library (New York: Oxford University Press, 1969) p. 260.
8 ibid., p. 259.
9 Kenkō Futaba, '*Nihon Bukkyō Shisōshi no Shōmondai*' ('Problems in the History of Japanese Buddhist Thought), *Kyoto Joshidaigaku Bukkyo bunka kenkyukiyo* 5 (1975), 1–28.
10 *Nihongi* op. cit., Part II, p. 131.
11 Futaba, op. cit., pp. 8–9.
12 Anesaki, op. cit., p. 61.
13 Joseph M. Kitagawa, *On Understanding Japanese Religion*, (Princeton: Princeton University Press, 1987, p. 298.
14 *Yuimakyō, gisho*, in *Dainihon Bukkyo Zensho*, vol. II, p. 26.
15 Shinshō Hanayama, '*Hokke gissho no kenkyā*, Tokyo: The Oriental Library, 1933), p. 469.
16 Nakamura, op. cit., p. 16.
17 ibid., p. 17.
18 de Bary, op. cit., p. 266.
19 ibid., p. 280.
20 Nakamura, op. cit., p. 40.
21 ibid., p. 53 (adapted).
22 Anesaki, op. cit., p. 113.
23 Junjirō Takakusu, *The Essentials of Buddhist Philosophy*, (Honolulu: University of Hawaii, 1947), p. 137.
24 ibid., p. 139.
25 ibid.
26 Five aggregates, that is, form (matter), perception, conception (idea), volition (will) and consciousness.
27 Takakusu, op. cit., p. 139.
28 ibid., p. 135 (adapted).
29 ibid. p. 135 (adapted).
30 ibid., p. 136 (adapted).
31 Anesaki, op. cit., p. 129 (adapted).
32 Takakusu, op. cit., p. 144.
33 Nakamura, op. cit., p. 50.
34 ibid., pp. 53–4.
35 Anesaki, op. cit., pp. 131–2.
36 ibid., p. 133.
37 ibid., p. 126 (adapted).
38 ibid., pp. 127–8.

39 Joseph M. Kitagawa, *Religion in Japanese History* (New York, 1966), pp. 111–12.
40 de Bary, op. cit., p. 327.
41 *Namu Amida Butsu*, meaning 'Adoration to Amida Buddha', is the formula provided for the purpose of calling the name of Amida, *nembutsu*.
42 Harper Havelock Coates and Ryugaku Ishizuka, *Hōnen: The Buddhist Saint* (Kyoto: The Society for the Publication of Sacred Books of the World, 1949), pp. 728–9.
43 De Bary, op. cit., pp. 331–2.
44 *Tannishō*, meaning 'Collection inspired by concern over heresy', is a collection of Shinran's sayings compiled probably by his disciple Yuienbo. *Tannisho, A Shin Buddhist Classic*, trans. Taitetsu Unno Honolulu: Buddhist Study Center Press, 1984, p. 6.
45 ibid.
46 Anesaki, op. cit., p. 182.
47 de Bary, op. cit., pp. 331–2.
48 *Tannishō*, op. cit., p. 8.
49 *Shōzōmatsu wasan, Shinran's Hymns on the Last Age* (Kyoto: Ryukoku University Translation Center, 1980), p. 96.
50 ibid, p. 94.
51 *Shōzōmatsu wasan*, op. cit., p. 37.
52 *The True Teaching, Practice and Realization of the Pure Land Way: A Translation of Shinran's Kyōgyōshinshō*, Shin Buddhism Translation Series, (Kyoto: Hongwanji International Center, Kyoto, 1983), vol. I, p. 166.
53 *Shōzōmatsu wasan*, op. cit., p. 97.
54 *Letters of Shinran, A Translation of Mattosho*, Shin Buddhist Translation Series 1 (Kyoto: Hongwanji International Center, 1978), pp. 82–3.
55 ibid, pp. 74–5.
56 Kitagawa, *Religion in Japanese History*, p. 124.
57 Masao Abe, 'Dogen', in *The Encyclopedia of Religion*, ed. M. Eliade, vol. IV (New York: Macmillan 1987), pp. 388–9.
58 *Kenzeiki. Soto shu Zenshu* (Tokyo, 1929–38), 17:16a.
59 *Bendowa*, trans. Norman Waddell and Masao Abe, *The Eastern Buddhist* (*EB*), NS, 4(1) (1971), 124–57.
60 ibid.
61 *Shōbōgenzō*, Iwanami-bunko edn (Tokyo, 1942), vol. II, p. 217.
62 *Fukanzazengi*, trans. Norman Waddell and Masao Abe, *EB* 6(2): 115–28.
63 *Bendowa*, op. cit., p. 129.
64 ibid., p. 144.
65 *Shōbōgenzō*, 'Bussho' (2) *EB* 9(1):88.
66 *Shōbōgenzō*, 'Gyōji', Iwanami-bunko edn, op. cit., vol. I, p. 122.
67 *Bendōwa*, op. cit., p. 145.
68 A note on the hermeneutics of Asian texts is in order here. Dōgen was interpreting a Chinese-language text composed of ideographs whose grammatical relationship with one another is not completely precise. In rendering the meaning of these ideographs in Japanese, Dōgen deliberately overlooked the traditional reading in favour of his alternative reading. Although Dōgen's new reading of the text is somewhat dubious from a strictly grammatical perspective, it remains a highly significant innovation in the development of Japanese Buddhist thought.
69 Masao Abe, 'Dōgen on Buddha-nature', *EB* 4(1):44.
70 ibid., p. 53.

71 'Being time: Dōgen's *Shobogenzo Uji*', *EB* 12(1):116.
72 ibid., p. 126.
73 ibid., p. 120 (adapted).
74 ibid., p. 120–1 (adapted).
75 See Masao Abe: *A Study of Dōgen, his Philosophy and Religion* (Albany, N.Y.: State University of New York Press, 1991).
76 Kitagawa, *Religion in Japanese History*, p. 119.
77 Quoted in Hajime Nakamura, *The Ways of Thinking of Eastern People*, p. 398.
78 See p. 761 above.
79 de Bary, op. cit., p. 347.
80 ibid.
81 Takakusu, op. cit., p. 182 (adapted).
82 Nakamura, *A History*, vol. I, p. 94.
83 See p. 753 above.
84 Anesaki, op. cit., pp. 192–3.
85 Takakusu, op. cit., p. 180 (adapted).
86 Anesaki, op. cit., p. 191.
87 ibid., p. 202.
88 Kitagawa, *On Understanding Japanese Religion*, pp. 211–12.
89 The following discussions are largely taken from Nakamura, *A History*, vol. II, pp. 2–37, 46–71.
90 Genryū Kagamishima, *Dōgen Zenji to sono Monryū* (*Zen Master Dōgen and his Followers*) (Tokyo: Seishin Shobo, 1961), p. 112.
91 ibid., pp. 106, 108.
92 ibid., pp. 120, 124.
93 *Roankyō*, part I.
94 Tominaga Nakamoto, *Emerging from Meditation*, trans. Michael Pye (Honolulu: University of Hawaii Press, 1990).
95 ibid., Ch. 8.
96 *Roankyō*, part I.
97 Nishida Nagao, *Nihon shukyo shisōshi no kenkyu* (*Studies of the History of Religious Thought in Japan*) (Tokyo, 1955), pp. 178ff.
98 *Ketsujō-shū*.
99 Nakamura, *A History*, vol. II, p. 27.
100 The Ten Virtues consist of: (1) not killing, (2) not stealing, (3) not committing adultery, (4) not lying, (5) not talking frivolously, (6) not slandering, (7) not being double-tongued, (8) not coveting, (9) not being angry and (10) not being heretical.
101 *Jūzen Hōgō* (*The Ten Buddhist Virtues*: a sermon preached in 1773), *Transactions of the Asiatic Society of Japan* 33(2):44.
102 *Byōsha Bōkoji ni shimesu* (*A Letter to a Certain Sick Layman*).
103 *Jūzen Hōgō*, op. cit., p. 53.
104 Nakamura, *A History*, vol. II, p. 119.
105 Kitagawa, *On Understanding Japanese Religion*, pp. 278–9.
106 ibid., p. 214.
107 ibid., p. 215 (adapted).
108 Torataro Shimomura, 'D. T. Suzuki's place in the history of human thought', in *A Zen Life: D. T. Suzuki Remembered*, ed. Masao Abe (New York: Weatherhill, 1986), p. 66.
109 ibid., p. 66, (adapted).

110 Abe, 'Editor's introduction', op. cit., p. xvi.
111 D. T. Suzuki, *Zen and Japanese Culture*, Bollingen Series 66 (New York: Pantheon, 1959), pp. 360–1.
112 D. T. Suzuki, *Introduction to Zen Buddhism* (London, 1948), pp. 59–60.
113 ibid., p. 60.
114 D. T. Suzuki, *Studies in Zen* (New York, 1955), p. 85.
115 ibid., p. 120.
116 Keiji Nishitani, *Religion and Nothingness*, trans. Jan Van Bragt (Berkeley/Los Angeles/London: University of California Press, 1982), p. 291.
117 Kitarō Nishida, 'The problem of Japanese culture', in *Sources of Japanese Tradition*, ed. W. Theodore De Bary *et al.* (New York: Columbia University Press, 1958), vol. II, pp. 355–6.
118 Nishida, *An Inquiry into the Good*, trans. Masao Abe and Christopher Ives (New Haven, Conn.: Yale University Press 1990). See Abe's Introduction, p. xv.
119 Nishida, *Last Writings: Nothingness and the Religious Worldview*, trans. David Dilworth (Honolulu: University of Hawaii Press, 1987), p. 67. I use Dilworth's translation in the following quotations.
120 ibid., p. 51.
121 ibid., p. 52.
122 ibid., p. 70.
123 ibid., p. 87.
124 See Hajime Tanabe, *Philosophy as Metanoetics*, trans. Takeuchi Yoshinori (Berkeley: University of California Press, 1986).
125 See Shin'ichi Hisamatsu, *Zen and the Fine Arts*, Tokiwa Gishin (Tokyo: Ko-dansha International, 1982). Masao Abe, 'Hisamatsu's philosophy of awakening', *The Eastern Buddhist* 14(1):26–42.
126 See Keiji Nishitani, *Religion and Nothingness*, trans. Jan Van Bragt (Berkeley: University of California Press, 1982).

FURTHER READING

Anesaki, Masaharu (1963) *History of Japanese Religion*, Rutland, Vt./Tokyo: Charles E. Tuttle.
de Bary, W. Theodore (ed.) (1969) *The Buddhist Tradition in India, China, and Japan*, The Modern Library, New York: Oxford University Press.
Kitagawa, Joseph M. (1966) *Religion in Japanese History*, New York.
—— (1987) *On Understanding Japanese Religion*, Princeton: Princeton University Press.
Nakamura, Hajime (1967) *A History of the Development of Japanese Thought*, 2 vols, Tokyo: Kokusai Bunka Shinkokai.

37

MORALS AND SOCIETY IN JAPANESE PHILOSOPHY

Takashi Koizumi

PERRY'S VISIT TO JAPAN

In the middle part of the nineteenth century, Japan still maintained its feudal system and continued its policy of national isolation under the Tokugawa government. However, on 3 June 1853, Commodore Matthew Calbraith Perry, the special envoy of the United States to Japan, visited Uraga with four war vessels to force Japan to open the country to the world and to negotiate for a supply of American whale-fishing vessels. Perry was also charged with negotiating with Japan to establish an intermediate trade base for trade between China and the United States. Uraga is located at the southern part of the Miura Peninsula about 50 kilometres to the south of Edo, capital of Japan and site of present-day Tokyo.

As the Tokugawa government had continued its policy of national isolation since the early seventeenth century, it had no experience in diplomatic affairs except for its relationships with Korea and Holland. As a result, it was at a loss when Perry suddenly came to Japan. The diplomatic impotence of the government created a strong distrust in the government on the part of the *samurai* in each domain. The *samurai* of the Chōshū, Satsuma and Tosa domains were particularly troublesome; they formed a unified front against the Tokugawa government for the purpose of realizing their policy of *sonnō-jōi* (reverence for the emperor and expulsion of foreigners) and conspired to overthrow the Tokugawa government, which gave in to Perry's demand to open Japan. The *samurai* of these rebellious Domains succeeded in establishing the new Meiji government in 1868.

The most intellectual *samurai* of the Tokugawa period were very impressed by the superiority of Western civilization (in the sciences and philosophy) to Eastern civilization. They studied Western science first in Dutch, then in English. However, such intellectuals were regarded as overly Westernized and were often exposed to the danger of assassination by extreme nationalists.

Meiji Ishin (the Meiji Restoration) was implemented in 1868 by the political leaders of several domains, mainly leaders from the Chōshū, Satsuma and Tosa domains, who now discarded the ideology of 'expulsion of foreigners' and actively introduced Western civilization into Japan.

Accordingly, Japanese scholars of the Western sciences came to be regarded as the most necessary element in introducing Western civilization. Among such scholars were Fukuzawa Yukichi[1] and Nishi Amane,[2] leading intellectuals of the time. These men offered new administrative ideas for the development of Japan. Let us examine Fukuzawa Yukichi's ideas first.

FUKUZAWA YUKICHI AND SELF-INDEPENDENCE

Fukuzawa Yukichi (1834–1901) was very deeply impressed by the superiority of Western civilization to Japanese. Of course, he did not think that every aspect was eminently superior; he had his own viewpoint from which he compared both civilizations and attempted to choose aspects from both to create a stronger Japanese civilization. In his book *Tsūzoku Kokken Ron* (*A Popular Theory of National Rights*), Fukuzawa noted:

> Thus, if we carefully observe the present conditions of both Japanese and Western societies and compare their merits and demerits, whether physical or spiritual, in some cases we will find that it is still necessary to change some aspects of the present conditions of Japanese society. In some other cases we will find that since our society has changed too much, we should minimize the change. In any event, it is the most difficult thing for us to choose the right way to go.[3]

Fukuzawa therefore insisted that

> since Japan has its own civilization and need not throw away what it has, we should do original things by utilizing the wisdom unique to our own civilization. We must incorporate the most useful aspects of Western civilization into our own. Additionally, we must abolish the useless aspects of our own civilization.[4]

In other words, Fukuzawa did not want Japanese civilization as a whole to be painted over with Western. Rather he sought to keep the best parts of Japanese civilization and graft on what was useful from the West.

What did Fukuzawa consider to be the best parts of Western civilization? He pointed out two important characteristics of it in his autobiography:

> We find there are teachings on morals, economics, culture and military sciences with their own merits and demerits both in the East and in the West. When reviewing teachings of both the East and the West by observing the overall national conditions from the standpoint of achieving the greatest happiness of the greatest number of people within a specific

> civilization, we have to conclude that the conditions of the East are inferior to those of the West. . . . If we compare Eastern Confucianism with the Western philosophy of civilization, we find that two aspects that can be found in the West, but not in the East are *Sūrigaku* (the sciences) and *Dokuritsushin* (the spirit of self-independence).[5]

For Fukuzawa, 'sciences' meant practical knowledge, in which he included the learning of Japan's forty-seven characters, phonetic alphabet, basic correspondence, counting, geography, physics, history, economics and morality,[6] all of which he considered to be very useful for individuals and society.

On the other hand, by 'the spirit of self-independence' he meant that one should regard oneself as being of irreplaceable worth, and that one should take the same attitude towards others. In his *Questions on Moral Education*, published in 1882, he writes that 'today under the philosophy of individual independence, one must first become independent, develop self-respect, regard oneself as pure and precious, and on this basis build relations with others and thus preserve discipline in society.'[7]

This concept of self-independence became his fundamental philosophy throughout his life. To Fukuzawa, Confucian philosophy was the obstacle that prevented Japanese society from achieving self-independence. In his essay entitled 'Words left behind in Nakatsu',[8] he gives a very unusual and interesting interpretation of Meng-tzu's [Mencius] five moral relationships (*gorin*) from the standpoint of self-independence.

Traditionally, the five moral relationships define the relationship between a father and his children, a lord and his subjects, man and wife, older and younger persons, and friends. The latter four are based upon the first and at the same time on the Confucian vertical social order.[9] But Fukuzawa writes:

> The fundamental basis of human morality is the relationship between man and wife. And following this relationship are the bonds between parents and children, brothers and sisters. When heaven brought forth human beings, the very first must have been a man and a woman. Man and woman both are individual human beings standing between heaven and earth; there is no reason to distinguish the relative importance or dignity of the two.[10]

Fukuzawa insists that the fundamental basis of all morality lies in morality between man and wife – both of whom are perfectly equal in human dignity and importance. It is surprising that Fukuzawa insisted on the equality between men and women at such an early period (1870) when Confucianism was still deeply rooted in Japanese society.

Furthermore, the above-mentioned statement implies another important point. Meng-tzu's rule that 'Man and wife shall be separate' means that a man should take care of business outside the home, while a wife should take care of household tasks alone. Fukuzawa gave quite a different interpretation of the statement: 'This word "separate" should be interpreted as "distinct". Thus, the meaning of the moral rule will be that each married couple is a couple distinct from all other married couples.'[11]

In other words, Fukuzawa stresses that a married couple is an independent unit and should be regarded as separate and independent from all other couples, including its own parental couples. The parental couple and its married children should be separate and independent from one another. To Fukuzawa, couples are independent and equal in dignity and importance.

Fukuzawa's interpretation of the relationship between a man and woman was very progressive for those days. His ideal of sexual equality had been expressed in several essays[12] where he attacked the traditional Confucian morality that was still strongly supported by the male-dominated society. His essays promoted the first Japanese feminist movement in the nineteenth century.

As we have seen, Fukuzawa emphasized intellectual education focused on Western sciences in order to attain self-independence for Japan. This was important to him because he realized that Japanese civilization lacked Western sciences, the spirit of self-independence, and the benefits that both gave to society.

However, Fukuzawa noticed *chuseishin to aikokushin* (the loyalty of Japanese people towards the emperor and Japan) and recognized it as the emotional and irrational element deeply rooted in the Japanese soul. He also realized the usefulness of such a national character in domestic and international politics and economics. In several essays on moral education,[13] we note that from 1882 he insisted that Japan base its national morality, identity and national character on loyalty towards the emperor and on patriotism. However, Fukuzawa clearly realized that patriotism is nothing but group-egoism, or biased love of a country as contrasted with love for all mankind.[14]

The international situation at the time was dominated by imperialistic European colonization activities, and Fukuzawa daringly proposed group-egoism as the means for Japan to maintain its independence. Then he planned to use the Japanese people's emotional loyalty towards the emperor and patriotism to spur the spirit of national defence. Specifically Fukuzawa and other leading Japanese intellectuals were concerned about the threat of European colonization of Japan.

Fukuzawa made a unique distinction between the subjective and the objective moral points of view.[15] By the subjective he meant achieving self-reliance, economic independence and spiritual self-independence. Additionally, he maintained that as a member of society one should expend one's surplus energy in such a way as to help other members of society to realize their own self-independence. Those people attaining spiritual self-independence should act in a leadership role.

Fukuzawa realized that it would be difficult for common people to attain a form of existentialist subjectivity. Of course, there were many people who could support themselves financially. However, they were unable to attain spiritual self-independence. Furthermore, there were other people who could not support themselves financially at all. Fukuzawa stressed that in either situation, the people could not obtain an existentially subjective moral point of view. He insisted that the few leaders in society should lead the common people to believe in some kind of religion which encouraged them to morality. These leaders should take an objective viewpoint in forcing the common people to learn morality. Thus we can say that

Fukuzawa took an authoritarian viewpoint concerning the moral education of the common people.

NISHI AMANE'S ATTEMPT TO CONSTRUCT A UNIFIED SCIENCE

Nishi Amane was the first Japanese philosopher to translate 'philosophy' into Japanese as '*tetsugaku*'. Nishi promoted Japan's modernization both as a philosopher of enlightenment and as a high-ranking bureaucrat of the early Meiji government.

After the Meiji Restoration in 1868, Nishi was invited to accept a bureaucratic post at the Army Ministry, while concurrently serving at the Translation Office and the Education Ministry. Besides these official duties, he opened a private school called the Ikueisha and taught young people Western sciences and philosophy in order to educate them as future leaders of Japan. His educational policies focused on teaching young students Western sciences in a unified and organic way in order to develop them for use in modernizing Japan.[16] This unified and organic understanding of Western sciences was regarded as philosophy by Nishi. Therefore, his philosophy may be said to be a practical unified science. In his book *Hyakuichi Shinron* (*A Unified Science of a Hundred Moral Theories*), he described the gist of his unified science as follows:

> When we seek to clarify the laws of nature and the laws of man and simultaneously establish doctrinal methodology while in quest of the above-mentioned laws of matter and of the human mind, we call such intellectual activities philosophy, which is translated into Japanese as *tetsugaku*.[17]

This is the first sentence in which the word '*tetsugaku*' appears in Japanese. Nishi attempted to construct a unified science by combining Japanese Confucianism with J. S. Mill's distinction between the laws of matter and the laws of mind, William Hamilton's distinction between science and art, and J. S. Mill's inductive methods.[18]

However, because Nishi Amane borrowed the ideas from nineteenth-century Western unified science and its methodology, he failed to construct a Japanese unified science. He understood that his failure was due to the theoretical impossibility of harmonizing physiology and psychology into the framework of unified science by applying unifying principles borrowed from Western philosophy. In his *Seisei Hatsuun* (*The Foundation of Physiology and Psychology*) (1873), he said, 'We can find neither the link between physiology and psychology, nor their unifying principles. On this point, we are astounded by the wide gulf between them.'[19] Given this failure he came to consider utilitarian ethics a possible solution to the practical issues he was confronted with in Japan.

Nishi Amane's utilitarian ethics

Nishi Amane translated J. S. Mill's *Utilitarianism* into Japanese in 1877 and regarded *saidai fukushi* (the greatest happiness principle) as one of the most profound revolutions in the history of ethics. He did not wholeheartedly agree with Mill's utilitarian ethics, which defined the greatest happiness as the ultimate object of life. However, he accepted this doctrine as a primary principle and offered his own reconstruction of this same principle in *Jinsei Sanpō Setsu* (*A Theory of Three Precious Objects in Human Life*) in 1874.[20] The reason Nishi was attracted to Mill's utilitarianism is that in his youth he sympathized with Confucian philosophy, the ultimate object of which was promotion of a better life for people (*hyakuichi shinron*).[21] He went on to clarify '*dainitō no ganmoku*' (the secondary principles), which are the means of realizing the primary principle. His idea of the secondary principles and their relationships to the primary principle are described in his *Jinsei Sanpō Setsu*.[22] The focus of the secondary principles was the three precious objects *mame*, *chie* and *tomi* (health, knowledge and wealth).

Since he regarded these three things as the foundation of happiness bestowed upon men by heaven, it was very natural for him that people seek after them and regard them as their own moral objectives that exert influence at both the individual and the social level. Therefore, they were the secondary moral principles not only for individuals, but also for society as a whole, and consequently the secondary moral principles in politics.

On the basis of these three moral objects Nishi sets forth three social and political rules as follows:

> Do not do anything to harm others' health and promote it if possible.
> Do not prevent others from having knowledge and promote it if possible.
> Do not ruin others' wealth and promote it if possible.[23]

Nishi sets negative imperatives at the beginning of these rules and places positive imperatives with the conditional phrase 'if possible' at their end. If we borrow present-day terminology, then we may say that the negative imperatives express negative utilitarianism, while the positive imperatives express positive utilitarianism.

According to Nishi, the negative utilitarian principles consist of two elements. One element is meant to prevent *san kaki-shippei*, *guchi* and *binbō* (the three evils of disease, idle complaint and poverty), which harm health, knowledge and wealth. Nishi defines this element as 'rights'. The other element obliges individuals to respect others' *sanpō* – *mame, chie* and *tomi* (the three treasures – health, knowledge and wealth) and to restrain *san akuma-kyōzoku*, *sagi* and *setto* (the three demons of brutal crime, deception and theft). Nishi defines this element as 'obligation'.[24]

He thinks that when men have fulfilled both rights and obligations, they will have attained the foundation of morality. Fulfilment of rights and obligations of this kind is a necessary condition for achieving basic human happiness.

Shōkyoku kō to sekkyoku kō (negative and positive principles)

Negative principles are the necessary conditions for the greatest happiness, but are not all that is required for human happiness. Fulfilling the requirement of the negative principles does not include any action based on positive principles that promotes the interests of others. Nishi insists that after the requirements of the negative principles have been satisfied, the positive principles must be fulfilled if man is to promote others' health, knowledge and wealth. Fulfilling the positive principles is then the sufficient condition for the greatest happiness. Nishi uses hypothetical imperatives in order to express the positive principles, saying 'Promote it if possible.'[25]

His point is very important for a reconstruction of consistent utilitarian ethics. Thus he can avoid a pragmatic paradox that positive utilitarianism is apt to involve. Suppose that, without assuming negative secondary principles, we apply positive utilitarianism to a certain situation in which we cannot attain the greatest happiness for the greatest number of people without sacrificing a few persons in society. This leads us to a pragmatic paradox in which the greatest happiness for the majority of society cannot be obtained without sacrificing the happiness of some.

Nishi invents a very clever system of utilitarianism by incorporating both negative and positive principles. He sets negative utilitarian principles as the necessary conditions for the greatest happiness and requires their fulfilment from the outset. Only after satisfying the necessary conditions does he require fulfilment of the positive utilitarian principles as the sufficient conditions for the greatest happiness principle. Thus he overcomes the pragmatic paradox.

Nishi's practical syllogism and its application

Since Nishi recognized the primary principle and used the secondary principles as a means to fulfil the former, he was aware of the distinction between rule-utilitarianism (the standpoint of legislative use in Mill's usage) and act-utilitarianism (the standpoint of jurisdictive use in Mill's usage). At the same time, Nishi was aware of the practical syllogism that Mill regarded as the logic of utilitarian principle application. Nishi dealt with this logic in his article entitled 'Ronri Sinsetsu' ('A new theory of logic') in 1884.[26]

According to Nishi, the syllogism's major premiss consists of the statement which expresses the social purpose of a country, the middle premiss consists of the means to that end, and the conclusion consists of the subject's choosing the particular means to that end. Nishi calls this procedure from the social purpose to the means achieving the subject's conclusion 'the orderly use of the practical syllogism', and the procedure from subject's choice to searching for the means and the social purpose 'the adverse use of it'. Furthermore, he calls the procedure of searching for both the social purpose and the conclusion by examining various means 'the procedure from the middle premiss to both the major premiss and the conclusion.' Nishi's account of the uses of the practical syllogism is comparable with R. M. Hare's in *The Language of Morals*.[27]

Now let us examine Nishi's applications of the practical syllogism to actual political, economic and military issues in the Japan of his day.

As Mill did in his *Utilitarianism*, Nishi regarded the happiness of all mankind as the ultimate object of life. Achieving the happiness of all mankind was, for Nishi, what Kant described as 'pacis aeternalis' or 'harmonia aeterna'.[28] However, Nishi thought it impossible to realize this utopian state in the nineteenth century. The reasoning behind this belief was that, despite being half way to this goal, the world was constantly plunged into international conflicts. Nishi predicted that all countries would make war against one another and that in the end there would remain only one country that would successfully incorporate every other country into its fold under the principle of the survival of the fittest.[29] This idea manifests Herbert Spencer's influence upon him.

Policies for promoting the wealth and military power of Japan

For Nishi, wealth may be compared to water in the reservoir, while military power may be compared to the embankment of the reservoir. Thus, wealth together with military power brings about national prosperity.[30]

Once national wealth is recognized as the immediate major premiss, the state can determine the means to achieve it. Critical to this is the choice of an appropriate political institution fitted to the national circumstances at that time. For Nishi, choosing the appropriate political institution depends upon the standard of civilization of the people. Thus, a nation or a state may choose radicalism, liberalism, conservatism, or theocracy according to the standard of civilization.[31] Nishi proposed in his 'Zuihitsu' ('An essay') that since we do not have any standard of civilization yet, we need an autocratic political system in order to attain national wealth.[32] In the essay entitled, 'Baku Kyūshō Kogi Ichidai' he also discussed the merits and demerits of democracy and took a very cautious attitude towards adopting democracy in Japan.[33]

On the other hand, in his 'Kenpō Sōan' ('A draft of the Constitution'),[34] which Yamagata Aritomo, Minister of the Army, asked him to write, Nishi proposed in 1881 a comparatively liberal democratic electoral system. He seemed there to assume a considerably developed standard of civilization when the so-called democratic rights movement was gaining popularity in various parts of Japan.

When Nishi realized that economic policy was the means to national wealth, he considered the laissez-faire policy to be the best one for Japan and proposed in his book *Tōei Mondō* (*A Dialogue under Lamplight*)[35] the abolition of all guild systems and insisted on unrestrained finance and interest policies.

Regarding military policies, Nishi predicted that every country would be involved in a struggle of the survival of the fittest, and said that this necessitated that each country devote itself to national defence. Accordingly, Japan must develop strong defence forces. In 1880, Yamagata Aritomo asked Nishi to write the famous draft of the 'Edict for Japanese soldiers',[36] promulgated on 4 January 1882, which became the spiritual foundation for Japanese soldiers until the end of the Second World War.

THE BACKGROUND OF THE 'EDICT FOR EDUCATION'

Fukuzawa Yukichi calls the period from 1868 to 1876 'Sōji Hakai' (the Age of Destruction),[37] and the period after 1877 'Kenchi Keiei' (the Age of Construction). The Seinan War broke out in 1877, and brought about various significant social, political, economic and ideological changes in Japan. The Imperial Army, consisting of farmers, workers and merchants under the conscription system of the Meiji government, defeated the rival army of the *samurai* under the leadership of Saigō Takamori.[38] The defeat of the *samurai* under Saigō further diminished their socio-political power. Additionally, the war expenditure totalled one-sixth of Japan's national budget and brought about 200 per cent inflation. This in turn caused the *samurai* class to lose its economic base, while the social status of farmers, workers and merchants appreciated considerably. Some conservative leaders came to fear these changes and view them as a crisis in which Japan faced spiritual bankruptcy, yet they created an evolution in the political consciousness of the people and were a catalyst for the democratic rights movement from 1878.

MOTODA EIFU'S (NAGAZANE'S) *KOKKYŌRON* (A THEORY OF NATIONAL MORALITY) AND THE PROMULGATION OF THE 'EDICT FOR EDUCATION'

Motoda Eifu (1818–91) was the tutor of Emperor Meiji and tried to establish a national morality based on Confucianism. He wrote 'Kyōgaku Taishi' ('The doctrine of education')[39] on the instruction of the emperor in 1879, in which he criticized the early Meiji educational trend that stressed knowledge and technology and yet disregarded the Confucian values of *jingi chūkō* (humanity, loyalty and filial piety). Motoda insisted that after having learned these primary human values, we should seek to gain knowledge and master technology.

Itō Hirobumi (1841–1909), the first Prime Minister of the Meiji government, wrote 'Kyōikugi' ('A discussion on education') in 1879,[40] in which he criticized Motoda's strongly conservative ideas. Itō insisted that the current moral confusion was caused not by changing from the Confucianist educational system to the Western system, but rather by social and political changes that evolved during the Meiji Restoration. Therefore he argued that the current moral confusion could not be overcome by educational reform alone. He claimed that the government should not assume the role of establishing a national morality, because the members of the government were not sufficiently wise and morally upright to do this. What the government should do was to protect Japanese history, literature, customs and language, and encourage students to be interested in the sciences.

Motoda argued against Itō's opinion by writing an essay entitled 'Kyōikugi Fugi' ('A comment on *A Discussion on Education*') in 1879,[41] in which he once again stressed the teaching of morals focusing on humanity, loyalty and filial piety. In 1882, he wrote 'Gakusei nitsuki Chokuyu' ('The edict for the educational system'),[42] and 'Chokuyu Taii' ('The gist of the edict'),[43] in which he insisted on abolishing educational trends biased in favour of Western sciences. He pressed for the teaching of Japanese history alone at elementary schools, so as to cultivate reverence towards the emperor and patriotism.

Motoda worked out the fundamental plan for the 'Kyōiku Chokugo' ('Edict for education') in his essay 'Kokkyō Ron' ('A thesis of national morality').[44] In this essay he claimed that the emperor should be dissociated from religion, and that since both the emperor and the people venerated and served Imperial Ancestors, national morality should be based on this reverence.

Motoda said that since the Imperial Ancestors epitomized and revered the qualities of wisdom, humanity and courage, and because the people also respected the same qualities, national morality should be based on these characteristics. Motoda insisted that the core of the national education system should consist of clarifying the duties that make up the relationship between the emperor and his subjects. Motoda emphasized that the educational system should stress the cultivation of filial piety, defend the Imperial system and promote humanity, augmented with Western sciences. It is clear that Motoda reversed the order of priority in Meng-tzu's *gorin* (five morals) in that he made the moral duties between the emperor and his subjects primary and relegated filial piety to a position of secondary importance. Thus Motoda laid the foundation for a very nationalistic strain of Japanese Confucianism in preparation for establishing the fundamental concept of the 'Edict for education' promulgated on 30 October 1890.

The opening statement of the 'Edict for education' is perfectly consistent with Motoda's idea in his 'Kokkyō Ron'.

> Our Imperial Ancestors have founded our empire on a basis broad and everlasting and have deeply and firmly implanted virtue; our subjects ever united in loyalty and filial piety have from generation to generation illustrated the beauty thereof.[45]

It goes without saying that the promulgation of this edict determined the direction of Japanese national education and morality from 1890.

PROMULGATION OF THE EDICT AND FUKUZAWA YUKICHI

At this time Japanese society consisted of two social classes, the ruling and the ruled. Fukuzawa Yukichi, Itō Hirobumi, Motoda Eifu and others belonged to the ruling class in the sense that they were in a position to settle on a plan for national education and morality. On the other hand, there were the ruled masses, who were obliged to follow any decision made by the ruling class. When the 'Edict for education' was promulgated, these masses were obliged to accept it as absolute authority. If they did not, then they were punished for their irreverence.

Fukuzawa was critical of both the edict and Confucianism because of his ideas of self-independence. Although he did not express his opinion directly, he criticized the government's unexpected change in educational policy implemented in 1881. In his essay entitled 'Kyōiku no Hōshin Henka no Kekka' ('The effects of change of educational policy'),[46] Fukuzawa claimed that the government was trying to revive regressive Confucianistic philosophy, abolish the foreign-language curriculum and restrict public education to the teaching of loyalty to the emperor, filial piety and patriotism. This educational policy led to social and political extremism which produced many 'criminals' who were guilty of irreverence towards the emperor and the country. Fukuzawa recommended that the government immediately undertake a policy of educational reform to correct the imbalance.

THE CASE OF UCHIMURA KANZŌ'S IRREVERENCE TOWARDS THE EDICT

The ruled masses had nothing to do with the formulation of the edict, and were only obliged to accept it as an object of reverence. But a few people were acutely aware of the edict's being in contradiction with their own faith. One of them was Uchimura Kanzō (1861–1930). In 1878 he was baptized by M. S. Harris, an American Methodist missionary.

When he went to the United States in 1884, he had several significant experiences.[47] One was that his patriotism underwent a radical change. While in Japan, he strove to make Japan into a strong country like its European counterparts or the United States, an ideal which was popular among Japanese intellectuals. In the United States, he worked as a male nurse at an asylum for mentally retarded children in Elwyn, Pennsylvania. He read the Book of Jeremiah and decided that he could learn from the prophet how to save his own country. Uchimura compared Japan to the powerless Kingdom of Judaea, which could be saved only by bowing in reverence to a righteous God. He was deeply impressed by the prophetic role of Jeremiah, who accused Judaea of injustice and strongly urged it to return to God. He was very conscious of his own role in pointing out Japan's unrighteousness and urged Japan to become righteous in the eyes of God. Uchimura regarded Jesus and Japan – 'my two J's' – as the two great factors of life.

In due course, he became conscious of the fact that his love for Jesus and Japan was tearing him apart. He felt that the tragedy he was experiencing was just what Jeremiah had experienced as a medium between God and the Kingdom of Judaea 2,600 years ago. In his essay 'Eremia Kansō' ('My impressions of Jeremiah') in *Seisho no Kenkyū* (*The Bible Studies*) in 1906, he noted, 'I have read through the Book of Jeremiah many times. . . . I feel that Jeremiah's experiences were just the same as my own.'[48] Reading the Book of Jeremiah while in America was a catalyst for his irreverence towards the edict.

The second significant experience was achieving faith in redemption during his meeting with Julius Hawley Seelye, president of Amherst College: 'Christ, paying all my debts, can bring me back to the purity and innocence of the first man before the Fall. Now I am God's child, and my duty is to believe Jesus.'[49]

Full of a patriotism acceptable to his Christian faith, Uchimura returned to Japan in 1888 and accepted a professorship of the First High School (college) in Tokyo in September 1890.

As we have seen, the 'Edict for education' was promulgated on 30 October shortly after he accepted his professorship. The president of the school planned a ceremony for receiving the edict on 9 January 1891, when the school began the winter term. At this ceremony, all teachers and students were supposed to go before the edict and bow to it. Uchimura interpreted the act of bowing before the edict as an act of worship, which obviously went against his Christian faith. Not quite sure what to do, Uchimura chose to behave in accordance with his Christian principles and did not bow. He said,

> I was not at all prepared to meet such a strange ceremony, for the thing was the new invention of the president of the school. As I was the third in turn to go up and bow, I had scarcely time to think upon the matter. So, hesitating in doubt, I took a safer course for my Christian conscience, and in the august presence of sixty professors . . . and over one thousand students, I took my stand and did not bow! . . . The anti-Christian sentiment . . . found a just cause . . . for bringing forth against me accusations of insult against the nation and its Head, and through me against the Christians in general.[50]

His refusal to bow before the edict resulted in the violent indignation of nationalistic professors and students attending the ceremony. Later, the school president persuaded him that this ceremony was not worship of the edict but merely an expression of respect for it. Uchimura fell ill with pneumonia and asked a friend to go before the edict and bow for him. Ultimately, Uchimura was forced to resign from the school. Most of the newspapers and magazines accused Uchimura of irreverence towards the emperor, while a small number of Christians defended him. Some Christians criticized him for his weak attitude.[51]

The case evolved from the violent clash between Christian faith and patriotism that existed in the soul of Uchimura Kanzō and in Japanese society as a whole. In other words, it was the collision between freedom of faith as a universal principle and patriotism as a particular principle. The result of this conflict was a victory for nationalism, while Christianity was branded an anti-nationalist religion. The edict became the fundamental principle of Japanese morality and education, and through it obedience was enforced upon the people. The edict itself had an absolute authority until the end of the Second World War. Because of his strong patriotism, Uchimura consistently took the Christian viewpoint in criticizing Japan's social injustice. He sharply pointed out the depth of Japan's sins, saying that 'it is clear at a glance' that God would judge 'Japan to be ripe for destruction' on account of its unrighteousness.

Uchimura has had a very strong impact upon the mind of modern Japan, for he established a critical viewpoint of his own country by looking at every nation not as an absolute entity but as a relative entity under the rule of God. Uchimura accused Japan of group-egoism from his Christian viewpoint. He expected that after the egoistic Japan had been destroyed, a new Japan would appear through God's grace. The resurrected Japan would be in a position to connect the East with the West spiritually and culturally. He believed that this was to be 'Nippon no Tenshoku' (Japan's calling),[52] decided by the redemptive God. He predicted that this future Japan would be the country in which Christianity would be grafted on to the *bushidō* (the way of the *samurai*) spirit and philosophy, and in which Christ and Paul would become incorporated into Japanese tradition. In Uchimura Kanzō we can see a typical example of a merging of Christian and Japanese traditions.

MAN, MORALITY AND COUNTRY IN WATSUJI TETSURŌ

We have seen that the 'Edict for education' had a decisive influence upon morality in Japan prior to the last war. Watsuji Tetsurō (1889–1960), one of the great representative moral philosophers of present-day Japan, developed a theory of national morality from his own ethical viewpoint. He also tried to base the 'Edict for education' on this same viewpoint.

Watsuji's ethics is not based on man as an individual but on *ningen* ('between men'), by which he meant the interpersonal relationship between men, *Zwischen den Menschen* or *das Zwischenmenschliche*, which was nothing but fundamental morality. He insisted that the concept of man as an individual being was merely an abstract concept derived from modern Western culture.[53]

By 'between' Watsuji meant *kōiteki-renkan* (connection-through-action or active association) by means of which men can communicate with one another. He insisted that there existed a moral foundation in human communities which should be allowed to develop naturally by incorporating the characteristics peculiar to each natural environment, people, culture and history, through 'connection-through-action'. Morality, therefore, would develop naturally in what he called *fūdo* (natural climatic and geographical characteristics). By *fūdo* Watsuji meant the people, nature, history and culture of each geographical area. All of these elements would be intimately connected through interaction and incorporated into a cultural unit by *kōiteki-renkan*.

According to Watsuji, the Japanese *fūdo* has a typhoon-like character which has in turn determined the Japanese people's character: in an abundant natural environment, the Japanese do not accept any restrictive religious or dogmatic principles, always endure the vicissitudes imposed by life and nature, and occasionally express violent emotion, but easily forget it over time.[54]

Watsuji specified the methods of cooperating of private entities by analysing *kazoku, bunka kyōdōtai, kokka* (the organization of families, cultural communities and countries) in a social context. He compared *chien kyōdōtai* (territorial communities) with cultural communities and found the latter to be relatively more public than the former. Cultural communities will transcend territorial communities because the former are diffusive and liberated, while the latter are concentrated and limited. Watsuji insisted that nations are public in the sense that they include other communities. Although cultural communities are closed and exclude heretics, snobs and savages, a country must be open and public because it includes all of them and anything else.

Watsuji thought that the only human community that could permit every human action would be mankind as a whole, but he notes that there has never existed any such community of mankind. He concluded that countries are the only public communities in the sense that they include and transcend all private beings. For example, the relationship between parents and children transcends that between man and wife, while maintaining the latter relationship. The interests of territorial communities transcend the interests of individual families, while looking after the latter. Cultural communities transcend territorial communities, while maintaining links to the latter. Thus, *kokka* (countries) transcend every individual community within themselves, while looking after the interests of each community.[55] Therefore countries are the ultimate communities in that each country is aware of all the developmental connections between all moral organizations and maintains all these connections at each respective stage. In other words, a country is the moral organization that incorporates every other moral organization within itself. Watsuji admitted that countries are closed in the sense that they exclude other countries; yet he insisted that countries are public, for they are the only moral organization including all other moral organizations.

Watsuji emphasized the importance of the 'Edict for education' as the basis for a national morality peculiar to Japan, and he provided a philosophical foundation for the edict in a theory of the *fūdo*. Since he recognized the state as the ultimate moral organization, his moral system is obliged to have a closed nature because his moral system excludes the moral systems of other countries. He thought that national morality would evolve a human morality common to all mankind. Furthermore, he objected to enforcing the so-called universal morality of mankind on each country, because what is called universal morality is itself nothing but a particular strain of a closed particular national morality. Accordingly, he insisted that the 'Edict for education' was the morality best fitted to the Japanese.[56]

Here we find Watsuji's weak point. Although a universal morality has yet to appear, we cannot deny that the possibility exists of establishing a universal morality over time through international association. Furthermore, in the latter part of the twentieth century, we have come to be aware that we live in a small world in which we all face the same political, economic, social and cultural problems. If we insist on protecting ethnic, political, economic and cultural independence on the basis of a narrow national egoism, we are apt to become involved in a dangerous adventure. We are now aware of the real possibility of communicating and cooperating with one another, and mankind as a whole faces many global issues including ecological crises, issues on the use of natural resources, world population problems and so forth. We have come to recognize the limitations of Watsuji's ethical system, which attempts to base morality on the nation alone. In present-day Japan, we have come to understand that Japan must share some common fundamental moral values with the rest of the world, while limiting the development of national morality in order to cultivate a universal morality.

NOTES

1 Fukuzawa Yukichi (1834–1901) was a leading enlightenment figure in the Meiji period, and founded Keio Gijuku.
2 Nishi Amane (1829–97) was the first philosopher of modern Japan and a high-ranking bureaucrat of the Meiji government.
3 Fukuzawa Yukichi, *Tsūzoku Kokken Ron* (1878), in *Fukuzawa Yukichi Zenshū* (*Collected Works of Fukuzawa Yukichi*) (Iwanami Shoten, 1959), vol. IV, p. 624. In the following notes *Fukuzawa Yukichi Zenshū* is abbreviated as *CWFY*.
4 ibid., p. 624.
5 Fukuzawa Yukichi, *Fukuō Jiden* (1899), *CWFY*, vol. VII, p. 167.
6 Fukuzawa Yukichi, *Gakumon no Susume* (*Commendation of Learning*, 1872), *CWFY*, vol. III, p. 30.
7 Fukuzawa Yukichi, *Tokuiku Ikan* (1882), *CWFY*, vol. V, p. 362; *Fukuzawa Yukichi on Education*, trans. Eiichi Kiyooka (University of Tokyo Press. 1985), p. 160. This is abbreviated as *FYE*.
8 Fukuzawa Yukichi, 'Nakatsu Ryūbetsu no Sho' (1870), *CWFY*, vol. XX; *FYE*, pp. 35–41.
9 Uchino Kumaichirō, *Mentzu* (Meiji Shoin, 1962), p. 184.
10 'Nakazu Ryūbetsu no Sho', *CWFY* vol. XX, p. 50.
11 ibid., p. 50.
12 Fukuzawa Yukichi, 'Nippon Fujin Ron' ('An essay on Japanese woman', 1885), *CWFY* vol. V, pp. 445–74; 'Danjo Kōsai Ron' ('An essay on friendship between man and woman', 1886), *CWFY*, vol. V, pp. 579–605.
13 Fukuzawa Yukichi, 'Teishitsu Ron' ('An essay on the mikado', 1882), *CWFY* vol. V. pp. 257–92; 'Tokuiku Yoron' ('An addition to questions on moral education', 1882), *CWFY*, vol. VIII, pp. 465–70.

14 Fukuzawa Yukichi, 'Bunmeiron no Gairyaku' ('An introduction to civilization', 1875), *CWFY*, vol. IV, p. 191.
15 Fukuzawa Yukichi, 'Tokuiku Yoron', *CWFY*, vol. VIII, pp. 465–6.
16 Nishi Amane, *Hyakugaku Renkan* (*Encyclopedia of Sciences*, 1870), *Nishi Amane Zenshū* (*Collected Works*), vol. IV (Munekata Shobō, 1981), p. 11. *Nishi Amane Zenshū* is henceforth abbreviated as *NAZ*.
17 Nishi Amane, *Hyakuichi Shinron* (*A New Theory of Unified Science*, 1874), *NAZ*, vol. I, (Munekata Shobō 1962), pp. 288–9.
18 Koizumi Takashi, 'Nishi Amane to Obeishisō tonodeai' ('Nishi Amane's encountering European and American thoughts') (Sanrei Shobō, 1989), ch. 3.
19 Nishi Amane, *Seisei Hatsuun* (*The Foundation of Psychology and Physiology*, 1873), *NAZ*, vol. I, pp. 64–5.
20 Nishi Amane, *Jinsei Sanpō Setsu* (*A Theory of Three Precious Objects of Life*, 1874), *NAZ*, vol. I, pp. 514–54.
21 Nishi Amane, *Hyakuichi Shinron*, *NAZ*, vol. I, p. 237.
22 ibid., p. 515.
23 ibid., p. 520.
24 ibid., p. 522.
25 ibid., p. 523.
26 *NAZ*, vol. I, pp. 574–85.
27 R. M. Hare, *The Language of Morals* (Oxford University Press, 1952).
28 Nishi Amane, 'Zuihitsu' ('An essay', 1869–1870), *NAZ*, vol. III (Munetaka Shōbo, 1966), p. 204.
29 Nishi Amane, 'Heibu Ron' ('An essay on military policy', 1878–81), *NAZ*, vol. III, pp. 22–7.
30 ibid., p. 54.
31 Nishi Amane, 'Seiryaku Ron' ('Political tactics', 1879), *NAZ*, vol. II, p. 291–2.
32 Nishi Amane, *Tōei Mondō* (*A dialogue under lamplight*, 1870), *NAZ* vol. II, p. 251.
33 Nishi Amane, 'Baku Kyūshō Kōgi Ichidai' ('A talk on the proposal of the Cabinet councillors', 1874), *NAZ*, vol. II, pp. 238–41.
34 Nishi Amane, 'Kenpō Sōan' ('A draft of the Constitution', 1881–2). *NAZ*, vol. II, pp. 197–237.
35 Nishi Amane, *Tōei Mondō*, op. cit., pp. 262–3.
36 Nishi Amane, 'Gunjin Chokuyu Sōkō' ('A draft of the edict for soldiers', 1880), *NAZ*, vol. III, pp. 109–13.
37 Fukuzawa Yukichi, 'Soji Hakai to Kenchikeiei' ('Destruction and construction', 1882?), *CWFY*, vol. XX, pp. 248–9.
38 Saigō Takamori (1827–77), a statesman of the last part of the Tokugawa period and of the early Meiji period, enforced the abolition of the feudal Domains. He died in the Seinan War in 1877.
39 Motoda Eifu, 'Kyōgaku Taishi', in *Kyōiku Chokugo Kanpatsu Kankei Shiryōshō* (*The Collection of Materials concerning Promulgation of the Edict for Education*), vol. I (Kokumin Seishin Bunka Kenkyūju, 1939), pp. 3–4. I abbreviate this collection as *KCKKS*.
40 Itō Hirobumi, *Kyōikugi*, 1879, in *KCKKS*, vol. I, pp. 5–9.
41 Motoda Eifu, '*Kyōikugi Fugi*', 1879, *KCKKS*, vol. I, pp. 10–14.
42 Motoda Eifu, 'Gakusei nitsuki Chokuyu', 1882, *KCKKS*, vol. I, pp. 22–3.
43 Motoda Eifu, 'Chokuyu Taii', *KCKKS*, vol. I, p. 24.
44 Motoda Eifu, 'Kokkyō Ron', 1884, *KCKKS*, vol. II, pp. 297–8.

45 Katayama Seiichi (ed.), *Shiryō Kyōiku Chokugo* (*The Materials on the Edict for Education*) (Kōryōsha Shoten, 1974), p. 7.
46 Fukuzawa Yukichi, 'Kyōiku no Hōshin Henka no Kekka', *CWFY*, vol. XIII, p. 575.
47 Uchimura Kanzō, 'How I became a Christian', in *Uchimura Kanzō Zenshū*, ed. Suzuki Toshirō *et al.* (40 vols, Iwanami Shoten, 1981–4), vol. III (1982), pp. 5–167. I abbreviate the *Zenshū UKZ.*
48 Uchimura Kanzō, 'Eremia Kansō', *Seisho no Kenkyū* (*The Bible Studies*) (1906).
49 Uchimura Kanzō, 'How I became a Christian', p. 117.
50 Uchimura Kanzō, *UKZ*, vol. XXXVI (1983), *Shokan* (*Letters*), pp. 331–2.
51 Ozawa Saburō, *Uchimura Kanzō Fukei Jiken* (*The Case of Uchimura Kanzō's Irreverence*) (Shinkyō Shuppansha, 1961).
52 Uchimura Kanzō, 'Nippon no Tenshoku' ('The vocation of Japan'), *Seisho no Kenkyū* (*The Bible Studies*) (November 1924).
53 Watsuji Tetsurō, *Ningen no Gaku toshiteno Rinrigaku* (*Ethics as the Science of Between-Men*) (Iwanami Shoten, 1934).
54 Watsuji Tetsurō, *Fūdo* (Iwanami Shoten, 1935), pp. 134–69. And see 'Rinrigaku' 2 ('Ethics'), in Watsuji Tetsurō, *Zenshū*, vol. XI (Iwanami Shoten, 1962), pp. 398–400.
55 Watsuji Tetsurō, 'Rinrigaku' 1 ('Ethics'), in Watsuji Tetsurō, *Zenshū*, vol. X (Iwanami Shoten, 1962), pp. 330–625.
56 ibid., pp. 592–625.

FURTHER READING

Blacker, Carmen (1969 (1964)) *The Japanese Enlightenment, A Study of the Writings of Fukuzawa Yukichi*, Cambridge: Cambridge University Press.

Furukawa, T. and Ishida, K. (eds) (1977) *Nipponshisōshi Kōza* (*Lectures on the History of Japanese Thought*), vols VI, VII, VIII, Yuzankaku.

Hikakushisōshi Kenkyūkai (ed.) (1982) *Ningen to Shūkyo* (*Man and Religion – the Religious Viewpoint of Modern Japanese*), Tōyōbunka Suppan.

Iida Kanae (1984) *Fukuzawa Yukichi*, Chūō Kōronsha.

Inoue Tetsujirō (1893) *Kyōiku to Shūkyō no Shōtotsu* (*The Conflicts between Education and Religion*), in Seki Kōsaku (ed.) *Inoue Hakase to Kirisuto Kyōto*, Misuzu Shobō, 1988.

—— (1974) 'Chokugo Engi' ('A commentary on the edict for education'), in *Material on the Edict for Education*, ed. Katayama Seiichi, Kōryōshoten.

Ishikawa Mikiaki (1932) *Fukuzawa Yukichi Den* (*A Life of Fukuzawa Yukichi*), Iwanami Shoten.

Ishizaka Iwao (ed.) (1985) *Fukuzawa Yukichi Tokushū* (*Essays on Fukuzawa Yukichi*), *Kindai Nippon Kenkyū* 2 (Studies on Modern Japan 2). Fukuzawa Memorial Centre for Modern Japanese Studies, Keio University.

Kamei Shunsuke (1977) *Uchimura Kanzō – The Signpost for the Meiji Mind*, Chūō Kōronsha.

Kanō Masanao (1974) *Fukuzawa Yukichi*, Shimizushoin.

Karaki Junzō, (1963) 'Exposition, Watsuji Tetsurō', in *Gendai Nippon Shisō Taikei* 28 (*The Collection of Present-day Japanese Thoughts*), Chikuma Shobō.

Katayama Seiichi (ed.) (1974) *Shiryō Kyōiku Chokugo* (*Material on the Edict for Education*), Kōryōsha Shoten.

Kawakami Tetsutarō (ed.) (1967) *Uchimura Kanzō Shū* (*Selections from Uchimura Kanzō*), *Meiji Bungaku Zenshū* 39, Chikuma Shobō.

Keio Gijuku (ed.) (1958–64) *Fukuzawa Yukichi Zenshū* (*Collected Papers of Fukuzawa Yukichi*), 21 vols, Iwanami Shoten.
Kiyooka Eiichi (1985) *Fukuzawa Yukichi on Education*, University of Tokyo Press English translation.
Koizumi Shinzō (1966) *Fukuzawa Yukichi*, Iwanami Shoten.
Koizumi Takashi (1989) *Nishi Amane to Oubei Shisō tonodeai* (*Nishi Amane Encountering European and American Thoughts*), Sanrei Shobō.
—— (1991) *Nakamura Keiu to Kirisuto Kyō* (*Nakamura Keiu and Christianity*), Hokuju Shuppansha.
Kokumin Seishin Bunka Kenkyūjo (The Institute for the Studies of National Mind) (ed.) (1939) *Kyōikuchokugo Kanpatsu Kankei Shiryōshū* (*The Materials concerning Promulgation of the Edict for Education*), Kokumin Seishin Bunka Kenkyūjo.
Minamoto Enryō (1986) *Jitsugaku Shisō no Keifu* (*A History of the Ideas of Practical Learning in Japan*). Kōdansha Gakujutsu Bunko.
Motoda Eifu (Nagazane) (1942) *Motoda Eifu*, ed. Kaigo Muneomi, Bunkyō Shoin.
Nakamura Hajime and Takeda Kiyoko (supervising), Mineshima Hideo and Koizumi Takashi *et al.* (eds) (1982) *Kindai Nippon Tetsugakushisōka Jiten* (*A Dictionary of Modern Japanese Philosophers and Thinkers*), Tokyo Shoseki.
Nishimura Shigeki (1976) *Nishimura Shigeki Zenshū* (*Collected Papers of Nishimura Shigeki*), Shibunkaku.
Ohkubo Toshiaki (ed.) (1962–82) *Nishi Amane Zenshū* (*Collected Works of Nishi Amane*), Munetaka Shobō.
—— (ed.) (1967) *Meiji Keimōshisōshū* (*Readings in Japanese Thoughts of the Meiji Enlightenment*), *Meiji Bungaku Zenshū* 3, Chikuma Shobō.
—— (1986–) *Ohkubo Toshiaki Rekishi Chosakushū* (*Ohkubo Toshiaki's Collected Essays on History*), 8 vols, Yoshikawa Kōbundō.
Ohnishi Hajime (1982) *Ohnishi Hajime Zenshū* (*The Works of Ohnishi Hajime*), Nippon Tosho Centre.
Ozawa Saburō (1961) *Uchimura Kanzō Fukei Jiken* (*The Case of Uchimura Kanzō's Irreverence*), Shinkyō Shuppansha.
Piovesana, Gino K., SJ (1963) *Recent Japanese Philosophical Thought, 1862–1962, A Survey*, Enderle Bookstore.
Sekine Masao (1967) *Uchimura Kanzō*, Shimizushoin.
Senuma Shigeki (ed.) (1974) *Meiji Tetsugakushisōshū* (*Readings in Meiji Philosophical Thought*), *Meiji Bungaku Zenshū* 80, Chikuma Shobō.
Suzuki Toshirō *et al.* (eds) (1981–4) *Uchimura Kanzō Zenshū*, 40 vols, Iwanami Shoten.
Takagi Hiroo (ed.) (1987) *Inoue Enryō no Kyōiku Rinen* (*The Educational Ideas of Inoue Enryo*), Tōyō University.
Takahashi Masao (1987) *Nishimura Shigeki*, Yoshikawa Kōbunkan.
Tomita Masabumi (ed.) (1966) *Fukuzawa Yukichishū* (*Selections from Fukuzawa Yukichi*), *Meiji Bungaku Zenshū* 8, Chikuma Chobō.
Tomita Masabumi and Tsuchihashi Shunichi (eds) (1981) *Fukuzawa Yukichi Senshū* (*Selections from Fukuzawa Yukichi*), 14 vols, Iwanami Shoten.
Watsuji Tetsurō (1962) *Zenshū* (*Collected Works of Watsuji Tetsurō*), Iwanami Shoten.

38

CONTEMPORARY JAPANESE PHILOSOPHY

John C. Maraldo

The appellation 'Japanese philosophy' is problematic in several senses. Many philosophers regard philosophy as a Western discipline imported into Japan a little over a century ago, and to this day restrict the term to investigations whose theme or method originates in the Western tradition. 'Japanese philosophy' in that case simply means Western philosophy as it is pursued in Japan. Others may apply the term to philosophically informed enquiries into pre-modern ('pre-philosophical') Japanese traditions. And some use the term to refer to pre-modern Japanese Confucianism, Buddhism, or other schools of thought; or again to contemporary treatises inspired by Eastern as well as Western sources. In the latter cases, the question arises as to what is 'Japanese' about past or contemporary thinking in Japan. In the former usage, which restricts 'philosophy' to an originally Western discipline, a similar question is raised about what is original in the work of philosophers in Japan; but the more important problem is the purported universality of a method of enquiry with Greek origins. The problem of the bounds of philosophy is today a central concern for philosophers world-wide, but it affects material for an encyclopedia of Asian philosophy in a special way, for 'philosophy' is not an Asian term and thus, for some writers, not an Asian conception at all.

This chapter seeks to sustain the problematic nature of Japanese philosophy rather than prematurely to define away the ambiguities. Indeed one may view contemporary Japanese philosophy as an attempt to come to terms with several issues that relate directly or indirectly to the question of the universality of philosophy. As discussed below, these issues do not follow in strictly chronological order; they often overlap with one another, or recede from view and then reappear at various times. Accordingly, this necessarily selective survey[1] will mention figures and works in more than one context. Although most of the issues appear in the common province of philosophy world-wide, some are peculiar to Japan's historical situation. The very meaning of 'philosophy' for the Japanese is of the latter sort. To place the beginning of modern Japanese philosophy roughly with the Meiji Restoration of 1868 is to see it as a result of the confrontation with Western thinking. Western studies (*yōgaku*) were not new to the Japan of the 1860s, but as they had been defined by Arai Hakuseki (1656–1725) they were limited for the most part to a study of the applied sciences and technology. When Nishi Amane (1829–97) was sent to Holland in 1862 by the Tokugawa government, he noted that the more theoretical disciplines such as economics, political science and legal theory were unknown in Japan. As for *hi-ro-so-hi*, the overarching theoretical discipline, the West stands first, Nishi later wrote in his *Hyakugaku renkan* (early 1870s), which he subtitled, in English, *Encyclopedia*. 'In our country there is nothing that deserves to be called philosophy; China too does not equal the West in this regard.'[2]

THE PROBLEM OF THE MEANING OF 'PHILOSOPHY' IN MODERN JAPAN

Nishi's statement is echoed in a famous verdict made thirty years later, by Nakae Chōmin (1847–1901), who shortly before his death wrote: 'Since olden times to this day there has been no philosophy in Japan.'[3] Soon afterwards Tanaka Odō (1867–1932) contested the view that there was no indigenous Japanese philosophy different from Indian and Chinese thought.[4] This controversy paralleled a slightly earlier one between Nishimura Shigeki (1828–1902) and Tori Koyata (1847–1905). Nishimura wrote in 1887 that if philosophy is taken as the investigation of the truths of heaven and earth, then sage-ancestors, scriptures and other expedients play no role in it as they do in Confucianism and Buddhism.[5] Tori refuted this view rhetorically, repeating Nishimura's terms: 'Are not Confucianism and Buddhism investigations of truth? Is not the basis of knowledge and action (*chikō*) also the basis of so-called truth?'[6] Nishi, Nishimura and Nakae are recognized today as leading Meiji-era intellectuals, while Tori and Tanaka have become as obscure as the rhetorical arguments they advanced.[7] More than anything else, however, it was the establishment of philosophy as an academic discipline, taught in the novel institutional setting of a university, that promoted philosophy as a Western discipline. In the thirty years between Nishi's and Nakae's verdicts, the meaning and scope of philosophy underwent significant development.

The question about the meaning and unprecedented nature of philosophy appeared first in Nishi's attempts to translate the Western term. He initially used the term *philosophia* untranslated, or transcribed it into Japanese syllabary, but soon attempted to find an equivalent in Chinese ideographs. Approximating the 'love of wisdom', he invented the term *kikyū tetsuchi*, 'quest for clear wisdom', then abbreviated it to *kitetsugaku* and finally, about 1874, to *tetsugaku*, the compound of two ideographs that has become standard in China and Korea as well as Japan. Nishi's understanding of philosophy likewise evolved, along with the range of his sources. En route to Europe, he wrote of it as a Western counterpart of Chinese social and political thought, a clarification of wisdom and virtue that surpasses Song Confucianism.[8] After returning and teaching new Western disciplines in Japan, when he coined the term *tetsugaku*, he took it in the sense of the queen of the sciences, the study that synthesizes and unifies 'the hundred learnings'. It was a rational, practical approach to knowledge that uses inductive logic, and deals with the principles of both the natural and the human world, of both nature and morality, the physical and the mental or spiritual.

The clear division between these two realms was itself one of the Western imports often hidden beneath the cover of traditional language, as in the title of a treatise Nishi composed about 1872 to explain the meaning of philosophy. *Seisei hatsuun* can be translated as the 'relationship of the physical and the spiritual', yet alludes to a saying of Mencius' opponent Kao-tzu, 'Our condition at birth (*sei*) is what we call nature (*sei*).' (The two ideographs have the same pronunciation but are written differently.) Nishi's title replaces an implied classical Chinese opposition between one's natural condition and imposed morality with a Western dichotomy between matter and spirit. Nishi's treatises are filled with such bricolage, old (Confucian and Buddhist) words given new, dissociated (Western) usages; *shūkyō* as the eventual translation for 'religion' is a case in point. To understand philosophy meant that one would have to create a new language to signify novel distinctions and conceptual frameworks.

In addition to this sort of bricolage and to neologisms like *tetsugaku*, early Meiji-era attempts to translate the language of philosophy included numerous terms left untranslated, transcribed into Japanese phonetic syllabary or written in the roman alphabet, as well as proper names written in ideograms read phonetically, to imitate the Western pronunciation, and divorced from the original meaning of the ideographs. This diversity is indicative of the creativity of the early translators of the Western discipline as well as their perplexity with its alien conceptions. A conception as basic to Western reasoning as the notion of contradiction, while certainly not unprecedented in Asian thought, was an occasion of consternation to early translators and of challenge to later philosophers who sought to differentiate Western and Eastern thinking.

In his 1886 comments on the compilation of philosophical lexicons and the reformation of language, Tsutomi, a former student of Nishi, mentions three translations of the 'principle of contradiction' (in English), which may be retranslated as 'collisionism', 'the principle of eating one's own words', and the 'principle of [what is in] question'.[9] Lexicographers eventually settled on *mujun* for 'contradiction', a Chinese term harking back to the classical Legalist Han Fei's story about the all-penetrating spear (*mu*) meeting an impenetrable shield (*jun*). Two editions of a philosophical dictionary begun in 1881 by the first Japanese professor of philosophy at Tokyo University, Inoue Tetsujirō (1855–1944), culminated in a new version in 1912 which endeavours 'to settle finally the Japanese equivalents of the European technical terms',[10] but still lists fourteen compounds for 'contradiction' in addition to the standard *mujun*. Inoue, along with about fifty others, also contributed to a monumental seven-volume *Tetsugaku dai jisho* (*Great Philosophical Lexicon*) in 1909–12, which was but one part of an effort to produce encyclopedias on medicine, manufacturing, education, economics and the arts, and so come to terms with Western conceptualizations.

Western philosophy can hardly be considered a contradiction to traditional Japanese thought, but was different enough to many early Meiji-era figures to anticipate the verdict by Nakae Chōmin cited above. For Nakae, the Japanese Confucians and Buddhists of old were nothing but antiquarians, the new universities even with their American and European professors offered only the history of (Western) philosophy, and contemporary Japanese 'philosophers' like Inoue and Katō Hiroyuki (1836–1916), former president of Tokyo University, were merely uncritical importers of occidental doctrines. Nakae implied that pure philosophy was the result of truly original thought that transcends practicality and gives life and actions their profound meaning.

Miyake Setsurei (1860–1945) was as harsh as Nakae in his judgement of native traditions if not of his contemporaries. His *Philosophical Trifles* of 1889 likewise belittles Confucians, Daoists and Buddhists, and proclaims that 'despite the name, there is no such thing as Eastern philosophy . . . if we do not confront the mirror [of Western philosophy] we shall not see the blemishes on our face. We must turn this mirror to illumine the appearance of eastern philosophy.'[11] For Miyake, the latter had degenerated into mere exegesis and needed to adopt the Western ability to explain with penetrating consistency and to establish causal relations and logical connections. Placing the difference between East and West in formal logic follows a persistent if contested pattern throughout modern Japanese thought.

THE QUESTION OF AN EASTERN LOGIC

Although no logician himself, Nishi Amane introduced the idea of formal reasoning repeatedly in lectures relying on J. S. Mill's *System of Logic*. His *Seisei hatsuun* states that the Japanese and Chinese have forgotten ways such as the inductive method of Mill and need to relearn this kind of logic. He attacks the 'deductive', i.e. philological methods of Confucian studies; but also criticizes the West for succumbing to 'objective contemplation'. The West must relearn Eastern 'subjective contemplation' (the Japanese terms are glossed in English), which seeks the inner principles of the heart or mind.[12] The Confucian Nishimura Shigeki later added that the East sought the mind within, the West without, in sciences like physiology; the former is holistic and synthetic, the latter analytic and precise though partial.[13] And the Buddhist Inoue Enryō, in his preface to *An Evening of Philosophical Conversation* (1886), emphasized the novelty of the Western discipline and clarified it as logical enquiry into the axioms of truth and the foundations of other disciplines.[14]

Even such authoritative works as Inoue Tetsujirō's *Philosophy of the Wang Yang-ming School in Japan* (1900), *Philosophy of the Ancient Learning School in Japan* (1902) and *Philosophy of the Chu Hsi School in Japan* (1906) implied by their subject matter that the 'philosophy' of these schools consists not in their logical argumentation but in their views on cosmology, politics, ethics, human relations and other topics. Inoue's successor at Tokyo Imperial University, Kuwaki Genyoku, had previously given a 'formal definition of philosophy' in 1900 that specified it, using English terms, as generalized, methodical or systematic, and rational; therefore a science, namely of universal, ultimate and unifying principles.[15] But perhaps the first really to practise critical thinking was the young Ōnishi Hajime (1864–1900), who authored a *Logic* in 1893 and, in other works and university lectures, took pains to introduce Western philosophy precisely and to reveal the obscure, eclectic or inconsistent views of his contemporaries. These examples show that the general agreement about the logical and 'scientific' character of (Western) philosophy cut across boundaries between those who repudiated native traditions and those who sought to renew them, and between academic and non-academic writers.

Nor is this differentiation merely a reflection of the Meiji *zeitgeist* and confrontation with the spirit behind Western technology. Long after Japanese engineers achieved technological feats and philosophers began to practise logical argumentation as second nature, many persisted in defining Western science (in the broad sense of *wissenschaft*) as rational, logical and object-orientated, as opposed to the intuitive and concrete character of an Eastern learning predominantly orientated to self-transformation. This is the view of Nishitani Keiji (1900–90), for instance, who reiterates that the classical law of contradiction abstracts from reality and cannot accommodate actual contradictions in it.[16] An example is the relationship in good government in which the *many* must autonomously negate their individual wills to form a unity, a *one*, that in turn must govern by negating its hegemony and granting autonomy to individuals. One might object that such relationships involve tension or disparity between entities, but not a contradiction between statements. Nishitani's point, however, is that the restriction to atomic propositions in abstract, formal logic is precisely what precludes an ability to grasp concrete, continually transforming reality and the relationship between things and human selves. He uses 'contradiction' in a broad, transformed sense.

Nishitani follows his teacher Nishida Kitarō (1870–1945) here, and via him, Hegel, but with a difference explained later in this chapter. Nishida's views on logic, nuanced and evolving as they are, consistently express the universalistic yet developmental character of logic. Foreign professors such as E. Fenollosa, L. Busse and R. Koeber at Tokyo Imperial University before and during Nishida's student days had replaced Mill's empirical logic with the logic of Hegel, Kant and Hermann Lotze as a model, so Japanese philosophers like Nishida began to understand logic in a wider sense and to maintain its cogency and naturalness for anyone's thinking. 'Logical understanding is the internal development of something universal', Nishida wrote at the beginning of his career,[17] signifying by 'universal' both what particulars have in common and what is logically accessible to everyone: hence not the way that only those in the West think.

Even when Nishida endeavours to differentiate tendencies in Western and Eastern thinking, as in his 1938 lectures on 'The problem of Japanese culture',[18] he states that it is not as if there is a Western logic and an eastern logic. 'Logic must be one.' But it takes different directions as the world develops historically; indeed it is the form in which the world functions historically and forms itself. Thus, although formal, abstract logic may be the same everywhere, logic as a form of concrete knowledge is inseparable from the particularities of historical life. By implication, 'concrete logic' would have to account for the historical lack of formal logic in pre-modern Japan, as well as for the possibility of novel developments after its introduction.

NISHIDA'S LOGIC OF PLACE AND TANABE'S LOGIC OF SPECIES

In Nishida's case that new development, universal in scope, involved the status of contradiction. 'Concerning my logic' – Nishida's very last writing, cut short by illness leading to death in 1945 – ends: 'Logic is the form of our thinking. To clarify what logic is we must proceed from the essence of our thinking.'[19] But that essence is not immutable. This fragment notes that the paradigm of logic found in Aristotle does not permit contradiction. Yet logic itself has a history and underwent a development that, in Kant's transcendental logic or Hegel's dialectical logic, for example, entailed a negation of what previously counted as logic. In Hegel's logic contradiction is the very form of self-development.

Nishida himself developed the logic of 'the self-identity of absolute contradictories' in order to account for the individual self as that which is capable of action and which entails change within identity, creativity out of conditioning, and plural individuality *vis-à-vis* the unity of the world. Nishida also called his contribution the logic of place (*basho*), which may be understood as an account of the relation between the individual and the universal. In conventional logic, in order to talk about things, we must have recourse to universals that necessarily refer to more than one instance of the 'same' thing, or at least that group similar things together. A problem arises, however, when we try to define metaphysically one individual thing in differentiation from others of like kind, by adding on specific differences, i.e. by predicating attributes of a subject of judgement. No matter how many attributes we predicate of the subject, according to Nishida we never reach the individual, and this is all the more true for unique human individuals.

How can we logically describe the true individual? Nishida first stepped back from conventional subject–predicate logic and tried to show how every judgement arises within a field of consciousness, how every subject is conceptualized or objectified according to the structures of consciousness. This is basically a Kantian and Fichtean move, which for Nishida can grasp the subjects and objects of judgements and get at the universal consciousness conceptualizing them, but not at the individual, acting self. Logic can reach individuals neither by adding innumerable predicates to a subject nor by seeing them as constituted by some consciousness-in-general (Kant's *Bewußtsein überhaupt*) which must somehow relate to individual (self-)consciousness.

In his mature stage, from the 1930s on, Nishida proposes that what underlies the individual is neither a group of predicates describing and objectifying it, nor general consciousness as the field in which it appears, but rather – nothing. Absolute nothingness. This is not to say that the individual is nothing in the sense that there are no such things. On the contrary, individuals are self-determining in each moment of their action and interaction; they are the 'self-determinations of nothingness'. There is nothing underlying them; they are not 'grounded' anywhere, but take place in the absence of a principle of sufficient reason.

On the other hand, the world in which individuals take place must be a *dialectical* universal, and in two senses. It must be not static but developing, self-forming and self-realizing (*jikaku-teki*) in interaction with and among individuals. And in its concrete reality, it must form identities that sustain, not sublate, contradictories. It itself is an 'absolutely contradictory self-identity', for it is a unity of individuals that remain absolutely different from one another. The individual likewise is such a self-identity and 'continuity of discontinuities' continually negating itself in interaction with others. But if the individuals that are the foci of the world's self-realization are without ground, then absolute nothingness must underlie the world too. The 'place' in which individuals and world take place is absolute nothingness.

Nishida's logic of place reveals influences from Hegel's notion of the whole as concrete universal and his view of logic, unlike formal logic, as inseparable from the content of experience. It also draws upon the Mahāyāna Buddhist notion of emptiness (*śūnyatā*) and logic of negation. But for Nishida, as for Kierkegaard, Hegel's universal subsumed the individual into something higher; and Buddhism as well as traditional Japanese thought lacked a full account of the individual. One of Nishida's major accomplishments, therefore, was an alternative metaphysic of individual selfhood that, uninformed by the twentieth-century 'linguistic turn' as it was, critically expanded insights both Western and Eastern.

In his last completed essay, 'The logic of place and a religious worldview' (1945), Nishida rephrases the contradictory self-identity of individuals and world in terms of an 'inverse correspondence' or 'contra-respondence' (*gyaku taiō*) between the Absolute (God) and the self. To face the Absolute is to die to oneself, and the realization of one's own death is the source of religious awareness. The Absolute for Nishida is of course not a God who is the ground of the world, nor is facing it anything like destruction before the dazzling countenance of Yahveh. As the absolute One it 'exists' through self-negation that allows for a plurality of individuals. Nevertheless its exact relation to absolute nothingness as conceived earlier, and the relation among individuals each related to the Absolute in an unmediated way, remained unresolved problems.

Tanabe Hajime (1885–1962), Nishida's younger colleague at Kyoto University, had criticized him for ignoring the historical and social dimension of human existence and seeing the individual self in a 'mystical' way as the unmediated self-realizing determination of absolute nothingness. Starting about 1934, Tanabe developed a 'logic of species' or social-cultural specificity that placed social entities between the individual and the genus or universal.[20] Tanabe thus emphasized more than Nishida had the social and historical conditioning of humans. The nation state had a special status: it was a kind of universal that could mediate conflict between the individual and the species. At least when it was successful at such mediation, the state embodied rationality, morality, law and social justice, and was the ultimate subject of history. In the development of his 'logic of historical reality' and 'logic of national existence', Tanabe hesitated simply to identify the nation state with the Absolute. Instead, by applying Mahāyāna Buddhist logic, he proposed that it was a particular manifestation of the formless Absolute, in theory not superior to any other state. In fact, however, in the early 1940s Tanabe affirmed the uniqueness and universal character of the Japanese nation state, unified by the emperor. It is a matter of controversy whether or not his final attempt, in 1947, 'The dialectic of the logic of species', counters the politically absolutist tendency of the former articles by positing 'absolute nothingness' as the basis of the nation state. In any case, by 1944, Tanabe experienced a change of heart (metanoia) and recognized his confusion of the ideal state with Japanese imperialism.

In his consummate work *Philosophy as Metanoetics* (1946), Tanabe sought to overcome the irrationality of history, which in his personal case meant the inability to act effectively against war, by an enjoinder to repentance. Metanoia or repentance (*zange*) calls not for regret over the past, but the surrender and death of the wilfully acting self. The ensuing renewal or 'resurrection' of the self cannot be willed but must be bestowed by an 'absolute Other-power'. This is an obvious allusion to Pure Land Buddhist faith, but Tanabe deflects any personalistic, devotional interpretation of Amida Buddha when he calls Other-power 'absolute nothingness'. The terminology in common with Nishida likewise discourages any equivalence when Tanabe insists that absolute nothingness must function as an absolute Other and thus as absolute mediation.

The difference between Nishida and Tanabe may be formulated in terms of the logic of relations. Nishida's logic of place allows members of a relationship, such as the relative and the absolute, the individual and the universal, or I and thou, to be mutually and freely self-determining, since they are immediately 'grounded' in absolute nothingness, the ultimate place. Nishida's mature logic repeats here his early conviction that pure experience allows an unmediated connection with the Absolute. Tanabe's logic, on the other hand, suggests that a relationship exists only in mediation with other relationships; its members are not simply mutually determining, but the relationship between them is determined by other relationships. The continual insertion of something in between every relation entails an absolute disruption of every attempt to grasp the whole logically. It would seem that for Tanabe, contradiction so infuses the actual world that one cannot possibly speak of its self-realizing (*jikaku-teki*) self-determination. In the end, it appears that this limit to logic also disrupted Tanabe's lifelong project to lay a foundation common to personal life and the objective realm of science.

THE PROBLEM OF SCIENCE AND RELIGION, THE OBJECTIVE AND THE PERSONAL

The attempt to reconcile the personal and the scientific that originated the philosophies of Nishida and Tanabe began in Nishi Amane's differentiation between subjective and objective, and is prefigured even in the late Tokugawa-era motto, 'Western technology, Eastern morality'. But before the original philosophies could arise, there needed to emerge a clearer sense of person and subjectivity, and of the epistemological problem of justifying objective knowledge. The attempt to grapple with such issues serves to demarcate the introduction and mere imitation of philosophy in Japan from its actual practice. The first philosophies introduced to Japan by Nishi, positivism and utilitarianism, had evolved in the West in response to a long history of metaphysics and epistemology; but in Japan philosophers practised the latter after they had embraced and then lost interest in the former.

The manner in which Nishi introduced positivism is indicative of how and why many philosophical currents found their way into Japan. Since it was Holland to which the shogunal government sent Nishi, he was bound to become familiar with the positivist rejection of metaphysics and the utilitarian economics that were championed by his teachers there, C. W. Opzoomer and S. Vissering. Had Nishi studied in Göttingen, with H. Lotze, for example, instead of Leiden, his understanding of philosophy would have been different. Still, Auguste Comte's system of positivism, which replaced the constructs of theology and metaphysics with empirical facts, and J. S. Mill's inductive logic and utilitarian ethics nurtured Nishi's enchantment with scientific progress and concern to technologically develop and commercially expand Japan. Nishi had long before shifted his interest from the orthodox Chu Hsi [Zhu Xi] school, which he considered excessively speculative, to the (Ogyū) Sorai school and the 'practical studies' (*jitsugaku*) embraced by advocates of opening the country and adopting Western technology. His personal interests reflected those of leaders who were to prevail in governing Japan, so that historical circumstances conjoined with philosophical dispositions in bringing to Japan positivism before German epistemology and idealism.

A positivistic attitude oblivious to epistemological issues suited many other leading figures of the Japanese enlightenment (*keimō*) and 'Meiji Six Society' (*Meiroku sha*) in the 1870s. The status of religion *vis-à-vis* public or objective knowledge in this development serves as a leitmotif in discerning an abiding problem. Most of these enlighteners were critical of institutional forms of religion, both their native Buddhism and foreign Christianity, as being authoritarian and antiquated, but tolerant enough to advocate separation of church and state and allow religion to function as a private preference. In this respect their notion of religion, for which they resurrected the term *shūkyō*, was the product of a secularized world. As enlighteners, they promoted a thoroughly rational understanding of the universe and human society. But unlike their European role-models, they had little appreciation of the problem of the epistemological basis of scientific, ethical and religious claims.

Fukuzawa Yukichi (1834–1901), in his *Outline of a Theory of Civilization* (1874), distinguished between public and private and between knowledge and virtue; but in a style more Confucian than he would like to admit, continued to name knowledge and virtue together and did not discuss the problem of justifying public virtue or public knowledge. Using another distinction from his *Encouragement of Learning* (1872), he wrote of the 'knowledge and virtue of the formless' (*mukei no chidoku*), i.e. of abstract and immaterial things as opposed to the (applied) sciences of the material (*yūkei no gakumon*); but this knowledge seems more a matter of self-cultivation than truth supported by adequate evidence or reasons. Similarly, Nishi's articles on *chishiki* (knowledge) in the journal *Meiroku zasshi* of 1874 reflect more the 'deductive', Confucian-style classification he had criticized than the scientific method he purported to explain. Nishi understood science as the inductive investigation of truth based on 'observation, experience and proof',[21] yet his own lectures were often dogmatic renditions of Comte's *Cours de philosophie positive*.

Katō Hiroyuki, who introduced modern notions of natural rights and social evolution before he advocated the supremacy of the state, remained throughout closer to scientism than critical enquiry when it came to metaphysics and religion. Philosophy should remain free of the supposed supernatural (= religion) and organize the true sciences that investigate the laws of nature. He was familiar with a work by Draper called *History of the Conflict between Religion and Science*,[22] yet was himself not interested in resolving that conflict.

To be sure, religion was a philosophical concern for early writers, but more as a problem of its autonomy than its epistemological justification. Nishi's articles on religion[23] defined it in terms of personal faith and relegated it to the private sphere deserving of a qualified political autonomy. Buddhist thinkers such as Inoue Enryō and Kiyozawa Manshi (1863–1903) wrote tracts on the philosophy of religion defending its independent nature.[24] From the 1920s on, Hatano Seiichi (1877–1950) continued this work by focusing on religious experience. He first attacked positivistic reductions of religion[25] and later argued that, though accessible to rational understanding and consisting of various types, religion is based upon an autonomous form of experience.[26]

By far the most influential philosophy of religion emerged from the 'Kyoto school', which counts Nishida and Tanabe as its founders. Nishida did not so much privilege religious experience as see a religious dimension to all experience, but the most significant difference from Hatano and earlier philosophers of religion was his acute epistemological awareness. This consciousness is discernible even in his maiden work, *An Enquiry into the Good* (1911), in which science is not an explicit topic. There Nishida defines the core of religion as the relation between human beings and God, where God functions not as a transcendent creator but as the unifying activity within oneself and without, in nature. The self experiences a 'religious demand' or need for a unity greater than that of individual life, and this unity is foreshadowed in immediate or 'pure experience', which precedes differentiations into experiencing subject and experienced object, spirit and matter. Pure experience is thus prior to the emergence of the individual self as well as of the objective world, and as such can be regarded as the sole (or seed) reality. This work, then, attempts to unify the subjective and the objective experiences of reality and, by implication, the personal and the scientific, in a prior experience that drives the demand for ever increasing unities.

Nishida's subsequent essays and especially his next major work, *Intuition and Reflection in Self-Consciousness* (1917), grapple with epistemological questions raised by his encounter with the works of Bergson and the Neo-Kantians. They relate immediate experience to the constitution of all knowledge, and root the variously constituted worlds of religion and art, morality, history, psychology, biology and physics all in the *a priori* of experiential unity. Seen from today's perspective, one should read these and later works up to Nishida's awakening to historical consciousness in 1931 as metaphysical attempts to account for and unify levels of knowledge, not as discussions of the justification of scientific truth-claims. Many of them were written in cross-fertilization with Tanabe's early efforts to unite the personal and the objective, philosophy and science, in an intuitive grasp of unity.[27]

Tanabe's turn to Hegel's dialectics about 1927 led to his critique of Nishida and to his own logic of species. Along with Marxist critiques, Tanabe's criticisms provoked Nishida's interest in the social, historical world mentioned above, but left the two philosophers alienated. Tanabe's efforts culminated in his metanoetic philosophy, in which truly philosophical problems were at the same time deeply personal ones. An abiding task of philosophy for him was the mediation of science and religion, two cultural phenomena which have grown independent and seemingly incompatible, but which can be viewed from the philosophical standpoint that considers things in their unity, holistically.[28] He continued to write on the philosophy of science, particularly the problem of historicism in mathematics and the natural sciences.[29] Nishida's attempts ended in a view that placed religion outside the grasp of philosophy and in the heart of the individual, who necessarily confronts death.[30] His late essays totally individualize religion and imply that religious experience is autonomous, but articulate no place for an independent, objective realm of science.

In recent years Nishida's viewpoint has been articulated and expanded by Ueda Shizuteru (1926–), a scholar of Meister Eckhart and mysticism, who has lectured widely in Germany and Switzerland. Together with Abe Masao (1915–), another third-generation Kyoto-school philosopher well known in North America, Ueda places the paradigm of religious experience in Zen.[31] It was Nishida's own student, Nishitani Keiji, however, who most radicalized the problem of the relation between science and religion.

NISHITANI KEIJI'S PHILOSOPHY OF RELIGION

'The problem of religion and science is the most fundamental problem facing contemporary man', Nishitani writes in his consummate work *What is Religion?* (1961).[32] Earlier works had specified the limits to Western philosophical attempts to resolve the problem. Empiricism and materialism cannot deal with the most pressing existential issues such as the meaning of life and death, and existentialism for its part deals with human subjectivity but not with the objectivity of nature, human society and history. Nishitani understood Nishida's philosophy up to 1935 as an attempt to come to terms with both the subjective and the objective.[33] Nishitani also wrote numerous essays on the relation between religion and society and politics;[34] but it was the problem of nihilism that most commanded his attention. The loss in modern (Western) history of a teleological worldview and internally ordered universe that culminates in the human person[35] left human endeavours to resolve religious issues in a state of disruption. Nishitani had personally experienced disruption and ensuing despair early in his own life.[36] His project became one of locating religion in a technological world that has dislodged religious solutions and even repressed religious questions.

What is Religion? argues that the mechanization of man occurs when humans act as if they stood outside the laws of nature in their attempt to master nature. In an ineluctable reversal they become even more subject. Yet Nishitani's analysis does not repeat Heidegger's pessimism regarding the technological thinking that seeks to know the causes of things in order to transform them for human use; nor does it simply avow the Eastern view of transforming the self or Nishida's 'acting at one with things', 'knowing something by becoming it.' Rather Nishitani suggests that, as beings both spiritual and physical, humans realize the laws of nature both intellectually and bodily, by embodying them in their own movements or in the making of machines. In the modern age especially, humans are thrown into an unaware nihilism when they act as desire-driven subjects, standing outside the world of causation, thinking that they are autonomous but in reality having no ground at all beneath them. The aware nihilism of Nietzsche and the existentialists, who propose that we stand steadfast on *nihilum* and affirm living in the midst of meaninglessness, is not an adequate solution. Nishitani radicalizes the problem by proclaiming that the self, the world and all things are indeed empty of autonomous being, but that by awakening to this very emptiness and interdependence we realize our freedom and utter uniqueness. This solution is explicitly a Buddhist one, but Nishitani refines the classical Mahāyāna philosophy of emptiness (*śūnyatā*) here by relating it to technology and to history. His recourse to 'emptiness' is an implicit critique of Nishida's 'absolute nothingness', in which lurks the danger of nihilism again: nothing underlying subject and substance, reason bankrupt, and no way to connect the objectivity of science with the personal dimension of religion. The 'field of emptiness' embraces the impersonal aspects of self, God and world that allow for objectivity, as well as the personal foundations of science in human conviction.

SOME MARXIST ANSWERS TO THE INCOMPATIBILITY OF RELIGION AND SCIENCE

Kawakami Hajime (1879–1946), a professor of economics at Kyoto Imperial University who introduced Marxist theory, became an even more indefatigable proponent of Marxism after his resignation in 1928 and prison sentence in 1933. But throughout his career he was also an advocate of a place for religion in life. The compatibility of materialism and religion was clear enough for him, but a source of constant perplexity and criticism for other Marxists. 'I am a materialist,' Kawakami wrote, explaining that 'sensation, consciousness and thought are only functions of organic matter.' But religion and science both have their legitimate spheres of knowledge. Religious truth is distinct from scientific truth because it arises from knowledge of our internal consciousness, the mind reflecting upon itself as in Zen meditation, and concerns the problem of the self and the meaning of personal life, not the nature of the social and material world. True religion is compatible with materialism because the mind it can know is only a function of matter. It is when religious leaders pretend to be able to solve social problems that religious institutions become corrupt. '[E]ven though one has studied Zen deeply, there is no reason to believe that one understands the theory of capital.'[37]

Miki Kiyoshi (1897–1945), the first philosopher to develop a Marxist existential humanism, revived his interest in the problem of religious truth at the end of his life in an incomplete essay on Shinran, the medieval founder of the True Pure Land sect of Buddhism. Religious truth, Miki argued, differs in character and dimension from scientific and philosophical truth, but like all truth must be based on objectivity.[38] The essence of religious experience, however, is interiority, and as such is subjective and psychological. Religion therefore transcends the subjective by basing itself on scriptures, the words of those like the Buddha whose self-confirmation of the truth is taken as a model. But since those models are historical and contingent, their objectivity and transcendence are problematic. They acquire an *a priori*, transcendental universality in something like the Original Vow of Amida. Miki's dialectical interpretation of Pure Land thought concludes with the qualification that religious truth must not transcend the world to rest on its own validity, but must function in actual life. By this he seems to mean the problem and salvation of the self as it is universalized in 'all sentient beings'. If the proper place of religion in the social world remains ambiguous here, Miki's rejection of personal experience as the basis of religion is unmistakable.

The position of another Marxist critic of the Kyoto school, Tosaka Jun (1900–45), is clearer. A student of Nishida, he was trained in phenomenology and Neo-Kantianism but soon turned to historical materialism. Although he was in prison while Nishida wrote his last essays on religion, he would most likely have upheld his 1931 critique of the 'bourgeois idealism' of Nishida's philosophy.[39] His materialist interpretation of 'scientific method', *Kagaku hōhōron*, in 1929, and his attack on the fascist tendency of 'Japanese ideology', *Nihon ideorogi ron*, in 1935, were implicit rejections of the relevance of personal religious experience.

ETHICS AND THE PROBLEM OF INDIVIDUALISM

Nishitani has suggested that it was a growing sense of inner self-awareness and doubt about the ordinary perspectives on life and the world that motivated the shift from positivism and utilitarianism to German philosophy in the mid-Meiji era.[40] From a contemporary perspective it seems remarkable that a strong sense of personal individuality may have been as novel to the Japanese as the discipline of philosophy.[41] It sounds slightly incredible, for example, that the future novelist Shimazaki Tōson should discover his self, 'something of which [I] had been unaware up to that time', in reading Rousseau's *Confessions* in 1892.[42] Tōson and novelists like Kitamura Tōkoku and Tayama Katai wrote in a unprecedented personal and confessional style that soon developed into the so-called *shi-shōsetsu* or 'I-novel' written from a first-person point of view.[43] In philosophy this development was manifested in Abe Jirō's (1883–1959) *Diary of Santarō* (1914), a kind of philosophical journal written in a genre that reflects the importance of the self as individual. This book was a best seller that remained far more influential than Abe's more critical works on Nietzsche's *Zarathustra* in 1919 and *Jinkaku shugi* (*Personalism*) in 1920.

Watsuji Testsurō (1889–1969) had turned the attention of his contemporaries to Nietzsche in 1915 and, two years earlier, to the radical individualism of Kierkegaard, in works named after these two thinkers. Watsuji's most lasting contributions came much later in the area of ethics and earned him a reputation equal to that of Nishida and Tanabe. Watsuji's philosophy may be understood as a response to the dual problems of individualism and the loss of traditional values, both initiated by Japan's encounter with the West. Watsuji's recovery of traditions and overcoming of individualism occurred, however, in a philosophy that was thoroughly inspired by his reading of Western philosophers and his personal experience in Europe. He pursued the first task in several works of intellectual history, ranging from *Guzō saikō* (*Revival of Idols*) in 1918, to *Genshi kiristokyō no bunkashiteki igi* (*The Cultural-historical Significance of Primitive Christianity*) in 1926, *Genshi bukkyō no jissen tetsugaku* (*The Practical Philosophy of Primitive Buddhism*) in 1927, and *Nihon seishin-shi kenkyū* (*Studies in the History of the Japanese Spirit*) in 1926 and 1934, and culminating in a two-volume work, *Nihon rinri shisō-shi* (*A History of Japanese Ethical Thought*) in 1954.

Watsuji's properly philosophical works regard ethics not as one branch of philosophy among others but as its very core, since human relations are the most important philosophical concern and ethics clarifies precisely the 'existential fundamentals of the condition common to human beings.'[44] The work in which Watsuji gives this definition, *Ethics as the Study of Human Being* (1934), begins with a hermeneutical analysis of the relevant Japanese terms that plays upon the connotations of the ideographs and defies exact translation: *rin-ri* (ethics, the reason underlying companionship), *nin-gen* (human being, the specific interrelation in and as which we exist), *sekken* (society or the world) and *son-zai* (existence, temporal preservation and spatial location). It continues with a critique of the ethical presuppositions of Aristotle, Kant, Hermann Cohen, Hegel, Feuerbach and Marx, and ends with an enquiry into the method of ethics that reflects Heidegger's analysis of the questioning of being in *Sein und Zeit*. In this and subsequent works, Watsuji seeks to overcome the subjective sense of ought inherent in modern Western ethics by drawing upon Eastern traditions, particularly the Confucian five relations and Buddhist self-negation. The absolute negation of the subject that forms the basis of moral laws in Watsuji's ethics lent itself to a rationalization of submission to the trans-individual nation, a position that Watsuji rescinded in the post-war period. His plays upon words and his concern to define the unique contribution of Japanese tradition are a transmutation of Heidegger's puns and proclamations of the superiority of Greek and German philosophy. But Watsuji must also be regarded as an original thinker and critic of Heidegger and traditional Japanese thought.

For Watsuji the human being is not an enclosed subject-self but a transcending self that exists by relating to that which is beyond itself. Following the convention of phenomenology, Watsuji used the term 'intentionality' to designate the structure of consciousness that always exceeds its interior and directs itself towards something. But he was critical of the emphasis in phenomenology, especially in Heidegger, on human temporality to the near exclusion of spatiality. An appreciation of spatial existence formed the basis of Watsuji's *Fūdo*, a study of the effects of environment on culture, conceived during his sojourn in Europe in 1927 and published in 1935. Philosophically more cogent than this work's rather idealized generalizations about monsoon, desert and pastoral cultures, and about the uniqueness of Japan, is Watsuji's insight into the ways human nature is rooted in and particularized by various environments. Spatiality as well as temporality underlies intentionality and the bestowal of meaning upon the world, and, contra Heidegger's individualistic *Dasein*, makes human existence fundamentally relational. 'Human being' in Japanese is *ningen*, where *nin* translates roughly as 'person' or 'people', and *gen*, also read *aida*, as 'the space in between'. The basic structure of being human is thus the 'we', the 'betweenness' or relationality (*aida gara*), of experience. Watsuji's works on ethics developed the inchoate ideas of *Fūdo* that emphasized not only man-in-relation but also the spatial foundation of that relation as a form of intentionality. In this sense his philosophy proceeds from a critique of a lack not only in Heidegger but also in traditional Confucian and Buddhist thought.

Although not directly concerned with ethical issues, the main works of Kuki Shūzō (1888–1941) can be read as meditations on the problem of individual life. *Iki no kōzō* (*The Structure of Iki*), first published in 1930, has become a classic if idiosyncratic work employing nearly untranslatable terminology to interpret an allegedly unique Japanese aesthetic value as a way of being. The focus on the concrete conditions of human existence and sense of the transience of life[45] received theoretical foundation in *Gūzen no mondai* (*The Problem of Contingency*), published in 1935.[46] This work derived types of contingency from the profound individuality of people and things that resists conceptualization as subsumption under general concepts, and frustrates logic as the necessary relation between reasons and conclusion. The 'possible nothingness' of individuals is disjunctive of any natural unity and disruptive of necessary relations between things; it accounts for the transience of human encounters or even the possibility of non-encounter, but for Kuki it also supports the imperative to act in such a manner that an encounter is not in vain.[47]

The concerns of Miki Kiyoshi, who studied with Heidegger and in Paris a few years before Kuki, overlapped the problems of ethics and individuality, the objective and the personal, logic and history. He eventually helped introduce Marxist thought and preceded Sartre in developing a Marxist existential humanism, but set his philosophical agenda in an early work on *The Study of Man in Pascal* in 1926. The concern there is the relativity and finitude of human existence. In the preface Miki describes his method of interpreting Pascal as a clarification of the experiences underlying concepts and of the concepts involved in experiences.[48] An implicit affirmation of the hermeneutical position opposed to any notion of 'pure experience', this work nevertheless posited a 'fundamental experience' (*Kisō keiken*) that reconciles the irrational and rationality, pathos and logos. Philosophical anthropology counts as the primary articulation of fundamental experience; ideology is a secondary form of discourse.

Miki's *Historical Materialism and Modern Consciousness*, published two years later, reflects the same method, but discovers in the particular anthropology and fundamental experience of the proletariat that underlie Marxism an invaluable recognition of the historicity of human existence and the centrality of praxis. *The Philosophy of History*, published in 1932, distinguishes three levels of history. Actual events constitute history as being (*sonzai*); and the narrative description of events is history as logos or discourse. Fundamental to both is history as fact (*jijitsu*, which Miki uses to translate the German *tatsache*), a dimension that is exhausted neither by objective being or event nor by subjective discourse. 'What enables the subjective to become objective being is the presupposition of subjectivity as fact.'[49] This facticity is the fundamental experience that gives rise to what ordinarily count as history and historiography. The seeming repetition of Heidegger's sense of historicity (*geschichtlichkeit*) here receives a critical Marxist twist when Miki emphasizes that human actions create new discourses that underlie ideologies. This theme is developed further in *Kōsōryoku no ronri* (*The Logic of the Imagination [Einbildungskraft]*), 1937–9, a systematic if incomplete work that explores forms of discourse such as myth and science and of practices such as institutionalization and technology. Technology in particular unites the objective knowledge of science and subjective human purpose. And since humans exist as bodies, human experience is not foremost a phenomenon of consciousness but occurs as embodied action in the objective world.

The interpretation of human being as an alternative to subjectivist ethics and radical individualism thus took different forms in Watsuji and Miki. Both adopted the global notion of *ningen*, but Watsuji focused on the rationality of human existence and ultimately gave the notion of the human a uniquely Japanese reading. Miki stressed the historicity and praxis of human beings and did not seek any ethnocentric privileging of the Japanese position. This difference is reflected in the events that befell them during the war period. Watsuji's philosophy was easily pre-empted by militarists, whereas Miki fell victim to police oppression and died in prison. To relegate these consequences to 'historical circumstance' would be to ignore the profound difference in their ethical philosophies.

ISSUES OF GLOBALISM, NATIONALISM AND JAPANISM

The nationalism of many significant philosophers like Nishida, Tanabe and Watsuji during the Pacific War is a perplexing issue precisely because our standpoint of judgement today is far removed from the constraints of a repressive regime. Some philosophers and critics like Kihira Tadayoshi (1874–1949) and Minoda Muneki (1894–1946), for example, were much more blatantly unconditional supporters of the 'national political essence' (*kokutai*) and military expansionism than others. The question of how to read nationalistic and jingoistic tracts is especially crucial in the case of philosophers related to the Kyoto school.[50] Again, some writings of these philosophers are more clearly political in nature than others. A symposium on 'The world historical standpoint and Japan' in which Kōsaka Masaaki (1900–69), Nishitani

Keiji, Kōyama Iwao (1905–93) and Suzuki Shigetaka (1907–88) participated,[51] for example, obviously treats the current political situation of Japan, whereas the language in their teacher Nishida's treatises on the state and Japanese culture is generally more abstract.[52] Some scholars have argued that such tracts must be read as camouflaged metaphysical critiques of narrow-minded government policies;[53] others read the purported philosophy of world history as a 'thinly disguised justification for Japanese aggression and continuing imperialism.'[54] What is indisputable is that these figures understood themselves as global thinkers, counteracting the Western domination of the world, whether military or cultural, and defending a special place for Japanese culture in world history. They were generally supporters of the emperor system and saw it as the unifying centre of Japan in the long history of that often decentralized country.

Related to the issue of political globalism and nationalism is the effort to determine the specificity of Japanese values. It would take several pages merely to list all the books on the 'Japanese spirit' (*nihon seishin*) and the so-called *nihonjin-ron* or treatises that purport the uniqueness of the Japanese. Philosophically significant, however, are works by two advocates of the centrality of Zen. Nishida's friend from high-school days, D. T. Suzuki (1870–1966), wrote *Zen and Japanese Culture* in 1938, a popular book among his Western readers, and *Nihonteki reisei* (*Japanese Spirituality*) in 1944. The latter work takes pains to distinguish *reisei* (spirituality) from *seishin* (spirit), but barely hints at the nationalist connotation that *seishin* had in the pre-war period. *Reisei*, for Suzuki, is quintessentially the non-discriminating wisdom of Mahāyāna Buddhism.[55] Nishida's student Hisamatsu Shinichi (1889–1980) wrote *Oriental Nothingness* in 1939, claiming in a historically oversimplified manner that the 'absolute nothingness' of the East, i.e. of Buddhist thought, is fundamentally different from and deeper than Western conceptions of nothingness opposed to being. Concerning the question of Japanism in general, Ueyama Shumpei (1921–) published a widely read, critical assessment, *Nihon no dochaku shisō* (*The Indigenous Thought of Japan*) in 1965, and today Umehara Takeshi (1929–) continues explorations in this vein.

The study of the human (*ningengaku*) also continued in the post-war period and through the 1960s. Mutai Risaku (1890–1974), a student of Nishida who developed his own philosophy, wrote of a new or 'third humanism' and even an 'anthro-humanism' (*ningen hūmanisumu*) that centred on the 'holistic man' (*zentaiteki ningen*). Miyake Gōichi's (1895–1952) anthro-ontology (*ningen sonzairon*) was published in 1966. Unlike Kyoto-school figures, these philosophers did not draw upon Japanese tradition, but gave original interpretations to the imported Western concept of humanism to demonstrate that the Japanese could also be global thinkers.

An oblique critique of the very possibility of a philosophy of man (*ningen ron*) is found in recent representatives of deconstruction and post-structuralism. The works of Nakamura Yūjirō (1925–) and Asada Akira (1957–), among others, have given philosophical definition and dispersion to the waves of post-structuralism and post-modernism that have inundated the not so post-modern print media in Japan. Nakamura has, for example, applied deconstruction to Nishida's philosophy, uncovering its unsystematic nature and discovering in it latent foils of the feminine and other configurations of alterity.[56] The theme of counter-reason was explored earlier in his *Knowledge of Pathos*[57] and *Theory of Sensus Communis*.[58] Nakamura's critique is implicitly directed not only at the rationalizing done in the name of an oriental reason or logic, but also at the very construction of a monolithic Japanese self and tradition. This interest is shared by the economic anti-theorist Asada, whose *Structure and Power: Beyond Semiotics* and other books[59] have been influential in advancing post-structuralist critiques of culture. Present controversy over the meanings of the post-modern and modernity, and whether these categories apply to Japan, indicates that critics can accord Japan a historical specificity (even if on the basis of its traditional lack of historical consciousness) without claiming some essential uniqueness for it.[60]

OTHER CONTEMPORARY ISSUES: PHILOSOPHY OF LANGUAGE, THE MIND–BODY PROBLEM, APPLIED ETHICS AND THE 'END OF PHILOSOPHY'

It will be evident from the foregoing survey that the influence of Anglo-American analytic philosophy has lagged behind the impact of European thinking on modern Japanese philosophy. Pioneering works in the late 1950s and early 1960s, such as Nagai Shigeo's *Analytic Philosophy*,[61] Sugihara Masuo's *Study of Modal Logic*[62] and Yamamoto Ichirō's *Philosophy of Language*,[63] were followed in the 1970s by Ōmori Shōzo's (1921) *Language, Perception, World*[64] and Hiromatsu Wataru's (1933–) *Mono, koto, kotoba*,[65] a careful analysis of concepts, both Japanese and European, relating to things, matters and words. Sakabe Megumi has furthered the analysis of Japanese concepts *vis-à-vis* Western ones in *The Philosophy of 'Fureru'*[66] and *Mirror on the Japanese Language: The Various Phases of Conceptualization*.[67]

Classical metaphysical problems also continue to engage the minds of philosophers in Japan. Philosophical materialism as opposed to idealism was novel to Meiji-era Japanese, as were dualisms based upon a mechanistic view of the universe and a strict dichotomy between matter and spirit. Tsuda Mamichi (1829–1903), Nishi Amane's companion traveller to Holland, introduced materialist views of reality in 1895 in his *Yuibutsuron* (*Theory of Materialism*), and Inoue Enryō attacked such views three years later in *Ha yuibutsuron* (*Dismantling Materialism*). Nakae Chōmin and Katō Hiroyuki were avowed materialists at the turn of the century, although the defence of historical materialism had to wait for figures like Kawakami Hajime. Nishitani Keiji claims that the abiding philosophy of nothingness of the East bears no relation to materialism or idealism, since it posits reality neither as matter nor as mind, but allows for the oneness of things and mind in the utter nihility of their independent being.[68] But the novelty of Western materialism is most evident in the treatment of the mind–body problem in Japan.

The very terms in Japanese for 'mind–body problem' (*shin-shin mondai*) reveal the alien character of this issue. *Shin*, also pronounced *kokoro*, is written with an ideogram signifying 'heart' that is as polysemous as the English 'mind' but covers a quite different range of meanings. It has traditional connotations of centre, core, marrow, vitality and sincerity as well as feeling, mood and mind in the nominal sense and the verbal sense of attending to something. The second *shin* of the compound, also pronounced *mi* and *karada*, connotes not only body but one's person, self, social status and even ability, or, in verbal constructions, a sense of 'putting oneself into' some activity. It clearly implies more a sense of embodied subjectivity than the English 'body'. The *shin-shin* used today to signify 'mind–body' is another example of palaeonymy in modern Japanese philosophy, for this usage excavates and mutates the medieval Buddhist *shin-jin* that is written with the same ideographs. The problem of translation is not alleviated if one employs more traditional compounds such as *seishin* and *shintai* for spirit and body, or *reikon* and *nikutai* for soul and flesh, respectively, since these terms too have native connotations quite different from their counterparts in European languages.

Many contemporary philosophers in Japan, however, write as if the mind–body problem were a universal and more or less univocal legacy. At the same time, their reliance upon Western formulations of the problem implies a decision to reject pre-modern Japanese and Asian thought as not philosophical. Some works do make original contributions when measured either against contemporary Anglo-American and Continental treatises or against the treatment of traditionally Japanese perspectives. An example of the former is *The Mind–Body Problem*, by Ōmori Shōzo *et al.*,[69] which extends linguistic analyses of Western-derived concepts and problems such as that of the knowledge of other minds or the source of action in will. Hiromatsu Wataru's *The Mind–Body Problem*[70] is cognizant of developments in physiology and artificial intelligence, but problematizes the philosophy of mind from his own perspective. Hiromatsu links the problems of other minds and intersubjectivity, and views the issues of self and other in the light of social philosophy and the philosophy of history. Ichikawa Hiroshi's (1931–) *The Body as Spirit*[71] is a development of Merleau-Ponty's phenomenological analyses that differentiates levels of intentionality based upon the degree of difference between posited object and positing self; the intentionality of moods, for example, is much weaker than that of reflective thinking. Ichikawa posits a pre-reflective consciousness separating self and object that permits intentional acts to occur, and that is acquired through the living body and the various kinds of space in which it lives.

An example of the recovery of Japanese perspectives is Yuasa Yasuo's (1925–) *The Body: Towards an Eastern Mind–Body Theory*.[72] This work goes beyond presentations of the thought of the medieval Buddhist figures Kūkai and Dōgen, as well as contemporaries like Nishida, Watsuji, Bergson and Merleau-Ponty, to argue that body–mind unity is not a given fact, but a continual achievement of bodily practices like meditation that bring the self to its full consciousness. Ichikawa's *The Structure of Mi: Beyond the Theory of the Body*[73] is another of a dozen or so books that represent the interest in this field.

If the metaphysical relation of body and mind is an imported issue in modern Japanese thought, the practical meaning of the body is a traditional issue that has helped shape current problems in medical ethics. In particular, the definition of brain death and the ethics of organ transplants have received relatively more attention in Japan because of the traditional understanding of the body as a holistic phenomenon that is not necessarily dead as soon as the brain ceases to function. The traditional conception of humans bound up with nature has perhaps retarded an interest in the kind of environmental ethics that evaluates human dominance over nature, environmental pollution, consumption of resources and similar social problems. The technology introduced since the Meiji Restoration has forced a new conception of nature, disconnected from seasonal change and local resources, that has yet to be fully examined. Katō Hisatake's *Environmental Ethics*[74] exemplifies the few works that have begun the examination. Yet the significance of books and articles in the new field of applied ethics cannot be measured adequately by their relatively small number compared with Anglo-American work. The public discussion of social ethical issues is reviving the kind of debates that engaged Meiji 'enlighteners' (*keimōka*) or later Marxists and their opponents. This philosophical discussion encourages a more open style of decision-making and has the potential to change medical and political practice.

The 'end of philosophy' proclaimed by Heidegger and echoed in post-analytic philosophers such as Richard Rorty has received a response in such works as *What is Philosophy? Its History and its Possibility*, edited by Takeichi Akira and Tsunetoshi Sōzaburo.[75] With chapters on virtually all philosophical fields and problem areas, this anthology laments in its preface the present lack of real controversy among Japanese philosophers. (Ethical problems, theoretical or applied, are not among the issues represented in this work.) If there is such a lack, with the possible exception of ethical controversies, it is perhaps a dual sign of the state of good health of academic philosophy in Japan and of its chagrin at failing to engage post-industrial society at large. Perhaps contemporary Japanese philosophy is not at all unique in the challenges it faces.

NOTES

Research for part of this chapter was generously supported by a grant from the Social Science Research Council and the American Council of Learned Societies, with funds provided by the Japan–United States Friendship Commission, the Ford Foundation and the National Endowment for the Humanities.

1 Two very active areas of research by Japanese philosophers are not taken into consideration here: works about Western philosophers, and post-war articles in philosophical journals.
2 Thomas Havens, *Nishi Amane and Modern Japanese Thought* (Princeton: Princeton University Press, 1970), pp. 108–9.
3 'Ichi nen yū han' ('One year and a half left'), cited in Funayama Shinichi, 'Nihon no kindai tetsugaku no hatten keishiki', in Nishitani Keiji (ed.), *Nihon no tetsugaku* (*Japanese Philosophy*) (Kyoto: Yūkonsha, 1967), p. 66.
4 'Katsudōteki ichi genron to "zoku ichi nen yū han"' ('Dynamic monism and "One year and a half left, continued"'), cited in Funayama, op. cit., pp. 66–7.
5 'Shitsugi' ('Doubts'), cited in Funayama, op. cit., p. 67.
6 In 'Nishimura shi shitsugi no shitsugi' ('Doubts about Nishimura's doubts'), cited in Funayama, op. cit., p. 68.
7 The controversy continues today, in the form of institutions if not words; departments of 'pure philosophy' in Japanese universities restrict themselves to the study of Western philosophers, while it is uncertain whether professors in departments of 'Chinese philosophy' and 'Indian philosophy' should count as philosophers or as historian-philologists. Umehara Takeshi, former director of the recently founded International Research Centre for Japanese Studies (Nichibunken) in Kyoto, has said that it is prejudiced and imbecile not to consider traditional Japanese thought as philosophy. See Funayama, op. cit., p. 68.
8 From a letter to Mastuoka Rinjirō, 12 June 1862. Cited by Saito Sumie, 'Nishiyō tetsugaku no dōnyū to keimō no tetsugaku' ('The introduction of Western philosophy and the philosophy of the enlighteners'), in Miyakawa Tōru and Arakawa Ikuo, *Nihon kindai tetsugaku shi* (History of Modern Japanese Philosophy) (Tokyo: Yūhikaku, 1976), p. 19.
9 'Tetsugaku jii hensan no koto o ronji awasete – yo no gengo kairyōka ni tsugu', in *Meiji tetsugaku shisōshū, Meiji bungaku zenshū* 80 (Tokyo: Chikuma Shobō, 1974), p. 86.
10 *Tetsugaku ji-i*, also entitled in English *Dictionary of English, German, and French Philosophical Terms with Japanese Equivalents* (Tokyo: Maruzen, 1912), preface.
11 'Tetsugaku kenteki' ('Philosophical trifles'), in *Miyake Setsurei shū* (Tokyo: Chikuma Shobō, 1967), p. 151.
12 'Seisei hatsuun', in *Meiji tetsugaku shisōshū*, pp. 4–5.
13 'Jishiki roku' ('A record of self-knowledge', 1899), in *Meiji tetsugaku shisōshū*, p. 23.
14 'Tetsugaku isseki wa', in *Meiji tetsugaku shisōshū*, p. 43.
15 'Tetsugaku gairon' ('Introduction to philosophy'), in *Meiji tetsugaku shisōshū*, pp. 192–3.
16 'Nishida Sensei no jinkaku to shisō' ('Nishida's personality and thought'), in *Nishitani Keiji Chosakushū*, vol. IX (Tokyo: Sōbunsha, 1987), pp. 59–63. See *Nishida Kitaro*, trans. Yamamoto Seisaku and James W. Heisig (Berkeley: University of California Press, 1991), pp. 47–9.
17 'Ronri no rikai to sūri no rikai' ('Understanding in logic and mathematics', 1912), in *Nishida Kitarō Zenshū*, vol. I (Tokyo: Iwanami Shoten, 1974), p. 251.
18 A small part is translated in *Sources of Japanese Tradition*, vol. II, compiled by Ryusaku Tsunoda, William Theodore De Bary and Donald Keene (New York: Columbia University Press, 1958), pp. 350–65. A Spanish translation by Agustín Jacinto Zavala has been published in *Estado y Filosofía* (Zamora, Mich./Mexico: El Colegio de Michoacán, 1985); and a French translation by Pierre Lavelle as *La culture Japonaise en question* (Paris: Publications Orientalistes de France, 1991).
19. 'Watakushi no ronri ni tsuite' ('Concerning my logic'), in *Nishida Kitarō Zenshū*, vol. XII (Tokyo: Iwanami Shoten, 1974), p. 266.
20. The article 'Shakai sonzai no ronri' ('The logic of social being', 1934) introduces Tanabe's new logic; and vols VI and VII of *Tanabe Hajime Zenshū* (Tokyo: Chikuma Shobō, 1963)

contain six other early essays on the logic of species.

21 *Nishi Amane, Katō Hiroyuki*, *Nihon no meicho* 34 (Tokyo: Chūō Kōron, 1984), p. 207.

22 Cited in his 'Jinken shinsetsu' ('New theory of human rights', 1882), in *Nishi Amane, Katō Hiroyuki*, p. 412.

23 'Kyōmonron', in *Meiroku zasshi*, 1874; see *Nishi Amane, Katō Hiroyuki*, pp. 186–98.

24 Inoue Enryō, *Shūkyō shinron* (*New Theory of Religion*) (Tokyo: Tetsugaku Shoin, 1888); Kiyozawa Manshi, *Shūkyō tetsugaku gaikotsu* (*Skeleton of a Philosophy of Religion*) (1892).

25 Hatano Seiichi, *Shūkyō tetsugaku no honshitsu oyobi sono kompon mondai* (*The Essence of the Philosophy of Religion and its Fundamental Problems*), 1920.

26 Hatano Seiichi, *Shūkyō tetsugaku* (*Philosophy of Religion*), 1935; *Shūkyō tetsugaku jōron* (*Introduction to the Philosophy of Religion*), 1940; *Toki to Eien* (*Time and Eternity*), 1943.

27 Especially Tanabe's *Kagaku gairon* (*Outline of Science*), 1918 and *Sūri tetsugaku kenkyū* (*A Study of the Philosophy of Mathematics*), 1925.

28 'Tetsugaku nyūmon II: Kagaku tetsugaku ninshikiron' ('Introduction to philosophy II: philosophy of science and epistemology', 1950), in *Tanabe Hajime Zenshū*, vol. XI, especially pp. 300–2.

29 *Sūri no rekishishugi tenkai* (*Development of Historicism in Mathematics*), 1954.

30 'Basho no ronri to shūkyōteki sekaikan' ('The logic of place and a religious worldview'), *Nishida Kitarō Zenshū*, vol. XI (Tokyo: Iwanami Shoten 1965), pp. 371–465.

31 See especially Ueda Shizuteru, *Zen bukkyō* (Tokyo: Chikuma Shobō, 1973); and 'Zettai mu no shūkyō tetsugaku' ('Absolute nothingness and the philosophy of religion'), in S. Ueda and K. Yanagawa (eds) *Shūkyōgaku no susume* (*An Encouragement of the Study of Religion*) (Tokyo: Chikuma Shobō, 1985).

32 *Shūkyō to wa nanika*, (translated as *Religion and Nothingness*) in *Nishitani Keiji Chosakushū*, vol. X (Tokyo: Sōbunsha, 1987), p. 53.

33 'Nishida tetsugaku – tetsugakushi ni okeru sono ichi' ('The place of Nishida's thought in the history of philosophy'), in *Nishitani Keiji Chosakushū*, vol. IX, pp. 95–123; translated in *Nishida Kitarō*, pp. 65–92.

34 See the essays in vol. IV of *Nishitani Keiji Chosakushū* (Tokyo: Sōbunsha, 1987).

35 See his 1949 work *Nihilisumu* (*Nihilism*); the English translation, by Graham Parkes and Setsuko Aihara, is *The Self-Overcoming of Nihilism* (Albany: State University of New York Press, 1990).

36 Described in 'The days of my youth', *FAS Society Journal* (Kyoto) (Winter 1985–6), 25–30.

37 From 'Gokuchū zeigo' ('Prison ramblings'), translated in *Sources of Japanese Tradition*, vol. II, pp. 366–7.

38 'Shinran', in *Miki Kiyoshi Zenshū*, vol. XVIII (Tokyo: Iwanami Shoten, 1969), pp. 483ff.

39 'Kyōto gaku ha no tetsugaku' ('The philosophy of the Kyoto school'), in *Tosaka Jun Zenshū*, vol. III (Tokyo: Keisō Shobō, 1966), pp. 171–6.

40 'Waga shi Nishida Kitarō sensei wo kataru' ('Speaking of Nishida, my teacher'), in *Nishitani Keiji Chosakushū*, vol. IX, pp. 19–20; translated in *Nishida Kitarō*, pp. 7–8.

41 The thesis of the novelty of a strong sense of individuality is as controversial as that about the novelty of philosophy. Furukawa Tesshi, for example, traces the rise of individualism in early Meiji figures such as Fukuzawa Yukichi and Uchimura Kanzō (1861–1930), the founder of 'non-church' Christianity, to the tradition of *bushidō*. See his article 'The individual in Japanese ethics', in Charles A. Moore (ed.), *The Japanese Mind* (Honolulu: University Press of Hawaii, 1967), p. 237.

42 'Rūsoo no Zange chū ni miidashitaru jiko' ('The self that I discovered in Rousseau's *Confessions*'), in *Tōson Zenshū*, vol. VI (Tokyo: Chikuma Shobō, 1967), p. 10.

43 There is controversy also over whether these 'novels' expressed or veiled the author's individuality, and whether they translated a Western genre or developed previous Japanese genres. For the former positions see Janet Walker, *The Japanese Novel of the Meiji Period and the Ideal of Individualism.* (Princeton: Princeton University Press, 1979); for the latter, see Edward Fowler, *The Rhetoric of Confession: Shishōsetsu in Early Twentieth-Century Japanese Fiction* (Berkeley: University of California Press, 1988). Walker notes, contrary to Nishitani's thesis, the influence of J. S. Mill's individualism and his theory of liberty on the formation of Japanese individualism (*kojinshugi*).

44 *Ningen no gaku to shite no rinrigaku* (Tokyo: Iwanami Zensho, 1984), p. 41. This work was expanded in Watsuji's three-volume *Rinrigaku* (*Ethics*); the volumes were published respectively in 1937, 1942 and 1949.

45 See also Kuki's essays 'Considerations on time' and '*Propos* on Japan', translated from the French by Stephen Light, in *Shūzō Kuki and Jean-Paul Sartre* (Carbondale, Ill.: Southern Illinois University Press, 1987). Kuki is credited with introducing the thought of Heidegger to his French tutor, Sartre.

46 This work has been translated into French by Omodaka Hisayuki as *Le Problème de la contingence* (Tokyo: Tokyo University Press, 1966).

47 I am grateful to Professor Sakabe Megumi for the analysis of Kuki's philosophy of contingency.

48 *Miki Kiyoshi Zenshū*, vol. I (Tokyo: Iwanami Shoten, 1966), p. 5.

49 *Rekishi tetsugaku*, in *Miki Kiyoshi Zenshū*, vol. VI (Tokyo: Iwanami Shoten, 1967), p. 28.

50 See the essays in James W. Heisig and John C. Maraldo (eds) *Rude Awakenings: Zen, the Kyoto School and the Question of Nationalism* (Honolulu: University of Hawaii Press, 1995).

51 *Sekaishiteki tachiba to Nippon*, published as a special issue of the journal *Chūō kōron* in 1943. The symposium participants view the ethics of war in the light of a war of different ethics; see pp. 214–19, and Horio Tsutomu, 'The *Chūōkōron* discussions, their background and meaning', in Heisig and Maraldo, op. cit., pp. 289–315; and John C. Maraldo, 'Questioning nationalism now and then', in Heisig and Maraldo, op. cit., especially pp. 351–6.

52 Nishida complained that his essay 'Kokutai', written in May 1943 at the behest of the Institute for National Policy, was excerpted out of context, simplified and distorted by Prime Minister Tōjō; the essay is in *Nishida Kitarō Zenshū*, vol XII (Tokyo: Iwanami Shoten, 1966), pp. 397–426; the complaint is in a letter to Watsuji, in vol. XIX (Tokyo: Iwanami, 1966), p. 245. For the essay on Japanese culture, see n. 16. An example of Tanabe's nationalism is his book *Kokkateki sonzai no ronri* (*The Logic of National Existence*), 1939.

53 For a study that mitigates Watsuji's position, see William LaFleur, 'Reasons for the rubble', in *Sengo nihon no seishinshi* (*A Postwar History of the Japanese Ethos*) (Tokyo: Iwanami Shoten, 1988). For a review of critical assessments of Tanabe see James W. Heisig, 'Tanabe's logic of the specific and the spirit of nationalism', in Heisig and Maraldo, op. cit., pp. 255–88. Karatani Kōjin offers a general critical assessment in *'Sentzen' no shisō* (*'Prewar' thoughts*), Tokyo: Shunjūsha, 1994.

54 With respect to 'The world historical standpoint and Japan', this is the verdict of Tetsuo Najita and H. D. Harootunian, 'Japanese revolt against the West: political and cultural criticism in the twentieth century', in Peter Duus (ed.) *The Cambridge History of Japan*, vol. VI (Cambridge: Cambridge University Press, 1988), p. 741.

55 *Nihonteki reisei*, Iwanami bunko edn (Tokyo, 1972), p. 17.

56 Nakamura Yūjirō, *Nishida tetsugaku no datsukōchiku* (*The Deconstruction of Nishida Philosophy*) (Tokyo: Iwanami Shoten, 1987).

57 *Patosu no chi* (Tokyo: Chikuma Shobō, 1982).

58 *Kyōtsū kankaku* (Tokyo: Iwanami Shoten, 1979).

59 *Kōzō to chikara: kigoron wo koete* (Tokyo: Keisō Shobō, 1983). See also *Tōsō ron* (*Theory of Escape*) (Tokyo: Chikuma Shobō, 1984).
60 See *Postmodernism and Japan*, ed. Masao Miyoshi and H. D. Harootunian (Durham, N. C., London: Duke University Press, 1989); and Shiro Kohsaka, 'Reaktionen auf "Die Postmoderne Kultur" [von Peter Koslowski] und die moderne Japans', in Eduard Zwerlein (ed.), *Postmoderne Kultur und Wirtschaft* (Idstein: Schulz-Kirchner Verlag, 1993).
61 *Bunseki tetsugaku* (Tokyo: Kōbundō, 1959).
62 *Yōsōronrigaku no kenkyū* (Tokyo: Sankibōbutsushorin, 1964).
63 *Kotoba no tetsugaku* (Tokyo: Iwanami Shoten, 1965).
64 *Gengo, chikaku, sekai* (Tokyo: Iwanami Shoten, 1971).
65 (Tokyo: Keisō Shobō, 1979).
66 *'Fureru' koto no tetsugaku* (Tokyo: Iwanami Shoten, 1983).
67 *Kagami no naka no nihongo – sono shikō no shujusō* (Tokyo: Tokyo daikagu shuppankai, 1989).
68 'Nishida Sensei no jinkaku to shisō', pp. 64–5.
69 *Shinshin no mondai* (Tokyo: Sangyōtosho, 1980); this work follows Ōmori's earlier explorations in *Mono to kokoro* (1976), whose title reflects more traditional Japanese concepts of things and heart/mind.
70 *Shinshin mondai* (Tokyo: Seidosha, 1989).
71 *Seishin to shite no shintai* (Tokyo: Keishō Shobō, 1975).
72 *Shintai – Tōyōteki shinshinron no kokoromi* (Tokyo: Sōbunsha, 1977).
73 *Mi no kōzō – shintairon o koete* (Tokyo: Seidosha, 1984).
74 *Kankyō rinrigaku no susume* (Tokyo: Maruzen, 1992).
75 *Tetsugaku to wa nani ka: sono rekishi to kanōsei* (Tokyo: Keisō Shobō, 1988).

FURTHER READING

Abe Masao (1985) *Zen and Western Thought*, Honolulu: University of Hawaii Press.

Bernstein, Gail Lee (1976) *Japanese Marxist: A Portrait of Kawakami Hajime*, Cambridge, Mass.: Harvard University Press.

Duus, Peter (1988) 'Socialism, liberalism, and Marxism, 1901–1931', in Peter Duus (ed.) *The Cambridge History of Japan*, vol. VI, Cambridge: Cambridge University Press.

Hatano Seiichi (1988) *Time and Eternity*, trans. Suzuki Ichirō, Westport, Conn.: Greenwood Press. A translation of *Toki to eien*.

Heisig, James W. and Maraldo, John C. (eds) (1995) *Rude Awakenings: Zen, the Kyoto School and the Question of Nationalism*, Honolulu: University of Hawaii Press.

Meiroku Zasshi: Journal of the Enlightenment (1976) trans. William R. Braisted, Cambridge, Mass.: Harvard University Press.

Najita, Tetsuo and Harootunian, H. D. (1988) 'Japanese revolt against the West: political and cultural criticism in the twentieth century', in Peter Duus (ed.) *The Cambridge History of Japan*, vol. VI, Cambridge: Cambridge University Press.

Nishida Kitarō (1973) *Art and Morality*, trans. David A. Dilworth and Valdo H. Viglielmo, Honolulu: University of Hawaii Press.

—— (1987a) *Intuition and Reflection in Self-Consciousness*, trans. Valdo H. Viglielmo with Takeichi Yoshinori and Joseph S. O'Leary, Albany: State University of New York Press.

—— (1987b) *Last Writings: Nothingness and the Religious Worldview*, trans. David A. Dilworth, Honolulu: University of Hawaii Press.

—— (1990) *An Inquiry into the Good*, trans. Masao Abe and Christopher Ives, New Haven, Conn.: Yale University Press.

Nishitani Keiji (1982) *Religion and Nothingness*, trans. Jan Van Bragt, Berkeley: University of California Press. A translation of *What is Religion? (Shūkyō to wa nanika)*.

—— (1990) *The Self-Overcoming of Nihilism*, trans. Graham Parkes and Setsuko Aihara, Albany: State University of New York Press.

—— (1991) *Nishida Kitarō*, trans. Yamamoto Seisaku and James W. Heisig, Berkeley: University of California Press.

Nitta, Y. and Tatematsu, H. (eds) (1979) *Japanese Phenomenology*, *Analecta Husserliana* 8, Dordrecht, Holland: D. Reidel.

Odin, Steve (1996) *The Social Self in Zen and American Pragmatism*, Albany: State University of New York Press.

Parkes, Graham (ed.) (1987) *Heidegger and Asian Thought*, Honolulu: University of Hawaii Press. This anthology has contributions by Japanese philosophers Nishitani Keiji, Yuasa Yasuo, Takeichi Akihiro, Mizoguchi Kōhei and Kotoh Tetsugaki.

Pincus, Leslie (1991) 'In a labyrinth of western desire: Kuki Shuzo and the discovery of Japanese being', in Masao Miyoshi and H. D. Harootunian (eds) *Japan and the World* (a special issue of *Boundary 2* 18 (3), Durham, N. C.: Duke University Press, pp. 142–56.

Piovesana, Gino G. (1969) *Contemporary Japanese Philosophical Thought*, New York: St John's University Press.

Rimer, J. Thomas (ed.) (1990) *Culture and Identity: Japanese Intellectuals during the Interwar Years*, Princeton: Princeton University Press.

Sakai, Naoki (1989) 'Modernity and its critique: the problem of universalism and particularism', in Maso Miyoshi and H. D. Harootunian (eds) *Postmodernism and Japan*, Durham, N. C.: Duke University Press.

—— (1991) 'Return to the West/return to the East: Watsuji Tetsuro's anthropology and discussions of authenticity', in Masao Miyoshi and H. D. Harootunian (eds) *Japan and the World* (a special issue of *Boundary 2* 18(3), Durham N. C.: Duke University Press.

Takeuchi Yoshinori (1983) *The Heart of Buddhism*, trans. James W. Heisig, New York: Crossroad.

Tanabe Hajime (1986) *Philosophy as Metanoetics*, trans. Takeuchi Yoshinori, Berkeley: University of California Press.

Unno, Taitetsu (ed.) (1990) *The Religious Philosophy of Nishitani Keiji*, Berkeley: Asian Humanities Press.

Unno, Taitetsu and Heisig, James W. (eds) (1990) *The Religious Philosophy of Tanabe Hajime*, Berkeley, Calif.: Asian Humanities Press.

Viswanathan, Meera (1989) 'An investigation into essence: Kuki Shūzō's *"Iki" no Kōzō*', *Transactions of the Asiatic Society of Japan* 4: 1–22.

Watsuji Tetsurō (1988) *Climate and Culture*, trans. Geoffrey Bownas, Westport, Conn.: Greenwood Press. A translation of *Fūdo*.

Yuasa Yasuo (1987) *The Body: Toward an Eastern Mind–Body Theory*, trans. Nagatomo Shigenori and T. P. Kasulis, Albany: State University of New York Press.

Part VI

ISLAMIC PHILOSOPHY

INTRODUCTION

It would not be an exaggeration to say that the history of Islamic philosophy is one of a constant process of accommodation. Although Islamic religion has undergone quite striking modifications and even bifurcations as have other religions, it has always had a strong emphasis on orthodoxy – much more so than, say, Christianity or Buddhism. In consequence, the history of Islamic philosophy is in large part one of an endeavour to place this orthodoxy alongside of philosophical currents of which intellectual honesty precludes an outright rejection. The obvious difficulty of this task explains the lengthy Islamic tradition of heretics, where the touchstone of heresy is the failure to satisfy religious authority that a satisfactory accommodation with dogma has been achieved.

Islamic religion was founded by the prophet Muḥammad (570–632), and the two-hundred-year period following his death involved the focusing and division of alternative othodoxies. Such sects as the Khārijites, Mu'tazilites and Ash'arites laid the foundation for Islamic philosophical discussion, differing as they did on such questions as the necessity of faith or of action for salvation, the relevance of reason to revelation, and the possibility of human freedom in the context of an omnipotent deity.

The major period of Islamic philosophy is undoubtedly that of the ninth to the twelfth centuries, when Islamic ideas met those of ancient Greece. Intense scholarship, involving the translation and assessment of the available Neoplatonic texts, juxtaposed Islamic and quasi-Aristotelian thought bringing the question of revealed and rational truths to the fore. The major figures during this period were al-Kindī (810–73) – the 'Father of Islamic Philosophy' – with al-Fārābī (870–950), Avicenna (980–1037), al-Ghazālī (1058–1111) and Averroes (1126–98). Al-Ghazālī indeed launched a strong attack on the previous emphasis on reason as against revelation, with his work *The Incoherence of the Philosophers*; Averroes, who had by then the original works of Aristotle as opposed to the Neoplatonic versions of the earlier thinkers, was able to counter this attack with his own work *The Incoherence of the Incoherence*.

An interesting development that stands out in Islam is Sufism, which is still predominant in Turkey, Iran and the Indian sub-continent. Sufis are still regarded as heretics by orthodox Islam since they proclaim the identity of man, truth and deity. This is in keeping with mystical ways of thinking found in other traditions like Buddhism and Christian gnosticism. Many Sufis composed their thoughts in verses or songs.

As Islam spread widely beyond its original home, into India and through to south and south-east Asia, its adaptation to indigenous systems of ideas was less marked than, for instance, that of Buddhism. In more recent centuries the ideas which have been making the greatest impact on Islam and Islamic philosophy are those from the West, essentially those of modern science and technology. Professor Hanafi's chapter 'Contemporary Islamic Philosophy' (Chapter 48) describes this recent attempt at accommodation, particularly in the context of Egypt, and similar efforts to accommodate science and technology within an orthodox Islamic culture can be found in countries such as Pakistan and Malaysia.

Islamic philosophy is in essence theocentric, and concerned at base with the relations between man and deity and between deity and cosmos. Figuring large are the problem of free will versus predestination, the nature of divine justice and the problem of evil, and at a more theoretical level the relation and priority between philosophical speculation and divine revelation.

B. C. and I. M.

39

THE ORIGINS OF ISLAMIC PHILOSOPHY

Ian Richard Netton

OVERVIEW

Viewed from the perspective of philosophical development and the history of ideas, the Near and Middle East at the end of late antiquity and the dawn of the rise of Islam (that is, *c.* AD 570) resembles nothing so much as an over-rich stew, whose constituents seethe uneasily within a bubbling cauldron. These constituents include Pythagoreanism, Gnosticism, Platonism, Aristotelianism and Neoplatonism. The history of Middle Eastern philosophy from the seventh century AD onwards is the history of that cauldron with the addition of a further vital ingredient, the religion of Islam. And the latter is by no means monolithic but multivalent in its character and thought.

It must be stressed right at the beginning, however, that the Middle Eastern version of Aristotle's thought, and that of other thinkers as well, often differed radically from the original.[1] As Peters notes,

> to say that Aristotle and Aristotelianism are two different things is to state the obvious. And yet the implications of that bald fact for the history of philosophy are so immense that to gloss it over with a passing reference is to distort the very premises of *falsafah* [Islamic philosophy].[2]

He goes on to add that

> the second Greek attempt at integrating Plato and Aristotle, the one worked out in the Neoplatonic schools of Athens and Alexandria, was completely successful in altering the original Aristotelian insight into the nature of the world, not only for the Arabs, but well beyond.[3]

The direct consequence of all this was, therefore, that nascent Islamic philosophical thought was permeated or infiltrated by, or amalgamated with, a species of Greek thought which had been subtly, or not so subtly, altered: Aristotle's ideas, for example, could become an un-Aristotelian mishmash, though still with the label 'Aristotelian' attached by their glossator or exegete.[4]

Three figures above all others from antiquity stand out as having had a profound and lasting impact on the development of Islamic philosophy: Plato, Aristotle and Plotinus. It must, however, be emphasized that the history of Islamic philosophy is not *just* the history of the influence of Greek thought upon Islamic, or the offspring of a culture clash between the Greek and Islamic intellectual domains. As I have shown elsewhere, Islamic philosophy, while naturally leaning upon and drawing from some of its antecedents, was 'more than capable of constituting a system of thought in its own right'.[5]

The homes of Greek learning in the Near and Middle East at the time of the rise of Islam in the seventh century AD were many: some were akin to the academies of medieval and modern times which we today call 'universities'. Examples included the philosophy school or schools of Alexandria in Egypt, and the medical centre of Gondēshāpūr near what later became called Baghdad. Ḥarrān, too, in northern Syria, was a third vital source of Neoplatonic and astral learning. This triangle of cities, to which Baghdad may be added from AD 830, provides a dramatic indication of the way in which late Greek thought had penetrated, and established itself within, the Fertile Crescent.[6]

Of course, in selecting for analysis, and concentrating upon, just the three cities of Alexandria, Gondēshāpūr and Ḥarrān I do not intend to imply that these were the *only* sources of influence on the development of Islamic philosophy. Far from it. However, in view of their cosmopolitan nature, and the diverse and eclectic intellectual milieux which they constituted, they do provide a very good indication of the sort of intellectual cauldron which the Near and Middle East had become during the period under discussion.

Alexandria

In his *Sword of Honour* Evelyn Waugh neatly referred to the city of Alexandria as an 'ancient asparagus bed of theological absurdity'.[7] His remark highlights succinctly the extraordinary intellectual diversity and eclecticism of one of the greatest cities of middle and late antiquity. All the great theological and philosophical 'isms' had taken root and flourished here – Judaism, Gnosticism, Platonism, Aristotelianism, Neoplatonism – not to mention Christianity and a host of other, more minor, divergences from the above-mentioned intellectual streams.[8] And certain names stand out, even above the multitude of philosophical celebrities who inhabited the Alexandrian milieu. Foremost among these is surely Plotinus (AD 204/5–270) himself, the founding father of Neoplatonism. There is no doubt that he both absorbed, and contributed to, the Alexandrian spirit of intellectual enquiry, having studied in Alexandria under his teacher Ammonius Saccas for eleven years.

The Alexandrian scholars before the Arab conquest in AD 642 occupied themselves with producing many commentaries on the works of Aristotle. Not all were favourable, but all bear witness to the importance which Aristotle had achieved in the Alexandrian school of philosophy. A good example of what was produced is the *œuvre* of the theologian, philosopher and grammarian John Philoponus, who flourished in the last part of the fifth century AD into approximately the second half of the sixth, and received from the Arabs the title of John the Grammarian, Yaḥyā al-Naḥwī. One of John's most important treatises was entitled *Contra Aristotelem*. The original of this treatise has been lost, but Simplicius quotes from it in his own work.[9] Philoponus' attack on Aristotle in his Alexandrian commentaries is full-blooded: he 'was particularly concerned to oppose Aristotle's doctrine of an eternal universe as well as the Stagarite's thesis that a dichotomy existed between heaven and earth. The Alexandrian maintained that only God was omnipotent and that God's creation of the world *ex nihilo* placed him automatically above nature'.[10] John Philoponus's theology and philosophy are of particular interest to us here because of their highly probable influence on the Arab philosopher al-Kindī, who will be discussed later in this chapter.[11]

So Aristotle was both revered *and* criticized in Alexandria before the Arab conquest. This is not surprising. The region was home not just to Aristotle's doctrines but to those of Plotinus as well. And Neoplatonism was the second part of the Alexandrian legacy to the Arabs, after Aristotelianism. Indeed, Peters stresses the predominant nature of Neoplatonic thought in Athens and Alexandria:

> It was the Neoplatonic synthesis compounded by Plotinus to which the immediate future belonged. Aristotelianism was a distinctly minor school, and it was by reason of Porphyry's introduction of at least certain elements of the Peripatetic doctrine into the curriculum of a thriving Neoplatonism that the former was saved from descending to the position of a curious fossil from the past.[12]

However, as if the intellectual milieu which the Arabs encountered were not already complicated enough, the Neoplatonism of seventh-century Alexandria was not necessarily always the exact version propagated by Plotinus. The latter, like Aristotle before him, had had his disciples, exegetes, glossators and elaborators. Plotinus taught a 'simple' doctrine of three major hypostases headed by the One or the Good, from which eternally emanated Intellect and Soul.[13] His followers, however, like Iamblichus (*c.* AD 250–*c.* 326) and Proclus Diadochus (AD 412–85), introduced a plethora of intermediaries into Plotinus' basic hypostatic scheme, endowing them with such names as 'henads' and 'monads'. Later Neoplatonic metaphysics were thus made complex far beyond anything Plotinus might have imagined.[14]

Proclus was carefully studied in pre-conquest Alexandria, as was that other major Neoplatonist and commentator on Aristotle, Porphyry of Tyre (AD 234–*c.* 305), author of a famous *Introduction* (*Eisagōgē*) to Aristotle's *Categories*. And not only were they studied in Alexandria. At a later stage both may be said to have been adopted by Islamic philosophy, because of the association with them of two Neoplatonic works whose real authorship is unclear: the famous *Theology of Aristotle* (*Theologia Aristotelis*) and *The Book of the Pure Good* (*Liber de Causis*).

It is clear from the most casual reading that the *Theologia Aristotelis* could not have been written by Aristotle, despite the Arabs' acceptance of it as part of his corpus. (It is, in fact, a padded-out version of books IV–VI of Plotinus' *Enneads* and imbued with the classical Plotinian language of emanation.) The *Liber de Causis* in its Arabic version reduced Proclus' 211 propositions in the *Elements of Theology* to 31, but the connection between the two works is still apparent. Like the *Theologia*, the Arabic *Liber de Causis* speaks the language of emanation, and surveys a variety of Neoplatonic subjects like Proclus's four chief hypostases of the One, Existence, Intellect and Soul.[15]

The influence of such doctrines reached far into the early development of Islamic and Arabic philosophy and had vast implications and repercussions. We find a similar multiplication of hypostases in the thought of later Islamic Neoplatonic thinkers like al-Fārābī (AD 870–950) and his better-known disciple Ibn Sīnā (AD 979–1037). The name of al-Kindī has been linked in some way with one of the translations of the *Theologia Aristotelis*,[16] and he is discussed alone. In short, the Alexandrian milieu had a profound impact on the future development of medieval Islamic philosophy.[17] It was an impact which was complemented by that of the two other points of the triangle of Aristotelian and Neoplatonic influence, Gondēshāpūr and Ḥarrān.

Gondēshāpūr

Despite its location near what later became known as Baghdad, Gondēshāpūr was much more a Byzantine city than a Persian, though it was to Persia that the city belonged. It was built by the Sāsānid ruler Shāpūr I (reg. AD 241–71), but its

> main title to fame lies in its importance as a cultural centre which influenced the rise of scientific and intellectual activity in Islam. Its importance was enhanced by its having been closely associated with a secular field of learning, namely medicine, and by its having been the foremost representative of Greek medicine.[18]

The curriculum in philosophy followed by the Academy had many elements in common with Alexandria's, and the city played a full role in a translation industry which translated numerous Greek classics into Pahlavi and Syriac.[19]

The city was also the chosen refuge of many Aristotelian and Neoplatonic scholars fleeing from persecution elsewhere. After the Christian Council of Ephesus in AD 431, which condemned the Nestorian Christological position, Nestorian scholars fled first to Edessa and then moved on to Gondēshāpūr. They were steeped in the thought of Aristotle but also knew their Porphyry, and Nestorian philosophy was thus already permeated by elements of Neoplatonism. Later, the Emperor Justinian closed the Athenian School of Philosophy in AD 529, and Gondēshāpūr was again the chosen refuge of such Neoplatonic philosophers as Damascius (died AD 553), a disciple of Proclus, and Simplicius (died AD 533).

The city of Gondēshāpūr, then, was renowned for much more than medicine, although its excellence in that field should not be overlooked. It was a centre which was at once Aristotelian, Neoplatonic, Nestorian and Byzantine. From it Greek thought would permeate Islam, together with a plentiful supply of physicians and scholars to the ʿAbbāsid caliphal courts.[20]

It is unclear exactly when Aristotle began to be translated into Arabic, but we know that such translations began to appear after the ʿAbbāsid revolution in AD 750, which overthrew the Umayyad Dynasty and brought the ʿAbbāsids to power; soon afterwards the new dynasty established its capital in Baghdad.[21] Peters notes that the ʿAbbāsid Caliph al-Manṣūr (reg. AD 754–75) made the Syriac Christian Jūrjīs ibn Bakhtīshūʿ, who had headed the hospital in Gondēshāpūr, his court physician in Baghdad in AD 765, and he believes that the latter date 'is probably the single most important one in the translation movement.'[22] Gondēshāpūr, with its translation from Greek into Syriac and Pahlavi, was thus the forerunner of what Peters calls 'the Baghdad translation movement',[23] in which Arabic was now the language into which Aristotle, Galen and many others were translated.

It should now be abundantly clear that the two cities of Gondēshāpūr and Alexandria, whose accumulated wisdom was to have such a profound impact on the development of Islamic philosophy, were intensely academic, rigorously intellectual and highly cosmopolitan in their outlook – akin, perhaps, if modern parallels be sought, to pre-war Berlin or post-war Paris. The intellectual apparatus generated and propagated by both Gondēshāpūr and Alexandria was of a calibre and strength to confront and often challenge the verities of a rising Islamic tradition which, whatever its virtues, manifestly lacked the philosophical structures, metaphysics and logic which were so highly developed within the Greek intellectual domain.

Ḥarrān

We turn finally to the contribution of Ḥarrān in northern Syria. Ḥarrān is interesting as much for its astrology as for its complex transcendent theology and Neoplatonism. The three areas merged in the pagan Sabaean sect (or sects) associated with that city; adherents of Sabaeanism continued to survive for some time after the rise of Islam both in Ḥarrān and Baghdad, and traces of them only finally disappeared from Baghdad at the end of the eleventh century AD. Their liturgical language was Syriac, and their theology, which included a devotion to astral spirits, seven of which looked after seven of the planets, had many points in common with Neoplatonism: particularly noteworthy was their stress on a transcendent deity. Indeed, in one form at least, they may fairly be described as a Neoplatonic pagan sect or group of sects.[24] Arab writers were fascinated by them, perhaps because of their 'exotic' appeal, and the great medieval Persian scholar and heresiographer al-Shahrastānī (AD 1086–1153), for example, gave much space in his work to expounding their dogmas.[25] The Sabaeans are important for Islam, not because of any great impact on the development of orthodox Islamic theology but because they were yet another channel of Neoplatonism to Islamic philosophy. They also gave to the Islamic world a number of important scholars including the redoubtable Thābit b. Qurra (died AD 901), famous as a translator into Arabic of Archimedes' works as well as the *Introduction to Arithmetic* by Nicomachus.[26]

To the city of Ḥarrān came finally the Alexandrian philosophers in the middle of the ninth century AD. At the beginning of the tenth century they continued their journey to Baghdad, thus further embellishing, from the intellectual point of view, a city which already possessed the great House of Wisdom founded by the 'Abbāsid Caliph al-Ma'mūn (reg. AD 813–33) in AD 832. Ḥarrān and Alexandria were thus linked physically as well as intellectually: Baghdad was their heir, and philosophy was ripe for development from the nascent Islamic faith.[27] That development may be characterized succinctly as having taken two forms or directions: an individual direction as epitomized in the life and works of 'the Father of Arab Philosophy', al-Kindī; and a group direction, as epitomized in the thought of that varied collection of Islamic thinkers who among other things tried to combine use of the text (the Holy Qur'ān) with use of reason, and who went by the collective umbrella name of Mu'tazila or Mu'tazilites. Both the individual and the group contributed in a formal and significant way to the elaboration of what became known as *falsafa*, Islamic philosophy. Both will be surveyed here.

ABŪ YŪSUF YA'QŪB IBN ISḤĀQ AL-KINDĪ (DIED AFTER AD 866)

Life

It is probable that al-Kindī was born near the close of the eighth century AD into a well-regarded civil service family; his father held the post of governor of Kūfa in Iraq under two caliphs.[28] Little is known of his early life in Kūfa. Later, following a classic Islamic pattern of travel in search of knowledge, he moved to the city of Baṣra in southern Iraq and then northwards to the capital of the Arab Empire, Baghdad.[29]

Atiyeh believes that here

> one can confidently assume, he met the various Syrian and Persian scholars who then formed the backbone of the new learning in the capital of the 'Abbāsid Empire. They must have been the ones who initiated him more thoroughly into the secrets of Greek philosophy and science. He quite possibly became one of the very few Muslim Arabs of his time who

> mastered both Greek and Syriac. His knowledge of Greek, Persian and Indian literatures earned him unique respect and fame throughout his stay in Bag͟hdād.[30]

However, al-Kindī's linguistic expertise in the fields of Greek and Syriac is open to question. Atiyeh himself admits elsewhere that 'it cannot be asserted categorically that al-Kindī knew Greek and Syriac, or that he ever translated any work from these languages.'[31]

Al-Kindī was a victim of the politico-religious circumstances of his age. Mu'tazilism (see below) became the prevailing religious 'unorthodoxy', adopted in the highest circles by three of the 'Abbāsid caliphs, al-Ma'mūn (reg. AD 813–33), al-Mu'taṣim (reg. AD 833–42) and al-Wāthiq (reg. AD 842–7). Indeed, al-Ma'mūn went so far as to impose Mu'tazilite doctrines by force, and leading religious scholars and jurists were subjected to a *miḥna* or inquisition in an attempt to gain their adherence.[32] The Mu'tazilite position was later rejected by al-Wāthiq's successor, al-Mutawakkil (reg. AD 847–61), who returned the *dār al-Islām* (House of Islam) to the orthodox fold.[33]

It was to be al-Kindī's later misfortune that, earlier in his life, he allied himself with the Mu'tazilite caliphs al-Ma'mūn and al-Mu'taṣim. They became his patrons: he belonged to the translation circle established by al-Ma'mūn; he was tutor to al-Mu'taṣim's son Aḥmad (and, indeed, dedicated his book *On First Philosophy* to al-Mu'taṣim); and he may well have worked at the court as a physician as well.[34] His fortunes were drastically reversed with the accession of al-Mutawakkil: was this a result of al-Kindī's alleged Mu'tazilite leanings or, more politically, simply the fact that he was associated with the *ancien régime*?[35] It is difficult to say with precision, but the details of his fall from grace may be reiterated briefly here.

Al-Kindī had clearly made several enemies, and among those whose hostility he had aroused were the sons of a certain Mūsā ibn Shākir. They worked as scholars in the service of the new caliph and apparently envied al-Kindī his excellent library. If we are to believe the evidence of Ibn Abī Uṣaybi'a, their intrigues resulted in the temporary confiscation of al-Kindī's library and the philosopher receiving a beating. Later, al-Kindī retrieved his books, but he never recovered the position which he had once occupied at the caliphal court under al-Mutawakkil's Mu'tazilite predecessors.[36] Atiyeh notes somewhat poignantly: 'His death must have been a quiet one, noticed only by those nearest to him. It was the death of a great man out of favour, yet at the same time that of a philosopher who loved solitude.'[37] Ivry's conclusion is that 'his misfortunes under al-Mutawakkil were apparently due more to personal intrigue or to a general change of intellectual orientation at court, than to his religious beliefs.'[38]

The environment in which al-Kindī worked, studied and wrote was, indeed, a philosophically exciting and personally stimulating one, at least before the reign of al-Mutawakkil. He served caliphs who had a genuine enthusiasm for intellectual enquiry and who had, in fact, turned the theological *status quo* upside down by the adoption of a new 'brand' of Islam. In such a climate, philosophy could develop and flourish. Of course, the new 'liberalism', which was really nothing of the sort, had its nastier side as well: the institution of an inquisition and the persecution of those who declined to hold the trendy unorthodox views espoused by caliph and court was one aspect of this. Naturally, the 'anti-Mu'tazilite' camp had its victims too: the great medieval Islamic jurist and theologian Aḥmad ibn Ḥanbal (AD 780–855) refused to accept Mu'tazilite doctrine and, in consequence, was imprisoned and beaten under the caliphates of al-Ma'mūn and al-Mu'taṣim. But while al-Kindī fell from favour with the accession of al-Mutawakkil, Ibn Ḥanbal was restored.[39] The careers of these two figures, al-Kindī and Ibn Ḥanbal, illustrate only too well the impact that the secular state could have on the intellectual or religious: the pendulum of power could thus affect theologian, philosopher and jurist as well as courtier and soldier. Al-Kindī was a philosopher both honoured *and* dishonoured in his own land.

The milieu was, above all, ripe for a sophisticated development of philosophy. The theological quarrels over Mu'tazilite dogmas had shown the need for a more intellectual approach to matters which had previously been held on faith merely because they were revealed in the Qur'ān, or because they were a part of the tradition (*ḥadīth*) from the Prophet Muḥammad. There was a need, too, for an enlarged philosophical vocabulary in Arabic which would facilitate the debates in such fields as metaphysics. In both these areas, al-Kindī made a substantial contribution. The following paragraphs will survey and assess this contribution; for al-Kindī is *deservedly* called 'the Father of Arab Philosophy'. He was the first major Muslim philosopher, and while he argued from a stance of theological (or Qur'ānic) conviction,[40] he was none the less sufficiently enamoured of the use of reason to ensure that the contribution which he made was substantial, lasting and very far from being perfunctory.

Philosophy

It is probable that in al-Kindī's mind there was no rigid division between philosophy and theology. It is useful to survey the principal aspects of his theology briefly in view of the implications which these had for his own philosophical development. However, 'al-Kindī, like so many philosophers before and after him, did not produce a tidy system: it is, therefore, no surprise that certain aspects of his idea of the deity should have ultimately conflicted with some of his philosophy'.[41]

Al-Kindī held fast to the God portrayed in the Qur'ān, certainly with aspects of Aristotle's Unmoved First Mover, but placing most stress on the Qur'ānic doctrine of *tawḥīd*, the absolute unity of God. Indeed, God's whole existence is bound up with the idea of his unity.[42] Al-Kindī stresses this doctrine of divine unity throughout his *œuvre*; one illustration must suffice here, taken from his *Epistle to 'Alī b. Jahm on the Unity of God*:

> So He is not many but One, without multiplicity. May He be praised and elevated high above the qualities which the heretics attribute to Him. He does not resemble His creation for multiplicity exists in all Creation but absolutely not in Him. For He is a Creator (*Mubdi'*) and they are the created.[43]

Al-Kindī's strict Qur'ānicism is in evidence elsewhere as well, in two fields which would constitute major problems for later Islamic philosophers: he believed that the world had been created by God *ex nihilo*, and he also accepted that the body as well as the soul would rise from the dead on the last day.[44] Thus, while his deity might have had aspects of Aristotle's, his view of the origins of the world and matter had little if anything in common with those of the Greek philosopher. Of course, it has been well observed by Atiyeh – and this is the major difference between the God of Aristotle and that of al-Kindī – that Aristotle's God is a mover, not a creator.[45]

Elsewhere, however, if we may now move from the theological to the more purely philosophical, al-Kindī shared many of Aristotle's concepts, in particular, his terminology. Al-Kindī's work is saturated with the thinking and writings of Aristotle. His vocabulary is frequently Aristotelian, with its use of such terms as substance and accidents, matter and form, potentiality and actuality, generation and corruption, and the four causes.[46] It is not, however, a slavish adherence: al-Kindī diverged from Aristotle, for example, in his development of substance and, unlike Aristotle, did not believe that this word should ever be used of God.[47] When we take this into consideration, as well as the purely theological divergences noted earlier, it is clear that a considerable amount of selectivity has been employed by al-Kindī in his use of Aristotelian material; and the key to why he made one choice rather than another probably rests in al-Kindī's Qur'ānicism rather than anything else.[48] The would-be philosopher in al-Kindī could never quite break free from the Qur'ānic theologian who also lurked in the recesses of his mind!

Of course, to absorb Aristotelian Greek thought into the mainstream of Arabic thinking required adequate linguistic tools. In particular, it required a philosophical vocabulary which could adequately render what Aristotle had to say in comprehensible Arabic. Al-Kindī did not always find such a vocabulary at hand, so he invented some of what he needed. His extension of the Arabic philosophical lexicon is one of his major contributions to the development of Islamic philosophy. As Fakhry states:

> Many of the terms that al-Kindī uses bear the mark of a greater reliance on translation from Greek or Syriac, and it is not surprising that in the course of time such terms were dropped and others were substituted for them . . . in some cases al-Kindī resorts to the use of unfamiliar or archaic terms such as '*ais*' and '*lais*' to express the antithetic concepts of being and nonbeing, and even coins verbs, participles and substantives from such terms. He creates even unlikelier terms still, such as '*hawwā*' and '*tahawwī*' (i.e. bring and bringing into being) from the third-person singular pronoun (*hua*), in an attempt to explain the concept of creation *ex nihilo*. Despite his inventiveness, however, it cannot be said that al-Kindī wrote with great grace or elegance.[49]

Apart from the Aristotelian, there is another important philosophical aspect of al-Kindī, and that is the Neoplatonic. Scholars do not usually, in any survey of Islamic philosophy, consider al-Kindī and his relationship with the doctrines of the Neoplatonists. 'From a strictly theological point of view it is clear that al-Kindī was much closer to the Qur'ān than to Plotinus.'[50] Yet there *is* a Neoplatonic dimension which deserves analysis, though that is certainly not to say that al-Kindī was a full-blooded partisan of Neoplatonism.

It is true that little of the famous *Theologia Aristotelis*, with which he was somehow associated, seems present in his writings.[51] It is true that he describes his deity in terms founded in the Qur'ān, though with some genuflection towards the thought of Aristotle: God, for example, is 'Unmoved' (*Ghayr mutaḥarrika*).[52] But elsewhere al-Kindī writes passages of negative prose about the deity which would not have looked out of place in the *Enneads* of Plotinus. It is in this use of a negative vocabulary in his approach to God that we find the strongest traces of Neoplatonism in the Arab author. The following constitutes an excellent example of this kind of writing, and also provides an extended example of the kind of metaphysics on which he loved to dwell:

> It is clear that the True One [God] is not an intelligible thing, nor matter nor a genus nor a species nor an individual nor a difference nor a property nor a general accident nor a movement nor a soul nor an intellect. [It is] neither a whole nor a part, [nor can It be described by the terms] 'all' nor 'some'. It is not [characterized as] One because of [Its] relation to something else. No! It is absolutely One and does not accept multiplication. . . . Thus the True One does not have any matter nor form nor quantity nor modality nor relation. It cannot be described by any of the intelligible things which remain, and It possesses neither genus nor difference nor individual nor property nor general accident nor movement. It cannot be described by anything which is not actually considered to be one. It is therefore, quite simply, pure unity, i.e. it is nothing but unity while every other one is [characterized by] multiplicity.[53]

The utter uniqueness, and indeed unknowableness, of God shines forth in true Neoplatonic fashion from this quotation. God is beyond the five Porphyrian predicables (and a sixth Kindian predicable of 'individual') as well as a variety of Aristotelian categories, the soul and the intellect.[54]

This is the best illustration of a 'Neoplatonic' al-Kindī. We would do well, however, not to exaggerate this aspect. Although the word 'emanation' is not totally absent from his writings, it is never developed in a full Plotinian manner. (The doctrine of creation *ex nihilo* saw to that.) There are, furthermore, no precise equivalents of Plotinus' Intellect and Soul in the thought of al-Kindī.[55] In other words, while bearing in mind that al-Kindī's thought *has* been tinged with Neoplatonism, our assessment must also balance this against the Aristotelian and Qur'ānic substrate which also underlies his writings. And if inconsistencies and even contradictions are perceived in al-Kindī's work, we should remember, as Walzer has warned, that there are dangers in trying 'to make al-Kindī more consistent than he may have been and to credit him with an achievement which he may not have been able to perform.'[56] Such inconsistencies and contradictions need not dismay us: they may happen in every philosopher. Al-Kindī absorbed many of the exciting intellectual currents of the age into his writings, not always successfully synthesizing them but none the less managing to lay the foundations of real philosophy in Islam. His contribution was enormous and paved the way for both al-Fārābī and Ibn Sīnā.

THE MU'TAZILA

Who were they?

The epithet 'Mu'tazila' (or 'Mu'tazilites') is best regarded as an 'umbrella' term denoting a group in medieval Islam which held certain beliefs in common but which also disagreed on other doctrinal details.[57] In this respect the term perhaps resembles the usage of the word 'Anglican' today. William Thomson has described the Mu'tazila in the following terms:

> This movement never produced a synthetic scheme of thought, nor even an eclectic system. Its *raison d'être* was not, in fact, the creation of a unified body of belief, but rather the interpretation of certain inherited doctrines in favour of a particular view of divine nature and human destiny, to which end the Mu'tazilites made use of a heterogeneous lot of ideas borrowed for the most part from the various schools of Greek thought which they had come to know.[58]

The origins of the name 'Mu'tazila', from which the English 'Mu'tazilite' is coined, are mainly shrouded in legend, and most accounts are probably not to be taken seriously. According to one of the most popular ones, which derives from al-Shahrastānī (see above), the saintly al-Ḥasan of Baṣra (died AD 728) was asked for his views on the grave sinner. Was that sinner to be considered as a Muslim believer or an unbeliever? Before al-Ḥasan could reply, one of those present, Wāṣil ibn 'Aṭā', responded that the grave sinner was not to be considered as either; rather he was in an 'intermediate position'. Wāṣil then withdrew and al-Ḥasan said: 'Wāṣil has withdrawn (Arabic: *i'tazala*) from us.' From this Arabic verb is derived the group name *Mu'tazila*, which means literally 'those who withdraw', or 'those who secede'.[59] W. M. Watt believes that 'there are strong reasons for rejecting this story',[60] though he admits that there do seem to have been connections between Mu'tazilism and al-Ḥasan's disciples.

The Mu'tazila may be loosely grouped into a southern Iraqi Baṣran branch and a Baghdad branch. Among their founders and leaders were Mu'ammar (died AD 830), Abū 'l-Hudhayl al-'Allāf (*c.* AD 748–53–*c.* AD 840–1 or later) and al-Naẓẓām (died AD 836 or 845) in Baṣra, and Bishr ibn al-Mu'tamir (died AD 825) in Baghdad.[61] Another of their great theologians and moralists was 'Imād al-Dīn Abū 'l-Ḥasan 'Abd al-Jabbār (*c.* AD 935–1024/5). Rather than give a brief, and inevitably unsatisfactory, sketch of *all* these thinkers, I shall survey the life and career of 'Abd al-Jabbār only in this biographical section. We shall then move to a survey of the major doctrinal positions of the Mu'tazila, an area where it is difficult to separate theology from philosophy, before concluding with a short survey of some relevant aspects of the thought of 'Abd al-Jabbār. He will be, as it were, our Mu'tazilite case study.

'Abd al-Jabbār was 'the leading Mu'tazilite of his time'.[62] He was born in or near Hamadhān, in western Iran, into a poor family. Here and in Iṣfahān he received a general education before studying theology in Baṣra, where he became a Mu'tazilite. He then spent a longer study period in Baghdad and so, like al-Kindī, and many others before and after him, he may be said to fit the classical medieval Islamic paradigm of the scholar travelling and wandering in search of both knowledge and the great teachers of the age who might impart that knowledge. After AD 970/1 he was invited by the Buwayhid Vizier Ibn 'Abbād (AD 938–995), a Mu'tazilite supporter, to come to one of the Buwayhid capitals, Rayy (near modern Tehran). The central Asian Buwayhids had established themselves as a major dynasty in Islam from AD 945 and held power both in Baghdad, where 'Abd al-Jabbār was previously living, and Rayy. It seems likely that 'Abd al-Jabbār taught law and Mu'tazilite theology before Ibn 'Abbād created him Chief Judge of Rayy in 977/8. However, on Ibn 'Abbād's death in AD 995, 'Abd al-Jabbār was deposed by the ruling Buwayhid prince, Fakhr al-Dawla (reg. AD 983–97), but may have been reinstated later. Hardly anything is known of the last thirty years of his life, but G. F. Hourani considers that his prolific writing output would have been impossible if a whole forty-five years of his life had been spent in the public office of Chief Judge. His most famous and largest written work was his *al-Mughnī fī Abwāb al-Tawḥīd wa'l-'Adl*, a title which Hourani translates as *Summa on the Headings of* [*God's*] *Unity and Justice*: it constituted a major discussion of Mu'tazilite theology.[63]

'Abd al-Jabbār appears to have achieved international fame somewhat late. Although, as we have already noted, he was well regarded by his academic and legal peers in his own age, it was only with the discovery of three-fifths of the text of *al-Mughnī* in a Yemeni mosque in 1951/2 that a widespread outside interest began in his thought and work. The huge value of *al-Mughnī*, and another work by 'Abd al-Jabbār entitled *Sharḥ al-Uṣūl al-Khamsa* (*The Exposition of the Five Principles*),[64] is that they constitute 'the earliest complete Mu'tazilite treatises'.[65] Although scholars were already aware of the essentials of Mu'tazilite doctrines, they are now provided with a full exposition. It is to some of these principal doctrines that this chapter will move in a moment; a final word remains to be said here about 'Abd al-Jabbār's status as a thinker, theologian, philosopher and Mu'tazilite.

The contemporary praise was not unfounded. Those who followed 'Abd al-Jabbār regarded him as the leading Mu'tazilite of his age and, indeed, his life coincided 'not only with the high water mark of Mu'tazilism, expressed in his own works, but also with the period of greatest originality and vitality in the general intellectual history of Eastern Islam'.[66] He was contemporary, for example, with the great al-Fārābī (AD 870–950) and even more famous Ibn Sīnā (AD 979–1037), both of whom are considered in detail in this encyclopedia. He managed to lead a fairly tranquil life, and Hourani sees this tranquillity reflected in his ethics, 'which displays confidence that man can know right and wrong by reason in a well-ordered manner, although not on the whole by inflexible rules'.[67] Hourani goes on:

> He answers his opponents with the cool patience of a thinker fully in command of a mature system of doctrines, without anxiety and with no premonition of the impending worldly defeat of the system by those opponents and their political backers, the Great Saljuq Sultans.[68]

He epitomized, in other words, the Mu'tazilite respect for reason.

The philosophy, theology and doctrines of the Mu'tazila

Classically, Mu'tazilite apologetic grouped its principles under five major headings: (1) The absolute unity of God (*al-Tawḥīd*); (2) The absolute justice (*al-'Adl*) of God; (3) God's promise and threat; (4) The intermediate position of Mu'tazilite theology regarding the position of the grave sinner; (5) Ordering what was good and forbidding what was objectionable.[69] Briefly, these principles may be elaborated as follows: (1) The doctrine of the absolute unity of God meant that God had no attributes separate from his essence: the Qur'ān, the word of God, was therefore created by God at a certain time (perhaps the time of revelation via the Angel Gabriel to Muḥammad) rather than being eternal as orthodox belief held. An eternal Qur'ān as the uncreated speech of God beside an eternal deity offended the Mu'tazilite sense of absolute monotheism. As a direct consequence of all this, the anthropomorphic vocabulary in the Qur'ān, which spoke, for example, of God's eye (XX: 40) and God's face (XXVIII: 88), was interpreted by the Mu'tazila in an allegorical or non-literal fashion. God's eye was God's knowledge and God's face was his essence, according to the exegesis of 'Abd al-Jabbār.[70] (2) The principle of God's justice really concerned the great debate over who was responsible for evil and the question of man's free will. The Mu'tazila held that man had complete free will and real choice in all his activities; and God was not responsible for evil. (3) The third principle of God's promise and threat was a corollary of the second: it implied that, in view of man's absolute authority over his own acts, God, in justice, was obliged to reward those who obeyed him with paradise, according to his promises in the Qur'ān, and punish those who disobeyed his commands with the hell-fire threatened in the Qur'ān. Other practical points of theology were also discussed under the heading of 'God's promise and threat'.

Principles (4) and (5) had distinctly political connotations: principle (4), which was the intermediate position of Mu'tazilite theology regarding the position of the grave sinner, meant, in effect, that he was not to be regarded either as a believer or an unbeliever: such a sinner occupied an intermediate status. This enabled the Mu'tazila to refrain from taking sides over controversial figures from the Islamic past. The final, fifth principle, of ordering what was good and forbidding what was morally objectionable, meant that justice as they saw it was to be maintained by the Mu'tazila by word and sword. The principle could be used to sanction criticism of, and revolt against, the unjust ruler.[71]

Of these five principles, it is clear that the Mu'tazila themselves regarded the first two as the most important: they referred to themselves as *Ahl al-'Adl wa 'l-Tawḥīd* ('The people of justice and unity'). But there is a much more important point to be made about the Mu'tazila: Peters points out that the real difference between the Mu'tazila and their opponents lay in their theological methods. The Mu'tazila, by dint of their familiarity with the intellectual legacy of Greece, revered the human intellect as 'a source of real knowledge'. Although the Holy Qur'ān was still, naturally, central to their concerns, none the less

> they fought for the right to use the intellect as an independent source and not only as an instrument to study the revealed sources. This fight was, however, not a goal in itself; their first aim remained to describe their believing synthetic view of God and the cosmos, a view which is in accordance both with revelation and with the data of the human intellect.[72]

In other words, though, as with al-Kindī, philosophy still remained subservient to the demands of theology, the impetus for a break between the two – and the ultimate establishment of philosophy in a position superior to theology by such later Islamic philosophers as al-Fārābī – had begun. Herein lies the real importance of the Mu'tazila for the development of philosophy in Islam. It was necessary above to cover the principles of their theology since these constituted their primary interests and preoccupations; but it is in the methodology used, and the Greek philosophical conceptions employed in their dialectic concerning many of these interests and preoccupations, that we detect the stirrings of real philosophical method. Islamic thinkers, in other words, epitomized in al-Kindī on the one hand, and the Mu'tazila on the other, under the impetus of Greek rationalism, were beginning for the first time to think *philosophically*, rather than just *textually* or *theologically*.

I should like to conclude this chapter by showing briefly how 'Abd al-Jabbār employs some of the conceptions, vocabulary, attitudes and methodology of the Greek tradition. Hourani has noted that by the time 'Abd al-Jabbār flourished, the Greek legacy had become remote and that it was mainly known via Neoplatonism.[73] This may have been true of the development of Mu'tazilism, but it certainly was not true of mainstream Islamic philosophy, which continued to know (and later, as in the case of Ibn Rushd (Averroes) (AD 1126–98), deeply revere) the thought of Aristotle. Aristotle's thought may sometimes have been mixed with that of Plotinus, as in the case of the philosophical Brethren of Purity (*fl. c.* tenth–eleventh centuries AD),[74] but it was never lost. And while it may indeed be true, as Hourani states, that 'the whole range of ethical intuitionism . . . seen in 'Abd al-Jabbār's work is not derived from suggestions in Aristotle's ethical writings' and that, while 'no medieval thinker could read the *Nicomachean Ethics* and not be marked by it indelibly . . . the marks are not in 'Abd al-Jabbār',[75] we cannot escape the very real presence of Aristotle's *vocabulary* and *concepts* in the work of 'Abd al-Jabbār. This is hardly surprising given the way in which the works of such contemporaries of his as al-Fārābī and Ibn Sīnā, as well as those of the Brethren of Purity, are laden with the vocabulary of classical Aristotelian metaphysics, albeit often Neoplatonized. A few examples from 'Abd al-Jabbār's usage must suffice here.

For this Mu'tazilite theologian, a *substance* (Arabic: *jawhar*), 'by its being pure materiality, from itself has only a small number of qualities, all related to the concept of "materiality".' 'Abd al-Jabbār's global view is that of a 'world composed of separate atoms which are brought together in composites to constitute material bodies.' And 'substances can be the "bearers" or "substrates" of accidents.' This is elaborated further in the thought of the thinker:

> Everything that comes into being in our world – and that, consequently, is produced and made, and in this way called by 'Abd al-Jabbār 'acts' or *af'āl* – shows an element of permanence and an element of change. The first we called 'substance' (*jawhar*), the second we call 'accident' (*'araḍ*).[76]

It is not difficult to see the long shadow of Aristotle over all this, and indeed many other elements of 'Abd al-Jabbār's vocabulary. He may be distant in time from Aristotle; he may not, indeed, express himself as Aristotle might have done; but he is as indebted in his technical terminology to the Greek philosopher as the majority of Islamic philosophers before and after him.

A final word remains to be said on methodology and philosophical approach. For 'Abd al-Jabbār philosophy (reason) was confirmed by theology (revelation).[77] Like other good Mu'tazilites he saw absolutely no clash between his rationalism and his religion,[78] the former deriving ultimately if indirectly from the Greek legacy to Islam, the latter coming obviously from the Holy Qur'ān. As Peters neatly stresses: "Abd al-Jabbār's theology is a permanent attempt to make a synthesis between the data of the human intellect and those of the Islamic revelation.'[79] He is often successful, and probably more so than he anticipated: the resemblance between his theory of ethics, for example, and British intuitionism has been remarked upon.[80] His approach to theology has been labelled 'phenomenal' or 'phenomenalistic', as well as theological: the former terms are used by Peters 'to emphasize the importance of perceived reality in 'Abd al-Jabbār's theology as well as his conviction that perception necessarily leads to . . . true and certain knowledge.' For Peters it is the combination of the phenomenal and the theological which constitutes a major element in the method of thought of 'Abd al-Jabbār.[81] It is clear that there are areas here where Plato and 'Abd al-Jabbār would firmly have parted company.

There are also areas where, despite the distance between them, 'Abd al-Jabbār and Greek philosophy, in the person of Aristotle, stand shoulder to shoulder. In the words of Hourani:

> With all their differences in time and outlook Aristotle and 'Abd al-Jabbār come rather close to each other when seen within the total range of ethical thinkers of the past and present. They are similar in intellectual style: in their prosaic, down-to-earth search for truth about practical life, at the expense, if need be, of a neat simplicity of theory. Both believe firmly in the objective reality of values. . . . Both teach reason as the method of deliberation. . . . Their 'reason' includes a number of mental processes, and it is invoked confidently by both because the challenges of modern empiricism had not yet arisen in epistemology.[82]

NOTES

1 See I. R. Netton, *Muslim Neoplatonists: An Introduction to the Thought of the Brethren of Purity (Ikhwān al-ṣafā')* (London: Allen & Unwin, 1982), p. 19.
2 F. E. Peters, *Aristotle and the Arabs: The Aristotelian Tradition in Islam* (New York: New York University Press/London: University of London Press, 1968), p. 3.
3 ibid., p. 8.
4 See Netton, *Muslim Neoplatonists*, p. 19.
5 I. R. Netton, *Allāh Transcendent: Studies in the Structure and Semiotics of Islamic Philosophy, Theology and Cosmology* (London: Routledge, 1989), p. x and *passim*.
6 ibid., p. 7.
7 *Sword of Honour* (London: Chapman & Hall, 1965), p. 395.
8 Netton, *Allāh Transcendent*, pp. 7–8.
9 See his *In Aristotelis de Caelo Commentaria*, ed. I. L. Heiberg, *Commentaria in Aristotelem Graeca*, vol. VII (Berlin: Reimer, 1894); see also Netton, *Allāh Transcendent*, pp. 65–6, 94 n. 197. See also a reconstruction of Philoponus' text in C. Wildberg (trans.), *Philoponus: Against Aristotle, on the Eternity of the World* (London: Duckworth, 1987).
10 Netton, *Allāh Transcendent*, p. 66.
11 See ibid., pp. 66–9.
12 Peters, *Aristotle and the Arabs*, p. 9; see also Netton, *Allāh Transcendent*, p. 8.
13 See Plotinus, *Enneads*, trans. A. H. Armstrong, The Loeb Classical Library (7 vols, London: Heinemann/Cambridge, Mass.: Harvard University Press, 1966–). (This contains the Greek text with facing English translation.)
14 See Netton, *Muslim Neoplatonists*, p. 36; Netton, *Allāh Transcendent*, pp. 10–11.
15 See Netton, *Allāh Transcendent*, pp. 9–13.
16 See Majid Fakhry, *A History of Islamic Philosophy*, 2nd edn (London: Longman/New York: Columbia University Press, 1983), p. 19; Netton, *Allāh Transcendent*, pp. 13, 59.
17 For a more elaborate survey of the significance of Alexandria, see Netton, *Allāh Transcendent*, pp. 7–13. For the late Alexandrian Syllabus, and especially the importance of Porphyry, see Dimitri Gutas, 'Paul the Persian on the classification of the parts of Aristotle's

philosophy: a milestone between Alexandria and Baghdād', *Der Islam* 60(2) (1983). See also Dimitri Gutas, 'The starting point of philosophical studies in Alexandrian and Arabic Aristotelianism', in William W. Fortenbaugh (ed.), *Theophrastus of Eresus: On his Life and Work*, Rutgers University Studies in Classical Humanities 2 (New Brunswick/Oxford: Transaction Books, 1985).

18 Aydin Sayili, 'Gondēshāpūr', in *Encyclopaedia of Islam*, new edition, vol. II (Leiden: E. J. Brill/London: Luzac, 1965), p. 1120; see also Netton, *Allāh Transcendent*, p. 14.

19 Netton, *Allāh Transcendent*, p. 14.

20 ibid., pp. 14–15.

21 Peters, *Aristotle and the Arabs*, pp. 58–9.

22 ibid., p. 59.

23 ibid.

24 See B. Carra de Vaux, 'Al-Ṣābi'a', in H. A. R. Gibb and J. H. Kramers (eds), *Shorter Encyclopaedia of Islam* (Leiden: E. J. Brill/London: Luzac, 1961), pp. 477–8; see also Netton, *Allāh Transcendent*, pp. 15–16.

25 See al-Shahrastānī, *Al-Milal wa 'l-Niḥal*, part 3, pp. 88ff., part 4, pp. 3–25, in *Al-Fiṣal fī 'l-Milal wa 'l-Ahwā' wa 'l-Niḥal li'l-Imām Ibn Ḥazm . . . wa ma'ahu Al-Milal wa 'l-Niḥal li 'l-Shahrastānī*, vol. I: parts 1–3, vol. II: parts 4–5 (Cairo: Maṭba'a Muḥammad 'Alī Ṣabīḥ, 1964). The Sabaeans were by no means monolithic: however, 'Shahrastānī probably understood Ṣābianism mainly in terms of its neo-Platonic variety' (Bruce B. Lawrence, *Shahrastānī on the Indian Religions*, Religion & Society 4 (The Hague/Paris: Mouton, 1976), p. 63).

26 See Netton, *Allāh Transcendent*, p. 16.

27 See ibid.

28 George N. Atiyeh, *Al-Kindī: The Philosopher of the Arabs* (Rawalpindi: Islamic Research Institute, 1966), p. 5.

29 ibid., p. 6.

30 ibid.

31 ibid., p. 14, n. 3; see also Netton, *Allāh Transcendent*, p. 45.

32 These events have been described in many places. See, for example, D. Sourdel, 'The 'Abbasid caliphate', in P. M. Holt, Ann K. S. Lambton and Bernard Lewis, *The Cambridge History of Islam* (Cambridge: Cambridge University Press, 1970), vol. I, pp. 123–4; Hugh Kennedy, *The Prophet and the Age of the Caliphates, A History of the Near East*, vol. I (London/New York: Longman, 1986), pp. 163–4.

33 See Sourdel, op. cit., p. 126; Kennedy, op. cit., p. 169.

34 Atiyeh, op. cit., pp. 6–7; Alfred L. Ivry, *Al-Kindi's Metaphysics: A Translation of Ya'qūb ibn Isḥāq al-Kindī's Treatise 'On First Philosophy' (fī al-Falsafah al-Ūlā)*, Studies in Islamic Philosophy and Science (Albany, N.Y.: State University of New York Press, 1974), pp. 3, 22, 55; al-Kindī *Rasā'il al-Kindī al-Falsafiyya* (henceforth abbreviated to *Rasā'il*), ed. M. A. H. Abū Rīda (2 vols, Cairo: Dār al-Fikr al-'Arabī, 1950–3), vol. I, p. 97.

35 See Netton, *Allāh Transcendent*, pp. 46, 55.

36 See Ibn Abī Uṣaybi'a, *Kitāb 'Uyūn al-Anbā' fī Ṭabaqāt al-Aṭibbā'* (Beirut: Dār Maktabat al-Ḥayāt, 1965), pp. 286–7; Atiyeh, op. cit., pp. 7–8; Ivry, op. cit., p. 3; Netton, *Allāh Transcendent*, p. 46.

37 Atiyeh, op. cit., p. 8.

38 Ivry, op. cit., p. 5; see also Netton, *Allāh Transcendent*, p. 46.

39 See H. Laoust, 'Aḥmad B. Ḥanbal', in *Encyclopaedia of Islam*, new edition, vol. I (Leiden: E. J. Brill/London: Luzac, 1960). pp. 272–7.

40 See Netton, *Allāh Transcendent*, pp. 47–51.

41 ibid., p. 46.
42 ibid., pp. 47–8.
43 *Rasā'il*, vol. I, p. 207; Netton, *Allāh Transcendent*, p. 48.
44 *Rasā'il*, vol. I, pp. 165, 373–4; Netton, *Allāh Transcendent*, p. 50.
45 Atiyeh, op. cit., p. 51.
46 See *Rasā'il*, vol. I, pp. 101, 126, 144, 150, 154.
47 See Netton, *Allāh Transcendent*, pp. 52–3.
48 ibid., p. 55.
49 Fakhry, op. cit., pp. 89–90.
50 Netton, *Allāh Transcendent*, p. 83.
51 ibid., pp. 58–9.
52 *Rasā'il*, vol. I, p. 165.
53 ibid., vol. I, p. 160 (my translation); for another translation see Ivry, op. cit., p. 112. See also Netton, *Allāh Transcendent*, pp. 59–60.
54 Netton, *Allāh Transcendent*, p. 60.
55 ibid., pp. 63–5.
56 Richard Walzer, 'New studies on Al-Kindi', in Richard Walzer, *Greek into Arabic: Essays on Islamic Philosophy*, Oriental Studies 1 (Oxford: Bruno Cassirer, 1962), p. 176.
57 See Netton, *Allāh Transcendent*, pp. 4–5.
58 William Thomson, 'Al-Ash'arī and his al-Ibānah', *The Muslim World* 32 (1942), 250.
59 W. M. Watt, *Islamic Philosophy and Theology: An Extended Survey* (Edinburgh: Edinburgh University Press, 1985), p. 47. See also al-Shahrastānī, op. cit., part 1, p. 72.
60 Watt, op. cit., p. 47.
61 See ibid.
62 ibid., pp. 106–7; see also George F. Hourani, *Islamic Rationalism: The Ethics of 'Abd al-Jabbār* (Oxford: Clarendon Press, 1971), pp. 5–7; J. R. T. M. Peters, *God's Created Speech: A Study in the Speculative Theology of the Mu'tazilī Qāḍī l-Qūḍāt Abū al-Ḥasan 'Abd al-Jabbār bn Aḥmad al-Hamaḏānī* (Leiden: E. J. Brill, 1976), pp. 8–10; S. M. Stern, "Abd al-Djabbār B. Aḥmad', in *Encyclopaedia of Islam*, vol. I, pp. 59–60.
63 Hourani, *Islamic Rationalism*, pp. 4–7; Peters, *God's Created Speech*, pp. 8–10; Stern, op. cit., p. 59; Watt, op. cit., pp. 106–7.
64 Ed. 'Abd al-Karīm 'Uthmān (Cairo: Maktabat Wahba, 1965). For the discovery of the text of *al-Mughnī*, which was edited in Cairo in sixteen volumes by a variety of editors between 1960 and 1969, See Watt, op. cit., p. 106; Hourani, *Islamic Rationalism*, pp. 4–5; Peters, *God's Created Speech*, pp. 25–7. See, however, D. Gimaret, who attributes ('convincingly' according to G. F. Hourani) the text of *Sharḥ al-Uṣūl al-Khamsa* to an author other than 'Abd al-Jabbār: D. Gimaret, 'Les uṣūl al-khamsa du qāḍī 'Abd al-Jabbār et leurs commentaires', *Annales Islamologiques* 15 (1979), 47–96; see also George F. Hourani, 'The rationalist ethics of 'Abd al-Jabbār', in George F. Hourani, *Reason and Tradition in Islamic Ethics* (Cambridge: Cambridge University Press, 1985), pp. 107–8.
65 Watt, op. cit., p. 107.
66 Hourani, *Islamic Rationalism*, p. 7.
67 ibid., p. 8.
68 ibid.
69 Peters, *God's Created Speech*, p. 5; Watt, op. cit., pp. 48–52.
70 'Abd al-Jabbār, *Sharḥ al-Uṣūl al-Khamsa*, p. 227; Netton, *Allāh Transcendent*, pp. 4–5.
71 Watt, op. cit., pp. 48–52, esp. p. 52.
72 Peters, *God's Created Speech*, pp. 5–6.

73 Hourani, *Islamic Rationalism*, p. 145.
74 The standard work in English on these Brethren of Purity (Arabic: Ikhwān al-Ṣafā' is Netton, *Muslim Neoplationists*.
75 Hourani, *Islamic Rationalism*, pp. 144–5.
76 Peters, *God's Created Speech*, pp. 119–21, 123.
77 ibid., p. 404.
78 See Hourani, *Islamic Rationalism*, p. 129.
79 Peters, *God's Created Speech*, p. 15.
80 See Hourani, *Islamic Rationalism*, p. 144.
81 Peters, *God's Created Speech*, pp. 403–5.
82 George F. Hourani, 'Deliberation in Aristotle and 'Abd al-Jabbār', in Hourani, *Reason and Tradition in Islamic Ethics*, p. 117.

FURTHER READING

Atiyeh, George N. (1966) *Al-Kindī: The Philosopher of the Arabs*, Rawalpindi: Islamic Research Institute.

El-Ehwany, Ahmed Fouad (1963) 'Al-Kindi', in M. M. Sharif (ed.) *A History of Muslim Philosophy*, Wiesbaden: Otto Harrassowitz, vol. I, pp. 421–34.

Encyclopaedia of Islam (1960–) New edition, eds H. A. R. Gibb *et al.*, Leiden: E. J. Brill/London: Luzac, 8 bound vols + fascs published so far.

Fakhry, Majid (1983) *A History of Islamic Philosophy*, 2nd edn, London: Longman/New York: Columbia University Press.

Hourani, George F. (1971). *Islamic Rationalism: The Ethics of 'Abd al-Jabbār*, Oxford: Clarendon Press.

—— (1985) *Reason and Tradition in Islamic Ethics*, Cambridge: Cambridge University Press.

Ivry, Alfred L. (1974) *Al-Kindi's Metaphysics: A Translation of Ya'qūb ibn Isḥāq al-Kindī's Treatise 'On First Philosophy' (fī al-Falsafah al-Ūlā)*. Studies in Islamic Philosophy and Science, Albany, N.Y.: State University of New York Press.

Kennedy, Hugh (1986) *The Prophet and the Age of the Caliphates*, *A History of the Near East*, vol. I, London/New York: Longman.

Netton, Ian Richard (1982) *Muslim Neoplatonists: An Introduction to the Thought of the Brethren of Purity (Ikhwān al-Ṣafā')*, London: Allen & Unwin.

—— (1989) *Allāh Transcendent: Studies in the Structure and Semiotics of Islamic Philosophy, Theology and Cosmology*, London: Routledge. (See esp. the chapter entitled 'Al-Kindī: the watcher at the gate', pp. 45–98.)

Peters, F. E. (1968) *Aristotle and the Arabs: The Aristotelian Tradition in Islam*, New York: New York University Press/London: University of London Press, 1968.

—— (1970) *The Harvest of Hellenism*, New York: Simon & Schuster.

—— (1973) *Allah's Commonwealth: A History of Islam in the Near East 600–1100 A. D.*, New York: Simon & Schuster.

Peters, J. R. T. M. (1976) *God's Created Speech: A Study in the Speculative Theology of the Mu'tazilī Qāḍī l-Quḍāt Abū al-Ḥasan 'Abd al-Jabbār bn Aḥmad al-Hamaḏānī*, Leiden: E. J. Brill.

Shorter Encyclopaedia of Islam (1961), eds H. A. R. Gibb and J. H. Kramers, Leiden: E. J. Brill/London: Luzac.

Stern, S. M., Hourani, Albert and Brown, Vivian (eds) (1972) *Islamic Philosophy and the Classical Tradition*, Oriental Studies 5, Oxford: Cassirer.

Valiuddin, Mir (1963) 'Mu'tazilism', in M. M. Sharif (ed.) *A History of Muslim Philosophy*, Wiesbaden: Otto Harrassowitz, vol. I, pp. 199–220.

Walzer, Richard (1962) *Greek into Arabic: Essays on Islamic Philosophy*, Oriental Studies 1, Oxford: Cassirer.

Watt, William Montgomery (1985) *Islamic Philosophy and Theology: An Extended Survey*, Edinburgh: Edinburgh University Press. (This is a second enlarged edition of his *Islamic Philosophy and Theology*, published by the same press in 1962 as no. 1 in the Islamic Surveys Series.)

Wolfson, Harry Austryn (1976) *The Philosophy of the Kalam*, Structure and Growth of Philosophic Systems from Plato to Spinoza 4, Cambridge, Mass./London: Harvard University Press. (Contains large sections dealing with Mu'tazilite doctrines.)

40

AL-FĀRĀBĪ

Harry Bone

The reputation of Abū Naṣr Muḥammad b. Muḥammad b. Tarkhān b. Awzalagh (Uzlugh) al-Fārābī (*c.* AD 870–950), referred to as Alfarabius and Avennasar in medieval Latin texts, has to some extent been overshadowed by his predecessor al-Kindī and his successors Ibn Sīnā (Avicenna) (d. AD 1037) and Ibn Rushd (Averroes) (d. AD 1198), both of whom relied extensively on his work. One biographical source acknowledges Ibn Sīnā's debt to al-Fārābī and claims he was 'the greatest of the Muslim philosophers, none of them reached his standing in his field' (Ibn Khallikān 1970?: 153). According to another well-known tradition Ibn Sīnā is said to have read Aristotle's *Metaphysics* forty times before reading al-Fārābī's *Intentions of Aristotle's Metaphysics* (*Fī Aghrāḍ Kitāb Mā Ba'd al-Ṭabī'a*) – only then, it is claimed, did the work become clear to him (al-Qifṭī 1903: 412).

The acclaim of the medieval biographers for al-Fārābī reflects the significance of the man who became known as 'the Second Teacher' – second, that is, to Aristotle. His work marked a watershed in the history of Islamic philosophy which was to change the course of Islamic thought and flow on into the rational currents of medieval Christianity and Judaism. For while al-Fārābī's predecessors, al-Kindī and the Mu'tazilites, had drawn on the Greek tradition, both in their methodology and their philosophical approach to theology, it was revelation which took precedence over reason – the authority of the Qur'ān was paramount, a text revealed by a God who knew the particulars of a world he had created *ex nihilo*. For al-Fārābī, however, it was through the reason (*'aql*) of the philosopher that one could know the true nature of man and the universe rather than the revealed text of the Qur'ān. Furthermore, God (Allāh) was no longer the omniscient creator who willed change on earth, but rather a modified Neoplatonic 'First Mover' who did not *will* the creation of the world at all, but rather *caused* it; al-Fārābī's God was the First Cause (*al-sabab al-awwal*) of an eternally emanating cosmos. With such a view of the cosmos, his theories of intellection, politics and prophecy, 'the Second Master' (after al-Kindī) was to change the face of his art by firmly establishing the Aristotelian, Platonic and Neoplatonic traditions in Islamic philosophy.

LIFE

The sources we have for al-Fārābī's life are scant and far from reliable. He was born in AD 870 in the district of Fārāb in Transoxiana, the son of an army commander who was probably of Turkish origin, although one source claims he was of Persian descent (Ibn Abī Uṣaybiʿa 1965: 603). He grew up in Damascus, where, according to the same source, he worked as a night watchman in a garden, during which time he is said to have devoted himself to 'philosophy and philosophical enquiry' by 'staying up late to read and write by the light of the watchman's lamp' (ibid.: 603). As a young man he travelled to Baghdad, where he settled for some years and studied and mastered Arabic among other languages, and engaged himself in the study of logic. He was to study under some of the great logicians of his day, the Christian Aristotelians associated with the Baghdad school such as Mattā b. Yūnus and the Nestorian Yuḥannā b. Haylān, and, despite his youth, he soon surpassed his contemporaries and became the scholar of his age (Ibn Khallikān 1970?: 154; Ibn Abī Uṣaybiʿa 1965 : 605).

Most of his works are said to have been written during this period, and his experience of the turmoil of tenth-century Baghdad may well have left a lasting impression on him and his thought. He lived through the chaotic and turbulent reigns of the caliphs al-Muqtadir (reg. AD 908–32), al-Qāhir (reg. AD 932–4) and al-Rāḍī (reg. AD 934–40), and thus witnessed firsthand the decline of the Islamic polity. It was also a time of religious sectarian conflict in the capital, the struggle for supremacy between the Shīʿites and Ḥanbalites, and increasing social disorder as the weakness of central authority led to outbreaks of civil unrest amongst the lower orders of the city.[1] Ibn Khallikān tells us that one of al-Fārābī's main 'political' works, *Al-Siyāsa al-Madaniyya* (*The Political Regime*), was begun in Baghdad (1970?:155), and his portrayal of perfect and imperfect political states in this and similar works may well have been informed by his own experience of this political and religious chaos, just as Plato before him had drawn on contemporary models in his attempt to reform the *polis* as the ideal political entity.[2]

From Baghdad he left for Egypt only to return to Aleppo in Syria to join the court of Sayf al-Dawla (AD 918–67), the Ḥamdānid prince famous for his love of literature and the arts, who was quite impressed by al-Fārābī. He honoured him and acknowledged his learning and understanding and gave him a daily grant of four dirhams. But we are also told that al-Fārābī did not take full advantage of this princely favour: he is said to have led an ascetic life, living only on what he needed to live on, and he dressed in the 'garb of the Ṣūfīs' (al-Qifṭī 1903: 279), no doubt out of place amongst the Ḥamdānid prince's entourage. But despite the favour he enjoyed at court, his association with Sayf al-Dawla was to be short-lived: he died in AD 950 at the age of 80 shortly after his return to Aleppo, although the details and circumstances of his death are as uncertain and open to question as those of his life.[3]

It is significant that in this last period of his life, al-Fārābī was living in a Shī'ite environment, the ideas of which are reflected so strongly in his conception of the ideal political community and its leader, and, as one scholar has suggested, it may be that in fleeing the collapsing capital for life in Aleppo under Sayf al-Dawla he was acting on the belief laid down in one of his political works that it is the duty of the virtuous person to flee the corrupt regime for life in the ideal one (Bin-'Abd al-'Ālī 1979: 23). Perhaps al-Fārābī considered the rule of Sayf al-Dawla to be the contemporary example closest to his conception of the excellent or virtuous city (*al-madīna al-fāḍila*).

WORKS

Al-Fārābī broke with his Islamic predecessors in that he was a philosopher first and a Muslim second. He saw himself as a bearer of the tradition of Plato, Aristotle and the Neoplatonists, the 'excellent philosophers' (*al-ḥukamā' al-afāḍil*), and it was to the classical Greek tradition, 'the sayings of the Ancients' (*aqāwīl al-qudamā'*), that he looked for authority rather than the revealed text. Al-Jurr has suggested that al-Fārābī viewed Socrates, Plato and Aristotle as a chain of infallible *imāms* (1982: 106), while Leaman has claimed that al-Fārābī may have considered philosophy like *ḥadīth* (the tradition of the Prophet), in that it is only genuine if it is transmitted from generation to generation (Leaman 1985: 14). Although both of these interpretations are open to question, they do express, in the language of Islam, the fundamental assumption underlying al-Fārābī's work: his belief in the essential *unity* of the philosophical tradition. This belief is no more explicitly explained than in his *Reconciliation of the Opinions of the Two Sages* (*Al-Jam' Bayna Ra'yay al-Ḥakīmayn*), in the introduction to which he states his intention of 'showing the conformity between what they [Plato and Aristotle] believed' (*Jam'*: 79).

This conception of the timeless unity of philosophy partly accounts for the wide scope of al-Fārābī's works – he was a prolific writer who wrote on a wide range of philosophical subjects – and presents modern scholars with unusual problems in trying to unravel the thought of al-Fārābī and some of his successors (see Mahdi 1991: 12). For a philosopher who tries to reconcile the essential differences between the thought of the 'Ancients' in general – his works are a synthesis of Platonic, Aristotelian and Neoplatonic ideas – and Plato and Aristotle in particular, may not only make it difficult for the modern scholar to determine conclusively the philosopher's own position on a given question, but also presents problems in verifying the authenticity of works attributed to him.

Thus, although more than one hundred works are attributed to al-Fārābī, not all are genuine (Walzer 1965: 780). Those that modern scholars have accepted as his include works on logic (such as his *Necessary and Existent Premises*),[4] physics (*On Vacuum*), metaphysics (*On the One*), politics (*The Principles of the Opinions of the People of the Virtuous City*; *The Political Regime*) and music, a facet of his writing which is often forgotten, his most famous work being his *Great Book of Music*.[5] But he was perhaps most famous as a commentator (*shāriḥ*): his summaries of the philosophies of Plato and Aristotle, his numerous commentaries on Aristotelian logic, such as his *Commentary on Analytica Posteriora*, and on major works such as the *Nicomachean Ethics* and *Metaphysics*, and his commentaries on Plato's political works (especially the *Laws*) played a major role in integrating the classical Greek tradition into the mainstream of Islamic philosophy.

We can begin to see how al-Fārābī managed to do this, to break with al-Kindī and the Mu'tazilites and put reason above revelation, by looking at his political works and his conception of the relationship between politics, philosophy and religion.

THE RELATIONSHIP BETWEEN POLITICS, PHILOSOPHY AND RELIGION

The science of politics is central to al-Fārābī's philosophy but is not confined to the city state – the *polis* of Plato and Aristotle. In attempting to reconcile Islam with his Greek predecessors he conceived of man in a society which looked beyond the temporal *polis*, as did the Islamic community (*umma*). He took Aristotle's First Cause, which he identified with Allāh, and an eternal Neoplatonic emanation, adapted from Plotinus, and looked at man's relation with his fellow-man in the light of man's relation to the cosmos. It is significant that most of one of his main 'political' works, *The Virtuous City* (*Al-Madīna al-Fāḍila*),[6] is devoted to expounding the nature and structure of the universe and the origins of man and knowledge, and it is by examining the structure of the cosmos and the nature and purpose of man's knowledge that we can begin to understand al-Fārābī's conception of politics, the science of sciences.

In adapting a Neoplatonic scheme of emanation he presents the heavens as a series of ten intellects eternally emanating from the First Cause, the last of which is the active intellect (*al-'aql al-fa''āl*), which serves to actualize the intellect of man in this world, the world below the moon.[7] The active intellect gives man 'the first intelligibles' (*al-ma'qūlāt al-ūlā*), primary knowledge, and these are 'only supplied to him in order to be used by him to reach his ultimate perfection, i.e. happiness' (*Madīna*: 205). We shall analyse the nature of al-Fārābī's happiness (*sa'āda*) below. The key point here is that, according to al-Fārābī, man cannot attain perfection, for the sake of which his inborn nature has been given to him, unless groups of people come together and cooperate (*Madīna*: 229). Thus al-Fārābī, like his Greek predecessors, believed that knowledge alone is not enough to achieve perfection and that organized human association, and therefore politics, is essential.

Thus, although al-Fārābī in the tradition of Plato and Aristotle upheld that man was essentially a political animal, he took the role of politics one stage further. He modelled his perfect state on Plato's *polis*: the *madīna* (city) was the smallest perfect society and the ruler (*ra'īs*) was to be a philosopher. But al-Fārābī viewed the perfect or virtuous city (*al-madīna al-fāḍila*) as a microcosm of the heavens. He maintained that 'the ruler of the *madīna* is similar to the First Cause by which the rest of the beings exist' and that 'the ranks of beings descend little by little' (*Siyāsa*: 84) in a strict hierarchy in the perfect state of the sublunar world, as does the eternal emanation of the heavens. Just as the First Cause regulates the existence of the cosmos, so the ruler of the *madīna*, the *ra'īs*, orders the ranks of the citizens.

As Galston has observed, al-Fārābī does not make clear exactly how the *ra'īs* rules the city, the specific activities the supreme ruler undertakes (1990: 128). How exactly is the *ra'īs* similar to the First Cause, and how in practice do the ranks of the *madīna* and the sublunar world reflect those of the world above the moon? What is clear, however, is that the world above the moon is necessarily harmonious, the heavens eternally emanating from the First Cause, whereas in the sublunar world of the *madīna* ultimate perfection is only achieved by 'certain voluntary actions, some of which are mental and others bodily actions' (*Madīna*: 206). The harmony of the *madīna* can only mirror that of the world above the moon if the ruler of the *madīna* guides the people to do right actions, actions which are in keeping with their hierarchical place in society. The science of politics, then, according to al-Fārābī

> investigates the various kinds of voluntary actions and ways of life; the positive dispositions, morals, inclinations, and states of character that lead to these actions and ways of life; the ends for the sake of which they are performed. . . . It explains that some of these ends are *true* happiness, while others are presumed to be happiness although they are not.
>
> (*Siyāsa*: 12 (Preface))

Politics is concerned first with defining true happiness, second with the enumeration of acts, ways of life, morals, etc. which should be found in the *madīna* by which the citizens may attain true happiness (*Milla*: 59; *Iḥṣā'*: 72).

The role of religion (*milla*) in maintaining the harmony of the *madīna* is fundamental, though temporal. Religion arises from the need to convey what the philosopher knows about the universe to the masses in a form they will understand. It is a way of transmitting truths about the cosmos, the principles of beings, the First Cause and the nature of true happiness, as well as the acts and ways of life, etc. by which happiness is attained, in symbolic form. Philosophers, or those who are close to the philosophers and trust their views, may understand these truths by demonstration – they are 'impressed on their souls as they really are' – whereas the majority understand them through symbols 'which reproduce them by imitation' (*Madīna*: 279). Those who perceive the principles of beings, as they are, are the wise (*al-ḥukamā'*), the philosophers, while those who know the imaginary representations of them and take them to be like that in reality are the believers (*al-mu'minūn*) (*Siyāsa*: 86). Religion, then, constitutes 'opinions and acts decreed and bound by conditions laid down for the masses by their first ruler' (*Milla*: 43).

This idea of having one truth for the masses and another for the elect, an idea that both Ibn Sīnā (d. 1037) and Ibn Rushd (d. 1198) were later to adopt,[8] is so significant in the history of Islamic philosophy because it enshrined the supremacy of reason over revelation. The 'truth' of religion was now specific to a certain age and culture, and thus, according to al-Fārābī, there may be many virtuous nations and cities whose religions differ, even though they are all pursuing one and the same end: true happiness (*Siyāsa*: 85–6). Al-Fārābī's religion is no more than an *imitation* of philosophy, which comes before philosophy in time 'just as a user of tools comes before the tools' (*Ḥurūf*: 132), and the relationship between religion, philosophy and politics is illustrated by his assertion in *The Attainment of Happiness* (*Taḥṣīl al-Sa'āda*) that 'the meaning of philosopher, first ruler, lawgiver and *imām* are all one' (*Taḥṣīl*: 93).

In the light of the above we can understand why al-Fārābī grouped (dialectical) theology (*'ilm al-kalām*) and jurisprudence (*fiqh*) together with politics in his *Enumeration of the Sciences* (*Iḥṣā' al-'Ulūm*). In al-Fārābī's scheme of things, theology is no more than a means by which man can support 'the fixed opinions and actions which the founder of the religion/religious community [*milla*] declared, and declare false through arguments anything that contradicts them' (*Iḥṣā'*: 75). Similarly, jurisprudence is a means by which man deduces those things which the lawgiver (*wāḍi 'al-sharī'a*) has not specified exactly, and so theology and jurisprudence play no role in establishing the *truth* but may even lead one further from it, as both sciences are founded on a religion, which is, by definition, only an imitation of the ultimate philosophical truth.[9] Thus, the theologian (*al-mutakallim*) can be said to be 'one of the elite, but in relation to the people of that religion (*milla*) only, while the philosopher's "eliteness" (*khāṣṣiyyatuhu*) is in relation to all people and all nations' (*Ḥurūf*: 133).

Philosophy, therefore, comes before religion, which is an imitation of it – opinions and actions drawn up for the masses. Politics is fundamental to al-Fārābī's thought because it is the means by which such opinions and actions may be put into practice in such a way that man achieves his ultimate perfection, happiness, the very reason why man is given his 'first intelligibles', and the means by which the hierarchy and harmony of the perfect human association under the *ra'īs* may reflect that of the heavens above. Politics essentially deals with the question of 'realization', as Mahdi has observed: 'to know is to realize a thing in a certain way, to realize it in the mind; but realization has yet another dimension, which is to see the thing exist in others and in cities and nations' (1981: 15). In the light of this, it is no surprise to learn from Ibn Abī Uṣaybi'a that one of al-Fārābī's main 'political' works, *Al-Siyāsa al-Madaniyya* (*The Political Regime*) was also known as *Mabādi' al-Mawjūdāt* (*The Principles of Beings*) (*Siyāsa*: 13 (introduction)).

HAPPINESS: THIS WORLD AND THE NEXT, THE FIRST AND LAST PERFECTION

Al-Fārābī's happiness (*sa'āda*) is ultimately not of this world. We have seen how man's first intelligibles are only given to him to be used by him to attain happiness – happiness is his ultimate perfection 'for the sake of which his inborn nature has been given to him' (*Madīna*: 229). The prophet, we are told, 'holds the most perfect rank of humanity and has reached the highest degree of happiness': his soul is 'as if it is united with the active intellect', and it is through this that he knows 'every action by which happiness can be reached' (*Madīna*: 245–7), the first condition for being a ruler. This is the most perfect rank of humanity: that man reaches the rank of the active intellect (*Siyāsa*: 32).[10] But what exactly is happiness (*sa'āda*), and what is it to be happy?

Happiness is the good which is pursued for its own sake (*Madīna*: 206) and in this respect is comparable with Aristotle's *eudaimonia*. Happiness is 'the absolute good' (*al-khayr 'alā 'l-iṭlāq*) and thus defines what is good and evil – anything that is of any use in attaining happiness is good 'not for its own sake but because of its use in attaining happiness' and, conversely, everything which hinders the attainment of happiness is evil (*Siyāsa*: 72). But the absolute good in al-Fārābī's cosmos transcends this world: ultimate happiness for man is that his soul 'reaches a degree of perfection in (its) existence where it is in no need of matter for its support' (*Madīna*: 205), life in the hereafter. And so al-Fārābī makes the distinction between the happiness of man in this world and supreme happiness (*al-sa'āda al-quṣwā*) in the life to come. It is, he maintains, what Socrates, Plato and Aristotle believed: that man has two lives and two 'perfections', a first and a last, the last being ultimate happiness in the hereafter (*Fuṣūl*: 120). We shall examine the varying degrees of happiness and how they are attained in the section entitled 'Class and *tafāḍul*: degrees of excellence and happiness' below.

JUSTICE: THE HARMONY OF WORLD AND HEAVEN

The attainment of happiness, then, is the central theme of al-Fārābī's political works, unlike Plato's *Republic*, where the quest is for justice (*dikaiosyne*). However, the concept of justice is fundamental to al-Fārābī's philosophy and is ultimately expressed in the order of the cosmos. While Plato conceived man in a *polis* in his search for justice, and looked for justice in man's society to illustrate the nature of justice in man, the justice of al-Fārābī, with his view of man as part of a cosmic order, was determined by the fact that 'the First is just, and its justice is in its substance' (*Madīna*: 97) and that justice expresses itself in the manner in which the natural material bodies are arranged. Justice (*'adl*) has connotations of 'balance' and moderation and could be translated literally as 'equitable composition'.[11] Al-Fārābī's justice, then, is seen in the order of all existents, the balance of the universe of which man is a part. So how is the universe 'balanced', and how is justice expressed in it?

Justice is seen in the hierarchy of existents in the world above the moon, and the world below. In the superlunar world the ranks of existents descend one by one from the First Cause down through the ten intellects to the active intellect, whereas in the sublunar world the hierarchy of existents is depicted in ascending order: from common prime matter (*al-mādda al-ūlā al-mushtaraka*) to the elements (*al-isṭaqisāt*), up to the minerals, plants and animals, culminating in the highest rank, the rational animal – man (*Madīna*: 113). The First is just and therefore 'each existent receives from the First its allotted share of existence in accordance with its rank' (*Madīna*: 97), and any 'possible existent (*mumkin*)' will be granted its existence according to its intrinsic merit (*Siyāsa*: 64). Thus, justice is ultimately expressed by the fact that the universe is arranged into ranks of existence in a fixed order 'which act in conformity with the First Cause and follow it' (*Madīna*: 236–9).

Justice is also expressed in the regulation of existents (*mawjūdāt*) themselves and is indeed needed to maintain the eternal pattern of change in the sublunar world. Such existents, according to al-Fārābī, consist of form (*ṣūra*) and matter (*mādda*). Form in a body is the bodily essence (*al-jawhar al-jismānī*) of it, like the shape of a bed present in a bed, while matter is like the wood of a bed (*Siyāsa*: 36). Thus, the eternal pattern of generation and corruption, the renewal of a species of existents in the world, is maintained because

> since forms are contrary to one another and since it is as natural for matter to have one form, as to have its contrary, each of these bodies has a rightful claim to its form and a rightful claim to its matter. . . . Justice herein is, then, that matter be taken from this and given to that [i.e. the two contrary forms], or vice versa, and that this take place in succession. But because full justice has to be meted out to these existents, it is not possible that one and the same thing should last perpetually as one in number, but its eternal permanence is established in its being one in species.
>
> (*Madīna*: 144–9)

Therefore justice not only allows for the renewal of existents, the succession of individuals which make up one class, but also regulates their constitution. Thus justice regulates this world, the world below the moon.

So how is justice expressed in the *madīna*? Al-Fārābī viewed the natural hierarchy of the universe as the ultimate paradigm which 'applies equally to the city and equally to every whole which is composed by nature of well-ordered coherent parts' (*Madīna*: 236–7).[12] The universe, then, is the macrocosm of which any other organic whole is a microcosm: just as the heavens descend from the First Cause down through the hierarchy of intellects to the active intellect, so the city descends from the *ra'īs* down through the hierarchy of classes to the lowest class, the body descends from the heart down through the hierarchy of limbs and organs to the spleen and subordinate organs, and the soul descends from the rational faculty down through the hierarchy of faculties to the nutritive faculty.

So justice in the soul and state is the harmony of its constituent parts in accordance with their ranks. But we have already observed that man's actions are voluntary and therefore such a harmony is not necessary like the justice expressed in the natural order of existents but voluntary. The harmony of the city depends on the ruler and that of the soul on the rational faculty, to rule the other parts.

Al-Fārābī contrasts his vision of true justice by arguing the case for natural justice in *Al-Madīna al-Fāḍila*, as Walzer has observed. Justice, says al-Fārābī, is 'identical with superiority gained by force', and 'the group which gains superiority over the other . . . is to be called happy and blessed. These are the things which are natural, either to every individual or to every group, and they follow closely the nature of the natural existents' (*Madīna*: 298–9). But we see later (ch. 18, 10ff.) that this is really injustice, as the balance is disturbed and the harmony breaks down. Walzer has remarked that this view is 'deliberately introduced in Chapter 18 as an antithesis to the metaphysical truth as explained in the first two chapters' (*Madīna*: 358 (Commentary)), and al-Fārābī himself has remarked elsewhere that 'the harmony and justice which they employ among themselves is not truly justice, but only something resembling justice, not being so' (*Fuṣūl*: 40 (Arabic text: 136)).

CLASS AND *TAFĀḌUL*: DEGREES OF EXCELLENCE AND HAPPINESS

The ranks of the soul and the virtuous city, the former ordered by justice by virtue of its nature, the latter owing to the rule of the ruler, are divided into five:

SOUL: 1. The rational faculty (*al-quwwa al-nāṭiqa*) 2. The representative (*al-quwwa al-mutakhayyila*) 3. The appetitive (*al-quwwa al-nuzū'iyya*) 4. The sensitive (*al-quwwa al-ḥāssa*) 5. The nutritive (*al-quwwa al-ghādhiya*).

MADĪNA: 1. The philosophers (*al-afāḍil*) 2. The interpreters (*dhawū al-alsina*) 3. The assessors (*al-muqqadirūn*) 4. The fighters (*al-mujāhidūn*) 5. The rich (*al-māliyyūn*).

It is significant, however, that the five classes are not mentioned in *Al-Madīna al-Fāḍila* but only in *Fuṣūl al-Madanī*, which, it has been suggested, was intended for a Muslim audience (Rosenthal 1958: 133). In most of al-Fārābī's other political works we are presented with a more cosmic view – the *madīna*'s hierarchy as a microcosm of the ultimate Neoplatonic paradigm – and hence the concept of *tafāḍul*, 'difference in excellence'. The parts of al-Fārābī's *madīna* 'are different by nature, and their natural dispositions are unequal in excellence' (*Madīna*: 232–3), and in the *Al-Siyāsa al-Madaniyya* we see that 'people differ in excellence (*yatafāḍalūn*) by nature in ranks according to the difference of excellence of the ranks of the kinds of arts (*ṣanā'i'*) and sciences for which they have been disposed' (ibid.: 77). This difference in excellence is significant not only because it is the basis for order in the city, but because it seems to determine, to some extent, the *kind* of happiness that a given individual attains. The prophet attains the highest form of human happiness, as we have seen, while the share of happiness other individuals attain is related to their class.[13]

Al-Fārābī's happiness, then, like Plato's, differs from that of classical Islam in that the highest degree of happiness one can attain is determined by one's innate disposition, and consequently one's rank in the *madīna*. Allāh, of course, rewards man by degrees, but man is rewarded for each action,[14] and each individual is equal before him in his reckoning (*ḥisāb*), and hence there is no 'ceiling' placed on the degree of happiness he may attain according to his intrinsic value.

Al-Fārābī's conception of class and *tafāḍul* raises further questions about the happiness of the citizens. First, what determines the happiness of a given individual, and how is it attained? We have already seen that religion (*milla*), the means by which the masses attain happiness, consists of both opinions (*ārā'*) and actions (*a'māl/af'āl*). But these are both subject to the class of the citizen: individuals attain happiness through certain things in common which all the citizens perform and understand, and other things which each class knows and does on its own (*Madīna*: 260–1). Thus, an individual in a given class has a specific art (*ṣanā'a*) which conforms to his or her place in the *madīna*, the microcosm, just as each existent fulfils its cosmic function in the ranks below the First Cause, the macrocosm.[15]

The happiness of individuals varies in *kind* in correspondence with a person's rank and art, as we have already noted, but it also varies in *quantity* and *quality*. The arts (*ṣanā'i'*) not only differ in kind by nature – dancing is different from the art of jurisprudence, for example – but the practitioners of a certain kind of art differ in that some may know *more* parts of a given art than another, and they may also know what they do know *better*. Similarly, 'the kinds of happiness are unequal in excellence in these respects' (*Madīna*: 266–9). Thus, individuals may improve their lot, their share of ultimate happiness, by practice. Just as practising acts of writing 'earns man the goodness of the art of writing, a disposition of the soul', so practising the actions aimed at attaining happiness strengthens the part of the soul prepared by nature for happiness (*Siyāsa*: 81). In other words, the 'happinesses' (*al-sa'ādāt*) which the masses attain differ in excellence not only in kind, according to their class, but also 'in quantity and quality according to the difference of excellence of the perfections which they acquire through their deeds in the city (*bi'l-af'āl al-madaniyya*)' (*Siyāsa*: 81).

Second, how are the 'happinesses' of the masses related to their respective classes? A citizen's happiness is individual in that it is dependent on the opinions (*ārā'*) and actions (*a'māl/af'āl*) of that citizen, but a citizen's soul does not attain ultimate happiness alone. For the souls of a given class are 'like one single soul which remains the same all the time' (*Madīna*: 260–1), and the happiness of a soul increases with successive generations (*Madīna*: 264–7). Similar souls (*al-anfus al-mutashābiha*) join together with each passing generation, and the more souls join together, the greater the enjoyment of each of them (*Siyāsa*: 82). Happiness, then, in this sense, is both individual and collective.

Third, apart from the fact that al-Fārābī considers association to be needed because man is not physically self-sufficient, if man can attain happiness as an individual, then is association and life in a state under a philosopher-*ra'īs* needed *in itself* or just as a means by which the masses may be guided? While al-Fārābī, like his Greek predecessors, stresses the need for association for the sake of physical survival, we have already noted the stress he places on the unity and harmony of the parts of the city, or, indeed, the harmony of any organic whole composed of constituent parts, as the most perfect arrangement. In this sense the perfect state is needed in itself. However, there are cases where an individual may attain happiness outside *al-madīna al-fāḍila*, as Galston has observed (1990: 176ff.). For example, an individual from a virtuous city who is forced to live and act like the people of an imperfect city, 'an ignorant city' (*madīna jāhiliyya*), remains good, and 'the fact that he persists in doing what he is forced to do does not produce in his soul a disposition which is contrary to the virtuous dispositions' (*Madīna*: 276–7). But al-Fārābī tells us that such an individual is a stranger (*gharīb*)[16] in the ignorant city and it is his duty to emigrate to a virtuous city, if one happens to exist at that time (*Milla*: 56; *Fuṣūl*: 72 (Arabic text: 164)).

This need for an individual to live in a virtuous state corresponds to the classical Islamic view of the relationship between a Muslim and the Islamic community, the *umma*:

> The community of Islam is the only valid context from which individual Muslims can respond to the divine commands. One cannot be a Muslim outside of the *umma*; it is, in that understanding, the vehicle for or context of individual salvation. The Qur'ān is absolutely clear that no person is responsible for any other at the day of resurrection, but contemporary Islam is also extremely careful to underscore the importance of the collective life.
>
> (Smith and Haddad 1981: 29)

It is, then, the attainment of happiness (*sa'āda*) which is the the ultimate end of al-Fārābī's political works, and the end of man himself: the culmination of his cosmic function. In this respect al-Fārābī's *sa'āda* is comparable with Aristotle's *eudaimonia* or Aquinas' *beatitudo*. It has been claimed that al-Fārābī's happiness is essentially theoretical and built on study and science and that an individual's actions are secondary (Madkour 1983a: 40). While this may be true of the philosopher/prophet, as we shall see in the next section, the masses attain happiness through both their opinions (*ārā'*) and actions (*a'māl/af'āl*). The masses may perfect their souls with practice: 'the more steadily a man applies himself to them [*af'āl*], the stronger and more excellent and more perfect becomes the soul, whose very purpose is to reach happiness' (*Madīna*: 262–3). And so the virtuous city (*al-madīna al-fāḍila*) under the philosopher-ruler (*ra'īs*) and true religion (*milla*) is the ideal context for the masses to fulfil their cosmic function.

PERFECT AND IMPERFECT SOCIETIES: THE ROLE OF THE *RA'ĪS*

But who is fit to be the *ra'īs* of the *madīna*? What makes them special, and what role do they play? And how does al-Fārābī's portrayal of perfect and imperfect rulers relate to his own religio-political tradition? To answer these questions, let us first look briefly at the different kinds of imperfect societies so that we may shed some light on al-Fārābī's view of the role of the ruler.

Al-Fārābī maintained that people have to associate with each other to form societies because man is not self-sufficient – human association is based on need, and man 'needs many things which he cannot provide for himself' (*Madīna*: 228–9), a view taken up by our philosopher's successors such as Ibn Sīnā (1938: 303–4). The fact that there are many things he needs necessitates that the society be of a certain size, and al-Fārābī took the *madīna* as the smallest possible perfect society, following the example of Plato's *polis*. Thus any society smaller than the *madīna* – the village, quarter, street or house – must be imperfect by virtue of its size.

Al-Fārābī divides his other imperfect states into four groups, the ignorant city (*al-madīna al-jāhiliyya*), the wicked city (*al-madīna al-fāsiqa*), the city that has deliberately changed its character (*al-madīna al-mubaddala*) and the one that misses the right path (*al-madīna al-ḍālla*) (*Madīna*: 252–3). There are four types of 'ignorant' city, which are ultimately derived from Plato, and the comparison between the two has been studied enough elsewhere to require no further explanation here.[17] However, it is worth noting al-Fārābī's use of the word *al-jāhiliyya*, the Islamic term usually used to mean the 'age of ignorance', the pagan age of the Arabs before the advent of Islam.[18]

Al-Fārābī's other imperfect states are described in Qur'ānic terms. The wicked city (*al-fāsiqa*) is the city whose views are those of the excellent. It knows God, happiness and the ranks of existents, etc. but the actions of the people are those of the people of the ignorant cities (*Madīna*: 256–9).[19]

The city that has deliberately changed its character (*al-mubaddala*) is the city whose people previously held the views of the people of the excellent city, but they have been changed and therefore perform different actions (*Madīna*: 258–9). Words with the root letters b–d–l are often used in the Qur'ān to denote moral change, evil changed to good,[20] or, as in this case, good changed to evil.[21]

The city which misses the right path (*al-ḍālla*) is that which aims at happiness after this life, but it is given useless beliefs and wrong representations of true happiness as the first ruler falsely pretended to be receiving revelation (*Madīna*: 258–9). The idea of going or being led astray (*ḍall/iḍlāl*) is a common Qur'ānic theme.[22]

Although al-Fārābī's imperfect states are drawn to some extent from Plato's conception of the imperfect *polis*, there are marked differences. First, Plato's imperfect states reflect the societies of his day, the Spartan timocracy and Athenian democracy (and the tyranny of Dionysius I of Sicily?) – man as a citizen of the *polis*; while al-Fārābī's states are described in moral and religious terms – man as part of a religion or religious community (*milla*). However, it is conceivable that al-Fārābī, too, drew on his political and religious background for his portrayal of imperfect societies. Perhaps the city which has deliberately changed its character was the declining caliphate al-Fārābī sought to reform, and perhaps he had Musaylima and the other false prophets[23] in mind for his conception of the city which misses the right path because its first ruler falsely pretends to be receiving revelation?

Second, although Plato describes his imperfect states as a chronological breakdown of unity, each with its corresponding character sketch, each one developing from its predecessor, al-Fārābī's are individual cities which are viewed in religious terms. In this we see our two philosophers' ultimate aims: for Plato, to illustrate the nature of justice (justice in the soul is analogous to justice in the *polis* and both must degenerate accordingly), and for al-Fārābī, to look beyond the *polis* to the attainment of happiness in the next world.

Finally, we notice that while the corresponding characters of Plato's imperfect states are only types to correspond to the societies themselves, and may not necessarily be ruled by such a man, al-Fārābī stresses the role of the ruler of his societies. While it is clear that Plato's ideal society must be ruled by a philosopher and his tyranny by a tyrant, the nature of the rulers in between is not clear. The oligarchy which becomes polarized between rich and poor will not necessarily be *ruled* by the oligarchic man with his 'dual personality'. However, al-Fārābī emphasizes the personality and role of the ruler.

In contrast, al-Fārābī's perfect states are of three sizes: the city (*al-madīna*), the nation (*al-umma*) and the union of all perfect societies in the inhabited world (*al-ma'mūra*) (*Madīna*: 228–9). Once again this reflects al-Fārābī's Islamic world-view – the nation representing the Islamic *umma* and *al-ma'mūra* the idea that the territory of Islam (*dār al-Islām*) may expand to take up the whole world. The people of the perfect state need to be governed by a philosopher, because they are not capable of knowing happiness and the things by which it is attained on their own. They need a teacher and a guide (*Siyāsa*: 78) who knows these things by himself. So, what is it to *know* happiness?

While it is beyond the scope of this chapter to explore the epistemology of al-Fārābī fully,[24] we may make some general observations about how the ruler of al-Fārābī's state acquires knowledge. First, al-Fārābī states that the ruler must be both naturally disposed towards knowledge and educated so that his reason may reach the level necessary to attain it. The ruler is potentially a ruler by virtue of his inborn nature (*al-fiṭra wa'l-tab'*), and he should develop this and 'acquire the attitude and habit of will for rulership' (*Madīna*: 239). His successor Ibn Sīnā, on the other hand, maintained that some individuals are able to apprehend universals (*kulliyāt*) at once by virtue of their natural innate power – 'holy reason', *al-'aql al-qudsī* (Fakhry 1983: 142). Al-Fārābī's potential ruler develops his reason, and thus his potential for knowledge, through education (*ta'līm*).

The only work in which education is dealt with in detail is *The Attainment of Happiness* (*Taḥṣīl al-Sa'āda*). In it he outlines the course of intellectual development of the ruler, which culminates in his attainment of the knowledge required to rule the state.[25] The education of the masses, on the other hand, is twofold: 'theoretical education' (*ta'līm*), which 'produces theoretical virtues in nations and cities', and practical education (*ta'dīb*), 'which produces moral virtues and practical arts in nations' (*Taḥṣīl*: 78).

Through education, the potential ruler develops his reason to such a degree that he 'receives Divine Revelation (*yūḥā ilayhi*), and God Almighty grants his revelation through the mediation of the Active Intellect (*al-'aql al-fa''āl*)'. If the emanation from the active intellect passes to the passive intellect (*al-'aql al-munfa'il*), he is 'a wise man and a philosopher (*ḥakīm/faylasūf*) and accomplished thinker', but if it passes on to his faculty of representation (*al-quwwa al-mutakhayyila*) he is a visionary prophet (*Madīna*: 244–5). Thus al-Fārābī explains the prophecy of Islam, or any other religion, in psychological terms – prophecy is essentially an intellectual process.

But in distinguishing between the visionary prophet and the wise man/philosopher, al-Fārābī departs from the Platonic conception of the philosopher, and distinguishes between the first ruler of the city and those who follow him. The first ruler, the visionary prophet, corresponds to Muḥammad, and the second, the wise man, may correspond to the successor of the prophet (*khalīfa*), or more likely, the Shī'ite *imām*. The twelve inborn qualifications (*khiṣāl*) of the first ruler are similar to Plato's.[26] But the qualifications for al-Fārābī's second ruler more closely reflect his Islamic, and specifically Shī'ite, background:

1 He will be a philosopher.
2 He will know the laws of the first ruler.
3 He will excel at deducing new laws by analogy.
4 He will be good at deliberating and at deducing new laws for new situations for which the first had not legislated.
5 He will be good at guiding the people by his speech to fulfil the laws of the first.
6 He will be of tough physique in order to shoulder the tasks of war.

(*Madīna*: 250–3)

The first ruler is called the 'lawgiver' (*wāḍi' al-nawāmīs*) or 'giver of tradition' (*wāḍi' al-sunna*) and the 'true king' (*al-malik fi'l-ḥaqīqa*), while the second is described as the 'the king of tradition' (*malik al-sunna*) who is a philosopher but not a prophet[27] – he follows the tradition and laws laid down by the first ruler and may adapt them or deduce new laws to meet new situations, as conditions 2–5 above show. However, al-Fārābī stresses that if his successor is also a true king in that he fulfils all the conditions of the first ruler, he may change a lot of what the first ruler ordained not because it is, in itself, wrong, but because what the first ruler ordained was what was best for his own time. He justifies this by claiming that the first ruler, if he had seen the situation, would have done the same (*Milla*: 49). This corresponds to the Islamic conception of prophecy (*nubuwwa*) in that each prophet through the centuries has brought a message (*risāla*) modifying that of his predecessor, although classical Islamic teaching states, of course, that Muḥammad is the final one, the 'seal of the prophets' (*khātim al-anbiyā'*).

The closest Islamic paradigm for the second ruler is the *imām* of Shī'ism. Najjar goes further and says that 'Al-Fārābī's political doctrine is eminently a theoretical justification of political Shī'ism' (Najjar 1961: 62). Although al-Fārābī believed in the essential unity of philosophy and its superiority to religion, as we have seen, there is no doubt that the political model he used to reconcile the two must be seen in the light of Shī'ite doctrine: his portrayal of the second ruler and the fact that revelation (*waḥy*) continues after the first, and his conception of two truths, one for the masses and one for the philosophers (cf. the Shī'ite concept of esoteric interpretation (*ta'wīl*)), all give a distinctly Shī'ite stamp to al-Fārābī's political writings.[28]

Although al-Fārābī has a specifically Islamic interpretation of the role of the ruler compared with Plato's philosopher-king of the *polis*, he is closer to Plato than Islam regarding the number of rulers in the perfect state. Plato envisages a state run by a group of philosopher-kings, a Guardian class which is self-maintaining and without which the state falls, and while al-Fārābī states that the first ruler must be one, he nevertheless maintains that if one single ruler who fulfils all the conditions to be second ruler cannot be found but there are two who between them fulfil the conditions, then they may be the rulers of city, as long as one of them is a philosopher. He goes on to say that if all these six qualities exist separately in different men and they are all in agreement, they may all be the rulers of the city, a far cry from the classical conception of the *imām* (*Madīna*: 252–3).

In conclusion, then, al-Fārābī's first ruler is, as a lawgiver, more than Plato's *nomothetes*. He is the founder of a religion or religious community (*milla*). Like his successor, Ibn Sīnā, al-Fārābī maintained that prophets had a natural disposition for rulership, a special quality which distinguishes them from the masses,[29] and that prophecy could be explained through the operation of the faculties of the soul. It is through these theories of intellection and politics that we can see most clearly the way al-Fārābī attempted to reconcile reason with revelation in Islam and firmly establish the Greek philosophical tradition in Islamic philosophy. As Mahdi has remarked, his legacy is not only seen in the thought of his Islamic successors, Ibn Sīnā (Avicenna) and Ibn Rushd (Averroes), but also in that of Judaism and Latin Christianity, Maimonides and the great 'Averroists' Albert the Great and Thomas Aquinas (Mahdi 1991: 10).

NOTES

1. For more on social conditions in Baghdad in the tenth and eleventh centuries, see Ashtor 1976: 183ff.
2. Walzer has suggested that we can see echoes of al-Fārābī's life in his *Al-Madīna al-Fāḍila* (*The Virtuous City*) and similar political works, where he refers to the life of the true philosopher forced to live in a 'defective state', the conditions of which may well have applied to his own life. Similarly, the description of the conditions of some of the imperfect political associations – the 'ignorant' states – may conceivably have been drawn from actual conditions in Baghdad around AD 900 (*Madīna*: 4 (introduction)), just as Plato's portrayal of the timocracy (see *Republic* 545dff.) and democracy (555bff.) reflect the characteristics of contemporary Sparta and Athens respectively.
3. One account by al-Bayhaqī claims that he was murdered on the road from Damascus to Ascalon, although this has been challenged by some scholars (see Netton 1989: 101 and 137 n. 26).
4. For a list of al-Fārābī's main works on logic see Fakhry 1983: 109.
5. For a more detailed taxonomy of al-Fārābī's works see Walzer 1965: 780–1.
6. Full title: *The Principles of the Opinions of the People of the Virtuous City* (*Mabādi' ārā' Ahl al-Madīna al-Fāḍila*).
7. For a diagrammatic representation of al-Fārābī's tenfold scheme of emanation see Netton 1989 : 116.
8. Compare Ibn Rushd's *Faṣl al-Maqāl*, where he makes the distinction between the people of knowledge (*ahl al-'ilm*) and the people of faith (*ahl al-īmān*) (1968 : 39).
9. See *Ḥurūf*: 131–2 for more on the relative validity of theology and jurisprudence.
10. The two accounts of how the philosopher attains the highest rank of humanity in *Al-Madīna al-Fāḍila* and *Al-Siyāsa al-Madaniyya* do not agree. Whereas in the former work the philosopher's soul is said to be 'as if it is united (*ka'l-muttaḥida*) with the Active Intellect', in the latter it is said to have 'joined' (*ittaṣalat*) with it (*Siyāsa*: 79). Furthermore, as Galston notes, although al-Fārābī refers to the highest rank of humanity as being 'on the level' or 'close' to the level of the active intellect in *Al-Siyāsa al-Madaniyya*, he refers to it as being 'below' the level of it in *Al-Madīna al-Fāḍila*. Galston has suggested that this difference may reflect the different emphasis of the two works: *Al-Siyāsa al-Madaniyya* might be declaring that some individuals are capable of complete transcendence while *Al-Madīna al-Fāḍila* might be saying 'that man cannot completely divorce himself from his bodily nature or, conditionally, that if man cannot thus divorce himself, then the human possibilities are limited in the manner described' (1990: 216–17).
11. See *Madīna*: 434 (commentary), where Walzer compares al-Fārābī's justice (*'adl*) to Platonic *isotes geometrike*, 'proportionate equality'.
12. This is a common theme in medieval Arabic philosophy. Cf. al-Tawḥīdī's view that man is an archetype of the universe. 'To know man is to know the microcosm (*al-'ālam al-ṣaghīr*), and to know the world is to know macro-humanity (*al-insān al-kabīr*).' Al-Tawḥīdī, Abū Ḥayyān, *Kitāb al-Imtā' wa'l-mu'ānasa*, vol. I, eds A. Amin and A. Zain (Cairo, 1953), 147 in al-Azmeh 1986 : 63.
13. As Galston has rightly noted, 'Nothing in the Farabian corpus makes a definitive assessment of Alfārābī's position possible. He does in one work claim that the city of excellence aims at the ultimate happiness of all, but he nowhere claims that it attains its purpose. On the contrary, although at times he speaks categorically of the citizens' happiness, at other times he speaks of gradations among the types of happiness (*sa'ādāt*) they possess.' Galston 1990:

174–5. However, the implication throughout most of al-Fārābī's works is that the *kind* of happiness an individual may attain is related, if not determined, by an individual's class.

14. the Lord would never destroy
the cities unjustly, while their inhabitants
were heedless. All have degrees according to
what they have done; thy Lord is not heedless of
the things they do.

Qur'ān 6, 132 (Arberry 1982: 137)

Whoso brings a good deed shall have ten the like
of it; and whoso brings an evil deed shall
only be recompensed by the like of it; they
shall not be wronged.

Qur'ān 6, 161 (Arberry 1982: 141)

15. Like the citizen of the *madīna*, each existent in the universe 'acts in conformity with (*yaḥtadhī ḥadhw*) the First Cause . . . according to its capacity, choosing its aim precisely on the strength of its established rank in the universe' (*Madīna*: 236–9). This is in line with classical Islam – Allāh does not burden man with more than he can bear.

God charges no soul save to its capacity;
standing to its account is what it has earned,
and against its account what it has merited.

Qur'ān 2, 286 (Arberry 1982: 43)

16. Plural *ghurabā'*. Individuals who lead a life at odds with their surroundings are variously called *ghurabā'* or *nawābit*, 'weeds'.
17. see *Madīna*: 451–2 (commentary).
18. Al-Fārābī often uses Islamic terminology in his writings, and it might be that the texts which have many Islamic terms and invocations were intended for a more 'popular', specifically Muslim, audience. However, as Kraemer notes, it is clear that al-Fārābī and his successors, in trying to reconcile Islam with the Greek tradition, often used Islamic vocabulary with Hellenic concepts in mind (Kraemer 1987: 290).

19. Whoso disbelieves after that, those –
they are the ungodly (*al-fāsiqūn*).

Qur'ān 24, 55 (Arberry 1982: 359)

20. 'Moses,
fear not; surely the Envoys
do not fear in My presence,
save him who has done evil,
then, after evil, has changed (*baddala*)
into good.'

Qur'ān 27, 10–11 (Arberry 1982: 383)

21. Hast thou not see those who exchanged (*baddalū*)
the bounty of God with unthankfulness,
and caused their people to dwell in
the abode of ruin?

Qur'ān 14, 28 (Arberry 1982: 249)

22. For example, Qur'ān 1, 7; 2, 198; 6, 77; 23, 106.
23. see Eickelman 1967 for more on the false prophets.
24. For more on Al-Fārābī's epistemology, see I. R. Netton, *Al-Fārābī and his School* (London, 1992).
25. For more on the education of the ruler, see Galston 1990: 160ff.
26. see *Madīna*: 444–6. As Walzer notes regarding the characteristics of the first ruler: 'We find a direct reference to its origin in *Taḥṣīl al-sa'āda* [*The Attainment of Happiness*] . . . : "In order to become a philosopher certain conditions are required which Plato has mentioned in his Republic (*fi'l-siyāsa*)"' (445).
27. Ibn Rushd makes a similar distinction in his *Tahāfut al-Tahāfut*:

> And the people of revelation (*ahl al-waḥy*) have always had wisdom, and they are the prophets, peace be upon them, and therefore it is the truest of all sayings [to say] that every prophet is wise, but not every wise man a prophet.
>
> (Ibn Rushd 1971 : 868–9)

28. See Najjar 1961 and *Madīna*: 16–18 (introduction) for a fuller account of the parallels between the politics of al-Fārābī and Shī'ism.
29. Cf. Ibn Sīnā 1938: 304.

REFERENCES

Works by al-Fārābī

Fuṣūl. *Fuṣūl al-Madanī* (*Aphorisms of the Statesman*), edited with an English translation, introduction and notes by D. M. Dunlop, Cambridge: Cambridge University Press, 1961.

Ḥurūf. *Kitāb al-Ḥurūf* (*The Book of Letters*), ed. M. Mahdi as *Alfarabi's Book of Letters*, Beirut: Dār al-Mashriq, 1969.

Iḥṣā'. *Iḥṣā' al-'Ulūm* (*The Enumeration of the Sciences*), in *Milla*.

Jam'. *Al-Jam' Bayna Ra'yay al-Ḥakīmayn Aflaṭūn al-Ilāhī wa Arisṭuṭālīs* (*The Reconciliation of the Opinions of the Two Sages*), ed. Albert Nasri Nadir, Beirut: Dār al-Mashriq, 1968.

Madīna. *Mabādi' ārā' Ahl al-Madīna al-Fāḍila* (*The Principles of the Opinions of the People of the Virtuous City*), edited with an English translation by R. Walzer as *Al-Fārābī on the Perfect State*, Oxford: Clarendon Press, 1985.

Milla. *Kitāb al-Milla* (*The Book of Religion*), ed. M. Mahdi as *Al-Fārābī's Book of Religion and Related Texts* (*Kitāb al-Milla wa Nuṣūṣ Ukhrā*), Beirut: Dār al-Mashriq, 1968.

Siyāsa. *Kitāb al-Siyāsa al-Madaniyya* (*The Political Regime*), ed. Fauzi Najjar. Beirut: al-Maṭba'ah al-Kāthūlīkiyya, 1964.

Taḥṣīl. *Kitāb Taḥṣīl al-Sa'āda* (*The Attainment of Happiness*), ed. Ja'far Āl Yāsīn, Beirut, Dār al-Andalus, 1981.

Other sources

'Abd al-Rāziq, M. (1945) *Faylasūf al-'Arab wa'l-Mu'allim al-Thānī*, Cairo: Maṭba'at 'Isā al-Ḥalabī.

Arberry, A. J. (1971) *Revelation and Reason in Islam*, London: George Allen & Unwin.
—— (1982) *The Koran Interpreted*, Oxford: Oxford University Press.
Ashtor, E. (1976) *A Social and Economic History of the Near East in the Middle Ages*, London: Collins.
Al-Azmeh, A. (1986) *Arabic Thought and Islamic Societies*, London: Croom Helm.
Badawī, A. R. (1973) *Rasā'il Falsafiyya li'l-Kindī wa'l-Fārābī wa Ibn Bājja wa Ibn 'Adī*, Benghazi: al-Jāmi'a al-Lībiyyah.
Bin-'Abd al-'Āli, A. S. (1981) *Al-Falsafa al-Siyāsiyya 'inda al-Fārābī*, Beirut: Dār al-Ṭalī'a.
Copleston, F. C. (1955) *Aquinas*, Harmondsworth: Penguin.
Corbin, H. (1964) *Histoire de la philosophie islamique*, vol. I, Paris: Gallimard.
Daiber, Hans (1986) *The Ruler as Philosopher, a New Interpretation of al-Fārābī's View*, Amsterdam: North-Holland.
Eickelman, D. (1967) 'Musaylima', *Journal of the Economic and Social History of the Orient* 10: 17–57.
Fakhry, M. (1983) *A History of Islamic Philosophy*, London: Columbia University Press.
Galston, M. (1990) *Politics and Excellence, The Political Philosophy of Alfarabi*, Princeton: Princeton University Press.
Ibn Abī Uṣaybi'a (1965) *'Uyūn al-Anbā' fī Ṭabaqāt al-Aṭibbā'*, Beirut: Dār Maktabat al-Ḥayāh.
Ibn Khallikān (1970?) *Wafayāt al-A'yān wa Anbā' Abnā' al-Zamān*, ed. Iḥsān 'Abbās, vol. V, Beirut: Dār al-Thaqāfa.
Ibn Rushd (Averroes) (1968) *Faṣl al-Maqāl*, Beirut: Dār al-Mashriq.
—— (1971) *Tahāfut al-Tahāfut*, vol. II, Cairo: Dār al-Ma'ārif.
Ibn Sīnā (Avicenna) (1938) *Al-Najāt*, Cairo: Muṣtafā al-Bābī al-Ḥalabī.
—— (1984) *Al-Shifā', al-Ilāhiyyāt (1)*, Qumm: Maktabat āyat Allāh al 'Uẓmā al-Mar'ashī al-Najafī.
Al-Jurr, K. (1982) *Tārīkh al-Falsafa al-'Arabiyya*, vol. II, Beirut: Dār al-Jāl.
Kraemer, J. L. (1987) 'The jihād of the Falāsifa', *Jerusalem Studies in Arabic and Islam* 10: 288–324.
Leaman, O. (1985) *An Introduction to Medieval Islamic Philosophy*, Cambridge: Cambridge University Press.
Madkour, I. (1934) *La Place d'al-Fārābī dans l'école philosophique musulmane*, Paris: Librairie d'Amérique et d'Orient.
—— (1983a) *Fi'l-Falsafa al-Islāmiyya*, vol. I, Cairo: Dār al-Ma'ārif.
—— (1983b) *Al-Kitāb al-Tadhkārī, Abū Naṣr al-Fārābī fī Dhikrā al-Alfiyya li-Wafātihi*, Cairo: al-Hay'a al-Miṣriyya al-'āmma li'l-Kitāb.
Mahdi, M. (1962) *Al-Fārābī's Philosophy of Plato and Aristotle*, translated with an introduction, New York: Cornell University Press.
—— (1963) 'Al-Fārābī circa 870–950', in Leo Strauss and Joseph Cropsey (eds) *History of Political Philosophy*, Chicago: Rand McNally.
—— (1981) 'Al-Fārābī and the foundation of philosophy', in Morwedge (ed.) *Islamic Philosophy and Mysticism*, New York: Caravan Books.
—— (1991) 'Philosophy and political thought: reflections and comparisons', *Arabic Sciences and Philosophy* 1: 9–29.
Marmura, M. E. (ed.) (1984) *Islamic Theology and Philosophy: Studies in Honour of George F. Hourani*, Albany: State University of New York Press.
Najjar, F. (1961) 'Fārābī's political philosophy and Shī'ism', *Studia Islamica* 14: 57–72.
Netton, I. R. (1989) *Allāh Transcendent, Studies in the Structure and Semiotics of Islamic Philosophy, Theology and Cosmology*, London/New York: Routledge.

Plato (1935) *The Republic*, Loeb Classical Library, 2 vols, London/Cambridge, Mass.: Heinemann/Harvard University Press.
Al-Qifṭī, A. Y. (1903) *Tārīkh al-Hukamā'*, Leipzig: Dieterich'sche Verlagsbuchhandlung.
Rahman, F. (1958) *Prophecy in Islam*, London: George Allen & Unwin.
Rosenthal, E. (1958) *Political Thought in Medieval Islam*, Cambridge: Cambridge University Press.
Sharif, M. M. (1963) *A History of Islamic Philosophy*, Wiesbaden: Otto Harrassowitz.
Smith, J. I. and Haddad, Y. Y. (1981) *The Islamic Understanding of Death and the Resurrection*, Albany: State University of New York Press.
Walzer, R. (1962) *Greek into Arabic: Essays on Islamic Philosophy*, Oxford: Bruno Cassirer.
—— (1965) 'Al-Fārābī', in *Encyclopaedia of Islam*, new edition, Leiden/London: E. J. Brill.

FURTHER READING

Fakhry, M. (1983) *A History of Islamic Philosophy*, London: Columbia University Press.
Galston, M. (1990) *Politics and Excellence, The Political Philosophy of Alfarabi*, Princeton: Princeton University Press.
Mahdi, M. (1962) *Al-Fārābī's Philosophy of Plato and Aristotle*, translated with an introduction, New York: Cornell University Press.
Walzer, R. (1965) 'Al-Fārābī', in *Encyclopaedia of Islam*, new edition, Leiden/London: E. J. Brill.
—— (1985) *Al-Fārābī on the Perfect State* (*Al-Madīna al-Fāḍila*, edited and translated with an introduction and commentary), Oxford: Clarendon Press.

41

AVICENNA

D. J. O'Connor

Abū 'Alī al-Ḥusain ibn 'Abd Allāh ibn Sīnā, the philosopher and scientist known to the medieval West as Avicenna, was born in AD 980 (AH 370) in a village near Bukhara in what is now the ex-Soviet republic of Uzbekistan. His mother was Turkish and his father Persian. There is fairly complete information about his life. The first thirty years are covered by his autobiography. His friend and secretary al-Juzajani has left an account of the rest of his life. If we may take his own account at its face value Avicenna was an extraordinarily precocious child with a keen analytical intelligence, a spectacular memory and an unquenchable thirst for knowledge. By the age of 14 he had absorbed whatever knowledge his teachers could offer him. But according to his own claims, he was largely self-taught, especially in medicine, natural history and logic. In his autobiography he says, with characteristic self-confidence: 'Medicine is not one of the difficult subjects, and therefore I excelled in it in a very short time.' At 16 he was directing the work of well-established physicians. His skill in contemporary medicine brought him a rich reward. The emir of Khurasan was treated by Avicenna for a serious illness and made a good recovery. His reputation as a physician was thus established in the highest levels of society. In consequence he was allowed to use the magnificent library of the Samanid royal family to perfect his knowledge of the science and philosophy of his time. He took all knowledge for his province, and his interests covered logic, mathematics, astronomy, natural history and medicine, and indeed anything which can be studied in a systematic way. This was the general practice of many of the savants of his day.

His introduction to the Samanid court diverted his energies from science and philosophy. A man of such obvious abilities was in demand as an adviser and administrator. This led him, unfortunately, into the dangerous and unstable power games of court life. From then onwards, his career was subject to the fluctuating fortunes of the emirs to whom he was a loyal servant. He was sometimes a refugee and at other times imprisoned. The last years of his life were spent in court at Isfahan. He died in 1037 (AH 426), weakened, it was said (by his secretary) by drink and sex. He never married.

Avicenna was an immensely productive writer. A modern bibliography by Dr Anawati lists 276 works – though not all of these are indisputably genuine. Most were written at night after a day's work in the service of his patrons. The two most famous (and most substantial) books were his celebrated textbook of medicine, the *Canon of Medicine* (*Qānūn fi'l Tibb*), and the *Book of Healing* (*Kitāb al-Shifā'*), which, in spite of its title, covers his own non-medical teaching on logic, mathematics, natural history and philosophy.

To survey critically the whole of Avicenna's philosophy in a short chapter would be an impossible task. In his philosophical works, he produces a very large number of arguments for the conclusions he advocates. The only thing to be done is to select the important arguments for important positions and see how they stand up to critical scrutiny.

Although we are concerned primarily with Avicenna's philosophy, it is worth while giving some attention to his *Canon of Medicine*. This impressive compilation has had an extraordinary history. Moreover, it has, as we shall see, some small relevance to his achievements in logic. It was translated into Latin by Gerard of Cremona in the twelfth century. Together with the works of Galen, it became the authoritative source of medical information throughout the Middle Ages and well into modern times. In the middle of the seventeenth century it was still used at the University of Montpellier when John Locke went there to improve his medical skills. And even in the twentieth century it is still a respected source of information in some parts of the Muslim East. But longevity is not a virtue in a textbook. Paracelsus indeed created a scandal by burning it in public along with the works of Galen at his university lectures at Basle in the sixteenth century. But this was just a characteristically flamboyant gesture to emphasize the need for a new start in medical science.

We have to recognize that serious medical science did not (and indeed could not) exist prior to the end of the nineteenth century. For it was in that century that the essential prerequisites were developed – physiology, antisepsis, microbiology and anaesthetics and their associated technologies. And prior to that, a scientific chemistry had to be developed. Indeed, even anatomy as a science was unknown before the work of Vesalius in the sixteenth century, because the dissection of corpses was forbidden by both Christian and Islamic authorities. So what did Avicenna's famous *Canon of Medicine* consist of?

There were five books, which covered anatomy, the human body in sickness and in health, pathology, symptoms and physical signs, materia medica and pharmacology, a complete pharmacopoeia, as then known, and the pathology of various organs. There is one philosophical issue of some consequence. The French Islamic scholar Madame Goichon has noted that, in a passage on experimentation in medicine, Avicenna sketches, probably for the first time, the experimental methods of agreement, difference and concomitant variations later familiar to students of logic in the works of Bacon, Hume and, especially, of Mill. This was an insight of some importance. But what does his work on medicine really amount to? The subsequent history of the *Canon* shows it to have been a remarkably useful compilation and a landmark in the history of medicine. And, no doubt, Avicenna taught practical first aid and elementary surgery. But like those of all physicians prior to the last hundred years, most of his cures may safely be attributed to a combination of 'the healing powers of nature' noted by Hippocrates and the placebo effect.

Kitāb al-Shifā' (*The Book of Healing*) contains the most systematic and continuous development of Avicenna's philosophy, along with what would nowadays be considered as natural science. It is a substantially Aristotelian work, with the reservations noted below. But it was in no way a slavish recapitulation of Aristotle's doctrines. Avicenna tried conscientiously to rethink Aristotle's problems for himself. And it is in these attempts that Avicenna's claim to distinction as an independent philosopher must be assessed. *Al-Shifā'* reached the West at a time when the known works of Aristotle were confined to his logic. The first Western glimpses of his physics, metaphysics and psychology were obtained through Avicenna's eyes. Of his more substantial philosophical works which have reached us, second in importance is *Directives and Reminders* (*Al-Ishārāt wa'l Tanbīhāt*). This is a four-part work covering logic, physics, metaphysics and mystical religion. A shorter and perhaps more useful survey of his philosophy is contained in *The Salvation* (*Al-Najāt*), written about 1027. Avicenna explains in the introduction to this book that some friends had asked him for a short summary of the philosophical knowledge required by an educated person. This included not only logic, metaphysics and psychology but also mathematics, astronomy, music and ethics. It has been shown (by A.-M. Goichon) to be a summary of *Kitāb al-Shifā'* and other works in the form of a clever mosaic of quotations. The book seems to have been left unfinished by Avicenna and to have been completed by his secretary.

It is important in this short overview of Avicenna's work to start with a clear idea of the influences and sources of his thinking. There were three main influences: the Islamic religion, Aristotle and the Neoplatonists. And these influences tended to drive his thinking in different directions. When a fanatical and authoritarian religion is let loose in a society, independent thought in any field will always be at risk. But the evidence of history is that Christianity proved far more dangerous to independent thought than did Islam. One important reason for this was that Christian theologians from quite early times had used philosophy as an intellectual support for theology. This had the result that variations and innovations in philosophy tended to destabilize religious beliefs. This was something that medieval Catholicism could not tolerate.

But in the Islamic world, philosophy had no such privileged status. It was the private interest of a few intellectuals, who could very well escape the notice of the religious authorities if they were prudent and sensible. Moreover, the theology of Islam was much simpler and less detailed than that of Catholicism. A Catholic philosopher could easily find that his novel doctrine about free will or substance or causality could make him a heretic in respect of the official doctrine about divine grace or transubstantiation or creation. The Muslim philosopher lived in a much freer intellectual world. Moreover, religious authority in the Islamic world was not organized and centralized as it became in Europe. Censorship depended upon the whims of local rulers. These could indeed be damaging. But they were sporadic and unpredictable compared with the ever-present authority of the Catholic Church.

There seems no reason to believe that Avicenna was not a sincere Muslim. It is true that some of his philosophical beliefs (for example, that the universe was not created by God *ex nihilo*) were not orthodox. They seem to be the consequence of the philosopher's professional tendency (first recommended by Plato) to follow the argument wherever it leads. Al-Ghazālī's criticisms of Avicenna in his book *The Incoherence of the Philosophers* were much concerned with the function played by God in Avicenna's metaphysical system. For example, Avicenna is accused of inconsistency in holding both (1) that the world is eternal and (2) that God created the world. He also denied the resurrection of the body and that God's knowledge extended to individual objects (which amounted to a denial of divine providence). All of these doctrines, said al-Ghazālī, 'are in violent opposition to Islam'. He concludes his book with the question: ought believers in such doctrines to be branded with infidelity and punished with death? His answer is that so far as the doctrines are concerned, the accusation of infidelity is inevitable. (He adds nothing about the death penalty, but as the philosophers concerned were dead already, the question hardly arose.) But during his lifetime Avicenna does not seem to have encountered any serious accusations of infidelity. He was, indeed, persecuted and imprisoned from time to time. But these misfortunes seem to have arisen more from imprudent political alliances than from charges of heresy.

Avicenna considered himself to be an interpreter and developer of the doctrines of Aristotle. Greek science, including the writings of Aristotle, had reached Islamic culture first via various Syrian Christian sects who had settled in Baghdad. Later, in the ninth century, schools of professional translators encouraged and even financed by some of the caliphs gave translations of Aristotle and his commentators and of the Greek scientists to the scholars of Islam. Avicenna discovered much of this work in the library at Bukhara.

Unfortunately, the work of Aristotle did not reach the Arab world in an uncontaminated form. Many of his commentators were Neoplatonists whose whole philosophical standpoint was totally alien to Aristotle's. If we may sketch these contrasting attitudes crudely for the sake of a brief exposition, the Neoplatonists were religious mystics whose doctrines were based on the less intelligible reaches of Plato's metaphysics and, in particular, his doctrine of the Form of the Good. Aristotle, by contrast, appears as a hard-headed empiricist, a scientist handicapped by his early Platonist education. Moreover, two works were transmitted as genuine Aristotelian writings which were, in fact, Neoplatonic documents. The more important was the so-called *Theology of Aristotle*. This consisted of edited extracts from books IV–VI of Plotinus' *Enneads*.

The particular Neoplatonist doctrine which caused trouble for the Arab Aristotelians was the doctrine of emanation. The traditional doctrine about creation, common to Christianity and to Islam, was the doctrine of creation out of nothing. Aristotle, by contrast, believed in the eternity of the universe. It did not need to be created: it was always there. But the Neoplatonists, starting with Plotinus (AD 205–70), held that the origin and structure of the universe could be explained by supposing that there was a perfect transcendent cause from which everything proceeded in a natural flow. This flow was described by Plotinus with the Greek words *aporroia* and *proodos*, which mean respectively 'outflow' and 'proceeding forth'. In Latin, these terms came to be translated as *emanatio*. They had been widely used by Greek philosophers of varying traditions from Plato to the Stoics. (The Stoic Emperor Marcus Aurelius talks of the self as an *aporroia* from the Governor of the Universe.[1]) The concept appears in Avicenna's predecessor al-Fārābī as the Arabic word *fayḍ*. It came to be an important concept in Islamic philosophy and the occasion of considerable intellectual difficulty.

Avicenna and those who thought like him probably saw this theory, vague and mystical as it was, as a way of reconciling Aristotle's doctrine of the eternity of the universe with the Qur'ānic doctrine of divine creation. Al-Ghazālī, as we have seen, saw this simply as a blatant contradiction. The theory of emanation could have served as a reconciliation of Aristotle with Islamic doctrine only if it could be presented in a clear and intelligible form and shown to meet the standard criteria for genuine explanation. But once we try to clarify the cognitive content of the theory, it is plain that it cannot meet these requirements. Reality streams forth from the One of Plotinus or the Islamic God as mist arises from a lake or the perfume from a rose, heat from red-hot iron or, to use a favourite Neoplatonic simile, light and heat from the sun. This emanation of reality from its transcendent source is not thought of, however, as a temporal process, as any physical emanation must be. Nor is it a process, like all physical emanations, whereby the source is diminished by the emanation. Such qualifications lessen any force that the metaphor has. Physical emanations are simply energy distributions and subject, like all such distributions, to the laws of thermodynamics.

But, in any case, what reason is there to believe that the metaphor has any explanatory force? A metaphor is a way of expressing an analogy. Analogies, as Avicenna himself recognized, can sometimes be genuine sources of explanation. But one condition for this is that the *explicandum*, what has to be explained, can be shown to be structurally similar to the *explicans*, that which explains. For example, the seventeenth-century explanation of the function of the heart in the circulation of the blood relied on a vivid and accurate analogy between the heart and a pump. Pumps and their workings were, of course, familiar to the scientists of the time. This kind of analogy, common in scientific explanation, can be very illuminating. But the emanation metaphor has no such force. Moreover, physics now shows us that the nature and working of the various types of physical emanation are entirely different from the creative emanation hypothesized by Plotinus (and for which, in any case, there is no independent evidence). This doctrine is the most important, though not the only, way in which Neoplatonist influences distorted Aristotle's legacy to the Arabs. (Though Avicenna adopted this theory, there is some evidence that he did not consider it to be genuinely Aristotelian. In a letter written towards the end of his life to a disciple Kiyā he wrote: 'despite the fact that the Theology is somewhat suspect.'[2])

LOGIC

Aristotle's logical works were entitled the *Organon* (instrument) by one of his later commentators. But of the six books comprising the *Organon* only one, the *Analytica Priora*, is concerned with logic in the modern sense of the word, namely the study of the structure of valid deductive arguments or the science of deductive proof. Aristotle's contribution to this science was the theory of the syllogism, including the modal syllogism. This comprised a fairly complete logic of class inclusion with an approximation, via the doctrine of reduction, to an axiomatic approach. And, most importantly, Aristotle was the first to see that the subject matter of an argument is irrelevant to its validity. This important fact can be elucidated by replacing the terms of an argument by arbitrary symbols, thus: 'If all A is B and all B is C, then all A is C.' And this has the important effect of *generalizing* the argument form so that any argument of this form will be a valid argument, given that the original argument is a valid one. This idea makes a genuine science of logic a possibility. Aristotle did not, however, supplement his logic of classes with the more fundamental logic of propositions. This was left largely to the Stoic logicians. Thus the Greek legacy of logic passed to the Arabs comprised a logic of propositions and a logic of classes together with a number of works which concerned semantics and the philosophy of language. These included Aristotle's *Organon*, Porphyry's *Eisagoge* and a large number of commentaries on the logic of Aristotle. Many of these works, though interesting and important, are not strictly speaking logic at all. The inclusion of some of these works in the *Organon* helped to fuel a rather futile debate in the West and to a lesser extent in Islamic lands as to whether logic was a preface to or a genuine part of philosophy. Avicenna seems to have concluded sensibly that it was both.

It is difficult to determine Avicenna's own contribution to the science of formal logic because the work of later Greek philosophers in this area has survived only in a very fragmentary form. So we cannot be sure how far any additions to the Aristotelian-Stoic legacy which appear in the work of Arab logicians are due to them or how much is later Greek work known to the Arabs but unknown to us. There is, however, one area in which Avicenna seems to have been an important innovator. It is clear that he developed, whether as inventor or as a disciple, an analogy between modal concepts like 'necessary' and 'possible' and temporal concepts like 'always' and 'sometimes'. He finds the connection between time and modality by defining his three modalities 'necessary', 'possible' and 'impossible' in terms of permanence and impermanence. This is not the best way of classifying modalities, nor is it Aristotle's. Indeed, by confusing purely logical concepts with empirical ones (necessary = permanent) he introduces rich sources of fallacy. But by developing this analogy he was able to develop and sketch a tense logic of a fairly primitive though (in his version) a very complex kind. (The best source for this, among his many logical writings, is the first part of *Kitāb al-Ishārāt wa'l-Tanbihāl*). Tense logic is an important branch of modern logic, though it did not develop until the publication of Arthur Prior's *Time and Modality* in 1957. Avicenna's pioneering work in this area has not been given the attention it deserves in spite of Professor Rescher's invaluable sketch in *Temporal Modalities in Arabic Logic*.[3] Avicenna's treatment of this branch of modal logic was criticized by later Arabian philosophers (especially Averroes) for gratuitous and pointless complexity. There is substance in this criticism, but it does not diminish the importance of his insights.

The other matter of consequence in Avicenna's logical work is a classification of the methods of proof. These are, in rising order of importance, analogy, induction and syllogism. Analogy is a weak form of proof in which we move from observed similarities between two things to postulate an unobserved but important similarity between them. Induction is the standard procedure of generalizing from experience which generates most of human common-sense knowledge. Its justification and its relevance to scientific enquiry are still a matter of controversy. But its efficacy as a method of producing belief (though not of testing knowledge) is much greater than Avicenna seems to have conceded. The lack of any developed natural sciences in the Middle Ages prevented a proper appreciation of the serious problems of induction. But we should remember that (as was mentioned above) he showed in his medical work some appreciation of methods of experimental enquiry such as Mill later systematized. Indeed, he may have been the first philosopher to write about them.

The devotion of medieval philosophers to syllogistic reasoning seems strange to philosophers of the twentieth century in view of the known limitations of that small part of formal logic. But these limitations are, after all, mainly a discovery of the nineteenth century. Aristotle's definition of 'syllogism' in the *Prior Analytics* is quite general and applies, in fact, to any valid argument form, syllogistic or not: 'An argument in which, certain things having been assumed, something other than these follows necessarily from their truth.' And Avicenna's own definition in *Al-Ishārāt* is substantially the same. But his description and classification of syllogisms seems both un-Aristotelian and very hard to follow. He is certainly not the most perspicuous of logicians, and his modern interpreters do not agree on exactly what he meant. In any case, the notion that all reliable knowledge is based on syllogistic reasoning is so easily refutable by counter-examples that it need not be taken seriously.

One of the unnecessary complications that Avicenna added to his formal logic was a system of quantifying predicates – distinguishing 'All A is some B' from 'All A is all B', etc. It is not clear if this was original to Avicenna. In any event, it is a blind alley in formal logic, as was soon appreciated when Hamilton tried to reintroduce it in the nineteenth century. Avicenna's work on topics in philosophical logic is considerable, though it is hard to determine how far it is original. Two subjects are worth a brief mention, universals and propositions. There is in the *Shifā'* an elaborate refutation of Plato's theory of forms and an explicit statement in the *Danesh-Name* that 'the universal qua universal exists only in the mind'. On the subject of propositions, he makes a distinction between the cognitive content of a statement and the statement itself considered as a belief or assertion. (In the Latin translation of his *Logica* the relevant terms are *imaginatio* and *credulitas*.[4])

METAPHYSICS AND NATURAL THEOLOGY

Among the thinkers of Islam in the Middle Ages there were two distinct approaches to natural theology. One, the *kalām*, took for granted the truth of Islam and tried to work out various lines of argument for the existence of God without consciously calling to its aid the work of Greek philosophers. Its practitioners were called *mutakallimūn*. *Kalām*, originally the Arabic word for 'speech', became the name of the movement which has been called 'Arabic scholasticism'. *Falsafa*, the Arabic word for 'philosophy', offered a different approach. *Falsafa* was an alien importation into Islamic culture and relied heavily on the work of Aristotle and the Neoplatonists in so far as it had reached the Islamic world. Avicenna was a leading representative of *falsafa*. The main trend of the arguments of the *kalām* was to justify the belief in the creation of the universe from nothing. Avicenna held to the Aristotelian belief in the eternity of the universe. And his main argument for the existence of God had therefore to take a different path from those of the *mutakallimūn*. Avicenna offers four proofs for the existence of God. Two of these, the argument from motion and the argument from causality, were well known in previous writers and have, in any case, been comprehensively demolished by later criticism. He also offers a very embryonic ontological proof which shows some evidence that he came close to anticipating Anselm (who was four years old when Avicenna died). But his main proof was sufficiently original to be known by some modern critics[5] as 'Avicenna's proof'.

What kind of a God did Avicenna try to defend? There is a difference between the Islamic concept of God and the Christian concept that must be borne in mind. Both concepts are of God as creator and providence, but the Islamic concept is that of a being of unspeakable and unimaginable power of whose nature we can know nothing. Some Christian theologians did indeed endorse this notion of God. Aquinas tells us that we can know nothing of God except that he exists and how everything else is related to him. But the Christian doctrine of the incarnation provides a way of softening this austere picture so that, in Christianity, the relation of man to God takes on a sort of cosmic cosiness. There is nothing of this in Islam.

Avicenna's proof starts from an analysis of the concept of being in two ways. The first is a distinction between necessary and possible being and results in a threefold classification of things: (a) necessarily existent in virtue of themselves; (b) possibly existent in virtue of themselves (that is, their own natures) but necessary through a cause; (c) possibly existent in virtue of their own natures. But class (c), Avicenna believes, does not contain any members. For Avicenna, everything that exists does so necessarily. Their necessity must be original or derivative.

But what does 'in virtue of its own nature' mean? This introduces Avicenna's second way of analysing being, into essence and existence. This was an important and influential distinction in metaphysics, and its elaboration is largely original with Avicenna. There is a hint of it in Aristotle,[6] but he does not develop the idea or put it to any use. The essence of X is that property or set of properties which make it, characteristically, an X. A cat, for example, may be large or small, black or white, furry or even without fur. These are inessential properties or 'accidents'. The characteristic common property which makes them all cats is, presumably, their common DNA. So too carbon may be graphite, soot or diamond. These are accidental variations. Their common essence is that all their atoms have six protons.

Now some essences are actually manifested in reality: that is, they exist. Some do not. A dragon is a large, winged, fire-breathing lizard. That is an essence; but that particular essence does not have existence. Cats might become extinct, like dinosaurs. Then their essence would no longer be exemplified in the real world; it would have no existence.

With these preliminaries, Avicenna's argument proceeds in two parts: (1) the analysis of the concept of being (necessary and possible, essence and existence) and (2) a proof that something actually corresponds to the concept of something necessarily existing by virtue of its essence. At this point, Avicenna proceeds to introduce an *empirical* premiss into his argument, so that it shall not be merely an exercise in conceptual analysis – a pre-Anselmian version of the ontological argument. His premiss is: Something exists (*anna hunā wujūdan*). This is a modest enough empirical basis, but it serves to make the argument's conclusion, if valid, apply to the real world.

He next claims that everything in category (b) above may be caused in two ways: something brought it into existence and sustains it in existence. This idea of a sustaining cause is an addition to earlier notions of causality and one which was to have an important impact in later Western philosophy. Although some possible beings may not have an originating cause because they exist from all eternity (angels and the heavenly bodies, for example), they must all have sustaining causes. Now it is not possible that the sum total of things in this category should be self-sustaining. It would, according to Avicenna, be a contradiction to suppose this.

Why? He does not explain. He seems to have believed that whatever can be said truly about each member of a class (for example that it is not self-sustaining) can also be said truly about the class itself. This is certainly not so. Indeed, on the contrary, it is generally the case that a predicate can be true of a class which is not true of the individual members of the class. (And, of course, vice versa.) However, Avicenna draws the unjustified conclusion that the totality of entities in category (b) must depend for a sustaining cause on a being existing in virtue of its own nature.

So his conclusion does not follow. God, as he conceives him, is a being whose essence includes existence – or rather, as he develops the concept, whose essence is nothing but existence. This raises an important question, which he does not discuss. Can existence be an essence? This is not just a modern problem, though much was made of it by Kant. That exact question was raised by Avicenna's predecessor, al-Fārābī: 'Does the proposition "man exists" have a predicate or not?' Al-Fārābī answers, not very clearly, 'In logic, yes, but in natural philosophy, no.'[7] Now it is certainly possible to give examples of predicative phrases, to wit, definite descriptions, whose essence (that is, whose descriptive content) entails existence: 'the man who shot President Lincoln', 'the meteorite which fell in Tunguska in June 1908', 'the football team which won the World Cup in 1966' and so on. By tying the predicate to a spatio-temporal location, we ensure an existential content for the phrase. But this is of no use to a philosophical theologian like Avicenna. He needs an essence which is *identical* with existence so that, as he says, a necessary being 'is a being such that, when it is assumed not to exist, an impossibility results.'[8]

It is interesting to examine what has happened here. Avicenna starts with what is almost a common-sense distinction between the essence (the *what*) and existence (the *that*). Existence in this relationship starts with a completely non-descriptive function. It has no content of its own and serves merely to energize, as it were, essences into the world of reality. So, in the premisses of this argument, essence gives the description of what is at issue; existence statements are merely certificates of instantiation of the predicates comprised in the essence. But in the conclusion of the argument, existence loses its former function and becomes itself an essence – but an essence, contrary to the original definition of 'essence', *without* any descriptive content. So the conclusion of the argument simply contradicts the assumptions of the premisses. This is the sort of thing that gives metaphysics a bad name.

SOUL, MIND AND KNOWLEDGE

Although Avicenna professed himself to be a follower of Aristotle, we have seen that the various influences on his thought made it impossible for him to be in all respects an Aristotelian. This is especially true in his philosophy of mind. Aristotle's philosophical psychology is difficult to make completely clear and consistent, as the text we have is both fragmentary and corrupt at crucial points. But it is clear that he makes a serious attempt to explain the nature and activities of the life principle (*psyche*) in a purely scientific and objective way. Plato had used the term *psyche* with the theological overtones of the English word 'soul'. The *psyche* was viewed as immaterial and immortal. Its relation to the body was that of a temporary inhabitant of a corruptible material organism. Part of its function was to control, guide and regulate the actions of the body. All of these notions were passed on via Neoplatonic philosophers to the Islamic world of al-Fārābī and Avicenna. However, they are very difficult to reconcile with the Aristotelian doctrine.

Aristotle explained that 'what has soul (*psyche*) in it differs from what has not in that the former displays life.' And he develops this idea consistently to speak of the various levels of soul in the plant and animal world. Powers of nutrition, reproduction, movement, sensation and the different types of mental operation are all discussed in detail and explained as various manifestations of form in matter. There is more form (organization and knowable detail) in a plant than in a stone, more in an animal than in a plant, more in an intelligent human being than in one of the 'lower' animals. They are lower in being lower down this 'ladder of nature', that is, with less organization and complexity. In Aristotle's view, therefore, the soul of man is the form, in the Aristotelian sense, of his body – its nature, structure, organization and manner of working. He uses a very striking simile to bring his theory clearly into focus: 'Suppose that the eye were an animal – sight would have been its soul.'[9] In other words, mind or soul is just the way the body works. The 'soul' (*psyche*) is just the body in action, and the various modes of consciousness (remembering, thinking, sensing, willing, etc.) are just aspects of the functions of the body. This thoroughly materialistic (or at least, functional) view of the soul–body relation is one which dominates Aristotle's treatment of the subject in the *De Anima* and elsewhere. The Platonic notion that body and soul can be brought at birth into an intimate but arbitrary conjunction is rejected. 'We can wholly dismiss as unnecessary the question whether body and soul are one: it is as meaningless as to ask whether the wax and the shape given to it by the stamp are one.'[10] He does in one passage allow himself a Platonic doubt as to whether the relation of soul to body may not be that of a sailor to his ship,[11] but, by and large, he sticks to his materialistic pattern.

It will be obvious that this view of mind and body, congenial as it may appear to the scientific taste of the twentieth century, was hardly consistent with the principles of tenth-century Islam. If Aristotle had not softened this bluntly functional account in some significant way it would have been very difficult for Avicenna to make any use of Aristotle's *De Anima* in formulating his own theory of the soul. But in the last book of the *De Anima* Aristotle introduces the famous distinction between the active and passive reason.

> Mind, as we have described it, is what it is by virtue of becoming all things, while there is another which is what it is by virtue of making all things. . . . Mind in this sense is separable, impassible, unmixed . . . This alone is immortal and eternal. (We do not, however, remember its former activity because while mind in this sense is impassible, mind as passive is destructible and without it nothing thinks.)[12]

If we take this at its face value, the active intellect is immortal, a necessary condition for all knowledge but without memory. And, of course, it is uncertain, so far as this passage goes, whether the immortality referred to is in any way personal. This mysterious and ambiguous passage (the Greek text itself can bear several interpretations) has been a source of controversy among Aristotle's interpreters from the fourth century BC to the present. It provided Avicenna with some tenuous evidence for a claim to be an Aristotelian in his theory of the soul. In his own *De Anima* (a twelfth-century Latin translation of the relevant part of the *Shifā'*), he treats all of Aristotle's topics in great detail and with considerable updating of the scientific parts.

We have several independent treatments of the philosophy of mind from Avicenna. Some of them are more detailed than others, but all are substantially consistent. The latest of them was a brief essay 'On the rational soul'[13] in which he refers to a more detailed essay on the same topic written some forty years earlier when he was a very young man. The essay is a summary account of his philosophy of mind and some ancillary parts of his philosophy. It states (but explicitly excludes proofs of) the following propositions: (1) the rational soul is a substance; (2) it subsists by itself; (3) it is free of any materiality; (4) it is not imprinted on any corporeal entity; (5) it survives the death of the human body. These are, of course, Neoplatonic rather than Aristotelian propositions, though some of them could be made consistent with Aristotle's account of the active intellect.

What proofs does Avicenna offer? The main source for a detailed account of his philosophy of mind is his own *De Anima*, referred to above. In the first chapter, he uses the famous 'man in space' fantasy which seems to have caught the medieval imagination. (He uses it again in *Al-Ishārāt.*) This is a bizarre thought experiment. Imagine a man brought into existence and suspended in space without any physical stimulation – light, heat, pressure, etc. What would be the first concept to impress itself on his mind in such an empirically impoverished environment? Avicenna asserts that it would be the concept of self, a self independent of any body or material accompaniments.

But this is a very feeble argument. In the first place, the enquiry into how concepts arise is now seen to be a matter for experimental psychology, a subject which did not exist in the tenth century. In any case, the precise conditions of the thought experiment are not clearly defined. Is the subject supposed to be a mentally developed adult or a new-born infant? In the first case, Avicenna is hypothesizing the sort of sensory deprivation experiments which have actually been carried out in recent years.[14] The results of these were hallucinations rather than concepts of self. In the second case, placing a new-born infant in a state of sensory deprivation has, I feel safe in asserting, never been tried. But if it were tried, how would we ever find out what was the first concept (if any) to occur in the subject's consciousness? If we attend closely to Avicenna's own words here ('created perfect'), he seems to be hypothesizing an adult with a full complement of mental powers and concepts. But if that is so, Avicenna is begging the question, for the concept 'self' would already be present to such a mind. And if the man had no mental contents at all, he would just be in the state of a new-born baby and no better off for all his physical development.

Such 'thought experiments' can prove nothing. In fact, developmental psychologists in the present century have traced the origins of the concept of self in children. They have shown that it is a concept which develops slowly with the individual's maturation and experience. 'It is essentially a product of an interactive process' between the individual and its environment.[15] Avicenna gives here, as usual, little thought to the possible empirical basis of what he regards as fundamental concepts.

What Avicenna is chiefly concerned with is to show that the self or soul is of such a nature that it is, of necessity, immortal. In the discussion in *Al-Ishārāt* he goes on to claim that we can know by intuition that our inner selves, souls, are not corporeal. And that which is incorporeal is necessarily simple, that is to say, is not compounded in any way. Because it is not compounded it has no parts into which it can be disintegrated. Thus the soul must, of its nature, be immortal.

This argument seems to have been of Neoplatonic origin and appears from time to time in medieval Western philosophy. But it is none the better for all its antiquity. In the first place, the concept of an incorporeal spiritual substance is an extremely vague one. If we reject Avicenna's appeal to intuition, we have no experience of such entities and we can define them only negatively. An immaterial substance is something which is a substance and which does not have the defining properties of matter. The only safe definition of matter seems to be 'whatever acts in accordance with the laws of physics'. Now no doubt there are plenty of things in the world which do not act in accordance with physical laws – theorems of mathematics, the meanings of words, the laws of physics themselves, poems and symphonies (distinct from their embodiments in print and sound) and countless other instances. Indeed, most of the things that make life interesting are immaterial in this sense. But they are not substances, unitary enduring things with a history and criteria for identification. What is important to note here is that the concept 'material substance' is a rich one because it has a very wide range of exemplars. The concept 'immaterial substance' lacks exemplars to give it any content. This is not to say that immaterial substances cannot exist. It is just that there is no positive evidence for their existence and therefore no possibility of acquiring cognitive content for the concept.

Second, why should we suppose that simple incorporeal substances, supposing such things to exist, must be immortal? Let us concede, just for the sake of the argument, that material substances can be destroyed only by breaking them up into their constituent parts. Can we then argue that immaterial substances cannot be destroyed because they have no constituent parts to be divided into? Clearly it would be absurdly sophistical to claim that a soul is so unlike a material substance that it has no parts and yet so like a material substance that it can be destroyed only by being separated into its parts. We have first to establish that dispersion into constituent parts is the only way in which *anything* can be destroyed. And this is not only unproved but, prima facie, a very doubtful proposition indeed.

Although Avicenna did believe strongly in the immortality of the human soul, he did not believe in the Qur'ānic doctrine of the resurrection of the body. At least, he held that such talk was only figurative or metaphorical. This raises a problem which he seems never to have considered. Whatever may be the difficulties about the resurrection of the body, it does at least seem to offer some clue to identifying the resurrected selves. The two standard criteria for personal identity are memory and physical similarity and continuity, an internal and an external criterion respectively. A purely spiritual substance provides neither criterion. In particular, what we now know about the workings of the brain and the physical basis of memory indicates that the latter is at least a necessary condition of memory. We have no reason at all to suppose that memory could be retained in a non-material substance. How, then, are these immortal souls to be identified and assigned correctly to their appropriate destinies in heaven or hell? (The Qur'ān says: 'All shall fully remember their past deeds.'[16]) How could there be just punishment or just reward without the possibility of identifying the selves to be punished or rewarded?

Avicenna seems to divert attention from this question. In part 8 of *Kitāb al-Ishārāt* he discusses the rewards and punishments of the soul after death without any recognition of the difficulties raised by the absence of memory in post-mortem souls. Although Avicenna was well aware of the functions of the brain in sensation (a big advance on Aristotle), he denied that any cerebral functions were required for intellectual processes.[17] And as to memory, he places powers of retention and recall squarely in specified parts of the brain.[18] To the question: what is the surviving soul a survivor of, and how can it know this? his philosophy of mind can give no answer.

And there are further difficulties arising from this part of his philosophy. He explains that the soul neither is 'imprinted' in the body nor does it 'inhere in it'. 'The way of its attachment to the body, then, must be the way required by its particular disposition which attracts it to govern and control this particular body, because the soul has an inherent inclination towards it.'[19] An individual soul does not pre-exist its body. (Avicenna devotes chapter 14 of the *De Anima* to refuting the transmigration doctrine of some Platonists.) It is created only when its matching body is brought into existence. But what is the nature of this matching which gives the soul its 'inherent inclination' towards its particular body? If the soul is a simple uncompounded substance as the argument for immortality presupposes, how can it 'match' anything, except perhaps another soul? Its 'particular disposition' must consist in some complex variety which requires a unique structure. It must therefore be explained how a simple substance can have a structure. This explanation is lacking in Avicenna's work.

If we now turn to the soul's functions, Avicenna tells us[20] that the soul 'has two activities; an activity in relation to the body which is its government and control, and an activity in relation to itself and its principles which is intellection.'[21] The first function involves difficult questions about causal connections between material bodies and immaterial selves, questions more familiar to modern philosophers than to Avicenna. His own theory of causality was substantially Aristotle's: any instance of cause and effect can be analysed into the four Aristotelian causes, material, efficient, formal and final. The main difficulty here (though there are others) is this: how can an efficient cause, which is essentially a transfer of energy, pass from an immaterial substance to a material one or vice versa? (A voluntary movement would be an example of the first and a sensation of pain an example of the second.) The second function of the soul – its intellectual processes – raises the whole question of Avicenna's theory of knowledge. In this, he was much more a Neoplatonist than a follower of Aristotle.

The human soul is regarded by Avicenna as something, in Aristotelian terms, 'in potency'. It has therefore to be brought into act by something which is already in act. This 'something' is the active intellect. This intellect is not anything human except in the sense that it is required to bring the human mind to its proper functioning. It is strange that Avicenna, who called on intuition and introspection to establish the alleged non-material nature of the self, did not note that we do seem to our own (perhaps mistaken) inner experience to be active in processes like imagination and reasoning. And such activities are an essential part of our intellectual lives. However, he held (contrary to experience, one would suppose) that the active intellect was required to infuse the human mind with the 'intelligibles', the first principles of reasoning and the intuitively necessary truths. He explains that the sun is to our eyes as the active intellect is to our souls. It makes intellectual activity possible just as the sun makes visual experience possible. And as the sun reveals colours to us, so the active intellect reveals the 'intelligibles'. 'This substance needs to be eternally intelligible in itself as well as intelligent in itself.'[22]

Thus Aristotle's mysteriously immortal necessary condition for thinking has become a unitary non-human mind on which we all depend for our intellectual life. The active intellect is not, of course, the divine mind. It is, however, an emanation from the divine mind and nearer to it than we are. This is both an obscure and an unnecessary theory which fits ill on its allegedly Aristotelian basis. Emanation and illumination are unexplanatory metaphors.

ACHIEVEMENT AND INFLUENCE

To give a just estimate of Avicenna's interest and importance is not easy. The sheer magnitude and detail of his work are daunting to anyone who wants to understand it. To cover the contemporary range of human knowledge from mathematics and music to astronomy, physics and natural history and to psychology, theology and metaphysics is astonishing enough. But to infuse into that detailed survey a great deal of original work puts him into a very select company indeed. The names of Aristotle and Leibniz come to mind as achievers on this scale. And when we consider the conditions in which he had to work – in his scanty leisure time at best and on long tiring journeys or in prison at worst, we can only wonder and admire.

But the question by which any scientific or philosophical work has to be tested is this: how much truth is there in it? And the answer to this question has to be far less flattering. It is the fate of much scientific achievement to be proved wrong. Most of pre-Galilean science has been shown to be almost entirely free of genuine discovery. The position is a little better in mathematics, but even here there was not, during the Middle Ages, much advance on the Greeks. The *Qānūn fi'l-Ṭibb* for all its fame and influence is of far less value nowadays than even the most modest twentieth-century textbook of medicine. In fact, it is now no more than an important document for historians of medical science.

Some historians of science have been less than fair to Avicenna. George Sarton, the greatest of them, said: 'His main concern was not so much to know facts as to systematise them; his curiosity was blunted by his synthetic tendencies.'[23] A proclivity for system-building was a failing of much medieval work. But it was not Avicenna's worst fault. He was more to blame for generalizing on far too little evidence in his scientific work and for ignoring the relevance of experience in philosophy. For example, although he rejected the wilder claims of the alchemists, he seems to have been convinced that all metals were combinations in varying proportions of sulphur and mercury. He can surely have had no evidence for this. As a scientist, he was markedly inferior to his contemporary al-Hazen, who made some genuine discoveries in optics.

In philosophy, he was seriously handicapped by having to try to bring Aristotle into harmony with Neoplatonism, though without quite realizing how alien to each other these two traditions were. Commentators and expositors often refer to Avicenna as the greatest of the Neoplatonists. No doubt this is an accurate description: though the scaffolding of his philosophical argument was usually Aristotelian, his final positions were Neoplatonic. This naturally results in a certain fatal loose-jointedness between premisses and conclusions. Averroes's greater achievements as a philosopher can be put down in part to his consistently Aristotelian point of view.

Avicenna's quality of mind, so far as it can be diagnosed from his writings, offers an interesting study. His outstanding feature is, of course, an extreme hunger for knowledge and for communicating that knowledge. In this he shows himself a genuine follower of Aristotle. This no doubt accounts for some of his beliefs being well ahead of any possible evidence for them. But he was not without a certain redemptive scepticism, a very desirable quality in any scientist or philosopher. He rejected many of the more absurd beliefs of his contemporaries in matters like alchemy, astrology and various magical practices. He was even sceptical, as we have seen, of the Aristotelian provenance of the *Theology of Aristotle*. When he has, for doctrinal reasons, to deal with something verging on the magical, namely prophecy, he links it up with his philosophy of mind and theory of knowledge to give it a respectable intellectual foundation.

One substantial achievement which has been justly credited to Avicenna is his work in devising a suitable philosophical vocabulary for the Arabic language. Earlier philosophers, al-Kindī and al-Fārābī, had made contributions to this. But it was especially important – and difficult – for a philosopher concerned with subtle nuances of the concept 'being' to have a terminology capable of expressing these nuances. The distinguished French scholar Anne-Marie Goichon has traced the details of Avicenna's work in this field.[24]

One feature of his mental make-up deserves comment. He was very conscious of the intellectual gap between those interested in science and philosophy in Islamic society and the unthinking mass of the populace. And he does not hesitate to point in a rather arrogant way to the distinction between these *illuminati* and the rest. Moreover, he hints more than once that his real philosophy is not all contained in his 'published' works. Such hints about esoteric doctrines occur in the works of other ancient and medieval philosophers, including Plato. But the evidence seems quite insufficient to justify any firm conclusions, though the nature of this 'oriental' philosophy has intrigued his commentators.

His religious beliefs have been a lasting source of interest to students of his philosophy. The question is an important and interesting one in view of the substantial parts of his writings given over to philosophical theology and to mystical religion. Doubts raised during his lifetime about his orthodoxy seem to have offended him. There is an extant poem by Avicenna which concludes:

> No belief in religion is firmer than mine own.
> I am the unique person in the whole world and if I am a heretic,
> There is not a single Musulman anywhere in the world.[25]

Certainly there are reports of his going regularly to the mosque to pray when he came across a difficult problem in his studies. And when he read the book by al-Fārābī which made Aristotle's metaphysics clear to him, 'I distributed much in alms to the poor in gratitude to Almighty God.' Perhaps the strongest evidence of his genuine religious feelings are the parts of *Kitāb al-Ishārāt* devoted to religious topics. At one point, we find the extraordinary passage: 'Consider how, when you perceive the closeness of God and meditate on his omnipotence, your skin shivers and your hairs stand on end.' These are not the words of a half-hearted believer.

The impact made by Avicenna's work in Islamic lands can be seen in the subsequent history of Islamic philosophy. Some attitudes were decidedly negative. We have already noted al-Ghazālī's comments. Averroes was also critical of much of Avicenna's work, though he expressed himself in more temperate and dispassionate tones. The extremity of Muslim disapproval is probably marked by the burning of his works in Baghdad in 1150 at the orders of Caliph Mustanjid. But he has clearly survived as one of the great intellectual leaders of the Eastern world.

In the West, though his impact has not been so lasting, he was a very important influence in the formation of medieval scholasticism. Translations into Latin, made in Toledo in the mid-twelfth century, were soon current in Europe at a time when the bulk of Aristotle's work, apart from his logic, was unknown there. The obscure thickets of Avicenna's teaching on essence and existence proved welcome hunting grounds for Western metaphysicians of the thirteenth century and beyond. There is an early work of St Thomas Aquinas, *De Ente et Essentia*, in which the name of Avicenna occurs ten times in the course of about forty pages. And here Aquinas is appealing to Avicenna for support for his own theories. There were, of course, reactions against these alien influences from time to time as various allegedly heretical doctrines were traced to foreign teachings. It was probably the victory of Aristotle over Neoplatonism during the development of scholasticism which prevented Avicenna from being a greater and more lasting influence in the West.

In the East, he is still remembered. There is a fine statue of him near the Intourist hotel in his native Bukhara.

NOTES

1 *Meditations* II.4.
2 Quoted in D. Gutas, *Avicenna and the Aristotelian Tradition* (Dordrecht, 1988), p. 63–4.
3 (Dordrecht, 1967).
4 G. Nuchelmans: *Theories of the Proposition* (Amsterdam/London, 1973).
5 e.g. H. A. Davidson, *Proofs for Eternity, Creation and the Existence of God in Medieval Islamic and Jewish Philosophy* (New York and Oxford, 1987), ch. 9.
6 *Posterior Analytics* 92b10.
7 N. Rescher, *Studies in the History of Arabic Logic* (Pittsburg, 1963), p. 39.
8 Davidson, op. cit., p. 290, quoting *Al-Najāt*, pp. 224–5.
9 *De Anima* 412b18.
10 ibid., 412b6.
11 ibid., 413a8.
12 ibid., 430a14–25.
13 See Gutas, op. cit. pp. 72ff.
14 See W. Heron, B. K. Deane and T. H. Scott, 'Visual disturbance after prolonged perceptual isolation', *Canadian Journal of Psychology* 10 (1956), 13–16.
15 K. Lovell, *An Introduction to Human Development* (London, 1968), p. 85.
16 Sura 89, verse 23.

17 *Al-Ishārāt*, part 7 (Abstraction).
18 *De Anima*, part 1, ch. 4.
19 *Al-Ishārāt* ch. 10.
20 ibid.
21 F. Rahman's translation in his *Avicenna's Psychology* (Oxford, 1952).
22 Chapter 16 (Rahman's translation).
23 *Introduction to the History of Science* (Baltimore, 1927), vol. I, p. 695.
24 See ch. 2 of her *La Philosophie d'Avicenne* (Paris, 1951) and *Lexique philosophique d'Ibn Sina* (Paris, 1938).
25 Barani's translation in Gutas, op. cit.

FURTHER READING

There is a very full bibliography in A.-M. Goichon's article 'Ibn Sina' in the *Encyclopaedia of Islam*, vol. III (London/Leiden, 1971). What follows is a short guide to further reading.

Texts

Kitāb Al-Shifā' (Cairo, 1952).
Al-Najāt (Cairo, 1938).
Al-Ishārāt wa'l Tanbīhāt, ed. Forget (Leiden, 1892).

Translations

In English: *Avicenna's Psychology*, trans. F. Rahman (Oxford, 1952). This is a translation of the psychological part of *Al-Shifā'*.
In French: *Al-Ishārāt*, trans. A.-M. Goichon, *Livre des directives et remarques* (Paris, 1951).
La Metaphysique du Shifā', trans. G. C. Anawati (2 vols, Paris, 1985).
In Latin: *Avicenna Latinus*: Three volumes of the twelfth-century Toledo translation of parts of *Al-Shifā'* (Louvain/Leiden, 1968–77).

Commentaries

There are many expositions of Avicenna's thought. The best of those easily available are:

S. M. Afnan, *Avicenna: His Life and Works* (London: Allen & Unwin, 1958).
A. Badawi, *Histoire de la philosophie en Islam* (Paris: Librairie Philosophique, J. Vrin, 1972), vol. II, pp. 595–695.

Both of these are clear expository studies, but neither of them is seriously critical. In general, Islamic philosophy tends to attract reverential exposition rather then critical assessment. This is a pity because, in the absence of criticism, it is impossible to assess or indeed to understand a philosopher's work.

D. Gutas, *Avicenna and the Aristotelian Tradition* (Leiden, New York: E. J. Brill, 1988) provides interesting and very valuable background reading.

The best critical study is recent: Lenn E. Goodman, *Avicenna* (London/New York: Routledge, 1992).

ACKNOWLEDGMENT

I am especially indebted to my former colleague, Professor Ian Netton, who read an early version of this chapter and corrected me on some important points. Any remaining errors are, of course, my own.

D. J. O'C.

42

ISLAMIC PHILOSOPHY SINCE AVICENNA

Oliver Leaman

There can be little doubt about the impact which Avicenna had on the intellectual world of Islam. The breadth of his views, the brilliance of his style, the boldness of his doctrines came to impress two sets of thinkers, philosophers primarily concerned with Aristotelian kinds of argument and those interested in developing his more mystical approach. Many religious thinkers in the Islamic world felt that his theories were damaging to the truths of Islam as represented in the Qur'ān, the *ḥadīth* (traditions) and the major orthodox schools of jurisprudence. No one expressed this fear more precisely and with such logical vigour than Abū Ḥāmid Muḥammad al-Ghazālī, a thinker of Persian origin who lived a turbulent life between AD 1058 and 1111. What is significant about the strategy of al-Ghazālī is that he does not argue that Avicenna's views are contrary to Islam and so must be disregarded, although he did think that those views were unacceptable on religious grounds. Al-Ghazālī argued that the development of philosophy in the Islamic world up to the time of Avicenna was based upon fallacious reasoning which must be replaced by sound reasoning, and once we employ correct reasoning we can see that the main tenets of religion rest on secure logical foundations. This is not to say that he thought that such foundations provide our justification for following the rules of Islam – this is naturally the role of revelation – but he sought to establish that there is nothing in logic which rules out religion. He had here at least two motives. One was to counter the doctrines of the philosophers in the Islamic world whose thought was dominated by a particular form of Aristotelianism, and especially the culmination of that thought as represented by the works of Avicenna. Second, he argued that it is not sufficient to criticize those philosophers on the grounds that their opinions are heterodox: one must rather show that their arguments fail by the standards which they themselves seek to establish, the standards of correct logical reasoning. In that case logic can be retained in the service of the correct explication of theological doctrine and does not have to be rejected by the orthodox Muslim.

Before he set up his assault upon philosophy he felt the need to describe as accurately as he could the actual detail of the philosophers' arguments, and the book in which he did so (*Maqāṣid al-falāsifa*) is so fair-minded and carefully constructed that it led to Christian Europe regarding al-Ghazālī as an orthodox *faylasuf*, an adherent of the sort of Greek-inspired thought which flourished for a time in the Islamic world. But the title of this book is suggestive of his real interests, since he was concerned to argue that the intentions of the philosophers are not as simple as their writings would have one believe. Although the philosophers argue that they are merely presenting a more sophisticated analysis of the nature of the world and our place in it than that available to ordinary Muslims, they in fact are intent on dismantling the religious notion of God, the afterlife and creation under the guise of merely explicating these notions. Al-Ghazālī's attack is most often studied in his magnificent *Tahāfut al-falāsifa* (*The Incoherence of the Philosophers*), which sets out to destroy the main foundations of philosophical analysis as represented mainly in the work of al-Fārābī and Avicenna. This book consists of a well-constructed extended argument designed to show that the philosophers do not succeed in what they say that they intend to show, that there is no incompatibility between Islam and the philosophical point of view. Al-Ghazālī's attack on philosophy was attacked in turn by the Andalusian philosopher Abū-l Walīd ibn Rushd (Averroes, AD 1126–98), who incorporated the text of al-Ghazālī's book in his own *Tahāfut al-tahāfut* (*The Incoherence of the Incoherence*, hereafter *TT*).

An important aspect of the argument between al-Ghazālī and the philosophers is the appropriate analysis of God's attributes. The title which al-Ghazālī gives to his 'Third Discussion' is very important in this respect. It goes 'The demonstration of their confusion in saying that God is the agent and the maker of the world and that the world is his product and act, and the demonstration that these expressions are in their system only metaphors without any real sense' (*TT* 147). Al-Ghazālī's argument here is that we can only call God a real agent if he can be taken to make decisions, carry them out and have the will and purpose to bring about particular changes in the world. God should be regarded as someone who acts rather like us, except that he has far greater knowledge and power. A meaningful deity can only be a real agent if he acts 'through will and through choice' (*TT* 156), so that

> our aim in this question is to show that you philosophers use those venerable names without justification, and that God, according to you, is not a true agent, nor the world truly his act, and that you are applying this word metaphorically – not in its real sense.
>
> (*TT* 171)

It is interesting to note here that al-Ghazālī distinguishes his line sharply from that of the theologians (*mutakallimūn*), who also attacked the philosophers, but who on the whole did not see the need for the application of rigorous arguments as part of that attack. Al-Ghazālī's approach does not depend upon the truth of Islam in order to operate successfully, as is the case with the arguments of the theologians. He is arguing for a particular account of meaning. If the name 'God' is to have its religious meaning, then we must be able to credit the holder of that name with a full list of qualities and powers, the sort of list which one finds, for instance, in the Qur'ān. Such a theory is not dependent for its truth upon the existence of God, or even on the existence of a particular kind of God, but merely on the meaning of 'God' within a religious community. This point will be expanded later.

In his very personal account of his intellectual biography, the *Munqidh min al-ḍalāl* (*The Deliverer from Error*), al-Ghazālī sums up his main critique of the philosophers:

> In the three questions . . . they were opposed to [the opinion of] all Muslims, viz. in their affirming (1) that men's bodies will not be assembled on the Last Day, but only disembodied spirits will be rewarded and punished, and the rewards and punishments will be spiritual, not corporal . . . they falsely denied the corporal rewards and punishments and blasphemed the revealed Law in their stated views. (2) The second question is their declaration: 'God Most High knows universals, but not particulars.' This also is out-and-out unbelief. . . . (3) The third question is their maintaining the eternity of the world, past and future. No Muslim has ever professed any of their views on these questions.
>
> (*Munqidh*, trans. McCarthy, pp. 76–7)

No summary of the highly sophisticated and challenging arguments which al-Ghazālī and Averroes exchanged can do justice to the quality of the thought, but it is possible to concentrate upon some of the most intriguing aspects of the discussion. Al-Ghazālī is totally opposed to the way in which Aristotelian philosophers insisted upon the existence of an eternal world. After all, an eternal world does not seem to require a creator, nor can it have a potential destroyer. Yet the Qur'ān is full of references to the creation of the world and also replete with threats of its eventual destruction should the deity think it necessary. The philosophers produced a large variety of arguments to establish the incoherence of God actually creating the world at a particular time. If at one time there was God and nothing else, what influenced him to create the world when he did? After all, there was nothing in existence apart from himself, and so what motive could he have had for creating it at all, and when he did?

In his defence of the Aristotelian position Averroes emphasizes the disanalogy between an eternal and a temporal agent. We can decide to do things, we can wait until a certain time before doing them, and we can wonder about our future actions, but such possibilities cannot arise for God. There is no gap for him between desire and action, and nothing stands in the way of his activity, and yet we are to think, if al-Ghazālī is correct, of God suddenly deciding to create the world. What distinguishes one time from another for God? For us times are distinct because they have different qualitative aspects, and this enables us to distinguish between them. For

God, though, in a putative form of existence before the creation of the world, all times are alike, and there is nothing to characterize one time over another as *the* time for creation to take place. Al-Ghazālī suggests that such an objection is based upon mental laziness (*TT* 37–8). Even human beings can choose between alternatives which appear to be identical. He gives the example of a hungry man being confronted by two dates, only one of which he can take. Since they are to all intents and purposes identical, it would seem to follow from the philosophers' arguments that he must stand there and starve because there is no difference between them. This example does not really work, though, since as Averroes points out, what is at issue here is a choice between eating and not eating, not really a choice between two dates. For al-Ghazālī's argument to work he would have to show that the chooser can establish a difference where none previously existed (*TT* 40–1).

What al-Ghazālī is trying to establish is some scope for divine action and decision-making which represents God as a real agent and not just as a cipher for natural events which would take place anyway. The difficulty is in prising apart God's will and his knowledge. God knows, given his omniscience, exactly how the universe should be organized to produce the optimal arrangement, and the philosophers insisted that there is no point in thinking of a gap in time existing between that conception and its instantiation. Since God is omnipotent he does not need to wait for the appropriate moment to create the universe: nothing exists which could oblige him to wait, and he does not need to take time to effect the creation. These are characteristics which are specifically human, and we should beware of associating God's properties with our own (*TT* 438). The way in which we choose and decide is actually a reflection on our deficiency, since it implies that we need time to work out what to do, and we do not immediately grasp the best possible action. Given God's nature, Averroes argues, we cannot think of his acting in any different way from that represented by the organization of the world. Al-Ghazālī objects that such a conception robs God of all freedom of action and decision, yet from an Aristotelian point of view this is not really the case. Like us, God has some essential features which specify that particular actions are appropriate and in accord with that nature. This does not imply a radical lack of freedom or ability to choose. It is just that we are certain kinds of creatures, and particular kinds of moral choice are in accord with our moral nature. It is just the same for God, who must take account of his nature when deciding how to create, and it is no criticism of his power to decide to insist that such decisions are to be linked to his nature as a perfect being.

Al-Ghazālī has a clever objection to the notion that there is conceptual difficulty in the idea of God creating the world *ex nihilo*. One frequent objection to this possibility is that if time is regarded as a measure of change, there can have been no time before the world was created, and hence the first change was initiated. There can thus be no start to time, or indeed end to time, since in either case time itself would be destroyed. We can think of time carrying on eternally because of the link between that notion and that of an eternal world. Al-Ghazālī wants to be able to think of God first existing without the world and without time, and then bringing both the world and time about, and any refusal to accept this formulation he dismisses as due to a defect in our imagination (*TT* 65–6). He takes up this point several times in his attack, accusing the philosophers of failing to be sufficiently imaginative in their conceptions of alternative possibilities which reflect more fully the range of alternatives open to God. He criticizes their arguments for the eternity of matter in this way. They argue that for change to take place, there must be something in existence in the first place to change into something else, so that God must have used material which he himself did not create. There must exist an eternal matter in terms of which we can think of change occurring. Al-Ghazālī rejects these arguments by suggesting again that it is solely due to a failure of our imagination that we are led to this belief in an eternal substratum to change. We can just think of nothing existing at one time, and then God bringing about change by creating *ex nihilo* in the way in which he chooses. And this is enough to prove that the sorts of divine powers which the Aristotelians refuse to countenance are perfectly conceivable, albeit with a little mental effort required.

What is at issue here is a difference in the theory of meaning. For al-Ghazālī abstract terms have a meaning which is independent of their reference in the external world. To be able to use such terms we need only represent to ourselves a series of pictures or images in which the events are characterized in certain ways. We can then talk about God realizing these states of affairs separately from any explanation of how they are linked to other states of affairs in the real world. So change can be brought about by sleight of divine hand, without the preconditions which are necessarily involved in analysing change which occurs in the external world, since the former kind of change is brought about miraculously by a divine agent. Yet Averroes' counter-argument is based on the principle that it is not sufficient to have a series of images in one's mind to prove the meaningfulness of the state of affairs corresponding to those images. For example, we can conceive of God creating the world at a particular time in the sense that we can form a picture of what this would be like, and yet this does not establish that we thereby know what we are talking about. A meaningful use of language is acquired through its connection with the framework in which it makes sense, and this framework is firmly connected to the way in which the world works. Al-Ghazālī is trying to defend the philosophical respectability of employing the notion of imagination so frequently used in the *kalām* (Islamic theology) to challenge the main tenets of Aristotelianism, as represented mainly by Avicenna.

A perfect example of this strategy can be found by looking at the debate over the nature of causation. On the model of causation which Avicenna presents, there is a necessary relation between the agent and his or her effect. The world and everything in it is entirely dependent upon an agent for their existence, and via the process of emanation the agent maintains everything in existence. The theological view which forms the basis of al-Ghazālī's critique is the Ash'arite doctrine that an act which comes into existence no longer has any connection with its agent. If it continues to exist it must be continually recreated by a divine power. The Ash'arites were so concerned to stress the power and purpose of the deity that they denied that the everyday world really consists of stable material objects, but asserted instead that in reality there exist atoms which are constitutive of such objects and which only exist instantaneously. It is only divine will which produces such atoms, connects them in certain ways and keeps on producing them so that we may enjoy existence in a world which is well adapted to our needs. Our impression that on occasions the occurrence of certain phenomena causes changes in the world is, strictly speaking, misleading, since those changes are produced by God, and the fact that they are preceded by particular events in our experience does nothing to show that they must lead to those effects.

Avicenna constructed a very different account of causal connection. According to him, while it is true that we cannot actually perceive the causal nexus, we can over a period of time observe regular connections which entitle us to make inferences about causal connections and future events. This causal nexus is necessary rather than contingent, since effects do not just happen to be brought about by their causes, nor are they events which just now and then follow other events. The effects follow their causes because they must do so, they are necessitated by them, and the whole of creation is a necessitated and necessitating series of events. One of the strengths of al-Ghazālī's opposition to this analysis is, of course, that we cannot actually observe the causal connection. All that we experience is a conjunction of discrete events. An association forms quite naturally in our minds, but this association does not have any basis in direct experience. Al-Ghazālī is concerned to show that God is the real agent of what seem to be purely natural events, and that there is no reality in the notion of a causal 'power' to compete with him for influence in the world of generation and corruption. He is not interested in challenging the idea of regularity in nature, since he is quite happy to accept that there is such regularity, so long as it is appreciated that the cause of that regularity is the influence of God. He gives the example of a piece of cotton and a flame. It is possible, he asserts, for a flame to come into contact with the cotton and yet for no fire to result, and also for the cotton to burst into flame without contact with fire (*TT* 517–18). It is certainly empirically true that in every case where a flame touches a flammable material, a fire will ensue (other things being equal), and this is a judgement which we are entitled to possess. Yet 'observation proves only a simultaneity, not a causation, and, in reality, there is no cause but God' (*TT* 518).

In his response to this critique of the concept of causation Averroes again appeals to a different and potentially preferable theory of meaning from that provided by al-Ghazālī. Al-Ghazālī's point is not just that when we see a cause and then an effect we cannot actually see the power which causes the burning of the cotton. His thesis is stronger than this. What we normally think of as agents and their effects are really only creations out of nothing which do not persist after their creation. They are nothing more than combinations of accidental properties consisting of atoms which exist for only a minute portion of time. The only power in the universe is to be found in the constant activity of God, who causes things to come into existence and if he wishes recreates them so that they stay in existence. On this approach it would indeed be the case that causal connection is a vacuous principle, since the 'agents' and their 'acts' are in existence for far too short a period of time for any significant connection to take place between them. Causal rules are acceptable provided that we understand by them a description of what God does and not what he must do. Only that sort of description can do justice to the notion of God as an agent. Al-Ghazālī's theory seems quite moderate. It does call for a change in our thinking of the nature of the external world and yet does not require any difference in our practical attitude to that world and its understanding. Yet Averroes claims that the theory is far from mild, and in fact leads to a denial of the possibility of knowledge of the world (*TT* 522). This appears to be a wildly disproportionate response to al-Ghazālī's theory.

Yet Averroes has a defence for his strong view, a defence which relies upon the connection between a term and its causal properties. If the connection is one of meaning, and not just of association, then accepting the term and denying its properties will be an exercise in contradiction. Al-Ghazālī gives the example of a decapitated person acting like a living human being, with the sole exception of being minus a head. He gets up, sits down, writes and so on (but presumably does not talk!), and while there is no doubt that such a thing has never happened, there is no difficulty in thinking of God bringing it about, should that be his will. We can imagine the state of affairs in which such a person acts quite normally, yet does not have a head. Indeed, such an image is the standby of many ghost stories. This shows, al-Ghazālī would argue, that the connection between a head and a human being is merely contingent, and that there is no necessity in the connection. Yet Averroes wonders whether the situation is really quite so simple. Would we call the decapitated being a person? How could we incorporate this change to our normal understanding of the world without having to incorporate vast alterations in our understanding of the processes of nature? This answer might seem to beg the question in its implication that there are fixed meanings for terms which presuppose the existence of relatively determined essences for empirical objects. But the argument is not that *all* properties of objects are crucial aspects of those objects' essences; rather, it is that an essential aspect of what x is is to be found in what x does, and how such activity relates to the activity of other things in the world around it. An advantage of such a claim is that it provides an account of how naming is possible. We can name objects because we can identify relatively stable entities with regular patterns of behaviour and lawlike connections with other such entities. This is not to suggest that our knowledge-claims are invariably correct, but rather that if we could not be sure on the whole that our names correspond with stable and fixed essences, then naming itself would become vacuous.

So it is very much Averroes' position that if a corpse did sit up and write theological texts (*TT* 535) we would be presented with a serious difficulty in understanding what was happening. It is rather like looking for an object which appears to have vanished completely off the face of the earth. We can think of the object as having completely vanished – one minute it was there, and the next it was gone, and there is no point in looking for it any more because it has no existence anywhere in our world. Yet if we think through that possibility we find that it throws into disarray our entire notion of the world and the objects within it. If God could just make things vanish and the dead move in animated ways, we should have to acknowledge that whole areas of our experience had become mysterious, and the process of looking for causes which is so important a part of our approach to our experience would become nugatory. We can indeed form a picture in our minds of such possibilities, but Averroes rejects the value of such a thought experiment, for 'only the masses rely on imagination, and he who is well trained in intellectual thought . . . renounces imagination' (*TT* 256–7). It is clear that al-Ghazālī and Averroes do not just differ on specific doctrines, but also on the way in which philosophy is to be conducted.

As well as trying to establish a role for the deity as a real agent, al-Ghazālī was concerned to provide God with real knowledge, knowledge of the ordinary events in the world which he created. This is a difficult issue for most of the *falāsifa*, since an immutable and eternal God cannot be understood to know that I am now sitting at the typewriter and that the sun is shining outside my window in a simple sense. Nor can he be simply aware of what I am going to do tomorrow if my freedom of action is to be preserved, yet if he does not know this he cannot enjoy the status of an omniscient being. Avicenna tried to avoid these difficulties by arguing that God is limited to knowing only very general and abstract features of the world, since any other sort of knowledge would diminish him as an eternal and immaterial being. Yet if this is all that he knows, then what is the point of prayer and the notion that God is aware of our actions, for which we will be rewarded and punished in the next life? Al-Ghazālī insists that any acceptable Islamic God must know the everyday events of our world. Averroes counters with the charge that this would make God into someone very similar to his creatures, and would provide him with knowledge which is to all intents and purposes beneath his dignity. God's knowledge is special because he is not limited to receiving sense-impressions from the world as is the case with finite creatures. On the contrary, he is the creator of the objects in the world, and he knows in a far more comprehensive way what they are and how they are constructed.

Can God know individuals? It would seem not, since the very best knowledge is abstract and universal, and since 'God thinks only himself, his essence must of necessity be intellect' (*TT* 462). The passages in the Qur'ān which refer to God seeing and hearing should not be taken literally, but rather as a way of informing the ordinary believer that God is not deprived of any sort of knowledge. We might expect Averroes to claim with Avicenna that God's knowledge is limited to universal judgements, yet he does not adopt this line, arguing instead that God's knowledge is neither universal nor individual, but more like the latter than the former. This is because of his perspicuous grasp of the nature of reality, a reality which he himself has constructed. Our knowledge is the effect of what he brings about, whereas his is produced by that which he himself brings about. On an Aristotelian account of knowledge, a knower is identical with the objects of knowledge. If God knows anything he knows everything, and from an epistemic point of view he is identical with everything he knows. The organization and structure of the universe are a reflection of God's thought. Through thinking about his own being, he will at the same time be thinking about the structure of the world which mirrors that essence. He cannot really be identical with contingent and accidental phenomena, yet his essence is not totally unconnected with such phenomena. They represent transitory instances of the necessary and essential relationships which he has established. He knows, for instance, the physical laws and the way in which they structure the universe, but it does not follow that he knows how those laws actually work. To understand the principle of gravity it is not necessary to observe every falling apple, or even any falling apple. The fall of a particular apple is only an appropriate object of knowledge of a sentient creature with sensory faculties and far beneath the dignity of the creator. Averroes challenges the view that this is to diminish God's knowledge, charging the theologians with misrepresenting the nature of God. He is very different from the sort of knowing subject which we represent, and any attempt at interpreting him as just like us but more so is guilty of failing to acknowledge the significance of the difference between God and ourselves.

The third charge which al-Ghazālī brought against philosophy is that it fails to allow the physical resurrection of human beings and the provision of physical rewards and punishments consequent upon their behaviour during their lives. Although the account of the soul which Aristotle provides is tentative at best, it does involve a description of the body–soul relationship which makes the idea of an afterlife difficult to grasp. The soul is the form of the living human being, an aspect of the being itself, and there is no point in talking about the matter existing without the form when we are considering organisms. It is difficult for Aristotelians to contemplate a purely spiritual existence for the soul. Persons are combinations of soul and body, and in the absence of the latter there are no persons left. The commentators have ever since argued fiercely over the appropriate interpretation of Aristotle's remarks on the soul, but the important point to make here is the difficulty in reconciling those remarks, how ever interpreted, with the ordinary notion of physical resurrection of people. As we become more involved with immortal and eternal knowledge, i.e. with universals and abstract principles, our mind becomes identical to a degree with those objects of knowledge, given Aristotle's account of knowledge. It follows that once we have perfected ourselves intellectually and know everything that there is to know about the formal structure of reality, there is no longer any 'us' around to do the knowing. Averroes seems to regard our progress in knowledge as equivalent to a lessening of our ties to our individual material and human characteristics, with the radical consequence that if anything survives death, it is the species and not the individual. As temporal and finite creatures we are destructible, but as members of a species we are permanent, though only the species is really free from destruction.

There is nothing in this doctrine which gives comfort to the supporter of the traditional religious view of the afterlife. Averroes' theory seems even more incompatible with Islam than the account of a spiritual afterlife for individual souls which Avicenna provides, and which forms the object of al-Ghazālī's derision. Averroes gives a *political* account of the religious language describing an afterlife in terms of providing ordinary believers with a motive for virtuous action and dissuading them from immorality (*TT* 585). Such an account would be regarded as missing the point by al-Ghazālī, who insists upon a literal understanding of the scriptural passages describing a very real and physical afterlife. Averroes does not totally rule out the possibility of such an afterlife, but it is fairly clear from his work that he treats it as a wildly improbable possibility. The only meaning which the notion can be given is political, and there is nothing irreligious about such an interpretation, according to Averroes. It is difficult for unsophisticated ordinary believers to understand that it is worthwhile to act virtuously and that their actions have a wider reference than their immediate community of acquaintances, so any religion which is going to succeed in capturing their adherence must speak to them in ways which they can understand and in a language which strikes an emotional chord. Highly graphic accounts of an afterlife, of God seeing everything which happens and of his creation of the world, ensure acceptance by the majority of the principles of religion, while more philosophical accounts will satisfy the intellectual questions of the more sophisticated. Yet each group is aware of the same truths. It is just that those truths are dressed up in different ways.

We have thus far seen that Averroes responds to al-Ghazālī's arguments by explaining what he sees as the strength of the Aristotelian position. Averroes is in the fortunate position of not having to agree with Avicenna all the time, and it is true to say that he criticizes the arguments of Avicenna almost as frequently as al-Ghazālī's counter-arguments. One reason for this is his well-founded suspicion that Avicenna's version of Aristotelianism is heavily influenced by Neoplatonism, whereas Averroes was intent on returning to as pure and uncorrupted a form of Aristotelianism as was possible during a period when philosophy as such was inevitably formulated in Neoplatonic terminology. Perhaps the most crucial site of dispute between Avicenna and Averroes is their differing views on the relationship between essence and existence. This has often seemed to be a technical and minor issue, of limited general interest, but in fact it represents a crucial dividing line between the metaphysical theories of the two protagonists. According to Avicenna, a state of affairs is possible if and only if something else acts to bring it into existence, with the deity being the sole exception. This results, according to Averroes, in our having to think of possible states of affairs as being non-existent by themselves, until their existence is brought about by their cause (*TT* 119). Avicenna argued that there are necessary causal relationships between states of affairs in the world, and the course of events only exists if something else necessitates it. The possible is that whose essence does not include its existence and so must depend upon a cause which makes its instantiation necessary, but only necessary relative to that cause. In this modal system there are really only two kinds of being, that necessary through another and that necessary in itself, so that the domain of the possible becomes conflated with the actual and the necessary.

Both Averroes and Avicenna maintain that there is a logical distinction between essence and existence, but the former accuses the latter of conflating the order of thought with the order of things, the logical and ontological orders. Avicenna does indeed start with the logical distinction between essence and existence and then proceeds via his theory of emanation to show how existence comes to essence from the necessarily acting Necessary Being. The overflow of causes and effects is simultaneous with its ultimate source both temporally and ontologically, since God's contemplative activity is eternal and the causal chain continues as long as does that activity. Emanation provides the ontological adhesive which relates cause and effect; it provides the essences which are to be instantiated with their existence and with their power to actualize other essences in their turn. Essences lie in wait for the nudge towards existence. Averroes argues that the theory of emanation to explain creation does do justice to the view that the contingent things of the world are dependent for their existence upon God, but that it overemphasizes that dependence. It demands an outside factor for the explanation of the existence of objects in the world, and might well be regarded as a form of modified occasionalism. It seems to be a rather apologetic reaction to the full-blooded Ash'arite occasionalism which represents the complete dependence of everything we think we experience in the world upon the individual will of God. In his attack upon philosophy al-Ghazālī can run rings around the account of emanation provided by Avicenna in support of his general claim that it is philosophically, as well as theologically, unsound. As Averroes points out many times, emanation is a profoundly un-Aristotelian doctrine, although a doctrine which in his time it was difficult to discard entirely. The existence/essence distinction put forward by Avicenna is perfectly acceptable to al-Ghazālī, with the modification that direct divine intervention is required to bring existence to the essences.

It is worth stressing again that what is at issue here is not just a difference in philosophical opinion, but rather a difference over how to do philosophy as such. In Averroes' opinion, Avicenna tends to give the game away by playing into the hands of the theologians, here representing the enemies of philosophy. Avicenna divides the world up into existing things and essences, into what we can think about and what really exists, into things which are necessary through another and possible in themselves. These distinctions throw doubt on the sort of realism and emphasis upon substance which are so important for Aristotle and his supporters. Aristotle views the world as one entity, as a single order of nature with no insuperable barriers to human understanding and investigation. The sorts of dichotomies which have become so characteristic of post-Cartesian philosophy (and Descartes may well have been influenced by Avicenna), between mind and matter, man and nature, civil and moral law and so on are on the whole absent in Aristotle and in Averroes. The latter suggests that where al-Ghazālī's attack upon philosophy is valid it succeeds because it draws attention to the defects of Avicenna's methodology, which consists largely of unsympathetic accretions to Aristotelian philosophy. Once we appreciate the full force of Aristotle's own arguments, he urges, al-Ghazālī's objections can be dismissed. Al-Ghazālī's demand for a philosophy which represents the deity as possessing the same sorts of properties as we have, but more powerfully, falls into the trap of regarding God as a Superman, as someone like us, but more so. A truly religious conception of the deity must do justice to the radical separation which exists between him and his creation.

The role of the philosopher in the community or state is a constant theme of Islamic philosophy. This stems from a discussion in Greek philosophy as to the best way of living. Aristotle seems to waver between the view that the prime constituent of the good life is intellectual thought and the alternative, a more broadly based basket of virtues. These two alternatives not only are incompatible but also have very different implications. The identification of a more social notion of happiness as living in accordance with a general combination of virtues would serve to make it more available to a general public, and yet would appear to treat intellectual excellence as merely one among many personal virtues. The choice of intellectual excellence as the supreme form of human well-being implies that the vast majority of the community, unable or disinclined to concentrate completely on intellectual thought, are deprived of the very best form of life. This is a particularly live issue for the *falāsifa*, since they could hardly accept that the ordinary unsophisticated Muslim who dutifully carries out his or her religious and social obligations without giving a thought to deeper philosophical issues is thereby denied the possibility of living as well as he or she could. Such a position would bring into question the responsibility of the deity who has created such a diverse range of abilities in his creatures and then watches the vast majority living an inferior form of life as compared with the intellectual élite. No religion such as Islam with its universalist ambitions could tolerate such a general restriction on human well-being.

Averroes thinks that he has a way out of this difficulty. First, he argues that philosophy and Islam are not incompatible; indeed, they are closely interconnected. If Islam is a rational faith (as it is always saying) and if it compels adherence by the use of rationally persuasive arguments, then it requires its audience to use their reason to determine how to live and what to believe. This does not mean that all believers must involve themselves in philosophy in order to work out their obligations and beliefs, since most believers are incapable of philosophical work. He frequently gives the example of law to explain his point here. Some people who are concerned with the development and interpretation of law, the lawyers and judges, study in detail the principles behind legislation and employ rational arguments to try to decide difficult cases. The majority of the population just behave within the confines of the law without really thinking about the principles behind the legislation. There is nothing wrong with that, and there is no requirement for everyone in the community to become lawyers. Different people have different attitudes to the law, some based upon deep understanding and some based upon casual acquaintance, and this difference does not interfere with the ability of everyone in the community to live in an organized and regulated society.

Any religion should be expected to present its message in a suitable form for the particular audience it is addressing. Averroes argues that Islam is an especially excellent religion because of its ability to present the issues it wishes to get over to the greatest variety of people. Some people will be attracted to Islam and strengthened in their faith if the philosophical arguments for being a Muslim are pursued and developed. Others cannot really follow such arguments, but can follow arguments which explain in simple terms what is wrong with other religions and what is right about Muslim practices. Still others will not even be able to grasp this, and so must be persuaded by rhetorical devices which maintain a weak connection with rational argument in their attempt at being generally persuasive. This might seem to be a patronizing way of dealing with the faith of different categories of believers, and some have seen it as a transparently thin disguise for Averroes' real view that philosophy alone reveals the truth and religion is suitable for the intellectually weak who can be expected to rest content with stories and doctrines which are, strictly speaking, false. Yet there is no need to agree with this interpretation. Averroes is pointing to the fact that there are a variety of ways of coming to know something, some of which are surer than others, but once the object is known it is part of one's knowledge, however that item of information may have been acquired. We know religious truths in different ways, but we really do know exactly the same thing in the end.

In many of his works, and particularly in the *Faṣl al-maqāl* (*The Decisive Treatise on the Harmony between Religion and Philosophy*), which is precisely concerned with this issue, Averroes argues that there is no way in which the highest form of reasoning, demonstrative reasoning, can clash with the principles of religion. Philosophers are best able to understand the allegorical passages in the Qur'ān given their training in logical reasoning (hardly a claim designed to assuage the hostility of the theologians!), and there is no general religious requirement that all scriptural statements have to be taken at their face value. One might become impatient here and wonder why this sort of interpretation is necessary at all. Is there not already in existence in the Islamic community a whole tradition of scholarship in law and theology which is directed at nothing else than the interpretation of such passages? Averroes is critical of this tradition. It is only those who are capable of demonstrative thought and of deciding on questions of interpretation involving allegory who should be given the task. If demonstration conflicts with the apparent sense of scriptural passages, then those capable of demonstration know that the passages must be interpreted allegorically so as to cohere with the demonstrative truths. Philosophers are careful when they do this not to offend the religious sensibilities of the less sophisticated, in sharp contrast to the practice of theologians. The latter frequently interpret passages so ineptly that they either throw doubt on the religion itself, or threaten the status of philosophy by raising suspicions in people's minds of the orthodoxy of the conclusions reached by philosophers. There are a variety of ways of communicating the truth to a variety of audiences, and some concepts are accurate concepts of objects while others are just symbols of such objects. Religion is presented for the easy comprehension of the masses, and where there is a hidden meaning it is up to the philosophers to discover it and keep it to themselves, and for the rest of the community to accept the literalness of scripture.

Averroes sets about the Ash'arite theory of moral language, which interprets rightness and wrongness entirely in conformity with the commands of God. The point of the theory, yet again, is to emphasize the power and authority of the deity over all things, even over the meaning of ethical terms. If what we ought to do is simply equivalent to God's commands, then we know everything that we need to know about moral behaviour and need seek no further guidance to our moral activity. Such a view would strike a mortal blow to the way in which philosophy attempts to provide logical explanations for particular beliefs, and it is hardly surprising that Averroes opposed it fervently. He argues that there is a dimension to moral notions which makes them far broader than merely being equivalent to divine commands, and that a whole level of difficult questions which it is important to ask, such as how evil can exist in a world created by a benevolent deity, just drop out of the frame established by the Ash'arites and al-Ghazālī. Since God created the world, and since 'good' and 'evil' are defined in terms of what he does and what he does not do, there is no meaning in the question of how evil in the world came about. If God created a state of affairs, it cannot be called evil.

If right actions are not simply equivalent to God's commands, what are they? Averroes follows an Aristotelian account here. Since all substances have natures, and these natures define their ends, we as substances also have natures and ends at which our actions point. The purpose of a knife is to cut and the purpose of a tree is to grow, but what is the purpose of a human being? One of our ultimate aims is to be happy and to avoid actions which bring unhappiness. There is something of a congruence here between Aristotelian and Islamic principles. Moral virtue leads to happiness because, if we do what we are supposed to do by our nature as people and as commanded by our God, we will be able to achieve happiness. This happiness may be defined in a variety of ways, ranging from a bundle of social and religious practices to an entirely contemplative ideal. The latter is available only to the very few, and neither religion nor philosophy would approve of it as the ultimate aim for all human beings. For both Aristotle and Averroes there is an essential social dimension to human happiness, which makes the identification of happiness with correct moral and religious behaviour much easier to establish. It is possible for someone to live entirely apart from the community and concentrate on intellectual thought, but this way of living is inferior to a life in which there is a concentration on intellectual thought combined with integration within society.

One of the characteristics of a religion such as Islam is that one would expect happiness and misery to be represented in some form in the afterlife, and Averroes does indeed refer to the importance of such a notion. Yet we have seen that he is very suspicious of the notion of an afterlife which has surviving individuals like us in it, and so one wonders how this notion is going to serve to encourage general moral behaviour. What ordinary believers may find difficult to grasp, thus requiring the religious language and imagery, is that our moral actions affect not only ourselves but the happiness of the whole community, and not just at a particular time, but as a species. When we behave badly we damage our own chances of human flourishing, and this affects our personal opportunities for achieving happiness. It also affects our relationships with other people, leading to a weakening of the whole notion of society. So while strictly speaking the misery consequent upon wrongdoing may not follow us personally after our death, it may well follow the community, and the significance of the notion of an afterlife is that it points to the wider terms of reference in which moral action participates. Religious law and language are capable of transmitting values and motives to the very widest audience possible. Any religion which is going to be successful employs language compatible with the psychology of its intended audience, and such a religion needs to be based on inspiration rather than reason. Only someone inspired (like a prophet) knows how to frame his language in such a way as to move people, and if he is a true prophet then he moves people in exactly the same direction as the philosopher sees with his use of demonstrative reason that they ought to go.

Averroes worked at a time when there was something of an atmosphere that philosophy produced in Andalus, Muslim Spain, must take a new direction. His predecessors, ibn Ṭufayl (d. 1185) and ibn Bājja (d. 1139), prepared the path with their generally rather critical attitude to the philosophy that arrived in Spain from the east of the Islamic empire. Although Averroes came to have relatively little influence in the Islamic world among the Muslim community, his thought is crucial to any understanding of the development of both Jewish and Christian philosophy in the Middle Ages and beyond, and not only because of the immense status of his commentaries on Aristotle. His fellow-countryman Moses Maimonides (AD 1135–1204) took an even more independent line with the philosophical tradition as it reached him. He argued that both al-Ghazālī and Averroes were mistaken in their account of the relationship between God and his properties. Al-Ghazālī insisted that enough ordinary sense be left in our grasp of the divine properties for it to be meaningful to identify the God of the philosophers with the God of religion. Averroes thought that he could do this by arguing that God is the exemplar or paradigm of the qualities which we identify with our finite experience, and so represents, for example, the height of wisdom, perfect knowledge, complete power and so on. Naturally, we cannot simply refer to God using the same sort of language we use about ourselves, and al-Ghazālī's insistence here upon precisely this point can be rejected as his desire for a Superman conception of the deity. Maimonides rejected both these accounts, and argued that there is no way in which we can directly refer to God at all. The idea that God can actually listen to individual prayers or be concerned with his creatures is laughable, and results from a too close identification of divine with human qualities. Yet, like Averroes, Maimonides does not reject such religious language totally. It has a point, and the point is to enable the majority of the community to conduct themselves in ways which are more likely to stimulate virtue and suppress vice. Only the philosophically sophisticated can really understand how to reconcile an incomprehensible deity with the need for strict observance of the religious law, which is largely the subject matter of his *Guide of the Perplexed*.

If a theme can be found for philosophy in the Islamic world, then it will relate to the issue of language and its appropriate analysis, and this is an especially live issue in the post-Avicennan intellectual world. Al-Ghazālī argues that language is a simple and transparent mirror of reality, and that religious language accurately describes the nature of religious reality. Averroes and Maimonides on the contrary point to the importance of equivocation and ambiguity in language, and relate this to a feature of our lives, namely that different people see things from different points of view. Our language is flexible enough to capture this diversity of view, and both Maimonides and Averroes try to show how it is possible for one thing to be described in a variety of ways, and how we can have diverse perspectives on the truth. Perhaps the most important contribution which this period of philosophy has made is in exploring the features of this elusive but crucial aspect of our language.

REFERENCES

Averroes *Faṣl al-maqāl* (*The Decisive Treatise on the Harmony between Religion and Philosophy*); page-references are to the Arabic in *Philosophie und Theologie von Averroes*, ed. M. J. Müller (Munich, 1859); all translations are from *Averroes on the Harmony of Religion and Philosophy*, trans. and int. G. Hourani (London: Luzac, 1961; repr. 1967 and 1976).

Tahāfut al-tahāfut (*TT*), ed. M. Bouyges, *Bibliotheca Arabica Scholasticorum*, *Série Arabe* 3 (Beirut: Imprimérie Catholique, 1930); page-references are to this edition; all translations are taken from *Averroes' Tahāfut al-tahāfut*, which includes al-Ghazālī's *Tahāfut al-falāsifa*, trans. and int. S. Van Den Bergh (2 vols, London: Luzac, 1954; repr. 1969 and 1978).

Al-Ghazālī (1980) *Al-munqidh min al-ḍalāl* (*The Deliverer from Error*), trans. R. McCarthy, *Freedom and Fulfillment*, Boston, Mass.: Twayne.

Leaman, O. (1985) *An Introduction to Medieval Islamic Philosophy*, Cambridge: Cambridge University Press.

—— (1988) *Averroes and his Philosophy*, Oxford: Clarendon Press; 2nd edition (1997) Richmond: Curzon Press.
—— (1990) *Moses Maimonides*, London: Routledge; 2nd edition (1997) Richmond: Curzon Press.

FURTHER READING

Genequand, C. (1984) *Ibn Rushd's Metaphysics*, Leiden: Brill.
Al-Ghazālī (1989) *The Remembrance of Death and the Afterlife*, trans. T. Winter, Cambridge: Islamic Texts Society.
Hourani, G. (1985) *Reason and Tradition in Islamic Ethics*, Cambridge: Cambridge University Press.
Kogan, B. (1985) *Averroes and the Metaphysics of Causation*, Albany: State University of New York Press.
Lerner, R. (1974) *Averroes on Plato's 'Republic'*, Ithaca, N.Y.: Cornell University Press.
Nasr, S. H. and O. Leaman (eds) (1996) *History of Islamic Philosophy*, London: Routledge.
Rosenthal, E. (1958) *Political Thought in Medieval Islam*, Cambridge: Cambridge University Press.

43

SUFI MYSTICISM

William Montgomery Watt

In the Islamic world a person who engaged in almost any form of mysticism came to be known as a Sufi (*ṣūfī*). The name is derived from the Arabic *ṣūf*, 'wool', the wearing of which was a custom of some of the early ascetics who were precursors of later Sufism. Sufism or *taṣawwuf* is not, of course, a form of philosophy, but mystical experiences gave some Sufis the confidence to go beyond the traditional theological basis from which they started and engage in speculations which were in a broad sense philosophical. To appreciate these properly, however, it is necessary to know something about the earlier history of the Sufi movement.[1]

There was undoubtedly a strain of mysticism in Muḥammad himself, but this has been so overlaid by later hagiography that it is difficult to make objective statements about it. His mystical strain may perhaps be surmised from some verses in the Qur'ān, but here the problem of interpretation raises difficulties. Later Sufism, however, was deeply indebted to meditations on the Qur'ān and the *ḥadīth* (the anecdotes about the sayings and doings of Muḥammad, formerly called 'traditions').

Later Sufis regarded the ascetic movement found in the eighth century as an early form of Sufism. The rapid conquests of the Arab armies during the seventh century meant that considerable wealth came into the hands of the ruling élite of the Islamic Empire, and many of those involved in government, administration or commerce came to lead somewhat luxurious lives. As a protest against the flaunting of wealth many serious-minded Muslims began to advocate the adoption of a degree of poverty combined with various forms of abstinence. One of the leaders of this movement was al-Ḥasan al-Baṣrī (d. AD 728), who was a teacher of theology in Basra with a circle of disciples. He warned people against the perils and afflictions of this world, and the uncertainty of its pleasures, in contrast to the unending joys of paradise. This is in accordance with one theme of Qur'ānic teaching: 'you [unbelievers] have chosen this present world, although the Hereafter – what is with God – is better and more lasting'.[2]

From Iraq the ascetic movement spread to many other parts of the Islamic world and was particularly strong in Khurasan (eastern Iran). If the stories can be believed, some Sufis went to incredible lengths in their practice of austerity. The transition to a more mystical approach comes with a woman ascetic, also of Basra, Ṛābi'a al-'Adawiyya (d. AD 801).[3] She is credited with being the first to speak of a selfless love for God. One of her sayings was:

> O God, if I worship thee in fear of Hell, burn me in Hell; and if I worship thee in hope of Paradise, exclude me from Paradise; but if I worship thee for thine own sake, withhold not thine everlasting Beauty.[4]

The ninth century saw a growth of Sufism throughout the Islamic world, with less emphasis on austerities and more on love and other forms of mystical experience. Some mystics came into a state of 'intoxication' in which they felt their union with God to be so close that one, Bāyazīd al-Bisṭāmī (d. AD 875), for example, is said when in a state of ecstasy to have cried out, 'Glory be to me! How great is my Majesty!' From such experiences there developed the conception of *fanā'*, 'annihilation (in God)' or 'passing away (into God)', with the implication that the created self has disappeared; and for some this became the goal of the mystical life. Towards the end of the ninth century many theologians became rather critical of the Sufis because of this and other deviations from strict orthodoxy as understood by the theologians. One of the leading Sufis of the time, however, al-Junayd of Baghdad (d. AD 910), worked out in various writings a more or less coherent account of Sufism as it had developed up to that point, but expressed this in a way which met some of the criticisms of the theologians. He saw the end of the mystical life not as ecstatic intoxication in which the self has been annihilated in God (*fanā'*), but as *baqā'*, remaining in God with a new life. The new life was sometimes described as one in which the qualities of the lover had been replaced by those of the Beloved. Many Sufis were fond of the *ḥadīth* in which God addressed Muḥammad with the words:

> my servant draws near to me by the performing of duties, and draws still nearer by works of supererogation until I love him; and when I love him, I am his ear so that he hears by me, I am his eye so that he sees by me, I am his tongue so that he speaks by me, and I am his hand so that he takes by me.[5]

Slightly younger than al-Junayd was one of the most remarkable of all the Sufis, al-Ḥusayn ibn-Manṣūr al-Ḥallāj (AD 857–922). He learned from al-Junayd and other Sufis of the time, but went his own way. In his earlier years his life was one of extreme asceticism, but in time he experienced mystical unitive states and became filled with love for God. This may have come about in 883, when he went on pilgrimage to Mecca and remained there in retreat for a year. Returning home to Tustar (in south-west Iran) he became a popular preacher to masses of ordinary people. In 887 he set out on what might be called an apostolic preaching journey through Iran to central Asia. This lasted five years. After a second pilgrimage to Mecca in 894, when he was followed by four hundred disciples, he made his home in Baghdad, but from 897 to 902 undertook another apostolic journey by India to central Asia and back through Iran, apparently hoping to convert the infidel Turks to Islam. Settling then in Baghdad, apart from a two-year sojourn in Mecca, he was mainly engaged in preaching a combination of mystical love and social reform. This was a period of political unrest in Baghdad, with coups and counter-coups, and some powerful people regarded al-Ḥallāj as a social agitator and charlatan. Al-Ḥallāj had also made enemies through his claim to have achieved a mystical union with God. He eventually fled from Baghdad, but at the end of 912 was arrested and imprisoned. Powerful friends secured the abandonment of his trial at this time, but in 922 he was again tried, and finally condemned and executed, apparently by a form of crucifixion.

From that day to this his case has been much discussed. Some Muslims thought his condemnation was justified; but others thought he had been wrongly condemned and was in fact a saint and martyr, with the result that he has had a great influence on following generations. The distinguished French orientalist Louis Massignon for some fifty years devoted a large part of his time to collecting material about al-Ḥallāj and studying it. The second enlarged edition of his main work, *The Passion of al-Ḥallāj, Mystic and Martyr of Islam*, appeared in English translation in four volumes in 1982.[6] The original French edition was published in 1922.

The best-known statement of al-Ḥallāj is the phrase spoken in reply to a question, 'Anā 'l-Ḥaqq', meaning 'I am the Truth [sc. God]' or perhaps rather 'My "I" is the Truth.' There are divergent accounts of when these words were uttered, and still more divergent interpretations. Presumably al-Ḥallāj did not mean that he had become identical with God. One possibility is that he felt that his personality or self had been annihilated in God or had passed away into him, so that in a sense he himself no longer existed. On such an interpretation the words would seem to be not far from what Paul meant when he said, 'I live, yet not I, Christ lives in me.'[7]

Some of the subtlety of the thought of al-Ḥallāj may be appreciated from his treatment of the theme of the primordial covenant (*mīthāq*) between God and the human race. This conception is based on a Qur'ānic verse (7.172) whose actual wording is: 'and when your Lord took from the sons of Adam, from their loins, their descendants, and made these bear witness about themselves, "Am I not your Lord?" They said, "Yes, we bear witness."' This is a verse much used by Sufis. It was interpreted to mean that before the the actual creation of Adam, God required from the whole human race this acknowledgement of his Lordship. Al-Ḥallāj took it to mean that both transcendent divinity (*lāhūt*) and humanity (*nāsūt*) were present in God before creation; and so it can be said that '*nāsūt* is the form assumed by the divine word prior to the whole of creation.'[8]

Somewhat similar ideas are found in the thinking of other Sufis, notably in that of Ibn-al-'Arabī, which will be described later. The doctrine of Ibn al-'Arabī came to be known as 'unity of being' (*waḥdat al-wujūd*), and that of al-Ḥallāj was then taken to exemplify the contrary position of 'unity of witness' (*waḥdat al-shuhūd*). This name indicates that God witnesses to himself in the heart of his servant, and that the servant welcomes into the emptiness of himself the Loving Guest, 'the essence whose Essence is Love', as al-Ḥallāj expressed it. When so understood, union with God comes about through acts of faith and love. God, or divine grace, works through the mind and will of the worshipper, but the worshipper remains himself. Thus his unity with God is something which can be seen or witnessed, but it is not a unity of being.

The period of a century or a century and a half after al-Ḥallāj has been called a period of consolidation in Sufism. More and more people were being attracted to the Sufi way of life, and many books were being written by Sufis. The books were often general descriptions of Sufi practice or collections of biographies of distinguished Sufis. What came to be regarded as the standard account of the theoretical structure of early Sufism is the *Risāla* or Epistle of al-Qushayrī (d. AD 1072). The author makes the distinction between the 'stations' (*maqāmāt*, sing. *maqām*) of the mystic way and the 'states' (*aḥwāl*, sing. *ḥāl*). A station is a stage or lasting condition which the mystic seeker reaches mainly through his own efforts, whereas the state comes to him as a gift from God. Al-Qushayrī mentions nearly forty stations, beginning with repentance Other important stations are abstinence (or asceticism) and renunciation, that is, even of lawful practices which distract the seeker from God. Among the states he includes gnosis or non-discursive knowledge (*ma'rifa*), love (*maḥabba*) and yearning (*'ishq*). Although al-Qushayrī was a Shāfi'ite jurist, there was still a degree of antagonism between the Sufis and many of the jurist-theologians.

In the second half of the eleventh century there appears the outstanding figure of Abū-Ḥāmid Muḥammad al-Ghazālī (AD 1058–1111). Born at Tus in eastern Iran, al-Ghazālī engaged in legal and theological studies, and then in 1091 at the early age of 33 became professor at the prestigious Niẓāmiyya college in Baghdad. It has to be borne in mind that the core of Islamic higher education was jurisprudence, and that theology was subordinate to this. Though Westerners may think of al-Ghazālī mainly as a theologian, his primary duty as professor would be to teach Shāfi'ite jurisprudence. After four years he abandoned his professorship to take up the life of a Sufi. He spent some time in Damascus, then made the pilgrimage to Mecca, then returned by stages to his home town of Tus, where he collected disciples in something like a monastery. In 1105 or early in 1106 he was prevailed upon to return to teaching in the Niẓāmiyya college in neighbouring Nishapur. At the end of 1109 (or perhaps later) he went back to Tus, and died there in December 1111.[9]

Western scholars have been attracted to al-Ghazālī by the charm of his *Deliverer from Error* (*Al-Munqidh min aḍ-ḍalāl*), an autobiographical work which is a kind of *apologia pro vita sua*.[10] Much attention has been paid to his part in the confrontation between Sunnite theology and the philosophy of Ibn Sīnā (Avicenna) and al-Fārābī. By private study he mastered the teaching of these men, and then wrote a critique of it, showing how at various points it contradicted Sunnite doctrine. At the same time, however, he greatly admired Aristotelian logic and other aspects of philosophy, and was partly responsible for introducing further philosophical ideas into the *Kalām* or rational theology of later centuries. It might have been expected that his interest in philosophy would later lead him into speculations in the field of mysticism, but it did not. As a Sufi his great achievement was the composition of a voluminous work, *The Revival of the Religious Sciences* (*Iḥyā' 'ulūm ad-dīn*). This consists of forty books or chapters, some of which are long enough to occupy a volume in an English translation. Through this work and through the example of his life he did much to heal the rift between the theologians and the Sufis. He showed how the life of a Sufi could be combined with the fullest performance of the ritual and liturgical duties of a Muslim, and indeed how these duties gave deeper meaning to that life. This was almost certainly an important factor in the increase of Sufi practice in the following centuries among various classes of Muslims. (To avoid confusion it should be mentioned that Abū-Ḥāmid al-Ghazālī had a brother, Aḥmad al-Ghazālī, also a Sufi, who had more profound experiences of mystical love and expressed these in poetry.)

Al-Ghazālī had many predecessors who collected disciples around them and shared a common life with these, besides giving them the individual spiritual direction which was regarded as essential if one was to make progress in the Sufi path. One such was Abū-Sa'īd ibn-Abī-l-Khayr (d. AD 1049), who drew up ten basic rules for his disciples, which were imitated in many later fraternities. These included such matters as maintaining ritual purity, observing the set times of prayer communally, rising for prayer at night, and keeping special times of the day for recollection, for reciting the Qur'ān and the like. Friendly relations were encouraged both with other Sufis and with the community in general.

In the later twelfth century, probably because such groups of disciples were increasing greatly in number, they began to have a permanent and more elaborate organization and are now called orders (sing. *ṭarīqa*). One of the earliest orders was the Suhrawardiyya, founded by 'Abd-al-Qādir as-Suhrawardī (d. AD 1168) and his nephew Shihāb-ad-dīn Abū-Ḥafṣ as-Suhrawardī (d. AD 1234), which had its original home in Baghdad. Another order originally centred in Baghdad was the Qādiriyya, which took its name from 'Abd-al-Qādir al-Jīlānī (d. AD 1166).

The Shādhiliyya order, founded in Egypt by Abū-l-Ḥasan 'Alī ash-Shādhilī (d. AD 1258), expanded especially in north Africa and Spain. The order best known to Westerners is probably the Mawlāwiyya or Mevlevi order (in its Turkish form), which takes its name from the great mystical poet and teacher Jalāl-ad-dīn ar-Rūmī (d. AD 1273), who was known as Mawlānā ('our master'). These are the whirling dervishes of Konya in Asiatic Turkey.

Gradually Sufi orders spread into nearly every part of the Islamic world. Old orders divided and new orders were founded. This multiplicity of orders enabled them to meet the religious needs of Muslims from various social classes and from different cultural backgrounds. Each order had its own special form of worship, usually called *dhikr*, meaning 'remembrance (of God)', since repetition of the divine name 'Allāh' was a prominent feature of the worship. There could also be dancing (such as whirling) or other bodily movements. The whole was designed to bring about a state of ecstasy in the participants, and even spectators were often deeply moved. Because the orders emphasized friendliness towards all men and humble service to needy members of the general community, the meetings for *dhikr* were friendly communal occasions. By encouraging mystical ecstasy and communal festivity the orders supplied something which was perhaps felt to be absent from the standard prayers (*ṣalāt*), and this may account for their growth in the centuries after their founding.

The orders usually had special buildings for their common life and common worship. These have various names, such as *khānqāh*, *zāwiya*, *ribāṭ*, and in Turkey *tekke*. Sometimes the dervishes (the members) had separate cells; sometimes there was a single large room. Many were married, because celibacy was not part of the Sufi tradition. In later times in addition to the full members there were attached to many orders a large number of ordinary people in a similar way to the 'third orders' of Christian monasticism. These people gained their living in normal ways, but attended the meetings for *dhikr* and often participated fully in the exercises. Through their preaching the orders did much to raise the religious and moral attitudes of these ordinary people.

About the same time as the Sufi orders were coming into existence the theosophical trend in Sufism was receiving fuller intellectual expression. An important contribution to this was made by a man known as Suhrawardī Maqtūl, 'the man from Suhraward who was killed' (AD 1153–91), because he died in prison. He is called 'the master of illumination' (*shaykh al-ishrāq*) because of his theory that what is comprehended intellectually as existence is experienced as light. He thought of God as the First Absolute Light, from whose rays all things are created and given life.

A slightly different form of theosophy was worked out by Ibn-al-'Arabī, 'the greatest shaykh' (AD 1165–1240). Muḥyī-d-dīn Abū-'Abd-Allāh Muḥammad ibn-'Alī ibn-al-'Arabī was born in Murcia in Islamic Spain. He probably met the philosopher Ibn-Rushd (Averroes), who was a friend of his father; and he was certainly influenced by the writings of Ibn-Masarra. After studying with various Sufi shaykhs in Spain and North Africa he spent from 1202 to 1204 in Mecca. From Mecca he went by Baghdad and Mosul to Konya. He made further travels in Syria and Iraq before in 1230 settling in Damascus, where he died ten years later. He was a prolific writer, and had apparently left over two hundred works on various subjects. His best-known Sufi works are *Al-Futūḥāt al-makkiyya* (*The Meccan Revelations*), in many volumes, and *Fuṣūṣ al-ḥikam* (*The Bezels of Wisdom*). In the latter he has chapters on each of twenty-eight prophets, including Muḥammad, and shows how each exemplifies an aspect of divine wisdom.

The theosophy of Ibn-al-'Arabī came to be known as 'unity of existence' (*waḥdat al-wujūd*) to distinguish it from the type of view represented by al-Ḥallāj as described above; which was now called 'unity of witness' (*waḥdat al-shuhūd*). The ideas of Ibn al-'Arabī were widely accepted in Sufi circles. He himself was something of a poet and often expressed his thought in varying ways. A more systematic exposition of *waḥdat al-wujūd* was given by some later thinkers, especially ash-Shabistarī (d. AD 1320) and 'Abd-al-Karīm al-Jīlī (d. *c.* AD 1408–17). The following brief description of *waḥdat al-wujūd* is based largely on Reynold A. Nicholson's *Studies in Islamic Mysticism*,[11] where the chief source is *Al-Insān al-kāmil* by al-Jīlī, though some attention is also given to *The Bezels of Wisdom* by Ibn al-'Arabī.

According to this view God is Pure Being (*wujūd*) or Absolute Essence (*dhāt*). He is sometimes spoken of as 'the dark mist' or 'blindness' (*'amā'*), a conception reminiscent of 'the cloud of unknowing' of an English mystic.

> The essence of God is unknowable *per se*; we must seek knowledge of it through its names and attributes. It is a substance with two accidents, eternity and everlastingness; with two qualities, creativeness and creatureliness; with two descriptions, uncreatedness and origination in time; with two names, Lord and slave (God and man); with two aspects, the outward or visible, which is the present world, and the inward or invisible, which is the world to come; both necessity and contingency are predicated of it, and it may be regarded either as non-existent for itself but existent for other, or as non-existent for other but existent for itself.[12]

To the Essence of God belong the names and attributes of God in their real nature, but not as they appear in existence. An attribute or quality (*ṣifa*) is what conveys knowledge of a thing to the understanding. Thus it is by its attributes that the Essence is manifested and made known. For the human understanding the forms of thought by which it apprehends the attributes are distinguished from the underlying reality, though ultimately attributes and Essence are identical. In the Qur'ān many names are given to God, such as the Merciful, the Seeing; and traditional Islam compiled a list of the ninety-nine most beautiful names.[13] Corresponding to the names there are attributes or qualities, such as mercy and sight; and these were much discussed by the theologians. In the thought of Ibn-al-'Arabī, however, the distinction between names and attributes is not always clear.

A key idea is that of the manifestation of the Essence or its theophany. One way of introducing this is to apply to the Absolute Essence the words of a *ḥadīth* in which God says to Muḥammad, 'I was a hidden treasure and I wanted to be known, so I created the world.'[14] Three stages of manifestation are distinguished. The first is Abstract Oneness (*aḥadiyya*), in which Being is conscious of itself as unity, that is, is conscious of the oneness of many particulars but not of their separateness. In the second stage this abstract unity is resolved into a pair of opposites. One is 'he-ness' (*huwiyya*), where Being in its inward aspect is conscious of itself as negating the many attributes; the other is 'I-ness' (*aniyya*), the outward expression of this, where Being is conscious of itself as the 'truth' of the many, revealing itself in their existence. The third stage is 'unity in plurality' (*wāḥidiyya*), where the many attributes are seen to be identical in the Essence with each other and with the One, or, more precisely, where Being identifies itself as One with itself as Many. This apparently implies a loss of the distinction between the attributes, so that mercy and vengeance become the same.[15]

There is also another manifestation of the Essence, namely divinity (*ilāhiyya*). This, said al-Jīlī,

> is a name for the sum of the individualisations of Being, *i.e.*, Being in the relation of Creator (al-Ḥaqq) to created things (*al-khalq*), and for their maintenance in their respective order in that sum.[16]

One aspect of divinity is mercifulness (*raḥmāniyya*). God showed his mercy by bringing the universe into existence, and his perfection is to be seen in every particle and atom of the universe. Mercifulness thus specially manifests the creative attributes (*aṣ-ṣifāt al-ḥaqqiyya*), whereas divinity shows both the creative and the creaturely (*khalqī*) attributes. Another aspect of divinity is Lordship (*rubūbiyya*), but in this case there is a necessary relation between God and his creatures, since 'Lord' (*rabb*) is a term requiring as its complement 'slave' or 'servant' (*'abd*), the word commonly used in theological Arabic for 'human being'.[17]

The conception of creation here is far from simple, and owes something to Neoplatonic emanation. God as the Merciful exists in all created beings, and indeed manifests himself in them, but he also causes then to appear in himself. This is not to be regarded as inherence or incarnation (*ḥulūl*), for that implies the presence of one thing in something else, and was associated in Muslim thinking with the Christian doctrine Muslims rejected; for Ibn-al-'Arabī and al-Jīlī the created things really were God's attributes. Neither is the relation of God with created things to be regarded as pantheism, as has sometimes been suggested by modern Western scholars, since there is also his transcendence (*tanzīh*), which only he can conceive and know. God as transcendent is the pure Essence without attributes and independent of created beings; but this is not, strictly speaking, God as object of worship, since that implies worshippers. God in respect of his divinity thus requires created beings. Their existence, however, is relative, not absolute, because it is Real Being limited and individualized by appearing as a relation of reality. Created beings are attributes of God, though the attributes are not something added to the Essence, but the relationship of the Essence as subject to the Essence as object. In knowing itself the Divine Essence knows all things as they are in itself, while distinguishing itself from the objects of its knowledge.

Al-Jīlī classifies the attributes of God as: (1) attributes of the Essence, such as One, Eternal, Real; (2) attributes of beauty (*jamāl*), such as Forgiving, Knowing, Guiding aright; (3) attributes of majesty (*jalāl*), such as Almighty, Avenging, Leading astray; (4) attributes of perfection (*kamāl*), such as Exalted, Wise, First and Last, Outward and Inward. He pays special attention to the seven attributes also singled out by the

Islamic theologians: life, knowledge, will, power, speech, hearing and sight. In some passages the attributes are said to be infinite in number.[18]

Ibn al-ʿArabī sometimes also speaks of five divine 'presences' (*ḥaḍarāt*), by which he seems to mean different levels of existence. The lowest of these is *nāsūt*, humanity or the corporeal world. Above this comes the *malakūt*, usually taken to be the world of the lower angels (from *malak*, 'angel'), but perhaps rather the domain of royalty (from *malik*, 'king'), since it immediately controls the corporeal world.[19] Next is the *jabarūt* or domain of power, sometimes called the archangelic world or the sphere of divine decrees and spiritual powers. After this comes the *lāhūt* or domain of divinity, which is presumably to be understood, as *ilāhiyya* was above in another context, as 'the sum of the individualizations of Being'. Finally there is the *hāhūt* (formed from the word *huwa*, 'he'), which is the Divine Essence in itself.[20] These five 'presences' are also the different levels of manifestation of the Absolute Essence.

The creation of the world is sometimes compared to the production of a mirror in which God is able to see himself. The created world apart from human souls is like an unpolished mirror, and the creation of Adam (the human essence) is thus the polishing of the mirror. In accordance with a *ḥadīth* (parallel to a Biblical text) the Sufis usually believe that Adam was created in his (God's) image. This interpretation of the *ḥadīth* was rejected by nearly all the mainstream Islamic theologians; one way of doing so, for example, was to say that, when God created him 'in his image', that meant 'in his [Adam's] proper image'. For the Sufis the creation of Adam in God's image means that the divine attributes belong to him in virtue of a necessity of his Essence. That the divine attributes are in the human essence also implies that the human person is a microcosm, the universe in little, or a prototype of the universe.

It was realized, of course, that in most human beings the attributes are not fully manifested, and that even in prophets and saints there are varying degrees of the capacity for manifesting the attributes. Moreover, while in one respect the Absolute has completely realized itself in human nature, it has also to return to itself, and this comes about by the mystical illumination of human beings. In this connection Ibn al-ʿArabī spoke of three journeys which lie before human beings. The first journey (*safar*) is 'the journey from God' in which each individual human essence as it was originally in the Absolute descends through various spheres and levels and becomes manifested, that is, created or born. At the end of this journey the human being is at his furthest from God. Many human beings never proceed further, and so remain more or less unaware of their relation to God. The second journey is 'the journey to God', which is the beginning of the return and the entry on the mystic path. How far a person progresses on this path depends on his innate disposition, on his finding competent spiritual guides, and on his fulfilling the necessary conditions. In speaking about the path in detail Ibn al-ʿArabī incorporates much of the teaching of earlier Sufis about stations, states and the like.

If the Sufi completes the second journey he has a unitive experience. The third journey is then 'the journey in God', which seems to be hardly a journey in the strict sense, since it is also described as *baqā'* or 'remaining' in God. Thus for Ibn al-'Arabī the unitive experience does not mean that the Sufi is identical with the Essence of God or united with it. All created beings are latent in the Divine Essence, and the unitive experience consists in the Sufi's becoming aware of his oneness with the divine attributes as their manifestation. This is the basic meaning of 'unity of being' or *waḥdat al-wujūd*.

Al-Jīlī distinguishes three stages of mystical illumination, of which two seem to correspond to the second of these journeys, and one to the third. The first stage is the illumination of the names, in which the mystic comes to understand the mystery conveyed by one of the names, and so in a sense becomes one with it. This is followed by the illumination of the attributes, in which the mystic becomes one with an attribute such as life or knowledge. Finally there is the illumination of the Essence, where the mystic, a prophet or saint experiencing ecstasy, becomes absolutely perfect and in some sense one with God. God is now, as it were, the mirror in which the mystic contemplates his own reality, and at the same time the mystic is a mirror in which God sees his names and attributes.

This last stage of illumination is frequently spoken of as that of the Perfect Person or Perfect Human Being (*al-insān al-kāmil*).[21] Those mystics who achieve the unitive experience may all be called Perfect Persons, but the Perfect Person *par excellence* is Muḥammad, standing above and beyond all other Perfect Persons. As the total manifestation or theophany of the divine attributes he is the microcosm or prototype of the universe, and in the creative process stands, as it were, between creator and creature. In this last respect much use is made of the term 'the reality (or idea) of Muḥammad' (*al-ḥaqīqa al-muḥammadiyya*). This reality of Muḥammad is manifested to some extent in all prophets and saints from Adam onwards, but its final and perfect manifestation is in Muḥammad himself, who is the seal or completion of the prophets (*khātam al-nabiyyīn*).[22] Al-Jīlī sometimes identifies the reality of Muḥammad with 'the Spirit' (*rūḥ*) which directs the creative process, and thus gives it a place in the work of creation comparable to that of the Logos in Christian thought.[23]

The above paragraphs give some idea of the central doctrines of the system of thought called *waḥdat al-wujūd*, though not of all its complexities. For example, Ibn al-'Arabī also developed a conception of saints in which there was a seal of the saints (*khātam al-awliyā'*) as well as a seal of the prophets, and he may even have supposed that he himself was this seal of the saints. He also holds the view that God determines the existence of each human being, but avoids sheer determinism by saying that God only determines this through what the person originally had it in him to become, and in this way each person may be said to determine his own destiny.

Many Western scholars have regarded Ibn al-'Arabī as a pantheist, but this is not altogether correct. He indeed saw all things as in some sense existing in God, but at the same time he never lost sight of the divine transcendence. What has also to be noticed, however, is the extent to which his interest was centred on contemplation and gnosis. Earlier Sufis like al-Ḥallāj had tried to express their love for God and their union with him through their activity, but Ibn al-ʻArabī seems to have been satisfied with a purely contemplative piety. Among recent scholars Henri Corbin and Seyyed Hossein Nasr have insisted on the non-pantheistic interpretation of his thought.

Ibn al-ʻArabī undoubtedly had a great influence on all later Sufis, even on those who rejected his theories. Many accepted his views to a great extent. Something like forty commentaries were written on his book *The Bezels of Wisdom*. Writers like al-Jīlī tried to give more coherent and systematic expositions of his thought or at least of aspects of it. Among the Sufis, however, there was no real intellectual development beyond the central thinking of *waḥdat al-wujūd*.

In the seventeenth century some of the ideas of Ibn al-ʻArabī found a place in a philosophical and theosophical movement among the Imāmites (Shīʻites) of Iran. One of the earliest names in this movement is that of Bahā'-ad-dīn al-ʻĀmilī (AD 1546–1622), often known as Shaykh-i-Bahā'ī, who was a prolific writer on many subjects. His father was an Imāmite scholar who had fled from Mount ʻĀmil in Syria because of persecution by the Ottoman Empire, which was Sunnite. The son may have influenced Mīr Dāmād (d. AD 1630), who wrote largely on logic and metaphysics and latterly lived mostly in Ispahan. These two were overshadowed by their pupil Ṣadr-ad-dīn Muḥammad ash-Shīrāzī (d. AD 1640), usually known as Mullā Ṣadrā, who concentrated on philosophy and was severely criticized by the theologians. He is said to have had a dream in which he saw his teacher Mīr Dāmād, who was also his father-in-law, and complained that he was being attacked for views similar to the teacher's; he was told that this was because he wrote in a way all could understand, whereas Mīr Dāmād had written so that only philosophers could understand. Mullā Ṣadrā's philosophy had in fact a large admixture of theosophy, based on Suhrawardī Maqtūl and Ibn al-ʻArabī, but the precise importance of these influences on his thinking has not yet been fully studied. A more extensive interest in the mystical element was shown by a pupil and son-in-law of Mullā Ṣadrā, Mullā Muḥsin-i-fayḍ al-Kāshī or al-Kashānī (d. AD 1679). After him, however, there were no important names until the tradition of Mullā Ṣadrā was revived by as-Sabzawārī (AD 1797–1878).[24] In the twentieth century the group who describe themselves as holding 'the perennial philosophy' have adopted some of the ideas of Ibn-al-ʻArabī, as can be seen from Frithjof Schuon's *Dimensions of Islam*.[25]

Apart from the influence of Ibn al-ʻArabī on the thinkers just mentioned, little need be said about the history of Sufism after him, since it had little relevance to philosophy. Even earlier a wonderful flowering of mystical poetry had begun, especially in the Persian language. Among the chief names are: Sanā'ī (d. AD 1131), Farād-ad-dīn ʻAttār (d. AD 1220), Jalāl-ad-dīn ar-Rūmī (d. AD 1273), Saʻdī (d. AD 1292), Ḥāfiẓ

(d. AD 1389) and Jāmī (d. AD 1492). While these abound in wonderful poetic imagery and imply a theosophical basis, they hardly contribute to the intellectual formulation of Sufism. The Sufi orders have continued up to the present with varying fortunes. At the beginning of the twentieth century some were distinctly decadent, and leaders with little real piety would impose on the ignorant masses. Since then there seems to have been some revival of genuine Sufism, but the extent of this is difficult to assess. One may note, however, that one of the most prominent Muslim thinkers of the early part of the century, Muḥammad Iqbāl (d. AD 1938), had been deeply influenced by al-Ḥallāj and Jalāl-ad-dīn ar-Rūmī.

NOTES

1 The following account is based mainly on A. J. Arberry, *Sufism: An Account of the Mystics of Islam* (London: Allen & Unwin, 1950), and Annemarie Schimmel, *Mystical Dimensions of Islam* (Chapel Hill: University of North Carolina Press, 1975).
2 87.17; cf. 28.60; etc.
3 See Margaret Smith, *Rābi'a the Mystic and her Fellow-Saints in Islam* (Cambridge: Cambridge University Press, 1928).
4 Arberry, op. cit., p. 42.
5 ibid., pp. 27, 58; Schimmel, op. cit., p. 43.
6 Translated by Herbert Mason (Princeton: Princeton University Press).
7 Galatians 2.20.
8 Massignon, op. cit., vol. III, p. 101.
9 W. M. Watt, *Muslim Intellectual*, (Edinburgh: Edinburgh University Press, 1963).
10 English translations in W. M. Watt, *The Faith and Practice of al-Ghazālī* (London: Allen & Unwin, 1955); and R. J. McCarthy, *Freedom and Fulfillment* (Boston, Mass: Twayne, 1980).
11 (Cambridge: Cambridge University Press, 1921, and reprinted).
12 ibid., p. 83; 'eternity' means without beginning and 'everlastingness' without end.
13 See *Encyclopaedia of Islam* (Leiden: E. J. Brill/London: Luzacy, 1954–), new edition art. '(al-) Asmā' al-Ḥusnā'.
14 Schimmel, op. cit., p. 268.
15 Nicholson, op. cit., pp. 95–7.
16 ibid., p. 97.
17 ibid., pp. 98–100.
18 ibid., pp. 100f.
19 Discussed in Frithjof Schuon, *Dimensions of Islam* (London: Allen & Unwin, 1969), pp. 142–58.
20 Schimmel, op. cit., p. 270; Seyyed Hossein Nasr (ed.), *Islamic Spirituality: Foundations* (London: SCM, 1989), p. 353.
21 Formerly, of course, the Perfect Man, but this is now considered sexist.
22 Sura 33.40; originally the phrase may have meant 'confirming previous prophets', but now all Muslims take it to mean 'the last of the prophets'.
23 Tor Andrae, *Die Person Muhammads in Lehre und Glauben seiner Gemeinde* (Stockholm: Norstedt, 1918), pp. 339–54, deals with Ibn-al-'Arabī; an interesting passage from al-Qayṣarī (d. AD 1330) is translated on pp. 343–5.

24 W. M. Watt, *Islamic Philosophy and Theology*, enlarged edn (Edinburgh: Edinburgh University Press, 1985), pp. 152f.

25 Schuon, op. cit.

FURTHER READING

Andrae, Tor (1987) *In the Garden of Myrtles: Studies in Early Islamic Mysticism*, Albany, N. Y.: State University of New York Press.

Arberry, A. J. (1935) *The Doctrine of the Sufis*, Cambridge: Cambridge University Press (translation of an early text).

—— (1950) *Sufism: An Account of the Mystics of Islam*, London: Allen & Unwin.

Corbin, Henri (1969) *Creative Imagination in the Sufism of Ibn 'Arabī*, Princeton: Princeton University Press.

Encyclopaedia of Islam (1954–) new edition, Leiden: E. J. Brill/London: Luzac; articles on (al-)Ḥallāj, Ibn al-'Arabī, etc.

Gilsenan, Michael (1973) *Saint and Sufi in Modern Egypt*, Oxford: Clarendon Press.

Keddie, Nikki R. (ed.) (1972) *Scholars, Saints and Sufis: Muslim Religious Institutions in the Middle East since 1500*, Berkeley: University of California Press; reprinted 1978.

Lings, Martin (1975) *What is Sufism?*, Berkeley/Los Angeles, University of California Press.

Massignon, Louis (1982) *The Passion of al-Ḥallāj, Mystic and Martyr of Islam*, trans. Herbert Mason, 4 vols, Princeton: Princeton University Press.

Nasr, Seyyed Hossein (1964) *Three Muslim Sages*, Cambridge, Mass.: Harvard University Press.

—— (ed.) (1989) *Islamic Spirituality: Foundations*, London: SCM.

Nicholson, Reynold A. (1921) *Studies in Islamic Mysticism*, Cambridge: Cambridge University Press; reprinted.

—— (1923) *The Idea of Personality in Sufism*, Cambridge: Cambridge University Press.

—— (1936) *The Kashf al-Maḥjūb of al-Hujwīrī* (translation), Gibb Memorial Series, London: Luzac; reprinted.

—— (1950) *Rūmī, Poet and Mystic*, London: Allen & Unwin.

Schimmel, Annemarie (1963) *Gabriel's Wing*, Leiden: Brill (a study of Muḥammad Iqbāl).

—— (1975) *Mystical Dimensions of Islam*, Chapel Hill: University of North Carolina Press.

Schuon, Frithjof (1969) *Dimensions of Islam*, London: Allen & Unwin.

Smith, Margaret (1928) *Rābi'a the Mystic and her Fellow-Saints in Islam*, Cambridge: Cambridge University Press.

—— (1935) *An Early Mystic of Baghdad*, London: Sheldon Press (the mystic is al-Muḥāsibī).

Watt, W. Montgomery (1953) *The Faith and Practice of al-Ghazālī*, London: Allen & Unwin (translations); reprinted, Oxford: Oneworld, 1995.

44

ISLAMIC PHILOSOPHY IN SOUTH AND SOUTH-EAST ASIA

John Bousfield

With the establishment of Islamic orthodoxy and Sunnism in particular by the tenth century AD the major intellectual thrust was against philosophy as such, the characteristic affirmation of human reason and the intricate reconciliation with Hellenism being vigorously repudiated. For many Muslims throughout the *ummah* the teachings of Imam al-Ghazālī, both in his *Tahāfut al-falāsifa* and more especially his *Iḥya' 'Ulum id-Dīn*, came to express the essence of a satisfactorily worked out religious life. The specification of orthodoxy and the maintenance of *sharī'a* in the face of deviant tendencies thus came to be a dominant feature of many of the urban centres of Islamic culture.

In both South and South-east Asia scholars have wanted to identify a countervailing trend towards heterodoxy and to elevate this to the status of a cultural essence. Nevertheless the simplest assessment of philosophical activity in these two cultural zones would be that little if any original work in Islamic philosophy or for that matter theology was produced at least until the rise of modernism in the nineteenth century, and that even then European-derived arguments were deployed in order to establish the rhetoric of the modernist position. It could be added that for much of the period from the tenth century onwards research on the texts in use both in the Islamic royal courts and the religious schools (*madrasa* and in South-east Asia a local rural variant, the *pondok pesantren*) has barely begun. So that while it is the case that academic philosophy has occupied a curricular place, if not a very significant one, in the traditional schools, the quality of the texts is as yet unknown. It would therefore be unwise to take for granted the inductively sound proposition that what has been in use consists of copies of Arabic (or, in north India, Persian) texts with at most marginal commentaries. In the case of legal and theological texts this was the case. Certainly in traditionalist schools in the main South-east Asian centres one could expect some teaching concerning basic Ash'arite orthodoxy and possibly some logic, but otherwise a typical al-Ghazālī-inspired mistrust of or hostility towards *falsafa* prevailed and still does. The modernist interest in philosophy is motivated by an interest in a package of rationalist activities seen as essential to the regeneration of Muslim society. This interest leads, as we shall note, to a taste for particular kinds of philosophy over others.

Now that caution has been duly expressed, however, it is essential that attention be drawn to a number of scene-setting features intrinsic to the Islamization process in both areas and at the same time that the attribution of certain mythical qualities to cultural activity there be challenged. By doing this it is possible to disclose the intellectual elaboration of a world-view which represents the philosophical core of Islamic culture as it was actively and creatively established in the two areas. It has been commonplace to find a characteristic syncretism at work everywhere and then to view with suspicion any signs of an assertive 'pure' Islam. In other words either Islam is said to have been assimilated and transformed within a rich and heady tradition or else its existence is acknowledged but treated as balefully negative. The relation between South Asia and South-east Asia was in turn often construed by contrasting two styles of syncretism, active and passive. In effect, Indic culture, the great Hindu–Buddhist complex, was for long considered to have had a hegemonic hold over South-east Asia. Thus the great states of mainland South-east Asia were 'Indianized' (with the exception of 'Sinicized' Vietnam). On the one hand the Indic tradition is 'Great', prototypical and paradigmatic. The syncretic process is at work in its very inception, and this in turn is intrinsically connected to the hallmarks of a sophisticated monism, tolerant ritual polytheism and the civilization of a hierarchical and differentiated caste society. Islam arrives on the scene in the eighth century as an ambiguous but potentially hostile outsider which cannot displace the great tradition without undergoing the processes of syncretism which will inevitably deprive it of its *tawḥīdic* uniqueness.

Syncretism in South-east Asia is given an altogether different character. Here the culture of small-scale societies was for long taken to be transformed by the cultural colonialism of India. The colonies take on a whole cultural package which includes a nicely mixed Hindu–Buddhist cosmology and an entire system of royal and brahminical administration. Thus within a 'Little' tradition a copied 'Great' tradition gets established. The sophisticated, literate and hierarchical culture is laid over the earlier, indigenous animist world. The latter survives, however, and so the layers of the cake start to permeate each other. Indeed it is an easy assimilation, where those aspects of the Indic tradition which fit are eagerly devoured, while the higher and purer elements are simply ignored, in the case of Buddhism and Islam, until much later. When Islam arrives it makes inroads in those areas dependent on trade and less able to sustain the conditions necessary for a highly differentiated and complex society relying on an agrarian base. The Islam which comes with the traders (from India, of course) is happily already heterodox and most un-legalistic. The mystical monism of the Sufis appeals directly and is consumed in the first instance as another part of the cake. Only later, much later, do the implications of a radical Islam sink in. By then Islam becomes a banner around which to concentrate anti-European sentiments. An essentially similar view is often expressed from the opposite perspective by Muslims who wish to repudiate any such syncretist associations.

To understand what we will identify as Islamic philosophy throughout these areas it is necessary to see the falsehood of this picture. In an important sense these areas are provinces of Islam. They look to the West Asian centres as sources of truth and inspiration. The institution of the *ḥajj* and the related practice of staying on in Mecca or Medina to study give substance to this, as does the daily locating of the *kibla* sustain it ritually. Beyond this there has always been a complex and ambiguous, if not actually ambivalent, relation with Arab culture, which comes to the fore whenever Pan-Islamism is at stake. The contentious issue of the Islamic purity of Arab ways often lies at the heart of calls to return to the *sunna* of the Prophet. The assertion of a spiritual Arabism formed part of the programme of 'renovation' of Shah Wali Allah of Delhi in the eighteenth century. Needless to say it is a position resented by others who feel that both the universality of their Islam and their own ethnic identity, Bengali, Malay, Bugis or whatever, have been denigrated. The nature of the provincial communities is in turn complex. But precisely when such a community is surrounded by others different in religion and possibly ethnicity, it often seeks to reproduce an exemplary purity, to establish itself as an 'exemplary centre' on a par with those of the spiritual heartland. A common epithet for an area whose people regard themselves as pious Muslims of the highest degree is 'Verandah of Mecca'; Aceh at the north tip of Sumatra and Patani and Kelantan, two northern Malay states, among other places in South-east Asia, had this title. Intellectual effort was often channelled as a result into *fiqh* and *ḥadīth* studies. The latter in particular was typically associated with puritan Sufis seeking to base all their practice on the primary sources of Islam in defiance sometimes of the authority of the *'ulamā'*. Both the followers of Aḥmad Sirhindī in the seventeenth century and those of Shah Wali Allah put studies of *ḥadīth* at the centre of their efforts. Adherence to a legal school in the case of Sunnīs carried with it more or less explicit adherence to a set of received doctrinal and theological positions. The Muslims of the Indonesian archipelago early on became followers of the Shāfi'ī school and have always found the thought of al-Ghazālī canonical. The situation is rather more complicated in India because of the presence of Shī'ī groups with their somewhat different jurisprudence and their avowedly esoteric philosophy, but again adherence among the Sunnīs to the Hanafi school carries with it a similar Ash'arite perspective. If any trend opposes this, it is again from the Traditionists, who usually favour the Hanbali school with its emphasis on a literal reading of the *ḥadīth*.

So one key feature of the provinces is a preoccupation with the specification of an orthodoxy of practice which displaces speculative theology and philosophy from the centre of activity. But to leave it there and abandon the pursuit of philosophical speculation would be to give a completely one-sided picture. The other aspect of provincialism is what we might call the freedom of the provinces. People can engage in a degree of free intellectual enterprise which permits an active appropriation of local traditions as well as imports from other centres. The process involves a high degree of bricolage but results in more than just derivative and uncritical copying of the mainstream. On the contrary new and original versions of ideas were developed both in India and in South-east Asia. In certain cases this led to the incorporation of Islamic elements into something quite distinctively regional like the *dīn-i-illāhi* of the Mogul Emperor Akbar (AD 1556–1605)[1] or the mystical paths which have resulted in the present day in the so-called *kebatinan* movements in Java.[2]

But the most important result is the encounter between *tawḥīd*, the absolute unity of divinity, and the paradoxical realm of an ontology based on experiences of existential monism developed to the highest order within the attempt to maintain orthodoxy. In other words, the other most consuming intellectual passion in these areas throughout the traditional, pre-colonial period was the great Sufi cosmology of *waḥdat al-wujūd*, unity of being, which had reached its maturity in the work of Ibn-al-'Arabī in the thirteenth century.[3] Versions of this travelled rapidly throughout the *umma* moving along the paths laid down by the *ṭarīqā*, the Sufi orders. The immense popularity of this cosmology at all levels has been commented upon – and not without ambivalence – by many Muslim scholars, Fazlur Rahman being an outstanding example. The reason is that if it was Sufism which prevented Islam from becoming a dry legalistic sect, the property of court-sponsored *'ulamā'*, it did so only by becoming a potentially degenerate folk religion. In fact, as we are about to see, the Sufi cosmology, making use of just about everything to hand in the more scholastic enterprises of theology and philosophy, provided a satisfactory account of reality for the ruling élites and in virtue of the same implications a folk cosmology of considerable force, containing as it does recipes for power. It has often been pointed out that the systems elaborated in the spiritual manuals of the period lasting from the thirteenth to the nineteenth century appear to be constructed out of Neoplatonism, Gnosticism, the Philosophy of Light, *ḥikmat al-ishrāq*, developed systematically during the same period by Suhrawardī, and the late thought of Ibn Sīnā as well as the esoteric systems of the Shī'īs.[4] The relations are probably not causal; rather all these identifiable trends in Islamic thought arose and developed together.

We will look now at what makes the cosmology so attractive and try to locate it in its context in the two cultural areas under consideration. But one most crucial aspect should be mentioned here because it is what gives it its philosophical appeal across time. It is a cosmology, an attempt to link being and existence, which, full of pleasure on the surface, is troubled, troubled at its very core. And it feeds on this anxiety.

The concept of *waḥdat al-wujūd*, usually translated as 'unity of being or existence', has a complementary concept in that of *waḥdat al-shuhūd*, 'unity of vision or experience'.

The decisive question is, what link holds between these? Those spiritually inclined, the Sufis, as well as those opposed to the pursuit of the esoteric, had to take up their position in relation to this. If an experience of unity or a vision of divinity which excludes all else is possible, in what sense can it be held to be legitimate or, to put it another way, valid, truth-bearing? One solution, popular really only with modernists, is to discount any claim to veracity in such experience. The mystical teaching is an illusion, a pathology. Instead of raising fundamental questions about the nature of God and his creation an 'empiricist' metaphysics rules out all unitarian possibilities. By and large in traditional Islam and Muslim societies the issue would not go away like this. It is not that the characteristic claims of the Sufis are false but rather that they are in a sense sinful: people should not be treading where only the prophets, if anyone, can go.

The cosmology, in its broadest outlines, elaborates a picture of the universe, but in doing so invokes a paradoxical metaphysics. This is intimately connected throughout to a 'descriptive psychology' which in its turn is linked to a programme of spiritual education. The whole forms a system which is self-supporting: the ordered series of experiences which constitute the fruits of the educative disciplines from one aspect verify the claims made in the cosmology. From another aspect it is the discursive provision of the metaphysics and its accompanying ontological commitment which provide the intentionality of the inner states, endow them with their meaning. It is indeed significant that something like a Husserlian phenomenology can be used in the analysis of this dimension of the system. The latter-day members of the tradition are enthusiastic about phenomenology and its existentialist variants because it seems to them that they themselves are already involved in the practice of gaining the level of transcendental consciousness and in that mode viewing the stream of ordinary consciousness. This is particularly true of the Javanese tradition, but there are also Malay Muslim mystics who construe part of their labour in this way.

It is also worth stating that the nature and source of these experiences are problematic within the tradition and not just to secular and academic commentators. This is not the place to discuss the grounds of mysticism in general: the question is specifically, why did Islamic intellectual endeavour centre on the possibility of experience of cosmic unity? One hypothesis has suggested that neither Ibn-al-'Arabī nor any of his successors were actually Muslims, even if they persuaded themselves that they were. They belonged instead to other traditions and simply tried to make the latter appear Islamic; they may even have wanted to have it both ways and synthesize Islam with Neoplatonism, the yogic and tantric traditions and so on. But this raises all the same problems as the emergence of Aristotelianism in a monotheistic context: what motivates the attempt to reconcile the irreconcilable? Another possibility, undoubtedly appealing to some of the Sufis, including Ibn-al-'Arabī and al-Jīlī, as well as their latter-day affines in Indonesia, is that the unity of being is disclosed at the heart of all human experience and will then have to be related to Islamic monotheism in some satisfactory way. At the highest level – and this is indeed a clear consequence of the system – everything that is, every idea that is conceived and every act is Islam. But, decentring this argument, all traditions are at the highest level equal. It is an important facet therefore of much of the Sufis' writings – and this is typical of the South and South-east Asian *shaikhs* – that Islam is taken to be the highest and most perfect of all religions. Indeed the writers are often overtly hostile to any alternatives. Finally one can argue with many scholars and sympathizers that there is something intrinsically Islamic in the system even at its most monist. This is the Sufis' own perspective, and recent historical work combined with a more empathetic approach has seemed to confirm early origins within the Islamic community of trends towards both asceticism and ecstatic religion. This would suggest that from the very formation of Islam there is the possibility of this way of thinking.

We must assume that the possibility of ecstatic experience characteristically involving temporary loss of selfhood or existence did not just arise rhapsodically in individuals. Here we have a cosmology which is represented as coming from the Qur'ān itself and the *sunna* of the Prophet. Constant emphasis is put on adherence to *sharī'a*. Yet at the same time the paradoxical monism to which I have alluded is derived from the agreed Qur'ānic base. A Wittgensteinian proposition has to be invoked to the effect that there must have been an available conceptual base embedded in the life of the community from which the sense of the elaborate system derives. This conceptual base, the 'certainties' of the communities, is not so much added to or mixed in with the pure version of Sunnī Islam; rather it is the basic framework in terms of which those features central to the 'tawḥīdic world-view' are encountered. This gives more access to the success of the cosmology in these parts of Asia than the simpler suggestion that basically monist cultures reinterpreted Islamic monotheism pantheistically. It will be argued below that the key to the success of the Sufi system is what it says of power. And that it is this very strength which also causes the central difficulty.

The basic cosmology, as already stated, spread throughout the Muslim communities from the thirteenth century. This is often said to have received particular impetus after the fall of Baghdad to the Mongols in 1258, when many *'ulamā'*, scholars and in particular Sufis fled and spread out along the various trade routes. The incursion of Islam into South-east Asia occurred later than in India, where there had been Islamic rulers since the eleventh century. Evidence suggests that there were Islamic courts at the end of the thirteenth century at the earliest. During the next three centuries Islamization was widespread throughout the Indonesian archipelago, and it is almost certain that the missionaries were Sufis. The two related areas of difference which might actually characterize the teachings of a *ṭarīqa* are first, how the assertion of the unity of being is understood, and second, how if it is rejected the unity of experience is put in its place. The three most important Indian intellectuals of the traditional period, 'Abd-al-Haqq Dihlawi (AD 1551–1642), Aḥmad Sirhindī (AD 1564–1624) and Shah Wali Allah (AD 1703–62), all placed this issue at the centre of their work. By and large all the Sufis, notwithstanding their metaphysical differences, share a particular view of authority, which will appear surprising if we think of 'orthodoxy' in contemporary terms.

The system is worked out in relation to and utilizing elements of the *Mu'tazila* viewpoint, *kalām* and *fiqh* as well as Aristotelianism and Neoplatonism. Bearing in mind that all the texts are spiritual manuals used in conjunction with techniques and disciplines which together constitute the path, it is nevertheless possible to identify the key elements of philosophical interest. The focus here will be on the 'existential monist' tradition, which was more popular in its pure or 'extremist' form in South-east Asia. The work of the well-known Sumatran mystic and prolific writer Hamzah Fanṣūri (d. *c.* AD 1605) will be taken as exemplary,[5] as well as the popular system of the 'Seven Grades', which is to be found in texts of both areas. The best-known of these is the *Tuḥfa al-mursala ila rūh al-nabi* (*The Gift Addressed to the Spirit of the Prophet*), written by a Gujarati, Muhammad ibn Faḍli'llah, around 1590.[6] It was loosely translated into Javanese in verse form as early as 1620. It is associated with the teachings of a number of orthodox *ṭarīqa* such as the Shattariyyah.

A radical essentialism which identifies essence and being, essence and attribute, and arguably will and necessity, is promoted against both the philosophers and the orthodox theologians. Against the *Mu'tazila* as well as moderate Ash'arites a radical determinism is derived without compromise from Qur'ānic indications of the pre-eternity of the Divine Decree. This is distilled into the theory of the unity of being in which the infinite Essence pours out the totality of the world without in any way being modified or reduced. Time is created infinitesimal moment by infinitesimal moment rather than creation occurring in time. While this echoes some of the radical atomism of the *mutakallimūn*, it is here intended to depict a tenseless eternal moment pregnant with 'infinitizing' activity. One is reminded of the way in which Levinas condenses Bergsonian duration into the absolute unique present.[7] Tenselessness is a syntactic feature of the Malay language, so that many of Hamzah's statements about the Essence eternally creating, the cosmic ocean for ever producing waves, can express an eternal present without metaphor. The self-disclosure of the Essence can only be to a witness, and that witness must be different from the Essence while being of and from the Essence. This is a key to Ibn-al-'Arabī's system, and Hamzah grasps it. There must be a real subject, in a location, for the Essence to be reflected and witnessed. So the theory of the unity of being invokes difference rather than denying it. Much in the system reminds us of that of Spinoza. It has, though, an organic feel to it, and the intellectual love of God is a pale reflection of *ma'rifah*, *gnosis*, which can include an experience of intense love modelled on the experience of physical passion.

Following Ibn-al-'Arabī, the texts establish the nature of the connection between the world as it appears to us, the 'hundreds and thousands', as the world and its particulars are called, and the essential unity of being. It has been argued that the Arab term *wujūd* does not have the meaning 'being'. What is meant is that the cognates of the term do not function in either predication or existential assertions. The term does not function in Arabic in a way analogous to the Greek term, *on*. The commentators Marijan Molé and Annemarie Schimmel have suggested that the term, although clearly selected to have the analogous meaning of an all-encompassing metaphysical category, has the more dynamic root meaning 'finding', 'to be found'. It thus opens up a narrative of God finding himself and being found, these two being one, *waḥdat al-wujūd* and *waḥdat al-shuhūd*.[8] It is open to question whether the term is used with these Heideggerian resonances in classical Arabic as opposed to having a hermeneutics imposed upon it. Nevertheless the idea that being is process and even agency, that it is disclosure and revelation, does make sense in this context, for, as I am claiming, an *a priori* monism of power, conceived dynamically, lies at the heart of the system. I should add that Hamzah, writing in Malay, translates *wujūd* with a word which does function in existential assertions and also implies a possessive relation between subject and object, *ada*. This term can be nominalized into *keadaan*, thus adding once again the sense of existence and in particular, being as opposed to non-being. It is of great importance that translation was occurring; not just because that implied a degree of cultural creativity not always acknowledged but also because translation is integral to the development of the system. Certainly both senses, of a total category and of dynamic self-disclosure, fit the scheme of being presented by Hamzah.

Following Ibn-al-'Arabī, an account is given in which the divine Essence pluralizes, particularizes and externalizes without any essential loss. In Hamzah's version the process, while a matter of divine will rather than necessity, is nevertheless also literally the outcome of a moving out of *aḥadiyya* (pure unity) or *kunī dhāt* (innermost essence, transcendent and beyond all names) to a state of *waḥda* (plurality in unity) or *ta'ayyun awwal* (the first determination) – in which Predispositions of the Essence and their intentional correlates, the Fixed Prototypes (*a'yān thābita*) of all that will ever be take up a place in relation to each other while still constituting and being constituted as a unity. The innermost hidden essence is best thought of as the outer limits of the thinkable, the transcendent aspect of the transcendent, while the stage of a determined unity is the transcendent thought of from the perspective of transcendence in relation to that which it transcends, i.e. as immanent. Although the system presents this as a process which looks like the emanationism typical of Neoplatonism and often treats the path as one of return to such a state, it is clear from the texts that some of the thinkers, including Hamzah, understand it as a matter of states of consciousness in relation to reality rather than as a quasi-organic process. In the pure system the stage of the first determination involves what we might call the priority of divine intentionality first:

> The first stage is fourfold: Knowledge, Being, Sight, and Light. All these are called the 'first determination', for by virtue of knowledge, the knower and the known become manifest; by virtue of Being, That which causes to be and That which becomes manifest; by virtue of Sight, the Seer and the Seen are manifest; by virtue of Light the Illuminator and the Illuminated are manifest. All these . . . acquire their names in the first determination.[9]

The second determination is the same unity, but now from the point of view of the content of these primordial intentionalities. These contents are like the forms of Plato, and they are in turn objects of possible transcendent experiences involving intense passion.

The other version popular in the area, that of the Seven Grades, similarly conceives three stages of unity before the process of particularization and externalization: *aḥadiyya*, transcendent unity; *waḥda*, the unity in which the Predispositions are not differentiated from one another but inhere in a state of dynamic potentiality and cosmic intimacy in which there is an identity among different realities; and *wāḥidiyya*, where the contents of divine consciousness and passion are differentiated from one another but still have the structure of the unity of consciousness. This second level or determination is that of unity in plurality. It is at the first stage when, so to speak, the knower and the known are 'true unity', that it is possible to talk of identity between beings. Only at this level am 'I' God, not once I am a creature. Ibn-al-'Arabī is frequently quoted:

> We were Lofty Letters unmoved,
> Attached to our Abode in the Mountain Peak. . . .
> I was with you within it,
> and we were all you and you were He.[10]

These primordial realities, the forms, thus come from God's knowledge, not vice versa. Or rather both divine knowledge and its contents emerge from a deeper structure of 'subjectless intentionality'. Moreover, being of the Essence, his living names, it is appropriate to attribute consciousness to them. Indeed as the most perfect realization of the attributes prefigured in the names (i.e. the Logos) we are there – already – but not as our outer selves. This first state of being is the first movement of divine passion. Hamzah glosses it thus:

> the things known to God are eternal, for the Primordial Potentialities are indeed the Predispositions of his Essence and they all are descriptions of none but Him.[11]

From this Hamzah derives both his monism and his typical radical determinism, discussed below.

We need first to glimpse at the next 'stages', where externalization and particularization occur. Hamzah says:

> The human spirit, the animal spirit and the vegetal spirit are the third determination. The fourth and fifth determinations are determinations ad infinitum, encompassing the realm of physical things in its entirety.[12]

He is quite clear that this creative externalization is without limit. The Sevener system is neater, if cruder. The four external grades are those of 'Spirits, Ideas, Bodies, and that of the Perfect Man.'[13] Of these the first three represent something like the Neoplatonic descent towards extension, divisibility, lack of subtlety and corruptibility. The fourth marks the outer limit of manifestation, where the whole macrocosm is distilled into the microcosm of the perfect mirror, witness, vicegerent of God and saint. Again, in reverse, the perfect man, *al-insān al-kāmil*, is the potential realization of the whole cosmic order, but only after a developmental path back to the grade of unity which is the Sufi path with its spiritual disciplines. The *Tuḥfa* makes it quite clear that what happens in the outer, manifest world is always an expression of the inner, hidden world of the Essence. The Javanese version makes use of Hindu images and concepts. The relation between the Reality and the world of appearance is said to be like that of Viṣṇu to Kṛṣṇa, who is the appearance of the former. Again, the world of creatures is depicted as the shadows of the puppets in the hands of the *dalang*, the master puppeteer of the Javanese shadow play.

Perhaps because of its neatness this system, developed at the end of the sixteenth century, spread rapidly throughout India and the Indonesian archipelago. It was associated with the teachings of several of the more 'orthodox' *ṭarīqa* (though it should always be added that this orthodoxy was open to contestation). Ironically, Hamzah's earlier and in many ways purer system, following as it does Ibn-al-'Arabī and al-Jīlī, came to be regarded as pantheistic and heterodox; yet Hamzah, perhaps more rigorously than the followers of the Sevener system, fights to preserve the transcendent nature of divinity in the system and to promote the obligations of *sharī'a*.

This period witnessed among the Sufis a preoccupation with avoiding the excesses of the very beast they had created and preventing a descent into the sin of pantheism. At the same time there was, especially during the period of Akbar in India, a sense that urgent measures were necessary as Islam moved into its second millennium. Mahdist notions were in the air.[14] In the main South-east Asian centres of Sumatra and Java, meanwhile, Sufism was in at the inception of Islamic kingdoms and was promoting ideas of power and leadership in the context of supplanting older, Hindu–Buddhist regimes.[15] In both areas the preoccupations led to a confrontation with the same problems.

Integral to the Sufi cosmology is the idea of a spiritual hierarchy of people based on their rank relative to the grades of being, their degree of return towards the Essence. The various ranks of high Sufis, such as *al-quṭb*, the 'pole', *al-ghawth*, the 'help', *al-badal*, the 'peg', all imply not just a being at the pinnacle of the hierarchy but also one standing at the centre, the axis of the world, and also linking the manifest with the Hidden, the source with the outcome.[16] This was of immediate interest and appeal to the millenarians, who were upset by the apparent religious excesses of Akbar's rule and sought regeneration in a leader of cosmic standing. It was also attractive to those rulers in Sumatra, the Malay peninsula, Java and so on who more in the manner of Akbar's court found a congenial new account of the style of power to which they were accustomed. Hamzah is typical of this appealing tension. He both extols the sense of universal justice inherent in *sharī'a* and praises his patron, the Sultan of Aceh, whom he describes as *al-quṭb* and as *al-insān al-kāmil*. As a member of the Qadiriyyah *ṭarīqa* he maintains that one must always check experience and intuition against their fit with the sources of Qur'ān and *ḥadīth* and reject their implication if they clash. The trick lies in the hermeneutics of the Sufis, who stayed rigorously close to sources but produced interpretations which already presupposed their system.

Now the source of power in the latter is the Essence itself. Even 'prior' to the divine command, '*Kun*!', 'Be!', the unity of being is, as we have seen, a state of tension, and indeed it is characterized as a state in which the potentialities yearn with such hunger to be liberated that the Essence, responding in a sense to itself, moves in an infinite wave of compassion and mercy, *ir-Raḥmān ir-Raḥīm*. The whole Essence pervades each of the predispositions and each of the fixed essences; and in a vast and infinite forking and fractal structure each attribute of divinity has every other within it and vice versa; and so on through the ever occurring and infinite particularizations. From the attribute of *al-Jamāl*, beauty, comes all that is good; from that of *al-Jalāl*, majesty, all that is evil (Hamzah translates with Malay words which do not necessarily have a moral sense or one of merit or sin).[17] There is no evasion in the system of the consequences of this. God would be imperfect if he created people who then sinned or created sinners and then decided to punish or forgive them. The whole is part of the Essence: sinners embody defiance (the primary sin is refusal to submit) and thus power; their obliteration embodies both the power of the Essence and the goodness of the Essence. But the whole Essence is embodied in everything – at the highest level of true unity, it must be remembered – and so there both are and are not sinners. Of those who suffer in hell one must ask, who suffers? and realize with al-Jīlī that such suffering is also, at the level of unity, pure joy.[18] So, good and evil are both separate and one, depending on the level of being occupied.

This is a problem. If these different grades of being cannot be separated at some point, this is a recipe for fatalistic mayhem. Undoubtedly this was a fear of many of the devout, including thinkers like Hamzah himself. At the same time it gave a new inflection to a more fundamental metaphysics in these areas. It has been argued by many that in much of South-east Asia reality is thought of as power, the key proposition being 'Power is'; moreover it is amoral, or rather it is pervasive, and is manifest both in what is experienced as good and in what is experienced as evil.[19] The latter in turn are relative: they are dual aspects of One Reality. There can only be good with evil and vice versa, as they mutually define each other and are relative to perspective. Good needs evil. There is either a state of balance or else there is disorder. Cosmic power can be reflected and focused in the outer world of appearance. In particular the ruler is a microcosmic focal point of both order and energy; royal majesty is exhibited in the visibility of power, and that is visible in what is most evil as well as what is most good and just. It is the style of rule which counts. This is displayed in texts of the courts, but also in what is known of many rulers. And it finds its most consummate legitimation in the work of the Sufi thinkers.

Balance, characteristic of the local cosmology, is supplanted by a hierarchy of subordination in which the ruler takes up a rank of Protector of Law. A similar transformation occurred with the incursion of Theravāda Buddhism. Evidence suggests that the rulers took the teachings seriously enough to seek preceptors among the ranks of the Sufis and to engage in the disciplines themselves. Not only rulers at the apex of their societies but also spiritual leaders of smaller rural communities took up this aspect of the system. Sufi *shaikhs* dispensed medicine and amulets and took up combat with sorcery. A remarkable case study of the Gayo, a highland tribe in Aceh, demonstrates that a whole series of ritual protections against sorcery enact Hamzah Fanṣūri's system.[20]

Whether by achievement or grace (not that the two are different in the system), energy from the Essence flows through these microcosmic pivots. It is clear that much of this part of the Sufi cosmology was taken over in its more developed form by the Indian thinkers. Both Aḥmad Sirhindī in the time of Akbar and Shah Wali Allah after the fall of the dynasty in the eighteenth century not only look to notions of spiritual hierarchy but imply that they are themselves the spiritual poles of the time. Both invoke a theory of sainthood which is most developed in Ibn-al-'Arabi's version. In this saints can occupy a rank as important as that of the Prophet.

There is much pleasure in the texts just as there is much at the end of the spiritual practices. The texts themselves occupy their place because they render visible the cosmology which daily life may not. They constitute a symbolic message. But there is also the trouble mentioned above. The radical determinism, not unique to Sufism, goes hand in hand with the assertion, present in the texts, that there is only one Reality: not only is there only one God, there is only God. Then the question of existence arises: what are the creatures? If the answer is that we too are God, Islam is denied. This worries some of the *shaikhs* as much as it angers the *'ulamā'*. Hamzah was accused of abject heresy by a successor at the court of Aceh, al-Rānīrī (d. AD 1666) from Gujarat.[21] The *wujūdiyya*, the 'existential monists', were accused by him of identifying God with his creatures. This was a familiar charge against Sufis, but one which in Aceh for a time could get them killed. None of the mainstream *shaikhs* conceded that they were pantheists, though there should be no doubt that in both India and the archipelago there was plenty of unrepentant or naïve monism.

For those concerned, only a number of solutions are available. Either one maintains that there is a substantial difference between God and his creatures or one denies that there are creatures. If there is a substantial difference, the Essence of God is undermined; that is familiar from Spinoza. If there is such a difference, the created substances can, in virtue of their substantiality, have power, i.e. free will. That denies the power of God. If the creatures do not have being, then they cannot be in a state of Islam. Either way there is paradox. The Sufis take the paradox head on. The solution of Aḥmad Sirhindī was to revive the 'true' tradition of *waḥdat al-shuhūd*, which is said to derive from al-Ḥallāj himself.[22] According to this an individual can reach a level of experience at which only God is present and there is no sense of individual existence. This is sometimes understood as God witnessing himself in the heart of the servant. After the experience the servant returns to 'ordinary' reality, albeit transformed. This position became associated especially with the Naqshbandiyya *ṭarīqa*, with whom Aḥmad Sirhindī was most associated. It is arguable and has been argued ever since whether this unity of witness does not simply avoid the ontological consequences of the system. On the other hand it apparently preserves the 'distance' between God and His witness, and that difference is necessary for the system to have any experiential base whatsoever. It should be added that the Naqshbandiyya nevertheless developed after Aḥmad an elaborate theory of the spiritual organs of the body which is highly reminiscent of *chakra* theory in the Hindu tradition. More or less pure and often very impure versions of this circulate even now throughout the areas.

The *shaikh* al-Rānīrī, mentioned already, exhibits this tendency. He directs his efforts against those who in his view take the claim that God and the universe are one to mean that they are identical. Now there are statements in Hamzah which do assert this unity. Al-Rānīrī interprets this to be an assertion of identity and argues thus:

> [God] is the Self-subsistent One, and He is the One Who gives subsistence to others. Hence, the World is not fit to be categorised as 'being' – it is called darkness, not-being . . . it is nothing but a shadow. . . . This is why [the Sufis] say that God and the Universe is One. They do not intend it to mean that the World and God are one being and identical. This is why they say that God and the Universe are neither the same nor different, for their identity and non-identity would require two entities existing per se.[23]

The great contemporary Sufi philosopher of Malaysia, Syed Naguib al-Attas, has in turn kept the argument alive by defending Hamzah against what seems a gratuitously hostile misinterpretation.[24] What is clear in al-Rānīrī's work is an 'orthodox' espousal of the atomism of the *mutakallimūn*.

Hamzah, as we have seen, does talk about a unity, but that unity is of God with himself, and it is only at the highest thinkable level that it can be asserted that contained in the Essence is the consciousness of man. He too denies that the world and the creatures have being. He says, 'Existence is a sin' above all others. What he seems to mean is that existence is both an illusion somehow sustained by the self (an argument not unlike that of some Buddhists) and that existence is not being. We can see that the Sufis are no less caught up in metaphysics than the Aristotelian philosophers were. The poignancy of their system lies in this attempt to preserve the possibility and legitimacy of a realm of supra-normal experience while at the same time preventing the consequences of their determinism and their potential amorality.

The argument and the attempts at reconciliation continued and still do. Shah Wali Allah, like Aḥmad Sirhindī, whom he considered a predecessor, attempted once again to synthesize the two alternatives of existential and testimonial monism,[25] arguing along lines familiar from the above discussion that these derive from different perspectives which are contingent upon advancement along the mystical path. *Waḥdat al-shuhūd* is a higher stage in which difference is experienced as well as unity. From Ibn-al-'Arabī he took the idea of a world beyond this, '*'ālam al-mithāl*, which is occupied by subtle bodies perceptible only to a kind of faculty of imagination which Henri Corbin calls the creative imagination and which is particularly interesting to Jungians.[26] Shah Wali Allah is said to have derived his own inspiration from this world, a not uncommon claim made by or about Sufi *shaikhs* today.

At a practical level it is appropriate to mention here what we have called the descriptive psychology of the Sufis which accompanies the system. On the face of it this is a complete misnomer, since the Sufis try to produce particular states and interpret them in the light of the system. In particular it is the various schemes of 'stations (*maqāmāt*) and states (*aḥwāl*)' along the path which concern us.[27] The former are developmental conditions which the Sufi reaches through spiritual exercise and which are specified in relation to the transformation of normal attitudes and moods into measures of proximity to God. The states are said to be the result of grace; they are not the inevitable outcome of the adept's work. In keeping with their emphasis on *al-jalāl*, divine majesty or rigour, there is no guarantee that a state is permanent; indeed the Sufi advances in the knowledge of his own impermanence; God denies as well as allowing, tests as well as blessing. The manuals of the *ṭarīqa* offer different lists both of the stations and the states and of their order.

Indeed what is presented is a very complex structure in which the state of an individual will differ according to their station; the latter in turn will have a different structure dependent on the degree of discipline, intellect, emotional propensities and so on of the individual. A typical progression of states might be faith, repentance, abstinence, renunciation, *tawakkul*, 'God-consciousness' – to which we will return in a moment – poverty, patience, gratitude, contentment, fear, hope, love, intimacy and union. It is quite important that there is disagreement about whether some are stations or states: fear and hope in this transcendental understanding are sometimes considered states. Contentment, *riḍā*, is a station in that it involves the active and conscious acceptance of all that is entailed by the Divine Decree, including suffering of the most abject kind. Yet it can be viewed also as a state, an end desired in itself. Fear, *khawf*, and hope, *rajā'*, are sometimes treated as stations and sometimes as states. It depends on whether they are acquired states or as achievements analogous to virtues. Two states worth mentioning are *basṭ* and *qabḍ*. The first is a state of ego-expansion, a joyous feeling of community with the whole of creation; the second is the opposite, a contraction into a state of abject loneliness and eventual loss of self. Now the disciple learns to reach these stations and be open to the states. It is a matter both of recognizing the contents of consciousness and of changing the perspective from which they are viewed. The Sufi must both be immersed in the pure temporal present, *waqt*, and maintain a kind of transcendental watch. *Tawakkul* is perfect trust in God and reliance on him alone. To gloss it as 'God-consciousness' captures the idea of a perspective which includes continued awareness of God's power; nothing passes without it being the occasion of both the reliance on God and the 'remembrance' of him. It thus requires the maintenance of an interpretative attitude to life in its smallest details.

It is in this sense that the scheme is here described as a descriptive psychology. Perhaps no different from those proto-phenomenological endeavours usually so-called, it would be more appropriate to call them descriptive and revisionary. This they have in common with the elaborate schema of Buddhist and tantric meditation techniques. There was an interest in translating works from these traditions during the time of Akbar which was undoubtedly part of his religious cult.

An emphasis on a pure, meditative grasp of experience in the present is central to the modern *kebatinan* movement in Java.[28] The term, which means 'inwardness' or 'hiddenness' – *ilmu kebatinan* is the science of the inner – has come to designate contemporary, non-Muslim mystical movements. Often syncretic in their declared aims, the various movements none the less have certain common features. The members regard themselves as the true descendants of the pure Javanese tradition, which includes Hindu and Buddhist elements as well as Islamic mysticism of the kind we have been discussing. Much of the terminology of the various movements is Sufi: the cosmology and accompanying psychology have much the same structure. In addition, however, Indic and Javanese terms are used and are not subsumed within an Islamic framework. It has also been suggested that a further ingredient is European theosophy encountered early this century.

At the core of the teachings lies a concept of the unity of being. One reality, *hakekat*, underlies the outer realm of sensory experience. This world is construed in terms of the metaphysics of power and balance mentioned above. Through ascetic disciplines and meditative exercise this unity can be experienced. Underlying everything is *rasa*, roughly 'intuitive feeling', and this is the major load-bearing concept in the system. It comes to mean the underlying sense of life which pervades reality. It is not just the stream of consciousness, although it has this connotation too. It is a deep sensibility of the essence which is the essence. Reality is consciousness. Thus an organic monism is developed which identifies experience with reality and which conceives the path of the mystic to be a movement to a transcendental level which turns out to be where the individual is already. This reminds us again of the relation between the 'natural attitude' and the 'transcendental ego' in Husserl's later phenomenology. There is indeed a growing interest in Java in this part of the European philosophical tradition.

Kebatinan is one outcome of the meeting of different traditions in South-east Asia. It will require more research to discover whether similar syncretist movements have occurred recently in South Asia. The orthodox *ṭarīqa*, while often promoting similar ideas, have nevertheless sought to dissociate their own memberships from the *kebatinan* movements. They have had other battles to fight as well. They were subjected to the critique of the Wahābist movement from the eighteenth century onwards but seemed well equipped in virtue of their system to argue for their purity and orthodoxy. A new assault on that system came later from the modernists. We have to ask whether modernism along with the new Wahābism changed the scene and undermined the traditional framework embodied best in the thought of the Sufis.

The modernists were concerned with a rejuvenation of Islamic practice which laid emphasis on social and educational reform.[29] They came to promote the view that Western science, technology and education were compatible with pure Islam. In general this required them to assert both that the Qur'ān is rational and that rationalism is thus compatible with its message. The founder of modernism in South Asia, Sayyid Ahmad Khan (AD 1817–98), took a neo-Mu'tazilite position, arguing both that the Qur'ān was entirely true and that it was interpretable in rationalist, scientific terms. An emphasis on justice and the possibility of human endeavour appealed to this new attitude, impressed by European achievements. The rationalist perspective combined with the conviction that Islam was superior ethically and spiritually. This superiority was of such a demonstrable nature that a programme of apologetics could be successful. To change traditional institutions in favour of European models was in no way to compromise or dilute Islam. In keeping with his approach to the interpretation of the Qur'ān there was scepticism concerning the *ḥadīth*, many of which were regarded as dubious. Even so the modernists shared with the more fundamentalist Wahābists a loathing for all in the tradition which was not seen as strictly Qur'ānic. The difference was that for modernists tradition was perceived to stand in the way of legitimate progress. Sufism did not in general avoid this critique.

The intellectuals of the movement were thus concerned primarily with reviving the meta-philosophical argument about the legitimacy of speculation, science and the nature of Qur'ānic truth. By and large their philosophical tastes did not lead them back to any interest in Aristotelianism. A neo-Ash'arite perspective, tempered with Mu'tazilite overtones, took empiricism and later pragmatism to be congenial at least in general terms. The potential agnosticism involved in going down this path is prevented only by the truth of revelation. If the latter is in turn obvious in rational, i.e. empirical terms, the modernists may be caught in an unpleasant circle. The emphasis on practical success only really counters this rhetorically.

Yet appearing through this exoteric and ethical orientation as if it just will not go away is the spirit of the system of the Sufis. Muḥammad Iqbal (AD 1877–1938), often considered the towering intellectual of his time in South Asian Islam, produced a modernist grounding of Islamic thought by making use of a range of European thinkers: Hegel, Bergson, Whitehead, Russell, Einstein and even Nietszche are called upon in the construction of his interpretation.[30] So also are Berkeley and J. S. Mill. What Iqbal dislikes is the 'hypothesis of pure materiality', which he takes to have been refuted not only by the philosophers but also by developments in physics. Instead he constructs a process metaphysics in which reality is the infinite working out of the infinite through the evolution of self-consciousness. In Hegelian fashion reality is the potentiality of the Infinite Self, which is articulated most perfectly in the actual developing consciousness of mankind. Recent work has been critical of Iqbal as a philosopher.[31] It is argued that he uses ideas drawn from a range of incompatible thinkers and that these are in turn either misunderstood or misused. From our point of view, however, what is of significance is that he ends with a form of pantheism, constructed on the back of the Hegelian tradition, which recapitulates in many ways the system which we have presented. What is missing is the commitment to the spiritual path with its own unique 'empiricism'.

In Indonesia, more than in Malaysia, where the inspiration of thinkers like Maududi has gripped the imagination of many younger Muslim intellectuals, modernism has maintained its hold, and while it is now politically not so important, it is well established as the alternative to the traditional world-view. Yet even here the modernists are obliged to deal with the problem of the Sufi metaphysics. As we might expect, an attempt is made to generate a non-esoteric understanding of the tradition relying on an extremely restricted version of *waḥdat al-shuhūd*.[32] More recently, however, there has been increasing interest among intellectuals in the universities and the Islamic colleges in the Sufi tradition. Work is being done which once again attempts to utilize recent developments in European philosophy such as the existentialist phenomenological movement to generate a modern version of what has been considered here to be a complex and subtle system. This movement is part of a confidence in the strength of Islam to offer the best solution to contemporary problems combined with a desire to rediscover what the Wahābist and modernist tendencies have often suppressed in the great tradition of Islam in these areas. In reply to the question, what is the satisfactory solution to the various theological and philosophical problems which the community must address, an Indonesian philosopher replied, 'That of Ibn 'Arabī'. Further research needs to be done in both South and South-east Asia, but it appears that a 'new Sufism' may well be at the forefront of the philosophical regeneration of the Islamic world-view. We can end with Hamzah Fanṣūri's conclusion:

> We must not think that the Law is insignificant, for God Most Exalted is called both the Outwardly Manifest and the Inwardly Hidden. His Outward Manifestation is His Law; His Inward Hiddenness is His Truth. . . . The Law is protected in the Truth, the Truth is embodied in the Law. When you are at one with the Law, you are at one with the Truth: when you are at one with the Truth, you are at one with Gnosis, but only God knows best![33]

NOTES

1 Schimmel 1982.
2 Mulder 1978.
3 Affifi 1939; also, Ibn-al-'Arabi 1980.
4 Fakhry 1970.
5 Al-Attas 1970; also Bousfield 1983.
6 Johns 1965.
7 Levinas 1978.
8 Schimmel 1975.
9 Al-Attas 1970: 435.
10 ibid., p. 372; Johns 1965: 43.

11 Al-Attas 1970: 373–4.
12 ibid., pp. 435–6.
13 Johns 1965: 59.
14 Schimmel 1982; also, Ahmad 1969.
15 Reid and Castles 1975.
16 Schimmel 1975.
17 Al-Attas 1970.
18 Nicholson 1921.
19 Anderson 1972.
20 Bowen 1987.
21 Al-Attas 1966.
22 Friedmann 1971.
23 Al-Attas 1966.
24 ibid.
25 These expressions derive from L. Massignon's work.
26 Baljon 1986.
27 Corbin 1969.
28 Mulder 1978; Stange 1980.
29 Ahmad and Von Grunebaum 1970; Ahmad 1967.
30 Iqbal 1958.
31 Raschid 1981.
32 Karim Amrullah (Hamka) 1976.
33 Al-Attas 1970: 414.

REFERENCES

Affifi, A. E. (1939) *The Mystical Philosophy of Muyid-Din-Ibnul' Arabi*, Cambridge: Cambridge University Press.

Ahmad, A. (1967) *Islamic Modernism in India and Pakistan*, Oxford: Oxford University Press.

—— (1969) *An Intellectual History of Islam in India*, Edinburgh: Edinburgh University Press.

Ahmad, A. and Grunebaum, G. E. von (1970) *Muslim Self-Statement in India and Pakistan 1857–1968*, Wiesbaden: O. Harrassowitz.

Anderson, B. R. O'G. (1972) 'The idea of power in Javanese culture', in C. Holt *et al.* (eds) *Culture and Politics in Indonesia*, Ithaca, N.Y.: Cornell University Press.

Al-Attas, S. M. N. (1966) *Rānīrī and the Wujudiyyah of 17th Century Aceh*, Malaysian Branch of the Royal Asiatic Society, Monograph III, Singapore: Malaysian Branch of the Royal Asiatic Society.

—— (1970) *The Mysticism of Ḥamzah Fanṣurī*, Kuala Lumpur: University of Malaya Press.

Baljon, J. M. S. (1986) *Religion and Thought of Shah Wali Allah Dihlawi*, Leiden: Brill.

Bousfield, J. (1983) 'Islamic philosophy in Southeast Asia', in M. B. Hooker (ed.) *Islam in South-East Asia*, Leiden: Brill.

Bowen, J. (1987) 'Islamic transformations: from Sufi doctrine to ritual practice in Gayo Culture', in R. S. Kipp and S. Rogers (eds) *Indonesian Religions in Transition*, Tucson: University of Arizona Press.

Corbin, H. (1969) *Creative Imagination in the Sufism of Ibn 'Arabī*, trans. R. Mannheim, Princeton: Princeton University Press.

Fakhry, M. (1970) *A History of Islamic Philosophy*, New York/London: Columbia University Press.
Friedmann, Y. (1971) *Shaykh Ahmad Sirhindi*, Montreal: McGill-Queen's University Press.
Hadiwijono, H. (1967) *Man in the Present Javanese Mysticism*, Amsterdam: Bosch & Keuning NV-Baarn.
Ibn-al-'Arabī (1980) *The Bezels of Wisdom*, trans. R. W. J. Austin, London: SPCK.
Iqbal, M. (1944) *The Reconstruction of Religious Thought in Islam*, Lahore: Javid Iqbal.
Johns, A. H. (1965) *The Gift Addressed to the Spirit of the Prophet*, Canberra: Australian National University Press.
Karim Amrullah, H. A. (Hamka) (1976) *Tasauf Moderen* (*Modern Sufism*), Jakarta: Yayasan Nurul Islam.
Levinas, L. (1978) *Existence and Existents*, trans. A. Lingis, The Hague: Nijhoff.
Mulder, N. (1978) *Mysticism and Everyday Life in Contemporary Java*, Singapore: Singapore University Press.
Nicholson, R. A. (1921) *Studies in Islamic Mysticism*, Cambridge: Cambridge University Press.
Raschid, M. S. (1981) *Iqbal's Concept of God*, London: KPI.
Reid, A. J. S. and Castles L. (eds) (1975) *Pre-Colonial State Systems in Southeast Asia*, Malaysian Branch of the Royal Asiatic Society, Monograph VI, Kuala Lumpur: Malaysian Branch of the Royal Asiatic Society.
Schimmel, A. (1975) *Mystical Dimensions of Islam*, Chapel Hill: University of North Carolina Press.
—— (1982) *Islam in India and Pakistan*, Leiden: Brill.
Stange, P. D. (1980) 'The Sumarah movement in Javanese mysticism', Ph.D. dissertation, University of Wisconsin, Madison.

45

LOGIC AND LANGUAGE IN ISLAMIC PHILOSOPHY

Oliver Leaman

The development of logic in Islamic philosophy is significant not so much for its contribution to philosophy but for the part it played in the structure of Islamic law and theology. Although we tend now to regard logic as a part of philosophy, within Islamic philosophy logic came to have a rather controversial position which fostered its transplantation into other bodies of theory. The introduction of logic into the Islamic world followed the same sort of pattern as that of philosophy itself. The tenth-century translators in Baghdad had available to them a large body of Syriac works covering wide areas of Greek thought, both practical and theoretical. They were impressed by Galen's insistence that to be a real physician (*ṭabīb*) one must master mathematical, natural, moral and logical sciences, and an energetic translation programme produced an Arabic philosophical curriculum rich in Greek, and especially logical, thought. With the decline of the political significance of Baghdad in the eleventh century and the growth in importance of Shiraz, Cairo and Cordoba, medical training along with logic was transported throughout the centres of learning in the Islamic world. But the link between medicine and logic was not broken in this diffusion of medical training, largely through the enormous respect in which Galen was held throughout the educated Islamic world.

Yet this positive role of logic was not universally acknowledged, as is revealed by the popular slogan *man tamanṭaqa tazandaqa* ('whoever is in favour of logic is in favour of heresy'). What was the nature of Arabic logic which was both so favoured and so reviled? It consisted of Aristotle's *Organon* supplemented by Porphyry's *Eisagōgē* and Stoic and Neoplatonic developments. A popular organization of logic was the *Eisagōgē* presented as an introduction to the *Organon*, generally consisting of the *Categories*, *Hermeneutics*, *Analytics*, *Apodeictics*, *Topics*, *Sophistics*, *Rhetoric* and *Poetics*. Many Muslims were suspicious of this conceptual machinery and its implications, and a famous debate took place in Baghdad in AD 932 before the vizier between the Christian translator Abū Bishr Mattā (*c.* AD 870–840) and the theologian (*mutakallim*) Abū Sa'īd al-Sīrāfī (AD 893–979) over the respective merits of logic by contrast with more traditional Islamic linguistic methods. Although heavily rigged in favour of the supporters of *kalām* against Greek thought, this is a very interesting debate, and it was to be replicated in different forms during the next few centuries, wherever philosophy was taken seriously in the Islamic world. Mattā argues for the priority of logic over natural language, in that logic can serve as a basis to the understanding of the structure of language itself, regardless of which particular language is at issue. Al-Sīrāfī counters with the argument that Greek logic is only useful in understanding the structure of the Greek language, and has no application to Arabic at all. The point which Mattā tries to make is that logic considers not the superficial details of a particular language and does not need to examine ordinary lexical meanings, but rather deals with the structure of all rational thought regardless of language. Al-Sīrāfī refuses to accept this point and, in between making fun of his opponent's lack of sophistication in his use of Arabic, argues that the philosophers do not even know the Greek language. They are restricted to using texts which they have only at third hand, from Greek to Arabic via Syriac. Mattā defends himself by expressing his confidence in the quality of existing translations, maintaining that it does not matter if some of the linguistic aspects of the original do not survive in translation so long as the basic semantic values are accurately reproduced from Greek to Arabic. Al-Sīrāfī, by contrast, is so impressed with the importance of natural language that he is not prepared to accept this point, insisting throughout on the vacuity of a logic being applied to anything but the language out of which it was produced.

The dispute has as a sub-text the suggestion that it is dangerous for Muslims to become over-enthusiastic about the 'new' Greek-inspired learning, a system of thought which has no direct connection with Islam or the language in which the Qur'ān is written. Al-Sīrāfī's very defensiveness implies that among educated circles of the time there was great interest in everything emerging in translation from the ancient Greek world (hence all the translations), an interest which has to be countered. After all, the implication of this fascination with all things Greek is that Islam itself is inferior to Greek philosophy and logic in its claim to make sense of reality and the place of human beings within the world. Al-Sīrāfī's approach is not entirely based upon xenophobia, though, and he does accept that a distinction can be drawn between the vagaries of speech and the permanence of linguistic expressions. Yet he transforms the Aristotelian view of the relation between logic and language, interpreting logic not as a way of reasoning but rather a way of speaking properly. Once this method of correct expression is learned it can be converted into a science, the science of grammar, and formulated in terms of abstract rules. These rules govern the techniques of correct expression, so that the proper role of the logician is to adjudicate over disputes concerning proper uses of a particular language. The ambitious claim that logic can extend over all languages is unacceptable, and even if it were true we could not know it to be true, since not all languages are available to us. The point of mastering the rules of a particular language is to be able to express clearly the rules of that language, to be able to argue rationally with opponents of differing legal, theological and religious points of view and thereby to determine the truth.

It is difficult to read accounts of this celebrated debate without feeling rather sorry for Mattā, who is so obviously taken to be cowed into silence by the brilliance of his opponent's debating skills. We might in response feel rather contemptuous about the way in which al-Sīrāfī seeks to harry Mattā with rather repetitive and dubious points. But there is more to the debate than might be thought. It is really a debate between the supporters of demonstrative as opposed to dialectical argument. The philosophers (*falāsifa*) were exponents of the desirability of working with entirely demonstrative premisses towards the goal of entirely demonstrative conclusions. Such premisses are taken to be certain and irreproachable, and if used as parts of a valid logical process they result in conclusions which share in their certainty. Dialectical reasoning, by contrast, employs as its premisses statements which are generally accepted as true, but not of the same logical rigour as demonstrative premisses. There is nothing wrong with dialectical reasoning. It follows exactly the same rules of valid reasoning as demonstrative reasoning, but the strength of its conclusions is inevitably compromised by the relative weakness of its premisses. For al-Sīrāfī there is something very suspect in anyone calling his premisses relatively weak, since they are often based upon truths established by religion, yet from a logical point of view they do not share the demonstrative strength of necessary propositions. Logicians did not discount the value of dialectical thinking; on the contrary, they argued in favour of its value in particular contexts. Theologians, on the other hand, often regarded logic as a useful aid to their work, but what they meant by logic is usually dialectic or defensive forms of argument. To a degree, the difference between philosophy and theology (*kalām*) is identical to the difference between necessary premisses and religious premisses.

Yet philosophers and theologians were often at each other's throats. The machinery of *kalām* (which literally means 'speech') consists of a question and answer process, whereby someone proposes a thesis and someone else queries it. The emphasis tends to be on the type of language used, and represents accurately the initial stages of Islamic theology as involved in defending its principles against the intellectual skills of the Jews, Christians and Manichaeans when the *dār al-Islām* (the realm of Islam) spread to the centres of civilization from Arabia. Once Islam became the established religion, there was the question of settling doctrinal differences and refuting heretics, which is often a matter of bringing out the inconsistencies in the doctrines of one's opponents, or proving that those doctrines have absurd consequences. *Kalām* is not a speculative science which tries to establish a proper theoretical and demonstrative understanding of the nature of God and his creation, according to the philosophers. It is not properly concerned with very general rules or truths, but rather with defending and justifying the dogmas established by a particular legislator or prophet within a particular religious and cultural context. Its general purpose is to strengthen faith and acceptance of the law by those who are not logically capable of following the justification on purely rational lines, and so must be satisfied with a form of justification which incorporates dialectical reasoning. If *kalām* would be satisfied with this important task it would not find itself in conflict with demonstrative philosophy. The proper role for *kalām* is the dialectical and rhetorical presentation of the dogmatic principles of a particular religion, and it cannot set out to establish logically the fundamental truths which are only imperfectly represented by religious principles. Yet the theologians are often over-ambitious and argue that the principles embodied in the system of religion are equivalent to the universal truths which the philosophers employ in their work, and in such cases great confusion and conflict arise. This is due to a total misunderstanding of the logical distinction between philosophy and theology.

This argument for a logical division of labour runs throughout the works of al-Fārābī, ibn Sīnā (Avicenna) and ibn Rushd (Averroes). Al-Fārābī suggests that over a period of time thinking becomes logically refined until we get to the stage of demonstrative reasoning or philosophy. Initially religion consists of dialectical and sophistical methods, which help get the religion going in the first place. The weakest form of reasoning is sophistical, which depends upon rules of persuading an audience to accept a view by poetic exaggeration and literary tricks, yet it is none the less a logical method. It does not proceed haphazardly, but in accordance with rules. Clearly, the popularization of a religion among the widest possible public is going to involve the employment of sophistical methods. They are gradually superseded by dialectical thinking, which can regulate logical moves from one premiss to others, but is incapable of establishing the acceptability of that premiss in the first place. This acme of logical thought can only be attained by demonstrative reasoning. The purpose of religion is to instruct the masses in practical and theoretical truths which they are on the whole incapable of assimilating in their pure state. There are more appropriate logical techniques for use where the masses are concerned, and these are naturally less rigorous than those applicable to the instruction of the intellectual élite.

It is difficult to overemphasize the significance of the distinction between demonstrative and dialectical thought in Islamic philosophy. This distinction enters into almost every aspect of this period of philosophy. A particular controversy at the time was formulated in terms of how it is best for human beings to live. Should they adhere to the moral and political virtues of everyday life to achieve the highest level of happiness, or should they rather seek to attain intellectual perfection? This choice is based upon the two methods of logical reasoning. Moral reasoning is not of the category of scientific or demonstrative reasoning, proceeding from necessarily true propositions to a necessarily true conclusion. Rather, it is better described as dialectical or probable, since it takes as its premisses the nature of a particular society and of the people in it, and then derives conclusions concerning how they might best live together under such conditions. Such reasoning would be without purpose were there to be no objects in existence which the concepts of society and its citizens could successfully describe. By contrast, purely demonstrative reasoning is entirely unconcerned whether any objects in fact instantiate the concepts it uses, since it operates at a level of abstraction where such considerations are vacuous. The contemplative thinker, given the opportunity to choose between these two different subject matters of necessary propositions as premisses or merely probable premisses, would obviously choose the former since he will then be dealing with a much higher level of truth than if he thinks about propositions which describe the contingent features of the world. For Avicenna and Maimonides, then, moral rules have no greater status than that of generally accepted views, important undoubtedly for all citizens if they are to live peaceful and virtuous lives, but incapable of transporting them to higher levels of human perfection, to the realm of demonstrative reasoning.

The *falāsifa* were concerned to delineate the limitations of dialectical reasoning in order to carve out for themselves a more significant role by contrast with the *mutakallimūn*, the dialectical theologians. The methodology of the latter was often based upon the work of al-Ash'arī (d. AD 935) and is based upon the *argumentum ad hominem*, the technique of defending one's position by attacking that of one's opponent. The rigour and clarity of Aristotelian logic were seen as a threat by many theologians, especially given its foreign origins, and a furious debate occurred in Islamic theology concerning the respective merits of the specifically Islamic dialectical techniques and the more precise Aristotelian methodology. Despite their frequent differences, both al-Ghazālī and Averroes were highly critical of the dialectic of the *mutakallimūn*, arguing that it fell far short of demonstrative reasoning and the attainment of certainty. This could result in doubt being cast upon religious principles, which are capable of a better defence than that provided by many theologians. As such, dialectic is a potentially dangerous method, since it can throw doubt in many people's minds, where no doubt should exist, when it sets out to defend religious positions in its characteristically haphazard manner.

The *mutakallimūn* were scathing about the language of logic. This language is frequently technical and difficult to grasp immediately. Since logicians go on endlessly about the value of clear thought, the theologians wondered why they are unable to express themselves clearly! The *mutakallimūn* suggest that any intelligent person can argue logically without having to study logic as such. Moreover, the study of logic can lead to the acceptance of doctrines which are inimical to religious belief. Yet those trained in the secular sciences – physicians, mathematicians, astronomers and philosophers – were convinced of the virtue of logic. It was part and parcel of the study of their particular disciplines. Logic was regarded as just another science both by al-Fārābī and the more eclectic Ikhwān al-Ṣafā' (Brethren of Purity) which has to be mastered along with everything else in the curriculum.

The precise nature of logic was a matter of particular controversy at the time. Was logic just a part of philosophy, a separate science (*'ilm*), a propaedeutic to the study of philosophy, a craft (*ṣināʿa*) or an instrument (*āla*)? This discussion is a reflection of an earlier Greek debate between Aristotelians and Platonists. The former were of the view that logic is only an instrument, while for the latter it is a part of philosophy and thus is related closely to some aspect of being. If logic is only an instrument, then it is possible to accept logic and at the same time reject the particular kinds of philosophy which it sets out to serve. This was precisely the line adopted by al-Ghazālī (d. AD 1111), who was hostile not just to *falsafa* but even towards astronomy and mathematics. Yet he produced several works on Aristotelian logic and commended it in many other places as the sole means of justification in one's claim to knowledge. Al-Ghazālī's efforts here did a great deal to 'naturalize' logic in Islamic theology and jurisprudence. A rearguard action two centuries later was mounted by ibn Taymiyya, who argued that logic emobodies metaphysical concepts and so is a part of philosophy. Since philosophy is a false and dangerous activity, he went on, both it and logic should be abandoned. Although his attack is skilful in the extreme, he was unable to sway the mass of support for al-Ghazālī's use of logic as a part of the appropriate analysis of the Islamic sciences. Logic, then, came to be accepted as an instrumental aspect of both theology and law, one which it is perfectly safe to use provided that one does not introduce along with the logic objectionable Peripatetic notions.

So the precise relationship between logic and philosophy turns out to be an important topic. In a typically sophisticated manner Avicenna presents a useful analysis of the relationship. He argues that logic has its own subject matter which is unique to it. Yet this subject matter consists of properties acquired by concepts when organized to attain or communicate knowledge, and so the purpose of logic is to assist in other scientific investigations. If philosophy is regarded as a conceptual enquiry, then logic is certainly an instrument of philosophy, since logic has an important place in the whole philosophical enterprise. Logic regulates and organizes the conceptual investigation so important in philosophy, and is therefore more than just a part of philosophy. On the other hand, if philosophy refers to all forms of theoretical thought, then logic is clearly a part of philosophy, in that it too is a form of theoretical thought. In his use of logical expressions, especially leading modal and predicate calculus expressions, Avicenna brings out the close links in Islamic philosophy between logic and philosophy, where the latter is understood as metaphysics. We shall see how close these links are when we examine his analyses of the essence/existence relationship, and the terms 'necessity', 'possibility' and 'actuality'.

According to Avicenna, existence is an element excluded from the analysis of the nature of anything other than the deity. Existence is an aspect of me, of me as an instantiated object, but it is not part of my essence, of me as a person. This is because I am contingent and only possible through the activities of a necessary being, and this necessary being is itself not limited in this way. Its existence is part of its essence unlike everything else in the universe. Existence is thus an addition to essence and logically distinct from essence, and is not part of the nature of a thing. This distinction between essence and existence is also largely accepted by the *kalām*, and seems quite acceptable. After all, we can quite easily distinguish between the qualities which a thing has and the existence of the thing. Yet Averroes furiously attacks this approach. He argues that objective knowledge of *p* is knowledge that *p* exists, and so existence is far from accidental to a thing, but rather the essence (or part of the essence) of the thing. He is quite happy to accept that there is a logical sense in which existence can be regarded as an attribute like other attributes, yet he also insists that when 'existence' is used as a non-logical term it refers to the existing thing and not to a property of it.

This might appear to be a rather trivial dispute over the primary sense of existence, with Avicenna going for the predicative sense as his paradigm of the concept itself, while Averroes prefers to identify essence and existence, using existence to refer to substance. There is more to the difference than this, though. Averroes is attempting to defend what he sees as the real Aristotelian position. For Aristotle it is matter taking a particular form which makes up a particular thing. If it were only matter which was involved in individuation, and not form, it would be possible to draw a clear contrast between the form in me – my status as a human being – and all my specific features, and refer to the latter as matter. I should then consist of matter which is made up of a collection of accidental predicates. For Aristotle, if I am fat and you are thin, these are not just accidents in matter, but different directions which rationality has taken, rationality being part of the essence of human beings. His notion of individuality as consisting of a fusion of form and matter, of the actual and the potential, led to much development in Islamic philosophy. Avicenna pursues this theory in a somewhat non-Aristotelian direction, arguing that essence is entirely indifferent with respect to existence. The essence of a thing, taken in itself and without its cause, would not exist, and so existence cannot be included within the essence of a thing.

This doctrine seems quite reasonable. Avicenna basically distinguishes between the existence of a thing and the essence of the thing, which is surely an important and useful distinction in any logical system. Yet the full fury of Averroes, and later Aquinas, was thrown against this thesis on account of its essentialism. The idea that existence is an accident implies that existence is related to essence as merely an additional aspect of a thing, whereas it is really (for Aristotelians) the very act of essence. Avicenna's position leads to a variety of theses highly objectionable to the *falāsifa*. For example, it leads to difficulties in establishing the doctrine of the existence of an eternal matter whose entire rationale is the impossibility of something being produced from nothing. Al-Ghazālī defended the theological view that something can come from nothing if God wants it to, since we can think of something coming from nothing, and so such a notion must be *possible*. We can think of things as possible without their being actual by showing that we can conceive of things independently of their actualization in the world. He could use Avicenna's distinction between essence and existence to claim that the notion of possibility is logically independent of the notion of actuality or existence, and so the eternal existence of matter as a substratum is not a necessary condition of our notion of possible change in the world. If the idea of possibility is just another universal concept which we have in our minds, then the link between possibility and actuality can be totally severed, and to find out if an idea is possible, we just have to try to think about it. If we can, then it is possible; if we cannot, then there is something logically wrong with it and we have to reject it.

Averroes responds to this position by arguing that what is important about the notion of possibility is its identification of states of affairs which are potentially actual, which might be actualized in the external world. He is using here what has been called Aristotle's 'Principle of Plenitude', according to which what is possible has happened or will happen at some time. Were it not possible to use the universal term 'blue' in the external world to pick out individuals, there would be no point in having a concept of blue. In just the same way, possibility as a concept has external relevance in so far as we can use that concept in selecting phenomena in the external world. We can talk about possible states of affairs in terms of their eventual transformation into actual states of affairs, and in terms of nothing else. The idea that there are essences which we can usefully discuss and yet which have no relation to the external world is vacuous. This is not to suggest that we cannot hold in our minds ideas and images which purport to represent states of affairs which are possible. We can do so, but this does nothing to prove that those states of affairs are really possible. We can think about nothing existing, and then think about God bringing the world about, without the prior existence of matter which Aristotelians argue is a necessary condition of all physical change. Yet Averroes would argue that this is not enough to prove that there are no conceptual links between change and matter, between an essence and its existence. To establish that there is such a conceptual connection one must show that it is impossible to make sense of the claim that something has changed without the prior existence of matter as a substratum, and to disprove the existence of such a connection it must be shown that we can make sense of the idea of material change without the presupposition of already existing matter. More is required than just the holding of certain pictures in one's mind in a certain order.

This brings us quite neatly to the conclusion that the existence/essence debate, which was so furiously rerun in Christian philosophy too, is not just about the appropriate analyses of existence and essence, important though they are, but is also and crucially about the proper understanding of how to do philosophy. There is an intimate connection between the interpretation of modal concepts and the proper way to conduct arguments. In spite of his distance from Aristotle, Avicenna sought to avoid the occasionalism of the Ash'arites. The latter emphasized the power of God by arguing that all existence and change in the universe is brought about by God's activity, so that a constantly acting deity maintains natural processes in operation. Avicenna argues that there are necessary causal relationships between states of affairs in the world, and what can take place can only happen if something else necessitates it. The possible is that whose essence does not include its existence and so must depend upon a cause which then makes its instantiation necessary, but only necessary relative to that cause. The Necessary Being from which all existence emanates is necessary in itself, having no cause and with an essence which entails its own existence. In Avicenna's modal system there are only two kinds of being, those necessary through another and that necessary in itself, so that the realm of the possible becomes conflated with the actual and the necessary. A state of affairs is only possible if something else brings it about (except for God, of course). This interpretation of modality produces a form of modified occasionalism, the doctrine that changes in the world are only made possible through the direct intervention of something else, i.e. God. As Averroes points out, this implies that we have to think of possible states of affairs as being non-existent by themselves, until their existence is brought about by their cause. Constructing a notion of possibility in terms of an external condition rather than through its inherent characteristics deprives the concept of any objective reference in the external world, and concedes far too much to the traditional theological understanding of the relationship between the possible and the actual.

Many commentators have argued that when Avicenna talks about the accidental nature of existence in metaphysics he is merely stressing the contingency of the created things in the world, the fact that they do not have to exist. Yet according to Averroes, and later Aquinas, this logical point has grave metaphysical consequences. At its heart lies a confusion between the essence of a thing and our thought of the thing. When Averroes stressed the need to distinguish between two meanings of existence, one referring to the true and the other to the opposite of non-existence, he suggested that the first is something in the mind, while the second refers to things in the world, the real world which exists outside the mind. Does Avicenna really confuse the order of thought and the order of things, the logical and ontological orders? He starts with a logical analysis of the relation of essence and existence and then proceeds via his theory of emanation to show how existence comes to essence from the necessarily acting Necessary Existent. The universe is eternal because of the unceasing nature of God's thought and the resulting overflow of causes and effects which eventually constitutes our world. Ontologically, the causal series is inseparable from God because it is his overflow. The theory of emanation provides the ontological framework which relates cause and effect, supplying also the essences which are to be instantiated with their existence and with their power to actualize other essences in their turn. It does indeed encourage the move from the logical distinction between existence and essence to the ontological distinction which Averroes finds so objectionable. Avicenna follows the path of dividing things up into existence and essence, into what we can think about and what really exists, into things which are necessary through another and those which are possible in themselves. This is to go against the sort of realism and emphasis upon the notion of substance which are so important a part of the philosophy of Aristotle and Averroes. It is the close link which Avicenna establishes between his philosophical approach and understanding of logic that underpins his original account of ontology. Logic is far from being a purely technical means of dealing with abstract arguments here; it is intimately connected with the entire thrust of Avicenna's philosophy.

It is time to relate the treatment of modal concepts to the theory of meaning. For al-Ghazālī and the *mutakallimūn*, it is the imagination which establishes the boundaries of the possible. Intellectual laziness leads us not to examine the radical possibilities which exist for alterations to our conceptual system, and we persist in thinking that the apparently fixed nature of that system is mirrored by the nature of things themselves. Yet if we examine our experience using only the notion of logical possibility, we shall soon discover that there are feasible alternative ways of looking at the world, alternatives which in fact are ruled out because God chooses to construct a certain framework of ideas in our minds which establish a pattern of regularity. There is nothing necessary about such a pattern, and we can imagine it not to hold, if we try. Averroes cannot accept such an approach to the issue of determining the meaning of propositions which challenge the fundamental aspects of our conceptual scheme. We can think about people without heads writing a book, or someone stepping inside a fire without being harmed, since these thought experiments do not involve logical impossibility. Yet more is involved in working out which notions are compatible than can be discovered by using nothing more than the concept of logical possibility. In such thought experiments, can we preserve the ordinary meanings of the terms we use if we countenance such radical changes to the customary behaviour of familiar terms? It is a fact that we burn when in contact with fire, and no doubt not an immutable fact, and yet such a fact significantly affects the meaning of the language we use. The feat of imagination which we might accomplish would not necessarily show that any genuine possibility exists in a radical transformation of any of our most basic beliefs about ourselves and our world.

We can see this more clearly if we examine the controversy over the nature of the divine attributes. This controversy has a long history in Islamic theology, but it came to have an important place in philosophy too. Al-Ghazālī's view of meaning, and especially the meaning of the divine attributes, places the emphasis upon univocity. That is, he understands that the terms we apply to God are the same terms which we apply to non-divine creatures, and that the behaviour which we credit to the deity differs only in scope from many of our ordinary activities. He goes into some detail on this by arguing that any attempt at interpreting the divine properties as equivocal or ambiguous or metaphorical is a roundabout way of undermining the very notion of God itself. So al-Ghazālī insists that God really does take decisions, carries out actions and is aware of everything which his creatures do in an uncomplicated sense, and that if he is to be God he must do all these things. Anything different would be to detract from his power and knowledge.

This is not just an issue affecting the nature of the divine attributes, but rather a dispute about the nature of meaning itself. In his *Categories* Aristotle distinguishes between two types of equivocal terms, pure and *pros hen* equivocals. The former share the name and only the name, while the latter indicate some similarity in the objects which forms the basis to the sharing of the name. Averroes tends to argue that the language we use to describe the properties of God is in the form of *pros hen* equivocals. If they were to be univocal (as al-Ghazālī has it) they would lead to an analysis in terms of a genus and species, which in turn would imply multiplicity within the unity of the divine essence. If they were to be entirely equivocal there would be nothing in common between our religious and ordinary language except the words themselves, and this would cut off the route by which we move from our understanding of the world to our understanding of God. The concept of God has a special status which defies description in terms of type and qualities. Were he to be thus definable, he would consist of a number of attributes which make up a plurality, in the same way in which we consist of thinking, wanting, hoping and so on. The terms we apply to God are ambiguous or equivocal: they are related analogically to the terms we apply to ourselves, but in a way which preserves the special status of the deity. God is the exemplar of all things, containing them in a complete way. God is paradigmatically a thing, while everything else – his creation – enjoys only a derivative degree of substance. When we talk about immaterial things such as God we use much the same sort of language as when we talk about everyday objects in the world, but these similarities in language should not obscure the fact that we are using the same terms in different ways, i.e. in analogical ways.

Averroes is pointing here to a doctrine of Aristotle's which uses the notion of focal meaning to show how an expression can have a primary sense in virtue of which its other senses can be explained. The aim is to be able to avoid the objection which al-Ghazālī and the Ash'arites made to the notion of God existing without attributes. All the predicates which we apply to the deity are applied to just one genus because that very special genus exemplifies in the most perfect way all those qualities. There exists just one God who brings about action, and all the characteristics which we may apply to him are much more complete predicates than those which we can apply to ourselves and to the objects in our world. God's properties cannot be separated from him in the way in which our properties can be distinguished from us, because they follow from his essence rather than merely being contingent parts of it. There is no longer, then, a problem in reconciling the essential simplicity of the concept of God with the fact that he has properties, because those properties are essential parts of him and aspects of his being, and they make possible the attribution of properties to things in the everyday world in general. We think of God possessing a variety of attributes because we tend to think of him as rather like us, but more so. Our intellect naturally analyses and separates aspects of things which are in reality impossible to separate. That does not matter provided that we understand that what really exist are unified things, and in the case of God the properties with which we endow him are an essential and indivisible constituent of this essence.

This discussion of the role of equivocation in language is not limited in its scope to reconciling the simplicity of God with the multiplicity of the properties ascribed to him. It serves to differentiate areas of investigation and argue that they are characterized by different logical criteria. Unlike most of his philosophical predecessors, but like his fellow-countryman Maimonides, Averroes places great emphasis on the notions of equivocation and ambiguity in our language. The relatively loose connection between similar names permits him to discuss the difficulties involved in grasping what those names mean. Their meanings are distinct depending upon the context within which they are used, although they are not entirely distinct. There is a thread of meaning connecting the different uses which extends from the divine paradigm to the temporal particular. If we regard these terms as clear and univocal, then we get into the sorts of problems we find in Avicenna when we have to explain how a simple deity could incorporate a multiplicity of attributes, and how the essence of a thing is independent of its existence. If like al-Ghazālī we condemn the suggestion that equivocation is a feature of the relationship between our language describing God and our language describing the ordinary world because this would detract from God's power and omniscience, then we are obliged to treat the deity as a kind of Superman. This seems to Averroes to be very suspect as a feasible role for an Islamic deity, once we get away from unsophisticated understandings of the meaning of 'God'. Averroes argues that equivocation is an inevitable aspect of our language, since that language has to cope with a wide variety of points of view using the same name. Averroes accepts with Aristotle that there can be no priority or posteriority within the same genus, and so is led to develop an account of meaning which is based upon the *pros hen* rather than the genus–species relation. In his stress on the validity of equivocation he moved away from his predecessors, but in the application to which he put this theory of meaning he fell in line with a popular philosophical analysis of language.

It is important to notice how a particular logical analysis, here of homonymy (i.e. use of the same name), leads to a particular approach to language and in turn to metaphysics. Averroes's whole philosophy is based upon the significance of different points of view, not just the distinction between God's point of view and the human point of view, but also between the standpoints of a whole variety of different human beings related to their capacities for forms of reasoning. He distinguishes between demonstrative, dialectical, rhetorical and sophistical people, who all use similar language to describe what is important to them, yet this language is neither univocal nor completely equivocal. There are links between different applications of the same name, and such links are sufficiently strong for it to make sense to say that these uses are of the same term. A doctor has a different view of disease from an ordinary patient, and an ordinary believer has a different view of the basis of his belief from a philosopher, yet all these views are to be respected. Such a variety of views is mirrored by the variety of language available to characterize a whole continuum of approaches, ranging from the entirely demonstrative to the most poetic and expressive. Equivocation in language must be accepted because it is an aspect of our lives as we live as different people in a community with a whole range of ends and interests available to us.

Although all views are to be respected, it is important to understand that the structure of argumentation produced by different people is often itself distinct and must not be confused. Thus the poet seeks to move an audience to action by the use of his imagery and metre, which is perfectly appropriate to poetry but would not do in metaphysics. The theologian argues on the basis of religious presuppositions, and this is unproblematic so long as he does not stray from those presuppositions into trying to judge far wider topics and arguments. Once he does so he throws doubt not only on the veracity of the positions he attacks but also on the religion which he defends. The philosopher seeks to establish via demonstrative argument universally valid conclusions which have very general application, yet it would be wrong for him to stray into the realm of religion or poetry and lay down rules for those activities. Once we clearly distinguish between the separate realms of discourse here we are in a position to accept a variety of forms of reasoning as helpful to a variety of human activities and purposes.

Among these activities and purposes are theology and law. Despite his fervent critique of Peripatetic philosophy, al-Ghazālī was an equally fervent adherent of the value of a logical approach to theological topics. He not only argued for logic, but even tried to make it accessible to a wider audience by simplifying it and using examples from Islamic law to illustrate it. Such an approach is tempting given the difficulty of deciding difficult theological and legal issues on the basis only of the Qur'ān, the *ḥadīth* and the *sunna*. Many aspects of the *sharī'a* are not sufficiently translucent to permit of an obvious answer to legal difficulties which occur. This leads to the necessity to decide what constitutes proof in legal debate, and how far analogy can be taken. Some argument forms in Sunnī legal theory are properly demonstrative, but this is rare. The arguments tend to be looser, based upon the similarity between terms mentioned in the premisses and those in the conclusion, with a relationship helped by the middle term in the argument. This middle term is often based upon the expressed intentions of the deity in the religious sources. For example, it might be held that either God or Muḥammad had laid down which actions are to be permitted or prohibited. Where we come across an action which is apparently unmentioned in the *sharī'a* we have to ask whether it is similar in meaning (*ma'nā*) to some act for which legislation is already established. The Qur'ān forbids the consumption of wine (and indeed a particular kind of wine). There is no mention of Guinness, so does this mean that Muslims can quite happily quaff Guinness and remain within the divine law? If we use a principle of analogy (*qiyās*) we can argue that since wine and beer are similar (i.e. they are both intoxicants), and since wine is forbidden, it follows that beer is also forbidden, and since Guinness is beer, Guinness is forbidden. For this sort of argument to work there must be a similarity (*'illa*) between the two objects in question which is based upon their common possession of a relevant property, in this case being an intoxicant rather than being a drink.

This method of legal argumentation was already quite highly developed when al-Fārābī presented elaborate versions of Aristotelian logic to display such argument forms more perspicuously, and over the next few centuries ever more complex versions were produced, defended and applied to particular controversial legal issues. The Greek origins of the logical structure of jurisprudence, *fiqh*, became invisible as al-Ghazālī reformulated legal logic as Islamic logic. As Sunnī Islam developed it was felt necessary to ground it in a sophisticated logical methodology in order to buttress it against theological opponents. We must not forget that the development of *sharī'a* was rarely without controversy, and the most potent form of attack upon a legal position is a demonstration that it is internally inconsistent. Particular legal schools were linked with theological movements, and both sought to characterize a valid interpretation of an Islamic way of life. Whatever arguments they could produce in favour of their views were welcome, but even more welcome was the use of logic to ensure the internal coherence of their legal and theological systems. In this respect at least the *falāsifa* were quite correct to characterize legal and theological reasoning as predominantly dialectical, and as such it incorporated a heavy dose of Greek logic thoroughly naturalized in Islamic dress.

It would be a mistake to think that the work on logic and language which took place within the context of Islamic philosophy was always done with at least one eye on wider theoretical and practical issues. A great deal of work went on regarding such technical issues as the number of the categories, their organization, the structure of the syllogism and the precise explication of the various Greek authors on logical thought and semantics. Since many of these works are no longer extant, have not been edited or are difficult to understand, given the very obscure intellectual climate which forms their background, it is perhaps natural to concentrate upon those aspects of logic and language which are linked more obviously to wider issues in Islamic culture. It is important to recognize how developments in logic and language made such issues more perspicuous, while at the same time refining the exact points of disagreement between different philosophers, and between philosophers and theologians. It is impossible to separate the conceptual investigation of logic and language in Islamic philosophy from everything else which went on within that philosophical tradition.

FURTHER READING

Abed, S. (1996) 'Language', in S. H. Nasr and O. Leaman (eds.) *History of Islamic Philosophy*, London: Routledge, pp. 898–925.

Averroes (ibn Rushd) (1961) *Faṣl al-maqāl* (*Averroes on the Harmony of Religion and Philosophy*), trans. and int. G. Hourani, London: Luzac; repr. 1967 and 1976.

Brunschvig, R. (1970) 'Logic and law in classical Islam', in G. von Grunebaum (ed.) *Logic in Classical Islamic Culture*, Wiesbaden: Harrassowitz.

Ess, J. van (1970) 'The logical structure of Islamic theology', in G. von Grunebaum (ed.) *Logic in Classical Islamic Culture*, Wiesbaden: Harrassowitz.

Al-Ghazālī (1980) *Al-qisṭās al-mustaqīm* (*The Correct Balance*), trans. and int. R. McCarthy, *Freedom and Fulfillment*, Boston, Mass.: Twayne, pp. 287–332.

Grunebaum, G. von (ed.) (1970) *Logic in Classical Islamic Culture*, Wiesbaden: Harrassowitz.

Ibn Sīnā (Avicenna) (1984) *Remarks and Admonitions: Part One: Logic*, trans. and int. S. Inati, Toronto: Pontifical Institute of Medieval Studies.

Inat, S. (1996) 'Logic', in S. H. Nasr and O. Leaman (eds.) op. cit., pp. 802–23.

Leaman, O. (1985) *An Introduction to Medieval Islamic Philosophy*, Cambridge: Cambridge University Press.

—— (1988) *Averroes and his Philosophy*, Oxford: Clarendon Press; 2nd edition (1997) Richmond: Curzon Press.

—— (1990) *Moses Maimonides*, London: Routledge; 2nd edition (1997) Richmond: Curzon Press.

Mahdi, M. (1970) 'Language and logic in classical Islam', in G. von Grunebaum (ed.) *Logic in Classical Islamic Culture*, Wiesbaden: Harrassowitz.

Netton, I. (1989) *Allāh Transcendent: Studies in the Structure and Semiotics of Islamic Philosophy, Theology and Cosmology*, London: Routledge.

Rescher, N. (1963) *Studies in the History of Arabic Logic*, Pittsburgh, Pa.: University of Pittsburgh Press.

—— (1964) *The Development of Arabic Logic*, Pittsburgh, Pa.: University of Pittsburgh Press.

Sabra, A. (1980) 'Avicenna on the subject matter of logic', *Journal of Philosophy* 77 (11): 746–63.

Zimmermann, F. (1981) *Al-Farabi's Commentary and Short Treatise on Aristotle's De Interpretatione*, London: British Academy.

46

KNOWLEDGE AND REALITY IN ISLAMIC PHILOSOPHY

Lenn E. Goodman

KNOWLEDGE

The watershed that Islam sets between itself and the prior condition of humanity, especially in Arabia, is marked in the stark Qur'ānic opposition between knowledge and ignorance. Repeatedly the Qur'ān attributes sin to oblivion of God's demands. Ignorance is culpable and bears a practical import as concrete in the here and now as its consequence will be in the hereafter. The past was the age of ignorance (*al-jāhiliyya*); connotatively, of barbarism and confusion: 'the unbelievers', we read, at a crucial juncture in Muhammad's career, 'got up in their hearts heat and passion, the heat and passion of Ignorance' (Qur'ān 48.26). Ignorance here is a positive force, to be calmed and quelled by God's presence. Faith imparts knowledge, for faith is trust, and trust in God gives certitude. Ignorance breeds only anxiety and self-seeking (see Qur'ān 3.154). Ignorance led the pagans to flaunt their finery (33.33); and ignorance still causes men to cavil at the rule of God, as if preferring some archaic, pagan rule by which to be judged (5.50).

Hundreds of times the Qur'ān equates knowledge with belief in God and recognition of his Prophet's message. Hundreds of times more the Prophet's hearers are reminded that God knows what they do not, all that is in land or sea, heaven and earth, the acts and intentions of every human being. Knowledge links the act of creation, by which God is known to man, the constant acts of God's governance, and the denouement of judgement, in which man must believe. The gift of knowledge is God's grace. For it is only through knowledge that man is lifted up, not above the beasts but above the damned.[1]

The salvific coloration imparted by the Qur'ān to the idea of knowledge never leaves it in Arabic usage. But neither does the idea that the means to salvation is knowledge.

Surveying the poetry of the *Jāhiliyya*, Franz Rosenthal finds there too a celebration not of ignorance but of knowledge. 'Is ignorance a match for knowledge?' one pre-Islamic poet asks. Another answers clearly: 'One who is ignorant of a thing is not like one who knows' – a thought that will be echoed in the next century in the Qur'ān (39.9).[2]

From the beginnings of recorded thought in Arabic, the idea of knowledge is practical, moral – not excluding the speculative, but not confined to it. The root idea, perhaps, is that of knowing the way. But when Greek philosophy, medicine and other foreign sciences enter the world of Arabic learning, they are assigned the word 'wisdom' (*ḥikma*), with its ancient Semitic overtones of craft; the word for knowledge (*'ilm*) is retained by Islam. So the sciences may be sacred or secular, Arab or foreign, shallow or profound, whereas 'wisdom' may be merely technical or pragmatic. The Greek equation of the technical and critical with the scientific and of wisdom with the speculative and supernal never does take hold. Rather, speculation may be exotic, subjective, suspect; but learning and knowing make one profound. The expectation remains even as the ways of knowing proliferate to include vast erudition in the sayings and practices of the Prophet (*ḥadīth*), legal and juridical learning (*fiqh*), or the byways of theological disputation (*kalām*). All of these are sciences (*'ulūm*, the plural of *'ilm*), and a Muslim cleric is simply (or not so simply) an *'ālim* (pl. *'ulamā'*), one who knows. Even mystic experience is described cognitively, as it is in many another tradition, as *gnosis* or intuition (*ma'rifa, dhawq*), imparting an understanding that surpasses ordinary knowledge, but not ceasing to be a way of knowing.

To Muslim theologians of the classic age, knowledge is an active faculty and a subjective content that matches an objective reality. When the more philosophically inclined among them speak of knowledge acquiring the form of things, taking things to be as they are, and indeed, having a propositional form and affirming what is in fact the case, we can see that Aristotle's influence has been at work. When the theologians speak more dialectically, of knowledge as a silencing or resting of the soul (*sukūn al-nafs*), they echo the discussions of the Stoics and the Sceptics, as they do when they speak of knowledge in the language of acquisition, perception and apprehension.

There is a rationalism inherent in the idea of knowledge, which Muslim theologians and mystics voice when they speak of clarity, certainty, discernment and discrimination as marks of knowledge. The Mu'tazilites, under Stoic influence, thought of knowledge as a species of belief, since conviction or commitment is among its necessary conditions. But more orthodox theologians rejected the view, since it would require God to have beliefs, an unacceptable predication.[3]

Just as the Stoics and Epicureans fought shy of Aristotelian conceptualism and Platonic realism, many Muslim thinkers offered reductionistic, anti-conceptual models of knowing, defining knowledge as 'mere remembering' or imaging (*khayāl*), or more metaphorically, as the shadow and shape of the object known. But if the appeal to shadow and shape was literal, it was clearly false; if it was metaphorical, the metaphor cried out for resolution and some reference to the actualities it intended to describe, as did the more commonplace metaphor of light for knowledge. Appeals to memory or imagination were, similarly, at best a *pis aller*. For memory still requires a subject, an object and a cognitive link between them. And that link is what we ask about when we enquire after knowledge.

Imaging, imagining or fantasy, similarly, require both subjective and objective unity if they are to be cognitive, and references to some image do not tell us how such unities are brought about – or how they are aligned and paired with one another. These purported models seem more to presuppose knowledge than to define or explain it. And an image or memory may prompt or precede only such knowledge as is conceptual, if any conceptual knowledge proves to be distinguishable. So the appeal to images, like the appeal to memory, either presupposes what it was intended to explain or denies it in whole or part. If that denial is to budge from the dogmatic, or if there is to be any movement at all beyond the inadequacy of a circular account, such stopgaps as these will not block the path to philosophy (as may have been the intent behind them) but will only demand admission to it.

The same, of course, is true of pragmatic, formalistic and functional definitions, which speak of knowledge as the overcoming of ignorance and doubt, or as the object of desire, or as the attribute that enables one to act in an orderly fashion (cf. Ryle on 'knowing how' and 'knowing that'). Heideggerians might be interested in al-Tirmidhī's claim that 'knowledge is the disclosure (*tajallī*) of things themselves'. But such remarks may resonate more roundly in our own surroundings than they did in their original Islamic setting. The idea that took hold, because it was capable of philosophical argument and articulation and because it answered to the need to connect knowing with God, was the idea of the active intellect.

The theory of the active intellect stems from Aristotle, who remarked in his *De Anima* (III. 5) that in all classes of things there is a matter, which is passive and potential, and an active, productive cause, analogous to the art which works up matter in a given medium. In the case of thinking, he argues, the prepared mind is the matter. In acquiring the concepts of things, it *becomes* those things in a certain way; and what actualizes the mind, i.e. renders it actually instead of merely potentially intelligent, as light renders actually visible what is in itself only potentially visible, is 'another, which is what it is by virtue of making all things', just as the human mind 'is what it is by virtue of becoming all things' (430a14–15).[4]

Scholars have debated for centuries whether the activating factor was an inner aspect or faculty of the individual human mind or an external and universal agency. The theory that there is such an external agency at work in all our conceptual thinking fascinated the great Muslim epistemologists al-Fārābī (AD 870–950) and Ibn Sīnā (Avicenna, AD 980–1037). But in deference to Aristotle's comprehensive efforts to overcome the dichotomy between immanent and transcendent causation, we should note that the seeming ambivalence of *De Anima* III. 5 may not be wholly unintended.

On the one hand, Aristotle would hardly hold that the mind simply actualizes itself, immediately after saying that whenever something is actualized it needs something else to actualize it. On the other hand, he makes a point of saying, in just this context, that the realized mind (and it alone) is separable from the body, pure, absolute, impassible, timeless and immortal. His own gloss of the apparent ambiguity of his intentions is couched in terms of Plato's theory that a disembodied intelligence would have no memory:

> Potential knowledge is prior in time to actual knowledge; but in absolute terms it is not prior even in time. The mind does not sometimes think and sometimes not think. When set free, it is just what it is and nothing more. This alone is immortal and eternal. We do not remember; for although the mind in this sense is impassible, as passive it is destructible. But without this nothing thinks.
>
> (430a20–6)[5]

What Aristotle is saying, as I read it, is that prior to our birth as individuals and knowing subjects, even beyond the confines of temporality altogether, the human intelligence was (and eternally is) impassible and absolute, timeless and immortal. We have no recollection of this state, since memory demands passivity. But pure, unmixed or disembodied intelligence is not only timeless but purely actual, as the divine intelligence is, its thought caught up in no progress from potency to act. The instance vindicates Aristotle's general claim of the priority of the actual to the potential. In our embodied state, we have no Platonic recollection of the pure knowledge that a timeless mind enjoys, since memory is no faculty of such a mind. So we must learn rather than simply strive to recollect what we once knew. But the timeless element within us remains the condition of all conceptual thought. Aristotle models how this is possible in a striking Homeric simile in his work on demonstration and discovery:

> out of sense perception develops what we call memory, and out of frequently repeated memories of the same thing comes experience. For multiple memories make up a single experience. From experience in turn, the universal, now stabilized in its fullness within the soul, the one standing over and against the many, as a single identity running through them all. Here arise the skill of the craftsman and the knowledge of the scientist – skill in the realm of what comes to be; and knowledge, in that of what is. In short, these states of knowledge are neither in us in their determinate form, nor derived from prior, higher states of knowledge. Rather, they emerge from sense perception – as in a battle a rout is stopped if one man makes a stand, and then another, until the company is regrouped. And the soul is so constituted as to be capable of this.[6]

Here Aristotle focuses on what the mind contributes of its own resources and how it marshals its powers and orders its experience so as to construct conceptual knowledge, developmentally, using the data of sense-experience as raw material. But the mind, of course, does not constitute itself or supply itself with sensory data. It does not innately possess pure concepts like Plato's idea of Sameness, which are necessary tools in the construction of universal knowledge. And it clearly cannot fabricate such tools out of mere sensations. So Aristotle does not seem to find it inconsistent in another passage to place emphasis on our need for external help:

> One does not deliberate after previous deliberation, itself presupposing deliberation, but there is some starting point; nor does one think after first thinking, and so ad infinitum. Thought, then, is not the starting-point of thinking, nor deliberation of deliberation. What then can be the starting-point except chance? So everything would come from chance. But perhaps there is a starting-point with none beyond it, which can act as it does by being the sort of thing it is. The object of our search is this: What is the commencement of movement in the soul? The answer is clear. As in the universe, so in the soul, it is god. For in a sense the divine element within us moves everything. The starting-point of reasoning is not reasoning but something greater. And what could be greater even than knowledge and intellect but god?[7]

Thus the active intellect is both external and divine, within us and proper to us. It activates thought by being what it is, and it makes the mind in principle identical with all that is known. The active intellect, as *the divine element within us*, realizes the mind as mind, actualizes it as the divine being that it truly and ultimately is, allowing it to cap the temporal process of mental development with the conceptual knowledge whose atemporal aspect bespeaks the ultimate immortality, impassivity and absoluteness of at least the one aspect of the human soul that shares the nature of divine intelligence.

All this was apparently a bit too ambiguous for Alexander of Aphrodisias (*fl.* AD 200), the sober Aristotelian commentator whose philosophical work so often took aim at Stoic fudging on the borderlines between divine transcendence and immanence. Alexander squarely identified the active intellect with God, specifically, the Prime Mover of the Aristotelian heavens. Yet at the same time he sees the active intellect at work in us from the very origin of the processes of thought, founding the potentialities that differentiate a conscious from an unconscious being. He rationalizes this internalization of its work by speaking of a *nous thyrathen*, a mind in us that is externally derived.

Other interpreters, responding to Aristotle's criticisms of Plato's freestanding forms but still loyal to the idea that both existence and knowledge in particulars must reflect the purity of ideal archetypes, housed the Platonic forms in the divine mind, establishing the tradition of Middle Platonism that we find represented in the Jewish philosopher Philo of Alexandria (*fl.* 20 BC–AD 40). Such work laid the foundations for the synthesis of Plotinus (AD 205–70), the founder of Neoplatonism, who identified the active intellect and the cosmic *Nous* of Aristotle with the Platonic realm of Being (as distinguished from Becoming), the realm of the forms. In drawing up this equation, Plotinus relied on Aristotle's identification of conceptual thought with what it knows. *Nous* for Plotinus was not the highest God. The One, Plato's Good, stood above it, infinite and absolute. But *Nous* mediated that absoluteness to the cosmos, through the temporalizing discursiveness of the universal Soul, the third of Plotinus' 'principial hypostases'. Themistius (fourth century AD) enriched the theory, by arguing that if the active intellect is analogous to light, as Aristotle urged, it must have an external source and it must enter into individual minds according to their receptivity. Thus Plato's God, the One or the Good, was firmly placed above divine Intelligence, while Aristotle's desire to see a god at work in the highest operations of the human mind was preserved.

Neoplatonists sought to preserve the absolute transcendence of the highest God from any compromising engagement with particularity. Thus the Christian philosopher John Philoponus (*c.* AD 490–570) reports that Marinus, a disciple of Proclus, the great systematizer of the Neoplatonism of Plotinus, treated the active intellect as *daimonion*, quasi-divine, not a fully fledged god – angelic in the language Philoponus himself preferred, language soon to be adopted by the philosophical translators who transposed the theories of pagan Greeks into a language acceptable in Islam. In one commentary preserved in Latin, Philoponus ascribes to anonymous thinkers the view that the active intellect is a being subordinate to God, 'closer to ourselves, which sheds its influence upon our souls and perfects them.'[8]

The Nestorian translator Ḥunayn ibn Isḥāq shows little interest in the theory of a hypostatic active intellect in his paraphrase of Aristotle's *De Anima*. The little-known philosopher Bakr of Mosul tries to combat such theories, arguing that it is the task of the individual human mind to make universal judgements, and that it contains innately the principles (Plato's forms) that enable it to do so. But Ḥunayn's son, Isḥāq, in translating Alexander's term *nous thyrathen*, the 'derived intellect', rendered in Arabic *al-'aql al-mustafād*, that is, the intellect acquired or received by emanation, makes it clear that this aspect or element of the mind is the active intellect as received by the individual. He calls it 'the received active intellect'.[9] So at the very entry of the theory into Islamic epistemology, the immanent and hypostatic aspects of the active intellect are present; and the identification of that intellect with God has been suppressed.

Al-Kindī (*c.* AD 801–67), the earliest Muslim philosopher of note, is attracted to the idea of a hypostatic active intellect, which he apparently identifies with the first of the disembodied intelligences that in Aristotelian cosmology govern the celestial spheres. The Jewish philosopher Isaac Israeli follows him in this schematism, as elsewhere in his thinking. Some forms, al-Kindī explains, representing what he takes to be the sound argument of Aristotle and the ultimate sense of Plato as well, have no matter or 'fantasy' to them (he transliterates the Greek term for an imaginative projection). Such forms and the knowledge they represent are attained by the soul's 'coming into contact' (*bāsharat*) with the higher intellect which eternally thinks them. By this means the human mind, only potentially intellectual at the start, becomes actually intellectual. Just as the mind acquires the form of sensory objects abstracted from their matter, and indeed, *becomes* the form of what it knows, since the unity of consciousness allows no difference between our thought and its object, so (and even more so) in intellectual apprehension, the mind becomes identical with its ideas. But it does not, al-Kindī insists, become identical with the active intellect.[10] For that intellect as such is not identical with the concepts grasped by the human mind – as though its reality were exhausted by the ideas that we human beings might come to apprehend.

The human soul, being the form of man within us, derives, al-Kindī argues, from the very substance of the creator, as light flows from the sun. It is simple, noble and perfect, of immense dignity. Its substance is spiritual, indeed divine, as is manifest from the nobility of its nature, its antipathy to all bodily appetites and passions. Thus, clearly it is immortal, not only distinct from the body but separable from it.[11] This does not mean, of course, that the soul is itself divine. It derives from God, but its being is not equivalent to his. Yet to understand the nature of the soul as a spiritual, i.e. intellectual, being does make clear not only why it is immortal but how it is capable of knowing. The theory is laid out clearly by al-Fārābī.

Like other philosophers who fell under the spell of Plato's arguments, al-Fārābī saw that the senses alone can never supply us with the universal and necessary laws that Aristotle found to be the heart of science. Indeed, sense-perception provides not even the concepts underlying the elemental terms of such judgements. Yet sense-experience is not irrelevant to our knowledge of the world. All human knowledge depends on sense-perception. The theory of the active intellect shows how conceptual knowledge is achieved, given the sketchy hints and clues provided by the senses. Knowledge, like being, is definiteness. Just as the Bestower of Forms sheds reality on particulars by imparting specificity to matter, so the active intellect gives actuality to our minds, making them intellects in fact and not merely in potential, by imparting the same forms to human intelligence. For the active intellect is the Bestower of Forms, the tenth disembodied intelligence, which emanates from the last of the celestial intelligences, which governs the sphere of the moon. It is responsible, by a kind of emanative delegation, for the governance of nature and for the rational enlightenment, mystical awakening and prophetic inspiration that attune human minds to the realities underlying sense-experience.[12]

The comparison of the active intellect with light was well established when Aristotle described its work on the analogy of light, which makes potential colours actual. In the same context, Aristotle said that the mind, thought of as passive, becomes all things, whereas the active intellect is what it is because it *makes* all things. So it was not difficult for a Neoplatonist like al-Fārābī to vindicate Aristotle's realism by ascribing to the same source the forms that make things what they are and the apprehensibility of those forms by human reason. Light, in the metaphorical, Neoplatonic sense, is the vehicle of that apprehension. Forms (that is, being in all its varieties) are actualized in things by the active intellect; they enter our minds from the same source, refracted through the materiality of things. The fulfilled human mind is aptly labelled 'derived' or 'acquired', since its enlightenment comes from without. And, insofar as its understanding is conceptual, it reflects not the particularity of things (their matter) but their specificity (form), the being they derive from the active intellect. To use a modern analogy, we might say that the disembodied intelligences of the spheres emanate from their divine source as electromagnetic radiation radiates from a star. The hypostatic intelligences in fact *are* that radiation, and human intelligence is induced in the potential intellect as a current is induced in a wire by a magnetic field, or as a magnetic polarity is induced in a piece of ferrous metal by the presence of such a field. That polarity or current is *our* intelligence, but at the same time it is our participation in the universal intelligence that radiates from the divine.

It is the work of the heavens, according to al-Fārābī's theory, to produce the bodies we observe in nature and to govern the rhythms of their motions. But the active intellect imparts their forms. In particular, it 'scans' the realm of nature; and, wherever it finds a being that has attained some measure of perfection and separation from matter, it purifies that being, which is, of course, a human mind, and brings it into propinquity with itself. It achieves this work by lighting up the traces of sensory data, transmuting them into concepts apprehensible to the mind, or (to put the matter developmentally) capable of rendering what is only potentially a mind actually effectual as a mind.

It is by such means, as al-Fārābī argues in his *Principles underlying the Beliefs of the Inhabitants of the Virtuous State* and in his *Civil Polity*, that we come to know the fundamental axioms of thought, 'the first common intelligibles', for example that the whole is greater than its part or that equals of the same quantity are equal to each other. Given these axioms, the human mind can construct not only such sciences as arithmetic and geometry but axiology and all the natural sciences. In his *Essay on the Intellect* al-Fārābī takes the primary truths for granted as givens and assigns our knowledge of the truths of practical reason to experience. But he ascribes to the influence of the active intellect our ability to grasp the forms embedded in particulars. These forms are the realities of things, by Aristotle's account as well as Plato's; and they are principles of value as well as intelligibility. But primary knowledge of them is by acquaintance (*ṣādafa*). It is not propositional. If the difference between al-Fārābī's view in the *Essay* and that of the other two works represents a change of mind rather than just a change in focus as to the multi-faceted activities of the active intellect, it may express an effort to find a level of activity for the active intellect still more elemental than that of axioms. For, as Aristotle showed, terms and concepts are the elements of propositions; and, as Plato firmly believed, what underlies our explicit knowledge, say, of the equals axiom, is an intuitive apprehension of the pure form of equality.

Individuals vary in their receptivity to primary concepts according to al-Fārābī; and some may specialize, in view of their innate receptivities. But it is possible not just in principle but in practice for one human being to receive all the primary concepts and to attain with their aid adequate knowledge of all things – of physical things like rocks and plants, by grasping conceptually (thus, scientifically) the forms or ideas which are their natures and which underlie (and underwrite the veracity of) the accounts of the senses; and of disembodied things like the celestial Intelligences, by direct acquaintance. For light itself is not invisible.

When the human disposition for thought, the material or passive intellect, which al-Fārābī also calls our rational faculty or power, becomes an 'actual intellect', it can serve in turn as the matter or substrate of the active intellect itself, which comes into contact (*ittiṣāl*) with it and is even described, in keeping with suggestions made by Plotinus (in the text known in Arabic as the *Theology of Aristotle*), Porphyry and Shī'ite theology, as uniting with it, dwelling within it, or raising it nearly to its own rank. The 'nearly' is important, if the ancient pagan legacy of the model, and its continuing pantheistic resonances in Sufi theory and Shī'ite immanentist theology, is to be kept under control and not allowed to swamp the monotheistic framework into which it is imported. But the elevation of the human mind by the active intellect is an essential feature of the theory. For it enables al-Fārābī to explain the possibilities of human immortality, mystical experience, and the comprehensive inrush of ideas that lays the foundation for prophecy.

Prophets, to be sure, require imagination and the gifts of poetry and rhetoric if they are to translate their comprehensive grasp of reality from conceptual terms into the symbols, myths, rituals and institutions that will give more ordinary human beings practical access to the truths to which their minds are opened up. But in content and form the knowledge underlying true prophecy does not differ from that of the mystic or that of the philosopher. The lower type of prophet, whose mind is not itself perfected, may work on the level of images, unselfconsciously influenced by the play of the active intellect upon the imagination. The higher type of prophet is a philosopher whose gifts enable him to translate conceptual knowledge into images, words and laws. But if the prophecy is real and not just a trick of the imagination, the ideas that inform it are the same as those of the philosopher, even when their spokesperson does not apprehend them conceptually. And prophets from different cultures, whose work is expressed in divergent systems of law and custom, myth and symbol, are all voicing the same message, if their inspiration is genuine and not self-serving, erroneous or perverse. The images may differ, just as languages may differ, but the truths they express are the same.

What had been a somewhat muddled sentence or two in al-Kindī's *Essay on the intellect*, and a somewhat qualified caution in al-Fārābī's discussions of the soul, becomes a guiding theme in Avicenna. The soul does not unite with the active intellect, and individual human minds retain their discreteness, even in their disembodied state. In the context of Platonic epistemology and psychology the question becomes an issue, since knowing is achieved through identity of an (intellectual) subject with its (intellectual) object, and immortality is attained by knowing. The soul, through knowledge, becomes or reverts to its primal status as an eternal, intellectual being, and thus sheds not only its links to physicality but also its particularity, its individuality.

Avicenna is insistent that the fulfilled, informed or enlightened soul, to remain a subject, and so remain capable of knowledge, must retain its individuality and distinctness from its object. Taking a hint from al-Fārābī, who had ascribed the differentiation of disembodied souls to differences they retained as a result of their once being linked to highly diverse bodies, Avicenna ascribes an origin and a history to every soul, by which each is differentiated from the rest, and by which all are differentiated sharply from the timelessness of the active intellect. He takes Porphyry to task for holding that the enlightened mind unites with the active intellect, arguing that if such a union were the endpoint of knowledge, then either the unitary active intellect would be hopelessly divided against itself or the individual who knew anything would know everything. The persistent temporality of human consciousness, which seems to lie at the core of Avicenna's famous Floating Man thought experiment, designed to model the mind's lack of dependence on the body or on any physical thing, reveals clearly that the human intellect may (to use the modern word) *intend* divinity, whether in the absolute form of the Transcendent or in the mediating form of the active intellect, but cannot merge with it.[13]

Avicenna's respect for al-Fārābī is probably not diminished by the need to clarify his predecessor's more sympathetic references to the idea of union. For, epistemically at least, union is clearly unnecessary. The illumination provided by the active intellect will suffice. And, as al-Kindī says in the passage that originates the whole discussion among the philosophers of Islam, a mind can be identical with its ideas without for that reason becoming identical with their source.

It is still widely supposed that Francis Bacon, in overthrowing the idols of the mind, set the inductive method firmly on the throne too long and too unquestioningly held alone by an aprioristic deductivism. But Aristotle credits Socrates with devising induction as a method, eliciting a common theme or pattern from the seemingly disparate materials of experience. And that method was intimately conjoined with the other great methodological achievements of Socrates: dialogue, dialectic, analysis and definition. Plato's theory of forms, all that it entailed for epistemology, ontology and psychology, was itself a product of the Socratic inductive method, as Plato's dialogues make abundantly clear. And it was Aristotle, not Bacon, who first broke clear of Plato's deductivism, replacing definitions and analysis with syllogistic, and proposing that the goal of the syllogism as a method of discovery was not its nominal conclusion but the middle term that links extremes, allowing intelligence to discover what seemingly disparate classes have in common and where things differ that are seemingly alike.

Avicenna himself, despite the seeming deductivism of his appeal to pure concepts, was an important contributor to the growth of inductive logic. Developing Aristotle's syllogistic logic, he incorporated modal values and propositional terms into the quantificational calculus of Aristotle, guided in part by the logical work of Galen, the medical writer who most influenced him as a physician and expositor of medical science. Galen had taken seriously the propositional calculus of the Stoics; and, following in Galen's tradition, Avicenna elaborates a hypothetical logic in which the Stoic theory of signs is absorbed. Thus Avicenna can model in his logic the pattern of a conditional with multiple antecedents and a common consequent: 'If this man has a chronic fever, a hard cough, laboured breathing, shooting pains, and a rasping pulse, he has pleurisy.'[14] Here the philosopher-physician lays the groundwork for the idea of a syndrome as he pioneers in the diagnosis of a particular disease.

Following up on the theory of signs in his medical writings, Avicenna clearly employs the methods of agreement, difference and concomitant variation, which are vital constituents of the scientific method.[15] Indeed, if we add modern ideas about quantifying probability to the hypothetical syllogistic of Avicenna, we can see the roots of risk-factor analysis and multi-factorial probabilistic modelling in his conditional logic. Yet neither the theory of signs nor the logic of hypotheticals leads Avicenna to the conception of a controlled experiment, any more than his interest in observation in medicine and in astronomy leads him to recognize the fundamental significance of quantitative precision in science, a significance that will one day all but eclipse the Aristotelian and ultimately Empedoclean concern with the qualitative.

Key elements of the inductive method are present in Avicenna. If they do not loom large in his epistemology, it is because he is not convinced of the sufficiency of brute empiricism (the empiricism of enumeration, unaided by thematic concepts) to provide us with the intellectual elements requisite for the construction of sound theories of nature. And, of course, he does not believe, any more than al-Fārābī does, that sound theories of nature are the sole or highest aims of the human quest for knowledge. What Avicenna pursues is an integrated theory of knowledge, and his achievements here complement those of our own notions of science, balancing our reliance on empiricism with a complementary faith in reason as the means to that totality without which no theory is lawlike, let alone universal and necessary. Reason in Avicenna is not an artefact of its own devising and thus has little fear of the varieties of relativism and subjectivism that dog the steps of modern epistemologies. It is the gift of divine agencies, and its development is achieved through our responses to their influence. Which is to say that all rationality is inspired and that reason extends not merely to matters of natural fact but to the values that invest all being and to the highest reaches of the heavens. For in understanding anything one will be apprehending its value, and in understanding *that* one will be, in effect, granted a share of the beatific vision.

The first human certainty, Avicenna argues, is that of the senses. But what the senses actually reveal is not merely phenomena but being. And the idea of being, which we attach to the objects put before us by the senses, is prior epistemically even to our sensations: it is a primitive, supplied to the mind from above. The second human certainty, again prompted by experience, is the recognition that being is not necessary in itself but contingent. This idea, aided by the recognition that whatever need not exist but does exist must have a cause, suffices to bring us to the recognition of the reality of a Necessary Being, the absolute condition of all that is conditioned.

Beyond the external senses, we possess 'internal' senses – 'estimation', for example, which apprehends the 'intention' or significance of things (not just 'grey mass in motion' but 'wolf approaching'), and the *sensus communis*, which integrates the data of the senses with one another. Other faculties regulate our receptivity to percepts, our retention of them and our ability to re-present or project them as images. Still other faculties combine and separate the elements of sensory images, to create imaginary or fantastic images and the images we behold in dreams. Avicenna assigns all of these faculties to the Aristotelian 'animal soul', since they are concerned with our sensibility and reactiveness, and since they all have counterparts in non-human animals. He even assigns them locations in the brain. His reliance on the language of faculty psychology does not mask the fact that his efforts here are descriptive rather than explanatory. But the analysis of functions is taken to a high pitch, especially when compared with theories that routinely identify memory, say, with image-making.

The rational soul makes use of the data of the senses, as integrated and interpreted by the intermediary faculties ('internal senses'), but it faces in two directions: downwards, towards the body, in its practical capacity as a governor; and upwards, towards the intellectual world of the disembodied Intelligences, in its speculative capacity, receiving pure concepts from the active intellect, or purifying the concepts of sensory particulars with the aid of the active intellect. While as yet unformed by any ideas, the rational soul is called potential or material, as children are said to have the potential to write, meaning that they are able to learn to write. Once opened up to the primary ideas or axioms, which are too fundamental to be taught and on which our ability to grasp more complex ideas depends, the rational soul is called *intellectus in habitu* or actual intelligence, since it is now capable of reasoning. But when actually contemplating the forms or ideas which it is capable of contemplating, it is called the acquired or derived intellect, since the ideas are induced in it by the active intellect.

The mind's responsiveness to ideas and active grasp of them is *ḥads*, intuition. When this is very strong, knowledge seems to flow from within the mind rather than emanating from beyond it. Taken to its highest degree, such responsiveness is that rare quality which in certain individuals is called a spirit divine. For both the sensitivity and the ideas to which such persons respond come to them from the divine and may affect both the rational soul itself and the imagination, as al-Fārābī explained. For this sensitivity to the ideas shed on us by the active intellect is the basis of prophecy:

> there might be a man whose soul has such an intense purity and is so firmly linked to the rational principles that he blazes with intuition, i.e. with the receptivity to inspiration coming from the active intellect, concerning everything, so that the forms of all things contained in the active intellect are imprinted on his soul, all at once or nearly so – not that he accepts them blindly, but rather, that he grasps them rationally, in terms of their logic, comprehending all the middle terms. For there is no certainty in accepting blindly ideas which are

> to be known by way of their causes. This is a kind of prophetic inspiration; indeed, the highest kind, and the one most fittingly called a divine power. It is the highest power a human being can reach.[16]

Prophets by this account are not freaks or charlatans but thinkers whose minds or imaginations are in contact with the rational source of all subjective and objective rationality in nature and beyond it. Mystics too are not creatures of paradox but human beings whose minds are filled with the comprehensive awareness that flows forth eternally from the timeless to the temporal. For the work of the faculty or power Avicenna speaks of is not confined to prophetic leaders. Purity of mind can bring one first glimpses and then enduring contact with the higher, intellectual realm. A mind continually lit up by that contact is called *'aql qudsī*, a sacred mind, by Avicenna, fusing the two highest values of Greek and Semitic thought, intelligence and holiness.

Despite his vehement criticism of Avicenna in *The Incoherence of the Philosophers*, al-Ghazālī (AD 1058–1111), who took upon himself the role of restoring Islamic faith and orthodoxy for the century that dawned in his lifetime, adopted Avicenna's explanation of the continued independence and individuality of the human soul after death, accepting the view that once it had a history even a disembodied mind was forever unique, and accepting Avicenna's argument that if two minds were one, as the old tradition of Platonic monopsychism suggested, then they would share the same consciousness. Thus, for al-Ghazālī, as for Avicenna, the fact that you and I know different things and the fact that consciousness is private are sufficient proof that our individuality can endure even after the destruction of the body which grounded that individuality throughout our natural lives.

Ibn Rushd (Averroes) does not share Avicenna's discomfort with monopsychism and the timeless unity of human rational souls with the hypostasis that is their source. But Ibn Bājjah, Maimonides, and Ibn Ṭufayl, who seek to reconcile al-Ghazālī with Avicenna, return to the Neoplatonic roots of the idea of monopsychism to devise a delicate theory of quasi-individuation for the disembodied soul. Ibn Ṭufayl argues that once matter is left behind, the categories of identity and difference are no longer relevant; disembodied minds are neither the same as nor different from one another, or from the source that has inspired them. Difference, he insists, is a matter of alienation, the failure of the mind to break free, through intellection, of the trammels of the body. The highest form of knowledge is the apprehension of God's unity. This experience, as Avicenna held, can become a lambent flame, rather than the vanishing sparks in which it is first beheld. In the light of that flame, all prior knowledge and experience, the reports of the senses, the discourse of reason, even philosophy itself, are revealed to be mere preparations for the consummatory vision, not set aside but transcended. Yet even the purest thought (here Ibn Ṭufayl agrees with Avicenna) would never make us identical with the Absolute that we behold.[17]

Where al-Ghazālī departs from Avicenna, epistemologically, is in the new meaning he assigns to intuition. It is no longer the Platonic rational intuition or the Aristotelian active receptivity of the intellect but is now the Sufi, experiential intuition (*dhawq*, literally 'taste') of the Ineffable, a direct and immediate experience of the divine. The practical exercises of Sufi spirituality and the somewhat ascetic discipline of Islamic pietism may prepare the mind for this experience, but it is not something that one's own acts can guarantee. It comes unbidden, by God's grace, and is known only to those who have experience of it. Its paradoxicality and ineffability mask the abyss at whose edge it plays. For its portent borders on pantheism, and only the sheerest and most subtly woven tissue of intellectual and linguistic discipline prevents the mystic, who 'sees God in all things', from plunging headlong into the blasphemous claim to identity with the godhead.

Mystic experience for al-Ghazālī is a form of knowing, self-certifying and self-sufficient. It validates and sustains religious faith, deriving from that faith in turn no further warrant, since it needs none, but only the categories, intellectual and practical, that interpret the significance of the experience itself and the meaning of the symbols the mystic will encounter in his quest for *gnosis* in nature, and in the supernal world beyond. Mystic experience voids the doubts of the sceptic, not by answering but by eclipsing them. Learning, especially in the form of traditions from the Prophet and his companions, is the key to the performance of God's will and the understanding that allows us to be guided in accordance with the intentions of our creator. But medicine, jurisprudence, even astronomy contribute to the pious life. Astrology, with its pagan assumptions and its purely conjectural claims, does not. Nor does the frivolous (secular) erudition of those who immerse themselves in poesy or the tribal genealogies of the Arabs. Here al-Ghazālī brings the ideal of knowledge in Islam full circle, back to the primal opposition between the teaching and the lore of the Prophet and the merely human knowledge and values of his predecessors. Both realms have been enlarged by conquest and the elaboration of culture. But the stark difference between them remains. And the portal al-Ghazālī opens between the two is conditional: nothing is of ultimate value but the vision of God's face. All things else are instrumental, or they are worthless distractions. The test of knowledge is its usefulness in bringing us closer to God, and the height of knowledge is not learning for its own sake but the immediate apprehension of God's presence.

BEING AND BECOMING

'Being' in Arabic is *kawn*. Given the verbal force typical in Arabic nouns derived from verbs, it is not surprising that this word develops the general connotations of 'becoming', in Plato's sense of coming to be, *genesis*. It naturally renders that term in Aristotle's phrase 'coming to be and passing away'; its Aristotelian opposite is *fasād*, 'corruption', again with verbal force, meaning rotting, wasting, decomposing. Thus Bashshār ibn Burd, the eighth-century AD poet of Basra, wrote: 'wa kullu shay'in li-kawnihi sababun', 'each thing must have a cause of its becoming'.[18] That all things must have a cause was a natural inference when the very being of things was conceptualized as their coming to be: the cause of their being was the cause of their origination. The prolific essayist al-Jāḥiẓ (*c.* AD 776–869) was writing in an easy and idiomatic Arabic when he asked, 'What is the cause of the being of cats, or the reason for the creation of swine?'[19] Al-Dimashqī (d. AD 1327), a cosmographer from the city whose name he bears, speaks of the completion of the *kawn* of the foetus,[20] meaning its development. The doxographer al-Shahrastānī (d. AD 1153) writes of foreknowledge of a thing before its existence (*kawnihi*), i.e. before its coming to be, before its occurrence as an event. There is nothing for Process philosophers to quarrel with here. Even Ibn Rushd writes that man's being, i.e. his coming to be, is from another man.[21]

But the tension between being and becoming is evident to readers of Arabic when they find Aristotle saying that, 'change is the opposite of complete (or total) being (*al-kawn al-kullī*).'[22] And this Platonic tension is never absent in Islamic discussions of being. True, the word 'being' was not discussed in Muslim sources before the translation of Greek materials into Arabic. But reflection on the nature of being as such, the subject of metaphysics, was well founded when the Qur'ān proclaimed: 'All things are perishing, except His face' (28.88). Islamic orthodoxy today easily finds in these words a denial of the ultimate adequacy of the claim to being made by all sensory things. The King Fahd Qur'ān comments: 'The only Eternal Reality is Allah. The whole phenomenal world is subject to flux and change and will pass away, but He will endure for ever.'[23] Plato's argument that change betokens impermanence and thereby entails both the reality of a creator and the insufficiency of what is created chimes perfectly with the Qur'ānic sense, which is complemented by the conception of the omnipresence and omnisufficiency of God, again spoken of by way of metonymy: 'whithersoever you turn, there is the Face of God' (Qur'ān 2.115). The face of God is what is seen by the blessed (Qur'ān 18.28, 30.38–9, 6.52, etc.), who, for their part, open their faces to him (Qur'ān 2.112, 3.20, 6.79, etc.).

Ordinary being, the being of things, in the Qur'ān is the act or work of God, 'Creator of the heavens and the earth; when He decreeth a thing He has but to say to it "BE!" and it is' (Qur'ān 2.117, cf. 3.47, 6.73, 16.40, 19.35, 36.82, 40.68). Here the idea of being is given voice not in the infinitive but in the imperative mood, and not in the abstract but the concrete: the imperative 'BE!' is the logos, vehicle of God's creative act. It is not confined to absolute origination but includes God's miracles (Qur'ān 21.69 – 'Fire, be coolness and safety for Abraham'), his ordinances (Qur'ān 5.8 – 'O believers, be you steadfast before God, witnesses for justice'; cf. 4.135, 39.66), and even his curses (Qur'ān 2.65, 7.166, 17.50).

Being, here, is relational: the absolute being of God is regnant (Qur'ān 13.16, 14.48, 38.65, 39.4, 40.16). Beneath it tremble the ephemera of nature, which God created, conditions, forms, shapes and rules. All creation owes him absolute allegiance. Men will burn in hell forever if they fail to confess him. Thus, in the traditions ascribed to the Prophet, we find the heading: 'He who accepts Islam on his deathbed, before the agony of death is a Muslim; but it is forbidden to plead for blessings upon polytheists. One who dies a polytheist is destined for Hell, and there are no means adequate to extricate him' (*Ṣaḥīḥ* Muslim, I x). Of Muḥammad, we read,

> 'The Apostle of God said to his uncle (as he lay dying), 'Profess that there is no god but God, and I will bear witness on the Day of Judgment that you did so.' He answered, 'But for fear of [my fellow tribesmen of] Quraysh condemning me for doing it out of fear, I would surely have given this pleasure to your eyes.' It was then that God revealed: 'Thou canst not guide whomever thou lovest; rather God will guide whom He pleaseth. He knoweth best who shall be guided.'
>
> (Qur'ān 28.56)

The scriptural sensitivity to the conditionedness of created being becomes a powerful theme in *kalām*, the multifarious enterprise of Islamic dialectical theology. For *kalām* schools, the central fact about being was its contingency. Examining the concept of being, the early *mutakallimūn*, practitioners of *kalām*, reasoned that the positing of one thing does not entail the existence of anything else, or even the persistence of the same thing beyond the instant of its positing. A substance (*jawhar*), they therefore reasoned, was an atom – by which purist *mutakallimūn* understood an unextended point. For any differentiation of such a point, as by extension in space, would mean that more was inferred than initially allowed. If God gave being to a thing, it had that being, for that moment. But it did not have more. Its being was *here*, not elsewhere; *now*, not later, or forever. If the beings we observe seem larger in bulk than a single point, that is because they are aggregates of atoms. If they seem to persist, that is because it is God's pleasure to re-create successor aggregates, moment by moment, more rapidly than we can apprehend. The properties of all substances (i.e. atoms) are themselves created and assigned or vouchsafed to them. All are 'accidental', none essential. For nothing in the positing of a 'being' implies anything about its nature. That is a separate matter. Logical atomism is here pushed to an extreme untested by Hume or Russell: God gives each 'substance' its character, just as he gives it its existence. So nothing acts of its own power, and no property ('accident') entails any other. In the words of the Qur'ān, 'There is no power but in God' (18.39; cf. 2.165).

Imagination, as Moses Maimonides remarks,[24] is the linchpin of the *kalām*, for what is possible is equated with what is imaginable. If there is no contradiction in an assumption, it is conceivable and therefore possible. Thus miracles are possible if they involve no contradiction. And indeed all events are on a par with miracles. For in *kalām* there is no sliding of what is into what it shall be, as in Aristotle, but each new state of the world is a new creation, whose sole connection to what went before is in the sheer will (or accustomed grace) of the creator.

The denial of power to any being but God made attractive to the early *mutakallimūn* the Megarian elenchus against potentiality. Where Aristotle argued that without a prior possibility no event would occur (since the outcome would be *ex hypothesi* impossible), Megarians held that potentiality violates Aristotle's own law of the excluded middle and its Parmenidean archetype in the principle of contradiction. For a thing either is or is not ϕ; to say that it is ϕ potentially is simply to fudge on the law of contradiction. *Kalām* occasionalists seem similarly to have held that potentialities to be real must be actual, and to be actual must be active. Thus even the tenth-century advocate of divine grace al-Ash'arī (AD 874–935), who allowed and required capacities, in virtue of the fact that an agent is sometimes capable and sometimes incapable of a given action, rejected the idea of durable dispositions. He insisted that capacities do not exist before the particular act they render possible: the inflammability that underlies the kindling of a piece of cotton is created at the very moment that the cotton burns. If the capacity existed sooner, al-Ash'arī argues, it would have gone out of existence instantly like everything else, leaving the kindling to occur by virtue of a non-existent capacity.[25] So even here there is the stark Megarian contrast of the existent with the non-existent. There is no latent potentiality to compromise or threaten the absolute creative act of God, in the beginning, and at every moment.

The radical contingency of being in the cosmology of the *kalām* seems to aim a sharp riposte at the seeming necessitarianism of Aristotle's naturalism. For Aristotle, knowledge was science, and the aim of science was to discover why things must be as they are. Necessities were everywhere. Matter was eternal, ungenerated and indestructible. Form too was immutable, although particulars could put off one form and take on another. Being was not the mere facticity of a thing but its essence (*to ti en einai*, the 'what it was to be that thing') – that is, its having the specific characteristics that made it a member of a natural kind and that could not be lost or altered without the destruction of that thing. Here destruction meant not annihilation, as in the *kalām*, but denaturing. For nothing real could be utterly destroyed. But for a thing to be real was for it to have its essence, and for it to be destroyed was for it to lose that essence. Species never lost their essences: they were eternal and immutable. So were the heavenly bodies. Thus species and celestial substances made a special claim upon the title of reality: changeless and indestructible, they were the most fitting and responsive objects of scientific study. The universality and necessity of the natural characteristics that pertained essentially to species (and to particulars insofar as they were members of species) and the immutable pattern of necessity visible in the invariant motions of the heavens were the realities correspondent to what true knowledge, scientific knowledge, most genuinely knows. They were also the marks in nature of the implicit workings of the divine Intelligence that animates the cosmos, not acting on it from without, like a *deus ex machina* in a bad play,[26] but working within it, through the inner powers and capacities, strengths and dispositions, energies and affinities that animate all things. Metaphysically brash the *mutakallimūn* may have been, but they were not naïve. They understood clearly what they were combating.

The earliest Muslim thinkers to call themselves philosophers, *falāsifa*, using the transliterated Greek term, sought accommodation with Greek cosmology, relying on the arguments and authority of Plato and of the Christian thinker Philoponus (AD 490–570) to counterbalance the vigorous eternalism of Aristotle and the strident anti-creationism characteristic of the pagan Neoplatonic reaction against Christian monotheism from Porphyry and Proclus to Simplicius and beyond. For al-Kindī (d. *c.* AD 867), the first major philosopher to write in Arabic and himself an Arab nobleman and a physician, creation was one variety of change, added to Aristotle's list: bringing something out of nothing.[27] Perfect being was found in God and shared with us, in the measure of our capacity, through our intellectual awakening to the Platonic forms, our sole enduring and inalienable possession.[28] The transitory being of sensory things depends on the higher and fuller being of the ideal and the divine. We know that God exists, because changeable things are transitory and transitory things cannot cause themselves.[29] Behind all change and perishing must lie the One, indivisible and unique, indescribable and eternal, whose constancy is the source of all mutability. No quantity can be infinite, so time itself must be of finite duration; and the bodies whose existence is presupposed by the very passage of time will perish in the change that marks its passing. For Aristotle is right that time is the measure of motion. Yet his own arguments against creation seem to al-Kindī better suited to service in its behalf: to posit motion in eternal bodies, he argues, is to assign the character of the transitory to the eternal. For 'that which is eternal does not move'.[30] Aristotle had reasoned that there is a paradox, an infinite regress, in the idea of the becoming of becoming; so change and the cosmos as a whole must be eternal. But al-Kindī turns the tables, insisting that what is eternal must be timeless and so rejecting the very idea of an eternal body, eternal motion, and *a fortiori*, an eternal cosmos.

Just as Plato in the *Timaeus* (28d) demands a perfect division of 'that which is always real and has no becoming' from 'that which is always becoming and is never real', so al-Kindī draws the distinction, with deference to the creationist cosmogony he finds in the Qur'ān. But he sidesteps the anti-naturalism of the *kalām* occasionalists, to reconcile monotheistic creationism with the naturalism of Aristotle – on the Platonic grounds that the world of the senses, known to us through the intellect, is no mere opposite but the expression of eternal ideas. Unity and intelligibility, he argues, *are* found in natural objects, not absolutely but derivatively. So even the lesser being that we know bespeaks the perfect being of God. As in Plato, unity and intelligibility are the marks by which we recognize being itself, when we cannot descry it in isolation.

Whatever unity we see in nature, al-Kindī argues, must have a cause. For natural objects are never without some degree of unity. And this is not ascribable to chance. For in nature neither unity nor multiplicity is ever found apart from the other. (And, as Aristotle reasoned, chance relationships are never uniform.) The unity we find in things, moreover, is not ascribable to their inner natures. For unity is never of the essence in an aggregate, a class or whole, insofar as it is an aggregate: even essential properties must be distinguished from that of which they are the properties. And so (*pace* Aristotle) their linkage in or as the essence of a thing cannot be accounted to the being of that thing. On the contrary, that being is due to their linkage, which must in turn be ascribed, in every case, to a higher source of unity. For

> everything which is an accident in one thing is essential in another . . . the unity which occurs in a thing by accident is acquired from that in which it occurs by essence. Thus there is a one, true, of necessity uncaused unity.[31]

To the Peripatetics and their followers, from Aristotle onwards, self-predication, the notion that the idea of man is itself described as 'man', seemed the great paradox and stumbling block of Platonism. But to al-Kindī, as to many a later thinker drawn within the orbit of Platonic thinking, the same thesis was the gateway and threshold to the *via eminentiae*. Man was man precisely because of what he derived from Above, where all of his perfections were most truly and most properly discovered.

As the translation of Greek texts advanced, the coherence of metaphysics and the consensus of the Aristotelians made powerful claims to authority. Greek naturalism gained a firm beachhead in Arabic through its association with Greek logic, and through its achievements in medicine, astronomy and technology. Aristotle's claims for the invariance of the celestial motions come to seem vindicated by observation and by the ancient Sanskrit records of the *Siddhānta*, made over into Arabic in the mid-eighth century and given a reliable text by the late ninth – along with the the *Almagest* and *Tetrabiblos* of Ptolemy.[32] The folly of ignoring cause and effect and the profit of studying their nexus become vivid and compelling in the work of physicians whose art is grounded in the Arabic translations of Greek texts. Avicenna will argue, using Greek geometry, that dimensionless atoms are demonstrably absurd, in view of the geometrical paradoxes they entail; and Maimonides will hold that such atomism not only breaks down the continuity of solid objects but, by positing a void, ignores the workings of scores of mechanical (including medical) devices whose operation would be impossible if a void were real. Yet the appeal of creation is not lost. And the Persian physician and philosopher Muḥammad ibn Zakariyā' al-Rāzī (d. AD 925 or 932) will fall back on a more Epicurean conception of atoms, assigning them solidity and size but retaining the void, still taking refuge in Plato against the Aristotelian notion that naturalism entails the eternity of the cosmos.

Only by positing that five things are eternal, al-Rāzī argues, can monotheists escape the claim of those who hold that the cosmos as a whole is eternal and in no need of external support – the view of the eternalists (*al-dahriyya*), advocates of what is conceived as a Stratonician kind of view, which seems, in the context of monotheist creationism, tantamount to atheism. The five eternals of al-Rāzī's cosmology are time, space, matter, Soul (the world soul) and God. Without all five of these, the world as we know it would not exist. Challenged by a more conventional creationist during one of the intellectual discussions that typically ornamented the courts of Muslim high officials of cultural pretensions, al-Rāzī declared:

> I hold that five things are eternal, but that the world has an origin. The cause of its origination was the longing of Soul to be incarnated in this world. It was this passion that moved her, and she did not know what disastrous consequences would befall her as a result of her embodiment. She thrashed about in bringing forth the world and set matter into a turmoil of chaotic and disordered motion, unable to achieve what she intended. But the creator, glory and exaltation be to him, pitied her and helped her to bring this world to its inception and to impose order and stability on its motions. He did so out of mercy for her, knowing that once she had tasted the troubles in which she had embroiled herself she would return peaceably to her own world; her thrashing about would cease, and her passionate yearning for embodiment would cool and be calmed. Thus she brought about the world's origin, with the help of the creator. Without that help she could not have done it; but without this cause the world would not have come to be. We have no stronger proof against the eternalists than this account. And if this is not how it happened, we have no argument at all against them. For we shall not be able to find any other explanation of the origin of the cosmos that will sustain proof and demonstration.[33]

Al-Rāzī descends into the maelstrom of quasi-gnostic descants on the cosmogony of Plato's *Timaeus* for reasons that remain transparent even through the sometimes hostile reports of his well-attested views. He remains convinced that God is the creator and that the natural order did not and could not simply cause itself. Indeed, no power but that of God was adequate to the origination of the cosmos. To argue that the cosmos was eternal would be, in effect, to argue that it was its own cause, that God was unnecessary and the natural order self-sustaining, a wholly untenable view in al-Rāzī's estimation. Yet Greek metaphysics has now penetrated Arabic thought to the extent that absolute creation seems here too much to expect of God. For the core idea of Greek metaphysics, from its foundation as an explicit enquiry in the thinking of Parmenides, was the idea that being *must* be, that there is somehow a contradiction in denying the existence of what is real. And that theme is respected in the thought of al-Rāzī. Each Democritean or Epicurean atom of his cosmos *must* exist, in the sense that it cannot fail to exist. The atoms are not created and cannot be destroyed. But they are powerless to order themselves. Their existence requires time and space. Yet in themselves they are inert. Motion will come to them only when imparted by Soul, the life principle. So, at the beginning, they exist without motion, and the time in which they endure is unending and unbegun, existing as an absolute, since there is, as yet, no motion to be its measure, and its passage does not in fact require a measure. Space too is absolute. For the motion of the atoms is made possible only by the paradoxical reality of the void, space understood not in relative terms, as in Aristotle, as the place of some body, but as extension, which might or might not be occupied by a body.

If God's creative wisdom is necessary to give being to the world we know, and if God's power is sufficient in ordering the natural world, al-Rāzī still must ask *why*

God would create the world. And he surveys the range of answers to that question with a jaundiced vision, dialectically compromised by some past history of debate with the gnostic view that creation is a disaster of cosmic proportions, an accident – indeed a tragedy, which the world itself has yet to overcome. Al-Rāzī himself does not share the gnostic view that finite being or even finitude is evil. But he does argue, in Epicurean fashion, that evils outweigh goods within this world – necessarily, since sufferings will always outrun the successes of the subtly ordered complexes of atoms that make up the objects of nature, including, of course, the human frame, which his ministrations as a physician made it his task to repair, working against the implacable corrosion and decay that will inevitably undermine all that robust health and medical art and skill can shore up. So it is a task for al-Rāzī to explain why God in his goodness would allow Soul, the life principle, to ally herself with, let alone ensare herself in, matter. In true gnosticism the answer to this question is given in terms of *tolma*, the audacity of the Soul, which is the reason for her fall. And al-Rāzī does adopt a version of the gnostic and Neoplatonic myth of the fall of the Soul. But in using such materials he must confront the monotheistic objection that surely a God great enough to form the cosmos would have the power, the goodness and the knowledge to prevent a presumed disaster. Al-Rāzī answers, again through the Platonic expedient of myth – or more precisely, through a carefully and self-consciously constructed allegory, which we find him addressing not to an imaginary but to an actual adversary:

'Tell me now', [his adversary asks,] 'What you say is that the Soul longed to be incarnated in this world, but lost control when she was bringing it forth and was assisted by God because he pitied her?'

'Yes'.

'And did God know what troubles she would suffer if she undertook to be embodied in the world?'

'Yes'.

'Would it not have been more in keeping with God's mercy to have hindered rather than helped her – to stop her from incarnating herself in the world, rather than cast her into all these calamities as you claim he did?'

'He could not stop her.'

'Are you implying that God is powerless?'

'What I said implies no such thing.'

'Didn't you just assert that he could not stop her? You said "He could not." Isn't that powerlessness?'

'I didn't mean that he couldn't because he was powerless to stop her. Let me give you an analogy to show you exactly what I mean. The only real analogue of the situation would be that of a man who has a little boy whom he loves tenderly, compassionately, and protectively. This son of his comes upon a garden and sees all the luxuriant flowers in it. There are also many thorns and stinging vermin in the garden, but the boy does not know of the harms it contains. He sees only the flowers and the richness of the place. Stirred by desire, his soul strains to get in. His father prevents him, because he knows about the harmful things the garden contains. The boy cries and presses, ignorant of the suffering

> that the thorns and vermin will cause him. So his father feels sorry for him. He is able to prevent him from going in but knows that he will not let up until he does go in and gets stung by a scorpion or pricked by a thorn. Then his passion will abate and his spirit will be at peace. So he lets him enter. And when he goes in he does get stung by a scorpion. He comes out again, and now his soul is not so eager any longer to go back, and he settles down.'[34]

Al-Rāzī's interlocutor finds the story puerile, contradictory and rather blasphemous, with its suggestions that the Sovereign of the universe was unable to keep order in his own household and was indeed a mere assistant at the world's creation. But for the philosopher this particular version of the myth of the fall of the soul has the advantage of discriminating clearly between the wisdom of God and the discursive intelligence of living beings, who are capable of learning only from experience. The liveliness of motion is beneath the dignity of God, whose impassivity is untouched by the vicissitudes concomitant with embodiment. But Soul is not immune to the attractive but ultimately noxious adventures of the flesh.

Existence in the barest sense, for al-Rāzī, does not depend on God. But order, peace and wisdom do. There is a kind of spontaneity, he argues, beyond the coercive force of nature and the compelling dictate of reason, without which the world would not exist.[35] Viewed in itself, creation is not an unqualified success. If God saw to it that the world was good, that was only by imposing some measure of his wisdom on what Soul had started, turning chaos into cosmos. Even then, such wisdom could be imposed only in the measure that time and space and matter could receive. For Soul, existence in the world was on the whole a loss – that is, when viewed strictly in the world's terms and without reference to what lies beyond the world. But in a larger sense, with reference to the larger life of the soul, worldly existence was, or rather is, a learning experience, necessary and appropriate to such timebound beings as we are, who can learn and find our true home in no other way.

Al-Rāzī's creationism serves his theism, but not in the straightforward *kalām* way of seeking a proof for the existence of God from the insufficiency of finite beings in accounting for themselves. Indeed the model of creation he puts forward does not prove but assumes the reality of God. Its aim, as I have argued elsewhere,[36] is to demonstrate, in the face of eternalist objections, that creation is indeed possible and not absurd. If creation is possible, then al-Rāzī can argue *a posteriori* for the reality of God as the source of order, form and intelligence in the cosmos. But to show convincingly that creation is possible he finds that he must concede the impossibility of transforming nothingness into being. He must adopt some version of *formatio mundi*, although not the Epicurean version, which would have material atoms simply arrange themselves. The order must come from God. Thus, where the *kalām* occasionalists sharply demarcate being from any proposed concomitants or successors, al-Rāzī admits the eternity of atoms but denies them any intrinsic capability of motion, let alone self-organization. Animation comes from Soul; form, from God.

By modelling creation as a drama played out among principles each of which is eternal and absolute but none of which alone could or would produce the observed effect, al-Rāzī not only differentiates the roles and responsibilities of each player in the drama but demonstrates, in the face of increasingly grave philosophical doubts and denials, the conceivability of creation itself. His model shows that creation is intelligible on assumptions that violate no law of logic and contradict none of the several posits or postulates that seem to al-Rāzī (and, he hopes, to his contemporaries) unabstractable from the natures of each of the players on his stage. God remains wise and good; matter, indestructible but inert; time and space, actual and undeniable even in the absence of motion; Soul, undying, active, animating, but irrational. Soul, of course, is the key mediating principle between God and nature. She is capable of incarnation and thus of self-alienation, but also open to inspiration and so, to redemption, not through the arbitrary and capricious favour claimed by scriptural religions, but through the universal revelation of reason, which God in his mercy vouchsafes to every human soul.[37]

Crucially, al-Rāzī's five eternals do not entail one another's being. They are not parts of a single inevitable system, a macrocosmic organism no aspect of which is conceivable without the rest. Their interaction is contingent, not upon God's will alone (which is invariant), but on the restiveness of the life principle, and the strange complementarity of its ignorance with God's supernal wisdom. So, although the five must be eternal, the world they constitute is not. Each of the five, even space, is real in a sense. But none of them alone would generate the world of nature. Being requires a dynamic. Only so does it acquire a history.

Al-Fārābī (*c.* AD 870–950), a trained logician and subtle commentator on Aristotle's *De Interpretatione*, has a clear idea of metaphysics. He does not expect cosmology or cosmogonic allegory to solve the problems of first philosophy. He understands perfectly that theology is only one component of first philosophy, belonging to it in so far as the study of being *qua* being commits us to an investigation of the 'first principles' or ontic foundations of being. And, unlike the thinkers of the *kalām*, he does not equate the positing of being with the bestowal of being by God. So he does not demand that one abstract away from the givenness of being as we know it all but the barest posit that can be conveyed by the reference of the term. Al-Fārābī is a committed defender of the eternity of the world. He knows intimately the arguments by which Aristotle defended his claim (directed against mythic modes of explanation) that it would be absurd to assign an origin to the entire cosmos and to time itself. He is capable of elaborate skirmishing with a creationist like John Philoponus.[38] To al-Fārābī the scriptural idea of creation is, like the sensuous rewards and punishments of the scriptural afterlife, a paradigm case of the sort of symbolism or myth that he ascribes to the poesy of prophets in their delicate and socially vital Platonic task of clothing in the rhetoric of pictorial imagination the truths apprehended on a conceptual plane by philosophical intelligence. The truth subtended by scripture's symbolic stories of creation is that of emanation, the ontic dependence of all being on the One. Al-Fārābī knows that the doctrine is not strictly Aristotelian. But he clearly believes that the metaphysics of Aristotle will not stand without it. For it is emanation that provides the dynamic, causal link between nature and the divine, not merely at the level of motion but metaphysically, at the level of being.

Aristotle chastised Plato for providing only a logical rather than a genuinely causal linkage between the forms and particulars. But Aristotle himself, in bringing the forms to earth and rendering them immanent, as the essences of the species of things, assigned a level of invariance and intelligibility to natural kinds that Plato never would have acknowledged there. And when Aristotle set about explaining the causal governance of nature by the divine, he was left only with an absolute Intelligence, *Nous*, whose thought had no identity or content but itself, whose causal efficacy was confined to the passive attracting of lesser intelligences, and whose response to the apprehension of its perfection was the ceaseless piloting of the spheres, in their rotary courses, in a vast and invariant choric dance. If Aristotle's aim was to transcend mythicism, his substitution of one pictorial symbolism for another had not taken him very far.

Successors were able to remedy the situation. Since Aristotle's principal objections against the Platonic forms were based on arguments that seemed to show that ideas cannot exist alone, finding a home for the forms was a powerful desideratum among Platonists. For monotheists like Philo (*c.* 25 BC–AD 40) it was natural to find that home in the mind of God, thus subordinating the ideas to God and resolving their claim to be divine principles themselves, as they so readily appear to be in Plato. Two further benefits followed directly: God's thought was no longer merely vacuous, as it seemed to be for Aristotle. For even in thinking himself God was now thinking all ideas. Second, since these ideas were no mere abstractions but the very plans and patterns of the world, the archetypes of creation, in knowing himself God knew nature, and, in projecting his ideas, God projected the natures of things, caused nature to be what it was, and exercised his sovereignty by governing nature and bestowing its character.

In Aristotle's theory of knowledge, that aspect of the mind called the active intellect is assigned the role of rendering actually understood concepts that are potentially intelligible, much as light makes it possible for visible objects to be seen. The Peripatetic systematizer and commentator Alexander of Aphrodisias (*fl.* AD 200) identified the active intellect with God and assigned to it the task of imparting forms to matter. Alexander thus ascribed the realization which all Aristotelian objects pursue to the action of God upon or within them. So now it could be understood how God's causal activity extended beyond the mere inspiring of the lesser intellects and induction of motion in the spheres. God's act was universal, extending to all teleological processes. God was the good that all pursued. And he moved things not merely as their goal or their ideal, but as the productive and energizing source of their activity.

Plotinus (AD 205–70), the founder of Neoplatonism, went further. Borrowing the Stoic idea of a divine energy that pervades, enspirits and animates the world, he discarded the Stoic materialist assumption that this spirit was a physical sort of energy and restored the Platonic equation of being with the intellectual. Yet the Stoic dynamic, of an animating intelligence that pervades nature, now understood in terms of the bestowal of form, being, unity, upon things in the measure of their receptivity, transformed the relationship of forms and particulars from a static logical connection of mere 'participation' to a dynamic causal relationship. At the same time, the idea of emanation, the vibrant radiation of form within all things, symbolized by the undiminished flowing of sunlight from the sun, allowed the adoption within Neoplatonism of an idea of divine creativity that did not depend on the suspect notion of scriptural monotheism (now engaged in increasingly strident polemics with the pagan philosophical tradition) that the world had an origin.

In the pantheon of Plotinus, Aristotle's *Nous* was no longer the supreme God. For intelligence, Plotinus argued, is not the very best of things. Above it stands pure unity, the Platonic Form of the Good, that is, God, the One. *Nous*, filled with the ideas, which are united under their most general exemplars but differentiated in their specificities, is not pure unity but a 'one many'. Yet because thought and thinker are identical, as Aristotle himself had observed, *Nous* is the ideas, that is, *Nous* is being. Its clarity and definiteness, its timeless knowledge, are the marks of being. Yet its existence, although eternal, is not self-sufficient or self-bestowed. The being of *Nous* is derived, imparted by the One, whose infinite power transcends even the determinacy of being.

The idea of emanation allows Neoplatonic philosophers to explain the differentiation of the One, how its generosity imparts being to *Nous*, to Psyche, the world soul, and to nature, whose temporality reflects the need of Psyche to think discursively and depart from the timeless and reflexive thinking of pure Intelligence. For if being is thought, creativity is productive thinking. Systematizers like Proclus did not hesitate to say that the One timelessly generates all that emanates from it in the same way that the point in geometry generates all figures, or that the number one generates (but clearly not in time) all numbers. For the simple was understood not as primitive but as ontically rich and potent. And indeed, in an intellectualist, Platonic ontology, logical relations were not really static at all but were causal and dynamic from the outset.

Al-Fārābī adopted and adapted all this. The active intellect, still a hypostasis, was no longer identified with God but was now merely the lowest and least in a train of disembodied intellects, descending from God, differentiated from him yet dependent on him and united to him by the focus of their thought upon him. Each of these bears responsibility for one of the celestial spheres:

> The active intellect is what ought to be understood by the 'Faithful Spirit' (Qur'ān 26.139) and the 'Holy Spirit' (Qur'ān 2.87). It is this which should be taken to be the vehicle of revelation to a man who is a prophet, and the intermediary between God on high and

a man who is inspired. Human felicity should be understood as the soul's coming within the active intellect's dominion, and the active intellect itself should be seen as man's overseer, giving any human being the very basis by which happiness is to be sought and attained, guiding him and showing him the way to his own well-being. Or, if God is taken to be the giver of these things to man, then we must understand that he does so through the active intellect. Alexander [of Aphrodisias] the Commentator says that it follows from the view of Aristotle that the active intellect governs not only man but also sublunary physical bodies, in concert with the celestial bodies, and that the celestial bodies in fact impart only motion, whereas the active intellect gives them the forms towards which they move.[39]

Al-Fārābī's interest in the allocation of governance over nature and man between the responsibilities of the active intellect and those of the spheres reflects a philosophical issue of critical importance to him. Proclus (AD 410–85) had criticized Aristotle for resting his theism on the Prime Mover argument, showing, in effect, that God was responsible for the motion but not the existence of the world. Plato seemed to Proclus to have found higher ground in the *Timaeus*. For even if the creation myth of that dialogue was not taken literally (and Proclus certainly did not take it literally), it referred through its symbols to the ontic dependence of nature on the forms and did not reduce the divine to a mere engine, active or passive, of the motions of the heavens. Simplicius, the eternalist adversary of Philoponus in the sixth century, reconciled the symbolism of the *Timaeus* myth with the Prime Mover argument by reminding those who might be worried by Proclus' critique that in an eternalist framework the creative force of emanation was not in the originating but in the sustaining of the world, and that precisely was the effect with which Aristotle's Prime Mover was charged. For the primary motions imparted to the spheres were the very principles of order in the cosmos, their regularities sustaining all natural regularities beneath them, from the cycles of the seasons to the rhythms of the generations in biology. So, if God was the Prime Mover, God was the creator in the only philosophically acceptable sense: the sustainer of the cosmic order, the imparter of all that differentiated cosmos from chaos.

Abū Bishr Mattā (d. AD 940), the Christian logician, humanist, translator and commentator, from whom al-Fārābī learned much, was aware of this Greek discussion and, in the spirit of Simplicius, papered over the disparity between the two approaches, arguing that if God was a cause of motion he was a cause of existence. For, as Simplicius had assumed, what it means for the cosmos to exist is for it to have the nature that it has, i.e. to move in the fashion that it does. The cosmos was traditionally identified with its largest parts, the celestial spheres. It was their motions that gave it its nature and determined the character of all processes beneath them, in the same sense that the motions of the members of an organism give it its nature, with the changes in the most important members (for example the heart, head, viscera and lungs) determining the complexion or general health of the whole. Drawing on Abu

Bishr's gloss, al-Fārābī, in summarizing Aristotle's *Metaphysics* book by book, simply substituted 'existence' for 'motion' at the crucial juncture, representing the famous teleological argument for the Prime Mover in Book Lambda as an argument for the ground of all existence and referring to the disembodied intellects not as the movers of the spheres but as the sources of the order in all things which emanate from them.[40]

Such glosses were profoundly dissatisfying to Avicenna (Ibn Sīnā, 980–1037). If the work of al-Razī showed anything, it showed that the imparting of motion, even of ordered motion, was not the imparting of being. And if the Proclean critique of Aristotle revealed anything, it revealed that the differences between Plato and Aristotle were real differences, demanding a choice between Plato's idea that nature is derivative from the true being of the eternal forms and Aristotle's affirmation that being itself is present, and inalienable, in the cosmos, in the heavenly bodies and in all natural kinds. Faced with this choice, Avicenna chose Plato. He agreed with al-Fārābī and the great majority of Neoplatonic Aristotelians that the world's origination was a myth whose literal sense would not withstand philosophic scrutiny. And he agreed that emanation was the deeper and philosophically robust meaning of that myth. But what emanation portends is not the imparting of motion.

Avicenna forged the great synthesis of Islamic philosophical metaphysics[41] by merging the naturalism of Aristotle and the emanation of Plotinus with the seemingly incompatible scriptural and *kalām* idea of the contingency of all finite being and of the cosmos itself. He achieved this synthesis through the recognition that the radical opposition between the *kalām* and Peripatetic views of being resulted from the application of rival assumptions which were not logically but only perspectivally opposed. When Aristotle argued that the being of a thing is its essence, that the properties of a thing are necessary (since without them it would not be what it was), and that the non-existence of those things which are real in the primary sense is self-contradictory, he was regarding being as a given, *assuming* its presence and seeking to discover its character. At the root of his thinking was the powerful suasion of Parmenides that non-existence is ultimately an absurdity, and that even becoming is problematic. When the thinkers of the *kalām* demanded that we infer no more from the posit of a substance than the bare fact of its existence, here and not elsewhere, now and not earlier or later, and by a power that could not possibly be its own, they were looking at being not as a fact but as a possibility which might or might not have been realized. Their inspiration, of course, was scripture, and the God's-eye view that scripture presents of the world as an artefact that need not have existed at all, need not have had the nature we discover, and surely need not continue for ever, or even for an instant longer than God pleases.

The two views were not irreconcilable. Considered in itself, Avicenna argued, any finite being is contingent. For it does not contain the sufficient grounds or basis of its own existence. It requires its causes to give it being and sustain it. Yet, considered in relation to those causes, it is necessary. They necessitate it. For the causes of a thing are the necessary and sufficient conditions of its existence. Natural science is the study of those causes. And, contrary to the anti-naturalism implicit in the *kalām*, such science is possible and indeed unavoidable. For no finite thing exists in isolation. Each exists embedded in a context that gives it definition and, in that profoundly Aristotelian sense, gives it being. But no causal sequence or system, Avicenna argues, using the premisses of Aristotle himself, can be extended to infinity. This does not mean, as al-Kindī and many another creationist assumed, that the sequence of seasons and generations does not go on forever. Avicenna was convinced that the world's age is infinite. But he was equally convinced, on good Aristotelian grounds, that the natural order itself is not self-sustaining. A finite, closed system, he reasoned, in which each member is both a cause and an effect, could never be a self-sufficient being. So even an eternal cosmos requires a cause, and on good Platonic and Neoplatonic grounds Avicenna sought the cause of the world's being (and not just its order) beyond the transient phenomena and events of nature, in the celestial intellects and spheres, and ultimately in God.

Avicenna anchored his idea of being in the distinction between essence and existence. The distinction itself was not radically new. It had been latent in Plato's differentiation of forms from particulars and acknowledged by Aristotle when he clearly differentiated the question of what a thing is from the question of whether such a thing exists. But in Avicenna the distinction acquired a new and central significance. For when Aristotle distinguished *what?* from *whether?* he pointedly confined the issue to the instantiation of specific essences. The existence of a given particular might be problematic – was there or was there not a man or a beast, say, that met a given description? But the existence of natural species and of the cosmos itself was unquestionable. Existence was not, as it became in Avicenna's philosophy, 'an accident superadded to the essence of a thing'. On the contrary, Aristotle had analysed existence in terms of essence when he declared that the being of a thing was its essence, its definiteness as a conceptually identifiable member of its kind.

For Avicenna, by contrast, with the seconding his philosophy received from the mythic vision of scripture and the imaginative vision of *kalām*, all being but that of God was problematic; none was self-sufficient. The cosmos and all natural kinds could conceivably have been other than we find them. All finite things are contingent, then, as the *mutakallimūn* held. Their natures and even their existence are not necessary, for there is no contradiction in the denial of any fact about them. Considered in itself, any determinate thing is contingent; and, if it does exist, it is necessary only in relation to the causes that give it being. If we posit a cause, as Aristotle habitually did, we must infer the effect. But if we wish to emphasize the dependence of effect on cause, then we can abstract from the cause and argue that without its action the effect would not exist. That is what Genesis does when it calls up within our minds the image of a world not yet created. True, the cosmos for Avicenna is eternal. But the conceptual force behind the scriptural image of creation, he believes, is captured in the idea of contingency. Even though the world is eternal, it is contingent, still dependent on its timeless cause. *Formatio mundi* is no acceptable alternative. For it preserves beings that are not only eternal but self-sufficient and self-subsistent, the matter, time and Soul of al-Rāzī, for example, not to mention al-Rāzī's scandalous space, positing the reality of non-existence. To make ultimates of the ingredients of nature was as much as to render them divine, and the real scandal of al-Rāzī's story was not that God became the mere midwife of the Soul, but that matter, Soul, time and space were made capable of existence on their own, without any help at all from God.

Fortunately, Avicenna could show that logic barred the way to such assumptions. For, as the *kalām* idea of possibility revealed, any determinacy in a being, whether its having a definite character or even its having rather than lacking existence, can be denied without contradiction and so must be regarded as contingent. Necessity is found only in what cannot be denied, that is, only in a being whose essence is identical with its existence and whose reality it is self-contradictory to deny. God is that being, the ultimate cause demanded by the very contingency of all lesser beings, since they are inadequate to explain or existentiate themselves. Thus, in a sense rejected by later monotheists but metaphysically far stronger than that allowed by al-Rāzī's myth of the world's formation, Avicenna's God can still be called creator – not that he originates the world, but in the sense that he and he alone is ultimately responsible for all that is.

Avicenna's insistence on the eternity of the cosmos, in the face of what he saw as compelling Aristotelian and Neoplatonic arguments, sat ill with defenders of scriptural creation. The difficulty was not simply a fundamentalist backlash in defence of scriptural literalism. For, as Maimonides (AD 1135–1204), the Jewish philosopher, jurist and physician, argued, rational theology has no trouble allegorizing scripture when its apparent sense seems to run up against the firm requirements of reason, as it does, for example, in the case of Biblical anthropomorphisms. Rather the difficulty was the tension between eternity and contingency. Al-Ghazālī (AD 1058–1111), the Muslim theologian who came through a crucible of spiritual doubts to speak out as the champion of Islam at the dawn of its sixth century, took to task the entire school of Neoplatonic Aristotelian philosophers, with Avicenna at their head, for assigning to God responsibility for a nature that was eternal. What is eternal, by Aristotle's own standards, al-Ghazālī insisted, needs no cause, and the Muslim philosophers were atheists in spite of themselves. For no meaning could be given to their notion that God was the 'author' (*Ṣāni'*) of the world if the world had no origin.

Maimonides softened the blow. He withheld al-Ghazālī's charge that the system of Avicenna was incoherent, and he did not accuse the philosophers of atheism. But he did regard their eternalism as problematic and ultimately untenable. It was a mistake, he argued, to try to prove or disprove creation apodeictically. Such efforts led only to the absurd overburdening of God in the *kalām*, making him responsible directly for every single action and event that will ever occur, and rendering otiose and vain all the apparent natural causes of the observed phenomena. The misguided effort to find demonstrative arguments *against* creation, on the other hand, led to the philosophers' needless battles with the mutability of nature and their projection on to the very act of creation of the notions of time, matter, change and potentiality that we extract from our examination of the settled order of nature as we find it today.

Yet although it was misguided to try to make a logical necessity or a metaphysical truth out of creation, Maimonides did not believe that there were no good reasons on either side of the debate between creation and eternity. Thus he did not reject the project of metaphysics itself as a human attempt to characterize being at large, particularly with regard to the crucial question of its grounding, that is, its self-sufficiency or contingency. Creation, he argued, was the more probable view, and preferable to eternalism on theological grounds as well: probable, because it made more sense to speak of the world's determinacy (including the determination of existence over non-existence) as requiring a cause if one conceived of a time before which the relevant determinations had not yet been made; preferable, because the only sort of cause that could be relied upon to make the necessary determinations without some prior basis for discrimination was a voluntary cause. Only by conceiving God as freely choosing the act of creation and assigning rather than simply accepting the nature of the world, Maimonides and al-Ghazālī agreed, could one understand how sheer unity would permit the emergence of multiplicity at all. The strict determinism that seemed to follow from the equation of being with necessity was objectionable enough if it made of emanation a mere automatism or a matter of mathematical implication. But, extended to its full extreme, such necessitarianism excluded change altogether. Far from requiring God's act, the view that things must be as and what they are froze emanation in its tracks and bound divine generosity and grace in isolated self-containment. The world without voluntary creation could not proceed from God, and Aristotle lay trapped within the monism of Parmenides.

The project of the philosophers, as Avicenna understood, had been from the beginning an explanatory one. Its aim had been to find the causal foundations and ontic groundworks of reality, that is, of the changing, multifarious and colourful world we observe. Thus even the stoutest efforts of the philosophers against creation did not debar the idea of emanation, which was, after all, a kind of continuous creation that curiously paralleled and seemed to mock the instant-by-instant creation of the *kalām*. But if the efforts of the philosophers to link nature to the divine were truly given their head and the unity and timelessness of the One were indeed to be regarded as projected forth from on high and precipitated down through the spheres with the true automatism of the logical, concretized as the natural, then change would have to be regarded as impossible, and the multiplicity we observe would have to be acknowledged, contrary to every explanatory impulse of the Neoplatonic Aristotelians, as an illusion.

Emanation (even from its inception in the thinking of Plotinus) absorbs some of the function and force of the idea of creation. But creationist thinkers in turn absorb much of the power of Aristotelian naturalism, and of the emanationist scheme itself, especially if they can assure themselves, as al-Ghazālī and Maimonides seek to do, of their ability to reconcile it with the free grace of God and the free choice of human subjects. Both al-Ghazālī and Maimonides, while criticizing Avicenna, avail themselves of his distinctive hybrid of necessity and contingency. What they value most in Avicenna is his recognition that the *mutakallimūn* were right in holding that determinate things could not determine themselves. But the very determinacy and lack of self-sufficiency to which *kalām* made its appeal demand an openness to causality and, even if only tacitly, lean on a commitment to naturalism. If any causes, whether natural or emanative, determine their effects, that will mean that they necessitate them: what is contingent in itself will be, as Avicenna held, necessary with reference to its causes. Surely, as Maimonides argued, it was better to integrate the observed or apparent causes of events, those that practice and observation correlate with specific outcomes, into a nexus between the ultimate causality of God and the final observed effect than to treat such observed concomitants of events as mere otiose bystanders to outcomes in which they play no role.

Al-Ghazālī, for his part, had no desire to defend the occasionalist notion that appearances have no real connection to what actually occurs. He accepted the idea that things have essences and that it is logically impossible for the members of a species to lack the properties of their genus – for a corpse, for example, to think, since consciousness presupposes life. Things are not as isolated from one another as the occasionalists of the *kalām* presumed; and indeed the arguments of Avicenna against the atomism of the *kalām* led al-Ghazālī to distance himself from that atomism, even as he relied on the creationism it had been meant to vindicate. As for Maimonides, he defended a vigorous naturalism and voluntarism, which rested on the idea that God delegates the power of action to his creatures, in stable patterns for the lower orders, but according to rational choice for moral agents, that is, human beings.

But the order of nature is not a matter of logical necessity. The connection observed between what is familiarly regarded as a cause and what is regarded as its effect, al-Ghazālī argued, in the face of a long tradition of Aristotelian essentialism and Neoplatonic logicism, is not a necessary one. For the two are discrete events, and neither entails the other. Thus God may intervene in nature to alter or contain the fixed natures of things, confining the power of fire so that it does not burn the flesh of Abraham, God's intimate, when that prophet is cast into the furnace by the tyrant Nimrod. There is no contradiction in such intervention, so it is not impossible. And God, of course, can create. The idea that time has a beginning is not incoherent. Maimonides, whose commitment to naturalism was warmer than al-Ghazālī's, was no less firm in his recognition that natural necessities are not necessities of logic. Following Avicenna's (and ultimately al-Fārābī's[42]) lead, he distinguished carefully between hypothetical and categorical necessities, arguing that the regularities observed in nature are indeed the results of a necessity, but not of an absolute requirement of the very logic of being. Rather, they are expressions of the essences and dispositions which God imparted at the creation. They are, in the words that later medieval scholastics would assign, with their distinctive flair for terminological niceties, 'ordinary', that is, ordained necessities, the stable outcomes of God's free determinations. Even miracles, Maimonides argues, can be accommodated to the naturalism of such creative ordination by adapting the midrashic conceit that ascribes the mouth of the fish that swallowed Jonah, the mouth of the earth that swallowed Korah and other portentous figures of scriptural history to the twilight of the sixth day of creation, as ordained departures from the otherwise unexceptioned course of natural history. But such events are marginal cases. The normal one deals with events whose course is uniform, in the phrase that Maimonides adopts from Aristotle, 'always or for the most part'. The Aristotelian Neoplatonists who took as their own the title of philosophers were wrong to imagine that such regularities or even necessities of nature could not have been otherwise. Such unwarranted assumptions stemmed simply from the projection of the familiar necessities of nature upon the formative, as yet unformed stages of existence.[43] The past was undetermined by the created determinants that now exist. We must conceive it so, if the very idea of determination is to have any meaning. The present is not fixed in logical necessity; and the future lies open.[44]

Of all the Muslim philosophers, it was Averroes (Ibn Rushd, AD 1126–98), the Cordovan philosopher, physician and *Qāḍī* of Seville, scion of a long line of *qāḍīs* and author of the great Arabic commentary on the *Metaphysics* and other works of Aristotle, who understood most clearly what Aristotle meant by his analysis of being. Averroes saw that being, for a committed Aristotelian, must mean the essence of a thing. And, bearing the brunt of al-Ghazālī's devastating critique of the philosophers in *The Incoherence of the Philosophers*, he saw that he must sever the dependence of Islamic philosophy on the synthesis of Avicenna if he was to save that philosophy for Aristotle. So, in his rebuttal to al-Ghazālī, *The Incoherence of the Incoherence*, he repeatedly isolated Avicenna as no true spokesman of Peripatetic philosophy, recognizing in effect that eternity was, as al-Ghazālī claimed, incompatible with Avicennan contingency, but opting for naturalism and eternalism, not contingency.

Avicenna was wrong, Averroes reasoned, to treat existence as an accident, which a given essence might have or lack. The differences among the Aristotelian categories are deeper than mere generic differences, variants on a single theme. Category differences do not merely differentiate the expressions of a single idea that we can recognize and study as being, in itself. For what is meant by the being of a time, a place, a habit or relation has nothing in common but only a structural relationship, a way of affirming but no common content of affirmation, with what is meant by the being of a particular substance or a species. When we say that metaphysics is the science of being *qua* being (*al-mawjūd bimā huwa mawjūd*), what we mean is that metaphysics seeks pure being.

Such knowledge, in its absoluteness, belongs to God alone, as he contemplates his own unique simplicity. We humans approach it when we consider the being of the disembodied Intelligences, which are as clear of matter, potentiality and otherness as any object that does not lie (as God does, in his indefiniteness) beyond being and (in his absoluteness) wholly or all but wholly beyond our comprehension.

In the end, Averroes will reject even emanation, for its presumption that being is an accident imparted to particulars. His natural theology will revert to Aristotle's reliance on the Prime Mover, abandoning al-Fārābī's effort to find a Neoplatonic meaning for the scriptural idea of creation. The purity of Aristotelian philosophy is thus restored. But al-Kindī's project of naturalizing Aristotelian metaphysics in Islam is lost. In the East, Persian philosophers will continue for centuries to work out the relations between Avicennan metaphysics and Sufi monism. And, in the Kabbalah, Jewish theosophists will continue for centuries to play out the metaphysical drama of Maimonidean theological voluntarism against a backdrop painted with the increasingly lifelike symbolisms of Neoplatonic, gnostic and Neopythagorean myth. Averroes' insights and arguments will take hold in the minds of many Jewish Maimonideans, and indeed Avicenna's doctrine of contingency will find a following among Jewish and Christian theistic voluntarists. But, in the Hebrew literature sprung from the long sojourn of Jewish thinkers in Islamic lands, philosophy after Averroes is increasingly on the defensive, for its perceived commitment to eternalism and its seeming inability to accommodate the will and personhood of God. And in Arabic writings, philosophy has yet to regain the assurance that it had in the Middle Ages. No Arabic writer after Averroes openly and confidently offers to declare, out of reason and critical thought alone, the true nature of being, the character of reality at large.

NOTES

1 See Hanna Kassis, *A Concordance of the Qur'ān* (Berkeley: University of California Press, 1983), pp. 239–54.
2 The poets are Bishr ibn Abī Khāzim and Nābighah al-Dhubyānī, both of the latter half of the sixth century; see F. Rosenthal, *Knowledge Triumphant: The Concept of Knowledge in Medieval Islam* (Leiden: Brill, 1970), pp. 14, 17.
3 For a generous survey of *kalām* and allied definitions and general descriptions of knowledge, see Rosenthal, op. cit., pp. 46–69.
4 *De Anima* III. 5; I follow the Oxford translation as emended by Jonathan Barnes in *The Complete Works of Aristotle* (Princeton: Princeton University Press, 1985).
5 Here I follow the old Oxford translation of J. A. Smith, which seems to me clearer than the Barnes version.
6 *Posterior Analytics* II. 19, 100a4–14.
7 *Eudemian Ethics* VII. 14, 1248a18–28.
8 See *Le Commentaire de Jean Philopon sur le troisième livre du Traité de l'âme d'Aristotle*, ed. M. Corte (Liège: Faculté de Philosophie et Lettres, Université de Liège/Paris: Droz, 1930), p. 30.

9 See J. Finnegan (ed.), 'Texte arabe du *Peri Nou* d'Alexandre d'Aphrodise', *Mélanges de l'Université St. Josef* 33 (1956), 157–202, see 186–7, 189, 194; Jean Jolivet, *L'Intellect selon Kindī* (Leiden: Brill, 1971), p. 38.

10 See al-Kindī, *Risāla fī 'l-'Aql*, Arabic text in R. J. McCarthy, 'Al-Kindī's treatise on the intellect', *Islamic Studies* 3 (1964), 122–4; French translation in Jolivet, op. cit., pp. 1–6.

11 'Statement on the Soul abstracted from the book of Aristotle and Plato and other philosophers [*sic*]', *Rasā'il al-Kindī*, ed. M. A. H. Abū Ridā, (Cairo: Dār al-Fikr al-'Arabi, (1950–3), p. 273.

12 See al-Fārābī, *Risāla fī 'l-'Aql*, ed. M. Bouyges (Beirut: Catholic Press, 1938).

13 Emil Fackenheim, Philip Merlan and others have suggested that in his 'Essay on love', Avicenna at least temporarily made an exception to his outspoken rejections of the doctrine of 'union' (*ittiḥād*). But, as I showed in *Avicenna* (London: Routledge, 1992), pp. 163–72, the suggestion rests on a mistranslation. Avicenna does not endorse *ittiḥād* but resolves the Sufi references to such union in terms of his own preferred idea of contact, *ittiṣāl.*

14 See Nabil Shehaby, *The Propositional Logic of Avicenna* (a translation from the *Shifā': al-Qiyās*) (Dordrecht: Reidel, 1973), pp. 54–5.

15 See A.-M. Goichon (trans.), *Ibn Sīnā: Livre des directives et remarques* (Paris: Vrin, 1951), pp. 56–9.

16 Avicenna, *Najāt*, trans. after Fazlur Rahman, *Avicenna's Psychology* (Westport, Conn.: Hyperion, 1951), pp. 36–7.

17 See Ibn Ṭufayl, *Ḥayy Ibn Yaqẓān* (Los Angeles: Gee Tee Bee, 1983; first published New York, 1972), pp. 150–5.

18 Bashshār ibn Burd, *Diwān*, ed. M. Tahir b. Ashur (Cairo, 1950–7), 1.242, line 5.

19 Al-Jāḥiẓ, *Tria Opuscula*, ed. G. van Vloten (Lugd. Bat., 1903), 102, line 12 = ed. Ch. Pellat, *Kitāb al-Tarbī wa-'l-Tadwīr* (Damascus, 1955), p. 27.

20 Dimashqī, *Kitāb Nuḥbat al-Dahr fī 'Ajā'ib al-Barr wa-'Baḥr*, ed. A. F. Mehren (St Petersburg, 1866), p. 78.

21 Ibn Rushd, *Tahāfut al-Tahāfut*, ed. Maurice Bouyges (Beirut: Catholic Press, 1930), 21, line 6.

22 Aristotle, *Kitāb al-āthār al-ulwīya*, translated by Yaḥyā ibn al-Biṭrīq in the eighth century, ed. A.-R. Badawi (Cairo, 1961), 92, line 4.

23 The Presidency of Islamic Researches, Ifta', Call and Guidance, *The Holy Qur'ān: English Translation of the Meanings and Commentary* (Riyadh: King Fahd Holy Qur'ān Printing Complex, n.d., *c.* 1990), p. 1148 n. 3421.

24 See Maimonides, *Guide to the Perplexed* 1.73 and my discussion in *Rambam: Readings in the Philosophy of Moses Maimonides* (New York: Viking, 1976), pp. 124–55.

25 Al-Ash'arī, *Kitāb al-Luma'*, ed. and trans. R. J. McCarthy (Beirut: Catholic Press, 1953), pp. 76–81.

26 See Aristotle, *Metaphysics* 1.4, 985a18.

27 Al-Kindī, *On First Philosophy*, trans. Alfred Ivry as *Al-Kindī's Metaphysics* (Albany: State University of New York Press, 1974), p. 73.

28 Al-Kindī, 'Essay on how to banish sorrow', eds H. Ritter and R. Walzer, in *Uno Scritto Morale Inedito di al-Kindī*, Reale Accademia Nazionale dei Lincei Series 6, vol. VIII, first fascicle (Rome, 1938).

29 Al-Kindī, *On First Philosophy*, p. 65.

30 ibid., p. 67.

31 ibid., p. 84.

32 See L. E. Goodman, 'The translation of Greek materials into Arabic', in *The Cambridge History of Arabic Literature*, vol. II, *Religion, Learning and Science in the 'Abbasid Period*

(Cambridge: Cambridge University Press, 1984), p. 482.

33 'Munāẓarāt bayna al-Razīyayn', in *Abi Bakr Mohammadi filii Zachariae Raghensis Opera Philosophica Fragmentaque quae Supersunt*, ed. Paul Kraus (Cairo: Fouad I University, 1939), p. 308.

34 ibid., pp. 309–10.

35 ibid., pp. 311–12.

36 See L. E. Goodman, 'Rāzī's myth of the fall of the soul and its function in his philosophy', in G. F. Hourani (ed.), *Essays on Islamic Philosophy and Science* (Albany: State University of New York Press, 1975), pp. 25–40.

37 See al-Rāzī, op. cit., pp. 295–300.

38 See al-Fārābī, *Against John the Grammarian*, trans. M. Mahdi, *Near Eastern Studies* 26 (1967), 253–60, and Mahdi's discussion, pp. 233–53.

39 Al-Fārābī, *K. Mabādi 'ārā' 'ahlu 'l-madīnatu 'l-fāḍila* (*The Book of the Principles Underlying the Beliefs of the People of the Virtuous State*), ed. R. Walzer as *Al-Farabi on the Perfect State* (Oxford: Oxford University Press, 1985), pp. 52, 54; the translation here is my own.

40 Al-Fārābī, *Maqālah fī aghrād mā ba'd al-tabī ah*, trans. T.-A. Druart, in 'Le Traité d'al-Fārābī sur les buts de la *Métaphysique* d'Aristote', *Bulletin de Philosophie Médiéval* 24 (1982), 43.

41 See L. E. Goodman, *Avicenna* (London: Routledge, 1992).

42 See L. E. Goodman, 'Al-Fārābī's modalities', *Iyyun* 23 (1972), 100–12; in Hebrew with English summary.

43 See L. E. Goodman, *Rambam* (New York: Viking, 1976), pp. 183–204.

44 See L. E. Goodman, 'Three meanings of the idea of creation', in David Burrell and Bernard McGinn (eds), *God and Creation* (Notre Dame: Notre Dame University Press, 1990) and the further discussion in L. E. Goodman, *God of Abraham* (Oxford: Oxford University Press, 1996), pp. 236–75.

FURTHER READING

Goodman, L. E. (1992) *Avicenna*, London: Routledge.

Ivry, A. (1974) *Al-Kindi's Metaphysics*, Albany: Suny – a translation of Al-Kindi's *On First Philosophy*.

Rosenthal, F. (1970) *Knowledge Triumphant: The Concept of Knowledge in Medieval Islam*, Leiden, Brill.

Shehady, N. (1973) *The Propositional Logic of Avicenna*, Dordrecht, Reidel.

47

MORALS AND SOCIETY IN ISLAMIC PHILOSOPHY

Lenn E. Goodman

Islamic ethics develops in three phases: scriptural, elaborated in the *ḥadīth*, a vast literature of traditions attributed to the Prophet; the legal system (*fiqh*) that builds on that foundation, incorporating matter from other Middle Eastern traditions and seeking, like them, to reduce normative and ritual praxis to law; and pietistic, articulated in the sayings, writings and practice of the Sufi orders and mosque community, which for centuries have popularized Islamic norms among highly diverse communities. To committed Muslims Sufism, the Islamic tradition of mystical *gnosis*, has seemed to spring organically from the spirit of the Qur'ān as a way of life rather than a mere conceptual option. Sufi orders disseminate and define an Islamic ethos, using channels of transmission and chains of authority that are at once literary, charismatic, transgenerational and trans-cultural. Penetrating but never dominating Islamic ethical thought have been three kindred but rival intellectual traditions: *falsafa* (philosophy), *adab* (literary tradition) and *kalām* (dialectical theology).

Falsafa, philosophy proper, arises from the Arabic translations of Greek philosophical and scientific classics sponsored by Arab princes and notables of the eighth to tenth centuries.[1] As its name suggests, *falsafa* was seen as an import, but its perspectives and even methods were deeply naturalized. *Kalām*, dialectical theology, may have begun in the confessional debates following the Islamic conquests, but it continued among hundreds of movements, sects, schisms, parties, factions and opinions that express the heterogeneity of backgrounds and commitments of the early adherents of Islam. Over the centuries *mutakallimūn*, practitioners of *kalām*, carried their debates from a primitive yet often conceptually radical doggedness about core theological values to a pitch of high scholastic seriousness about a wide range of theological issues, whose ramifications in ethics included sustained critical discussions of theistic subjectivism, determinism, the sanctions of sin and the anatomy of action. *Adab* was the literary tradition of the administrative class, which looked past the boasts and lampoons of pre-Islamic poetry to the urbane mores of the court and chancery. Arabic prose was its creation; it valued culture, refinement and statesmanship. Reason in Islamic law meant analogy with precedent; in *kalām* it meant dialectical, hypothetical inference; in *falsafa*, rational intuition and the deductive syllogism; but in *adab* reason meant deference to experience, the learning and wisdom of the nations to which Islam had made its adherents the rightful heirs.

Qur'ānic ethics is presumptive, much as Qur'ānic narrative is allusive.[2] Ecstatic visions and legislative oracles appear against a moral background to which the voice of revelation responds powerfully, sometimes violently. Muḥammad's meditations and his abhorrence of the rude ways of his contemporaries fed his visionary pronouncements of divine judgement and led to his adoption of a monitory role modelled on the Hebrew prophets. His moral vision distinctively mixes puritan revulsion and earthy permissions: gambling, alcohol, fornication and faithlessness are condemned, with powerful apocalyptic sanctions. Those who submit to God will be supernally rewarded; the heedless, who give the lie to the Prophet and reject God's word, will suffer transcendently. The permissions include the well-known admission of four wives and unspecified concubines – provided the wives are treated fairly. Rejection of the Jewish dietary restrictions (except the one on pork) aids the Prophet in distinguishing Islam from the religion of his Jewish contemporaries among the Arabs, with whom he had for a time sought followers; so does shifting the direction of prayer from Jerusalem to Mecca. Arab culture is accommodated in the adoption of the Kaaba as a sacred site, adaptation of the Arab pilgrim festival and sacrifices, conciliatory references (later withdrawn) to pagan goddesses, and the unquestioning acceptance of familiar spirits, the *jinn*. But the Biblical and rabbinic heritage remains evident in the effort to regulate inheritances, prayer and blood payments, and the punishment of adultery – which last requires four eyewitnesses to the overt act, in view of the gravity of the offence and its penalty.

Like Biblical Judaism, Qur'ānic Islam does not sharply divide law from morals, ritual symbolism from spiritual commitment. Like Biblical Christianity, it does not sharply distinguish matters of faith from matters of allegiance. It speaks to an embattled community of believers – at first a beleaguered minority, later a militant and triumphalist authority – so it does not count spirituality in the first instance as a personal or private matter. Hence the communal character of Islamic mysticism and the legalist, rigourist tone of its devotional and ethical requirements. Unlike the ethics of Plato or Marx, but like the scriptural ethics of the sister religions, Qur'ānic ethics does not relativize its means to the ends it seeks, or countenance violation of its standards in pursuit of its aims. It is an ethics not of virtues but of imperatives. It does not in the first intention seek to foster a certain kind of human character but prescribes a way of life through commands and prohibitions whose fulfilment will define an ethos but whose performance is an end in itself. This is not to say that Qur'ānic ethics is inflexible or without its tensions; but the exceptions to scripturally derived rules must be built into the rules themselves, and any inner contradictions must remain implicit – and so almost invisible to the faithful. Obedience to God's will is the clearest mark of faith, and faith is the basis of justification.

Rationalists of the Mu'tazilite school of *kalām* argued on Stoic lines that God, being benevolent, is properly conceived as making his will known through revelation and requiting human actions by punishment and reward. But the rival Ash'arite school was largely successful in claiming greater orthodoxy when it held that God has no obligations to mere creatures: all events including human decisions about allegiance or rebellion are created by God, and even if God rewarded disobedience and punished faithfulness, we would still be obligated to obey our lord; God would still be just, since there is no injustice to a chattel. The Qur'ān, to be sure, is no systematic theology, and many of the problems that vexed the *mutakallimūn* were unseen by the Prophet, whose rhetoric of divine omnipresence and absolute control on the one hand and human moral accountability and responsibility on the other allowed him to come down firmly on both sides of the divide between free will and determinism, and many another issue where *mutakallimūn* were to see grounds for disagreement. But the Ash'arites were surely not mistaken in seeing in the Qur'ān a powerful predestinarianism that was stifled by the Mu'tazilites.[3]

Just as Islam did not confine itself to its original Arab audience, Islamic ethics does not confine itself to its Qur'ānic base. The medium of *ḥadīth* absorbed a wide range of folk and traditional materials now heard from the mouth of the Prophet (whereas God is the speaker in the Qur'ān). Moral attitudes, advice, restrictions and interpretations that might have sounded out of place in the oracular Qur'ān here find an authority second only to that of revelation. A *ḥadīth* is literally a piece of news, in this case, about the sayings and doings of the Prophet and his circle, as relayed by his companions and the generations of traditionists. Hundreds of thousands were collected by the early scholars of Islam. Expanded and winnowed, the corpus became the basis of a core half-dozen authoritative collections whose reports, classified by theme, remain a source of ethical and ritual exemplars and precepts. Indeed, Sunnī Islam takes its name and claim to orthodoxy from the ideal of adhering to the practice (*sunna*) of the Prophet; and Shī'ī Islam, while placing greater emphasis on personal and familial charisma, also upholds the idea of the precedent of the Prophet and stoutly maintains its own set of *ḥadīths*. By no means all *ḥadīth* material is authentic in the literal sense. The *ḥadīth* speaks with many and sometimes contradictory voices and is far from representing a cult of personality – unless allowance is made for the projection of a prophetic persona, itself an artefact of the *ḥadīth*. But *ḥadīth* does authentically express the spirit of the Islamic community in its formative centuries and remains a source of inspiration to Muslims. Its contents may echo the Gospels, Talmud, Persian wisdom literature or pre-Islamic Arab proverbs, but the process of selection and elaboration yields a coherent tenor, in which the standards of the idealized persona are spelled out: there is a push towards the puritan and supererogatory, rigour becomes an ideal in a way that no revealed scripture acting alone could enunciate, and the expressions of liberality or good humour assigned to the Prophet acquire striking emphasis, as marks of the release of tension and self-demand. Pietist ideals of saintliness and devotion appear here, embroidering the full tapestry of life around the Qur'ānic pronouncements, much as Talmudic or monastic traditions seek to transform every instant of life into a focal point of reverence, as if introducing a new set of categories.

From the sea of *ḥadīth* one cannot extract a single essence, but the salt flavour of the whole is still detectable in every part. There are treatments of faith, knowledge, purification (including how to wipe one's shoes and clean one's teeth), prayer, funerals, charity, visiting the sick, fasting, trade, marriage, divorce, pilgrimage, freeing slaves, paying debts of guilt and honour, fighting the holy war (*jihād*), permitted and forbidden foods, clothing and ornaments, modes of address, sitting, standing, laughing, sneezing, yawning and sexual intercourse. Bukhārī's collection reports the words of the Prophet: 'None of you truly has faith if he does not desire for his brother what he desires for himself.' From the same source:

> The Prophet of God said, 'Help your brother Muslim whether he be oppressor or oppressed.' People asked, 'Messenger of God, if he is oppressed we shall help him, but how shall we help him if he is the oppressor?' He replied: 'Prevent him from oppressing.'

The *ḥadīth* looks back to the Biblical and rabbinic formulations of the Golden Rule but also ahead to later conditions, for which the Prophet's authoritative teaching as a paragon of moral wisdom is never found wanting.[4]

Both Bukhārī and Muslim report the often-cited words ascribed to Muḥammad: 'Whoever obeys me obeys God. . . . Whoever obeys the Commander of the Faithful obeys me.' In the same vein: 'Hear and obey, though an Abyssinian with a head like a raisin be placed over you.' But in a tradition as richly diverse as the *ḥadīth*, even so categorical a command will not go unqualified. So the caveat is heard, still in the voice of the Prophet: 'But only so long as one is not ordered to disobey God.' In that case, 'there is no hearing and no obeying'. Sometimes the Prophet of the *ḥadīth* adopts a world-weary tone: authority, he advises, is 'a good suckler but a poor weaner'. Yet the thrust is always pragmatic, addressed to the exigencies of experience. The tension between the demands of allegiance and those of perceived principle is not to be erased. But when a synthesis is attempted it leans towards constituted authority: government (*al-sulṭān*) is the shadow of God on earth; all of his servants who are downtrodden shall turn to it. When it is just it shall be rewarded and the flock must be grateful; when it is oppressive, the burden redounds to it and the flock must bear it patiently. Like Hobbes, Muslim jurists sometimes sound like Calvin: they too know the horrors of civil war and anarchy: 'If anyone sees something hateful in his commander', the Prophet is made to say, 'let him bear it patiently. For no one breaks with the community by so much as a handsbreadth without dying the death of the *jāhiliyya*' – the barbarous days of ignorance before the dispensation of Islam. 'If two khalifs are given the oath, kill the second!'

These standards, to be sure, left and still leave gaps broad enough to march armies through, yet they weave a network of norms that spreads into the personal realm and back again to the communal. They are powerfully seconded by the predestinarian voice in the Qur'ān. There is no fatalism normatively, if fatalism means that individual acts and choices make no difference in the scheme of things. The most predestinarian Muslim theologians held vigorously to Qur'ānic accountability; when they held that God creates our acts, they meant that God acts through us – creating motion, sin or sickness *in us*, not in himself, yet acting all-powerfully none the less, as in the Qur'ānic paradigm: 'When you shot it was not you who shot but God' (8.17). Man is accountable, the Ash'arites argued, because he *appropriates* a choice, not because he 'makes' it. Morally each person is responsible, but – here is the surreptitious, distinctively medieval sting – each in his own sphere: every one of you is a shepherd and must answer for his flock, the Prophet urges – the Imam for the people, a man for his household, a woman for her husband's house and children, a slave for his master's goods. As so often in popular thought, there is little concern for formal coherence with other contexts, and the most distinctive message is in the sub-text that gives definition to the terms 'we', 'you' and 'they'.

A fundamental aim of Islamic law and principles of jurisprudence is to ordain what is good and prohibit what is wicked. Ibn Taymiyya (d. AD 1328), whose name is still a watchword of Muslim fundamentalists, explains that *jihād* is the logical completion of this obligation and that the broad moral command to institute morality has the same prescriptive status as *jihād* – a powerful, positive obligation, 'among the most important duties we are ordered to perform', falling on individuals to the extent of their ability and on the institutions of an Islamic society systematically. The first four caliphs, writes the jurist al-Māwardī (d. AD 1058), needed no courts of equity, for in their day the sway of faith was strong and mere admonitions sufficed to halt wrongdoing – aided, in the case of wild Bedouin, perhaps, with a little strong-arming. But as society grew more complex and outrages by the great against the small became more frequent, such courts were established, with their judges, jurisconsults, guards and bailiffs, scribes and witnesses. The statutory penalties were exacted for apostasy, fornication, theft, wine-drinking and the rest.

The demand to ordain what is right and prohibit wickedness extends beyond the realm of statute, into the marketplace, mosque and private home. Responsible for public morals is the *muḥtasib*, a man of incorruptible character, fit to serve as the tongue of the *qāḍī*, ensuring that what can be mended need not be endured. He sees that beggars are kept from the mosque and ensures that no beast is left to foul its entrance, regulates schoolmasters and their discipline, polices the cemeteries against drinking, depravity and trysts, keeps storytellers and riffraff out of people's homes, and ensures that milk is sold only by honest people, undiluted, and from wooden or crockery vessels, not copper, lest it engender noxious verdigris. He sees that market vegetables are washed in the river – not in ponds or pools – and poultry sold with tails plucked, rabbits, skinned – to reveal spoilage. Eggs must be tested when sold; abattoirs, enclosed and sanitary, with proper notation of the beasts' title. Market women are not to turn town gardens into brothels. Sales of grapes must be regulated, lest they be used for wine. The professions, especially medicine, must be kept clear of impostors; the baths and bathmen too, covered up. A Muslim may not massage a Jew or Christian or do his menial work. The *muḥtasib* must ensure that Muslim women are not debauched in churches, those dens of wine and fornication, that Jews butcher no meat for Muslims (although they say God's name in slaughter, as Islam requires), that Christian priests are circumcised – by force if necessary, since they are hypocrites to claim to follow the *sunna* of Jesus and yet go uncircumcised. Villagers must have their long hair cut or shaved on coming into town, and country youths must be disarmed; church bells may not sound in Muslim lands, and learned books may not be sold to Jews or Christians. Usury must be suppressed, and foreign currency kept from circulation – lest it cause inflation. Schools must be managed by men of proven piety; daggers, banned from manufacture: 'for no one buys them but ruffians, good for nothings, and wicked men.' Prostitutes from licensed houses (a telling admission this, in view of the Qur'ānic outrage against fornication) must wear veils when they go abroad and must be kept from teaching their wiles to married women and from attending wedding parties, even when invited. Catamites must be expelled from the city. Christians, Jews, tax farmers and police agents must be identifiable by their dress and not allowed to dress as dignitaries – and the protected minorities (*dhimmī*s) must wear a badge to distinguish and disgrace them as 'the party of Satan' (Qur'ān 58.20). Boxing and martial arts must be forbidden to boys, since they foment quarrels; and frivolities like chess and backgammon, to everyone, since they are modes of gambling and distractions from the thought of God and our ultimate destiny.

The category defining the charge of the *muḥtasib* is that of the wicked or disreputable (*munkar*, literally, 'unspeakable'; cf. the Latin *nefas*), a wide-ranging congatherum of moral, sumptuary, communal and quasi-ritual concerns. It is the *muḥtasib*'s job (somehow) to prevent anal intercourse and other wicked practices and to see that the Qur'ānic demand for public humiliation of the tolerated minorities is implemented – much as we might delegate to local authorities implementation of some equal-opportunity and non-discrimination concerns. Fair trade, public health and safety and private decency all come under the same general heading, of public policy. The idea that private morals or private dealings are somehow beyond the reach of law or detailed regulations derived from its unwritten spirit is not an axiom of Islam – or of most traditional polities. But the catalogue of the *muḥtasib*'s somewhat idealized functions is also evidence of the variety of abuses, from privilege to peccadilloes to outrages against public piety and private decency that fell into the shadow between norms and empiric practices.

Kalām is less concerned with positive prescriptions than with the metaphysic of morals and the underlying issues of theodicy. Many a *mutakallim* was a *faqīh* or jurisprude, but only one to my knowledge was a *muḥtasib*, al-Sarakhsī (AD 835–99), disciple of the philosopher al-Kindī and author of works on literature, geography, art history, the pagan Sabians and other topics, including two works on frauds, which may have justified his claim to his post, held for less than a year before he fell out of favour.[5] Generally, normative issues were left to the legal schools; *mutakallimūn* did not find here the theological conundrums that goaded their dialectic. But *kalām* philosophy of action remains fascinating today even to philosophers who do not share the original motivating itch. The Mu'tazilites preserved free will and responsibility and held human reason competent to judge justice and injustice. On both counts they were condemned by contemporaries for seeming to tie God's hands: to limit his power by assigning acts and capabilities to mere creatures, and to demean his sovereignty by holding God accountable to human notions of goodness. Mu'tazilites might claim to know the moral truth, but their views, the Ash'arites could claim, were mere opinion: better to rely on God's good pleasure than a will-o'-the-wisp like human ideas of objective right.[6]

The Mu'tazilites and their philosopher successors held that Ash'arites made God an arbitrary despot, and there is some evidence that Ash'arite theology was influenced by deference to authority. But other values too were at stake. Al-Ash'arī (d. AD 932), the founder of the school, defended Mu'tazilite theodicy for years before his conversion to 'orthodoxy', but came to see it as a refusal to take seriously the facts of natural evil and divine authority. In urging God's freedom to act and choose at his pleasure, the Ash'arites were also defending human moral perceptions in a way, refusing to discover concealed goods, as the Mu'tazilites were prone to do, behind every apparent evil – insisting on acceptance of the world as it is. For centuries Muslim theologians argued (even against the great al-Ghazālī) that this world is not the best God might have made, but the one he chose to make. Ash'arism even motivated al-Ghazālī's celebrated critique of the Neoplatonic rationalists' deductivist account of causality and led to the conception of a more open universe and a more empirical mode of discourse about nature than was accepted among the *falāsifa*.[7]

Mu'tazilites held that a man acts and chooses by God-given powers – so he alone is responsible for his choices. Naturally the doctrine commends itself to moralists. It was complemented by a sophisticated theory of degrees of freedom: by our own choices we may limit our future effectiveness and capabilities for choice. A development of Stoic theory, the thesis about natural accountability was adopted by Jewish philosophical ethicists like Saadiah (AD 882–942) and Maimonides (AD 1135–1204).[8] But again the Ash'arite alternative deserves notice. Ash'arites conceded that we act by capacities, scotching the Aristotelian objection that it is impossible to do what one has no capacity to do. But they held that God creates our capacities at the very moment of our action; they have no prior existence (as mere dispositions) and are not polyvalent. Ash'arī argued that if the capacity for an action pre-dated the act, the act would already have taken place; and if capacities were polyvalent, they would yield opposing acts. Grounded in a strikingly Megarian, non-Aristotelian logic of possibility – a rigid insistence that only the actual is real – Ash'arī's dogged offensive never quite loses its *ad hoc* tang; but as a welcome by-product it generated a kind of behaviourism that put a brake on spiritual militancy: radical predecessors of the Mu'tazilites had held that a grave sinner must be unfaithful to Islam and so must be slain in this world and damned in the next. The Ash'arites responded that such inferences again tie God's hands, placing arbitrary, merely human restrictions on divine grace. They used their theory of created capacities to combat the notion that a person can be judged humanly for anything more than he actually has done: behavioural conformity is all that man can enforce; deeper levels of faith, beneath the husk of lip-service, are judged by God alone.[9]

Sufism, like *kalām*, develops a dialectical duality, but not between rationalistic voluntarism and the diverse shades of predestinarianism and theistic subjectivism. Rather, the polarity is between expansiveness (*inbisāṭ*) and constraint (*inqibāḍ*) – an elation that engulfs the cosmos, and an anguish bordering on self-extinction. These moods occur naturally but are deepened by the meditative practices of *taṣawwuf* (Sufi practice); they ground Sufi life styles classically described as drunken and sober. Sober Sufism seeks a discipline that will control the excesses of the rival extremes, find the proper place for each in the dialectic of moods and hierarchy of Sufi states, using each tendency to limit the other and give it its proper measure. But intoxicated Sufism rejects moderation in search of absoluteness, neither a dying unto self nor a rebirth to eternal life in God but dissolution of the boundaries between self and God. Here pantheism takes the colours not of naturalism familiar to us, say, in Wordsworth, but of a more personal immanentism called incarnationist by the heresiographers.

Mysticism is individualist in its Hellenistic and Romantic phases, but the ancient forerunners and medieval heirs of the tradition organized their quest on corporate lines – Sufi orders in the Islamic case, following the rule and example of charismatic leaders and the train of their successors. These orders are nodes of religious activities ranging from the *dhikr* and *samā'* – meditative repetitions of the epithets of God, and contemplative concerts, accompanied by the vertiginous, ecstatic dancing of the dervishes – to the feats of self-mortification and wonder-working of the *faqīr* (mendicant), to the exploits of militant and military orders, to the missionary outreach that spread Islam deep into Asia, Africa and the Pacific, far beyond the reach of the original Arab armies of conquest.[10]

The use of hashish was not excluded for many Sufis. And the construction placed upon personal expansion did not exclude an antinomian tendency, rationalized as a transcendence of merely human norms but also expressing rebelliousness against highly structured societal restrictions. In Sufi art and poetry, wine-drinking or gazing into the faces of beardless acolytes (lovely as the moon, where a still more perfect light appears) bore a potent ambiguity as symbols of ecstatic abandon, foci of poetic paradox, sensuous licence and libertinage, which could still claim sacred privilege. Puritan moralists and jurists condemned all this but never wholly put a stop to the abuses or quenched their lambent aura of sanctity – any more than they succeeded in halting all veneration at the shrines of Sufi saints.[11]

Al-Ghazālī (AD 1058–1111) promoted sober Sufism in the institutional and intellectual mainstream, following a pietist reading of Sufi themes. Mystic monism was made a groundwork to the life of reliance upon God. Thus he argues in his monumental *Iḥyā' 'Ulūm al-Dīn*, *Revival of the Sciences of the Faith*, that the highest monotheism – kernel of the kernel, in his image – is a monism which sees nothing in existence but God (4.305). Al-Makkī (d. AD 996) pioneered this approach, drawing ethical implications from the monistic teachings of Sufis like al-Junayd (d. AD 910), who was, along with al-Muḥāsibī,[12] one of the two great teachers of orthodox and sober Sufism:

> Junayd relates on the authority of Yaḥyā ibn Abī Kathīr: it is written in the Torah, 'Cursed is he whose trust is in a creature no better than himself' (cf. Psalms 118:8). Junayd says this applies to anyone who says, 'If it hadn't been for so and so I'd have died.' It is said that for a man to say, 'If things hadn't worked out as they did—' is idolatry. And it is said, 'Many a time has "If only—" begun the work of the Devil'. . . . If you trust God as he ought to be trusted, God will provide for you as he does for the birds that start out each day empty and return full. The hills will shower you with their bounty. Jesus said, 'Behold the birds of the air: they sow not, neither do they reap, neither do they store away, yet God provides for them day by day' (Matthew 6:27).[13]

As the promiscuous use of Jewish, Christian and Muslim sources shows, Makkī's is a cosmopolitan pietism. Its themes are borne along not only by al-Ghazālī but by Baḥyā[14] and numberless other Jewish, Christian and Muslim mystics who a find practical meaning for the unity which monistic mystics experience in giving one's will to God's plan and placing all desires, hopes and fears in God's control, with perfect acceptance and reliance.

Among the philosophers proper, the *falāsifa*,[15] we find a vibrant interest in ethics, especially in the earlier writers, before issues of logic, cosmology and metaphysics come to dominate the work of the more systematic thinkers. Al-Kindī (d. AD 867) steps gingerly into ethical philosophy by way of a psychological prescription against anxiety and grief, with the Platonizing advice to attach one's desires only to the permanent, intellectual goods, which alone are ever truly ours[16] – a striking contrast, yet recognizably akin, to the advice mystic pietists were giving at the same time about the proper focus of human hopes and longings. The insouciant al-Rāzī (d. AD 925 or 932), like al-Kindī a physician, re-reduces the ethical counsels of Plato to a somewhat ascetic Epicureanism, urging that to maximize pleasure is to minimize desire.[17] Al-Fārābī (*c.* AD 870–950), Avicenna (Ibn Sīnā, AD 980–1038) and Averroes (Ibn Rushd, AD 1126–98), the three greatest philosophers of Islam, develop the ethics of Aristotle and politics of Plato in the context of the cosmology of the spheres, physiology of the humours, and metaphysics of the hypostatic active intellect. Their ethical work is eclipsed by their achievement in metaphysics and logic, complemented in al-Fārābī by a sophisticated philosophy of language and culture, in Averroes by a magisterial philosophy of nature, and in Avicenna by a powerful synthesis of Greek rationalism with Islamic mysticism.[18] But in the century before Avicenna's death, we find a number of philosophical figures trained in Arabic letters and Greek sciences, imbued with the values of the court, chancery and military camp, the culture of *adab* alongside and interpreting the religion of Islam.[19] These men, friends, colleagues, masters and disciples, made genuine inroads towards a humanistic ethical literature and ideal. Miskawayh (AD 936–1030), one of the most articulate, was an ethicist of stature. His *On the Refinement of Character* is rightly called 'the most influential work on philosophical ethics' in Islam.[20] Its contents were taken over by al-Ghazālī in the *Iḥyā* and so incorporated into orthodoxy, but altered in ways that are prophetic for subsequent ethical thinking in Islam.[21]

Miskawayh was born in Rayy near present-day Tehran; he died in his nineties at Isfahan. Reputedly of Zoroastrian background, he was – like al-Fārābī and the Sincere Brethren of Basra[22] – a Shī'ite. He was a vocal advocate of Persian culture in its struggle with Arab hegemony over Iran. As a youth he served the *wazīr* al-Muḥallabī and became librarian and boon companion to the powerful *wazīr* Ibn al-'Āmīd, at his side 'day and night' for seven years. Ibn al-'Āmīd was a lover of learning; and Miskawayh, with his training in the ancient sciences, presided over ten camel loads (2–5 tons) of manuscripts. The minister told him how relieved he was to learn that his trove had survived the sacking of his palace by Khorasanian raiders: 'All my treasures can be replaced but these.' After his patron's death, Miskawayh continued in service to his headstrong son; and, on this master's deposition, served the monarch 'Aḍud al-Dawla as a courtier and legate. He later served monarchs at Baghdad and Rayy, finally retiring as court physician to the Khwarizmshah, ruler of Khiva on the Oxus. The story is told that he was so provoked by the young Avicenna that he threw a copy of his ethical work at him across the room – out of character for the refined bibliophile, but the story may have emphasized the one area in which Miskawayh surpassed his formidable successor.

Miskawayh's teacher was the Jacobite Christian Yaḥyā ibn 'Adī (d. AD 974), a translator and commentator of Plato and Aristotle and a disciple of translators, a logician and teacher of many Christians and Muslims including Miskawayh's Boswell al-Tawḥīdī. It was from Ibn 'Adī that Miskawayh learned philosophical argumentation, defending logic against the charge of a *mutakallim* that it was (as its name suggests) just a way of ordering words: Miskawayh retorted that if that much could be derived from etymology, one could equally conclude that a *mutakallim* was a mere talker. Naturally Miskawayh defended the Greek sciences against all forms of parochialism, but the heart of the cosmopolitanism he imbibed from Ibn 'Adī is voiced when Ibn 'Adī's ethics urges that man's highest perfection is in the universal love of humankind as a single race: the basis of our unity and man's crowning glory is the divinely imparted rational soul, which all men share, and by which indeed all are one (for in a Neoplatonic ontology only the accident of matter differentiates individuals; in our essential rationality we are one person). The goal of ethics is control of our natural irascibility, allowing expression to our deeper unity in acts of love and compassion.[23] Miskawayh's loyalty to his teacher's ideals is evident in the assignment of the same title to both men's ethical works, *On the Refinement of Character*.

His writings include a compendious annalistic history, *The Experience of Nations and Outcomes of their Endeavours*. It follows the exhaustive annals of al-Ṭabarī down to the author's times and then (for the years AD 951–83) notably emphasizes first-hand experience and eyewitness reports of military, diplomatic and court events. As a court favourite and minister Miskawayh accompanied Ibn al-'Āmīd in the field and once was sent to inventory a fortress taken from the rival Ḥamdānid dynasts, which had been betrayed by its venal commander. Ordered to humiliate the loyal slave officer in charge, who had been captured, Miskawayh, neither a paragon nor a hypocrite, sent the man back to the conquering prince for his fate to be settled.

Miskawayh's learning was not incidental to his court function. His masters shared his belief that statesmen could profit from the histories and comportment of past rulers and from other ancient lore in which he was adept. He wrote two treasuries of the ancient sciences and books on ethics, happiness and moral education besides his vivid work on history and writings on logic, the natural sciences, divinity, arithmetic, alchemy and cooking. There is also a rewarding set of his replies to the questions of Tawḥīdī. Towards alchemy, he took a revealing stand: alchemy is an esoteric science, taught by hints, so that only philosophers have access to it. Its secrets are thought dangerous: if they fell into the hands of the ignorant, men would abandon cooperation, pursue power only in the form of domination, and pleasures only of the lowest sort. The charge, reflective of the pietist anxiety over *homo faber*, is still made against technology today, and Miskawayh's reply is worthy of a Bacon or Descartes: real alchemy is simply a branch of mineral science (sc. chemistry) and should not be confined to an esoteric élite. For those who learn are no longer ignorant. Since mastery of alchemy depends on philosophical understanding, we can be confident that its practitioners will not misuse it. Here we see a transcendent faith in learning, in the organic interconnectedness of the natural and human sciences, and in the transparency of the human will and social organization to the goods that illuminate their course. Our word for what Miskawayh placed his faith in here is 'humanism', very much in the Socratic tradition that does not isolate act from understanding. Miskawayh's word is *adab* – 'manners', 'culture', the root of *ta'dīb*, 'education', 'discipline', 'refinement'. His faith, unlike that of al-Makkī, al-Junayd or al-Ghazālī, relies on positive connections in nature at large and in human nature in particular – between cause and effect, discipline and conduct: whether in science or in ethics, his discourse is fraught with 'if only's and 'were it not for's.

Adab in its narrowest sense means 'literature', a prime vehicle of the refinement Miskawayh sought and counted on. That he wrote on the pure style in poetry as well as on usage and manners reveals the nexus of values he most cherished. But *adab* was much more than literature and went far beyond mere usage. Combining and universalizing what had been central themes of Plato and Aristotle, Miskawayh saw the humane and humanizing manners and mores of a universal human culture as crucial to our fulfilment as individuals and as a species. *Adab* is, he wrote, the nourishment that gives substance to the mind as food gives substance to the maturing body; it is the content of wisdom – knowledge tested by experience about the good life and its means of attainment. Without it, reason is not reason.[24] Here the sum of human culture, actively assimilated and lived by, provides the material values without which Aristotelian phronesis would be a mere formal virtue. Like al-Makkī, whose spiritual vade-mecum was entitled *Food for Hearts*, Miskawayh seeks sustenance for the inner, moral man. But, unlike al-Makkī, he does not find that sustenance in the devotional posture of the heart but in the intellectual focus of the mind and governance of emotion by reason. He informs reason not with the *sunna* of the Prophet but with *paideia*, the *adab* of humanity.

In his traditional pious foreword, setting out the task of ethics in the context of Islam, Miskawayh follows the Mu'tazilite/Shī'ite voluntaristic reading of the Qur'ān, quoting one of its characteristic oaths: 'By the soul and that which shaped it and breathed into it its wickedness and impiety' – the lines might give comfort to predestinarians; but Miskawayh reads on – 'he who keeps it pure prospers, and he who corrupts it fails!' Miskawayh reads the verses (91.7–10) as mandating a Socratic tendance of the soul: one might forge the same metal into a perfect or a worthless sword (35). The creator affords the matter of our humanity, but to work up that material through art and culture is our charge. Society, Miskawayh argues, is a necessary means to this end: each of us is necessary to someone else's perfection, and all of us must cooperate to provide the material base necessary to humanize our existence (14). From here higher and more intellectual plateaux are sought, each of us advancing in the measure of his capacities and all of us complementing the weaknesses of the rest (118, 123, cf. 64). The social virtues, then, of friendliness, affability and cooperativeness are necessary to human well-being, as Aristotle argued; and ascetics are mistaken in seeking perfection outside human society: the life of the anchorite or vagabond stunts our humanity and thwarts our nature. Such men are neither temperate nor just; they lack the social theatre in which such virtues are developed (25–6, 139). In the spirit of Ibn 'Adī, and in perfect agreement with Aristotle, Miskawayh argues that love is the basis of all society – friendship being a more intimate and fellowship a more diffuse form of love. Humanity itself is named from fellowship (deriving the Arabic *insān*, 'man', 'humanity', from *uns*, 'fellowship'), and not, as one poet pretended, from *nisyān*, 'forgetfulness'. Even public worship is designed to foster fellowship, neighbourhood by neighbourhood, city by city, and (through the Pilgrimage to Mecca) among the Islamic community throughout the world. It was with this thought in mind – that religion does not isolate but unites humanity – that the wise King Ardashir of Persia (reg. 226–41) called religion and monarchy twin brothers (125–8).

Piety, in Miskawayh's catalogue of virtues, is defined not in theological terms (as devotion is further on, as honouring God and his elect, 21–2) but eudaimonistically, as the performance of acts of virtue which enhance and perfect the soul (19). And the virtues in general are defined in the Aristotelian manner, as means towards happiness, varying in their applications in diverse situations, as assayed by experience and addressed by way of art (22). The virtues, then, are not, as scripture might seem to suggest, matters of strict adherence to behavioural rules. Popular religion, in fact, is a mere attempt to trade abstemiousness in this world for sensory goods in the next – as though a transcendent God could legitimately be placed in the service of human appetites and passions (39–40). Like al-Rāzī,[25] Miskawayh follows Galen in arguing that all sensory pleasures presuppose prior lack and pain. He goes on to argue that the ethics of the common mass is (in our terms) conflicted – as a result of an inner contradiction in their thinking: philosophers understand that what is most divine is what furthest transcends the material conditions of both pleasure and pain. But popular morality simultaneously celebrates the successful hedonist and abhors the conditions of his success – responding with awe, therefore, to the seeming ascetic, whose way of life the common man in no way desires to share. Without philosophy to reconcile the conflicting ascetic and hedonic impulses of our nature and direct them towards the higher and purer pleasures of the intellectual life, the vulgar live a life of mingled self-indulgence and shame, not even knowing the source of their embarrassment, let alone the character of its remedy (41, 43, 113, 136).

Like al-Fārābī,[26] Miskawayh regards religion as a mode of poetry and practice that platonically instils the proper ethos in a people. He does not seek literal truth in scriptural rhetoric, just as he does not find categorical commandments in religious laws. Rather, he sees religious symbolism as a hortatory exercise and observance of the laws as a means of inuring the character to virtue. He evinces more concern about a young man's drinking companions than about the fact that young men will violate the religious law by drinking (53). Before coming to philosophy, Miskawayh confesses, he himself was acculturated less in the salubrious ethos of the Qur'ān than in the morals of the pre-Islamic poets like Imru' al-Qays and Nābighah, who flaunt the raffish ethos of the desert. When the romantic ideals of passion and self-assertion are held up to admiration by one's parents and the spirit of such poets is what is most admired by one's prince, it is difficult to free oneself from their grip; and only gradually, Miskawayh admits, did he break free of the sensuous and wanton values of the *jāhiliyya* poets and wean himself – with the aid of philosophy – from the way of life their songs instilled (45–6).

Manners, he argues, make the man. By nature a boy is bad – a liar, cheat and tattletale, spiteful, meddlesome, importunate, jealous and malicious – a danger to others and even more to himself. But by training, suitable reading, well-placed praise and private reproof (lest he become shameless under the blast of condemnation before his fellows), proper diet and discipline, decent demeanour, comportment, dress, companions, and play that is neither exhausting nor debilitating, he can be made a man (51–5). Courtesy (*adab* again) is not external but organic to morals – as means serve ends in an organism. Even among the lesser animals, the highest are those that come closest to culture: the sexually reproducing species and those that nurture and train their young (and so are amenable to domestication). Man is the highest of the animals because in him the capacity for education is clearest, allowing human intelligence to reclose the arcing circle from creator to creatures, reuniting with its source (61–2).

Some of the ancients carried the recognition that happiness depends on transcendence of the physical so far that they denied that happiness was attainable in this life. It is in this sense, evidently, that Miskawayh reads the notion rejected by Aristotle that no man is to be called happy while he lives. It would be disgraceful, Miskawayh insists, to hold that a living man who performs good deeds, holds sound beliefs, serves his fellow-men and thus in all ways acts as God's deputy is not objectively happy. To be sure, intellectual perfection reaches higher than mere moral perfection of our worldly nature; and only intellectual perfection, as Aristotle allowed, endures beyond the grave. But the moral virtues are necessary means to the higher intellectual end; the spiritual goal which is the ultimate aim of philosophy is not attainable by any other means (Sufis take note!). There are no shortcuts to felicity that bypass the avenues of moral and intellectual self-perfection. For the key premiss of all mysticism and *gnosis*, as of all asceticism which pursues a spiritual goal, is that the soul requires purification. And clearly, Miskawayh argues, again citing Aristotle (now on the need for experience), purification is not achieved without living through the stages of our natural human development – undergoing the discipline and acculturation that Miskawayh takes to be the object of our existence in this world (74–83). A school is not life, but life is a school.

The fate of Miskawayh's ethics is emblematic of that of Greek philosophy under Islam: an immense legacy is absorbed; orthodoxy does not reject it, but builds from the inherited materials, much as the early Islamic builders appropriated the structures and stones of Greek basilicas that had once been pagan temples, and later used the designs and architectural principles to construct new, distinctively Islamic structures. No sentence of Miskawayh's ethics is left unexamined when al-Ghazālī takes over the work. But Miskawayh's distinctive humanism is systematically expunged. Richard Walzer and H. A. R. Gibb showed the heavy dependence of al-Ghazālī's *Iḥyā'* on Miskawayh, and others have detailed the diffusion of that influence in later authors like the pivotal Naṣīr al-Dīn al-Ṭūsī (AD 1201–74), the Shi'ite polymath who defected to the conquering Mongol forces in 1247.[27] But in emphasizing Miskawayh's formative role and al-Ghazālī's openness to philosophical ethics, Walzer and Gibb overstated al-Ghazālī's dependence, overlooking his selective preferences for other philosophers' ideas when they better served his purposes, and neglecting to assay the material impact on his and later Islamic thought of his displacement of Miskawayh's most distinctive themes in favour of those he drew from traditional Islamic sources and the Sufi pietists like al-Muḥāsibī and al-Makkī – as though an archaeologist were so thrilled to discern the lineaments of a Greek temple in a mosque that he neglected to observe the Muslim worship going on inside. Al-Ghazālī appreciates the edifying conclusions he finds among the fruits of philosophy but discards the fruit along with the argumentative branch that had supported it when the conclusions are not to his taste. Next to his deracinating of philosophical theses, excising their argumentative nerve, al-Ghazālī's grafting of ancient doctrines on to the authority of some Islamic sage is positively innocuous.

Sensitive to Miskawayh's polemic against Sufi austerity, al-Ghazālī suppresses Miskawayh's Aristotelian rejection of the life of solitude as sub- or superhuman – although closely following him in what comes before and after. He rejects the social rationale of public worship and suppresses the platonizing proposal that happiness requires a youthful study of mathematics to accustom us to truth and truthfulness. In all, Abul Quasem finds that about a third of Miskawayh's ethics was unacceptable and dropped as quietly as the rest was used.[28] My own appraisal of the clear basis of selection is that whatever was outspokenly humanistic or secular was dropped by al-Ghazālī, just as he broke with *falsafa* where he found it excessively naturalistic. Walzer and Gibb advert to al-Ghazālī's changes in the ethics but call the discarded elements of *adab* 'merely formal and superficial'.

Al-Ghazālī follows Miskawayh and Platonic tradition in identifying wisdom, courage and temperance as the virtues of the rational, irascible and appetitive faculties, and in treating justice as the master-virtue integrating the other three; he follows the later Greek and prior Islamic tradition in listing the remaining virtues under the cardinal four. But Miskawayh sees the intellectual virtues subsidiary to wisdom cognitively, as intelligence, retentiveness, reasonableness (conformance of our notions to reality), quickness and strength in inference, and lucid grasp of abstract concepts and theoretical ideas. Al-Ghazālī takes a far more spiritual tack: in place of intelligence he lists excellence in deliberation, following al-Fārābī in insisting, as Aristotle had, that practical wisdom is not mere cleverness in finding means to ends but a virtue that apprehends what is most conducive in the pursuit of noble aims. For memory and lucidity he substitutes discernment in controversy (cf. *Nicomachaean Ethics* VI. 10) and penetration. In place of reasonableness he puts insight into truth without recourse to proof – a virtue of holy men. He caps his list in the *Iḥyā'* with an intellectual virtue not found in his earlier ethical work: self-scrutiny, of the subtle movements and hidden evils of the soul, a pietist virtue *par excellence*. Without it we would never know our own motives, and even with it they may remain opaque. Where Aristotle relies on reason, the virtue of practical wisdom, to locate the appropriate in concrete circumstances and direct us towards the doable good, al-Ghazālī argues that without prayer and God's help we mortals would never find the right, let alone acquire it in our characters. Al-Ghazālī follows the *falāsifa* in reading the *fātiḥa*, the opening prayer of the Qur'ān, as invoking God's aid in finding the mean when it beseeches God (1.6) to 'show us the Straight Path'. But he departs sharply from them when he insists that we are given no means of finding and hewing to that path for ourselves: all of us, as the Qur'ān is traditionally held to imply, will spend part of eternity in hellfire.

Under temperance Miskawayh lists modesty, composure (the ability to keep one's soul at rest when the passions are stirring), liberality, integrity, contentment, gentility, orderliness, personableness, being accommodating, dignity and godliness – all virtues of a courtier. He defines contentment as moderation in food and drink; integrity, in terms of licit and illicit gain; godliness, as steadiness in fair doings, by which the soul is perfected. Al-Ghazālī lists modesty and liberality under temperance, following Miskawayh, al-Fārābī and the moralist Ibn Abi Dunya – but not Aristotle, who treats modesty as a surrogate for virtue appropriate to the young. He also lists patience here, the virtue of Job and other prophets and the fruit of steadfastness, the ability to bear sufferings and losses. Following Miskawayh and Avicenna, al-Ghazālī defines patience broadly as a resistance to all passions, of pleasure or pain; he reserves this Qur'ānic virtue for special discussion among our avenues to salvation. Under temperance he adds a form of self-restraint, forgoing some of our due, using a definition from Miskawayh, but adding that such virtues are relevant only for those still attached to worldly things. Similarly with thrift and orderliness. Even with liberality we see the same thrust: al-Ghazālī dwells on the dangers of preoccupation with our livelihood, to the detriment of concern with our ultimate destiny. If one must choose between poverty and generosity, he argues, citing Muḥāsibī, one must prefer poverty, as the less entangled with worldly things.[29]

Al-Ghazālī parallels Miskawayh in defining godliness in terms of good action done for the sake of the perfection in it – but adds: and for the sake of coming nearer to God, thus rendering Miskawayh's eudaimonism theological, in keeping with Plato's famous remark that we perfect ourselves as human by becoming as like to God as humanly possible. God alone is truly generous, giving without expecting a return, but men approximate such liberality if they are generous for God's sake or for the sake of their eternal reward. In his properly ethical writings al-Ghazālī follows Miskawayh and Avicenna in defining contentment as a virtue of moderation. But in the *Iḥyā'* he seizes on the Aristotelian proviso that virtues must be exercised in the right way, to expand the virtue of contentment into an ascetic principle demanding that we not seek to provide for our needs beyond a single day – a month at most – and give away all that we have beyond that. The Aristotelian social virtues – affability, good humour and cheer – are made over to conform to the ideals of sobriety and sedateness: one should not laugh unreservedly but emulate the Prophet, who preferred smiling to laughter.[30] Jesting leads to falsehood: Muḥammad 'did jest, but he only spoke the truth'. The saintly Ḥasan al-Baṣrī, al-Ghazālī reports with admiration, did not laugh for thirty years.

Miskawayh expatiates on liberality, the brightest virtue in a courtier's milieu, on which his fortunes most depend. It includes altruism, magnificence, charitableness, bounty (spending more than one really should, a favourite virtue of the Arab poets[31]), appreciativeness of achievement, and the self-denial whose ambivalent reception we saw in al-Ghazālī. Al-Ghazālī expands on the dangers of speech, listing twenty evils of the tongue. He recognizes the Aristotelian mean of cheerfulness and good humour between the glum or morose and the clownishness of the buffoon, but presents the virtue of exchanging pleasantries at a party and expressing satisfaction with the casual remarks of acquaintances as a duty and a chore. Seclusion is to be preferred, and we must look to the model of the Prophet to see how such occasions may be borne with good address. Likewise with tact: we must learn to forgo contention and find the mean between pettishness and obsequiousness. But al-Ghazālī complements this advice by reverting to Aristotle for a virtue that neither Miskawayh nor Avicenna listed, righteous indignation, here defined as grief at undeserved good or ill fortunes. This must be sharply distinguished from envy and spite, which are strictly forbidden but very similar in appearance. The true guide in distinguishing the virtue from the vice is the motive or intention – worldly versus other-worldly goals. A similar canonization of intention is used in Spinoza's distinction between piety and ambition, which seeks men's approbation, where true piety (also called humanity by Spinoza) seeks their genuine well-being. As Spinoza intimates, this subtle difference of intention demarcating virtues from vices runs all through the list of moral strengths and weaknesses. And the pietist theme of scrutiny of our intentions remains central in the ethics of Kant.

Al-Ghazālī follows Miskawayh in defining delicacy or gentility as an inner attachment to what is fair or fine, and in defining personableness in terms of dress, the one aspect of outward appearance beyond demeanour that one can regulate oneself – with clear effect upon one's mood. Miskawayh says simply that personableness is a love of complementing the soul with fair adornments. One can picture him interviewing would-be assistants and explaining the importance of self-presentation, the signs that properly or improperly chosen clothing give about the inner man. But al-Ghazālī puts *greater* emphasis on clothing. The *Iḥyā'* devotes a full chapter to the Prophet's mode of dress: he wore whatever came to hand, saying that he was just a slave and so dressed as a slave; our ideal clothing is of the coarsest stuff, affording just the necessary coverage and sturdy enough to last no longer than a day and a night – again the theme of trusting God, now elevated to ritual proportions. Few but the most saintly will attain the ideal, but lavish clothes are never acceptable. The mean, presentability without luxury or ostentation, becomes a compromise not between excess and deficiency but between a vice and an ideal.

Under courage Miskawayh lists great-spiritedness (disdain for the trivial, ability to bear both honour and humiliation), dauntlessness (confidence in a crisis), fortitude (in sufferings, especially those that cause terror), *ḥilm*, Aristotle's gentleness (now assimilated to the Roman *clementia*, from which it takes its name), steadiness (valuable in defending one's womenfolk or the religious law), gallantry (eagerness to do great deeds and win glory), and perseverance (sustained command of the soul over the body, applying it like a tool to a task). Al-Ghazālī's riposte uses the Aristotelian notion that every virtue has its proper sphere to urge that the Realm of Islam is not the proper arena for the courage that is a mean between recklessness and cowardice and quotes God himself in support: 'Muḥammad is the Apostle of God, and those who are with him are strong against unbelievers but merciful among themselves' (Qur'ān 48.29). Al-Ghazālī's interest in courage is much less military: fear is a virtue when applied to God; its proper object is hellfire. Like others of Sufi persuasion, he shifts the focus away from warfare, where Aristotle had found its paradigm case, and on to 'the greater *jihād*', against the passions. He omits the martial arts from education and uses sports to strengthen the body rather than to teach courage.

Among the sub-virtues, al-Ghazālī adds magnificence, perhaps because courage is needed in making great expenditures, adopting Aristotle's notion that magnificence is shown in honouring the divine and in public works – mosques, roads, hospitals and bridges – although the involvements needed to support such activities are not compatible with the self-denying life of the other-worldly ideal.[32] In defining 'dauntless', al-Ghazālī follows Aristotle's definition of courage as a mean in facing danger and death – he says, between recklessness and helplessness or desertion. But he redefines gallantry to make goodness and eternal life its object rather than glory. He adds nobility and benevolence to the virtues listed under courage, the former taken from Miskawayh's anatomy of liberality, and the latter defined (as Spinoza will define humanity) as wanting for all men what one desires for oneself.[33]

Ḥilm[34] is crucial for al-Ghazālī, as for Miskawayh and Ibn 'Adī, because it masters anger. It can be simulated, but its true nature is to cool the blood, whose heat is necessary to life but harmful in excess. We are attuned, al-Ghazālī argues, to be aroused to defend ourselves and our own, but if our claims go beyond bare necessity, we must curb our ire and possessiveness over all that is extraneous: self-control serves abstemiousness and resignation. But dignity, which for Miskawayh means little more than grave demeanour, as in the ethics of Yaḥyā, is redefined by al-Ghazālī as self-respect grounded in recognition of self-worth and as a mean between vanity and abjectness. Still, al-Ghazālī insists, like most medieval ethicists, that humility, not pride, is our proper virtue.

In describing greatness of soul, al-Ghazālī goes back to Aristotle: the great man is not overly excited by honours. Recognizing the problem for his ideal of renunciation inherent in acceptance of Aristotle's principle that externals are needful in the exercise of virtue, he expands on the dangers of love of fame and condemns the quest for honours. Seeking God in place of worldly regard, some, he explains (the Sufis), pursue apparent humiliation and disgrace. But seclusion, isolation and migration to lands where one is unknown are the recommended alternatives. Al-Ghazālī alludes here to his own story; for these were the cures he adopted when his own reputation threatened to overwhelm him: humility and obscurity must displace the quest for worldly greatness. It is always ambiguous, as al-Ghazālī knows, how far such efforts can succeed in extinguishing the sort of worldliness he found even in the spiritual leaders of his day, and how far even the closest self-scrutiny will be deluded, mistaking for spirituality mere sublimation of social instincts and acquisitive urges, finding a new sphere for emulousness or a new vocabulary of selflessness to voice the old ambitions. Aristotle thought that great men do claim the honours due them. Cicero confessed that none of his sacrifices had been made without the hope of fame – and they did go beyond Aristotle, in that Cicero courted and suffered the martyrdom Aristotle sidestepped. The spiritual benefits of al-Ghazālī's transvaluation of classical values remain invisible in the nature of the case, but the material harm of devaluing glory is visible in every land that other-worldliness has touched.

Al-Ghazālī is attracted to the Aristotelian idea of the mean. He readily finds proof-texts in Qur'ān and *ḥadīth* to give it an Islamic standing and subtly uses Aristotle's caveats about appropriateness and context to naturalize the theory of virtues far more effectively than Miskawayh could do by treating it as an exotic offshoot of the rare and foreign plant Philosophy. The worries of his fellow-Ash'arites about capacities and dispositions resident and fixed in human character are quietly forgotten, as is the fact that the ethical focus of the Qur'ān and *ḥadīth* is not on virtues but on commands. But to achieve his naturalization of the Greek theory al-Ghazālī had to modify both form and content: virtue is redirected to positive practice, and the mean is often made second best to an ascetic extreme, an alternative combated by Aristotle and many medieval successors. The mean is retained by al-Ghazālī, but used as seems appropriate: he follows Aristotle in rejecting Plato's claim that justice is no mere compromise and agrees with Miskawayh in calling it a mean between doing and suffering wrong – yet retaining Plato's notion that justice is the sovereign virtue, the result of using wisdom to give proper scope to all the rest. Because justice comprises all the other virtues al-Ghazālī does not, as Miskawayh does, assign it sub-virtues at the level of family, household, community and friends. His is not an assertive, rights-claiming theory, although his ethical writings do differentiate a political and a distributive justice, overseen by the conscientious ruler.[35]

George Hourani wrote that al-Ghazālī's definition of obligation in terms of personal interest entails that the 'the concept of "obligation" as essentially connected with social justice is absent from al-Ghazālī's ethics'.[36] But the adoption of an egoistic stance is a feature of all classical ethics in the Socratic tradition, which seeks dialectically to show the advantageousness of moral standards; the tendency is heightened by al-Ghazālī's Ash'arite polemic against Mu'tazilite deontology: obligation arises out of interests, and God, having no needs, has no obligations. Stoic philosophers and their Mu'tazilite heirs can be convicted of inconsistency on the point, in assigning moral responsibilities to the divine – even if we might deem it a generous or well-meaning inconsistency. However, al-Ghazālī's relative lack of interest in what we would call social obligations is not an essential feature of his philosophy and does not lead to his complete ignoring of questions, say about social justice. Rather it expresses his assumption that the religious law adequately addresses our social responsibilities and his suspicion that programmes of socio-political activism would represent at best an unwholesome worldliness, if not a sanction of disorder and upheaval. Like Miskawayh, al-Ghazālī does not reject the Aristotelian idea that justice is a social virtue involving give and take – in Islamic terms, proper and improper acquisition. But he is prepared, as Miskawayh was, in some measure to bracket the more radical claims of Socrates about the preferability of suffering injustice to committing it – despite the Islamic admiration for martyrdom and the disclaiming of worldly ends. Islam is a polity, not merely a path of other-worldly quest, and that must be acknowledged in any Islamic ethics, even if the recognition does lead to conflicts and tensions.

Al-Ghazālī follows pietist and mystic tradition in placing love of God ahead of knowledge, making it the fruit of wisdom and turning Aristotle's highest single good into a this-worldly means to an other-worldly aim. He does place speculative wisdom, whose true object is knowledge of God, above practical wisdom, as Aristotle does. But he treats practical wisdom as a mean, between the over-cleverness of guile (which uses cunning to attain base aims) and the stubborn witlessness of stolidity (which bars the lower passions from their natural goals). Yet despite the attractiveness of the idea of the mean, which anchors him in an Aristotelian social and biological naturalism, al-Ghazālī answers an insistent pressure from a realm whose claims are transcendental and whose goals are given specificity by rejection of the very appetites and impulses that a worldly eudaimonism like Miskawayh's seeks to channel and modulate but never to deny. This cross-pressure of the other-worldly, which defines itself not as the fulfilment of our natural drives but as their antithesis, is a source of ambivalences in al-Ghazālī's ethical scheme and a commanding motive to him in the suppression of the humanism he finds in Miskawayh, leading him to search al-Fārābī, Avicenna, Aristotle or Plato, dig into the *ḥadīth* or plumb the verses of the Qur'ān for alternative interpretations of the virtues, by which to formulate an ideal more closely attuned to his own Islam.

The resultant ideas of the virtues do take root. Through them, Greek concepts of the mean and the good life, translated into an idiom that effectively masks their foreignness, survive to afford the ethical framework for generations of later Muslim thinkers. The skeleton is strikingly preserved – Aristotle's profound and profoundly original conceptualization of the virtues. But, like the mosaics in Byzantine basilicas, the faces are deleted or plastered over; where the spiritual lineaments of late Greek piety and *paideia* could once be seen, the space is filled with painted sayings from the Prophet and his Book. The humanism of a Miskawayh, like the intellectualism of an al-Fārābī, Avicenna or Aristotle, or the even the prudential and ascetic hedonism of an al-Rāzī, do not survive. The prescriptive fountainhead of later Islamic ethics draws on pietism and Sufism, the canonical sources, occasionally the rhetoric and dialectic of *kalām*. The sub-surface engineering is Greek, but the classic motifs seen at the surface are subtly altered to suit their present place, and the waters that flow forth show no signs to those who drink them of how far they have travelled: to the drinker they seem wholly local. The free spirit of Miskawayh, the musky flavour that his name suggests might have been imparted to al-Ghazālī's ethics, Miskawayh's more independent views and speculative excursions, are gone; rarely in the later history of Islamic ethics will their like recur.

In al-Ghazālī, as in Aristotle and Miskawayh, the aim of ethics remains the perfection of the individual, but the social and cultural dimensions critical in defining and refining our humanity are supplanted by the very ideal of isolation that Aristotle rejected and Miskawayh combated. The perfected individual is no longer the man who directs his practical affairs by the implicit habituation and acculturation of reasonableness and whose highest aim is contemplation of nature and its transcendental meaning, but the spiritual seeker, who has almost cut away the middle term and reached directly for the divine. His discipline is not strictly of moderation and self-refinement but of ascesis; and his contemplation is gnostic and ecstatic – a quest rather of the heart than of the understanding, leading not to mastery in this world or a naturalist's inductive synthesis of its categories but to detachment from it and ever closer attachment to the supernal world of the divine.

We cannot romanticize Miskawayh as the last best hope of a cosmopolitan humanism in Islam. The reasons for the acceptance of al-Ghazālī's ethics and rejection of its more secular, humanistic model were many and powerful and not simply founded in narrowness, or ignorance. Miskawayh's courtier ethic, like his life, shows the biases of his nature and his role. As in his historiography so in his ethics, he is a conspicuous ego. He was criticized in his time for name dropping and trouble making; and penchants for both, alongside a certain tendency to flatter, are still visible in his writing – even though a penchant for trouble can be a virtue in a philosopher where it is not in a courtier. The flaws of his ethics – its tendency to promote conformity and breed a cohort of refined time-servers – were as visible to his successors as the personal faults that favoured such biases were to his contemporaries; it was in part a recognition of such biases that led al-Ghazālī and others to seek authenticity and depth in the canon of tradition and take refuge in Islam from an ethic that had come to seem as empty and superficial as the wisdom of the courtier Polonius seems to us.

Al-Ghazālī too has his faults, again mirrored in his ethics. The exile and isolation he made a virtue were in part necessities for him; in part, desertions, in his terms, when the patron who had sponsored his polemics against the Ismāʿīlīs fell to assassination, the tactic that gave them their best-known name in the West. Al-Ghazālī's meditative ethics is itself escapist in part. It renounces worldly aims on the eudaimonistic grounds that it knows of something better. But it does not attain perfect selflessness for any living subject of its counsels, and it does in effect tend to leave the world's wounds to fester. Scholars of Islamic thought, Christian Arabs seeking a philosophical base for pluralism, Pakistani or Egyptian modernists in quest of an Islamic activism, may look back longingly to Miskawayh and his ideals of culture, community and individuality. One feels a sense of loss in their care in detailing al-Ghazālī's recasting of Miskawayh's Aristotelian ethics into a Sufi mould. Pietism, to be sure, is not as likely a medium as courtesy for the founding of a new humanism – whether secular or theistic. Yet courtliness has had its say and its day in the Islamic world, and we have the work of Spinoza and of Kant to show us that even mysticism and pietism can ground a humanistic ethics if a philosopher of clear enough intelligence undertakes the task of construction.

NOTES

1 For the translation movement, see my chapters in the *Cambridge History of Arabic Literature*, vols I and II (Cambridge: Cambridge University Press, 1983, 1990).

2 For the nature of Qur'ānic discourse, see John Wansbrough, *Quranic Studies* (Oxford: Oxford University Press, 1977). For the moral range of the Qur'ān, see T. Izutsu, *Ethico-Religious Concepts in the Qur'ān* (Montreal: McGill University Press, 1966); Daud Rahbar, *God of Justice: A Study of the Ethical Doctrines of the Qur'ān* (Leiden: Brill, 1960); Fazlur Rahman, *Major Themes of the Qur'ān* (Minneapolis: Bibliotheca Islamica, 1989); Frederick Denny, 'Ethics and the Qur'ān: community and world view', in R. Hovanisian (ed.), *Ethics in Islam* (Malibu, Calif.: Undena, 1985).

3 Cf. George Hourani, 'Ethical presuppositions of the Qur'ān', in his *Reason and Tradition in Islamic Ethics* (Cambridge: Cambridge University Press, 1985), pp. 23–48.

4 The *Ṣaḥīḥ* or canon of *ḥadīth* gathered by Muslim is translated by A.-H. Siddiqi in four volumes published by Ashraf in Lahore, 1976; James Robson's translation of the widely used collection *Mishkāt al-Maṣābiḥ* is reprinted by the same publisher in two volumes (n.d.). Perhaps the best general introduction to Islam as a system of ideas is John Williams's sourcebook, *Themes of Islamic Civilization* (Berkeley: University of California Press, 1971); it contains many of the *ḥadīths* cited here and the long passage about the *muḥtasib* summarized below.

5 He was stripped of his wealth, beaten, imprisoned and left to die. See Franz Rosenthal, *Aḥmad b. aṭ-Ṭayyib as-Sarakhsī* (New Haven, Conn.: American Oriental Society, 1943), pp. 23–5.

6 For a modern analysis, see George Hourani's *Islamic Rationalism: the Ethics of 'Abd al-Jabbar* (Oxford: Oxford University Press, 1971), and my review in the *Middle East Journal* 25 (1971), 543–5.

7 For Ash'arism and the open universe, see my 'Three meanings of the idea of creation', in D. Burrell and B. McGinn (eds) *God and Creation* (Notre Dame: Notre Dame University Press, 1990); for the Ash'arite critique of optimism, Eric Ormsby, *Theodicy in Islamic Thought: The Dispute over al-Ghazālī's Best of All Possible Worlds* (Princeton: Princeton University Press, 1984); for the political background of *kalām*, W. Montgomery Watt, *The Formative Period of Islamic Thought* (Edinburgh: Edinburgh University Press, 1973).

8 Saadiah's critique of Ash'arism emerges brilliantly in his exegesis of the Book of Job; he

assigns the Ash'arite view that God may do as he pleases to the as yet unenlightened Job. See my Saadiah's *Book of Theodicy* (New Haven, Conn.: Yale University Press, 1988).

9 See Ash'arī's *Kitab al-Luma'*, trans. R. J. McCarthy, *The Theology of al-Ash'arī* (Beirut: Catholic Press, 1953). The inference that one cannot pry open a heart to test sincerity is from al-Ghazālī's *Iḥyā''Ulūm al-Dīn*, XXXV 2 (Cairo, 1967), 4. 305–6.

10 For the theory and practice of Sufism, see al-Hujwiri, *Kashf al-Maḥjūb* (*Drawing back the Veil*), trans. R. A. Nicholson, Gibb Memorial Series, 1967 (London: Luzac, 1911); for *inbisāṭ*, R. C. Zaehner, *Mysticism, Sacred and Profane* (London: Oxford University Press, 1971); for the orders, J. S. Trimmingham, *The Sufi Orders in Islam* (London: Oxford University Press, 1971); for the *samā'*, Bruce Lawrence, *Notes from a Distant Flute* (Tehran: Imperial Iranian Academy of Philosophy, 1978).

11 For hashish, see Franz Rosenthal, *The Herb: Hashish versus Medieval Muslim Society* (Leiden: Brill, 1971); for the dialectic of mystic licence, see my Halmos Lecture, 'Sacred and secular: rival themes in Arabic literature', University of Tel Aviv, 1988.

12 See Margaret Smith, *Al-Muhasibi (781–857), an Early Mystic of Baghdad* (Amsterdam: Philo Press, 1974 (1935); A. H. Abdel-Kader, *The Life, Personality and Writings of al-Junayd*, Gibb Memorial Series, (London: Luzac, 1962).

13 *Qūt al-Qulūb* (*Sustenance for Hearts*) (Cairo, 1961), 2.7, emended by the AH 1310 edn, 2.4.

14 See my article in the *Journal of the History of Ideas* 44 (1983), 115–30.

15 The best one-volume history of philosophy in Islam is Majid Fakhry's *A History of Islamic Philosophy* (New York: Columbia University Press, 1983). See also S. H. Nasr and O. Leaman, *History of Islamic Philosophy* (London: Routledge), 2 vols.

16 See al-Kindī's 'Essay on how to banish sorrow', eds H. Ritter and R. Walzer, *Uno Scritto Morale Inedito di al-Kindi* (Rome: Academia dei Lincei, 1938).

17 See my 'The Epicurean ethic of Muḥammad b. Zakariyā' al-Rāzī', *Studia Islamica* 34 (1971), 5–26.

18 See Charles Butterworth, 'Medieval Islamic philosophy and the virtue of ethics', *Arabica* 34 (1987), 221–50, and 'Ethics and classical Islamic philosophy: a study of Averroes' commentary on Plato's *Republic*', in Hovanisian, op. cit.

19 For the period see Roy Mottahedeh, *Loyalty and Leadership in an Early Islamic Society*, (Princeton: Princeton University Press, 1980); for the intellectual milieu, Joel Kraemer, *Humanism in the Renaissance of Islam: The Cultural Revival during the Buyid Age* (Leiden: Brill, 1986), and *Philosophy in the Renaissance of Islam* (Leiden: Brill, 1986).

20 The work is translated by Constantine Zurayk (American University of Beirut, 1968); the pages of this edition are cited parenthetically in what follows. The testimonial is from Richard Walzer and H. A. R. Gibb's article on ethics in the *Encyclopaedia of Islam* (Leiden: Brill, 1960), s. v. *akhlāq*; cf. M. A.-H. Ansari, *The Ethical Philosophy of Miskawayh* (Aligarh: Aligarh Muslim University, 1964).

21 For al-Ghazālī's appropriation of Miskawayh's ethics, see Richard Walzer's *Greek into Arabic* (Oxford: Cassirer, 1963), pp. 220–35 and the article *akhlāq* cited in the preceding note; for necessary qualifications to this account, M. Abul Quasem, 'Al-Ghazālī's rejection of philosophic ethics', *Islamic Studies* 13 (1974), 111–27, *The Ethics of al-Ghazālī, a Composite Ethics in Islam* (privately printed in Peninsular Malaysia, 1975); and M. A. Sherif, *Ghazali's Theory of Virtue* (Albany N. Y.: State University of New York Press, 1975).

22 See my translation of their *The Case of the Animals vs Man* before the King of the Jinn (Boston: Twayne, 1978).

23 See Kraemer's *Humanism in the Renaissance of Islam*, p. 115.

24 See Franz Rosenthal, *Knowledge Triumphant: The Concept of Knowledge in Medieval Islam* (Leiden: Brill, 1970), 284–7, 320.
25 See my article 'Razi's psychology', *Philosophical Forum* 4 (1972), 26–48.
26 See his *K. Mabādi'ārā' 'ahlu 'l-Madīnatu 'l-Fāḍila*, trans. with commentary by Richard Walzer as *Al-Farabi on the Perfect State* (Oxford: Oxford University Press, 1985); and *Fuṣūl al-Madanī*, trans. D. M. Dunlop as *Aphorisms of the Statesman* (Cambridge: Cambridge University Press, 1961).
27 See G. M. Wickens trans. *The Nasirean Ethics* (London: Allen & Unwin, 1964); W. Madelung, 'Naṣīr al-Dīn Ṭūsī's ethics between philosophy, Shi'ism, and Sufism', in Hovanisian, op. cit., pp. 85–101.
28 Quasem, op. cit., pp. 119–20.
29 See Sherif, op. cit., p. 69.
30 ibid., p. 185.
31 See Andras Hamori, *On the Art of Medieval Arabic Literature* (Princeton: Princeton University Press, 1974), pp. 11, 23.
32 Al-Ghazālī expands on his reservations about the dangers of self-aggrandizing motives in building mosques and other forms of public benefaction in his *Kashf wa 'l-Tabyīn fī Ghurūr al-Khalq Ajma'īn*, ed. M. al-Bābi (Cairo, 1960); see W. N. Arafat, 'Al-Ghazālī on moral misconceptions', *Islamic Quarterly* 14 (1970), 60–1.
33 See Sherif, op. cit., p. 183, citing al-Ghazālī's *Maqṣad.*
34 See the important article by Charles Pellat in the *Encyclopaedia of Islam.*
35 Sherif, op. cit., p. 72, citing *Maqṣad.*
36 *Journal of the American Oriental Society* 96 (1976), 69. The remark, in the abstract of his essay, is not repeated in the version printed in *Reason and Tradition.* But Hourani retains passages taking Ghazālī to task for diverging from the tendency of recent philosophers to 'connect obligation essentially with the interests of others . . . a view . . . now so prevalent that it has become a question whether one can ever have an obligation to oneself', *Reason and Tradition*, p. 141.

FURTHER READING

Al-Fārābī (1985) *K. Mabādi 'ārā' 'ahlu 'l-Madīnatu 'l-Fāḍila*, trans. R. Walzer, as *Al-Farabi on the Perfect State*, Oxford: Oxford University Press.

Amin, Osman (1979) 'Stoic ethics in classical Arabic culture', *Actas del V Congreso International de Filosofia Medieval*, Madrid: Editora Nacional, 1.89–94.

Arkoun, Mohammed (ed.) (1986) *L'Islam, morale et politique*, Paris: Desclée de Brouwer/ UNESCO.

Fakhry, Majid (1975) 'The Platonism of Miskawayh and its implications for his ethics', *Studia Islamica* 42 (1975), 39–57.

Hourani, George F. (1985) *Reason and Tradition in Islamic Ethics*, Cambridge: Cambridge University Press.

Hovanisian, R. (ed.) (1985) *Ethics in Islam*, Malibu, Calif.: Undena.

Ibn Ṭufayl (1983) *Ḥayy Ibn Yaqẓān*, trans. L. E. Goodman, Los Angeles: Gee Tee Bee.

Ikhwān al-Ṣafā' (1978) *The Case of the Animals vs Man before the King of the Jinn*, trans. L. E. Goodman, Boston: Twayne (reissued, Los Angeles, Gee Tee Bee).

Laoust, Henri (1970) *La Politique de Gazālī*, Paris: Geuthner.

Lazarus-Yafeh, Hava (1975) 'Place of the religious commandments in the philosophy of al-Ghazzālī', in her *Studies in al-Ghazzālī*, Jerusalem: Magnes Press.
Marmura, M. E. (1969) 'Ghazālī on ethical premises', *Philosophical Forum* NS 1 (1969), 393–403.
Nadvi, H. H. (1974) 'Al-Bīrūnī and his *K. al-Jamāhir fī Ma'rifat al-Jawāhir*: ethical reflections and moral philosophy', *Islamic Studies* 13 (1974), 253–68.
Schacht, J. (1966) *An Introduction to Islamic Law*, Oxford: Clarendon Press.

48

CONTEMPORARY ISLAMIC PHILOSOPHY

Hassan Hanafi

HISTORY, GEOGRAPHY, CIRCUMSTANCES, AND TRENDS

Contemporary Islamic philosophy requires first the definition of three words: 'contemporary', 'Islamic' and 'philosophy'.

There is no consent among scholars on what 'contemporary' should include. Does it include the nineteenth century, or does it refer only to the twentieth, since the nineteenth century more properly belongs to 'modern' Islamic philosophy? According to other scholars there is no such distinction to be drawn between contemporary and modern. The two terms are best used indiscriminately. Both begin with the first intellectual contact of the Muslim world with the West as it appears in thinkers such as al-Ṭaḥṭāwī (1801–73) in Egypt and Aḥmed Khan (1817–98) in India.

The term 'Islamic' covers most of the intellectual production in the Muslim world, and is wider and more accurate than the term 'Arabic' in 'contemporary Arabic philosophy', often used within the Arab world and in orientalism. Sometimes both terms are used interchangeably. 'Arabic' may of course refer not only to geography but also to language: many writings in the Muslim world are in Arabic, though others are written in English, French, Persian, Urdu and so on. The contemporary Muslim world was once one political entity, the Ottoman Empire, with relative independence of what are now Arab and Muslim national states.

Some regions were more active than others for geographical and historical reasons. Egypt, Syria, Turkey and India were more intellectually productive than the rest of the Muslim world. Egypt received the first cultural shock through the French expedition (1798–1801), before the French colonization of Algeria in 1830 and the British invasion of Aden in 1839. Syria was also in direct contact with Western culture through missionaries and Syrian Christians. Turkey was the metropole of the Muslim world and the centre of the caliphate, in direct contact with the West, eager to swallow the Ottoman Empire and through the young Turks to adopt the West as a model of modernization. Each centre stretched out to a wider area: Egypt in North Africa; Syria included Lebanon and Jordan; Turkey covered northern Iraq to central Asia; India expanded westwards including Iran, Pakistan and Afghanistan; and eastwards including Malaysia, Indonesia and the Philippines.

Arguably, Egypt was the centre of Muslim intellectual creativity. It lies at the heart of the Muslim world. North Africans passed through Egypt during their pilgrimage. For Turkey, Egypt may be, through the rule of Muḥammad Ali, the natural heir of the Ottoman Empire. Most Syrian intellectuals acquired their reputation once they journeyed to Egypt. For Sudan, Egypt is the northern gate to the West and to modernity. Islamic reform took place in Egypt and widely spread out eastwards to Malaysia and Indonesia. Egypt, during the rule of Muḥammad Ali, was the model of modernization in all Africa and Asia until Japan during the Meiji era. Ethnic homogeneity, social cohesion, central power, historical legacy and religious education made Egypt the cradle of contemporary Islamic philosophy.

The term 'philosophy' in Islam does not have a strict sense. It refers neither to a method nor to a system. It has a very wide sense including religious reform, socio-political thinking and secular scientific thought. The word 'thought' is more adequate than the word 'philosophy'. In many Arab universities, the subject matter is called 'thought', not 'philosophy', since it is said that the latter lacks theoretical rigour. It is still somehow similar to Montaigne's *Essais* and to the popular writings of the French Enlightenment. Systematic contemporary philosophy is absent since tradition plays, even now, the role of epistemology, ontology and axiology. God exists, the world is created and the soul is immortal: these three major philosophical propositions are still taken as unquestionable. There is no 'coupure éspistémologique' between the past and the present which permits a philosophical radical beginning as happened during the Renaissance in the West.

Historical circumstances led to the birth of contemporary Islamic philosophy. The French expedition to Egypt led by Napoleon Bonaparte was the first cultural shock. Scholars accompanying the army founded the 'institute', published newspapers, brought printing presses for Arabic and French, collected data and wrote a 'Description of Egypt'. A new modern world was seen and used as a mirror in which to see one's self. Missionaries, especially in Syria and Lebanon, founded new schools and colleges as well as scientific and literary societies. Orientalism also helped in the publication of classical texts and the study of the history of the Muslim world. New schools were founded. Several missions were sent to Europe to study modern sciences. Many writers visited Europe and wrote about their journeys. Printing expanded, and the press afforded new opportunity for the publication of new ideas and the popularization of culture. Translations from Western languages into Arabic gave Arabs and Muslims the opportunity to become acquainted with modern thought.

It is difficult to classify contemporary Islamic thinkers. Some scholars just mention them selectively and chronologically (A. Amin). Others classify them according to their professions: Khedival family, kings and princes, generals, administrators and politicians, businessmen and pious people, the pioneers of scientific renaissance, journalists, literary men (G. Zeidan). The spectrum here is extremely wide, and includes all men of reputation. Another scholar classifies thinkers into six groups: liberal and radical thinkers, reformers defending the Ottoman league, reactionaries also defending the Ottoman league, reformers defending Pan-Arabism and Pan-Islamism, Arab nationalists, and reformers calling for Ottoman decentralization (M. M. Musa). In this classification trends already appear, such as Pan-Islamism, Pan-Arabism, Arab nationalism, liberalism, reformism and radicalism. Another classification begins directly with four trends: religious, political, social and scientific (A. al-Muhafza). Another classification puts major thinkers into three groups: pioneers in literature, pioneers in culture and education, and pioneers in secular scientific thought (H. Sharabi). A final classification tries to distinguish between three groups: traditionalists or conservatives, modernists or pro-Westerners, and syncreticists (M. J. al-Ansari).

It is clear, however, that there are three major trends in contemporary Islamic thought: religious reform, socio-political thought and secular scientific thought. The first begins with religion, the second with the state and the third with science. At the same time, all thinkers orientate themselves on three fronts: old Islamic tradition, new Western tradition, and the present reality of the Arab and Muslim world, where these two traditions interact.

Religious reformers defend Islamic tradition after its renewal, criticize the metaphysical foundations of Western tradition such as materialism and atheism, and accept its practical achievements: freedom, democracy, social justice and scientific progress. On the other hand, secular scientific thought criticizes the petrified tradition and defends the Western one as a model of modernization. The third trend, namely socio-political liberalism, takes an eclectic stand *vis-à-vis* both traditions, Islamic as well as Western, reading each through the eyes of the other. Islam is a liberal religion, and Western liberalism is not that far from Islamic ideals. The purpose here is the foundation of the modern state linked to the past through continued tradition and to the present through Western modernity.

RELIGIOUS REFORM

Religious reform goes back to Ibn Taymiyya (1262–1327) and his efforts to purify Islam of mystical deviations, theological stagnation and legal formalism. Moral change of political power and mutual consultation (*shūrā*) with the people led to social change.

Subsequently, religious reform was launched by socio-religious and political movements. They were at first from a traditional type, *salafiyya*. The Wahhābī movement in Higaz founded by M. ibn ‘Abd Al-Wahhāb (1703–92) simply called for the purification of Islam and the return to Islamic doctrines like the unity of God, which appears in theory as transcendence and in practice as the rejection of superstitions and all forms of associations and intercessions between man and God. Al-Shawkani (1759–1839) in Yemen almost made the same call: purification of Islam, and rejection of imitation and deviations as well. In Iraq, the two Alusis Mahmoud (1802–53) and Shukry (1856–1924) repeated the same prescription with some mystical influence. In Libya, M. A. al-Sanusy (1787–1859) and his son al-Mahdi (1859–1902) shared the same goals: the return to the purity of early Islam, the rejection of imitation and the acceptance of mystical teachings. In Sudan, M. ben A. al-Mahdi (1844–85) reiterated the same guidelines: purification of Islam, reunification of the four schools of law, rejection of deviations, and struggle against political corruption. These *salafiyya* reform movements had an impact at the practical level through socio-political activism. Their theoretical contribution was, however, minimal: philosophy was still banned since al-Ghazālī's ‘refutation’ in the *Tahāfut* and the legal opinions prohibiting philosophy such as that of Ibn al-Salah.

Since previous religious movements were essentially efforts to renew the self and to restore its purity in history, another reformist school was more open to the West. New circumstances arose, for example the occupation of the Muslim world by Western powers. The scene was this: the backwardness of the self, and progress of the West. The question arose, why did the Muslims decline while the West progressed? Al-Afghani (1839–97) was the pioneer of this movement. The Islamic world declined because Muslims lost their faith. They have to liberate themselves from fanaticism; faith and science can be accommodated. The return to the authentic Islamic tradition helps in the affirmation of the self and the rejection of the imitation of the West. However, Muslims have to be open to modernity without imitation. Islam is capable of giving Muslims nowadays the prerequisites of renaissance against Renan's opposition between Islam and science. Islam is a huge modern project of liberation of the Muslim world from external colonialism and internal despotism. Predestination as passive behaviour is a misinterpretation of the Islamic belief in destiny. Muslims form one community in one Pan-Islamic political entity sharing wealth and free citizenship. A. al-Nadim (1845–96) combined revolutionary theory with revolutionary practice defending freedom, democracy, citizenship and patriotism. M. Abdu (1849–1905), Afghani's disciple, continued his master's mission, concentrating on the ethical and educational foundation of reform, the purification of Islam from all forms of deviation, reviewing Islamic doctrinal systems in the light of modern science, the defence of Islam against Western influences, and the reform of higher education. His disciple M. R. Reda (1865–1935) continued in the same way declaring the independence of thought and the freedom of reason in practising science, the rejection of superstitions and non-Islamic social customs, the return to pure Islam as presented in Islamic scriptures, the refutation of all anti-Islamic doctrines such as atheism, materialism and nihilism, the re-education of Muslims and the spreading of Islam throughout the world. Ch. Arsalan (1869–1946) continued to ask the same question: why had Muslims declined while others progressed? His agenda was twofold: first, Muslim glory in the past not only on the southern Mediterranean shore but also on the northern shore, in Europe; second, Muslim crisis in the present and how to solve it. H. al-Banna, Reda's disciple (1906–46), conceived Islam as a whole edification of the individual and of the community. He implemented al-Afghani's dream, founding an Islamic revolutionary party to realize the Islamic revolutionary project: Islam versus imperialism from outside and despotism inside. The Muslim Brethren was a hugely popular organization capable of acquiring power just before the 1952 army revolt in Egypt. Sayed Qutb (1906–66) was the most prominent thinker of the Brethren before being jailed and tortured in 1954. His 'signposts on the road' opposing Islam to *jāhiliyya* and calling for the total destruction of the actual Muslim states to build a new ideal society is, even now, the motto of Muslim activist groups.

In this reformist modernist school there has been a gradual decline in radicalism from the pioneers to the present generation. Only Adib Ishak (1856–85), the Christian disciple of al-Afghani, continued the ascending radical line of the thought of his master, looking for causes of the Muslim decline and of the Western progress. While M. Abdu suffered a set-back after the defeat of the Orabi revolution, R. Reda suffered another set-back after the take-over of the young Turks in 1924, changing the caliphate to a secular liberalist Western model, and switched from modernist reform to *salafiyya* conservatism. Internal circumstances can be behind such set-backs, as in the case of S. Qutb. He began as a poet, literary critic and writer on social affairs and switched after prison and torture, since 1954, from social revolution to *coup d'état*, from open political and social struggle to underground secret organization, from openness and dialogue to closeness and monologue.

A third branch of religious reform is linked to the internal circumstances of the Muslim world, namely the destiny of the caliphate to be preserved, a symbol of Islamic unity, but reformed to cope with modernity; or abolished for other alternatives, such as Arab nationalism for the Arab world or regional nationalism for Turkey. Al-Sayadi (1849–1909) defended the Ottoman Empire in the name of unity of the Muslim world. R. al-Azm (1867–1925) defended a reformed Ottoman Empire given the importance of social relations, the affirmation of self-identity and the need for decentralization. A. al-Maghribi (1867–1956) called for a modern democratic and socialist Ottoman Empire. T. al-Gazairi (1852–1920) called for decentralization legitimizing Arab and Ottoman leagues. A. al-Zahrawi (1855–1916) shared the same ideal in order to keep ethnic diversity within Islamic unity. S. al-Quasimi (1887–1916) stood for Arab renaissance based on decentralization, nationalism, freedom, education, democracy and science. His brother G. al-Quasimi (1865–1914) shared the same ideals: a critique of Ottoman despotism and a call for freedom, democracy, and a parliamentary system based on a constitution. Religion is viable once based on patriotism, science, education and expertise. Arabism is identical to Islam, since Arabs were the first carriers of Islam.

Al-Kawakibi (1848–1902) is the prominent figure who represents this dual legitimacy between Ottoman and Arab leagues. He studied the nature of despotism and how to overcome dictatorship, trying to find the links between despotism on the one side and religion, masses, wealth and so on on the other. He also described the indifference of the Muslim masses, trying to trace its religious, political, ethical and social causes. In North Africa, religious reform followed the modernist school founded by al-Afghani and represented by A. ben Badis (1887–1914) and A. al-Ibrahimi (1889–1965) in Algeria, A. al-Fasi (1910–74) in Morocco and A. ben Ashour (d. 1868) in Tunisia. Islam and nationalism are identical without the intercession of Arab nationalism, which may be distinct from Pan-Islamism or regional nationalism, as in Syria.

In Asia, religious reform was initiated in India by A. Khan (1817–98), who introduced Muslims there to modern Western culture. A. Ali (1849–1928) also tried to express the spirit of Islam as a rational, ethical and human world-view. M. Iqbal (1873–1938) expressed his new Islamic philosophy in prose, though mostly in poems. The affirmation of the self, *khūdī*, as subjectivity in the individual and in the community is a manifestation of divinity in human life. 'God', *khodā*, is from the same root. In subjectivity, man and God are unified. Subjectivity is true creativity, internal spiritual life similar to mystical experience. It opposes all forms of external domination and internal imitation. The West, on the other hand, is material, conceptual and hegemonic. The philosophy of life of Bergson and Nietzsche and the practical idealism of Fichte may lie behind Iqbal's philosophy.

Religious reform takes a defensive position *vis-à-vis* Islamic tradition and a critical stand *vis-à-vis* Western culture, for the last three generations since R. Reda: M. Iqbal, Qutb and actual Muslim groups. The tradition begins with divine revelation in the Qur'ān, continues through the prophetic tradition and arrives at the legal schools. Since it was successful in the past in changing society and in founding a state and even an empire, it is also thought capable, nowadays, of doing the same. Sometimes it is called integrism or fundamentalism, a predictable reaction to Westernization and to the failure of modern ideologies of modernization.

Religious reform continued to be a major source of inspiration for modern Islamic philosophy, although it was not an academic and rigorous philosophy in itself: it was still rhetoric, popular and activist. It has subsided now and become history. New generations are now succeeding in transforming this zeal into a more rigorous religious thought as a transitional step towards philosophy as a rigorous discipline.

SOCIO-POLITICAL THOUGHT

Socio-political thought is the second trend in modern Islamic thought beginning with the state. Two distinctive schools can be recognized: regional nationalism and Arab nationalism.

Al-Ṭaḥṭāwī (1801–73) in Egypt is the father of Egyptian nationalism. He conceived a modern national state based on liberalism, and the ideas of enlightenment. The fatherland is the place for all citizens to live in and to build by freedom, thought and factory. The ideals of the French Revolution – liberty, equality and fraternity – are at the very basis of civil society. The common welfare is preserved as a common goal. Labour is the only source of value. Agriculture, industry and commerce are the main sources of the nation's wealth. The separation of powers lays the ground for the parliamentary system. The education of women and girls is as much a national duty as that of men and boys. Western political ideals were assimilated into Islamic culture and justified by Islamic sources as if they were coming from within Islamic tradition, not from without. Egyptian nationalism and Islam are identical. Love of one's country is an article of faith. A. Mubarak (1824–93) continued on this mission, concentrating on education and city planning. He also, like al-Ṭaḥṭāwī, compared the Western life style with the traditional one. A. F. Zaghloul (1863–1914) gave an account of the English constitution and wrote on the causes of the progress of the British, on principles of law and on social solidarity. His brother S. Zaghloul (1857–1927) led the Egyptian liberal revolution on the borderline between religious reform and constitutional liberalism. A. L. al-Sayed (1872–1963) renewed al-Ṭaḥṭāwī's effort with more linkage to Western sources of liberalism in Greece. M. H. Heikal (1888–1956) and M. Fahmy (d. 1958) tried to find philosophical sources for liberal nationalism. T. Hussein (1889–1973) was the most prominent figure representing this trend. The ideal type of culture for Egypt is Western liberal culture. Egypt is more linked historically and culturally to Western Mediterranean culture than to the eastern one.

In Syria, the same trend appeared with A. F. al-Shidiaq (1805–87). Cultural liberalism is not absolute, since it is limited by socialism under the influence of Christian socialism in England. His critique of religious authority and sacerdocy made him a new Christian Voltaire of the East in spite of his defence of the caliphate against Orabi's revolution. In Tunisia, Kh. al-Tunsi (1810–90) played the same role as al-Ṭaḥṭāwī in Egypt. He compared political systems, in both the Muslim and European worlds, extending his remarks not only to Egypt but also to the whole Muslim world. Positive aspects of Western political systems such as freedom, democracy and progress are Islamic ideals. Modern sciences, urbanism, agriculture and industry are major components of Islamic culture, not a monopoly of the West. In Turkey, Medhat Pacha (1822–83), called 'the father of liberals', reformed caliphate regions in Balcan, Baghdad, Syria and Izmir, and he participated in the downfall of the sultans for constitutional rule based on democracy and mutual consultation between the ruler and the ruled.

Arab nationalism was another school of socio-political thought, especially in Syria and Lebanon, more radical and completely secular. R. Hassoun (1825–80) and F. Marrash (1835–74) borrowed from Western thought liberty, equality, justice, social and political democracy, and liberation from medieval despotism. They criticized socio-political circumstances in the Ottoman Empire, urging the Arabs to liberate themselves from the Turkish yoke. Hassoun asked the help of the Russians and the British, while Marrash based his call for liberation on the evolutionist theory looking for the origins of creatures, societies, states and civilizations. G. D. al-Halabi (1836–92) shared these same ideals.

Arab nationalism sometimes leant on nationalism more than on liberalism, motivated by the desire to separate from the Ottoman Empire and to find a unifying alternative in Arabism without falling into the sectarianism already threatening Lebanon. Most of the representatives of this trend were Lebanese Christians such as N. al-Yazigi (1800–71), B. al-Bustani (1819–83), I. al-Yazigi (1847–1906), N. Azouri (d. 1916), S. al-Bustani (1856–1925) and N. Fares (b. 1856). They were all against religious fanaticism, calling for a return to the Arab heritage of tolerance and brotherhood. The study of Arabic language and literature flourished, and new Arabic dictionaries were compiled. All Arabs belonged to the same fatherland. Knowledge was a deep motivation in all human beings unifying all Arabs if sectarianism separate them: a new common education was necessary for the masses as well as for the élite to form a new secular and national society. Arab societies participated in the formulation and in the realization of this trend. In practice, new secret societies were founded for fear of Turkish persecution of calls for Arab independence. Their political blueprint included: the independence of Syria unified with most of Lebanon, Arabic as the official language of the country, cancellation of censorship, and national military service. The Arab League or the League of the Arab Nation, founded in 1904 by N. Azouri, was the first to call for one independent modern Arab state, based on secular nationalism and science. Many other societies continued calling for Arab nationalism. The first Arab congress, held in Paris in 1913, formalized the whole movement in such principles as the reform of the Ottoman Empire, Arab autonomy within the Empire, and sharing in its rule, central authority in each Arab region, Arabic as the official language, and national military service.

The movement continued this century, finding new incentives from history in the writings of S. al-Husari (1879–1968) and from culture by M. Aflaq (1910–89). Al-Husari combined history with sociology and education. He showed the origins of regional nationalism and its limits, arguing with its representatives in Egypt and Lebanon, and distinguishing between Arab nationalism and European nationalism. Aflaq identified Arab nationalism with Islam as the Arab religion. Arab nationalism is based on three principles: unity, socialism and freedom. An apolitical party, the Arab Socialist Renaissance Party, was founded in order to implement the ideology in practice. The party now, in two opposing factions, rules in Syria and Iraq.

The major motivation in socio-political thought was the establishment of independent modern states or one Arab state because of the weakness of the central power in Istanbul. However, the same phenomenon of degradation of religious reform existed also in socio-political thought, a gradual weakness from the first to the fifth generation, from al-Ṭahṭāwī to the New Wafd Party in Egypt, from Kh. al-Tunsi to the New Destour Party in Tunisia, from N. Azouri to the practice of the Arab Socialist Renaissance Party in Syria and Iraq. Al-Ṭahṭāwī conceived the modern state as the vehicle of modernization through public-sector and state socialism. The New Wafd Party preserved the old liberalism conceived as a capitalist, *laissez-faire* economy depending largely on the private sector. Al-Tunsi imposed modern ideas of enlightenment on Islamic law, while the New Destour Party broke Islamic law by fast-breaking in Ramadan and reformed family law. N. Azouri called for one independent Arab state, and the practice of the Arab Socialist Party made foes of two Arab nations adhering to the same ideology, Syria and Iraq.

Another observable phenomenon is that of set-backs in the life of the same author who begins as a liberal secularist, and ends as a conservative religious defender because of external or internal factors, socio-political circumstances or traditional and historical elements. Al-Ṭahṭāwī pursued his line of thought till the end in spite of his exile to Sudan. However, A. Abdel Razek (d. 1927) and Kh. M. Khaled, on the borderline between reformism and liberalism, repented their early secularism and returned to the rule of Islam and the necessity of an Islamic state.

The importance of socio-political liberalism appears as a linkage between the three main currents in modern Islamic thought. Religious reform adopted liberal ideals. Liberalism was grafted on to Islamic law. Scientific secularism is a liberal model. It is clear that socio-political liberalism extends over the two other currents, deriving its sources from Islamic tradition or from Western culture. It expresses a real need for the Muslim world in transition from tradition to modernity. Some authors are on the borderline between religious reform and socio-political liberalism, such as K. Amin (1862–1908), the disciple of M. Abdu and champion of women's rights, and al-Aqqad (1889–1964), the disciple of S. Zaghloul, the Egyptian nationalist leader and Islamic writer.

The cultural stand of socio-political thought is eclecticism. It selects from Islamic tradition and Western culture what satisfies present needs. The tradition is neither absolutely positive, as is the case in integrism, nor absolutely negative, as viewed by Western secularism. In the tradition, there are different alternatives: anthropomorphism and transcendence, predestination and free will, faith and reason. The same alternatives exist in the West. The criterion of choice is the needs of the present societies. If they need reason and free will they find the satisfaction of their needs, first in their own tradition, and second in Western tradition, reading that tradition into its own. Contemporary Islamic philosophy is, mainly, the outcome of such dialectics between the tradition of the self and the modernity of the other.

SECULAR SCIENTIFIC THOUGHT

Secular scientific thought is the third trend in modern Islamic thought, carried on, first, by Arab Christians from Lebanon, Syria and Egypt and then followed by Muslim thinkers, especially in Egypt. Sh. Shmayel (1850–1917), a Lebanese doctor, is the founder of this trend. He popularized Darwin's theory of evolution as interpreted by Buchner, a combination of Darwinism and materialism. He was a partisan of a decentralized Ottoman administrative party. However, he adopted a natural philosophy derived from the natural sciences, as only the sciences are capable of making progress in human societies. Philosophy, education, art, sociology, psychology, anthropology, economics, law, even metaphysics, including religion and religious sciences – especially theology – are all, on his view, natural sciences. Natural philosophy is useful for society. It offers a philosophical view of the origin of the universe, helping man to understand his situation in the cosmos; it also has a practical use in making progress such as occurred in the West; and it has a political use in promoting knowledge of one's rights and duties. Shmayel attacked despotism and called for revolution, and he advocated a socialist society and an international community based on freedom and justice. Even language can be universal, as in the case of scientific language. A modern state can never be founded on political despotism or religion. Authority in society emerges from social contract, the basis of an ideal republican electoral regime as opposed to a royal absolute or relative despotism.

F. Anton (1872–1922) shared the same ideas derived from natural philosophy. He translated Renan's *Life of Jesus*, some parts of his *Origins of Christianity* and conversations between Nietzsche and Tolstoy. He defended secularism and a separation between religion and state. The purposes of these two authorities are different and even contradictory. Religion aims at cult and virtue according to scriptures forcing others to adopt its doctrines and values, while the state protects individual freedoms granted by the constitution. Religion admits distinction between religions, while the state considers all religions as equal. Religions concern the afterlife, while the state concerns this world. A religious state is weak, since it uses religion for popular consent, while the secular state is strong in the face of hard realities. Religious authority ends in war, while a secular state is more eager for peace. Like Shmayel, who tried to find indigenous sources for his natural philosophy in the Qur'ān, F. Anton found them in Averroes as interpreted by Renan, a rationalist materialist philosopher. Reform socialism as a transitional form of socialism is viable. However, scientific socialism in the future is the only means leading to freedom, equality, justice, brotherhood, prosperity, happiness, mutual understanding, tolerence, solidarity, and peace for all nations.

Secular scientific thought was popularized by Y. Sarrouf (1852–1927) in agriculture, industry, engineering, medicine and mathematics, with particular emphasis on botany and local plants. The development of modern technology in the West was compared with its position in the Arab and Muslim world. Linguistic, literary and religious sciences are not enough for social development and historical renaissance. Others like S. al-Bustani (1856–1925), A. al-Rihani (1876–1940) and N. Haddad (1870–1954) popularized natural science, history and scientific theories. S. Musa (1887–1958) continued the tradition and visualized all modern thinkers in Western culture as masters and educators: Darwin, Weissmen, Marx, Nietzsche, Voltaire, Freud, Renan, Dewey. None of them comes from the Islamic tradition. He popularized modern ideas to effect a cultural shock in traditional Islamic culture, for example the psycho-socio-historical origin of the concept of God, psychoanalysis and evolution. I. Mazhar (1891–1962) also propagated Darwin's theory, applying it in religion and criticizing all syncretic reformist trends. Z. N. Mahmoud (1904–93) began as a logical positivist, thinking that logical positivism would help in knowing how to use language and how to practise analytical and scientific methods. Afterwards he began to apply logical positivism to modernize Islamic traditions and Arabic thought, criticizing the Arabic language as leaning towards subjectivity. Arabic thought postulates a conceptual dualism between heaven and earth, the other world and this world, religion and science. Arabic thought can be modernized once it becomes more rational, scientific and open to dialogue. F. Zakaria (b. 1927), on the borderline between scientific and liberal thought, stresses the importance of scientific thought against mythical and religious thought and defends the natural stand of man in the cosmos. The model of scientific thought is also natural science.

In secular scientific thought the same phenomenon of gradual deradicalization occurred from the previous first generation to the current fifth, from Sh. Shmayel to F. Zakaria, from the propagation of scientific thought from within and without to the propagation of scientific thought only from without and the criticism of it within, from linking civilization and modernity to the Qur'ān (Shmayel) and to Averroes (F. Anton), Ibn Ṭufayl and Ikhwān al-Safā' to linking modernity only to logical positivism, scientific determinism and Reichenbach. The same phenomenon of set-backs also occurs. Shmayel, Anton, Haddad and Musa pursued their secular scientific thought from the beginning till the end. I. Mazhar turned back from Darwinism to Islam. Z. N. Mahmoud switched interest from the propagation of logical positivism to the critique of tradition and the renewal of Arab thought, from the outside to the inside, at least changing data with a consistent rational, analytical and scientific view. F. Zakaria also switched interest from the propagation of Western scientific thought to the critique of Islamic fundamentalism.

Secular scientific thought takes a critical and even an opposing stand to tradition. Tradition is obsolete, related to the past. It does not correspond any more to the needs of present Muslim societies. It is better to adopt modern culture, usually identical to the Western one, the universal culture assimilated by all peoples and societies. Between religious reform and scientific secularism there are certain dialectics of negation and affirmation. Religious reform defends the tradition and criticizes the West; scientific secularism, on the contrary, criticizes tradition and defends the West. Both are radical stands in spite of their differences in negation and affirmation; each is a reaction to the other.

The three major trends in modern Arab and Islamic thought deal with three fronts. First is the tradition still persisting after fourteen centuries providing the masses with their theoretical world-view and practical norms. Second is the West, a new challenge for tradition, a second source of knowledge and action for almost two centuries, especially for the élite. This second separate and outside source created secularism in secular scientific thought and modernism in religious reform and in socio-political thought. Third is the reality of the Muslim world, its needs and exigencies, which are behind the reform of tradition or the initiation of modernity.

These three fronts are also three dimensions of time. The tradition is anchored in the past and coming out of it. Western modernity is aiming at the future, projecting its hopes and ideals forward. The reality of the Muslim world is the present, open to the legacy of the past and tending towards the possibilities of the future.

Since tradition is deeply rooted in time, it assumes more importance in contemporary Islamic thought than does Western tradition. That is why these three fronts are unequal in length and consequently in depth of consciousness. The first is longer, deeply rooted in national consciousness. The second is shorter in time and consequently lies on the surface of national consciousness. The third is absent from it given the cultural alienation of national consciousness, once to the past and once to the future. From the first front comes mostly mass culture, from the second comes that of the élite, and from the third comes only the suffering and pains expressed by poets and writers.

PROFESSIONAL PHILOSOPHICAL CURRENTS AND RESEARCH PROJECTS TODAY

There are two kinds of philosophical activity in the contemporary Muslim world. First, there is professional philosophy pursued by teachers of philosophy in universities, mostly through textbooks. Emerging from an era of ignorance when philosophy was still condemned as it was in the days of al-Ghazālī and Ibn al-Salah as useless and a threat to faith, philosophy began to find its way into modern Arab and Muslim thought, introducing reason and real-life experiences as criteria for thinking, through contacts with the West. Philosophy became a subject in the high-school curriculum, including logic, psychology, ethics and sociology. Students were sent abroad to study at postgraduate level. The foundation of universities and departments of philosophy helped in transforming philosophy into a discipline.

Philosophy began with a triple mission: editions of texts, philosophical studies in different languages, and translations from Western philosophy. Many ancient Arabic texts were edited, covering whole areas of philosophy, theology, mysticism and jurisprudence. Histories of philosophy were written for Greek, medieval and modern Western philosophy as well as for Islamic philosophy.

It is difficult to speak about philosophical schools, trends or even currents in this professional philosophy. However, the choice of texts translated, authors to be written about, systems to be treated or methods to be adopted reveals certain states of mind or attitudes which might be classified as follows:

1. Rationalism was advocated by some teachers valuing reason versus tradition, mysticism and superstition, finding their roots in ancient Mu'tazilism and Averroism and in Western rationalism, Cartesianism (Tawil, Qasim, Iraqi). It can be extended to Spinozism (Hanafi) or Hegelianism (Imam).

2. Idealism or spiritualism was adopted by certain teachers (O. Amin, Z. Arsouzi), a certain rationalism tinted with intuitionism called 'consciencism', *Jowaniya*, or immanentism, *Rahmaniya*, from the word *wom*, giving priority to inside versus outside, to intuitionism versus abstraction, similar to Bergsonism or to Cartesianism newly interpreted through Bergson.

3. Materialism or Marxism was also adopted as a reaction to the excess of spiritualism and idealism, which sometimes reached the limits of superstition and irrationalism. Since in traditional societies materialism is seen as atheism, anarchism and nihilism, it was difficult for this to be adopted directly. Marxism or dialectical materialism was a better choice since it is linked to social science and to methodology (M. Wahba).

4. Scientism was also advocated as an efficient tool for the reform of superstitions and unscientific societies. Science is usually natural, scientific method, philosophy of science, scientific logic, logical positivism, methodology, mathematics, and the scientific world-view, etc. (A. M. Mosharafa, M. Nazif, H. Tukan, Z. N. Mahmoud, A. Sabra, Abu Rayan, M. Th. al-Findi, F. Zakaria, M. Zeidan, S. Qonsou), a useful alternative to rhetoric and passion.

5. Neo-Thomism was adopted by some Christian teachers combining reason and nature, God and grace, predestination and free will, reason and mystery, transcendence and anthropomorphism (Y. Karam, Ch. Malek, G. Sh. Anawati), a philosophy of equilibrium acceptable enough in a believing society.

6. Neo-realism was also chosen as a combination between idealism and realism, between spiritualism and naturalism, between time, space and deity (Y. Heweidi). S. Alexander, R. B. Parry and other new realists became well known.

7. Phenomenology was also used as philosophy and as method (H. Hanafi), a reconstruction of Western human sciences and an analysis of real-life experiences to solve the methodological crisis of deductive and inductive methods and the subsequent crisis in human sciences between formalism and empiricism.

8. Existentialism finally appeared in the writings of some teachers (Z. Ibrahim, A. Badawi), whether believing in existentialism – Kierkegaard, Jaspers, Marcel – or rejecting it – Heidegger, Merleau-Ponty, Nietzsche. The loss of the individual and the desire for human freedom are two major motivations for such choice.

Second, there are also important research projects, which are gaining more and more popularity among philosophers trying to link the three trends in modern Arab and Muslim thought and the professional philosophy of university teachers. They are thinkers and teachers, reformers and academicians, practitioners and theoreticians, citizens and scholars. After the defeat of 1967, they went beyond professional philosophy as an academic career to conceive systematic research projects as a means to victory, critical of the self and of the other. Most of them, if not all, began with a method or a doctrine from the West, using it as a tool or as a link by and through which past tradition or actual crisis is analysed or seen. Each thinks, more or less, that his methodological or doctrinal choice is motivated by the needs of his time and the desire to contribute to the new renaissance of the Arab and Muslim world after the several set-backs which it suffered since the colonization of the last century and the recolonization of this century.

It is difficult to enumerate such projects, since some of them are total and some are partial. Many of them are still linked to professional philosophy, such as *Jowaniya* (O. Amin) or ethical idealism (T. Tawil), logical positivism (Z. N. Mahmoud), Neo-Thomism (Y. Karam) and existentialism (Badawi, Z. Ibrahim). However, six major integral research projects came to the forefront of professional philosophy and are still stimulating major intellectual activity. The authors are still alive except one (H. Muruwa, who was assassinated in Lebanon).

1. *Critique of Arab Mind* by al-Gabri is the most spectacular project, since reason inherited from the past is dependent on scripture (Ash'arism) or internal illumination (mysticism). The critique would free reason from literalism and irrationalism in order to become pure demonstrative and scientific reason. *Arab Mind* has as its genesis eloquence (*bayan*), theosophy (*'irfān*) and demonstration (*burhān*). It also has a similar triadic structure, whether in epistemology or in politics (belief, tribe, spoils), similar to the old-fashioned racial classification of people's minds. *Modernization of Arab Mind* by H. Sa'ab refers essentially to the Islamic tradition still adopted in national culture.

2. *Critique of Epistemological Mind* by M. Arkoun is written in French concentrating on linguistics and theory of knowledge and applied to scripture and tradition. Linguistics as a science was found helpful in showing the degree of progress in philosophy. From linguistics came a new renaissance of human and social sciences. The Qur'ān is a language, an Islamic tradition, and as a whole a corpus. The Arab mind needs to know how to read itself and how to read its tradition. It needs epistemology, not ontology or axiology. The '*Double Critique*' of A. al-Khatibi is directed not only at Islamic tradition but at the Western one also. Critique is a double-edged weapon working two ways, in the self and in the other. Comparative linguistics is also a means of affirming that Arabic language is at the very source of all other languages. Consequently, Arabism is an absolute value (A. F. Khesheim).

3. *Project of a New Vision of Arabic Thought* by T. Tizini is a history in twelve volumes of Arabic thought written from a historical materialistic viewpoint describing

the genesis of this thought, coming from below, not jumping from above, born on earth, not descending from heaven. *Materialistic Trends in Arabic Islamic Philosophy* by H. Muruwa comprises two volumes: classical Islamic philosophy discovering materialistic trends from within, not from without. *Critique of Religious Thought* by S. G. Azum criticizes religion obstructing scientific thought and used as the opium of the people. *Contemporary Arab Ideology* exposes Arab or liberal Marxism, a certain kind of Marxism adapted to the historical circumstances of the Arab world. Liberalism is still at a transitional historical stage, from tradition to modernism, liberty as a means, social justice as an end. The middle class is still the vehicle of modernization via its class consciousness and it can express the interests of peasants and workers, not necessarily the bourgeois class sold to the haute bourgeoisie.

4. The *Islamic Personalism* of Lahbabi tries to discover the human being from within Islamic tradition, not only from without. Since the individual is absent in tradition as well as in mass culture and socio-political practice, it may be possible to rediscover him in philosophy, ethics, mysticism or jurisprudence. Since human liberty is a struggle for liberation, an *a posteriori* acquisition, not an *a priori* concept, Bergson was linked to Mounier. Muslim personality is a historical being, created in the past and tending to the future (H. Djait).

5. *Tradition and Modernism* by H. Hanafi is another project conceiving modernization from within, not from without, parting from the inherent potentiality of the tradition to modernize itself. If the actual need of the Arab and Muslim world is to deepen its spiritual legacy, there is use of authentic research and criticism of the stereotyped images of Western orientalism. The project contains three parts: first, the reconstruction of classical sciences, rational scriptural sciences (theology, philosophy, mysticism and jurisprudence), pure scriptural sciences (Qur'ān, *tafsīr*, *ḥadīth*, *sīra* and *fiqh*) and pure rational sciences, mathematical and physical sciences as well as human and social sciences. Second, a critique of Western tradition and the foundation of a new science of 'occidentalism' in opposition to 'orientalism', in which the West is taken as an object of research. Third, a theory of interpretation which permits reading reality in the texts and the texts in reality for a new hermeneutics departing from holy scriptures.

6. *Social Dialectics* by Abdel Malek is a socio-cultural and political project based on such major concepts as specificity, historical supervalue, time, state, army, endogenous intellectual creativity and national renaissance. The Arab and Muslim world is a part of the world order, a cultural circle distinct from two other cultural circles, the India–China circle and the Western European and American circle. In the first circle, ancient civilizations and states arose in China and Egypt. The state is a tool of modernization. The army is the crux of the state and the charismatic leader is its soul. Intellectuals, philosophers, writers and scientists are components of the state. The ideology is national renaissance, the transformation of this cultural circle to political ideology against Western hegemony and for cultural independence. Linked to the East, the Arab and Muslim world makes one bloc against the West.

Philosophy in the Muslim world during the past two centuries has been in three stages: first, modern Islamic thought and its three trends and five generations; second, contemporary Arab and Muslim professional philosophy since the foundation of modern universities, mostly linked to Western philosophy; third, present research projects combining the first and second stages. Ideologies of renaissance: religious reform, socio-political thought and scientific secularism with professional philosophy, for a second hopeful renaissance.

LIMITS OF CONTEMPORARY ISLAMIC PHILOSOPHY

Contemporary Islamic thought is still out of touch with contemporary Islamic realities. It does not sufficiently face the major challenges of the Muslim world. The distance between theoretical apparatus and hard reality is still too big in spite of all the efforts of religious reform, socio-political liberalism and secular scientific thought. The weapon used is much weaker than the enemy faced. There are seven hard Muslim realities which are still refractory to modern Islamic thought.

1. A first challenge is the decolonization and liberation of occupied territories by Western and Eastern powers, including the Zionist occupation of Palestine. It is not enough to call for liberation of occupied territories as a religious duty. Land can also be a part of the credo, since God is God of heaven and earth. Hitherto, the Ash'arite creed has been repeated, the theory of essence, attributes and acts of God which was conceived against classical religious sects, dualism and trinitarianism during the early centuries of Islam; yet a theology of land can be more efficient for the liberation of the occupied territories. Hitherto, land has appeared as a value in liberation in poems, songs and theatre: not yet in theology, philosophy, jurisprudence or mysticism. The old tradition helps in such a new effort since physics is not distinct from metaphysics in theology and philosophy; since God and the world are one in mysticism; and since divine revelation is applied in society as law. Romanticism of the land in Western culture can also provide a second source of inspiration.

2. The freedom of all Muslim peoples against internal oppression and despotic rule is a second major challenge. Muslims have been colonized by foreigners from outside and dominated by their princes and kings from inside. The greatest gain in contemporary Islamic philosophy was the opportunity to criticize traditional fatalism and to reject predestination (al-Afghani, Iqbal), to switch from *Kasb* theory (al-Ash'arī), a certain kind of occasionalism, to *libre arbitre* theory (Mu'tazilites) as M. Abdu did in his *Treatise on Unity*. A complete and radical theory of free choice is not yet conceived, a choice based on rational wavering between alternatives or on self-determination. Unity of God (*tawḥīd*) is not yet equal to freedom. In Islamic tradition, there are components of freedom in theology (Mu'tazilism) and in law, in the obligation of

revolt against an unjust ruler. Theories of freedom in Western culture are multiple and appeal to the needs of the Muslim world.

3. Social justice has been strongly advocated in contemporary Islamic thought. Socialism, according to al-Afghani, is the essence of religion. Violence is permitted from the peasants. M. al-Siba'i in Syria wrote *Socialism in Islam*; S. Qutb in Egypt wrote *Social Justice in Islam*. In *The Struggle between Islam and Capitalism* al-Ṭaḥṭāwī advocated a state-orientated economy and a strong public sector. Sh. Shmayel, S. Musa and I. Mazhar defended socialism and even Marxism. However, religious thought is accepting socialism as a social and moral practice, not as a theory. As a theory, it is considered as materialism, nihilism and Communism (al-Afghani). It is also state socialism, not popular socialism (al-Ṭaḥṭāwī), and Marxism as Western political ideology (S. Musa). Socialism, up to now, is not part of the Islamic creed, linked to the eminent ownership of God. Productive activity such as agriculture and industry cannot be in private ownership. Public welfare has absolute priority over individual interests. Different kinds of socialism are offered by Western culture and can be taken as auxiliary examples for strengthening one's self.

4. The unification of the Muslim world has always been advocated in the name of Pan-Islamism in religious reform, Pan-Arabism in scientific secularism and the new caliphate in socio-political liberalism. However, sectarian and civil wars followed. The concept of unity, till now, as a part of belief has not been included as a basis for political unity. Precedents existed: the unity of Arabia, the unity of central Asia and the unity of India. Western culture provides other examples from the link between the metaphysics of unity and political unity in Germany.

5. Westernization is still overwhelming in the Muslim world. A crisis of identity is evident in many areas. All modern thinkers tackle the issue of tradition and modernity and agree on the importance of the dialectic between the self and the other. Most of the appeals stay on the level of slogans and pure intentions. Therefore, the reconstruction of the tradition and its renewal preserve national character from the split between religious conservatism and Western secularism. De-Westernization helps in the liberation of the self from its domination by the other. It brings back the West to its natural borders and proper size. The preservation of identity is completed by the de-alienation of the self. In contemporary Islamic thought, till now, the West has been seen as a model of modernization. The rejection of imitation as a source of knowledge in Islamic tradition and the reasons for creativity in Western culture can be new components for self-identity.

6. Development has not yet been a major issue in modern Islamic thought. It is left to economists and planners. Any striving for development was limited because the notion itself is absent from national culture, the heir of Islamic tradition. Islam is still conceived as a religion of eternal felicity under the influence of al-Ghazālī and the commonplace notion of religion inherited from world religions. Nature, till now,

has been private. Physics, inherited from past tradition, has been inverted metaphysics. The notion of development has been borrowed from developmental philosophy in the West. It did not mobilize the masses. However, a similar notion can be mined from the tradition: the development of revelation in different phases, from Judaism, to Christianity, to Islam; the development of law from the Torah, to the Gospels, to the Qur'ān; internal development: of the *sharī'a* itself, known as abrogation; external development of *fiqh* through reasoning, *ijtihād*. Futurology can be done by the reconstruction of eschatology from the other world to this world. Self-reliant development has also been absent in contemporary Islamic thought because of its absence in the inherited tradition based essentially on reliance of the whole world, man, society and nature, on God. However, in the Islamic tradition naturalism exists within Mu'tazilism. In Western tradition, self-reliance became a whole tradition.

7. Finally, the lack of mass mobilization was the stumbling block in the way of development. Planning was the monopoly of the state, implemented by bureaucrats and imposed on the masses. Mass participation was absent, since democracy itself was absent from political regimes. However, mass mobilization can be achieved by traditional components such as the feeling of the message, individual responsibility, community vocation, doing good in the world, a sense of solidarity, people as the origin of power, and an active élite. Revolt of the masses and education of the masses are major concepts in Western political culture.

FURTHER READING

Amin, Osman (1958) *Lights on Contemporary Moslem Philosophy*, Cairo: The Renaissance Bookshop.

Al-Azmeh, Aziz (1986) *Arabic Thought and Islamic Societies*, London: Croom Helm.

Falaturi, A. (1990) *Muslim Thought for Teachers*, Cologne.

Hanafi, Hassan (1995) *The Anguish of Thought and Homeland*, 3 vols, Alexandria: Dar al-Mar'ifa.

Hourani, Albert (1991) *Islam in European Thought*, Cambridge: Cambridge University Press.

GLOSSARY

PERSIAN PHILOSOPHY

Abbreviations Av. = Avestan MP = Middle Persian (Pahlavi) Skt = Sanskrit
OP = Old Persian P = Persian

asha (Av.): that which is ordered, right, as it ought to be; a principle which should rule all aspects of existence, opposite of *drug*; = *arta* (OP); *ṛta* (Skt).

ashavan (Av.): a person 'possessing *asha*', hence behaving as a human being should, being just, truthful, righteous, destined for eternal bliss.

asn xrad (MP): innate intellect of man.

ātash bahrām (MP, P): sacred temple fire of the highest grade.

athaurvan (Av.): priest.

axw (MP): will.

dād (MP, P): law.

daēnā (Av.): an entity formed by a person's thoughts, words and acts. Surviving his death, it leads him to heaven or hell.

daēva (Av.): a god of old Indo-Iranian religion, in Zarathushtra's usage restricted to war-gods seen as bellicose, hence evil, divinities.

dastvar (MP): a term often used in Pahlavi texts to translate Avestan *ratu*.

dastvarīh (MP): religious authority, the function of the *dastvar*.

dēn (MP): religion or religious tradition.

dregvant (Av.): a person 'possessing *drug*', hence behaving as a human being should not, wicked, deceitful, destined for hell and final extinction.

drig(h)u (Av.), *driyōsh* (MP): a righteous poor man.

drug (Av.): that which is crooked, opposite to *asha*, especially in the moral sphere; deceit, the 'lie', wickedness; = *drauga* (OP), *druh* (Skt).

druǰ (P): devil.

frashegird (MP): renovation of physical creation.

frawahr (MP): higher spiritual part of man.

gāhāmbār (MP): seasonal religious gathering.

gētīg (MP): physical being.

gumēzishn (MP): mixture, mixed state of existence.

khshathra (Av.): the power to rule; dominion, kingship; the place where rule is exerted, kingdom, especially Mazdā's kingdom to come on earth.

khvarenah (Av.): *khvarrah* (MP): a force connected primarily with fire, sun and water, which brought fertility, growth and well-being; the concept was also associated with the blessings of good kingship, and with *khvēshkārīh*.

khvarrah (MP): *see khvarenah*.

khvēshkārīh (MP): one's 'proper function', duty.

kibla (Arabic): direction of prayer for Muslims; mark for this direction (*see also under* Islamic philosophy).

mainyu (Av.): a force inherent in each thing, tangible or intangible, animate or inanimate; such a force conceived as divine spirit; a god; = *mēnōg* (MP).

manthra (Av.): a priestly utterance regarded as divinely inspired and truly spoken, hence possessing power.

mar (MP): scoundrel.

mēnōg (MP): spiritual being; = *mainyu* (Av.).

Mithra (Av.): divinity, Lord of the Covenant.

pasu-vīra (Av.): cattle-and-men, the pastoral community.

paymān (MP): the proper measure of anything, as opposed to excess or deficiency.

ratu (Av.): a divine or human being who is responsible for the proper development of a phenomenon, group or species, and is in authority over it.

s(e)raosha (Av.): hearkening, in the sense both of man's hearkening to the words of God, prophet or priest, and of divine hearkening to man's prayers.

spenta (Av.): possessing power; of divinities, having power to aid, beneficent, bounteous, holy; of things, filled with (good) power, holy.

tan ī pasēn (MP): the future body, received by the blessed after the last judgement.

tkaēsha (Av.): teacher.

weh dēn (MP): the 'good religion', Zoroastrianism.

yasna (Av.): act of worship.

yazad (MP): *see yazata*.

yazata (Av.), *yazad* (MP): 'divinity', a term used for all divine beings who receive worship.

Zarathushtrōtema (Av.): the one who is most like Zarathushtra; the ideal representative of Zarathushtra on earth; according to some sources every age must have its *Zarathushtrōtema*.

INDIAN PHILOSOPHY

Abbreviations Skt = Sanskrit Pa. = Pali

abhāva (Skt): negation, negative statement, non-existence (seventh category of Vaiśeṣika). *See also under* Buddhist philosophy.
abhidharma (Skt): the standard term for Hīnayāna Buddhist philosophical systems. *See also under* Buddhist philosophy.
abhidhēyatva (Skt): nameability.
abhihitānvayavāda (Skt): Kumārilabhaṭṭa's theory according to which words in a sentence perform a dual function – they are meaningful *qua* words, and also as part of the sentence in which they occur.
abhrānta (Skt): non-erroneous.
abhyudaya (Skt): material prosperity, high status, happiness in life.
ācāra (Skt): custom, common morality.
adhyāsa (Skt): superimposition, imposition of false characteristics on to an experienced phenomenon.
adṛṣṭa (Skt): invisible store of results of performed actions.
Advaita Vedānta (Skt): non-duality, a school of Vedānta philosophy that teaches the oneness of God, Soul and universe, whose chief exponent was Śaṅkarācārya.
āgama (Skt): testimony, tradition, traditional treatise, scripture.
āgami karma (Skt): results of actions to be experienced in a future life.
ahaṅkāra (Skt) (also *ahaṁkāra*): ego sense, self-sense, individuation.
ahiṃsā (also *ahiṁsā*) (Skt): abstinence from doing injury to others.
ajīva (Skt): inanimate substance in Jaina philosophy; there are two kinds: (1) the formless (*arūpi*): time (*kāla*), space (*ākāśa*), motion (*dharma*) and rest or inertia (*adharma*); and (2) substance with form (*rūpi*) called *pudgala*.
ājīva (Skt): livelihood.
ākāṅkṣā (Skt): grammatical completeness.
ākāra (Skt): ideas, images.
ākāśa (Skt): space, ether, sometimes added as fifth to the four 'great elements' (*mahābhūtās*: earth, water, air, fire) which form the material reality.
akhyāti (Skt): error as a creation of truncated memory.
amṛta (Skt): the concept of immortality, the natural state of the Vedic gods.
ānanda (Skt): bliss.
anekānta (Skt): having more than one end or conclusion.
anekāntika (Skt): ambiguous, vague, imprecise, not pointed.
anekāntavāda (Skt): theory of the multi-faceted nature of reality.
anitya (Skt): impermanence. *See also under* Buddhist philosophy.
anṛta (Skt): that which is opposed to *ṛta*, the moral order of the Vedas.
aṇu (Skt): atom.

anubhava (Skt): pure immediate experience.

anuloma (Skt): in the proper order (marriage between individuals of the right castes).

anumāna (Skt): inference.

anupalabadhi (Skt): non-apprehension.

anuvartamāna (Skt): continuation or persistence; reality as equivalent to persistence of being.

anvitābhidhānavāda (Skt): Prabhākaramiśra's theory according to which the verb is the primary constituent of a sentence and other words derive meaning in virtue of being related to it.

anyathākhyāti (Skt): error conceived as a misplaced perception of an object.

aparokṣa (Skt): immediately evident; direct knowledge as distinguished from mediate knowledge (*parokṣa*).

apṛthaksiddhi (Skt): inseparable existence; in Viśiṣṭādvaita the term is used to describe the inseparable relation that exists between a substance and its attribute.

āptavacana (Skt): reliable verbal testimony.

arahat (Skt): perfected one (*see arhant under* Buddhist philosophy).

ārambhavāda (Skt): the view which regards each effect as a new beginning.

Āraṇyakas (Skt): the third category of the Vedic literature, containing esoteric speculations on the ritual propounded in the *Brāhmaṇas*.

arhant (also *arahant*) (Skt): *see arahat*.

arhat (Skt): *See arahat*.

artha (Skt): object, wealth, material possessions.

arthāpatti (Skt): contextual interpretation of apparently incomplete and/or inconsistent expressions occurring in the scriptures (Veda); presumption.

arthaśāstra (Skt): a treatise on the science of management of wealth and property of a state.

āsana (Skt): right posture.

asat (Skt): 'non-being' or 'unreal'; in some Vedic hymns, the formless chaos out of which the cosmos emerges.

āśramadharma (Skt): the duties of stages in life.

āśrava (Skt): inflow, influx, influence; mental bias or canker; cankers that keep one bound to the world of *saṁsāra*; used particularly in Jainism and Buddhism; = *āsava* (Pa.).

asteya (Skt): non-stealing.

astitva (Skt): existence, objectivity.

asura (Skt): the other group of divine beings, alongside the *deva*, in early Vedic literature, subsequently their opponents, finally demons.

ātman (Skt): self (as reflexive pronoun); the self; the inmost essence of man, in the *Upaniṣads* seen as identical with *Brahman*, the inner essence or source of the whole of reality; in the *Ṛgveda* its meaning was 'breath' or 'breath of life'; in Buddhism it is used only negatively in statements denying self, essence or substance to phenomena, but it is never positively defined, asserted or denied. Hence, *anātman/anatta* – insubstantial, without self: the doctrine of *anātman/anatta* asserts the insubstantiality of all *saṁsāric* entities of phenomena; some schools of Buddhism, such as Theravāda, assert non-existence of any self, essence or substance in the ultimate sense, claiming that even *nibbāna* is *anatta*; = *atta* (Pa.).

avidyā (Skt): ignorance, nescience – especially concerning ultimate spiritual truths; = *avijjā* (Pa.).

avyakta (Skt): 'unmanifest', *prakṛti* or matter in its unevolved state.

āyatana (Skt): level, sphere, basis. *See also under* Buddhist philosophy.

bādha (Skt): sublation, where a new experience undermines or refutes an earlier experience or other cognitive state.

bādhita (Skt): sublated or negated, truth is determined by its non-sublation. What is sublated is falsified.

bhakti (Skt): devotion or loyalty to any cause, especially in later Hinduism the attitude of emotional surrender to a personal deity. The '*bhakti*' period roughly designates the past millennium of Indian thought.

bhaktimārga (Skt): the way of devotion for the attainment of *mokṣa*.

bhakti yoga (Skt): the route to spiritual perfection through adoration or devotion.

bhava (Skt): existence.

bhedābheda (Skt): identity in difference.

bhūyodarśana (Skt): repeated observation, say, of smoke-with-fire occurrences.

bimbapratibimbabhāva (Skt): the relation between the original and its reflection. An analogy to explain the appearance and the unreality of the individual.

bodhi (Skt): enlightenment, awakening.

brahmacāri (Skt): pupil, disciple, apprentice, usually celibate, but in Vrātya and later Tantric tradition ritual cohabitation was not excluded.

brahmacārya (Skt): continence in things of sense – enjoyment; the capacity to walk in the ways of Brahman or truth.

Brahman (Skt): originally probably the sacred power underlying religious acts, then the sacrificial power maintaining the universe, finally the cosmic First Cause or Absolute; the inmost essence of the universe identical with the inmost self of each individual, *ātman*; the ultimate reality for Vedāntins.

Brāhmaṇa (Skt): the second category of the Vedic literature, the prose discussions of the sacrificial ritual and its background.

brāhmin (also *brāhman*, *brāhmaṇa*) (Skt): the priest caste; the first caste in the system of four castes.

buddha (Skt): enlightened, awakened; the Buddha; the Enlightened One or the Awakened One as the world teacher of the doctrine of liberation. *See also under* Buddhist philosophy.

buddhi (Skt): intellect.

buddhivṛtti (Skt): modification of the intellect as a result of stimulation by an object through the sense-organs.

Cārvāka (Skt): the school of materialists or sceptics; also known as Lokāyata.

catuṣkoṭi (Skt): *see under* Buddhist philosophy.

cit (also *chit*) (Skt): pure immediate consciousness.

damyatā (Skt): self-control.

darśana (Skt): seeing, viewing; world-view; a philosophical system.

dāsa (Skt): the term used to describe the dark-complexioned natives of ancient India.

dātta (Skt): generosity.

dayādhvam (Skt): compassion.

deva (Skt): the benevolent deities of the Vedas, opposed by the *asura*; later used generically for the lower gods, in contrast to *Īśvara*; God.

dharma (Skt): the principle of order and stability in Hindu thought, thus including religion, law and morality; the teaching about the ultimate reality as presented by the Buddha; in Jainism motion as one of the inanimate substances of phenomenal reality; in Vaiśeṣika, property; = *dhamma* (Pa.) (*see also under* Buddhist philosophy).

dharmabhūtajñāna (Skt): attributive consciousness in Viśiṣṭādvaita. The consciousness which reveals physical objects and mental states to a knowing subject.

dharmasūtra (Skt): ancient Indian treatises that explain the relation of individuals in a society.

dharmibhūtajñāna (Skt): Substantive consciousness in Viśiṣṭādvaita. The consciousness which constitutes the very nature of the knowing subject.

dharmin (Skt): substratum of properties.

dhātu (Skt): element (material or immaterial); a designation for ultimate categories of reality (*see also under* Buddhist philosophy).

doṣa (Skt): malice, hate; = *dosa* (Pa.).

dravya (Skt): substance, the category of substance as the substratum of qualities; also the first category of Vaiśeṣika.

dṛṣṭa (Skt): perception.

dṛṣṭānta (Skt): paradigm, example, analogy.

dṛṣṭi (Skt): vision, view, viewing = *diṭṭhi* (Pa.) (*see also under* Buddhist philosophy).

duḥkha (Skt): unhappiness, suffering, unsatisfactoriness = *dukkha* (Pa.) (*see also under* Buddhist philosophy).

Dvaita (Skt): the Vedānta system of Madhvācāryā.

gṛhasta (Skt): a family man; a householder.

guṇa (Skt): attribute, quality, characteristic, strand or constitutent of *prakṛti* in Sāṅkhya; second category in Vaiśeṣika philosophy.

haoma (P): *see soma*.

hetu (Skt): reason; in Nyāya logic, second member of the five-step syllogism; middle term, also known as *liṅga*.

hetvābhāsa (Skt): logical fallacy, bad argument.
indriya (Skt): sense, sense-faculty.
iśvara, *Īśvara* (Skt): the supreme deity of developed Hinduism (whether conceived of as Viṣṇu, Śiva or Kṛṣṇa); God.
iśvara-praṇidhāna (Skt): devotion to God.
jātaka (Skt): *see under* Buddhist philosophy.
jāti (Skt): real universal.
jīva (Skt): animate substance, soul, spirit-monad, conscious individual.
jīvanmukta (Skt): living enlightened being.
jñāna (Skt): 'knowledge', especially in the sense of insight into religious truths, so *jñānamārga*, 'the way of knowledge', knowledge gained through contemplation or by spiritual vision.
jñānamārga (Skt): the path of knowledge for the attainment of *mokṣa*.
jñāna yoga (Skt): the route to spiritual perfection through knowledge.
jñeyatva (Skt): knowability.
kāla (Skt): time.
kalpa (Skt): cycle of time.
kāma (Skt): desire, pleasure, love, egoistic attachment.
kāraṇa (Skt): cause.
karma (Skt): action, motion (third category in Vaiśeṣika), deed; often used to refer to the 'doctrine of *karma*' as the natural law of retribution for man's actions operating throughout successive lives in the sense of 'as you have sown so you will reap'; = *kamma* (Pa.) (*see also under* Buddhist philosophy).
karmamārga (Skt): the path of action, one of the three important pathways to achieve *mokṣa*.
karmaphala (Skt): accumulated results of action.
karma yoga (Skt): the route to spiritual perfection through performing one's duty.
keśin (Skt): the long-haired one; a wandering renunciate referred to in the *Ṛg Veda* and the *Atharva Veda* as an accomplished sage who has reached immortality and is outside the mainstream of the Vedic tradition.
kevala (Skt): alone, sole, absolute, perfect knowledge.
kṣatriya (Skt): a member of the second caste (*varṇa*), the aristocratic and warrior élite, in the system of four castes.
līlā (Skt): a game or frolicsome sport of the divine creator.
lobha (Skt): desire, craving, lust.
lokasaṁgraha (Skt): the welfare of the whole society; interconnectedness of society; maintenance of the world.
Mādhyamika (Skt): the school of Mahāyāna Buddhism stemming from Nāgārjuna.
māgadha (Skt): relating to or living in the country of Magadha (present-day Bihar and West Bengal); ancient designation for a Vrātya master.
mahā (Skt): great; usually used as the first component in compounds.

mahat (Skt): literally 'the great one', the first product of evolution of *prakṛti* in Sāṅkhya.

Mahāyāna (Skt): *see under* Buddhist philosophy.

maithuna (Skt): embrace of two lovers; sexual union; ritual cohabitation in Vrātya and Tantric practice.

manas (Skt): mind, intellect, inner sense.

mantra (Skt): hymn; syllable or short sentence, pronounced or murmured for the purpose of meditation.

manusmṛti (Skt): the famous treatise on duties of individuals in relation to various social institutions.

māyā (Skt): phenomenal, cosmic illusion.

Mīmāṁsā (Skt): a philosophical system whose name actually means 'Vedic exegesis'.

mithyā (Skt): false. Something which cannot be categorically determined to be either absolutely real or totally fictitious.

moha (Skt): delusion.

mokṣa (Skt): liberation, redemption, salvation, the ultimate purpose of beings according to most Indian systems. Also known as *mukti*.

nāma (Skt): name; mentality; *nāmarrūpa* designates the psycho-physical compound forming the human personality.

nāstika (Skt): 'the one who says "is not"', i.e. denies the existence of something. It frequently denotes Lokāyatas and others who deny or doubt the existence of other worlds, but it is also applied to all non-orthodox doctrines which deny the authority of the Vedas such as Jainism and Buddhism.

naya (Skt): a viewpoint, a perspective (in Jainism).

nayavāda (Skt): theory of the limited, perspectival nature of much of human knowledge.

nirguṇa Brahman (Skt): *Brahman* without attributes, a term used to describe the Absolute, unqualified *Brahman. See saguṇa Brahman.*

nirvāṇa (Skt): the ultimate state of liberation from the round of rebirths (*saṁsāra*) which can be realized also during one's lifetime on earth; the Buddhist concept of liberation from suffering; = *nibbāna* (Pa.) (*see also under* Buddhist philosophy).

nirvikalpa pratyakṣa (Skt): indeterminate perception.

nirvikalpa samādhi (Skt): meditative trance where the distinction between the knower and the known disappears.

niskāmakarma (Skt): desireless action.

nitya (Skt): eternal.

nivṛtti (Skt): withdrawal from action, disengagement.

nivṛtti mārga (Skt): one of the two paths to realizing spiritual perfection. The life of the recluse who has no involvement.

niyama (Skt): daily observances which have the purpose of clearing the body and mind of obstruction.

niyati (Skt): fate, destiny.

nyāya (Skt): logic.
Nyāya-Vaiśeṣika (Skt): sister systems of realistic Indian thought.
om (also *aum*) (Skt): the most sacred word of the Vedas. It is a symbol both of the Personal God and the Absolute.
padārtha (Skt): category, word meaning.
pañca śīla (Skt): the fivefold virtues.
pāpa (Skt): the demerit that occurs to a person doing wrong action, evil.
parādhīnaviśeṣāpti (Skt): the acquisition of distinctions in the primary matter as subject to the will of God. The name of the Dvaita theory of creation.
paramāṇu (Skt): atom; *aṇu*.
parāmarśa (Skt): application of *vyāpti* (invariable concomitance) to a particular case in the justification process.
pariṇāmavāda (Skt): theory of the real transformation of material cause into its effect.
paṭiccasamuppāda (Pa.): *see under* Buddhist philosophy.
paryāya (Skt): mode, modification, transitory state.
pradhāna (Skt): the inferred one, *prakṛti* in its unmanifest state.
prajñā (Skt): wisdom = *paññā* (Pa.) *(see also under* Buddhist philosophy).
prakṛti (Skt): primal nature, the known in the Sāṅkhya and Yoga schools.
pralaya (Skt): periodic cosmic dissolution.
pramā (Skt): knowledge.
pramāṇa (Skt): means of knowing.
prāmāṇya (Skt): justification.
prameya (Skt): object of knowledge.
prāṇa (Skt): 'breath' in Vedic thought, often used to designate the vital self, life-force.
prāṇāyāma (Skt): control of the breath in a particular posture (*āsana*) of the body to purify the mind and prepare it to enter a trance-like state.
prārabdhakarma (Skt): the result of past deeds which are experienced in the present life.
prasaṅga (Skt): context (of communication).
prataḥ-prāmāṇyavāda (Skt): the Nyāya theory which maintains that a belief is to count as knowledge only when it is justified and true.
pratiloma (Skt): against the proper order (marriage between individuals of different castes).
pratītyasamutpāda (Skt): dependent origination; a chain of ten or twelve links (*nidānas*) which explains, in Buddhist terms, the process of *saṁsāric* (phenomenal) existence = *paṭiccasamuppāda* (Pa.).
pratiyogi (Skt): counter-correlate.
pratyabhijñā (Skt): recognition; apperception.
pratyakṣa (Skt): perception.
pratyāhāra (Skt): withdrawal of the senses.
pravṛtti (Skt): positive activity.
pravṛtti mārga (Skt): one of the two paths to realizing spiritual perfection and positive

involvement in good actions.

pudgala (Skt): individual, person; in Buddhism it refers to the phenomenal personality only, while in a Hindu context it may designate also the individual transmigrating self; the extinct Buddhist school of Pudgalavāda also advocated continued existence of the *pudgala* as bearer of individual identity through successive lives; in Jainism: matter, material body; category of existence which implies shape (*see also under* Buddhist philosophy).

puṁścalī (Skt): female attendant in fertility rites of Vrātyas.

puṇya (Skt): the merit that accrues to a person on doing good action.

puruṣa (Skt): 'person', in various senses, from the primeval person of the *Ṛg Veda* to the spiritual entity in Sāṅkhya (and Yoga) thought, consciousness.

puruṣārtha (Skt): human value and ideal.

rājanya (Skt): the ruling caste, *kṣatriya*.

ṛṣi (Skt): sage, wise man, seer.

rajas (Skt): passion – one of the three constituents of *prakṛti* (matter) in Sāṅkhya, productive of activity and pain.

ṛta (Skt): the Vedic term for the principle of order in the universe in both its natural and moral aspects. Also associated with *dharma* in later Indian philosophy.

rūpa (Skt): shape, form; bodily form; material form; material body.

saccidānanda (Skt): combination of the words *sat*, *cit*, *ānanda*, existence, knowledge, bliss. A name of *Brahman*, the ultimate reality.

saguṇa brahman (Skt): qualified *Brahman*, the Absolute conceived as the creator, preserver and destroyer of the universe, corresponds to *īśvara*, or the personal God.

sāhacarya niyama (Skt): regular association, say, of smoke with fire.

sakṛddarśana (Skt): single observation, say, of smoke–fire occurrence leading to the knowledge of *vyāpti*, for example where there is smoke there is fire.

sākṣin (Skt): witness.

samādhi (Skt): concentration, absorption; a higher mental state reached through meditation, sometimes regarded also as a state of higher cognition.

sāmānya (Skt): universal, class character, the fourth category of Vaiśeṣika.

sāmānya lakṣaṇa pratyāsatti (Skt): intuition or extraordinary perception which enables one to have knowledge of generality (*vyāpti*).

sāmānyatodṛṣṭa (Skt): analogical reasoning.

samavāya (Skt): inherence, inseparability.

sambandha (Skt): connection relation.

saṃhitās (Skt): the collected hymns comprising the first part or category of each of the four Vedas.

saṃjñā (Skt): perception = *saññā* (Pa.) (*see also under* Buddhist philosophy).

Sāṅkhya (Skt): classical Indian philosophical system closely related to Yoga.

saṃsāra (also *saṁsāra*) (Skt): global flow, the phenomenal process of reality, usually used, in the context of the lives of individuals, in the sense of the round of rebirths.

saṁskāra (Skt): volitional dispositions.
samyak (Skt): right, correct = *sammā* (Pa.).
saṁyoga (Skt): contact, conjunction.
saṅkalpa (Skt): thought, intention, resolution = *saṇkappa* (Pa.).
saṅkhāra (Pa.): *see under* Buddhist philosophy.
sannyāsa (Skt): renunciation.
saṅtoṣa (Skt): contentment.
sapakṣa (Skt): thesis to be justified; paradigm which shows the application of its relevant *vyāpti*.
saptabhaṅgī (Skt): the Jain seven-step logic.
śarīra (Skt): physical body, also bodily remains after cremation = *sarīra* (Pa.).
śarīraśarīribhāva (Skt): body–soul relation. In Viśiṣṭādvaita used as an analogy to describe the relation that exists between God, the souls and the world.
śāstra (Skt): teaching, laws, science.
sat (Skt): being, real, existence.
satkāryavāda (Skt): the view that regards each effect as pre-existing in the cause.
sattva (Skt): real, existent – one of the three constituents of *prakṛti* (matter) in Sāṅkhya, productive of pleasure, happiness, bliss.
satya (Skt): truth.
satyāgraha (Skt): adherence to the truth.
savikalpa pratyakṣa (Skt): determinate perception.
śauca (Skt): cleanliness, removal of pollution.
siddha (Skt): a perfected being, usually regarded as possessing magic powers.
śīla (Skt): ethics, morality, rules of conduct; = *sīla* (Pa.).
skambha (Skt): support, the framework on which the universe is erected, a form of the *axis mundi* or cosmic tree.
skandha (Skt): compound, constituent, aggregate, group; = *khandha* (Pa.).
smṛti (Skt): traditional sacred texts (*see also under* Buddhist philosophy).
soma (Skt): the deified personification of a plant central to Vedic ritual (cf. *haoma* in early Iranian ritual), from which the juice was pressed and drunk.
sparśa (Skt): contact, touch = *phassa* (Pa.).
śruti (Skt): reliable verbal testimony.
śūdra (Skt): the labour caste; the fourth caste.
sūtra (Skt): discourse, treatise = *sutta* (Pa.).
svabhāva (Skt): essence, essential character.
svabhāvavādins (Skt): the naturalists.
svadharma (Skt): one's own duty, duty specific to one's caste.
svarga loka (Skt): heaven.
svarūpa (Skt): self identity.
svataḥ prāmāṇya (Skt): intrinsic validity of experience. The view that knowledge is intrinsically valid while falsity is extrinsic to knowledge.

svataḥ prāmāṇyavāda (Skt): the Mīmāṁsaka theory which maintains that the conditions which make beliefs possible make them true also. The theory is motivated by the desire to defend the scriptures (Veda).

svatantra/paratantra (Skt): independent/dependent. In Dvaita, God alone is the one independent real; all else is dependent upon him.

swarāj (Skt): complete independence, self-rule.

syād (Skt): possibly, perhaps, somehow.

syādvāda (Skt): view that something may be so or otherwise, depending on the conditions; the Jaina view that the perspectival knowledge can best be expressed through the *syād* operator. (*See also naya.*)

tamas (Skt): darkness – one of the three constitutents of *prakṛti* (matter) in Sāṅkhya, ignorance, productive of apathy, confusion and indifference.

tāṇhā (also *taṅhā*) (Skt): thirst, selfish craving.

tapas (Skt): austerity.

tarka (Skt): argumentation of the *reductio* type; counterfactual conditional in relation to empirical generalization (*vyāpti*), induction, reasoning.

tathāgata (Skt): 'thus gone' or 'thus arrived'; in Buddhist tradition: a designation for the *buddhas* and possibly other accomplished beings or *arahats* who reached final liberation.

tātparya (Skt): (the speaker's) intention as a factor in understanding the meaning of sentences.

Theravāda (Skt): the oldest surviving school of Buddhism, which is rooted in the Pali canon.

tīrthaṅkara (Skt): 'ford-maker'; the designation for accomplished Jain teachers who teach how to get across the stream of *saṁsāra* and reach liberation.

triratna (Skt): the Three Jewels of right behaviour; in Jainism refers to right faith, right knowledge and right conduct.

trivarga (Skt): the three golden aims of life, i.e. pertaining to *dharma*, *artha* and *kāma*.

tṛṣnā (Skt): thirst for possession of things.

upādāna (Skt): grasping, clinging, attachment (in Buddhism).

upādhi (Skt): limiting adjunct – in Advaita pure being-consciousness is as though particularized because of conditioning by a limiting adjunct; a condition which vitiates a generalization (*vyāpti*), makes it illicit; in Vaiśeṣika refers to artificial classification.

upamāna (Skt): comparison.

Upaniṣad (Skt): the fourth category of the Vedic literature, the most esoteric and speculative.

vāc (Skt): speech.

vāca (Skt): *see vāc*.

Vaiśeṣika (Skt): orthodox school allied with Nyāya.

vaiśya (Skt): the merchant caste.

vanaprastha (Skt): the third *āśrama* in the life of man, where one devotes one's time to meditation; forest dweller.
varṇa (Skt): very often the word is used to mean a caste, colour.
varṇasaṃkara (Skt): literally mixture of colour. Here mixture of castes leading to destruction of *dharma*.
vedanā (Skt): feeling (*see also under* Buddhist philosophy).
Vedas (Skt): the earliest religious literature of India, in four collections (*Ṛgveda, Sāmaveda, Yajurveda, Atharvaveda*) and four categories (*Saṃhitas, Brāhmaṇas, Āraṇyakas, Upaniṣads*).
vibhava (Skt): enhanced existence, wealth, prosperity; final beatitude; end of existence; death; annihilation.
vidyā (Skt): knowledge.
vijñāna (Skt): consciousness, conceptualizations = *viññāna* (Pa.).
Vijñānavāda or *Yogācāra* (Skt): one of the major Mahāyāna Buddhist philosophical schools.
vipakṣa (Skt): contrary thesis, opposite thesis; paradigm which shows inapplicability of the relevant *vyāpti*.
viśeṣa (Skt): particularity; individual character, the fifth category of Vaiśeṣika.
Viśiṣṭādvaita (Skt): the Vedānta system of Rāmānuja and the Śrivaiṣṇavas.
vivartavāda (Skt): theory of the merely apparent transformation of cause into its effect.
vrātya (Skt): one bound by a vow (*vrata*); designation for early non-Vedic, Indo-Aryan fraternities forming a loose confederation in the east of northern India, the ancient Magadha, with their own religious, mythological and philosophical tradition partly overlapping with the Vedic one; designation for the primordial cosmogonic power which manifested itself in individualized form as the cosmic Ekavrātya, also called Mahādeva.
vyākaraṇa (Skt): grammar, grammatical philosophy.
vyāpti (Skt): universal connection, generalization, invariable concomitance.
vyāvartamāna (Skt): non-continuance or exclusion.
yajña (Skt): sacrifices to various gods enjoined in the Vedas.
yakṣa (Skt): a localized manifestation of the divine, especially in popular Hinduism; tree or other nature spirits.
yama (Skt): abstention, restraint; one of the stages of *samādhi* in Yoga.
yathārthatā (Skt): truth.
yoga (Skt): disciplining of mind and body to achieve spiritual perfection; classical Indian philosophical system closely related to Sāṅkhya.
yogyatā (Skt): logical compatibility of words in a sentence.
yuga (Skt): the span of time calculated according to the Indian scheme of cycle of time (*kalpa*).
yugadharma (Skt): the principle of righteousness to be acted upon in accordance with the time and its social requirements.

BUDDHIST PHILOSOPHY

Abbreviations Pa. = Pali Skt = Sanskrit Sin. = Sinhalese Tbt. = Tibetan
Bur. = Burmese

abhāva (Skt): negation, absence, non-existence.

abhidhamma (Pa.): philosophical elaboration of basic Buddhist concepts. In its collected form constitutes the *Abhidhamma Piṭaka*, the third section of the threefold Buddhist scriptures, the *Tipiṭaka* (Pa.) or *Tripiṭaka* (Skt).

abhidharma (Skt): *see abhidhamma.*

abhiññā (Pa.): one of the six 'super knowledges' acquired by the Buddha, the six super knowledges are: retrocognition, clairvoyance, clairaudience, telepathy, magical powers and knowledge of destruction of *āsavas* = *abhijñā* (Skt).

abhrānta (Skt): *see under* Indian philosophy.

abhyudaya (Skt): *see under* Indian philosophy.

adhimokṣa (Skt): ascertainment, decisive knowledge.

adṛṣta (Skt): unseen power of *karma*, dictating the nature of rebirth.

advaya (Skt): non-dual.

adveṣa (Skt): non-malevolence.

āgama (Skt): a name for the discourse section in the Sanskrit language; now only extant in Chinese and Tibetan.

āgama jñāna (Skt): knowledge derived from the scriptures.

ahiṃsā (Skt): causing no injury, non-violence, humaneness.

āhrīkya (Skt): irreverence, lack of modesty.

aja (Skt): unborn.

ajāta (Skt): *see aja.*

ākāśa (Skt): space.

ākhyāna (Skt): linguistic expression, explanation.

ālaya vijñāna (Skt): in Yogācāra, the storehouse consciousness that is the source and substratum of other consciousness and the external world.

alobha (Skt): non-greediness.

amataṃ padam (Pa.): immortal place, an epithet for *nirvāṇa.*

anāgata (Skt): future, what has yet to come.

anapatrapā (Skt): *see anapatrāpya.*

anapatrāpya (Skt): not feeling awful towards sins, not being embarrassed about misdeeds.

anātman (Skt): *see anattā.*

anattā (Pa.): the doctrine that there exists no permanent, independent partless self underlying impermanent phenomena, a fundamental teaching of Buddhism.

anitya (Skt): impermanent.

anityatā (Skt): extinction, impermanence.

anucakka (Pa.): wordly power as opposed to the power of righteousness, *dhammacakka*.

anukampā (Skt): sympathy, a fundamental Buddhist virtue.

anumāna (Skt): inference, means of correct knowledge along with perception and *āgama*.

anupalabdhi (Skt): mode of knowing absence or non-existence.

anyathābhāva (Skt): alteration, change.

apatrapā (Skt): *see apatrāpya*.

apatrāpya (Skt): awfulness with regard to sins, embarrassment about misdeeds.

apoha (Skt) in Pramāṇavāda, the nominalistic principle whereby class membership is apprehended through the exclusion of what is other than a member of the correct class.

apramāda (Skt): making endeavours to acquire good virtue, conscientiousness.

aprāpti (Skt): non-acquisition, opposite of *prāpti*.

apratisaṅkhyā nirodha (Skt): the extinction of the manifestations of the elements because of lack of productive causes without the action of discriminative knowledge. (*See also pratisaṅkhyā nirodha*.)

arahant (Pa.): *see arhant*.

arhant (Skt): a perfected one; a worthy one; in Theravāda (Hīnayāna), anyone who has achieved *nirvāṇa* – enlightened *sthaviras*, in Mahāyāna, one liberated from *saṃsāra*, not yet a fully enlightened *buddha*.

arhat (Skt): *see arhant*.

arthakriyātva (Skt): efficiency, as a criterion of something (relatively) real.

arūpadhātu (Skt): the immaterial plane of existence, abode for subtle spirits without a material body.

ārya (Skt): noble, holy. One who has acquired the *dharma* eye (*dhammacakku*) and is on the supermundane (*lokottara*) path; Arya(n), said of the Four Truths.

āsaṃjñika (Skt): a force which transfers an individual into the realm of the unconscious trance.

āsaṃjñi samāpatti (Skt): the highest level of meditative absorption, a force stopping consciousness and producing the annihilation trance.

asaṃskṛta dharma (Skt): unconditioned *dharmas*, which in *abhidharma* tradition include space and cessation.

āsava (Pa.): influx, a defiling mental tendency. Usually listed as a sense-desire, desire for becoming, desire for wrong views, ignorance.

āśraddhya (Skt): non-believing.

āsrava (Skt): *see āsava*.

āśraya parāvṛtti (Skt): basic transformation, as a result of which the defiled mind disappears and the world is seen as it is.

asura (Skt): demon.

atadvyāvṛtti (Skt): *see apoha*.

atīta (Skt): past, what has gone.

ātman (Skt): the self; according to the *Upaniṣads* it refers to the immutable blissful basis of both the cosmos and ourselves, anything in or by itself. (The existence of a permanent self is denied in Buddhism.)

ātmasaṃvedana (Skt): *see svasaṃvedana.*

auddhatya (Skt): agitated and disturbed state of mind.

avatār (Skt): the descent of a deity to the earth in an incarnate form.

avidyā (Skt): ignorance.

avijjā (Pa.): *see avidyā.*

avijñapti (Skt): non-expression.

avijñapti rūpa (Skt): unmanifested matter which is the vehicle of moral qualities.

āyatana (Skt): regions, fields, sources. According to Buddhism our individual existence of twelve regions – these are the six sensitive regions (vision, hearing, smell, taste, touch and mind) and the six regions of objects corresponding to the former.

bags chags (Tbt): latency out of which subject and object arise simultaneously; any latent disposition; *see also vāsanā.*

bala (Skt): strength, one of the perfections in the qualities and practices of the *bodhisattva.*

bauddha (Skt): follower of the Buddha, a Buddhist.

bhagavan (Skt): Lord, God the supreme Being, an epithet of the Buddha (from *bhaga*, god).

bhāva (Skt): existence, i.e. the five *skandhas* (q.v.), considered composite (*saṃskṛta*), impermanent (*anitya*) and without a self (*anātman*), in a word *duḥkha* (q.v.).

bhikkhu (Pa.); a Buddhist monk, one who receives a shares of householders' food.

bhikkhunī (Pa.): nun; *see also bhikkhu.*

bhikṣu (Skt): *see bhikkhu.*

bhikṣuṇī (Skt): *see bhikkhunī.*

bodhi (Skt): *see under* Indian philosopy.

bodhisatta (Pa.): *see bodhisattva.*

bodhisattva (Skt): the Buddha prior to his enlightenment; being who is to become fully enlightened (*saṃbodhi*); in Mahāyāna, an altrustic aspirant to buddhahood, who may also serve as a saviour figure, one who teaches and leads others to and on the path to enlightenment.

Bön (Tbt.): a tradition often described as the pre-Buddhist religion of Tibet; after the eleventh century a heterodox alternative to Buddhism.

brāḥmana (Skt): refers to Hindu schools.

brahmavihāra (Skt): Brahma abidings or sublime virtues of loving kindness (*mettā*), compassion (*karuṇā*), sympathetic joy (*muditā*) and equanimity (*upekkhā*).

bstod tshogs (Tbt): devotional corpus, hymns to the Buddha.

buddha (Skt): in Hīnayāna, a supreme *arhant*; in Mahāyāna, the goal of all paths, a condition of omniscience, omnibenevolence and immense power.

cakkavattin (Pa.): a universal monarch who is expected to rule according to the wheel of the *Dhamma* and thus betrays in his rule the elements of righteousness and justice. The term is also expressly applied to the Buddha, who turns the wheel (*cakka*) of *Dhamma*.
cakravartin (Skt): *see cakkavatin.*
cakṣur indriya (Skt): visual sense organ.
catuṣkoṭi (Skt): fourfold negation: whereby an entity is examined as *x*, non-*x*, both *x* and non-*x* and neither *x* nor non-*x*.
cetanā (Skt): volition, used to signify both thinking and willing.
cetayitvā (Skt): the deliberate decision to do something, acting by deciding.
chanda (Skt): desire.
chos lugs (Tbt.) sect, order, school, religious or doctrinal system.
cintā (Skt): reflection.
cittā (Skt): mind.
cittamātra (Skt): in Yogācāra, the theory that all entities in the conditioned cosmos are inseparable from the consciousness experiencing them, are 'mind-only'.
dāna (Skt): giving, understood as a formal religious act in Theravāda Buddhism and as a general, social virtue in Mahāyāna.
dēvāle (Sin.): a shrine within a Theravādin temple complex devoted to a god.
devātideva (Skt): a god above gods, epithet applied to the Buddha.
dhamma (Pa.): the teaching of the Buddha (usually as *Dhamma*); one of the fundamental elements of existence as described by Buddhist philosophers; phenomenon; objective as well as subjective duty.
dhammacakkhu (Pa.): *see dharmacaksu.*
dharma (Skt): *see dhamma.*
dharmacaksu (Skt): *dharma* eye or spiritual vision which marks the starting point of the Noble Path. Includes seeing the impermanence of the world and the possibility of release from it.
dharmakāya (Skt): *dharma* body or aspect. In Hīnayāna, the Buddha's teachings; in Mahāyāna, the qualities of a *buddha*'s mind and/or a *buddha*'s non-dual *gnosis* or empty nature.
dharmi (Skt): locus of property.
dharmin (Skt): substratum, subject of inference: for instance the hill is the subject when it is proven to possess fire (the predicate).
dhātu (Skt): element, sphere, realm.
dhyāna (Skt): absorptive meditation – one of the perfections; first stage of meditation; = *jhāna* (Pa.).
dravya (Skt): substance, substantiality.
dravyasiddha (Skt): substantially established.
dṛṣṭānta (Skt): *see under* Indian philosophy.

dṛṣṭi (Skt): literally view, but mostly in a pejorative sense of clinging to a view (which in itself may be correct), a dogmatic attitude, a dogma; as such tantamount to ignorance (*avidyā*) = *ditthi* (Pa.).

duḥkha (Skt): unsatisfactoriness, suffering, mental and physical, the first noble truth; relates to the five *skandhas* (q.v.).

dukkha (Pa.): *see duḥkha.*

dūṣaṇa (Skt): proof.

dūṣaṇābhāsa (Skt): wrong refutation.

dvairūpya jñāna (Skt): doctrine of the twofold form of knowledge: the view that advocates that every cognition is produced with a twofold form – that of itself (*svābhāsa*) and that of the object (*viṣayābhāsa*).

dveṣa (Skt): aversion.

gamaka (Skt): reason or necessary mark (in logic).

gamya (Skt): object of inference (in logic).

gandha viṣaya (Skt): olfactory sense-data.

ghrāṇa indriya (Skt): olfactory organ.

grāhya (Skt): perceivable, as opposed to *grāha*(*ka*), grasping, grasper.

grub mtha' (Tbt.): doxographies, an important genre of literature in which a wide range of philosophical positions are catalogued and evaluated.

gsar ma (Tbt.): new sects, basing their practices on texts translated in the second dissemination of Buddhism in Tibet.

gter ma (Tbt.): treasures, discovered texts.

gter ston (Tbt.): text discoverers, discoverers of *gter ma.*

guṇa (Skt): attribute, quality, adjectivality.

gźan stoṅ (Tbt.): other empty.

hetu (Skt): reason, as where smoke is the reason for stating that there is fire.

hetuvidyā (Skt): logic.

Hīnayāna (Skt): literally Lower Vehicle – the term applied to Pali Buddhist tradition by those of the Sanskrit tradition, who called themselves the Great Vehicle (*Mahāyāna*).

hrī (Skt): modesty.

icchantika (Skt): one incapable of attaining enlightenment.

indriya pratyakṣa (Skt): sense-perception; has the *svalakṣaṇa*, something evident, as its object.

īrṣyā (Skt): jealousy.

jāla (Skt): web, net.

jarā (Skt): decay.

jātaka (Skt): story of one of the Buddha's previous lives.

jāti (Skt): origination, class character, universal, generic property.

jhāna (Pa.): *see dhyāna.*

jihvā indriya (Skt): taste organ.

jina (Skt): conqueror, victor, an epithet for the Buddha.
jīva (Skt): soul.
jīvita (Skt): life force.
jñāna (Skt): intuitive cognition, mostly as a result of the culmination of *prajñā* (q.v.).
kalpanā (Skt): abstract construction, mental construction.
kāmadhātu (Skt): the plane of desire, generally said to be inhabited by living beings of gross matter such as human beings.
kamma (Pa.): *see karma.*
kāraṇa (Skt): instrumental cause.
karma (Skt): action which is intentional, which can be good or bad and has consequences influencing and conditioning one's rebirth and destiny as a human being. It can be understood in terms of rewards and punishments, as well as the development of character.
karmavipāka (Skt): maturation of actions and the attendant consequences.
karuṇā (Skt): compassion, one of the four sublime states (*brahmavihara*).
kāruñña (Pa.): *see karuṇā.*
kaukṛtya (Skt): repentance.
kausīdya (Skt): mental indolence.
kāya indriya (Skt): tactile sense organ.
kevala (Skt): abstractions; can also mean alone.
khandha (Pa.): *see skandha.*
kleśa (Skt): vices, the root causes of suffering, especially desire, aversion, ignorance, which can be eliminated through full cognizance of the nature of the *dharma.*
krodha (Skt): anger.
kṣaṇa (Skt): atomic moments; according to the Sarvāstivādins conditioned *dharmas* were said ultimately to be atomic moments.
kṣaṇikatva (Skt): in Sautrāntrika and subsequent schools, the theory of 'momentariness', whereby conditioned *dharmas* are durationless, instantaneous events.
kṣūnti (Skt): patience, one of the perfections.
kun gźi rnam śes (Tbt.): *see ālayavijñāna.*
kun rdzob bden pa (Tbt.): *see saṃvṛti satya.*
lakṣaṇa (Skt): characteristics, used in many different contexts.
lam rim (Tbt.): stages of the path, literature that sought to collate the essential doctrines and practices required for progressing on the path to enlightenment.
laukika (Skt): worldly, mundane, ordinary.
liṅga (Skt): reason, mark, as where smoke is a mark that there is fire.
lokiya (Pa.): *see laukika.*
lokottara (Skt): higher supermundane, relating to higher practice and experience on the path.
lokuttara (Pa.): *see lokottara.*

lta ba (Tbt.): view, a school's or person's position regarding a range of religious questions – for instance rebirth and nature of reality; = *dṛṣṭi* (Skt).
mada (Skt): complacency, self-satisfaction.
madhyama pratipad (Skt): middle way, between extremes.
mahākaruṇā (Skt): supreme compassion.
mahāprajñā (Skt): supreme wisdom.
mahāpurisa (Pa.): *see mahāpuruṣa.*
mahāpuruṣa (Skt): great man.
Mahāyāna (Skt): Great Way or Vehicle, which aims to offer liberation to all beings and is exemplified in the *bodhisattva* path.
Maitreya (Skt): a great *bodhisattva* destined to be the next *buddha*. The supreme example of loving kindness (cf. *maitrī* (Skt), *mettā* (Pa.)).
maitrī (Skt): kindliness.
māna (Skt): arrogance.
mānasa pratyaksa (Skt): mental perception.
maṇḍala (Skt): regular pattern used for meditation.
manasikāra (Skt): attention.
Mañjuśrī (Skt): a great *bodhisattva*; the supreme exemplar of wisdom (*prajñā*).
mārga (Skt): plan, way, path.
mati (Skt): intelligence; *see also prajñā.*
mātsarya (Skt): stinginess.
māyā (Skt): deceit, illusion, deception.
med dgag (Tbt.): non-affirming negation = *prasajyapratiṣedha* (Skt).
mettā (Pa.): *see maitrī.*
middha (Skt): drowsiness.
moha (Skt): infatuation, ignorance; *see also avidyā.*
mrakṣa (Skt): hypocrisy, concealing one's own sins.
mtshan ñid (Tbt.): defining characteristics or mark, the field of knowledge that is concerned with identifying defining characteristics; refers to scholastic philosophy; *see also laksaṇa.*
muditā (Skt): joy.
nairātmya (Skt): the theory that everything is non-self or *anattā*.
nāma (Skt): linguistic determination, name.
nāmakāya (Skt): the force imparting significance to words.
ñāna (Pa.): *see jñāna.*
nāstika (Skt): refers to non-orthodox schools in Indian philosophy – that is, those which rejected the Vedas.
neyārtha (Skt): any teaching of the Buddha that is provisional and requires further interpretation for its purport to be understood.
nibbāna (Pa.): *see nirvāṇa.*
nigamana (Skt): conclusion (in logic).

nikāya (Pa.): sect of the *sangha*. A body of monks sharing a common ordination, tradition and code (*prātimokṣa* (Skt), *pātimokkha* (Pa.)) of discipline (*vinaya*). Also a name for the discourse sections (*sūtra* (Skt), *sutta* (Pa.)) of the Pali canon.

nirākārajnāñavāda (Skt): theory that knowledge has no form of its own, that it merely reflects or contains something unreal.

nirmāṇakāya (Skt): transformation aspect of the *trikāya* doctrine; refers to the historical Buddha and his predecessors and the future *buddha*, Maitreya.

nirvāṇa (Skt): the Buddhist *summum bonum*, a peaceful, undefiled state transcending the cycle of rebirths that is *saṃsāra*; extinction, the locus where the *kleśas* are extinct, where emptiness is fully realized and where *prapañca* disappears; also the end of rebirth, 'blowing out' the fires of greed, hate and ignorance, or extinguishing the influxes. Usually equated with enlightenment or liberation.

nītārtha (Skt): any teaching of the Buddha that is definitive, requiring no further interpretation for its purport to be understood. *See also neyārtha.*

nitya (Skt): durable, permanent, eternal (as opposed to *anitya*).

ṅo bo ñid sku (Tbt.): *see svabhāvikakāya.*

paccekabuddha (Pa.): human beings who can gain enlightenment but are incapable of teaching it. Also refers to those who gain enlightenment without relying on a teacher = *pratyekabuddha* (Skt).

pada kāya (Skt): the force of imparting significance to sentences.

pakṣa (Skt): subject of inference (in logic).

Pali: the Indian language in which Theravāda discourses were preserved.

paññā (Pa.): *see prajñā.*

paramārthasatya (Skt): the ultimate or absolute truth, namely emptiness *śūnyata* or *nirvāṇa*, i.e. liberation (*mokṣa*) as opposed to *saṃvṛti* or *vyavahāra satya* (q.v.). The ultimate truth may vary from system to system.

paramattha (Pa.): ultimate = *paramārtha* (Skt).

pāramitā (Skt): the perfections, or supreme virtues and qualities cultivated by a *bodhisattva*; these are charity, morality, patience, concentration and wisdom.

parasparāpekṣātaḥ sat (Skt): dependent being, for instance 'long' and 'short', 'thin' and 'fat', which exist in dependence upon each other.

paratantra (Skt): in Yogācāra, the dependent nature.

parijñana (Skt): full realization.

parikalpa (Skt): intellectual systematization.

parikalpita (Skt): the imaginary nature, utterly unreal, one of the three natures (*svabhāva*) in Yogācāra.

parīkṣā (Skt): critical investigation.

pariniṣpanna (Pa.): the absolute nature, the complete absence of self-existence in the dependent nature, consummate nature.

paṭiccasamuppāda (Pa.): *see pratītyasamutpāda.*

pātimokkha (Pa.): *see prātimokṣa.*

phassa (Pa.): *see sparśa.*

phyag rgya chen mo (Tbt.): the great seal – a state of enlightened awareness in which phenomenal appearance and noumenal emptiness are the unified, crowning experience of Buddhist practice. Also a meditation tradition in which the true nature of mind is revealed.

pirit (Pa.): recital of some of the discourses of the Buddha found as a text by the monks. *Pirit* was chanted on auspicious occasions, at times of sickness, at funerals and at the giving of alms.

pirivena (Pa.): institution of learning the *Dhamma*, the Pali language and related subjects which grew around some of the more central temples in Sri Lanka.

piṭaka (Pa.): a collection of Buddhist teachings, there being three such – *vinaya, sutta* and *abhidhamma* – known collectively as the *Tipiṭaka.*

pradāśa (Skt): insisting on objectionable things.

prajñā (Skt): wisdom or insight that perceives the true nature of reality however defined by a particular school; analytical insight into the nature of the *dharma.*

prajñapti (Skt): designations or fictitious entities – i.e. not substantial entities.

prajñaptisat (Skt): provisional being, entities that are transitory like clothes, men and women.

pramā (Skt): outcome of a process of knowing (*pramāṇa*).

pramāda (Skt): laziness, non-practice of virtues.

pramāṇa (Skt): mode of knowing, one of the sources of authoritative cognition; most Buddhists recognize two: perception (*pratyakṣa*) and inference (*anumāna*).

pramāṇa phala (Skt): *see pramā*; outcome of the process of knowing.

pramāṇavyavasthā (Skt): theory of separation of *pramāṇas.*

praṇidhāna (Skt): resolution of a *bodhisattva.*

prapañca (Skt): the expanded world, created by *vikalpas* and reflected in language; conceptual proliferation; the empirically perceived world.

prāpti (Skt): acquisition, a force which effects the acquisition of elements in an individual existence.

prasajyapratiṣedha (Skt): non-affirming negation.

prasaṅga (Skt): especially in Mādhayamika, a consequential argument employing the *catuṣkoṭi* or other dialectical form that allows an opponent's position to self-destruct; (the absurd logical) implication in any assumption of the existence of own-being (*svabhāva*).

praśrabdhi (Skt): mental dexterity, mental suitability for any action.

pratibhāsa (Skt): sensation.

pratibhāsa pratīti (Skt): mental reflex, concept.

pratigha (Skt): hatred, opposition.

pratijñā (Skt): statement of a thesis, proposition.

prātimokṣa (Skt): the code of rules governing the individual life of the monk or nun.

It is to be recited every fortnight at *uposatha* by the whole community after confessing transgressions against it.

pratisaṅkhyā nirodha (Skt): the extinction of defilements through the action of discriminative knowledge.

pratiṣedha (Skt): negation.

pratītyasamutpāda (Skt): literally, dependent origination 'arising on the grounds of a preceding cause'. The Buddhist theory that all events arise through specifiable causes and conditions; refers to the twelve factors that account for the genesis of suffering.

pratyakṣa (Skt): perception, perceptual knowledge, one of the two *pramāṇas*.

pratyutpanna (Pa.): present, what has come up.

pṛthagjana (Skt): profane, common being, a person who is unenlightened.

pudgala (Skt): in Pudgalavādin schools, a continuing person who is neither permanent nor impermanent, neither identical with nor separate from the aggregates.

puggala (Pa.): *see pudgala.*

puñña (Pa.): *see puṇya.*

puṇya (Skt): *see under* Indian philosophy.

rāga (Skt): attachment by mind, desire.

raṅ bźin (Tbt.): *see svabhāva.*

raṅ stoṅ (Tbt.): self-empty.

rasa viṣaya (Skt): taste sense-data.

rdzogs-chen (Tbt.): the Great Completeness – the practice/attachment in the highest of the nine Vehicles among the corpus of Buddhist teaching identified by *Rñiṅ-ma-pa*.

rnam pa (Tbt.): image, aspect cast by the object towards the perceiving consciousness according to the Sautāntrika, Yogācāra and Madhayamika schools = *ākāra* (Skt).

rñiṅ ma (Tbt.): old sect basing its practices on texts translated in the first dissemination period of Buddhism in Tibet.

rūpa (Skt): physical body, material form, one of the five *skandhas*.

rūpadhātu (Skt): the material plane of existence, plane where ethereal beings live.

rūpakāya (Skt): a *buddha*'s physical body.

rūpa viṣaya (Skt): sense-data.

sa bon (Tbt.): seed = *bīja* (Skt).

śabda viṣaya (Skt): auditory sense-data.

sādhya (Skt): a predicate, to be proved.

sahabhāva (Skt): related, coexistence.

sākāra (Skt): having a form, aspect.

sākāra jnānavāda (Skt): theory that knowledge has a form of its own (as opposed to *ninākāra jnānavādā*).

Śākya (Skt): name of the tribe to which Gautama, the founder of the Buddhist tradition, belonged.

Śākyamuni (Skt): literally, sage of the *Śākyas*, another name for the Buddha.

samādhi (Skt): concentration, trance, state of hypnosis.

sāmānya (Skt): universals.

sāmānyalakṣaṇa (Skt): object of conceptualization, mental constructs, generalized reality, the object of *anumāna*.

saṃbhogakāya (Skt): enjoyment aspect of the *trikāya* doctrine. *Buddhas* at this level are foci of worship and will help the faithful in various ways. They also serve as objects of meditation, a glorified form of a *buddha* available to advanced meditators.

sambodhi (Skt): supreme enlightenment.

saṃjñā (Skt): ideation, ideas, one of the five *skandhas* = *saññā* (Pa.).

saṃkalpa (Skt): evaluations.

saṃprayukta (Skt): accompanying, said of *saṃskāra*.

saṃsāra (Skt): the involuntary running on from life to life, transcendence of which is the principal goal of Indian religious philosophies; the process of birth and death to which an individual (i.e. the five *skandhas*) is and always has been subject; it is a consequence of *karma* and *kleśa* and can be abolished only through *jñāna*, which again depends on *prajñā*.

saṃskāra (Skt): volition, *karmic* energies, one of the five *skandhas* = *saṅkhāra* (Pa.).

saṃskṛta dharma (Skt): conditioned phenomena.

saṃvṛti satya (Skt): conventional truths, relative reality where everything is conditioned and in constant ferment.

sangha (Skt): originally the community of Buddhist monks, nuns, laymen (*upāsaka*) and laywomen (*upāsikā*); now generally the order of ordained monks, nuns and novices.

saṅkhāra (Pa.): *see saṃskāra*.

saññā (Pa.): perception, the recognition of objects, one of the five *skandhas*.

sānta (Skt): coming to rest, quiescent.

sārūpya (Skt): conformity of knowledge with object.

sarvatraga (Skt): universal.

śāstra (Skt): a treatise that either comments on a *sūtra* or another *śāstra* or treats some topic independently.

śāthya (Skt): fraudulence.

satya (Skt): truth, reality.

satyadvaya (Skt): in Mādhayamika the 'Two Truths', the ultimate nature of any *dharma*, emptiness, and its conventional reality, which is not thereby negated.

sayadaw (Bur.): Buddhist monk.

sems (Tbt.): mind = *citta*, *manas* (Skt).

sems ñid lhan skyes (Tbt.): co-emergent mind.

sīla (Pa.): *see śīla*.

śīla (Skt): morality in general, moral precepts.

skandha (Skt): the five 'aggregates' that Buddhists say comprise a person. They are matter, sensation, perceptions, mental formations and consciousness = *khanda* (Pa.).

smṛti (Skt): conscious memory; attentive mindfulness = *sati* (Pa.).

snaṅ ba lhan skyes (Tbt.): co-emergent appearances.

sparśa (Skt): sensation caused by contact between objects, sense-organ and consciousness.

spraṣṭavya viṣaya (Skt): tactile sense-data.

śraddhā (Skt): faith, considered a prerequisite for Buddhist practice and philosophical understanding; belief.

śramaṇa (Skt): recluses who left home and wandered in search of truth; also refers to non-Hindu schools.

srāvaka (Skt): hearer (of the Buddha's teaching).

śrotra indriya (Skt): auditory organ.

sruta (Skt): study, literally listening.

sthiti (Skt): subsistence.

stoṅ gzugs (Tbt): body that is utterly immaterial; empty form.

stūpa (Skt): memorial shrine.

styāna (Skt): sloth, indolence, inactive temperament.

śubha (Skt): pleasure.

śuci (Skt): attractive.

sugata (Skt): well gone, one of the epithets of the Buddha.

sukha (Skt): pleasure, opposite *duḥkha*.

śūnya (Skt): empty (of independent existence).

śūnyatā (Skt): in Mahāyāna, especially Mādhayamika, the emptiness of self-existence that is the ultimate nature of all *dharmas*.

sūtra (Skt): a canonical text, usually in dialogue form, said to contain the Buddha's actual words as recorded during his earthly career.

sutta (Pa.): *see sūtra*.

svabhāva (Skt): literally own-being; in Sarvāstivāda, the fundamental and permanent (independent) nature of a thing (*bhāva*) or a *dharma*. According to Nāgārjuna the true *svabhāva* of things is that they have no such permanent and independent *svabhāva*.

svabhāvānumāna (Skt): analytical entailment.

svabhāvikakāya (Skt): Buddha's nature body; a *buddha*'s emptiness and the non-dual *gnosis* of emptiness.

svalakṣaṇa (Skt): thing-in-itself; own defining characteristic, unique particular, evident.

svaprakāśa (Skt): self-luminous nature of knowledge.

svasaṃvedanapratyakṣa (Skt): self-perception.

svātantra (Skt): an 'independent', formal inference through which one attempts to establish one's own position or demolish that of one's opponent.

tantra (Skt): a complex programme of initiation and ritual designed to bestow enlightenment and supernormal powers with greater speed than is possible via the exoteric path.

tarka (Skt): argumentation, logic.

tathāgata (Skt): thus gone, one of the epithets of the Buddha.

tathāgatagarbha (Skt): in Mahāyāna, the matrix of enlightenment – that is, the capacity of any being to achieve full buddhahood.

tattva (Skt): fundamental fact, truth, emptiness, non-origination.

tattvajñāna (Skt): true knowledge of the nature of reality, generally regarded as the primary aim of philosophy.

Theravāda (Skt): the form of Buddhist teaching practised today mainly in Sri Lanka and South East Asia; literally, the teaching or doctrine of the elders (*thera*).

trikāya (Skt): three bodies: refers to the Mahāyāna doctrine of buddhahood as *trikāya*, where there are three levels, *saṃbhogakāya*, *nirmāṇakāya* and *dharmakāya*.

trisvabhāva (Skt): in Yogācāra, the three natures into which reality is divisible – the dependent nature (*paratantra*), imaginary nature (*parikalpita*) and absolute nature (*pariniṣpanna*).

tṛṣṇā (Skt): thirst or grasping, which is a condition of suffering.

tshad ma (Tbt.): *see pramāṇa*.

upalabdhi (Skt): knowledge acquired through perception, observation.

upamāna (Skt): analogy.

upanāha (Skt): faculty of resentment.

upanaya (Skt): application.

upāsaka (Skt): a lay devotee, a devout or faithful lay person.

upāyakauśalya (Skt): skilful means; the devices and stratagems employed by *buddhas* and *bodhisattvas* to bring beings to the path and liberation.

upekkhā (Pa.): *see upekṣā*.

upekṣā (Skt): equanimity, indifference.

uposatha (Pa.): days on which communal confession of offences take place in the *sangha*.

vāda (Skt): doctrine.

vāsanā (Skt): traces generally left by actions; said to 'perfume' the mental series.

vedanā (Skt): feeling (pleasant, unpleasant, neutral), one of the five *skandhas*.

vicāra (Skt): subtle investigation.

vicikitsā (Skt): doubting.

vihiṃsā (Skt): causing injury.

vijñāna (Skt): knowledge that is gained through experience; scientific knowledge, consciousness, one of the five *skandhas*; = *viññāṇa* (Pa.).

vijñaptimātratā (Skt): the consciousness-only school of Buddhist idealism; the world as concept only.

vikalpa (Skt): discursive thought, concept.

vinaya (Skt): the section of the Buddhist scriptures dealing mainly with the *sangha*, the rules for its common life, code of conduct for the monk.

viññāṇa (Pa.): *see vijñāna*.

vipāka (Skt): fruition, as of *karma*.
viparyāsa (Skt): inverted view, the mistaken belief that there is anything pure, good, permanent or independent, the main *modus operandi* of *vikalpa*.
vīrya (Skt): energy – one of the perfections; courageousness in action.
vitarka (Skt): reflection.
vohāra (Pa.): conventional; = *vyavahāra* (Pa.).
vyañjanakāya (Skt): the force imparting significance to articulate sounds.
vyavahāra satya (Skt): relative, conventional, practical truth; usually synonymous with *saṃvṛtisatya*, and opposed to absolute truth, or *paramārthasatya*.
yakkha (Skt): ghostly being of light.
yāna (Skt): vehicle; *see Hīnayāna* and *Mahāyāna*.
yogi jñāna (Skt): mystical perception.
yongs grub (Tbt.): *see pariniṣpanna*.

CHINESE PHILOSOPHY

Abbreviations: C. = Chinese J. = Japanese Skt = Sanskrit

bagua (C.): the eight trigrams.
bian (C.): dialectic in Ming Jia.
bianyi (C.): changes.
bie (C.): separation, variation.
Bing Jia (C.): the Military Strategy School.
buyi (C.): constancies, unchanging.
Chan (C.): a School of Buddhism (cf. *Zen* (J.) *in* Japanese philosophy).
Chun Jiu (C.): the Spring and Autumn period.
daiji (C.): the original great ultimate.
dao (C.): way, social norms.
Dao Jia (C.): the School of Daoism.
dayi (C.): essential meaning.
de (C.): virtue, potency.
di (C.): substance.
ding (C.): political and social stability.
ding-yu-yi (C.): stabilization through unification.
fa (C.): law.
fan (C.): reversion.
faxiang (C.): *Dharma*-characteristics in Chinese Buddhism (*see Dharma* (Skt) *in* Buddhist philosophy).
faxing (C.): *Dharma*-essence in Chinese Buddhism (*see Dharma* (Skt) *in* Buddhist philosophy).
foxing (C.): *buddha*-nature (*see buddha* (Skt) *in* Buddhist philosophy).

fu (C.): reverting.
geyi (C.): matching of Buddhist terms with Daoist terms (cf. *ko-i*) (J.)).
gongan (C.): public cases, *Chan* puzzles (cf. *koan* (J.)).
gua (C.): form.
gui (C.): spirit from the past, ghost.
he (C.): harmony, correspondence.
housheng (C.): improving life.
hua (C.): transformation.
Huayan Jia (C.): Wreath, Garland Sūtra School.
jia (C.): philosophical school.
jian (C.): whole, universal.
jianai (C.): universal love.
jianyi (C.): direct presentation of changes.
jiji (C.): completion, fullness.
jing (C.): reverence and piety.
junzi (C.): morally ruling person.
kong (C.): emptiness, zero, nothingness.
li (C.): ritual, rite, pattern, objective order, idea.
li kan (C.): the trigrams for fire and water.
lian (C.): virtue of honesty.
ling (C.): command, order, decree.
liuqi (C.): the six vapours (in medicine), the six factors in nature (wind, cold, heat, humidity, dryness and fire).
liyong (C.): developing utilities, utilizing, making use of.
luan (C.): chaos.
ming (C.): command, understanding, name, enlightened.
Ming Jia (C.): the School of Names.
minsheng (C.): livelihood.
ming shi (C.): name and object.
mo (C.): magical power, demon, evil spirit.
mou (C.): the parallel form of dialectic.
neng (C.): energy.
Nung Jia (C.): the Agronomy School.
pu (C.): divination.
puci (C.): oracle inscriptions.
qi (C.): blending of *yin* and *yang*.
quan (C.): comprehensive observation.
ren (C.): the virtue of humanity, benevolence, person, human being.
renai (C.): universal love.
renwei (C.): artificiality.
ru (C.): master of ceremonies.

Sanlun (C.): 'Three Treatises' in Chinese Mādhyamika Buddhism.
shangdi (C.): supreme divinity.
sheng (C.): creativity, growth.
shengren (C.): sage, ideal person, holy person.
shi (C.): actuality, reality, position, situation, divination.
shu (C.): skills, methods, arts, technique.
ti (C.): fraternal duty.
tian (C.): heaven.
tianming (C.): mandate of heaven.
tianzi (C.): will of heaven, Son of Heaven (Emperor).
tiyong (C.): substance and function.
wei (C.): intangible, minute.
weiji (C.): incompletion, before completion.
Wei Shi Jia (C.): the Consciousness Only school.
Wei Xin Jia (C.): the Mind Only school.
wu (C.): void, nothingness.
wuhua (C.): perpetual transformation.
wuwei (C.): the principle of non-action, non-intervention.
wuyu (C.): desireless condition, having no desires.
wuxing (C.): the five powers of nature (metal, wood, water, fire, earth).
Wu Xin Jia (C.): the No-mind School.
xiangdong (C.): wilful conformity.
xiao (C.): the virtue of filial piety, the imitation form of dialectic.
xiaoren (C.): small person, person of mean character.
xin (C.): heart-mind, confidence, faith.
xing (C.): practice, nature, the virtue of integrity, faithfulness, spontaneous tendency.
Xinxue (C.): the doctrine of mind, mind-monism.
xu (C.): fate.
xue (C.): learning.
yang (C.): bright, the masculine principle in nature (symbolizing male, sun, brightness, positivity).
yi (C.): changes, changes and transformation, invisible, righteousness.
Yijing (C.): *The Book of Changes.*
yin (C.): shady, the feminine principle in nature (symbolizing female, moon, darkness, negativity).
Yinyang Jia (C.): the School of Yin and Yang.
yong (C.): function, usefulness.
you (C.): being, existing.
youwei (C.): efficiency, intervention, action.
yuan (C.): round, perfect, encompassing, comprehensive, the analogy form of dialectic.
Zhanguo (C.): the Warring States Period.

zhengde (C.): rectifying one's virtues.
zhengming (C.): correction of names
zhi (C.): knowledge, intelligence, wisdom, intention, refutation (a method in inference).
zhong (C.): centrality, loyalty.
Zhong Heng Jia (C.): the Diplomatic School.
zhou (C.): drawing out (a method of inference).
ziwei (C.): each for himself.
zong (C.): ancestor.

JAPANESE PHILOSOPHY

Abbreviations J. = Japanese C. = Chinese Skt = Sanskrit

aida gara (J.): 'The in-between' (lit: relation). An ontological concept in the philosophy of Watsuji Tetsurō that signifies the fundamental relationality of human existence.
aikoku (J.): patriotism.
bakufu (J.): military government; Japan's feudal government.
bunka kyōdōtai (J.): cultural communities.
bushidō (J.): way of the *samurai* (*bushi*).
chi, jin, yū (J.): wisdom, humanity and courage.
chien kyōdōtai (J.): territorial communities.
chokuyu taii (J.): the Gist of the Edict written by Motoda Eifu in 1882.
chūkun aikoku (J.): loyalty and patriotism.
daigaku (J.): government university.
daimyō (J.): feudal lord.
daini to no ganmoku (J.): the secondary principles.
darani (J.): *dhāraṇī* (Skt) incantation (cf. *mantra* (Skt) *under* Indian philosophy).
dō (J.): = *michi*, way (cf. *dao* (C.)).
dokuritsushin (J.): the spirit of independence.
ekō (J.): merit-transference, ritual for the dead.
fūdo (J.): natural climatic and geographical characteristics.
gakusei ni tsuki chokuyu (J.): Imperial Edict for the Educational System (1882).
gi (J.): reason, meaning, justification, principle.
gimu (J.): (legal) obligation, duty.
giri (J.): (social) obligation, debt.
gunjin chokuyu (J.): the Edict for Japanese soldiers (1882).
hō (J.): religion (cf. *dharma* (Skt) *under* Buddhist philosophy).
hyakuichi shinron (J.): a unified science of a hundred moral theories in 1874.
ie (J.): family, household.

igaku (J.): heterodox learning, studies.

iki (J.): 'freshness', the nearly untranslatable aesthetic term, interpreted by Kuki Shūzō to define a basic cultural difference that refers to a purportedly unique, 'artfully natural' style manifested in certain Japanese female attire and comportment, and in architectural and musical patterns.

jikaku; *jikaku-teki* (J.): 'self-consciousness', 'self-awareness' or 'self-realization'. The modern philosophical usage draws upon both the colloquial sense of one's awareness of a social role or responsibility and the Buddhist sense of awakening to one's true self; *jikaku-teki* is the adjectival form.

jin (J.): virtue of humanity.

jinen (J.): suchness, things-as-they-are.

jingi chūkō (J.): humanity, justice, loyalty and filial piety.

jinsei (J.): benevolent government.

jinsei sanpō setsu (J.): theory of three precious objects in human life.

jissō (J.): true state.

jitsugaku (J.): practical studies.

kaji (J.): enfolding power.

kami (J.): sacred; god, spirit, tutelary deity.

kazoku (J.): family, families.

keimō (J.): Enlightenment. The term refers both to the eighteenth-century European and the Meiji-era movements to replace dogmatic, authoritative ideology with rational, scientific thinking.

kenchi keiei (J.): the age of construction.

kenpō sōan (J.): a draft of the Constitution by Nishi Amane.

kō (J.): filial piety.

kōan (J.): Zen riddle for meditation.

kōiteki-renkan (J.): connection-through-action or active association.

kokka (J.): countries.

kokutai (J.): 'national polity' or 'national political essence'. The concept of imperial rule backed by filial piety and loyalty that was first formulated in the Tokugawa era and later used to support a strong nationalist and anti-individualist ideology in the Pacific War period.

kunshin no gi (J.): justice between a lord and his subjects.

mame, chie, tomi (J.): health, wisdom and wealth.

mappō (J.): era of degenerate *dharma* (*see under* Buddhist philosophy).

matsuri (J.): religious cult.

meiji ishin (J.): the Meiji restoration of 1867/8; the restoration of the administration of Japan to the emperor.

meiroku sha (J.): Meiji Six Society. A group of 'Enlightenment' figures, including Nishi Amane, Nishimura Shigeki, Kato Hiroyuki, Tsuda Mamichi and Fukuzawa Yukichi.

michi (J.): way, *dao*; = *dō*.

mondō (J.): question and response between Zen master and disciple.

mono; koto; kotoba (J.): (concrete) 'things'; (abstract) 'things', 'matters' or 'affairs'; and 'words' or 'language', respectively. *Kotoba* can be written with different ideographs, all of which differ from *koto* as things or matters, but the evident pun suggests that words are things having meaning.

mujō (J.): impermanence.

mujun (J.): contradiction.

nembutsu (J.): invocation of Amida Buddha.

nihonjin-ron (J.): theory of Japaneseness. Popular literature advocating the unique or special characteristics of the Japanese people.

ningen (J.): man, human being. This compound of two ideographs connotes the interpersonal realm and suggests that communality is prior to individuality in the definition of the human.

ningengaku (J.): human studies, the study of the human, the general term for (philosophical) anthropology.

ninjō (J.): human feeling.

nippon no tenshoku (J.): Japan's calling.

on (J.): personal obligation, benefit, debt.

rangaku (J.): Dutch learning.

reisei (J.): spirituality.

rinri (J.): 'ethics'. Consisting of two ideographs signifying the principles of companionship, this pre-modern term has a more restricted and academic use than *dōtoku*, 'morality'.

rōjū (J.): member of the *shōgun's* Council of Elders.

rōnin (J.): masterless *samurai*.

ronri; ronrigaku (J.): logic. The first term is more general and denotes any reasoned way of thinking; the second term serves as an equivalent to formal logic, also called *keishiki ronri*.

sadō (J.): way of tea.

saidai fukushi (J.): the greatest happiness.

samurai (J.): warrior retainer = *bushi*.

san akuma (J.): three demons – crime, deception and theft.

san kaki (J.): three evils – disease, idle complaint and poverty.

sanpō (J.): three precious objects – health, knowledge and wealth.

satori (J.): awakening.

seishin (J.): 'spirit'. Can also be translated as 'mind', 'soul' and, in adjectival form, 'mental', 'spiritual'.

sekkyoku kō (J.): positive principles, constructive principles.

shidō (J.): *see bushidō*.

shin; *kokoro* (J.): Heart or mind (the same ideograph). Often opposed simply to the body in contemporary Japanese thought, but in classical Japanese thought paired not only with body but also with words (*kotoba*) as a transformation of mind (*kokoro*).

shin; *shintai*; *karada*; *mi* (J.): body. *Shin*, *karada* and *mi* are three readings of the same ideograph; *mi* also refers to one's status or station in life. The *tai* of *shintai* can also be read *karada*, or in other contexts can denote 'substance'.

shingaku (J.): heart/mind learning.

shingon (J.): true word, *mantra* (Skt).

Shintō (J.): = *kami no michi*, way of the gods.

shōbō (J.): era of right *dharma* (*see under* Buddhist philosophy).

shōgun (J.): military commander; rulers of Japan 1192–1868.

shokuzai (J.): redemption, atonement.

shōkyoku kō (J.): negative principles, destructive policies.

Shōwa (J.): reign period 1925–89.

shugendō (J.): mountain cult of *yamabushi*, a blend of Buddhist, Shintō and folk religious practices.

shūkyō (J.): 'religion'. The term that became the standard translation of the Western category introduced in the Meiji era.

sōji hakai (J.): the Age of Cleansing and Destruction.

sonnō-jōi (J.): reverence for the emperor and expulsion of foreigners.

sonzai (J.): being or existence. The two ideographs for *son* and *zai* connote temporal and spatial presence respectively. *Sonzairon* is ontology.

surigaku (J.): mathematical sciences.

taika (J.): 'Great Reform', constitutional transformation of AD 645.

Tendai (J.): sect of Buddhism imported from China by Saichō (767–822).

tetsugaku (J.): philosophy.

tō (J.): = *dō* (J.).

Tokugawa (J.): shōgunal reign period 1600–1868.

uji (J.): clan, family, local community.

uji (J.): identity of being and time.

yamatai (J.): name of earliest Japanese court.

yōgaku (J.): 'Western learning'. The study of Euro-American medical, scientific and technological texts and of European texts on social sciences and humanities from the last days of the Tokugawa period to the early Meiji period.

zazen (J.): seated meditation.

zen (J.): meditation (cf. *dhyāna* (Skt) *under* Indian philosophy).

zōbō (J.): era of semblance *dharma* (*see under* Buddhist philosophy).

ISLAMIC PHILOSOPHY

Abbreviations Ar. = Arabic G. = Greek M. = Malay In. = Indonesian
P. = Persian

(The Arabic article *al-* is ignored in the alphabetical arrangement.)

'abd (Ar.): slave, servant, often used (with the force of 'creature') for human being in theological Arabic.

abdāl (pl.) (Ar.): *see badal.*

ada (M., In.): exist, be, have.

adab (Ar.): polite letters, courtesy, culture.

'adl (Ar.): justice, word much used by *Mu'tazila* (q.v.) in their references to God.

afāḍil (Ar.): the virtuous, epithet of one of the ranks in the virtuous city propounded by al-Fārābī.

af'āl (pl.) (Ar.): acts, deeds (*fi'l* (s.)).

af'āl al-madaniyya (Ar.): deeds in the city.

aḥadiyya (Ar.): absolute unity, the unknowable essence of God.

aḥwāl (pl.) (Ar.): states (e.g. of ecstasy) which come to the mystic from God (*ḥāl* (s.)).

āla (Ar.): instrument, tool.

'ālam al-mithāl (Ar.): the world of images, symbols or ideals, seen or reached through the imagination.

'ālim (Ar.): the clerics, orthodox lawyers, theologians.

'amā' (Ar.): the dark mist, blindness, mystical condition.

a'māl (Ar.): actions, works; = *af'āl.*

anfus al-mutashābiha (Ar.): similar souls.

anna huna wujūdan (Ar.): something exists, a premiss used by Avicenna in his proof for God's existence.

aniyya (Ar.): I-ness.

'aql (Ar.): reason.

'aql al-fa''āl (Ar.): active intellect; for al-Fārābī and Avicenna it serves to actualize the intellect of man in this world in allowing us to think conceptually.

'aql al-mustafāḍ (Ar.): derived intellect, intellect acquired or received by emanation.

'aql al-munfa'il (Ar.): passive intellect.

'aql al-qudsī (Ar.): holy reason, sacred intelligence, intellect, natural innate power.

aqāwil al-qudamā' (Ar.): the saying of the Ancients – generally refers to the classical Greek tradition.

ārā' (Ar.): opinions.

'araḍ (Ar.): accident, a translation of the Greek Aristotelian word *sumbebēkos.*

Ash'arite: deterministic and theistic subjectivist school of Islamic *kalām.*

a'yānu'l-thābita (Ar.): fixed essences, archetypes, the forms.

'ayn (Ar.): eye, essence.
aysa (also *ais* or *ays*) (Ar.): term used especially by the Arab philosopher al-Kindī to indicate the concept of being.
badal (Ar.) (pl. *abdāl*): the peg, position of the Sufi hierarchy as a substitute for the *quṭb*.
baqā' (Ar.): the mystical state of perdurance (immortality) in God.
basṭ (P.): expansiveness, exhilaration, one of the states of the mystical path, a state of intense joy.
bāṭin (Ar.): inner, hidden, esoteric.
bayan (Ar.): eloquence.
burhān (Ar.): demonstration, demonstrative reasoning.
dahriyya (Ar.): eternalism, the doctrine of those who hold that the cosmos is eternal, materialists, atheists.
dalang (M., In.): shadow puppeteer.
ḍall (Ar.): errancy, being led astray.
dār al-Islām (Ar.): the realm, domain or territory of Islam.
dhāt (Ar.): essence, identity.
dhawq (Ar.): literally taste; refers to the Sufi experiental intuition.
dhawū al-alsina (Ar.): the interpreters, one of the five ranks of the virtuous city propounded by al-Farabi.
dhikr (Ar.): literally mention, recollection; Sufi meditative practice focused on God's spoken names and epithets, ritual of focusing the mind on God or the gathering at which this is done through the frequent mention or remembrance of God.
dhimmī (Ar.): of or pertaining to the minorities tolerated under Islam, principally Jews and Christians, the 'People of the Book'. Payment of special taxes historically exempted *dhimmī* from forced conversion.
dīn (Ar.): religion, specifically Islam as a comprehensive way of life.
fāḍila (Ar.): virtuous, excellent.
falsafa/falāsifa (Ar.): philosophy/philosophers, derived from the Greek *philosophia*.
fanā' (Ar.): the mystical state of annihilation (in God), absorption or passing away (into God).
faqīh (Ar.): Muslim jurist, practitioner of *fiqh*, Islamic jurisprudence.
faqīr (Ar.): literally poor mendicant, mystic or ascetic.
fasād (Ar.): corruption.
fātiḥa (Ar.): the opening prayer (*sūra*) of the Qu'rān.
faylasuf (Ar.): philosopher.
fiqh (Ar.): jurisprudence in Islam, divided up into different and competing schools of interpretation and practice.
fiṭra wa'l-tab' (Ar.): innate, intrinsic, inborn nature.
gharīb (Ar.): stranger.
ghawth (Ar.): help, aid, position in Sufi hierarchy sometimes highest, sometimes second.

ghayr muttaḥarrika (Ar.): unmoved, used by the Arab philosopher al-Kindī of God (Aristotle's unmoved first mover).

ḥaḍārat (Ar.): presence; Ibn al-'Arabī speaks of five divine presences (see *nāsūt*, *malakūt*, *jabarūt*, *lāhūt* and *hāhūt*), which are also the different manifestations of the Absolute Essence.

ḥadīth (Ar.): Traditional Islamic accounts, ascribed to ancient and oral authority, of the sayings and doings of the Prophet Muḥammad and his companions. The corpus of *ḥadīth* forms a key basis of normative practice.

ḥads (Ar.): intuition.

hāhūt (Ar.): divine essence in itself, ipseity.

ḥajj (Ar.): the pilgrimage to Mecca.

hakekat (In.): reality, the 'Truth', from the Arabic *ḥaqīqa*.

ḥakīm (Ar.): philosopher, wise man, accomplished thinker (pl. *ḥukamā'*).

ḥāl (Ar.): a state or lasting condition of the Sufi path held to come as a gift from God (pl. *aḥwāl*).

ḥaqīqa al muḥammadiyya (Ar.): the reality (or idea) of Muḥammad as an agent in creation.

ḥaqq (Ar.): used as a name of God, literally the truth.

hawwā (Ar.): word created by the Arab philosopher al-Kindī indicating 'to bring into being' (by creation *ex nihilo*).

ḥikma (Ar.): wisdom, science.

ḥikmat al-ishrāq (Ar.): Philosophy of Light, associated with Suhrawardī.

ḥilm (Ar.): virtue of clemency, mildness, generally from a position of strength (cognate with the Latin *clementia*).

ḥukamā' (Ar.): the wise, philosophers.

ḥukamā' al-afāḍil (Ar.): the excellent philosophers, the tradition of Plato, Aristotle and the Neoplatonists.

ḥulūl (Ar.): inherence, immanence, incarnation.

huwiyya (Ar.): he-ness.

idlāl (Ar.): *see ḍall.*

ijtihād (Ar.): independent reasoning.

ilāhiyya (Ar.): divinity.

'illa (Ar.): cause, ground of analogy, similarity.

'ilm (Ar.): knowledge, science (pl. *'ulūm*).

'ilm al-kalām (Ar.): dialectical or philosophical theology.

imām (Ar.): Muslim leader in many senses, such as a prayer leader. The rightful *imām* of all Muslims is classically regarded as the legitimate *khalīfa* or Commander of the Faithful. Thus discussions of the *imāmate* are discussions of political legitimacy.

inbisāṭ (Ar.): expansiveness in the emotional dialectic of Sufism; = *basṭ*.

inqibāḍ (Ar.): anguish, constraint in the emotional dialectic of Sufism.

insān (Ar.): man, humanity.

insān al-kāmil (Ar.): the perfect man, microcosm.
irfān (Ar.): theosophy.
'ishq (Ar.): yearning.
isṭaqisāt (Ar.): elements.
ittiḥād (Ar.): union, as with God or other supernatural being, such as the active intellect.
ittiṣāl (Ar.): contact, communion; Greek *haphē*; Hebrew *devequt*.
jabarūt (Ar.): a heavenly sphere, that of divine power.
jāhiliyya (Ar.): the age of ignorance, the pre-Islamic age regarded in Islam as the epoch of benightedness.
jalāl (Ar.): majesty, divine majesty.
jamāl (Ar.): beauty, divine beauty.
jawhar (Ar.): substance; the equivalent Greek Aristotelian philosophical term is *ousia*; cf. Latin *substantia*.
jawhar al-jismānī (Ar.): bodily essence, form in a body, substantial form.
jihād (Ar.): the obligation of holy war on behalf of Islam.
jinn (Ar.): the collective designation of the supernatural beings known as genies, invisible beings made from flame.
jowaniya (Ar.): inside, used as an Arabic translation of the Kantian term 'transcendentalism'.
kalām (Ar.): literally talk or speech, Islamic dialectical or philosophical theology, apologetics, especially associated with medieval atomism (*see also mutakallim*).
kamāl (Ar.): perfection.
kawn (Ar.): existence, development, coming into being.
kawn al-kullī (Ar.): complete or universal being.
keadaan (M., In.): existence, being, word translating *wujūd* (Ar.).
kebatinan (M., In.): from *bāṭin* (Ar.): generic term for Javanese mysticism.
khalīfa (Ar.): anglicized as caliph, prophet, literally deputy or successor, title of heads of the Islamic states.
khalq (Ar.): creation, created things.
khalqī (Ar.): creaturely.
khānqāh (Ar.): special Sufi building for common life and worship.
khāṣṣiyyat (Ar.): éliteness.
khātam al-awliyā' (Ar.): seal of the saints.
khātam al-nabiyyīn, *khatim al anbiyā'* (Ar.): seal or completion of the prophets.
khawf (Ar.): fear, one of the stations of the path.
khayāl (Ar.): mere remembering, imaging.
khayr 'alā 'l-iṭlāq (Ar.): the absolute good.
khiṣāl (Ar.): qualifications: generally refers to inborn qualifications.
khodā (P.): God.
khūdī (P.): self, subjective in the individual.

kibla (*qibla*) (Ar.): direction of the *Ka'ba* in Mecca, to be faced during prayer.
kulliyyāt (Ar.): universals.
kun (Ar.): 'Be!', the Divine Creative Command.
kunī dhāt (Ar.): absolute essence.
lāhūt (Ar.): divinity or its sphere.
lais or *lays* (Ar.): term used especially by the Arab philosopher al-Kindī to denote the concept of non-being. The Arabic verb *laysa* means 'It is not . . .'
mādda (Ar.): matter.
mādda al-ūlā al-mushtaraka (Ar.): common prime matter.
madīna (Ar.): city.
madīna al-ḍālla (Ar.): the errant city that misses the right path.
madīna al-fāḍila (Ar.): the excellent or the virtuous city.
madīna al-fāsiqa (Ar.): the wicked city.
madīna al-mubaddala (Ar.): the city that has deliberately changed its character.
madīna jāhiliyya (Ar.): the ignorant city.
madrasa (Ar.): traditional Islamic college.
maḥabba (Ar.): love.
malakūt (Ar.): a heavenly sphere, usually that of the angels.
malik al-sunna (Ar.): the king of tradition.
malik fi'l-ḥaqīqa (Ar.): the true or rightful king.
māliyyūn (Ar.): the rich or propertied.
ma'mūra (Ar.): the inhabited world.
ma'nā (Ar.): meaning, the basic semantic component in logical theory.
man tamanṭaqa tazandaqa (Ar.): whoever is in favour of logic is in favour of heresy.
manṭiq (Ar.): logic, generally representing Greek logic as developed in Islamic philosophy and theology.
maqām (Ar.): a state or lasting condition of the Sufi path, reached by human effort (pl. *maqāmāt*).
ma'qūlāt al-ūlā (Ar.): the first intelligibles, the primary objects of knowledge.
ma'rifa (Ar.): *gnosis*, mystical knowledge, intimate knowledge.
mawjūdāt (Ar.): existents.
miḥna (Ar.): inquisition or ordeal, used to refer to the testing instituted by the Arab Caliph al-Ma'mūn (reg. AD 813–33) to enforce adherence to the *Mu'tazilite* (q.v.) doctrine.
milla (Ar.): religious community, people of a particular religion, religion (cf. Turkish *millet*).
mīthāq (Ar.): covenant, especially that of God with the human race before creation.
mubdi' (Ar.): term used of God to denote his function as a creator *ex nihilo*; the contrast is with Neoplatonic emanation.
muḥtasib (Ar.): literally accountant, Muslim inspector of markets and morals; a man of incorruptible character fit to serve as the tongue of the *qāḍī* (cf. Latin *censor*).

mujāhidūn (Ar.): the fighters, the (holy) warriors, those engaging in *jihād*.
mu'minūn (Ar.): the believers.
mumkin (Ar.): possible existent.
munkar (Ar.): literally 'rejected' or 'unspeakable', the evil or disreputable, which it is the Qur'ānic obligation to suppress (cf. Latin *nefas*).
muqqadirūn (Ar.): the assessors, one of the ranks in al Fārābī's virtuous city.
murīd (Ar.): follower, disciple, Sufi novice (pl. *murīdūn*).
mutakallim (Ar.): literally 'speaker', Islamic philosophical or dialectical theologian, practitioner of *kalām* (cf. Latin *loquentes*) (pl. *mutakallimūn*).
Mu'tazila (Ar.): literally those who withdraw; a rationalist group of theologians in medieval Islam.
Mu'tazilite (Ar.): Anglicized Arabic word used to refer to individual member of *Mu'tazila* (q.v.).
Naqshbandiyya (Ar.): name of one of the major Sufi orders.
nāsūt (Ar.): humanity, sphere of corporeality.
nubuwwa (Ar.): prophecy.
on (G.): being.
pesantren (In.) term for *pondok* (sometimes *pondok pesantren* is used).
pondok (M.): rural Islamic school named after the cluster of huts used as dormitories by the students.
qabḍ (Ar.): withdrawal into a state of abject loneliness and eventual loss of self (opposite of *basṭ*).
qāḍī (Ar.): an Islamic judge.
qibla (Ar.): *see kibla*.
qiyās (Ar.): analogy, a theoretical tool used in Islamic theology, law and philosophy.
Qur'ān (Ar.): the sacred scripture of Islam taken to be the word of God as revealed to Muḥammad and containing the chief foundations of Islamic law and morality.
quṭb (Ar.): the pole, a cosmically significant individual according to the Sufi doctrine.
quwwa al-ghādhiya (Ar.): the nutritive faculty.
quwwa al-ḥāssa (Ar.): the sensitive faculty, the power of perception.
quwwa al-mutakhayyila (Ar.): the faculty of representation or imaging.
quwwa al-nāṭiqa (Ar.): the rational faculty, reason.
quwwa al-nuzū'iyya (Ar.): the appetitive faculty.
rabb (Ar.): lord, sovereign, also a name for God.
Raḥīm (Ar.): the Merciful, one of the Divine names.
Raḥmān (Ar.): the Compassionate, one of the Divine names.
raḥmāniyya (Ar.): mercifulness, compassion.
ra'īs (Ar.): head, ruler.
rajā' (Ar.): hope, one of the mystical stations.
rasa (M., In.): intuitive feeling.

ribāṭ (Ar.): special Sufi building for common life and worship.
riḍā' (Ar.): contentment, one of the mystical stations.
risāla (Ar.): message, letter.
rubūbiyya (Ar.): lordship (cf. *rabb*).
rūḥ (Ar.): spirit (in many senses).
sa'āda (Ar.): happiness, felicity.
sa'āda al-quṣwā (Ar.): supreme happiness, ultimate felicity (generally refers to happiness in the life to come).
sabab al-awwal (Ar.): the First Cause, God as the First Cause (of an eternally emanating cosmos).
ṣādafa (Ar.): acquaintance.
safar (Ar.): journey.
salafiyya (Ar.): a movement calling for a return to the *salaf*, the early Companions of the prophet.
ṣalāt (Ar.): the formal Muslim prayers or worship.
samā' (Ar.): literally hearing, Sufi ecstatic concert evoking the name of God in musical *dhikr* and poetry, often accompanied by ritualized whirling dance.
ṣanā'i' (Ar.): arts, crafts.
sānī (Ar.): 'maker' or 'author', a term applied to God by eternalist philosophers to suggest the world's dependence on the divine act without suggesting any commitment to the rejected doctrine of the world's temporal origination.
sawiya (Ar.): special Sufi buildings for common life or worship.
shaikh, *shaykh* (Ar.): Islamic leader, spiritual leader.
sharī'a (Ar.): Islamic, i.e. religious law.
shāriḥ (Ar.): commentator.
Shī'ī (Ar.): (Anglicized version *Shī'ite*) of or pertaining to the branch of Islam holding the true successors of the Prophet Muḥammad to have been of the house of his kinsman 'Alī. Shī'ism is characterized by a more charismatic view of leadership than the rival Sunnī tradition.
shuhūd (Ar.): vision, contemplation, experience.
shūrā (Ar.): a way of electing the *imām* by the scholars of the people, usually equated with democracy.
ṣifa (Ar.): attribute, quality.
ṣifāt al-ḥaqqiyya (Ar.): creative attributes.
ṣinā'a (Ar.): craft (pl. *ṣanā'i'*).
sīra (Ar.): biography of the Prophet.
sufi (*ṣūfī*) (Ar.): an Islamic mystic.
sunna (Ar.): tradition, custom, standard practice, especially that of Muḥammad.
Sunnī (Ar.): of or pertaining to the branch of Islam upholding the legitimacy of the historical sequence of the Prophet's early successors (*khalīfa*), who were selected from the ranks of his closest lieutenants. Sunnī Islam claims legitimacy through

adherence to the practice (*sunna*) of the Prophet Muḥammad and his closest followers, a key determinant of normative practice in Islam of all branches.

sūra (Ar.): chapter of the Qu'rān.

ṣūra (Ar.): form, shape, image.

ta'ayun awwal (Ar.): the first determination of the essence.

ṭabīb (Ar.): physician, educated not only in medicine but in the whole of philosophical and scientific thought.

ta'dīb (Ar.): enculturation, discipline, practical education which is said to produce moral virtue and practical acts in nations (cf. Greek *paideia*).

tafāḍul (Ar.): difference in excellence.

tafsīr (Ar.): interpretation, commentary of the Qu'rān.

tahawwī (Ar.): word invented by the Arab philosopher al-Kindī to indicate bringing into being (by creation *ex nihilo*).

tajallī (Ar.): disclosure, manifestation.

ta'līm (Ar.): theoretical education which produces theoretical virtues in nations and cities.

tanzīh (Ar.): transcendence, freedom from impurity or corporeality.

ṭarīqa (Ar.): a Sufi order, literally a path.

taṣawwuf (Ar.): Sufi practice and discipline.

tawakkul (Ar.): trust in God, one of the stations, total God-consciousness.

tawḥīd (Ar.): divine unity or assertion of unity; much used by the *Mu'tazila* (q.v.) in their references to God.

ta'wīl (Ar.): interpretation, sometimes esoteric.

tekke (Turkish): special Sufi buildings for common life and worship.

'ulamā' (Ar.): see *'ālim*.

umma (Ar.): community, especially the Muslim community.

uns (Ar.): fellowship.

wādi' al-nawāmīs (Ar.): the lawgiver.

wādi' al-sharī'a (Ar.): the lawgiver.

wādi' al-sunna (Ar.): the giver of tradition, the giver of the *sunna*.

waḥda (Ar.): plurality in unity.

waḥdat al-shuhūd (Ar.): unity of witness, vision.

waḥdat al-wujūd (Ar.): unity of being or existence (a name given to the system of Ibn al-'Arabī).

Wahhābī (Ar.): follower of M. ibn 'Abd al-Wahhāb – a Muslim reformist of fundamentalist tendency.

wāḥidiyya (Ar.): unity, term used specifically to designate unity in diversity by Sufi thinkers.

waḥy (Ar.): revelation.

waqt (Ar.): time, occasion, *kairos*.

wazīr (Ar.): the chief minister of an Islamic state, often, in effect, the ruler, although notionally a counsellor to the reigning monarch, and actually subject to deposition should he fall out of favour.

wujūd (Ar.): pure being; *see also dhāt*.

wujūdiyya (Ar.): existentialism.

zāwiya (Ar.): special Sufi building for common life and worship.

INDEX